THE VICTORIA HISTORY
OF THE
COUNTIES OF ENGLAND

———

A HISTORY OF
YORKSHIRE EAST RIDING

VOLUME VII

OXFORD
UNIVERSITY PRESS

Great Clarendon Street, Oxford ox2 6DP

Oxford University Press is a department of the University of Oxford.
It furthers the University's objective of excellence in research, scholarship,
and education by publishing worldwide in

Oxford New York

Athens Auckland Bangkok Bogotá Buenos Aires Cape Town
Chennai Dar es Salaam Delhi Florence Hong Kong Istanbul Karachi
Kolkata Kuala Lumpur Madrid Melbourne Mexico City Mumbai Nairobi
Paris São Paulo Shanghai Singapore Taipei Tokyo Toronto Warsaw

with associated companies in Berlin Ibadan

Oxford is a registered trade mark of Oxford University Press
in the UK and certain other countries

Published in the United States
by Oxford University Press Inc., New York

© University of London 2002

British Library Cataloguing in Publication Data
Data available

Library of Congress Cataloging in Publication Data
Data available

ISBN 0-19-722797-X

Typeset and Printed by The Charlesworth Group
Huddersfield, England

THE VICTORIA HISTORY
OF THE
COUNTIES OF ENGLAND

EDITED BY A.J.FLETCHER

DIEU ET MON DROIT

THE UNIVERSITY OF LONDON
INSTITUTE OF
HISTORICAL RESEARCH

INSCRIBED TO THE

MEMORY OF HER LATE MAJESTY

QUEEN VICTORIA

WHO GRACIOUSLY GAVE THE TITLE TO

AND ACCEPTED THE DEDICATION

OF THIS HISTORY

A HISTORY OF THE COUNTY OF

YORK

EAST RIDING

EDITED BY G. H. R. KENT

VOLUME VII

HOLDERNESS WAPENTAKE
MIDDLE AND NORTH DIVISIONS

PUBLISHED FOR

THE INSTITUTE OF HISTORICAL RESEARCH

BY

OXFORD UNIVERSITY PRESS

2002

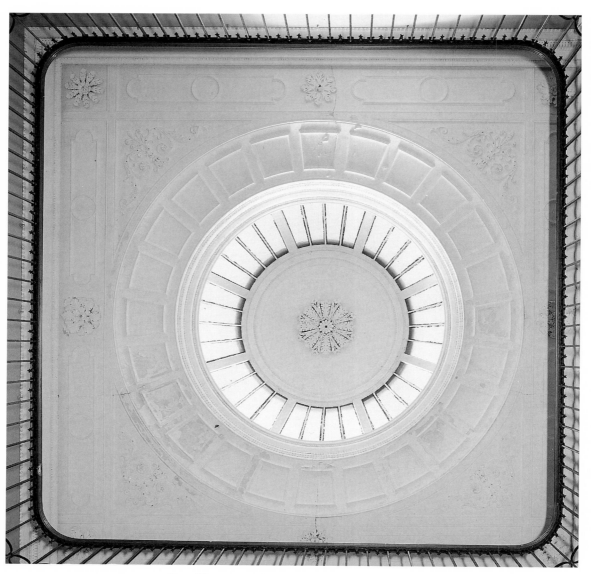

RISE HALL, LOOKING UP INNER STAIRCASE HALL

CONTENTS OF VOLUME SEVEN

LIST OF PLATES

LIST OF TEXT FIGURES

xi

LIST OF MAPS

The maps were drafted by the authors of the respective articles; except for those on pp. 00, which are by Catherine Pyke, they were all drawn by K. J. Wass. The basic framework of most of the maps is taken from the Ordnance Survey 6-inch map of *c.* 1850; the sources, which sometimes also include the 6-inch map, are otherwise given below. The maps are listed below in the order in which they appear in the volume, not in one alphabetical sequence; parish names are indicated by the use of capitals, and maps of parts of parishes have been indented.

LIST OF MAPS

EDITORIAL NOTE

The Victoria History of the County of York will eventually comprise five distinct sets, of which three, those treating the whole shire generally, the North Riding, and the city of York, are complete. That for the West Riding has yet to be started. The East Riding set, of which this volume is a part, is in progress. Those who wish to learn more of the structure, aims, and progress of the History as a whole may consult the *General Introduction* (1970) and *Supplement* (1990). The present volume deals with the history of much of Holderness wapentake, completing the survey of that part of the Riding begun in volume V of the East Riding series.

Dr. K. J. Allison, the county editor for the East Riding, retired in 1990 and was succeeded by the present editor, Dr. G. H. R. Kent, formerly assistant editor. Between 1991 and 1994 Dr. John Walker served as assistant editor, and Dr. T. N. Cooper held the post jointly with that of lecturer in the Department of History at Hull University for three years from 1996 to 1999. Central editing of the volume was done by Professor C. R. Elrington and his successor as General Editor, Dr. C. R. J. Currie, both of whom have introduced various changes in the arrangement and presentation of the material.

Thanks are due to many other people in connection with this volume. Dr. David Connell of the Burton Constable Foundation was enthusiastic and indefatigable in his support during the lengthy investigation of the building history of Burton Constable Hall, and Mr. John Chichester-Constable and his daughter, Mrs. Rodrica Straker, patiently answered questions about the family's estate in Holderness. Other owners, who made records available and allowed their houses to be visited and photographed, included Mr. Oliver Marriott of Grimston Garth, Mr. Rupert Russell of Wassand Hall, and Mr. Hugh Bethell at Rise. Mr. Bethell's agent, Mr. Andrew Johnson, and Mrs. A. Dyson at the estate office at Rise Park were especially helpful. Dr. J. E. Crowther, Mr. and Mrs. M. Sewell, Mr. and Mrs. J. Gelsthorpe, and Dr. J. E. S. Walker helped with the account of Hornsea, Mr. P. Butler with that of Garton, and Mr. and Mrs. R. E. Walgate of Scarborough with Swine. Professor D. M. Woodward kindly supplied information about Trinity House, Hull, and its holdings in Holderness. Further afield, the duke of Rutland, the marquess of Exeter and Lady Victoria Leatham, and the earl of Shaftesbury kindly allowed access to records kept respectively at Belvoir castle near Grantham, Burghley House near Stamford, and St. Giles's House at Wimborne in Dorset. All of those mentioned above, together with many named in the footnotes, are thanked most sincerely for their invaluable help.

The illustration of the volume was facilitated by a joint undertaking in the late 1990s by the Victoria County History and the Royal Commission on Historical Monuments, English Heritage from 1997, to improve the coverage of the East Riding in the National Monuments Record at Swindon. Special thanks are due in this respect to Bob Skingle, English Heritage's photographer in York, and to the owners of buildings recorded. Mr. Ben Chapman of Withernsea has also generously allowed the use of postcards from the Chapman Social History Archive. The expansion in the illustration of the volume is due largely to the Architectural Editor, Ms. Elizabeth Williamson, whose encouragement and assistance is gratefully acknowledged.

A final debt is to the public bodies and their staffs, without whom the history could not have been written. The financial support established by the former East Riding county council before its abolition in 1974, and recently continued by its successor, the East Riding of Yorkshire council, is gratefully acknowledged, together with the recent contribution, financial and otherwise, of the University of Hull. Both bodies have assisted the project in other ways. The archive and library services provided at Beverley by the council and its predecessors have contributed hugely to the volume, while much material has been made available from the archives collection in the Brynmor Jones Library at the university. Particular thanks are due to the former county archivist, Mr. Keith Holt, his assistant, Mrs. C. A. Boddington, and to Mrs. Helen Clark and the searchroom staff; to Ms. Pamela Martin, Mrs. Jenny Stanley, and the staff at Beverley Reference Library, and at the university to Mr. Brian Dyson and Ms. Helen Roberts. The staffs at the other repositories much used for the History, the Borthwick Institute of Historical Research at York and the Public Record Office in London, and the former Holderness Borough council and its officers, are also warmly thanked for their assistance.

LIST OF CLASSES OF DOCUMENTS
IN THE PUBLIC RECORD OFFICE

USED IN THIS VOLUME
WITH THEIR CLASS NUMBERS

CHANCERY

		Proceedings
C	1	Early
C	2	Series I
C	3	Series II
C	5	Six Clerks Series, Bridges
C	44	Common Law Pleadings, Tower Series
C	54	Close Rolls
C	60	Fine Rolls
C	66	Patent Rolls
C	78	Decree Rolls
C	94	Survey of Church Livings

		Inquisitions Post Mortem
C	133	Series I, Edw. I
C	134	Edw. II
C	135	Edw. III
C	138	Hen. V
C	139	Hen. VI
C	140	Edw. IV
C	141	Ric. III
C	142	Series II
C	143	Inquisitions ad quod damnum

COURT OF COMMON PLEAS

		Feet of Fines
CP 25(1)		Series I
CP 25(2)		Series II
CP 40		De Banco Rolls
CP 43		Recovery Rolls

CROWN ESTATE COMMISSIONERS

CRES 35	Files
CRES 38	Title Deeds
CRES 39	Surveys and other records

EXCHEQUER

King's Remembrancer

E 123	Entry Books of Decrees and Orders, Series I
E 126	Entry Books of Decrees and Orders, Series IV
E 134	Depositions taken by Commission
E 142	Ancient Extents
E 150	Inquisitions post mortem, Series II
E 178	Special Commissions of Inquiry
E 179	Subsidy Rolls, etc.

Augmentation Office

E 303	Conventual Leases
E 309	Enrolments of Leases
E 310	Particulars for Leases
E 311	Transcripts of Leases
E 315	Miscellaneous Books
E 317	Parliamentary Surveys
E 318	Particulars for Grants

Pipe Office

E 367	Particulars and Warrants for Crown Leases

MINISTRY OF EDUCATION

ED 7	Public Elementary Schools, Preliminary Statements
ED 49	Elementary Education Endowment Files

HOME OFFICE

	Various
HO 67	Acreage Returns
HO 107	Population Returns
HO 129	Ecclesiastical Returns

RECORDS OF JUSTICES ITINERANT

JUST 1	Eyre Rolls, Assize Rolls, etc.

COURT OF KING'S BENCH

KB 138	Writs and Returns

EXCHEQUER

Office of the Auditors of Land Revenue

LR 2	Miscellaneous Books
LR 4	Accounts (Woods)

OFFICE OF LAND REVENUE

LRRO 1	Maps and Plans

MAPS AND PLANS

MPE 1	Maps and plans from Office of Land Revenue
MPI 1	Maps and plans from Crown Estate Commissioners' records

MINISTRY OF TRANSPORT

MT 10	Board of Trade Harbour Department: Correspondence and Papers

COURT OF REQUESTS

REQ 2	Proceedings

GENERAL REGISTER OFFICE

RG 6	Society of Friends' Registers and Certificates

	Census Returns
RG 9	1861
RG 10	1871
RG 11	1881
RG 12	1891
RG 31	Places of Religious Worship Returns

SPECIAL COLLECTIONS

SC 2	Court Rolls
SC 6	Ministers' and Receivers' Accounts
SC 11	Rentals and Surveys, rolls
SC 12	Rentals and Surveys, portfolios

COURT OF STAR CHAMBER

STAC 4	Proceedings

STATE PAPER OFFICE

SP 46	Supplementary volumes

NOTE ON ABBREVIATIONS

Among the abbreviations and short titles used the following may require elucidation:

abp.	archbishop
acct.	account
Acreage Returns, 1905	Board of Agriculture, Acreage Returns of 1905, from a MS. copy in possession of the Editor, Victoria History of the East Riding
Acts of P.C.	*Acts of the Privy Council of England* (H.M.S.O. 1890–1964)
Add. Ch., MS.	Additional Charter, Manuscript
App.	Appendix
Arch.	Archaeological
Aveling, *Post Reformation Catholicism*	H. Aveling, *Post Reformation Catholicism in East Yorkshire, 1558–1790* (East Yorkshire Local History Series, xi)
B.I.H.R.	University of York, Borthwick Institute of Historical Research
B.L.	British Library (used in references to documents transferred from the British Museum)
Baines, *Hist. Yorks.* (1823)	E. Baines, *History, Directory and Gazetteer of the County of York*, volume ii, East and North Ridings
Beverley Chapter Act Bk. i–ii	*Memorials of Beverley Minster: the Chapter Act Book of the Collegiate Church of St. John of Beverley, 1286–1347* (Surtees Society, vols. xcviii, cviii)
Bd. of Educ., List 21	*Board of Education, Public Elementary Schools, and Certified Efficient Schools in England* (1908–38)
Boulter, 'Ch. Bells'	W. C. Boulter, 'Inscriptions on the Church Bells of the East Riding', *Yorkshire Archaeological Journal*, volume ii (1873)
Bridlington Chart. ed. W. T. Lancaster	*Abstracts of the Charters and other documents contained in the Chartulary of the Priory of Bridlington* (1912)
Bulmer, *Dir. E. Yorks.* (1892)	T. Bulmer & Co., *History, Topography and Directory of East Yorkshire*
Cal. Chart. R.	*Calendar of the Charter Rolls preserved in the Public Record Office* (H.M.S.O. 1903–27)
Cal. Close	*Calendar of the Close Rolls preserved in the Public Record Office* (H.M.S.O. 1892–1963)
Cal. Fine R.	*Calendar of the Fine Rolls preserved in the Public Record Office* (H.M.S.O. 1911–62)
Cal. Inq. Misc.	*Calendar of Inquisitions Miscellaneous (Chancery) preserved in the Public Record Office* (H.M.S.O. 1916–68)
Cal. Inq. p.m.	*Calendar of Inquisitions post mortem preserved in the Public Record Office* (H.M.S.O. 1904–95)
Cal. Inq. p.m. Hen. VII	*Calendar of Inquisitions post mortem, Henry VII* (H.M.S.O. 1898–1955)
Cal. Pat.	*Calendar of the Patent Rolls preserved in the Public Record Office* (H.M.S.O. 1891–1986)
Cal. S.P. Dom.	*Calendar of State Papers, Domestic Series* (H.M.S.O. 1856–1972)
ch.	church
Char. Com.	Charity Commission
Chron. de Melsa	*Chronica monasterii de Melsa*, ed. E. A. Bond (Rolls Series xliii, 1866–8)
Close R.	*Close Rolls of the Reign of Henry III preserved in the Public Record Office* (H.M.S.O. 1902–75)
Coll.	College
Com.	Commission, Commissioners
Complete Peerage	G. E. C[ockayne] and others, *Complete Peerage* (2nd. edn. 1810–59)
Compton Census, ed. Whiteman	*Compton Census of 1676: a critical edition*, ed. A. Whiteman (British Academy Records of Social and Economic History, new ser. x, 1986)
Crockford	*Crockford's Clerical Directory*
ct.	court
D.N.B.	*Dictionary of National Biography*
Directories	*Post Office* (later *Kelly's*) *Directory of Yorkshire: North and East Ridings with the City of York* (1872) and later editions; and see entries under Baines, Bulmer, *Slater's*, and White
Dugdale, *Mon.*	W. Dugdale, *Monasticum Anglicanum*, ed. J. Caley and others (6 vols. 1817–30)
E.R.A.O.	East Riding of Yorkshire Archive Office, formerly Humberside Archive Office, Beverley

NOTE ON ABBREVIATIONS

E.Y.C.	*Early Yorkshire Charters*, vols. i– iii, ed. W. Farrer (1914–16); vols. iv–xii, ed. Sir Charles Clay (Yorkshire Archaeological Society, Record Series, Extra Series, 1935–65)
Educ. Enq. Abstract	*Abstract of Answers and Returns relative to the State of Education in England*, H.C. 62 (1835), xliii
Educ. of Poor Digest	*Digest of Returns to the Select Committee on the Education of the Poor*, H.C. 224 (1819), ix (2)
English, *Holderness*	B. English, *The Lords of Holderness, 1086–1260* (1979)
Feud. Aids	*Inquisitions and Assessments relating to Feudal Aids preserved in the Public Record Office* (H.M.S.O. 1899–1920)
Geol. Surv.	Geological Survey
H.M.S.O.	Her (His) Majesty's Stationery Office
H.U.L.	Archives in the Brynmor Jones Library, University of Hull
Hearth Tax	*Yorkshire Hearth Tax Returns* (Hull University, Studies in Regional and Local History, no. 7, 1991)
Herring's Visit. i–v	*Archbishop Herring's Visitation Returns, 1743* (Yorkshire Archaeological Society, Record Series, vols. lxxi, lxxii, lxxv, lxxvii, lxxix)
Hist. MSS. Com.	Royal Commission on Historical Monuments
Hodgson, *Q.A.B.*	C. Hodgson, *Queen Anne's Bounty* (2nd edition, 1845, with supplement, 1864)
Inventories of Ch. Goods	*Inventories of Church Goods* (Surtees Society, volume xcvii)
L. & P. Hen. VIII	*Letters and Papers, Foreign and Domestic, of the Reign of Henry VIII* (H.M.S.O. 1862–1932)
Lawrance, 'Clergy List'	N. A. H. Lawrance, TS. list of beneficed clergy in Holderness wapentake up to the Restoration, in the archives in the Brynmor Jones Library, University of Hull
Lond. Gaz.	*London Gazette*
med.	medieval
O.N.S.	Office of National Statistics, Birkdale (formerly General Register Office, later Office of Population Censuses and Surveys)
Orange, 'Meaux Cart.'	G. V. Orange, 'Cartulary of Meaux [British Library, Lansdowne MS. 424]: a critical edition' (Hull University Ph.D. thesis, 1965)
P.N. Yorks. E.R. (E.P.N.S.)	*The Place-names of the East Riding of Yorkshire and York* (English Place-name Society volume xiv, 1937)
P.R.O.	Public Record Office
par.	parish
parl.	parliament
Pevsner, *Yorks. E.R.*	N. Pevsner, *The Buildings of England: Yorkshire: York and the East Riding* (1972)
Pevsner and Neave, *Yorks. E.R.*	N. Pevsner and David Neave, *The Buildings of England: Yorkshire: York and the East Riding* (2nd edn., 1995)
Plac. de Quo Warr. (Rec. Com.)	*Placita de Quo Warranto in Curia Receptae Scaccarii Westm. asservata*, ed. W. Illingworth and J. Caley (Record Commission, 1818)
Poor Law Abstract, 1804	*Abstract of Returns relative to the Expense and Maintenance of the Poor*, H.C. 175 (1803–4), xiii
Poor Law Abstract, 1818	*Abstract of Returns relative to the Expense and Maintenance of the Poor*, H.C. 82 (1818), xix
Popham, 'Wassand Estate'	J. Popham, 'Wassand Estate', volume 3 (part of a landscape management plan, copy in E.R.A.O.)
Poulson, *Holderness*	G. Poulson, *The History and Antiquities of the Seigniory of Holderness* (2 volumes, 1840–1)
Proc.	*Proceedings*
R.C.H.M. *Nonconf. Chapels*	Royal Commission on Historical Monuments, *Inventory of nonconformist chapels and meeting-houses in the north of England* (H.M.S.O. 1994)
R.D.B.	The former Registry of Deeds, Beverley, now part of the East Riding of Yorkshire Archive Office
Rec.	Record(s)
Reg. Corbridge, i–ii	*Register of Thomas Corbridge* (Surtees Society, volumes cxxxviii, cxli)
Reg. Giffard	*Register of Walter Giffard* (Surtees Society, volume cix)
Reg. Gray	*Register, or Rolls, of Walter Gray* (Surtees Society, volume lvi)
Reg. Greenfield, i–v	*Register of William Greenfield* (Surtees Society, volumes cxlv, cxlix, cli, clii, cliii)
Reg. Langley, ii	*Register of Thomas Langley, bishop of Durham* (Surtees Society, volume clxvi)
Reg. Romeyn, i–ii	*Registers of John le Romeyn and Henry of Newark* (Surtees Society, volumes cxxiii, cxxviii)
Rep.	*Report*
9th Rep. Com. Char.	*Report of the Commissioners for Inquiry concerning certain Charities in England and Wales*, H.C. 258 (1823), ix
Rep. Com. Eccl. Revenues	*Report of the Commissioners appointed to Inquire into the Ecclesiastical Revenues of England and Wales* [67], H.C. (1835), xxii

NOTE ON ABBREVIATIONS

3rd Rep. Poor Law Com.	*3rd Annual Report of the Poor Law Commissioners for England and Wales*, H.C. 546 (1837), xxxi
Returns relating to Elem. Educ.	*Returns relating to Elementary Education*, H.C. 201 (1871), lv
Review of Char. *Rep.*	Humberside County Review of Charities, 1978–80, *Report* of the Review Co-ordinator to Humberside County Council
Rolls Ser.	Rolls Series
Rot. Hund. (Rec. Com.)	*Rotuli Hundredorum temp. Hen. III & Edw. I*, ed. W. Illingworth and J. Caley (Record Commission, 1812–18)
Shaftesbury MSS.	Manuscripts of the earl of Shaftesbury at St. Giles' House, Wimborne St. Giles, Dorset
Sheahan and Whellan, *Hist. York & E.R.*	J. J. Sheahan and T. Whellan, *History and Topography of the City of York, the Ainsty Wapentake, and the East Riding of Yorkshire*, volume ii, East Riding (1856)
Slater's Royal Nat. Com. Dir. Yorks.	*Slater's Royal National Commercial Directory of the County of Yorkshire* (1864 and 1887 editions)
Soc.	Society
T.E.R.A.S.	*Transactions of the East Riding Antiquarian Society*
Tax. Eccl. (Rec. Com.)	*Taxatio Ecclesiastica Angliae et Walliae auctoritate P. Nicholai IV circa A.D. 1291*, ed. S. Ayscough and J. Caley (Record Commission, 1802)
Test Ebor. i–vi	*Testamenta Eboracensia* (Surtees Society, volumes iv, xxx, xlv, liii, lxxix, cvi)
Trans.	*Transactions*
V.C.H.	*Victoria County History*
Valor Eccl. (Rec. Com.)	*Valor Ecclesiasticus temp. Hen. VIII auctoritate regia institutus*, ed. J. Caley and J. Hunter (Record Commission, 1810–34)
Visit.	*Visitation*
W.Y.A.S.	*West Yorkshire Archive Service, Bradford*
White, *Dir. E. & N.R. Yorks.* (1840)	W. White, *History, Gazetteer and Directory of the East and North Ridings of Yorkshire* (1840)
White, *Dir. Hull & York* (1846)	F. White & Co., *General Directory of Kingston-upon-Hull and the City of York* (1846)
White, *Dir. Hull & York* (1858)	F. White & Co., *General Directory and Topography of Kingston-upon-Hull and the City of York* (1858)
Y.A.J.	*Yorkshire Archaeological Journal*
Y.A.S.	Yorkshire Archaeological Society, Leeds
Yorks. Ch. Plate	*Yorkshire Church Plate*, begun by T. M. Fallow, completed and edited by H. B. McCall, Yorkshire Archaeological Society Publications, Extra Series, volume i (1912)
Yorks. Chantry Surv. ii	*The Certificates of the Commissioners appointed to survey the Chantries, Guilds, Hospitals, etc. in the County of York*, ii (Surtees Society, volume xcii)
Yorks. Deeds, i–x	*Yorkshire Deeds* (Yorkshire Archaeological Society, Record Series, volumes xxxix, l, lxiii, lxv, lxix, lxxvi, lxxxiii, cii, cxi, cxx)
Yorks. Fines, i–iv	*Feet of Fines of the Tudor Period* (Yorkshire Archaeological Society, Record Series, volumes ii, v, vii, viii)
Yorks. Fines, 1218–31; 1232–46; 1246–72; 1272–1300, 1300–14; 1327–47; 1347–77; 1603–14; 1614–25	*Feet of Fines* (Yorkshire Archaeological Society, Record Series, volumes lxii, lxvii, lxxxii, cxxi, cxxvii, xlii, lii, liii, lviii)
Yorks. Hund. and Quo Warr. R. 1274–94	*Yorkshire Hundred and Quo Warranto Rolls 1274–94* (Yorkshire Archaeological Society, Record Series, volume cli)
Yorks. Inq. i–iv; *Hen. IV–V*	*Yorkshire Inquisitions* (Yorkshire Archaeological Society, Record Series, volumes xii, xxiii, xxxi, xxxvii, lix)

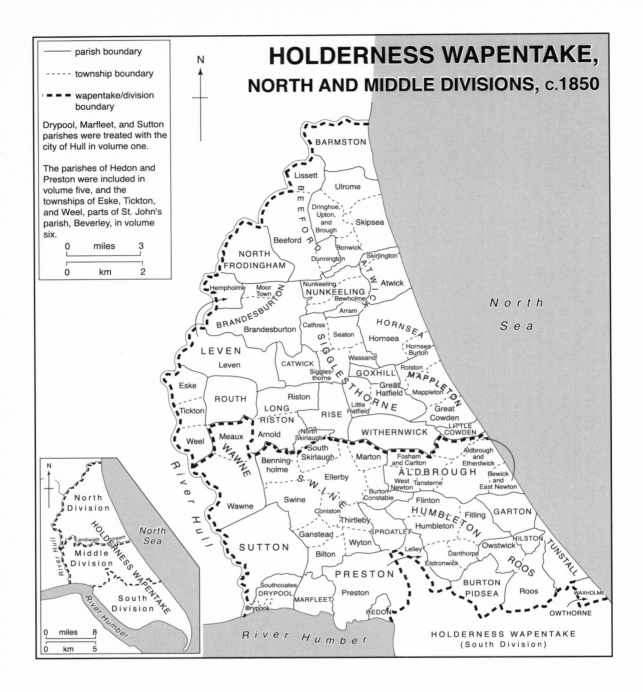

HOLDERNESS WAPENTAKE,
NORTH AND MIDDLE DIVISIONS, c.1850

— parish boundary

- - - township boundary

■ ■ ■ wapentake/division boundary

Drypool, Marfleet, and Sutton parishes were treated with the city of Hull in volume one.

The parishes of Hedon and Preston were included in volume five, and the townships of Eske, Tickton, and Weel, parts of St. John's parish, Beverley, in volume six.

0 miles 3

0 km 2

N

North Sea

BARMSTON

Lissett

Ulrome

Dringhoe, Upton, and Brough

Skipsea

Beeford

Bonwick

Dunnington

Skirlington

BEMFORD

NORTH FRODINGHAM

Hempholme

Moor Town

Nunkeeling

NUNKEELING

Bewholme

Atwick

ATWICK

BRANDESBURTON

Arram

Brandesburton

Catfoss

HORNSEA

LEVEN

Seaton

Hornsea

Hornsea Burton

Leven

Wassand

SIGGLESTHORNE

Siggles-thorne

CATWICK

GOXHILL

Rolston

MAPPLETON

Eske

ROUTH

Riston

Great Hatfield

Mappleton

Tickton

LONG RISTON

RISE

Little Hatfield

Great Cowden

Weel

Meaux

Arnold

North Skirlaugh

WITHERNWICK

LITTLE COWDEN

WAWNE

South Skirlaugh

Marton

Fosham and Carlton

Aldbrough and Etherdwick

Benning-holme

SWINE

Ellerby

ALDBROUGH

Bewick and East Newton

West Newton

Tansterne

Wawne

Swine

Coniston

Burton Constable

Flinton

HUMBLETON

Fitling

GARTON

Thirtleby

Humbleton

SPROATLEY

HILSTON

SUTTON

Ganstead

Wyton

Lelley

Danthorpe

Owstwick

ROOS

TUNSTALL

Bilton

Elstronwick

PRESTON

BURTON PIDSEA

Roos

WAXHOLME

Southcoates

DRYPOOL

MARFLEET

Preston

OWTHORNE

Drypool

HEDON

HOLDERNESS WAPENTAKE
(South Division)

River Humber

North Sea

N

North Division

HOLDERNESS WAPENTAKE

River Hull

Lambwath stream

Middle Division

South Division

River Humber

0 miles 8

0 km 5

xx

HOLDERNESS WAPENTAKE
(Middle and North Divisions)

AN account of the former wapentake has been given in an earlier volume.[1] The history of the whole of South division, including Waxholme township, which was in Middle division but part of Owthorne parish, together with that of Hedon and Preston from Middle division, has similarly been dealt with elsewhere.[2] Extensions to the boundaries of the borough of Kingston upon Hull in the 19th and 20th centuries have taken in, from Middle division, the whole of Drypool and Marfleet parishes, most of Sutton on Hull, and parts of Bilton and Wawne. The history of the first three of those parishes has accordingly been treated along with that of the rest of the city of Hull.[3] Eske township, in North division, has been dealt with as part of the borough and liberties of Beverley.[4] The present volume covers the rest of Middle and North divisions.

The North and Middle divisions shared with the other part of the wapentake an undulating plain bounded on the east by the North Sea. The western boundary of the two divisions was the river Hull and its tributaries, a stream flowing east to the sea marked the northern limit of the wapentake, and other watercourses draining west and south-west to the Hull and Humber defined its internal divisions. Much of the land lies between 10 and 20 m. above sea level, but the ground at Nunkeeling reaches 30 m. and in the Hull valley and the flat margins of the Humber estuary it scarcely exceeds sea level. Most of the area is covered with glacial deposits, chiefly boulder clay but also locally important concentrations of sand and gravel.

Alterations to the natural drainage were made by monastic houses and lay lords in the Middle Ages, and later there were piecemeal attempts to improve the area's poor drainage, but it was not until the formation of drainage boards in the later 18th century that flooding began to be controlled. The improvement finally enabled the remaining wastes to be added to the farm land, as well as causing the virtual disappearance of one of Holderness's characteristic features, its meres, permanent but fluctuating lakes of which only that at Hornsea now remains.

Several of the parishes were very large and contained a number of settlements, the largest being Swine, which in the 19th century, after earlier losses to adjoining places, contained nearly 15,000 a. divided between thirteen townships. The area also includes the smallest parish in the wapentake, Goxhill with just over 800 a. The differences may reflect landownership before the Conquest, as well as possible variations in the number of churches built by early lords on their holdings. There is no apparent explanation in the pattern of landownership which obtained in the larger parishes in the mid 11th century. Aldbrough, later of 6,400 a., thus comprised, besides Ulf's manor, sokeland belonging to Morkar's manors of Kilnsea and Easington, while Humbleton, of a similar size, was a dependency of Morkar's manors of Kilnsea and Withernsea and the archbishop of York's manor of Swine.

[1] *V.C.H. Yorks. E.R.* v. 1–5.
[2] Ibid. v, *passim.*
[3] Ibid. i. 6–8 and *passim.*
[4] Ibid. vi. 278–81.

After the Conquest there were two chief holdings, those of the archbishop of York and the count of Aumale. The latter lordship passed to the Crown and then eventually, in the 16th century, to the Constable family of Halsham in south Holderness and Burton Constable, which later held much land in Holderness, including a compact estate of several thousand acres in and around Burton Constable. In the Middle Ages large landowners in the area included several religious bodies, notably the abbeys of Meaux and Thornton, in Lincolnshire, foundations of William le Gros, count of Aumale, and the priories of Swine, Nunkeeling, and Bridlington. The connection with Lincolnshire, evident in the holdings of Aumale tenants like the Goxhills of Sproatley, may have been reinforced by Thornton's long possession of the manors of Humbleton and Garton and its other estates in Holderness. Much of the land formerly belonging to religious bodies, as well as some otherwise held by the Crown, was sold in the 16th and 17th centuries. The Bethells, whose interest in the area resulted from their position as Crown officers, built up an extensive estate in North and Middle Holderness from the 16th century: Rise manor was leased and, in the 17th century, bought, and other purchases and acquisitions by marriage enlarged the family's holding there and in many other places. By the mid 19th century the estate in Holderness comprised almost 14,000 a., with much land in Riston and Arnold, Catfoss, Ellerby, and Leven parish, where the manor formerly belonging to Beverley minster had been bought in the 18th century. A smaller estate in Sigglesthorne and Hornsea parishes was created by another family called Constable, later the Strickland-Constables, a local gentry family who bought Wassand manor in the 16th century, and later acquired much of Seaton; by the 20th century the estate comprised some 2,000 a. in Wassand, Seaton, and Hornsea, besides Hornsea mere. The Thompsons of Scarborough, purchasers of Thornton abbey's manor of Humbleton in the 17th century, and their heirs, the Hothams, created an estate of c. 2,500 a. in that parish, while from the 18th century the Kirkbys of Hull built up another compact estate based on Roos manor which passed to their heirs, the Sykes of Sledmere. The estate around Wassand Hall remains largely intact, but sales, especially in the 20th century, have extinguished or reduced the other large holdings. The Chichester-Constables, successors to the Constables, remain as landowners in Holderness, but part of Burton Constable has lately been given to a trust to ensure the survival of the Hall and park there. The decline of the old estates has to some extent been accompanied by the creation of large farming concerns managing considerable areas with few farms.

North and Middle Holderness remains a predominantly rural area of nucleated settlement in villages and hamlets. While several of the larger villages have had some commercial pretensions, only one settlement developed into a market town, that of Hornsea, formerly belonging to St. Mary's abbey, York. The settlements of the area were usually sited on the higher ground, often on the better-drained sand and gravel deposits, although there is evidence for earlier, prehistoric lake-dwelling at Ulrome. The common plan was a long street-village, sometimes with discrete ends. The number of medieval villages and hamlets has been reduced, some places, like Monkwith, in Tunstall, and Cleeton, in Skipsea, being eroded by the sea, and others, like the subsidiary settlements of Ellerby township, in Swine, being reduced to one or two farmhouses. Conversely, the opening of a railway from Hull in 1864 accelerated the development of Hornsea, both as a coastal resort and seaside suburb of Hull, besides creating the hamlet of New

Ellerby close to one of the stations. Many of the other settlements also grew and changed their character in the 19th and especially the 20th century, to a great extent losing their connection with agriculture and becoming enlarged dormitory settlements of the city of Hull and the towns of Beverley, Bridlington, and Driffield. In Wawne and Bilton, in Swine, the process has gone further, and parts of those places have been taken into the city of Hull and covered with houses.

Brick is the predominant building material, but most of the churches, and some domestic and farm buildings, are of stone, either imported limestone or boulders from the fields and shore. At least one house, at Beeford, represents an earlier building tradition, being constructed of mud. The churches include one of more than local significance, the Perpendicular chapel at Skirlaugh, and at Goxhill a charming Gothick building with early Victorian fittings. Noteworthy secular buildings in the area formerly included the Norman castle at Skipsea, the head place of the lordship of Holderness, now represented by impressive earthworks. Later buildings of note include Burton Constable Hall, the seat of the Constables, lords of Holderness, a medieval house which was largely rebuilt in the 16th century, and later remodelled in Classical and Jacobean-revival styles, and Grimston Garth, in Garton, a large, Gothick summer residence built near the cliff in the 18th century. Those houses, and that of the Bethells at Rise, stand in parks, and the woods there and close to Wassand Hall in Sigglesthorne provide a welcome variety in a landscape largely cleared of its old woodlands. On a smaller scale Italianate villas were put up at Woodhall in Ellerby and at Wyton, in Swine, in the earlier 19th century, and groups of houses were built or remodelled for the middle classes at Wyton and Burton Pidsea. At Swine the village and outlying farmhouses were rebuilt by the Crown in the 1860s, and there was similar building in other places dominated by a single landowner, among them Burton Constable, Rise, Wassand, and Wawne. Hornsea's role as in part a detached suburb of Hull was reflected in the urban, even metropolitan, style of its buildings from the later 19th century, and more recent building and lay-outs there and elswhere have diluted still further local characteristics in building.

Travel between settlements was difficult before the area was drained. Some of the medieval improvements to streams seem to have been prompted primarily by the need for better communication, and the Hull's importance for transporting goods was evident from the extension of the system in the 19th century by canals, including that at Leven. The chief roads running through North and Middle Holderness were those from Beverley and Hull to Bridlington, and from Hull to Aldbrough. Stretches of those roads were improved by turnpike trusts in the 18th and 19th centuries. Other roads run through the coastal settlements between Withernsea and Bridlington, and connect that route to the inland road to Bridlington. Otherwise the area is served by minor and field roads. A railway line linking Hull and Hornsea, and serving several villages between those places, was operated from 1864 to 1965.

The chief occupation of the area was for long agriculture, which remains significant but now employs only a fraction of the population. The inadequate drainage of much of Holderness caused large areas to be left unimproved as marshland, or carrs, and moors until comparatively recently. Though waste, the unimproved grounds contributed to the local economy, providing, besides rough grazing, fish, fowl, reeds for thatching, and crops of furze, or whins, for fuel. The abundance of grazing, notably in the south of the Hull valley, and the location there of the Cistercian houses of Meaux and Swine, may have made sheep-and dairy-farming more important in the Middle Ages than later.

Evidence for changes in land use and agricultural practice in Holderness are, on the whole, poorly documented. The extension of the farmed land into the waste in the 13th century is perhaps clearest in the immediate proximity of Meaux abbey in Wawne parish, and that house's records also document the later retreat from demesne farming. The inclosure of the open fields and other commonable lands, and the sometimes related conversion of tillage to pasture, was a lengthy process. Several places dominated by one landowner, whether a religious house, as at Nunkeeling and in the hamlets of Leven parish, or a lay lord like the Constables at Burton Constable, were apparently inclosed before the mid 16th century, and piecemeal inclosures at Little Cowden, in Mappleton, and other places were also reported in 1517. The sale of former monastic and other Crown estates in the 16th and 17th centuries prompted a rash of inclosures, some initiated presumably by purchasers like the Micklethwaites at Swine, who inclosed land there in the 1650s, and the Bethells, who inclosed Rise in 1660. At Wawne Sir Joseph Ashe, member of a London mercantile family, probably inclosed, as well as instigating an ambitious drainage scheme. There is good evidence for some twenty places in North and Middle Holderness being inclosed in whole or in part in the 17th century; the areas involved cannot always be determined, but at Brandesburton and Burshill over 3,000 a. were dealt with in the 1630s. Inclosures by agreement continued into the 18th century, the second of Flinton's inclosures dating from 1752. The lengthy process was completed in the later 18th and 19th century by inclosures under Acts of Parliament, but the proportion of land left to be dealt with was almost certainly less than in other parts of the riding. Of the c. 100,000 a. comprised in the area, only some 38,000 were then inclosed by Act. That the number of smaller tenants was reduced and holdings consolidated during the process is suggested at North Frodingham, inclosed in the early 19th century: one of the c. 55 allottees and his partners then received land for many newly-purchased holdings, and later the large village had only some 20 farms. After inclosure was completed, the area developed as a major producer of cereal crops; also significant in the 20th century was the intensive rearing of pigs and poultry.

There was little employment in the area unconnected with agriculture, but one or two local tradesmen at Burton Pidsea and Marton achieved wider renown in the 19th and 20th centuries as makers of agricultural machinery. Bricks were made from the local clay in small works in several parishes, and the extraction of sand and gravel expanded from small beginnings to large-scale working in the 20th century, most notably in Catwick and Brandesburton. Occupations for those living along the coast have included fishing from Hornsea, and the removal of gravel from the sea shore. More recently seasonal work has been provided by holiday makers on the caravan sites and leisure facilities which developed after the Second World War. Some small-scale industrial and commercial concerns have also made use of the sites of former airfields at Lissett in Beeford and Catfoss, in Sigglesthorne.

MIDDLE DIVISION

ALDBROUGH

THE village of Aldbrough lies 18 km. north-east of Hull and 2 km. from the sea, which forms the eastern parish boundary.[1] About 1 km. north is Little Cowden, which lost its church to the sea by the 17th century and was later associated for ecclesiastical and civil purposes with Aldbrough;[2] by the 19th century, however, Little Cowden formed a township with its larger neighbour Great Cowden, mostly in Mappleton parish, and its history is dealt with under Mappleton. The extensive ancient parish of Aldbrough included the hamlets of Bewick, Carlton, Etherdwick, Fosham, East Newton, West Newton, Ringbrough, and Tansterne. There may have been another settlement east of the village at Thorpe Garth, where land north of the farmhouse was called Old Garths in the 19th century.[3] Apart from East and West Newton, the lesser settlements may always have been small, and Carlton was reduced by inclosure, which by 1517 had resulted in the eviction of six inhabitants and the decay of a house.[4]

The names Aldbrough, Bewick, Etherdwick, Fosham, and Newton are Anglian, and Carlton and Tansterne Anglo-Scandinavian hybrids. Aldbrough means 'old stronghold', Bewick 'dairy farm near the bees', Carlton perhaps 'peasants' farms', and Etherdwick 'Ethelred's dairy farm'. Fosham, sometimes Fosham garth, meaning 'homestead on the ditch' probably alludes to Lambwath stream which forms much of the northern parish boundary and divides the North and Middle divisions of the wapentake. The precise meaning of Tansterne is uncertain but the name refers to a pool there. The name Ringbrough, also occasionally used with the suffix 'garth', may be an Anglian and Scandinavian hybrid and means 'circular stronghold'. From the 12th century the prefix 'East' was used to distinguish one of the Newtons, which was then and later also known as Newton next to Aldbrough, Aldbrough Newton, and Ringbrough Newton. The other Newton was named Newton Constable from the 13th century after its owners and West Newton from the 16th century. 'Totele' recorded in 1086 is believed to be the later Thorpe Garth; the name Thorpe, signifying hamlet, occurs from the 12th century, sometimes with the suffixes 'next to Aldbrough' or 'in Aldbrough', and may be Scandinavian.[5]

In 1852 the ancient parish of Aldbrough contained 6,398 a. (2,589 ha.), of which 2,544 a. (1,029 ha.) were in Aldbrough and Etherdwick township, 1,440 a. (583 ha.) in Bewick and East Newton township, 1,232 a. (498 ha.) in Fosham and Carlton township, 392 a. (159 ha.) in Tansterne township, and 792 a. (320 ha.) in West Newton hamlet. West Newton hamlet and the larger settlement of Burton Constable, in Swine, together formed the township of West Newton.[6] By 1871 the townships of Aldbrough and Etherdwick, Fosham and Carlton, and Tansterne were combined as Aldbrough township, and Bewick and East Newton was called East Newton township. In 1885 a detached area of East Newton township called Scarshaws was transferred to Withernwick.[7] The parish was also reduced by coastal erosion, up to 4 yd. a year being lost in the late 18th and 19th centuries.[8] The civil parishes, formerly townships, had been reordered by 1891, when Aldbrough had 4,904 a. (1,985 ha.) and East Newton 607 a. (246 ha.). In 1935 Aldbrough, then of 4,886 a. (1,977 ha.), and an unchanged East Newton were united to form a new Aldbrough civil parish, with a total area of 5,494 a. (2,223 ha.), and West Newton with Burton Constable civil parish, formerly West Newton township, was added to Marton to form Burton Constable civil parish.[9] By 1991 Aldbrough civil parish had been reduced to 2,178 ha. (5,382 a.).[10]

In 1377 there were 117 poll-tax payers at Aldbrough, 37 at East Newton and Ringbrough, 9 at Bewick, and 4 at Tansterne; Carlton, Fosham, and Thorpe presumably contributed to the Aldbrough figure. In 1672 Aldbrough village and East Newton had 57 houses assessed for hearth tax and 30 discharged, and 9 more were assessed at Carlton and Fosham. At West Newton and Burton Constable, in Swine, together there were 105 poll-tax payers in 1377 and 16 houses in 1672. Etherdwick was similarly taxed with Flinton, in Humbleton, 85 poll-tax payers being recorded in 1377 and 28 houses in 1672.[11] The parish was said to have 100 families in 1764.[12] The population of the parish, excluding East and West Newton, rose from 555 in 1801 to 802 in 1821 and 845 in 1841, before falling sharply in the later 19th century. Numbers recovered slowly from 680 in 1901 to 741 in 1931. East Newton had 24 inhabitants in 1801; numbers thereafter fluctuated, reaching 41 in 1841 and standing at 25 in 1931. After the union of Aldbrough and East Newton civil parishes the combined population increased slowly to 835 in 1961 but was 930 in 1971, 1,069 in 1981, and 1,339 in 1991, of whom 1,353 were usually resident. At West Newton and Burton

---

[1] This article was written in 1991.
[2] Below, local govt.; church.
[3] E.R.A.O., DDX/252/2.
[4] *Trans. R. Hist. S.* N.S. vii. 249.
[5] *P.N. Yorks. E.R.* (E.P.N.S.), 59–61; *V.C.H. Yorks.* ii. 266, 326; G. F. Jensen, *Scand. Settlement Names in Yorks.* 113, 119, 121, 136, 166.
[6] O.S. Map 6″, Yorks. CCXII, CCXIII, CCXXVIII (1855 edn.). The discrepancies in the sums result from rounding up.

[7] *Census*, 1871, 1891.
[8] T. Sheppard, *Lost Towns of Yorks. Coast*, 160–1; Poulson, *Holderness*, ii. 8.
[9] *Census*, 1891, 1931 (pt. ii); below, Swine, Burton Constable, intro.
[10] *Census*, 1991.
[11] P.R.O., E 179/202/60, mm. 36, 46, 52, 77, 84, 86; *Hearth Tax*, 60.
[12] B.I.H.R., V. 1764/Ret. 1, no. 13.

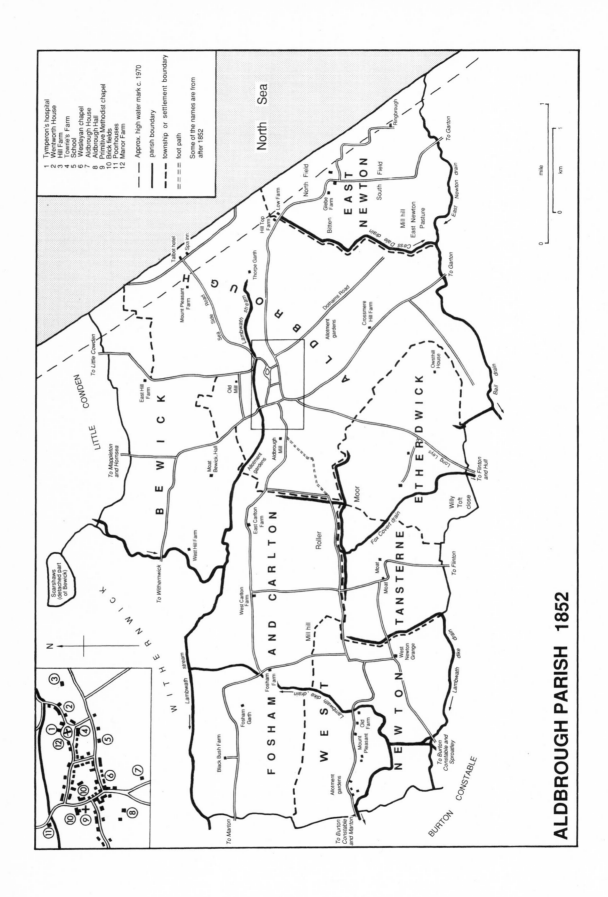

ALDBROUGH PARISH 1852

North Sea

Legend:
1 Tymperon's hospital
2 Wentworth House
3 Hill Farm
4 Towrie's Farm
5 School
6 Wesleyan chapel
7 Aldbrough House
8 Aldbrough Hall
9 Primitive Methodist chapel
10 Brick fields
11 Poorhouses
12 Manor Farm

— — — Approx. high water mark c. 1970
———— parish boundary
– – – – township or settlement boundary
═══ foot path

Some of the names are from after 1852

Constable the population rose from 172 in 1801 to 239 in 1851 but had fallen to 141 by 1931.[13]

The parish is largely on boulder clay and most of the ground lies between 7 m. and 15 m. above sea level.[14] Deposits of sand and gravel produce higher ground, notably in the north and on the coast, where the land exceeds 20 m. and ends in an unbroken line of steep cliffs. The village and most of the hamlets were sited on the higher ground, and sand and gravel has been extracted.[15] Lower alluvial land borders the main drains on the north-west and southern boundaries. The commonable lands at Aldbrough were inclosed in 1766 and those at East Newton in 1772; the other settlements were inclosed earlier, Etherdwick, and possibly Carlton, by agreement in the 17th century.

Aldbrough is drained chiefly by Lambwath stream and other drains flowing west from the coast towards the river Humber. The streams defining the southern boundary include that recorded as insufficient in 1367[16] and later represented by East Newton and Bail drains. 'Prestmare', 'Marsknooke', and several other field-names recorded at Aldbrough in 1616 suggest the former poor drainage of parts of the parish.[17] Land in the parish depended on Keyingham fleet for an outlet to the river: 16 a. at Aldbrough and 7 a. at Tansterne drained into the fleet in 1618,[18] and under the Keyingham Level Drainage Acts of 1772 and later[19] Lambwath stream, the southern boundary drains, and several cross drains were improved. After 1845 low ground assessed to the drainage included 80 a. at Aldbrough, 49 a. at East Newton, 25 a. at Etherdwick, 10 a. at Carlton, and 5 a. at Tansterne.[20] The drainage at Tansterne was aided by a wind pump by 1942.[21]

From Aldbrough village roads leading north-west to Mappleton and south-east to Garton have been upgraded and improved as parts of the Holderness coast road. In 1937 the road was straightened north of the village and Bail bridge carrying it over the southern boundary drain was widened.[22] Another road running south-west to Flinton has been incorporated in a principal road to Hull. Bridges carrying the Hull road were in disrepair in the mid 14th century, when the inhabitants of Etherdwick were among those held responsible.[23] Lesser roads from the village lead north-east to the shore, east to East Newton and Ringbrough, and west to Carlton, Fosham, Tansterne, and West Newton. That to East Newton was realigned, probably at the inclosure of East Newton in 1772, and a road to

Tansterne awarded in 1766 was later discontinued.[24]

ALDBROUGH village stands on a ridge of high ground which falls sharply to the north into the valley of Lambwath stream, and its church is further elevated by the circular mound on which it stands. Aldbrough has a linear plan comprising two parallel streets connected by cross lanes. The main street was formerly the northern one, comprising Church Street and North Street. Church Street, leading west from the church and broadening to form a triangular area in which a small green survives, was the market place. Much of the ground between Church Street and the southern street was unbuilt in the mid 18th century and may once have formed part of a larger green.[25] The northern street has, however, been regarded as the back street since the late 19th century.[26] The southern street comprises the broad High Street and an eastern continuation, called Chapel and Back Streets respectively in 1851. The busiest street is the westernmost cross lane, which forms part of the parish's principal road; it was called Johnson's Lane in the 18th century and later Hornsea Road. Already in the 18th century the village extended west beyond the main road along Carlton Lane, then West Lane, and there was some infilling and extension of the village by the mid 19th century.[27] Many more houses were added in the village and on its western and southern sides in the mid and late 20th century. The new housing included c. 130 council houses, mostly in the Headlands Drive and Wentworth Grove estates, built in the 1950s and 1960s respectively.[28] Houses were later built on ground excavated for brickmaking on either side of Hornsea Road, those on the west side standing well below the main road and Carlton Lane. The district council built a sewage works on Headland Road c. 1951, and several pumping stations and a sewage works on Carlton Lane were added c. 1970.[29] The tradition that there was a castle at Aldbrough is based on a misreading of a charter of 1115, the castle referred to there being almost certainly that of Skipsea. Castle hill was named in the mid 19th century, and Castle Park, a housing estate recently built in 1991, continues the tradition.[30]

The village buildings date mostly from the 19th and 20th centuries and include a few farmhouses. Almost all are of brick, presumably the result of brickmaking in the village;[31] boulder construction is found mostly in cottage foot-

[13] V.C.H. Yorks. iii. 493; Census, 1911–91.
[14] Geol. Surv. Map 1", drift, sheet 73 (1909 edn.).
[15] O.S. Map 6", Yorks. CCXIII (1855 edn.); O.S. Map 1/2,500, Yorks. CCXII. 12 (1891 edn.).
[16] Poulson, Holderness, i. 124.
[17] P.R.O., E 178/4870.
[18] E.R.A.O., DDCC/54/53.
[19] V.C.H. Yorks. E.R. v. 55–7.
[20] E.R.A.O., DDPK/3/8; cf. O.S. Map 6", Yorks. CCXII, CCXIII, CCXXVIII (1855 and later edns.).
[21] R.D.B., 649/239/205.
[22] Ibid. 584/604/466; E.R.C.C. Mins. 1936–7, 158, 268; 1937–8, 159.
[23] Public Works in Med. Law, ii (Selden Soc. xl), p. 312.
[24] E.R.A.O., IA. Aldbrough; O.S. Map 6", Yorks.

CCXII (1855 edn.).
[25] Market Place was named in 1827: H.U.L., DDCV(2)/62/51. For 18th-cent. references in this para., E.R.A.O., IA. Aldbrough.
[26] P.R.O., HO 107/2365; O.S. Map 1/2,500, Yorks. CCXIII. 9 (1891 edn.); inf. from Mr. R. N. Jackson, Aldbrough, 1991.
[27] O.S. Map 6", Yorks. CCXIII (1855 edn.).
[28] R.D.B., 585/103/80; 750/111/94; 875/651/476; 910/444/379; 1026/328/293; 1393/344/310; 1398/534/462.
[29] Ibid. 875/651/476; 1534/251/220; 1602/311/269; 1607/294/264; 1635/294/240.
[30] E.Y.C. iii, pp. 30–2; Poulson, Holderness, ii. 3, 5, 24; below, church; O.S. Map 6", Yorks. CCXIII (1855 edn.).
[31] Below, econ. hist.

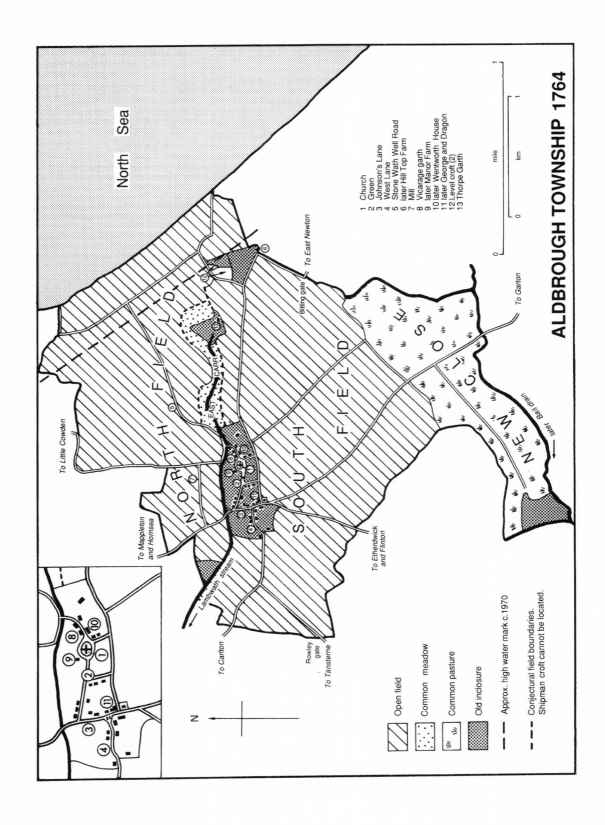

North Sea

ALDBROUGH TOWNSHIP 1764

1 Church
2 Green
3 Johnson's Lane
4 West Lane
5 Stone Wath Well Road
6 later Hill Top Farm
7 Mill
8 Vicarage garth
9 later Manor Farm
10 later Wentworth House
11 later George and Dragon
12 Level croft (2)
13 Thorpe Garth

mile
km

To East Newton

Bitting gate

To Garton

later Bail drain

NORTH FIELD

SOUTH FIELD

NEWCOMMON

CARR

EAST

To Little Cowden

To Mappleton
and Hornsea

To Etherdwick
and Flinton

Lambwrath stream

To Carlton

Rowley
gate

To Tansterne

N

Open field
Common meadow
Common pasture
Old inclosure

Approx. high water mark c.1970

Conjectural field boundaries.
Shipman croft cannot be located.

ings and boundary walls. Of the few noteworthy buildings, Tymperon's hospital is treated below.[32] The **L**-shaped George and Dragon may have been built *c.* 1700 and was remodelled in the 19th century, when its pedimented, Tuscan doorcase was moved. Wentworth House was probably the house of Matthew Wentworth, who married the widow of Thomas Michelbourne (d. 1632),[33] and later belonged to James Bean (d. 1767), a returned planter of Jamaica. Bean rebuilt[34] or remodelled the house, which retains a mid 18th-century staircase. The house, with a stuccoed façade, was altered and enlarged again in the 19th century and *c.* 1970, when it was taken over by an Evangelical charity as a conference and retreat centre.[35] It was an hotel in 1998. Aldbrough Hall was built on the southern edge of the village after 1764 by Christopher Scott (d. by 1794); it was demolished *c.* 1970 but its wooded grounds survived in 1991.[36] A conservation area in the village was formed in 1974.[37]

Up to five houses at Aldbrough were licensed in the later 18th century.[38] The George, later the George and Dragon, was named from 1806 and from it a coach service to Hull ran in 1820;[39] it still traded in 1991. The second house in the village, the Elm Tree, was recorded as a beerhouse in 1910.[40] Other houses have included the Bricklayer's Arms, in Cross Street, which was named from the 1820s until 1872; *c.* 1900 it was taken over by the elderly Hull marine artist W. D. Penny and was later called the Artist's Rest. Also in Cross Street was the Holderness hotel, which was mentioned from the 1870s until the 1930s.[41] An Oddfellows' lodge was founded in 1839 and suspended in 1845, and by 1860 it had been closed or had left the order. A branch of the Druids, founded in 1891 and recorded until 1937, met at the Holderness hotel and by the 1930s at the Artist's Rest.[42] A church hut was erected on the vicarage garth east of the church in 1921 and removed in 1937 to build a parish hall, called Stamford Hall after Edward Stamford, a major contributor.[43] The Y.M.C.A. had a hut in Nottingham Road, south of Church Street, until it was demolished *c.* 1930. Another hut, beside Hornsea Road, was later used by a

youth club; it was demolished *c.* 1995 but in 2000 it was proposed to build a new hall for the club, which had continued to meet in Stamford Hall and the new village hall.[44] The parish council provided the 6-a. War Memorial Recreation Ground south of the village in 1948; a village and sports hall was opened there in 1993.[45] Village women used a library at the school in 1921 and a county branch library was later held in Cross Street.[46]

By the mid 19th century allotment gardens were provided at Aldbrough on land belonging to the poor, to Towrie's charity,[47] and to the vicar, the last, off the Carlton road, containing 6 a. in 1901. There were also gardens at West Newton.[48] Aldbrough Floral and Horticultural Society was founded in 1880.[49]

Aldbrough has attracted visitors since the 19th century. There was a beerhouse near the sea in 1832[50] and sea bathing was established by 1836. Robert Raikes (d. 1837) began the building of a large hotel, which was probably that trading by 1844 as the Talbot hotel, later described as a temperance establishment. The Spa inn was also mentioned from 1846, and by 1851 there were three lodging houses near the sea and another in the village. A regular omnibus service from Hull was run during the season in the 1840s, and those catering for visitors *c.* 1850 included an omnibus operator, three 'hackney men', and a bathing-machine proprietor. Aldbrough failed as a spa, largely perhaps because of the poor access to its beach and the lack of a railway.[51] The Talbot, also known as Sea View, was closed *c.* 1915. A few years later, however, many bungalows were built along the cliff, mostly for week-enders from Hull,[52] who were entertained in an amusement hall, several tea rooms, and in the former Spa inn, then called the Royal hotel. A new Royal hotel was built further inland *c.* 1930 and still traded in 1991 as the Double Dutch; both of the 19th-century hotels have been demolished.[53] Sea Side Road, which leads south-west to the village, was also loosely built-up with bungalows by the 1950s, when the cliff-side houses, including those built on a site established by the district council for holiday houses and caravans in the 1930s, had

32 Below, charities.

33 E.R.A.O., DDRI/9/15.

34 Cf. R.D.B., AI/349/697; H.U.L., DDLG/11/34. E.R.A.O., DDRI/9/15; ibid. IA. Aldbrough; memorial in ch.

35 Inf. from Mr. A. Dent, Wentworth Ho., 1991.

36 R.D.B., CU/444/515; below, manors; O.S. Map 6", Yorks. CCXIII (1855 edn.); O.S. Map 1/2,500, Yorks. CCXIII. 9 (1891 edn.); inf. from Mrs. M. Oliver, Aldbrough, 2000.

37 Inf. from Devt. Dept., Holderness B.C., 1990.

38 Para. based on E.R.A.O., QDT/2/7, 9; directories.

39 R.D.B., CK/435/722; *Hull Advertiser*, 2 June 1820.

40 E.R.A.O., NV/1/2.

41 Ibid.; O.S. Map 1/2,500, Yorks. CCXIII. 9 (1891 edn.); inf. from Mr. J. D. Creasser, Aldbrough, 1992; inf. from Mr. A. G. Credland, Hull Museums and Art Galleries, 1992.

42 D. [R. J.] Neave, *E.R. Friendly Soc.* (E. Yorks. Loc. Hist. Ser. xli), 42.

43 R.D.B., 678/489/388; B.I.H.R., V. 1912–22/Ret.; E.R.A.O., PE/76/35; datestone; below, church.

44 R.D.B., 1415/420/362; E.R. Educ. Cttee. *Mins.*

1929–30, 37; 1953–4, 9; inf. from Mr. R. N. Jackson, Aldbrough, 1991–2; inf. from Mrs. M. Oliver, Aldbrough, 2000.

45 R.D.B., 792/215/172; name in gate; inf. from Mrs. Oliver.

46 B.I.H.R., V. 1912–22/Ret.; E.R.A.O., PE/76/24, s.a. 1939.

47 Below, charities.

48 E.R.A.O., PE/76/28; O.S. Map 6", Yorks. CCXII (1855 edn.).

49 Bulmer, *Dir. E. Yorks.* (1892), 302.

50 T. Sheppard, *Lost Towns of Yorks. Coast*, 161.

51 P.R.O., HO 107/2365; K. L. Mayoh, 'Comparative Study of Resorts on Coast of Holderness' (Hull Univ. M.A. thesis, 1961), 2, 30–2, 38, 42, 63; White, *Dir. E. & N.R. Yorks.* (1840), 256; White, *Dir. Hull & York* (1846), 355–6; below, manors (Etherdwick); O.S. Map 6", Yorks. CCXIII (1855 edn.). Rest of para. based on directories.

52 O.S. Map 1/2,500, Yorks. CCXIII. 5, 9 (1891 and later edns.); B.I.H.R., V. 1931/Ret.

53 R.D.B., 356/187/148; O.S. Map 1/2,500, Yorks. CCXIII. 5, 9 (1891 and later edns.); O.S. Map, TA 23 NE (1956 edn.); a window in the Double Dutch bears the earlier name; inf. from Mr. J. D. Creasser, Aldbrough, 1992.

to be moved away from the cliff.[54] The caravan site accommodated 350 static and 50 touring caravans in 2000, when one or two of the farms also had small sites.

Beacons have been sited on the high ground close to the sea. Three were recorded at Aldbrough in 1588 and later one. It was taken down in the early 1780s and rebuilt by the early 19th century, when it was reported as partly washed away by the sea. The restored beacon was finally removed from Bunkers hill, close to the northern parish boundary, c. 1830 and its site has been lost.[55] There were coastguards at Aldbrough in 1851 and a coastguard station with two houses was built on the cliff by 1879; it operated until c. 1945. The houses were demolished in 1977.[56] Volunteers manned a rocket life-saving station at Aldbrough in the early 20th century.[57] Military installations built c. 1940 and standing close to the cliff edge in 1991 included a partially destroyed brick tower at Ringbrough.

WEST NEWTON was recorded as Newton in 1086. The hamlet formerly stood along the south side of a single street,[58] and earthworks in vacant garths there indicate that it used to be more closely built; in the later 19th century a pair of estate houses and in the mid 20th century eight council houses were added on the north side,[59] but there were still fewer than 20 houses in 1991. The older buildings, which include several farmhouses, date from the 18th century. Mount Pleasant farm retained its 19th-century farm buildings in 1993. There was a licensed house in the later 18th century and the Gate tavern was named in the 1820s.[60]

EAST NEWTON. Newton, later East Newton, hamlet was also recorded from 1086. It may have comprised an east-west street with a parallel back lane,[61] and by the 18th century there was a green.[62] Only three houses remained in 1852 and in 1991, when two had been rebuilt.

OUTLYING BUILDINGS in the parish include the scattered farms of the other townships. At Aldbrough Thorpe Garth Farm and Hill Top Farm existed at inclosure in 1766; farmsteads were built later on former common land at Crossmere hill, where an 18th-century dovecot survives, and, by 1852, at Mount Pleasant. Hill Top Farm was rebuilt c. 1990. Close to Hill Top Farm and just in East Newton township stands the single-storeyed Low Farm, a 19th-century, lobby-entrance house probably built on former common land.[63]

MANORS AND OTHER ESTATES. In 1066 Ulf held *ALDBROUGH*. He had 9 carucates described as in Aldbrough, and berewicks of the manor, which extended into several parishes, included 1½ carucates at East Newton and 2 bovates at 'Totele', probably Thorpe Garth. Sokeland included 6 carucates at Bewick, 5 carucates and 6 bovates at 'Totele', 3 carucates at Fosham, 1½ carucates at East Newton, and 1 carucate at Ringbrough. All the land passed to Drew de Bevrère by 1086 and later formed part of the Aumale fee.[64] Drew also succeeded to sokeland in Aldbrough belonging to Morkar's manors of Kilnsea and Easington. That of Kilnsea comprised 2 carucates at Etherdwick, 1 carucate at Tansterne, and 1 carucate at Ringbrough, and 2 carucates more at Ringbrough were soke of Easington.[65]

Much of the Aumale fee passed to the Ros family of Roos and Helmsley (Yorks. N.R.), later Barons Ros of Helmsley, whose estate included all 6 carucates at Thorpe and 3 carucates at Fosham by the mid 13th century. Robert de Ros was named as undertenant in 1284–5,[66] and William de Ros, Lord Ros, as a lord of Aldbrough and its members in 1316.[67] The estate, later reckoned to include land in Etherdwick, East Newton, and Ringbrough, descended in the Ros family and its successors as part of Roos manor;[68] most of the land was evidently held by freeholders of that manor but 37 a. of copyhold were awarded at inclosure in 1766.[69]

An early undertenant of the Ros family was John of Beverley, or of Aldbrough, lord of Aldbrough and Thorpe, who was succeeded in turn by his son Reynold and daughter Agnes of Kelk. In 1284 Agnes's heir William of Sunderlandwick gave *THORPE* manor to his son John.[70] It was probably the same estate which was later held by a cadet branch of the Ros family resident at Gedney (Lincs.) and from the late 17th century was usually called *THORPE-GARTH WITH ALDBROUGH*. Robert son of Robert de Ros of Helmsley was granted free warren at Thorpe and Gedney in 1297,[71] and at his death by 1311 held 1 carucate and rents of

54 *Hull Daily Mail*, 20 Apr. 1978; O.S. Map 6″, TA 23 NE., NW. (1956 edn.); inf. from Mr. Creasser.
55 E.R.A.O., LT/9/54; QSF. Mich. 1779, D.8; Christ. 1780, D.9; Christ. 1784, D.1; J. Nicholson, *Beacons of E. Yorks.* 10, 28; A. Bryant, *Map of E.R. Yorks.* (1829).
56 P.R.O., HO 107/2365; *Kelly's Dir. N. & E.R. Yorks.* (1879), 338; *Hull Daily Mail*, 10 Feb. 1977; O.S. Map 1/2,500, Yorks. CCXIII. 5 (1891 and later edns.); O.S. Map 6″, TA 23 NE. (1956 edn.) showing the station; inf. from Mr. R. N. Jackson, Aldbrough, 1992.
57 Inf. from Mr. Creasser.
58 *V.C.H. Yorks.* ii. 216; O.S. Map 6″, Yorks. CCXII (1855 edn.).
59 R.D.B., 808/330/261; O.S. Map 1/2,500, Yorks. CCXII. 11 (1891 edn.).
60 E.R.A.O., QDT/2/7, 9.
61 *V.C.H. Yorks.* ii. 266; O.S. Map 6″, Yorks. CCXIII

(1855 edn.).
62 R.D.B., L/76/151.
63 E.R.A.O., IA. Aldbrough; O.S. Map 6″, Yorks. CCXIII (1855 edn.).
64 *V.C.H. Yorks.* ii. 266, 326.
65 Ibid. 264–6, 326; *V.C.H. Yorks. E.R.* v. 24, 69.
66 *Cal. Inq. p.m.* iv, p. 352; *Kirkby's Inquest*, 74, 375; *Complete Peerage*, s.v. Ros.
67 *Kirkby's Inquest*, 304.
68 P.R.O., C 142/48, no. 161; C 142/139, no. 103; C 142/218, no. 52; H.U.L., DHO/7/41; *Cal. Inq. p.m.* viii, pp. 330–1, 343; xv, p. 233; *Yorks. Fines, 1614–25*, 168; *N. Country Wills*, i (Sur. Soc. cxvi), pp. 186–7.
69 R.D.B., AH/1/1.
70 B.L. Cott. MS. Otho, C. viii, ff. 78 and v., 83v.; *Bridlington Chart.* ed. W. T. Lancaster, 307; Poulson, *Holderness*, ii. 31; below, church.
71 *Cal. Chart. R. 1257–1300*, 469; below, this section.

£5 in Aldbrough and Thorpe by knight service of William de Ros, Lord Ros. Robert's son James was a minor and it was presumably as his guardian that John de Ros of Gedney was named as the other lord of Aldbrough in 1316.[72] James had entered by 1332 and in 1343 Sir James Ros, probably the same, was named as Lord Ros's undertenant. The estate then comprised 3 carucates, evidently including the tenants' land, and was held of Sir James by Robert de Ros,[73] perhaps Sir Robert de Ros who died in 1381 and was succeeded in turn by his brothers Nicholas (d. 1397) and Sir James Ros.[74] As Thorpe manor, it descended to Sir Robert Ros (d. 1441), who left daughters, Margery wife of John Wittalbury and Eleanor.[75] Eleanor married John Paulet (d. 1492),[76] and the same estate, then called the manors of Aldbrough and Thorpe-garth, passed successively to John's son Sir John (d. 1525) and grandson Sir William Paulet, who was created Baron St. John in 1539 and in 1546 exchanged the estate with the Crown.[77] There were then a dozen houses and almost 2 carucates, all held by tenants.[78] The manor house and land were let to John Thorpe in the 1550s, to Robert Thorpe in 1587, and to Robert and his sons John and Thomas in the early 17th century.[79] The Crown sold Thorpe manor in 1611 to John Eldred and William Whitmore.[80] It was held by Alexander Thorpe in 1613, and later belonged to the Towrie, or Towry, family. In 1615 William Towrie devised it to his son Francis and he to his brother George in 1624.[81] Samuel Bower evidently had the manor by 1698,[82] and his daughters, Priscilla, wife of John Dowbiggin, and Frances, wife of Richard Smith, had succeeded him by 1720. Priscilla Dowbiggin sold her moiety to Hugh Andrew in 1746, and in 1751 he bought the other from Richard Smith and his son William.[83] At inclosure in 1766 Andrew (fl. 1772) received 225 a.[84] He was succeeded by his widow Mary, who married John Mackley, and she (fl. 1797) by her niece Elizabeth Collier.[85] Robert Harrison bought Thorpe Garth in 1803. He (d. 1821) was succeeded by his daughter Ann (d. 1836) and then by his grandson Robert Harrison,[86] who had 185 a. at Aldbrough in 1845. Harrison's assignees in bankruptcy sold the manor and the 145-a. Thorpe Garth farm in 1859 to Hannah

and Sarah Starkey, who then charged it with a rent to augment a church living in Huddersfield.[87] By 1892 the estate belonged to Lewis Starkey (d. 1910), who was succeeded by his son (Sir) J. R. Starkey (d. 1940) and he by Sir William Starkey, Bt. The farm, then of 137 a., was sold to H. G. Fisher in 1952 and to G. E. Caley in 1963.[88] Caley, who already had c. 200 a. formerly belonging to his father Henry and including Mount Pleasant farm, Aldbrough,[89] gave a half share of his estate to his wife Kathleen in 1966, and they bought the 59-a. Top farm at East Newton in 1968.[90] Thorpe Garth farm belonged to Mr. A. P. Leake in 1992.[91]

The chief house, which was recorded in 1311, was decayed in 1382 but was evidently rebuilt or repaired.[92] It was again rebuilt c. 1850.

Sir Richard Hastings held land at Aldbrough in 1428,[93] and George Hastings, Lord Hastings, settled a manor of *ALDBROUGH*, held under Roos manor as ¼ knight's fee, in 1527 on John Docwray and his wife Margaret. Docwray (d. 1531) was succeeded by his widow.[94] The estate, which extended into Cowden, may have passed to Sir Thomas Stanhope, who held 2 carucates and 2½ bovates of the Ros fee at Aldbrough in 1558. As Aldbrough manor the estate was conveyed in 1586–7 by John and Jerome Markham to Ralph Bowes and sold in 1602 by Sir Jerome Bowes and Jerome Markham to (Sir) William Gee.[95] Comprising two farms at Aldbrough and extending into East Newton and Great Cowden, in Mappleton, the estate descended from Sir William (d. 1611) in the Gees of Bishop Burton to William Gee,[96] who divided and sold it c. 1705. Richard More (fl. 1710) bought land from Gee and from several other proprietors, and devised an estate at Aldbrough including six houses and 1 carucate and 5 bovates to Nicholas More. In 1720 More sold the estate to Hugh Sleigh, from whom Thomas Scott bought it in 1728.[97] Scott's son Christopher bought more land in 1741 and later,[98] and at the inclosure of Aldbrough in 1766 and East Newton in 1772 he received 463 a.[99] After his death by 1794 much of the estate was sold, mostly in 1809,[1] when John Dodsworth bought four houses and 177 a. at Aldbrough. Shortly before Dodsworth had bought a large estate at Carlton, and c. 50 a. at

[72] *Cal. Inq. p.m.* v, pp. 137–8; *Feud. Aids*, vi. 164.
[73] *Cal. Inq. p.m.* viii, pp. 330–1, 343; below, econ. hist.
[74] *Cal. Inq. p.m.* xv, p. 233; xvii, p. 331.
[75] P.R.O., C 139/106, no. 24.
[76] Ibid. C 142/8, no. 70; *Cal. Close*, 1447–54, 86–7; *V.C.H. Yorks. E.R.* ii. 233.
[77] H.U.L., DHO/7/23; *L. & P. Hen. VIII*, xxi (2), p. 243; *Complete Peerage*, s.v. Winchester.
[78] P.R.O., SC 11/762; H.U.L., DDSY/56/1.
[79] P.R.O., E 310/32/196, f. 7; E 310/28/166, f. 65.
[80] Ibid. C 66/1903, no. 9.
[81] H.U.L., DHO/7/44; Poulson, *Holderness*, ii. 31.
[82] P.R.O., CP 43/460, rot. 224.
[83] R.D.B., G/379/839; R/496/1207–8; U/433/819.
[84] Ibid. AH/1/1; AR/187/365.
[85] Ibid. BY/147/228; BY/274/426.
[86] P.R.O., CRES 38/2102 (deed 1859).
[87] R.D.B., CF/207/324; HW/379/466; HW/380/467; B.I.H.R., TA. 870VL.
[88] R.D.B., 136/537/463; 136/538/464; 891/513/424; 912/492/416; 1317/486/443; E. Walford, *Co. Fam. of U.K.*

(1879), 984; Bulmer, *Dir. E. Yorks.* (1892), 300.
[89] R.D.B., 831/202/168; 1071/192/172.
[90] Ibid. 1489/202/164; 1489/203/165; 1489/204/166; 1489/205/167; 1588/287/234.
[91] Inf. from Mrs. M. Leake, Aldbrough.
[92] P.R.O., SC 11/762; *Cal. Inq. p.m.* v, p. 138; xv, p. 233; xvii, p. 331.
[93] *Feud. Aids*, vi. 273. [94] P.R.O., C 142/56, no. 85.
[95] H.U.L., DDSY/56/1; *Yorks. Fines*, iii. 69; iv. 192.
[96] P.R.O., C 142/332, no. 165; H.U.L., DDGE/6/21–2, 25–6, 51; J. Foster, *Pedigrees of Yorks.* iii. An estate in this or another Yorks. Aldbrough passed to Sir Wm's. dau. Jane, but no more is known of it: P.R.O., C 60/472, no. 46.
[97] R.D.B., D/95/149; F/414/898; F/415/899; K/440/927; E.R.A.O., DDCK/1/1.
[98] R.D.B., Q/339/859; AE/444/832; AU/562/934; BH/231/399; Poulson, *Holderness*, ii. 18.
[99] R.D.B., AH/1/1; AQ/46/6.
[1] Ibid. BU/108/156; BX/212/339; CL/70/124; CO/200/321; CO/203/325; CO/206/329; CO/211/336; CO/286/453; CO/294/466.

Aldbrough from Robert Harrison.[2] In 1813 c. 90 a. at Aldbrough were sold to John Hall;[3] the rest of the land there descended with the Carlton farm.

Kirkstall abbey (Yorks. W.R.) had a manor of *ALDBROUGH*, possibly in origin part of the abbey's rectorial estate. The Crown sold the manor to John Eldred and William Whitmore in 1611; it was then wholly held by tenants and included a dozen houses and c. 1 carucate.[4] The grant was repeated in 1614 with a minor change, evidently in connection with a dispute, settled in 1616, between Eldred and Whitmore and the lay rector over the ownership of land formerly belonging to Kirkstall.[5] The estate in 1611 included next to the church a house[6] which was presumably the later Manor Farm and later belonged to the Tymperon family. In 1654 Henry Tymperon also bought part of the rectorial estate. William Tymperon, by will proved in 1729, devised the manor for a charity benefiting the parish, and his trustees were awarded 196 a. at inclosure in 1766.[7] In 1952 the trustees sold 200 a., comprising practically all of the estate. Manor farm, of 157 a., was bought by F. D. Slingsby.[8] M. F. Bradshaw (d. 1965) and K. F. Bradshaw bought the farm with 95 a. in 1959, and K. F. Bradshaw, who added the 90-a. Dairy farm in 1971, still owned both farms in 1992.[9]

The Esthall or Hall family held an estate at Aldbrough by knight service of the Ros family of Helmsley. William of Esthall was named as a mesne lord there in 1311, and in 1343 Thomas of Esthall held 1 carucate.[10] It was perhaps the same estate, then extending into Etherdwick and East Newton, which Philip Hall sold to Sir John Routh in 1400 and which presumably later descended with Tansterne.[11]

William Hautayn of Fosham was recorded in 1304, and in 1343 John Hautayn held all 3 carucates of Fosham by knight service of William de Ros, Lord Ros of Helmsley.[12] In 1367 *FOSHAM* manor was settled on Thomas Disney and his wife Maud, apparently in her right, and John Disney had succeeded by 1397.[13]

The heir of the same or another John Disney was evidently Maud, wife of John Elrington, on whom the manor was settled in 1467.[14] Simon Elrington (d. by 1501) was succeeded by his son Thomas,[15] and the same or another Thomas Elrington (d. 1566) by his son Edward,[16] who sold Fosham to William Barnes or Barne in 1577–8.[17] In 1617 and 1620 Barnes's heir William Barnes sold the estate to Robert Wright and his son George.[18] George Wright was the owner in the 1670s.[19] In 1727 George Wright, probably another, conveyed the manor to his son George, who sold it to James Bean in 1751.[20] Bean (d. 1767) left it to his great-nephews John and Joseph Fox, Joseph releasing his share to John in 1786.[21] John Fox (d. after 1833) was succeeded by his sons John (d. by 1848) and Joseph as joint tenants.[22] There were c. 260 a. in 1849, when the estate was divided between Joseph and John's trustees. John Fox's part, comprising the manor and the 122-a. Fosham Garth farm, descended to Thomas Fox.[23] In 1888 his estate was foreclosed upon and sold to D. P. Garbutt, who sold it to J. W. P. Garbutt in 1911.[24] In 1919 W. G. R. Chichester-Constable bought the farm and it later descended with the estate at West Newton.[25] Joseph Fox's share, comprising Black Bush farm, had passed by 1874 to Thomas Dent (d. 1900), possibly his nephew, whose trustees sold it in 1901 to Henry North (d. 1967). North's daughters Dorothy Maltas and Rose Kirk sold the 174-a. farm to Norman Caley and his wife Mary in 1968, and it later descended with their estate in West Newton.[26]

John Disney was licensed to have divine service in his house at Fosham in 1397.[27] The manor house, which occupied a moated site, had three hearths in 1672, and was rebuilt by George Wright the younger by 1727.[28] In the later 19th century Fosham Garth Farm was rebuilt near Black Bush Farm and the old house was demolished.[29]

Another estate at Fosham descended from John More (d. by 1709) to his widow Ruth and son Nicholas (d. 1720), and belonged in 1745 to Nicholas's sisters; it was soon afterwards foreclosed upon by Elizabeth Bowes and Frances

[2] Ibid. CN/108/176; CO/384/594; below, this section (Carlton).
[3] R.D.B., CU/444/515.
[4] P.R.O., C 66/1903, no. 9.
[5] Ibid. C 66/1988, no. 3; ibid. E 134/12 Jas. I Hil./5; C 178/4870.
[6] Ibid. C 66/1903, no. 9.
[7] R.D.B., L/150/295; AH/1/1; *9th Rep. Com. Char.* 829–31; *V.C.H. Yorks. E.R.* vi. 269; below, this section (rectory); charities.
[8] R.D.B., 910/444/379; 911/52/48; 911/376/319; 912/374/316; 913/376/315; E.R.A.O., accession 1681 (1953–4).
[9] R.D.B., 1133/72/63; 1538/493/423; 1702/481/418; inf. from Mr. K. F. Bradshaw, Aldbrough, 1992.
[10] B.L. Add. Ch. 62354; *Yorks. Inq.* ii, p. 72; iii, p. 47; *Cal. Inq. p.m.* v, p. 144; viii, pp. 330–1, 343; *Test. Ebor.* i, pp. 100–1.
[11] P.R.O., CP 25(1)/279/149, no. 7; below, this section.
[12] *Yorks. Inq.* iv, p. 63; *Cal. Inq. p.m.* viii, pp. 330, 343.
[13] *Yorks. Fines, 1347–77*, p. 227; *Yorks. Deeds*, ix, p. 123; *Reg. Waldby* (Borthwick Texts and Cals.), 17.
[14] P.R.O., CP 25(1)/294/74, no. 45.

[15] Ibid. C 1/406, nos. 9–10.
[16] Ibid. C 142/150, no. 160.
[17] *Yorks. Fines*, ii. 114. Barne was a tenant of the manor in 1558: H.U.L.,DDSY/56/1.
[18] P.R.O., C 5/13/7; *Yorks. Fines, 1614–25*, 79, 156.
[19] E.R.A.O., DDCC/1/1; P.R.O., E 179/205/504.
[20] R.D.B., K/295/603; U/467/892.
[21] Ibid. AI/349/697; BM/87/147; memorial in ch.; Poulson, *Holderness*, ii. 26.
[22] R.D.B., GM/37/55; GN/167/219.
[23] Ibid. GO/239/269; HH/102/117; NC/18/28; O.S. Map 6", Yorks. CCXII (1855 edn.).
[24] R.D.B., 26/468/422 (1888); 28/315/300 (1889); 138/245/216.   [25] Ibid. 201/283/233.
[26] Ibid. LK/43/52; 32/177/160; 32/264/243 (both 1901); 1532/555/489; 1594/281/235; P.R.O., HO 107/2365; below, this section.
[27] *Reg. Waldby*, 17.
[28] R.D.B., K/295/603; P.R.O., E 179/205/504; Poulson, *Holderness*, ii. 26.
[29] O.S. Map 6", Yorks. CCXII (1855 edn.); O.S. Map 1/2,500, Yorks. CCXII. 11 (1891 edn.).

Faceby.[30] Elizabeth bought the moiety of Frances (d. by 1763) in 1771, when the estate comprised 258 a.[31] It passed to Dorothy Bowes and after her death was sold in 1824 to Anthony Wilkinson,[32] who was succeeded by his son John.[33] In 1847 Anne Raikes (d. 1848) and her son Robert Raikes bought it,[34] and in 1862 the Raikes trustees sold nearly 280 a. at Fosham to Sir Thomas Constable, Bt. The farm later descended with West Newton.[35]

Low Fosham Farm dates from the late 18th century and is a stuccoed building with a pantile roof, to which single-storeyed side screen walls were added in the later 20th century.[36]

In 1149 or 1150 William le Gros, count of Aumale, granted an estate at Bewick to John of Meaux in exchange.[37] By 1182 John of Meaux had been succeeded by his son Robert, whose widow Maud was granted a carucate and rents at Bewick for dower by their son (Sir) John in 1196.[38] John added 1 carucate at Bewick and 1 carucate at Thorpe by exchange with Michael Darcy and Meaux abbey respectively.[39] His son Godfrey had 3 carucates at Bewick in the mid 13th century; by the 1280s the Aumale under-tenant was Godfrey's son (Sir) John (d. by 1308), who was granted free warren there and elsewhere in Aldbrough in 1299,[40] and whose estate in 1303 was called *BEWICK* manor.[41] At the death by 1311 of John's son Godfrey most of Bewick manor and 1 carucate and 2 bovates at Aldbrough, described as a member of Bewick, were held of the honor of Aumale by knight service; the rest of the manor, with 2 bovates at Bewick, was said to be held by like service of the provost of Beverley.[42] Godfrey's son Sir John died c. 1377 and his heirs sold the manor in 1379 to Sir Ralph Hastings.[43] John de la River also conveyed to Sir Ralph a share of the manor, including 2 carucates and 1 bovate and comprising ⅐ knight's fee.[44] The manor was later held in turn by Sir Richard Hastings (d. 1436) and his brother (Sir) Leonard (d. 1455), before descending in the Hastings family, later Lords Hastings, to George Hastings, Lord Hastings

(fl. 1527).[45] It was sold to the Savoy hospital, London, and after the hospital's suppression was granted in 1553 to the city of London in support of other hospitals there[46] and was assigned to St. Thomas's hospital, Southwark. In the 16th and 17th centuries the manor was often held by the Moore family as lessees.[47] The hospital was awarded 47 a. in Aldbrough township at inclosure in 1766,[48] and the estate comprised just over 800 a., mostly in three farms at Bewick, in 1845 and 844 a. in 1910.[49] The hospital governors sold 93 a. to the Air Ministry in 1951 and 694 a. in the parish to Mr. R. H. Leonard and his wife Susan in 1972.[50] In 1992 the Leonard family still owned the estate.[51]

The site of the manor and its houses were worth little in the 15th century.[52] The manor house may have been rebuilt in 1636.[53] It had 12 hearths in 1672, when John Moore lived in it.[54] The present house, called Bewick Hall, is an 18th-century building which was remodelled in the later 19th century and incorporates materials from an earlier house. Its **L**-shaped plan comprises a four-bayed main block with rear wing. The medieval house was believed to have stood on a moated site west of Bewick Hall which has not survived; another, possibly secondary, site immediately north of Bewick Hall was still moated in 1991.[55]

The sokeland of Kilnsea manor at Etherdwick and Tansterne was evidently given to a butler of the count of Aumale. Beatrice, daughter of Amand the butler (d. by 1218) and widow of Geoffrey de Friboys, held all 3 carucates there in 1240.[56] Later at least part of the butler's fee was held by Geoffrey Berchaud (d. by 1276) as the count of Aumale's tenant, and Simon Constable was named as the tenant at Etherdwick and Tansterne in 1284–5.[57] At the death of John Constable in 1349 the estate comprised 2½ carucates at Tansterne and 2 carucates at Etherdwick. It descended in the Constables with Burton Constable manor.[58]

TANSTERNE was held of the Constables by the Rouths and their successors. The manor

[30] E.R.A.O., DDCC/1/8, 13.

[31] Ibid. DDCC/1/15, 22; R.D.B., AP/142/235.

[32] E.R.A.O., DDCC/1/31, 34; R.D.B., DR/274/329.

[33] B.I.H.R., TA. 870VL.

[34] R.D.B., GG/81/100; GP/330/366; IA/48/61; below, this section (Etherdwick).

[35] R.D.B., IK/74/84; J. Foster, *Pedigrees of Yorks.* iii; below, this section.

[36] Inf. from Mr. Caley, Low Fosham, 1992.

[37] *E.Y.C.* iii, pp. 89–90; for fam., *Chron. de Melsa* (Rolls Ser.), i. 81; *Y.A.J.* xliii. 101–11.

[38] *E.Y.C.* iii, p. 106; xii, p. 92.

[39] Hist. MSS. Com. 78, *Hastings,* i, p. 169; below, this section.

[40] *Kirkby's Inquest,* 75, 371; *Cal. Inq. p.m.* iv, p. 352; *Cal. Chart. R. 1257–1300,* 476; Hist. MSS. Com. 78, *Hastings,* i, p. 171.

[41] *Yorks. Fines, 1300–14,* p. 39.

[42] *Cal. Inq. p.m.* v, pp. 143–4.

[43] Ibid. vii, p. 293; *Cal. Close, 1377–81,* 245, 247; 1405–9, 222; Hist. MSS. Com. 78, *Hastings,* i, p. 174; *Test. Ebor.* i, pp. 100–1.

[44] P.R.O., CP 25(1)/278/141, no. 27.

[45] H.U.L., DHO/7/12, 14, 20; *N. Country Wills,* i (Sur. Soc. cxvi), pp. 69–72, 75–6; Hist. MSS. Com. 78, *Hastings,*

i, p. 297; Greater Lond. R. O., H 1/ST/E 67/1/48; *Complete Peerage,* s.v. Hastings.

[46] *Cal. Pat. 1547–53,* 283–4; *Valor Eccl.* (Rec. Com.) i. 359.

[47] Greater Lond. R. O., H 1/ST/E 67/1/48, 177; H 1/ST/E 67/3/59; H 1/ST/E 67/13/22; H 1/ST/E 67/31/4.

[48] R.D.B., AH/1/1; Poulson, *Holderness,* ii. 23–4; below, this section.

[49] E.R.A.O., NV/1/2; B.I.H.R., TA. 870VL.

[50] R.D.B., 883/376/320; 1801/128/112; 1814/495/433.

[51] Inf. from Mr. R. H. Leonard.

[52] H.U.L., DHO/7/12, 14.

[53] Dated brick in present ho. For this and following detail, Dept. of Environment, *Buildings List* (1987).

[54] P.R.O., E 179/205/504.

[55] Sheahan and Whellan, *Hist. York & E.R.* ii. 357; Poulson, *Holderness,* ii. 24; O.S. Map 6", Yorks. CCXII (1855 edn.); H. E. J. le Patourel, *Moated Sites of Yorks.* 110.

[56] *Kirkby's Inquest,* 375; *Chron. de Melsa* (Rolls Ser.), i. 412; *Yorks. Fines, 1232–46,* p. 82; English, *Holderness,* 92.

[57] *Kirkby's Inquest,* 74; *Cal. Inq. p.m.* iv, pp. 353, 355; *V.C.H. Yorks. E.R.* v. 25.

[58] P.R.O., C 142/48, no. 161; ibid. CP 40/291, rot. 57d.; H.U.L., DHO/7/42; DHO/8/47; *Cal. Inq. p.m.* ix, pp. 219–20; J. Foster, *Pedigrees of Yorks.* iii.

and land at Etherdwick was settled on (Sir) John of Routh in 1306, when he was granted free warren at Tansterne.[59] John (d. by 1311) left a son Amand.[60] By 1376–7 another Amand of Routh had the manor and an estate enlarged with 1½ carucate at Carlton and 2 bovates at Etherdwick belonging to his wife Christine, probably as heir to the Hothams.[61] Another grant of free warren was made for Carlton, Etherdwick, and Tansterne to Amand and Christine's son Sir John Routh in 1386;[62] he bought land at Aldbrough, Etherdwick, and East Newton in 1400 and was recorded again in 1428.[63] His widow Dame Agnes was succeeded at Tansterne and Etherdwick by Sir John's son John in 1435.[64] The estate later passed to John's brother Brian (d. 1483) and then to his daughter Elizabeth and her husband Sir John Cutt (d. 1521); c. 1500 it comprised a manor of Aldbrough, with many houses and c. 1½ carucate, half of Carlton manor, with 2 bovates there, Tansterne manor and a house called Tansterne Garth, and nearly 1 carucate and other land, houses, and rents at Etherdwick, East and West Newton, and Ringbrough. The moiety of Carlton was at West Carlton.[65] The Cutts' son John (d. 1528) was succeeded by his son John.[66] Sir John Cutt, probably the same, sold the estate to John Michelbourne and his son Richard in 1549,[67] and it was later held in undivided moieties. John Michelbourne gave his moiety in 1552 to his son Thomas (d. 1582), who devised it to his sons John and Thomas. John died c. 1585 and Thomas later enjoyed the whole moiety.[68] The other moiety descended from Richard Michelbourne (d. 1583) to his son Richard (d. 1607) and the latter's son Sir Richard.[69] At the partition of the family's estate in 1614 Sir Richard ceded the manors of Aldbrough, Carlton, and Tansterne, and land at Etherdwick, to Thomas. Sir Richard's share, at Ringbrough and East Newton,[70] was sold in 1614 and 1621.[71]

Thomas Michelbourne (d. 1632) was succeeded by his son Thomas[72] and he (d. by 1655) by his sister Mary and her husband (Sir) Hugh

Bethell (d. 1679).[73] Bethell's estate, which included the rectory, descended to his nephew Hugh Bethell (d. 1717), and from him to his son Hugh (d. 1752), whose son Hugh (d. 1772) was awarded 237 a., besides 91 a. for tithes, at the inclosure of Aldbrough in 1766.[74] That Hugh's brother William sold the estate at Aldbrough, of c. 360 a., in many lots, William Meadley buying 67 a. in 1785 and 235 a. in 1799.[75] William Bethell (d. 1799) was succeeded in the rest of the estate by a distant kinsman Richard Bethell, who had all 387 a. of Tansterne and 258 a. at Carlton in 1845.[76] Richard (d. 1864) was succeeded by his nephew W. F. Bethell (d. 1879), and he by his son G. R. Bethell.[77] Bethell died in 1919 and his executors and beneficiary Bethell Bouwens later sold the estate, R. S. Wright buying the 316-a. West Carlton farm in 1920 and Alfred Smith 246 a. in Tansterne Grange farm in 1930.[78] West Carlton farm descended from Wright (d. 1939) to his widow Emily (d. 1950), then to C. R. Wright (d. 1976), who was succeeded by his widow Gwen. In 1978 David Maltas bought the farm which was later farmed by Maltas Farms Ltd. and in 1992 was of 333 a.[79] Tansterne Grange farm was sold to C. L. Knapton in 1943, Henry Mitchell in 1944, H. R. Sellers in 1949, B. A. and M. A. North in 1953, E. N. Wright in 1961, and in 1974 to Caley Partners (Farmers) Ltd., the owners in 1992.[80]

Tansterne manor house probably occupied the extensive moated site there; a smaller moated site survived further east in 1991.[81] In the earlier 17th century the Michelbournes lived at West Carlton, presumably in a successor to the 14th-century house.[82] The house had 10 chimneys in 1686, when Mary Bethell's second husband Christopher Hildyard let it.[83] It fell down in the mid 18th century, and was rebuilt further west in the earlier 19th century.[84]

Amabel widow of Sir William of Etherdwick was dowered there in the 13th century.[85] Part of the estate may have passed to the Rouths

[59] E.R.A.O., DDCC/111/6; Yorks. Fines, 1300–14, p. 57; Cal. Chart. R. 1300–26, 70.
[60] P.R.O., CP 40/291, rot. 57d.; E.R.A.O., DDCC/111/6.
[61] Yorks. Fines, 1347–77, pp. 201–3.
[62] Cal. Chart. R. 1341–1417, 301. For the Rouths, also E.R.A.O., PE/147/26.
[63] Feud. Aids, vi. 273; above, this section. The church formerly contained 15th-cent. memorials to the Rouths: Poulson, Holderness, ii. 12.
[64] E.R.A.O., DDCC/18/1, s.v. 15 July 1435; below, Routh, manors.
[65] For identification cf. E.R.A.O., DDRI/9/20; O.S. Map 6", Yorks. CCXII (1855 edn.); below, econ. hist.
[66] P.R.O., C 141/4, no. 45; C 142/36, no. 67; C 142/48, no. 161; Yorks. Fines, i. 25.
[67] Yorks. Fines, i. 140. For the Michelbournes, Suss. Arch. Colln. l, 67–101.
[68] P.R.O., CP 40/1154, Carte rot. 15; ibid. C 142/214, no. 221.
[69] P.R.O., C 142/214, no. 205; Yorks. Fines, 1603–14, 143–4.
[70] E.R.A.O., DDRI/35/33; Yorks. Fines, 1614–25, 11.
[71] Yorks. Fines, 1614–25, 10, 174; H.U.L., DDMC/107/15.
[72] E.R.A.O., DDRI/9/6; Miscellanea, i (Y.A.S. Rec. Ser. lxi), 106.

[73] E.R.A.O., DDRI/9/18, 19; DDRI/35/57, 62; Foster, Pedigrees of Yorks. iii, s.v. Bethell.
[74] R.D.B., I/447/972; AH/1/1; below, this section.
[75] R.D.B., AY/126/219; AY/197/296; AY/332/542; AZ/382/632; BC/388/615; BH/572/978; BI/465/729; BZ/228/357.
[76] E.R.A.O., DDCC(2)/Box 8/17, survey 1779; B.I.H.R., TA. 870VL.
[77] R.D.B., NH/190/280; 182/428/364; Burke, Land. Gent. (1937), 151–2.
[78] R.D.B., 209/582/492; 211/331/288; 228/25/20; 229/22/21; 399/316/263.
[79] Ibid. 627/175/138; 872/78/72; inf. from Mr. T. R. Maltas, West Carlton Farm, 1992.
[80] R.D.B., 658/394/349; 679/507/422; 683/33/28; 807/522/432; 953/564/495; 1212/287/253; inf. from Caley Partners Ltd., 1992.
[81] O.S. Map 6", Yorks. CCXII (1855 edn.); H. E. J. le Patourel, Moated Sites of Yorks. 116.
[82] E.R.A.O., DDRI/9/18; below, this section (Carlton).
[83] Ibid. DDRI/9/20; P.R.O., E 179/205/504; J. Foster, Pedigrees of Yorks. iii, s.v. Bethell.
[84] Map of Carlton and Tansterne, 1728, at Rise Park Estate Off., 1991; Poulson, Holderness, ii. 25; O.S. Map 6", Yorks. CCXII (1855 edn.).
[85] Yorks. Deeds, v, p. 41.

by the marriage of William of Routh and Maud, relative of Thomas of Etherdwick,[86] and it was perhaps the rest which Sir Alexander Grimston held of the Constables before 1447.[87] Robert Gray and his wife sold a manor of *ETHERDWICK* to William Wintringham in 1575.[88] In 1598 Wintringham's son John sold the manor house of Etherdwick with three other houses, 13 closes, and 1 carucate and 2½ bovates there to William Green, vicar of Burton Agnes. Green (d. 1600) was succeeded by his brother Thomas,[89] and Thomas by his son Francis, whose son Mark was allotted 348 a. at inclosure in 1651[90] and sold much of the land then and in 1652.[91] Thomas Green and others sold the manor in 1686–7 to William Wilberforce,[92] whose grandsons Christopher and William Wilberforce were dealing with it in 1753. Christopher (d. *c.* 1755) left his interest to William's son Robert, who had the whole estate by 1759.[93] Robert (d. 1768) was succeeded by his son William Wilberforce, the philanthropist (d. 1833), whose son William sold the estate, of 165 a., to Robert Raikes in 1836.[94] Raikes also assembled an estate at Aldbrough. The purchaser of most of the Bethell estate there, William Meadley (d. by 1827), devised his estate to his nephew William Speck, who sold 172 a. to Raikes in 1830 and 1833. Raikes bought *c.* 70 a. more at Aldbrough in 1831[95] and died in 1837. He was succeeded in Etherdwick, and in 262 a. at Aldbrough, by his widow Anne (d. 1848) and then by their daughter Ann Lutwidge (fl. 1871).[96] Ann's son Charles Lutwidge (d. 1907) left the estate to E. F. Lowthorpe-Lutwidge. In 1918 William Tasker bought Mount Pleasant farm at Aldbrough, of 107 a., and G. H. Gibson a 171-a. farm at Etherdwick; in 1920 W. E. Campkin bought the 125-a. Hill farm, Aldbrough.[97] The farm at Etherdwick, later named as Stud farm, was sold to W. H. Clark in 1923[98] and in 1942 by the mortgagee to Henry Caley. After his death in 1946 Caley's estate, which comprised 500 a. in the parish, including Mount Pleasant farm, and land in Humbleton,[99] was sold in several lots.[1] Caley's son R. H. Caley bought 160 a., including most of Stud farm, in 1949. He died in 1974 and in 1991 his daughters Mrs. Jean Megginson and Mrs. Wendy Thomas owned the farm, then of

c. 193 a.[2] The chief house had eight hearths in 1672.[3]

All 3 carucates at East Newton were evidently given with Etherdwick and Tansterne to the count of Aumale's butler,[4] and at least part of the land later passed to the Constables.[5] In the late 13th century, however, most of East Newton was held by Thomas of Newton (d. by 1287), whose heir was his neice Beatrice wife of Robert Darcy; his estate then included ½ carucate of demesne and 1½ carucate occupied by tenants, and was held by knight service of the king as part of the Aumale fee.[6] It has not been traced later.

A manor of *CARLTON*, comprising 2 carucates, was held in 1066 by Sven and by Drew de Bevrère in 1086, when Drew's undertenant there was Ralph.[7] By the mid 13th century the Whittick family held the Aumale fee at Carlton, then put at 2 carucates and 7 bovates, by knight service. William Whittick, undertenant in the 1280s, was succeeded by 1303 by Walter Whittick and he or another Walter (d. by 1332) by William Whittick. Parts of the estate were probably subinfeudated by the 14th century when the Whittick holding comprised only 1½ carucate and when other parts of Carlton were held by William of Withernwick and John of Routh.[8]

It was perhaps the Whittick estate which belonged to Sir John Melton by 1454, when the rental was apparently nearly £7 a year.[9] Later sometimes called a manor, it descended from another Sir John Melton (d. 1544) to his daughter Lady (Dorothy) Darcy (d. 1557) and then in the Darcy family to John Darcy, Lord Darcy.[10] Lord Darcy sold it in 1606 to Philip and Leonard Gill,[11] and in 1627 Leonard had 258 a. at Carlton.[12] It was probably the same estate, then a farm of nearly 300 a., mostly at Carlton, which the devisees of Samuel Wright sold to John Dodsworth in 1808.[13] Dodsworth, who also bought land at Aldbrough, was dead by 1820, and in 1822 his son John and trustee Daniel Sykes conveyed the estate to Daniel's brother Henry, apparently for Daniel who had it at his death in 1832.[14] Daniel was succeeded by his nephew H. S. Thornton, who had 281 a.

[86] B.L. Cott. MS. Otho, C. viii, f. 85v.
[87] E.R.A.O., DDCC/18/6.
[88] *Yorks. Fines,* ii. 77.
[89] H.U.L., DDLG/11/20; P.R.O., C 142/268, no. 133; *Yorks. Fines,* iv. 105; *V.C.H. Yorks. E.R.* ii. 116.
[90] H.U.L., DDLG/11/21; Poulson, *Holderness,* ii. 30.
[91] H.U.L., DDLG/11/22; E.R.A.O., DDHB/45/181.
[92] P.R.O., CP 25(2)/805/2–3 Jas. II Hil. no. 43; R.D.B., FB/92/106.
[93] R.D.B., W/383/777; Z/274/638; AB/295/529; H.U.L., DDSY/6/38.
[94] R.D.B., BM/87/147; FB/92/106; FB/219/236; *D.N.B.* s.v. Wilberforce.
[95] H.U.L., DDCV(2)/62/48, 51; R.D.B., EI/302/338; EM/159/146; ET/272/297; above, this section.
[96] Ibid. FF/82/95; KS/370/497; B.I.H.R., TA. 870VL; K. J. Allison, *Hull Gent Seeks Country Residence 1750–1850* (E. Yorks. Loc. Hist. Ser. xxxvi), 43; J. Foster, *Pedigrees of Yorks.* iii.
[97] R.D.B., 98/354/336 (1907); 190/456/392; 190/548/473; 227/308/258; E. Walford, *Co. Fam. of U.K.* (1879), 657.

[98] R.D.B., 264/442/372; 402/77/69.
[99] Ibid. 401/452/388; 652/537/462; 754/291/245.
[1] Ibid. 813/88/70; 814/249/198; 814/600/492; 828/579/479; 831/202/168.
[2] Ibid. 831/207/170; inf. from Mrs. W. Thomas, Etherdwick, 1992.
[3] P.R.O., E 179/205/504.
[4] *Kirkby's Inquest,* 374.
[5] P.R.O., C 141/4, no. 45; C 142/48, no. 161.
[6] *Cal. Inq. p.m.* iv, pp. 353, 355; *Yorks. Inq.* ii, p. 72.
[7] *V.C.H. Yorks.* ii. 268.
[8] *Kirkby's Inquest,* 75, 244, 375; *Cal. Inq. p.m.* iv, pp. 226, 353; vii, p. 306.
[9] Shaftesbury MSS., M 220 (acct. 33–4 Hen. VI).
[10] P.R.O., C 142/70, no. 60; C 142/116, no. 57; C 142/273, no. 82; ibid. E 150/241, no. 39.
[11] *Yorks. Fines, 1603–14,* 54–5, 62.
[12] Below, econ. hist.   [13] R.D.B., CM/572/875.
[14] Ibid. DI/174/220; DN/188/217; EP/251/296; cf. J. Foster, *Pedigrees of Yorks.* ii, s.v. Thornton of Birkin; iii, s.v. Sykes of Sledmere; above, this section (Aldbrough).

at Carlton and 85 a. at Aldbrough in 1845.[15] Thornton died by 1891 and later his grandchildren H. G. Thornton and Evelyn Thornton, who married C. H. Notley, held the estate in undivided moieties.[16] Norman Cardwell bought East Carlton farm with 370 a. in the parish in 1919 and gave it to his wife Evelyn in 1966.[17] F. A. Porter & Sons bought the farm in 1978 and still owned it in 1992.[18]

A house was recorded on the Whittick estate in the 14th century.[19] The present East Carlton Farm was rebuilt in the late 18th or early 19th century;[20] the walled garden, among trees some distance away, presumably belonged to an earlier house.

Another estate at Carlton, comprising 1½ carucate and including a chief house, was held of the Whitticks, Withernwicks, and Rouths by Sir John of Carlton (d. 1304), who was succeeded by his granddaughter Avice and her husband Richard of Hotham.[21] It probably descended from the Hothams to Christine wife of Amand of Routh, and was presumably the half of Carlton manor later included in the estate of the Rouths and their successors.[22]

At *RINGBROUGH*, Baldwin held 2 carucates from Drew in 1086.[23] That estate and other land passed to the Scrutevilles, or Ringbroughs. About 1150 Alan de Scruteville obtained 60 a. in Aldbrough by exchange with William le Gros, count of Aumale,[24] and Sir William de Scruteville was given land at East Newton by Meaux abbey in the earlier 13th century.[25] By the mid 13th century the Scrutevilles had all 4 carucates at Ringbrough.[26] The estate evidently passed to Sir William's daughter Emma and her husband John de Ros. The undertenant of the Aumale fee at Ringbrough in 1284–5 was another John de Ros.[27] He (d. by 1319) was succeeded by his son (Sir) Richard, who at his death in 1351 held Ringbrough manor in chief as ¹⁄₁₂ knight's fee and nearly a carucate at Aldbrough by knight service of the Lords Ros of Helmsley. Sir Richard was succeeded by his grandson Richard de Ros.[28] The manor, which extended into Garton, may have belonged to Richard's son John by the 1370s,[29] and it was possibly as his heir that Grace wife of Sir Philip Tilney and

her husband were dealing with it in 1389. The lady of Ringbrough was mentioned in the early 15th century,[30] and in 1422 the manor was conveyed to Philip Tilney.[31] Elizabeth Tilney's son John Bourchier, Lord Berners, sold the reversion of the estate to Sir John Skevington in 1523. Skevington obtained possession in 1524 and died in 1525, leaving a son William (d. 1551). The estate may have descended to William's son William but soon afterwards belonged to John Skevington. In the 16th century it included, besides the demesne at Ringbrough and land in Garton, a dozen houses and almost 1½ carucate at Aldbrough and East Newton.[32] The same or another John and William Skevington were dealing with the estate in 1601,[33] and in 1656 Ursula Skevington, widow, and Sir John Skevington, Bt., sold it to William Bower.[34] William Bower, probably another, and John Bower conveyed Ringbrough to Edward Bower in 1696,[35] and John, perhaps the same, sold the manor with land at East Newton in 1719 to Richard Woolfe (d. by 1746). Woolfe's son, the Revd. Nicholas Woolfe, sold Ringbrough in 1748 to Thomas Grimston, who already had an estate there.[36] Ringbrough, which was reduced by coastal erosion, later descended in the Grimstons.[37] Charles Grimston had 183 a. in East Newton and Ringbrough township in 1845.[38] In 1856 the estate comprised, besides the manor, 169 a. in Ringbrough farm, c. 1915 about 150 a., and in 1967 only 127 a. With the estate at Grimston, in Garton, Ringbrough passed to Boston Deep Sea Fisheries Ltd., which sold it to M. J. and Bessie Meadley in 1967.[39] The farm belonged to their son Mr. M. S. Meadley in 1991.[40]

The manor house was recorded in 1351–2 and again, as Ringbrough Hall, in the 16th century;[41] the farmhouse was rebuilt in the 18th century.[42]

In 1086 the archbishop of York had a berewick of 3 carucates in Newton and land at 'Santriburtone', later Burton Constable, in Swine. Land in both was later held of the archbishop by the counts of Aumale, and of them by the Constable family.[43] All 3 carucates were confirmed to Robert Constable, who succeeded his uncle and namesake c. 1200.[44] (Sir) Simon

[15] B.I.H.R., TA. 870VL.
[16] R.D.B., 43/434/397; 43/435/398; 43/436/399 (all 1891); 100/26/22 (1898).
[17] Ibid. 201/149/120; 1490/385/342.
[18] Inf. from Mrs. Joan Porter, Carlton, 1992.
[19] Cal. Inq. p.m. vii, p. 306.
[20] Cf. Poulson, *Holderness*, ii. 70.
[21] Cal. Inq. p.m. iv, p. 226.
[22] *Yorks. Fines, 1300–14*, p. 54; above, this section (Tanstern).
[23] *V.C.H. Yorks.* ii. 266, 326.
[24] *E.Y.C.* iii, pp. 71, 91–2; *Yorks. Fines, 1218–31*, p. 154 n.; *Chron. de Melsa* (Rolls Ser.), i. 83.
[25] *Chron. de Melsa*, i. 415; G. V. Orange, 'Cart. of Meaux' (Hull Univ. Ph.D. thesis, 1965), pp. 446–7. Cf. *Chron. de Melsa*, ii. 38–9.
[26] *Kirkby's Inquest*, 374.
[27] *Feud. Aids*, vi. 40; *Cal. Inq. p.m.* iv, p. 356; below, Routh, manors.
[28] *Cal. Inq. p.m.* vi, p. 98; ix, p. 440.
[29] *Yorks. Fines, 1347–77*, pp. 179–80.

[30] B.I.H.R., CP. F. 148; P.R.O., CP 25(1)/289/55, no. 189.
[31] *Y.A.J.* xvi. 97; Poulson, *Holderness*, ii. 32.
[32] H.U.L., DHO/7/26, 35; E.R.A.O., DDCC/1/2; *Yorks. Deeds*, iv, pp. 5–10; Poulson, *Holderness*, ii. 32; below, Garton, manors.
[33] *Yorks. Fines*, iv. 168.   [34] *Yorks. Deeds*, iv. 10–11.
[35] P.R.O., CP 25(2)/895/8 Wm. III Trin. no. 54.
[36] R.D.B., F/437/944; R/493/1199; T/100/197; H.U.L., DGN/6/5; P.R.O., C 142/210, no. 124.
[37] R.D.B., AQ/46/6; cf. J. Foster, *Pedigrees of Yorks.* iii.
[38] B.I.H.R., TA. 252M.
[39] R.D.B., HL/351/352; 31/20/19 (1889); 155/36/31; 155/37/32; 185/114/93; 549/398/315; 721/247/221; 793/70/59; 1478/132/123; 1496/112/104; E.R.A.O., NV/1/40; below, Garton, manors.
[40] Inf. from Mrs. K. Meadley, Ringbrough.
[41] P.R.O., C 135/112, no. 37; *Yorks. Deeds*, iv. 7 n., 10.
[42] Date on building: inf. from Mrs. Meadley.
[43] Below, Swine, Burton Constable, manor.
[44] E.R.A.O., DDCC/135/51, no. 22; Burton Constable Hall, DDCC/141/68, cart. p. 40 (a).

Constable was granted free warren at Newton in 1285,[45] and at his death in 1294 the estate at *NEWTON CONSTABLE* included 1 carucate and 5 bovates held of the Crown as successor to the counts of Aumale and 1 bovate of a mesne lord; another carucate at Newton or Burton Constable was held by Constable's undertenants.[46] It was regarded as a member of Burton Constable manor in 1336 but later as a separate manor, held as ½₀ knight's fee.[47] The estate, which had been enlarged by purchase by the mid 15th century and after the acquisition of Lambwath manor in 1549 extended into Carlton and Fosham,[48] continued to descend in the Constables.[49] In the late 18th and mid 19th century it contained all of West Newton and *c.* 100 a. at Carlton and Fosham.[50] Sir Thomas Constable, Bt., bought nearly 280 a. at Fosham from the Raikes trustees in 1862, and W. G. R. Chichester-Constable *c.* 120 a. there from J. W. P. Garbutt in 1919,[51] and in 1963 the Chichester-Constables had 773 a. at West Newton and 505 a. at Carlton and Fosham.[52] In 1965 J. R. J. Chichester-Constable sold Fosham farm, Fosham Garth farm, Mount Pleasant farm, and Old farm, containing in all 760 a., to Norman Caley Ltd., and the 232-a. Grange farm to Edward, John, and Terence Porter,[53] who farmed as F. A. Porter & Sons. Norman Caley Ltd. still owned the farms at Fosham and West Newton in 1992, besides another purchase, Black Bush farm, Fosham, and F. A. Porter & Sons retained Grange farm.[54] A farm of *c.* 100 a. at West Newton remained part of the Burton Constable estate in 2000.[55]

The house with six hearths recorded at West Newton in 1672 was perhaps the manor house.[56] It may have stood near Mount Pleasant Farm but had gone by the mid 19th century.[57] The site of another house on the estate, Old Farm, may formerly have been moated but no trace of a moat remains visible.[58]

After the appropriation of the church in 1228 the *RECTORY* belonged to Aumale abbey. It was worth £24 a year in 1291.[59] It was administered as a member of Burstall priory, in Skeffling, with which it was seized by the Crown during the French wars and sold to Kirkstall abbey in 1396.[60] After the Dissolution the Crown let the rectory in 1550 to Richard Thorpe, and in 1575 to his sons Robert, John, and Stephen Thorpe.[61] In 1607 the Crown sold the rectory to Martin White,[62] and he to another Richard Thorpe. Thorpe (d. 1613) was succeeded by his son John. After dispute with the owners of another part of Kirkstall's former estate at Aldbrough, the glebe land of the rectory was decreed in 1616 to comprise 1 bovate. The rectory also then included a parsonage house and corn and hay tithes.[63] John Thorpe (d. 1640) was succeeded by his cousin Richard Thorpe, who in 1650 held the rectorial estate in Aldbrough, Bewick, Carlton, Etherdwick, Fosham, and Tansterne, all of which was worth £44 10s. net.[64] Thorpe sold part or all of the land in 1654 to Henry Tymperon, along with corn and hay tithes at Aldbrough and Etherdwick which his heir later bought back.[65]

After Thorpe's death *c.* 1660 the rectory passed to his sister-in-law, Mary, wife of Sir Hugh Bethell. Sir Hugh (d. 1679) devised it to Anne Johnson, who married Matthias Crouch, for her life, and then to his nephew Hugh Bethell, who succeeded *c.* 1700 and died in 1717.[66] It later descended with the other estate of the Bethells.[67] At the inclosure of Aldbrough township in 1766 Hugh Bethell had all the corn tithes, a few hay tithes, some mortuaries, and a composition of £2 a year paid since the 17th century for the tithes of the common pasture. For all those dues he was then awarded 91 a. and £32 10s. a year.[68] The land at Aldbrough was sold *c.* 1790 with the rest of William Bethell's estate there.[69] The tithes of 36 a. at Bewick were commuted at the inclosure of Withernwick in 1814,[70] and by 1845 corn and hay tithes from 258 a. at Carlton and all 387 a. at Tansterne were merged in the landed estate of Richard Bethell, who was then awarded a rent charge of £273 10s. for his remaining tithes at Bewick, Carlton, Etherdwick, and Fosham.[71]

Richard Thorpe sold the corn and hay tithes of West Newton and the tithes of the land alongside Lambwath stream to Sir Henry Constable in 1610,[72] and in 1650 their net value was £10.[73]

45 *Cal. Chart. R.* 1257–1300, 308.
46 P.R.O., C 133/68, no. 9; *Cal. Inq. p.m.* iii, pp. 114–16.
47 H.U.L., DHO/7/42; *Cal. Inq. p.m.* viii, p. 24; *Hen. VII*, ii, pp. 60–2.
48 H.U.L., DHO/8/47; E.R.A.O., DDCC/18/6; below, Swine, Marton, manors.
49 E.R.A.O., DDCC/134/23.
50 Ibid. DDCC/111/39; DDCC(2)/Box 8/17, survey 1779; B.I.H.R., TA. 59L, 870VL.
51 R.D.B., IK/74/84; 201/283/233.
52 Ibid. 1295/284/255.
53 Ibid. 1408/334/291; 1409/294/272.
54 Inf. from Mr. N. Caley, West Newton, and Mrs. Joan Porter, Carlton, 1992.
55 Inf. from Mr. R. Wastling, Grange Farm, Thirtleby, 2000.
56 P.R.O., E 179/205/504.
57 Sheahan and Whellan, *Hist. York & E.R.* ii. 358.
58 E.R.A.O., DDCC(2)/Box 8/17, survey 1779; inf. from Mr. Caley, 1992.
59 *Tax. Eccl.* (Rec. Com.), 304.
60 *Cal. Inq. Misc.* vi, p. 52; *Cal. Pat.* 1391–6, 585; *V.C.H. Yorks. E.R.* v. 133.

61 *Cal. Pat.* 1566–9, p. 263; 1572–5, p. 549.
62 P.R.O., C 66/1705, [no. 11 from end].
63 Ibid. E 134/12 Jas. I Hil./5; E 178/4870; H.U.L., DHO/7/44; B.I.H.R., CP. H. 4913.
64 P.R.O., C 142/609, no. 77; *T.E.R.A.S.* iv. 51; below, this section.
65 E.R.A.O., DDRI/35/68; P.R.O., CP 25(2)/614/1654 Mich. no. 61; CP 25(2)/754/18–19 Chas. II Hil. [no. 5]; above, this section (Aldbrough).
66 P.R.O., E 134/4 Anne East./10; E 134/4 & 5 Anne Hil./2; Foster, *Pedigrees of Yorks.* iii.
67 R.D.B., I/447/972; BZ/323/520; above, this section (Tansterne).
68 R.D.B., AH/1/1. The pasture tithes were much disputed in the 17th and early 18th cent.: P.R.O., E 126/18, ff. 516, 609v.; E 134/3 Anne Mich./5; E 134/4 Anne East./10; E 134/ 4 & 5 Anne Hil./2; B.I.H.R., CP. H. 1267, 1270, 1384, 4913, 5039.
69 Above, this section (Tansterne).
70 R.D.B., CQ/245/16.   71 B.I.H.R., TA. 870VL.
72 E.R.A.O., DDCC/58/15.
73 Lamb. Pal. Libr., COMM. XIIa/17/237; *T.E.R.A.S.* iv. 51.

They descended in the Constables with West Newton manor,[74] and by 1845 they had been merged.[75]

The tithes of East Newton and half of those of Ringbrough were worth £14 net in 1650, when they were said, probably erroneously, to belong to John Constable, viscount Dunbar. The impropriator Richard Thorpe (d. 1613) had married William Towrie's daughter, and by 1663 the corn and hay tithes of East Newton and half of the same at Ringbrough belonged to Robert Towrie, who gave them to the vicarage.[76] The other half of the tithes at Ringbrough were probably held with the manor there; John Grimston's estate was expressly excluded from the commutation of tithes in 1772, and by 1845 the moiety had been merged in the landed estate.[77]

Corn and hay tithes at Carlton and Fosham also belonged to the Constables, and some had been extinguished by 1779. Of those remaining in 1845, the tithes from 108 a. at Carlton and Fosham were merged in the landed estate of Sir Thomas Constable, Bt., who was then awarded a rent charge of £2 9s. 6d. for the rest, from c. 530 a. at Fosham. Other proprietors at Fosham had by then also merged tithes on c. 40 a. in their estates.[78]

A chantry endowed with the corn tithes of Etherdwick was probably that of St. German in Aldbrough church.[79] After its suppression the tithes were apparently confused with the former estate of another chantry, in Rise church, and with that they were granted to Giggleswick (Yorks. W.R.) grammar school in 1553.[80] In 1650 they were worth £4 a year, and in 1845 the school was awarded £80 a year for them.[81]

The remaining rent charges awarded in 1845 were for hay tithes; Henry Broadley received £6 a year for 128 a. at Etherdwick, H. S. Thornton £1 from Carlton, and Henry Stephenson 1s. from Etherdwick.[82]

William the butler had given land at East Newton to Thornton abbey (Lincs.) by 1190, and other donors added 2 bovates at Aldbrough by 1312 and an estate at Etherdwick by 1350.[83] After the Dissolution the estate, which included 3½ bovates at East Newton, was granted to the short-lived Thornton college.[84] The Crown sold

houses and land at Aldbrough, East Newton, and Etherdwick as part of Thornton's manor of Garton in 1611 to John Eldred and William Whitmore.[85]

In 1634 William Greame bought 2 bovates at Etherdwick formerly belonging to Thornton college,[86] and his son Robert sold them in 1645 to his brother John.[87] At inclosure in 1651 John Greame was allotted 64 a.[88] He was succeeded in 1665 by his son Robert (d. 1708),[89] who had bought 77 a. from Hugh Bethell and his wife Mary in 1657[90] and settled Etherdwick on his son John in 1699.[91] John Greame (d. 1746) devised the estate to his son John[92] (d. 1798), who bought 64 a. more at Etherdwick in 1792[93] and left the estate to his nephew John Greame (d. 1841).[94] John's son Yarburgh Greame, later Yarburgh (d. 1856),[95] was succeeded by his sister Alicia (d. 1867) and her husband George Lloyd (d. 1863),[96] who left a son the Revd. Yarburgh Lloyd, later Lloyd Greame (d. 1890).[97] In 1915 Lloyd Greame's son Y. G. Lloyd Greame sold Etherdwick farm, of 245 a., to Frederick Nettleton, from whom R. E. Williams bought it in 1920.[98] In 1926 the mortgagee sold the farm to W. J. Richardson (d. 1929), whose children sold it to J. W. Frankland in 1929. Later called Etherdwick Grange farm, the land remained in Mr. Frankland's family in 2000.[99]

About 1170 William le Gros, count of Aumale, gave 1 carucate at Thorpe to (Sir) William de Cauz,[1] who sold it to Meaux abbey between 1182 and 1197. The abbey granted it in exchange to Sir John of Meaux between 1197 and 1210.[2] Hugh Darcy gave his land at Bewick to Meaux abbey between 1221 and 1235 but the estate has not been traced later.[3]

William de Forz, count of Aumale, gave 2 bovates at East Newton and Sir William de Scruteville land at Thorpe to Nunkeeling priory in the late 12th or earlier 13th century. Other gifts were received from William of Routh and Stephen Hatfield,[4] and the priory also had 6 bovates at Aldbrough as a chantry endowment.[5] Part of the priory's former estate at East Newton, which included 5 bovates, was sold by the Crown in 1611 to John Eldred and William Whitmore.[6]

74 E.R.A.O., DDCC/111/231; J. Foster, *Pedigrees of Yorks.* iii.
75 B.I.H.R., TA. 59L.
76 P.R.O., E 178/4870; *T.E.R.A.S.* iv. 51; below, church.
77 R.D.B., AQ/46/6; B.I.H.R., TA. 252M.
78 B.I.H.R., TA. 870VL.
79 Below, church.
80 The chantry was called St. Mary's 'in the parish church of Rise and Aldbrough': *Cal. Pat.* 1553, 68–9; *V.C.H. Yorks.* i. 461.
81 *T.E.R.A.S.* iv. 53; B.I.H.R., TA. 870VL.
82 B.I.H.R., TA. 870VL; R.D.B., BZ/323/520.
83 *E.Y.C.* iii, pp. 41–2; *Cal. Pat.* 1307–13, 448–9; *Cal. Inq. p.m.* ix, pp. 251–2.
84 *L. & P. Hen. VIII*, xvii, pp. 29–30; P.R.O., E 310/33/198, f. 36.
85 P.R.O., C 66/1903, no. 9.
86 H.U.L., DDLG/11/1.
87 Ibid. DDLG/11/3, 10.   88 Ibid. DDLG/11/5.
89 Ibid. DDLG/52/14. For the fam., F. F. Johnson, *Sewerby Ho. and Park, passim.*
90 H.U.L., DDLG/11/7.
91 Ibid. DDLG/50/7.
92 Ibid. DDLG/11/30.
93 R.D.B., BQ/391/613.
94 H.U.L., DDLG/11/14; DDLG/52/39.
95 Ibid. DDLG/11/15–16.
96 Ibid. DDLG/11/17; E. Walford, *Co. Fam. of U.K.* (1879), 640.
97 H.U.L., DDLG/11/45.
98 E.R.A.O., NV/1/2; R.D.B., 168/335/298; 216/206/172.
99 R.D.B., 279/292/253; 333/395/306; 391/190/159; 392/45/32; inf. from Mrs. Thomas, Etherdwick, 2000.
1 *E.Y.C.* iii, p. 115.
2 *Chron. de Melsa* (Rolls Ser.), i. 220, 310; Hist. MSS. Com. 78, *Hastings*, i, pp. 166–8.
3 *Chron. de Melsa*, i. 419; G. V. Orange, 'Cart. of Meaux' (Hull Univ. Ph.D. thesis, 1965), pp. 442–3.
4 B.L. Cott. MS. Otho, C. viii, ff. 84–5, 85v.
5 H.U.L., DDSY/56/1; below, church.
6 P.R.O., C 66/1903, no. 9; ibid. E 310/27/158, f. 32; E 310/27/160, f. 22; *Valor Eccl.* (Rec. Com.), v. 115.

Donors including Ralph and Robert of Etherdwick gave St. Sepulchre's hospital, Hedon, c. ½ carucate, other land, and rent at Etherdwick and Aldbrough.[7] After the suppression the estate passed to the Constables of St. Sepulchre's Garth.[8]

Either St. Giles's hospital, Beverley, or Warter priory had an estate at Aldbrough, which was granted to Thomas Manners, earl of Rutland, in 1536.[9] Land at East Newton formerly belonging to a chantry in Beverley minster was sold to Francis Phillips and Richard Moore in 1608.[10]

About 250 a. at Aldbrough and Etherdwick belonged to Hull Royal Infirmary until 1924, when they were sold; from 1925 Headlands farm and most of the land were included in the larger estate of Henry Caley.[11]

ECONOMIC HISTORY. COMMON LANDS AND INCLOSURE. *Aldbrough.* Aldbrough village had 10 ploughlands in 1086,[12] and in the 17th and 18th centuries the open fields there were still reckoned to contain 80½ bovates belonging to the village, besides 8 bovates of Bewick hamlet. North and South fields were named in 1616.[13] Leys of odd lands recorded in Sea field, or fields, presumably part of North field, in the early 18th century may reflect the disruption of the tillage by coastal erosion.[14] Common meadow land probably lay mostly in the carrs bordering Lambwath stream: in 1616 meadow in South field included some in East carr, and later in the century hay was grown in West carr in South field.[15] On the eve of inclosure grazing in the open fields was mostly stinted at the rate of 3 gates in South field and 1½ gates in North field for each bovate held; each householder also had 2 gates in the harvested field and unlimited pasturage there during the winter. The fallow field was opened for summer grazing by cattle on 1 May. The village's common pasture was New close, which may formerly have been arable and was described as including 'lands and leys' as late as the 18th century; the pasture was overstocked c. 1680, and the stint was accordingly reduced from 2½ to 2 beast gates or 1 horse gate a bovate, enjoyed from 1 May to Michaelmas.[16]

The open fields and common pasture at Aldbrough were inclosed by an award of 1766

under an Act of 1764. Allotments totalled 1,793 a., of which more than 781 a. were from South field, more than 544 a. from North field, and 302 a. from New close. Hugh Bethell was allotted 328 a., including 91 a. for tithes, Christopher Scott 321 a., Hugh Andrew 225 a., and the Tymperon trustees 196 a. There were also two allotments of 100–129 a., two of 50–99 a., ten of 5–49 a., and eleven of under 5 a.[17]

Bewick. Bewick was evidently inclosed early, but stinted pasture was mentioned there in the early 17th century.[18]

Carlton. At Carlton there were 2 ploughlands and 20 a. of meadow in 1086, when one plough was worked there.[19] In 1517 Sir John Cutt was reported to have converted tillage to pasture with the loss of a plough.[20] Most of the remaining commonable lands there seem to have been inclosed by agreement in 1627, when nearly 500 a. were divided between two proprietors; Thomas Michelbourne then received 200 a. in West field and 36 a. in a pasture close called Rowley, later Roller, and Leonard Gill 200 a. in East field and 58 a. in Rowley pasture.[21] A stinted summer pasture in Innams close nevertheless remained in 1631.[22]

Etherdwick. A common field of Etherdwick was mentioned in the 13th century.[23] By an agreement of 1648 between the five freeholders the commonable lands of Etherdwick were inclosed in 1651, the lack of grazing for stock to manure the more extensive tillage being given as a reason for inclosure. Mark Green was allotted 348 a., Thomas Michelbourne 77 a., and John Greame 64 a.; the other two allotments are unknown. Of the recorded allotments 128 a. came from Oxdale, 90 a. from Mill field, 86 a. from Bracken Hill field, 70 a. from Mayrod Hill and Leys, 43 a. from the moor, 37 a. from Wildertofts, and 35 a. from the infield.[24]

Fosham. At Fosham part of the tillage lay west of Black Bush Farm where ridge-and-furrow survived in 1991.

West Newton. At West Newton in 1086 there were 2 ploughlands and 20 a. of meadow.[25] The open fields there almost certainly lay north and south of the hamlet, and ridge-and-furrow was evident north of the street in 1991.

7 *Yorks. Deeds*, v, p. 41; Hist. MSS. Com. 78, *Hastings*, i, p. 163; Dugdale, *Mon.* vi. 654–5.
8 *Valor Eccl.* (Rec. Com.), v. 110; *V.C.H. Yorks. E.R.* v. 194; *Cal. Pat.* 1547–8, 170, 250; 1553, 87–8.
9 *L. & P. Hen. VIII*, xi, p. 207; xvi, p. 325.
10 P.R.O., C 66/1752, no. 4; *Cal. Pat.* 1572–5, p. 178.
11 R.D.B., 292/486/403; 292/487/404; 292/513/425; 292/543/447; 292/544/448; 294/195/160; 299/137/117; 314/481/371; above, this section (Etherdwick).
12 *V.C.H. Yorks.* ii. 266.
13 B.I.H.R., TER. H. Aldbrough 1685 etc.; R.D.B., AH/1/1; P.R.O., E 178/4870.
14 R.D.B., F/414/898; F/415/899.
15 B.I.H.R., TER. H. Aldbrough 1685 etc.; P.R.O., E 178/4870.
16 R.D.B., F/415/899; AH/1/1; P.R.O., E 126/18, f. 516;

E 134/3 Anne Mich./5; E 134/4 Anne East./10; E 134/4 & 5 Anne Hil./2; H.U.L., DDCV/2/1, s.v. 1734.
17 4 Geo. III, c. 39 (Priv. Act); E.R.A.O., IA.; R.D.B., AH/1/1, which incorrectly records one of Wm. Wright's allotments: E.R.A.O., DDPK/29/2; cf. also R.D.B., BZ/228/357.
18 B.I.H.R., CP. H. 5039.
19 *V.C.H. Yorks.* ii. 268.
20 *Trans. R. Hist. S.* N.S. vii. 249.
21 E.R.A.O., DDRI/35/37; map of Carlton and Tansterne, 1728, at Rise Park Estate Off., 1991; O.S. Map 6", Yorks. CCXII (1855 edn.).
22 B.I.H.R., CP. H. 4913.
23 *Yorks. Deeds*, v, p. 41.
24 H.U.L., DDLG/11/4–5, 21.
25 *V.C.H. Yorks.* ii. 216.

Ringbrough and East Newton. Ringbrough and East Newton may each have had their own common lands in the Middle Ages, but they seem later to have been managed together. In the 1330s North and South fields were mentioned at Ringbrough, but other land of the hamlet then and later lay in the fields of East, or Ringbrough, Newton. East Newton pasture included gates for Ringbrough in 1719.[26]

The open fields at East Newton were named in 1726, when their pasturage was evidently stinted at the rate of 32 sheep gates in North field and 28 in South field for each bovate held; in the common pasture the rate was then 8 gates a bovate. By the 1760s the stints had been reduced to 8 sheep gates in South field, 3 in North field, and 4 gates in the pasture.[27] The common meadows lay in an area called Bitting or Bitten.[28] The commonable lands of East Newton were inclosed by an award of 1772 under an Act of 1770. There were 507 a. to be dealt with, and 10 a. of old inclosures were involved in exchanges. Allotments totalled 496 a., of which 85 a. were from North field, more than 64 a. from the pasture, and more than 24 a. from Bitten. Ridge-and-furrow survived near the northern boundary and south of the hamlet in 1991. Alice Etherington received 145 a., Christopher Scott 142 a., and the vicar 80 a. for glebe land and tithes. There were three other allotments of 20–79 a.[29]

Tansterne. The tillage of Tansterne was also reduced by early inclosure, Alexander Pudsey having converted 40 a. to pasture by 1517.[30] An open field probably lay south of the settlement's garths where ground was occupied as South Field close in 1728.[31]

TENURES AND FARMS TO C. 1800. *Aldbrough.* Thorpe manor was divided between 14 tenants in the mid 16th century; eight men held nearly 2 carucates, mostly in holdings of 1–2 bovates each, and there were four cottagers with no open-field land and two freeholdings of unknown size. Tenants on the manor of Aldbrough formerly belonging to Kirkstall abbey owed poultry rents in the 17th century.[32]

Bewick. In 1379 Bewick manor included eleven holdings of 1–3 bovates and seven of only a few acres each.[33]

West Newton. Ploughing and most carting works owed by the Constables' tenants at West Newton had been commuted for fowls, eggs, and money rents by the 1540s.[34] About that date the tenants

occupied 14 houses, 2 carucates and 3 bovates, and other land; most of the dozen holdings were of 2 bovates each.[35]

WARRENS AND FISHERIES. In the early 14th century Bewick manor included fish ponds and one or two warrens,[36] evidently on land south of the manor house later called Cony Garth hill.[37] Other fisheries at Aldbrough, Bewick, Carlton, and Fosham belonged to the Crown as lord of Holderness in the mid 14th century; they were presumably sited in Lambwath stream or mere.[38]

LATER AGRICULTURE. Aldbrough parish had 2,356 a. under crops in 1801.[39] In 1845 there were 4,264 a. of arable land and 1,938 a. of grassland in the parish, and 7 a. of woodland at West Newton.[40] At Aldbrough, East Newton, and Fosham there were 3,380 a. under crops and 1,714 a. of permanent grassland in 1905,[41] and the parish was still divided fairly equally between arable and grassland in the 1930s, when the grassland lay mostly south and west of the village and in the north-west of the parish alongside Lambwath stream.[42] In 1987 of 1,307 ha. (3,230 a.) returned under Aldbrough civil parish, 1,137 ha. (2,810 a.) were arable land and 147 ha. (363 a.) grassland; there were then more than 14,000 pigs, nearly 700 sheep, and some poultry and cattle.[43]

The land of Aldbrough village was usually worked by a dozen farmers in the 19th and earlier 20th century, of whom up to three had 150 a. or more in 1851 and the 1920s and 1930s.[44] East and West Newton had nine farms in 1851, fairly evenly divided between larger and smaller units, but by the mid 20th century smaller farms predominated in both.[45] Over the same period Bewick, Carlton, Etherdwick, Fosham, and Tansterne each had up to three farms, all or most of them of 150 a. or more. Half a dozen cowkeepers worked in the parish in the late 19th century, and later there were one or two dairy farmers. Market gardening has also been pursued at Aldbrough, and there and at West Newton a few smallholdings had been provided by the 1930s. In 1987 of 18 holdings returned under Aldbrough, two were of over 200 ha. (494 a.), two of 100–199 ha. (247–492 a.), two of 50–99 ha. (124–245 a.), three of 10–49 ha. (25–121 a.), and nine of under 10 ha.[46]

MARKET. A market on Tuesdays and a fair on the eve and feast of St. Bartholomew (24 August) were granted to James de Ros for his manor of Aldbrough in 1332.[47] The market place

26 R.D.B., F/437/944; *Y.A.J.* xiii. 45–6; *Yorks. Deeds*, iv, p. 10.
27 B.I.H.R., TER. H. Aldbrough 1726; E.R.A.O., DDKI/3/1.
28 H.U.L., DDCV/2/1, s.a. 1741.
29 10 Geo. III, c. 71 (Priv. Act); R.D.B., AQ/46/6.
30 *Trans. R. Hist. S.* N.S. vii. 247.
31 Map of 1728.
32 P.R.O., SC 11/762; ibid. C 66/1903, no. 9.
33 Ibid. CP 25(1)/278/141, no. 27.
34 E.R.A.O., DDCC/18/2.
35 P.R.O., C 142/65, no. 61; E 150/240, no. 12.
36 *Cal. Inq. p.m.* v, p. 144; *Cal. Pat.* 1307–13, 370.
37 O.S. Map 6", Yorks. CCXII (1855 edn.).
38 H.U.L., DHO/9/16; *Cal. Pat.* 1343–5, 586; below, Swine, Marton, econ. hist.
39 P.R.O., HO 67/26/12.
40 B.I.H.R., TA. 59L, 252M, 870VL.
41 Acreage Returns, 1905.
42 [1st] Land Util. Surv. Map, sheets 33–4.
43 Inf. from Min. of Agric., Fish. & Food, Beverley, 1990.
44 Para. based on P.R.O., HO 107/2365; directories.
45 R.D.B., 1295/284/255.
46 Inf. from Min. of Agric., Fish. & Food.
47 *Cal. Chart. R.* 1327–41, 288.

was in Church Street.[48] The tolls were later owed to the lords of Holderness.[49] By the late 18th century the market had been discontinued and the fair was mainly for cattle; William Constable was entitled to 1*d.* for each beast sold and 1*d.* for each stall in 1779, when the tolls were let for 13*s.* 4*d.* a year.[50] The fair was held on 4 September in 1792.[51] It ceased to be held *c.* 1880, but a hiring fair was briefly revived later.[52]

INDUSTRY, TRADE, AND PROFESSIONAL ACTIVITY. Aldbrough had the usual occupations of a small commercial centre in the 19th and earlier 20th century, and one or two craftsmen and shopkeepers were also recorded at West Newton in the earlier period.[53] There were one or two brewers and maltsters at Aldbrough in the mid 19th century, and from 1878 Ralph Jackson, later Messrs. Ralph Jackson & Sons, was brewing and malting at a works on Hornsea Road, which was called Brewer's Street by 1851; the works had closed by 1923.[54] Bricks were made at Aldbrough by the beginning of the 19th century, and one or two brick-and tile-makers were recorded in the 1840s; there was later only one concern, with a works at the west end of the village,[55] which was closed *c.* 1915.

In the late 13th century income from wrecks and fish sales was paid to the lords of Holderness by a reeve at Ringbrough.[56] Aldbrough was included in a list of ports in 1565,[57] and there was still a little coastal trade in the earlier 19th century,[58] when lime-burning was carried on near the coast.[59] Cobbles, sand, and gravel have been taken from the shore at Aldbrough: dealers in stone and gravel were recorded there in 1851,[60] and Sir Thomas Constable, Bt., lord of Holderness, successfully defended his rights over the shore in 1864, and in 1870 licensed three Aldbrough men to take cobbles at the rate of 6*d.* a ton.[61] In the 1920s and early 1930s a few boats fished from Aldbrough, more than 13,000 crabs and nearly 400 lobsters being caught in 1930.[62]

Omnibus proprietors were recorded at Aldbrough in 1892,[63] and East Yorkshire Motor

Services Ltd. had a garage there *c.* 1935. There have also been haulage contracting and agricultural and motor engineering concerns in the parish,[64] and a firm of motor engineers still operated in the village in 1991.

MILLS. A windmill stood by the 14th century on land of Bewick manor in Aldbrough North field.[65] The same or a rebuilt mill was called Old mill from 1685;[66] it ceased to be used *c.* 1905 and was later demolished.[67] A windmill at Carlton or Aldbrough formed part of the Michelbournes' estate in the mid 16th century, and was possibly mentioned again in 1671.[68] Another mill was built beside the Carlton road after 1764, and later called Aldbrough mill.[69] It was assisted by steam by 1889, ceased to be used *c.* 1930, and has been demolished. A third mill at Aldbrough may have existed *c.* 1840.[70]

Other windmills were recorded at Ringbrough in 1351, at Fosham in 1577-8, and at Etherdwick from 1600 until its removal by 1753. The last stood near the boundary with Aldbrough village. The site of the Ringbrough mill was later commemorated by Mill hill west of the farm,[71] and that at Fosham by Mill field closes.[72] There was perhaps also a water mill at West Newton, where land called Mill dam was mentioned in the 14th century.[73]

LOCAL GOVERNMENT. In the Middle Ages breaches of the assize of ale at Aldbrough were presented in Roos manor court and officers appointed there included ale- and bread-tasters for the village.[74] By the 14th century Ringbrough manor court was held infrequently.[75] That of the Aldbrough manor formerly belonging to Kirkstall abbey was mentioned in 1611,[76] and court papers, including presentments, pains, and call rolls, survive for Tymperon's manor, evidently the same, for 1732-59.[77] The court, which had view of frankpledge, met annually and was almost entirely concerned with agricultural regulation at Aldbrough and East Newton. Besides 2 affeerors and a pinder, 2 constables and 2 bylawmen were appointed for

48 Above, intro.
49 H.U.L., DHO/7/42; DHO/8/47.
50 E.R.A.O., DDCC(2)/Box 8/17, survey 1779.
51 *1st Rep. Com. Mkt. Rights and Tolls* [C. 5550], p. 216, H.C. (1888), liii.
52 Bulmer, *Dir. E. Yorks.* (1892), 301, 303; *Kelly's Dir. N. & E.R. Yorks.* (1872), 310.
53 Para. based on directories.
54 R.D.B., CK/435/722; MN/252/402; 89/228/214 (1897); 265/249/211; 265/573/496; P.R.O., HO 107/2365; O.S. Map 1/2,500, Yorks. CCXIII. 9 (1891 edn.).
55 O.S. Map 6″, Yorks. CCXIII (1855 edn.); R.D.B., CO/206/329; *Hull Advertiser*, 25 Dec. 1813.
56 H.U.L., DHO/9/16-17.
57 *Acts of P.C.* 1558-70, 289.
58 *Hull Advertiser*, 17 Apr. 1835.
59 O.S. Map 6″, Yorks. CCXIII (1855 edn.).
60 P.R.O., HO 107/2365.
61 E.R.A.O., DDCC/136/167, 170, 173.
62 N.E. Sea Fisheries Cttee. *Mins.* 1921-3, 111; 1931-3, 150, and *passim*.
63 Bulmer, *Dir. E. Yorks.* (1892), 304.
64 Directories.
65 Greater Lond. R. O., H 1/ST/E 67/1/48; H.U.L.,

DHO/7/12, 14; *Cal. Inq. p.m.* v, p. 144; above, this section.
66 E.R.A.O., DDRI/1/1; ibid. IA. Aldbrough; B.I.H.R., TER. H. Aldbrough 1685, etc.; O.S. Map 6″, Yorks. CCXIII (1855 edn.).
67 Directories; O.S. Map 1/2,500, Yorks. CCXIII. 9 (1910 edn.).
68 P.R.O., CP 25(2)/755/23 Chas. II Mich. [no. 43]; *Yorks. Fines*, i. 231.
69 E.R.A.O., IA. Aldbrough; O.S. Map 6″, Yorks. CCXII (1855 edn.).
70 Directories.
71 Ringbrough: P.R.O., C 135/112, no. 37; O.S. Map 6″, Yorks. CCXIII (1855 edn.); Etherdwick: P.R.O., CP 25(2)/805/2-3 Jas. II Hil. no. 43; ibid. C 142/268, no. 133; R.D.B., U/128/243; W/383/777; Fosham: *Yorks. Fines*, ii. 114.
72 R.D.B., DR/274/329; Poulson, *Holderness*, ii. 26; O.S. Map 6″, Yorks. CCXII (1855 edn.).
73 Burton Constable Hall, DDCC/141/68, cart. p. 3 (a).
74 Burghley Ho., near Stamford (Lincs.), MS. 37/18 (Roos ct. rolls), s.vv. Oct. 1299, Oct. 1404, Oct. 1416.
75 *Y.A.J.* xiii. 46.
76 P.R.O., C 66/1903, no. 9.
77 H.U.L., DDCV/2/1-2; above, manors.

Aldbrough, and a constable and sometimes also 2 bylawmen for East Newton and Ringbrough. Bewick manor court was mentioned in the 16th and 17th centuries, but there is no record of its business.[78] The grant in 1611 of Thorpe Garth manor included a court, and a meeting was said to have been held c. 1800.[79] The agriculture and drainage of West Newton were regulated in Burton Constable court in the 15th century, when officers elected there included a messor for West Newton. Later officers of the court, which had view of frankpledge, were 1–2 bylawmen for West Newton, appointed in the mid 16th century, the constable, and an aletaster.[80]

Surviving parish records include overseers' accounts for 1681–9 and 1732–65 and a volume for 1650–1823 containing appointments of parish officers, summary accounts, and church and poor rates.[81] The overseers' accounts are largely concerned with the administration of Towrie's charity. The poor were employed in spinning and weaving linen in the mid 18th century, when those relieved included residents at East and West Newton, which later relieved their own poor. At East Newton three persons received permanent and one occasional poor relief in 1802–3, and at West Newton four people were relieved permanently in 1802–3 and c. 15 occasionally in 1812–15. In the rest of the parish permanent relief was given to 47 people in 1802–3 and to c. 20 between 1812 and 1815; in the same periods 5 and c. 20 persons were relieved occasionally.[82] Poorhouses were maintained by the overseers in the village, and possibly also at East and West Newton.[83] Two cottages at the north end of the village were later maintained by the parish council and c. 1900 were occupied rent-free; they were demolished in 1937.[84] Aldbrough, East Newton, and West Newton with Burton Constable joined Skirlaugh poor-law union in 1837[85] and remained in Skirlaugh rural district until 1935. Aldbrough and East Newton, as part of the new civil parish of Aldbrough, and West Newton with Burton Constable, as part of the enlarged parish of Burton Constable, were then taken into Holderness rural district. Aldbrough and Burton Constable civil parishes became part of the Holderness district of Humberside in 1974.[86] In 1996 Aldbrough and Burton Constable parishes became part of a new East Riding unitary area.[87]

A cemetery for Aldbrough and East Newton on the Carlton road was provided by the rural district council in 1922, parts being consecrated in 1923 and 1961.[88]

The E.R. constabulary, established in 1857, had a constable based at Aldbrough.[89]

CHURCH. According to an 11th-century inscription in Aldbrough church, it was built by Ulf, perhaps the tenant of Aldbrough in 1066.[90] The church was not, however, recorded again until 1115 when, with other churches in Holderness, it was given to Aumale priory, later abbey (Seine Maritime).[91] Aumale abbey appropriated the church in 1228 and a vicarage had evidently been ordained by 1252.[92] In 1396 Aumale abbey sold the church to Kirkstall abbey (Yorks. W.R.), which then appropriated it.[93] Chapels belonging to the church were recorded at Carlton, Ringbrough, Tansterne, and Thorpe in 1309.[94] There may also have been a chapel at Bewick where, in return for 20 a. given to Aldbrough church, Robert of Meaux (d. by 1196) was licensed to build a chapel and hear mass.[95] After the loss to the sea of Little Cowden (Colden) church that living was annexed to Aldbrough and the parishes were later often regarded as one.[96] In 1962 detached parts of the parish of Aldbrough with Colden Parva in Great Cowden were annexed to Mappleton and the detached part of Mappleton parish was transferred to Aldbrough with Colden Parva.[97] Aldbrough with Colden Parva was united with the benefices of Mappleton with Goxhill and Withernwick in 1979.[98]

The patronage of the vicarage belonged to Aumale abbey and from 1396 until the Dissolution to Kirkstall abbey. During war with France Aumale's estate was seized by the Crown, which presented repeatedly between 1344 and 1369, and turns granted by Kirkstall were exercised by Edward Gower in 1465 and Alice Midgley in 1547. After the Dissolution the Crown retained the patronage.[99] The archbishop of York was granted the advowson in 1558,[1] but the grant was apparently ineffective except for collations by the archbishop in 1613 and 1614.[2] From 1979 the Crown had one turn in three in the patronage of the united benefice.[3]

The vicarage was worth £6 13s. 4d. a year in 1291 and £13 15s. in 1535.[4] The improved

78   Greater Lond. R. O., H 1/ST/E 67/1/48; H 1/ST/E 67/3/59.
79   P.R.O., C 66/1903, no. 9; H.U.L., DHO/7/44; Poulson, *Holderness*, ii. 5.
80   E.R.A.O., DDCC/18/1, s.v. Apr. 1434; DDCC/18/2–3.
81   Ibid. PE/76/35–8, 53; ibid. DDCC/1/1.
82   *Poor Law Abstract, 1804*, pp. 592–3; *1818*, pp. 520–3.
83   B.I.H.R., TA. 252M, 870VL; E.R.A.O., DDCC/141/86.
84   R.D.B., 584/604/466; *Kelly's Dir. N. & E.R. Yorks.* (1905), 414; O.S. Map 6″, Yorks. CCXIII (1855 edn.).
85   *3rd Rep. Poor Law Com.* 170.   86   *Census.*
87   Humberside (Structural Change) Order 1995, copy at E.R.A.O.
88   R.D.B., 257/110/90; B.I.H.R., CD. 716, 866.
89   A. A. Clarke, *Country Coppers: Story of E.R. Police,* 18–19.
90   Below, this section.

91   *E.Y.C.* iii, pp. 30–1, 35–7; *V.C.H. Yorks. E.R.* v. 18.
92   *Reg. Gray*, pp. 22, 268.
93   *Cal. Inq. Misc.* vi, p. 52; *Cal. Papal Reg.* v. 16; *Cal. Pat.* 1391–6, 585.
94   *Reg. Greenfield*, v, pp. 236–7.
95   *Reg. Pontissara* (Cant. & York Soc.), 740–1; above, manors (Bewick).
96   Below, Mappleton, churches.
97   B.I.H.R., OC. 774. Part of Aldbrough with Colden Parva was, probably mistakenly, left detached.
98   B.I.H.R., OC. 942.
99   Ibid. Bp. Dio. 3, E.R., p. 169; Lawrance, 'Clergy List', Holderness, 1, pp. 2–4; *Cal. Pat.* 1343–5, 348; *Cal. Inq. Misc.* vi, p. 52; *Rep. Com. Eccl. Revenues*, 912–13.
1   *Cal. Pat.* 1557–8, 420.
2   Lawrance, op. cit. p. 4.   3   B.I.H.R., OC. 942.
4   *Tax. Eccl.* (Rec. Com.), 304; *Valor Eccl.* (Rec. Com.), v. 118.

annual value in 1650 was £30.[5] The net income averaged £185 a year in 1829–31,[6] and was £390 in 1884.[7]

Tithes in Carlton worth 10s. a year were given c. 1100 by Arnulf de Montgomery to Sées abbey (Orne), but were evidently resumed on Arnulf's deprivation in 1102.[8] In 1535 nearly all of the vicar's income came from offerings and hay, wool, lamb, and small tithes.[9] In 1706 the tithes and offerings were worth £28.[10]

In Aldbrough village the hay tithes of 80 bovates when fallow and of the balks were compounded for an annual payment of 7d. a bovate by the mid 17th century. Hay tithes from 8 bovates at Aldbrough belonging to Bewick hamlet were relinquished by the vicar to Hugh Bethell, the impropriator at Bewick, c. 1700, and the Bethells as impropriators also successfully claimed some rape tithes and mortuaries in Aldbrough village.[11] At inclosure in 1766 the vicar was awarded 24 a. for the hay tithes of the open fields and some closes; later the commutation was claimed to extend to the tithe of potatoes grown on former open-field land but the vicar successfully disputed that. The land allotted was retained in 1978.[12] The hay tithes of the rest of the old inclosures at Aldbrough, together with the small tithes of the village and most of the hamlets, were commuted for a rent charge of £184 in 1845.[13]

Robert Towrie by will of 1663 devised all the corn and hay tithes of East Newton and half of the same tithes from Ringbrough to augment the vicarage.[14] At the inclosure of East Newton in 1772 the vicar was awarded 75 a. for the great tithes.[15] His half of the great tithes at Ringbrough with the small tithes of East Newton, and presumably also those of Ringbrough, were commuted for a rent charge of £32 in 1845.[16]

At West Newton the vicar was owed 3s. 4d. and venison annually from Venison close, presumably for tithes, from the late 17th century. The small tithes there were commuted for a rent charge of £20 in 1845.[17]

The Towrie augmentation also included ¼ bovate at East Newton; the gift also mentioned a house there but only a garth was recorded from 1685.[18] At inclosure in 1772 the vicar was awarded 5 a. there for glebe, besides the 75 a. for tithes,[19] and a farmhouse was built there c. 1800.[20] Glebe farm was sold in 1968.[21]

A vicarage house recorded in 1535 was later lost; its garth east of the churchyard was recorded from 1685, and a building, evidently not the house, stood there in 1764.[22] In the 19th and early 20th century the vicar or his assistant occupied various houses in the village, among them Aldbrough House, Wentworth House, and Tymperon's House.[23] In 1935 a vicarage house was built in Sea Side Road on land bought from the Tymperon trustees.[24] That house was sold c. 1979 and the incumbent of the united benefice lived at Mappleton until a new benefice house was built in Carlton Drive c. 1983.[25]

In the 13th century Agnes of Kelk founded a chantry in a chapel added to Aldbrough church by her father. As an endowment she gave 6 bovates in Aldbrough to Nunkeeling priory, which was to provide services. The chantry was later transferred to the priory.[26]

By 1300 there was evidently also a chantry in Holy Trinity chapel in Aldbrough church endowed with tithes in Etherdwick, Tansterne, and other places in Holderness. The chantry was probably connected with the abbey of St. Mary and St. German at Selby (Yorks. W.R.): it was named as St. German's chantry in 1341, the tithes were called St. German's, and, whereas Aumale abbey, patron of the vicarage, had the presentation of the chantry priest, the abbot of Selby apparently nominated the presentee until he granted that right to Sir John of Carlton (d. 1304) or one of his predecessors. The Crown exercised the presentation during war with France in the mid 14th century and later it belonged to Carlton's successors in the nomination, the Fauconbergs. The 'advowson', presumably comprising the right both to nominate and to present, was sold by the Fauconbergs to the Nevilles in 1408, and later descended with Rise manor.[27] It was perhaps the same chantry which was called Etherdwick chantry in 1535, when the endowment comprised the corn tithes of Etherdwick worth just over £2 a year. Another chantry at Aldbrough was then said to be worth £1 6s. 8d.[28] The Etherdwick tithes seem later to have been confused with the property of a chantry in Rise church.[29] In 1521 there were guilds dedicated to St. Peter and St. Mary, and a guild house at Aldbrough was mentioned in 1566.[30]

[5] T.E.R.A.S. iv. 51.
[6] Rep. Com. Eccl. Revenues, 912–13.
[7] B.I.H.R., V. 1884/Ret. 1.
[8] E.Y.C. iii, pp. 27–8.
[9] Valor Eccl. v. 118.
[10] B.I.H.R., Bp Dio. 3, E.R., p. 169.
[11] Ibid. TER. H. Aldbrough 1685–1743; P.R.O., E 134/1655 East./5.
[12] R.D.B., AH/1/1; B.I.H.R., CONS. CP. 1835/8; above, manors (rectory); inf. from York Dioc. Bd. of Finance, 1981.
[13] B.I.H.R., TA. 870VL.
[14] Ibid. TER. H. Aldbrough 1685–1726; 9th Rep. Com. Char. 752.
[15] R.D.B., AQ/46/6.
[16] B.I.H.R., TA. 252M.
[17] Ibid. TER. H. Aldbrough 1685, etc.; ibid. TA. 59L.
[18] Ibid. TER. H. Aldbrough 1685, etc.; above, this section.
[19] R.D.B., AQ/46/6.
[20] B.I.H.R., TER. H. Aldbrough 1786, 1809.
[21] Ibid. TA. 252M; R.D.B., 1574/343/287.
[22] B.I.H.R., TER. H. Aldbrough 1685, etc.; Valor Eccl. (Rec. Com.) v. 118; E.R.A.O., IA. Aldbrough.
[23] B.I.H.R., V. 1884/Ret. 1; E.R.A.O., PE/76/41, letter 1933; PE/76/49; R.D.B., MP/269/382; 35/309/297 (1901); O.S. Map 1/2,500, Yorks. CCXIII. 9 (1910 edn.); 9th Rep. Com. Char. 829–31; directories; inf. from Mr. A. Dent, Wentworth Ho., 1991.
[24] R.D.B., 518/534/401; E.R.A.O., PE/76/41.
[25] B.I.H.R., OC. 942; inf. from Mr. R. N. Jackson, Aldbrough, 1991–2; Crockford (1989–90).
[26] B.L. Cott. MS. Otho, C. viii, ff. 78 and v., 83v., 85v.; cf. above, manors (Thorpe).
[27] Lawrance, 'Clergy List', Holderness, 2, pp. 179–80; Reg. Corbridge, i, p. 158; Reg. Greenfield, iii, p. 230; Cal. Inq. p.m. iv, p. 226; Cal. Pat. 1340–3, 185; 1348–50, 427; below, Rise, manor.
[28] Valor Eccl. (Rec. Com.), v. 118, 146.
[29] Above, manors (rectory); below, Rise, church.
[30] B.I.H.R., Prob. Reg. 9, f. 166v.; P.R.O., E 310/31/183, f. 59.

Godfrey de Lucy, bishop of Winchester 1189–1204, was rector *c.* 1190.[31] The church was frequently exchanged, and was disputed on at least one occasion, *c.* 1350.[32] William Mooke, vicar from 1528, was a York prebendary, and Aldbrough was later often held by non-residents with other benefices;[33] curates were employed to do the duty.[34] About 1645 Lord Fairfax replaced the delinquent vicar John Hutton with John Fenwick, but both men were contesting the Easter offerings and tithes in the early 1650s; competing celebrations of communion were held in the church and a house during the dispute which led to a division of tithes. Parishioners later refused payment, and both Hutton and Fenwick were accused of using the prohibited Book of Common Prayer and Fenwick of inviting preachers disaffected to the government, including Hutton, and of tippling.[35] The incumbent lived at Humbleton in 1743 and at Hull in 1764, in which year service was weekly and communion was celebrated four times, usually with *c.* 55 recipients.[36] By 1865 two Sunday services were held, an evening school for boys was tried unsuccessfully later in the decade, and in 1884 there was also a children's service.[37] Celebrations of communion were monthly in the later 19th century, generally with *c.* 20 recipients. In the earlier 20th century sevices were held in a church hut,[38] and youth clubs, including the Y.M.C.A., were provided.[39] Communion was then weekly but very few received. The church hut was removed from Aldbrough to West Newton and opened in 1939 as a chapel-of-ease dedicated to St. Mary. It was used for services, including communion, at first weekly and later fortnightly; up to 10 people usually took communion there in the 1960s but it was closed soon afterwards.[40]

The church of *ST. BARTHOLOMEW*, so called in 1310,[41] is built of boulders and ashlar; it comprises chancel with north chapel, aisled and clerestoried nave, south porch, and massive, three-stage, west tower. A stone sundial reset in the south aisle wall has an Anglo-Scandinavian inscription recording that Ulf built the church for himself and for the soul of Guneware,[42] and the long and narrow nave probably preserves the plan of Ulf's earlier 11th-century church. The chancel has remains of two 11th-century windows in the north wall, a pre-Conquest, sculpted, monolithic window head in the south wall, and possibly reset, 12th-century chevron above the south door.[43] The lower stages of the tower are of *c.* 1200. Nave, chancel, and tower are all of similar width. The aisles were added in the 12th century and their walls were rebuilt in the 14th, when the south aisle was extended eastward for a short distance alongside the chancel. The chancel was also remodelled in the 14th century and the north chapel added then, perhaps for Sir John Meaux of Bewick (d. *c.* 1377).[44] The chapel was later used for the village school.[45] The top stage of the tower was remodelled in the 15th century and the clerestory added in the 16th.[46]

The chancel was in disrepair in 1568.[47] The church was repaired and the chancel screen taken down in 1720.[48] In 1870–1 the church was substantially rebuilt to designs by William Perkin of Leeds. The work included the renewal of the chancel arch, the restoration of the nave arcades, aisles, and clerestory, and the reroofing of the whole church. During rebuilding, services were held in the school.[49] The tower was restored in 1907 and again *c.* 1920, when the bells were repaired.[50] Later restoration, mostly effected in 1949–50, included the fitting out of the chancel chapel as a Lady chapel.[51]

In 1353 Sir John Meaux of Bewick alleged that the sea threatened his ancestors' remains in the church and was licensed to re-inter them in Haltemprice priory, near Cottingham, in which he founded a chantry in 1377, shortly before his own death.[52] He nevertheless requested burial in Aldbrough church, in St. Mary's aisle, evidently the chancel chapel where two 14th-century tomb chests bearing stone effigies of a man and a woman are believed to commemorate him and his wife.[53] The size of the man's effigy led to the tomb being called Giant Morrell's and its location Morrell's or Morrill's aisle.[54] Above the knight hangs a replica of the medieval helmet associated

---

[31] *Reg. Pontissara*, 740–1; above, manors (Bewick).

[32] B.I.H.R., CP. E. 64; Lawrance, op. cit. pp. 2–3; *Cal. Pat. 1367–70*, 310.

[33] B.I.H.R., V. 1764/Ret. 1, no. 13; Lawrance, op. cit. p. 4; *Rep. Com. Eccl. Revenues*, 912–13; *Herring's Visit.* i, pp. 192, 221.

[34] E.R.A.O., PE/76/53, s.a. 1747, 1749; ibid. DDCC/1/1; B.I.H.R., Bp. Dio. 3, E.R., p. 169; ibid. ER. V./Ret. 1, f. 38v.; ibid. TER. H. Aldbrough 1773, 1809; Baines, *Hist. Yorks.* (1823), ii. 149; *Rep. Com. Eccl. Revenues*, 912–13.

[35] P.R.O., E 134/1655 East./5; E 134/1655 East./19.

[36] B.I.H.R., V. 1764/Ret. 1. No return was made in 1743: *Herring's Visit.* i, pp. 192, 221.

[37] *1st Rep. Com. on Employment of Children, Young Persons, and Women in Agric., App. Pt. II* [4068-I], p. 366, H.C. (1867–8), xvii. Rest of para. based on B.I.H.R., V. 1865/Ret. 1, no. 13; V. 1868/Ret. 1, no. 13; V. 1871/Ret. 1, no. 12; V. 1877/Ret. 1, no. 12; V. 1884/Ret. 1; V. 1912–22/Ret.; V. 1931/Ret.

[38] E.R.A.O., PE/76/35.

[39] Above, intro. (Aldbrough village).

[40] E.R.A.O., PE/76/19 (2); PE/76/24, letter 1939; PE/76/55; above, intro. (Aldbrough village); inf. from Mr. R. N. Jackson, Aldbrough, 1992.

[41] *Cal. Inq. p.m.* vii, p. 293.

[42] J. Lang, *Corpus of Anglo-Saxon Sculpture*, iii, 123–4; *Y.A.J.* xxi. 256–8; A. L. Binns, *E. Yorks. in the Sagas* (E. Yorks. Loc. Hist. Ser. xxii), 20; Poulson, *Holderness*, ii. 6, all illus.

[43] Illus. in Poulson, *Holderness*, ii. 1, 15.

[44] Above, manors (Bewick); below, this section.

[45] Below, educ.

[46] For unrestored building, *T.E.R.A.S.* xxiii. 29 (reprod. of watercolour in ch.), 31; Poulson, *Holderness*, ii. 11–15, illus.

[47] *Cal. Pat. 1566–9*, p. 263.

[48] B.I.H.R., ER. V./Ret. 1, f. 38v.; *Y.A.J.* xxiv. 109, 132–3.

[49] B.I.H.R., Ch. Ret. i; ibid. V. 1871/Ret. 1, no. 12; ibid. Fac. 1870/1; E.R.A.O., PE/76/19 (1); PE/76/24, acct.; PE/76, accession 1435, corresp. 1870–5.

[50] E.R.A.O., PE/76/35, s.vv. 1904, 1922; *Kelly's Dir. N. & E.R. Yorks.* (1909), 425.

[51] B.I.H.R., Fac. 1943/44; E.R.A.O., PE/76/19 (3); PE/76/24, corresp. 1939–50, acct. 1946; photo. in ch.

[52] B.I.H.R., Reg. 11, f. 7v.; *Y.A.J.* xliii. 107; Dugdale, *Mon.* vi. 521; Hist. MSS. Com. 78, *Hastings*, i, p. 173.

[53] *Y.A.J.* xxvi. 230–1.

[54] B.I.H.R., TER. H. Aldbrough 1685, etc.; Poulson, *Holderness*, i. 475 (illus.); ii. 12, 20.

with his tomb;[55] since 1978 the original helmet has been at the Tower of London.[56]

The fittings include choir stalls of the 1930s by J. Wippell & Co. Ltd.[57] Bells from Ravenser Odd chapel, in Easington, were bought after its destruction in the 14th century for Aldbrough church,[58] and there were three bells in 1552 and later.[59] The plate includes a cup with cover made in 1662 and a paten of 1701.[60] The registers of burials begin in 1570 and those of baptisms and marriages in 1571; they are largely complete.[61]

The churchyard was closed in 1923 and replaced by a cemetery on the Carlton road.[62] A lich-gate was added in 1952 as a war memorial.[63]

The parish clerk was entitled to four sheaves from each bovate at Great Cowden belonging to Aldbrough parish until inclosure in 1772, when a rent charge of nearly £2 a year was substituted.[64]

NONCONFORMITY. Roman Catholicism was fostered by the Constables, who were seated just outside the parish at Burton Constable, in Swine. The family's tenants at West Newton were served by the chaplain at Burton Constable, and in the later 17th century by a priest partly supported by the Constables and resident at Marton, in Swine. Recusants and non-communicants recorded under Aldbrough sometimes included the Burton Constable household: John Constable, viscount Dunbar, and his wife were, for instance, included among 29 persons named between 1664 and 1666. Numbers rose to c. 50 in the later 18th century,[65] and in 1764 the parish had 12 Roman Catholic families.[66]

Protestant dissenters in 1676 were said to number 50.[67] Most may have been Friends. The monthly meeting was occasionally held at Aldbrough in the later 17th century, and John Raines of Aldbrough was a prominent Friend in 1678, as were later the Fosters of Bewick.[68] In 1764 six Quaker families lived in the parish.[69] A meeting house at the west end of the village was registered in 1778,[70] but no more is known of

the congregation. Thomas Thompson, a leading Hull Methodist, and others registered a house in Aldbrough in 1781,[71] and the Wesleyans built a chapel in 1803.[72] It was perhaps remodelled in 1828, and was later often said to have been built then.[73] The chapel, in High Street, was rebuilt on an enlarged site in 1888,[74] and an adjoining schoolroom, put up in 1835, was reconstructed in 1907. The chapel was closed in 1939.[75] An unidentified protestant congregation registered a house in Aldbrough in 1791, and another in 1802.[76] The Primitive Methodists built a chapel in Hornsea Road in 1850, added a schoolroom in 1899,[77] and enlarged the chapel in 1907.[78] The chapel was closed in 1961, on the opening of a new Methodist church in High Street.[79] After their closure the former Wesleyan chapel was used by a dairyman, and the Primitive Methodist buildings as a shop.

At West Newton a chapel registered by the Wesleyans in 1907 was closed in 1933. The building, north of the street, was later demolished.[80]

EDUCATION. Towrie's charity employed a teacher from the 1680s, and in 1741 books and fuel for the school were also provided.[81] In 1818 there was a school for boys and another for girls at Aldbrough, each attended by c. 60 children; c. 17 pupils in each were paid for from the charity, at a cost of c. £20 a year in 1823.[82] In 1833 the charity was supporting 26 of the 45 boys at an Aldbrough school,[83] probably that for boys held in the church until its removal by 1840,[84] and in 1855 c. 35 boys were taught at the charity's expense. The trustees built a new school for boys and girls on their land in Headlands Road in 1862,[85] and 20 boys and 20 girls were taught free there, along with fee-paying pupils, in 1868.[86] There were 70 pupils on inspection day in 1871,[87] and 90 in 1877,[88] when the Church school received £52 a year from the charity.[89] An annual government grant was received from 1882–3, and in 1896 a class-

55 Y.A.J. xliii. 109–11; T.E.R.A.S. xxii, p. xx; Test. Ebor. i, pp. 100–1. For re-sitings of the man's tomb, E.R.A.O., PE/76/19 (3); PE/76/24, plan [1940s]; Poulson, Holderness, ii. 12–13.
56 Sunday Times, 28 May 1989; Hull Daily Mail, 31 Jan. 1989; inf. from Mr. R. N. Jackson, Aldbrough, 1992.
57 E.R.A.O., PE/76/35, s.v. 1930; PE/76, accession 1435, design.
58 Chron. de Melsa, iii. 79; V.C.H. Yorks. E.R. v. 30.
59 Inventories of Ch. Goods, 37; Boulter, 'Ch. Bells', 82.
60 Yorks. Ch. Plate, i. 210.
61 E.R.A.O., PE/76/1–4, 7.
62 Ibid. PE/76/29; above, local govt.   63 Plaque.
64 R.D.B., AQ/61/8; B.I.H.R., TER. H. Aldbrough 1768, 1773.
65 E.R.A.O., DDCC/111/34; Aveling, Post Reformation Catholicism, 54, 67; Herring's Visit. iv, p. 206.
66 B.I.H.R., V. 1764/Ret. 1, no. 13.
67 Compton Census, ed. Whiteman, 600.
68 H.U.L., DQR/17/3, 37, 43, 64, 72; E.R.A.O., DDQR/17.
69 B.I.H.R., V. 1764/Ret. 1, no. 13.
70 E.R.A.O., QSF. Christ. 1778, D.9; P.R.O., RG 31/7, no. 50; H.U.L., DQR/17/49.
71 B.I.H.R., Fac. Bk. 2, p. 272; V.C.H. Yorks. E.R. i. 313–14.

72 B.I.H.R., Fac. Bk. 3, p. 349; P.R.O., HO 129/522/3/2/6; R.D.B., HG/54/61.
73 Directories; T. Allen, Hist. Co. York, iv. 251.
74 R.D.B., 25/440/318 (1888); Kelly's Dir. N. & E.R. Yorks. (1889), 321; (1893), 355.
75 R.D.B., 91/16/15 (1897); E.R.A.O., MRH/1/33, letter 1933; date stone on sch.; inf. from Mr. H. Colley, Aldbrough, 1992.
76 B.I.H.R., Fac. Bk. 2, p. 477; 3, p. 294.
77 P.R.O., HO 129/522/3/2/5; datestones.
78 Kelly's Dir. N. & E.R. Yorks. (1909), 426.
79 O.N.S. (Birkdale), Worship Reg. nos. 506, 68476; datestone; inf. from Mr. Colley.
80 O.N.S. (Birkdale), Worship Reg. nos. 42311, 45087; O.S. Map 1/2,500, Yorks. CCXII. 15 (1910 edn.); inf. from Mr. Colley.
81 E.R.A.O., PE/76/53; below, charities.
82 Educ. of Poor Digest, 1075; Baines, Hist. Yorks. (1823), ii. 149.   83 Educ. Enq. Abstract, 1078.
84 Poulson, Holderness, ii. 12–13; T. Allen, Hist. Co. York, iv. 249.
85 P.R.O., ED 7/135, no. 2; ED 49/8506.
86 B.I.H.R., V. 1868/Ret. 1, no. 13.
87 Returns relating to Elem. Educ. 472–3.
88 B.I.H.R., V. 1877/Ret. 1, no. 12.
89 P.R.O., ED 7/135, no. 2.

room was added to meet the requirements of the Education Department.[90] A Scheme of 1906 separated the educational part of the charity from the rest as the Towrie Educational Foundation, which was endowed with the school buildings and a quarter of the net income, to be spent on prizes, scholarships, or evening classes for children of the parish.[91] Attendance at the school, which took infants, was usually c. 100 from 1906 until the mid 1930s when it fell to c. 80.[92] The Towrie trustees transferred the school to the county council, and sold the council land to rebuild and extend it, in 1928,[93] and they provided a school playing field in 1940.[94] During rebuilding in 1929 pupils were taught in the Y.M.C.A. hut and the Wesleyan Sunday school.[95] Additional space was provided by the use of the youth club hut from 1953, and by the transfer of senior pupils to South Holderness County Secondary School in 1954.[96] A new wing, providing nursery and infant accommodation, a hall, and offices, were built on land bought from the Towrie trustees and opened in 1979. In 1991 there were 166 juniors and infants and 40 part-time nursery pupils on the roll.[97] In 1983 a Scheme reunited the two parts of Towrie's charity, and made one of its objects the promotion of young people's education,[98] and c. 1990 the school received about £200 a year which was spent on books and school visits.[99]

In 1833 there were three other schools at Aldbrough in which 25 boys and 50 girls were taught at their parents' expense.[1] An infants' school recorded in 1851 had 30 pupils in 1865, and 29 children attended two dames' schools in the 1870s. At West Newton there was a schoolmistress in 1851, and a mixed school with 14 pupils in 1871;[2] it was perhaps the same school which received a grant from Towrie's charity in 1892.[3]

CHARITIES FOR THE POOR. John Thorpe (d. 1640) devised land in Aldbrough to his uncle George Towrie charged with £2 10s. a year for the poor of the parish, but no more is known of it.[4] Robert Towrie by will dated 1663 left a farm at Aldbrough for the poor of the parish; the income was to be spent in raising children, apprenticing boys, and relieving the old.[5] The

charity took effect in 1681, and in the 1840s its management was disputed in Chancery.[6] The income, c. £20 a year in the late 17th and 18th century, was mostly used to provide clothing, fuel, cash doles for those not on poor relief, and schooling for children.[7] About three boys a year were apprenticed in the early 19th century. The trustees received 115 a. at inclosure in 1766,[8] and the farmhouse was rebuilt opposite the church, apparently on a new site, in 1789,[9] and later refronted. Another house at Aldbrough, said in 1729 to be partly used as an almshouse, may have been supported by the charity,[10] and in 1803 two cottages, nos. 32 and 34 Church Street, were built by the trustees, and later occupied rent-free.[11] In 1823 the farm, of c. 130 a., was let for £200 a year. The estate was reduced to c. 115 a. in 1901 and 98 a. in 1955, and the annual gross income fell from nearly £150 c. 1900 to £104 in 1955.[12] In 1906 a Scheme assigned three quarters of the net income to provide cash payments, goods, and services for elderly parishioners and young persons; the educational branch of the charity might apprentice boys.[13] Before and after the charity's reorganization, eleemosynary expenditure was usually in the form of cash doles; in the early 20th century up to £100 a year was given to some 40 persons, and sixty gifts of 6s. each were made at Christmas in 1954.[14] In 1983 a Scheme reunited the educational and eleemosynary branches of Towrie's charity, and made one of its objects the relief of needy residents of Aldbrough and Burton Constable civil parishes.[15] In 1985–6 the gross income of the charity from land, including some at East Newton, and stock was nearly £6,000 a year; Christmas boxes of £10 each were then given to 154 persons, and c. £90 was spent on transport for the old.[16]

William Tymperon, by will proved in 1729, devised his estate at Aldbrough for an almshouse in Beverley. Two inhabitants of Aldbrough were to be housed in the hospital, which when established took only women.[17] Under a Scheme of 1824 a three-roomed almshouse was built soon afterwards at Aldbrough for three almswomen, who were each to receive 6s. a week, clothes, and coal. The new house was evidently for almspeople from Aldbrough, and the Beverley hospital was reserved for residents of that town[18] until

[90] Ibid. ED 49/8506; *Rep. of Educ. Cttee. of Council, 1882–3* [C. 3706-I], p. 752, H.C. (1883), xxv.
[91] P.R.O., ED 49/8506; 1983 Scheme in possession of trustees, 1992.
[92] *Bd. of Educ., List 21* (H.M.S.O., 1908 and later edns.).
[93] R.D.B., 371/39/32; 373/530/438; E.R. Educ. Cttee. *Mins.* 1927–8, 33, 38–9, 183; 1928–9, 42, 165.
[94] R.D.B., 631/558/451; 649/194/167; E.R. Educ. Cttee. *Mins.* 1938–9, 87; 1939–40, 222; 1940–1, 20–1.
[95] E.R. Educ. Cttee. *Mins* 1929–30, 37; datestone on sch.
[96] E.R. Educ. Cttee. *Mins.* 1952–3, 226; 1953–4, 9, 145; above, intro. (Aldbrough village).
[97] E.R. Educ. Cttee. *Mins.* 1965–6, 44; plaque in sch.; inf. from the head teacher, Aldbrough, 1992.
[98] Scheme in possession of trustees.
[99] Inf. from the head teacher.
[1] *Educ. Enq. Abstract*, 1078.
[2] B.I.H.R., V. 1865/Ret. 1, no. 13; V. 1877/Ret. 1, no. 12; P.R.O., HO 107/2365; *Returns relating to Elem. Educ.* 472–3.
[3] Bulmer, *Dir. E. Yorks.* (1892), 303.
[4] P.R.O., C 142/609, no. 77.
[5] Para. based on *9th Rep. Com. Char.* 752.
[6] *Hull Advertiser*, 17 Nov., 15 Dec. 1843; cf. E.R.A.O., DDCC/1/1, s.v. 1746.
[7] E.R.A.O., PE/76/53; B.I.H.R., V. 1764/Ret. 1, no. 13; above, education. [8] R.D.B., AH/1/1.
[9] Datestone; E.R.A.O., IA. Aldbrough.
[10] R.D.B., M/5/7.
[11] White, *Dir. E. & N.R. Yorks.* (1840), 256; 1983 Scheme in possession of trustees, 1992.
[12] E.R.A.O., accession 1681; R.D.B., 648/549/458.
[13] P.R.O., ED 49/8506; 1983 Scheme.
[14] E.R.A.O., accession 1681.
[15] Scheme. [16] E.R.A.O., CCH. 79.
[17] *9th Rep. Com. Char.* 829–31; para. based on *V.C.H. Yorks. E.R.* vi. 269.
[18] E.R.A.O., PE/76/48; PE/76, accession 1435, accts. 1841–60; T. Allen, *Hist. Co. York*, iv. 251; *Kelly's Dir. N. & E.R. Yorks.* (1872), 310; O.S. Map 6", Yorks. CCXIII (1855 edn.).

1911, when it was laid down that one or two of the inmates at Beverley might again come from Aldbrough.[19] Tymperon's hospital at Aldbrough, close to the church, is a single-storeyed building which echoes the earlier Beverley house in the round-headed, blank arcading of its façade.[20] In the early 20th century repairs and the support of the widowed occupants usually cost *c.* £60 a year.[21] Most of the land at Aldbrough was sold in 1952[22] and the hospital at Beverley in 1953, and a new Scheme was obtained in 1957.[23] The endowment then comprised, besides the almshouse, *c.* 1 a. at Aldbrough and just over £14,000 stock. The charity was divided into an almshouse charity and a payment of £100 a year for Aldbrough Sunday school and education in Beverley. The almshouse branch allowed contributions from the almspeople, who were to come from Aldbrough or Beverley. The Scheme also established a building improvement fund, and *c.* 1962 the hospital at Aldbrough was renovated and remodelled as two dwellings.[24] Tymperon's hospital was still maintained in 1991 but stood empty in 1998.

At inclosure in 1766 the overseers of the poor received nearly 14 a.,[25] and by 1852 the field, on Dothams Road, was divided into allotment gardens, which were transferred to the parish council in 1894.[26] There were *c.* 25 tenants on Poor's Field in the early 20th century and still 7 in 1935–6, but later the land was used agriculturally. Tenants' rents produced *c.* £16 a year, which was mostly spent on flour and coal, 87 people benefiting in 1900–1 and 30–40 a year in the mid century.[27] About 1980 the income of £40 was applied with that of Towrie's charity as Christmas doles.[28] Land belonging to Towrie's charity was also let as allotment gardens by 1852 when some of the holdings adjoined Poor's Field.[29] In 1901 the charity had 16 gardens of 1 a. each and 11 of ½ a. or ¼ a.[30]

James Bean (d. 1767) left 2*s.* a week for bread but the rent was lost *c.* 1800.[31] Land in Fitling, in Humbleton, belonged to the poor of West Newton from the 18th century.[32]

BURTON PIDSEA

THE small commuter village of Burton Pidsea stands in the north-western corner of its parish, some 9 km. east of Hull and 5 km. south-west of the North Sea at Grimston, in Garton.[33] The area of the parish was 2,303 a. (932 ha.) in 1852 and has not been changed.[34]

The common Anglian name Burton, or settlement, was used without qualification in 1086 and later, but the personal name Gamel occurs as a suffix in the 12th century and Pidsea has been used since the 13th, both before and after Burton.[35] Gamel was presumably the name of a local landowner.[36] Pidsea is a compound Anglian word referring to a mere which in 1260 belonged jointly to the lord of Burton Pidsea and the Ros family, lords of the adjoining parish of Roos.[37] Pidsea mere was thus on the boundary between the two parishes, possibly in the later Ing carr;[38] it seems to have disappeared after the early 17th century, and the name Pidsea was later applied to the east end of the village.[39] The church belonged to York minster and, perhaps for that reason, or in reference to its dedication, the village has occasionally been called Burton St. Peter.[40]

There were 238 poll-tax payers at Burton Pidsea in 1377,[41] and 56 houses were assessed for hearth tax and 9 discharged in 1672.[42] About 44 families were said to live in the parish in 1743 and 47 in 1764.[43] From 272 in 1801 and 299 in 1811, the population rose sharply to 378 in 1821, then flutuated upwards to 394 in 1851 and 408 in 1861. Thereafter numbers fell, particularly in the 1890s, to 285 in 1901.[44] The population had increased to 326 by 1911 but then fell back to 299 in 1931. There were still only 336 inhabitants in 1951, but numbers increased markedly from the 1960s with the growth of the village, to 430 in 1971 and 925 in 1981. Of 968 usually resident, 933 were counted in 1991.[45]

In the north and centre of the parish the gently undulating land lies mostly between 8 and 15 m. above sea level, but alongside the main drains, and notably in the southern half of the parish, there are extensive areas of lower ground, falling to *c.* 5 m. in the south-western corner of Burton Pidsea. Except for alluvium, chiefly in the valleys of the drains, and small deposits of gravel in and to the south of the village, the parish is on boulder clay.[46] The lower, alluvial

[19] H.U.L., DDCV/15/607.
[20] Cf. *V.C.H. Yorks. E.R.* vi, plate facing p. 269.
[21] E.R.A.O., accession 1681 (accts. 1900–55).
[22] Above, manors (Aldbrough).
[23] Inf. from Messrs. Crust, Todd & Mills & Co., 34 Lairgate, Beverley.
[24] E.R.A.O., PE/76, accession 1435, plans.
[25] R.D.B., AH/1/1.
[26] O.S. Map 6″, Yorks. CCXIII (1855 edn.); *Return of Allotments and Smallholdings*, H.C. 182, p. 359 (1903), lix.
[27] E.R.A.O., accession 1681.
[28] Review of Char. *Rep.* 101.
[29] *1st Rep. Com. on Employment of Children, Young Persons, and Women in Agric., App. Pt. II* [4068-I], p. 366, H.C. (1867–8), xvii; below, this section; cf. E.R.A.O., IA.; O.S. Map 6″, Yorks. CCXIII (1855 edn.).
[30] E.R.A.O., accession 1681.
[31] *9th Rep. Com. Char.* 752–3; memorial in ch.
[32] Below, Humbleton, manors [Fitling].
[33] This article was written between 1997 and 1999. Material for it was collected by Dr. T. N. Cooper.
[34] O.S. Map 6″, Yorks. CCXXVIII, CCXLII (1855 edn.); *Census*, 1991.
[35] Para. based on *P.N. Yorks. E.R.* (E.P.N.S.), 16, 55–6.
[36] Cf. *Cal. Close*, 1346–9, 306; *V.C.H. Yorks. E.R.* v. 191.
[37] *Yorks. Inq.* i, pp. 79, 83; below, Roos, manors.
[38] O.S. Map 6″, Yorks. CCXXVIII, CCXLII (1855 edn.).
[39] Typescript recollections at H.U.L., DDMM/29/66.
[40] *Kelly's Dir. N. & E.R. Yorks.*(1889), 362.
[41] P.R.O., E 179/202/60, m. 76.
[42] *Hearth Tax*, 60.
[43] B.I.H.R., V. 1764/Ret. 1, no. 106; *Herring's Visit.* i, p. 117.
[44] *V.C.H. Yorks.* iii. 494.
[45] *Census*, 1911–91; below, this section [village].
[46] Geol. Surv. Map 1″, drift, sheet 73 (1909 edn.); Geol. Surv. Map 1/50,000, sheet 81 (1991 edn.).

land was used as grassland and the higher ground for the open fields. The commonable lands were inclosed in 1762.[47]

The parish boundaries were formed very largely by streams flowing southwards towards the river Humber. The north-western boundary drain, then called Burton foss, was defective in 1367, as were those running along the western, southern, and south-eastern boundaries.[48] A newly-made dike in Roos and Burton Pidsea said in 1387 to be blocking existing watercourses and causing flooding in Burton Pidsea was perhaps a realignment of the eastern boundary stream.[49] Regulation of some drains in the parish later belonged to Burstwick manor court.[50] Much of the water draining from the parish found its way into the Humber through Keyingham fleet.[51] In the early 17th century, when the insufficiency of the fleet was complained of by Burton Pidsea and other townships in the level,[52] 440 a. in the parish was found to depend for its drainage on that stream.[53] The poorly-drained nature of parts of Burton Pidsea is perhaps reflected by reference to a boat-stake there in 1650, and boats had to be used to survey the flooded carrs for inclosure in the early 1760s.[54] The drainage of Keyingham level was made more effective under Acts of 1772 and later,[55] nearly 600 a. of low grounds in Burton Pidsea being assessed to the work of the drainage board after 1845.[56] In Burton Pidsea the eastern boundary drain, which carried water to Stone Creek, in Paull, was evidently improved as Owstwick and Halsham drains, and those running along the north-western and western sides of the parish, towards Hedon haven, as Burton Pidsea, Burton West, and Burstwick drains. Besides by a drain, a stretch of the southern boundary was also marked by an embankment, called Black bank.[57]

The main road is that running east-west between Roos and Lelley, in Preston, which passes along the northern edge of Burton Pidsea village. At the western boundary, West,[58] or Burton, bridge, which was out of repair in 1367,[59] carries the road over the drain. The only other road leading beyond the parish boundary is that which runs south from the village to Burstwick. It was made, or more likely straightened, at inclosure in 1762[60] and was called Greens Lane by the 1820s.[61] Another road from

the village, possibly once part of its back lane,[62] leads south-eastwards, and a field road also gives access to the south of the parish. The latter was made at inclosure in 1762, probably by extending an existing short lane between the village and its windmill; it led to land called Holme flatt and was called Holme Lane in 1829[63] and Mucky Lane by the 1850s.[64] Other roads made at inclosure included that leading northwards from the main road to the north-eastern corner of the parish, which survives as part of a footpath to Owstwick.[65]

BURTON PIDSEA village was a long, loosely built settlement, extending diagonally across the parish from north-west to south-east, in the 18th century.[66] Its garths separated the two open fields and at the southern end a street led into the common pasture. The church was in the north of the village. Its position suggests that the early chief street may have been that leading along the northern and eastern sides of the garths. That street was, moreover, awarded as a road in 1762, whereas a parallel way bordering the south and west of the village, presumably the back lane, was then confirmed merely as a private road. The latter street, formerly Townside Road[67] but now known as Back Lane and Carr Road, later became the more important of the two, and the northern and eastern street mostly interrupted fieldroads and paths.[68] The two streets, and the extension of one of them, now part of the main road, were linked by several side lanes. One of them, formerly called Kirkholme[69] and now Church Street, was given a new, northern stretch at inclosure in 1762. The westernmost lane, then, and probably also in 1367,[70] called West Lane, was Buck Lane in the 19th and earlier 20th century and later Jubilee Lane, after a cottage there.[71]

Since the 18th century building has mostly taken place in the north of the village, close to the main road, with the result that the southern farms now have the air of outlying houses. Apart from the medieval church and a few boundary walls, which are of boulders, the village is brick-built. What was probably once a small green near the church had evidently been encroached upon before inclosure in 1762, and other buildings were probably added there later in the cent-

47 Below, econ. hist.
48 Poulson, *Holderness*, i. 123, 125, 127.
49 *Cal. Pat.* 1385–9, 325.
50 E.R.A.O., DDCC/15/36, s.vv. 24 Apr., 15 May 1650.
51 Poulson, *Holderness*, i. 127.
52 E.R.A.O., CSR/14/1.
53 Ibid. DDCC/54/53.
54 Ibid. DDCC/15/36, s.v. Feb. 1650; Poulson, *Holderness*, ii. 37.
55 *V.C.H. Yorks. E.R.* v. 55, 57.
56 E.R.A.O., DDPK/3/8.
57 *V.C.H. Yorks. E.R.* v. 7–8, 57; O.S. Map 6″, Yorks. CCXXVII, CCXXVIII, CCXLI, CCXLII (1855 edn.).
58 E.R.A.O., DDCC/15/36, s.v. 20 Feb. 1649; O.S. Map 1/10,000, TA 23 SW. (1979 edn.).
59 Poulson, *Holderness*, i. 123; A. Bryant, *Map of E.R. Yorks.* (1829).
60 E.R.A.O., DDCK/32/5.
61 A. Bryant, *Map of E.R. Yorks.* (1829).
62 Below, this section [village].
63 E.R.A.O., DDCK/32/5; A. Bryant, *Map of E.R.*

Yorks. (1829).
64 O.S. Map 6″, Yorks. CCXXVIII, CCXLII (1855 edn.).
65 E.R.A.O., DDCK/32/5; O.S. Map 6″, Yorks. CCXXVIII (1855 edn.); O.S. Map 1/10,560, TA 23 SE. (1956 edn.).
66 Para. based on inclosure award and map at E.R.A.O., DDCK/32/5.
67 E.R.A.O., DDCC(2)/80, s.v. 11 Jan. 1837; R.D.B., 147/221/188.
68 Carr Road was called Mill Lane in 1852, perhaps in error for the nearby lane to the former mill site: O.S. Map 6″, Yorks. CCXXVIII (1855 edn.); O.S. Map 1/10,560, TA 23 SE. (1956 edn.); O.S. Map 1/10,000, TA 23 SE. (1982 edn.).
69 E.R.A.O., DDCC(2)/80, s.v. 9 Apr. 1806.
70 It may alternatively then have been used for part of the main road. Poulson, *Holderness*, i. 123–4.
71 O.S. Map 6″, Yorks. CCXXVIII (1855 edn.); O.S. Map 1/10,560, TA 23 SW. (1956 edn.); O.S. Map 1/10,000, TA 23 SW. (1979 edn.).

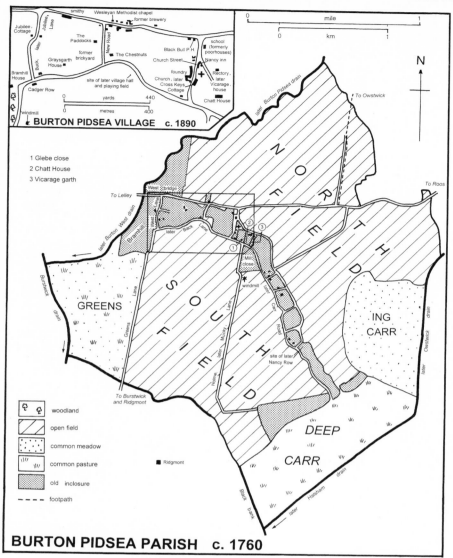

BURTON PIDSEA VILLAGE c. 1890

1 Glebe close
2 Chatt House
3 Vicarage garth

woodland

open field

common meadow

common pasture

old inclosure

- - - - footpath

BURTON PIDSEA PARISH c. 1760

ury. That later used as the Nancy inn, possibly once two houses and partly of one storey with attics, is believed to date from the 18th century, as is the single-storeyed Cross Keys Cottage, Church Street, formerly three dwellings. At the north end of the street poorhouses were put up, perhaps on waste ground.[72]

The development of the northern part of the village, which was recognised as enjoying a good 'prospect',[73] continued in the earlier 19th century, with the building, or rebuilding, of several houses there.[74] Isaac Raines, surgeon and apothecary of Burton Pidsea, probably lived in the house he bought in 1806, before building Graysgarth House in 1818 on the site of another house and parcels of land amounting to 2 a. which he purchased in that year and in 1819. The house,

of grey brick with a slate roof, has a porch supported by two pairs of Tuscan columns and flanked by bows rising through both storeys, and stone, heraldic shields at first-floor level. Called Burton Hall in 1852,[75] the house was extended to the west in red brick in the later 20th century. Isaac Raines's son-in-law William Clapham (d. 1860) was responsible for Chatt House, an extensive enlargement, probably of c. 1840.[76] Evidently also about 1840 Edward Baxter, farmer of c. 1,500 a. and racehorse breeder, and his neighbour William Harland, another of the larger farmers, remodelled their houses, later called the Paddocks and the Chestnuts respectively.[77] As part of their improvements, both men obtained the replacement of one of the side lanes by New Road, c. 200 m. further west, in 1843,[78]

[72] Cf. E.R.A.O., DDCK/32/5 (map); O.S. Map 6″, Yorks. CCXXVIII (1855 edn.). For descriptions of the buildings in this and the next para., Pevsner and Neave, *Yorks. E.R.* 379; Dept. of Environment, *Buildings List* (1987).

[73] Baines, *Hist. Yorks.* (1823), ii. 184.

[74] Houses existed on or near the sites of all the larger houses, except Bramhill House, *c.* 1760: cf. E.R.A.O., DDCK/32/5.

[75] E.R.A.O., DDCC(2)/80, s.vv. 15 Oct. 1806, 25 Mar. 1818, 14 Apr. 1819; R.D.B., DC/401/539; Poulson, *Holderness*, ii. 44–5; *Kelly's Dir. N. & E.R. Yorks.* (1905), 471; A. Bryant, *Map of E.R. Yorks.* (1829); O.S. Map 6″, Yorks. CCXXVIII (1855 edn.).

[76] Below, manors [Routh].

[77] Typescript recollections at H.U.L., DDMM/29/66; P.R.O., HO 107/2364.   [78] E.R.A.O., HD/48.

when Baxter built and dated a brick and boulder wall along his side of New Road. Harland presumably then made the undated, lower, boulder wall opposite.[79] The Paddocks, a red-brick house with a stuccoed parapet, bow windows, and a large porch supported by square pillars, was enlarged with a side wing in the 20th century. Its outbuildings have tie beams with Baxter's initials and the date 1829. The more modest Chestnuts is an 18th-century house refronted and reroofed in slate; the façade is of rendered brick with quoins and has a porch supported by fluted wooden pillars with foliated capitals. The only one of the larger houses certainly built on a new site was Bramhill House. Thomas Ford, farmer, mortgaged its site, Bramer Hill close, and other lands in 1844 for £3,000, and the house was evidently built soon afterwards.[80] That part of Burton Pidsea had been called 'Bramhulle' in the 13th century and 'Braimehills' in the 17th.[81] The large house, of grey brick with a slate roof, faces south to take advantage of the view across the falling ground in the south of the parish and beyond. The south façade has a heavy stone porch with square pillars which leads from the house into the remains of a small, well treed park.[82] Other work of the mid 19th century included the rebuilding by Edward Baxter of a house on Carr Road as five cottages for old people; the terrace, now occupied as one house, was named Nancy Row after Baxter's racehorse.[83]

There was also a little building north of the main road, now Main Street, a Wesleyan chapel being put up there in 1847 and a brewery by the 1850s,[84] but the village remained small until the mid 20th century. The rural district council then built c. 20 houses, Bengey Cottages, on the north side of Main Street,[85] and later, c. 1970, laid out the Glebelands estate, comprising some 70 bungalows, on the opposite side of the road.[86] Many private houses were also added then and later. Piecemeal 'ribbon' development occurred along both sides of Main Street, but more typical were the small estates made off Main Street, Jubilee Lane, and Back Lane. The earlier buildings were mostly modest, but in the late 20th century many so called executive-style houses were put up in the former grounds of the 19th-century houses: c. 45 houses were built on land belonging to the Chestnuts; about the same

number of larger, mock-Georgian houses in Barley Garth, in the former grounds of the Paddocks; six in Gray's Croft, alongside Graysgarth House, and about 25 in and off Jubilee Lane, among them a row of half-timbered detached houses on part of Graysgarth farm.[87] The increased size of the village led to the provision of a sewage works beside Burton Pidsea drain in the 1960s,[88] and by the 1970s electricity and gas stations and a telephone exchange had also been built in Burton Pidsea.[89]

In the later 18th century there were up to four alehouses in the village. The Black Bull was named in the 1820s, rebuilt in or shortly before 1845, and still traded in 1999.[90] Cross Keys Cottage is believed to have operated as an alehouse until its closure as a disorderly house in the mid 19th century.[91] Drink was also served at the blacksmith's, whose house was named by 1852 the Nancy inn, after the renowned racehorse of that name which Edward Baxter bred in Burton Pidsea in the late 1840s. The Nancy inn remained in 1999.[92] A lodge of the United Ancient Order of Druids, founded in Burton Pidsea in 1863 and recorded until 1938, met at the Black Bull.[93] A village fair held on the 12th of July seems to have been discontinued in the 1850s[94] but then revived, extended to include the 11th July, and combined with the annual feast day of the friendly society branch. The latter celebrations included a parade through Burton Pidsea with the village brass band. Other social events in the 19th century included ploughing matches and a weekly game of football, which began at the church door immediately after Sunday morning service.[95] A village or Church hall, with reading and billiard rooms, was proposed in 1910,[96] and a 'memorial hall' c. 1920; neither was built then and Burton Pidsea continued to rely for a meeting place on the school until the Memorial Hall was finally put up beside Back Lane in or soon after 1954 on part of a 3-a. site. The rest of the ground has been used for a playing field and a children's playground. Principal users of the hall have included the Women's Institute and of the field the local football and cricket clubs.[97] In the 1960s a youth club was also held in the village.[98]

OUTLYING HOUSES. Houses built away from the old village garths on former commonable

79 Besides the date, the wall included Baxter's initials, but pointing had made the latter indecipherable in 1999: A. Lazenby, *Cobble Stones of Holderness*, 119 (illus.).

80 E.R.A.O., DDCC(2)/80, s. vv. 19 Mar. 1844, 28 June 1862; O.S. Map 6", Yorks. CCXXVIII (1855 edn.). Elsewhere the house is said to have been built in 1843: Sheahan and Whellan, *Hist. York & E.R.* ii. 359.

81 P.R.O., SC 6/1078/11, m.7; E.R.A.O., DDCC/20/2; ibid. DDCK/32/5.

82 O.S. Map 6", Yorks. CCXXVIII (1855 edn.).

83 R.D.B., 63/309/287 (1904); W. G. B. Page, *Life of Thos. Mercer*, 23, 31; O.S. Map 1/10,000, TA 22 NE. (1975 edn.).

84 O.S. Map 6", Yorks. CCXXVIII (1855 edn.); below, econ. hist.; nonconf.

85 R.D.B., 585/104/81; 710/498/414; 808/258/206.

86 Ibid. 1428/566/499; 1428/567/500; 1482/206/182; 1509/504/438.

87 O.S. Map 1/10,000, TA 23 SW. (1979 edn.); Humb. C.C. *Mins.* 1978–9, D 519.

88 R.D.B., 1452/54/47.

89 Ibid. 1832/414/340; O.S. Map 1/10,000, TA 23 SW. (1979 edn.); TA 23 SE. (1982 edn.).

90 E.R.A.O., QDT/2/7, 9; ibid. DDCC(2)/80, s.v. 1 May 1845.

91 Local inf.

92 W. G. B. Page, *Life of Thos. Mercer*, 23, 31; Sheahan and Whellan, *Hist. York & E.R.* ii. 359; O.S. Map 6", Yorks. CCXXVIII (1855 edn.).

93 Typescript recollections at H.U.L., DDMM/29/66; D. [R. J.] Neave, *E.R. Friendly Soc.* (E. Yorks. Loc. Hist. Ser. xli), 47.

94 White, *Dir. Hull & York* (1851), 546; Sheahan and Whellan, *Hist. York & E.R.* ii. 359.

95 Typescript recollections at H.U.L., DDMM/29/66; *Hull Times*, 29 Mar. 1913.

96 E.R.A.O., PE/75/47.

97 R.D.B., 988/326/287; B.I.H.R., V. 1912–22/Ret.; V. 1931/Ret.; inf. from Mr. R. Wray, Graysgarth Farm, Burton Pidsea, 1999.

98 E.R. Educ. Cttee. *Mins.* 1960–1, 127.

land included Thimble Hall in North field, put up by 1829 and perhaps renamed, or replaced soon afterwards by, Buzzard Nest. One or two houses, called Greens Farm in 1829 and Salmond Cottage in the 1850s, were similarly put up in the south of the parish.[99]

MANORS AND OTHER ESTATES. In 1066 Morkar's manor of Withernsea included 7 carucates of sokeland at Burton Pidsea; they had passed to Drew de Bevrère by 1086[1] and were later part of the Aumale fee.[2] The estate, sometimes called *BURTON PIDSEA* manor, was a member of Burstwick, the chief manor of the fee in Holderness.[3] With Burstwick manor, it descended from the counts of Aumale to the Crown and its grantees, reverted to the Crown in 1521 on the execution of Edward Stafford, duke of Buckingham, and then passed by grant to Henry Neville, earl of Westmorland, in 1558 and sale in 1560 to Sir John Constable. The Constables, later viscounts Dunbar, and their successors retained the estate.[4] In the mid 15th century the estate at Burton Pidsea comprised, besides freeholdings, 72 houses, 5 carucates and 1 bovate, and 287 a.[5] Little or none of the land was held in demesne from the 13th century,[6] and the only allotment made to William Constable at inclosure in 1762 was of a few perches, presumably for his consent as lord of the manor.[7] The rest of his estate then comprised some 1,210 a. of copyhold of Burstwick manor.[8] The land was enfranchised at various dates, 210 a. being freed in 1857 and 124 a. in 1904, for instance.[9] The nearness of Burstwick and apparent lack of demesne land in Burton Pidsea probably account for there being no manor house on the Aumale estate there.

A reputed manor of *BURTON PIDSEA*, with free fishing in Pidsea mere, was bought from Richard Bean and his wife Elizabeth by George South in 1550.[10] South (d. by 1575) devised his land in Burton Pidsea to his son John.[11] He had evidently been succeeded by his son, Sir Francis South, by 1606, and in 1610 the latter sold the so-called manor to Walter Aire.[12]

After the ordination of a vicarage,[13] the *RECTORY* belonged to the dean and chapter of York minster. In 1650, during its confiscation by the Commonwealth, the rectory was valued at £108 net, most of the income coming from the tithes and Easter offerings.[14] At inclosure in 1762 the tithes were commuted for rents totalling some £143 a year, and 168 a. was then awarded for the 4 bovates of glebe land.[15] The dean and chapter let the rectory for terms of three lives from the 17th century. James Clapham of Hull, mathematician, was involved in the renewal of the lease to Isabella Hutchinson in 1713, possibly for William Clapham, an officer of the Church court at York, who is said to have obtained the lease about that date. The rectory thereafter descended in the Claphams or their relatives[16] to another William Clapham, who in 1854 bought the freehold of the land from the Ecclesiastical Commissioners, in whom the dean and chapter's estate had been vested in 1852.[17] It later descended with Clapham's other land.[18]

The rectory house comprised five low rooms and a large chamber in 1650 and had 2 hearths in 1672.[19] It was recorded again in 1743[20] and, as the 'glebe homestead', c. 1760, when it stood south of the church beside the later Carr Road.[21] By the 1830s the house had been demolished and two cottages built adjoining its site.[22]

A small freeholding in Burton Pidsea belonged to Brian Routh (d. 1483),[23] and later descended like Tansterne, in Aldbrough, to the Cutts[24] and the Michelbournes.[25] It was sold to Thomas Chatt in 1647,[26] and probably passed later to Philip Chatt.[27] William Clapham seems to have succeeded him by the 1690s.[28] Besides a house, 'late Chatt's', the Claphams assembled a small estate in Burton Pidsea, largely of copyhold, by piecemeal purchases. At inclosure in 1762 William Clapham's son George was awarded 6 a. and his son George 82 a.[29] By 1785, when the latter George conveyed the estate to his son William, the copyhold had been enlarged to c. 170 a.[30] William (d. 1835) left most of the holding to his son Leonard (d. 1839), and the rest to his other son William, who succeeded his

[99] E.R.A.O., DDCC(2)/80, s.v. 22 July 1892; DDCK/32/5 (map); A. Bryant, *Map of E.R. Yorks.* (1829); O.S. Map 6", Yorks. CCXXVIII, CCXLII (1855 edn.).
[1] *V.C.H. Yorks.* ii. 265. [2] *Yorks. Inq.*, i, p. 78.
[3] *Cal. Pat.* 1338–40, 148; 1557–8, 39; *Abbrev. Plac.* (Rec. Com.), 190.
[4] E.R.A.O., DDCC/111/21; DDCC/141/66; H.U.L., DCC/2/63; *V.C.H. Yorks. E.R.* v. 9–10; *Cal. Pat.* 1557–8, 39.
[5] P.R.O., C 139/93, no. 44, m. 4.
[6] Ibid. SC 12/17/5; E.R.A.O., DDCC/111/34; *Yorks. Inq.* i, p. 78; below, econ. hist.
[7] E.R.A.O., DDCK/32/5.
[8] Ibid. s.v. survey of 1761.
[9] R.D.B., HQ/221/277; 63/309/287 (1904).
[10] *Yorks. Fines*, i. 147.
[11] *N. Country Wills*, ii (Sur. Soc. cxxi), p. 229.
[12] *Yorks. Fines, 1603–14*, pp. 53, 137.
[13] Below, church.
[14] Lamb. Pal. Libr., COMM/XIIa/17/157–9; *T.E.R.A.S.* iv. 55.
[15] E.R.A.O., DDCK/32/5; ibid. DDIV/2/6.
[16] Lamb. Pal. Libr., COMM/XIIA/17/158–9; E.R.A.O., DDIV/2/6; York Minster Libr., R 2, Burton Pidsea nos. 1–2;

B.I.H.R., TER. H. Burton Pidsea 1786, 1809, 1817; Poulson, *Holderness*, ii. 44.
[17] R.D.B., GZ/374/429, 431; HF/161/224; *Lond. Gaz.* 10 Sept. 1852, pp. 2436–51.
[18] Below, this section [Routh].
[19] Lamb. Pal. Libr., COMM/XIIa/17/157; P.R.O., E 179/205/504. [20] *Herring's Visit.* i, p. 118.
[21] E.R.A.O., DDCK/32/5, s.vv. schedule of ancient inclosures, inclosure map.
[22] R.D.B., GZ/373/428.
[23] P.R.O., C 141/4, no. 45.
[24] Ibid. C 142/48, no. 161.
[25] Ibid. C 142/214, nos. 205, 221; ibid. CP 40/1154, Carte rot. 12; *Yorks. Fines*, i. 140, 357; above, Aldbrough, manors (Tansterne).
[26] P.R.O., CP 25(2)/525/23 Chas. I Trin. [no. 18].
[27] Ibid. E 179/205/504; Poulson, *Holderness*, ii. 42.
[28] Poulson, *Holderness*, ii. 42; above, manors (rectory).
[29] R.D.B., AF/34/7; E.R.A.O., DDCC(2)/80, s.v. 4 Nov. 1761; 2 June 1762; 17 May 1769. For the family, Poulson, *Holderness*, ii. 44.
[30] E.R.A.O., DDCC(2)/80, s.v. 18 May 1785. Cf. ibid. s. vv. 16 Oct. 1799; 15 Oct. 1800; 5 Apr. 1809.

brother.[31] In 1854 William Clapham bought the rectorial estate, of *c.* 170 a., which had long been held by his family as lessees.[32] Clapham (d. 1860) was succeeded by his son W. S. Clapham, who in 1872 sold Chatt House with 171 a. of copyhold and 194 a. of freehold to his relative Henry Cautley, a Leeds worsted manufacturer.[33] Cautley (d. 1897) left the estate in undivided half shares to his sons Edmund (d. 1944) and H. S. Cautley, later Baron Cautley.[34] In 1946 Lord Cautley and another sold the 368-a. Chatt House farm to Thomas Harrison.[35] Harrison already had Manor farm and *c.* 250 a. in the parish,[36] and about 200 a. was added by other purchases *c.* 1950.[37] In 1969 he sold Manor farm with 620 a. in Burton Pidsea to the Equitable Life Assurance Society.[38] In 1997 R. C. Lewis, Mr. Harrison's step-son, re-purchased the land in Burton Pidsea, which is farmed by T. Harrison (Farmers) Ltd. Chatt House and *c.* 20 a. were held separately by the family in 1999.[39]

Philip Chatt had two houses in Burton Pidsea in 1672, neither apparently large,[40] and a house 'late Chatt's' but then belonging to George Clapham stood south-east of the church in the 1760s.[41] The Claphams' house was described in the 1780s as 'lately rebuilt',[42] and it was later extensively enlarged, it is said in 1839 by William Clapham.[43] Clapham's enlargement comprises a square block in grey brick with stone dressings under a slate roof. The south front has a prominent, semicircular, stone porch with Doric pilasters and entablature, and to the rear part of the older, red-brick house remains. A stable block, now converted into living accommodation, extends east from the house, and further away stands a square, red-brick dovecot, of two storeys with a pyramidal, louvred roof; both are contemporary with the remodelling of the house.

At inclosure in 1762 there were eight proprietors with over 100 a. each in Burton Pidsea,[44] and some of those holdings were later enlarged

by purchase to form sizeable estates. Richard Howard, a Hull merchant, was awarded 172 a. in 1762, and in 1812 his daughter Ann sold an estate by then enlarged to *c.* 275 a. to Charles Howard and Marmaduke Prickett. The purchasers then also bought 60 a. from another proprietor.[45] Howard conveyed his half shares in the purchases to Prickett between 1816 and 1837.[46] Transactions in the 1820s added *c.* 60 a. to the estate,[47] and Prickett (d. 1860 or 1861) was succeeded in nearly 400 a. by the Revd. Thomas Prickett (d. 1902).[48] The estate was sold by the Pricketts in 1912, Charles Wray buying Red House farm, of 231 a., and V. H. Lear 158 a.[49] In 1913 Red House, later Manor, farm was re-sold to William Thompson (d. 1943), who was succeeded by his great-nephew, Thomas Harrison. Manor farm later descended with Harrison's other land in the parish.[50]

A manor house, presumably the chief house of one of the freeholdings,[51] is believed to have stood south of the village, on or near a site which may formerly have been moated, and a farmhouse there was called Red House in the mid 19th century and later, for an unknown reason, Manor Farm.[52] Manor Farm is an 18th-century house; its outbuildings include a two-storeyed dovecote, also of the 18th century, with a pyramidal roof.[53]

Another of the larger holdings was based on the estate of the Burtons. Richard Burton who was awarded 145 a. at inclosure in 1762[54] may have been Richard Burton (d. 1765), and Richard Burton (d. 1784), who was succeeded in 156 a. in Burton Pidsea by his sister Mary and her husband Napier Christie Burton, his great-nephew.[55] In the mid 1790s the estate was evidently sold to Thomas and John Turner, from whom Abraham Dunn bought it in 1799.[56] It was sold to Robert Sayle in 1806.[57] Sayle (d. by 1832) left the estate, together with *c.* 50 a. of copyhold, to his nephew Edward Baxter,[58] who already had a farm of some 30 a. in Burton

[31]   Ibid. s.v. 11 Jan. 1837; 23 Oct. 1839.

[32]   R.D.B., GZ/374/429; HF/161/224; above, this section (rectory).

[33]   R.D.B., KO/297/415; KQ/249/314; KS/118/166; KX/301/395; E.R.A.O., DDCC(2)/80, s.vv. 19 May 1870; 23 May 1870; 13 Feb. 1872; B.I.H.R., TER. H. Burton Pidsea 1871. Mary, daughter of William Clapham (d. 1835), married a Henry Cautley: Poulson, *Holderness*, ii. 44.

[34]   E.R.A.O., DDCC(2)/80, s.v. 4 Apr. 1898; *Who Was Who, 1941–50*.

[35]   R.D.B., 718/174/145.

[36]   Ibid. 652/36/29; below, this section [Howard].

[37]   R.D.B., 748/100/86; 953/493/430; 954/501/439; 1024/499/438.

[38]   Ibid. 1893/192/123.

[39]   Inf. from Mr. R. C. Lewis, Burton Pidsea, 1999.

[40]   P.R.O., E 179/205/504.

[41]   E.R.A.O., DDCK/32/5, s.vv. schedule of ancient inclosures, inclosure map; ibid. DDCC(2)/80, s.v. 2 June 1762.

[42]   E.R.A.O., DDCC(2)/80, s.v. 18 May 1785.

[43]   Sheahan and Whellan, *Hist. York & E.R.* ii. 359; Poulson, *Holderness*, ii. 42, 44; O.S. Map 6", Yorks. CCXXVIII (1855 edn.). The admission of William Clapham in that year refers to the house in the usual way, however, and the work may have been done later: E.R.A.O., DDCC(2)/80, s.v. 23 Oct. 1839.

[44]   Below, econ. hist.

[45]   R.D.B., AF/34/7; CT/104/178; CT/174/285; E.R.A.O., DDCC(2)/80, s.v. 8 July 1812.

[46]   R.D.B., DB/72/95; DS/35/54; E.R.A.O., DDCC(2)/80, s. vv. 17 Apr. 1816; 25 Oct. 1837.

[47]   R.D.B., DU/29/34; E.R.A.O., DDCC(2)/80, s.vv. 12 July 1826; 10 Jan. 1827.

[48]   R.D.B., IF/38/51; IX/125/170; 52/12/12 (1903).

[49]   Ibid. 143/354/312; 147/221/188; 147/222/189; 147/291/256; 147/310/273.

[50]   R.D.B., 153/312/264; 697/296/245; 740/409/338; above, this section [Routh]; inf. from Mr. R. C. Lewis, Burton Pidsea, 1999; below, Humbleton, manors [Fitling].

[51]   Above, below, this section.

[52]   A. Bryant, *Map of E.R. Yorks.* (1829); O.S. Map 6", Yorks. CCXXVIII (1855 edn.); O.S. Map 1/2,500, Yorks. CCXXVIII. 13 (1890 edn.).

[53]   Pevsner and Neave, *Yorks. E.R.* 379; Dept. of Environment, *Buildings List* (1987).

[54]   R.D.B., AF/34/7.

[55]   Ibid. BI/240/381; BR/599/974; BR/600/975; CF/312/505; *V.C.H. Yorks. E.R.* iv. 69.

[56]   E.R.A.O., QDE/1/6/4; R.D.B., BZ/306/495; CB/287/471.

[57]   R.D.B., CL/488/772; CL/71/127.

[58]   E.R.A.O., DDCC(2)/80, s.v. 22 Apr. 1835; ibid. QDE/1/6/4.

Pidsea[59] and added *c.* 40 a. by purchase in the 1830s.[60] Baxter (d. 1855) was succeeded by his son William[61] and he (d. 1877) by his nephews Hugh (d. 1879), Edward, and William Baxter, as tenants in common. In 1892 William and Edward Baxter conveyed the 282-a. estate to F. R. Pease,[62] who sold it, as Paddocks farm, to Thomas and James Robinson in 1904.[63] Charles Wray bought the farm in 1911, and sold 158 a. in 1933, Paddocks farmhouse with 117 a. to R. C. Connor in 1944, and The Paddocks with 4 a. of grounds to C. H. Ross, a Hull butcher, in 1945.[64] The farm was divided and sold, mostly in 1953, 75 a. being bought by Thomas Harrison.[65] The Paddocks was bought by the present owner, Raymond Beal, in 1971.[66]

Land in Burton Pidsea and Roos was held by the St. Quintins, and of them by the Ros family in the 13th century. In 1202 Herbert de St. Quintin's tenant, Robert de Ros, occupied the whole 6-carucate holding, of which 2 carucates were evidently in Burton Pidsea.[67]

Another early estate in Burton Pidsea was that of 1 carucate which William le Gros, count of Aumale (d. 1179), granted to Richard son of Seberin.[68]

A count of Aumale granted Gamel of Burton, his son Robert, and their heirs an estate in Burton Pidsea, including ½ carucate.[69] The same or another Robert of Burton was the tenant in 1260,[70] and it was evidently the same holding which descended from Nicholas Ward (d. by 1323) in turn to his sons Robert[71] and Henry of Burton.[72] Henry (d. by 1343) left a daughter Beatrice,[73] on whose death in 1349 Adam or Henry Ward's daughter Maud was her heir.[74] The estate was perhaps recorded again in 1377 and *c.* 1390.[75]

Two bovates of the Aumale fee in Burton Pidsea were held in the 13th and 14th centuries in return for service as an officer of the lord's court at Barrow-on-Humber (Lincs.). Another tenure by serjeanty involved 1 bovate held for keeping South park, in Burstwick.[76]

Thornton abbey (Lincs.) had 5 bovates in Burton Pidsea in the early 16th century.[77] After the abbey's dissolution, the land passed briefly to Thornton college by Crown grant of 1542 and then reverted to the Crown, which sold it in fee farm to John Eldred and William Whitmore in 1611.[78] Thornton abbey's tenant at Burton Pidsea was William Buckton (d. 1506), of Hackness (Yorks. N.R.), who settled his interest in the land on his sons, Robert and Ralph.[79] No more is known of the estate. At their suppression in 1540, the Knights Hospitaller had ½ carucate and other land in Burton Pidsea, then occupied by a freeholder.[80]

ECONOMIC HISTORY. COMMON LANDS AND INCLOSURE. The open fields lay on either side of the village in North and South fields, which were named in 1610.[81] Reference to 'forland' in the 13th century may indicate an earlier expansion of the tillage by the taking in of waste land.[82] An area called the Greens was possibly also part of the tillage, but by the 17th century it seems to have been used primarily as common meadowland and pasture: selions of arable land, meadow, and pasture in the Greens were conveyed in 1649, but other land there was then described as 'meadow or pasture in the far land', and the following year six tenants were appointed to measure and divide meadowland in the Greens.[83] In 1690 a stint agreed in Fitling manor court, which participated in the agricultural regulation of Burton Pidsea, allowed one pasture gate in winter for each 3 a. held in South field and the Greens, and the same stint was to be applied in South field the following summer, while the Greens was being 'aired'.[84] It was perhaps, too, the Greens which was called Pasture field in 1728.[85] Other common meadowland lay in Ing carr, where '1/2 bovate of meadow' was recorded in 1503, and in Lambert dikes, Southdales, and Turf carr, the last presumably at some time having also been used as a turbary.[86] The chief common pasture was Deep carr, which was stinted in 1381.[87] On the eve of inclosure in the mid 18th century Deep carr contained 197 beast gates.[88] The stint there then seems to have been three cattle, or half that number of horses, for each bovate held.[89]

Under an agreement of 1760 and Act of 1761, the commonable lands were inclosed by award of 1762.[90] Allotments made totalled 1,994 a., of which 775 a. came from North field, 597 a. from

59 E.R.A.O., DDCC(2)/80, s.v. 26 Oct. 1831.

60 Ibid. s. vv. 22 Apr. 1835; 11 Jan. 1837; R.D.B., EU/386/388.

61 E.R.A.O., DDCC(2)/80, s.v. 26 Jan. 1856.

62 Ibid. s.v. 22 July 1892; R.D.B., NN/94/139; 52/508/474 (1892).

63 R.D.B., 63/311/288 (1904).

64 Ibid. 132/224/206; 471/437/373; 472/74/58; 472/135/105; 677/416/324; 691/486/407.

65 Ibid. 953/493/430; 954/280/245; etc.

66 Ibid. 1694/217/184; *Reg. of Electors* (1999).

67 *Yorks. Fines, John* (Sur. Soc. xciv), pp. 76–7; below, Roos, manors (Roos).

68 English, *Holderness*, 172.

69 *Cal. Close, 1346–9,* 306.

70 *Yorks. Inq.* i, pp. 77–8.

71 *Cal. Fine R. 1319–27,* 214.

72 *Cal. Pat. 1324–7,* 264.

73 *Cal. Inq. p.m.* viii, pp. 281–2.

74 Ibid. ix, p. 254; *Cal. Fine R. 1347–56,* 178.

75 *Yorks. Fines, 1347–77,* p. 204; *Cat. Anct. D.* ii, C.

2018; *Cal. Close, 1389–92,* 343.

76 P.R.O., SC 12/17/5; *Yorks. Inq.* i, pp. 77, 79; *Cal. Inq. p.m.* ix, p. 80.

77 *Cal. Inq. p.m. Hen. VII,* iii, pp. 165–6.

78 P.R.O., SC 6/Hen. VIII/2022, m. 79; ibid. C 66/1903, no. 9, mm. 17, 25–6; *L. & P. Hen. VIII,* xvii, p. 29.

79 *Cal. Inq. p.m. Hen. VII,* iii, pp. 165–6.

80 *V.C.H. Yorks.* iii. 261; *Miscellanea,* iv (Y.A.S. Rec. Ser. xciv), 99.

81 E.R.A.O., DDCC/20/5.

82 P.R.O., SC 6/1079/15, m. 5.

83 E.R.A.O., DDCC/15/36, s. vv. 12 Dec. 1649; 9 Jan. 1650; 5 June 1650.

84 Ibid. DDX/595/42.   85 Ibid. DDX/595/83.

86 Ibid. DDCC/15/18, s.v. Jan. 1503; DDCC/20/2.

87 Ibid. DDCC/15/2, s.v. Sept. 1381.

88 Ibid. DDCK/32/5; ibid. DDCC/20/2, 5.

89 Cf. R.D.B., AF/14/6; E.R.A.O., DDIV/2/6.

90 R.D.B., AF/14/6; AF/34/7 (agreement and award); E.R.A.O., DDCK/32/5 (copy of award with plan); 1 Geo. III, c. 37 (Priv. Act).

South field, 235 a. from Ing carr, 199 a. from Deep carr, and 189 a. from the Greens.[91] There were 43 proprietors, eight of whom received over 100 a. each; they included only three 'local' owners, William Mair of Burton Pidsea, Francis Farrah of Fitling in Humbleton, and John Storr of Hilston. Richard Howard, a Hull merchant, received 172 a., the dean and chapter of York 168 a. for the rectorial glebe and rents of £143 a year for the tithes, Mair 156 a., Richard Burton of Hull Bank in Cottingham, 145 a., Farrah 140 a., Storr 125 a., James Pearson 118 a., and the Mottram family 116 a. There were also six allotments of 50–99 a., ten of 20–49 a., fourteen of 5–19 a., and five of under 5 a.

THE DEMESNE AND TENURES. The Aumale estate at Burton Pidsea seems to have produced c. £45 a year in the mid 13th and early 14th centuries.[92] The assized rents of the free and bond tenants and the cottars were apparently worth £23 in 1269–70, and in 1304–5 they were charged at £37.[93] The bondmen were said to have held 5 carucates in Burton Pidsea in 1260.[94] Both they and the cottars were obliged to work on the demesne, and hens and geese were also owed, but those duties may have been commuted for cash payments by the later 13th century.[95] The unfree tenants also owed tallage, valued at £4 a year c. 1270, merchet,[96] chevage,[97] and entry fines.[98] In the early 17th century, apparently after some dispute and the ruling that the fines were uncertain, some copyholders paid the lord of Burstwick manor sums for confirmation of their estates and a statement of their obligations and rights: the entry fine payable on a change of tenant was declared to be a year's rent; leases for less than two years did not require the lord's licence and no fine was payable; leases for terms above two years or for life were charged at the rate of ½ year's rent. Those tenancies were perhaps distinguished later as 'copyhold freed', as opposed to the majority which were 'copyhold in bondage'. Of the 1,994 a. allotted at inclosure in 1762, 40 a. was copyhold freed of Burstwick manor and 1,170 a. copyhold in bondage; the remaining 784 a. was freehold.[99]

The demesne land farmed as part of Burton Pidsea in the mid 13th century, and later leased to tenants there, seems to have been mostly at Ridgmont, in Burstwick parish. Demesne lands called 'Bramhulle' and 'Holm', perhaps those later described as 'demesne lands called forland',

were probably in Burton Pidsea, but they had already been let for 14s. a year by 1268.[1] At Ridgmont the demesne belonging to Burstwick manor was said to comprise 240 a. of arable land and just over 100 a. of meadow in 1260,[2] c. 700 a. in 1340,[3] 10½ bovates and 200 a. in the 15th century,[4] and 800 a. extending into Burton Pidsea in the later 16th century.[5] In the mid 13th century the demesne was being exploited directly, and corn sales contributed to the cash income of Burton Pidsea, just over £11 being charged in 1269–70, for instance. The grazing of the stubble at Ridgmont was sold in 1268, but other pasture there and at 'Estholm' was then being used for the countess's sheep.[6] Some 150 a. of demesne land was sown and about 40 a. of meadow mown in 1267–8.[7] Permanent staff on the demesne included two ploughmen and a harrower, but most of the work was apparently done by hired labourers.[8] Direct exploitation of the estates based on Burstwick manor was being reduced or given up by the 1280s, and in 1287 Burton Pidsea tenants occupied 230 a. of arable land, 117 a. of meadow, and 99 a. of pasture at Ridgmont for rents of c. £21 a year.[9] In the 15th century the land held by Burton Pidsea men was put at 234 a. of arable land, 28 a. of meadow, and 99 a. of pasture.[10] The former demesne lands in Ridgmont were conveyed in the Burstwick court rolls, mostly as Burton Pidsea lands. The transfers involved bovates, and Ridgmont field was referred to in 1548. Meadow in 'Hestham', perhaps the earlier 'Estholm', was recorded in 1551, and there seems to have been a stinted pasture in Ridgmont called Rush carr.[11]

FISHERIES. In 1260 the two halves of Pidsea mere belonged respectively to the count of Aumale, lord of Burton Pidsea, and to (Sir) William de Ros, lord of Roos, but both lords enjoyed the fishing of the whole mere. The count's eel fishery, then said to be worth 5s. a year, was presumably in the mere.[12] Pidsea mere fishery was let, apparently for 10s. a year about 1270, for 15s. in 1318–19, and for £1 before 1471, when the rent had to be reduced for lack of takers to 10s.[13] The fishery, then belonging to the Crown as successor to the count of Aumale, had allegedly been fished illegally c. 1300.[14] In 1335 William de Ros, Lord Ros, was licensed to inclose his half of Pidsea mere, but in 1344 his widow complained that the bondmen of Burton Pidsea had recently made ditches from the mere

91 For the areas of the commonable lands at inclosure, cf. E.R.A.O., DDCK/32/5.

92 The accounts of the 1260s deal with half of the manor and the total charge is conjectural.

93 P.R.O., SC 6/1078/12, m. 5; SC 6/1079/17, m. 8d.

94 Yorks. Inq. i, p. 78.

95 P.R.O., SC 12/17/5.

96 Ibid. Tallage was sometimes called an 'aid': P.R.O., SC 6/1078/11, m. 7; SC 6/1078/13, m. 4.

97 Ibid. SC 6/1082/3, m. 7; SC 6/1084/5, m. 2d.; E.R.A.O., DDCC/15/1.

98 P.R.O., SC 6/1078/11, m. 3.

99 E.R.A.O., DDCC/20/2, 5–6; R.D.B., AF/34/7.

1 P.R.O., SC 6/1078/11, m. 7; SC 6/1082/3, m. 7. Holm flatt was later mentioned as part of South field: R.D.B., AF/34/7.   2 Yorks. Inq. i, pp. 77–8.

3 V.C.H. Yorks. E.R. v. 14.

4 P.R.O., C 139/93, no. 44, m. 4.

5 E.R.A.O., DDCC/111/21.

6 P.R.O., SC 6/1078/11, m. 7; SC 6/1078/12, m. 5.

7 Ibid. SC 6/1078/11, m. 7.

8 Ibid. SC 6/1078/11, m. 7 and d.

9 Ibid. SC 6/1079/15, m. 7; SC 6/1082/3, m. 7.

10 Ibid. SC 6/1084/5, m. 2 and d.

11 E.R.A.O., DDCC/15/1, s. vv. Oct. 1368; June 1369; DDCC/15/2, s.v. Nov. 1381; DDCC/15/9, s.v. Nov. 1460; DDCC/15/23, s.vv. June 1548; Jan. 1551.

12 Yorks. Inq. i, pp. 79, 83; Complete Peerage, s.v. Ros.

13 P.R.O., SC 6/1078/11, m. 7; SC 6/1080/9, m. 3; SC 6/1084/5, m. 2d.; SC 12/17/5.

14 Cal. Pat. 1292–1301, 624–5; Abbrev. Rot. Orig. (Rec. Com.), i. 125.

and were drawing water and fish from it.[15] Further destruction of the fishing led to tenants of Roos manor being forbidden in 1403 from keeping their ducks on the mere.[16] A reputed manor of Burton Pidsea included free fishing in the 'water of Pidsey' in 1550,[17] but that description, and the mere itself, seems to have been lost in the 17th century.[18] Fishing, presumably in other waters, and fowling in Burton Pidsea were held by a lessee of the lord of the manor in the early 18th century.[19]

LATER AGRICULTURE. There was said to be c. 695 a. under crops in 1801, and 1,121 a. of arable land and 1,018 a. of grassland were returned in 1905.[20] Most of the parish was given over to crops in the 1930s, when the grassland was concentrated close to the village and in the south-east of the parish.[21] In 1987 the area returned for the civil parish, 961.6 ha. (2,376 a.), evidently included some land elsewhere; there were then 927.9 ha. (2,293 a.) of arable land and only 26.3 ha. (65 a.) of grassland. Livestock included nearly 12,600 pigs, almost 500 poultry, and 180 sheep.[22] In the 19th century and earlier 20th there were usually about ten farms in Burton Pidsea, of which seven in 1851 and three to five in the 1920s and 1930s were of 150 a. or more.[23] A cowkeeper was recorded in 1851, and from the late 19th century there were up to four in Burton Pidsea. There has also been some market gardening since the 1930s, and about 60 a. bought for that purpose in the 1950s[24] was still so used in 1999. There was a poultry farm by 1929 and four of them were recorded in 1937, when Burton Pidsea also included two small-holdings. Nine holdings were recorded in 1987, of which one was of 500–699 ha. (1,236–1,727 a.), one of 100–199 ha. (247–492 a.), one of 50–99 ha. (124–245 a.), three of 10–49 ha. (25–121 a.), and three of less than 10 ha.[25]

INDUSTRY AND TRADE. The number and type of tradesmen working in Burton Pidsea in the 19th and 20th centuries were typical of a largely agricultural village. Edward Baxter, the largest farmer and proprietor of the village mill in the mid 19th century, was, however, also a brick and tile maker, and a renowned breeder of horses.[26] The last activity is perhaps reflected in a saddler being employed c. 1850 and in the early 20th century, when there was also a horse

breaker in the village.[27] As a brick and tile maker, Baxter was recorded from 1840 until 1858. His works were close to the Paddocks, the house he is believed to have rebuilt for himself c. 1840, and they may have been established primarily to supply materials for that house, although the yard presumably also provided bricks and tiles for other building operations then under way in the village.[28] The site of the brick and tile works was evident as a low-lying field in 1999. In 1840 Peter Drew, a beer-house keeper in Burton Pidsea, was also brewing, and he had established Providence Brewery, on the north side of Main Street, by 1852. The business seems to have been given up in the 1870s. As the Old Brewhouse, the building remained in 1999.[29] William Stamford, wheelwright, had an iron foundry by 1846, and his successor, John Stamford, employed six men in 1851, and was also casting brass and making agricultural machines by 1872. Edward Stamford sold the concern in 1919 to the Holderness Plough Co. Ltd.,[30] which was succeeded by Seward Agricultural Machinery Ltd. The business was sold in 1998, and the premises stood empty and unused in 1999.[31] One or two other agricultural engineering concerns seem to have worked in the village. Edward Caley, engineer to an Owstwick steam threshing company in 1892, was later recorded simply as an agricultural engineer under Burton Pidsea; in 1921 he was managing the Holderness Plough Co. Ltd., but Caley & Ayre were then separately listed as agricultural engineers. The latter concern had been renamed Caley & Townsend by 1933, and another agricultural engineer, William Stephenson, hitherto a cycle agent, was recorded from 1929. Commerce was largely the concern of one or two shopkeepers, and of the carriers to Hull, one of whom dealt in coal c. 1900.[32] In 1999 a garage and shop was operated in Main Street, and an automobile engineer, a joiner, and a plumber and heating engineer worked from other premises there; another shop and Post Office traded in Church Street.

MILLS. There was a windmill at Burton Pidsea from the 1260s.[33] It was perhaps the same windmill which stood in South field in 1616[34] and the later 18th century.[35] It had been demolished by 1852, but its hill was still evident in 1999. The old mill was evidently replaced in

[15] Cal. Pat. 1343–5, 398; 1358–61, 476.
[16] Burghley Ho. MS. 37/18, s.v. Oct. 1403.
[17] Yorks. Fines, i. 147.
[18] P.N. Yorks. E.R. (E.P.N.S.), 55.
[19] E.R.A.O., DDCC/111/34.
[20] P.R.O., HO 67/26/88; Acreage Returns, 1905.
[21] [1st] Land Util. Surv. Map, sheet 33–4.
[22] Inf. from Min. of Agric., Fish. & Food, Beverley, 1990; cf. above, intro. [area].
[23] For this and the following, P.R.O., HO 107/2364; directories.
[24] R.D.B., 954/280/245.
[25] Inf. from Min. of Agric., Fish. & Food.
[26] P.R.O., HO 107/2364; R.D.B., FE/243/239; White, Dir. Hull & York (1851), 546; above, intro. [inns].
[27] Directories.
[28] P.R.O., HO 107/2364; O.S. Map 6", Yorks. CCXXVIII (1855 edn.); White, Dir. E. & N.R. Yorks.

(1840), 258; White, Dir. Hull & York (1858), 546; above, intro. [village].
[29] Typescript recollections at H.U.L., DDMM/29/66; White, Dir. E. & N.R. Yorks. (1840), 258; Kelly's Dir. N. & E.R. Yorks. (1872), 343; P. Aldabella and R. Barnard, Hull & E. Yorks. Breweries (E. Yorks. Loc. Hist. Ser. l), p. 22 (illus.); O.S. Map 6", Yorks. CCXXVIII (1855 edn.).
[30] R.D.B., 197/567/486; P.R.O., HO 107/2364; directories.
[31] Inf. from Paul Seward & Co. Ltd., 1998.
[32] Directories.
[33] P.R.O., SC 6/1078/11, m. 7; SC 6/1084/5, m. 2d.; SC 12/17/5; E.R.A.O., DDCC/15/23 (bill on roll). Yorks. Inq. i, p. 79.
[34] E.R.A.O., DDCC/20/6.
[35] Ibid. DDCC/15/48, p. 96; T. Jefferys, Map of Yorks. (1772).

1834 by a tower mill and mill house on a new site beside Greens Lane.[36] The mill was assisted by steam power by 1889 but it ceased to grind in or shortly before 1901, when its machinery was dismantled. The miller, nevertheless, remained in business, dealing in roller-ground flour supplied from mills in Hull.[37] The mill was later disused[38] but the five-storeyed tower remained in the garden of Mill House in 1999.

LOCAL GOVERNMENT.
Burton Pidsea business was conducted in Burstwick manor court, rolls of which survive for 1368–1925.[39] Besides the conveyancing of copyhold in Burton Pidsea and of former demesne land in Ridgmont, the court dealt with debt pleas, affrays, and breaches of the ale assize in Burton Pidsea.[40] Officers appointed in the court between the 14th and 18th centuries included 2 constables, 2 ale-tasters, 2 mill-reeves, 1–4 reeves, or penny-graves, and a pinder, all for Burton Pidsea. Bylawmen at Ridgmont were also mentioned in 1547, and 4 were regularly elected for Burton Pidsea in the 17th and 18th centuries.[41]

The manor of Fitling, formerly belonging to the Hospitallers, extended into Burton Pidsea,[42] and agriculture, drainage, and the testamentary affairs of its tenants there were regulated by the court at Fitling. Three bylawmen and a pinder appointed in 1690 at a court held in Burton Pidsea were probably for that village,[43] and two bylawmen for Burton Pidsea were sworn in 1700.[44]

Account books of the parish overseers of the poor survive from 1786.[45] Burton Pidsea built and maintained poorhouses; they were repaired for £35 in 1830 and a datestone of that year, bearing the initials of Edward Baxter and Robert Clapham, the overseers, survives in the wall of the successor building, the school.[46] In the early 19th century 12–15 people there were on permanent out-relief; 18 in 1802–3 and 5–7 between 1812 and 1815 were also helped occasionally.[47] Burton Pidsea township, later civil parish, evidently joined Patrington poor-law union in 1836[48] and remained in Patrington rural district until 1935, when it was incorporated into the new rural district of Holderness. The civil parish became part of the Holderness district of Humberside in 1974[49] and, in 1996, of a new East Riding unitary area.[50]

Ridgmont, in Burstwick parish, was closely connected with Burton Pidsea in the Middle Ages,[51] and in the 19th century it lay within the constablewick of Burton Pidsea.[52]

CHURCH.
A church at Burton Pidsea was recorded, as that of Burton Gamel, c. 1160. By then William le Gros, count of Aumale, or one of his ancestors, had given it to Aumale abbey (Seine Maritime).[53] In 1228 the abbey ceded the church to the archbishop of York, who assigned it to York minster in 1230.[54] Burton Pidsea was thereafter in the patronage and peculiar jurisdiction of the dean and chapter of York.[55] A vicarage was ordained, perhaps twice, apparently in or before 1291 and certainly in 1301.[56] Following its augmentation in the 1860s with tithe rents formerly belonging to the rectory, the living was sometimes called a rectory.[57] In 1961 Burton Pidsea vicarage was united with that of Humbleton with Elstronwick, but the two parishes remained distinct. The dean and chapter of York and the Crown, as patron of Humbleton, present alternately to the united benefice.[58]

In 1291 the vicar was said to have all the oblations, mortuaries, and personal tithes, and some other tithes.[59] Under the ordination of 1301 he was assigned the whole altarage, or £4 a year from the lessee of the rectory or the dean and chapter,[60] and for long afterwards almost all of the vicar's income came from a salary paid out of the rectory. It was £6 a year in 1535,[61] £15 in 1650,[62] and £25 from the 1660s.[63] In 1743 the living was said to be worth only £26 10s. a year in all.[64] In 1809 the dean and chapter augmented the vicarage with the grazing of the churchyard, and from 1818 the curate serving Burton Pidsea also received £10 a year from the parish for providing another Sunday service.[65] The living was augmented with a parliamentary grant of £200 in 1810 and in 1818 and 1838 with sums of £200 from Queen Anne's Bounty.[66]

36 R.D.B., EY/73/78; EY/74/79; O.S. Map 6″, Yorks. CCXXVIII (1855 edn.).

37 Typescript recollections at H.U.L., DDMM/29/66; directories; *Hull Times*, 29 Mar. 1913.

38 O.S. Map 1/10,560, TA 23 SW. (1956 edn.).

39 E.R.A.O., DDCC/15/1–62; DDCC(2)/80.

40 Ibid. DDCC/15/2, s.vv. Sept. 1381; Jan. 1382; DDCC/15/9, s.v. Oct. 1460.

41 Ibid. DDCC/15/1, s.v. Oct. 1368; DDCC/15/9, s.v. Oct. 1460; DDCC/15/18, s.v. Oct. 1502; DDCC/15/23, s.vv. Dec. 1547; Nov. 1548; DDCC/15/36, s.v. Oct. 1655; DDCC/15/41, s.vv. Oct. 1690; July 1701.

42 Ibid. DDX/595/138 etc.   43 Ibid. /114.

44 Ibid. /51. Cf. ibid. /48, 54, 83; above, econ. hist.

45 Ibid. PE/75/91–2.

46 Ibid. /92, pp. 129, 132, 135; O.S. Map 6″, Yorks. CCXXVIII (1855 edn.); below, educ.

47 *Poor Law Abstract, 1804*, pp. 592–3; *1818*, pp. 520–1.

48 The township is not listed in *3rd Rep. Poor Law Com.* 169.   49 *Census*.

50 Humberside (Structural Change) Order 1995 (copy at E.R.A.O.).

51 *Cal. Pat. 1338–40*, 193; above, econ. hist.

52 *V.C.H. Yorks. E.R.* v. 17.   53 *E.Y.C.* iii, pp. 35–6.

54 *Reg. Gray*, pp. 22, 47–8; *V.C.H. Yorks.* iii. 25.

55 Lawrance, 'Clergy List', Holderness, i, pp. 26–8; Poulson, *Holderness*, ii. 38. The probate records of the peculiar are divided between the Borthwick Institute and the Minster Library; they are briefly described in the *Borthwick Guide*, 158–61.

56 York Minster Libr., L 1/10, f. 535; L 2/2(a), f. 95.

57 R.D.B., KI/356/494; below, this section [income].

58 E.R.A.O., PE/68/24; *Crockford* (1961–2), 566.

59 The information comes from Torre's manuscripts compiled in the 17th century: York Minster Libr., L 1/10, f. 535. No ordination has been found.

60 York Minster Libr., L 2/2(a), f. 95.

61 *Valor Eccl.* (Rec. Com.), v. 112.

62 *T.E.R.A.S.* iv. 55.

63 B.I.H.R., V. 1662–3/CB. 1, f. 316v.; ibid. TER. H. Burton Pidsea 1716–1871.

64 *Herring's Visit.* i, p. 118.

65 E.R.A.O., PE/75/3; B.I.H.R., TER. H. Burton Pidsea 1809; Poulson, *Holderness*, ii. 39.

66 Hodgson, *Q.A.B.* p. cccxliii. B.I.H.R., TER. H. Burton Pidsea 1817 dates one of the grants 1811.

Some of the money was used to buy nearly 5 a. in Aldbrough in 1812 and 3 a. in Burton Pidsea in 1822,[67] and between 1829 and 1831 the income averaged £42 a year net.[68] In 1868 the rectorial tithe rents, amounting to nearly £143 a year, were annexed to the living by the dean and chapter's successors, the Ecclesiastical Commissioners, who later that year gave £64 a year from the Common Fund.[69] The rental of the glebe land bought in Aldbrough and Burton Pidsea was £13 a year in 1871,[70] and the total net income in 1883 was £215.[71] Some 2½ a. in Burton Pidsea was sold for redevelopment with houses between 1965 and 1967,[72] and the land at Aldbrough had also been disposed of by 1970.[73]

At ordination in 1301 the vicar was given ½ a. of the glebe on which to build a house at his own cost.[74] The vicarage house, then comprising three low rooms, was demolished in the 1650s, apparently by the lessee of the rectorial tithes.[75] Its garth, extending between the two streets on the east side of the later Chatt House, was the only vicarial glebe until the 19th century. The land was let for 10s. a year in 1716, 15s. in 1777, and £1 in 1809.[76] In 1868 the Ecclesiastical Commissioners granted £1,400 towards the building of a new house, and in 1869 a 4-a. site between the main road and the church was bought from William Clapham's trustees and the 1/2-a. site of the former house was exchanged with them for an equivalent strip of ground alongside the new site.[77] The house was built largely in 1869; the stable was added and lesser works of completion done to designs by William Botterill of Hull in or soon after 1871.[78] The tall, Gothic-influenced house is of red brick with crested slate roofs and heavy, stone, bay windows. From 1948 Burton Pidsea was served from Sproatley and later from Humbleton, whose vicarage house was designated the residence of the united benefice in 1961.[79] That house was replaced by a new vicarage built in Gray's Croft, Burton Pidsea, in 1980–1.[80] The redundant vicarage house at Burton Pidsea and its 4 a. of grounds were sold to T. N. Stephenson in 1950.[81]

Land called 'Gildehustede' was recorded in the mid 13th century,[82] in the mid 16th the ten-ants of Burton Pidsea had a guild house there, and later that house and 1 a. were let by the Crown;[83] the 'guildhall' and an adjoining croft had evidently passed to Sir Henry Constable, viscount Dunbar, by the earlier 17th century, when he sold them to Richard Wadworth.[84] The church had lights in honour of St. Mary and St. Zita in 1465,[85] and an image of St. Mary may have been the object of local pilgrimage in the earlier 16th century. There was also an obit endowed with a house, 2 bovates, and other land.[86]

Five vicars were inducted between 1412 and 1426, two of them explicitly by exchange,[87] and the living was being served by a curate c. 1530.[88] In 1567 Burton Pidsea church still had Roman Catholic fittings and paraphernalia,[89] and c. 1600 few sermons were preached there.[90] Ralph Cornwall, vicar of Burton Pidsea from 1662 and also vicar or curate of Skipsea, was accused of drunkeness, brawling, and profanity c. 1665.[91] The charge in 1663 that a man acted as parish clerk without licence, took away the church keys, and offended the vicar, was presumably part of the same controversy.[92] Cornwall was still in office in 1671 but had evidently resigned or been removed by 1679.[93] The lack of a house and poverty of the living[94] led to vicars' often holding other preferments, living elsewhere, and employing curates in the 18th and earlier 19th century. In 1764 the vicar lived at Burton Agnes, where he was curate, and Burton Pidsea was served for him by the curate at Aldbrough.[95] A service was held at Burton Pidsea on two Sundays out of three in the mid 18th century; Holy Communion was then administered three or four times a year, with an average of c. 25 receiving at Easter.[96] Jonathan Dixon, curate from 1781 and vicar from 1786 until his death in 1831, also served Humbleton, Garton, Tunstall, and Elstronwick churches.[97] Service at Burton Pidsea became weekly in 1818, when the church was once again in the charge of a curate.[98] One of the curates employed at Burton Pidsea c. 1850 obtained a library of 136 volumes for the parish, but it had been dispersed by the early 20th century.[99] George Trevor, canon of York minster, chaplain of Sheffield parish church,

[67] R.D.B., CT/180/295; DL/222/254.
[68] *Rep. Com. Eccl. Revenues*, 922–3.
[69] *Lond. Gaz.* 14 Aug. 1868, p. 4514; 17 Nov. 1868, p. 5930.   [70] B.I.H.R., TER H. Burton Pidsea 1871.
[71] Ibid. V. 1884/Ret. 1.
[72] R.D.B., 1428/566/499; 1509/504/438.
[73] B.I.H.R., ADM. (1970–2).
[74] York Minster Libr., L 2/2(a), f. 95.
[75] Lamb. Pal. Libr., COMM/XIIa/17/160; B.I.H.R., V. 1662–3/CB. 1, ff. 316v.–317; ibid. D/C. CP. 1669/5.
[76] A 'small homestead' not mentioned in the terriers apparently stood there c. 1760: E.R.A.O., DDCK/32/5, s. vv. schedule of ancient inclosures, inclosure map; B.I.H.R., TER. H. Burton Pidsea 1716–1809; above, last para.
[77] R.D.B., KI/356/494; KI/357/495; *Lond. Gaz.* 15 May 1868, p. 2808.
[78] E.R.A.O., PE/75/44–5; B.I.H.R., TER. H. Burton Pidsea 1871; ibid. MGA. 1871/1; date above door.
[79] E.R.A.O., PE/68/24; *Crockford* (1949–50), 248; (1955–6), 222; (1973–4), 251.
[80] Inf. from the vicar, 1999.
[81] R.D.B., 853/161/137.   [82] P.R.O., SC 12/17/5.
[83] Ibid. E 311/35, no. 29; E.R.A.O., DDCC/15/23 (bill on roll).   [84] E.R.A.O., DDCC/20/8.
[85] B.I.H.R., Prob. Reg. 4, f. 115; Prob. Reg. 10, f. 51v.; D. H. Farmer, *Oxford Dictionary of Saints*, 418–19.
[86] B.I.H.R., CP. G. 223; *Y.A.J.* xliv. 192.
[87] Lawrance, 'Clergy List', Holderness, 1, pp. 26–7.
[88] B.I.H.R., CP. G. 223.
[89] Ibid. V. 1567–8/CB. 1, f. 192.
[90] Ibid. V. 1600/CB. 1B, f. 139; J. S. Purvis, *Tudor Par. Doc. of Dioc. York*, 57.
[91] B.I.H.R., CP. H. 2561; Lawrance, 'Clergy List', Holderness, 1, p. 28; 2, p. 141; below, Skipsea, churches (Skipsea).
[92] B.I.H.R., V. 1662–3/CB. 1, f. 317.
[93] Ibid. D/C. CP. 1671/17; Poulson, *Holderness*, ii. 38.
[94] Above, this section.
[95] B.I.H.R., V. 1764/Ret. 1, no. 106; TER. H. Burton Pidsea 1777; *Herring's Visit.* i, p. 118; *Rep. Com. Eccl. Revenues*, 922–3.
[96] B.I.H.R., V. 1764/Ret. 1, no. 106; *Herring's Visit.* i, p. 118.   [97] Poulson, *Holderness*, ii. 38.
[98] Ibid. 39; E.R.A.O., PE/75/3.
[99] P.R.O., HO 129/521/1/25/44; E.R.A.O., PE/75/67, s.v. 1853; B.I.H.R., V. 1912–22/Ret.; Sheahan and Whellan, *Hist. York & E. R.* ii. 359.

and from 1868 rector of Burton Pidsea, increased the Sunday services to two. Celebrations of communion, still only quarterly in 1865, soon afterwards became monthly; communion was fortnightly c. 1920, and weekly by 1931. The number of communicants rarely exceeded 12 and on non-festal Sundays in 1931 averaged 5. The congregation in general was said to be growing 'rapidly' in 1868 and 'slightly' in 1877, but in 1931 it averaged only 25. A children's service had been adopted by 1900, but then and later the parish was felt to suffer from its lack of a hall or reading room. In 1931 special services were held on St. Peter's day and for the parades of the friendly society and the golfers of Withernsea Golf Club.[1] Burton Pidsea was served with Sproatley, Humbleton, and Elstronwick between 1948 and 1953, and thereafter with Humbleton and Elstronwick, with which churches it was united in 1961.[2] In 1999 a service and a celebration of Holy Communion were provided alternately in Burton Pidsea church on Sundays.[3] R. M. Lamb, vicar 1886–1921, was an authority on bee-keeping,[4] and Deryck Goodwin, physicist and vicar from 1986 to 1990, served as the diocesan advisor on church lighting.[5]

The church's dedication to ST. PETER AND ST. PAUL was recorded in 1542,[6] but in 1465 and frequently thereafter it was named in honour of ST. PETER alone.[7] The building, which is set on a mound above the street, is mostly of boulders with ashlar dressings. The original plan of chancel, nave, and west tower has been enlarged to form a near rectangle by the addition of four-bayed north and south aisles embracing the tower, a south chapel alongside the chancel, and a second chapel, or room, now a vestry, on the north side of the chancel. The nave and the core of the tower are probably 12th-century, and an early 13th-century lancet with dogtooth ornament is reset in the east wall of the vestry.[8] The chancel has an early 14th-century, two-light window with geometric tracery and a square head. The south chapel, apparently dedicated to the Virgin and presumably housing her image and light,[9] was added in the mid 14th century; its east window is of three lights with flowing tracery and the two-bayed arcade to the chancel has double-chamfered arches with an octagonal, central pier and simple chamfered capitals. The south aisle was probably built with the south chapel, the eastern respond of the aisle's arcade being identical in design to that of the chapel. The rest of the south

arcade was rebuilt, that aisle widened, the north aisle added, and the chancel arch reconstructed as part of a large-scale renovation completed by 1442, when a commission was issued for the re-consecration of the 'newly built' church.[10] All the arches have two chamfered orders with a hood mould on polygonal piers with moulded capitals. The aisles extend alongside the tower, whose walls have been pierced to provide north and south tower arches; the eastern tower arch was rebuilt last, its capitals varying slightly from those of the arcades. The 15th-century aisle windows are of three super-mullioned lights with two-centred heads; the west windows, which have two lights with reticulated tracery, are probably reset, perhaps from the nave. The south door also has a two-centred head with traceried spandrels in a square frame; the north door, now blocked, is plain.

In or about the earlier 16th century a clerestory was made in the south wall of the nave; a third, upper stage was added to the tower; the south side of the church and the tower were embattled, and the south chapel was given new, three-light windows with depressed heads. The chancel was decayed c. 1600,[11] and soon afterwards the east window of the north aisle and the tower window were given straight mullions, presumably replacing older tracery, and the former was partly filled with early brickwork. Early brick is also present in the south porch, of uncertain, presumably 15th-century, origin but rebuilt in brick in the 18th or early 19th century,[12] and in the north 'chapel', also of unknown date. Other changes made by 1831 included the blocking up of the south chapel arches to form a schoolroom, the removal of the battlements from the nave, the replacement of the pinnacles on the south aisle buttresses, and the installation of a west gallery. In 1838 William Clapham, lessee of the rectory, repaired and ceiled the chancel, and rebuilt its east wall in brick incorporating a new three-light window, possibly replacing a trefoiled window of the late 13th or early 14th century. His work evidently also included the rebuilding of the east wall of the nave and at least part of the north chapel.[13] The church was restored to designs by R. S. Smith of Hull from 1866. The building was refloored, reseated, and refitted; the ceiling of the chancel was taken down and the chancel arch, which it had cut across, repaired; the porch was renewed, and the north chapel remodelled as a vestry. Other work probably included the opening up of the south chapel and the removal of the gallery. Much of the work had been done by 1868,

[1] B.I.H.R., V. 1865/Ret. 1, no. 96; V. 1868/Ret. 1, no. 92; V. 1871/Ret. 1, no. 92; V. 1877/Ret. 1, no. 90; V. 1884/Ret. 1; V. 1900/Ret. no. 65; V. 1912–22/Ret.; V. 1931/Ret.; Hull Times, 29 Mar. 1913; above, intro. [social inst.].

[2] E.R.A.O., PE/68/24; Crockford (1955–6), 222.

[3] Notice board at church.

[4] Hull Times, 29 Mar. 1913; Kelly's Dir. N. & E.R. Yorks. (1889), 362; memorial in church.

[5] Crockford (1991–2), 275; The Times, 14 Apr. 1997.

[6] Test. Ebor. vi, p. 169.

[7] B.I.H.R., Prob. Reg. 4, f. 115; Prob. Reg. 10, f. 51v.; York Minster Libr., L 1/10, f. 535; P.R.O., HO 129/521/1/25/44. Crockford (1948), 1592 has St. Peter and

St. Paul with St. Peter, but in 1992 the dedication was simply to St. Peter: ibid. (1991–2), 848.

[8] In the 19th century, before rebuilding, the window was apparently in the same position; its original location is unknown. For the church before restoration, Poulson, Holderness, ii. 39–41, illus. facing p. 11; T. Allen, Hist. Co. York, iv. 252.

[9] Poulson, Holderness, ii. 40; above, this section.

[10] B.I.H.R., Reg. 19, f. 81.

[11] Ibid. V. 1600/CB. 1B, f. 139; V. 1615/CB. 1, f. 219.

[12] Pevsner and Neave, Yorks. E.R. 379; Poulson, Holderness, ii. 41.

[13] Poulson, Holderness, ii. 40–1; Allen, op. cit. iv. 252; Y.A.J. xxiv. 125–6.

but in 1871 the sanctuary was being floored with encaustic tiles and the chancel roof was still unfinished.[14] The south chapel was repaired by Joseph Raines in memory of his wife in 1884,[15] further work done in the chancel in 1892 by Henry Cautley, owner of the former rectorial estate,[16] and the tower repaired and re-roofed in 1930.[17] The church was repaired again by Community Rural Aid Ltd. under the auspices of the Manpower Services Commission and re-dedicated in 1987,[18] and the nave was re-roofed in 1998.

At inclosure in 1762 the churchwardens were allotted just over 1 a. for church repairs. In 1871 rent of £3 10s. a year was received for the land,[19] which was sold in 1969.[20]

A small extension to the churchyard was consecrated in 1907.[21]

The church has a late-medieval, octagonal font, and a pulpit, partly of alabaster and marble, which was installed at the restoration of the church c. 1870.[22] Wooden boards displaying the Lord's Prayer, the Creed, and the Ten Commandments, possibly those ordered to be set up in 1663,[23] were returned to the church in 1987 and 1988 from Chatt House and a local workshop.[24] The south aisle and south chapel contain several memorials in stained glass and stone to the Raines family, the most notable being a Gothic wall memorial by W. D. Keyworth of Hull to Isaac Raines (d. 1846) and his wife Ann (d. 1853). In the north aisle a matching pair of marble tablets by Bailey & Furness and G. Bailey, both of Hull, commemorate William Harland (d. 1862) and others of his family (d. 1843 and 1859), and in the chancel there are floorstones, stained-glass windows, and mural memorials to the Clapham family, rectorial lessees, and their successors, the Cautleys.[25] There were three bells in 1552 and later; new or recast bells were obtained in 1677, and two of that peal were recast in 1891.[26] The plate includes a cup and paten cover, made in Hull in 1638, and other pieces given to the church by the dean of York in 1868, evidently to mark the restoration.[27] The registers of baptisms, marriages, and burials begin c. 1715 and are practically complete.[28] Transcripts from 1600 also survive.[29]

In the 18th and 19th centuries the parish clerk also served as sexton. Besides his fees, the clerk received each year 10d. from every house, 5d. from each cottage, and a corn render from each bovate. The last due was commuted into money rents at the rate of 1s. 9d. a bovate and amounting in all to £5 5s. 8d. at inclosure in 1762.[30]

NONCONFORMITY. As was commonly the case in Holderness, Roman Catholic fittings and furnishings were found in the church at Burton Pidsea in 1567, and Michael Bolton, vicar, is said to have resigned or been deprived in 1579 and later to have died a Catholic in Hull. There seem, nevertheless, to have been few Roman Catholics in the parish, c. 10 people or one or two families being so recorded in the early and mid 18th century. Nevertheless they probably included Leonard Sisson, 'gentleman' and lessee of the rectory, and his family, recorded as non-communicants c. 1600,[31] and c. 1720 Cuthbert Constable, lord of Burton Pidsea, and three other proprietors there were Roman Catholic.[32]

Twelve Quakers were presented for non-attendance at church in 1663, among them Philip Chatt, his wife, and a servant,[33] and the Holderness monthly meeting was held at Burton Pidsea in 1669.[34] In 1764 there was said to be only one Quaker family in the parish;[35] it was perhaps a branch of the Stickneys, prominent Friends who lived just outside Burton Pidsea at Ridgmont.[36]

Thomas Thompson, a leading local Methodist, secured the registration for dissenting worship of Richard Hastings's house in the west end of the village in 1784, and that or other houses, also in the occupation of Hastings, were licensed in 1790 and 1791.[37] The same or another Richard Hastings obtained the registration of a Wesleyan chapel in 1820.[38] It was replaced by a new chapel built on the north side of Main Street in 1847.[39] That building was extended about 1859[40] and restored in 1909. The chapel was closed in 1970 and the building demolished after 1980.[41]

It was perhaps another Richard Hastings who was a prominent member of the Primitive

[14] B.I.H.R., Fac. Bk. 5, pp. 136–8; Fac. 1866/4; ibid. Ch. Ret. i; ibid. V. 1871/Ret. 1, no. 92.
[15] Wall tablet in chapel.
[16] Kelly's Dir. N. & E.R. Yorks. (1893), 399.
[17] B.I.H.R., FAC. 1930/1/26; E.R.A.O., PE/75/28.
[18] Plaque on porch.
[19] E.R.A.O., DDCK/32/5; ibid. PE/75/67; B.I.H.R., TER. H. Burton Pidsea 1781, 1871.
[20] R.D.B., 1591/268/239.
[21] B.I.H.R., CD. Add. 1907/3.
[22] Ibid. TER. H. Burton Pidsea 1871; Pevsner and Neave, Yorks. E.R. 379.
[23] B.I.H.R., V. 1662–3/CB. 1, f. 316v.
[24] Ibid. TER. 1126.
[25] Pevsner and Neave, Yorks. E.R. 379. The arms of the Claphams were formerly also displayed in stained glass in the east window, made in 1838: Poulson, Holderness, ii. 40–2.
[26] B.I.H.R., TER. 142; E.R.A.O., PE/75/26–7; Inventories of Ch. Goods, 41; Boulter, 'Ch. Bells', 83.
[27] Yorks. Ch. Plate, i. 232.
[28] E.R.A.O., PE/75/1 (opening entries difficult to read); ibid. PE/75/2–3, 6.
[29] B.I.H.R., D/C. PRT. Burton Pidsea.

[30] Ibid. TER. H. Burton Pidsea 1764–1871; E.R.A.O., DDCK/32/5; G. T. J. Miles and W. Richardson, Hist. Withernsea with S. Holderness, 139.
[31] B.I.H.R., V. 1567–8/CB. 1, f. 192; V. 1600/CB. 1B, f. 139; V. 1764/Ret. 1, no. 106; Aveling, Post Reformation Catholicism, 11, 13, 68; Herring's Visit. i, p. 117.
[32] E.R.A.O., DDCC/111/34; ibid. QDR/2/1, 6, 47.
[33] B.I.H.R., V. 1662–3/CB. 1, f. 316v.; above, intro. [village].   [34] E.R.A.O., DDQR/17.
[35] B.I.H.R., V. 1764/Ret. 1, no. 106.
[36] J. T. Ward, E. Yorks. Landed Estates in the Nineteenth Cent. (E. Yorks. Loc. Hist. Ser. xxiii), 10.
[37] B.I.H.R., DMH. 1784/5; 1790/27; 1791/24; V.C.H. Yorks. E.R. i. 313.
[38] P.R.O., RG 31/5, no. 3463.
[39] Ibid. no. 4657; P.R.O., HO 129/521/1/25/45; R.D.B., GK/350/355; Sheahan and Whellan, Hist. York & E.R. ii. 359.
[40] R.D.B., IA/137/175; O.S. Map 6", Yorks. CCXXVIII (1855 and later edns.).
[41] D. [R. J.] and S. Neave, E.R. Chapels and Meeting Houses (E. Yorks. Loc. Hist. Soc.), 48; inf. from Mr. R. Wray, Graysgarth Farm, Burton Pidsea, 1999.

Methodists at Burton Pidsea in the mid 19th century. He fitted up a room for worship by the congregation in the 1840s and was the 'chapel' steward in 1851.[42] The room had evidently been closed by 1859, when its fittings were being distributed.[43] The congregation later met in a cottage, but services had apparently ceased by 1893.[44]

EDUCATION. Parents sent c. 50 children to day schools in Burton Pidsea in 1818,[45] and in 1833 there were three schools there, attended by 25 boys and 34 girls.[46] Former poorhouses in Church Street were remodelled or rebuilt as a school and master's house[47] in 1860. The parish school, which opened that year, was supported largely by school pence, but the parish subscribed £20 a year and provided the house in return for the master keeping its accounts, and his fees as a land surveyor were also used for the school. Average attendance at the mixed school was 30 in 1866.[48] The school was run according

to the National plan by 1872, when the site and buildings were conveyed to the vicar and churchwardens; that year has since been regarded mistakenly as the building date.[49] An annual government grant was first received in 1869.[50] In 1877 the school also accommodated infants and had an average attendance of 60.[51] It was transferred in 1909 to the county council, which in 1910 enlarged the site, remodelled the school, and improved the house.[52] Average attendance was usually c. 70 between 1906 and the 1930s but stood at 82 in 1913–14 and 55 in 1937–8.[53] The senior pupils were transferred to Withernsea High School at its opening in 1955.[54] Burton Pidsea primary school was enlarged and altered to provide three classrooms in the early 1960s,[55] a playing field was laid out in 1964,[56] and in 1975 classrooms for 75 infants were built.[57] There were 101 on the roll in 1990 and 69 in 1998.[58]

CHARITIES FOR THE POOR. None known.

GARTON

THE village of Garton lies close to the sea, some 17 km. ENE. of Hull, and the parish is best known for Grimston Garth, an 18th-century mansion standing in well wooded parkland east of the village.[59] A group of houses belonging to the chief estate stands at the north entrance to the park, forming the modern hamlet of Grimston; the medieval Grimston, now depopulated, was situated c. ½ km. to the north-west. The name Garton, perhaps meaning 'farmstead in or near a triangular piece of land', may be an Anglian and Scandinavian hybrid. From the 14th century the village was often distinguished from Garton on the Wolds by the suffix 'in Holderness'. The name Grimston may mean 'Grim's farmstead', and it is also a hybrid. The suffix 'Garth', apparently referring to the enclosure in which the manor house stood,[60] has also been used for the hamlet from the 16th century.[61]

The ancient parish of Garton comprised the greater part of Garton with Grimston township

and several detached parts in Owstwick township; in 1852 it contained 2,064 a. (835 ha.), of which 1,614 a. (653 ha.) were in Garton with Grimston and 450 a. (182 ha.) in Owstwick. Most of Owstwick was in Roos parish, and its history is treated below with that of Roos. The rest of Garton with Grimston township, 209 a. (85 ha.) in 1852, was also in Roos parish;[62] the boundary of the Roos part, which lay in Grimston, was defined in 1701.[63] The area of Garton with Grimston township, later civil parish, had been reduced by coastal erosion to 1,790 a. (724 ha.) by 1911.[64] In 1935 Garton with Grimston civil parish, with the same area, was added to Fitling civil parish, in Humbleton, to form East Garton civil parish, with a total area of 3,320 a. (1,344 ha.).[65] By 1991 that area had been reduced by erosion to 1,327 ha. (3,279 a.).[66]

There were 48 poll-tax payers at Grimston in 1377 but no return survives for Garton.[67] In 1672 Garton and Grimston together had 18 houses assessed for hearth tax and 4 discharged.[68] The

42 White, *Dir. Hull & York* (1858), 546. It was registered as a chapel in 1843 but was elsewhere said to have been built in 1844: P.R.O., RG 31/5, no. 4568; ibid. HO 129/521/1/25/46.
43 E.R.A.O., MRW/2/5, s.v. 15 June 1859. Cf. MRW/2/18.
44 Ibid. MRW/2/16; *Kelly's Dir. N. & E.R. Yorks.* (1889), 362.
45 *Educ. of Poor Digest*, 1078.
46 *Educ. Enq. Abstract*, 1081.
47 E.R.A.O., PE/75/88; O.S. Map 6", Yorks. CCXXVIII (1855 edn.).
48 P.R.O., ED 7/135, no. 27; ED 7/147, no. 197; B.I.H.R., V. 1865/Ret. 1, no. 96. Reg. from 1868 at E.R.A.O., PE/75/85.
49 E.R.A.O., PE/75/86, 88; *Kelly's Dir. N. & E.R. Yorks.* (1889), 362. Bulmer, *Dir. E. Yorks.* (1892), 397, gives 1868.
50 *Rep. of Educ. Cttee. of Council, 1869–70* [C.165], p. 668, H.C. (1870), xxii.
51 B.I.H.R., V. 1877/Ret. 1, no. 90.
52 E.R.A.O., PE/75/86, 90; E.R. Educ. Cttee. *Mins.* 1908–9, 234; 1909–10, 46, 178; 1910–11, 166, 197, 244, 326.

53 *Bd. of Educ., List 21* (H.M.S.O., 1908 and later edns.).
54 E.R. Educ. Cttee. *Mins.* 1952–3, 226–7; *V.C.H. Yorks. E.R.* v. 167.
55 E.R. Educ. Cttee. *Mins.* 1960–1, 160.
56 Ibid. 1958–9, 251; 1960–1, 130–1; 1964–5, 103.
57 Ibid. 1972–3, 196; inf. from the headteacher, 1998.
58 Inf. from Educ. Dept., Humbs. C.C., 1990; inf. from the headteacher, 1998.
59 This article was written in 1989.
60 E.R.A.O., PE/13/2 (1657); directories; below, manors.
61 *P.N. Yorks. E.R.* (E.P.N.S.), 58; Camden, *Brit.* (1695), 740. G. F. Jensen, *Scand. Settlement Names in Yorks.* 114–15, 119, 127–8, 203.
62 O.S. Map 6", Yorks. CCXXVIII (1855 edn.); *Census*, 1881.
63 E.R.A.O., DDCK/24/2. For the disputed boundary see P.R.O., E 134/28 Chas. II East./4.
64 *Census.*
65 Ibid. 1931 (pt. ii).   66 Ibid. 1991.
67 P.R.O., E 179/202/60, m. 19.
68 *Hearth Tax*, 60.

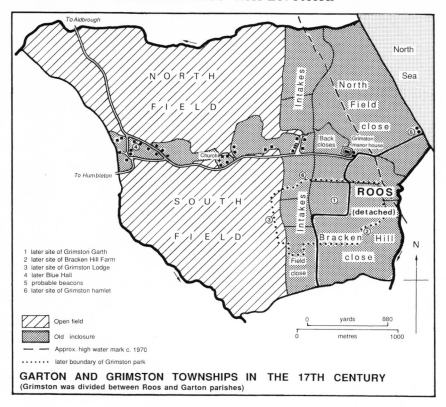

1 later site of Grimston Garth
2 later site of Bracken Hill Farm
3 later site of Grimston Lodge
4 later Blue Hall
5 probable beacons
6 later site of Grimston hamlet

▨ Open field

▨ Old inclosure

— — Approx. high water mark c. 1970

········ later boundary of Grimston park

GARTON AND GRIMSTON TOWNSHIPS IN THE 17TH CENTURY
(Grimston was divided between Roos and Garton parishes)

parish contained *c.* 22 families in 1743 and 24 in 1764.[69] From 105 in 1801 the population of Garton with Grimston township rose to 179 in 1841, was stable at *c.* 160 until the 1880s, and then fell to 121 in 1901. Numbers later rose to 144 in 1931. The population of the larger East Garton civil parish was 229 in 1931 and hardly changed until the 1960s, when it began to fall; 193 were counted in 1971 and 181 of the usually-resident 193 in 1991.[70]

Most of the township is on boulder clay and lies at more than 15 m. above sea level, rising to over 22 m. near the coast and resulting in an almost unbroken line of steep cliffs. Lower land, *c.* 13 m. above sea level, in the north and west is partly alluvial, and there are several pockets of sand and gravel.[71] The open fields of Garton extended from the higher ground into the lower areas, which also provided common grazing.

A stream rising on the high ground near the cliffs and flowing westwards towards the river Humber defines the northern township boundary; it was said to be neglected in 1367. Another drain described as insufficient in 1367 was probably that which formed the boundary with Tunstall.[72] In 1618 the grounds drained by Keyingham fleet included 12 a. in Garton,[73] and under the Keyingham Level Drainage Acts of 1772 and later[74] the northern stream was improved as East Newton and Bail drains.[75]

Lesser drains within the level included those running along much of the western boundary of Garton. After 1845 some 24 a. of low grounds in Garton were assessed to the drainage.[76] Keyingham Level Drainage Board still existed in 1998.[77]

The coast road from Hornsea to Withernsea runs through the west part of the township, leading northwards to Aldbrough and southwards to Hilston and Roos, and a minor road leads westwards to Fitling and Humbleton. The Aldbrough road is carried over the northern boundary drain by Bail bridge.[78] Roads formerly leading from the east end of Garton village northwards to Ringbrough and East Newton, in Aldbrough, and southwards to the Roos road were later partly represented by field roads and paths.[79]

GARTON village has a linear plan, its garths lying east–west across the township and form-erly separating the open fields to north and south. The main street is formed by the Ald-brough road and a side road to Grimston. In the 17th century a dozen houses stood on both sides of the street and in a southern back lane at the west end of the village, and the church and half a dozen houses lay north of the street at the east end. Other garths were already empty.[80] Houses removed by the mid 19th century included

69 B.I.H.R., V. 1764/Ret. 1, no. 208; *Herring's Visit.* ii, p. 12. 70 *V.C.H. Yorks.* iii. 494; *Census,* 1911–91.
71 Geol. Surv. Map 1″, drift, sheet 73 (1909 edn.).
72 Poulson, *Holderness,* i. 123–4.
73 E.R.A.O., DDCC/54/53.
74 *V.C.H. Yorks. E.R.* v. 55–7.
75 O.S. Map 6″, Yorks. CCXIII (1855 and later edns.).
76 E.R.A.O., DDPK/3/8.

77 Inf. from Environment Agency, Hull, 1998.
78 O.S. Map 6″, Yorks. CCXIII (1855 and later edns.).
79 T. Jefferys, *Map of Yorks.* (1772); A. Bryant, *Map of E.R. Yorks.* (1829); O.S. Map 6″, Yorks. CCXIII, CCXXVIII (1855 and later edns.).
80 E.R.A.O., DDCC/42/2 (a damaged and faded map of Garton and Grimston, prob. 17th-cent.); Hull Univ., Dept. of Geog., R.A.F. air photographs, run 24A, no. 3150.

several at the west end of the street.[81] Of the older buildings still standing in 1989 only Blue Hall Farm is noteworthy.[82] A dozen houses date from the 20th century, including eight council houses and one or two rebuilt farmhouses.[83]

GRIMSTON. The main street of Garton continues eastwards to Moat Farm, formerly Grimston manor house. Two houses at Grimston were recorded as decayed in 1517 as the result of inclosure.[84] In the 17th century half a dozen houses stood in a side lane west of the manor house;[85] their site was later known as Old Garths.[86] It was evidently proposed in 1785 to build cottages along with the new mansion at Grimston,[87] and a few stood beside the road leading into Grimston park by 1852.[88] A school was added in 1860,[89] and about the same date a lodge and three more cottages.[90] Some of the cottages have decorative bargeboards.

There were 1–2 licensed houses in the parish in the late 18th century. At Grimston the Stag's Head, presumably named from the Grimston family crest, or the Nag's Head was recorded in the 1820s, and it was probably the beerhouse mentioned in 1840.[91] A reading room at Garton was provided in 1887 in a cottage belonging to the church.[92] The former school at Grimston was used as a parish hall from 1961, and later meetings were held in the Methodist church in Fitling, in Humbleton.[93]

OUTLYING BUILDINGS include two farmhouses, Bracken Hill and Turmar Farm. Land called Bracken hill was recorded in the 15th century, and there was an old inclosure of that name in the 17th century. Bracken Hill was built there, possibly by 1772, and it was named in the 1820s, together with No Man's Friend, later Turmar Farm.[94]

High ground near the cliffs has been used for beacons. Three were recorded at Grimston in 1588,[95] and two structures shown on a 17th-century map were presumably the beacons commemorated by the name Beacon field.[96] A beacon was maintained on Beacon Hill in the early 19th century.[97] Thomas Grimston (d. 1821) raised and led forces of yeoman cavalry from Holderness between 1794 and 1814.[98]

MANORS AND OTHER ESTATES. In 1066 Morkar held 4 carucates at Grimston as soke of Withernsea manor. By 1086 the estate had passed to Drew de Bevrère,[99] and, like Withernsea, it later became part of the Aumale fee.[1] William de Ros was the tenant in the mid 13th century, and Grimston later descended in the Ros family, later Lords Ros of Helmsley (Yorks. N.R.), and their heirs, the Manners family, earls of Rutland, and the Cecils, Lords Ros, as a member of Roos manor.[2]

Grimston was held of the Ros family by the Grimstons.[3] Early tenants may have included Gilbert of Grimston, witness c. 1150 to a deed by William le Gros, count of Aumale, and Ralph of Grimston and his son Thomas, who were recorded in the early 13th century.[4] Roger of Grimston was named as a lord of Garton in 1316.[5] William of Grimston had succeeded by 1325, and held all 4 carucates by knight service in 1343.[6] Thomas of Grimston, undertenant by 1351,[7] was evidently succeeded by Sir Gerard of Grimston, and he by his son William by 1386.[8] The same or another William was lord of Grimston in 1415,[9] and Thomas Grimston (d. by 1462) was licensed to have an oratory there in the 1450s.[10] As the manor of GRIMSTON, later GRIMSTON GARTH,[11] the estate descended from Walter Grimston (d. 1544) to his son Thomas, and then possibly to Marmaduke Grimston, who was named as the tenant of the 4 carucates, held as 1 knight's fee, in 1558.[12] Walter's son Thomas or another Thomas (d. 1572) was succeeded by his son Thomas (d. 1586) and that Thomas's son Sir Marmaduke (d. 1604), whose heir was his brother Thomas.[13]

The estate, by then including a manor of GARTON, presumably part of the property formerly belonging to Thornton abbey,[14] passed

[81] B.I.H.R., TA. 263s; O.S. Map 6″, Yorks. CCXXVIII (1855 edn.).
[82] Below, manors.
[83] R.D.B., 827/50/43.
[84] Trans. R. Hist. S. N.S. vii. 246; below, econ. hist.
[85] E.R.A.O., DDCC/42/2.
[86] O.S. Map 6″, Yorks. CCXXVIII (1855 edn.); Hull Univ., Dept. of Geog., R.A.F. air photographs, run 24A, nos. 3147–8.
[87] E.R.A.O., DDGR/43/5 (11 Aug. 1785).
[88] O.S. Map 6″, Yorks. CCXXVIII (1855 edn.).
[89] Below, educ.   [90] P.R.O., RG 9/3601.
[91] E.R.A.O., QDT/2/7, 9; Baines, Hist. Yorks. (1823), ii. 209; White, Dir. E. & N.R. Yorks. (1840), 259.
[92] E.R.A.O., PE/13/18; Bulmer, Dir. E. Yorks. (1892), 410.
[93] Below, educ.; inf. from Mrs. J. A. Roberts, Garton, 1991.
[94] B.I.H.R., CP. F. 148; E.R.A.O., DDCC/42/2; T. Jefferys, Map of Yorks. (1772); Baines, Hist. Yorks. (1823), ii. 375; A. Bryant, Map of E.R. Yorks. (1829).
[95] J. Nicholson, Beacons of E. Yorks. 9.
[96] E.R.A.O., DDCC/42/2. For Beacon field see P.R.O., E 134/28 Chas. II East./4; O.S. Map 6″, Yorks. CCXXVIII (1855 edn.).
[97] E.R.A.O., LT/9/54; ibid. DDGR/35/38; Nicholson, op. cit. 37–8; O.S. Map 6″, Yorks. CCXIII (1855 edn.); A.

Bryant, Map of E.R. Yorks. (1829).
[98] R. W. S. Norfolk, Militia, Yeomanry and Volunteer Forces of E.R. 1689–1908 (E. Yorks. Loc. Hist. Ser. xix), 15, 24, 33, 45, 49.
[99] V.C.H. Yorks. ii. 265.
[1] V.C.H. Yorks. E.R. v. 163.
[2] P.R.O., C 142/160, no. 59; C 142/218, no. 52; C 142/301, no. 65; Kirkby's Inquest, 243, 374; Feud. Aids, vi. 39; Cal. Inq. p. m. iv, pp. 352, 354; viii, pp. 342–3; Complete Peerage, s.v. Ros; below, Roos.
[3] For the fam. see Foster, Pedigrees of Yorks. iii; Burke, Land. Gent. (1937), 986–7. Much of the pedigree given there is incorrect.
[4] E.Y.C. iii, p. 90; Chron. de Melsa (Rolls Ser.), i. 359.
[5] Yorks. Fines, 1272–1300, p. 139; Feud. Aids, vi. 164.
[6] H.U.L., DDSY/52/4; Cal. Inq. p. m. viii, p. 343.
[7] Cal. Inq. p. m. ix, p. 440.
[8] Cal. Close, 1385–9, 269.
[9] Yorks. Deeds, ix, p. 123.
[10] Test. Ebor. iii, p. 251 n.
[11] P.R.O., CP 43/236, rot. 55.
[12] Ibid. C 142/69, no. 142; H.U.L., DDSY/56/1.
[13] P.R.O., C 142/160, no. 59; C 142/210, no. 124; C 142/301, no. 65.
[14] Below, this section.

from Thomas Grimston (d. 1618) to his nephew Marmaduke Grimston (d. 1623).[15] Later reckoned a single manor, *GARTON WITH GRIMSTON*, it descended in the family[16] to Marmaduke Grimston (d. 1879), whose heirs were his daughters Florence, who married Edward Byrom, and Rose, who married George Hobart and in 1912 assumed the additional name Grimston. The family estates were held in undivided moieties[17] until 1918. The manor house and *c.* 1,210 a. in Garton with Grimston township then formed the bulk of the share assigned to Mrs. Hobart Grimston and her daughter Armatrude, wife of Sir Max Waechter.[18] Lady Waechter, who took the additional name de Grimston on her mother's death in 1927, gave the estate to her cousin Norman R. Grimston in 1946, and he sold it in 1948 to St. Andrew's Steam Fishing Co. Ltd.[19]

The company later sold much of the estate. Grimston Garth mansion, with nearly 100 a., and the 106-a. Bracken Hill farm were bought in 1949 by Joan Little, who sold the farmhouse with 65 a. to Harold Cox the same year.[20] Moat farm with 119 a. was bought by Frank Beadle in 1955, and the 231-a. Poplar farm by Frank Long in 1957.[21] In 1966 the remaining *c.* 600 a. were conveyed to Boston Deep Sea Fisheries Ltd., which in 1967 sold the 329-a. Church farm to Frank Long and the 273-a. Turmar farm to Claude Cox.[22] Grimston Garth and part of the grounds were sold by Mrs. Little in 1964 to Reckitt & Sons Ltd., which transferred the premises in 1970 to Reckitt & Colman Products Ltd. In 1972 the house was bought by Mr. Oliver Marriott, the owner in 1989.[23]

A chief house at Grimston was implied in the licence for an oratory in the 15th century,[24] and Grimston Garth was recorded as a seat of the Grimstons in 1586.[25] The manor house, which had seven hearths in 1672,[26] is said to have been burned down during the lifetime of William Grimston (1640–1711).[27] A substantial house nevertheless survived in 1772.[28] In the 18th century it seems not to have been used by the Grimstons, who stayed at Hilston when visiting their Holderness estate.[29] The manor house, or a replacement on its moated site, was later known successively as Grimston Garth Farm and Moat Farm; it was superseded in 1956 by a

new house standing outside the moat. Part of the old house stood in outbuildings on the still moated site in 1989, when a smaller moat near by surrounding an earthwork called the Mount also survived.[30]

A new Grimston Hall or Garth[31] was built by Thomas Grimston (d. 1821) between 1781 and 1786 about ½ km. south of the medieval site and a similar distance from the cliffs. It was used as a summer residence by the family, who also lived at Kilnwick.[32] The castellated house was designed by John Carr of York and built of brick with stone dressings, all of which was originally colour-washed.[33] The main block is triangular with a circular tower at each corner. The dining and drawing rooms are hexagonal and occupy the two principal floors within the triangle, with the hexagonal bedroom lantern and the tops of the towers rising one more storey. Two-storeyed wings, which also end in circular towers, adjoin the north side and enclose a narrow open court; they provided offices on the ground floor and bedrooms above. Much of the original Gothick plaster decoration and woodwork survives on the ground floor. The other principal rooms were decorated in a restrained Georgian style. The house may have been remodelled *c.* 1832,[34] and minor alterations were made *c.* 1860 to designs by W. D. Keyworth of Hull.[35] Those 19th-century changes included the addition of a three-storeyed tower against the eastern service wing and the enclosing of the service court. The house, which was not used by the family in the late 19th century, was restored by Lady Waechter de Grimston in the 1920s,[36] when the drawing room was provided with elaborate overdoors and oriental wallpaper. Further restoration, begun in the 1970s and continuing in 1990, involved the removal of the additions of the 1920s and most of those of the 19th century. The house lies close to the northern edge of a landscaped park of about 1 sq. km. which may have been laid out by Thomas White in 1782.[37] Work was continuing on the outbuildings in 1787,[38] presumably the low Gothick stable court just north of the house. To the west Grimston Lodge, a tall castellated gatehouse, was built and possibly designed by John Earle of Hull in 1812,[39] and a lodge in Grimston hamlet was described as newly built in 1861.[40]

[15] P.R.O., C 142/401, no. 126; C 142/708, no. 96.

[16] Ibid. C 142/401, no. 126; ibid. CP 25(2)/893/2 Wm. & Mary Trin., no. 23; R.D.B., H/641/1298; X/290/667; BF/270/465; HZ/331/425; H.U.L., DGN/11/8.

[17] R.D.B., 155/36/31; 155/37/32.

[18] Ibid. 185/114/93. The acreage within the township has been calculated from O.S. Map 1/2,500, Yorks. CCXIII. 13–14; CCXXVIII. 2, 6 (1910 and 1927 edns.).

[19] R.D.B., 549/398/315; 721/247/221; 793/70/59.

[20] Ibid. 806/300/243; 819/198/163.

[21] Ibid. 1018/246/226; 1068/210/185.

[22] Ibid. 1478/132/123; 1495/542/461; 1498/198/177.

[23] Ibid. 1381/219/191; 1662/122/102; inf. from Mr. O. Marriott, Grimston, 1989.   [24] *Test. Ebor.* iii, p. 251 n.

[25] Camden, *Brit.* (1695), 740.

[26] P.R.O., E 179/205/504.

[27] Poulson, *Holderness*, ii. 62.

[28] T. Jefferys, *Map of Yorks.* wrongly shows it on the S. side of the road.

[29] E.R.A.O., DDGR/42/1 (28 Oct. 1751).

[30] O.S. Map 6″, Yorks. CCXXVIII (1855 and later

edns.); A. Bryant, *Map of E.R. Yorks.* (1829); inf. from Mrs. B. Beadle, Grimston, 1991.

[31] O.S. Map 6″, Yorks. CCXXVIII (1855 edn.); A. Bryant, *Map of E.R. Yorks.* (1829).

[32] E.R.A.O., DDGR/35/38; H.U.L., DGN/11/8.

[33] For acct. and illus. of the ho. see *Trans. E. Yorks. Georgian Soc.* i (2), 25–8; ii (1), 23; ii (3), 43–9; M. E. Ingram, *Leaves from Fam. Tree,* 104–25, and facing 132; *Country Life,* 17 Oct. 1952, pp. 1186–8; Pevsner and Neave, *Yorks. E.R.* 445–7.

[34] E.R.A.O., DDGR/44/29 (14 Apr. 1832).

[35] Ingram, op. cit. 116–17.

[36] *Kelly's Dir. N. & E.R. Yorks.* (1879), 400; (1893), 428; (1929), 503.

[37] E.R.A.O., DDGR/43/2 (11 June 1782); D. [R. J.] Neave and D. Turnbull, *Landscaped Parks and Gardens of E. Yorks.* (E. Yorks. Georgian Soc. 1992), 31–2.

[38] E.R.A.O., DDGR/43/7 (13 Feb. 1787).

[39] Ibid. DDGR/43/32 (letter and sketch, 19 Aug. 1812; 16 Dec. 1812); O.S. Map 6″, Yorks. CCXXVIII (1855 edn.); H. Colvin, *Biog. Dict. Brit. Architects 1600–1840,* 278.

[40] P.R.O., RG 9/3601.

Fig. 1. Grimston Garth

The archbishop of York had a berewick of 2 carucates at Grimston in 1086.[41] His fee there was mentioned again in the 13th century.[42] By the mid 16th century 140 a. were held of the archiepiscopal manor of Cawood (Yorks. W.R.) by the Grimstons and later descended with Grimston manor.[43]

In 1066 Morkar held 6 carucates in Garton as soke of Easington manor. The estate passed to Drew de Bevrère, whose tenant Baldwin held it in 1086, and it later became part of the Aumale fee.[44] In the mid 13th century William of Etherdwick and William de Stutville held 5 carucates and 2 bovates of the estate.[45]

Some of the Aumale fee evidently passed to the Ros family, and descended as an appurtenance of Roos manor.[46] Another part was held by a cadet branch of the Ros family as a member of Ringbrough manor, in Aldbrough, with which it descended.[47] In 1351 at Garton 1 carucate of demesne and rent were held as 1/48 knight's fee, and there were 4½ bovates at Grimston.[48] In the 16th century the estate at Garton and Grimston included half a dozen houses and was wholly held by tenants.[49]

A large part of Garton evidently passed to Thornton abbey (Lincs.). By 1190 one Maurice

had given 2 bovates there,[50] and gifts were later received from Geoffrey of Gunthorpe and William le Bret, and probably from Thomas Nuthill, who was licensed to grant premises at Grimston in 1392.[51] By the mid 13th century 6 bovates were held in Garton, and in 1316 the abbot was named as one of its lords.[52]

After the Dissolution the former abbey's manor of *GARTON WITH GRIMSTON* was granted to the short-lived Thornton college in 1542.[53] By the college's suppression the estate passed to the Crown, which sold houses and land at Garton in the 1590s. The rest of the estate was granted, as the manor of *GARTON*, to John Eldred and William Whitmore in 1611;[54] no more is known of it.

The manor house and 5 bovates were granted in fee farm in 1590 to Edmund Downing and Roger Rante,[55] and two houses with lands to John Wells and Henry Best in 1595.[56] Both holdings passed to Sir Henry Constable, who evidently sold them to Marmaduke Grimston in 1595–6.[57]

It was perhaps the same estate, reputed a manor of *GARTON*, which by the late 17th century belonged to Henry Constable (d. 1700),[58] a junior member of the Constables of Burton Constable. Henry was succeeded by the senior line,[59] and in 1774 William Constable sold

41 *V.C.H. Yorks.* ii. 216.
42 *Kirkby's Inquest,* 374.
43 P.R.O., C 142/160, no. 59; C 142/301, no. 65.
44 *V.C.H. Yorks.* ii. 265–6, 326; *V.C.H. Yorks. E.R.* v. 24.
45 *Yorks. Fines, 1232–46,* p. 94; *Kirkby's Inquest,* 374.
46 H.U.L., DHO/8/51; P.R.O., C 142/218, no. 52.
47 H.U.L., DHO/7/26, 35; *Feud. Aids,* vi. 40; *Kirkby's Inquest,* 244; *Cal. Inq. p.m.* iv, p. 354; vi, p. 98; *Y.A.J.* xii. 250; *Yorks. Deeds,* iv, pp. 5–6, 8–9; above, Aldbrough, manors (Ringbrough).
48 *Cal. Inq. p.m.* ix, p. 440.
49 E.R.A.O., DDCC/1/2.   50 *E.Y.C.* iii, pp. 41–2.
51 *Cal. Chart. R.* 1300–26, 9–10; *Cal. Pat.* 1391–6, 152; *Yorks. Fines, 1232–46,* p. 85.

52 *Kirkby's Inquest,* 374; *Feud. Aids,* vi. 164.
53 P.R.O., SC 6/Hen. VIII/2022, m. 79; *L. & P. Hen. VIII,* xvii, pp. 29–30.
54 P.R.O., C 66/1903, no. 9.
55 Ibid. C 66/1349, mm. 11–12; E 310/27/158, f. 58; E 310/29/175, f. 61.
56 Ibid. C 66/1435, mm. 37–46.
57 E.R.A.O., DDCC/42/1. No evidence has been found of Constable ownership in Garton in the mid 17th century.
58 List of E.R. gentry compiled *c.* 1680 at B.L. Add. MS. 40132/109, reference supplied by Dr. S. Neave; Poulson, *Holderness,* ii. 59.
59 E.R.A.O., DDCC/111/34, 222, 231; Foster, *Pedigrees of Yorks.* iii.

the estate, then comprising 535 a. in three farms, to John Wright.[60] In 1785 Wright sold two of the farms, amounting to 384 a., to John Graves, evidently as trustee for Thomas Grimston.[61] The land later descended with the rest of the Grimston family's estate, some being used for the new park.[62]

The farm remaining with John Wright (d. by 1792), of 152 a. and later called Blue Hall farm, was devised to his son Samuel and sold to Thomas Walker in 1795 and Samuel Stocks in 1822.[63] Stocks died before 1856, when his trustee D. B. Kendell had the farm.[64] Kendell died in 1902, and the next year the estate was vested in the Revd. Samuel Hall, who had married Helen Kendell.[65] Hall died in 1942, and the farm was sold in 1943 to Bernard Hartley (d. 1961), from whose representatives Rudolph Sprinz bought it in 1964.[66] Mr. Sprinz was the owner in 1989.[67] The house was sold separately in 1990.[68]

The manor house recorded from 1718 was presumably Blue Hall, which was so called in 1749, evidently from the colour of its roof tiles.[69] The house, which is of red brick, was built in the later 17th century and has an L-shaped plan. The main west front was of three storeys and five bays with a central entrance. A two-storeyed service range ran eastwards behind its south end. The upper floor of the main range and the east end of the service wing were demolished in the 19th century, when the fenestration was also altered. The house was again remodelled in 1992–3, and the west front later looked early 19th-century in style, though the interior has panelled rooms and other fittings of the late 17th century and a possibly refixed staircase of that period with heavy, turned balusters.[70] There are remains of possible moats, and there may also have been a walled forecourt to the west front.

Tenants of Thornton abbey included the Gowers, who had a so-called manor of GARTON. Thomas Gower (d. 1522) held a chief house and 80–100 a. of the abbey by fealty, besides 20–30 a. under Burstwick manor by military service, and his family later also held land of Roos manor. Thomas Gower was succeeded in turn by his sons George (d. 1535) and

Gilbert.[71] The latter (d. 1586) defended his right to the manor in 1572, and was succeeded by his grandson Marmaduke,[72] who sold all or part of the estate, then extending into Fitling, to Marmaduke Grimston (d. 1604).[73] After the purchase the Grimstons, who already had part of Thornton's former estate,[74] held the reputed manor of the Crown under either Humbleton manor or Thornton manor.[75] It later descended with Grimston manor.

After the appropriation of the church c. 1222, the *RECTORY* also belonged to Thornton abbey, which had 3 bovates of glebe by 1260.[76] Like Thornton's manor, the rectorial estate passed in the 16th century to Thornton college and then to the Crown. In 1604 corn and hay tithes in Garton and lamb, wool, and other tithes at Grimston were granted to Sir Henry Lindley and John Starkey.[77] They were later sold to Richard and Miles Dodson, and then to Thomas Swann,[78] whose son, also Thomas, sold them in 1635 to John Chambers. In 1650 the tithes were valued at £18 net a year.[79] They were paid by composition in the 17th century.[80] John Chambers (d. 1655) was succeeded by his widow Margaret, who in 1671 released her life interest to their son Henry.[81] In 1679 the tithes were sold to Henry Maister.[82] The rectorial tithes later comprised only those on corn, hay, and wool.[83] Maister (d. c. 1699) was succeeded in the direct male line by William (d. 1716), Henry (d. 1744), and Henry (d. 1812).[84]

In 1808 Henry Maister sold most of the tithes to the landowners: those on 1,043 a. to Thomas Grimston, on 194 a. to William Jackson, and on 100 a. to John Wilson.[85] The tithes on 1,512 a. were merged in 1843.[86] Those remaining with Henry Maister passed to his nephew Arthur Maister (d. 1833)[87] and Arthur's son, the Revd. Henry Maister, who was awarded a rent charge of £16 for those from 77 a. in 1843.[88]

Meaux abbey had a small estate at Grimston. Gifts made between 1210 and 1220 included a bovate given by Robert the butler. Further grants were made in the mid 13th and late 14th century.[89] Part of the estate was tenanted by the

[60] R.D.B., AS/358/602.
[61] Ibid. BI/383/607; E.R.A.O., DDGR/43/4 (28 Aug. 1784). The sale was confirmed in 1792: R.D.B., BQ/561/847.
[62] O.S. Map 6", Yorks. CCXXVIII (1855 edn.).
[63] R.D.B., BQ/561/847; BR/394/640; BW/226/314; DN/87/94.
[64] Sheahan and Whellan, *Hist. York & E.R.* ii. 360.
[65] R.D.B., 49/64/59 (1902); 52/438/416; 52/439/417 (1903); 566/333/266.
[66] Ibid. 658/509/454; 661/429/371; 1234/273/233; 1380/293/266.   [67] Inf. from Mr. P. Butler, Garton, 1990.
[68] Inf. from Dr. S. Neave, Beverley, 1995.
[69] E.R.A.O., DDCC/111/34; B.I.H.R., TER. H. Garton 1749; T. Jefferys, *Map of Yorks.* (1772).
[70] Pevsner and Neave, *Yorks. E.R.* 433.
[71] H.U.L., DHO/7/28; DHO/8/51; P.R.O., C 142/57, no. 58; C 142/58, no. 27.
[72] E.R.A.O., PE/13/1; P.R.O., C 2/Eliz. I/N 3/38; *Visit. Yorks. 1584–5 and 1612*, ed. J. Foster, 144.
[73] E.R.A.O., DDWH, box 2, bdl. 5 (abstract of deeds).
[74] P.R.O., C 142/69, no. 142; C 142/210, no. 124.
[75] Ibid. C 142/301, no. 65; C 142/708, no. 96.
[76] Below, church; *Cal. Chart. R. 1300–26*, 9–10.

[77] P.R.O., C 66/1662, mm. 6, 10. An earlier grant was evidently ineffective: ibid. C 66/1349, m. 11.
[78] Ibid. C 78/332, no. 12; E 134/10 Jas. I Hil./4. The following acct. is based on an abstract of 17th-cent. deeds: E.R.A.O., DDX/188/35.
[79] P.R.O., CP 25(2)/522/11 Chas. I Mic. pt. 2 [no. 33]; *T.E.R.A.S.* iv. 53–4.
[80] P.R.O., E 134/29 Chas. II East./7; *Yorks. Royalist Composition Papers*, iii (Y.A.S. Rec. Ser. xx), p. 75.
[81] *Abstracts of Yorks. Wills, Commonwealth* (Y.A.S. Rec. Ser. ix), p. 73.
[82] Tithes from 80 a. may then have been sold separately: E.R.A.O., DDBV/18/1.
[83] B.I.H.R., TER. H. Garton 1716; R.D.B., CN/243/372.
[84] R.D.B., GY/16/23; *V.C.H. Yorks. E.R.* v. 152.
[85] R.D.B., CM/468/736; CN/56/90; CN/243/372.
[86] Ibid. FU/256/286; FU/257/289; FU/258/290; FU/258/291.
[87] M. E. Ingram, *Maisters of Kingston-upon-Hull, 1560–1840*, 120.   [88] R.D.B., GY/16/23; B.I.H.R., TA. 263s.
[89] *Chron. de Melsa* (Rolls Ser.), i. 359; ii. 22–3; iii. 195–6, 244.

Grimston family in the 14th century. All of it was evidently later lost to the abbey by sale and by erosion, which was said in 1401 to have destroyed 21 a.[90]

ECONOMIC HISTORY. COMMON LANDS AND INCLOSURE. Garton and Grimston both had their own common lands.

Garton. In the 17th century the open fields of Garton comprised 597 a. in North field and 489 a. in South field.[91] Both fields then included unspecified areas of meadow land and pasture. The fields were inclosed probably *c.* 1650, when a related agreement about tithes was said to have been made, and certainly by 1676.[92] The new closes included one of 50 a., mentioned in 1699, described as the westernmost part of Great, presumably North, field.[93] The location of the former tillage was also evident later from traces of ridge and furrow, and from the characteristic long, serpentine shape of some closes, which clearly followed the earlier groupings of strips.[94]

An area called the Bail,[95] in the north-western corner of the township, was used as a stinted pasture after the inclosure of the open fields. Beast gates there were referred to in 1677 and 1705,[96] but it apparently ceased to be used in common soon after. A close in the Bail was recorded in 1716,[97] and later in the century *c.* 70 a. lay in six Bail closes.[98]

Grimston. At Grimston the common lands included North field and other open-field land south of the hamlet.[99] The inhabitants of Grimston may once have enjoyed grazing rights in neighbouring Tunstall.[1] North field was evidently reduced by piecemeal inclosure. In 1517 Margaret Grimston was reported to have taken 40 a. of tillage for pasture and put down two ploughs;[2] part of the ground may have lain immediately west of the manor house, where inclosures called Back closes in the 17th century were later known as Great Parks.[3] By the 17th century the whole of the township lay in closes, the largest of which was the 226-a. North field. Another 100 a. lay in two closes described as 'intakes in the North field'.[4] In 1609 North field belonged to Thomas Grimston and was described as a pasture close.[5] North field had been divided by 1676, when Beacon field close was mentioned.[6] Closes lying south of the hamlet in the 17th century included three intakes, comprising 119 a., and the 129-a. Bracken Hill close. Ridge and furrow survived in 1989 in Grimston park.[7]

LATER AGRICULTURE. In 1801 Garton parish as a whole had 523 a. under crops.[8] In the smaller area of Garton with Grimston township there were 1,122 a. of arable and 596 a. of grassland in 1843,[9] and 1,150 a. and 545 a. respectively in 1905.[10] By the 1930s the predominance of arable over grassland was less marked.[11] In 1987 in East Garton civil parish 673.5 ha. (1,664 a.) were returned as arable land and 199.6 ha. (493 a.) as grassland; over 9,000 pigs, more than 600 cattle, and *c.* 170 sheep were then kept.[12] Much tree planting was done by the Grimstons,[13] both near the manor house and in the north-west part of the township, where the 24-a. Bail wood existed by 1829.[14] The township contained 72 a. of woodland in 1843[15] and 84 a. in 1905.[16]

In the 19th and 20th centuries there were usually 8 farmers in the township, of whom 6 in 1851 and 7 in the 1920s and 1930s had 150 a. or more.[17] Holdings of up to 10 a. were let with their cottages to half a dozen tenants on the Grimston family's estate in the 19th century.[18] Some market gardening was pursued in the late 19th century, and there were 2–3 cowkeepers in the late 19th and early 20th century and a poultry farmer in the 1920s and 1930s.[19] In 1987 of 18 holdings returned at East Garton three were of 100–199 ha. (247–492 a.), five of 50–99 ha. (124–245 a.), three of 10–49 ha. (25–121 a.), and seven of under 10 ha.[20]

INDUSTRY. Bricks were burnt locally for the building of the new manor house at Grimston in the 1780s,[21] and there was a brick and tile works near Turmar Farm in the mid 19th century.[22] Gravel was extracted from the shore in the 1860s.[23] An animal breeding station was kept at Grimston by Reckitts in the 1960s and 1970s,[24] and in 1989 the premises were occupied

[90] Ibid. i. 416 n.; iii. 244–5, 253, 285, 293.
[91] Para. based on the undated 17th-cent. map: E.R.A.O., DDCC/42/2.
[92] P.R.O., E 134/28 Chas. II East./4; E 134/29 Chas. II East./7.
[93] E.R.A.O., DDWH Box 2, bdle. 5 (abstract of deeds).
[94] Hull Univ., Dept. of Geog., R.A.F. air photographs, run 24A, no. 3149; run 334A, nos. 4123–7; run 334B, nos. 3131–3.
[95] *P.N. Yorks. E.R.* (E.P.N.S.), 58.
[96] E.R.A.O., DDX/188/1; P.R.O., E 134/29 Chas. II East./7.
[97] B.I.H.R., TER. H. Garton 1716.
[98] R.D.B., AS/358/602; BF/495/819.
[99] Two paras. based on 17th-cent. map: E.R.A.O., DDCC/42/2. B.I.H.R., CP. F. 148.
[1] Below, Tunstall, econ. hist.
[2] *Trans. R. Hist. S.* N.S. vii. 246.
[3] O.S. Map 6″, Yorks. CCXXVIII (1855 edn.).
[4] The intakes and those S. of the hamlet (below) were prob. from the fields of Grimston rather than those of Garton.
[5] P.R.O., C 142/708, no. 96.
[6] Ibid. E 134/28 Chas. II East./4.

[7] Also Hull Univ., Dept. of Geog., R.A.F. air photographs, run 334A, nos. 4121–2; run 334B, nos. 3129–31.
[8] P.R.O., HO 67/26/169.
[9] B.I.H.R., TA. 263s.
[10] Acreage Returns, 1905.
[11] [1st] Land Util. Surv. Map, sheets 33–4.
[12] Inf. from Min. of Agric., Fish. & Food, Beverley, 1990.
[13] E.R.A.O., DDGR/43/5 (11 Aug. 1785); DDGR/43/41 (13 Jan. 1821); DDGR/44/2 (9 Apr. 1827; 10 Jan. 1833).
[14] A. Bryant, *Map of E.R. Yorks.*
[15] B.I.H.R., TA. 263s.
[16] Acreage Returns, 1905.
[17] P.R.O., HO 107/2364–5; directories.
[18] P.R.O., HO 107/2365; R.D.B., HZ/331/425.
[19] Directories.
[20] Inf. from Min. of Agric., Fish. & Food.
[21] E.R.A.O., DDGR/43/7 (13 Feb. 1787).
[22] *Kelly's Dir. N. & E.R. Yorks.* (1872), 368; O.S. Map 6″, Yorks. CCXXVIII (1855 edn.); P.R.O., HO 107/2365.
[23] P.R.O., RG 9/3601; E.R.A.O., DDCC/136/170.
[24] Local inf.

by laboratory animal consultants and agricultural feed and pharmaceuticals firms.[25]

MILLS. One or two windmills stood in Garton c. 1600.[26] A mill near the southern boundary was commemorated in the 17th century by Mill Field close, and later by Millfield or Windmill hill, and ground in the south-west is called Mill hill.[27] Blue mill, near Blue Hall farm, was evidently built in the mid 1820s and worked until c. 1880; the tower survived in 1989.[28]

LOCAL GOVERNMENT. A court was included in the grant of the manor of Garton in 1611,[29] and view of frankpledge belonged to the manor of the Constable family in the 18th century.[30] Inhabitants of Grimston were presented in Roos manor court for breaches of the assize of ale in the Middle Ages.[31]

Churchwardens' accounts exist from 1754.[32] Permanent poor relief was given to 16 people in 1802–3 and 3–5 in 1812–15 and 2–4 were relieved occasionally in the early 19th century.[33] Cottages built on land belonging to the church were used as poorhouses in the mid 19th century.[34] Garton with Grimston joined Skirlaugh poor-law union in 1837[35] and remained in Skirlaugh rural district until 1935 when it was taken into Holderness rural district as part of the new civil parish of East Garton, which became part of the Holderness district of Humberside in 1974.[36] In 1996 East Garton parish became part of a new East Riding unitary area.[37]

CHURCH. The church recorded on an estate in Garton and Ringbrough, in Aldbrough, in 1086[38] was probably at Garton, and a church certainly existed there by 1190, when it belonged to Thornton abbey (Lincs.) as the gift of Hanelaci of Bydon.[39] It was appropriated to the abbey c. 1222.[40] A vicarage was apparently ordained by the mid century, when Hugh, vicar of Garton, was mentioned,[41] but it was not recorded until 1308.[42] Garton was united with

Hilston in 1927 and with Roos with Tunstall in 1974.[43]

The advowson belonged to Thornton abbey until the Dissolution,[44] and in 1542 it was granted to the short-lived Thornton college.[45] Elias Asby presented in 1546 as grantee of Thornton abbey but the patronage was thereafter resumed by the Crown. A grant of the advowson of 'Garton' to the archbishop in 1558 evidently did not take effect.[46] After the union of 1927 the Crown had two turns in four in the patronage of the new benefice.[47] In 1956 the Crown's turns were transferred to the archbishop, who was the sole patron from 1960.[48] At the further union of 1974 one turn in three was given to the archbishop.[49]

The church was worth £6 13s. 4d. in 1291.[50] Thornton abbey was cited for the insufficiency of the vicar's portion in 1308.[51] The living was worth just over £6 gross in 1535[52] and the improved annual value in 1650 was £10 net.[53] Augmentations from Queen Anne's Bounty were received in 1767 and 1787, of £200 on each occasion,[54] and the average net value in 1829–31 was £97 a year.[55] A grant of £125 from the Common Fund was made in 1863 to meet a benefaction of like amount[56] and in 1884 the net value of the living was £100.[57]

Most of the income came from tithes.[58] By the late 17th century they were mostly paid by composition[59] and in the early 18th century some were withheld as allegedly due to the rectory.[60] Except for those due from the vicarial glebe, which had been merged, the tithes were commuted in 1843; rent charges of £68 and £19 16s. were awarded respectively for those of Garton with Grimston township and that part of Owstwick township which lay in Garton parish.[61]

There was only 1 a. of glebe in 1535 and c. 5 a. in the earlier 18th century.[62] The augmentations were used to buy 5 a. in Cottingham in 1768 and 7 a. in Etherdwick, in Aldbrough, c. 1800.[63] An acre in Cottingham was sold in 1846 and nearly £6 a year was later received as interest on the purchase money.[64] Three acres

25   Inf. from Bantin & Kingman Ltd., Grimston, 1989.
26   E.R.A.O., DDWH Box 2, bdle. 5 (abstract of deeds); *Yorks. Fines, 1614–25*, 119.
27   E.R.A.O., DDCC/42/2; O.S. Map 6″, Yorks. CCXXVIII (1855 and later edns.); A. Bryant, *Map of E.R. Yorks.* (1829).
28   P.R.O., HO 107/2365; A. Bryant, *Map of E.R. Yorks.* (1829); directories.
29   P.R.O., C 66/1903, no. 9.
30   E.R.A.O., DDCC/105/79; DDCC/111/34, 234.
31   Burghley Ho., 37/18.
32   E.R.A.O., PE/13/17–21.
33   *Poor Law Abstract, 1804*, pp. 592–3; *1818*, pp. 522–3.
34   Below, church.
35   *3rd Rep. Poor Law Com.* 170.
36   Census.
37   Humberside (Structural Change) Order 1995, copy at E.R.A.O.
38   *V.C.H. Yorks.* ii. 266.
39   *E.Y.C.* iii, pp. 41–2.
40   *Reg. Gray*, p. 144 n.; *Reg. Romeyn*, i, p. 215.
41   W. H. Turner and H. O. Coxe, *Cal. Chart. and R. in Bodl.* 609.
42   *Reg. Greenfield*, v, p. 226.
43   *Lond. Gaz.* 4 Nov. 1927, pp. 6972–3; B.I.H.R., OC. 880.

44   Lawrance, 'Clergy List', Holderness, 1, pp. 45–7.
45   *L. & P. Hen. VIII*, xvii, pp. 29–30.
46   *Cal. Pat. 1557–8*, 420. It was perhaps Garton on the Wolds: *V.C.H. Yorks. E.R.* ii. 221 n.
47   *Lond. Gaz.* 4 Nov. 1927, pp. 6972–3.
48   Ibid. 3 July 1956, p. 3888; below, Hilston, church; Tunstall, church.
49   B.I.H.R., OC. 880.
50   *Tax. Eccl.* (Rec. Com.), 304.
51   *Reg. Greenfield*, v, p. 226.
52   *Valor Eccl.* (Rec. Com.), v. 112.
53   *T.E.R.A.S.* iv. 53–4.
54   Hodgson, *Q.A.B.* p. cccxlv.
55   *Rep. Com. Eccl. Revenues*, 936–7.
56   *Lond. Gaz.* 12 June 1863, pp. 3020–1.
57   B.I.H.R., V. 1884/Ret. 1.
58   *Valor Eccl.* v. 112.
59   E.R.A.O., PE/13/2 (note dated 1695–6); B.I.H.R., TER. H. Garton 1716 etc.
60   B.I.H.R., TER. H. Garton 1716, 1726.
61   Ibid. TA. 42L, 263s.
62   Ibid. TER. H. Garton 1716–64; *Valor Eccl.* v. 112.
63   R.D.B., AL/144/262; B.I.H.R., TER. H. Garton 1809.
64   B.I.H.R., TER. H. Garton 1849.

FIG. 2. GARTON CHURCH IN THE EARLIER 19TH CENTURY

in Garton were sold in 1925 and *c.* 2 a. in 1962.[65] In 1978 there were still 4 a. of glebe in Cottingham and 7 a. in Aldbrough.[66] A vicarage house was recorded from 1308, when it was inadequate.[67] It was no more than a cottage in the 18th and earlier 19th century[68] but by 1889 a new house had been built nearby.[69] It was sold in 1962.[70]

Lights in the church included a plough light in 1515.[71]

In the 17th and 18th centuries vicars were not appointed and Garton was served by licensed curates[72] who had other parishes too. In 1743, for instance, John Browne also officiated at Aldbrough, Humbleton, and Elstronwick, in Humbleton, and lived at Humbleton.[73] The incumbent of Garton with Hilston lived at Garton from 1927 until 1947. From 1948 Garton with Hilston was served by the incumbent of Roos with Tunstall.[74] There was a chaplain at Garton in 1525–6 who received £4 net a year,[75] perhaps the £4 which the impropriator was said in 1716 to have formerly paid for a monthly sermon. By 1716 and still in 1857 the vicar received £2 for the duty.[76] An assistant curate was employed in the 1830s.[77]

There was a service on two Sundays out of three in 1743 and 1764, and communion was celebrated thrice a year, with *c.* 20 recipients.[78] Two weekly services were held by 1865 but in

the 1870s and in 1884 there was only one. Communion was celebrated about every eight weeks in 1865, monthly by 1868, every six weeks in 1884, and monthly again *c.* 1920, with usually a dozen recipients in the 19th and early 20th century. A weekly celebration was held in either Garton or Hilston in 1931, when generally only five people received at Garton.[79] A parochial library was mentioned *c.* 1920.[80]

The church of *ST. MICHAEL*, so called by 1468,[81] is built of boulders with ashlar dressings and consists of chancel with south chapel, nave with south aisle and porch, and west tower. The north wall of the nave, and perhaps that of the chancel, survive from a 12th-century church. The tower was added and the chancel extended or rebuilt in the earlier 13th century. The south aisle and chapel were added in the 14th century, when new windows and a doorway were put into the north wall. In the 16th century the aisle and chapel were refenestrated and the porch, which is mostly of brick, was added. The church was in disrepair in 1578 and in the later 17th century.[82]

A mausoleum was built on the north side of the chancel by Charles Grimston *c.* 1820[83] and two windows were inserted on the south side of the nave to form a clerestory by 1840.[84] The mausoleum was evidently removed and the clerestory windows blocked up in the mid

[65] R.D.B., 320/496/382; 1262/99/75.

[66] Inf. from York Dioc. Bd. of Finance, 1981.

[67] *Reg. Greenfield*, v, p. 226.

[68] B.I.H.R., TER. H. Garton 1716 etc.

[69] O.S. Map 6″, Yorks. CCXXVIII (1855 edn.); ibid. 1/2,500, Yorks. CCXXVIII. 2 (1891 edn.).

[70] R.D.B., 1262/99/75.

[71] P.R.O., E 311/35, no. 29; *Test. Ebor.* iii, p. 252 n.; G. C. Homans, *Eng. Villagers of Thirteenth Cent.* (1970), 361.

[72] Lawrance, 'Clergy List', Holderness, i, pp. 47, 73; *Herring's Visit.* ii, p. 13; Poulson, *Holderness*, ii. 55. For an earlier curate see B.I.H.R., V. 1567–8/CB. 1, f. 203v.; V. 1578–9/CB. 1, f. 72.

[73] *Herring's Visit.* ii, p. 13.

[74] *Crockford*.

[75] *Y.A.J.* xxiv. 76.

[76] B.I.H.R., TER. H. Garton 1716, 1857.

[77] *Rep. Com. Eccl. Revenues*, 936–7.

[78] B.I.H.R., V. 1764/Ret. 1, no. 208; *Herring's Visit.* ii, p. 13.

[79] B.I.H.R., V. 1865/Ret. 1, no. 202; V. 1868/Ret. 1, no. 184; V. 1871/Ret. 1, no. 183; V. 1877/Ret. 1, no. 181; V. 1884/Ret. 1; V. 1912–22/Ret.; V. 1931/Ret.

[80] B.I.H.R., V. 1912–22/Ret.

[81] *Test. Ebor.* ii, p. 200 n.

[82] B.I.H.R., V. 1578–9/CB. 1, f. 72; V. 1693–4/CB. 1, f. 48; ER. V./CB. 3, f. 100; ER. V./CB. 4, ff. 3v., 201v.; ER. V./CB. 5, f. 2v. For the church before restoration see B.I.H.R., Fac. 1887/2.

[83] E.R.A.O., DDGR/37/21; Poulson, *Holderness*, ii. 50 (illus.), 58.

[84] Poulson, *Holderness*, ii. 58 and illus. facing.

century,[85] when new corbel stones were also put up.[86] Restoration work in 1887, to designs by Smith & Brodrick of Hull, included the replacement of the east window and one in the nave and the insertion of another in the chancel.[87] Another window was made in the nave in 1929[88] and at about the same date the chancel and nave roofs were rebuilt.[89]

The Grimston family is commemorated in several windows and by two hatchments. The fittings include a mutilated chancel screen, which was reported in 1567.[90] A carved Calvary was mounted on the screen c. 1929.[91] Part of a late medieval cross head stands in the porch.

Land in Garton given to the church was among concealed lands let by the Crown c. 1590.[92] Nearly 3 a. in Kirk Field close were said in 1716 to have been given for buying bread and wine for communion, but by 1743 the income was used for church repairs. The annual income was 12s. in 1716[93] and £2 2s. by the 1830s.[94] Cottages for the poor were built and gardens made there in or shortly before 1837.[95] The endowment was later known as the Church Land and Cottages. By a Scheme of 1910 expenditure was allowed for the upkeep of church and cottages and for the support of services. The cottages and the land then produced an income of nearly £16[96] but that sum was reduced by the demolition of the cottages; the land, then comprising under 2 a., was let for £4 a year in the mid century and £40 in 1990.[97] In 1932 N. J. Miller, vicar of Garton 1886–90, left £500 for the fabric of Garton and Hilston churches.[98] The Friends of St. Michael's were established in 1975 and later maintained the churchyard.[99]

There were two bells in 1552[1] but later only one.[2] The plate includes a service given in 1834.[3] The registers of baptisms, marriages, and burials date from 1582 and are complete, except for 1661.[4]

NONCONFORMITY. Religious conservatism in Garton was revealed by the visitations of 1567

and 1582.[5] The number of Roman Catholics recorded then and later rarely exceeded half a dozen; members of the Grimston family were, however, named in the 16th century, and a private chaplain was kept by Henry Constable of Garton (d. 1700).[6] Two families were Roman Catholic in 1743 and 1764.[7]

Four recusants named in 1669 and 10 protestant dissenters recorded in the parish in 1676 may have been Friends.[8] Quakers from Garton attended a meeting house at Owstwick. In 1743 there were three Quaker families, evidently including two from Grimston, and in 1764 five.[9]

The Wesleyan Methodists built a chapel at Garton in 1826[10] which later also served Fitling, in Humbleton.[11] It was abandoned as unsafe in 1934, and later demolished. A new chapel, later the Methodist church, was built just beyond the parish boundary in Fitling in 1935.[12] In 2000 its congregation was small, but the building was also then used as a centre for meetings by various religious groups.[13]

An unidentified building at 'Garton' was registered for worship in 1827.[14]

EDUCATION. In 1604 the curate of Garton kept a school,[15] and a school was recorded in the parish in 1743 and 1764, when it was supported by subscription.[16] A school in Garton in which 37 children were taught at their parents' expense in 1818[17] was presumably that to which Thomas Grimston subscribed in 1819.[18] It was replaced by a school supported by Charles Grimston, which was evidently begun c. 1832 and in 1833 was attended by 3 boys and 8 girls, all said to be taught at their parents' expense.[19] The school was held in the church c. 1840.[20]

A Church school was built at Grimston on a site given by Marmaduke Grimston and opened in 1860.[21] It was supported by Marmaduke Grimston and other subscribers,[22] by school pence, and from 1861–2 by an annual govern-

---

[85] B.I.H.R., Fac. 1887/2 does not show them.
[86] Bulmer, *Dir. E. Yorks.* (1892), 410.
[87] E.R.A.O., PE/13/18; B.I.H.R., Fac. 1887/2; notice and watercolour showing church before restoration, both in church.
[88] B.I.H.R., Fac. Bk. 11, pp. 10, 32.
[89] Ibid. Fac. 1928/2/18; photo. *c.* 1925 in ch.; *Kelly's Dir. N. & E.R. Yorks.* (1909), 517; (1933), 474.
[90] B.I.H.R., V. 1567–8/CB. 1, f. 203v.; *Y.A.J.* xxiii. 457; xxiv. 132–3; undated watercolour in church shows it before restoration.   [91] B.I.H.R., Fac. 1929/2/19.
[92] P.R.O., E 311/35, no. 29.
[93] B.I.H.R., TER. H Garton 1716; *Herring's Visit.* ii, p. 12.   [94] E.R.A.O., PE/13/18.
[95] Below, charity.
[96] E.R.A.O., PE/13/23; ibid. accession 1681.
[97] B.I.H.R., TER. 530; inf. from Mr. K. S. Burrell, Garton, 1990; below, charity.
[98] *Kelly's Dir. N. & E.R. Yorks.* (1933), 474; below, Hilston, manor.
[99] E.R.A.O., Reg. of Char.; inf. from Mr. O. Marriott, Grimston, 1989.   [1] *Inventories of Ch. Goods*, 36.
[2] G. R. Park, *Ch. Bells of Holderness*, 49.
[3] B.I.H.R., TER. 530; *Yorks. Ch. Plate*, i. 253.
[4] E.R.A.O., PE/13/1–3, 5.
[5] B.I.H.R., V. 1567–8/CB. 1, f. 203v.; V. 1582/CB. 1, f. 210v.; Aveling, *Post Reformation Catholicism*, 21, 68; above, church.

[6] B.I.H.R., V. 1582/CB. 1, f. 211; Aveling, *Post Reformation Catholicism*, 54, 68; Poulson, *Holderness*, ii. 59; *Compton Census*, ed. A. Whiteman, 600.
[7] B.I.H.R., V. 1764/Ret. 1, no. 208; *Herring's Visit.* ii, p. 12.
[8] *Compton Census*, 600; *Depositions from York Castle* (Sur. Soc. xl), p. 168.
[9] B.I.H.R., V. 1764/Ret. 1, no. 208; H.U.L., DQR/17/41, 68; *Herring's Visit.* ii, p. 12; iv, p. 236; below, Roos.
[10] P.R.O., HO 129/522/1/2; White, *Dir. E. & N.R. Yorks.* (1840), 259; O.S. Map 6", Yorks. CCXXVIII (1855 edn.). It was registered in 1827: B.I.H.R., DMH. Reg. 1, pp. 545–6.
[11] E.R.A.O., MRH/1/47.
[12] Ibid. MRH/1/48; R.D.B., 523/57/44; 523/58/45; O.N.S. (Birkdale), Worship Reg. no. 1723; datestones.
[13] Inf. from the Revd. Arnold Johnson, Hornsea, 2000.
[14] B.I.H.R., DMH. Reg. 1, p. 547.
[15] Ibid. V. 1604/CB. 1, f. 80.
[16] Ibid. V. 1764/Ret. 1, no. 208; *Herring's Visit.* ii, p. 12.
[17] *Educ. of Poor Digest*, 1081.
[18] E.R.A.O., DDGR/43/39 (23 Dec. 1819).
[19] Ibid. DDGR/44/29 (23 Apr. 1832); *Educ. Enq. Abstract*, 1085; Poulson, *Holderness*, ii. 59.
[20] White, *Dir. E. & N.R. Yorks.* (1840), 259; Bulmer, *Dir. E. Yorks.* (1892), 410.
[21] R.D.B., HY/169/232; E.R.A.O., PE/13/27; SGP. 29; SL/43/1; crest and date on building.
[22] B.I.H.R., V. 1865/Ret. 1, no. 202.

ment grant.[23] Average attendance was 24 in 1860,[24] and on inspection day in 1871 there were 35 children at the school,[25] which was later said to take children from Owstwick township.[26] Closure recommended in 1905 because of the small roll was resisted,[27] and between 1906 and 1938 there were usually about 20 pupils in attendance.[28] Controlled status was granted to the school in 1950.[29] In 1954 the senior pupils were transferred to Withernsea High School,[30] and in 1960 the school was closed, the remaining pupils being transferred to Withernsea.[31] The school was sold for a parish hall in 1961,[32] but later the building was resold and converted into two houses.

CHARITY FOR THE POOR. John Lamplough by will proved in 1896 left £50, with which nearly £40 stock was bought the next year. In the 1920s and 1930s the income of £1 a year was spent on fuel, clothing, and medical services, or used to make occasional money payments.[33] In 1989 the income was added to the balance of c. £25.[34]

In or shortly before 1837 half a dozen cottages were built and gardens made on land at Garton belonging to the church.[35] A reading room was later housed in one of the cottages,[36] which were rebuilt in 1894.[37] The cottages were occupied until the mid 20th century but have since been demolished.[38]

HILSTON

THE village of Hilston lies 19 km. ENE. of Hull and 1 km. from the sea.[39] The name Hilston may be an Anglian and Scandinavian hybrid, and probably means 'Hildolf's farm'; the modern form was used by the 14th century.[40] In 1852 the ancient parish contained 553 a. (224 ha.). Hilston civil parish was united with those of Owstwick, Roos, and Tunstall to form a new Roos civil parish in 1935.[41]

Hilston and Owstwick, in Roos, together had 116 poll-tax payers in 1377.[42] Hilston had five houses assessed for hearth tax in 1672.[43] There were seven families in the parish in 1743 and 1764.[44] From 37 in 1801 the population of Hilston rose to 54 in 1861 before falling to 29 in 1901; it was only 27 in 1931.[45]

The parish is largely on boulder clay and mostly lies at over 15 m. above sea level, rising to more than 23 m. on the northern and southern boundaries and 27 m. at Hilston Mount. A small valley runs across the middle of the parish, close to the village, and lower land there is covered with sand and gravel.[46] The commonable lands, whose location is unknown, were evidently early inclosed.

Hilston is drained by streams flowing west towards the river Humber. That rising in Tunstall and running across the parish was in disrepair in 1367, as was a drain which evidently formed the boundary with Tunstall and Grim-

ston, in Garton.[47] A small area of the parish relied on Keyingham fleet for its drainage to the river: it was put at c. 6 a. in 1618, and 10 a. of low ground were assessed to the drainage of the level after 1845.[48]

The principal road in Hilston is that from Roos to Garton which passes the west end of the village and has been upgraded and improved[49] as part of the main Holderness coast road. From the east end of the village street roads run southeast to Roos and Tunstall and north-east to Hooks Farm in Tunstall. Another minor road, leading from the main road south-west to Owstwick, was perhaps recorded in 1669 as Burncroft Lane;[50] the land north of it was called Bryndcroft, meaning 'burnt enclosure', in the 13th century and Burncrofts later.[51] Much of the western parish boundary and part of the eastern are formed by the main and minor roads.

HILSTON village lies in the valley, the proximity of high ground and water presumably determining the choice of site and the relief the linear plan of the settlement. There were only six houses in 1783.[52] Two council houses were built in the mid 20th century,[53] but in 1990 there were still only ten houses, including a newly built farmhouse. The older houses include Mayfield and Mount Farms and Hilston Cottage.[54] A licensed house at Hilston was recorded c. 1755.[55]

23   *Rep. of Educ. Cttee. of Council, 1861–2* [3007], p. 621, H.C. (1862), xlii.
24   P.R.O., ED 7/135, no. 60.
25   *Returns relating to Elem. Educ.* 472–3.
26   *Kelly's Dir. N. & E.R. Yorks.* (1889), 447.
27   E.R. Educ. Cttee. *Mins.* 1905–6, 191, 260; 1906–7, 13, 40, 122.
28   *Bd. of Educ., List 21* (H.M.S.O., 1908 and later edns.).
29   E.R. Educ. Cttee. *Mins.* 1949–50, 275.
30   Ibid. 1952–3, 227; 1953–4, 145.
31   E.R.A.O., SL/43/3; E.R. Educ. Cttee. *Mins.* 1959–60, 4.
32   R.D.B., 1223/28/26.
33   E.R.A.O., PE/13/23; ibid. accession 1681.
34   Inf. from Mr. Marriott, 1989.
35   B.I.H.R., TA. 263s; ibid. TER. H. Garton 1849; E.R.A.O., PE/13/18; O.S. Map 6", Yorks. CCXXVIII (1855 edn.).
36   Above, intro.   37   B.I.H.R., TER. 744.
38   Inf. from Mr. P. Butler, Garton, 1990.

39   This article was written in 1990.
40   *P.N. Yorks. E.R.* (E.P.N.S.), 57–8; G. F. Jensen, *Scand. Settlement Names in Yorks.* 128.
41   O.S. Map 6", Yorks. CCXXVIII (1855 edn.); *Census* 1931 (pt. ii).
42   P.R.O., E 179/202/60, m. 48.
43   *Hearth Tax*, 60.
44   B.I.H.R., V.1764/Ret. 1, no. 33; *Herring's Visit.* ii, p. 86.
45   *V.C.H. Yorks.* iii. 494; *Census*, 1911–31.
46   Geol. Surv. Map 1", drift, sheet 73 (1909 edn.).
47   Poulson, *Holderness*, i. 122–3.
48   E.R.A.O., DDCC/54/53; DDPK/3/8.
49   R.D.B., 1647/367/323.
50   H.U.L., DDSY/27/35; O.S. Map 6", Yorks. CCXXVIII (1855 edn.).
51   *Chron. de Melsa* (Rolls Ser.), i. 416; *P.N. Yorks. E.R.* 58.
52   Poulson, *Holderness*, ii. 83.
53   R.D.B., 585/102/79.
54   Below, manor.
55   E.R.A.O., QDT/2/9.

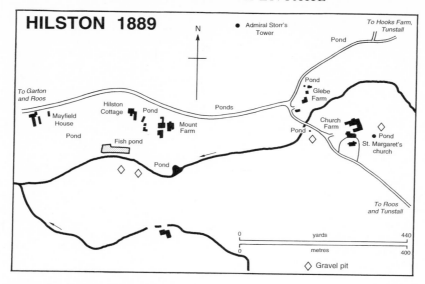

HILSTON 1889

Hilston is known for Admiral Storr's Tower which stands north of the village on a knoll called Hilston Mount. The octagonal brick building is *c.* 50 ft. high and has a semicircular staircase turret on its northern side. It was built in 1750 by Joseph Storr (d. 1753) and was called the Mount in 1810 but by 1852 was named after Storr's son, Rear Admiral John Storr. It may have been intended as a watch tower and was reputedly a well known landmark for sailors; it served as a hospital for troops camped on the coast in 1794–5 and later as a cottage, but was disused in 1990.[56]

MANOR AND OTHER ESTATES. In 1066 Murdoch held a manor of *HILSTON*, evidently comprising 4⅔ carucates; it had passed to Drew de Bevrère by 1086[57] and later formed part of the Aumale fee.

Two carucates in Hilston, with land at Tansterne, in Aldbrough, Benningholme, in Swine, and elsewhere in Holderness, were evidently granted to a butler of the count of Aumale.[58] Beatrice, daughter of Amand the butler (d. by 1218)[59] and widow of Geoffrey de Friboys, held all of her father's fee in 1240 but John de Surdeval had a share by 1252, presumably as heir of another daughter, Hawise, wife of Alan de Surdeval.[60] The estate was later held by Geoffrey Berchaud (d. by 1276) and his son

John. Geoffrey Berchaud's heir was said to have a mesne lordship in Hilston in 1287.[61] By then, though, Berchaud's holding had evidently passed to Simon Constable, probably by purchase from Geoffrey Vernon, and in 1285 he was granted free warren at Hilston.[62] His estate was enlarged by exchange with Nunkeeling priory.[63] At the death of Sir John Constable in 1349 he was mesne lord of the 2 carucates at Hilston.[64]

William of Routh (fl. *c.* 1250) held part of the butler's fee.[65] He was succeeded by Amand of Routh (fl. 1304),[66] and Amand by John of Routh[67] (dead in 1311), custody of whose son Amand was claimed by Robert Constable as overlord.[68] By the 1370s the estate had apparently been enlarged with 5¼ bovates belonging to Christine, wife of another Amand of Routh.[69] Hilston descended like Tansterne in the Rouths[70] and their successors the Cutts[71] and Michelbournes.[72] About 1500 the estate comprised 4 houses, 6 bovates, and other land and was held as *HILSTON* manor under Burton Constable manor, in Swine.[73] At a partition of the estates of the Michelbournes in 1614, Thomas Michelbourne released his moiety of Hilston to Sir Richard Michelbourne, thereby reuniting the manor.[74] Sir Richard sold much of the estate in 1614 and 1616. The rest descended to his son William who conveyed it to another son Henry in 1642;[75] no more is heard of it.

Sir Richard Michelbourne sold two houses, 3

56 R.D.B., CR/74/95; O.S. Map 6″, Yorks. CCXXVIII (1855 edn.); date and arms on bldg.; Poulson, *Holderness*, ii. 78 (illus.), 79–80, 83; T. Jefferys, *Map of Yorks.* (1772).
57 *V.C.H. Yorks.* ii. 265. Cf. Owstwick entries ibid. 264–5, 326.
58 *Kirkby's Inquest*, 374; above, Aldbrough, manors (Tansterne); below, Swine, Benningholme, manors.
59 English, *Holderness*, 92.
60 *Yorks. Fines, 1232–46*, p. 82; *1246–72*, p. 88; *Chron. de Melsa*, i. 412.
61 B.L. Cott. MS. Otho C. viii, f. 81v.; *Cal. Inq. p.m.* ii, p. 107; iv, p. 355.
62 E.R.A.O., DDCC/46/1; *Kirkby's Inquest*, 74; *Cal. Chart. R. 1257–1300*, 308; Poulson, *Holderness*, ii. 79, 223, where the release is probably misdated.
63 E.R.A.O., DDCC/111/4.
64 *Cal. Inq. p.m.* ix, pp. 219–20.

65 *Yorks. Fines, 1232–46*, p. 82; *1246–72*, p. 88.
66 *Cal. Inq. p.m.* iv, p. 145.
67 *Yorks. Fines, 1300–14*, p. 57.
68 P.R.O., CP 40/291, m. 57d.
69 *Yorks. Fines, 1347–77*, pp. 201–2.
70 P.R.O., C 141/4, no. 45; E.R.A.O., DDCC/18/1, s.v. 15 July 1435; *Cal. Chart. R. 1341–1417*, 301; above, Aldbrough, manors (Tansterne).
71 P.R.O., C 142/36, no. 67; C 142/48, no. 161; *Yorks. Fines*, i. 25.
72 P.R.O., C 142/214, nos. 205, 221; ibid. CP 40/1154, Carte rot. 15; *Yorks. Fines*, i. 140; *1603–14*, 143–4; *1614–25*, 62. For the Michelbournes, *Suss. Arch. Colln.* l. 67–101.
73 P.R.O., C 141/4, no. 45; C 142/48, no. 161.
74 E.R.A.O., DDRI/35/33; *Yorks. Fines, 1614–25*, 11.
75 E.R.A.O., DDRI/35/50.

bovates, and other lands to Frances, widow of Thomas Hardy, in 1616. She conveyed her purchase to her son Thomas Hardy in 1619.[76] The Hardys also bought land belonging to Thorpe manor in Aldbrough.[77] Jane, daughter of Thomas Hardy, presumably the younger, and wife successively of John Carlile (d. by 1669) and James Hewitt (d. by 1675) was succeeded in or after 1675 in part of the estate by her son James Hewitt (d. 1749) and in the rest by her son Randolph Carlile. On Carlile's death c. 1745 his share passed to Hewitt. The reunited estate descended to Hewitt's son Randolph,[78] who sold it as the manor or reputed manor of Hilston to Thomas Dixon the younger in 1770.[79] It was mortgaged to the Revd. Mark Sykes in 1772 and sold to him in 1780.[80] Hilston later descended like an estate in Owstwick[81] to Sir (Tatton) Mark Sykes, Bt. (d. 1919). In 1916 Church farm, with 126 a. in Hilston, was sold to Albert Clark and in 1920 the Sykes trustees sold the 85-a. Mayfield farm to William Wood.[82] Clark (d. 1924) devised Church farm to his wife Sarah (d. 1955); it passed to their son John Clark, who had bought c. 70 a. in Hilston, including Glebe farm, in 1954.[83] John Clark (d. 1977) was succeeded by his son J. R. Clark, the owner in 1991.[84] Wood sold Mayfield farm in 1927 to Charles Maltas (d. 1945) and his wife Alice (d. 1950), from whose executor George Clappison bought it in 1959.[85] It was sold in 1981 to D. C. Betts and his wife and in 1988 to John Waddleton and his wife, the owners in 1991.[86] Church Farm may have been the house of Mrs. Carlile and her second husband James Hewitt, which stood at the east end of the village and in 1672 had five hearths.[87] It was recorded again in 1750.[88] The house was extensively remodelled in the later 20th century, and by 1990 a new farmhouse had been built near it.

In 1614 Sir Richard Michelbourne sold a house, 1¼ bovate, other land, and the advowson to Marmaduke Marchant, rector, and 1¾ bovate and closes to John Storr.[89] Most of Marchant's purchase seems to have passed to the Storrs, in 1657 John Storr, probably another, being confirmed in a house and c. 70 a. and Jane Hardy in the advowson and an acre.[90] Storr (d. 1657) was succeeded in turn by his sons John (d. 1677) and Joseph (d. 1728),[91] and Joseph's son Joseph (d. 1753) was dealing with more than 243 a. in Hilston in 1739.[92] He was succeeded by his son, Rear Admiral John Storr (d. 1783), and John by his cousin G. W. Thompson[93] (d. by 1808). Thompson's son G. L. Thompson sold the estate in several lots in 1810. Joseph Foster then bought 120 a. and another purchase, of 95 a.,[94] was added to his estate c. 1820.[95] Foster (d. c. 1835) left Hilston to his son James[96] (d. by 1845). The estate, comprising Hilston Cottage and Mount farm, was evidently devised in shares,[97] the residuary heirs being the Revd. William Foster and his sister Catherine's son, the Revd. N. J. Miller, who held it in moieties.[98]

N. J. Miller (d. 1932) was succeeded in his moiety by his daughter Dorothy Ward (d. 1966), and she by her goddaughters Mrs. Kathleen Graham and Miss Undine Moir,[99] who sold their share, comprising Mount Farm and c. 100 a., in 1976 to William Grant (Paull) Ltd.[1] The other moiety, of 109 a., may have descended from William Foster (d. 1880) to his son W. H. Foster (d. 1900) and then apparently passed to James A. Foster (fl. 1937).[2] He was succeeded by his son W. G. Foster, who sold Hilston Cottage and 7 a. to T. W. Kirtley in 1957[3] and the rest of his half, amounting to some 50 a., to William Grant (Paull) Ltd. c. 1980. The estate was thus re-united by the company, which retained the farm in 1992.[4]

A house was included in the sale to Marchant in 1614, and in 1672 John Storr had a house of four hearths.[5] It was perhaps the same house which was illustrated c. 1720 as Storrs Hall; it was then of two storeys and comprised a five-bayed central block flanked by projecting gabled wings of two bays.[6] In 1754 the Storrs evidently remodelled or rebuilt their house, south of the street. It was demolished c. 1800 and Old Hall grounds were named in 1829.[7] A groom's cottage enlarged after the demolition[8] is probably the

76 Ibid. DDCC/18/3, s.v. Apr. 1616; H.U.L., DDSY/27/4, 7–8; *Yorks. Fines, 1614–25*, 62.
77 Below, this section.
78 E.R.A.O., PE/17/1; H.U.L., DDSY/27/35; DDMC/94/1; B.I.H.R., TER. H. Hilston 1716, 1749; Poulson, *Holderness*, ii. 403.
79 R.D.B., AO/142/150.
80 Ibid. AR/97/191; BC/496/774; H.U.L., DDSY/27/41.
81 R.D.B., CD/197/291; J. Foster, *Pedigrees of Yorks.* iii; *Kelly's Dir. N. & E.R. Yorks.* (1901), 496; below, Roos, manors [Owstwick].
82 R.D.B., MM/355/564; 176/338/298; 226/444/368; Burke, *Peerage* (1925), 2174.
83 R.D.B., 292/170/149; 313/255/211; 992/130/116; 1001/314/272; 1021/123/97.
84 E.R.A.O., PE/17/7; inf. from Mrs. V. Clark, 1991.
85 E.R.A.O., PE/17/7; R.D.B., 343/249/215; 843/73/63; 1133/150/137.
86 Inf. from Mr. Waddleton.
87 H.U.L., DDSY/27/35; P.R.O., E 179/205/504.
88 R.D.B., U/172/325.
89 E.R.A.O., DDCC/18/3, s.v. Apr. 1615; *Yorks. Fines, 1614–25*, 23; Lawrance, 'Clergy List', Holderness, 1, p. 59.
90 P.R.O., CP 25(2)/614/1656–7/Hil. no. 63.
91 E.R.A.O., DDX/595/82–3.
92 B.I.H.R., TER. H. Hilston 1716; R.D.B., P/272/699;

Poulson, *Holderness*, ii. 79; below, this section; Roos, nonconf.
93 R.D.B., BD/232/362; BR/2/2; memorial in ch.
94 R.D.B., CN/367/582; CR/24/31; CR/74/95; CR/75/96; CR/416/559.
95 Ibid. CZ/452/692; DO/243/261; EX/243/275.
96 Ibid. IY/324/465.
97 Ibid. GB/103/113; HC/256/329; HL/357/356; II/333/424.
98 Ibid. MA/25/41; NG/339/482; N. J. Miller, *Winestead and its Lords*, p. ix; Bulmer, *Dir. E. Yorks.* (1892), 422.
99 R.D.B., 465/80/59; 465/81/60; 1577/126/105; 1577/127/106; Miller, op. cit., p. ix; inf. from Miss M. Maltas, Roos, 1991.
1 Inf. from Mr. K. Grant, Roos, 1992.
2 E.R.A.O., PE/17/7; R.D.B., NG/339/482; 94/100/98 (1897); 370/4/3; *Kelly's Dir. N. & E.R. Yorks.* (1937), 467; memorial in church.
3 R.D.B., 1085/71/68; inf. from Miss Maltas.
4 Inf. from Mr. Grant.
5 P.R.O., E 179/205/504; E.R.A.O., DDCC/18/3, s.v. Apr. 1615.
6 *Sam. Buck's Yorks. Sketchbk.* 328.
7 Poulson, *Holderness*, ii. 83; T. Jefferys, *Map of Yorks.* (1772); J. Tuke, *Map of Holderness* (1786) in Poulson, *Holderness*, ii, facing p. 1; A. Bryant, *Map of E.R. Yorks.* (1829).
8 J. Featherstone, *Hilston and its Churches*, 5.

present Mount Farm, which comprises a range of one storey with attics, possibly of the 17th century, and extensions of the late 18th and 19th century. The successor to Old Hall as the chief house on the estate was sold with 4 a. of grounds to Joseph Foster in 1810.[9] It was called Hilston Cottage by the 1850s, when it was the house of the Revd. William Foster.[10] Hilston Cottage was possibly built c. 1700; it was extended later in the 18th century and again between 1846 and 1889.[11]

An estate extending into Owstwick belonged to a cadet branch of the Ros family. Robert son of Robert de Ros of Helmsley (Yorks. N.R.) had a grant of free warren in Hilston in 1297 and, as Robert de Ros of Gedney (Lincs.), he held a chief house, 6 bovates, and other land in Hilston at his death by 1311.[12] The estate descended to Robert's grandson Sir James Ros (fl. 1397)[13] and then to Sir Robert Ros (d. 1441), who left daughters.[14] It was evidently the same estate which was held in turn by Sir John Paulet (d. 1525) and his son Sir William, created Baron St. John in 1539.[15] As an appurtenance of Thorpe manor in Aldbrough, it passed by exchange from Lord St. John to the Crown in 1546.[16] Comprising 6¼ bovates and several houses in the mid century, it was sold in 1611 to John Eldred and William Whitmore, from whom Thomas Hardy bought two houses and 4¼ bovates in 1612.[17] That estate presumably passed to his widow Frances and was later held with the rest of the family's lands.[18]

Beatrice de Friboys gave some 2 bovates and other land in Hilston to Nunkeeling priory which later in the 13th century exchanged the estate with Sir Simon Constable.[19] Gaudin of Aseby gave another bovate, of which no more is known.[20] The Knights Hospitaller also had land there by the late 13th century.[21] After the suppression the estate, comprising a house and 2 bovates, was briefly held by the refounded order from 1558, before reverting to the Crown.[22] After 1210 Amand the butler (d. by 1218) gave to Meaux abbey a bovate and two tofts in Hilston of which the location was later unknown.[23] In the Middle Ages tithes in Hilston formed part of the endowment of St. German's chantry in Aldbrough church.[24]

ECONOMIC HISTORY. The tillage probably lay in fields on either side of the village called North and South fields.[25] An area called the Hooks, in Tunstall, evidently extended into Hilston and may have been used as pasture with the inhabitants of Tunstall and Grimston, in Garton.[26] Common pasture in Hilston was mentioned in 1657 but the commonable lands had evidently been inclosed by agreement by 1669, when Mrs. Carlile's estate was entirely in closes, among them Oxgang close and another of c. 70 a.[27]

In 1801 there was reckoned to be 188 a. under crops in the parish. The areas of arable and grassland in Hilston were recorded respectively as 379 a. and 108 a. in 1846[28] and in 1905 as 298 a. and 181 a.[29] In the 1930s the two land-uses were more equally balanced, the grass-land lying mostly around the village.[30] There were usually four farmers in Hilston in the 19th and earlier 20th century, of whom one in 1851 and two in the 1920s and 1930s had 150 a. or more.[31]

LOCAL GOVERNMENT. Churchwardens' accounts survive for 1741–1914.[32] There was said to have been a poorhouse in 1783 but no other evidence of it has been found.[33] In the early 19th century four people received permanent out-relief and one person was being relieved occasionally in 1802–3.[34] Hilston joined Patrington poor-law union in 1836 and remained in Patrington rural district until 1935 when it was taken into Holderness rural district as part of the new civil parish of Roos, which became part of the Holderness district of Humberside in 1974.[35] In 1996 Roos parish became part of a new East Riding unitary area.[36]

CHURCH. Re-used stonework suggests that a church was built in the 12th century[37] but it was not recorded until 1252.[38] The church may originally have been a chapel of Roos: it was called a chapel c. 1270, when one man served both places, and the rector of Roos later enjoyed a small pension from Hilston.[39] Hilston rectory was united with Tunstall in 1877 and, on further regroupings of the benefices, with Garton in 1927, and with Roos with Tunstall in 1974.[40]

9 R.D.B., CP/20/32; CR/75/96; HL/357/356.
10 B.I.H.R., TA. 33M; O.S. Map 6″, Yorks. CCXXVIII (1855 edn.).
11 B.I.H.R., TA. 33M; O.S. Map 1/2,500, Yorks. CCXXVIII. 6 (1891 edn.).
12 Cal. Chart. R. 1257–1300, 469; Cal. Inq. p.m. v, pp. 137–8.
13 Cal. Inq. p.m. xi, p. 165; xv, p. 233; xvii, p. 331.
14 P.R.O., C 139/106, no. 24.
15 H.U.L., DHO/7/23; Complete Peerage, s.v. Winchester.   16 L. & P. Hen. VIII, xxi (2), p. 243.
17 P.R.O., SC 11/762; ibid. E 310/30/177, f. 75; E 310/30/182, f. 45; ibid. C 66/1903, no. 9; H.U.L., DDSY/27/1–3.
18 H.U.L., DDSY/27/8; above, this section.
19 E.R.A.O., DDCC/11/4; B.L. Cott. MS. Otho C. viii, f. 82; below, Mappleton, manors [Nunkeeling priory].
20 J. Burton, Mon. Ebor. 386.
21 E.R.A.O., DDCC/46/1.
22 H.U.L., DDSY/27/2; Misc. iv (Y.A.S. Rec. Ser. xciv), 99; Cal. Pat. 1557–8, 321.

23 Chron. de Melsa, i. 359–60; above, this section.
24 Reg. Corbridge, i, p. 158; above, Aldbrough, church [chant.].   25 R.D.B., P/272/699.
26 Below, Tunstall, econ. hist.
27 H.U.L., DDSY/27/35; P.R.O., CP 25(2)/614/1656–7 Hil. no. 63.
28 B.I.H.R., TA. 33M; P.R.O., HO 67/26/208.
29 Acreage Returns, 1905.
30 [1st] Land Util. Surv. Map, sheets 33–4.
31 P.R.O., HO 107/2364; directories.
32 E.R.A.O., PE/17/23. 33 Poulson, Holderness, ii. 83.
34 Poor Law Abstract, 1804, pp. 592–3; 1818, pp. 522–3.
35 3rd Rep. Poor Law Com. 169; Census.
36 Humberside (Structural Change) Order 1995, copy at E.R.A.O.   37 Below, this section.
38 Yorks. Fines, 1246–72, p. 88.
39 Reg. Giffard, pp. 109, 281, 289; Tax. Eccl. (Rec. Com.), 304; Feud. Aids, vi. 330.
40 B.I.H.R., OC. 880; Lond. Gaz. 11 May 1877, pp. 3076–7; 4 Nov. 1927, pp. 6972–3.

John de Surdeval granted $\frac{1}{3}$ of the advowson to William of Routh (or Rue) in 1252.[41] The Rouths later had the whole advowson and presented rectors from c. 1275;[42] the patronage descended with their manor to the Michelbournes.[43] Sir William FitzWilliam presented in 1535 during the minority of his ward John Cutt and Ralph Ellerker as grantee of one turn in 1545.[44] Like the manor, the advowson was held in undivided parts by the Michelbournes[45] and presentations were made by Richard and Thomas Michelbourne jointly between 1559 and 1574. Richard Michelbourne and Sir Richard Michelbourne, presumably the son and grandson of Richard,[46] presented in 1603 and Thomas Sherlock for unknown reason in 1607.[47] In 1614 the entire advowson fell to the share of Sir Richard Michelbourne,[48] who then sold it to Marmaduke Marchant, rector.[49] Marchant was named as patron in 1650 but by a fine of 1657 the patronage was assured to Jane Hardy, widow (d. 1668).[50] For unknown reason Stephen Clark and his wife Jane presented in 1684. The patronage thereafter descended with the Hardy estate to the Sykes family. Randolph Hewitt granted a turn to Henry Munby, who presented in 1759.[51] The advowson and the landed estate descended differently in the 19th century, the patronage passing to the Revd. Christopher Sykes, later rector, after whose death in 1857 it evidently reverted to the senior representative of the Sykes family.[52] From the union of benefices in 1877 the former patron of Hilston had every alternate presentation.[53] The right was later held by the Sykes trustees,[54] who after the union of 1927 had one turn in four.[55] That turn was transferred in 1960 to the archbishop of York, who thereby became the sole patron.[56] At the further union of 1974 one turn in three was given to the archbishop.[57]

A pension payable out of the church was recorded in 1291 and later[58] but the value of the living in the Middle Ages is unknown. The living was worth £5 in 1535 and the improved annual value in 1650 was nearly £25.[59] The average net value in 1829–31 was £50 a year.[60] The income was £81 net in 1877, when a further sum of £60 a year from the Common Fund was granted to the united benefice.[61]

The Easter offerings and nearly all of the tithes were paid by composition of £9 14s. a year in the earlier 18th century and just over £13 by 1764. Two bovates of the Storr estate were reckoned to be tithe-free when in hand and otherwise to owe tithe in kind.[62] Except for those of the glebe, which were declared to have been merged, all the tithes were commuted for a rent charge of £12 19s. in 1846.[63]

There were c. 45 a. of glebe land from the early 18th century.[64] The land was sold as Glebe farm in 1919.[65] The rectory house had five hearths in 1672.[66] It was dilapidated in 1714 and 'very slender and weak' in 1780, when it was rebuilt.[67] It later served as the farmhouse of Glebe farm, with which it was sold in 1919.[68]

The poor living was often held by lesser clergy, many of those presented in the 14th and 15th centuries being chaplains and vacancies by resignation then being common.[69] John Bolton, rector, was deprived as a papist in 1562,[70] and puritan incumbents were ejected in 1607[71] and 1662.[72] Possibly also puritan was Marmaduke Marchant, rector from 1607 until his death by 1660, who was with the parliamentary forces in Hull in 1643.[73] From the mid 17th century Hilston was usually held with other benefices[74] and served by incumbents living outside the parish, in the 19th and 20th centuries at Garton, Tunstall, or Roos.[75] Christopher Sykes, patron of Hilston and Roos, presented himself to both livings in 1819 and lived at Roos.[76] From 1948 Garton with Hilston was served by the incumbent of Roos with Tunstall.[77] Assistant curates were employed in the late 18th and earlier 19th century.[78]

41 Yorks. Fines, 1246–72, p. 88.
42 P.R.O., C 141/4, no. 45; Lawrance, 'Clergy List', Holderness, 1, pp. 56–8; Yorks. Fines, 1300–14, p. 57; Reg. Giffard, p. 289.
43 Yorks. Fines, i. 25, 140.
44 Lawrance, op. cit. p. 58; B.I.H.R., ADM. 1545/2.
45 Yorks. Fines, i. 231; 1603–14, 143–4.
46 Above, manor.
47 Lawrance, op. cit. pp. 58–9; B.I.H.R., ADM. 1603/18.
48 E.R.A.O., DDRI/35/33.
49 Ibid. DDCC/18/3, s.v. Apr. 1615; Yorks. Fines, 1614–25, 23; above, manor.
50 P.R.O., CP 25(2)/614/1656–7 Hil. no. 63; E.R.A.O., PE/17/1; Lawrance, op. cit. p. 59; T.E.R.A.S. iv. 53.
51 B.I.H.R., Bp. Dio. 3, E.R., p. 166; R.D.B., U/172/325; AA/146/303; AO/142/150; BC/496/774.
52 B.I.H.R., Inst. AB. 18, pp. 315–16; ibid. 22, p. 164; Foster, Pedigrees of Yorks. iii.
53 Lond. Gaz. 11 May 1877, pp. 3076–7; Burke, Peerage (1925), 2174.
54 B.I.H.R., BA. TP. 1914/2; R.D.B., 212/102/85.
55 Lond. Gaz. 4 Nov. 1927, pp. 6972–3.
56 B.I.H.R., OC. 759; above, Garton, church; below, Tunstall, church.
57 B.I.H.R., OC. 880.   58 Above, this section.
59 Valor Eccl. (Rec. Com.), v. 119; T.E.R.A.S. iv. 53.
60 Rep. Com. Eccl. Revenues, 942–3.
61 Lond. Gaz. 11 May 1877, pp. 3076–7; 25 May 1877, p. 3343.

62 B.I.H.R., TER. H. Hilston 1716 etc.
63 Ibid. TA. 33M.
64 Ibid. TER. H. Hilston 1716 etc.
65 R.D.B., 199/230/195; O.S. Map 1/2,500, Yorks. CCXXVIII. 7 (1910 edn.).
66 Cf. P.R.O., E 179/205/504; Lawrance, op. cit., p. 59.
67 B.I.H.R., TER. H. Hilston 1781; H.U.L., DDSY/27/13; E.R.A.O., PE/17/1.
68 B.I.H.R., TA. 33M; above, this para.
69 Lawrance, op. cit. pp. 57–9.
70 B.I.H.R., Inst. AB. 1, f. 48; 2 (2), f. 12d.; HC. Misc. (ex CP. G. 1599); HC. AB. 9, f. 63; Aveling, Post Reformation Catholicism, 11.
71 R. A. Marchant, Puritans and Ch. Courts in Dioc. York 1560–1642, 262.
72 Calamy Revised, ed. A. G. Matthews, 62; V.C.H. Yorks. E.R. v. 46.
73 Lawrance, op. cit. p. 59; Miscellanea, i (Y.A.S. Rec. Ser. lxi), 155.
74 B.I.H.R., V.1764/Ret. 1, nos. 33, 208; /Ret. 2, no. 60 (Garton and Humbleton); V. 1868/Ret. 1, no. 219 (Tunstall); E.R.A.O., PE/44/21 (Roos); Lawrance, op. cit. pp. 59, 78 (Keyingham); Herring's Visit. i, p. 177; ii, p. 87 (Drypool).
75 B.I.H.R., V.1764/Ret. 1, no. 33; V. 1868/Ret. 1, no. 219; directories; but see Herring's Visit. ii, p. 86.
76 B.I.H.R., Inst. AB. 18, pp. 315–16; below, Roos, church.   77 Crockford.
78 E.R.A.O., PE/17/3; P.R.O., HO 129/521/1/27/48.

FIG. 3. HILSTON CHURCH IN THE EARLIER 19TH CENTURY

The quarterly sermons were neglected at Hilston in 1575.[79] Except for one Sunday a month, when the incumbent served elsewhere, two weekly services were held in 1743 but in 1764 there was only one weekly service on two Sundays out of three. Communion was then celebrated four times a year, with up to 20 recipients.[80] There was still only one weekly service in the mid 19th century. Communion was held monthly in 1865, seven or eight times a year later in the century, and fortnightly c. 1920, with usually half a dozen recipients in the mid 19th century and 16 c. 1920. A weekly celebration was held in either Hilston or Garton in 1931, when generally only three people received at Hilston.[81] In 1900 some 80 parishioners of Garton were said to attend Hilston church.[82] During the rebuilding of the church in the 1860s and again in the mid 20th century, services were held in private houses.[83]

The church of ST. MARGARET has been rebuilt twice. The medieval church, which was probably of 12th-century origin, was built mostly of boulders and consisted of chancel and nave with wooden bell turret.[84] The chancel was out of repair in 1596[85] and in 1830 the church was damp and neglected.[86] It was demolished and rebuilt to designs by J. L. Pearson in 1861–2, chiefly at the expense of Sir Tatton Sykes, Bt. It was built of boulders faced inside with ashlar, and comprised chancel with north vestry and organ chamber, nave, and west tower with square spire.[87] The church was extensively damaged by a bomb in 1941 and was rebuilt in 1956–7 to designs by Mr. Francis Johnson of Bridlington. The new church is of brick and consists of sanctuary, nave with west gallery, and west tower surmounted by an octagonal lantern. A Norman doorway, with two orders of chevron ornament, was re-used for the entrance of both the 19th- and 20th-century rebuildings, and the present building also incorporates some 19th-century stained glass.[88] In 1932 the Revd. N. J. Miller left £500 for the fabrics of Garton and Hilston churches.[89]

There were two bells in 1552 but later only one,[90] which was damaged in 1941 and replaced at the rebuilding with one from Wharram Percy church.[91] The plate includes a service given in 1860.[92] The registers of burials begin in 1654, of marriages in 1662, and of baptisms in 1663; they are largely complete.[93] An addition to the churchyard was consecrated in 1863.[94]

PROTESTANT NONCONFORMITY. Friends from Hilston were part of the Owstwick meeting in the later 17th century, and the monthly meeting for Holderness was held at Hilston in 1686.[95] Prominent Friends included John Storr of Hilston (d. 1677), who left a rent charge in Hilston to the poor of the monthly meeeting.[96] There were two Quaker families in the parish in 1743 and one in 1764.[97] An unidentified protestant congregation registered a house in 1816.[98]

EDUCATION. Children from Hilston went to school in Roos.[99]

CHARITIES FOR THE POOR. None known.

79 *Abp. Grindal's Visit. 1575*, ed. W. J. Sheils, 73.
80 B.I.H.R., V.1764/Ret. 1, no. 33; *Herring's Visit.* ii, p. 86.
81 B.I.H.R., V. 1865/Ret. 1, no. 243; V. 1868/Ret. 1, no. 219; V. 1871/Ret. 1, no. 219; V. 1877/Ret. 2, no. 26; V.1912–22/Ret.; V.1931/Ret., s.v. Garton.
82 Ibid. V.1900/Ret., no. 137.
83 Featherstone, *Hilston*, 11.
84 Poulson, *Holderness*, ii. 82, illus. facing p. 58.
85 B.I.H.R., V. 1595–6/CB. 3, f. 172v.
86 E.R.A.O., PE/17/24.
87 B.I.H.R., Fac. 1861/3; TER. 79; Featherstone, *Hilston*, 8; *Hull Advertiser*, 22 June 1861; *Hull Packet & E.R. Times*, 1 Aug. 1862; Bulmer, *Dir. E. Yorks.* (1892), 422.
88 B.I.H.R., CD. 852; Featherstone, *Hilston*, 8, 11–12, illus.; *Hull Packet & E.R. Times*, 1 Aug. 1862; date on bldg.
89 *Kelly's Dir. N. & E.R. Yorks.* (1933), 474; above,

manor.
90 B.I.H.R., TER. H Hilston 1770 etc.; ibid. ER. V/CB. 5, f. 247; Boulter, 'Ch. Bells', 84; *Inventories of Ch. Goods*, 48; *Hull Packet & E.R. Times*, 1 Aug. 1862.
91 Featherstone, *Hilston*, 12.
92 *Yorks. Ch. Plate*, i. 261–2.
93 E.R.A.O., PE/17/1–2, 4. Transcripts from reg. survive from 1601 at B.I.H.R. (microfilm copy at E.R.A.O., MF/7/8).
94 R.D.B., IH/70/90; B.I.H.R., CD. 339.
95 E.R.A.O., DDQR/17.
96 Below, Roos, nonconf.
97 B.I.H.R., V.1764/Ret. 1, no. 33; *Herring's Visit.* ii, p. 86.
98 B.I.H.R., Fac. Bk. 3, p. 753.
99 Ibid. V. 1865/Ret. 1, no. 243; directories; below, Roos, educ.

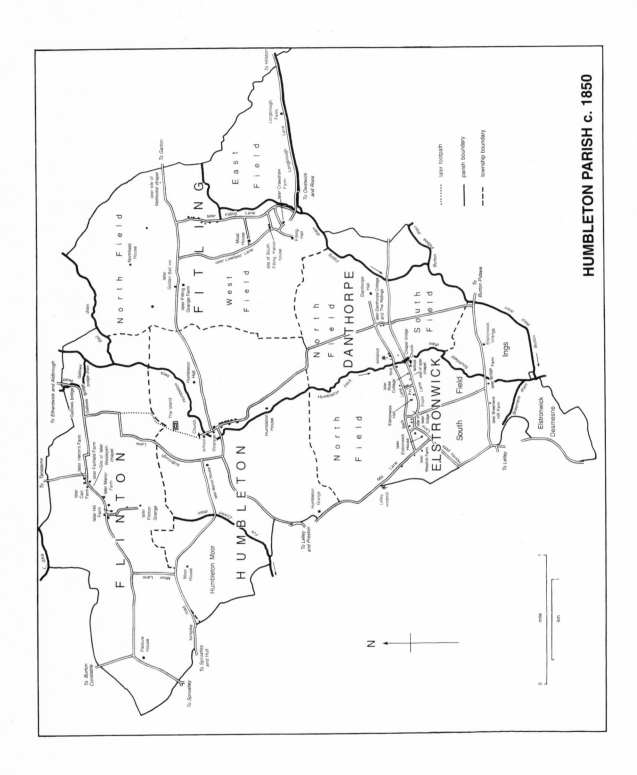

HUMBLETON PARISH c. 1850

later footpath
parish boundary
township boundary

HUMBLETON

THE large irregularly-shaped ancient parish of Humbleton comprised five settlements, with Humbleton village standing in its northern half.[1] The small village is c. 8 km. ENE. from the edge of Hull city and some 6 km. from the North Sea at Grimston, in Garton. Elstronwick, of much the same size as Humbleton, is situated just over 2 km. to the south and adjoining Elstronwick to the east is the hamlet of Danthorpe. The remaining settlements of Fitling and Flinton stood respectively 2 km. east and NNW. of Humbleton. The origin and meaning of the name Humbleton, recorded as Humeltone in 1086, is obscure; it may originally have been an Anglian name, indicating a settlement where bindweed grew, which was altered later by the substitution of the similar Scandinavian word for the hop plant.[2] Elstronwick is an Anglian name, meaning 'Elfstan's dairy farm'; some of the spellings, which have included Astenewic in 1086 and later Elsternwyk or Elsternwick, suggest a Scandinavian modification of the name Elfstan.[3] Also Anglian are the names Fitling, meaning 'the settlement of Fitela and his people', and Flinton, perhaps referring to a place where flints were found.[4] Danthorpe, 'village of the Danes', is believed to have been an isolated Danish settlement in a predominantly English area.[5] Parish and township boundaries were formed in part by streams, but in Elstronwick and Flinton limits were also marked by field roads, called 'pale walks',[6] and Longbrough Lane ran along part of the southern boundary in Fitling.[7]

The demesne land of Elstronwick manor was, or became, part of the demesne of the superior and adjacent manor of Burstwick,[8] and in 1813, at the inclosure of Elstronwick, 140 a. of that township, described as former demesne land of one or other of the manors, was regarded as part of Burstwick parish.[9] That division of Elstronwick township between Humbleton and Burstwick parishes was not mentioned later, however. In 1852 the ecclesiastical parish of Humbleton comprised 6,296 a. (2,548 ha.), of which 1,477 a. (597.7 ha.) lay in Humbleton township, 1,529 a. (618.8 ha.) in Fitling, 1,399 a. (566.2 ha.) in Flinton, 1,155 a. (467.4 ha.) in Elstronwick, and 736 a. (297.9 ha.) in Danthorpe.[10] The townships later became civil parishes. A detached part of Lelley, in Preston, comprising 3 a., was transferred to Elstronwick between 1881 and 1891.[11] In 1935 Humbleton and Flinton civil parishes

were combined to make a new parish of Humbleton, and an enlarged parish of Elstronwick was formed from Elstronwick and Danthorpe civil parishes and the 805-a. (325.8-ha.) Lelley civil parish. Fitling civil parish was then added to that of Garton with Grimston to form East Garton civil parish.[12] In 1991 the areas of Humbleton and Elstronwick civil parishes were virtually unchanged at 1,165 ha. (2,879 a.) and 1,091 ha. (2,696 a.) respectively.[13]

Humbleton parish probably had more than 300 poll-tax payers in 1377 and about 100 houses in 1672.[14] The 42 burials recorded in 1588–9 presumably included victims of plague, and there were similarly high numbers of deaths between 1656 and 1659.[15] In 1743 the parish was said to have 79 families.[16]

In Humbleton village there were 97 poll-tax payers in 1377, and 15 houses there were assessed for hearth tax and 5 discharged in 1672.[17] Flinton and Etherdwick, in Aldbrough, together had 85 poll-tax payers in 1377 and 28 houses in 1672.[18] From 89 in 1801, the population of Humbleton township, later civil parish, rose to 160 in 1831, stood at c. 140 in the mid century, rose in the 1870s to 160 in 1881, but then fell to 124 in 1901. Numbers had risen to 145 by 1931. Flinton's population of 105 in 1801 increased to 126 in 1831, fell to 108 in 1851, recovered to 125 in 1861, and then declined to 83 in 1901. In 1931 there were 93 inhabitants. The population of the enlarged civil parish of Humbleton, which would thus have been 238 in 1931, declined to 202 in 1971 and 188 in 1991.[19]

Elstronwick and Danthorpe had 100 poll-tax payers in 1377, and 24 houses were assessed and 10 discharged at Elstronwick and 8 charged at Danthorpe in 1672.[20] Elstronwick township had 126 people in 1801, 154 in 1821 and 157 in 1851, 94 in 1891, 123 in 1901, but only 95 in 1931. From 51 in 1801, the population of Danthorpe fell in the 1820s to 37 in 1831, was usually c. 60 in the later 19th century, and stood at 52 in 1931. The enlarged civil parish of Elstronwick would have had 259 inhabitants, mostly in Lelley, in 1931; there were only 241 inhabitants there in 1971, but 280 by 1981 and 301 in 1991.[21]

At Fitling there were 74 payers in 1377, and 24 houses were recorded there in 1672.[22] In 1801 Fitling had 127 inhabitants. Numbers declined to 103 in 1831, recovered to 131 in 1841 and 143 by 1871, but then fell sharply in the 1880s to

[1] This article was written in 1997–8.

[2] *P.N. Yorks. E.R.* (E.P.N.S.), 54–5; G. F. Jensen, *Scand. Settlement Names in Yorks.* 114.

[3] *P.N. Yorks. E.R.* 53; Jensen, op. cit. 139; Poulson, *Holderness*, ii. 63.   [4] *P.N. Yorks. E.R.* 53–4.

[5] Ibid. 53; Jensen, op. cit. 57, 189.

[6] E.R.A.O., DDCC/142/4; ibid. DDHI, accession 1141 (inclosure map); *V.C.H. Yorks. E.R.* v. 196.

[7] O.S. Map 6", Yorks. CCXII–CCXIII, CCXXVII–CCXXVIII (1855 edn.).

[8] P.R.O., C 66/641, m. 16.

[9] R.D.B., CQ/218/15.

[10] O.S. Map 6", Yorks. CCXII–CCXIII, CCXXVII–CCXXVIII (1855 edn.).

[11] *Census*, 1881–91; O.S. Map 1/2,500, Yorks. CCXXVII. 13 (1910 edn.).

[12] *Census*, 1931 (pt. ii).

[13] Ibid. 1991.

[14] Below. The inclusion of figures for Etherdwick, in Aldbrough parish, make it impossible to be more precise.

[15] E.R.A.O., PE/68/1–2.

[16] *Herring's Visit.* ii, p. 88.

[17] P.R.O., E 179/202/60, m. 31; *Hearth Tax*, 60.

[18] P.R.O., E 179/202/60, m. 36; *Hearth Tax*, 60.

[19] *V.C.H. Yorks.* iii. 494; *Census*, 1901–91.

[20] P.R.O., E 179/202/60, m. 34; *Hearth Tax*, 60.

[21] *V.C.H. Yorks.* iii. 494; *Census*, 1901–91.

[22] P.R.O., E 179/202/60, m. 81; E 179/205/504.

105 in 1891 and again in the 1920s to 85 in 1931.[23]

The parish is covered with boulder clay, apart from some alluvium alongside the main drains and a few scattered deposits of sand and gravel.[24] The undulating land lies mostly between 8 and 15 m. above sea level. Slightly higher ground is found in the east and north-west of the parish, in Fitling and Flinton respectively, and there is lower land in the south, beside the main drains in Danthorpe and Elstronwick. Humbleton seems to have been inclosed in the early 17th century and c. 1700. Fitling was dealt with in 1640, Flinton in 1675 and 1752, Danthorpe in 1735, and Elstronwick in 1813.[25]

The drainage is southwards towards the river Humber, chiefly by Humbleton beck and Fitling drain. Humbleton beck is fed by a stream called Bail drain, which forms the northern boundary of Fitling, and then flows down the middle of the parish through the villages of Humbleton and Elstronwick, where it becomes Southfield drain. Fitling drain runs alongside that settlement, through Danthorpe, and then along the southern parish boundary, as Burton West drain, to join Humbleton beck's continuation, Southfield drain. Besides Humbleton beck and Fitling and Bail drains, streams later called Gallows Bridge drain, Braemere drain, Fox Covert drain, Burton Pidsea drain, and Lambwath dike were all recorded as insufficient in 1367.[26] Lambwath dike has been known variously as Coom Hill sewer and Hell, or L, dike, the last two perhaps abbreviations of Lambwath.[27] Formerly water from the parish was carried into the Humber by way of Keyingham fleet. In 1618 grounds dependent on the fleet for their drainage included 60 a. in Bramer, lying in both Elstronwick and Lelley, 30 a. in Humbleton, 20 a. in Flinton, and 16 a. in Fitling.[28] Under the Keyingham Level Drainage Acts of 1772 and later, the drains of Humbleton parish were improved and water from the parish was evidently diverted away from Keyingham fleet into Burstwick drain and an outfall in Hedon, probably at the remaking of that drain in the early 19th century. After 1845 low ground assessed to the Keyingham Level Drainage included 129 a. in Elstronwick, 38 a. in Fitling, 26 a. in Danthorpe, 21 a. in Flinton, and 15 a. in Humbleton.[29]

The only main road runs through the north of the parish, passing through Flinton village. A lane running along the boundary between Humbleton and Flinton townships westwards to Sproatley was provided with a new link to Flinton village, later called Moor Lane, at inclosure in 1752,[30] and in 1767 the boundary lane was turnpiked as part of the Wyton branch of the Hull to Hedon road; the trust was discontinued in 1878.[31] That road to Flinton and one from there leading east have since been improved as part of the Aldbrough to Hull road. The parish is otherwise served by minor roads. From Humbleton roads lead north to Flinton, Etherdwick, and Aldbrough, east to Fitling, south to Elstronwick and Danthorpe, south-west to Lelley, and west, across Humbleton moor, to Sproatley. A road between Humbleton and Etherdwick was recorded in the 1360s, when two bridges carrying it at 'Gerardebrigge' had been allowed to fall into disrepair by Humbleton, Etherdwick, and Flinton townships.[32] Another road, leading north from Church bridge at Humbleton, was then said to have been neglected by the lord of the manor; the road, which now exists only as a footpath, may then have been part of the way to Etherdwick, which now leaves the village by a different route. Parts of the present Etherdwick road were called Aldbrough Lane and Gallows Bridge Road by the mid 19th century.[33] Also recorded as defective in the mid 14th century was West bridge in Elstronwick, which perhaps carried the road between Lelley and Burton Pidsea over a lesser drain.[34]

HUMBLETON village stands mostly on the eastern side of Humbleton beck, its north-south street, built on both sides, running parallel with, and close to, that watercourse. At the northern end of the street, however, the church and a former school stand on a small hill on the other side of the beck, and c. 300 m. away to the north there is a moated site, which was probably occupied by the medieval manor house; the village street evidently once continued further north, to the moated site and then perhaps on to Etherdwick.[35] Humbleton Hall and Manor Farm stand respectively a short distance east and west of the village.

The buildings are, apart from the church, of brick. The village, described as 'small and mean' in the 1850s,[36] was largely rebuilt in the later 19th century by the Hotham family, the chief landowner. Older cottages, with pantiled roofs, dormer windows, and some string coursing, remain near the church. Apart from a school and master's house, built in 1878, the Hothams put up nine houses in the village street, three of them c. 1890.[37] Four of the houses, standing in a terrace, were remodelled as two in 1997,[38] and another two are now also one house. In the mid 20th century the district council added 20 houses and bungalows along the east side of the street, and provided a water treatment works for

[23] V.C.H. Yorks. iii. 494; Census, 1901–31.

[24] Geol. Surv. Map 1", drift, sheet 73 (1909 edn.).

[25] Below, econ. hist.

[26] Poulson, Holderness, i. 123–5, 127, 129; O.S. Map 6", Yorks. CCXXVII–CCXXVIII (1855 edn.).

[27] E.R.A.O., DDHI, accession 1141 (Flinton inclosure map); DDCC/141/70; O.S. Map 6", Yorks. CCXII (1855 edn.).   [28] E.R.A.O., DDCC/54/53.

[29] Ibid. DDPK/3/8; ibid. QDA/4, 14; V.C.H. Yorks. E.R. v. 55–7, 170.

[30] E.R.A.O., DDCC/142/4; ibid. DDHI, accession 1141 (inclosure map); O.S. Map 6", Yorks. CCXXVII (1855 edn.).

[31] K. A. MacMahon, Roads and Turnpike Trusts in E. Yorks. (E. Yorks. Loc. Hist. Ser. xviii), 24, 70; 7 Geo. III, c. 71; Kelly's Dir. N. & E.R. Yorks. (1872), 508.

[32] Public Works in Med. Law, ii (Selden Soc. xl), pp. 312–13; Poulson, Holderness, i. 130.

[33] O.S. Map 6", Yorks. CCXII, CCXXVII (1855 edn.).

[34] Poulson, Holderness, i. 125.

[35] O.S. Map 6", Yorks. CCXXVII (1855 edn.); above, this section [roads]; below, manors (Humbleton).

[36] Sheahan and Whellan, Hist. York & E.R. ii. 369.

[37] Below, educ.; H.U.L., DDHO(3)/49/51, 81.

[38] Datestone.

the village,[39] and the development of the street's western side with private houses was continuing in 1998. Apart from the houses belonging to the Hotham estate, other noteworthy buildings are Humbleton Hall, the former vicarage house,[40] and, at the south end of the village, Humbleton House, which dates from *c.* 1795[41] but probably stands on the site of South End, or Gartham's, Farm, mentioned in 1622.[42]

In the later 18th century there was usually one licensed house at Humbleton.[43] A parochial lending library was run from the school at Humbleton in the 19th and early 20th century,[44] and a men's institute was being held above the stables of the vicarage house in the 1930s.[45] The village had no general meeting place until the former school, closed in 1959, was adopted for that purpose.[46] A recreation club for Humbleton was founded in 1946, and the following year a playing field, including tennis courts, was laid out on 2 a. provided by the trustees of Heron's charity.[47] The adjoining 3-a. school playing field, also belonging to the trustees, was added after the closure of the school in 1959, and in 1963 a pavilion built on the school field in the early 20th century was replaced with a new building.[48]

Outlying buildings include Humbleton Grange, which William Thompson built shortly before 1690;[49] the present house was formerly a single-storeyed building which was heightened to two storeys in the 19th century and later extended. The Thompsons had evidently also built a farmhouse on the newly-inclosed moor by 1709; later called Moor House, or Farm, it was joined after 1852 by one or two other houses.[50]

The straggling loosely-built village of ELS-TRONWICK extends across the middle of the former township. Beyond the beck, which was the eastern boundary, the band of settlement is continued by the even more scattered buildings of Danthorpe. Almost all of Elstronwick's buildings formerly stood between the southern and northern lanes, which were linked by short side lanes. Perhaps the only early exception was the medieval chapel, later church, which was sited on the south side of the southern lane, close to the beck. Part of the northern lane is called Back Lane, and stretches of the southern one have

been known as Front Lane, Church Lane, and Honeypots Lane.[51] It was presumably the westernmost cross lane which was called West Lane in the 17th and 18th centuries.[52] The open fields flanking the village were inclosed in 1813, and by the mid 19th century a nonconformist chapel and two houses had been built beyond the lanes on former commonable land.[53] There has been no further development south of the southern lane, but *c.* 15 houses have since been added along the northern edge of the village and beside the westernmost side lane, most of them in the 20th century.[54]

The buildings are, apart from the church, of brick. They include several farms which, with unbuilt areas of grassland, contribute to the village's open character. The earliest building is probably the single-storeyed Rose Cottage, which has a lobby-entry plan and may date from the beginning of the 18th century.[55] Elstronwick Hall is also 18th-century in origin, but was much enlarged between 1852 and 1889 by the addition of a southern block of red brick with stone dressings. The Hall and its grounds of 12 a., together with a farm and several cottages in Elstronwick, belonged to the Dickinsons, owners of much of Roos parish, and either J. T. Dickinson (d. 1875) or his brother George would seem to have been responsible for the enlargement.[56] The remodelling of the Hall was evidently accompanied by the building of Wrights Cottages, a pair of 'estate' houses in Back Lane, and a lodge cottage at the western end of the small park. The latter is of red brick with prominent yellow-brick quoins and has a projecting middle bay under a cross gable decorated with bargeboards.[57] Elstronwick House is probably also of the 18th century. Houses built in the 20th century include six council houses in Back Lane.[58]

There were one or two beerhouses at Elstronwick in the later 18th century, and the Crown and Anchor was named in the 1820s and still traded in 1998.[59] By the early 20th century a charitable endowment of *c.* 10 a. lying south of Elstronwick church had been divided into allotment gardens and let.[60] A playing field for the children of Elstronwick and Danthorpe was provided off Back Lane in 1971.[61]

Outlying buildings in Elstronwick include Elstronwick Grange, put up during or soon after

[39] R.D.B., 605/333/282; 605/334/283; 908/127/112; 913/518/433; 923/544/460; 1393/347/313.
[40] Below, manors (Humbleton [Thompson, Stringer]); churches (Humbleton).
[41] Pevsner and Neave, *Yorks. E.R.* 568.
[42] H.U.L., DDHO/36/5 (f). Below, manors [Humbleton, Kirkstall abbey].
[43] E.R.A.O., QDT/2/9.
[44] B.I.H.R., V. 1912–22/Ret.; *Educ. Enquiry Abstract,* 1088.
[45] B.I.H.R., V. 1931/Ret.
[46] E.R.A.O., PE/68/accession 2023; below, educ.
[47] The purchase by the trustees was completed in 1952: R.D.B., 908/465/397.
[48] Inf. from Mr. H. Jackson, Humbleton, 1999; inf. from Heron's Educational Foundation, 1999; below, educ.
[49] Cf. H.U.L., DDHO/36/39; O.S. Map 6", Yorks. CCXXVII (1855 edn.). Below, econ. hist. [brick-making].
[50] H.U.L., DDHO/36/47; O.S. Map 6", Yorks. CCXXVII (1855 edn.).

[51] O.S. Map 6", Yorks. CCXXVII (1855 edn.); *Reg. of Electors* (1998).
[52] H.U.L., DAS/7/3, s.v. Apr. 1652; DAS/7/5, s.v. Sept. 1728.
[53] O.S. Map 6", Yorks. CCXXVII (1855 edn.); below, nonconf.
[54] O.S. Map 1/2,500, Yorks. CCXXVII. 12 (1891 edn.); O.S. Map 1/2,500, TA 2232–2332 (1975 edn.).
[55] Pevsner and Neave, *Yorks. E.R.* 404.
[56] O.S. Map 6", Yorks. CCXXVII (1855 edn.); O.S. Map 1/2,500, Yorks. CCXXVII. 12 (1891 edn.); R.D.B., 192/390/343; 614/294/238; Bulmer, *Dir. E. Yorks.* (1892), 439.
[57] O.S. Map 6", Yorks. CCXXVII (1855 edn.); O.S. Map 1/2,500, Yorks. CCXXVII. 12 (1891 edn.); Pevsner and Neave, *Yorks. E.R.* 404.
[58] R.D.B., 912/173/147; 1250/508/455; 1665/377/343.
[59] E.R.A.O., QDT/2/7, 9; directories.
[60] P.R.O., ED 49/8539; E.R.A.O., IA. Elstronwick.
[61] R.D.B., 1742/461/374; Char. Com. reg., no. 523237.

inclosure in 1813.[62] Evidently of the same date is the uninhabited Bridge Farm, of one storey with an attic.[63]

DANTHORPE was sited on the same axis as Elstronwick and now forms a thinly-built extension of that village. From their shared boundary, the beck, Danthorpe hamlet extended eastwards to Fitling drain, another southward-flowing stream. Its early buildings probably all stood between two lanes which crossed the beck, by Chapel bridge and a ford, to join those in Elstronwick. In 1928 the district council replaced the ford with a bridge and improved the road there.[64] Chapel bridge was a wooden footbridge in 1998, and stretches of both the northern and southern lanes have been mere footpaths or field roads since the mid 19th century. One of the short cross lanes by then continued north and south, to Humbleton and Burton Pidsea respectively. One or two houses standing on the north side of the northern lane by the 1850s had probably been built following inclosure in the 18th century.[65] A few more have been built there and elsewhere since the mid 19th century, but the hamlet still has only about 15 houses.[66] The buildings are of brick, and almost all of them date from the 19th and 20th centuries. Danthorpe Hall, at the easten end of the settlement, is, however, 17th-century in origin.[67] Other early houses include Danthorpe Cottage and The Ridings on the Humbleton road; comprising two single-storeyed ranges of cottages,[68] later infilled and given dormer windows, the older part has side-sliding sashes to the ground floor. Among the recent houses is a pair built by the district council.[69]

FITLING has a north-south alignment, roughly parallel to Fitling drain, which flows to the east of the settlement. Most of the scattered buildings, which include several farms, are served by a street and a parallel back lane, known respectively as Fitling Lane and Lowfield Lane,[70] both c. 2 km. long, and by the side lanes which connect them. One of the side lanes is continued by roads to Humbleton and Garton. The village has two groups of houses, one including Fitling Hall at the southern end of the lanes and the other at the north end, close to the Humbleton–Garton road. There were formerly manors of North and South Fitling, but the location of the chief house of North Fitling

manor is not close to the northern group of houses.[71] The early plan of the village was probably modified by the building of new farms on former commonable land after its inclosure in the 17th century.[72] Later additions there included the now-demolished Longbrough Lane House, built by 1829; Northfield House, of 1820, apparently built by Simon Horner, and the large Fitling Grange Farm, which the Sykes family put up c. 1850.[73]

The buildings are of brick, and practically all of them date from the 19th and 20th centuries. Crawshaw Farm is thought to be of c. 1700,[74] and other houses, including a pair of cottages in a side lane, evidently date from the Hothams' ownership of much of Fitling in the later 19th century. Fitling Hall is discussed below.[75]

The carrier to Hull also sold beer at the Golden Ball inn, on the Humbleton to Garton road, from the late 19th century; the house traded until the 1950s.[76] The Methodist church has occasionally been used as a meeting place for Fitling.[77]

The brick-built village of FLINTON, comprising some 20 houses, stands on either side of an east-west street, now part of the Sproatley-Aldbrough road, and in side lanes leading north and south from the street. The houses include those of several farms, and the outbuildings of Manor Farm are prominent. Carr Farm and the former Fairfield Farm, both unoccupied in 1998, and Hill Farm House, formerly Hill Farm, are all believed to have been built, or rebuilt, in the mid 18th century.[78] The other houses date from the 19th century, Heron's Farm being rebuilt c. 1815,[79] or the 20th. Additions of the latter period include eight council houses[80] and the recently-rebuilt Fairfield and Hill Farms. Unusually, few houses were built out of the village following inclosure in the 17th and 18th centuries. One of the exceptions, Pasture House, in the west of the township, was put up by 1844.[81]

A beerhouse was recorded occasionally at Flinton in the later 18th century.[82]

MANORS AND OTHER ESTATES. In 1066 the sokelands of Morkar's manor of Kilnsea included 4 carucates at Elstronwick, 3½ or 4½ carucates at Flinton, 3 carucates at Foston ('Fostun'), which may have been in Humbleton,

[62] R.D.B., CQ/218/15; CW/211/306; IX/214/287; E.R.A.O., IA. Elstronwick; H. Teesdale, *Map of Yorks.* (1828); O.S. Map 6″, Yorks. CCXXVII (1855 edn.).

[63] Dept. of Environment, *Buildings List* (1987); E.R.A.O., IA. Elstronwick.

[64] Notice on bridge; E.R.A.O., RDSK/12, p. 39; RDSK/13, p. 39; R.D.B., 354/448/377.

[65] O.S. Map 6″, Yorks. CCXXVII–CCXXVIII (1855 edn.); E.R.A.O., DDCK/32/26; below, econ. hist.

[66] O.S. Map 1/2,500, Yorks. CCXXVII. 12, CCXXVIII. 9 (1890–1); O.S. Map 1/2,500, TA 2232–2332 (1975 edn.).

[67] Below, manors (Danthorpe).

[68] O.S. Map 1/2,500, Yorks. CCXXVIII. 9 (1890 edn.).

[69] R.D.B., 664/284/240.

[70] *Reg. of Electors* (1999).

[71] Below, manors (Fitling).

[72] Below, econ. hist.

[73] H.U.L., DDHO(3)/9/13; A. Bryant, *Map of E.R. Yorks.* (1829); O.S. Map 6″, Yorks. CCXXVIII (1855 edn.); Sheahan and Whellan, *Hist. York & E.R.* ii. 371; below, manors (Fitling).

[74] Dept. of Environment, *Buildings List* (1987).

[75] Below, manors (Fitling).

[76] R.D.B., 1152/520/467; O.S. Map 1/25,000, TA 23 (1953 edn.); directories.

[77] Above, Garton, intro.

[78] Dept. of Environment, *Buildings List* (1987).

[79] *9th Rep. Com. Char.* 766.

[80] R.D.B., 590/488/388; 806/118/100.

[81] Cf. E.R.A.O., DDHI, accession 1141 (inclosure map); ibid. PE/68/T.5; O.S. Map 6″, Yorks. CCXXVII (1855 edn.).

[82] E.R.A.O., QDT/2/9.

and 1 carucate at Humbleton. He also held 6 carucates at Fitling and 2 carucates and 6 bovates at Danthorpe as soke of his manor of Withernsea. By 1086 Drew de Bevrère had both manors and their dependent lands,[83] and they were later part of the Aumale fee. The only other tenant recorded in 1086 was the archbishop of York, who held 1 carucate at Danthorpe and 6 bovates at Flinton as berewicks of his manor of Swine.[84]

Much of the Aumale fee in the parish was held by the Scures family.[85] At Humbleton William de Scures gave the village with its church to Thornton abbey (Lincs.), it is said in the 1150s or 1160s and certainly by 1190.[86] Thornton abbey was granted free warren in Humbleton in 1301, and was recorded as one of the two lords of Humbleton and its members in 1316.[87] Its manor of *HUMBLETON* was mentioned in 1334.[88] The house's estate there was probably enlarged by the gift of Thomas of Nuthill and others in 1392.[89]

In 1614 the Crown granted Humbleton manor, formerly belonging to Thornton abbey, to William Whitmore and Edmund Sawyer in fee farm; it then included several houses at Humbleton and land there and at Danthorpe, Elstronwick, Fitling, and Flinton.[90] Later that year Whitmore, Sawyer, and Sir Arthur Ingram sold the manor to William Thompson of Scarborough and his son Francis, who quickly re-sold some farms at Flinton to the tenants.[91] The Thompsons, four of whom sat in parliament for Scarborough in the 17th and earlier 18th century,[92] enlarged their estate in Humbleton by buying up leasehold there: a Crown lease of one farm was acquired in 1617,[93] and Francis's son Stephen bought others, including that of the manor house and farm from Robert Rawson in 1624.[94] In 1628 the manor was settled on William Thompson (d. by 1638) and Francis (d. by 1657), with reversion to Stephen (d. 1677).[95] The fee-farm rent for Humbleton, sold by Parliament in 1651,[96] reverted at the Restoration to the Crown, which in 1662 released practically all of it to the Thompsons in return for Scarborough castle.[97] Humbleton manor continued to descend in the Thompsons from father to son, being held by William Thompson (d. 1691 or 1692),[98] Francis Thomp-

son (d. 1693), and William Thompson (d. 1744).[99] It then passed to the last William's cousin, William Thompson (d. 1756), who was succeeded in turn by his sons William (d. 1766) and Lillingston (d. 1771). Under a settlement of 1764, Sir Charles Hotham, Bt., cousin of William Thompson (d. 1766), inherited Humbleton and substituted Thompson for his own surname.[1] After his death in 1794, the estate descended in the Hothams with the baronetcy and later also the barony. In the late 18th century the manorial estate was reckoned to comprise 556 a. in Humbleton, Danthorpe, and Flinton,[2] and Beaumont Hotham, Lord Hotham, had c. 700 a. at Humbleton in the 1840s.[3] The holding in Humbleton township was enlarged in 1866 by the purchase of Humbleton Hall with 337 a., and elsewhere in the parish the Hothams bought much land in the 1870s and 1880s.[4]

Frederick Hotham, Lord Hotham, sold 2,560 a. in the parish between 1908 and 1919. In Humbleton township 1,035 a. was disposed of: Ryby Wright bought Manor House farm, with 447 a. in Humbleton, C. F. H. Knapton the 246-a. Moor farm, both in 1911, and James Wood Humbleton Hall with 318 a. in Humbleton and 68 a. in Flinton in 1912.[5] Ryby Wright died in 1936, and his executors divided and sold Manor House farm that year. The farmhouse and 391 a. were bought by the trustees of Ann Watson's charity of Sutton on Hull,[6] who still owned Manor farm in 1999, besides another farm in Humbleton, of 415 a.[7]

The medieval manor house may have occupied a moated site north of the church.[8] Thornton abbey, or its tenant, had evidently allowed the road there to fall into disrepair by 1367,[9] and reference in the 16th century to the 'site or chief house of the manor of Humbleton called le Hallgarth' suggests that the medieval house may also have been allowed to fall down.[10] The manor house was recorded again as Hallgarth in the 17th and early 18th century,[11] and was later said to have stood south-west of the church.[12] Stephen Thompson's house had eleven hearths in 1672,[13] and about 1720 William Thompson exchanged land with the vicar to improve the prospect from his house and make a new approach road at the west end of the churchyard.[14] The house was demolished in the late

[83] *V.C.H. Yorks.* ii. 264–5, 326.
[84] Ibid. 210 n., 216, 325–6.
[85] Below, this section (Fitling, Flinton).
[86] *E.Y.C.* iii, pp. 41–2; Poulson, *Holderness*, ii. 63.
[87] *Cal. Chart. R.* 1300–26, 9; *Feud. Aids*, vi. 164.
[88] H.U.L., DHO/5/47.   [89] *Cal. Pat.* 1391–6, 152.
[90] P.R.O., C 66/1999, no. 3.
[91] H.U.L., DDHO/36/10–11; DDHO/70/2.
[92] J. Foster, *Pedigrees of Yorks.* iii; *Hist. Parl., Commons*, 1660–90, i. 485–6; iii. 551–2, 554–5; memorial in church.
[93] H.U.L., DDHO/36/15.
[94] Ibid. DDHO/36/19, 22; cf. DDHO/36/1.
[95] Ibid. DDHO/36/20.
[96] P.R.O., C 54/3636, no. 29.
[97] H.U.L., DDHO/57/58.
[98] Ibid. DDHO/36/39; DDHO/71/38. Cf. Foster, op. cit.; *Hist. Parl., Commons*, 1660–90, iii. 554–5.
[99] H.U.L., DDHO/36/36, 42; DDHO/57/58.
[1] Ibid. DDHO/71/33.
[2] Ibid. DDHO/70/37, 39; DDHO/71/37; DDHO(3)/

53/17; J. Foster, *Pedigrees of Yorks.* iii.
[3] E.R.A.O., PE/68/T.2.
[4] R.D.B., IX/153/205; below, this section (Humbleton, Fitling, Flinton).
[5] R.D.B., 134/484/418; 137/171/148; 138/444/384 etc.; below, this section (Fitling, Flinton).
[6] R.D.B., 544/210/169; 544/504/392; 547/491/393; 547/608/490; 548/163/119; 549/52/42; 550/245/177; 552/434/343.
[7] Inf. from Ann Watson's Trust, Sutton on Hull; Dee, Atkinson, & Harrison, Driffield; below, this section [Humbleton, Kirkstall].
[8] H. E. J. le Patourel, *Moated Sites of Yorks.*, 113.
[9] Cf. Poulson, *Holderness*, i. 125; O.S. Map 6", Yorks. CCXXVII (1855 edn.).
[10] *Cal. Pat.* 1566–9, p. 139.
[11] P.R.O., C 66/1999, no. 3; H.U.L., DDHO/36/47.
[12] Poulson, *Holderness*, ii. 70; T. Jefferys, *Map of Yorks.* (1775).   [13] P.R.O., E 179/205/504.
[14] E.R.A.O., PE/68/3, confirmation of 1724; cf. O.S. Map 6", Yorks. CCXXVII (1855 edn.).

18th century.[15] A farmhouse standing opposite the Thompsons' house, on the west side of Aldbrough Lane, by the 1770s was later variously called Lane House, Manor House, or Manor Farm.[16]

William Thompson sold part of his estate in Humbleton in 1708 to Sir John Newton, Bt., and Thomas Hutton, acting for John Stringer (d. by 1709) and his wife Elizabeth, née Pelham. By the marriage of their daughter Anne to John FitzWilliam, viscount Milton, later Earl Fitz-William, the estate passed to the FitzWilliams.[17] In 1811 William Wentworth-FitzWilliam, Earl FitzWilliam, sold c. 330 a. in Humbleton with land in Fitling to Thomas Moxon (d. 1813), who devised the holding to his brothers Richard, George, and John. Moxon or his brothers built a new house, later called Humbleton Hall, before 1824, when the old farmhouse on the estate, opposite the vicarage house, was occupied as two cottages. The Moxons and their assignees in bankruptcy sold the estate in 1824 to Galen Haire (d. 1834). When Haire's son John sold the property to John Smith in 1858, Humbleton Hall was let to Talbot Clifford Constable and another tenant. The estate descended from Smith (d. 1863) to his son Alfred, from whom Beaumont Hotham, Lord Hotham, bought it in 1866, thereby reuniting it with the manor.[18]

Humbleton Hall was built by the Moxons between 1811 and 1824. The house is of red brick with slate roofs, but colour wash has been applied to the five-bayed south front, which has a central Tuscan porch flanked by shallow two-bayed bows rising through both storeys and, to either side, curved screen walls.[19]

A farm in Humbleton, formerly belonging to Kirkstall abbey (Yorks. W.R.) as an appurtenance of its manor of Aldbrough, was granted by the Crown in 1611 and again in 1614 to John Eldred and William Whitmore.[20] They sold it in 1614 to Edmund Sawyer, from whom Marmaduke Rawson bought it in 1615.[21] Called Gartham's farm, after previous tenants, or South End farm, it was devised by Rawson to his son Robert.[22] The estate was almost certainly that which descended later from Christopher Shutt to his son William (fl. 1734), grandson James (d. 1787), and great-grandson, also James. The last

James Shutt (d. 1800)[23] left it to James Bell, who conveyed it to his father, Robert Bell of Roos, in 1810. Bell was apparently succeeded c. 1825 by his son Robert, who had c. 410 a. in Humbleton in the 1840s,[24] and c. 1870 the estate was held for Alwin Shutt Bell and others, as heirs of Robert Bell, M.D.[25] By 1887 the farm belonged to Ada Shutt Worthington, widow.[26] In 1924 Mrs. Worthington's heirs, Adela Worthington, Sarah Birney, and Georgina Gilliat, sold Humbleton House farm, then of 350 a. in Humbleton and 68 a. in Elstronwick, to G. T. Butterworth (d. 1931).[27] The premises were conveyed in 1941 to Herbert Butterworth, who the following year sold them to Ann Watson's charity of Sutton on Hull. The farm formed part of the trust's large estate in Humbleton in 1999.[28]

The carucate at Danthorpe belonging to the archbishop of York[29] was assigned to his church at Beverley, and was later held of its provost.[30]

Beverley minster's estate at Danthorpe and land of the Aumale fee there were held by a family named after the place. Sir Alan of Danthorpe probably held the estate before his son (Sir) John,[31] who in the mid 13th century was said to hold 2 carucates and 6 bovates there, possibly representing the entire Aumale fee in Danthorpe.[32] The John of Danthorpe recorded as the tenant of 3 carucates and 6 bovates in Danthorpe and 'Pundagh' in 1284–5 was possibly Sir John's son, John,[33] who in 1287 held 1½ carucate at Danthorpe of the count of Aumale.[34] About 1300 the Danthorpe family's estate there included just over 1 carucate of demesne held of the provost of Beverley, some land held of John of Meaux, and the manor of *DANTHORPE*, held as ⅟₄₈ knight's fee of the king as the count of Aumale's successor and comprising 7⅔ bovates of demesne and 5 bovates occupied by free and bond tenants. John of Danthorpe, an idiot, died in 1301, leaving as heirs his nephew William Berchaud, similarly incapacitated, and niece Joan Glede.[35] The estate was partitioned between them in 1303.[36] Joan married Robert of Hedon, who was named as one of the lords of Elstronwick and its members in 1316, presumably on account of Danthorpe.[37] She (d. by 1335) was succeeded by her son John in rents and more than 1 carucate at Danthorpe, besides half shares

15   Poulson, *Holderness*, ii. 70; below, churches [Elstronwick fabric]; T. Jefferys, *Map of Yorks.* (1775); J. Tuke, *Map of Holderness* [1786], printed in Poulson, *Holderness*, ii, facing p. 1; A. Bryant, *Map of E.R. Yorks.* (1829) shows Old Hall Grounds.

16   T. Jefferys, *Map of Yorks.* (1775); Sheahan and Whellan, *Hist. York & E.R.* ii. 370; O.S. Map 1/2,500, Yorks. CCXXVII. 4 (1891 edn.).

17   *Complete Peerage*.

18   H.U.L., DDHO/36/59, 68, 78, 82 (indenture and deeds schedule of 1811–66); R.D.B., IX/153/205; above, this section.

19   Pevsner and Neave, *Yorks. E.R.* 568; Min. of Housing, *Buildings List* (1965); Dept. of Environment, *Buildings List* (1987).

20   P.R.O., C 66/1903, no. 9; C 66/1988, no. 3; *Cal. Pat. 1563–6*, p. 406.

21   H.U.L., DDHO/36/5 (d).

22   Ibid. DDHO/36/23; DDHO/36/5 (b, c, f).

23   R.D.B., M/470/778; CB/81/120; memorial in

Humbleton church.

24   R.D.B., CE/163/250; CP/503/771; E.R.A.O., QDE/1/6/18; ibid. PE/68/T.2; Poulson, *Holderness*, ii. 70.

25   R.D.B., IU/44/64; LA/122/180; H.U.L., DAS/7/8, p. 108.

26   R.D.B., 20/437/406; 20/439/408 (1887).

27   Ibid. 293/475/385; 447/215/164.

28   Ibid. 647/271/221; 655/208/180; inf. from Ann Watson's Trust; Dee, Atkinson, & Harrison, Driffield, 1999.

29   *V.C.H. Yorks.* ii. 210 n., 216, 325–6.

30   *Yorks. Inq.* iv, p. 18; *Cal. Inq. p.m.* v, p. 144.

31   *Kirkby's Inquest*, 245 n.; *Rolls of Justices in Eyre for Yorks. 1218–19*, (Selden Soc. lvi), pp. 126–7.

32   *Kirkby's Inquest*, 375.   33   *Feud. Aids*, vi. 40.

34   *Cal. Inq. p.m.* iv, pp. 353, 355; *Yorks. Inq.* iii, pp. 123–4.

35   *Yorks. Inq.* iii, pp. 123–4; iv, pp. 17–18, 25–7; *Cal. Pat. 1301–7*, 123; *Kirkby's Inquest*, 245.

36   *Cal. Close, 1302–7*, 92–8.

37   *Feud. Aids*, vi. 164.

in Danthorpe and Pundagh manors.[38] John of Hedon was granted free warren at Danthorpe in 1348,[39] and he or another John was recorded at Danthorpe in 1367.[40] William Berchaud (d. by 1335) was succeeded in his share of the Danthorpes' lands in Danthorpe and Pundagh by his kinsman Geoffrey Redemar.[41] The immediate successors of John of Hedon and Geoffrey Redemar are unknown.

In 1391 a third share in Danthorpe manor, evidently then belonging to Joan, wife of Stephen Parkinson, was conveyed by them to John of Hutton.[42] It was presumably the same manor, then extending into Owstwick, in Roos, which was held, as part of the former Aumale fee, under Burstwick manor by knight service in the 16th century. It was conveyed by William Fleming to John and George Wright in 1534, and descended from John Wright (d. 1540) to his son Robert.[43] On Robert's death in 1594, the estate included four houses and 2 carucates.[44] His son William Wright, William's wife Anne, and son Robert sold it to Robert Thorpe in 1608.[45] Thorpe (d. 1611) was succeeded in Danthorpe manor by his brother William (d. 1620), and he by his son John (fl. 1640).[46] In the earlier 18th century the Thorpes' estate comprised c. 350 a.[47] Another John Thorpe had the manor by 1706. He (d. by 1717) was evidently succeeded by his son John,[48] who was allotted 214 a. at inclosure in 1735 and died that year or the next. John's heirs, his uncle Ingleby Thorpe[49] and cousin James, sold the manor to Roger Hall in 1744. Hall, a Hull merchant, had himself been awarded 106 a. at the inclosure of Danthorpe in 1735 and then also held the estate of St. John's college, Cambridge, as its lessee.[50] The manorial estate, comprising four farms by 1745,[51] was sold by Hall to Henry Etherington, another Hull merchant, in 1753.[52] The rest of Hall's estate at Danthorpe, comprising a 132-a. farm, was sold by him to James Shaw, from whom Etherington bought it in 1754.[53] Etherington (d. 1760)[54] was succeeded by his son Henry, later Sir Henry Etherington, Bt.,[55] who bought two farms with c. 90 a. in all in 1783 and 1787,[56] and in 1788 had 627 a. in Danthorpe.[57] Under a settlement of 1813, Sir Henry's estates passed at his death without issue in 1819 to his

wife's great-niece, Mary Coventry, viscountess Deerhurst, later countess of Coventry, and her heirs. Mary (d. 1845)[58] was succeeded by her son Henry Amelius Coventry, who sold Danthorpe manor with 608 a. to William Marsdin in 1870.[59] As the Danthorpe Hall estate, it was sold in 1878 to W. H. Wilson-Todd.[60] In 1910 Sir William P. Wilson-Todd, Bt., sold the estate to Henry Dixon, who also bought the 112-a. farm of St. John's college, Cambridge, in 1920.[61] Dixon died in 1935, and in 1936 his executors sold the estate in lots.[62] Herbert Johnson, who bought Danthorpe Hall with 457 a., died in 1960, and his son and successor, Herbert B. Johnson, in 1991. In 1998 the Hall was held by Mr. Johnson's trustees and the farm belonged to H. B. Johnson & Co. Ltd.[63]

The Danthorpes held their chief house at Danthorpe of the provost of Beverley.[64] In 1672 Mr. Thorpe lived in a house there with nine hearths,[65] presumably that later called Danthorpe Hall. The present building, of pebble-dashed brick with grey-brick quoins and slate and pantiled roofs, comprises a late 17th-century house enlarged about a century later with a rear wing, and again in 1840 with an eastern cross wing.[66] The 17th-century part has brick panels with pediments and dentilled coursing in the 'Artisan Mannerist' style, and inside some contemporary oak panelling. The garden is planted with shrubs and trees, and includes a small lake. The extensive farm buildings, which may date from the late 18th century, comprise three ranges around a large yard and a smaller separate block.[67]

Tibbald Hautayn (fl. c. 1225), his successor, Hamo Hautayn (fl. 1258–9), and another Tibbald (fl. c. 1300) held an estate in Danthorpe, put at 1 carucate and 3 bovates in the early 14th century, as military tenants of the Danthorpes. Most of the land was by the mid 13th century held of the Hautayns by knight service by the Marfleet family.[68]

William of Danthorpe gave 1 bovate in Danthorpe to Aumale abbey (Seine Maritime), which regranted it to William's son Adam in the earlier 13th century.[69]

[38] *Cal. Inq. p.m.* vii, p. 459; *Cal. Fine R. 1327–37*, 447.
[39] *Cal. Chart. R. 1341–1417*, 94.
[40] Poulson, *Holderness*, i. 123.
[41] *Cal. Inq. p.m.* vii, p. 471; *Cal. Fine R. 1327–37*, 454–5.
[42] P.R.O., CP 25(1)/278/146, no. 51.
[43] H.U.L., DHO/8/37; *L. & P. Hen. VIII*, xvii, p. 256; *Yorks. Fines*, i. 69, 139.
[44] P.R.O., C 142/243, no. 46.
[45] *Yorks. Fines, 1603–14*, 88.
[46] E.R.A.O., DDCC/70/3–4; P.R.O., C 142/379, no. 31.
[47] E.R.A.O., QDB/3, pp. 6–7, 58–9.
[48] Cf. P.R.O., CP 25(2)/984/5 Anne Mic. no. 9; E.R.A.O., QDB/2, pp. 13–15; QDB/3, pp. 6–7, 13–20.
[49] R.D.B., N/436/907; E.R.A.O., QDB/3, pp. 58–9.
[50] R.D.B., N/436/907; E.R.A.O., DDWH/bundle 5 (St. John's lease 1731); ibid. QDB/3, pp. 109–15; QDB/4, pp. 47–9.
[51] R.D.B., R/343/837.
[52] Ibid. W/413/833.
[53] Ibid. X/3/8.
[54] For the Etheringtons, *N. Ferriby Monumental Inscriptions* (E. Yorks. Fam. Hist. Soc.), p. 74.
[55] R.D.B., AY/383/640; H.U.L., DRA/337.
[56] R.D.B., BH/51/93; BL/337/517.

[57] Ibid. BM/542/855.
[58] Ibid. CX/11/11; CW/460/645; *N. Ferriby Monumental Inscriptions* (E. Yorks. Fam. Hist. Soc.), p. 74; *Complete Peerage*, s.vv. Coventry, St. Albans.
[59] R.D.B., KP/372/486; Burke, *Peerage & Baronetage* (1890), 338.
[60] R.D.B., NO/417/605; H.U.L., DDHO(3)/7/3, 5; Bulmer, *Dir. E. Yorks.* (1892), 438.
[61] R.D.B., 127/312/286; 225/217/175.
[62] Ibid. 536/358/282; 538/224/176; 540/237/178; 540/314/233; 541/309/224; 545/373/303 etc.
[63] Ibid. 540/237/178; 1213/426/373; 1213/427/374; 1213/428/375; inf. from Andrew M. Jackson & Co., Hull, 1999.
[64] *Yorks. Inq.* iv, p. 18.
[65] P.R.O., E 179/205/504.
[66] *Kelly's Dir. N. & E.R. Yorks.* (1901), 508.
[67] H.U.L., DDHO(3)/7/5 (illus.); Pevsner and Neave, *Yorks. E.R.* 404.
[68] H.U.L., DHO/16/32; *Cal. Close, 1302–7*, 97–8; *Bracton's Note Bk.* ed. Maitland, iii, p. 658.
[69] H.U.L., DHO/16/32; Poulson, *Holderness*, ii. 70; *Bracton's Note Bk.* iii, p. 658.

An estate at Danthorpe was bought from William Thorpe by John Lambert, and then, in 1530 or 1531, conveyed to St. John's college, Cambridge.[70] The college was awarded 105 a. for its commonable lands there at inclosure in 1735,[71] and in 1875 its farm was of 112 a.[72] In 1920 Henry Dixon, who already had the manorial estate at Danthorpe, bought the college's farm.[73]

A manor of *ELSTRONWICK* descended with the lordship of Holderness and with Burstwick manor,[74] of which it was regarded a member. It thus passed from Drew de Bevrère to the counts of Aumale, then to the Crown[75] and its grantees, including Margaret de Gavaston, countess of Cornwall, recorded as lady in 1316.[76] After the execution of Edward Stafford, duke of Buckingham, in 1521, it reverted to the Crown, and later passed by grant to Henry Neville, earl of Westmorland,[77] and sale to his son-in-law, Sir John Constable (d. 1579).[78] The manor thereafter descended in the Constables, later viscounts Dunbar, and their successors.[79] In the mid 15th century the manor comprised 14 houses, 1 carucate and 2 bovates, 162 a., and freeholdings.[80] Five bovates of demesne land were recorded in the 16th century, when they were regarded as part of the Burstwick demesne,[81] and 140 a. of demesne land had been sold by the early 19th century. The copyhold also became an appurtenance of Burstwick manor, 210 a. at Elstronwick being awarded as copyhold of Burstwick manor at inclosure in 1813.[82]

Nicholas de Stutville[83] and his descendents held 2½ carucates of the Aumale fee at Elstronwick; the estate was held of them as a member of their manor of Cottingham by the service of ¼ knight's fee. In 1287 Stutville's estate was said to be held by the heir of Hugh Bigod (d. 1266),[84] husband of Nicholas de Stutville's daughter Joan, but it otherwise descended in Joan's descendants from her marriage to Hugh Wake, passing from the Wakes[85] to the Plantagenets[86] and Holands, both earls of Kent.[87] For unknown reasons, the Wakes were said in 1323 to hold Elstronwick by knight service of the archbishop,

who seems in turn to have been the tenant of Sir William de Ros.[88]

The estate was held under the Stutvilles and their heirs by the Pattishall family. In the mid 13th century the tenant was John of Pattishall, probably (Sir) John of Pattishall (d. 1290).[89] He was evidently succeeded by his son Simon of Pattishall (d. 1295), and in 1312 rents from Elstronwick amounting to just over £12 a year were settled on Simon's son (Sir) John and his wife Mabel.[90] In 1316 Simon of Pattishall was given as one of the lords of Elstronwick, apparently in error,[91] and c. 1350 the Pattishalls were said to share the fee with the heirs of Richard son of Maurice.[92] Sir John of Pattishall (d. 1349) was, nevertheless, succeeded in all 2½ carucates by his son (Sir) William[93] (d. 1359), and he by his sister Catherine, wife of (Sir) Robert de Tudenham.[94] Later described as *ELSTRONWICK'S* or *TUDENHAM'S* manor, the estate descended in turn to Sir John de Tudenham (d. 1392), his son Robert (d. 1405), and grandson, also Robert.[95] In 1448 Sir Thomas Tudenham sold the manor to Edward Grimston,[96] and in 1535 another Edward Grimston sold it to Hugh Oversall (d. 1538). He was succeeded in the manor, then sometimes called Tudenham's in Elstronwick, by his son John.[97] In 1576 it was sold by another Hugh Oversall to James Clarkson and Michael Warton,[98] who in 1590 died seized of the manor, sometimes also called *OVERSALL'S*.[99] It then descended in the Wartons and their heirs like Beverley Water Towns manor. In the late 17th century the demesne seems to have comprised only 2½ bovates and was then occupied by tenants. On the partition of the estates of Sir Michael Warton (d. 1725) in 1775, Elstronwick manor fell to the share of Michael Newton; besides freehold and copyhold rents, it then comprised c. 100 a. and a few garths.[1] In 1813 Newton's heirs sold Elstronwick manor to the Hull banker, Thomas Thompson.[2] Thompson (d. 1828) devised the manor to his son, J. V. Thompson (d. 1856), for life, and then to the latter's children as common tenants.[3] In 1865 Thompson's children sold their estate, William Watson buying the manor and John Stamford the land.[4] From Watson (d. 1879), the manor descended in turn to his son

70   Poulson, *Holderness*, ii. 71.
71   R.D.B., N/436/907.
72   H.U.L., DDHO(3)/7/2.
73   R.D.B., 225/217/175; above, this section.
74   *V.C.H. Yorks. E.R.* v. 9–10.
75   *Abbrev. Plac.* (Rec. Com.), 190.
76   *Feud. Aids*, vi. 164; *Cal. Pat.* 1338–40, 148, 383; 1354–8, 13, 185; *Cal. Chart. R.* 1327–41, 470–1; *Cal. Close*, 1377–81, 178.
77   P.R.O., C 66/641, m. 16; *Cal. Pat.* 1557–8, 39.
78   H.U.L., DCC/2/63; DHO/8/47.
79   E.R.A.O., QDR/2/12; ibid. DDCC/111/39, 231; H.U.L., DHO/7/42; J. Foster, *Pedigrees of Yorks.* iii.
80   P.R.O., C 139/93, no. 44, m. 4.
81   Ibid. C 66/641, m. 16.
82   R.D.B., CQ/218/15. Cf. P.R.O., C 142/409, no. 161; Poulson, *Holderness*, ii. 72.
83   *Cal. Inq. p.m.* ix, p. 289.
84   Ibid. iv, p. 356.
85   Ibid. ii, pp. 258, 260; ix, pp. 201, 205–6.
86   Ibid. ix, p. 289; x, pp. 41, 47, 49.
87   Ibid. x, pp. 410–11; xvi, p. 111; xvii, pp. 299, 309; xix,

pp. 221–2; *Complete Peerage*, s.v. Wake; *V.C.H. Yorks. E.R.* iv. 67–8.
88   *Kirkby's Inquest*, 415.
89   Ibid. 375; *Cal. Inq. p.m.* ii, p. 260.
90   *Yorks. Fines, 1300–14*, p. 97. For the Pattishalls, *Complete Peerage*, s. vv. Pateshulle, Grandison.
91   *Feud. Aids*, vi. 164.
92   *Cal. Inq. p.m.* ix, pp. 205–6; x, p. 49.
93   Ibid. ix, pp. 288–9.
94   Ibid. x, pp. 410–11; *Cal. Fine R.* 1356–68, 119–20.
95   *Cal. Inq. p.m.* xvii, pp. 117–18; xix, p. 6.
96   P.R.O., CP 25(1)/280/159, no. 57; cf. *Cal. Papal Reg.* x. 305.
97   H.U.L., DHO/8/36; *Yorks. Fines*, i. 72.
98   *Yorks. Fines*, ii. 91.
99   P.R.O., C 142/224, no. 31; Poulson, *Holderness*, ii. 73.
1   H.U.L., DDCB/4/94–5; *V.C.H. Yorks. E.R.* vi. 210; *Yorks. Royalist Composition Papers*, ii (Y.A.S. Rec. Ser. xviii), p. 55.
2   R.D.B., CW/211/306; CW/213/307; CX/29/20.
3   H.U.L., DAS/7/30.
4   R.D.B., IW/206/285; IX/214/287.

James (d. 1909), James's widow Margaret (d. 1920), and their son James.[5]

William de Forz (d. 1241), count of Aumale, gave 1 carucate and 3 bovates in Elstronwick, and the tenants of the land, to (Sir) Peter de Fauconberg on his marriage with the countess's sister Margaret.[6]

It seems to have been part of that Fauconberg fee, comprising a toft and 1 bovate at Elstronwick, which was given to Nunkeeling priory, together with a bondman, probably in the 13th century.[7] A farm of 1 bovate at Elstronwick, presumably the same, was held by the priory at its dissolution; it was sold by the Crown in 1558 to John and William Butler.[8] It was also proposed in 1386 to grant land at Elstronwick to Nunkeeling priory as part of the endowment of a chantry in Elstronwick chapel,[9] but there is no evidence for such a grant.

Besides its estate in Humbleton, Ann Watson's charity owned the 181-a. Yew Tree farm at Elstronwick from 1947 until 1950,[10] and the 46-a. Lilac Tree farm there from 1946 until 1958.[11]

In the mid 13th century Giles of Goxhill held 1½ carucate at Elstronwick and Walter of Etherdwick a small holding there.[12]

The 6 carucates belonging to the Aumale fee at Fitling were evidently held by the Scures family. A tenant of William de Scures (fl. mid 12th century), one Sir Roger, and his wife, gave their 3-carucate holding to the Knights Hospitaller.[13] The order was one of the two lords of Fitling in 1316,[14] and its manor of *FITLING* formed part of the preceptory of Holy Trinity, Beverley, until the suppression of the Hospitallers in the 16th century.[15] In 1338 the estate in Fitling included a house and more than 165 a.[16] The manor, which had no demesne by the 16th century,[17] was sold by the Crown to Edward Rotherham and Edward Bates in 1614.[18] Thomas Edmundson was lord of the manor

from 1616 to 1622, and John Rawson from 1622 to 1655.[19] Rawson was allotted 359 a. for tithes and his commonable lands at the inclosure of Fitling in 1640.[20] He sold Fitling manor to Thomas Chatt in 1655.[21] John Chatt was lord in 1661, but Thomas Chatt's daughter, Frances Truslove, widow, later Frances Kemp, and her son Edward Truslove held the manor from 1662 to 1667, and Edward was then sole lord until 1686. In that year Joseph Storr bought the manor, which then extended into Burton Pidsea, Owthorne, and Tunstall,[22] and at other times was said to have dependent holdings in many other places in Holderness, including Humbleton, Danthorpe, Garton, and Owstwick, in Roos.[23] Including a chief house and c. 95 a. in Fitling held in demesne, the manor descended from Joseph Storr (d. 1728) to John Storr, recorded as lord later that year,[24] and then, with the Storrs' estate in Hilston, to G. L. Thompson, who sold it to Simon Horner in 1810.[25] The manor thereafter descended with Horner's other land in Fitling.[26] It was presumably the manor known also as *SOUTH FITLING*, to distinguish it from the nearby North Fitling manor, based on Moat House.[27]

The chief house of the Trusloves had only three hearths in 1672.[28] The two buildings occupying the site in the 19th century were evidently rebuilt by the Hothams as a pair of cottages c. 1900, and one was later called Hall Farm Cottage.[29]

The rest of the Scures's holding, put at 2 carucates and 7 bovates in the mid 13th century,[30] passed from Sir Robert de Scures, like Riston manor, to the Hildyards.[31] (Sir) Robert Hildyard, the tenant in the 1280s,[32] was succeeded by his son Robert and grandson Thomas (d. by 1322).[33] Amand of Fitling, recorded as the other lord of Fitling in 1316, may have been the Hildyards' tenant there.[34] Thomas Hildyard's daughter Catherine (d. by 1385), wife of Sir Peter Nuthill, was succeeded in the estate by her son Peter (fl. c. 1405), and it later descended like Nuthill manor, in Burstwick, before evidently passing back to the Hildyards. Described as

5 Ibid. MX/6/12; H.U.L., DAS/7/37.
6 B.L. Harl. Ch. 50. D. 39 print. *The Genealogist* N.S. xxxvi. 203. Cf. *Complete Peerage*, s. vv. Aumale, Fauconberge.
7 B.L. Cott. MS. Otho C. viii, f. 85v. The damaged source mentions Sir Peter de Fauconberg. The donor was Evelyn wife of Giles of [?Goxhill].
8 *Valor Eccl.* (Rec. Com.), v. 115; *Cal. Pat.* 1557–8, 383.
9 H.U.L., DHO/6/120; below, churches.
10 R.D.B., 744/108/89; 851/5/4; 851/6/5; above, this section (Humbleton).
11 R.D.B., 739/258/215; 1119/91/76.
12 *Kirkby's Inquest*, 375.
13 *Cal. Close*, 1346–9, 135–6; *Kirkby's Inquest*, 375.
14 *Feud. Aids*, vi. 164.
15 *Cal. Pat.* 1338–40, 125; *Cal. Close*, 1346–9, 135–6.
16 *Knights Hospitallers in Eng.* (Camd. Soc. lxv), 49.
17 *Miscellanea*, iv (Y.A.S. Rec. Ser. xciv), 96–100.
18 P.R.O., C 66/2043, no. 3.
19 The descent to 1698 comes partly from E.R.A.O., DDX/595/92. A William Rawson had held 2 bovates as a customary tenant on the manor in 1539–40: *Miscellanea*, iv. 97.
20 E.R.A.O., DDCC/39/3; below, this section, rectory (Fitling).

21 P.R.O., CP 25(2)/614/1655 East. no. 29. Ellen Rawson, John's widow, was recorded as lady in error in 1656 and 1657: E.R.A.O., DDX/595/20.
22 E.R.A.O., DDX/595/20–39; ibid. DDCC/39/4; P.R.O., CP 25(2)/805/2 Jas. II Mic. [last].
23 E.R.A.O., DDX/595/1–56, 138.
24 Ibid. DDX/595/82–3.
25 R.D.B., P/272/699; P/388/995; BD/232/362; BR/2/2; BZ/432/694; CN/367/582; CP/20/32; CP/586/887; above, Hilston, manor. For the Storrs, Poulson, *Holderness*, ii. 77, 79–80.
26 Below, this section [Lloyd].
27 R.D.B., DR/216/250; E.R.A.O., DDX/698/8; below, this section (N. Fitling).
28 P.R.O., E 179/205/504.
29 E.R.A.O., DDX/698/8; O.S. Map 1/2,500, Yorks. CCXXVIII. 5 (1891 edn.); *Reg. of Electors* (1999).
30 *Kirkby's Inquest*, 375.
31 Below, Long Riston, manors; *Chron. de Melsa* (Rolls Ser.), i. 96–8. For the Hildyards, J. Foster, *Pedigrees of Yorks.* iii.
32 *Cal. Inq. p.m.* iv, pp. 353, 355; *Feud. Aids*, vi. 40.
33 *Cal. Inq. p.m.* vi, pp. 185–6; Poulson, *Holderness*, ii. 77.
34 *Feud. Aids*, vi. 164.

FITLING manor in the 16th century, it was held in turn by Peter Hildyard (d. 1502), his widow Joan, Peter Hildyard (fl. 1535), Martin Hildyard (d. 1544 or 1545),[35] and Sir Christopher Hildyard (d. 1602).[36] The manor then passed to Sir Christopher Hildyard (d. 1634), who shortly before his death bought other land in Fitling, formerly belonging to Thornton abbey, from the Thompsons; the whole was inherited by his son Henry,[37] who at inclosure in 1640 was allotted 352 a.[38] In 1662 Henry Hildyard and his son Henry settled part of the estate, comprising four farms and 240 a., on themselves in tail; no use was then specified for the manor and the rest of the demesne, amounting to 227 a.,[39] possibly because that part was then exchanged for a manor of Routh with John Chatt.[40] John Chatt sold Fitling manor to Thomas Walker the elder in 1671.[41] It seems to have been the same manor which Sir John Hotham, Bt. (d. 1689), left to his wife Elizabeth (d. 1697), and which descended with the baronetcy, and later also with the barony, to Beaumont Hotham, Lord Hotham. Comprising a farm of *c.* 220 a.,[42] the estate was sold by Lord Hotham in 1819 or 1820 to Horner Reynard,[43] and thereafter descended with Reynard's other land in Fitling.[44] The manor was also known as *NORTH FITLING* manor in the mid 19th century to distinguish it from the nearby manor of South Fitling.[45]

The Hildyards' manor house occupied a moated site in 1662,[46] and in 1830 the part of Horner Reynard's estate which had been bought from Lord Hotham was identified as Moat House and the 229 a. of adjoining closes.[47] Moat House, of one storey with an attic and thought to date from the 18th century or earlier,[48] was demolished in the later 20th century.

Part of the Hildyards' estate retained by them in the 17th century[49] may have passed to Sir Richard Lloyd (fl. 1702).[50] His grandson, Richard Lloyd, with the children of Arthur Barnardiston, sold several houses and more than

170 a. in Fitling to Francis Farrah, probably one of the tenants, in 1713.[51] Farrah (d. by 1726) and his widow Frances apparently bought more land there.[52] The estate descended to Farrah's grandson, also Francis Farrah, who had succeeded Francis Farrah (d. 1763), probably his father.[53] He died in or soon after 1772, leaving his brother Robert as heir.[54] In 1785 Robert Farrah sold *c.* 300 a. in Fitling in three farms to Simon Horner, a Hull merchant.[55] Horner's purchase was later identified as including the 146-a. Northfield House farm; the rest was presumably the 151-a. 'ancient estate' based on Fitling Hall, described in the same source.[56] Horner bought another 31 a. in Fitling in 1786,[57] and a manor of Fitling with *c.* 95 a. from G. L. Thompson in 1810.[58] The family's holding was evidently also enlarged with the Hothams' manor of North Fitling, which Horner Reynard, nephew of the elderly Simon Horner, bought in 1819 or 1820.[59] In 1823 Simon Horner's estate was described as comprising the manors, or reputed manors, of North Fitling and South Fitling, the latter presumably that bought from Thompson.[60] After his death in 1828, the whole estate passed to Horner Reynard (d. 1834).[61] His son, Edward Horner Reynard, had 648 a. in Fitling in the 1840s.[62] In 1853 he sold the manor, manors, or reputed manors of Fitling and the land to James Foord.[63] Foord (d. by 1859) left the manor to his nephew, the Revd. Richard Foord,[64] from whom trustees for the Hotham family bought the estate in 1871.[65] Further purchases by the trustees in Fitling added a farm of 115 a. in 1872,[66] another of 90 a. in 1873,[67] the 227-a. Fitling Grange farm in 1874,[68] and a 116-a. farm in 1881.[69] Between 1908 and 1911 the Hothams sold 1,210 a. in Fitling. In 1910 Thomas Clapison bought 302 a. in Fitling Grange and Moat House farms, and the Moore family the 210-a. Northfield House farm. Fitling Hall with 227 a. in Fitling was sold to William Thompson in 1911.[70] Thompson (d. 1943) was succeeded by his great-nephew, Thomas Harrison, who

35 P.R.O., C 142/57, no. 58; E.R.A.O., DDCC/112/120; *V.C.H. Yorks. E.R.* v. 11; Poulson, *Holderness*, ii. 77.
36 *Yorks. Fines*, iv. 21.
37 P.R.O., C 142/530, no. 155; *Yorks. Royalist Composition Papers*, i (Y.A.S. Rec. Ser. xv), pp. 102–4; above, this section (Humbleton).
38 E.R.A.O., DDCC/39/3.
39 H.U.L., DDHO/70/55.
40 P.R.O., CP 25(2)/752/14 Chas. II Mic. nos. 41, 80; Poulson, *Holderness*, i. 393; below, Routh, manors (Routh).
41 P.R.O., CP 25(2)/755/23 Chas. II Mic. [12 from end].
42 H.U.L., DDHO/70/37, 39; DDHO/71/9, 20; DDHO/74/9; below, next para.; J. Foster, *Pedigrees of Yorks.* iii. It was held by the Storr family in the 1720s: H.U.L., DDHO/15/4.
43 R.D.B., FD/31/26; E.R.A.O., QDE/1/6/11.
44 Below, this section [Lloyd].
45 R.D.B., FD/31/26; above, this section [Hospitallers].
46 H.U.L., DDHO/70/55.
47 E.R.A.O., DDX/698/8. The suggestion that the formerly moated site was the location of the chief house on the Hospitallers' estate at Fitling thus seems erroneous: H. E. J. le Patourel, *Moated Sites of Yorks.*, 112. O.S. Map 1/2,500, Yorks. CCXXVIII. 5 (1891 edn.).
48 Min. of Housing, *Buildings List* (1965).
49 Above, this section (Fitling).
50 E.R.A.O., DDX/595/53.
51 Ibid. DDCC/39/4; R.D.B., E/146/257.
52 R.D.B., D/313/516; E/143/250; I/323/719.
53 Ibid. AE/119/236; AM/305/493.
54 Ibid. AU/253/416; AR/154/304.
55 Ibid. BH/574/981; BI/57/89; BI/407/637.
56 E.R.A.O., DDX/698/8; O.S. Map 6", Yorks. CCXXVIII (1855 edn.).
57 R.D.B., BL/277/422.
58 Ibid. CP/586/887; above, this section [Hospitallers].
59 Above, this section. The relationship comes from a letter written by the 89-year old Horner in 1823: deeds relating to Heron's charity in possession of Mr. M. Craven, Hessle, 2000.
60 R.D.B., DR/216/250; above, this para.; above, this section [Hospitallers].
61 E.R.A.O., QDE/1/6/11; ibid. DDX/698/8; R.D.B., EH/366/412. For the death dates, E.R.A.O., PE/72/18.
62 E.R.A.O., PE/68/T.4; R.D.B., FD/31/26; FD/32/27; FD/34/29; GD/256/299.
63 R.D.B., HA/49/55.
64 Ibid. HX/388/456.
65 Ibid. KX/45/51.
66 Ibid. KY/86/114; H.U.L., DDHO(3)/9/8.
67 R.D.B., LE/288/397.
68 Below, this section [Fitling, Kirkby].
69 R.D.B., NI/280/407. Cf. H.U.L., DDHO(3)/9/14.
70 R.D.B., 121/267/244; 121/280/255; 137/372/334 etc.

sold Fitling Hall farm to George Butcher in 1946, and in 1999 it belonged to G. A. Butcher & Sons.[71]

Simon Horner enlarged Fitling Hall in 1819, adding a grey-brick block with a three-bayed south front to the existing red-brick house.[72] In 1879 the Hothams restored the house, which stood among trees in a small park.[73]

In 1729 Christopher Kirkby (d. c. 1733) bought a farm in Fitling[74] which descended like land in Owstwick, in Roos, to the Sykes of Sledmere.[75] A small farm was bought in 1787,[76] another farm, from trustees of the Mitford family, in 1855, and more land in 1865. The enlarged estate, then of 227 a. and called Fitling Grange farm, was sold by Christopher Sykes's trustees to John Hotham, Lord Hotham, and the Hotham trustees in 1874,[77] and later descended with the rest of that family's holding in Fitling.[78]

Meaux abbey was licensed to acquire land in Fitling in 1431,[79] and at its dissolution the house had two farms there, each of 2 bovates, which were let for just over £3 a year.[80] By 1770 the overseers of the poor of Marton, in Swine, and West Newton, in Aldbrough, shared a small estate in Fitling, later reckoned to comprise c. 12 a. In 1910 the holding was recorded as that of the poor of Marton. No more is known of it, or of the respective charities.[81] An acre or so in Fitling also belonged to the poor of Sproatley,[82] and Towrie's charity, in Aldbrough, seems to have had land in Fitling.[83] That of Leonard Chamberlain, benefiting Hull, had c. 60 a. in Fitling in the 1840s and in 1910; the land was later sold.[84]

The Scures family evidently held all or most of the Aumale fee in Flinton. In the mid 13th century (Sir) Robert de Scures had 2 carucates there,[85] and his heir, (Sir) Robert Hildyard, was recorded as a tenant at Flinton in 1284–5.[86]

William de Scures's gift to Thornton abbey in the mid 12th century had included 1 carucate and 5 bovates in Flinton and 7s. rent.[87] The abbey's estate there was enlarged by Ralph of Gloucester and William le Vergaunt, whose gifts were confirmed c. 1250;[88] possibly by Walter de la Gaunge in 1314,[89] and by Robert Forman and others in 1443.[90] With the rest of Thornton's estate in the parish, that at Flinton passed to the Crown and, as part of Humbleton manor, was included in the grant to Whitmore and Sawyer in 1614; the Flinton rental was then nearly £13 a year.[91]

Part of Thornton abbey's estate at Flinton was held by Thomas of Flinton in 1283,[92] and it was perhaps on that account that Herbert or Robert of Flinton was returned as one of the two lords of Humbleton and its members in 1316.[93] The Flintons' estate passed to Herbert of Flinton's son-in-law, Walter Grimston,[94] and the Grimstons later held all or much of the abbey's land at Flinton in socage. As *FLINTON* manor, the estate was settled in 1440 on Thomas Grimston (d. by 1462) and his wife, with remainder to their son Walter, whose son Thomas had evidently succeeded by 1481.[95] Walter Grimston (d. 1544) held a chief house, seven others, 420 a., and a windmill there, wholly or mostly of the Crown as the abbey's heir.[96] The manor descended from father to son to Thomas Grimston (d. 1572), Thomas Grimston (d. 1586), and Sir Marmaduke Grimston (d. 1604). The last mentioned enlarged the estate, buying a 5-bovate holding in 1585 and the rectorial tithes in 1587.[97] Sir Marmaduke was succeeded by his brother Thomas[98] (d. 1618). Part of the estate was later held by Thomas's relict for life, and the rest by his nephew, Marmaduke Grimston (d. 1623). Marmaduke's son William, a minor,[99] bought a further 5 bovates in 1634,[1] and he had succeeded to Flinton by 1642.[2] In 1657 he sold the manor, then including c. 3 carucates of open-field land, and the tithes, to William Dobson, a Hull alderman.[3] By 1668 the estate had passed under Dobson's will to his daughter Esther and her husband, Christopher Hildyard.[4] Hildyard was awarded 397 a. at the inclosure of the east part of Flinton in 1675,[5] and his grandson, Sir Robert Hildyard, Bt., 512 a. for his lands and tithes when the rest of the township was dealt

[71] Ibid. 697/296/245; 735/362/288; inf. from G. A. Butcher & Sons.
[72] R.D.B., EH/366/412; datestone 1819 SH on house.
[73] H.U.L., DDHO(3)/49/18; O.S. Map 1/2,500, Yorks. CCXXVIII. 5 (1891 edn.).
[74] R.D.B., DDSY/19/13.
[75] Ibid. DDSY/108/5; DDSY/110/23, 30; below, Roos, manors (Roos and Owstwick); J. Foster, *Pedigrees of Yorks.* iii, s.v. Sykes.
[76] H.U.L., DDSY/19/24.
[77] Ibid. DDHO(3)/9/13, 16, 18.
[78] Above, this section.
[79] *Cal. Pat.* 1429–36, 142.
[80] P.R.O., SC 6/Hen. VIII/4612, m. 3d.
[81] H.U.L., DRA/337; E.R.A.O., NV/1/45; ibid. PE/68/T.4; R.D.B., AM/392/634; AM/393/635; BH/574/981; Bulmer, *Dir. E. Yorks.* (1892), 304.
[82] Below, Sproatley, charities.
[83] H.U.L., DDHO(3)/9/8; above, Aldbrough, charities.
[84] E.R.A.O., NV/1/45; PE/68/T.4; *V.C.H. Yorks. E.R.* i. 338; inf. from secretary to trustees, 1999.
[85] *Kirkby's Inquest*, 375.
[86] *Feud. Aids*, vi. 40; below, Long Riston, manors; *Chron. de Melsa* (Rolls Ser.), i. 96–8.

[87] *E.Y.C.* iii, pp. 41–2; above, this section (Humbleton).
[88] *Cal. Chart. R.* 1300–26, 9–10.
[89] *Cal. Pat.* 1313–17, 110.
[90] Ibid. 1441–6, 99–100.
[91] P.R.O., C 66/1999, no. 3; *Cal. Pat.* 1560–3, 358.
[92] *Abbrev. Plac.* (Rec. Com.), 275.
[93] *Feud. Aids*, vi. 164.
[94] J. Foster, *Pedigrees of Yorks.* iii, s.v. Grimston.
[95] P.R.O., CP 25(1)/292/69, no. 244; *Test. Ebor.* iii (Sur. Soc. xlv), 251–2.
[96] P.R.O., C 142/69, no. 142.
[97] E.R.A.O., DDHI, accession 1141 (deeds 1585, 1587); below, this section (rectory).
[98] P.R.O., C 142/160, no. 59; C 142/210, no. 124; C 142/301, no. 65; *Yorks. Fines, 1603–14*, 29; *1614–25*, 12.
[99] P.R.O., C 142/708, no. 96; C 142/401, no. 126.
[1] E.R.A.O., DDHI, accession 1141 (deed 1634).
[2] P.R.O., CP 43/236, rot. 55.
[3] Ibid. CP 25(2)/615/1657 East. no. 41; E.R.A.O., DDHI, accession 1141 (deed 1657, particulars of estate [1657]).
[4] P.R.O., CP 25(2)/761/19–20 Chas. II Hil. [last but one]; Poulson, *Holderness*, ii. 75; J. Foster, *Pedigrees of Yorks* iii, s.v. Hildyard.
[5] E.R.A.O., DDHI, accession 1141 (award 1675).

with in 1752.[6] With Winestead, Flinton manor passed on the death of Sir Robert D'Arcy Hildyard, Bt., in 1814 to his neice, Anne Catherine Whyte, later Hildyard. In 1802 the 1,126-a. estate lay in four farms.[7] Mrs. Hildyard sold much of it in lots in 1848.[8] Flinton manor with 653 a. in three farms was bought by Sir Thomas A. C. Constable, Bt.,[9] and descended, like Burstwick, to the Chichester-Constables,[10] who had some 630 a. at Flinton in 1963.[11] By 2000 most of the land had been sold, the c. 120-a. Hill farm alone remaining part of the Burton Constable estate.[12] Another farm, of 153 a. and later named as Manor farm, was bought from Mrs. Hildyard in 1848 by Robert Wright.[13] He (d. by 1881) was succeeded by his son William (d. 1886),[14] whose trustees, William's widow Jane and sons Ryby and J. C. Wright, sold the farm in 1896 to Edwin Wiley.[15] It was sold by Mabel Wiley in 1924 to Henry Caley (d. 1946), and then passed in turn to his son John and grandson Francis Caley, the owner in 1999.[16]

The manor house contained a chapel in 1481.[17] The present Manor Farm dates from the late 18th century, and is of brick with a slate roof; it incorporates a probably earlier pedimented porch, said to have been refixed from a house in Beverley, and inside has original stairs and doors and a reused contemporary fireplace.[18]

The 307-a. Flinton Hall farm, not sold by Mrs. Hildyard in 1848, was conveyed to trustees in 1853, and may have been held later for her daughter Esther Goad. It was eventually sold in 1874 to John Hotham, Lord Hotham, and the Hotham trustees.[19] Frederick Hotham, Lord Hotham, sold the farm with 238 a. to the Richardson family in 1910, and 68 a. with Humbleton Hall to James Wood in 1912.[20]

Robert Constable had ½ carucate in Flinton c. 1210,[21] and a small estate there later descended in the Constables.[22] It comprised 46 a. held of the Crown's manor of Humbleton, and presumably formerly of Thornton abbey, in the mid 16th century; a cottage and 1½ bovate in the early 18th, and c. 35 a. in the late 18th and earlier 19th century.[23] The holding probably descended later with Flinton manor.[24]

The 6 bovates in Flinton belonging to the archbishop of York in 1086[25] were evidently assigned to his church of Beverley. Tenants of the provost at Flinton included Thomas of Flinton in the later 13th century.[26] As part of St. John's fee, the 6 bovates with a house and other land there were held by knight service as a manor of FLINTON in the 16th century. Together with land in Fitling, held of the Hildyards, Flinton manor passed from George Flinton (d. 1536) to his widow Margaret, and then possibly to his son Edward.[27] Probably the same was an estate comprising 2 houses, 5½ bovates, and 40 a. in Flinton, held as ⅟₁₀₀ knight's fee by William Green and later by his brother Edward (d. 1615).[28] The tenant of Beverley Chapter manor at Flinton was Thomas Hewitt in 1655 and Sir Robert Hildyard, Bt., in the 1730s. The holding presumably later descended with the Hildyards' larger estate in the township.[29]

Bridlington priory was given ½ carucate and tofts in Flinton by Alan of Flinton c. 1165, when the gift was confirmed by Geram of Normanby, presumably Alan's lord.[30] The land was held of the priory by the Twyer family in the 14th century,[31] and by the St. Quintins in the 16th.[32]

The RECTORY belonged to Thornton abbey until its dissolution in the 16th century, and then by a Crown grant of 1542 to Thornton college for its brief existence.[33] After the suppression of the college, the rectory reverted to the Crown.

HUMBLETON. Corn and hay tithes in Humbleton, held under a lease to Robert Rawson for £6 16s. a year, were granted by the Crown in fee farm to Francis Morrice and Francis Phillips in 1609,[34] and re-sold by them the same year to Marmaduke Rawson.[35] The wool and lamb tithes of Humbleton and other townships had been sold in fee farm by the Crown in 1604 to Sir Henry Lindley and John Starkey.[36] They re-sold them in 1607, also to Marmaduke Rawson, who was probably the tenant.[37] Rawson (d. by 1630) was succeeded by his son Robert,[38] and in 1650 Jane Rawson had tithes in Humbleton township worth £20 a year.[39] Marmaduke

[6] Ibid. DDCC/142/4.
[7] Ibid. DDCC/111/299; DDCC/142/4; V.C.H. Yorks. E.R. v. 151; J. Foster, Pedigrees of Yorks. iii.
[8] E.R.A.O., DDCC/40/20.
[9] R.D.B., GN/95/125.
[10] V.C.H. Yorks. E.R. v. 10.
[11] R.D.B., 1295/284/255.
[12] Inf. from Mr. R. Wastling, Grange Farm, Thirtleby, 2000.   [13] R.D.B., GN/31/39.
[14] Ibid. NH/133/188; NS/28/43; 14/490/476 (1886).
[15] Ibid. 82/139/127 (1896).
[16] Ibid. 280/316/274; 754/291/245; inf. from Mr. Caley, 1999.
[17] Test. Ebor. iii (Sur. Soc. xlv), 251 n.
[18] Dept. of Environment, Buildings List (1987).
[19] H.U.L., DDHO(3)/10/2–3. R.D.B., HA/29/38; LL/166/228; J. Foster, Pedigrees of Yorks. iii, s.v. Hildyard.
[20] R.D.B., 121/278/253; 138/444/384.
[21] E.R.A.O., DDCC/40/1.
[22] Ibid. DDCC/111/16; H.U.L., DHO/7/42; DHO/8/47; Cal. Inq. p.m. Hen. VII, ii, pp. 60–2.
[23] P.R.O., E 150/240, no. 12; C 142/65, no. 61; E.R.A.O.,

QDR/2/12; ibid. PE/68/T.5; ibid. DDCC(2)/Box 8/17, p. 47.
[24] Above, this section.
[25] V.C.H. Yorks. ii. 216.
[26] E.R.A.O., PE/129/150, f. 17.
[27] P.R.O., C 142/58, no. 44; C 142/151, no. 34.
[28] Ibid. C 142/353, no. 53.
[29] Ibid. E 317/Yorks./17; H.U.L., DDCV/16/5; above, this section.
[30] E.Y.C. iii, p. 65; Bridlington Chart. 304–5, 343.
[31] Yorks. Inq. iv, pp. 65–7; Cal. Inq. p.m. vii, pp. 424–5.
[32] P.R.O., C 142/49, no. 55; ibid. SC 6/Hen. VIII/4430, m. 13.
[33] L. & P. Hen. VIII, xvii, pp. 29–30.
[34] P.R.O., C 66/1810, mm. 11–42. Cf. H.U.L., DDHO/36/1; Cal. Pat. 1566–9, p. 139.
[35] H.U.L., DDHO/36/4.
[36] P.R.O., C 66/1662, mm. 1–10.
[37] H.U.L., DDHO/36/53. Cf. B.I.H.R., CP. G. 368; Cal. Pat. 1560–3, 358; 1572–5, p. 304.
[38] H.U.L., DDHO/36/5 (f, h); P.R.O., CP 25(2)/520/6 Chas. I Hil. [no. 36].
[39] T.E.R.A.S. iv. 52.

Rawson's grandchildren sold their tithes in Humbleton and the other townships, except for those of their farm and another in Humbleton, to Stephen Thompson, lord of Humbleton manor in 1665.[40] Thompson (d. 1677) left his tithes to his grandson, the Revd. Stephen Thompson, whose heir, also Stephen Thompson, sold them to William Thompson in 1720, thereby reuniting them with the manor.[41] William Thompson had by then 'sold' some of the tithes from his own estate, which were paid by composition, together with part of the land.[42] The Thompsons' heir, Beaumont Hotham, Lord Hotham, merged tithes from 685 a., and three other owners those from c. 415 a. prior to commutation by award of 1844 and apportionment of 1846; the tithes remaining unmerged, from 333 a., were then commuted for a rent charge of £75 a year payable to Galen Haire's trustee.[43]

DANTHORPE. The rectorial estate at Danthorpe was worth £4 a year in the 1540s.[44] The corn tithes there, and possibly those of hay too, were granted by the Crown to George Lowe and Edmund Sawyer in 1615, and sold by them the same year to Edward Bee and Richard Cooper. Stephen Thompson bought the tithes from Bee in 1641,[45] and in 1650 he had tithes worth £15 a year in Danthorpe.[46] The wool and lamb tithes there descended like those of Humbleton township, passing from the Crown to the Rawsons and then, in 1665, to Stephen Thompson.[47] The Danthorpe tithes, then including those on hay, later descended with the tithes in Humbleton in the Thompsons and their heirs.[48] William Thompson was awarded rents amounting to £30 a year for tithes at the inclosure of Danthorpe in 1735,[49] and a rent charge of that amount was confirmed to his heir, Beaumont Hotham, Lord Hotham, when all the tithes of the township were commuted by award of 1844 and apportionment of 1845.[50]

ELSTRONWICK. In the 1540s Thornton college's rectorial estate in Elstronwick was let for just over £7 a year.[51] The corn and hay tithes of Elstronwick, formerly belonging to the college,

were granted in fee farm by the Crown to Edmund Downing and Roger Rante in 1591,[52] possibly for William and Anne Hildyard, whose heir, Sir William Hildyard, sold them, with land in Elstronwick, to Thomas Appleyard in 1609.[53] He was succeeded in turn by his sons, Christopher (fl. 1639),[54] Thomas (fl. 1647),[55] and Sir Matthew Appleyard, the last being recorded as one of the impropriators at Elstronwick in 1650.[56] Sir Matthew's son Matthew had the estate in 1653,[57] Matthew Appleyard, presumably another, in 1716,[58] Francis Appleyard in 1720,[59] and Christopher Appleyard, probably Sir Matthew's grandson, in 1759.[60] The Appleyards' interest evidently passed to John Bell (d. 1809), who owned the rectorial estate at Elstronwick, except for the tithes of the closes belonging to Burstwick parish. At inclosure in 1813 his trustees were awarded 23 a. for his glebe land and 40 a. for some of the tithes; Frances Bell, his widow, was then allotted 88 a. for the rest of Bell's corn and hay tithes.[61]

The tithes of the rest of Elstronwick, formerly demesne land and later regarded as part of Burstwick parish, descended with Burstwick rectory from Burstall priory to its successors, Kirkstall abbey (Yorks. W.R.), the Constables, later Lords Dunbar, and their heirs.[62]

FITLING. The wool and lamb tithes of Fitling passed, like those in Humbleton, to Marmaduke Rawson in 1607.[63] The corn tithes there, then let for nearly £5 a year, were sold in fee farm by the Crown to Francis Morrice and Francis Phillips in 1609,[64] and evidently also passed to the Rawsons. A modus of 3d. a year was paid from each bovate for the hay growing in the open fields in the 1540s, and then and later the hay tithes were let for 12s. a year in all.[65] John Rawson held undefined tithes at Fitling by 1616,[66] and he or another John Rawson received 100 a. for the corn, wool, and lamb tithes at inclosure in 1640.[67] In 1650 the impropriators were William Rawson and Richard Wood, a Hull alderman, and the annual value of the tithes was put at £25.[68] The tithes were evidently reckoned to have been sold to the other proprietors in 1640, and they remained

[40] H.U.L., DDHO/36/5 (f, h), 30; above, this section (Humbleton manor). Cf. P.R.O., CP 25(2)/520/6 Chas. I Hil. [no. 36].
[41] H.U.L., DDHO/36/48–9, 55; B.I.H.R., TER. H. Humbleton 1716.
[42] H.U.L., DDHO/36/59.
[43] E.R.A.O., PE/68/T.2.
[44] P.R.O., SC 6/Hen. VIII/2022, m. 79.
[45] H.U.L., DDHO/28/3.
[46] T.E.R.A.S. iv. 53; Yorks. Royalist Composition Papers, i (Y.A.S. Rec. Ser. xv), pp. 4, 6.
[47] P.R.O., C 66/1662, mm. 1–10; H.U.L., DDHO/36/30, 53; above, this section (Humbleton rectory).
[48] H.U.L., DDHO/36/48–9, 55.
[49] R.D.B., N/436/907.
[50] E.R.A.O., DDCK/32/26.
[51] P.R.O., SC 6/Hen. VIII/2022, m. 79.
[52] H.U.L., DDGE/6/10.
[53] P.R.O., CP 25(2)/521/8 Chas. I Mic. pt. 3 [no. 26]; Yorks. Fines, 1603–14, 114.
[54] P.R.O., CP 25(2)/524/15 Chas. I Mich. pt. 1, [no. 7].
[55] Ibid. CP 25(2)/525/23 Chas. I East. [no. 37].
[56] T.E.R.A.S. iv. 53. Cf. Yorks. Royalist Composition

Papers, i (Y.A.S. Rec. Ser. xv), p. 6.
[57] P.R.O., CP 25(2)/613/1653 East. [fifth from end].
[58] B.I.H.R., TER. H. Humbleton 1716.
[59] Ibid. ER. V./Ret. 2, f. 14v.
[60] P.R.O., CP 25(2)/1257/32 Geo. II East. no. 567a. For the Appleyards, Poulson, Holderness, ii. 364–5.
[61] R.D.B. CQ/218/15; for the Bells, Poulson, Holderness, ii. 74; memorials in Elstronwick church.
[62] E.R.A.O., QDR/2/12; ibid. DDCC/14/44; P.R.O., E 310/33/200, f. 65; Cal. Pat. 1377–81, 617; 1575–8, p. 52; T.E.R.A.S. iv. 53; V.C.H. Yorks. E.R. v. 13, 18.
[63] P.R.O., C 66/1662, mm. 1–10; H.U.L., DDHO/36/53; above, this section (Humbleton rectory).
[64] P.R.O., C 66/1810, mm. 11–42. Ibid. SC 6/Hen. VIII/2022, m. 79.
[65] Ibid. E 318/42/2263; ibid. SC 6/Hen. VIII/2022, m. 79; B.I.H.R., CP. G. 368.
[66] Yorks. Fines, 1614–25, 65.
[67] E.R.A.O., DDCC/39/3. The Rawsons had been lessees of the corn, hay, wool, and lamb tithes in the 16th century: B.I.H.R., CP. G. 368; Cal. Pat. 1572–5, p. 304.
[68] P.R.O., C 94/3, f. 68. Cf. Yorks. Royalist Composition Papers, i (Y.A.S. Rec. Ser. xv), p. 6.

uncommuted until dealt with by awards of 1844 and 1848 and apportionment in the latter year. Most of the corn, hay, wool, and lamb tithes, from 1,459 a. in all, were merged by eleven proprietors before commutation; those remaining, from just 18 a., were then commuted for a rent charge of £2 16s. a year.[69]

FLINTON. Thornton college's rectorial estate in Flinton was let for just over £5 a year in the 1540s.[70] The corn and hay tithes of Flinton were granted by the Crown in fee farm to Roger Manners in 1578, and sold by him to (Sir) Marmaduke Grimston in 1587.[71] They later descended with Flinton manor in the Grimstons and their successors.[72] William Grimston's tithes there were worth £20 a year in 1650 and £35 in 1657.[73] At inclosure in 1752, Sir Robert Hildyard, Bt., released his right to corn and hay tithes from the lands of the other proprietors in return for an unspecified area of land.[74] The wool and lamb tithes of Flinton had been sold in 1604 by the Crown to Sir Henry Lindley and John Starkey,[75] who re-sold them in 1607 to Marmaduke Rawson.[76] They later passed, with those in Humbleton, to the Thompsons and their heirs, the Hothams.[77] The tithes of Flinton township were commuted by award of 1844 and apportionment of 1845. Beaumont Hotham, Lord Hotham, was awarded a rent charge of £24 10s. 9d. a year for the wool and lamb tithes. The corn and hay tithes had all been merged before commutation, mostly by Mrs. Hildyard.[78]

The gorse tithes of Humbleton and Flinton were included in the grant to Francis Morrice and Francis Phillips in 1609.[79] Some were later bought by Marmaduke Rawson, and sold in 1637 by his son Robert to Stephen Thompson.[80]

ECONOMIC HISTORY. COMMON LANDS AND INCLOSURE. *Humbleton.* The open fields at Humbleton lay east and west of the village, and evidently included common meadow land.[81] East field may have been divided into a northern and southern field: a list of 'closes or grounds', apparently made in the mid 17th century, includes, besides the 56-a. West field, South field and High South field, both of c. 65 a.[82] The chief common pasture was Humbleton moor.[83] Beast gates 'in both winter and summer' and the right to crop gorse there were let by the Crown,

as lord of the manor, in the 16th and 17th centuries.[84] By the 17th century Humbleton moor may have comprised two parts, Great moor, of 219 a., and 74 a. near the later Humbleton Grange Farm variously known as Gartham, Gardam, or South moor.[85]

Much of the township may have been inclosed by the early 16th century, when the manorial closes were let for over £3 a year.[86] Of the commonable lands remaining, the open fields and some of the pastures were probably inclosed after the sale of the manor in the early 17th century. By 1622 Southend farm had been 'enclosed, diked, and fenced from the townfields of Humbleton';[87] a South moor close, of c. 40 a., was recorded in 1634,[88] and by 1654 the manorial estate included a West field close, of 80 a., and another close containing c. 70 a.[89] The rest of the pasture land was dealt with c. 1700, Great moor being described as 'newly inclosed' in 1709.[90]

Danthorpe. North and South fields were named c. 1300, and the latter was said to contain 15 bovates. The common meadow land lay in the fields; in the northern field there were pieces at Mikelmargote, Dankeldale, Wandales, Forlands, and West Langdale, and in South field at West Foss.[91] The common pasture of the township was called New close in 1640 and later. It evidently lay in the east of the township, adjoining Fitling's Infield.[92] New close was also described as a 'whinny' pasture, presumably on account of the whins, or furze, growing there, and it was perhaps because of the furze crops that entitlement in the pasture was expressed both in terms of beast gates and area, the seigneurial holding including 22 beast gates or c. 30 a.[93]

Danthorpe was inclosed in 1735 by agreement between the eight proprietors. North field then contained 247 a., South field 199 a., and New close 70 a. John Thorpe, lord of the manor, was allotted 214 a., Roger Hall 106 a., and St. John's college, Cambridge, 105 a.; there were five other allotments, ranging from 3 a. to 43 a.[94] Ridge and furrow was evident in front of Danthorpe Hall in 1998.

Elstronwick. From the 17th century there were two open fields in Elstronwick, lying north and south of the village and containing in all 32 bovates.[95] Each bovate comprised on average 24 a.,

[69] E.R.A.O., PE/68/T.4.
[70] P.R.O., SC 6/Hen. VIII/2022, m. 79.
[71] E.R.A.O., DDHI, accession 1141 (deed 1587); *Cal. Pat.* 1578–80, p. 1.
[72] P.R.O., C 78/332, no. 12; CP 25(2)/761/19–20 Chas. II Hil. [last but one]; E.R.A.O., PE/68/3, s.v. note of 1765; *Yorks. Fines, 1614–25,* 12.
[73] E.R.A.O., DDHI, accession 1141 (particulars of estate, [1657]); *T.E.R.A.S.* iv. 53. Cf. *Yorks. Royalist Composition Papers,* i (Y.A.S Rec. Ser. xv), p. 6.
[74] E.R.A.O., DDCC/142/4.
[75] P.R.O., C 66/1662, mm. 1–10.
[76] H.U.L., DDHO/36/53. Cf. *Cal. Pat.* 1572–5, p. 304.
[77] H.U.L., DDHO/36/30, 48–9, 55; DDCV(2)/53/3; above, this section (Humbleton rectory).
[78] E.R.A.O., PE/68/T.5.
[79] P.R.O., C 66/1810, mm. 11–42.
[80] H.U.L., DDHO/36/54.
[81] Ibid. DDHO/36/15; *Cal. Pat.* 1566–9, p. 139.
[82] H.U.L., DDHO/36/26.
[83] *Cal. Pat.* 1563–6, pp. 158–9. Cf. P.R.O., SC 6/Hen. VIII/2022, m. 81.
[84] H.U.L., DDHO/36/1, 15, 19; P.R.O., E 310/29/172, f. 33.
[85] H.U.L., DDHO/36/26, 47. For the name Gartham, *Cal. Pat.* 1563–6, p. 406.
[86] *Cal. Pat.* 1566–9, p. 139.
[87] H.U.L., DDHO/36/5 (f).
[88] Ibid. DDHO/36/23.
[89] Ibid. DDHO/71/38.　　[90] Ibid. DDHO/36/47
[91] *Cal. Close,* 1302–7, 96–8.
[92] E.R.A.O., DDCC/39/3.
[93] Ibid. QDB/3, pp. 6–7; R.D.B., N/436/907.
[94] R.D.B., N/436/907.
[95] P.R.O., E 134/8 Chas. I Mich./43; B.I.H.R., TER. H. Humbleton 1726; below, this section.

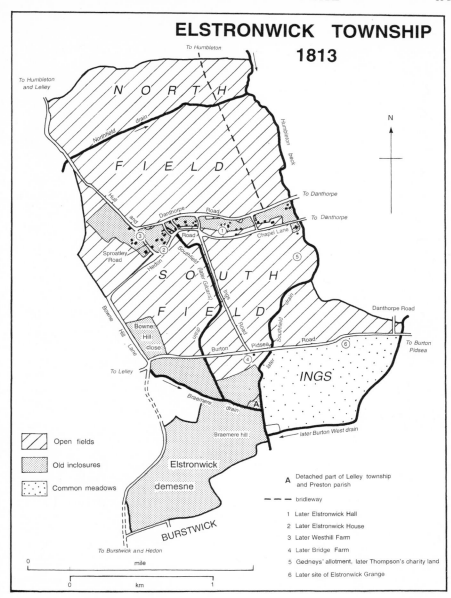

**ELSTRONWICK TOWNSHIP
1813**

Open fields

Old inclosures

Common meadows

A Detached part of Lelley township
   and Preston parish
- - - bridleway
1 Later Elstronwick Hall
2 Later Elstronwick House
3 Later Westhill Farm
4 Later Bridge Farm
5 Gedneys' allotment, later Thompson's charity land
6 Later site of Elstronwick Grange

evenly divided between the two fields, and 4 a. in a meadow called Ings.[96] The 'fields' evidently also included other meadow land and pieces of pasture: in the mid 17th century among the grounds on the north side of the village were a ley at Danke hill and a 'wand', probably a measured piece of meadow land, in the Maske, while to the south leys were mentioned in Manmer carr and West carr, and wands at Burton ends and in Ricgaite marre, Howle carr, and Ings.[97]

Elstronwick was inclosed in 1813 under an Act of 1806.[98] Allotments totalled 893 a., of which 400 a. came from North field, 362 a. from South field, and 119 a. from Ings; old inclosures involved in exchanges accounted for the remaining 12 a. One or more families called Bell

received the largest allotments. Robert and James Bell, both of Roos, were awarded 177 a. and 74 a. respectively, the trustees of John Bell (d. 1809) 145 a., Frances Bell, his widow, 93 a., and John Bell the younger 44 a.[99] Susanna Houblon and the other heirs of Michael Newton, lords of Elstronwick manor, were allotted 99 a., and the vicar of Humbleton received 51 a. for his glebe and tithes. There were two other allotments of c. 55 a., one of 26 a., six of 5–20 a., and two of less than 5 a.

Fitling. Fitling's East field was recorded in 1367 and again, with West field, in 1611.[1] A very small area of the tillage had been inclosed for pasture by Peter Hildyard in the late 15th century,[2] and in 1640 the rest was inclosed by agreement

96 Poulson, *Holderness*, ii. 72.
97 H.U.L., DAS/7/3, s.vv. 16 Oct. 1649; 3 Oct. 1653.
98 46 Geo. III, c. 9 (Local and Personal, not printed); R.D.B., CQ/218/15; E.R.A.O., IA. Elstronwick.

99 For the Bells, memorials in Elstronwick church.
1 P.R.O., E 178/4832; Poulson, *Holderness*, i. 123.
2 *Trans. R. Hist. S.* N.S. vi. 288–9; vii. 253.

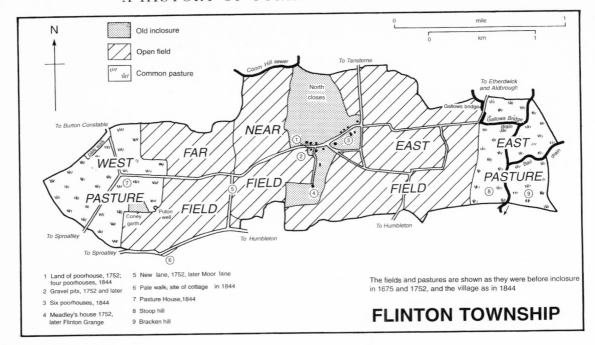

N

Old inclosure
Open field
Common pasture

0 mile 1
0 km 1

Coom Hill sewer
To Tansterne
North closes
To Etherdwick and Aldbrough
To Burton Constable
Gallows bridge
Gallows Bridge drain
NEAR
FAR
EAST
EAST
WEST
FIELD
FIELD
PASTURE
PASTURE
FIELD
Bail drain
To Sproatley
Coney garth
Puton well
To Humbleton
To Humbleton
To Sproatley

1 Land of poorhouse, 1752; four poorhouses, 1844
2 Gravel pits, 1752 and later
3 Six poorhouses, 1844
4 Meadley's house 1752, later Flinton Grange

5 New lane, 1752, later Moor lane
6 Pale walk, site of cottage in 1844
7 Pasture House, 1844
8 Stoop hill
9 Bracken hill

The fields and pastures are shown as they were before inclosure in 1675 and 1752, and the village as in 1844

FLINTON TOWNSHIP

between the 'lords of the manors and freeholders'.[3] More than 1,237 a. were allotted.[4] There were then four fields, of which West field contained 413 a., North field 398 a., East field 380 a., and Infield more than 47 a. The Infield lay in the south of the township, adjoining Danthorpe. Before inclosure the tillage included narrow, and presumably also broad, lands.[5] Allotments were made to c. 20 proprietors in 1640.[6] John Rawson and Henry Hildyard, both lords of manors, received 359 a. and 352 a. respectively, and William Kendall 195 a. There were besides one allotment of 63 a., four of 20–49 a. each, ten of 5–19 a., and one of 2 a. The remaining allotment was of more than 49 a. It had been alleged in 1600 that a farmer kept a flock of 200 sheep in Fitling,[7] and by 1662 at least 200 a. of arable land there had been 'lately' converted to pasture.[8]

The common meadows and pastures were evidently regarded as parts of the fields, and were not separately described in 1640. The 'main ings of Fitling' had been mentioned in the 1540s, but it was then denied that hay was grown anywhere in the township except on the arable strips, presumably when that ground was being fallowed.[9] That there were some common meadows is, however, suggested by later references to a 'wandale', or measured strip of meadow land, in Aldbrough Foss, and to leys and other land in the Green, or Greens,[10] and Inholmes.[11] The chief of Fitling's common pastures was probably

that called Fitling moor in 1611 and, probably anachronistically, Fitling Great pasture in 1709. It seems to have lain in the north-west of the township, adjoining Flinton's pasture on Bracken hill.[12] Moorland in or near West field was only referred to incidentally at inclosure in 1640,[13] but Moor and Bracken Hill closes were recorded later in the century. In 1653 the former West field included land in a close called Bracken Hill, and between 1725 and 1729 a Bracken Hill close containing c. 100 a. was divided into smaller fields.[14]

Flinton. In 1397 Flinton's fields were named as East and West fields, and strips also then lay in 'each field of Monkplattes'.[15] A pasture said to belong to Thornton abbey seems to have provided stinted grazing for other proprietors in 1443,[16] and there were later two common pastures in Flinton, at the east and west ends of the township. East pasture, which included Bracken hill, seems to have lain against Fitling's main common pasture.[17]

By 1517 the tillage at Flinton had been reduced by the inclosure of c. 65 a., all or most of which had been converted to pasture.[18] Larger-scale inclosures were effected in the 17th and 18th centuries. The eastern half of Flinton was dealt with by agreement of 1674 and award of 1675. East field then contained 395 a., and East pasture, which was said to be 'already inclosed', 163 a. Christopher Hildyard was

3 The following is based on E.R.A.O., DDCC/39/3–4. Cf. Poulson, *Holderness*, ii. 78.
4 The source is damaged and the detail of one of the allotments is missing.
5 Cf. below, Withernwick, econ. hist.
6 One or two allottees may have been named twice: cf. Elizabeth Meadley, Elizabeth Iveson.
7 B.I.H.R., CP. H. 53.
8 H.U.L., DDHO/70/55.
9 B.I.H.R., CP. G. 368.
10 R.D.B., E/146/257; P.R.O., E 310/28/166, f. 18.

11 E.R.A.O., DDCC/39/4.
12 H.U.L., DDHO/36/47; P.R.O., E 178/4832.
13 E.R.A.O., DDCC/39/3; O.S. Map 6", Yorks. CCXXVII, CCXXVIII (1855 edn.).
14 E.R.A.O., DDCC/39/4; H.U.L., DDHO/36/27; DDSY/19/6, 12.
15 E.R.A.O., DDCC/111/15.
16 *Cal. Pat.* 1441–6, 99–100, 147.
17 O.S. Map 6", Yorks. CCXXVII, CCXXVIII (1855 edn.); above and below, this section.
18 *Trans. R. Hist. S.* N.S. vi. 288–9; vii. 250.

awarded 397 a., Robert Buck 63 a., and there were two allotments of just under 50 a. Seven 'cotcher' gates, enjoyed by cottagers in East field when it was fallowed every other year, were then extinguished.[19] The rest of the township was inclosed under an agreement of 1751 by award of 1752. There were then two open fields, Near, or Hither, and Far fields, comprising 42½ bovates and odd lands, and presumably representing the earlier West field. Besides tillage, the fields included pieces of grassland.[20] Among the old inclosures was the 4-a. Coney garth, which had evidently been taken in from West pasture. The allotments totalled 605 a., of which 243 a. came from Far field, 196 a. from Near field, and 166 a. from West pasture. Sir Robert Hildyard, Bt., lord of the manor and tithe-owner, was awarded 512 a.; there was also one allotment of 55 a., one of 25 a., one of 10 a., and two of less than 5 a.[21]

WOODLAND. Humbleton manor included an unknown area of woodland in the mid 16th century.[22] In Fitling a 5-a. close adjoining the manor house's moat was called the Wood in 1662, and in 1786 c. 30 a. in the south-west corner of the township lay in Great and Little Wood closes.[23] Humbleton township was described as well-wooded in the mid 19th century,[24] but the area of woodland returned was only 13 a. for the whole parish in 1905 and 6.4 ha. (16 a.) for Humbleton and Elstronwick civil parishes in 1987.[25]

TENURES AND FARMS TO c. 1800. *Humbleton.* Tenants on Humbleton manor owed poultry rents, and in the 16th and 17th centuries holdings were charged with harvesting works called sickle boons, presumably by then long commuted.[26]

Danthorpe. In 1086 one ploughland and a bordar were recorded on the archbishop's estate at Danthorpe.[27] Much of the land there was held in demesne c. 1300.[28]

Elstronwick. On the chief manor of Elstronwick most of the income of £8 in 1324–5 came from the rents of the free and customary tenants, and a small sum from chevage levied on the latter.[29] The demesne was concentrated in the south of the township, adjoining or close to that of

Burstwick manor.[30] It was probably farmed from Burstwick, and indeed was sometimes later described as part of the superior manor's demesne.[31] Direct exploitation of much of 'Burstwick's' demesne had been given up by the end of the 13th century, and in the 1320s tenants of Elstronwick were among those leasing c. 300 a. of former demesne land; in 1341–2 their share was specified as 4–5 bovates, for which they paid £6 a year.[32] The grounds were said to have been let at first as copyhold[33] but by the 1650s they were freehold; the former demesne was then said to have been 'lately inclosed', and comprised Elstronwick Great and Little Burstwick fields, and Bramare, Bownehill, and Sandwath closes,[34] of which Bramare was used as meadow.[35] In 1813 those closes contained 140 a.[36]

In the early 19th century Elstronwick manor included c. 360 a. of copyhold.[37] Most of the land was enfranchised between 1866 and 1935.[38]

Fitling. The Hospitallers' manor included no demesne land in 1539–40, when, besides unquantified land, free tenants held 8 houses and almost 1 carucate, customary tenants 4 houses and ½ carucate, and tenants at will the chief house, 2 others, and 1 bovate.[39]

Flinton. The archbishop had ½ ploughland at Flinton in 1086, and three villeins and a bordar then worked one plough on the holding.[40] Flinton lay in ten holdings in the 1650s, one farm including 1 carucate, two 4 or 5 bovates each, five 1–2 bovates each, one ½ bovate, and one holding having no open-field land.[41]

LATER AGRICULTURE. In 1801 the parish, including Elstronwick chapelry, was reckoned to have c. 1,880 a. under crops,[42] and the parish was later chiefly given over to arable farming. Humbleton, Danthorpe, Fitling, and Flinton townships together had 3,618 a. of arable land and 1,388 a. of grassland in the 1840s,[43] and in 1905 the whole parish was said to contain 3,715 a. of arable land and 1,840 a. of grassland.[44] The area returned for Humbleton and Elstronwick civil parishes in 1987 evidently also included land of a neighbouring parish or parishes; of the 2,326.7 ha. (5,749 a.), 2,208.6 ha. (5,458 a.) were arable land, including 40.8 ha. (101 a.) used for vegetables, and 93.2 ha. (230 a.)

[19] E.R.A.O., DDHI, accession 1141.
[20] Ibid. DDCC/141/70.
[21] Ibid. DDCC/142/4; copy at R.D.B., B/381/55. Map at E.R.A.O., DDHI, accession 1141.
[22] E.R.A.O., DDCC/139/65.
[23] Ibid. DDX/698/8; H.U.L., DDHO/70/55; R.D.B., BL/277/422.
[24] Sheahan and Whellan, *Hist. York & E.R.* ii. 369.
[25] Acreage Returns, 1905; inf. from Min. of Agric, Fish. & Food, Beverley, 1990.
[26] H.U.L., DDHO/36/15; P.R.O., C 66/1999, no. 3; ibid. E 310/31/185, f. 18; E 318/42/2263.
[27] *V.C.H. Yorks.* ii. 216.
[28] *Yorks. Inq.* iii, pp. 123–4.
[29] P.R.O., SC 6/1080/10, m. 8.
[30] O.S. Map 6", Yorks. CCXXVII (1855 edn.).
[31] E.R.A.O., DDCC/14/44. Reference to 1 bovate of demesne land 'of Ridgmont in Elstronwick' may mean that the Elstronwick demesne was farmed from Ridgmont, in Burstwick: E.R.A.O., DDCC/15/1, s.v. Oct. 1368.
[32] P.R.O., SC 6/1079/14, m. 1; SC 6/1079/17, m. 2; SC 6/1080/10, m. 1; SC 6/1082/3, m. 7.
[33] E.R.A.O., DDCC/139/7.
[34] Ibid. DDCC/14/44.
[35] Ibid. DDBV/16/1. For the name, *P.N. Yorks. E.R.* (E.P.N.S.), 53.
[36] R.D.B., CQ/218/15.
[37] Ibid. CQ/218/15; CW/211/306; H.U.L., DAS/7/28. Cf. Poulson, *Holderness*, ii. 72.
[38] H.U.L., DAS/7/8, p. 171 etc.; R.D.B., 301/35/24; 494/638/500.
[39] *Miscellanea*, iv (Y.A.S. Rec. Ser. xciv), 96–7.
[40] *V.C.H. Yorks.* ii. 216.
[41] E.R.A.O., DDHI, accession 1141 (particulars of estate [1657]).
[42] P.R.O., HO 67/26/139, 228.
[43] E.R.A.O., PE/68/T.2, 4–5; ibid. DDCK/32/26.
[44] The total area returned seems to omit c. 700 a. of the parish: Acreage Returns, 1905; above, intro. [area]. Cf. [1st] Land Util. Surv. Map, sheet 33–4.

grassland. More than 16,000 pigs and *c.* 820 sheep were then kept.[45] In 1998 Heron's farm at Flinton was given over to the rearing of game birds.

In the mid 19th century there were nearly 40 farms in the parish, including seven small holdings.[46] Danthorpe had three farms, Humbleton and Flinton each had about six, but Fitling, which had been held by many proprietors since at least the 17th century,[47] and Elstronwick had eleven farms each. Fourteen of the farms were of 150 a. or more in 1851, and Hall farm at Danthorpe was then of over 600 a. and was later the only farm recorded there. In the 1920s and 1930s half of the *c.* 30 farms were of 150 a. or more. Houses for smallholders or cowkeepers had been built in Humbleton village by the Hothams *c.* 1890,[48] and two cowkeepers were recorded there in 1892 and two smallholders in the 1920s and 1930s. At Elstronwick and Fitling there were up to five cowkeepers, and a smallholder worked in Elstronwick in 1937. There had been a market gardener at Elstronwick and two 'gardeners' at Flinton in 1851, and *c.* 50 a. in Danthorpe was used for market gardening in the 1930s and 1940s.[49] In 1987 twenty holdings were recorded under Humbleton and Elstronwick civil parishes; of those, five were of 200–499 ha. (494–1,233 a.) each, three of 100–199 ha. (247–492 a.) each, two of 50–99 ha. (124–245 a.) each, five of 10–49 ha. (25–121 a.) each, and five of less than 10 ha. each.[50]

MARKET. A market was evidently held at Humbleton in the mid 16th century, perhaps in continuance of one established by Thornton abbey. Timber from the Crown's woods there was then said to have been offered for the building of a market hall for the fishermen and butchers frequenting it.[51]

INDUSTRY, TRADE, AND PROFESSIONAL ACTIVITY. In 1687 a Drypool brickmaker agreed to make 200,000 bricks at Humbleton for Francis Thompson, who was to provide the kiln.[52] Brick garth and Brickyard close at Humbleton were recorded later.[53] Brick-making in Danthorpe is also suggested by the field-names Brick close and Brick garth.[54] Small amounts of sand and gravel have been dug from

pits in Humbleton, Elstronwick, Fitling, and Flinton.[55] Commercial activity probably depended largely on the carriers to Hull, but Humbleton, Elstronwick, Fitling, and Flinton also each had a shop in the 19th century; only that in Humbleton was still listed in 1937.[56] A small shop later run at Elstronwick was given up *c.* 1995,[57] but the associated Post Office remained in 1999. Threshing machines were made in Humbleton and exported to Russia *c.* 1850.[58] A haulage contractor worked from Elstronwick in the 1930s,[59] and in 1999 there was a scrapyard there. An architectural practice was being conducted at Flinton in 1998.

MILLS. *Humbleton.* In 1367 the dam of an existing or former water mill on Humbleton beck was mentioned.[60] The name Mill close, recorded in 1709,[61] may relate to that mill or to the windmill which, before the 16th century, stood on Mill hill south-west of the church.[62]

Danthorpe. A mill at Danthorpe which had fallen down or been demolished by 1300[63] was evidently rebuilt on the same or another site, a windmill being recorded there in 1335[64] and again *c.* 1600.[65] In 1852 Danthorpe windmill stood on the north side of the hamlet, close to the beck.[66] It was later assisted by steam. In or soon after 1892 the mill evidently ceased to operate, and was demolished.[67] The miller's house remained in 1998.

Elstronwick. There was a mill at Elstronwick *c.* 1300,[68] and presumably in 1502, when a mill-reeve was elected for the village.[69] Mill bridge, located on the north side of the village in 1720, was perhaps named from the mill just over the boundary in Lelley, in Preston.[70]

Fitling. The Hospitallers had a windmill at Fitling in 1338,[71] the same or another was recorded in 1607,[72] and *c.* 1670 the miller was allegedly taking excessive tolls.[73] Mill, or Mill field, close was mentioned from 1669.[74]

Flinton. There was a windmill on the Twyers' estate at Flinton in 1334,[75] and one on the manor of the Grimstons in the 16th and 17th centuries.[76]

45 Inf. from Min. of Agric, Fish. & Food, Beverley, 1990; cf. above, intro. [areas].
46 Para. based on P.R.O., HO 107/2365; directories.
47 E.R.A.O., DDCC/39/3–4; DDX/595/53.
48 H.U.L., DDHO(3)/49/51, 81.
49 R.D.B., 538/224/176; 538/225/177; 650/143/126; 768/164/138.
50 Inf. from Min. of Agric, Fish. & Food.
51 E.R.A.O., DDCC/139/65.
52 H.U.L., DDHO/36/36. The bricks were probably for the building of Humbleton Grange Farm: ibid. DDHO/36/39.
53 Ibid. DDHO/36/47, 82.
54 Ibid. DRA/337; R.D.B., 127/312/286.
55 B.I.H.R., TER. H. Humbleton 1716; O.S. Map 6″, Yorks. CCXXVII, CCXXVIII (1855 edn.).
56 Directories.   57 Local inf.
58 P.R.O., HO 107/2365; *Hull Advertiser*, 10 Aug. 1849.
59 Directories.
60 Poulson, *Holderness*, i. 124.
61 H.U.L., DDHO/36/47.

62 P.R.O., E 318/42/2263; O.S. Map 6″, Yorks. CCXXVII (1855 edn.).
63 *Yorks. Inq.* iii, p. 124.
64 *Cal. Inq. p.m.* vii, p. 459.
65 P.R.O., C 142/243, no. 46; E.R.A.O., DDCC/70/3; *Yorks. Fines, 1603–14*, 88.
66 O.S. Map 6″, Yorks. CCXXVII (1855 edn.).
67 Directories; O.S. Map 1/2,500, Yorks. CCXXVII. 12 (1891 and 1910 edns.).
68 P.R.O., SC 6/1079/13; SC 6/1079/17, m. 8d.
69 E.R.A.O., DDCC/15/18.
70 H.U.L., DAS/7/5, s.v. May 1720; O.S. Map 6″, Yorks. CCXXVII (1855 edn.); *V.C.H. Yorks. E.R.* v. 197.
71 *Knights Hospitallers in Eng.* (Camd. Soc. lxv), 49.
72 *Yorks. Fines, 1603–14*, 65.
73 E.R.A.O., DDX/595/20, 26, etc.
74 H.U.L., DDSY/27/11; R.D.B., X/387/894; 127/312/286.
75 *Cal. Inq. p.m.* vii, pp. 424–5.
76 P.R.O., C 142/69, no. 142; E.R.A.O., DDHI, accession 1141 (deed 1657).

LOCAL GOVERNMENT. In the 1290s the abbot of Thornton claimed jurisdiction and freedom from royal taxation in Humbleton and Flinton under a charter of Richard I, and the profits of the ale assize by prescription.[77] The former abbey's manor court of Humbleton was referred to in the 16th and 17th centuries.[78]

ELSTRONWICK. The view of frankpledge and other regulation at Elstronwick belonged to Burstwick manor court, for which rolls survive from 1368–1925.[79] Besides the transferring of copyhold, the court was concerned with debt pleas, affrays, and breaches of the ale assize in Elstronwick.[80] Officers elected in the court at Burstwick for Elstronwick, and sometimes also for neighbouring Lelley, in Preston, included 1–2 constables, 2 aletasters, 1–2 mill-reeves, and 1–2 reeves, or pennygraves. The pinder at Elstronwick was also mentioned in 1547, and 2 bylawmen were appointed in 1655.[81] The office of pennygrave was performed by the holders of bovates in rotation in the 18th century.[82]

A court was also kept on the manor belonging to the Wartons and their successors. Surviving records include court rolls for 1647–1935.[83] View of frankpledge was also claimed for the Wartons' court; its other business included the supervision of the ale assize, and the regulation of agriculture and drainage in Elstronwick. The court met twice a year in the 17th and early 18th century; by the mid 18th century there seems to have been little business apart from conveying copyhold, however, and meetings were then and later held every few years, and after 1862 not at all. In the earlier 19th century the meeting place was a house in the village.[84] Up to 4 bylawmen, 2 overseers of highways, 2 aletasters, 2 affeerors, 1–2 pennygraves, 1 pinder, and 1 constable were appointed in the court.

FITLING. The view of frankpledge in Fitling was claimed to belong both to the Hildyards' manor[85] and to that of the Hospitallers' successors. Estreats, other brief records of court proceedings, and call rolls of the latter manor survive from 1582 to 1753.[86] The court had testamentary jurisdiction over its tenants, and its records include some wills and inventories;[87] presumably on that account, the court was occasionally said to be that of the 'fee franchise'.[88] The other business of the court, which was generally held at the manor house, included breaches of the bread and ale assize, and the usual regulation of drainage and agriculture. Meetings were evidently held twice a year in the 17th and 18th centuries. Officers appointed in the court included 1 constable for Fitling, 2 affeerors, and, in 1622, 4 bylawmen. After the inclosure of Fitling in 1640, agricultural regulation in Burton Pidsea may have become the court's chief concern.[89] Stocks recorded in 1700 were perhaps in Fitling, and the township was also said to be where the sheriff's tourn in Holderness met.[90]

FLINTON. A minute of proceedings in Flinton manor court in 1717 suggests that the court, which had leet jurisdiction, was then primarily concerned with local drainage. Two affeerors were sworn there.[91]

DANTHORPE. A manor court was said to have been held in Danthorpe Hall every three or four years until c. 1820.[92]

Surviving parish records include churchwardens' accounts for Humbleton from 1734,[93] chapelwardens' accounts for Elstronwick from 1753,[94] accounts of the surveyors of highways from 1798,[95] and Elstronwick constables' accounts from 1767.[96] There is also a book containing assessments and accounts of the overseer of the poor and the chapelwarden from 1654 to 1707.[97]

Humbleton, Fitling, and Flinton each had a poorhouse in the mid 18th century,[98] and in the 1840s the respective overseers held seven cottages at Humbleton, four cottages and garths at Fitling, ten cottages at Flinton, and a garden at Danthorpe.[99] At Elstronwick 4 paupers were relieved in the mid 17th century, and a poorhouse was built c. 1655;[1] the house was evidently replaced later by three cottages.[2] In 1802–3 permanent out-relief was given to 4 people there and 9 were helped occasionally; between 1812 and 1815 the numbers were respectively 10–11 and 2–3. Flinton relieved 9 regularly and 1 occasionally in the earlier period, and respectively 10–11 and up to 6 between 1812 and 1815. Humbleton and Fitling townships each relieved up to 8 people, and Danthorpe 1–2 in the early 19th century.[3] In 1837 Humbleton and the other townships joined Skirlaugh poor-law union.[4]

77 *Yorks. Hund. and Quo Warr. R.* (Y.A.S. Rec. Ser. cli), 215–16.
78 P.R.O., SC 6/Hen. VIII/2022, m. 81d.; ibid. C 66/1999, no. 3.
79 E.R.A.O., DDCC/15/1–62; DDCC(2)/80; P.R.O., SC 6/1084/5, m. 2.
80 E.R.A.O., DDCC/15/2, s.vv. Sept. 1381; Jan. 1382; DDCC/15/9, s.v. Nov. 1460; DDCC/15/23, s.v. Aug. 1547.
81 Ibid. DDCC/15/2, s.v. Sept. 1381; DDCC/15/9, s.v. Oct. 1460; DDCC/15/18, s.v. Oct. 1502; DDCC/15/23, s.v. Oct. 1547; DDCC/15/36, s.v. Oct. 1655; DDCC/15/41, s.vv. Oct. 1690; July 1701.
82 Poulson, *Holderness,* ii. 72.
83 H.U.L., DAS/7/3–8.
84 Poulson, *Holderness,* ii. 73.
85 H.U.L., DDHO/70/55.
86 E.R.A.O., DDX/595/1–142.
87 See also, ibid. DDX/595/144–5.

88 Ibid. DDX/595/54.
89 Above, Burton Pidsea, econ. hist., loc. govt.
90 Poulson, *Holderness,* ii. 77.
91 H.U.L., DDMC/34/1.
92 Ibid. DDHO(3)/7/5; Poulson, *Holderness,* ii. 72.
93 E.R.A.O., PE/68/71–2.
94 Ibid. PE/68/89.   95 Ibid. PE/68/78.
96 Formerly at E.R.A.O., DDX/360/1, returned to G. R. Norrison, Burstwick.
97 H.U.L., DAS/7/1.
98 E.R.A.O., PE/68/71; ibid. DDHI, accession 1141 (inclosure map); R.D.B., AM/393/635.
99 E.R.A.O., PE/68/T.2, 4–5; ibid. DDCK/32/26; Poulson, *Holderness,* ii. 70.
1 H.U.L., DAS/7/1.
2 Below, educ.; charities.
3 *Poor Law Abstract, 1804,* pp. 592–3; *1818,* pp. 520–3.
4 *3rd Rep. Poor Law Com.* 170.

They remained in Skirlaugh rural district until 1935, when, as the enlarged civil parishes of Humbleton, Elstronwick, and East Garton, they were incorporated into the new rural district of Holderness. From 1974 they were parts of the Holderness district of Humberside.[5] In 1996 Humbleton, Elstronwick, and East Garton parishes became part of a new East Riding unitary area.[6]

CHURCHES. In 1086 there was a church and a priest at 'Foston', which may have been in Humbleton parish,[7] and there was certainly a church at Humbleton by the 12th century. The living became a vicarage. Chapels were built at Fitling and Elstronwick in the Middle Ages. Fitling chapel seems to have had only a short existence, but Elstronwick chapel, later church, survived the religious changes of the 16th century, and was later held with Humbleton.[8] In 1961 the benefice of Humbleton with Elstronwick was united with that of Burton Pidsea, but the two parishes were left separate.[9]

HUMBLETON. The first certain reference to Humbleton church is found in William de Scures's gift of Humbleton village and its church to Thornton abbey (Lincs.), which was made probably in the 1150s or 1160s and certainly before 1190.[10] The church was appropriated to Thornton in or about 1222,[11] and a vicarage was ordained, apparently between 1291 and 1301, when the vicar was first mentioned.[12]

The patronage of Humbleton vicarage belonged to Thornton abbey until its dissolution in 1539,[13] and thereafter to the Crown. The archbishop of York had collated in 1483, by lapse, and did so again in 1613, and in 1538 and 1540 turns were exercised by grantees of the abbey.[14] The Crown and the dean and chapter of York, as patron of Burton Pidsea, were given alternate presentations to the united benefice in 1961.[15]

Humbleton church was valued at £16 a year in 1291.[16] In 1308 Thornton abbey was called to account by the archbishop over the insufficiency of the vicar's portion.[17] The net value of the vicarage was given as £7 a year in 1526,[18]

and £10 1s. 0½d. in 1535, after payment of a pension of 13s. 4d. to Thornton abbey.[19] In 1650 the improved annual value was £13 6s. 4d.[20] The poor living was augmented in 1748, 1771, and 1802, on each occasion with £200 Bounty money by lot,[21] and was also assisted from local charities. William Tymperon, by will proved in 1729, charged his estate at Aldbrough with the payment of £4 a year to the incumbent at Humbleton; that sum was increased to £10 by Chancery decree of 1824 and to £15 by 1853, reduced to £12 10s. in 1928, but restored to £15 by the 1950s.[22] The incumbent also received £1 a year from Heron's charity for an annual sermon, and the same amount from the constable of Humbleton.[23] The net income averaged £230 a year between 1829 and 1831,[24] and was £198 c. 1920.[25]

Before the 18th century practically all of the income came from tithes and offerings. The vicarial tithes included the wool and lamb tithes at Elstronwick, and also some hay tithes there.[26] The tithe of rape was released to the vicar in the 18th century, after being claimed by one of the lay rectors.[27] At the inclosure of Elstronwick in 1813, the vicar received 45 a. for his tithes, which then apparently included all except those of corn and hay.[28] The tithes of the other townships were commuted by the Tithe Commissioners, in Humbleton by award of 1844 and apportionment of 1846 for a rent charge of £50 a year; in Danthorpe by award of 1844 and apportionment of 1845 for a rent charge of £22; in Fitling by award of 1844 and supplementary award and apportionment of 1848 for a rent charge of £29 18s., and in Flinton by award of 1844 and apportionment of 1845 for a rent charge of £50.[29]

The glebe comprised the vicarage house and a little ground at Humbleton, and c. 5 a. of open-field land at Elstronwick, for which two pasture gates were enjoyed when the land was fallow.[30] At the inclosure of Elstronwick in 1813, the vicar was awarded 6 a. for his glebe interests there, besides 45 a. for his tithes.[31] Bounty money had been used to buy 4 a. at Burton Pidsea in 1804,[32] and a farm was later made from that land and the allotments in Elstronwick; it was sold in 1911.[33] Bounty money was also used to buy c.

5 *Census*.
6 Humberside (Structural Change) Order 1995, copy at E.R.A.O.
7 *V.C.H. Yorks.* ii. 265.
8 Below, this section.   9 E.R.A.O., PE/68/24.
10 *E.Y.C.* iii, pp. 41–2; Poulson, *Holderness*, ii. 63.
11 *Reg. Gray*, p. 144 n.
12 *Tax. Eccl.* (Rec. Com.), 304; *Reg. Corbridge*, i, p. 168.
13 D. Knowles and R. N. Hadcock, *Medieval Religious Houses Eng. and Wales*, 176.
14 Lawrance, 'Clergy List', Holderness, i, pp. 71–3; list of incumbents in D. Bowes, *St. Peter's Church, Humbleton*, (1984), [22–3]. A grant of the advowson to the archbishop of York in 1558 was evidently ineffective: *Cal. Pat. 1557–8*, 420.
15 E.R.A.O., PE/68/24. Bowes, op. cit. erroneously has the Lord Chancellor presenting successively three times between 1964 and 1975: cf. B.I.H.R., ADM. (1970–2).
16 *Tax. Eccl.* (Rec. Com.), 304.
17 *Reg. Greenfield*, v, p. 226.   18 *Y.A.J.* xxiv. 65.
19 *Valor Eccl.* (Rec. Com.), v. 118.
20 *T.E.R.A.S.* iv. 52. Cf. *Yorks. Royalist Composition*

Papers, i (Y.A.S. Rec. Ser. xv), p. 6.
21 Hodgson, *Q.A.B.* p. cccxlvi.
22 B.I.H.R., TER. H. Humbleton 1809, 1825, 1853; E.R.A.O., accession 1681; ibid. PE/68/65; *9th Rep. Com. Char.* 829–31; above, Aldbrough, charities.
23 B.I.H.R., TER. H. Humbleton 1809; below, educ. The sermon had been discontinued by the 1890s: P.R.O., ED 49/8562.
24 *Rep. Com. Eccl. Revenues*, 944–5.
25 B.I.H.R., V. 1912–22/Ret.
26 Ibid. TER. H. Humbleton 1716; P.R.O., E 310/31/185, f. 18; *Valor Eccl.* v. 118; *Cal. Pat. 1575–8*, p. 543.
27 E.R.A.O., PE/68/3.
28 B.I.H.R., TER. H. Humbleton 1809; R.D.B., CQ/218/15.
29 E.R.A.O., PE/68/T.2, 4–5; ibid. DDCK/32/26.
30 B.I.H.R., TER. H. Humbleton 1716–64; *Valor Eccl.* v. 118.
31 B.I.H.R., TER H. Humbleton 1809; R.D.B., CQ/218/15.
32 E.R.A.O., DDCC/15/55, pp. 86–7.
33 R.D.B., 136/340/285.

15 a. at Fitling in 1763 and 16 a. at Bewholme, in Nunkeeling, in 1781,[34] and in 1850 the glebe at Humbleton was further enlarged by the exchange of tithe rents there for 9 a.[35] The land at Fitling, then of 17 a., was sold in 1954,[36] but in 1978 there remained 17 a. at Bewholme and 8 a. at Humbleton.[37]

The vicarage house was recorded from 1650.[38] In 1716 it was described as a mud-built house providing, besides chambers, four ground-floor rooms.[39] Jonathan Dixon, vicar, rebuilt the house in brick and tile in 1796, and re-laid the garden,[40] and his successor, John Jadis, vicar from 1832, had partly rebuilt, and probably enlarged, the house by 1849, when it had 14 rooms.[41] The mid 19th-century work includes the south front, in cream brick with slate roofs, Gothic windows, and decorative bargeboards on the gables.[42] The house was designated the residence of the united benefice in 1961, and was so used until 1980–1, when a new house was built in Burton Pidsea.[43] The former vicarage house at Humbleton was later sold.

The poor living was served with other churches in the 16th century, William Mysyn, vicar 1516–38, also holding the rectory of Little Cowden, and George Brook, vicar 1577–80, being curate at Winestead. In the 1590s some parishioners were accused of being 'cattle charmers' and witches.[44] Changes of vicar were relatively frequent then, and after 1613 there were no institutions until 1789, Humbleton being served in the interim by curates.[45] The quarterly sermons were lacking in 1575.[46] In 1743 the resident curate, John Browne, also served Garton, Aldbrough, and Elstronwick chapel. He then provided a weekly service at Humbleton, except for every third Sunday, and quarterly celebrations of Holy Communion, at which generally c. 60 received.[47] Browne was followed in 1761 by his son and namesake (d. 1787), who also held, besides the curacy of Garton, Hilston rectory.[48] Humbleton, Elstronwick, and Garton continued to be served together for some years after institutions were resumed in 1789.[49] By 1877 communion was celebrated eight times a year at Humbleton, but the number of communicants in the later 19th century was usually less than 10.[50] Communion was weekly in 1931.[51] Humbleton with Elstronwick and Burton Pidsea were held together before their formal union in

1961.[52] In 1998 there was a service or a celebration of Holy Communion each Sunday at Humbleton.[53]

In 1568 the Crown granted Hugh Counsell and Robert Pistor 1 bovate in Elstronwick, allegedly concealed and said to have been given to support a chantry priest in Humbleton church, and in 1570 they had a similar grant of land in Humbleton or Elstronwick, supposedly given for a light in Humbleton church.[54]

The present dedication of Humbleton church, to *ST. PETER*, was used in 1486 and 1536, but an alternative, *ST. PETER AND ST. PAUL*, was recorded in the mid 16th century.[55] The church stands on a small elevation, and comprises chancel with south chapel, aisled and clerestoried nave, and three-stage west tower embraced by continuations of the aisles. Much is of boulders, but the south aisle and clerestory are built of fine ashlar, and the chancel is largely of brick. The nave, the core of the lower stages of the tower, and probably the western part of the chancel date from before the Conquest. The scar of the early building's roof and a tower buttress relating to that roof are visible on the west wall of the nave. A narrow pointed lancet window at the west end of the chancel was made in the late 12th or early 13th century. The church was renovated and enlarged in the earlier 13th century, the south aisle being added, the chancel arch rebuilt, and the chancel lengthened. The four-bayed south arcade was then constructed outside the south wall of the nave; the south-east corner of the earlier nave is visible next to the easternmost respond of the arcade. Both the arcade and the chancel arch have pointed arches of two chamfered orders and octagonal moulded capitals, shafts, and water-holding bases. The work in the chancel included the making of a window, of two trefoiled lights with rudimentary bar tracery. An order to the parishioners to repair and reroof the nave in 1301[56] seems to have led to further remodelling and enlargement. The north aisle was built and both aisles extended westwards to flank the tower, the tower arch was enlarged, and the clerestory and the upper stages of the tower were added. The north arcade and the tower arches are similar to the 13th-century renovations but are 14th-century in style. The west window may have been inserted slightly later. The north aisle

[34] Ibid. AB/391/702; BD/168/257; B.I.H.R., V. 1764/ Ret. 2, no. 60; ibid. TER. H. Humbleton 1781, 1809.
[35] B.I.H.R., TER. H. Humbleton 1853.
[36] R.D.B., 993/470/412.
[37] Inf. from York Dioc. Bd. of Finance, 1981.
[38] *T.E.R.A.S.* iv. 52.
[39] B.I.H.R., TER. H. Humbleton 1716.
[40] Ibid. TER. H. Humbleton 1809.
[41] Ibid. TER. H. Humbleton 1849; Poulson, *Holderness*, ii. 66.
[42] Pevsner and Neave, *Yorks. E.R.* 568; Dept. of Environment, *Buildings List* (1987).
[43] E.R.A.O., PE/68/24; inf. from the vicar, 1999.
[44] B.I.H.R., V. 1590–1/CB. 1, ff. 129v.–130.
[45] Lawrance, 'Clergy List', Holderness, 1, pp. 35, 47, 72–3; 2, p. 169; B.I.H.R., Inst. AB. 16, p. 145; Poulson, *Holderness*, ii. 66.
[46] *Abp. Grindal's Visit. 1575*, ed. W. J. Sheils, 73.

[47] *Herring's Visit.* i, pp. 192, 221; ii, pp. 13, 88.
[48] Memorial in Humbleton church. B.I.H.R., V. 1764/ Ret. 1, nos. 33, 208; V. 1764/Ret. 2, no. 60; ibid. Fac. Bk. 2, p. 411; Poulson, *Holderness*, ii. 66 n.
[49] B.I.H.R., Inst. AB. 16, pp. 145, 216, 254.
[50] Ibid. V. 1865/Ret. 1, no. 274; V. 1868/Ret. 1, no. 243; V. 1871/Ret. 1, no. 248; V. 1877/Ret. 2, no. 59.
[51] Ibid. V. 1931/Ret.
[52] E.R.A.O., PE/68/24; *Crockford* (1955–6), 222; (1961–2), 566.   [53] Noticeboard at church.
[54] P.R.O., C 3/34/50; C 66/1046, mm. 1 sqq.; C 66/1063, mm. 1 sqq.; *Cal. Pat.* 1566–9, pp. 225–7; 1569–72, pp. 38, 42.
[55] B.I.H.R., Reg. 28, f. 106 and v.; Reg. 29, f. 165v.; ibid. Prob. Reg. 16, f. 17; *Test. Ebor.* iii (Sur. Soc. 45), 251 n. The date of the feast of dedication was changed in 1348, when neither date fell on days commemorating St. Peter or St. Paul: Poulson, *Holderness*, ii. 65.
[56] *Reg. Corbridge*, i. p. 168.

FIG. 4. HUMBLETON CHURCH IN THE EARLIER 19TH CENTURY

was refenestrated in the late 14th or early 15th century. Another substantial remodelling was evidently nearing completion in 1555. It involved the making or enlargement of the south chapel, and the widening of the south aisle, the walls of which were rebuilt in ashlar and provided with large windows under depressed four-centred heads.[57] A niche, perhaps once including a piscina, in the easternmost bay of the south aisle suggests that there was formerly an altar there. The embattling of the clerestory and the tower, which formerly also had pinnacles, and the refacing of the clerestory with ashlar were probably done at the same time. It may also have been then that the unusual stone staircase to the tower was constructed; it begins in the nave, passes through the south-eastern corner of the tower, and then continues through a turret built onto the south wall.

The church was decayed in the later 16th century,[58] and in the 17th the chancel was repaired in brick and given new south and east windows, and a new south door, all with square openings. It was then decreed, after dispute, that of each pound spent in maintaining the fabric the inhabitants of Humbleton, Fitling, and Flinton should pay 14s. and those of Elstronwick and Danthorpe 6s., presumably because of the latter townships' charges in maintaining Elstronwick chapel.[59] In 1744 the south porch was renewed in rendered brick.[60] A room had been formed from the west end of the north aisle

before 1767, when another was made at the west end of the south aisle,[61] and in 1791 a west gallery was built in the nave. The south chapel was also closed off to serve as a vestry, and by the mid 19th century the chancel arch had been disfigured by an earlier lowering of the chancel roof.[62] In 1888–9 much of the church was restored by J. L. Pearson, largely at the cost of John Hotham, Lord Hotham; the work included the opening up of the tower and the western ends of the aisles by the demolition of walls there, the removal of the gallery, and reseating and refitting.[63] In 1906 the chancel was restored for Lord Hotham, probably by John Bilson of Hull, who then designed a new pulpit and choir stalls.[64] The south porch, which was rebuilt in the early 20th century,[65] was removed in 1990.

During the 19th-century restoration a new font was installed; the medieval octagonal one it replaced is kept in the nave. Several windows were reglazed with stained glass, the choir stalls replaced, and other improvements made in the 1930s, and in 1956 oak vestry screens were fitted.[66] Above the east window hangs a copy of Raphael's *Transfiguration* by Ann Dixon, daughter of a past vicar, which was given in 1816.[67] The church formerly had stained glass depicting the arms of families associated with the parish, like the Staffords and the Constables.[68] The Thompsons, lords of the manor, are commemorated in the north aisle by an alabaster bust of William Thompson (d. by 1638),

[57] B.I.H.R., CP. G. 3543.
[58] Ibid. V. 1578–9/CB. 1, f. 70v.; V. 1590–1/CB. 1, f. 130; *Abp. Grindal's Visit. 1575*, ed. W. J. Sheils, 73.
[59] E.R.A.O., PE/68/1; B.I.H.R., CP. G. 3543.
[60] Cf. B.I.H.R., V. 1590–1/CB. 1, f. 130.
[61] E.R.A.O., PE/68/71.
[62] *Y.A.J.* xxiv. 153–4; Sheahan and Whellan, *Hist. York & E.R.* ii. 369. For the church before restoration, Poulson, *Holderness*, ii. 67–8, illus. facing p. 67. Cf. Pevsner and Neave, *Yorks. E.R.* 568.

[63] E.R.A.O., PE/68/76/1; B.I.H.R., Fac. 1887/13; Bulmer, *Dir. E. Yorks.* (1892), 437.
[64] Plaque in church; B.I.H.R., Fac. 1905/49; Fac. 1906/51.
[65] *Hull Times*, 18 Apr. 1914. The datestone of the 1744 porch is kept in the church.
[66] B.I.H.R., Fac. 1934/2/1; Fac. 1937/1/15; Fac. 1937/2/10 etc.; E.R.A.O., PE/68/19, 22; plaque on stalls.
[67] E.R.A.O., PE/68/T.10; *Kelly's Dir. N. & E.R. Yorks.* (1872), 507; Bulmer, *Dir. E. Yorks.* (1892), 438.
[68] Poulson, *Holderness*, ii. 68.

the upper part of a formerly larger figure,[69] and by an early 18th-century wall tablet detailing his descendents. Another mural memorial, in the chancel, is for James Shutt (d. 1787) and his family.

Humbleton church had three bells in 1552 and later.[70] The plate includes a cup of 1740 and a paten of 1700, both given in memory of Susannah Thompson in 1740; another paten made in 1719; a flagon of 1739, given by Arabella Thompson in 1740, and a salver of *c*. 1755, given by Robert Raines of Flinton in 1758.[71] The registers of baptisms, marriages, and burials begin in 1577. The record is mostly complete, but registrations of marriages are lacking for some years, notably in the earlier 17th century.[72] The parishioners were paying the clerk £5 8s. 8d. a year in 1809 and £7 6s. 8d. in 1849.[73]

ELSTRONWICK. A chapel had been built at Elstronwick, and a chantry with one priest founded there, by the 14th century. The vicar of Humbleton, who was said to be responsible for maintaining the chantry, may have neglected it before 1324, when he and the inhabitants of Elstronwick were in dispute about it. The archbishop of York then licensed the inhabitants to support their own chaplain there to say mass three days a week, baptize, and church women.[74] In 1386 Robert Franks, clerk, proposed to found another chantry there, for Richard of Ravenser, John Franks, and others; the endowment, in Elstronwick and elsewhere in Holderness, was to be given to Nunkeeling priory, which was to provide a chaplain to celebrate four days a week.[75] In 1526 two chaplains, each receiving £4 a year, were serving in the chapel.[76] The chapel's function as a chapel of ease was confirmed in 1536, when the right to bury at Elstronwick was granted and the chapel was consecrated anew, together with its yard.[77]

All or part of the chapel's landed endowment may have been recorded in 1535 as 'glebe lands in Elstronwick' belonging to Humbleton vicarage.[78] The endowment evidently passed to the Crown on the suppression of chantries. A succession of transactions in the late 16th and 17th centuries dealt with what seem to have been parts of it. In 1578 land at Elstronwick, lately belonging to the chapel there and allegedly concealed, was granted by the Crown to John Farnham, who then resold the *c*. 6 a. to Sir John Constable.[79] It was perhaps Elstronwick chapel

and another part of its endowment which the Crown sold to John Eldred and William Whitmore in 1611; the premises comprised 'the site of the chapel of Humbleton' and *c*. 5 a. in Elstronwick, all then let to the vicar of Humbleton, and were erroneously said to have formerly belonged to Thornton college.[80] Later that year another grant was made, to Francis Morrice and Francis Phillips, which included 5 a. in Elstronwick, also held by the vicar and said to have been given for a priest serving Elstronwick 'church'.[81] At least part of the chapel's endowment seems to have been secured for the parish; in the 1660s the chapel's glebe comprised *c*. 2 a. worth £1 a year, and later the incumbent of Humbleton and Elstronwick had *c*. 5 a. of openfield land in Elstronwick.[82]

Whatever the fate of its lands, Elstronwick chapel continued in use. The curacy was held separately from Humbleton vicarage in 1552.[83] In 1575 the quarterly sermons were found to have been neglected at Elstronwick.[84] The chapelry was later annexed to Humbleton.[85] In 1743 the curate at Humbleton 'frequently' held a service in Elstronwick chapel every third Sunday, and he celebrated communion there three times a year, when usually about 27 people received.[86] There was a weekly service in the chapel by the mid 19th century, and eight celebrations of communion a year by 1877; usually about 12 people took communion there in the later 19th century.[87] In 1931 communion was weekly.[88] In 1998 a service or a celebration of communion was provided at Elstronwick each Sunday.[89]

Dedicated to *ST. LAWRENCE* by 1386,[90] the largely-rebuilt church comprises chancel and nave with western bell turret. The nave is of coursed cut cobblestones, the chancel of boulders, and the roofs and the wooden bell turret are covered with slate. The medieval chapel was built at unknown date before 1324.[91] Its chancel was probably remodelled in the earlier 14th century, the east window being of that period. The other windows, some of which have been remade or replaced, suggest by their tracery that the chapel was refenestrated later that century and in the next. Some work may have followed the promulgation in 1431 of an indulgence for those helping to repair the building.[92] It was later neglected,[93] before being extensively repaired and remodelled in 1791 by Jonathan Dixon, vicar, for the parishioners at Elstron-

[69] Illus. in Poulson, *Holderness*, ii. 63. J. Foster, *Pedigrees of Yorks*. iii for death date.
[70] *Inventories of Ch. Goods*, 47; Boulter, 'Ch. Bells', 84.
[71] B.I.H.R., TER. H. Humbleton 1777, 1786; *Yorks. Ch. Plate*, i. 274–5.
[72] E.R.A.O., PE/68/1–4, 6–7. Transcripts survive from 1600: B.I.H.R., PRT. Hold. D. Humbleton.
[73] B.I.H.R., TER. H. 1809, 1849.
[74] Ibid. Reg. 9A, f. 353v.
[75] H.U.L., DHO/6/120; Poulson, *Holderness*, ii. 74.
[76] *Y.A.J.* xxiv. 76.
[77] B.I.H.R., Reg. 28, f. 106 and v.
[78] *Valor Eccl.* v. 118.
[79] E.R.A.O., DDCC/17/23; *Cal. Pat.* 1575–8, pp. 405–7.
[80] P.R.O., C 66/1903, no. 9.
[81] Ibid. C 66/1908, no. 1. Cf. *Y.A.J.* xliv. 192.

[82] B.I.H.R., TER. H. Elstronwick n.d., 1685; Humbleton 1716.
[83] *Inventories of Ch. Goods*, 40, 47.
[84] *Abp. Grindal's Visit. 1575*, ed. W. J. Sheils, 73.
[85] B.I.H.R., TER. H. Elstronwick n.d., 1685; Humbleton 1685 etc.; Poulson, *Holderness*, ii. 66.
[86] *Herring's Visit.* i. 192; ii. 88.
[87] B.I.H.R., V. 1865/Ret. 1, no. 274; V. 1868/Ret. 1, no. 243; V. 1871/Ret. 1, no. 248; V. 1877/Ret. 2, no. 59.
[88] Ibid. V. 1931/Ret.
[89] Notice at church.
[90] H.U.L., DHO/6/120.
[91] B.I.H.R., Reg. 9A, f. 353v.
[92] *Cal. Papal Reg.* viii. 388.
[93] B.I.H.R., ER V./CB. 1, f. 77; ER V./CB. 4, f. 131v.; ER V./CB. 5, f. 152v.; ER V./Ret. 2, f. 14v.

FIG. 5. ELSTRONWICK CHURCH AFTER REMODELLING IN 1791

wick. The chapel was partly rebuilt, reglazed, and rerooofed; the north and south doorways were blocked up, and a new entrance made in the west end; the bell turret was added, and the north wall was given a new window. Inside, pews and a west gallery were fitted. The new entrance incorporated an Ionic pilastered doorcase, said to have been brought from the Thompsons' house at Humbleton.[94] The building was, nevertheless, described in the mid 19th century as small and mean with blocked or altered windows.[95] It was virtually rebuilt and refitted in 1874–5 at the expense of J. T. Dickinson, the tithe-owner, his wife, and brother George, of Roos.[96] The stepped floor of the sanctuary retains its Victorian tiles.

There are many memorials to members of the Bell family, impropriators in Elstronwick. The mutilated wall tablets of John Bell (d. 1809) and Henry Carr (d. 1848) are by John Earle of Hull.[97] Stained glass in the west and east windows commemorates respectively J. T. Dickinson (d. 1875) and his mother-in-law.

In 1552 and later Elstronwick chapel had one bell.[98] The plate there includes a cup of 1816 and pewter vessels.[99] Baptisms, marriages, and burials were entered in the Humbleton registers.[1]

FITLING. Fitling chapel was recorded in 1347. It was then alleged that the chapel had included a chantry for one priest until c. 1300, when the Hospitallers, whose manor of Fitling was the supposed endowment, discontinued it. The beneficiaries of the alleged chantry had been the counts of Aumale, lords of Burstwick manor.[2] Nothing more is known about Fitling chapel.

NONCONFORMITY. A rood screen with painted images remained in Humbleton church in 1567, but was defaced soon afterwards.[3] There is otherwise little evidence of Catholicism in the parish before the later 17th century.[4] One or two families were presented at Flinton in 1581, and Margaret Ellerker and two others at Elstronwick in 1633, and in 1676 there were said to be 27 papists in the parish.[5] Besides the Constables, lords at Elstronwick,[6] prominent Roman Catholics included the Thorpes, who lived at Danthorpe Hall: John Thorpe was regularly recorded as a recusant c. 1670,[7] and a priest was serving the neighbourhood from Danthorpe Hall in the 1720s and, despite complaint, evidently also in 1735, when another John Thorpe, his wife, a priest, and eight others were presented as papists.[8] Numbers of Roman Catholics remained small, however, three families being recorded in 1743, five in 1764,[9] and 24 individuals in 1780.

Twelve protestant dissenters were returned under Humbleton in 1676,[10] and in the mid 18th century the parish included two Quaker families.[11]

HUMBLETON. A house at Humbleton was registered for protestant worship in 1806.[12] A Primitive Methodist chapel was built there in 1860[13] and fitted out from a closed chapel at Burton Pidsea.[14] It was closed c. 1995,[15] and had been converted to a house by 1998.

ELSTRONWICK. At Elstronwick a room was used for worship by a congregation of protestants from 1816.[16] In 1853 the Primitive Methodists built a chapel there,[17] which was still used in 1998.

FITLING. Inhabitants of Fitling have attended a Wesleyan Methodist chapel in Garton and its successor, now the Methodist church, which was built nearby, but in Fitling, in 1935.[18]

94   E.R.A.O., PE/68/89; Poulson, Holderness, ii. 74; above, manors (Humbleton). The doorway was later removed. An earlier 'bell house' was mentioned c. 1710: B.I.H.R., CP. I. 552.
95   For the church before restoration, Poulson, Holderness, ii. 74.
96   B.I.H.R., Ch. Ret. ii; Bulmer, Dir. E. Yorks. (1892), 439; plaque in church.
97   Pevsner and Neave, Yorks. E.R. 404; Poulson, Holderness, ii. 74; above, manors (rectory).
98   E.R.A.O., PE/68/89, s.v. 1791; Inventories of Ch. Goods, 40; Boulter, 'Ch. Bells', 83.
99   Yorks. Ch. Plate, i. 245.
1   Above, this section.
2   Cal. Close, 1346–9, 135–6; Cal. Inq. Misc. ii, p. 499.
3   J. S. Purvis, Tudor Par. Doc. of Dioc. York, 32, 176.
4   Para. based on Aveling, Post Reformation Catholicism, 67.
5   Aveling, op. cit. 31; Compton Census, ed. Whiteman, 600.
6   E.R.A.O., QDR/2/12.

7   Depositions from York Castle, (Sur. Soc. xl), 121, 168, 181.
8   E.R.A.O., QDB/2, pp. 13–15; QDB/3, pp. 6–7, 58–9; Aveling, op. cit. 47; Herring's Visit. iv, pp. 213–14.
9   B.I.H.R., V. 1764/Ret. 2, no. 60; Herring's Visit. ii, p. 88.
10   Compton Census, ed. Whiteman, 600.
11   B.I.H.R., V. 1764/Ret. 2, no. 60; Herring's Visit. ii, p. 88.
12   B.I.H.R., Fac. Bk. 3, p. 410.
13   Bulmer, Dir. E. Yorks. (1892), 438. It was registered in 1861: O.N.S. (Birkdale), Worship Reg. no. 13201. Illus. in R.C.H.M. Nonconf. Chapels, 196.
14   E.R.A.O., MRW/2/5, s.v. 15 June 1859.
15   D. [R. J.] and S. Neave, E.R. Chapels and Meeting Houses (E. Yorks. Loc. Hist. Soc.), 52; inf. from Mrs. Kirk, Humbleton, 1999.
16   B.I.H.R., Fac. Bk. 3, p. 751.
17   Date on building. It was registered in 1854: O.N.S. (Birkdale), Worship Reg. no. 5097. Cf. E.R.A.O., MRW/2/18, s.v. 1855; R.D.B., 72/319/301 (1895).
18   Above, Garton, nonconf.

FLINTON. At Flinton houses were registered for a group of protestants in 1791 and 1795.[19] That congregation was probably Wesleyan: there were 10 Wesleyan members at Flinton in 1838,[20] and Wesleyan Methodists built a chapel there in 1855. The chapel was closed c. 1970,[21] and in 1979–80 was rebuilt as a garage.[22]

EDUCATION. HUMBLETON. There may have been a school at Humbleton in the 1660s, when John Fenwick, curate, was licensed to teach.[23] Francis Heron by will[24] dated 1719 devised his estate in Flinton and Sutton on Hull to his wife for life, and thereafter mostly for education in Humbleton parish.[25] Ten pounds a year was to be spent in teaching reading and writing to poor children of the parish, and employing a schoolmaster; £1 paid to the minister at Humbleton for an annual sermon on charity, and the rest of the income invested and used to apprentice boys of Humbleton, Fitling, and Flinton townships, those of Flinton always taking precedence. The charity became effective on the death of Heron's widow in 1734, but was interrupted in the 1740s when someone claiming to be Heron's heir took possession of the property. In 1790 the endowment comprised a farm of almost 60 a. at Flinton and 1 a. at Sutton.[26] The land at Sutton was sold in 1934 and 1948. The rental was £70 a year in the 1820s, £100 in 1879, and thereafter some £80 until that sum was increased to £195 in 1959.[27] Besides rents, the charity had £100 stock in the early 20th century.[28] The trustees still held Heron's farm, then of 65 a., in 1999.[29]

In 1734, the year in which the charity began, the lord of the manor licensed the parishioners to build a school on waste ground in Humbleton,[30] but the school was being held in the church later in the century.[31] It had c. 20 pupils in 1743, and in 1764 the charity was paying for 12 children to be taught reading, writing, arithmetic, and, if appropriate for them, classics.[32] The stipend of the master had been raised to £15 before 1810, when another £5 was added in return for an increase in the number taught from 12 to 18, of whom 6 each came from Flinton, Humbleton, and Sutton.[33]

The enlargement of the school was being considered in the 1820s,[34] and in 1830 the trustees built a new school with master's house on a site adjoining the churchyard given by Beaumont Hotham, Baron Hotham.[35] The new school was attended by upwards of 30 boys and girls from all five townships in Humbleton parish, who were taught by the master in return for his accommodation and the stipend, then of c. £40 a year.[36] Infants were taken by 1865,[37] and at inspection in 1871 the Church school had 25 boys and 4 girls in attendance.[38] By the mid 1870s average attendance was 42 and the master's salary £60 a year.[39] A school district comprising Humbleton and the other townships of the parish had been formed in 1872, but the building was soon after reckoned insufficient.[40]

Another school, designed by William Harker of Beverley and also comprising a master's house, was built and opened in 1878.[41] John Hotham, Baron Hotham, provided its site beside the village street and largely paid for its construction, the old school, later Ivy, now Church, Cottage, being granted to him in partial recompense. Fees were introduced, but by Scheme of 1876 the trustees were enabled to spend £40 a year on prizes, scholarships, and exhibitions for children from Humbleton. The charity was paying the mistress £70 a year by 1896, when the school had 93 pupils and the accommodation was described as 'miserable'.[42] The building was improved in the early 20th century, chiefly by the addition of a classroom in the 1920s.[43] Heron's trustees also bought 3 a. next to the school in 1911 for a playing field, part of which was later used to teach gardening to the pupils.[44] Average attendance at Heron's endowed school was c. 80 in the early 20th century, and about 60 in the 1930s.[45] In 1954 the senior pupils were transferred to South Holderness County Secondary School.[46] The junior and infants' school was closed in 1959, when the remaining pupils were moved to Sproatley school.[47] The former school was subsequently used as a village hall.[48]

The provision of apprenticeships evidently ceased to be an object of the trust. By the early 19th century the share of the income available for apprenticeships was used, when candidates were lacking, for those going into service, 3–6

[19] B.I.H.R., Fac. Bk. 2, p. 479; Fac. Bk. 3, p. 83.

[20] E.R.A.O., MRH/1/12.

[21] Ibid. MRH/1/32; O.N.S. (Birkdale), Worship Reg. no. 6517; R.D.B., 39/360/345; 39/361/346 (1890); Kelly's Dir. N. & E.R. Yorks. (1872), 508; R.C.H.M. Nonconf. Chapels, 196; O.S. Map 1/10,560, TA 23 NW. (1956 edn.).

[22] Neaves, op. cit. 50; datestone on garage reading WESLEYAN HOUSE 1855–1979.

[23] Restoration Exhibit Bks. and the Northern Clergy 1662–4, ed. W. J. Sheils, 64.   [24] E.R.A.O., PE/68/3.

[25] Para. based on 9th Rep. Com. Char. 765–6.

[26] Lease of 1751 and deed of 1790 in possession of Mr. M. Craven, Hessle, 2000.

[27] P.R.O., ED 49/8562; inf. from charity records supplied by Heron's Educational Foundation, 1999.

[28] E.R. Educ. Cttee. Mins. 1903–4, 350.

[29] Inf. from Heron's Educational Foundation, 1999;

[30] E.R.A.O., PE/68/71.

[31] Ibid. PE/68/71, s.v. 1767; Poulson, Holderness, ii. 67; plan of church in B.I.H.R., Fac. 1887/13.

[32] B.I.H.R., V. 1764/Ret. 2, no. 60; Herring's Visit. ii, p. 88.

[33] 9th Rep. Com. Char. 765–6.   [34] Ibid. 766.

[35] The site was conveyed in 1838. P.R.O., ED 49/8562; O.S. Map 6", Yorks. CCXXVII (1855 edn.); Poulson, Holderness, ii. 69; Bulmer, Dir. E. Yorks. (1892), 438; White, Dir. E. & N.R. Yorks. (1840), 263.

[36] Educ. Enquiry Abstract, 1088; White, Dir. E. & N.R. Yorks. (1840), 263.

[37] B.I.H.R., V. 1865/Ret. 1, no. 274.

[38] Returns relating to Elem. Educ. 472–3.

[39] P.R.O., ED 7/135, no. 86; ED 49/8562.

[40] Ibid. ED 49/8562.

[41] E.R.A.O., SL/67/1, p. 19; Pevsner and Neave, Yorks. E.R. 568; Bulmer, Dir. E. Yorks (1892), 438.

[42] P.R.O., ED 49/8562.

[43] E.R. Educ. Cttee. Mins. 1904–5, 152; 1908–9, 52; 1922–3, 55.

[44] R.D.B., 137/125/104; Kelly's Dir. N. & E.R. Yorks. (1921), 544.

[45] Bd. of Educ., List 21 (H.M.S.O., 1908 and later edns).

[46] E.R. Educ. Cttee. Mins. 1952–3, 226; 1953–4, 145; V.C.H. Yorks. E.R. v. 201.

[47] E.R. Educ. Cttee. Mins. 1958–9, 206; 1959–60, 78.

[48] Inf. from Mrs. Powell, Humbleton, 1999.

being so helped in the early 1820s,[49] and apprenticeships were not mentioned in the Scheme of 1876.[50] After the closure of the school, a new Scheme was obtained for the charity in 1964. The Heron Educational Foundation was then established to make grants towards the secondary or higher education of young people resident in the parish, or to help provide vocational training for them. About 1980 the income of £1,000 a year was usually spent in grants to secondary pupils, or in generally supporting education in the parish.[51]

The L.E.A. provided a winter evening school at Humbleton in the 1920s.[52]

ELSTRONWICK. Land at Elstronwick assigned to the poor passed soon after inclosure in 1813 to Thomas Thompson, lord of the manor, because of the inadequacy of the overseers' title and failure of the donor's heirs.[53] In 1817 he conveyed the 9 a. and three cottages, or poorhouses, to trustees as an endowment for a school at Elstronwick.[54] In 1818 they built a cottage in Church Lane, later Ivy Cottage,[55] to house the school and schoolmistress. The charity had an income of £18 a year in the early 1820s, when the mistress was paid £11 10s. from it for teaching 18 boys and girls of 5 to 12 years old; reading and probably writing were taught, and the girls were also instructed in knitting and sewing. In 1833, when the school had 20 pupils, the schoolmistress received £20 a year, besides her accommodation.[56] By the mid 19th century the school was small, took only infants, and in 1865 was said to be 'very inefficient' because of the mistress's age.[57] The older children then went to school at Humbleton.[58] Only three boys were in attendance at Elstronwick at inspection in 1871,[59] and the school was hardly bigger at its closure in 1903. The landed endowment of the charity, then comprising c. 10 a., the former school, and the three cottages, together with c. £100 stock, produced a net income of £13 10s. in 1912. The three cottages were later demolished, but in 1999 the trustees still had Ivy Cottage, the old school, and the land. By Scheme of 1914 the Educational Foundation of Thomas Thompson was created to assist Elstronwick children, or those attending a school there or in the neighbourhood, and to aid their

further education.[60] The income was later used, with help from the local education authority, to transport children from Danthorpe and Elstronwick to Humbleton school in winter. Unspent income had accumulated to c. £150 by 1922, when the making of grants in aid of further education was being considered.[61] About 1980 the income of c. £200 was used generally to promote the education and welfare of children in the parish.[62]

FITLING AND FLINTON. In 1871 those schoolchildren from Fitling and Flinton not attending Humbleton school went instead to Garton and Sproatley schools respectively.[63]

CHARITIES FOR THE POOR. The poor of Elstronwick had the profits from ½ bovate by 1652.[64] Later called Town Lands, it was let for just over £2 a year in 1704.[65] Three cottages were later built on part of the land by the overseers, and let to poor labourers. At inclosure in 1813, the overseers' title was not recognized, and the 9 a. allotted was awarded instead to the heirs of the Gedneys, trustees in the 17th century, and then, by their lack, was forfeited to the lord of the manor, Thomas Thompson. He used the land to endow a school at Elstronwick. A provision that any income left after school expenses be used for Christmas doles in Elstronwick seems not to have been effective, and was removed by Scheme of 1908.[66]

William Meadley (fl. mid 17th century) was believed to have charged a garth at Flinton with the payment of 10s. a year to the poor, and in the 1820s the proprietor of the land distributed that sum among widows of Flinton each Easter.[67] The charity was evidently later lost.

There may have been an endowed almshouse in Humbleton. A list written apparently in the mid 17th century records Bead House close there, then of 26 a., and Bead House closes were mentioned again in 1866.[68]

Mrs. Arabella Thompson was said to have left £10 to the poor of Humbleton township in 1740, and Mrs. Susannah Thompson £20 to those in Humbleton parish by 1764, when the interest on the bequests, of £1 4s., was distributed by the minister and overseers.[69]

49 9th Rep. Com. Char. 766; above, this section.
50 P.R.O., ED 49/8562.
51 Review of Char. Rep. 107; Humb. Dir. of Char. 84.
52 E.R. Educ. Cttee. Mins. 1921–2, 133.
53 Below, charities.
54 Accounts from 1868 to 1893 are at E.R.A.O., PE/68/95, and those for 1903–5 at ibid. accession 1681.
55 O.S. Map 1/2,500, Yorks. CCXXVII. 12 (1891 edn.); inf. from Miss M. A. Kirk, Correspondent, Thomas Thompson's Educational Foundation, Elstronwick, 1999.
56 9th Rep. Com. Char. 766–7; Educ. Enquiry Abstract, 1088.
57 B.I.H.R., V. 1865/Ret. 1, no. 274; V. 1877/Ret. 2, no. 59.
58 P.R.O., ED 49/8539.
59 Returns relating to Elem. Educ. 472–3.

60 P.R.O., ED 49/8539; Kelly's Dir. N. & E.R. Yorks. (1897), 486; (1905), 528; inf. from the Correspondent, Miss M. A. Kirk, Elstronwick, 1999.
61 E.R. Educ. Cttee. Mins. 1914–15, 152, 233, 304–5; 1915–16, 137; 1922–3, 55.
62 Review of Char. Rep. 104; Humb. Dir. of Char. 83.
63 Returns relating to Elem. Educ. 472–3.
64 H.U.L., DAS/7/3, s.vv. Apr. 1652; Oct. 1668.
65 Ibid. DAS/7/1.
66 P.R.O., ED 49/8539; 9th Rep. Com. Char. 766–7; above, educ.
67 9th Rep. Com. Char. 767; Bulmer, Dir. E. Yorks. (1892), 440.
68 H.U.L., DDHO/36/26, 82.
69 B.I.H.R., V. 1764/Ret. 2, no. 60.

ROOS

THE village of Roos, lying some 19 km. east of Hull and 3 km. from the sea, has since the Second World War become increasingly a commuter settlement.[70] The parish includes the hamlet of Owstwick. The name Roos, meaning marsh or moorland, is possibly British, while Owstwick may be an Anglian and Scandinavian hybrid, and perhaps means 'eastern dairy farm', relative to Elstronwick, in Humbleton.[71] The settlement of 'Andrebi', recorded in 1086, may have lain in Roos, but has not been identified later.[72] In 1852 the ancient parish contained 3,623 a. (1,466 ha.), of which 2,528 a. (1,023 ha.) comprised the township, later civil parish, of Roos, 886 a. (359 ha.) were in Owstwick township, and 209 a. (85 ha.) lay detached in Garton with Grimston township. The rest of Owstwick township, amounting to 450 a. (182 ha.), and 1,614 a. (653 ha.) of Garton with Grimston township made up the ancient parish of Garton;[73] the history of Owstwick township is dealt with here and that of Garton with Grimston township under Garton. In 1935 Roos civil parish and all 1,338 a. (542 ha.) of Owstwick civil parish were united with Hilston and Tunstall civil parishes to form a new civil parish of Roos, with a total area of 5,721 a. (2,315 ha.).[74] By 1991 the area had been reduced, presumably by coastal erosion, to 2,283 ha. (5,641 a.).[75]

There were 149 poll-tax payers at Roos in 1377 and 116 at Owstwick and Hilston together.[76] In 1589, when Roos was visited by plague, 45 burials were recorded in three months.[77] Roos had 49 houses assessed for hearth tax and 8 discharged in 1672; at Owstwick 15 houses were assessed and 2 discharged.[78] There were 65 families in the parish in 1743 and c. 63 in 1764.[79] From 272 in 1801 the population of Roos township rose to 599 in 1851 but fell to 418 in 1911. Numbers increased to 455 in 1921 but fell again to 404 in 1931. In Owstwick the population rose from 109 in 1801 to 165 in 1811, before falling to 103 in 1851 and 80 in 1901. It rose to 114 in 1911 but fell to 81 in 1931. House-building at Roos largely accounted for the increased population of the enlarged civil parish, which rose from 631 in 1961 to 769 in 1971 and 907 in 1981. In 1991 there were usually 1,071 residents but only 1,043 were present.[80]

The parish is mostly on boulder clay[81] and much of the ground lies at over 7 m. above sea level, rising to more than 23 m. at the north end

of Roos township. The higher ground was occupied by the open fields and common pasture of Roos. Lower ground in the south and west is alluvial; part of it was used as common meadow but much was early inclosed. Commonable lands in Owstwick were inclosed in 1649 and those remaining at Roos in 1786.

The parish is drained by watercourses which flow south-west towards the river Humber and form parts of the boundaries of both Roos and Owstwick. They were in disrepair in 1367, when that forming the southern boundary of Roos township was recorded as part of Keyingham fleet.[82] A new drain in Roos which caused flooding c. 1387 was perhaps a realignment of the fleet.[83] The grounds drained by the fleet included 400 a. in Roos and 50 a. in Owstwick in 1618.[84] Roos petitioned in 1623 for the improvement of the fleet,[85] which by 1719 also served parts of the parish that formerly drained to Hedon haven.[86] The drains in Owstwick and Roos were improved under the Keyingham Level Drainage Acts of 1772 and later, and after 1845 low ground assessed to the drainage included 580 a. in Roos and 63 a. in Owstwick.[87]

Roads leading from Roos village north to Garton and east to Withernsea have been upgraded as parts of the main Holderness coast road. The Withernsea road is known as Pilmar Lane. Minor roads from the village lead south to Halsham, west to Owstwick and Burton Pidsea, east to Tunstall, and north to Hilston. From Owstwick roads lead east to Hilston, north to Fitling, west to Danthorpe, and south to Roos village and Burton Pidsea. The last mentioned road was straightened c. 1800 and was later known as New Road; it probably supplemented a road further west which was stopped up by the mid 19th century. Another minor road, Longbrough Lane, forms part of the northern boundary of the township.[88] Licence granted in 1845 to the surveyors of highways of Roos to take materials from Tunstall beach was then disputed.[89]

Roos village has a linear plan and two centres of settlement, known by the 16th century as the north and south ends,[90] with the church and manor house at the southern extremity. Both location and layout were probably influenced by the small stream called Roos or Town beck, which flows south through the village.[91] Before inclosure most of the houses stood on the west

70   This article was written in 1990.
71   *P.N. Yorks. E.R.* (E.P.N.S.), 56, 58–9; G. F. Jensen, *Scand. Settlement Names in Yorks.* 135, 142, 247.
72   *V.C.H. Yorks.* ii. 265.
73   O.S. Map 6″, Yorks. CCXXVIII (1855 edn.); *Census*, 1881.
74   *Census*, 1931 (pt. ii).
75   Ibid. 1991.
76   P.R.O., E 179/202/60, mm. 15, 48.
77   *Reg. Par. All Saints, Roos*, i, transcr. R. B. Machell (Hull, 1888), 26–8.
78   *Hearth Tax*, 60.
79   B.I.H.R., V. 1764/Ret. 2, no. 215; *Herring's Visit.* iii, p. 33.

80   *V.C.H. Yorks.* iii. 494; *Census*, 1911–91.
81   Geol. Surv. Map 1″, drift, sheet 73 (1909 edn.).
82   Poulson, *Holderness*, i. 122–3, 127.
83   *Cal. Pat.* 1385–9, 325.
84   E.R.A.O., DDCC/54/53.
85   Ibid. CSR/14/1.
86   Ibid. CSR/4/144.
87   Ibid. DDPK/3/8; *V.C.H. Yorks. E.R.* v. 55–7.
88   T. Jefferys, *Map of Yorks.* (1772); C. Greenwood, *Map of Yorks.* (1817); A. Bryant, *Map of E.R. Yorks.* (1829); O.S. Map 6″, Yorks. CCXXVIII (1855 and later edns.).
89   E.R.A.O., DDCC/1/62.
90   H.U.L., DDSY(3)/3/3.
91   E.R.A.O., PE/44/20, p. 49; R.D.B., KZ/259/359.

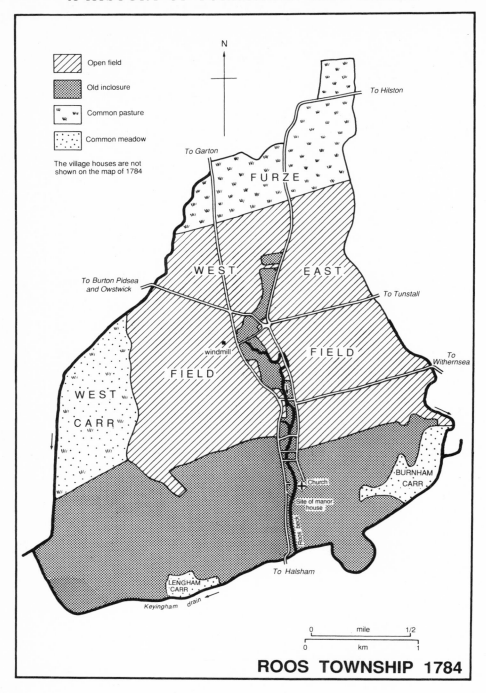

ROOS TOWNSHIP 1784

Legend:
- Open field
- Old inclosure
- Common pasture
- Common meadow

The village houses are not shown on the map of 1784

side of the main street, in a back lane to the west, and in several cross lanes. It may have been the back lane, now called Rectory Road, which was named as Westgate in 1626.[92] After inclosure houses began to be built on the east side of the main street, and the growth of the village became more rapid from the mid 20th century with much infilling and the building of small estates behind the streets. Many of the more recent houses are of a 'superior' kind. A dozen council houses were built on Pilmar Lane c. 1950 and c. 40 more added there in the 1960s, and eight also built at North End.[93] A sewage treatment works was built in 1965.[94] Outlying houses include Roos Furze and Glebe Farm, both built between 1786 and 1829; Sunderland Cottage was added in the later 19th century and Glebe Farm rebuilt c. 1881.[95]

92 H.U.L., DDSY(3)/3/5.

93 R.D.B., 585/101/78; 692/490/415; 1366/252/234; 1482/212/183; O.S. Map 6″, TA 23 SE. (1956 edn.); O.S. Map 1/2,500, TA 2830–2930 (1975 edn.).

94 R.D.B., 1616/385/320; inf. from Holderness B.C., Skirlaugh, 1990.

95 Bryant, *Map E.R. Yorks.* (1829); O.S. Map 6″, Yorks. CCXXVIII, CCXLII (1855 edn.); O.S. Map 1/2,500, Yorks. CCXXVIII. 11; CCXLII. 2 (1891 edn.); E.R.A.O., accession 1217 (Glebe Farm, mortgage). For the name Sunderland, below, econ. hist.

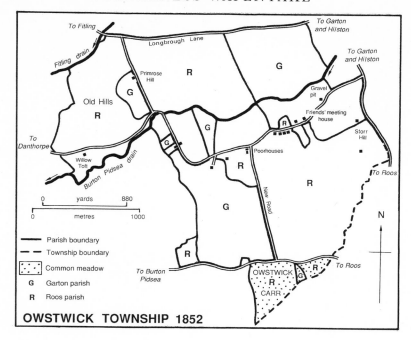

OWSTWICK TOWNSHIP 1852

The village houses, which mostly date from the 19th and 20th centuries, include several farmhouses. Among terraced cottages in the main street are six built in 1827.[96] Most of the noteworthy houses, including the former rectory, stand in the back lane. The Elms is an early 19th-century, stuccoed house which was enlarged in the later 19th and mid 20th century.[97]

There were one or two licensed houses at Roos in the later 18th century. The Crooked Billet or the Board was recorded in the 1820s,[98] and the Roos Arms has existed since at least 1840. There were also one or two unnamed beerhouses in the 19th and earlier 20th century. In 1892 one of the beerhouses was called the Black Horse and a house traded under that name in 1990.[99] A lodge of the Independent Order of Oddfellows was founded at Roos in 1839 but had been closed or had left the order by 1850; a branch of the National United Order of Free Gardeners had been moved to Roos from Withernsea by 1885 and was mentioned until 1948.[1] A reading room was provided in a cottage belonging to the church from 1885 until 1899,[2] and a rifle club met c. 1910.[3] A village institute was built in 1915 by Edward Milsom, rector, and his wife.[4] A playing field behind Main Street was provided c. 1980 and a sports pavilion was added in 1990.[5] A small wood called the Bog has been managed as a nature reserve since 1986.[6]

OWSTWICK. The dozen houses in the hamlet of Owstwick lie along one street, but there was formerly a back lane to the south.[7] The hamlet may also have had 'ends', for the east and west parts were referred to in the 16th century.[8] The buildings include two council houses and several farmhouses, one or two lying away from the hamlet.[9] Owstwick Hall, standing east of the hamlet, was built in the early 19th century by Joseph Storr (d. by 1834); it was called the Cottage in 1829 and Storr Hill later.[10]

MANORS AND OTHER ESTATES. In 1066 Murdoch and Swarger held 3 carucates and 5 bovates comprising two manors of ROOS and there were 3 ⅓ carucates of sokeland belonging to Morkar's manor of Kilnsea; all had passed to Drew de Bevrère by 1086, when his man Fulk occupied land on the manors.[11] Roos later became part of the Aumale fee. Four carucates of that fee in Roos were held as a mesne lordship by the St. Quintin family in the 13th and earlier 14th century[12] before descending to Henry Fitz-Hugh, Lord FitzHugh (d. 1425).[13]

Roos was for long held in demesne by the Ros or Roos family, which is believed to have been named from its estate there. The first known member was Peter de Ros (probably d. by 1130),

96   Stone on terrace.
97   *Trans. E. Yorks. Georgian Soc.* i (1), 32; inf. from Mr. D. R. Harris, Cottingham, 1990.
98   E.R.A.O., QDT/2/7, 9; Baines, *Hist. Yorks.* (1823), ii. 383.
99   Directories.
1   D. [R. J.] Neave, *E.R. Friendly Soc.* (E. Yorks. Loc. Hist. Ser. xli), 65.
2   E.R.A.O., PE/44/20, p. 54; below, charities.
3   E.R.A.O., PE/44/20, p. 93; *Hull Times*, 7 June 1913.
4   E.R.A.O., PE/44/20, pp. 50, 83, 93; *Kelly's Dir. N. & E.R. Yorks.* (1921), 583; local inf.

5   Inf. from Roos Playing Fields Assoc., 1990.
6   Inf. from S. Holderness Countryside Soc., 1990.
7   Jefferys, *Map Yorks.* (1772).
8   H.U.L., DDSY/52/22.
9   R.D.B., 588/637/491.
10   Ibid. EY/379/408; Bulmer, *Dir. E. Yorks.* (1892), 489; A. Bryant, *Map of E.R. Yorks.* (1829); O.S. Map 6", Yorks. CCXXVIII (1855 and later edns.).
11   *V.C.H. Yorks.* ii. 264, 269, 326.
12   *Yorks. Fines, John* (Sur. Soc. xciv), pp. 76–7; *Cal. Inq. p.m.* iv, p. 354; ix, pp. 25, 27.
13   *Yorks. Inq. Hen. IV–V*, p. 177; English, *Holderness*, 150; *Complete Peerage*, s.v. FitzHugh.

whose son Robert succeeded *c.* 1158 to Helmsley (Yorks. N.R.); the family took the title Baron Ros of Helmsley in the late 13th century.[14] The estate in Roos was mentioned in 1202, when another Robert de Ros held land there of Herbert de St. Quintin.[15] At the death of Robert's grandson Robert in 1285 it was described as the manor of *ROOS*. Part of the manor, including 1 carucate and 3¼ bovates of demesne land and evidently extending into Burton Pidsea and Tunstall, was held of the king as successor to the count of Aumale as 1 knight's fee; the remaining 4 carucates were held of the St. Quintins.[16] In 1301 a grant of free warren was made to William de Ros, who was named as sole lord of Roos in 1316.[17] The land held of the St. Quintins was said to comprise ¹⁄₁₂ knight's fee in 1343.[18]

The manor was held in dower by Margery widow of William de Ros from 1343 to 1363[19] and by Beatrice widow of Thomas de Ros from 1384 to 1415.[20] John de Ros's widow Margery held ⅓ from 1421 and the remainder was enjoyed from 1430 by Thomas de Ros's widow Eleanor, later duchess of Somerset.[21] After the attainder of Thomas de Ros in 1461 the issues and reversion of Roos were granted to George Plantagenet, duke of Clarence,[22] who succeeded to Eleanor's ⅔ share in 1467.[23] On the attainder of Clarence in 1478 that part reverted to the Crown,[24] which succeeded to the remaining ⅓ share on the death later that year of Margery, dowager Lady Ros.[25] Sir John Constable had the keeping of ⅔ of the manor from 1462 until his death[26] *c.* 1474, and later in the 1470s prominent Yorkists were granted parts of the manor, apparently as undertenants of Clarence or the Crown.[27]

John de la Pole, earl of Lincoln, had a grant of the manor in 1484[28] but that became void in 1485 on Henry VII's accession and the reversal of the attainder on Thomas de Ros. The Ros estates nevertheless remained with the Crown[29] because of the incapacity of the heir Edmund de Ros (d. 1508), custody being granted to Sir Thomas Lovell, husband of Edmund's sister Isabel.[30] On the death of Isabel by 1512 George

Manners, son of Edmund's other sister, succeeded as Lord Ros. He evidently also inherited Roos, his entry being recorded in 1513, when he died.[31] George's son and successor Thomas was made earl of Rutland in 1525.[32] After Thomas's death in 1543 his brother Sir Richard Manners held the manor during the minority of Thomas's son, Henry Manners, earl of Rutland (d. 1563),[33] who left Roos for life to John Manners, his second son who succeeded as earl in 1587 and died in 1588.[34] John's elder brother Edward, earl of Rutland (d. 1587), devised the reversion to his daughter Elizabeth, Lady Ros.[35] Elizabeth (d. 1591) was succeeded by her husband William Cecil, later earl of Exeter[36] (d. 1640), and he in turn by his nephew David Cecil, earl of Exeter (d. 1643), and David's widow Elizabeth (d. 1688); John Rastall, recorded as lord between 1649 and 1654, may have held Roos for the dowager countess.[37] The manor descended to John Cecil, earl of Exeter (d. 1700),[38] whose son William sold it in 1709 to Mark Kirkby.[39]

Kirkby (d. 1718) left Roos to his son Mark[40] (d. 1748). At the partition of Kirkby's estates in 1750 it fell to the share of his sister Isabel Collings, who by will proved in 1764 devised it to her nephew the Revd. Mark Sykes, later the first baronet (d. 1783).[41] Sykes, who was rector of Roos from 1735 to his death, had bought a small estate in Roos and Owstwick in 1741.[42] He was succeeded by his son Sir Christopher Sykes, Bt. (d. 1801), who left the manor with 970 a. in Roos to a younger son, Christopher Sykes, later also rector of Roos. The estate was enlarged with 65 a. bought by 1824.[43] The Revd. Christopher Sykes (d. 1857) was succeeded by his daughters Lucy, wife of the Revd. Charles Hotham, and Penelope, wife of Edward York.[44] Mrs. Hotham and Mrs. York sold 1,021 a. in Roos to J. T. Dickinson and his brother George in 1871; the manor was not included in the sale.[45] J. T. Dickinson (d. 1875) left his interest to his brother, who devised the estate in 1900[46] to trustees for his grandson M. W. Dickinson (d. 1943).[47] A small part of it was sold in 1937.[48] In

14 For the fam., *Complete Peerage*; *E.Y.C.* x, pp. 144–6; *V.C.H. Yorks. N.R.* i. 491–2.

15 *Yorks. Fines, John*, pp. 76–7.

16 *Cal. Inq. p.m.* ii, p. 345.

17 *Cal. Chart. R.* 1300–26, 21; *Kirkby's Inquest*, 304.

18 *Cal. Inq. p.m.* viii, p. 341.

19 Ibid. xi, pp. 400–1; *Cal. Pat.* 1343–5, 24.

20 *Cal. Inq. p.m.* xvi, p. 16; *Yorks. Inq. Hen. IV–V*, pp. 107–8.

21 H.U.L., DHO/7/11, 17; P.R.O., C 140/66, no. 35; *Yorks. Inq. Hen. IV–V*, pp. 174, 177.

22 *Cal. Pat.* 1461–7, 226, 454–5.

23 H.U.L., DHO/7/17.

24 *Complete Peerage*, s.v. Clarence; *Cal. Pat.* 1476–85, 88, 90, 212.   25 P.R.O., C 140/66, no. 35.

26 *Cal. Pat.* 1461–7, 230.

27 Ibid. 1467–77, 437, 457–8; 1476–85, 72, 124.

28 Ibid. 1476–85, 388.

29 Ibid. 1485–94, 66.

30 Hist. MSS. Com. 24, *Rutland*, iv, p. 560.

31 Belvoir Castle, near Grantham (Lincs.), Roos ct. roll (Apr. and Oct. 1513).

32 P.R.O., C 142/44, no. 153.

33 Belvoir Castle, Roos ct. roll (1547); *Complete Peerage*, s.v. Rutland; *Hist. Parl., Commons, 1509–58*, ii. 563–4.

34 P.R.O., C 142/139, no. 103; C 142/150, no. 160; *N. Country Wills*, i (Sur. Soc. cxvi), pp. 184, 186–7.

35 P.R.O., C 142/218, no. 52; *N. Country Wills*, ii (Sur. Soc. cxxi), pp. 117–18.

36 H.U.L., DHO/7/41; P.R.O., C 142/515, no. 76; for the Cecils, *Complete Peerage*, s.v. Exeter.

37 P.R.O., C 142/710, no. 4; ibid. CP 25(2)/527/7 Chas. I Mic. [no. 13]; E.R.A.O., DDBV/38/1; *T.E.R.A.S.* iv. 53.

38 P.R.O., CP 25(2)/899/8 Wm. III Hil. no. 9.

39 H.U.L., DDCV/134/2–3;; DDSY(3)/3/7; Poulson, *Holderness*, ii. 91.

40 R.D.B., G/242/545; *Y.A.J.* iii. 97 n.

41 H.U.L., DDSY/108/5; DDSY/110/23; for Sykes fam., Foster, *Pedigrees of Yorks.* iii; Burke, *Peerage* (1925), 2174.

42 H.U.L., DDCV/125/4; DDCV/133/24–5, 27; below, church.

43 H.U.L., DDSY/110/30; DDSY(3)/4/52; R.D.B., CD/198/292; DS/63/89.

44 R.D.B., KF/336/459.

45 Ibid. KX/3/4.

46 Ibid. LW/202/296; 40/231/220 (1902); window in church.

47 R.D.B., 251/39/33; 733/504/408; B.I.H.R., CD. Add. 1952/1.

48 R.D.B., 577/301/241; 584/396/301; 585/552/424.

1947 William Grant (Paull) Ltd. bought the 421-a. Elms farm and the 251-a. Sunderland farm, besides a further 83 a.,[49] and the 223-a. North farm was bought in 1947 by the trustees of Ann Watson's charity, Hull;[50] both estates were still in the same hands in 1990.[51]

The manor of Roos was bought in 1871 by Thomas Crust, who had purchased 75 a. of freehold in 1869[52] and between 1871 and 1877 added copyholds amounting to 182 a.[53] The estate, which later comprised c. 290 a. of freehold, descended like Tickton, in Beverley, to Crust's daughter Marian Nolloth and her successors, the Riggs.[54]

A manor house was recorded in the 13th and 14th centuries.[55] It was probably disused in 1416, when a new house at its east gate, garths, and part of the 'great grange' there were let,[56] and only its site was mentioned in 1421.[57] Earthworks marking the site of the so-called castle[58] survived near the church in 1990, when one side of the moat was still wet. The Revd. Christopher Sykes and his daughter Lucy and her husband lived at the rectory house.[59]

In 1066 Murdoch had a manor of *OWST-WICK*, evidently comprising 2 ⅓ carucates, and Morkar had 3 carucates of soke there belonging to his manor of Kilnsea. Both estates had passed to Drew de Bevrère by 1086[60] and later formed part of the Aumale fee.

It may have been Morkar's estate which passed to the Brus family, who held 3 carucates at Owstwick in the 13th century. The estate was held of the Bruses by the Merlays and of them by the St. Quintins.[61] Herbert de St. Quintin was confirmed as the tenant of rent and the service of ¼ knight's fee there in 1202[62] and the estate was held by his successors until the 14th century.[63]

It was similarly perhaps Murdoch's estate which was granted to a butler of the count of Aumale. Amand the butler (d. by 1218) gave land in Owstwick to Meaux abbey in the early 13th century,[64] and in 1240 his daughter Beatrice, widow of Geoffrey de Friboys, held 1 carucate and 1 bovate there of the count of

Aumale. By 1252 the estate was evidently held jointly by Beatrice and John de Surdeval, presumably the heir to Beatrice's sister Hawise de Surdeval.[65] As at Hilston and Tansterne, in Aldbrough, the butler's fee at Owstwick evidently passed in turn to the Berchauds[66] and the Constables, whose tenants were the Rouths. Amand of Routh was one of the lords named in 1316.[67] The Rouths' successor Sir Richard Michelbourne sold the small estate to Nicholas Kitchen in the early 17th century.[68] It has not been traced further.

By the 13th century much of Owstwick belonged to a family of that name. Stephen of Owstwick (d. c. 1288) held a chief house and 2 carucates from the Crown by knight service and 1 carucate and 1 bovate more from John of Aseby.[69] Stephen's son Stephen sold at least 1 carucate and 1 bovate to John Ughtred c. 1297.[70] John was succeeded soon after by his daughter Joan.[71] She married (Sir) Thomas de la Rivers, who was named as a lord of Owstwick in 1316.[72] In 1326 and 1328 the Rivers family sold the 1 carucate and 1 bovate to William son of Henry of Melton,[73] evidently for William Melton, archbishop of York, who c. 1336 gave (Sir) William Melton the so-called manor of *OWSTWICK*.[74] It was held as ¹⁄₄₀ knight's fee at Sir William Melton's death in 1362, when he was succeeded by his son William.[75] The estate later belonged to Sir John Melton (fl. 1455),[76] Margery Melton in dower in 1510,[77] Sir John Melton (d. 1544), and the latter's daughter Dorothy, wife of George Darcy, Lord Darcy, before descending in the Darcy family to John Darcy, Lord Darcy (d. 1635).[78]

It was perhaps the same manor of Owstwick, including a chief house, which Charles Laughton (d. 1638) devised to his son Charles, and a Mr. Laughton had 263 a. there in 1648.[79] Joshua Laughton and his son Charles had the estate in 1712 but by 1726 part at least had passed to Christopher Kirkby and presumably later descended with his other lands in Owstwick.[80]

Another estate in Owstwick extended into Hilston and belonged to a cadet branch of the

---

⁴⁹ Ibid. 742/537/455; 742/538/456; 743/231/194; 750/176/145.

⁵⁰ Ibid. 744/109/90; *V.C.H. Yorks. E.R.* i. 346.

⁵¹ Inf. from Mr. A. Grant, Roos, 1990; inf. from clerk to trustees, Sutton-on-Hull, 1990.

⁵² R.D.B., KI/319/439; KX/35/39.

⁵³ H.U.L., DDCV/134/16, pp. 200, 208, 226, 249, 253, 315.

⁵⁴ Ibid. DDCV/134/16; R.D.B., 1/275/234 (1885); 23/14/10 (1900); 61/362/343 (1903); *V.C.H. Yorks. E.R.* vi. 304.

⁵⁵ *Cal. Inq. p.m.* ii, p. 345; viii, p. 341.

⁵⁶ Burghley Ho., near Stamford (Lincs.), MS. 37/18.

⁵⁷ H.U.L., DDSY/56/1; *Yorks. Inq. Hen. IV–V*, p. 177.

⁵⁸ O.S. Map 6″, Yorks. CCXXVIII (1855 and later edns.).

⁵⁹ Below, church.   ⁶⁰ *V.C.H. Yorks.* ii. 264–5, 326.

⁶¹ *Yorks. Inq.* i, pp. 201–2; *Cal. Inq. p.m.* ii, pp. 188–9; *E.Y.C.* iii, p. 69 n.

⁶² *Yorks. Fines, John*, p. 73.

⁶³ P.R.O., CP 40/291, m. 57d.; H.U.L., DHO/16/91; *Yorks. Fines, 1232–46*, p. 162.

⁶⁴ English, *Holderness*, 92; *Chron. de Melsa* (Rolls Ser.), i. 359–60.

⁶⁵ P.R.O., C 141/4, no. 45; *Chron. de Melsa*, i. 412; *Yorks.*

Fines, 1232–46, p. 82; *1246–72*, p. 88.

⁶⁶ B.L. Cott. MS. Otho C. viii, ff. 81v., 82.

⁶⁷ E.R.A.O., DDCC/18/1, s.v. 15 July 1435; P.R.O., C 141/4, no. 45; ibid. CP 40/291, m. 57; *Feud. Aids*, vi. 164; *Cal. Chart. R. 1257–1300*, 308; above, Aldbrough, manors (Tansterne); Hilston, manor.

⁶⁸ E.R.A.O., DDCC/18/3, s.v. Apr. 1616.

⁶⁹ *Yorks. Inq.* ii, pp. 73–4.

⁷⁰ Ibid. iii, pp. 36–7; *Cal. Pat. 1292–1301*, 230.

⁷¹ *Yorks. Inq.* iii, pp. 90–1.

⁷² *Feud. Aids*, vi. 164; *V.C.H. Yorks. N.R.* ii. 104–5.

⁷³ *Yorks. Fines, 1327–47*, p. 7.

⁷⁴ *Cal. Inq. Misc.* iii, p. 46.

⁷⁵ *Cal. Inq. p.m.* xi, p. 285.

⁷⁶ P.R.O., CP 25(1)/281/161, no. 5; Shaftesbury MSS., M 220 (acct. 33–4 Hen. VI).

⁷⁷ Ibid. C 142/25, no. 121.

⁷⁸ Ibid. C 142/70, no. 60; C 142/273, no. 82; ibid. E 150/241, no. 39. For the fam., *Complete Peerage*.

⁷⁹ E.R.A.O., DDCC/69/1; DDCC/111/26.

⁸⁰ B.I.H.R., TER. H. Roos 1685, 1726; H.U.L., DDSY/52/50; below, this section.

Ros family. Robert son of Robert de Ros of Helmsley (Yorks. N.R.) had a grant of free warren there in 1297 and, as Robert de Ros or Roos of Gedney (Lincs.), he held 1 carucate and 1 bovate at his death by 1311.[81] The estate descended to Robert's grandson Sir James Roos (fl. 1397) and then to Sir Robert Roos (d. 1441), who left daughters.[82] It was evidently the same which was held in turn by Sir John Paulet (d. 1525) and his son Sir William, who was created Baron St. John in 1539.[83] The Paulets had 1 carucate and 1½ bovates, a few acres, and several houses in Owstwick, held as appurtenances of Thorpe manor in Aldbrough. The estate passed by exchange in 1546 from Lord St. John to the Crown, which sold it to John Eldred and William Whitmore in 1611.[84] It has not been traced further.

Other lay estates at Owstwick in the Middle Ages included that of William de la Twyer, who was named as a lord in 1316.[85]

The largest modern estate in Owstwick was that which passed from the Towrys to the Sykes family. A Mr. Towry had 254 a. there in 1648[86] and much of the estate was sold in 1658 by George Towry to Robert Witty (d. by 1688).[87] In 1694 it was sold to Mark Kirkby[88] (d. 1718), who left it to his son Christopher (d. c. 1733),[89] from whom it evidently passed to his brother Mark. The estate, which comprised 2 carucates and 3½ bovates,[90] descended with Roos manor until 1801, when Sir Christopher Sykes, Bt., left it with 26 a. in Roos to a younger son, later Sir Tatton Sykes, Bt. (d. 1863).[91] The estate, which extended into Burton Pidsea, passed to Sir Tatton's second son Christopher Sykes (d. 1898), and then reverted to Christopher's brother Sir Tatton Sykes, Bt. (d. 1913), whose son Sir (Tatton) Mark Sykes, Bt.,[92] sold it. In 1916 one farm, with 451 a. in Owstwick, was bought by Thomas Cook, and Grange farm, with 247 a., by Thomas Newton; in 1918 the 138-a. Primrose Hill farm was bought by T. E. Kirk.[93] In 1937 Cook's farm was sold to Thomas Cook the younger, who with Thomas K. Cook bought the 204-a. Elms farm in 1948.[94] In 1952 Kenby, formerly Cook's, and Elms farms, comprising

600 a., were conveyed to T. Cook & Son (Farmers) Ltd., which added c. 30 a. in 1959. The company still owned the farms in 1990.[95]

The great tithes of the part of Owstwick township lying in Garton parish remained with the Crown after the suppression of Thornton college (Lincs.).[96] Corn tithes there were granted to Francis Morrice and Francis Phillips in 1611.[97] The tithes were valued at £3 a year net in 1650, when all apparently belonged to George Towry,[98] who sold some of them in 1654.[99] In 1716 the impropriator was not known and the tithes were said to belong to the landowners by default.[1] Those on 428 a. were merged before the remaining tithes, on 22 a., were commuted in 1843 for a rent charge of £4 8s. payable to Hannah Sewell.[2]

Meaux abbey was given 2 bovates at Owstwick by Gilbert le Aungell between 1210 and 1220 and 4 bovates by Hugh of Rysome between 1221 and 1235, and by the mid century it had more than 1 carucate there.[3] The abbey was granted free warren in 1293,[4] and in 1316 the abbot was named as a lord of Owstwick.[5] In 1396 the estate comprised 6 bovates, 4 houses, and other land, all then divided between ten tenants who owed rents amounting to just over £3 a year.[6] In 1610 the Crown sold the abbey's estate, comprising 4 bovates, closes, and several houses, besides free rents, to Edward Bates and Henry Elwes.[7] A house and 1½ bovate were resold in 1613 and another house and land in 1629.[8]

Thornton abbey (Lincs.) had 2 bovates at Owstwick in 1288.[9] After the Dissolution its former estate descended with Garton and was sold in 1611;[10] no more is known of it.

Nunkeeling priory briefly had a small estate at Owstwick by grant of Beatrice de Friboys in the 13th century.[11]

Nine freeholdings in Owstwick were in 1702 reputed part of a manor of Fitling formerly belonging to the Knights Hospitaller.[12]

Clare college, Cambridge, had an estate in Owstwick by 1783.[13] The college sold Willow Toft farm, of 55 a., in 1901 to Mary Cook (d. 1921), who evidently devised it to Annie Cook (d. 1943). It was sold in 1943 to J. R. Ellis and

[81] *Cal. Chart. R.* 1257–1300, 469; *Cal. Inq. p.m.* v, pp. 137–8.
[82] P.R.O., C 139/106, no. 24; *Cal. Inq. p.m.* xi, p. 165; xv, pp. 232–3; xvii, p. 331.
[83] H.U.L., DHO/7/23, where it is said to be held of Roos manor; *Complete Peerage*, s.v. Winchester.
[84] P.R.O., SC 11/762; ibid. C 66/1903, no. 9; *L. & P. Hen. VIII*, xxi (2), p. 243.
[85] *Feud. Aids*, vi. 164.
[86] E.R.A.O., DDCC/69/1.
[87] H.U.L., DDSY/52/28, 33, 35.
[88] Ibid. DDSY/52/36–7, 39.
[89] R.D.B., G/242/545; *Y.A.J.* iii. 97 n., 98 n.
[90] H.U.L., DDSY/56/41; DDSY/101/52 (25 Feb. 1783).
[91] Ibid. DDSY/108/5; DDSY/110/23, 30; B.I.H.R., TA. 42L; R.D.B., CD/197/291; Foster, *Pedigrees of Yorks.* iii; Burke, *Peerage* (1925), 2174.
[92] R.D.B., GY/151/168; IP/395/499; Burke, *Peerage* (1970), 2603.
[93] H.U.L., DDSY/97/34; R.D.B., 176/487/431; 177/200/173; 185/548/450.
[94] R.D.B., 260/346/301; 567/289/219; 776/72/60.

[95] Ibid. 930/34/32; 930/36/34; 1141/80/68; inf. from T. Cook & Son.
[96] P.R.O., E 310/40/10; above, Garton, manors.
[97] P.R.O., C 66/1908, m. 13.
[98] *T.E.R.A.S.* iv. 53–4.
[99] P.R.O., CP 25(2)/614/1654 East. no. 34.
[1] B.I.H.R., TER. H. Garton 1716.
[2] Ibid. TA. 42L.
[3] *Chron. de Melsa*, i. 359–60, 416; ii. 23–4.
[4] *Cal. Chart. R.* 1257–1300, 427.
[5] *Feud. Aids*, vi. 164.
[6] B.L. Cott. MS. Vit. C. vi, ff. 207v.–208.
[7] P.R.O., C 66/1882, no. 4; ibid. SC 6/Hen. VIII/4612, m. 3d.
[8] B.L. Add. Ch. 65790; H.U.L., DDSY/52/24.
[9] *Yorks. Inq.* ii, p. 74; Poulson, *Holderness*, ii. 101.
[10] Above, Garton, manors.
[11] B.L. Cott. MS. Otho C. viii, f. 82; E.R.A.O., DDCC/111/4; below, Mappleton, manors.
[12] E.R.A.O., DDX/595/53.
[13] H.U.L., DDSY/56/41; DDSY/101/52 (25 Feb. 1783); B.I.H.R., TA. 42L.

in 1948, when of 76 a., was bought by Henry James, the owner in 1990.[14]

Two carucates at 'Andrebi' were soke of Morkar's manor of Withernsea in 1066; elsewhere the estate is said to have been held as a manor by Ramkel before passing to William Malet. By 1086 it belonged to Drew de Bevrère. No more is known of it.[15]

ECONOMIC HISTORY. AGRICULTURE BEFORE 1800. *Roos.* The open fields of Roos township were named as East and West fields *c.* 1640.[16] They included common meadow land and comprised 490 a. and 565 a. respectively *c.* 1750.[17] The rest of the common meadows were in West, Burnham, and Langham or Lengham carrs, which comprised 240 a., 57 a., and 11 a. respectively.[18] The carrs also included waste land called Sunderlands in 1343, and in the 17th century faggots of furze in Dean Sunderlands were let with other parts of the demesne.[19] Common pasture was provided mostly by the Furze, 163 a. of which was in East Furze and 107 a. in West Furze. As in neighbouring Tunstall, the pasture may once have been part of the tillage, and in 1685 'dales', 'lands', and 'falls' were recorded in East and West Furze, and earlier and later areas there were measured in acres, 'bands', or wands, and paces.[20] In 1663 West Furze was, however, said to be stinted at the rate of 1 beast gate a bovate and 1 'foot', or ¼ gate, for each toft; in East Furze 1 gate was enjoyed for every 3 a. held, possibly as grassed strips in that pasture.[21]

Pasture rights were closely regulated by the 17th century. In 1638 the stint in the fallow field was 3 gates a bovate from March until May and 6 from May until Michaelmas; horses and cattle were to be removed on May Day and the number of sheep in both periods was limited to 4 a gate. It was also ordered that year that no sheep should be put into the Furze until Michaelmas.[22] About 1750 each toft had, besides ¼ beast gate in the Furze in summer, ½ gate in West carr, and 1 beast gate or 5 sheep gates in the fields throughout the year.[23]

By the 1780s there were 873 a. of old inclosures in Roos township, most of them lying near the southern boundary; one close there contained 291 a. and another 78 a. The closes were often flooded,[24] and the Furze was also said to be mostly wet land or covered with whins.[25] The remaining commonable lands in Roos were inclosed by an award of 1786 under an Act of 1783.[26] There were 1,594 a. to be dealt with. Allotments totalled 1,554 a. and 10 a. of old inclosures were involved in exchanges. East field contained more than 395 a., West field over 170 a., the Furze more than 153 a., Burnham carr 51 a., and Lengham carr 8 a. The rector was allotted 337 a. for tithes and glebe, Sir Christopher Sykes, Bt., lord of the manor, 201 a., Benjamin Ganton 173 a., and Edmund Bramston 166 a. There were also four allotments of 50–99 a., ten of 20–49 a., thirteen of 5–19 a., and thirteen of under 5 a. each. Apart from the manorial and rectorial allotments, only 66 a. were freehold.

At Roos in 1558 the manor included some 40 bovates: the largest holding was of 3½ bovates and there were three of 3 bovates each, fourteen of 1 or 2 bovates, and twenty-two of less than a bovate; ten holdings included no open-field land. The manor-house site and the demesne were then let for nearly £23, copyhold rents produced almost £26, and free rents a few shillings.[27]

Owstwick. At Owstwick the open fields were named as North and South fields in 1320.[28] Both fields extended to the western boundary of the township.[29] An intake (*avenam*) recorded in 1288, and references later to foreland and odd land, suggest the enlargement of the cultivated area there by assarting.[30]

In 1648 there were 937 a. in the open fields, 140 a. in 'Audills', presumably Old Hills, and 97 a. of old inclosures. Of the 20 owners one had 263 a. and another 254 a., and there were five holdings of 50–99 a., ten of 5–49 a., and three of under 5 a.[31] An inclosure by agreement made in 1649[32] probably dealt with most of the remaining commonable lands. The new closes may have included the 80-a. Carr close mentioned in 1669.[33] Some land apparently remained uninclosed, for in 1668 parcels of meadow were said to lie dispersed in Owstwick carr,[34] and as late as the 1720s a close included a strip.[35] Meadow land in the carr was consolidated by purchase in the late 18th century.[36]

[14] R.D.B., 37/150/148 (1901); 247/212/174; 257/299/250; 663/391/348; 666/16/14; 790/418/350; inf. from Mr. M. James. The name Willowtofts was used in 1323: H.U.L., DDSY/52/3. [15] *V.C.H. Yorks.* ii. 265, 296.
[16] H.U.L., DDCV/134/1 (1635); DDSY(3)/3/6 (1642).
[17] Para. based on H.U.L., DDSY(3)/7/51 (undated survey of *c.* 1750); B.I.H.R., TER. H. Roos n.d. etc. Most of the areas in the survey seem to be expressed in acres, stengs, and a lesser measure, possibly a 'hand'. Occurrences of the last are few and have been ignored in the calculations.
[18] Cf. H.U.L., DDSY/101/52 (20 Mar. 1783). Langholm leys were recorded in 1343: *Cal. Inq. p.m.* viii, p. 341.
[19] H.U.L., DDCV/133/33; *Cal. Inq. p.m.* viii, p. 341; O.S. Map 6", Yorks. CCXLII (1855 edn.).
[20] Below, Tunstall, econ. hist. H.U.L., DDSY(3)/7/51 gives 16 p[aces] to the 'band'; there were evidently the same number of 'bands' in an acre.
[21] E.R.A.O., DDBV/38/1 (Oct. 1663).
[22] H.U.L., DDCV/134/1 (Apr. 1635, Oct. 1638).
[23] Ibid. DDSY(3)/7/51; B.I.H.R., TER. H. Roos 1764.
[24] B.I.H.R., TER. H. Roos 1786; R.D.B., BG/103/9; E.R.A.O., PE/44/32 (map); H.U.L., DDSY/101/52 (24 [Feb.] 1783); Belvoir Castle, Roos ct. roll (1511).
[25] H.U.L., DDSY/101/52 (21 Mar. 1783).
[26] R.D.B., BG/103/9; E.R.A.O., PE/44/32 (map); 23 Geo. III, c. 17 (Priv. Act). For correspondence about the inclosure, H.U.L., DDSY/101/52–3.
[27] H.U.L., DDSY/56/1.
[28] Ibid. DDSY/52/2(b).   [29] Ibid. DDSY/52/3.
[30] Ibid. DDSY/52/8; *Yorks. Inq.* ii, p. 74; *Cal.Inq. p.m.* v, p. 138.
[31] E.R.A.O., DDCC/69/1; O.S. Map 6", Yorks. CCXXVIII (1855 edn.).
[32] E.R.A.O., DDCC/139/26; DDGR/42/1 (28 Sept. 1751); ibid. DDX/7/2.
[33] H.U.L., DDSY/108/1.
[34] Ibid. DDCV/125/1; O.S. Map 6", Yorks. CCXXVIII (1855 edn.).
[35] B.I.H.R., TER. H. Roos 1716, 1726.
[36] R.D.B., EY/379/408; EY/383/410.

AGRICULTURE AFTER 1800. The parish had 949 a. under crops in 1801.[37] Owstwick township contained 885 a. of arable and 432 a. of grassland in 1843,[38] and there were 2,172 a. under crops and 1,592 a. of permanent grass in Roos and Owstwick together in 1905.[39] Roos wood was recorded c. 1740, and in the mid 19th century there was c. 50 a. of woodland in Roos township, mostly in plantations in the former carrs, but little remained in 1987.[40] In the 1930s grassland was mostly near the settlements and on the lower ground in the south and south-west of Roos.[41] The area returned under Roos in 1987 was slightly larger than the civil parish; there were then 2,180 ha. (5,387 a.) of arable land and 222.7 ha. (550 a.) of grassland, and over 89,000 poultry, more than 13,000 pigs, and c. 600 each of cattle and sheep were then kept.[42]

There were usually a dozen farmers in Roos township and half a dozen in Owstwick in the 19th and earlier 20th century,[43] of whom in each township two in 1851[44] and three or four in the 1920s and 1930s had 150 a. or more. In 1987 of 30 holdings returned at Roos, three were of over 200 ha. (494 a.), five of 100–199 ha. (247–492 a.), six of 50–99 ha. (124–245 a.), seven of 10–49 ha. (25–121 a.), and nine of under 10 ha.[45] A few men were employed at Roos as cowkeepers and market gardeners in the late 19th and early 20th century. Two or three cattle dealers and up to three horsebreakers were also recorded, and a horse show was held c. 1900.[46] There was an abbattoir in the north end of the village in 1990.

TRADE AND INDUSTRY. A brickworks at Roos existed by 1823 but was closed c. 1880, and gravel was extracted at Owstwick in or before the 1850s.[47] In the later 19th century James Blenkin, blacksmith, built up a business at Roos making and hiring agricultural machines, which employed up to 20 men, but it was in decline by 1913.[48] In the later 20th century premises at Owstwick were occupied in turn by an agricultural seed business and a farm machinery agency.[49] The numbers of craftsmen and tradesmen in Roos in the 19th and 20th centuries have reflected the large size of the village,[50] which still supported several shops in 1990.

MILLS. A windmill recorded in the 13th century was probably at Roos, and there was a

mill there in 1403[51] and a windmill from the 16th century.[52] The windmill stood in West field in the later 18th century;[53] it was disused in 1908 and was demolished then or soon after. Milling continued elsewhere in Roos at a steam mill for a few years.[54] At Owstwick two mills were recorded in the 13th century,[55] and there was a windmill there in 1588;[56] one or more mills were commemorated in the names Mill Field close, recorded in 1811, and Mill Field House, later Primrose Hill Farm, named in 1829.[57]

LOCAL GOVERNMENT. Franchises of Roos manorial court included infangthief, which was claimed by grant from Henry II and allowed in 1242 by the count of Aumale on condition that such cases were heard in the presence of his bailiff of Holderness. Gallows and the assize of bread and of ale were also claimed c. 1280.[58]

Court rolls survive for nearly 20 years between 1298 and 1422[59] and for 15 years in the 16th and early 17th century,[60] and the record is virtually complete from 1635 to 1935.[61] Other papers include copies of the roll from 1458.[62] The jurisdiction of the court included view of frankpledge and the assize of bread and of ale, and chevage was claimed from tenants in the 15th century. In the late 13th and the 14th century the court met about every three weeks but by the 15th century only two or three sessions a year were held. Meetings became more frequent in the 18th century, after the sale of the manor to a local family. Only one meeting a year was usual from the 1870s and the court last met in 1887. It was kept in a tenant's house in the 17th century.[63] Officers regularly appointed included 2 constables, 2 aletasters, 2 affeerors, and 4 bylawmen, and 2 mill-graves were recorded in the 15th and 16th centuries. A warrener answerable for strays and 2 pig-reeves were employed in 1416; in the 1630s there were 2 pinders, one for the sown field and one for the fallow, but later only one.

Part of Owstwick may have belonged to the Hospitallers, and testamentary jurisdiction there was an appurtenance of the order's former manor of Fitling, in Humbleton, in the 18th century.[64]

Churchwardens' accounts survive for 1666–1755 and 1796–1953.[65] In the early 19th century permanent poor relief was given to 11–20 people

37 P.R.O., HO 67/26/350.
38 B.I.H.R., TA. 42L.   39 Acreage Returns, 1905.
40 R.D.B., KA/348/468: H.U.L., DDSY/56/34; O.S. Map 6″, Yorks. CCXXVIII, CCXLII (1855 edn.); inf. from Min. of Agric., Fish. & Food, Beverley, 1990.
41 [1st] Land Util. Surv. Map, sheets 33–4.
42 Inf. from Min. of Agric., Fish. & Food.
43 Directories.
44 P.R.O., HO 107/2364.
45 Inf. from Min. of Agric., Fish. & Food.
46 Directories; Hull Times, 7 June 1913.
47 Directories; O.S. Map 6″, Yorks. CCXXVIII (1855 edn.).
48 Directories; Hull Times, 7 June 1913.
49 R.D.B., 1400/445/397; inf. from Rob. D. Webster Ltd., 1990.   50 Directories.
51 Burghley Ho. MS. 37/18; Cal. Inq. p.m. ii, p. 345.
52 H.U.L., DDSY/56/1; DDCV/134/1 (Apr. 1636); DDCV/134/6 (May 1742).
53 Jefferys, Map Yorks. (1772).
54 Directories; O.S. Map 1/2,500, Yorks. CCXXVIII. 14 (1910 edn.); Hull Times, 7 June 1913.
55 Chron. de Melsa (Rolls Ser.), ii. 24; Cal. Inq. p.m. iii, p. 355; Yorks. Inq. ii, p. 74.
56 H.U.L., DDSY/52/22.
57 R.D.B., CS/9/20; Bryant, Map E.R. Yorks. (1829).
58 Yorks. Fines, 1232–46, pp. 110–11; Plac. de Quo Warr. (Rec. Com.), 189; Rot. Hund. (Rec. Com.), i. 106.
59 Burghley Ho. MS. 37/18.
60 Belvoir Castle, Roos ct. rolls (1509–47); H.U.L., DDSY(3)/3/1–4 (1539–1624).
61 H.U.L., DDCV/134/1–17; DDSY(3)/3/6; E.R.A.O., DDBV/38/1.
62 H.U.L., DDSY(3)/3/7.
63 Ibid. DDCV/133/34.
64 E.R.A.O., DDX/595/51–2, 55; above, manors [Knights Hospitaller].
65 E.R.A.O., PE/44/23, 25–7.

in Roos township and 8–11 were relieved occasionally. In Owstwick township, which relieved its own poor, 9–16 received permanent and 3–4 occasional relief.[66] There were poorhouses at Owstwick.[67] Roos and Owstwick joined Patrington poor-law union in 1836[68] and remained in Patrington rural district until 1935 when they were taken into Holderness rural district as part of the new civil parish of Roos, which became part of the Holderness district of Humberside in 1974.[69] In 1996 Roos parish became part of a new East Riding unitary area.[70]

CHURCH. There was a church at Roos by 1086.[71] It was given to Kirkham priory by 1232, presumably by the Ros family which was related to the founder of the priory.[72] Roos, which remained a rectory, was united with Tunstall in 1927[73] and with Garton with Hilston in 1974.[74] In the Middle Ages Roos church may have had chapels at Hilston, which has long been a separate parish, and at Grimston. The garth of the chapel of Grimston was claimed to be in Roos parish in the 15th century.[75]

The advowson belonged to Kirkham priory until the Dissolution.[76] A turn granted to John of Lockton before his forfeiture in 1385 led to several apparently unsuccessful attempts by the Crown to present in his stead.[77] Assignees of the priory presented in 1508 and 1539.[78] In 1541 the advowson was granted to Thomas Manners, earl of Rutland,[79] and it later descended with the manor until the 19th century. The Crown presented in 1572, apparently by lapse, and in 1588 during the minority of Lady Ros.[80] At the death of the Revd. Christopher Sykes in 1857 the patronage evidently reverted to the senior representative of his family and was transferred by the Sykes trustees to Edward Milsom, rector, and his family in 1920.[81] When Roos was united with Tunstall in 1927, the former patron of Tunstall was given a share in the patronage of Garton with Hilston, united at the same time,

and the patronage of Roos with Tunstall was declared to belong wholly to the former patrons of Roos.[82] The advowson of Roos with Tunstall passed in, or by, 1928 to an Anglo-Catholic body, the Society for the Maintenance of the Faith,[83] which at the further union of 1974 was given two turns out of three.[84]

The church was worth £13 6s. 8d. net in 1291[85] and £19 net in 1535.[86] In 1650 the improved annual value of the rectory, comprising glebe lands, rents, and tithes in Roos, Owstwick, and Grimston, was £83 net.[87] The average net income was £602 a year in 1829–31[88] and the income was £441 net in 1883.[89]

In the early 17th century the tithe of hay growing in the fields of the parish was compounded for at the rate of 3d. a bovate.[90] In Roos township the tithes included a modus of 1d. a bovate for whins growing on the common pasture.[91] The tithes of Roos were commuted at inclosure in 1786, when the rector was allotted 214 a. and rents of £43 7s. 2d. for the tithes of old inclosures.[92] In Owstwick township a composition of 6s. 8d. a bovate was paid by the 1670s for the tithes of the tillage when it was fallow.[93] In 1843 the tithes of Owstwick were commuted for a rent charge of £167 13s. 8d.[94] By the 1670s the tithes at Grimston were paid by a composition of £1 13s. 4d., presumably charged on Five Nobles close, just over the boundary in Tunstall.[95] That composition was still paid in 1843, when the tithes of 205 a. were commuted for a rent charge of that amount.[96] There were four bovates of glebe, besides several tofts and crofts, at Roos from the later 17th century,[97] and at inclosure in 1786 the rector was allotted 123 a. for glebe, besides more for tithes.[98] Two acres were sold in 1892, the 219-a. Glebe farm in 1918, and 6 a. in 1968.[99] In 1978 there were still 119 a. of glebe.[1]

The rectory house had five hearths in 1672.[2] Repaired in the 1690s, it was rebuilt between 1784 and 1798,[3] but was replaced by a 'handsome mansion' in white brick, built in 1820 by Christopher Sykes, who also enlarged the

[66] *Poor Law Abstract, 1804*, pp. 592–5; *1818*, pp. 522–3.

[67] B.I.H.R., TA. 42L; O.S. Map 6″, Yorks. CCXXVIII (1855 edn.).

[68] *3rd Rep. Poor Law Com.* 169.

[69] *Census.*

[70] Humberside (Structural Change) Order 1995, copy at E.R.A.O.

[71] *V.C.H. Yorks.* ii. 269.

[72] Ibid. iii. 219; *Reg. Gray*, p. 54; *Complete Peerage*, s.v. Ros.

[73] *Lond. Gaz.* 4 Nov. 1927, pp. 6972–3.

[74] B.I.H.R., OC. 880.

[75] Ibid. CP. F. 148; above, Hilston, church.

[76] Lawrance, 'Clergy List', Holderness, 2, pp. 118–20.

[77] Ibid. p. 119; *Cal. Inq. Misc.* vi, p. 98.

[78] Lawrance, op. cit. p. 120.

[79] *L. & P. Hen. VIII*, xvi, pp. 505–6.

[80] Lawrance, op. cit. p. 121; R.D.B., G/242/545; H.U.L., DDSY/108/3, 5; DDSY/110/23; Poulson, *Holderness*, ii. 94.

[81] B.I.H.R., BA. TP. 1914/2, 1920/7.

[82] *Lond. Gaz.* 4 Nov. 1927, p. 6972.

[83] Cf. B.I.H.R., BA. TP. 1928/1; Ch. of Eng. *Yr. Bk.* (1930), p. 516.

[84] B.I.H.R., OC. 880.

[85] *Tax. Eccl.* (Rec. Com.), 304.

[86] *Valor Eccl.* (Rec. Com.), v. 119.

[87] *T.E.R.A.S.* iv. 53.

[88] *Rep. Com. Eccl. Revenues*, 962–3.

[89] B.I.H.R., V. 1884/Ret. 2.

[90] Ibid. CP. H. 1222.

[91] Ibid. TER. H. Roos 1764 etc.

[92] R.D.B., BG/103/9; H.U.L., DDSY(3)/3/10. The rents were payable from 1784.

[93] B.I.H.R., TER. H. Roos 1743 etc.; P.R.O., E 134/29 Chas. II East./7. Relatively small areas elsewhere in the par. may have been included in the composition.

[94] B.I.H.R., TA. 42L.

[95] P.R.O., E 134/28 Chas. II East./4; for the close, E.R.A.O., DDCC/42/2. The payment was later for Bracken Hill farm, Garton: B.I.H.R., TER. H. Roos 1764 etc.

[96] B.I.H.R., TA. 263s.

[97] Ibid. TER. H. Roos n.d. etc.

[98] R.D.B., BG/103/9.

[99] Ibid. 49/462/417 (1892); 190/174/155; 1569/223/170.

[1] Inf. from York Dioc. Bd. of Finance, 1981.

[2] P.R.O., E 179/205/504; cf. Lawrance, 'Clergy List', Holderness, 2, p. 121.

[3] P.R.O., C 5/147/31; E.R.A.O., PE/44/3; PE/44/20, pp. 12–13; B.I.H.R., TER. H. Roos n.d., 1764, 1786, 1809, 1817. For plan of old ho., E.R.A.O., PE/44/21.

grounds.[4] The grounds were further enlarged in 1868 and 1872.[5] The house was considered too grand for a rectory and was sold in 1892 to George Dickinson and renamed Roos Hall.[6] It was destroyed by fire in 1937[7] and Elm Farm was later built on the site. A new rectory house, c. ½ km. to the north-west, was built in 1892–3 in a Queen Anne style to designs by Temple Moore.[8] In 1968 a new house was built and the old one sold.[9]

Rectors were often non-resident in the Middle Ages and later. Robert Corbridge, rector from 1301, was absent for study for at least 13 years.[10] Pluralist incumbents included John Pigot, rector from 1399,[11] and John Manners, a member of the seigneurial family, rector from 1539 until his death in 1563.[12] Nicholas Cook was presented for non-residence in 1567.[13] Anthony Stevenson, rector from 1645, was ejected in 1662; he was 'well skilled in physic' and treated the poor free.[14] The living was later held by several members of the Sykes family, patrons and lords of the manor. Dr. Mark Sykes, later Sir Mark Sykes, Bt., rector 1735–83, often lived elsewhere.[15] Christopher Sykes presented himself to the living in 1819 and then nominated as his successor his son-in-law Charles Hotham, rector 1841–66.[16] From 1948 the incumbent of Roos and Tunstall also served Garton with Hilston.[17] A curate was recorded in the mid 16th century[18] and an assistant curate was employed in the 18th[19] and 19th centuries.[20]

Service was weekly in 1743 and 1764. Communion was then celebrated four or five times a year, usually with c. 30 recipients in 1764.[21] By 1865 two Sunday services were held and c. 1920 they were daily. Communion was held monthly in the later 19th century, with c. 25 recipients, twice each Sunday c. 1920, and weekly in 1931.[22] A reading room in Ivy Row was converted in 1899 to a mission chapel and the next year

licensed for services, including Holy Communion.[23] The chapel was still used occasionally in 1990.[24]

There was a medieval guild in the church[25] and lights there were endowed with houses and lands in Tunstall and Hollym.[26] A parochial library was established by 1840.[27] A class for young men was held on Sundays in the mid 1860s and a men's society flourished in 1913.[28] In the late 19th and early 20th century a church dedication festival or fair was held in June or July.[29]

The church of *ALL SAINTS*, so called by 1347,[30] consists of chancel with two-storeyed north vestry and transeptal south organ chamber, aisled and clerestoried nave, and west tower, flanked by continuations of the aisles, with west porch. It is built mostly of boulders with ashlar dressings, except for the clerestory which is of brick and the chancel and porch which are of ashlar. The plan accords with an origin in or before the 11th century but the earliest features are the 13th-century nave arcades, of three bays. The tower arch also is 13th-century. The vestry, of the 14th century, has a prominent round turret containing stairs to the upper room; it may have been intended for a chantry chapel and there was apparently a chaplain in the mid 15th century.[31] Remodelling of the chancel is shown by a north window of similar date to the vestry and by a 15th-century piscina. All the other windows, including those of the tall clerestory, are of the 15th or early 16th century and have been much restored. A bequest of £1 for the tower in 1442 was presumably for the reconstruction of the upper part.

A painted screen discovered in the church in 1567 may have stood until 1720.[32] The church was reseated in 1803–4[33] and a west gallery rebuilt in 1835–6.[34] There was an extensive rest-

[4] B.I.H.R., TER. H. Roos 1849; R.D.B., DS/63/89; White, *Dir. E. & N.R. Yorks.* (1840), 266; Sheahan and Whellan, *Hist. York & E.R.* ii. 375; O.S. Map 6″, Yorks. CCXLII (1855 edn.). For plan probably of the ho., E.R.A.O., PE/44/20, p. 14. Watercolour in church, showing it painted pink, is reprod. in *Trans. E. Yorks. Georgian Soc.* iv (2), frontispiece.
[5] E.R.A.O., PE/44/20, p. 49; R.D.B., KZ/230/317; 48/503/461 (1891).
[6] R.D.B., 49/462/417 (1892); E.R.A.O., DDX/215/12; *Kelly's Dir. N. & E.R. Yorks.* (1893), 480.
[7] R.D.B., 614/294/238.
[8] E.R.A.O., DDX/215/12; ibid. PE/44/20, pp. 86–7, 89.
[9] Inf. from the rector, Roos, 1990; R.D.B., 1569/223/170.
[10] *Reg. Corbridge*, i, pp. 152 n., 159; ii, p. 179; *Reg. Greenfield*, iii, p. 148 and n.
[11] Lawrance, 'Clergy List', Holderness, 2, pp. 119–20; *Cal. Papal Reg.* v. 396, 594–5; xiv. 8–9.
[12] B.I.H.R., CP. G. 1098, 1121; H.U.L., DDSY(3)/3/2; Lawrance, op. cit. p. 120; Poulson, *Holderness*, ii. 95; *Dean and Chapter Wills* (Y.A.S. Rec. Ser. xxxviii), 40.
[13] J. S. Purvis, *Tudor Par. Doc. of Dioc. York*, 30.
[14] E.R.A.O., PE/44/1, s.vv. 1662, 1668; *Calamy Revised*, ed. A. G. Matthews, 462.
[15] E.R.A.O., PE/44/3 (list of rectors); PE/44/20, p. 10; B.I.H.R., V. 1764/Ret. 2, no. 215; monument in church.
[16] B.I.H.R., Inst. AB. 18, pp. 315–16; ibid. 20, p. 365; E. window in church; above, manors (Roos).
[17] *Crockford*.

[18] *Inventories of Ch. Goods*, 45; *Royal Visit. of 1559* (Sur. Soc. clxxxvii), 99.
[19] B.I.H.R., TER. H. Roos 1764; E.R.A.O., PE/44/3 (list of rectors).
[20] B.I.H.R., V. 1865/Ret. 2, no. 428; V. 1868/Ret. 2, no. 378; *Educ. of Poor Digest*, 1089; directories.
[21] B.I.H.R., V. 1764/Ret. 2, no. 215; *Herring's Visit.* iii, p. 33. A total of 100 communicants was recorded in 1743.
[22] B.I.H.R., V. 1865/Ret. 2, no. 428; V. 1868/Ret. 2, no. 378; V. 1871/Ret. 2, no. 383; V. 1877/Ret. 2, no. 201; V. 1884/Ret. 2; V. 1912–22/Ret.; V. 1931/Ret.
[23] E.R.A.O., PE/44/20, pp. 54, 85b.
[24] B.I.H.R., V. 1912–22/Ret.; V. 1931/Ret.; O.S. Map 1/2,500, TA 2830–2930 (1975 edn.); inf. from Mrs. N. Kirkwood, Roos, 1990.
[25] Poulson, *Holderness*, ii. 97.
[26] H.U.L., DHO/10/6 (feodary's acct.); *Cal. Pat.* 1572–5, pp. 321–2.
[27] White, *Dir. E. & N.R. Yorks.* (1840), 266; Sheahan and Whellan, *Hist. York & E.R.* ii. 375.
[28] B.I.H.R., V. 1865/Ret. 2, no. 428; *Hull Times*, 7 June 1913.
[29] E.R.A.O., PE/44/20, p. 63; *Hull Times*, 7 June 1913.
[30] B.I.H.R., Reg. 10, f. 321.
[31] *T.E.R.A.S.* x. 8–9.
[32] E.R.A.O., PE/44/23; Poulson, *Holderness*, ii. 96; Purvis, *Tudor Par. Doc.* 31.
[33] E.R.A.O., PE/44/25.
[34] Ibid.; B.I.H.R., Fac. Bk. 4, pp. 379–81. For earlier gallery, B.I.H.R., TER. H. Roos 1777.

oration by L. N. Cottingham in 1842,[35] when the porch was added. Medieval window tracery in the garden of the Chestnuts, Rectory Road, in 1990 may have been taken from the church. The roofs were renewed in the 1860s[36] and the organ transept was added in 1881 to designs by F. S. Brodrick of Hull.[37] In the late 19th and early 20th century the church was again remodelled and refitted by Temple Moore, whose fittings include a chancel screen given in 1894, a wooden Calvary mounted on it c. 1915, and the reredos in the chancel.[38] A pulpit of 1615, removed in 1842, was put back in 1885.[39] Fragments of medieval and later stained glass survive in the chancel and clerestory windows.[40]

There were three bells in 1552 and later, but two more were added in 1911.[41] The plate includes a cup made in 1570, a paten made in 1627 and given by Sir Mark Sykes, Bt., rector 1735–83, and a paten given in 1899.[42] The registers of baptisms and burials begin in 1571 and of marriages in 1572; they are largely complete.[43]

A mausoleum for the Sykes family, built on the chancel in 1784, was taken down and an entrance to the vault made instead in the churchyard, probably at the restoration of 1842.[44] Additions to the churchyard were consecrated in 1869 and 1952, and about the date of the earlier enlargement an avenue of yews was planted alongside the path to the west porch.[45] The churchyard includes a stone Calvary, put up in 1968.[46]

Benefactions for the fabric were evidently made by the 17th century,[47] and the church later had 9 a. in Roos, Ryhill, in Burstwick, and Tunstall, besides rent charges in Owstwick, all known in 1823 as the Church Lands charity. The annual income rose from c. £5 in 1720 to over £10 in 1809 and £33 in 1861; it declined later but stood at c. £40 in 1930.[48] Cottages for the poor were built on part of the land at Roos by 1842.[49] In 1989 the sums of £371 and £100 were paid from the charity for the maintenance of Roos and Tunstall churches respectively.[50]

FIG. 6. OWSTWICK: QUAKER MEETING HOUSE

NONCONFORMITY. Religious conservatism was apparent at Roos in the 16th century but there is little evidence of Roman Catholicism.[51]

There was evidently a Quaker meeting at Owstwick in the 1650s, when William Dewsbury and James Nayler visited it,[52] and the 12 recusants recorded under Roos in 1669 and the 16 protestant dissenters in the parish in 1676 were probably all Friends.[53] A meeting house at Owstwick was built c. 1670 and a burial ground provided,[54] and Owstwick became the usual venue for the monthly meeting for Holderness in the late 17th century.[55] Prominent Friends included John Whitehead (d. 1696) and Marmaduke Storr (d. 1678), both of Owstwick, and other members of the Storr family of Owstwick and Hilston. John Storr of Hilston (d. 1677)[56] founded a charity for the poor of the monthly meeting and in 1745 a cottage at Owstwick was bought for an almshouse.[57] A meeting place was also licensed at Roos in 1716[58] and a house registered there in 1782 may have been for the Friends.[59] There were six Quaker families in the parish in 1743, when the Owstwick meeting was declining, and four in 1764, when there was a Sunday congregation of c. 15 but no regular teacher.[60] Owstwick monthly meeting was united with that of North Cave in 1784[61] and meetings evidently ceased at Owstwick c. 1790.[62] Burials continued until the mid 19th century.[63] The former meeting house was later used as a cottage and a Church Sunday school; it was

[35] E.R.A.O., PE/44/20, pp. 3, 53, 70–1; tablet and paintings (before and after restoration) in church; Sheahan and Whellan, Hist. York & E. R. ii. 374; D.N.B. s.v. Cottingham.

[36] E.R.A.O., PE/44/26, s.v. 1861–2; B.I.H.R., V. 1868/Ret. 2, no. 378.

[37] E.R.A.O., PE/44/20, pp. 64–5.

[38] Ibid. pp. 68, 83–5; notes in church; E.R.A.O., accession 1217 (invoice 1916); Hull Times, 7 June 1913.

[39] E.R.A.O., PE/44/20, p. 80; PE/44/26, s.v. 1885; Kelly's Dir. N. & E.R. Yorks. (1893), 480.

[40] Y.A.J. xxvi. 240–1; Poulson, Holderness, ii. 97–8.

[41] B.I.H.R., TER. H. Roos 1764 etc.; Inventories of Ch. Goods, 45; G. R. Park, Ch. Bells, Holderness, 58–9; notes in church.

[42] E.R.A.O., PE/44/20, p. 63; Yorks. Ch. Plate, i. 304–5.

[43] E.R.A.O., PE/44/1–4, 7. The first reg. (1571–1679) is print. Reg. Par. All Saints, Roos, i, transcr. R. B. Machell (Hull 1888).

[44] E.R.A.O., PE/44/20, p. 1; Poulson, Holderness, ii. 96; O.S. Map 6", Yorks. CCXLII (1855 edn.).

[45] B.I.H.R., CD. Add. 1869/3, 1952/1; Pevsner and Neave, Yorks. E.R. 660; illus. in M. and B. Chapman, Holderness in old picture postcards, 57.

[46] E.R.A.O., accession 1217 (faculty; terrier).

[47] Ibid. DDCC/69/1; H.U.L., DDCV/133/6.

[48] H.U.L., DDSY/56/15; E.R.A.O., PE/44/20, pp. 55–6; ibid. accession 1681; B.I.H.R., TER. H. Roos 1764–1861; ibid. V. 1764/Ret. 2, no. 215; R.D.B., BG/103/9; Herring's Visit. iii, p. 33; 9th Rep. Com. Char. 774.

[49] Below, charities.

[50] Inf. from the rector, Roos, 1990.

[51] Purvis, Tudor Par. Doc. 31; Aveling, Post Reformation Catholicism, 13, 68.

[52] F. Fletcher, 'Quakerism in E. Yorks.' (Hull Univ. B.A. dissertation, 1985), 6.

[53] Depositions from York Castle (Sur. Soc. xl), p. 169; Compton Census, ed. A. Whiteman, 601. Some of those named in 1669 appear in Quaker reg.: P.R.O., RG 6/1363.

[54] H.U.L., DQR/17/40; P.R.O., RG 6/1363; Poulson, Holderness, ii. 103 with illus.

[55] E.R.A.O., DDQR/17.

[56] P.R.O., RG 6/1363; H.U.L., DQR/17/40–1; D.N.B. s.v. Whitehead.

[57] H.U.L., DQR/17/64, 66, 75; ibid. DDSY/52/52.

[58] P.R.O., RG 31/7, no. 29.

[59] Ibid. RG 31/5, no. 621; B.I.H.R., Fac. Bk. 2, p. 287; H.U.L., DQR/17/68.

[60] B.I.H.R., V. 1764/Ret. 1, no. 208; Ret. 2, no. 215; Herring's Visit. ii, p. 12; iii, p. 33; iv, p. 236.

[61] E.R.A.O., DDQR/23.   [62] Ibid. DDQR/20, 23.

[63] Bulmer, Dir. E. Yorks. (1892), 489.

ruinous by the mid 20th century[64] and was later demolished. A house in Roos was licensed by an unspecified group of dissenters in 1795.[65] Wesleyan Methodists registered houses at Roos in 1805 and 1806 and a barn there in 1808,[66] and they built a chapel in Main Street in 1808.[67] The chapel was closed c. 1977[68] and later demolished. It was probably one of the poorhouses at Owstwick which was converted to a chapel by Wesleyan Methodists by 1892.[69] It was closed c. 1980 and was derelict in 1990.[70]

It was evidently Primitive Methodists who registered a building in Roos for worship in 1821.[71] They built a chapel in 1826[72] which was replaced by another, in Pilmar Lane, in 1868–9.[73] The chapel was enlarged with a schoolroom in 1897; it was closed c. 1970 and later demolished.[74]

EDUCATION. An unlicensed schoolmaster was recorded at Roos in 1604 and another master was mentioned in 1654.[75] Jane Hogg (d. 1766) left £6 a year for a schoolmaster at Roos but the endowment was evidently lost c. 1800.[76] Three schools with an average of 30 pupils each were recorded in 1818 and there were two schoolmasters in 1823.[77] In 1833 there were four schools in the parish at which 77 pupils were taught at their parents' expense.[78]

Lucy Hotham had built a girls' school near the rectory house by 1840,[79] and about that date others for boys and infants were provided in buildings at the junction of Main Street and Pilmar Lane.[80] The schools were supported by Mrs. Hotham and her husband Charles, rector, by school pence, and by 1848 by an annual government grant. Average attendance was then 55 boys and 52 girls.[81] The schools were soon afterwards united with the National Society.[82] In 1866 they were reorganized as one school at Pilmar Lane, where existing buildings were remodelled and a new main room built in 1872.[83] The former girls' school was later demolished.

Children from outside the parish had attended schools in Roos since the early 19th century,[84] and the National school also served the parishes of Hilston and Tunstall and was supported by a voluntary rate levied in those parishes and in Roos. Owstwick children attended until the township withdrew from the school district in 1888;[85] they later went to Grimston and Burton Pidsea.[86] There were usually 70 pupils in attendance at Roos Church of England school in 1906–7, more than 90 between 1910 and 1927, and again c. 70 in the 1930s.[87] The village institute, built on part of the school site in 1915, was used by the school.[88] Senior pupils were transferred to Withernsea County Secondary School in 1948, and in 1950 the school was granted Controlled status.[89] Another classroom was provided c. 1963 but the institute was again used from 1967. A new school was built in Main Street and opened c. 1980,[90] and the old school was later used as a house. There were 73 pupils on the roll in 1990.[91]

CHARITIES FOR THE POOR. George Green (d. 1672) left 10s. a year for the poor of Roos parish.[92] In 1675 Reginald Marriott gave 6s. 8d. a year and an unknown donor a like amount; both sums were charged on land in Roos. In 1823 the income from all three charities was distributed by the churchwardens with the sacrament money. A rent charge of £1 8s. from land in Roos, spent on bread, was believed in 1823 to be the gift of Thomas Dixon.[93]

By a Scheme of 1911 all those charities were united, the income to be used for food, fuel, clothing, and other goods, help in sickness, or for money payments, and it was spent in doles

64 White, Gen. & Com. Dir. Hull (1882), 338; Bulmer, Dir. E. Yorks. (1892), 489; G. T. J. Miles and W. Richardson, Hist. Withernsea with S. Holderness, 137; O.S. Map 6″, Yorks. CCXXVIII (1855 and later edns.).

65 B.I.H.R., Fac. Bk. 3, p. 83.

66 Ibid. pp. 403, 425, 435, 471.

67 Ibid. p. 484; P.R.O., HO 129/521/1/24/43; V.C.H. Yorks. E.R. i. 313; O.S. Map 6″, Yorks. CCXXVIII (1855 edn.).

68 O.N.S. (Birkdale), Worship Reg. no. 12449.

69 Bulmer, Dir. E. Yorks. (1892), 489; O.S. Map 6″, Yorks. CCXXVIII (1855 and later edns.); above, local govt.

70 D. [R. J.] and S. [A.] Neave, E.R. Chapels and Meeting Hos. (E. Yorks. Loc. Hist. Soc., 1990), 55.

71 B.I.H.R., DMH. Reg. 1, pp. 295–6; P.R.O., RG 31/5, no. 3594.

72 T. Allen, Hist. Co. York, ii. 429; Hull Times, 7 June 1913; O.S. Map 6″, Yorks. CCXXVIII (1855 edn.). P.R.O., HO 129/521/1/24/42 gives the date 1836 in error.

73 R.D.B., KF/141/186; KK/379/515; E.R.A.O., MRW/2/40; O.S. Map 1/2,500, Yorks. CCXXVIII. 15 (1891 edn.).

74 O.N.S. (Birkdale), Worship Reg. no. 19113; Miles and Richardson, Withernsea, 137.

75 B.I.H.R., V. 1604/CB. 1, f. 76v.; Reg. Par. All Saints Roos, i. 114.

76 H.U.L., DDSY/56/27; B.I.H.R., TER. H. Roos 1786; Poulson, Holderness, ii. 98. For the schoolmaster, E.R.A.O., PE/44/20, p. 8.

77 Educ. of Poor Digest, 1089; Baines, Hist. Yorks. ii. 383.

78 Educ. Enq. Abstract, 1094.

79 White, Dir. E. & N.R. Yorks. (1840), 266. E.R.A.O., accession 1217, G. W. Wilbraham, 'Educ. in Roos', gives the location, near Dent's Garth, for which see O.S. Map 1/10,000, TA 22 NE. (1975 edn.).

80 P.R.O., ED 7/135, no. 143; E.R.A.O., accession 1217, Wilbraham, 'Educ. in Roos'; H.U.L., DDCV/134/15, pp. 378, 406, 408; O.S. Map 6″, Yorks. CCXXVIII (1855 edn.).

81 B.I.H.R., V. 1865/Ret. 2, no. 428; Sheahan and Whellan, Hist. York & E.R. ii. 375; Mins. of Educ. Cttee. of Council, 1847–8 [998], pp. cxxx–cxxxi, H.C. (1847–8), l.

82 Mins. of Educ. Cttee. of Council, 1850–1 [1357], p. cxcv, H.C. (1851), xliv.

83 R.D.B., KF/336/459; E.R.A.O., SGP. 68; ibid. accession 1217, acct. bk. and Wilbraham, 'Educ. in Roos'; Bulmer, Dir. E. Yorks. (1892), 489.

84 B.I.H.R., V. 1865/Ret. 2, no. 428; Educ. of Poor Digest, 1089.

85 E.R.A.O., accession 1217, acct. bk. and Wilbraham, 'Educ. in Roos'.

86 Kelly's Dir. N. & E.R. Yorks. (1889), 447; (1925), 606.

87 Bd. of Educ., List 21 (H.M.S.O., 1908 and later edns.).

88 E.R.A.O., accession 1217, Wilbraham, 'Educ. in Roos'; above, intro.

89 E.R. Educ. Cttee. Mins. 1947–8, 114; 1949–50, 227, 277.

90 Ibid. 1963–4, 84; 1966–7, 147; 1969–70, 122–3; 1970–1, 52; local inf.

91 Inf. from Educ. Dept., Humbs. C.C., 1990.

92 E.R.A.O., PE/44/20, p. 8.

93 Ibid. PE/44/1; B.I.H.R., TER. H. Roos 1786 etc.; 9th Rep. Com. Char. 773–4.

of 5s. or 10s. until the mid century.[94] The income was later allowed to accumulate and in 1990 there was a balance of nearly £40.[95]

In 1672 William Gibson gave £1 and that sum and another gift[96] later comprised a town stock of £6, the interest on which was added to the other charities until the early 1820s, when the stock was spent.[97]

By 1842[98] six cottages for the poor stood with gardens on ground at Roos belonging to the Church Lands charity. Two of the cottages were later made into one and used successively as a reading room and a mission chapel.[99] The others were occupied until the mid 20th century, and were later demolished.[1]

SPROATLEY

THE village of Sproatley is situated some 4 km. north-east of the city of Hull and 8 km. south-west of the North Sea at Aldbrough. Just to the north, across the parish boundary in Swine, is Burton Constable Hall and its park,[2] but the estate's influence on the character of Sproatley has been much diluted by the recent development of the village as a dormitory for Hull. The name Sproatley is Anglian, and may mean a clearing in which brushwood is growing.[3] The area of the parish was 1,372 a. (555.3 ha.) in 1852, and has not been changed.[4] In the south of the parish the boundaries are mostly formed by watercourses. In the north, the parish was formerly separated from the grounds of Burton Constable Hall by a pale walk which was extinguished at inclosure in 1763, when another way, to Lelley, ran along part of the eastern boundary.[5]

There were 129 poll-tax payers at Sproatley in 1377,[6] and 29 houses there were assessed for hearth tax in 1672 and 8 discharged.[7] There were just over 30 families in the parish in 1743 and 1764.[8] From 232 in 1801, the population of Sproatley rose sharply in the 1810s and 1840s to stand at 357 in 1821 and 463 in 1851. It later declined, to 331 in 1881 and 272 in 1911. Numbers recovered to 325 in 1951, but then fell back to 264 in 1971. A rapid growth in the population followed Sproatley's development as a dormitory village for commuters working in Hull; by 1981 there were 1,289 inhabitants, and 1,442 were usually resident in 1991, when 1,424 were present.[9]

The parish is covered by boulder clay, except in the south where there is alluvium alongside the drains, and a large deposit of sand and gravel.[10] The land lies mostly between 15 and 23 m. above sea level. A ridge rising above 23 m. provided the village with its site, and there is

also a little higher ground in the north-west corner of the parish; south and east of the village the ground falls to c. 9 m. The north-west of the parish was used as a common pasture, and the rest very largely for the village's open fields and commonable meadows. Sproatley was inclosed in 1763.[11]

Sproatley is drained largely by a sequence of streams which flow westwards along the southern boundary towards Old fleet and outfall into the river Humber. The southern drains were insufficient in 1367, when another stream running down the western boundary was also mentioned.[12] From the village lesser streams carry water south and south-eastwards to the boundary drains, and another minor watercourse drains westwards into Thirtleby, in Swine. Improvements to the drainage under the Keyingham Level Drainage Acts of 1772 and later evidently included work on the southern streams, later known as Lelley, Sproatley, and Nuttles drains.[13]

From Sproatley village, roads lead north to Burton Constable and West Newton in Aldbrough, east to Flinton in Humbleton, south to Preston and Hedon, south-west to Wyton in Swine and Hull, and north-west to Thirtleby in Swine. The roads to Wyton and Flinton were added to the Hull–Hedon turnpike trust at its renewal in 1767; the trust was discontinued in 1878,[14] but those roads have since been improved as parts of the Hull–Aldbrough road. From the late 19th century Sproatley was served by buses running along it between Hull and Aldbrough and Garton.[15] Roads called Wringland and Castlegate were recorded in 1367; the latter, leading to Lelley,[16] was perhaps the way running along the eastern parish boundary which was awarded at inclosure in 1763 but apparently abandoned as a highway by 1827.[17]

94 E.R.A.O., PE/44/20, after p. 76; ibid. accession 1217, accts. 1921–51.
95 Inf. from the rector, Roos, 1990.
96 Possibly Mat. Shore's gift of £5 in 1702: E.R.A.O., PE/44/20, p. 2.
97 E.R.A.O., PE/44/1; 9th Rep. Com. Char. 774.
98 E.R.A.O., PE/44/20, pp. 70–1; P.R.O., HO 107/2364.
99 E.R.A.O., PE/44/20, p. 54; above, intro., church.
1 E.R.A.O., PE/44/27; inf. from Mrs. Kirkwood, 1990. Cf. R.D.B., 1443/110/100 (almsho.); O.S. Map 1/2,500, Yorks. CCXXVIII. 15 (1891 edn.) (poor ho.); O.S. Map 6", TA 23 SE. (1956 edn.) (Ivy Cott.).
2 This article was written in 1999.
3 P.N. Yorks. E.R. (E.P.N.S.), 52.
4 O.S. Map 6", Yorks. CCXXVII (1855 edn.); Census 1981, 1991.
5 R.D.B., AC/221/10; E.R.A.O., DDCK/35/1 (a); DDCC(2)/12; below, this section [drains].

6 P.R.O., E 179/202/60, m. 30.
7 Hearth Tax, 60.
8 B.I.H.R., V. 1764/Ret. 3, no. 51; Herring's Visit. iii, p. 123.
9 V.C.H. Yorks. iii. 494; Census, 1921–91.
10 Geol. Surv. Map 1", drift, sheet 73 (1909 edn.).
11 R.D.B., AC/221/10.
12 Poulson, Holderness, i. 128–9.
13 O.S. Map 6", Yorks. CCXXVII (1855 edn.); V.C.H. Yorks. E.R. v. 55–7.
14 K. A. MacMahon, Roads and Turnpike Trusts in E. Yorks. (E. Yorks. Loc. Hist. Ser. xviii), 24, 70; 7 Geo. III, c. 71; O.S. Map 6", Yorks. CCXXVII (1855 edn.).
15 Directories.
16 Poulson, Holderness, i. 130–1; cf. O.S. Map 6", Yorks. CCXXVII (1855 edn.).
17 E.R.A.O., DDCC(2)/plan 22; R.D.B., AC/221/10; Hull Central Libr., Sproatley incl. plan.

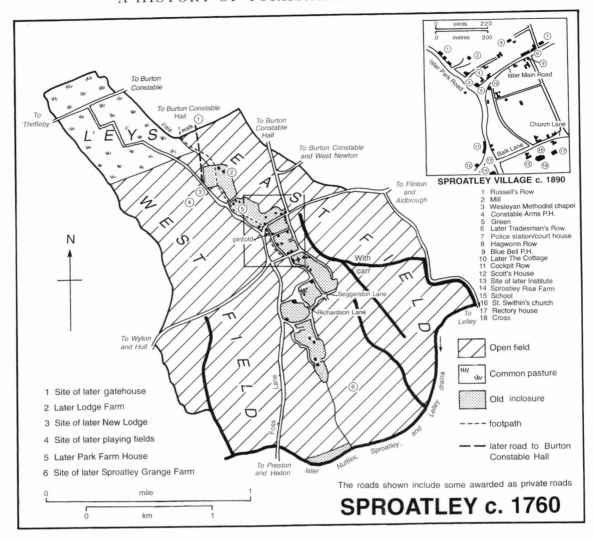

SPROATLEY VILLAGE c. 1890

1 Russell's Row
2 Mill
3 Wesleyan Methodist chapel
4 Constable Arms P.H.
5 Green
6 Later Tradesman's Row
7 Police station/court house
8 Hagworm Row
9 Blue Bell P.H.
10 Later The Cottage
11 Cockpit Row
12 Scott's House
13 Site of later Institute
14 Sproatley Rise Farm
15 School
16 St. Swithin's church
17 Rectory house
18 Cross

1 Site of later gatehouse
2 Later Lodge Farm
3 Site of later New Lodge
4 Site of later playing fields
5 Later Park Farm House
6 Site of later Sproatley Grange Farm

Open field
Common pasture
Old inclosure
footpath
later road to Burton Constable Hall

The roads shown include some awarded as private roads

SPROATLEY c. 1760

A footpath between Sproatley church and Burton Constable was awarded at inclosure in 1763, but soon afterwards it was evidently replaced by the new main drive to the Hall; a gatehouse was built just across the boundary on the new route c. 1785.[18]

SPROATLEY village was built along the ridge of higher ground lying roughly north-west to south-east through the centre of the parish.[19] To either side of the line of garths, almost 2 km. long, lay the open fields of the settlement, and to the north-west its chief common pasture. The thinly-built village was served by lanes running alongside and across the garths. Among the side lanes was one which was continued by the roads to Aldbrough and Hull; at its western end, at the foot of the slope, the lane crossed a small green, which still exists. Another of the side lanes, Church Lane, was extended to the Preston

road by the making, or improvement, almost certainly at inclosure in 1763, of the way later named Balk Lane. A medieval cross stood in the garths south of the church before its removal in the 19th century to the rectory-house garden or the churchyard.[20] After inclosure the village was extended onto lower, formerly commonable, land by the building near the junction of the Hull and Preston roads of two houses, later called Scott's House and Sproatley Rise, and a terrace of cottages, Cockpit Row. Thomas Simpson built the six cottages, probably soon after 1814, when he sold the adjacent site to Joseph Scott 'gardener', and certainly by 1822,[21] and Scott's House and Sproatley Rise had both been put up by 1827.[22] There was also building in the old garths, notably beside the main side lane, now Main Road, where Tradesman's Row and other cottages had been put up by the 1850s.[23] The still small village was then little changed until the

18 R.D.B., AC/221/10; Hull Central Libr., Sproatley incl. plan; O.S. Map 6", Yorks. CCXXVII (1855 edn.); below, Swine, Burton Constable, manor [park].
19 The following is based on the incl. map at Hull Central Library and the award at R.D.B., AC/221/10. Another map, evidently of the same period, differs in its detail: E.R.A.O., DDCC(2)/12.
20 O.S. Map 1/2,500, Yorks. CCXXVII. 7 (1890 edn.);

below, church [churchyard].
21 E.R.A.O., DDCC/88/177; R.D.B., CY/70/108; O.S. Map 6", Yorks. CCXXVII (1855 edn.).
22 E.R.A.O., DDCC(2)/plan 22; O.S. Map 1/2,500, Yorks. CCXXVII. 7 (1890 edn.); Dept. of Environment, Buildings List (1987).
23 O.S. Map 6", Yorks. CCXXVII (1855 and later edns.); below, this section.

later 20th century. Some 30 council houses were put up in Chestnut Grove and Church Mount *c.* 1950,[24] and from the 1970s the village was greatly enlarged by the building of private housing estates. Some 100 houses were then built between Main Road and Balk Lane, in Gallands Road and its side streets; *c.* 120 more to the north of Main Road, in Mill and Hall Roads, and more than 200 houses to the west of the village green, most of them in Westlands Road.[25]

The village is brick-built. Most of the buildings are recent, and the majority of them are bungalows. A few larger modern houses stand in Ash Grove, off Westlands Road, in Raleigh Drive, off Burton Constable Road, and in Church Lane.

The oldest of the other buildings is perhaps The Cottage, formerly two houses,[26] opposite the Constable Arms; the **L**-shaped building, of brick and pantiles, comprises a range of one storey with an attic, built on a lobby-entry plan, and a rear wing, and is thought to date from the early 18th century.[27] Lodge Farm is a rebuilding of a near-by farmhouse, bought by the Constables in 1774.[28] The Constable Arms was probably also built or rebuilt in the 18th century,[29] and the adjacent row of cottages has a datestone marked I.T. 1782. Park Farm House may also be 18th-century in origin; the house has been heightened from one storey to two, and the gables of both phases have tumbled-in brickwork. Nineteenth-century buildings include the church, rectory house, and school, all then rebuilt; the police station, an addition of 1849,[30] and a second lodge for Burton Constable Hall and park, the neo-Jacobean New Lodge, which was put up on the northern edge of Sproatley village in the 1860s.[31] The part of the village near the church was also improved in 1860 by the planting of an avenue of chestnut trees along Church and Balk Lanes by Sir Thomas Constable, Bt., and the rector, the Revd. C. J. Wall.[32] Besides Cockpit and Tradesman's Rows,[33] the 19th-century cottages also include Russell Row[34] and Jalna, a lodge-like building, both in Park Road. Most of the houses in the village belonged to the Chichester-Constables in 1910.[35] Housing was allegedly very poor *c.* 1920, when 18 of the cottages were said to be unfit for families.[36] The Burton Constable estate built a group of unusual houses, the slate-roofed Chichester Bungalows on Main Road, in 1937.[37] A conservation area

for the older parts of Sproatley village was established in 1987.[38]

The number of licensed houses in Sproatley declined from five in 1754 to two in the 1780s, when one of them was named as the Blue Bell.[39] That house belonged from 1835 to the Revd. Thomas Galland (d. 1843), a Wesleyan Methodist minister in the West Riding and owner of the adjacent land, and after 1847 to Sir Thomas Constable, Bt., and his successors.[40] A second house, the Constable, sometimes Constables', Arms may have been one of the two beerhouses operating in 1840, and it was named from 1846. It was also part of the Burton Constable estate.[41] Both houses still traded in 1999. Allotment gardens were provided on the Burton Constable estate in Sproatley, possibly by 1802, when the new tenants of 9 a. were described simply as 'labourers'.[42] By the 1850s a field beside the Hull road belonging to Sir Thomas Constable, Bt., perhaps the same ground, had been divided into 28 allotment gardens of a rood each.[43] The allotments were used until *c.* 1920.[44] Sproatley Floral and Horticultural Society was newly formed in 1837, when it met at the Blue Bell.[45] A friendly society branch, the Burton Constable Lodge of the United Ancient Order of Druids, was founded in 1861, and had 212 members in 1910 and 124 in 1938.[46] The annual Sproatley feast was presumably organised by the friendly society, and other social events in Sproatley included the meetings of the local hunt.[47] A village meeting place, Sproatley Institute, was opened in 1912.[48] Outside, in the junction of the Preston and Hull roads, those who served between 1914 and 1918 are commemorated, and a Second World War memorial was placed inside the Institute, which has since been called Sproatley Memorial Village Hall. The cruciform building, with a small louvred spire at its centre, was of corrugated iron until the mid 1990s, when that shell was replaced by one of steel.[49] Sproatley Cricket Club had been founded by 1897, and there was also a cycling club in 1901.[50] Land off Park Road belonging to the Burton Constable estate was leased *c.* 1975 for a village playing field, and a football pitch, tennis courts, and a children's play area were later laid out there. A shelter provided about 1980 was replaced in 1996–7 by a sports pavilion funded largely by grants from the Lottery and the Sports and Arts Association.[51]

[24] R.D.B., 742/290/243.
[25] Ibid. 1684/573/494; 1740/196/165; 1760/423/352; 1826/286/241; 1882/272/213.
[26] Local inf.
[27] Pevsner and Neave, *Yorks. E.R.* 709.
[28] E.R.A.O., DDCC/88/99; DDCC/141/71, plan of Sproatley no. 1; O.S. Map 1/2,500, Yorks. CCXXVII. 3 (1910 edn.).
[29] Dept. of Environment, *Buildings List* (1987).
[30] Below, this section, church, educ.
[31] Below, Swine, Burton Constable, manor [park].
[32] E.R.A.O., PE/130/44.
[33] Above, this section.
[34] E.R.A.O., DDCC/88/92; DDCC(2)/plan 22; O.S. Map 1/2,500, Yorks. CCXXVII. 3 (1890 edn.).
[35] E.R.A.O., NV/1/46.
[36] B.I.H.R., V. 1912–22/Ret.   [37] Local inf.
[38] Inf. from Development Dept., Holderness Borough Council, 1990.

[39] E.R.A.O., QDT/2/7, 9; ibid. DDCC/88/185; DDCC(2)/80, s.v. 1782.
[40] Ibid. DDCC/88/90, 143; R.D.B., GG/230/282; 633/441/344.
[41] E.R.A.O., NV/1/46; R.D.B., 747/225/191; directories.
[42] E.R.A.O., DDCC/141/12.
[43] Ibid. DDCC(2)/plan 31; ibid. NV/1/46; O.S. Map 6", Yorks. CCXXVII (1855 edn.). Cf. *Hull Advertiser*, 4 Oct. 1856.
[44] Inf. from Mr. H. P. Garthwaite, Sproatley, 2000.
[45] *Hull Advertiser*, 14 July 1837.
[46] D. [R. J.] Neave, *E.R. Friendly Soc.* (E. Yorks. Loc. Hist. Ser. xli), 67.
[47] H.U.L., DX/169/36.
[48] Ibid.
[49] Pevsner and Neave, *Yorks. E.R.* 709; local inf.
[50] *Kelly's Dir. N. & E.R. Yorks.* (1897), 539; (1901), 562.
[51] Datestone; *Hull Daily Mail*, 2 Sept. 1997; inf. from R. Wastling, Thirtleby Grange Farm, 2000.

A police station and magistrates' room for the Middle Division of Holderness was built in 1849 on the edge of the village, the site, at the junction of the Burton Constable and Aldbrough roads, being given by Sir Thomas Constable, Bt. Designed by H. F. Lockwood of Hull, the building is largely of cream brick with slate roofs, and comprises a central block, of two storeys and three bays, flanked by a single-storeyed wing to the west and on the eastern side by a recessed wing of two low storeys. The main block has a round-arched stone doorcase and round-headed windows, and the yard contains a small stable in red brick.[52] The removal of the petty sessions for the Middle Division from Hedon to the new station at Sproatley was opposed unsuccessfully,[53] and sessions were subsequently held at Sproatley, in 1872 every three weeks and later monthly.[54] The magistrates last met at Sproatley in 1995.[55] A superintendent was based at Sproatley before and after the formation of the E.R. constabulary in 1857, and later also a constable, but in 1893 the policing of South and Middle Holderness was amalgamated, and Hedon station became the headquarters of the new area.[56] The police station was discontinued c. 1970. The police house continued in occupation and part of the premises were later used briefly as a clinic,[57] but in 1999 the whole building stood empty.

OUTLYING BUILDINGS include Sproatley Grange Farm, built by the Constables soon after inclosure in 1763,[58] and one or two houses put up beside Hull Road in the 20th century. A waste tip begun in disused gravel pits near Sproatley Grange Farm in the 1970s was extended in the early 1990s.[59]

MANORS AND OTHER ESTATES. In 1066 Basinc, Forni, and Thor held three manors of *SPROATLEY* comprising 4 carucates; Earl Tosti 1 carucate in Sproatley as sokeland of his manor of Burstwick, and Morkar 5 bovates of sokeland there belonging to his manor of Withernsea. All of those lands may have been the same as the manor of Sproatley comprising 6 carucates which William Malet was said to have held in succession to Thorsten; the holdings at the Conquest and Malet's estate had, moreover, all passed to Drew de Bevrère by 1086.[60] Drew's estate later descended with the lordship of Holderness and with Burstwick manor,[61] of which Sproatley was a member. The holding, occasionally described as *SPROAT-LEY* manor, thus passed to the counts of Aumale,[62] then to the Crown and its grantees, of whom Margaret de Gavaston, countess of Cornwall, was recorded as lady of Sproatley in 1316.[63] In 1521 it was forfeited by Edward Stafford, duke of Buckingham, to the Crown, which granted it to Henry Neville, earl of Westmorland, in 1558.[64] He sold it to his son-in-law, Sir John Constable, in 1560, and Sproatley thereafter descended, with the seigniory of Holderness, in that family, later viscounts Dunbar, and their successors.[65]

The Constables, who already held land in Sproatley,[66] made other purchases there. In 1555, before the acquisition of the manor, a half share in a 5-bovate farm in Sproatley was conveyed to Lady (Joan) Constable and her son Sir John;[67] Sir John and his son, Sir Henry Constable, later bought land in Sproatley to extend the grounds of Burton Constable Hall,[68] and in the 1660s several farms were bought from Christopher Ridley's heirs.[69] By 1693 Robert Constable, Lord Dunbar, had, besides the manor, more than 3 carucates in the parish,[70] and William Constable was awarded 567 a. for his commonable land at inclosure in 1763.[71] The later Lodge farm, with c. 125 a., was bought from James Dealtry in 1774,[72] but 122 a. was sold to John Raines in 1778, and in 1779 Constable had 593 a. in all in Sproatley.[73] Sir Thomas Constable, Bt., enlarged the estate,[74] by buying in 1847 the Galland family's holding, of nearly 200 a., and in 1853 a 114-a. farm formerly belonging to Ripley school (Yorks. W.R.).[75] In 1912 the Chichester-Constables had, besides the manor, 934 a. in Sproatley.[76] Grange farm with 346 a. was sold to Rawsons (Partners) Ltd. in 1964, and c. 40 a. for private housing estates in the earlier 1970s,[77] and c. 550 a. remained part of the Burton Constable estate in 2000.[78]

52 E.R.A.O., DDCC/accession 1730; ibid. QAP/5/58–9, 69, 75 (plans); datestone; illus. in A. A. Clarke, *Country Coppers: Story of E.R. Police*, 114.
53 *Hull Advertiser*, 17 Nov. 1848; 5 Jan. and 6 Apr. 1849.
54 Directories.
55 Inf. from Hull & Holderness Magistrates' Courts, Hull, 2000.
56 E.R.A.O., QAP/5/60; Clarke, op. cit., 18–19, 46; *Kelly's Dir. N. & E.R. Yorks.* (1889), 459; Bulmer, *Dir. E. Yorks.* (1892), 511.
57 E.R. Police Cttee. *Mins.* 1965–8, 111; Humbs. C.C. *Mins.* 1977–8, D 105; inf. from Mr. and Mrs. H. P. Garthwaite, Sproatley, 2000.
58 E.R.A.O., DDCC/141/71, plan of Sproatley no. 2; R.D.B., AC/221/10; Hull Central Libr., Sproatley incl. plan; O.S. Map 6″, Yorks. CCXXVII (1855 edn.).
59 *Hull Daily Mail*, 13 July 1992; Humbs. C.C. *Mins.* 1976–7, E 1920.
60 *V.C.H. Yorks.* ii. 264–5, 269, 296.
61 *V.C.H. Yorks. E.R.* v. 9–10.
62 *Cal. Inq. p.m.* iv, pp. 349–54.
63 P.R.O., C 139/93, no. 44, m. 4; *Feud. Aids*, vi. 164; *Cal. Pat.* 1338–40, 148, 383; 1354–8, 13, 185; *Cal. Close*, 1377–81,

178; *Cal. Chart. R.* 1327–41, 470–1; *Cal. Fine R.* 1337–47, 244.
64 P.R.O., C 66/639, m. 3; E.R.A.O., DDCC/141/66; *Cal. Pat.* 1557–8, 39.
65 H.U.L., DCC/2/63; DHO/7/42; DHO/8/47; E.R.A.O., QDR/2/12; ibid. DDCC/111/231; J. Foster, *Pedigrees of Yorks.* iii; Burke, *Land. Gent.* (1952), 514.
66 Below, this section [Constable].
67 In 1650 it was partitioned between the then owners, John Constable, Lord Dunbar, and Christopher Ridley: E.R.A.O., DDCC/88/4, 18.
68 Below, econ. hist.; below, Swine, Burton Constable, manor [park].   69 Below, this section [Sutton].
70 P.R.O., E 178/6867.   71 R.D.B., AC/221/10.
72 Ibid. AS/299/511; E.R.A.O., DDCC/88/99; DDCC/141/71, plan of Sproatley no. 1; DDCC(2)/Box 8/17; O.S. Map 1/2,500, Yorks. CCXXVII. 3 (1910 edn.).
73 R.D.B., AZ/180/280; E.R.A.O., DDCC(2)/Box 8/17.
74 E.R.A.O., DDCC/111/39.
75 R.D.B., GG/230/282; HB/32/41.
76 Ibid. 232/171/146.
77 Ibid. 1382/261/239; 1532/251/222; 1684/573/494; 1760/423/352; 1826/286/241; 1882/272/213.
78 Inf. from R. Wastling, Thirtleby Grange Farm, 2000.

In 1086 Drew's man Roger occupied part of the estate formerly belonging to Basinc and his fellow tenants. He is believed to have been Roger de Montbegon, and Ernald de Montbegon held land in Sproatley of the count of Aumale in the 12th century.[79] It may have been the Montbegons' holding which was later occupied by a family named from its estate in Goxhill (Lincs.). Ralph of Goxhill, and apparently also his brother Erneis, gave Sproatley church and land in Sproatley to Bridlington priory in the earlier 12th century.[80] Erneis had a son Robert (d. by 1185), he a son Adam of Sproatley or Goxhill (d. by 1205), and Adam a son (Sir) Walter, who was known by his mother's surname, de Ver.[81] In 1210 or 1211 Walter de Ver obtained 1 carucate and 3½ bovates in Sproatley by exchange with Saer of Sutton for land there and in Goxhill.[82] Walter was dead in 1213, when his relict was claiming dower in 6 bovates and other land in Sproatley.[83] Walter's son, (Sir) Simon de Ver (d. c. 1264), was claiming 1 carucate there in 1230,[84] and his son, Simon, was later said to have held 6 or 7 carucates of the Aumale fee in Sproatley.[85] The younger Simon, a rebel against the Crown in the 1260s, divided and sold his estate. His manor of *SPROATLEY* was bought by Roger Darcy, who, apparently under pressure, re-sold it to the king in 1275 or 1276, in which latter year a de Ver widow also released her right in land in Sproatley to the king.[86] The Crown's estate may later have been subsumed in the chief manor.[87] Much of de Ver's land was, however, sold to the Constable, Gilt, and Lund families,[88] and by the 1280s free tenants occupied most of the holding and only 1 carucate and 2 bovates was held by the king in demesne.[89] Some land seems to have been retained by the de Vers, one or more John de Vers of Sproatley being recorded in the late 13th and mid 14th centuries.[90]

Robert of Goxhill was apparently enlarging the site of his house in the 12th century,[91] and the chief house formerly belonging to Sir Simon de Ver was mentioned in 1293.[92]

Simon de Ver granted Roger of Lund 5 bovates and the services of the tenants of 5½ bovates in Sproatley, which estate Roger had given to his nephew, or grandson, Simon of Lund by 1287.[93]

Robert Gilt, a Hedon burgess, bought an estate in Sproatley, comprising almost 1 carucate and 2 bovates, other land, and bond tenants, from Simon de Ver in 1270, and by 1287 he had granted that holding to his son Hugh.[94] Hugh (d. by 1323) was succeeded by his son, Roger Gilt (d. 1349), who held almost 2 carucates and other land in Sproatley,[95] and Roger probably by another Hugh Gilt (Gyk) of Sproatley, who was licensed to choose a confessor in 1358.[96] A Robert Gilt had granted his chief house and other property in Sproatley to Robert Goxhill by 1391, when the estate was given by Goxhill to his son John.[97] Another John Goxhill (d. 1529) held a little land in Sproatley.[98]

Simon de Ver sold c. 50 a. in Sproatley to Simon Constable in 1276,[99] and an estate there, probably the same, descended from Sir John Constable (d. 1489) to his brother Ralph.[1] It was presumably later held with the manor.[2]

In 1287 John of Preston held 1 carucate of the Aumale fee in Sproatley.[3] It was perhaps another John of Preston who by 1334 had died holding the estate and leaving his heir a son John.[4] The land later passed to a John of Preston's daughter Isabel (d. 1349), whose heir was Gillian Stedeman.[5]

In 1210 or 1211 Saer of Sutton granted 1 carucate and 3½ bovates in Sproatley to Walter de Ver, receiving in exchange ½ carucate and tofts there, and other land in Goxhill (Lincs.).[6] The land in Sproatley evidently descended like Sutton manor in the Suttons, later Lords Sutton, and then to the heirs of Agnes Sutton by Sir Ralph Bulmer.[7] By the attainder of Sir John Bulmer, it passed in 1537 to the Crown. The farm, with ½ carucate of open-field land and several closes, seems later in the century to have been occupied, or claimed, by the heirs of Sir John's son, Sir Ralph Bulmer (d. 1558),[8] and Sproatley premises continued to be recorded, apparently in error, as appurtenances of Sutton

[79] *V.C.H. Yorks.* ii. 172, 269.
[80] *E.Y.C.* ii, pp. 439–41, 446; iii, pp. 34–5, 40, 60, 62–3. For the Goxhills and their successors, the de Vers, ibid. ii, pp. 54–5; iii, pp. 61–3 and n.; W. Farrer, *Honors and Knights' Fees,* ii. 209.
[81] *Rot. de Ob. & Fin.* (Rec. Com.), 324.
[82] *Yorks. Fines, John* (Sur. Soc. xciv), pp. 165–6.
[83] *Cur. Reg. R.* vii. 1, 250.
[84] *Reg. Antiquissimum* (Lincs. Rec. Soc.), ii, p. 212; *Close R.* 1227–31, 394; 1247–51, 537.
[85] The de Ver fee there was also put at 12 carucates, almost certainly in error. *Cal. Inq. p.m.* iv. pp. 354, 357; *Feud. Aids,* vi. 41.
[86] *Yorks. Fines, 1272–1300,* p. 9; *Cal. Close,* 1272–9, 166, 169; W. Farrer, *Honors and Knights' Fees,* ii. 209; Poulson, *Holderness,* ii. 274–5.
[87] Above, this section.
[88] Below, this section.
[89] *Cal. Inq. p.m.* iv. p. 357; *Feud. Aids,* vi. 41; *Cal. Inq. Misc.* i, p. 400; *Yorks. Inq.* ii, pp. 58–9.
[90] P.R.O., E 142/86(2); *Cal. Inq. p.m.* vii, p. 385; *Cal. Fine R.* 1347–56, 402.

[91] *Bridlington Chart.* ed. W. T. Lancaster, 308.
[92] *Cal. Inq. Misc.* i. p. 447.
[93] P.R.O., KB 138/91; *Yorks. Inq.* ii, pp. 58–9; *Cal. Pat.* 1281–92, 145; Poulson, *Holderness,* ii. 274.
[94] B.L. Harl. Ch. 80. H. 7; *Yorks. Inq.* ii, p. 59.
[95] *Cal. Inq. p.m.* ix, p. 294; Poulson, *Holderness,* ii. 275.
[96] *Cal. Papal Reg.* iii. 599.
[97] Poulson, *Holderness,* ii. 275.
[98] P.R.O., C 142/49, no. 41.
[99] *Yorks. Fines, 1272–1300,* p. 8; *Cal. Inq. p.m.* iii, pp. 114–16; Poulson, *Holderness,* ii. 274–5.
[1] *Cal. Inq. p.m. Hen. VII,* i, p. 276; ii, pp. 60–2.
[2] H.U.L., DHO/8/47; above, this section.
[3] *Cal. Inq. p.m.* iv, p. 356.
[4] Ibid. vii, pp. 413–14.
[5] Ibid. ix, pp. 302–3; *Yorks. Fines, 1327–47,* p. 89.
[6] *Yorks. Fines, John* (Sur. Soc. xciv), pp. 165–6.
[7] *Complete Peerage,* s.v. Sutton; *V.C.H. Yorks. E.R.* i. 461, 472.
[8] P.R.O., SC 6/Hen. VIII/4335; ibid. E 310/32/192, f. 63; *L. & P. Hen. VIII,* xvi, p. 465; *V.C.H. Yorks. E.R.* i. 461. *Yorks. Fines,* i. 328, 371; ii. 51; Poulson, *Holderness,* ii. 275.

manor.[9] A Crown grant of the estate to Hugh Counsell and Robert Pistor in 1570 seems also to have been ineffective.[10] The holding, then including three houses, 1 carucate and 1 bovate, and other land in Sproatley, was granted by the Crown in 1616 to Edward Mercer and Christopher Ridley the younger of Beverley.[11] Ridley (d. by 1664) became the sole owner of the premises granted in 1616, besides holding other land in Sproatley.[12] Part of his estate, including some of the Bulmers' former land and comprising in all about 1 carucate, descended to his daughters, Deborah Monckton and Rebecca Pickard, who, with their husbands, sold their interests in 1664 and 1666 to John Constable, Lord Dunbar.[13] The rest, a 5-bovate farm, passed to Ridley's other daughters, Anne and Margaret, who in 1668 sold their shares to Robert Constable, Lord Dunbar.[14] The purchases later descended with the chief estate in the Constables and their heirs.[15]

The archbishop of York held 1 bovate in Sproatley as a berewick of his manor of Swine in 1086.[16]

The Ingilbys, later knights and baronets, held land in Sproatley by the 16th century, and later used it to endow Ripley school (Yorks. W.R.).[17] At inclosure in 1763 Sir John Ingilby, Bt., trustee of the school, was awarded 151 a. for its commonable lands in Sproatley.[18] William Raines bought the 161-a. estate in 1853,[19] and then re-sold it in lots. Sir Thomas Constable, Bt., bought the farm, later Park farm, with 114 a.[20]

Before he made his gift of the church, Ralph of Goxhill gave Bridlington priory 2 bovates in Sproatley, and later in the 12th century the house held 4 bovates of the Aumale fee there, apparently besides the glebe land of Sproatley church.[21] Ralph's nephew, Robert of Goxhill, gave 2 tofts in exchange for another belonging to Sproatley church, and his grandson, Sir Walter de Ver, added another bovate and 3 tofts.[22] The priory's former estate in Sproatley, then comprising 3 bovates, was granted by the Crown in 1601 to John Thynne and Henry Best, who then sold it to Sir Henry Constable.[23]

A chantry in Thearne chapel, in Beverley, was endowed with a cottage, a close, and 1 bovate in Sproatley. After the chantry's suppression, the Crown let the premises in Sproatley, and in 1586 it granted them in reversion to Sir Christopher Hatton.[24]

The Suddaby family c. 1600 charged land in Sproatley with a rent, or rents, for the poor of Bishop Wilton, and sums were paid in consequence until the mid 19th century.[25]

ECONOMIC HISTORY. COMMON LANDS AND INCLOSURE. The tillage lay on either side of the village, in East and West fields, which were named from the later 13th century.[26] The area of arable land was said to have been reduced by conversion to pasture in the 1480s, two houses falling into disrepair and eight people being ejected as a result.[27] A description of commonable lands made in 1650 may reflect internal divisions within the two fields, rather than a re-ordering of the common lands: land on the east side of the village, adjoining Humbleton and Lelley in Preston, and to its west, extending to Wyton, was then said to lie in South field; grounds bordering Thirtleby in Swine in the west and Flinton in the east were parts of North field, and next to Flinton and Humbleton there was a possibly small East field.[28] East and West fields were named again soon afterwards, moreover,[29] and on the eve of inclosure in the mid 18th century they contained 119 bovates and odd lands.[30] A meadow adjoining East field called Wadinfal, mentioned c. 1275, may have been common,[31] and in 1650 meadow in the lower and Town carrs, and in Wyton Scarf, was recorded.[32] Later the bovaters shared grassland in Rake carr, their shares in that meadow determining the number of pasture gates each enjoyed after mowing. Rake carr adjoined the southern boundary, close to the later Sproatley Grange Farm, and was evidently regarded as part of East field.[33] The lack of ridge and furrow on land alongside a stream in East field locates another probable meadow.[34]

The chief common pasture was the Leys,[35] which had almost certainly once been cultivated occasionally. In the 1570s and 1580s several owners sold their 'ley lands' in East Leys pasture, and at least one strip in or bordering that pasture, to Sir John Constable and his son (Sir) Henry, who then inclosed the land, amounting

9 P.R.O., CP 25(2)/805/1 & 2 Jas. II Hil. [no. 47]; CP 25(2)/894/4 Wm. & Mary Trin. [no. 1]; CP 25(2)/983/2 Anne Hil. [no. 63].
10 Cal. Pat. 1569–72, p. 38.
11 E.R.A.O., DDCC/88/17. Cf. Yorks. Fines, 1614–25, 143, 184.   12 P.R.O., E 134/15 Chas. II Mic./25.
13 E.R.A.O., DDCC/88/24, 25, 25b, 26.
14 Ibid. DDCC/88/21, 28.
15 Above, this section.
16 V.C.H. Yorks. ii. 210 n., 325.
17 Poulson, Holderness, ii. 276; Yorks. Royalist Composition Papers, ii (Y.A.S Rec. Ser. xviii), pp. 179–80; V.C.H. Yorks. i. 493.   18 R.D.B., AC/221/10.
19 Ripley School Estate Act, 14 & 15 Vic. c. 23 (Private) at H.U.L., DDCV(2)/83/4; R.D.B., HB/29/37.
20 H.U.L., DDCV(2)/62/60–1; R.D.B., HB/29/38; HB/32/41; E.R.A.O., DDCC(2)/plan 22.
21 E.Y.C. iii, pp. 34–5, 40, 62–3. The distinction between the priory's estate and the glebe is, however, unclear: cf. below, church.
22 Bridlington Chart. ed. W. T. Lancaster, 3–6, 308–9.
23 P.R.O., SC 6/Hen. VIII/4430, m. 28d.; ibid. E 310/30/177, f. 59; E.R.A.O., DDCC/88/14–15.
24 P.R.O., C 66/1272, mm. 12–22; Cal. Pat. 1388–92, 185; 1572–5, p. 178; Valor Eccl. (Rec. Com.), v. 135; V.C.H. Yorks. E.R. vi. 300.
25 E.R.A.O., DDCC/88/83, 95, 106–7.
26 Ibid. DDCC/88/1; for the dating, see above, manors [de Ver]. Cf. Cal. Inq. Misc. i. p. 447.
27 Trans. R.H.S. n.s. vi. 288–9; vii. 253.
28 E.R.A.O., DDCC/88/18.
29 B.I.H.R., TER. H. Sproatley 1662–3.
30 R.D.B., AC/221/10.   31 E.R.A.O., DDCC/88/1.
32 Ibid. DDCC/88/18.
33 R.D.B., AC/221/10; E.R.A.O., DDCC/141/71, plan of Sproatley no. 2.
34 Hull Univ., Dept. of Geog., Fairey surveys, run 365B, no. 2138.   35 R.D.B., AC/221/10.

to over 30 a., in Burton Constable park.[36] In 1650 the reduced Leys pasture contained grass-land, or leys, belonging to bovates, and lands covered with furze, or gorse, bushes, lying together in areas called falls.[37] In the mid 18th century the Leys was stocked one year according to the number of bovates held, and the next by reference to each proprietor's acreage in the pasture. Those without open-field land seem to have depended for their grazing on the fallow and other pasture afforded by the open fields.[38]

Sproatley was inclosed in 1763 under an Act of 1762.[39] Allotments totalled 1,237 a., of which 571 a. came from West field, 536 a. from East field, and 130 a. from the Leys. The totals for East field and the Leys included an extinguished field road. William Constable, lord of the manor, received 567 a., and there were two allotments of c. 150 a. each, one of 118 a., three of 50–99 a., one of 33 a., and three of less than 10 a. Most of the land was freehold, but 71 a. was awarded as 'copyhold free' and 16 a. as 'copyhold bond'.[40]

THE DEMESNE AND OTHER FARMS. The largest estate in Sproatley had land for 4 ploughs in 1086, when there was one plough on the demesne and another worked by 4 villeins. Forty acres of meadowland was also recorded on the holding, which was said to have been worth £2 10s. a year before the Conquest but only £1 in 1086.[41] Between the 14th and 16th centuries the estate produced an income of some £11–12 a year.[42] The assized rents of the free and customary tenants were worth c. £5, and smaller sums were recorded for the tenants' poultry renders, tallage, chevage, and court fines. In the late 16th and early 17th century some of the copyholders at Sproatley paid the lord of Burstwick manor sums for confirmation in their holdings and definition of their rights and obligations, particularly with regard to wood growing on their farms, and their entry and court fines.[43] The land governed by such agreements was perhaps that later termed 'copyhold free'. Poultry may still have been rendered to the Constables in the early 18th century, when their tenants in Sproatley also owed the duty of carrying coal and wood to Burton Constable Hall.[44]

Five bovates of demesne land, a *cultura* called Milldale, of about 1 bovate, and the chief house were occupied by a tenant at will in 1292, and from the early 14th century that farm was leased for £4 a year.[45]

PARK. By the 1290s the Crown also had a park at Sproatley, which was then enlarged by almost 30 a., mostly obtained by the exchange of demesne land with six freeholders. The park may have been in the north-west of Sproatley, adjoining Woodhall in Ellerby and Thirtleby. The lord of those places, Sir Herbert de St. Quintin, gave 7 a. for enclosure in the park, in return for which the Crown assigned him pieces of the lands obtained from the other five freeholders but not required for the park, ground which Sir Herbert seems to have intended adding to his woods in Ellerby and Thirtleby.[46] A parker was employed in the early 1300s, when there was said to have been poaching in the park, and the king's free warren in Sproatley was allegedly breached again in 1345.[47] Grazing for horses, cattle, and sheep in the park was being leased c. 1305, and in 1306–7 the whole park was let to Hugh Gilt for £2 5s. a year. Between the mid 14th century and early 16th rents amounting to almost £2 a year were received for 61 a. in the park, perhaps its total area.[48]

EARLY WOODLAND. In the early 13th century Walter de Ver's estate in Sproatley included an evidently large wood.[49] It may have included ill-drained scrub: 52 a. of woodland bought from Simon de Ver by Simon Constable in 1276 was later decribed as a mere.[50] It was perhaps the rest of the de Ver woodland which formed part of the Crown's estate in the 1292, when the grazing there was valued at £1 a year. That woodland may have been cleared for cultivation soon afterwards.[51]

FISHING. The fishing of With carr, east of the village, and North carr, which was probably in the north-eastern corner of the parish, belonged to Walter de Ver in the early 13th century.[52]

LATER AGRICULTURE. In 1801 Sproatley was reckoned to have almost 500 a. under crops.[53] The division between arable land and grassland was fairly even in the earlier 20th century, 707 a. and 456 a. respectively being returned in 1905, for instance.[54] Some of the grassland was used from the later 19th century by one or two cowkeepers, or dairymen, and in 1909 one of the farms specialized in poultry.[55] A nurseryman was working in Sproatley in 1892,[56] and a century later there were nurseries in

36 E.R.A.O., DDCC/88/2, 5–7, 10–12.
37 Ibid. DDCC/88/18.
38 R.D.B., AC/221/10.
39 2 Geo. III, c. 44 (Priv. Act); R.D.B., AC/221/10 (award); Hull Central Libr., Sproatley incl. plan. Cf. related plans at E.R.A.O., DDCK/35/1 (a); ibid. DDCC(2)/12.
40 Below, next section.
41 V.C.H. Yorks. ii. 269.
42 P.R.O., SC 6/1079/17, mm. 8d., 15d.; SC 6/1082/7, mm. 1–2; SC 6/1084/5 m. 1d.; SC 6/Hen. VII/1028, mm. 1d.–2; E.R.A.O., DDCC/141/66.
43 E.R.A.O., DDCC/88/101–2, 105. Cf. above, Burton Pidsea, econ. hist.
44 E.R.A.O., QDR/2/12.
45 P.R.O., SC 6/1079/14, m. 4; SC 6/1079/17, mm. 8d., 15d.; SC 6/1082/7, mm. 1–2; SC 6/1084/5, m. 1d.; SC 6/Hen. VII/1028, mm. 1d.–2; Cal. Fine R. 1272–1307, 314.
46 P.R.O., E 142/86(2); below, Swine, Ellerby, econ. hist.
47 Cal. Pat. 1292–1301, 624; 1301–7, 107; 1343–5, 586.
48 P.R.O., SC 6/1079/17, mm. 8d., 11d.; SC 6/1082/7, mm. 1–2; SC 6/1084/5, m. 1d.; SC 6/Hen. VII/1028, mm. 1d.–2.
49 Yorks. Fines, John (Sur. Soc. xciv), p. 165.
50 Yorks. Fines, 1272–1300, p. 8; Cal. Inq. p.m. iii, p. 116.
51 P.R.O., SC 6/1079/14, m. 4; Cal. Inq. Misc. i. p. 447; Cal. Fine R. 1272–1307, 314.
52 Yorks. Fines, John, p. 165: cf. E.R.A.O., DDCC/88/18.
53 P.R.O., HO 67/26/400.
54 Acreage Returns, 1905; [1st] Land Util. Surv. Map, sheets 33–4.
55 Directories.
56 Bulmer, Dir. E. Yorks. (1892), 512.

Boggle Lane and on Hull Road.[57] In 1987 of 395.7 ha. (978 a.) returned for Sproatley civil parish, 331.4 ha. (819 a.) were arable and 47.7 ha. (118 a.) grassland. Nearly 1,000 pigs and almost 500 sheep were then kept.[58] One of the proprietors, John Raines (d. by 1808), was said to have planted c. 1,000 trees in Sproatley,[59] and 21 a. of woodland were also returned in 1905 and 1.3 ha. (3 a.) in 1987.[60]

The largest estate in Sproatley, that of the Constables, comprised more than 3 carucates divided into nine farms in 1693.[61] In 1779 the almost 600-a. estate was, apart from 30 a. in hand, let to 19 tenants; the largest farm was of 231 a., and there were two others of c. 130 a. each, one of 49 a., and 15 holdings of under 10 a. each.[62] In the 1820s the estate in Sproatley comprised two holdings of c. 200 a. each, one of 121 a., one of 33 a., four of 5–9 a. each, and some 20 smaller tenancies.[63]

The whole parish usually contained six farms in the 19th century and the earlier 20th; four were of 150 a. or more in 1851, and all or most were larger farms c. 1930. There were two holdings of under 20 a. in 1851, and several smallholdings were recorded in the earlier 20th century.[64] The area returned for Sproatley in 1987 was divided between five holdings, three of 100–199 ha. (247–492 a.) and two of under 5 ha. (12 a.).[65]

INDUSTRY AND TRADE. Predominantly an agricultural place, Sproatley also provided employment for craftsmen and tradesmen in the 19th century and earlier 20th.[66] The requirements of Burton Constable Hall probably account for the numbers involved and the nature of some of the occupations. In 1851, for instance, residents in Sproatley included seven shoemakers, eight dressmakers, a milliner and a straw-bonnet maker, a carver and gilder, eight grooms, a groom cum whipper-in, a coachman, and three gardeners. A few men then employed as brick and tile makers probably worked in the yard in Burton Constable.[67] Less usual occupations also included rope-making, recorded in 1823. Shops in 1897 included a grocer's, a grocery cum drapery, and probably two butchers', and a tailor then kept the post office. A cycle shop had been opened by 1921, and a garage by 1929. Commercially, the village was also served during the period by up to three carriers to Hull. In 1999 a post office and grocery shop, a butcher's, and a joinery concern were trading in Sproatley.

Sand and gravel was dug from pits in the south of the parish before the 1970s, when more commercial extraction was begun there and the older workings were approved as a waste tip. Some sand was evidently also taken from a pit in the north of Sproatley, close to Lodge Farm.[68]

MILLS. A windmill at Sproatley was recorded in the later 13th century,[69] and a mill, perhaps the same, in 1391.[70] In the 19th century corn was ground in a windmill to the east of Park Road.[71] John Rank, the miller in 1840, was presumably a member of the Hull milling family.[72] The mill was evidently given up c. 1895.[73]

LOCAL GOVERNMENT. The court rolls of Burstwick manor[74] record conveyances of copyhold in Sproatley, the election of a rent collector for the village, orders to repair buildings on holdings, and brief references to the view of frankpledge in Sproatley; the copyhold there was not extensive and the evidence is therefore relatively slight.

Churchwardens' accounts survive from 1801,[75] and a book of accounts of the late 18th and early 19th century apparently includes those of an overseer of the poor, churchwarden, assessor and constable, and surveyor of highways.[76] Permanent out-relief was given to c. 10 people in Sproatley in the early 19th century, and about 15 others were then helped occasionally.[77] From 1824 to 1834 the care of the poor was undertaken by a select vestry appointed for the parish. During that period medical help was provided to individuals, and at least one person was maintained in Sutton parish's workhouse.[78] Sproatley joined Skirlaugh poor-law union in 1837,[79] and remained in Skirlaugh rural district until 1935, when it was incorporated into the new rural district of Holderness. It became part of the Holderness district of Humberside in 1974,[80] and of a new East Riding unitary area in 1996.[81]

CHURCH. Sproatley church had been built by the earlier 12th century.[82] The living, which remained a rectory, was united with that of Preston in 1980, but the two parishes were left separate.[83]

Ralph of Goxhill, and perhaps also his brother Erneis, gave Sproatley church to Bridlington

57 Reg. of Electors (1999).
58 Inf. from Min. of Agric., Fish. & Food, Beverley, 1990.
59 Poulson, Holderness, ii. 280; below, educ.
60 Acreage Returns, 1905; inf. from Min. of Agric., Fish. & Food, Beverley, 1990.
61 P.R.O., E 178/6867.
62 E.R.A.O., DDCC(2)/Box 8/17.
63 Ibid. DDCC/111/39; DDCC/141/86.
64 Ibid. NV/1/46; P.R.O., HO 107/2365; directories.
65 Inf. from Min. of Agric., Fish. & Food.
66 The following is based on P.R.O., HO 107/2365; directories.
67 Below, Swine, Burton Constable, econ. hist.
68 E.R.A.O., DDCC/141/71, plans of Sproatley, nos. 1 and 2; O.S. Map 1/2,500, Yorks. CCXXVII. 7 (1890 edn.); Humbs. C.C. Mins. 1976–7, E 1920.

69 Yorks. Inq. ii, pp. 58–9.
70 Poulson, Holderness, ii. 275.
71 O.S. Map 1/2,500, Yorks. CCXXVII. 3 (1890 edn.).
72 V.C.H. Yorks. E.R. i. 256; White, Dir. E. & N.R. Yorks. (1840), 267.
73 Directories.
74 E.R.A.O., DDCC/15/1–62; ibid. DDCC(2)/80.
75 Ibid. PE/130/54.   76 H.U.L., PR/8.
77 Poor Law Abstract, 1804, pp. 594–5; 1818, pp. 522–3.
78 Vestry book at E.R.A.O., PE/130/68; V.C.H. Yorks. E.R. i. 440.
79 3rd Rep. Poor Law Com. 170.   80 Census.
81 Humberside (Structural Change) Order 1995 (copy at E.R.A.O.).
82 E.Y.C. ii. pp. 439–41, 446.
83 B.I.H.R., OC. 964.

priory in the earlier 12th century; the first reliable confirmations indicate that the gift had been made by 1140.[84] The priory, or its grantees, presented to Sproatley until the house's dissolution in the 16th century, except in 1446, when the archbishop of York collated by lapse, and possibly also in 1495, when Agnes Constable presented for an unknown reason.[85] After the dissolution, the advowson belonged briefly to the Crown, before being granted to Edward Fiennes, Lord Clinton and Saye, in 1553.[86] It had passed to the Constables by 1570, and, except for a short confiscation by the Commonwealth in the mid 17th century,[87] remained with them and their successors until the later 19th century. Ralph Rand, trustee of the Roman Catholic Robert Constable, viscount Dunbar, presented in 1714, and later in the 18th century and in the early 19th the patronage was exercised, probably for the Constables, by their grantees and relatives, George Brudenell, earl of Cardigan and later duke of Montagu (d. 1790), and his son, James Brudenell, earl of Cardigan (d. 1811).[88] A turn was later evidently sold to a Mrs. Wall, who in 1858 presented C. J. Wall, then the curate.[89] In 1878 the advowson was sold to J. B. Barkworth, from whom D. B. Kendell, son-in-law and trustee of Samuel Stocks, bought it in 1883.[90] Stocks had had c. 175 a. in Sproatley in 1827, and in 1844 he was described as a retired cotton manufacturer living in the West Riding.[91] Kendell, who evidently presented a relative, Samuel Hall, in 1889,[92] died in 1902. He was succeeded in turn by his widow Frances[93] (d. by 1908) and Anna Kendell (d. 1929), presumably their daughter, who left the advowson to her niece, Jeannie Peirson.[94] In 1953 Mrs. Peirson transferred the advowson to the archbishop of York,[95] who, since 1980, has been the sole patron of the united benefice.[96]

The annual value of Sproatley church was put at £10 in 1291[97] and at £7 0s. 10d. net in 1535.[98] In 1650 the improved net value was £60 a year.[99] Net income averaged £230 a year between 1829 and 1831,[1] and was £283 in 1883.[2]

The Goxhill family's gift of the church included land, variously said in the mid 12th century to comprise 4–6 bovates.[3] Including the

rectory house, the glebe was worth £2 a year gross in 1535.[4] There were said to be 4½ bovates of glebe land in the 1680s, but other references in the later 17th and earlier 18th century put the open-field glebe at 9 or 10 bovates, and it was for 9 bovates that 73 a. was allotted to the rector at inclosure in 1763. The total area of glebe land, including the churchyard and the rectory house garden, was later c. 80 a.,[5] and the rental was £170 a year in 1878.[6] Two acres was sold in 1924,[7] 1 a. in 1933,[8] and the rectory house with 77 a. to Geoffrey Hope in 1946.[9]

The tithes were worth £7 9s. gross a year in 1535,[10] and at inclosure in 1763 the rector was awarded annual composition rents amounting to £105 for them.[11]

The rectory house was mentioned in the early 13th century,[12] and again, as decayed, in 1578.[13] George Bewe, rector, repaired and altered the house in 1661, and in the 1670s he planted the grounds and the churchyard with trees.[14] The house then had three hearths.[15] In 1764 it was partly built of brick and tile and partly of clay walls covered with thatch, and included a dining room, hall, and parlour on the ground floor, and three bedrooms and two attic rooms.[16] It was repaired and enlarged in 1793 or 1794,[17] and in 1809 there were six ground-floor rooms and six bedrooms.[18] It was said in 1828 to have been 'lately improved and enlarged',[19] and an earlier 19th-century illustration shows a three-bayed house with an off-centre doorway with Gothic moulding above it, and to the side a three-bayed wing, presumably of service rooms.[20] Brick walling of the 18th-century house remains in the back of the present building. In 1869 the house was again remodelled and enlarged. The work was done by John Atkinson & Son, probably to designs by Alfred Brown of Hull, and involved the extension of the north-western part of that house, internal re-arrangement of the north-eastern rooms, and much alteration to the south front, which was given a new entrance, a large bay, and new windows.[21] The house was altered in 1899 by John Bilson, who hung tiles on parts of the red brickwork of the south front, and incorporated Queen Anne features there, including a porch surmounted by a balustrade. Lesser

[84] *E.Y.C.* ii. pp. 439–41, 446; iii. pp. 60, 62–3.
[85] For this and the following, Lawrance, 'Clergy List', Holderness, 2, pp. 142–5; Poulson, *Holderness*, ii. 278.
[86] *Cal. Pat.* 1547–53, 167–8.
[87] H.U.L., DHO/8/47; *T.E.R.A.S.* iv. 55; B.I.H.R., CP. H. 2516.
[88] E.R.A.O., QDB/1, p. 139A; ibid. DDCC/88/70; DDCC/111/224, 229, 259; *Complete Peerage*, s.v. Cardigan.
[89] List of rectors in church; Sheahan and Whellan, *Hist. York & E.R.* ii. 376.
[90] The family name is sometimes spelt Kendall. R.D.B., MS/197/255; NR/241/341.
[91] E.R.A.O., DDCC(2)/plan 22; *Hull Advertiser*, 12 July 1844.
[92] R.D.B., 566/333/266; E.R.A.O., PE/130/2.
[93] R.D.B., 49/64/59 (1902); 52/439/417 (1903); B.I.H.R., Fac. 1910/21.
[94] B.I.H.R., BA. TP. 1908/3; 1929/5.
[95] Ibid. OC. 719.
[96] Ibid. OC. 964.
[97] *Tax. Eccl.* (Rec. Com.), 304.
[98] *Valor Eccl.* (Rec. Com.), v. 117.
[99] *T.E.R.A.S.* iv. 55.

[1] *Rep. Com. Eccl. Revenues*, 968–9.
[2] B.I.H.R., V. 1884/Ret. 2.
[3] *E.Y.C.* iii. pp. 40, 60; *Bridlington Chart.* ed. W. T. Lancaster, 344.
[4] *Valor Eccl.* (Rec. Com.), v. 117.
[5] B.I.H.R., TER. H. Sproatley 1662–3, n.d., 1716, 1726, 1781, 1853; R.D.B., AC/221/10.
[6] E.R.A.O., DDCC/14/33.
[7] P.R.O., ED 49/8604; R.D.B., 286/436/367.
[8] R.D.B., 482/112/81.
[9] Ibid. 717/168/137.
[10] *Valor Eccl.* (Rec. Com.), v. 117.
[11] R.D.B., AC/221/10.
[12] *Bridlington Chart.* ed. W. T. Lancaster, 309.
[13] B.I.H.R., V. 1578–9/CB. 1, f. 71.
[14] E.R.A.O., PE/130/1; B.I.H.R., CP. H. 2516.
[15] P.R.O., E 179/205/504.
[16] B.I.H.R., TER. H. Sproatley 1764.
[17] Ibid. MGA. 1794/2.
[18] Ibid. TER. H. Sproatley 1809.
[19] *Hull Advertiser*, 18 July 1828.
[20] Poulson, *Holderness*, ii. 274.
[21] B.I.H.R., MGA. 1869/2; ibid. Ch. Ret. iii.

changes were made in 1907 by Brodrick, Lowther, & Walker.[22] The rectory house was sold in 1946,[23] and rectors later lived in Preston.[24] The Old Rectory was being restored in 1999.

Early clergy may have included Benedict the chaplain of Sproatley, recorded c. 1200.[25] From the 14th to the 17th century the living was evidently often held by non-resident pluralists.[26] John of Carnaby (Kerneteby), rector from 1310, was also official of the archdeacon of the East Riding[27] and was abroad in 1322, and the preferments of John Bransby, B.Th., rector 1528–34, included the mastership of the college of Sutton on Hull and the rectory of Settrington. In the 17th and 18th centuries Sproatley was similarly held with other, but more local, churches. A curate was employed at Sproatley in 1721.[28] George Goundril, rector from 1740, lived at Sproatley, but he was also curate of Nunkeeling, c. 15 km. distant, in 1743 and vicar of Swine, where he employed an assistant curate. In 1743 he provided a service at Sproatley each Sunday in winter and two on alternate Sundays in summer, besides a daily service when at home. In the mid 18th century Holy Communion was celebrated three to four times a year, with c. 45, about half of the total number of confirmed parishioners, usually receiving.[29] Charles Wapshare, rector from 1806 to 1858, lived on his other rectory in Berkshire and employed curates, one of whom, Joseph Hatfield, had the church rebuilt about 1820;[30] he also interested himself in the erosion of the Holderness coast, taking many measurements in the 1830s.[31] C. J. Wall, curate by 1851 and rector from 1858 to 1889,[32] resided, and at the end of his incumbency, when he was rebuilding the church, also employed a curate. One service was held each Sunday at Sproatley in 1851,[33] but by 1865 there were two, and in the late 19th and early 20th century morning prayers were also read daily. Communion was monthly by the 1860s, fortnightly by 1884, and weekly in the earlier 20th century. In 1884 of the 743 confirmed Anglicans in the parish, 25 usually received, and in 1931 up to 12 communicated. A winter night school for men was tried in the 1860s, and later a library was run from the school; neither was very suc-

cessful.[34] The church was 'High Anglican' c. 1930.[35] Sproatley was held with, and served from, Preston before the union of the two benefices in 1980.[36] In 1999 there was usually a service, or a celebration of communion, in the church each Sunday.[37]

The church was dedicated to *ST. SWITHIN* by the early 13th century.[38] Little is known about the medieval church. Its steeple was recorded in 1552,[39] and the chancel was rethatched in the 1660s and repaired in 1670.[40] In general, though, the building seems to have been poorly maintained in the 16th and 17th centuries.[41] In the early 19th century the curate, Joseph Hatfield, had the small 'much decayed' building demolished, and a larger church built on its site. The old church was said to have been 'lately taken down' in December 1819,[42] and rebuilding was complete in 1820. Services were held in the interim in an old schoolroom in the rectory house.[43] The new church was apparently dedicated to *ALL SAINTS*, but by 1840 it seems once again to have been *ST. SWITHIN'S*.[44] It was a plain building, of cream brick with slate roofs and round-headed sash windows, comprising chancel, aisled nave, and short west tower. The tower, of three stages with parapet and pinnacles, was flanked by two small porches. Inside, to comply with the conditions of a grant from the Church Building Society, a large west gallery was built to provide free seating.[45] The cost was otherwise largely met by subscriptions, including one from Francis Constable.[46] William Hutchinson of Hull is recorded as 'planning the new church', but he may have been merely the surveyor, and other evidence suggests that the design was by Peter Atkinson of York.[47] In 1885 and 1886 most of the church was taken down and rebuilt again at the promotion of the rector, C. J. Wall. The rebuilding was in a 15th-century style by Smith & Brodrick of Hull. A north porch was added in place of the western ones; a northern organ chamber was also built onto the chancel, and inside the west gallery was removed. During the rebuilding services were held in the school.[48]

The church contains part of the incised coffin lid of a medieval priest,[49] and in the chancel a

22 Pevsner and Neave, *Yorks. E.R.* 709.
23 R.D.B., 717/168/137.
24 B.I.H.R., OC. 964.
25 *E.Y.C.* iii, p. 63.
26 For the following, Lawrance, 'Clergy List', Holderness, 1, pp. 4, 20; 2, pp. 143–5, 151; Le Neve, *Fasti, 1300–1541, Northern Province*, 61, 75. Lawrance's list is incomplete: cf. B.I.H.R., CP. E. 133.
27 *Reg. Greenfield*, v, p. 269.
28 E.R.A.O., PE/130/61.
29 B.I.H.R., V. 1764/Ret. 3, no. 51; *Herring's Visit.* iii, pp. 123–4; Poulson, *Holderness*, ii. 278.
30 B.I.H.R., TER. H. Sproatley 1809; E.R.A.O., PE/130/2; *Rep. Com. Eccl. Revenues*, 968–9; Poulson, *Holderness*, ii. 278; White, *Dir. E. & N.R. Yorks.* (1840), 267; *Educ. of Poor Digest*, 1094; below, this section [fabric].
31 E.R.A.O., PE/130/7.
32 Ibid. PE/130/2; P.R.O., HO 129/522/1/7/5; Sheahan and Whellan, *Hist. York & E.R.* ii. 376.
33 P.R.O., HO 129/522/1/7/5.
34 B.I.H.R., V. 1865/Ret. 2, no. 510; V. 1868/Ret. 2, no. 465; V. 1884/Ret. 2; V. 1912–22/Ret.; V. 1931/Ret.

35 Ibid. V. 1931/Ret.   36 *Crockford* (1965–6).
37 Notice at church.   38 *E.Y.C.* iii, p. 63.
39 *Inventories of Ch. Goods*, 38.
40 E.R.A.O., PE/130/1; B.I.H.R., CP. H. 2516.
41 B.I.H.R., V. 1567–8/CB. 1, ff. 194v.–5; V. 1578–9/CB. 1, f. 71.; ER V./CB. 2, f. 59.
42 E.R.A.O., PE/130/38. Perhaps as early as 1818: *Educ. of Poor Digest*, 1094.
43 E.R.A.O., PE/130/26, 27, 38, 54; *Educ. of Poor Digest*, 1094.
44 White, *Dir. E. & N.R. Yorks.* (1840), 267; Poulson, *Holderness*, ii. 278, which was probably anachronistic.
45 B.I.H.R., Fac. 1819/14; E.R.A.O., PE/130/26; Poulson, *Holderness*, ii. 278–9; photographs and an apparent painting of the rebuilt church displayed there in 1999.
46 E.R.A.O., PE/130/25, 54.
47 Ibid. PE/130/54; H. Colvin, *Biog. Dict. of Brit. Architects 1600–1840*, 73, 442.
48 B.I.H.R., Fac. 1885/18; Fac. Bk. 6, p. 560; E.R.A.O., PE/130/36–7; donations and payments listed in ibid. PE/130/5; Bulmer, *Dir. E. Yorks.* (1892), 510.
49 Poulson, *Holderness*, ii. 279 (illus.).

late 19th-century white marble memorial depicting a young girl commemorates a rector's sister. An oak altar by John Bilson of Hull was installed in 1910 in memory of the patroness of the living, Frances, daughter of Samuel Stocks and wife of D. B. Kendell.[50] A stone font, in the form of a small bowl on a baluster support, was evidently fixed in the rebuilt church c. 1820, replaced in 1879,[51] and then used as an ornament in the garden of the rectory house, later the Old Rectory, where it remained in 1999. The organ is said to have been built c. 1710 by 'father Smith' for Temple Newsam house, near Leeds, bought c. 1825 by J. Kendell, and given to the church in 1886, during the restoration, by his son, D. B. Kendell, the patron.[52] In the early 20th century Samuel Hall, rector, and his wife provided oak panelling in the chancel, and also gave several pieces of their work as woodcarvers.

The church has two 14th-century bells, which were restored in the late 1980s,[53] and a set of eight tubular bells, presented to the rebuilt church by the rector in 1888.[54] A clock was placed in the tower in 1898.[55] Elizabeth Biggs, or Briggs, daughter of George Bewe (d. 1680), rector, gave two salvers, which were later exchanged for another salver which serves as a paten. The salvers were given or exchanged in 1739. The plate also includes a cup of 1796 and a 19th-century flagon.[56] The registers of baptisms begin in 1657, and of marriages and burials in 1669; with the possible exception of some marriages c. 1750, they are complete.[57]

A little land, hitherto occupied by the school, was added to the churchyard and consecrated in 1869,[58] and another small addition was made in 1927.[59] The large yard, shaded by many mature trees, is entered through a lich-gate, of massive timber covered with slate, which was built in 1899 to commemorate Queen Victoria's reign to a design by John Bilson.[60] A memorial incorporating a draped urn and enclosed still within iron railings marks the vault of William Wilkinson of Hull (d. 1834) and his relatives. The base and part of the shaft of a medieval cross, formerly standing in the south of the village, may have been removed to the rectory-house garden by the 1840s, and they were later kept in the churchyard, their location in 1999.[61] Stonework said to come from the same or another cross was kept in the garden of the former rectory house in 1999. The churchyard also contains a rock thought to have been deposited during the Ice Age; it was restored and fenced by Sproatley W.I. for European Heritage Year in 1975.[62]

Besides 1s. from each house and 5d. from each cottage at Easter,[63] the parish clerk was entitled to three sheaves of wheat from each bovate, and grazing in the open fields and pastures, until inclosure in 1763, when he was allotted 8 a. instead.[64] The allotment was called Amen field in the late 19th century, when it was leased for £12 a year.[65]

NONCONFORMITY. Despite the lordship of the Constables and the proximity of Burton Constable Hall, Roman Catholicism seems to have had little influence in Sproatley. The rector was still saying requiem masses, and a holywater stoup had been kept in the church, in 1567, and 16 recusants at Sproatley were named in 1669. Fewer Roman Catholics were usually recorded in the parish, however, before the later 18th century, and they then numbered only about 20.[66]

There were said to be no protestant dissenters in the parish in 1743 and 1764.[67] The Wesleyan Methodists built a chapel on the east side of Park Road in 1804.[68] In 1818 it was alleged that the schoolmaster, who was Methodist, had established a Sunday school, and was refusing to allow children and teachers to attend Anglican services,[69] but in the mid century most of the chapel's congregation was said also to attend church.[70] The chapel was largely rebuilt in 1904, and, as Sproatley Methodist Church, was still used in 1999.[71]

EDUCATION. Bridget Biggs, daughter of George Bewe (d. 1680), rector of Sproatley,[72] left the reversion of an estate in Sheffield, Penistone, and Ecclesfield (all Yorks. W.R.) for education in Sproatley by her will of 1733 or 1734.[73] The churchwardens and overseers of the poor, supervised by the rector and the vicar of Holy Trinity, Hull, were to use the rents to build a school, and were to pay a master and mistress to teach 10 boys reading, writing, and arithmetic and 10 girls reading, writing, and sewing. The

[50] B.I.H.R., Fac. 1910/21; plate on altar.

[51] Plaque on present font.   [52] Plate on organ.

[53] Inf. from churchwarden, 1999.

[54] *Inventories of Ch. Goods*, 38; Boulter, 'Ch. Bells', 85; G. R. Park, *Ch. Bells of Holderness*, 59–60; plaque in tower.

[55] Plaque.

[56] B.I.H.R., TER. H. Sproatley 1764, 1809; E.R.A.O., PE/130/1, s.v. 1668; *Yorks. Ch. Plate*, i. 318–19; Lawrance, 'Clergy List', Holderness, 2, p. 145; below, educ.

[57] One or two earlier registrations have also been entered: E.R.A.O., PE/130/1–3, 6. There are transcripts from 1600: B.I.H.R., PRT. Hold. D. Sproatley.

[58] B.I.H.R., CD. Add. 1869/5; E.R.A.O., PE/130/45; P.R.O., ED 49/8604.

[59] R.D.B., 347/560/459.

[60] Pevsner and Neave, *Yorks. E.R.* 709.

[61] Illus. in Poulson, *Holderness*, 274; Bulmer, *Dir. E. Yorks.* (1892), 511; O.S. Map 1/2,500, Yorks. CCXXVII. 7 (1890 edn.).

[62] Bulmer, *Dir. E. Yorks.* (1892), 511.

[63] B.I.H.R., TER. H. Sproatley 1764.

[64] R.D.B., AC/221/10.

[65] *Kelly's Dir. N. & E.R. Yorks.* (1897), 538.

[66] B.I.H.R., V. 1567–8/CB. 1, ff. 194v.–195; V. 1764/Ret. 3, no. 51; Aveling, *Post Reformation Catholicism*, 13, 67; *Depositions from York Castle* (Sur. Soc. xl), pp. 121, 168, 182.

[67] B.I.H.R., V. 1764/Ret. 3, no. 51; *Herring's Visit.* iii, p. 123.

[68] B.I.H.R., Fac. Bk. 3, p. 371; datestone on chapel. O.S. Map 6", Yorks. CCXXVII (1855 edn.) apparently shows the chapel on the opposite side of Park Road.

[69] *Educ. of Poor Digest*, 1094.

[70] B.I.H.R., V. 1865/Ret. 2, no. 510; V. 1868/Ret. 2, no. 465.

[71] Datestones; D. [R. J.] and S. Neave, *E.R. Chapels and Meeting Houses* (E. Yorks. Loc. Hist. Soc.), 57; local inf.

[72] B.I.H.R., V. 1764/Ret. 3, no. 51; E.R.A.O., PE/130/1, s.v. 1671; Lawrance, 'Clergy List', Holderness, 2, p. 145.

[73] Para. based on *9th Rep. Com. Char.* 776–8; *Educ. of Poor Digest*, 1094.

rest of the income was to be spent on apprentice-ships and the like. The charity had taken effect by 1742, when a house for the master and mistress was built in the north-west corner of the churchyard and on adjacent waste ground.[74] About 30 children were said to attend the school in 1743,[75] and in 1764 the schoolmaster was paid £25 a year for teaching reading, writing, and arithmetic to the 20 boys and girls taught free, and the mistress £20 for instructing the 10 girls in knitting, sewing, and other 'female accomplishments'.[76] A schoolroom was added in 1777.[77] Mrs. Biggs's charity was enlarged by John Raines's bequest of £200,[78] received in 1808. The numbers taught free were increased then, and again in 1818 and 1819, in return for an increase in the teachers' stipends. In 1818 the school was said to be attended by 14 boys and 10 girls, and 16 boys and 15 girls were apparently taught free c. 1820.[79] Besides their shares of the schoolhouse, the master received £33 a year and the mistress £24 from Biggs's and Raines's charities c. 1820, when the poorly-built schoolroom, the lack of oversight by the non-resident rector, and the conduct of both the overseers and the master, who also kept a shop, were all causing concern. In 1833 the charity school was attended by 40 boys and 30 girls, of whom 18 in each department were then paid for by the trustees, and the rest were taught either at their parents' expense or freely by the teachers.[80]

In 1868 the school was rebuilt on adjacent glebe land, part of the former site, also belonging to the rectory, being then returned to the churchyard.[81] The new school, incorporating houses for the master and mistress, was designed by R. G. Smith of Hull. His building, of red and cream banded brickwork with Gothic windows, a small bell-turret, and an ornate metal weather vane, was re-roofed in slate and one of the houses adapted as an infants' classroom in the 1880s, both to designs by Smith & Brodrick of Hull.[82] In the 1860s the boys' department was attended by 41 boys and 6 senior girls and the girls' school by 33 girls and 13 'little boys'.[83] At inspection in 1871 there were 41 boys and 26 girls in attendance.[84] In 1873 average attendance was 38 for the boys and 30 for the girls, 14 of each sex then being supported from the charity funds.[85] Average attendance was usually c. 65

between 1906 and 1938.[86] In 1921 the buildings were improved[87] and the school became a Non-Provided school under the county council.[88] The trustees of the school charity provided a playing field in 1924, and in 1933 they further enlarged the site.[89] The senior pupils were transferred to South Holderness County Secondary School at its opening in 1954, and Sproatley Endowed School was thereafter a primary school.[90] The first phase of a new school, built beside Balk Lane and near the existing building, was opened in 1974; it comprised accommodation for 60 pupils and a school hall.[91] The old school continued in use, and two mobile classrooms were also employed to cope with the growing numbers.[92] The second instalment, providing five more classrooms, was completed, and the old school vacated, in 1979,[93] and an office for the headteacher was added in 1984. The bad state of Marton school led to its staff and pupils being moved in January 1984 to Sproatley school, which was again enlarged with a mobile classroom; Marton school was officially closed at the end of that year, and its pupils integrated into Sproatley school. There were 228 on the roll at Sproatley in 1990, and 204 in January 2000.[94] The redundant school buildings were sold in 1987,[95] and in 1999 they were occupied as two houses, called The Old Classrooms and The Old School House.

The value of Biggs's charity was increased by the discovery of coal on the estate.[96] The rental was c. £55 a year in the mid 18th century,[97] and nearly £90 a year c. 1820, when another £9 was received from Raines's bequest.[98] In 1884 the income comprised just over £100 a year in rents, and £230 interest on £7,335 stock and cash in hand.[99] The landed estate in the West Riding was mostly sold in the later 19th and early 20th century; in the East Riding 54 a. in Hollym was bought in 1899,[1] and in or soon after 1912 a farmhouse and other buildings were put up there. Following the change in the school's management in 1921, a Scheme was obtained in 1922 creating the Sproatley School Foundation to maintain the school and provide vocational training, or access to secondary education, for its pupils. The endowment then comprised, besides the school, the farm at Hollym, let for £71 a year; some unsold land in the West Riding, let for £22, and over £11,000 stock pro-

---

74 B.I.H.R., TER. H. Sproatley 1764; O.S. Map 6″, Yorks. CCXXVII (1855 edn.). Earlier dates, of 1739 and 1740, are given in B.I.H.R., V. 1764/Ret. 3, no. 51; Baines, *Hist. Yorks.* (1823), ii. 391.

75 *Herring's Visit.* iii, p. 123.

76 B.I.H.R., V. 1764/Ret. 3, no. 51.

77 The end of the school appears in a view of the old church kept in the church in 1999.

78 P.R.O., ED 49/8603; Poulson, *Holderness*, ii. 270–1.

79 The two sources differ regarding the free pupils.

80 *Educ. Enquiry Abstract*, 1096.

81 P.R.O., ED 7/135, no. 172A; ED 49/8604; E.R.A.O., PE/130/67; B.I.H.R., Ch. Ret. iii.

82 P.R.O., ED 49/8603; Pevsner and Neave, *Yorks. E.R.* 709; O.S. Map 1/2,500, Yorks. CCXXVII. 7 (1890 edn.).

83 B.I.H.R., V. 1868/Ret. 2, no. 465.

84 *Returns relating to Elem. Educ.* 472–3.

85 P.R.O., ED 7/135, no. 172A.

86 *Bd. of Educ., List 21* (H.M.S.O., 1908 and later edns.).

87 E.R.A.O., PE/130/67; E.R. Educ. Cttee. *Mins.*

1920–1, 106, 244.

88 P.R.O., ED 7/135, no. 172A; ED 49/8604; E.R. Educ. Cttee. *Mins.* 1920–1, 155; 1921–2, 103.

89 P.R.O., ED 49/8604; R.D.B., 286/436/367; 482/112/81.

90 E.R. Educ. Cttee. *Mins.* 1952–3, 226; 1953–4, 145.

91 Ibid. 1970–1, 52; 1971–2, 89; 1972–3, 43. This and the rest of the para. is based on inf. from the headteacher, Sproatley, 2000.

92 Humbs. C.C. *Mins.* 1976–7, E 1592; 1977–8, F 152.

93 Ibid. 1977–8, F 195.

94 Inf. from Educ. Dept., Humbs. C.C., 1990.

95 Inf. from Sproatley School Foundation, 2000.

96 P.R.O., ED 49/8603; E.R.A.O., PE/130/67.

97 B.I.H.R., V. 1764/Ret. 3, no. 51; ibid. TER. H. Sproatley 1770; *Herring's Visit.* iii, p. 123.

98 *9th Rep. Com. Char.* 777.

99 The rest of the para. is based on P.R.O., ED 49/8603–4.

1 R.D.B., 12/140/138 (1899).

ducing more than £250 a year. Medical help for pupils,[2] grants for further education, and extra books for the school were later provided from the income, which c. 1980 was said to be £1,400 a year.[3]

Part of the income of Bridget Biggs's charity was used in the early 19th century to provide a few apprenticeship premiums of £4–8 each, and more clothing allowances of up to 4 guineas for those going into service.[4] The provision of apprenticeships was given up in 1850,[5] and in the late 19th and early 20th century the income was spent in cash grants to pupils on leaving school and on completion of the first year's work.[6] In 1933 the trustees were also proposing to provide boys and girls with training in domestic work and handicraft.[7]

Other schools in Sproatley have included one begun by the parish clerk in 1702,[8] a girls' school with 20–30 pupils in 1818, and a small boarding school for boys kept by the Revd. Joseph Hatfield, curate, in the early and mid 19th century.[9]

In the 1870s the schoolmaster tried an evening school but it was unsuccesssful.[10]

CHARITIES FOR THE POOR.

Elizabeth Berrier by will of 1686 gave c. 1½ a. in Fitling in Humbleton for the poor of Sproatley. Ten shillings a year was, however, to be paid during his life to Benjamin Hardy, then rector, for a sermon on Mrs. Berrier's birthday. The rent of the land was £1 6s. a year in 1764, and just over £2 a year in 1821, when nine payments of 3–11s. were made to widows and the old.[11] Alice Johnson left £1 a year in Lelley in Preston; it was not known where the sum was charged in 1764, but in the early 19th century it was being collected and distributed in doles of 2–8s.[12] The two charities were administered together in the early 20th century. Berrier's charity had by then been converted into a rent charge, of £2 a year, and the joint income of £3 was used to help the sick, either in the form of cash doles or goods such as tea and coal. There were usually about 20 recipients.[13] In the later 20th century the rent charge from Lelley ceased to be collected and that charity was lost.[14] Berrier's charity became a relief in need trust benefiting parishioners of Sproatley by Scheme of 1982, which also allowed it to be administered with a larger charity for Burton Constable in Swine.[15]

SWINE

THE ancient parish of Swine was the largest in Holderness, even after the probable early loss of land to Sutton parish and the separation in the 17th century of Drypool chapelry.[16] In 1852–3 it still had 14,695 a. (5,947 ha.), and at its greatest extent it was above 5 miles (8 km.) long and broad;[17] in 1867, however, the chapelries of Bilton and Skirlaugh were made separate parishes, leaving Swine ecclesiastical parish with just over 7,000 a. (2,833 ha.).[18] The parish was situated in the centre of the Middle division of Holderness wapentake, and most of its land was in that division. Its northern end extended into the North division across Lambwath stream, which, as well as forming much of the parish boundary there, also separated the two divisions.

Apart from Swine village, the ancient parish included almost twenty villages or hamlets, half a dozen of which are now represented by isolated farmhouses and may always have been very small. By contrast, the former hamlet of Bilton, at the southern end of the parish, has grown into a virtual suburb of Hull, the built-up area of which lies c. 3 km. south-west of Swine village.

The boulder clay which covers most of the parish produces a gently-rolling landscape in the eastern half, where the ground is over 15 m. above sea level, reaching 27 m. at Ellerby. Along the northern parish boundary the higher ground falls sharply into the valley of Lambwath stream, but in the west and south it shelves down into the Hull and Old fleet valleys to less than 8 m. above sea level, falling as low as 3 m. at Swine village. Scattered sand and gravel deposits include those chosen as sites for Coniston and Thirtleby.[19]

The parish was drained by Lambwath stream, which continued south-westwards across the parish towards the river Hull, and by southern boundary streams carrying water into Old fleet and eventual outfall into the Humber. Lambwath, perhaps meaning 'lamb ford', is an Anglo-Scandinavian hybrid name.[20] Early in the 13th century Meaux abbey made a drain from Lamb-

[2] E.R.A.O., PE/130/67.
[3] Review of Char. Rep. 112.
[4] 9th Rep. Com. Char. 778. Accounts relating to the school and apprenticing in the early 19th century are included in H.U.L., PR/8.　　[5] P.R.O., ED 49/8604.
[6] Kelly's Dir. N. & E.R. Yorks. (1889), 459; P.R.O., ED 49/8604.
[7] E.R. Educ. Cttee. Mins. 1933–4, 74.
[8] E.R.A.O., PE/130/1.
[9] Educ. of Poor Digest, 1094; Hull Advertiser, 18 Jan. 1812; 18 July 1828.
[10] B.I.H.R., V. 1877/Ret. 3, no. 82; P.R.O., ED 7/135, no. 172A.
[11] B.I.H.R., V. 1764/Ret. 3, no. 51; E.R.A.O., PE/130/54, 60–1; 9th Rep. Com. Char. 778–9; above, Humbleton, manors [Fitling].
[12] B.I.H.R., V. 1764/Ret. 3, no. 51; E.R.A.O., PE/

130/54; 9th Rep. Com. Char. 776.
[13] E.R.A.O., accession 1681.
[14] Review of Char. Rep. 112.
[15] Humbs. Dir. of Char. 35; Review of Char. Rep. 102, 112–13; Char. Com. reg. no. 512673; below, Swine, Burton Constable, charity.
[16] This article was written mostly in 1993–4. Below, Swine, manors [Suttons], church.
[17] O.S. Map 6″, Yorks. CCXI, CCXII, CCXXVI, CCXXVII (1855 edn.).
[18] Below, Swine, church; Bilton, church; S. Skirlaugh, church.
[19] Geol. Surv. Map 1″, drift, sheets 72–3 (1909 edn.).
[20] P.N. Yorks. E.R. (E.P.N.S.), 70. Lambwath stream and its mere are, however, close to Langthorpe, in Ellerby, which is thought to mean 'Lambi's village': ibid. 48; below, Marton.

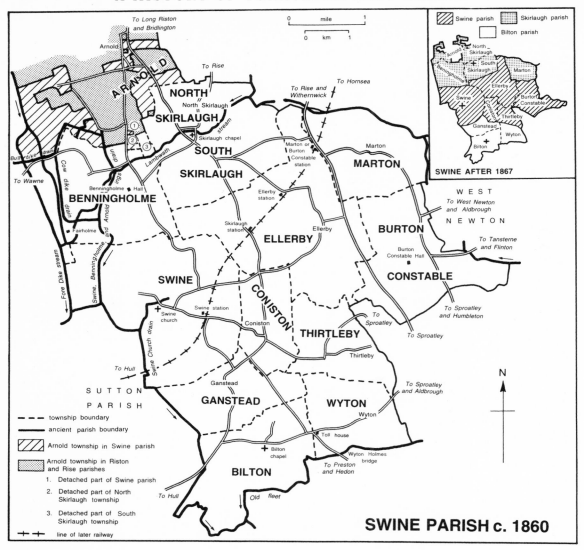

SWINE PARISH c. 1860

wath stream across Benningholme to the abbey mill; it was later called Monk dike and part of its course may be followed by Bull Dike drain. Other drains made or improved by the abbey probably included those along the western boundary called Moor dike and Forge, later Forth or Fore, dike.[21] Poor drainage is evident from the names Benningholme, Fairholme, and Marton,[22] where 'mere' field-names were common in 1322.[23] There were permanent pools at Swine, Wyton, and Bilton in 1367,[24] and two remained at Swine in 1735, after the failure of the plan of Joseph Micklethwaite, Viscount Micklethwaite, to drain c. 140 a. of low grounds there with windmills.[25] Inadequate drains caused flooding, and low ground in the south of the parish was also vulnerable to inundation from the river Humber; in the mid 17th century

lands in the parish were rated to the maintenance of protective banks at Drypool.[26] A drain awarded in 1778 to drain Long Riston and Arnold carrs had evidently still to be made in 1783, when a revised award extended it through the existing Cowdike drain in Benningholme.[27] As elsewhere in the Hull valley,[28] effective drainage of the marshy, low grounds, or carrs, only began after the formation in 1764 of the Holderness Drainage Board, notably by the cutting of a new outfall to the Humber in the 1830s. Other new drains included Swine, Benningholme, and Arnold ings drain, which was made in the earlier 19th century.[29] Just over 1,720 a. of low grounds in the west of the parish were rated to the drainage in 1775[30] and some 2,000 a. in the 1830s.[31] Nevertheless, flooding remained a problem, particularly on the higher ground

[21] Chron. de Melsa (Rolls Ser.), i. 354–7; ii. 82, 84–5; O.S. Map 6″, Yorks. CCXI, CCXII, CCXXVI, CCXXVII (1855 edn.); Poulson, Holderness, i. 128–30; J. A. Sheppard, Draining of Hull Valley (E. Yorks. Loc. Hist. Ser. viii), 3.
[22] P.N. Yorks. E.R. (E.P.N.S.), 46, 49; Chron. de Melsa, i. 357.   [23] Yorks. Deeds, ix, p. 121.
[24] Poulson, Holderness, i. 128.
[25] R.D.B., N/394/864; E.R.A.O., CSR/4/211; CSR/19/96.

The meres were shown in 1618: Shaftesbury MSS., P 144.
[26] E.R.A.O., CSR/12/9; CSR/16/1; CSR/20/68.
[27] H.U.L., DSJ/62; below, Long Riston, intro.
[28] For the following, V.C.H. Yorks. E.R. vi. 278–9.
[29] Cf. E.R.A.O., PE/104/52; O.S. Map 6″, Yorks. CCXI (1855 edn.).
[30] E.R.A.O., DDCC/143/135 (with map 1781).
[31] Ibid. QDA/12A (map, 1833), 12B, 13 (with map, 1838).

in the narrow Lambwath valley between Ald-brough and Rise parishes. Attempts to enlarge the Lambwath drain were blocked repeatedly by the Holderness Drainage Board, which feared the overloading of its system. About 1830 the Lambwath proprietors petitioned unsuccess-fully to have their 'unhappy valley' included in a new Holderness Drainage Bill, claiming that normal rainfall resulted in 400 a. being flooded for two or three weeks, and that heavier falls covered all 600 a. or more to the east of Rise with 2–3 ft. of water, besides overflowing to the west.[32] The Holderness Board's responsibilities were later exercized by the Yorkshire Ouse and Hull River Authority, which widened Swine Church drain c. 1970,[33] by the National Rivers Authority, and in 1998 by the Environment Agency.[34]

The ancient parish had more than 3,275 a. under crops in 1801, when much of the land in the south was occupied by pastures.[35] In the mid 19th and early 20th century there was generally almost twice as much arable land as grassland, 9,935 a. and 5,360 a. respectively being recorded in 1905.[36] Grassland and woods were, however, relatively predominant in and around Burton Constable, where in 1963 the Chichester-Constables had a compact estate of c. 5,000 a.[37] Otherwise the grassland was generally dispersed among the arable land, with slightly larger areas in the low-lying parts of Benningholme, Bilton, Ganstead, and Swine.[38] Proximity to Hull and Beverley has encouraged dairying and, perhaps to a lesser extent, market gardening and nursery-ing,[39] but in 1994 the area was overwhelmingly arable.

The main roads of the parish are those from Hull leading north to Bridlington by way of Ganstead, Coniston, and South Skirlaugh, and north-eastwards through Bilton and Wyton to Aldbrough. Minor roads connect the other settlements, including Swine village, with the main routes. The Bridlington road crosses Lambwath stream by a bridge, for which Swine priory was responsible in 1367.[40] The road was much improved after designation as a main road in 1921.[41] The Lambwath stream bridge was rebuilt by the county council in 1926,[42] and the road was widened and straightened in the later 20th century; much work was done in Skirlaugh village, by-passes were made for Coniston and Ganstead,[43] and another bridge, carrying the road over a drain in Ganstead, was widened in

1954.[44] The Aldbrough road was carried over Old fleet and a tributory stream respectively by Wyton Holmes bridge, recorded in 1367, and Bilton bridge, mentioned from the 13th or 14th century.[45] In 1745 the Aldbrough road as far as Wyton and a side road thence leading south to Preston and Hedon were turnpiked, and in 1767 the rest of the Aldbrough road in the parish was included in the Hull–Hedon trust, which was discontinued in 1878.[46] Wyton Holmes toll house stood in the junction of the Aldbrough and Preston roads until its demolition c. 1950.[47] Mile stones remain beside both the Aldbrough and Preston roads. The Aldbrough road was staightened at Wyton c. 1850,[48] and in 1884 the part between Hull and the western boundary of Wyton was declared a main road.[49]

The Hull–Hornsea railway line, opened in 1864,[50] crossed the parish. Swine station was built between the village and Coniston, Skir-laugh station beside the Bridlington road be-tween Coniston and South Skirlaugh, Ellerby station north-west of that hamlet, and Marton or Burton Constable station west of Marton.[51] Ellerby station was closed for passengers in 1902 but continued as a goods depot until its closure in 1959; Burton Constable station was renamed Ellerby in 1922. Skirlaugh station was closed to passengers in 1957 and entirely in 1963, and Swine and Ellerby to goods in 1963 and entirely in 1964.[52] The line was closed in 1965;[53] the track has been lifted and its course designated a foot-path. Station and other buildings were used as houses in 1994.

In the mid 19th century Swine parish lay, for the purposes of civil government, in thirteen townships, later civil parishes, of which Arnold and West Newton also contained parts of neigh-bouring ancient parishes. The number of civil parishes was later reduced by amalgamation, mainly in 1935, and there was further adjust-ment in 1952. Those changes are detailed below, where treatment is according to the earlier arrangement of townships, beginning with the history of Swine village itself.

The small village of Swine, formerly the site of a Cistercian priory and in the 19th century mostly rebuilt by the Crown, lies near the west-ern boundary of the extensive parish, only 3 km. north and north-east of the built-up area of Hull. Its name is Anglian and alludes to a creek, possibly of the river Humber.[54]

32 Ibid. DDCC/143/11, 34, 62, 66, 69–70.
33 R.D.B., 1680/493/428.
34 Inf. from Environment Agency, Willerby, 2000.
35 Benningholme and Marton townships made no returns: P.R.O., HO 67/26/47, 394, 404.
36 B.I.H.R., TA. 568L; E.R.A.O., PE/104/99, 104; Acreage Returns, 1905.
37 R.D.B., 1295/284/255. The Woodhall estate at Ellerby and part of Burton Constable were evidently omitted and have been added.
38 [1st] Land Util. Surv. Map, sheets 33–4.
39 Below, various townships, econ. hist.
40 Poulson, Holderness, i. 129.
41 E.R.A.O., CCO/202.   42 Datestone.
43 P.R.O., CRES 38/2187; E.R.C.C. Mins. 1965–6, 225–6; 1966–7, 228; 1967–8, 21; 1969–70, 23; 1970–1, 27–8, 428; 1972–3, 32, 162; below, Ganstead, intro.

44 Datestone.
45 Y.A.J. vi. 117–18; Poulson, Holderness, i. 131.
46 K. A. MacMahon, Roads and Turnpike Trusts in E. Yorks. (E. Yorks. Loc. Hist. Ser. xviii), 24, 70; O.S. Map 6", Yorks. CCXXVI–CCXXVII (1855 edn.).
47 E.R.A.O., QDB/9, p. 150; postcard of Wyton toll house in possession of Mr. C. Ketchell, Hull, 1995; O.S. Map 6", Yorks. CCXXVII (1855 and later edns.).
48 R.D.B., FG/452/23.
49 E.R.A.O., QAH/1/48.
50 K. A. MacMahon, Beginnings of E. Yorks. Rlys. (E. Yorks. Loc. Hist. Ser. iii), 17–19, 31.
51 O.S. Map 6", Yorks. CCXII, CCXXVII (1855 edn.).
52 C. R. Clinker, Reg. Closed Passenger Stns. and Goods Depots (1978), 45, 124, 132, 161.
53 Hull Daily Mail, 30 Apr. 1965.
54 P.N. Yorks. E.R. (E.P.N.S.), 51.

There were 2,286 a. (925 ha.) in Swine township.[55] In 1935 Swine civil parish was combined with that of Benningholme and Grange as the new civil parish of Swine, with an area of 3,792 a. (1,535 ha.).[56] There were 240 poll-tax payers at Swine in 1377,[57] the village had at least 40 houses in 1536,[58] and 30 were assessed for hearth tax in 1672.[59] Of the 171 families recorded under the parish in 1743 and 144 in 1764,[60] a substantial minority presumably lived in Swine township, but during the 19th century its population of c. 200 was overtaken by other places in the parish. The population, 204 in 1801, rose to 231 in 1831, fell to 180 in 1871, recovered to 212 in 1921, and fell again to 176 in 1931. Swine and Benningholme together had 269 inhabitants in 1931. That population continued to decline after their union in 1935, to 222 in 1961, 185 in 1971, and 167 in 1981. In 1991 the usual population was 182, of whom 173 were present.[61]

Early roads in Swine included Skirlaugh gate and West Carr gate, both recorded in 1454–5, when wine was carried to the village from Hull along navigable drains by way of 'Fishhouse'.[62] There was evidently a road to Wawne in 1618 but that to Benningholme seems to have been made in the earlier 19th century.[63]

SWINE village formerly stood on a long street leading south-eastwards to Coniston. On the south side of the street the buildings, which included the church, the manor house, and the priory, extended for only about ½ km. but on the north side houses were spaced all the way to the Coniston boundary. A few more stood in northern side lanes,[64] one of which, leading towards the main road and Benningholme, was called Dancing Lane in the 1850s.[65] Many cottages were said to have been demolished at Swine in the earlier 17th century,[66] and the priory buildings[67] had been removed by 1700, when the village was described as 'very mean and inconsiderable'.[68] The priory site was marked in 1994 by traces of fishponds and other earthworks, some in the misnamed Abbey Garths. In 1994 the village comprised a dozen houses set back behind the grass verges of its street; most of the buildings, one or two with tile-hung walls, dated from the Crown's re-

building of the village and outlying farms in the 1860s.[69] The Crown sold half a dozen houses c. 1965,[70] and in 1967 a sewage disposal works which the Crown Estate Commissioners had built for the village was adopted by Holderness rural district council.[71] Swine village was designated a conservation area in 1991.[72] Part of a village cross survived in Coniston Lane.[73]

There were up to three licensed houses at Swine in the later 18th century but only one in the 1820s, then called the White Lion or the Black Bull, its later name.[74] The Black Bull was evidently closed c. 1870.[75]

OUTLYING BUILDINGS. The reduction of the village in the 17th century was in part compensated for by the building of outlying farmhouses following inclosure in the 1650s. By 1735 the Micklethwaites had put up Kelwell, Hill, Carr House, Woodhouse, Great Stanks, and Bridge House Farms, Sleightings Farm, beside the Ellerby road, and possibly other outlying houses.[76] Like those in the village, the outlying farmhouses were rebuilt by the Crown in the 19th century, and a few cottages have been added since then.

Roman coin hoards have been found in the township.[77] The origins of an embanked enclosure on the northern boundary, described in the early 19th century,[78] are unknown.

MANORS AND OTHER ESTATES. In 1066 and 1086 the archbishop of York had *SWINE* manor, comprising 7 carucates and 7 bovates there and berewicks at Danthorpe, in Humbleton, Marfleet, Skirlaugh, and Sproatley.[79] Swine was evidently held of the archbishop with Winestead by the Verlis.[80] The first known tenants were Richard de Verli (fl. 1115) and Hugh (fl. later 12th cent.).[81] The same or another Hugh de Verli (d. by 1227) left as heirs two sisters, one of whom, Agnes de Verli, wife of Sir Alexander of Hilton (d. 1242), was succeeded by her son (Sir) Robert of Hilton. Robert, who was granted free warren in Swine in 1256,[82] was then co-tenant with Nicholas de Piselegh, who had married Verli's other sister Amabel.[83] He evidently later succeeded to the whole manor, and

55 O.S. Map 6″, Yorks. CCXI, CCXII, CCXXVI, CCXXVII (1855 edn.).
56 Census, 1931 (pt. ii).
57 P.R.O., E 179/202/60, m. 80.
58 Ibid. E 315/401, pp. 375–6.
59 Ibid. E 179/205/504, mm. 18–19.
60 B.I.H.R., V. 1764/Ret. 3, no. 66; Herring's Visit. iii, p. 127.
61 V.C.H. Yorks. iii. 494; Census, 1901–91.
62 Shaftesbury MSS., M 220 (acct. 33–4 Hen. VI). The roads and Fishhouse garth are shown on a map of 1618: Shaftesbury MSS., P 144.
63 Cf. E.R.A.O., PE/104/52; O.S. Map 6″, Yorks. CCXI (1855 edn.).
64 Shaftesbury MSS., P 144.
65 O.S. Map 6″, Yorks. CCXXVI (1855 edn.).
66 R.D.B., F/213/456.
67 Y.A.J. ix. 328–30.
68 De la Pryme's Diary (Sur. Soc. liv), 225–6.
69 Datestones.
70 R.D.B., 1278/24/22; 1430/517/454; 1564/197/170;

1607/303/272; 1648/45/34; 1676/205/168; 1681/338/292.
71 Ibid. 1545/80/62.
72 Inf. from Devt. Dept., Holderness B.C., 1991.
73 Illus. Poulson, Holderness, ii. 197.
74 E.R.A.O., QDT/2/7, 9; Baines, Hist. Yorks. (1823), ii. 394.
75 P.R.O., CRES 38/2117; O.S. Map 6″, Yorks. CCXXVI (1855 edn.); Kelly's Dir. N. & E. R. Yorks. (1872), 551–2.
76 R.D.B., N/394/864. Cf. Shaftesbury MSS., P 144; E.R.A.O., PE/104/52.
77 P. Whitting, Coins, Tokens and Medals of E. R. Yorks. (E. Yorks. Loc. Hist. Ser. xxv), 67, 75.
78 T. Thompson, Hist. of Church and Priory of Swine (Hull, 1824), 213–19; O.S. Map 6″, Yorks. CCXI (1855 edn.).
79 V.C.H. Yorks. ii. 210.
80 V.C.H. Yorks. E.R. v. 151.
81 E.Y.C. iii, p. 108; 'Meaux Cart.' pp. 465–6.
82 Cal. Chart. R. 1226–57, 454; Reg. Gray, p. 253; Complete Peerage, s.v. Hylton.
83 Kirkby's Inquest, 389.

entailed it on a younger son Sir William of Hilton (d. c. 1290) and William's wife Maud.[84] Maud married secondly Sir Robert de Tilliol,[85] who in her right was named joint lord of Swine in 1316.[86] She died in 1343 and was succeeded in the manor by her son Sir Robert Hilton.[87] He was followed about 1351 by his son Sir Robert, whose widow Maud held the manor in 1363.[88] The manor then descended from father to son to two further Sir Robert Hiltons, (fl. 1393)[89] and died c. 1430.[90] After the death in 1459 of the last Sir Robert's brother, Sir Godfrey Hilton, who seems to have held Swine manor for life, it fell to the share of one of Robert's daughters and coheirs,[91] Elizabeth wife of (Sir) John Melton, Lord Lucy.[92] In 1472 Melton (d. 1474) settled more than 2 carucates at Swine on his grandson and heir John and John's wife.[93] The latter John, later Sir John Melton, Lord Lucy (d. 1510),[94] was succeeded by his son Sir John, Lord Lucy (d. 1544), whose heir was his daughter Dorothy (d. 1557), wife of Sir George Darcy, Lord Darcy.[95] Swine later descended in the Darcys.[96] In 1639 Anne Savile, sister and heir of John Darcy (d. 1635), Lord Darcy, sold Joseph Micklethwaite the manor,[97] in which Lord Darcy's widow and her husband Sir Francis Fane had an interest for her life.[98] In 1653 Joseph (d. 1658) and his son John (d. 1660) acquired the former priory's manor of Swine, and in 1681 John's son Joseph bought the rectorial estate there and at Ganstead.[99] From the last Joseph the estate descended in turn to his sons Thomas (d. 1718) and Joseph Micklethwaite, later Viscount Micklethwaite.[1] Lord Micklethwaite, who enlarged the estate by purchase in 1720,[2] died in 1734, leaving nearly 2,200 a. in Swine to Ann Ewer.[3] She (d. 1739 or 1740) devised it to her nephew Anthony Ewer (d. by 1756),[4] who was succeeeded by his daughter Elizabeth, later wife of Sir Francis Wood, Bt.[5] From Lady Wood (d. 1796), the estate descended to an Ewer relative, Cropley Cooper, later earl of Shaftesbury (d. 1851).[6] In 1866 Cropley's son Anthony Cooper, earl of Shaftesbury, sold Swine manor with 2,165 a. in ten farms to the Crown,[7] which had bought Benningholme manor and 1,578 a. in 1859 and in 1870 added just over 600 a. more at Oubrough and Dowthorpe.[8] In 1995 the Crown's Swine estate comprised 1,869 ha. (4,618 a.), of which 933 ha. (2,306 a.) belonged to farms in the former township of Swine but evidently included a small area elsewhere.[9]

Hugh de Verli's house at Swine was recorded in the later 12th century.[10] In the mid 15th century the manor house of the Meltons included a hall, outer hall, great chamber, and 'knight chamber';[11] it seems to have stood on the east side of the church.[12] The amalgamation of the chief manor of Swine and the former priory's estate in 1653 makes later identification of the manor house uncertain. The 'mansion house of Swine' whose contents were sold by John Micklethwaite to John Dalton in 1660[13] was perhaps the manor house, and it may have been the same house, the largest in Swine, which had 13 hearths in 1672.[14] By the mid 19th century Swine Hall, standing near the church, was regarded as the 'old manor house'; it was probably demolished in or soon before 1868, when a vicarage house was built on the site.[15]

In the late 13th century deer were taken from Robert of Hilton's park at Swine.[16] The park, which had evidently been disparked by the mid 15th century,[17] may have lain south and west of the church around Giant hill, an artificial mound thought to date from the 14th or 15th century and possibly made as a look-out for hunting and fowling;[18] in 1618 the mound stood in a large close called the Pighill and Appleyard which adjoined Park close.[19]

Swine manor evidently included land held of the Hiltons by the Sutton family and later reckoned part of Sutton parish. Saer of Sutton (d. by 1290) was succeeded in Bransholme and other land by his son John, Lord Sutton (d. by 1338),[20] and John's daughter-in-law Aline (d. 1363) was said to have c. 400 a. in Swine, includ-

[84] Poulson, *Holderness*, ii. 198. For the Hilton descent in general, ibid. 197–9.

[85] *Complete Peerage* s. vv. Hylton, Lascelles.

[86] *Feud. Aids*, vi. 164; *Cal. Inq. p.m.* vi, p. 166.

[87] *Kirkby's Inquest*, 389 n.; 416, 440; *Cal. Inq. p.m.* viii, pp. 292–3.

[88] *Cal. Inq. p.m.* xi, p. 406.

[89] *Cal. Close*, 1392–6, 136.

[90] *Feud. Aids*, vi. 273; *Hist. Parl., Commons, 1386–1421*, iii. 379–81.

[91] *Cal. Pat.* 1429–36, 275; Poulson, *Holderness*, ii. 199; *Hist. Parl., Commons, 1386–1421*, iii. 377–9.

[92] Poulson, *Holderness*, ii. 199. The Melton pedigree there is confused; cf. *Complete Peerage*, s.v. Lucy.

[93] P.R.O., C 140/49, no. 27; Poulson, *Holderness*, ii. 199.

[94] E.R.A.O., DDX/31/514; P.R.O., C 142/25, no. 121.

[95] P.R.O., C 142/70, no. 60; E 150/241, no. 39; *Complete Peerage*, s.v. Darcy; *L. & P. Hen. VIII*, x, pp. 139, 247.

[96] P.R.O., C 142/116, no. 57; E.R.A.O., DDX/31/515.

[97] P.R.O., CP 25(2)/524/15 Chas. I East. [third from end]; *Dugdale's Visit. Yorks.* (Sur. Soc. xxxvi), 310.

[98] E.R.A.O., DDX/31/517; *Yorks. Royalist Composition Papers*, i (Y.A.S. Rec. Ser. xv), pp. 215–16.

[99] Below, this section; for the Micklethwaites, Poulson, *Holderness*, ii. 201; *Complete Peerage*.

[1] P.R.O., CP 43/378, rot. 27; CP 43/466, rot. 244.

[2] Below, this section [Thornton abbey].

[3] R.D.B., N/394/863–4.

[4] P.R.O., CRES 38/2118 (deeds 1740, 1756).

[5] Ibid. /2117 (deeds schedule 1866); /2118 (deed 1779).

[6] Ibid. /2117 (deeds schedule 1866); /2119 (1796 deeds); *Complete Peerage*.

[7] P.R.O., CRES 38/2117.

[8] Below, Benningholme, manors [Benningholme grange], Ellerby, manors [Oubrough grange].

[9] Inf. from Crown Estate Office, London.

[10] *E.Y.C.* iii, p. 108.

[11] B.L. Harl. Roll M. 41; Shaftesbury MSS., M 220 (acct. 33–4 Hen. VI).

[12] Poulson, *Holderness*, ii. 210.

[13] Shaftesbury MSS., E/G/514.

[14] P.R.O., E 179/205/504; above, this section.

[15] P.R.O., CRES 38/2117; O.S. Map 6", Yorks. CCXXVI (1855 edn.); below, church.

[16] *Cal. Inq. Misc.* i, p. 394.

[17] B.L. Harl. Rolls M. 41–2.

[18] *Y.A.J.* xlv, 142–8, pl. 1.

[19] Shaftesbury MSS., P 144. Cf. E.R.A.O., PE/104/52. Part of Pighill and Appleyard had once been tilled: Hull Univ., Dept. of Geog., Fairey Surveys air photographs, run 365B, nos. 2142–3.

[20] *Cal. Inq. p.m.* iii, pp. 2–3; for the fam., *Complete Peerage*.

ing the site of the Suttons' house, Bransholme castle.[21] Bransholme descended, with Sutton manor, to Thomas Sutton, Lord Sutton,[22] and then to his heirs.[23] The formerly moated Castle hill[24] remained in 1994.

Besides the church, Swine priory received gifts of land at Swine from Nicholas de Chevincourt and Thomas Riston.[25] The house was surrendered in 1539,[26] and much of its landed estate in the parish, including the priory site, was granted to Sir Richard Gresham in 1540 and returned to the Crown by exchange in 1544.[27] In 1557 Sir John Constable and his son Henry bought the priory site with 572 a. of demesne land in Swine, 297 a. in Oubrough grange, and land called Ganstead Inholmes, all of which was to be held in chief as 1/40 knight's fee.[28]

Henry Constable sold the priory estate at Swine in 1583 to Robert Dalton (d. 1626), who was succeeded in turn by his son Thomas (d. 1639) and grandson John.[29] John exchanged it in 1653 with Joseph Micklethwaite (d. 1658) and his son John (d. 1660); the *PRIORY* manor then included the priory site, a chief house, and *c.* 3½ carucates.[30] The estate later descended with Swine manor.[31]

Thornton abbey (Lincs.) was named as joint lord of Swine and its members in 1316,[32] and premises in Swine, appurtenant to the abbey's manor of Woodhouse, in Arnold, were granted after Thornton's dissolution to its short-lived successor, Thornton college, in 1542.[33] It may have been the abbey's estate at Swine which belonged to William Whitmore and then to Francis and Samuel Barlow. The Barlows sold it in 1718 to Joseph Banks and Michael Pierrepoint, from whom Joseph Micklethwaite, Viscount Micklethwaite, bought it in 1720.[34] It evidently later descended with Swine manor.[35]

The *RECTORY* belonged to Swine priory until its dissolution. In 1546 the Crown granted it to Sir Richard Gresham.[36] He (d. 1549) devised it to his daughter Elizabeth (d. 1552) and then in turn to his sons Sir John (d. by 1563) and Sir Thomas (d. 1579).[37] It later descended with Sir Thomas's share of Nunkeeling manor,[38] George Feilding, earl of Desmond, and Leices-

ter Devereux, viscount Hereford, being named as impropriators for the co-heirs in 1650,[39] and Lord Hereford's executors selling the rectory in lots in 1681.

Much of Swine rectory was bought in 1681 by Arthur Thornton, the purchaser at Nunkeeling, and descended with that estate to William Thornton,[40] who sold many of the tithes in the mid 18th century. The parsonage house, glebe lands, and all the tithes and dues of Swine township were, however, sold as another lot in 1681, to Joseph Micklethwaite.[41] His title descended with Swine manor to Cropley Cooper, earl of Shaftesbury, who in 1848 was awarded a rent charge of £13 6s. for the few unmerged tithes in Swine.[42]

ECONOMIC HISTORY. COMMON LANDS AND INCLOSURE. The open fields of Swine township were called North, South, East, and West fields in the mid 15th century. East field, which included land at North croft, was by 1618 part of North field, and South field was known by the mid 16th century as Mill field. The boundary between North and East fields would seem to have been the Skirlaugh road, on either side of which a different rotation was followed in the 15th century. West field had an outlying part south of the village in 1618, when other ground, called Gildums Arable, may have been a detached part of Mill field.[43] The commonable lands also included meadow land in Town ings and stinted pasture in West and North carrs, and perhaps also in a cow pasture called the Firth or Frithes in the 15th century.[44] Town ings presumably lay south of the village, where 'meadow doles' were recorded in 1618 and later Ings closes, and the Firth to its north, where land which may then have been tilled was named 'common pasture' and 'cow gate' in 1618.[45]

Swine priory may have been engaged in the wool trade *c.* 1200,[46] wool was stored in the church *c.* 1300,[47] and before 1517 the house was said to have inclosed arable land for pasture with the loss of one plough.[48] The remaining commonable lands in Swine were mostly inclosed by agreement between Joseph Micklethwaite and the other proprietors in or soon after the Micklethwaites' acquisition of the former

[21] For 'castle', *Yorks. Inq.* iv, p. 147 n.; *Cal. Pat.* 1350–4, 218.

[22] *Cal. Inq. p.m.* xi, pp. 406–7.

[23] *Yorks. Inq. Hen. IV–V*, pp. 159–60; *V.C.H. Yorks. E.R.* i. 471.

[24] O.S. Map 6″, Yorks. CCXXVI (1855 and later edns.); *T.E.R.A.S.* xxiii. 57–8; *V.C.H. Yorks.* ii. 23.

[25] Burton, *Mon. Ebor.* 254; Poulson, *Holderness*, ii. 204, 229 n. (for Chevincourt); below, church.

[26] *V.C.H. Yorks.* iii. 182.

[27] *L. & P. Hen. VIII*, xvi, pp. 95–6; xix (1), p. 279.

[28] *Cal. Pat.* 1555–7, 300–1; below, Ellerby, manors [Oubrough grange]; Ganstead, manor [Swine priory].

[29] P.R.O., C 66/1335, mm. 21–2; C 142/444, no. 79; C 142/583, no. 5.

[30] E.R.A.O., DDRI/35/6.

[31] Above, this section.

[32] *Feud. Aids*, vi. 164.

[33] *L. & P. Hen. VIII*, xvii, pp. 29–30; below, Long Riston, manors (Woodhouse).

[34] P.R.O., CRES 38/2118 (deed 1740).

[35] Above, this section.

[36] P.R.O., E 315/401, pp. 384–5; E 318/11/528, mm. 10–11, 17; *L. & P. Hen. VIII*, xvi, p. 723; xxi (1), pp. 573–5.

[37] P.R.O., C 3/77/44; C 142/93, no. 50; B.I.H.R., CP. G. 1312; *D.N.B.* s. vv. Gresham, Sir Ric., Sir Thos.

[38] Below, Nunkeeling, manors; E.R.A.O., DDRI/30/1; DDCC/111/25; P.R.O., C 142/396, no. 137.

[39] *T.E.R.A.S.* iv. 51.

[40] E.R.A.O., DDRI/30/1.

[41] Ibid. DDX/31/518.

[42] Ibid. PE/104/103; above, this section (Swine manor).

[43] B.L. Harl. Rolls M. 41–2; Shaftesbury MSS., P 144; Poulson, *Holderness*, ii. 206.

[44] B.L. Harl. Rolls M. 41–2; P.R.O., E 315/401, pp. 383–4; E.R.A.O., PE/104/75.

[45] Shaftesbury MSS., P 144; E.R.A.O., PE/104/52. For ridge and furrow there, Hull Univ., Dept. of Geog., R.A.F. air photograph, run 334A, no. 4152.

[46] *Cur. Regis R.* i. 144; iii. 177.

[47] *Reg. Greenfield*, iii, p. 134.

[48] *Trans. R.Hist.S.* N.S. vi. 288–9; vii. 249.

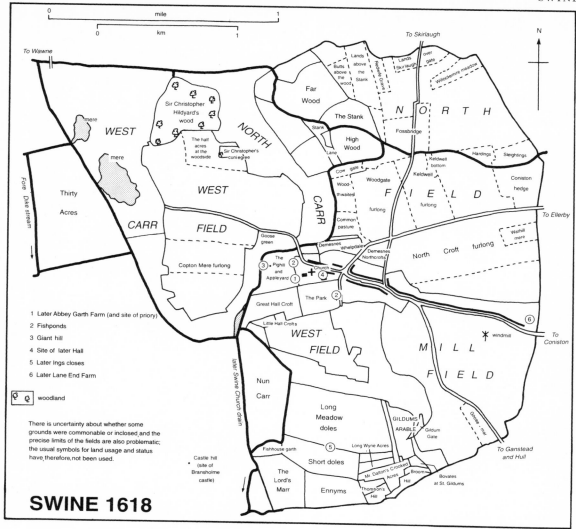

The map has the following labels:

SWINE 1618

1 Later Abbey Garth Farm (and site of priory)
2 Fishponds
3 Giant hill
4 Site of later Hall
5 Later Ings closes
6 Later Lane End Farm

woodland

There is uncertainty about whether some grounds were commonable or inclosed, and the precise limits of the fields are also problematic; the usual symbols for land usage and status have, therefore, not been used.

priory's estate in 1653.[49] Great ings, comprising *c.* 130 a., remained commonable, however;[50] after mowing, the meadows were grazed, from August to November in 1729 and from May until Christmas in 1760, at the rate of a gate for each 2 a. held there.[51]

THE MANOR. The income from Swine manor in 1447–8 was *c.* £60 gross.[52] Tenants' rents totalled £44. The cottagers also owed a small sum as 'boonsilver' in lieu of works, and they and the tenants at will rendered fowls, 'lakehens' and 'tethering' hens, the latter paid for the right to tether horses in the lord's meadow, perhaps Hall croft, after mowing. Wood sales were worth £6 and leases of pasturage *c.* £4. The rest of the income came mostly from sales of meadow, hay, rushes, hides, and fleeces, and from fines for infringments of the ale assize and other court perquisites. The demesne was then farmed directly under the supervision of a manorial reeve, a hayward, a

forester, a mill- and wood-reeve, and two supervisors of pasturage (*agistati*), whose responsibilty presumably extended to the manor as a whole. A small, permanent staff was enforced by casual labourers, of whom as many as 410 were hired for the harvest of 1448. The demesne had been leased by 1544.[53]

At the end of the 15th century 16 tenants at will on Swine manor held nearly 2 carucates between them, and 44 cottagers occupied 13 a. of meadow and pasture gates.[54] In 1735 the manor, then of *c.* 2,200 a. and comprising practically the whole township, lay in 14 holdings, of which three farms were of just over 200 a. each, six of 150–199 a., three of 100–149 a., and two of under 30 a.[55]

WOODLAND. The manorial demesne included extensive woodlands north of the village, part of them named in the 15th century as the Stanks.[56] Much of the woodland had been cleared and divided into closes by 1618, when

49 Shaftesbury MSS., E/G/510, 512–13; E.R.A.O., DDX/31/517; ibid. DDRI/35/6; ibid. PE/104/75; above, manors (priory).   50 R.D.B., N/394/864.
51 P.R.O., CRES 38/2118 (pains).
52 Para. based on B.L. Harl. Rolls M. 41–2; Shaftesbury

MSS., M 220 (acct. 11–12 Hen. VII).
53 Shaftesbury MSS., M 220 (rental 36 Hen. VIII).
54 Ibid. (acct. 11–12 Hen. VII).
55 R.D.B., N/394/864.
56 B.L. Harl. Roll M. 41.

field names included the Stank, Stank Lane, High Wood, and Far Wood. There then remained a large wood, called Sir Christopher Hildyard's wood, and nearby the smaller Sir Christopher's 'cuniegree'.[57] In 1735 the 'woodground remaining unstubbed called Swine wood' comprised 14 a.; it was felled between 1781 and the early 19th century.[58] Other old inclosures at Swine included Thirty Acres pasture, which was part of the priory's demesne.[59]

FISHERIES. The fishing of a stream between Fairholme and Swine mere, presumably part of Lambwath stream, was released to Swine priory in 1236,[60] in the 14th century fisheries at Swine belonging to the priory and to the Crown were said to have been trespassed upon,[61] and a fishery on Swine manor was let in the 1440s.[62]

LATER AGRICULTURE. Of 1,373 ha. (3,393 a.) returned under Swine civil parish in 1987, 1,240 ha. (3,064 a.) were arable land, 107 ha. (264 a.) grassland, and 12.1 ha. (30 a.) woodland; more than 14,000 pigs, 300 sheep, and 200 cattle, and nearly 30,000 poultry, were then kept.[63] One or two market gardeners and a cowkeeper worked at Swine in the later 19th and earlier 20th century,[64] and in 1987 vegetables were grown on 20.3 ha. (50 a.) of Swine civil parish.[65]

In the mid 19th century there were a dozen farmers at Swine, and later that century and in the earlier 20th usually 7–8; most of the farms were of 150 a. or more.[66] In 1995 there were eight holdings on the Crown's estate at Swine; the largest was of 170 ha. (420 a.), three were of 121–162 ha. (300–399 a.), three of 81–121 ha. (200–299 a.), and one of 28 ha. (69 a.).[67]

INDUSTRY. Gravel has been dug at Swine,[68] the Swine estate included a brick kiln in 1866,[69] and there was a small engineering concern in the village in 1993.

MILLS. Swine manor included a windmill in the 1440s,[70] and there was possibly another on the priory's estate in 1536, when a millhouse was recorded.[71] In 1618 a windmill stood south of the lane to Coniston in Mill field.[72] There was also a water mill on a small stream on the boundary with Benningholme into the 19th century,[73] but no more is known of it.

LOCAL GOVERNMENT. Swine manor court was held twice a year in the mid 15th century.[74] Surviving records include an estreat of 1536, a record of a session in 1624,[75] by-laws made in the court between 1729 and 1764,[76] and brief minutes for 1759–64.[77] The jurisdiction of the court included the view of frankpledge and the ale assize, but it was mostly concerned with drainage and the regulation of common grazing by the 18th century, and then seems to have met only once a year. Two affeerors, a constable, and a pinder were appointed in the court c. 1760, and a pinder as late as 1866.[78] Courts were also held at Swine by the priory.[79]

A poorhouse was maintained at Swine.[80] Nine people were relieved permanently and 5 occasionally in the township in 1802–3, and 8–15 were on permanent and 9–11 on occasional relief between 1812 and 1815.[81] Swine joined Skirlaugh poor-law union in 1837,[82] and the township, later civil parish, remained in Skirlaugh rural district until 1935. As part of an enlarged civil parish of Swine, it was then included in the new Holderness rural district, and at reorganization in 1974 was taken into the Holderness district of Humberside.[83] In 1996 Swine parish became part of a new East Riding unitary area.[84]

CHURCH. There was probably a church at Swine in 1086, when a priest was recorded on the manor,[85] and certainly one c. 1150, when the Verlis gave it to Swine priory at that house's foundation.[86] The priory was cited before the archbishop for failing to provide a perpetual vicar for the parish church in 1308–9,[87] and an ordination for Swine church, which does not survive, was made soon afterwards, the first known vicar being presented in 1323.[88] Another ordination was made in 1539, just before the priory's surrender.[89] The ancient parish included chapels at Bilton, Drypool, Ganstead, Marton, Skirlaugh, and Wyton. Ganstead chapel may have been abandoned before the 16th century and Marton in the 17th; Wyton chapel was lost c. 1660. Drypool chapelry became a separate parish in or soon after the mid 17th century and those of Bilton and Skirlaugh in 1867. Thereafter the reduced parish comprised Swine township, Burton Constable,

57 Shaftesbury MSS., P 144.
58 R.D.B., N/394/864; E.R.A.O., DDCC/143/135 (map); Thompson, Swine, 214; O.S. Map 6″, Yorks. CCXI (1855 edn.).
59 Poulson, Holderness, ii. 206.
60 Yorks. Fines, 1232–46, p. 43.
61 Cal. Pat. 1324–7, 226, 233; 1343–5, 586.
62 B.L. Harl. Roll M. 41.
63 Inf. from Min. of Agric., Fish. & Food, Beverley, 1990.
64 P.R.O., HO 107/2365; directories.
65 Inf. from. Min. of Agric., Fish. & Food.
66 P.R.O., HO 107/2365; directories.
67 Inf. from Crown Estate Office, London.
68 P.R.O., CRES 38/2118 (pains).
69 Ibid. /2117.
70 B.L. Harl. Roll M. 41.
71 P.R.O., E 315/401, p. 376.
72 Shaftesbury MSS., P 144.
73 Poulson, Holderness, ii, pl. facing p. 216.
74 B.L. Harl. Roll M. 41.

75 Shaftesbury MSS., M 220.
76 P.R.O., CRES 38/2118.
77 H.U.L., DDCV/160/1.
78 P.R.O., CRES 38/2117.
79 Ibid. SC 6/Hen. VIII/4529.
80 E.R.A.O., PE/104/52.
81 Poor Law Abstract, 1804, pp. 594–5; 1818, pp. 522–3.
82 3rd Rep. Poor Law Com. 170.
83 Census.
84 Humberside (Structural Change) Order 1995, copy at E.R.A.O.
85 V.C.H. Yorks. ii. 210.
86 Rob. de Verli's grant may merely have been one of confirmation by the then parson but he was later regarded as the founder: E.Y.C. iii, pp. 75–6; V.C.H. Yorks. iii. 178; Valor Eccl. (Rec. Com.), v. 114; Tax. Eccl. (Rec. Com.), 304.
87 Reg. Greenfield, v, pp. 198–9.
88 Lawrance, 'Clergy List', Holderness, 2, p. 154.
89 B.I.H.R., Reg. 28, ff. 133v.–134; V.C.H. Yorks. iii. 182.

Coniston, Ellerby, and Thirtleby. A mission chapel was built at Ellerby in 1889.[90]

The patronage of Swine vicarage remained with the priory in the Middle Ages.[91] After the Dissolution the Crown granted the advowson to Sir Richard Gresham in 1546,[92] and it later descended with the rectory in the Greshams and their successors, the Crown presenting in 1625 during the minority of Bridget Stanhope, later Feilding.[93] (Sir) William Thornton evidently sold the advowson c. 1700. In 1705 Ann Tadman presented John Moorhouse, and he (d. 1740) and his heirs later had the advowson, it falling to Sarah Brown at partition in 1791.[94] The patronage was bought by William Wilberforce (d. 1833), the philanthropist, and descended to his son William.[95] Later in the mid century it was vested in G. T. Woodroofe, the family's lawyer, because of their Roman Catholicism, and Woodroofe and his successors kept the patronage until the 1970s, when it was evidently returned to the Wilberforces. In 1994 the joint patrons were W. J. A. Wilberforce and Baroness de Stempel.[96]

Swine church was valued at £53 6s. 8d. in 1291.[97] On the eve of the Dissolution the priory was paying the vicar a stipend of £5 6s. 8d. a year, besides providing him with board valued at £2 13s. 4d.; about £8 may also have been spent on the salaries and board of the parish priest and a deacon.[98] By the ordination of 1539 the vicar was to receive £13 6s. 8d. a year from the rectory, besides his house and grazing or fodder for two horses.[99] By 1546 the vicar's stipend had been increased to £14 13s. 4d. and an allowance of £2 made for providing bread and wine for services in the parish.[1] After the loss of Marton chapel, the share of the tithes there previously enjoyed by its chaplain passed to the vicar; they were evidently compounded for £13 6s. 8d. a year by the late 17th century[2] and in 1849 were commuted for a rent charge of £18.[3] That charge was annexed to Skirlaugh benefice in 1867.[4] The vicar also received a modus of 3s. 4d. a year for tithes at Ellerby, a rent charge of that amount being substituted in 1849.[5] The

vicarage was augmented with £200 from Queen Anne's Bounty to meet a benefaction of that sum in 1783, with a Parliamentary grant of £1,200 in 1816, and with another £200 of Bounty money to meet benefactions totalling £200 in 1842.[6] Further benefactions, comprising the 4-a. parsonage site[7] and £1,050, had been received by 1867, when £40 a year to meet them was granted from the Common Fund.[8] The annual net income was £102 between 1829 and 1831 and c. £165 in 1882.[9]

The augmentations were used to buy almost 20 a. at South Skirlaugh in 1785 and the same at Thorngumbald, in Paull, in 1827.[10] The land at South Skirlaugh was sold in 1925.[11]

At the Dissolution the vicar shared one of the priory's houses, formerly used for visitors, with four or five priests serving the parish and priory churches, and, as the 'Guest Hall', that house was assigned to him by the ordination of 1539.[12] Another house seems to have been used later, however, when the vicarage house was described as a small building north of the church. The house, which was in disrepair in 1567 and again c. 1700, had evidently been abandoned by the vicar by 1717, when it was used as an alehouse,[13] and was demolished before 1726. There was later no house, and the vicar was living at Coniston, presumably in a rented house, in 1842–3, when a vicarage house was built with Bounty money and benefactions on the glebe land at South Skirlaugh.[14] That house was replaced by another in Swine village, built in 1868 with aid from the Common Fund on 4 a. granted by the Crown.[15] A new vicarage house was built nearby about 1967, when the redundant house was sold, as Priory House, with nearly 3½ a.[16] After 1868 Holyrood House, the former vicarage house at South Skirlaugh, was used as a farmhouse; it was sold in 1925.[17]

In the 14th century Swine priory mostly presented members of its community or of other religious houses as vicar, but later, presumably because of the removal of the canons from Swine, secular priests were appointed.[18] The medieval church included a chantry[19] and a

90   Below, Bilton, Ellerby, Ganstead, Marton, S. Skirlaugh, and Wyton, (all) church; *V.C.H. Yorks. E.R.* i. 297–8, 460 (Drypool).

91   For the following, Lawrance, 'Clergy List', Holderness 2, pp. 154–6; Poulson, *Holderness*, ii. 208–9.

92   *L. & P. Hen. VIII*, xxi (1), p. 575.

93   Above, manors (rectory); below, Nunkeeling, manors; *Complete Peerage*, s.v. Desmond.

94   P.R.O., CRES 38/2125 (abstract of title, Oubrough); below, Ellerby, manors [Oubrough grange].

95   *Clergy List* (1850); Burke, *Land. Gent.* (1952), 2714–16; Poulson, *Holderness*, ii. 264.

96   E.R.A.O., PE/104/39; *Crockford*.

97   *Tax. Eccl.* (Rec. Com.), 304.

98   *Valor Eccl.* (Rec. Com.), v. 112; *Miscellanea*, ii (Y.A.S. Rec. Ser. lxxiv), 100–1.

99   B.I.H.R., Reg. 28, ff. 133v.–134.

1   P.R.O., E 318/11/528, m. 10; E.R.A.O., DDCC/111/31.

2   B.I.H.R., TER. H. Swine n.d. etc.; P.R.O., E 318/11/528, m. 10; below, Marton, church.

3   E.R.A.O., PE/104/104.

4   Below, S. Skirlaugh, church.

5   E.R.A.O., PE/104/105.

6   Hodgson, *Q.A.B.* pp. clxxiv, ccxxxi, cccl.

7   Below, this section.

8   *Lond. Gaz.* 22 Nov. 1867, p. 6229.

9   B.I.H.R., V. 1884/Ret. 2; *Rep. Com. Eccl. Revenues*, 970–1.   10   R.D.B., BI/275/424; EB/355/357.

11   Ibid. 310/87/69.

12   B.I.H.R., Reg. 28, ff. 133v.–134; *Y.A.J.* ix. 330; *Miscellanea*, ii (Y.A.S. Rec. Ser. lxxiv), 100–1.

13   B.I.H.R., V. 1693–4/CB. 1, f. 49v.; ER. V./CB. 10, f. 77v.; ER. V./CB. 12, f. 141; J. S. Purvis, *Tudor Par. Doc. of Dioc. York*, 34.

14   E.R.A.O., DDX/215/14; B.I.H.R., TER. H. Swine n.d., 1716, 1726, 1849; O.S. Map 6", Yorks. CCXII (1855 edn.); above, this section [income].

15   B.I.H.R., NPH. 1867/3; ibid. Ch. Ret. iii; *Lond. Gaz.* 22 Nov. 1867, p. 6229; *Kelly's Dir. N. & E. R. Yorks.* (1872), 551.   16   R.D.B., 1506/458/377.

17   Ibid. 310/87/69; 881/29/24; Bulmer, *Dir. E. Yorks.* (1892), 509.

18   Lawrance, 'Clergy List', Holderness, 2, pp. 154–5. The canons were mistakenly thought to have been withdrawn earlier: *V.C.H. Yorks.* iii. 180.

19   *Miscellanea* ii (Y.A.S. Rec. Ser. lxxiv), 100–1; below, this section [fittings].

FIG. 7. SWINE CHURCH 1784

guild[20] of St. Mary. A chapel of unknown purpose stood in the churchyard in the 1440s.[21] One of the chapels at Swine was endowed with two houses and an acre in 1548.[22] At the Dissolution the vicar was assisted by a parish priest and a deacon.[23] Robert Read, vicar from 1540, married and was deprived in 1554.[24] Sermons were lacking in the mid 16th and early 18th century.[25] In the mid 18th century the incumbent lived at Sproatley, one of his other livings, and employed a curate to reside and do his duty at Swine. One Sunday service was then held in the parish church and Holy Communion was celebrated three or four times a year, with 70–80 recipients.[26] Curates were again employed in the earlier 19th century,[27] but the archbishop ordered a vicar to reside in 1836 and later removed him for refusing to comply.[28] There was still only one Sunday service in the parish church in 1865 but two services were provided by 1868, and celebrations of communion were monthly by 1871, fortnightly in 1884, and weekly by the early 20th century; in the later 19th century only a dozen usually received. Mission services at Coniston and Ellerby and cottage lectures were adopted in the 1870s and 1880s to meet the problem of a still-large parish

with a marginally-placed church, and a mission chapel was built at Ellerby in 1889.[29] William Cobby was vicar from 1875 to 1930.[30] In 1994 when the living was vacant there were regular celebrations of communion but few other services.

The church of *ST. MARY*, so called from the 12th century,[31] was formerly a cruciform building, the eastern arm of which was occupied by the parish church and the part west of the crossing tower by the priory church. That unusual disposition of priory and parish churches is also found, however, at Nunkeeling.[32] The nuns' church was evidently demolished soon after the Dissolution, apart from some fragments which remained in 1784;[33] its site and that of the claustral buildings was occupied in 1998 by the large yard and outbuildings of the neighbouring farm.

The parish church comprises a structurally-undivided chancel and clerestoried nave, with north chapel and south vestry to the chancel, and aisles, south porch, and west tower to the nave. It may have been rebuilt late in the 12th century, following the completion of the priory church and tower, whose western arch was of slightly

[20] B.I.H.R., Prob. Reg. 2, f. 564; *Test. Ebor.* v, p. 238; *Cal. Pat.* 1575–8, p. 486; Poulson, *Holderness*, ii. 210; *Y.A.J.* xliv. 189.

[21] B.L. Harl. Roll M. 41.   [22] *Y.A.J.* xliv. 190.

[23] *Miscellanea*, ii (Y.A.S. Rec. Ser. lxxiv), 100–1.

[24] A. G. Dickens, *Marian Reaction in Dioc. of York: The Clergy* (St. Anthony's Hall Publ. xi), 26.

[25] B.I.H.R., ER. V./CB. 12, f. 80; J. S. Purvis, *Tudor Par. Doc. of Dioc. York*, 34, 117.

[26] B.I.H.R., V. 1764/Ret. 3, no. 66; *Herring's Visit.* ii, p. 204; iii, pp. 124, 127–9, 131.

[27] *Educ. of Poor Digest*, 1095; *Rep. Com. Eccl.*

Revenues, 970–1.

[28] B.I.H.R., Inst. AB. 20, pp. 212, 312.

[29] For the following B.I.H.R., V. 1865/Ret. 2, no. 527; V. 1868/Ret. 2, no. 480; V. 1871/Ret. 2, no. 487; V. 1877/Ret. 3, no. 98; V. 1884/Ret. 2; V. 1900/Ret. no 375; V. 1912–22/Ret.; below, Ellerby, church.

[30] Memorial in ch.   [31] *E.Y.C.* iii, p. 75.

[32] Below, Nunkeeling, churches.

[33] For the priory church in the 16th cent., *Y.A.J.* ix. 328–9; *T.E.R.A.S.* iv, p. xx. For views of the reduced building in the late 18th cent., H.U.L., DP/159/1; Poulson, *Holderness*, i, plate facing p. 386.

earlier date.[34] Part of a 13th-century window head, with nailhead on its former external face, survives in the chancel, and is evidence for alterations to the east end at that date. In a dispute with the priory *c.* 1300 the parishioners made good their claim to a chapel called the North Crouch, which was situated in the north transept and housed St. Andrew's altar.[35] Both aisles of the parish church were rebuilt, and presumably widened, in the 14th century, a monolithic window head, reused in the south aisle wall, providing evidence for an earlier church on the site. The north aisle was also then extended eastwards to form the chapel, which was probably used as a burial place for the lords of the manor and was later called the 'lord's aisle'.[36] The tower was heightened at about the same time.[37] In the 15th century the east end was remodelled, principally by the insertion of new windows into the end of both aisles and the east and south sides of the chancel. The fabric was neglected after the Dissolution,[38] and the chancel roof had been lowered and part of the east window stopped up by the end of the 18th century.[39] In 1787 the truncated tower was rebuilt on a smaller base but slightly higher using much of the old stone.[40] The church was restored in the early 1870s.[41] A west gallery built in 1722 was then removed, the south vestry evidently rebuilt,[42] and it was perhaps then that the fittings were rearranged to bring the easternmost bay of the nave into the chancel. The north aisle and chapel were restored in the 1980s,[43] and in 1994 the church was being repaired by Community Action volunteers.[44]

The fittings include eight stalls with misericords of *c.* 1500; they were evidently moved from the priory church at its destruction and were formerly more numerous and canopied.[45] The north chapel is divided from the aisle by a screen put up in 1531 by the Darcys and later mutilated. The screen bears a now incomplete inscription referring to St. Mary's chantry, which was founded by Walter Skirlaw, bishop of Durham (d. 1406)[46] and presumably held in the chapel. Also of the 16th century is the low, chancel screen, which was cut down in the 18th

century.[47] A 14th-century chest tomb bearing effigies of a knight and lady, all of stone, is built into the south aisle wall. The north chapel, now called the Hilton chapel, has three similar tombs, of alabaster and representing three knights and two ladies of the 14th and 15th centuries; all are believed to commemorate Hiltons, and they almost certainly include the tomb of Sir Robert Hilton (d. *c.* 1430) and his wife.[48] The tombs in the chapel have been rebuilt and renovated in the present century.[49] The chapel formerly also contained brasses commemorating John Melton (d. 1458) and his wife.[50] Stone coffins discovered during the 19th-century restoration[51] were kept in the aisles in 1994. The church also has a pulpit of 1619, a small font, comprising a late 18th-century bowl of Coade stone with Gothick ornament on a possibly medieval shaft, and an iron chest, with the initials J. M., possibly those of one of the Micklethwaites.[52]

There were two bells in 1552 and later four, which were refounded or replaced in 1800 by James Harrison of Barton upon Humber (Lincs.).[53] The plate includes a cup of 1570,[54] a paten of 1681, and a flagon and a remade cup, both of 1819.[55] The registers begin in 1706 and are complete; transcripts survive from 1600.[56]

Land on the south side of the church was added to the churchyard in 1923 and consecrated in 1924.[57]

The parish clerk of Swine was entitled to sheaves of wheat from Arnold, Benningholme, and Coniston, besides his Easter dues. At inclosure in 1790 an annual rent of £1 12s. was substituted for those from Coniston, and the Benningholme sheaves had been compounded for a rent of £1 1s. by 1857.[58]

NONCONFORMITY. The Daltons of Swine were Roman Catholic, and 25 papists were recorded under the village in the 1660s and 17 in 1735.[59] Eight protestant dissenters were recorded under Swine in 1676,[60] when the prominent Quaker John Whitehead lived in the parish.[61] In Swine township unidentified prot-

---

34 Poulson, *Holderness*, i, plate facing p. 386.

35 *Reg. Greenfield*, iii, pp. xlv, 134; v, pp. xlix, 232–3; Poulson, *Holderness*, i, plate facing p. 386 shows the ruined transept abutting onto the tower and the priory church.

36 B.I.H.R., V. 1590–1/CB. 1, f. 124v.; below, this section [fittings].

37 Poulson, *Holderness*, i. plate facing p. 386.

38 B.I.H.R., V. 1590–1/CB. 1, f. 124 and v.; V. 1693–4/CB. 1, f. 49v.; ER. V./CB. 5, f. 102; ER. V./CB. 12, f. 80; J. S. Purvis, *Tudor Par. Doc. of Dioc. York*, 34.

39 H.U.L., DP/159/1.

40 B.I.H.R., Fac. Bk. 2, pp. 370–1; T. Allen, *Hist. Co. York*, iv. 262–3; Poulson, *Holderness*, i, plate facing p. 386.

41 B.I.H.R., Ch. Ret. iii; rainwater heads of 1872.

42 Its late 15th-cent. ceiling was apparently refixed. Bulmer, *Dir. E. Yorks.* (1892), 519; Poulson, *Holderness*, ii. 211.

43 E.R.A.O., PE/104/89/3; rainwater heads.

44 Inf. from Mr. F. Gritt, Swine, 1994.

45 *Y.A.J.* ix. 329; li. 153–5; *De la Pryme's Diary* (Sur. Soc. liv), 226; Poulson, *Holderness*, ii. 211.

46 *Valor Eccl.* (Rec. Com.), v. 114; *Reg. Langley*, ii (Sur. Soc. clxvi), pp. 81–90; below, S. Skirlaugh, church.

47 B.I.H.R., ER. V./Ret. 1, f. 35; ER. V./Ret. 2, f. 12; *Y.A.J.* xxiv. 172–6 (illus.).

48 *T.E.R.A.S.* iv, pp. xxii–xxiii; *Test. Ebor.* ii, pp. 16–17, 23–5. Illus. in Thompson, *Swine*, 92, 102, 104; Poulson, *Holderness*, i. 489; ii. 49; Y.A.S. excursion leaflet, 1906, (copy in Beverley Public Libr.).

49 B.I.H.R., Fac. Bk. 12, p. 22; E.R.A.O., PE/104/89/3, s.v. 22 Oct. 1985; *Y.A.J.* xxxiv. 239.

50 Thompson, *Swine*, 92–3, 109–10; *Complete Peerage*, s.v. Lucy.   51 Bulmer, *Dir. E. Yorks.* (1892), 519.

52 Poulson, *Holderness*, ii. 211; local inf.

53 B.I.H.R., TER. H. Swine 1764, etc.; *Inventories of Ch. Goods*, 46; Boulter, 'Ch. Bells', 86.

54 Its lost lid evidently bore the presentation date of 1571.

55 B.I.H.R., TER. H. Swine 1764, etc.; *Yorks. Ch. Plate*, i. 323–4.

56 E.R.A.O., PE/104/1–2, 5–6; B.I.H.R., PRT. Hold. D. Swine.

57 B.I.H.R., CD. 710; R.D.B., 277/179/146.

58 R.D.B., BG/291/39; B.I.H.R., TER. H. Swine 1764, etc. For Arnold, below, S. Skirlaugh, church.

59 Aveling, *Post Reformation Catholicism*, 47, 67; *Cal. Cttee. for Compounding*, iv, p. 3076.

60 *Compton Census*, ed. Whiteman, 600.

61 *D.N.B.*

estants registered buildings in 1804, 1811, 1816, and 1827.[62] They probably included Independents, who fitted up premises there c. 1800, encouraged by Fish Street chapel, Hull.[63] A house at Swine used by that congregation later passed to Wesleyan Methodists, who were in turn succeeded in 1846 by the Primitives. The last mentioned congregation numbered c. 30 in 1851.[64] The location of the house and further history of the congregation are unknown. A Wesleyan chapel being built at Swine in 1892 was probably opened in 1894.[65] It was closed in 1940,[66] evidently sold in 1957,[67] and used as a house by 1993.

EDUCATION. A schoolroom built at Swine with the bequest of Ellen Dunn (d. 1691), a servant of the Micklethwaites,[68] was presumably that later standing on the north side of the street.[69] An unlicensed schoolmaster was teaching in Swine in 1693,[70] and in 1743 the school had over 20 pupils and was supported by the villagers.[71] The boys' school recorded c. 1820 was probably the same; it then received £6 from £200 stock given in 1798 by Mrs. Elizabeth Lamb, a native of Swine, for the teaching of six children of Swine township and £5 5s. from the earl of Shaftesbury to support five pupils.[72] The school had 25 pupils, including the 11 taught

free, in 1833. Twenty girls were then taught at their parents' expense in two other schools at Swine.[73] Swine school was closed following the earl of Shaftesbury's sale in 1866, but in 1868 the Crown built a new school with master's house on another site and opened it as a National school for boys and girls, including infants.[74] It was supported by subscription and from 1869 by an annual government grant.[75] On inspection in 1871 there were 28 pupils, among them children from Coniston, Ellerby, Ganstead, and Thirtleby.[76] Between 1906 and the early 1930s average attendance usually exceeded 50, and a classroom was added in 1934.[77] Numbers fell soon after to an average of 38 in 1937–8,[78] and in 1954 senior pupils were transferred to South Holderness County Secondary School.[79] Swine school was closed in 1968, the pupils being transferred to the new school at Skirlaugh at its opening.[80] The teacher's house had been sold in 1960;[81] the school building, which was returned to the Crown in 1973, was used for a village hall before being converted into a house.[82]

Lamb's charity became Lamb's Educational Foundation by Scheme of 1933, when its area was redefined as Swine (civil) parish. The income, then £5 but £9 c. 1980, could be spent in assisting children in secondary education, and that object was met after 1933 by grants or payment of pupils' travelling expenses.[83]

BENNINGHOLME

THE half a dozen, dispersed farmhouses and cottages of Benningholme mostly stand on the higher ground, overlooking the valley of Lambwath stream, c. 3 km. NNW. of Swine village. Granges of Swine priory were established at Benningholme and, on lower-lying ground, at Fairholme, in the south-west corner of the township.[84] The name Benningholme, meaning 'Benna's water meadow', is an Anglo-Scandinavian hybrid, as may be Fairholme, or 'fair water meadow'.[85]

Benningholme township, later Benningholme

and Grange civil parish, was of 1,471 a. (595 ha.)[86] until it was enlarged by the transfer of c. 35 a. (14 ha.) from South Skirlaugh in 1885.[87] In 1935 it and Swine civil parish were combined as the new civil parish of Swine.[88]

Benningholme had 69 poll-tax payers in 1377[89] and 17 houses assessed for hearth tax in 1672.[90] The hamlet comprised a dozen houses, then closely-built, in 1772.[91] The population grew from 78 in 1801 to 108 in 1841 and thereafter fluctuated, reaching 120 in 1881 and standing at 93 in 1931.[92]

[62] B.I.H.R., Fac. Bk. 3, pp. 362, 585–6; ibid. DMH. Reg. 1, p. 545; P.R.O., RG 31/5, no. 2983.

[63] C. E. Darwent, Story of Fish St. Ch., Hull (1899), 129, 135.

[64] P.R.O., HO 129/522/2/5/3.

[65] Bulmer, Dir. E. Yorks. (1892), 519; Kelly's Dir. N. & E.R. Yorks. (1897), 541; O.S. Map 1/2,500, Yorks. CCXXVI. 4 (1910 edn.).

[66] E.R.A.O., MRH/1/55.

[67] Only the site was then mentioned: R.D.B., 1066/371/336.

[68] Thompson, Swine, 160.

[69] P.R.O., CRES 38/2117.

[70] B.I.H.R., V. 1693–4/CB. 1, f. 49v.

[71] Herring's Visit. iii, p. 127.

[72] P.R.O., ED 49/8609; Educ. of Poor Digest, 1095; 10th Rep. Com. Char. 663; Thompson, Swine, 160–1; Scheme in possession of Dr. I. A. Derham, Ganstead, 1995. N. Wright, John Day, a Village Poet.

[73] Educ. Enq. Abstract, 1097.

[74] P.R.O., ED 7/135, no. 179; ED 49/8609; E.R.A.O., SL/106/1; ibid. SGP. 76; datestone.

[75] B.I.H.R., V. 1868/Ret. 2, no. 480; Rep. of Educ. Cttee.

of Council, 1869–70 [C.165], p. 678, H.C. (1870), xxii.

[76] Returns relating to Elem. Educ. 472–3.

[77] E.R. Educ. Cttee. Mins. 1934–5, 39, 160.

[78] Bd. of Educ., List 21 (H.M.S.O., 1908 and later edns.).

[79] E.R. Educ. Cttee. Mins. 1953–4, 145.

[80] E.R.A.O., SL/106/4; E.R. Educ. Cttee. Mins. 1965–6, 148; below, S. Skirlaugh, educ.

[81] R.D.B., 1199/378/329.

[82] Ibid. 1887/496/412; inf. from Mrs. J. Stott, N. Skirlaugh, 1995.

[83] P.R.O., ED 49/8609; Scheme in possession of, and inf. from, Dr. I. A. Derham; Review of Char. Rep. 113.

[84] Below, manors.

[85] P.N. Yorks. E.R. (E.P.N.S.), 46; G. F. Jensen, Scand. Settlement Names in Yorks. 153.

[86] O.S. Map 6″, Yorks. CCXI (1855 edn.).

[87] Census, 1891; O.S. Map 1/2,500, Yorks. CCXI. 8, 12 (1891 edn.).

[88] Census, 1931 (pt. ii); above, Swine township, intro.

[89] P.R.O., E 179/202/60, m. 42.

[90] Hearth Tax, 60.

[91] T. Jefferys, Map of Yorks. (1772).

[92] V.C.H. Yorks. iii. 494; Census, 1901–31.

The scattered houses of BENNINGHOLME hamlet include four cottages of 1904 and a house of the 1960s, all built by the Crown[93] which owns the place. Benningholme Hall and the other older houses are discussed below.[94]

MANORS AND OTHER ESTATES. In 1066 Ulf held 2 carucates and 5 bovates at BENNINGHOLME as soke of his manor of Aldbrough. The estate had passed to Drew de Bevrère by 1086 and later formed part of the Aumale fee.[95]

Two carucates at East Benningholme, with other land in Holderness, were evidently granted by a count of Aumale to his butler.[96] In 1221 Amand the butler's daughters Beatrice de Friboys and Hawise de Surdeval, their overlord William de Forz, count of Aumale, and others were disputing Benningholme manor.[97] Land at East Benningholme was given to Swine priory by Hawise and to Nunkeeling priory by Beatrice.[98] In 1252 the butler's fee was evidently held by Beatrice and John de Surdeval, presumably Hawise's heir.[99] The Surdeval share seems to have descended to John de Surdeval, named as a lord at Benningholme in 1316,[1] and then to his son Amand (fl. mid 14th century).[2]

Much of the butler's fee was held by Geoffrey Berchaud (d. by 1276) and then by his son John.[3] Geoffrey Berchaud's heir was recorded as tenant of the count of Aumale at Benningholme and in other parts of the fee in 1287,[4] but by that date Simon Constable seems to have bought Berchaud's interest and possibly another share of the butler's fee from Geoffrey Vernon and Gillian de Friboys's daughter Joan Verder.[5] Constable held 3 bovates in demesne at Benningholme in 1287,[6] and the lordship of 2 carucates there later descended in his family.[7]

The Rouths held a manor of Benningholme under the Constables. William of Routh had land at Benningholme in 1250, and Sir Amand

of Routh's manor was recorded c. 1300.[8] John of Routh (d. by 1311) was succeeded by his son Amand, who was named as a lord of Benningholme in 1316.[9] By 1377 the estate seems to have been enlarged with land belonging to another Amand's wife Christine.[10] It later descended, like Tansterne, in Aldbrough,[11] in the Rouths,[12] before passing to the Cutts[13] and Michelbournes.[14] In 1483 the estate, sometimes called a manor, was said to comprise only six houses and 2¼ bovates at Benningholme.[15] In 1552 John Michelbourne settled his moiety of Benningholme manor on his son John, but it evidently later passed under that settlement to another son Thomas and then once again descended with Tansterne.[16] At the partition of the Michelbournes' estate in 1614, Sir Richard Michelbourne received Benningholme manor with lands in Swine and Coniston.[17] Two houses, 3½ bovates, and other land were sold shortly afterwards.[18] Sir Richard Michelbourne died in 1638, and in 1647 his sons sold the rest of the estate at Benningholme, comprising 3 houses, 2 bovates, other land, and pasture rights, as an appurtenance of Routh manor, to Thomas Chatt (d. by 1661).[19] The estate has not been traced further.

Another manor of BENNINGHOLME was held by Sir Peter Buckton in 1401, and Peter Buckton, presumably another, was recorded as a tenant of the Constables at Benningholme in 1447.[20] The manor descended to William Buckton (d. 1506), who left it to his sons Robert and Ralph Buckton; it then comprised 1½ carucate.[21] It was perhaps the same manor which William Layton and Ralph Holtby granted to Lancelot Holtby (d. 1561). Holtby's son George[22] sold it to James Wayte and John Metcalfe in 1585.[23] That manor, held of the Constables and comprising ½ carucate in Benningholme, was sold by Metcalfe to William Thompson in or shortly before 1617, by him in 1625 to Alexander Emerson, father and son, and by the younger Emerson in 1629 to Sir John Lister and his son Hugh[24] (d. by 1678), who was probably succeeded by his son John.[25] From John's son

93   Datestones.
94   Below, manors [Benningholme Hall, Benningholme Grange].
95   V.C.H. Yorks. ii. 266.
96   Kirkby's Inquest, 373; Yorks. Fines, 1232–46, p. 82; above, Hilston, manor.
97   Cal. Pat. 1216–25, p. 310; Pipe R. 1221 (P.R.S. N.S. xlviii), 137; Yorks. Fines, 1218–31, p. 54; Chron. de Melsa. (Rolls Ser.), i. 412.
98   Burton, Mon. Ebor. 252; below, this section [Nunkeeling].
99   Yorks. Fines, 1246–72, p. 88. B.L. Cott. MS. Otho C. viii, f. 83.
1   Feud. Aids, vi. 164.
2   Cal. Inq. p.m. xiii, pp. 252–3; Kirkby's Inquest, 116 n.
3   B.L. Cott. MS. Otho C. viii, f. 81v.; Cal. Inq. p.m. ii, p. 107.   4   Cal. Inq. p.m. iv, p. 355.
5   B.L. Cott. MS. Otho C. viii, f. 82v.; Poulson, Holderness, ii. 223; Feud. Aids, vi. 40.
6   Cal. Inq. p.m. iv, p. 357.
7   P.R.O., C 142/214, no. 205; ibid. CP 40/291, m. 57; Cal. Inq. p.m. v, p. 138; ix, pp. 219–20; xvii, p. 331; Hen. VII, iii, p. 166; J. Foster, Pedigrees of Yorks. iii.
8   B.L. Cott. MS. Otho C. viii, f. 83; Poulson, Holderness, i. 392; ii. 223.

9   P.R.O., CP 40/291, m. 57; Feud. Aids, vi. 164.
10   Yorks. Fines, 1347–77, pp. 201–2.
11   Above, Aldbrough, manors.
12   P.R.O., C 141/4, no. 45; Cal. Chart. R. 1341–1417, 301; Feud. Aids, vi. 273.
13   P.R.O., C 142/48, no. 161.
14   Yorks. Fines, i. 140.
15   P.R.O., C 141/4, no. 45.
16   Ibid. CP 40/1154, Carte rot. 12; ibid. C 142/214, no. 205; C 142/214, no. 221.
17   E.R.A.O., DDRI/35/33; Yorks. Fines, 1614–25, 10–11.
18   E.R.A.O., DDCC/18/3, s.v. Apr. 1615.
19   Ibid. DDRI/35/50; H.U.L., DDMC/6/1; P.R.O., CP 25(2)/525/23 Chas. I Trin. [no. 18]; Suss. Arch. Colln. l. 78–9.
20   E.R.A.O., DDCC/18/6; Cal. Chart. R. 1341–1417, 408; Test. Ebor. i. pp. 360–1.
21   Cal. Inq. p.m. Hen. VII, iii, pp. 165–6.
22   P.R.O., C 142/134, no. 196.
23   Yorks. Fines, iii. 47.
24   P.R.O., CRES 38/2103 (deeds 22 July 1625, 13 June 1629); E.R.A.O., DDCC/18/3, s.v. Oct. 1617.
25   For the following, P.R.O., CRES 38/2103 (abstract of Greens' title); CRES 38/2104 (agreement 1796).

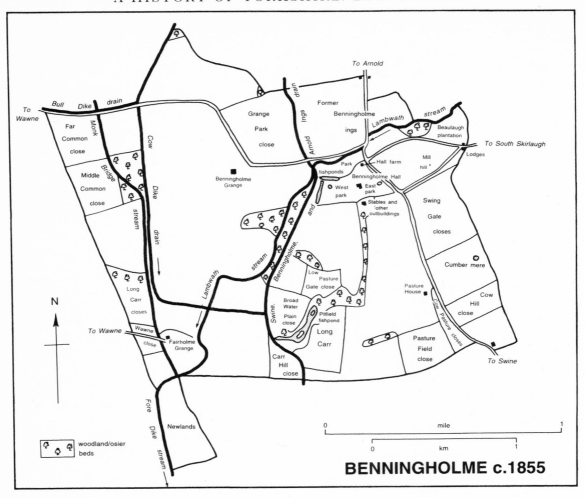

BENNINGHOLME c.1855

Lutton (fl. 1714)[26] the manor descended in turn to Lutton's son William (d. 1760),[27] his widow Grace (fl. 1796), and their daughter Harriet Green. The Greens sold the manor with c. 285 a. to Robert Harrison in 1807,[28] and it later descended with Harrison's larger estate.[29]

In 1625 the manor house site was recorded as Hall garth.[30] The manor house sold in 1807[31] was replaced as the chief house by Benningholme Hall, built by Robert Harrison (d. 1821)[32] and provided with grounds of c. 30 a. which included a small lake, islands, and a temple.[33] The white-brick house has a five-bayed entrance front with an Ionic porch and windows set in blank arches, and a garden façade with bows rising through both storeys and a cast-iron verandah to the ground floor. A red-brick, northern wing was demolished and a smaller, south

wing added in 1974.[34] Hall Farm which stood nearby was probably the old manor house; of two storeys with attics and dating from the 18th century or earlier, it was demolished c. 1985.[35]

Peter of Benningholme gave Swine priory land at West Benningholme, and the house had a grange there by 1235[36] and was named as one of the lords at Benningholme in 1316.[37] After the Dissolution, the Crown let Benningholme grange to Sir Richard Gresham in 1541 and in 1554 sold it, as ¼₀ knight's fee, to Lady (Joan) Constable and her son Sir John Constable.[38] It comprised 236 a. in 1578.[39] Benningholme grange and land formerly belonging to the priory at Ganstead[40] descended to Sir Henry Constable, viscount Dunbar, who settled them on a younger son Matthew.[41] Matthew forfeited

26 R.D.B., E/242/426.

27 Ibid. T/131/246; T/132/247.

28 Ibid. CM/97/159.

29 Below, this section [Benningholme grange].

30 P.R.O., CRES 38/2103 (deed 22 July 1625).

31 R.D.B., CM/97/159.

32 Below, this section [Benningholme grange].

33 E.R.A.O., DDX/252/2; Sheahan and Whellan, *Hist. York & E.R.* ii. 384–5.

34 Inf. from Mr. and Mrs. C. W. Fewson, Benningholme, 1994.

35 O.S. Map 6″, Yorks. CCXI (1855 edn.); Min. of Housing, *Buildings List,* (1965); inf. from Mr. Fewson, 1994.

36 *Chron. de Melsa* (Rolls Ser.), i. 413; Burton, *Mon. Ebor.* 253; Poulson, *Holderness,* ii. 203.

37 *Feud. Aids,* vi. 164. 'Belagh' grange, or pasture, recorded in the 1530s, may also have been at Benningholme, near the later Beaulaugh plantation: P.R.O., E 315/401, p. 381; *Valor Eccl.* (Rec. Com.), v. 114; O.S. Map 6″, Yorks. CCXI (1855 edn.).

38 *L. & P. Hen. VIII,* xvi, p. 723; *Cal. Pat.* 1553–4, 145–7; J. Foster, *Pedigrees of Yorks.* iii.

39 Burton Constable Hall, DDCC/141/68 (survey); microfilm copy at E.R.A.O.

40 Above, Swine, manors (priory).

41 E.R.A.O., DDCC/133/12, 19.

his estate to the Commonwealth for treason[42] but regained it before his death in 1667, when his brother John Constable, viscount Dunbar, gave it to another brother Henry (d. 1700). Henry left his estate, which also included a former grange of the priory at Fairholme,[43] to his nephew William Constable, later viscount Dunbar.[44] The granges descended with the rest of the Constable family's estate to William Constable, who sold the Benningholme and Fairholme estate, then comprising 690 a. in four farms, to Thomas Harrison in 1769.[45] Harrison had bought another estate at Benningholme, of 439 a., in 1767.[46] He died in 1795 or 1796,[47] and his estate passed to Robert Harrison, who bought another farm with at least 94 a. at Benningholme in 1800[48] and Benningholme manor in 1807.[49] Harrison (d. 1821) devised his Holderness estates to his daughter Ann (d. 1836), with remainder to his grandson Robert Harrison. In 1859 Robert Harrison's assignees in bankruptcy sold his estate in Swine parish to the Crown; it then comprised, besides Benningholme manor, 1,578 a. there and at Fairholme, North and South Skirlaugh, and Arnold, mostly in four farms.[50] The Benningholme estate later descended with the Crown's manor of Swine, bought in 1866.[51] In 1995 the Crown had 602 ha. (1,487 a.) at Benningholme.[52]

Benningholme Grange farmhouse is modern; the earlier house was demolished in 1967,[53] but its outbuildings, including an 18th-century cottage, remain.

Swine priory's grange of Fairholme was recorded from the early 13th century.[54] The Crown sold it in 1558 to William Edrington and Edward Beseley,[55] from whom the 70-a. estate passed, perhaps in 1594, to Marmaduke Langdale (d. 1611)[56] and later to Henry Constable (d. 1700). Thereafter Fairholme descended like Benningholme grange.[57]

William de Ros, later Baron Ros of Helmsley (Yorks. N.R.), held 1 carucate at Benningholme as mesne lord in 1287,[58] and the lordship later descended like Roos manor in the Ros family and their successors.[59] The land was evidently

subinfeudated to a cadet of the Ros family, together with Thorpe manor, in Aldbrough, with which it later descended.[60] In the 1550s the estate included only 2¼ bovates.[61] It has not been traced beyond its sale to John Eldred and William Whitmore in 1611.[62]

Peter Hildyard's manor of BENNING-HOLME, mentioned in the 1370s, and the manor of 'Swine' left by Martin Hildyard (d. 1544 or 1545) were perhaps the same,[63] but no more is known of it.

Beatrice de Friboys gave Nunkeeling priory 2½ bovates and other land at East Benningholme in the earlier 13th century, and in 1535 its estate there was valued at just over £3 10s. a year.[64] After the Dissolution, a house, 3 bovates and other land, and pasturage there were granted to Sir Richard Gresham in 1540,[65] and the estate later descended with Nunkeeling manor.[66]

Meaux abbey was given 1 bovate, 10 a., all of 'Tyrnyngholmum', and three tofts at East Benningholme by Amand the butler between 1210 and 1220; part of that estate was later granted to Sir Simon Constable.[67] After the Dissolution, the abbey's land at Benningholme descended with its manor of Arnold to the Micklethwaites.[68]

Thornton abbey was recorded as a lord at Benningholme in 1316, perhaps for land attached to its manor of Woodhouse, in Arnold.[69]

The rectorial tithes of Benningholme Grange were sold by William Thornton to Cuthbert Constable in 1738 and by William Constable to Thomas Harrison, with the landed estate there, in 1769.[70] Harrison already had other tithes in Benningholme township,[71] and, at the inclosure of Benningholme ings in 1778, he was awarded 6 a. and a rent charge of £3 for his tithes there.[72] Robert Harrison merged the remaining tithes in his Benningholme and Fairholme estate in 1843.[73]

ECONOMIC HISTORY. COMMON LANDS AND INCLOSURE. Little is known of the commonable lands of Benningholme. The tillage was

[42] Ibid. DDCC/6/2, 4; DDCC/111/216; Cal. Cttee. for Compounding, iv, pp. 3109–10.
[43] Below, this section [Fairholme].
[44] E.R.A.O., DDCC/111/219; DDCC/134/17; J. Foster, Pedigrees of Yorks. iii.
[45] E.R.A.O., DDCC/6/8–10.
[46] R.D.B., AI/223/451.
[47] Ibid. BW/347/482.
[48] Ibid. CB/248/401; P.R.O., CRES 38/2119 (s.vv. 1799, 1800).
[49] Above, this section; P.R.O., CRES 39/42; ibid. MPI 1/535.
[50] P.R.O., CRES 38/2102 (deed 1859); E.R.A.O., DDX/252/2.
[51] Above, this section.
[52] Inf. from Crown Estate Office, London.
[53] Local inf.
[54] Chron. de Melsa (Rolls Ser.), i. 357.
[55] Cal. Pat. 1557–8, 390.
[56] P.R.O., C 142/337, no. 81; Yorks. Fines, iv. 15.
[57] E.R.A.O., DDCC/134/17; above, this section.
[58] Cal. Inq. p.m. iv, p. 352; Complete Peerage.
[59] H.U.L., DDSY/56/5; P.R.O., C 142/218, no. 52; Yorks. Fines, 1614–25, 168; above, Roos, manors.

[60] P.R.O., C 139/106, no. 24; ibid. C 142/43, no. 56; Cal. Chart. R. 1257–1300, 469; Cal. Inq. p.m. v, pp. 137–8; xvii, p. 331; above, Aldbrough, manors (Thorpe).
[61] P.R.O., SC 11/762.
[62] Ibid. C 66/1903, no. 9.
[63] Public Works in Med. Law, ii (Selden Soc. xl), pp. 345–6; Test. Ebor. vi, pp. 215–16.
[64] B.L. Cott. MS. Otho C. viii, ff. 81v.–83; Valor Eccl. (Rec. Com.), v. 115.
[65] L. & P. Hen. VIII, xvi, pp. 95–6; Burton, Mon. Ebor. 386.
[66] P.R.O., CP 25(2)/756/24 Chas. II Trin. [no. 37]; ibid. C 142/765, no. 47; Cal. Pat. 1547–8, 331–2; 1569–72, p. 65.
[67] B.L. Cott. MS. Vit. C. vi, f. 205v.; Chron. de Melsa (Rolls Ser.), i. 355; ii. 150.
[68] E.R.A.O., DDRI/35/6; L. & P. Hen. VIII, xix (2), p. 78; Cal. Pat. 1569–72, p. 453; below, Long Riston, manors.
[69] H.U.L., DDSY/110/8; Feud. Aids, vi. 164.
[70] E.R.A.O., DDCC/6/8, 10; R.D.B., AO/151/158; above, Swine, manors (rectory).
[71] R.D.B., AI/223/451.
[72] Ibid. BB/73/13.
[73] P.R.O., CRES 38/2104.

reduced by Sir John Cutt, who inclosed land there and at Skirlaugh for pasture before 1517,[74] but West field was named in 1616, and in 1748 East, Great, and Little fields were recorded. The location of some of the open-field land is evident from the ridge and furrow which survives near Benningholme Hall and Pasture House Farm.[75] Some grassland lay in the fields, but most of the commonable meadow land was in the ings,[76] which after mowing were grazed between August and March.[77] Rough grazing was provided largely by the carrs, or marshlands. In the earlier 13th century Swine priory and Meaux abbey resolved a dispute over marshland lying between their two houses by agreeing to inclose part of the waste, leaving the rest as a common pasture for both houses and their tenants.[78] The common pastures, which were overcharged c. 1600,[79] also included a pasture in the south of the township;[80] High and Low pastures, mentioned in 1767, were presumably divisions of the southern pasture.[81]

Swine priory's intake from the carrs adjoined its grange at Benningholme, and Fairholme grange may have been established to exploit it;[82] Newland near Fairholme was named in 1367.[83] Other early inclosures made from the commonable lands probably included a 67-a. pasture close called New field, which was shared by two farmers in 1653.[84]

Much of the commonable land remaining in the 18th century was then inclosed. Out carr, or Wawne common, c. 400 a. extending alongside Benningholme grange from Arnold in the north to Newlands in the south, was presumably all or part of the medieval common pasture. It was partitioned by the owner of the former granges, William Constable, and the lord of Wawne manor, in 1751 or 1752, and soon after divided into closes. The ditch and bank made then to separate Constable's eastern half from the rest was later part of the Benningholme-Wawne boundary.[85] Benningholme ings were inclosed with the adjoining meadows of Arnold in 1778 under the Long Riston and Arnold inclosure Act of 1771; they then comprised 95 a. Thomas Harrison received 57 a., Mrs. Lister 24 a., and there were three other allotments of under 10 a.[86] Despite the inclosures, some pasture in Benningholme seems to have remained commonable into the 19th century.[87]

Benningholme Grange had its own pinfold in 1554,[88] but it is not known whether its grounds constituted an agricultural system separate from the rest of the township. Ridge and furrow evidence shows that Park, or Grange Park, close, so called since the 17th century, was once part of the open fields, and there is no other record of a park there.[89]

FISHERIES. Fisheries at Benningholme included one in Out dyke, let by John Constable in 1551,[90] and another in a former turbary, at Benningholme Turf pits;[91] it was perhaps the same pool which was called Pitfield Fish pond in 1852.[92] Possibly another pool was the 'broad water', from which rushes, or 'dumbles', and fish were taken without licence in the 17th century.[93] There were over 100 a. of willow beds and other woodland at Benningholme in the 1850s,[94] but much had been cleared by the early 20th century.[95]

FARMS. There were usually three or four farmers at Benningholme in the 19th and earlier 20th century; in 1851 all four farms exceeded 200 a. and the largest was of nearly 500 a. Two smallholdings were also recorded c. 1930.[96] In 1995 three of the Crown's farms at Benningholme were of over 121 ha. (300 a.), the largest holding being of 296 ha. (732 a.), and there was one small farm.[97]

MILL. Nothing is known of the mill which stood on Mill hill in the north-east of the township.[98]

LOCAL GOVERNMENT. View of frankpledge at Benningholme and the regulation of agriculture there belonged to Burton Constable court in the 16th and 17th centuries. Officers appointed in the court included a constable, an aletaster, a pinder, and a bylawman for Benningholme.[99] Fourteen people were relieved permanently in the township in 1802–3, and between 1812 and 1815 there were 6–8 on permanent and 5–8 on occasional relief.[1] Benningholme township, later civil parish, joined Skirlaugh poorlaw union in 1837[2] and remained in Skirlaugh rural district until 1935. As part of Swine civil parish, Benningholme was taken into the new

---

74 *Trans. R. Hist. S.* N.S. vi. 288–9; vii. 249.
75 For other ridge and furrow, Hull Univ., Dept. of Geog., R.A.F. air photographs, run 333A, nos. 4208–11.
76 P.R.O., CRES 38/2103 (deed 11 Nov. 1616); R.D.B., T/132/247.   77 E.R.A.O., DDRI/22/103.
78 *Chron. de Melsa* (Rolls Ser.), i. 356, 413. Hull Univ., Dept. of Geog., R.A.F. air photograph, run 334A, no. 4156.
79 E.R.A.O., DDCC/18/3, s.vv. Oct. 1596, Apr. 1597, Oct. 1616.
80 P.R.O., CRES 38/2103 (deed 11 Nov. 1616); E.R.A.O., DDCC/143/135; O.S. Map 6", Yorks. CCXI (1855 edn.).   81 R.D.B., AI/223/451.
82 *Chron. de Melsa* (Rolls Ser.), i. 356, 413. Hull Univ., Dept. of Geog., R.A.F. air photograph, run 334A, no. 4156.
83 Poulson, *Holderness*, i. 130; O.S. Map 6", Yorks. CCXI (1855 edn.).
84 E.R.A.O., DDCC/111/216.
85 E.R.A.O., DDCC/6/8, 10; ibid. QDB/4, pp. 132–4; above, manors [Benningholme grange]; below, Wawne, econ. hist.

86 11 Geo. III, c. 92 (Priv. Act); E.R.A.O., accession 2980, inclosure award and plan.
87 R.D.B., CM/97/159.
88 E.R.A.O., DDCC/18/2.
89 Ibid. DDCC/111/216; O.S. Map 6", Yorks. CCXI. (1855 edn.). For the tillage near the grange, Hull Univ., Dept. of Geog., R.A.F. air photograph, run 333A, no. 4211.
90 E.R.A.O., DDCC/18/2.
91 Ibid. DDCC/6/4; *Yorks. Fines*, ii. 87; iii. 47.
92 O.S. Map 6", Yorks. CCXI (1855 edn.).
93 E.R.A.O., DDCC/18/3, s.vv. Oct. 1617, Oct. 1634.
94 P.R.O., CRES 38/2102; E.R.A.O., DDX/252/2.
95 Acreage Returns, 1905; E.R.A.O., NV 1/13.
96 P.R.O., HO 107/2365; directories. Cf. P.R.O., CRES 39/42; ibid. MPI 1/535.
97 Inf. from Crown Estate Office, London.
98 O.S. Map 6", Yorks. CCXI (1855 edn.).
99 E.R.A.O., DDCC/18/2–3.
1 *Poor Law Abstract, 1804*, pp. 592–3; *1818*, pp. 520–1.
2 *3rd Rep. Poor Law Com.* 170.

Holderness rural district in 1935 and the Holderness district of Humberside at reorganization in 1974.[3] In 1996 Swine parish became part of a new East Riding unitary area.[4]

ROMAN CATHOLICISM. There may have been a dozen papists at Benningholme in the 1580s, but any other record of recusancy there was presumably made under Swine.[5]

BILTON

THE expanded village of Bilton, now barely separate from Hull's suburbs, lies *c.* 4 km. southeast of Swine village. The name, meaning Billa's farm, is probably Anglian.[6]

Bilton township, later civil parish, contained 1,204 a. (487 ha.),[7] of which 485 a. (196 ha.) were lost in 1930 and 7 a. (3 ha.) in 1935 to Sculcoates civil parish. The remaining 713 a. (289 ha.) were added in 1935 to Ganstead and Wyton civil parishes and 3 a. (1.2 ha.) of Preston civil parish to form a new parish of Bilton with 2,317 a. (938 ha.).[8] Extensions to Hull claimed 60 a. (24 ha.) more in 1955 and *c.* 100 a. (41 ha.) in 1968, leaving Bilton with 872 ha. (2,155 a.). In 1984 some 8 ha. (20 a.) were added to Bilton civil parish from Coniston, and in 1991 Bilton's area was 879 ha. (2,172 a.).[9]

The 69 poll-tax payers recorded under Bilton in 1377 may have included inhabitants of neighbouring Ganstead, which was not noticed separately.[10] In 1672 Bilton had 26 houses assessed for hearth tax.[11] During the 19th century the population was *c.* 100, and in 1911 there were still only 89 inhabitants. Thereafter numbers began to grow as a consequence of suburban development, to 127 in 1921 and 219 in 1931, when the combined population of the areas united in 1935 was 435. The new civil parish had 1,249 inhabitants by 1951 and 2,380 in 1961, of whom *c.* 450 lived in the area taken into Hull in 1968. The reduced parish, nevertheless, had a population of 2,452 in 1971; in 1991 there were usually 2,305 residents but only 2,259 were then present.[12]

In the mid 19th century the few farmhouses and other buildings of BILTON village stood along a single street leading south to the church and in side lanes to Wyton and Hull, later parts of the Hull–Aldbrough road.[13] The street was called Back Lane, possibly in relation to the main road, in the late 19th and earlier 20th century, but by 1954 it had been renamed Lime Tree

Lane.[14] The growth of the village in the earlier 20th century was achieved in part by the infilling of the street and the building of 44 council houses off it, in Highfield Crescent, *c.* 1950. Away from the village, the north side of the main road was lined with bungalows and houses, and a side road from it, Holmes Lane, was similarly developed.[15] The pace of building quickened later, when much of the land behind the ribbons of houses was covered by housing estates.[16] In 1994 the engulfing of the old street was being completed by the building of houses on Old Hall farm. The south side of the main road remains much less built-up, except in the west, where land on either side, lost to Hull in the 1960s, has been used for more housing estates and a suburban superstore.[17] Older buildings include Old Hall Farm, under renovation in 1994, the outbuildings of High Farm, by then converted into housing, and the former school, no. 189 Main Road, and another 'estate' building, both with decorative bargeboards. In 1927 Hull corporation built a pumping station near the village which was transferred to the Yorkshire Water Authority in 1979,[18] and *c.* 1955 the corporation put up an automatic telephone exchange at Bilton.[19]

A house was licensed at Bilton in the later 18th century,[20] but later the village had no public house. A village hall, built north of the main road in the early 1930s,[21] was replaced in 1985 by a hall for Bilton, Ganstead, and Wyton; the new hall was built on part of the 7-a. Memorial Playing Field, which had been bought by the parish council to commemorate the Second World War dead in 1948 and enlarged in 1953.[22] The former village hall, adjoining the playing field, was used as a sports clubhouse in 1994.[23] Other meeting places then included the British Legion hall, rebuilt in 1969,[24] and a wooden Church hall, erected by 1949.[25] Another hall built in 1936 for the recreation of the village men has been used since 1953 by an amateur

3 *Census.*
4 Humberside (Structural Change) Order 1995, copy at E.R.A.O.
5 Aveling, *Post Reformation Catholicism*, 67.
6 *P.N. Yorks. E.R.* (E.P.N.S.), 46–7.
7 O.S. Map 6″, Yorks. CCXXVI, CCXXVII (1855 edn.).
8 *Census*, 1931, (pts. i–ii).
9 Ibid. 1961, 1971, 1991; E.R.A.O., Holderness (Parishes) Order 1983; O.S. Map 1/2,500, Yorks. CCXXVII. 6 (1890 edn.).
10 P.R.O., E 179/202/60, m. 51.
11 *Hearth Tax*, 60.
12 *V.C.H. Yorks.* iii. 494; *Census*, 1901–91.
13 O.S. Map 6″, Yorks. CCXXVII (1855 edn.).
14 R.D.B., 986/290/248; O.S. Map 1/2,500, Yorks. CCXXVII. 9 (1891 edn.); O.S. Map 6″, TA 13 SE. (1956 edn.); O.S. Map 1/10,000, TA 13 SE. (1970 edn.).
15 R.D.B., 825/246/199; O.S. Map 1/10,560, TA 13 SE.

(1956 edn.); O.S. Map 1/10,000, TA 13 SE. (1985 edn.).
16 O.S. Map 1/10,560, TA 13 SE. (1968 edn.); O.S. Map 1/10,000, TA 13 SE. (1985 edn.).
17 O.S. Map 1/10,560, TA 13 SW. (1969 edn.); O.S. Map 1/10,000, TA 13 SE., SW. (1984–5 edns.); above, this section [area].
18 Hull Corp. *Mins. Water and Gas Cttee.* 1926–7, 27, 31, 60; 1927–8, 26, 57; inf. from Hull Corp., 1995.
19 Hull Corp. *Mins. Telephones Cttee.* 1950–1, 31; 1952–3, 9, 40; 1953–4, 31; 1954–5, 34.
20 E.R.A.O., QDT/2/9.
21 B.I.H.R., V. 1931/Ret.; R.D.B., 450/435/345.
22 R.D.B., 787/86/66; 933/194/165; board on field; inf. from Mr. J. Willingham, Bilton, 1995.
23 Notice on building; inf. from Miss B. Jackson, Bilton, 1995.
24 Notice on building.
25 E.R.A.O., PE/7/23/2.

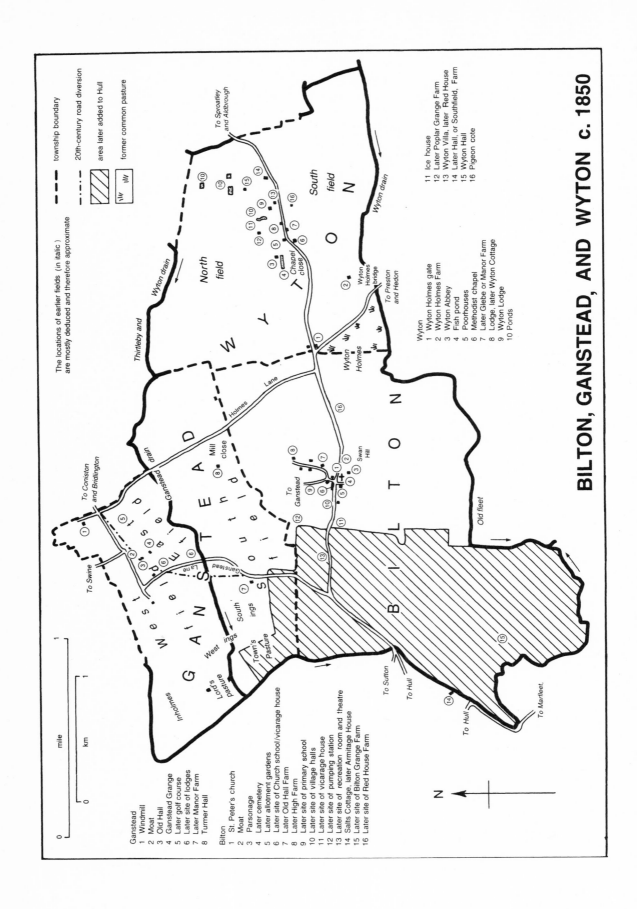

BILTON, GANSTEAD, AND WYTON c. 1850

township boundary

20th-century road diversion

area later added to Hull

former common pasture

The locations of earlier fields (in italic)
are mostly deduced and therefore approximate

Ganstead
1 Windmill
2 Moat
3 Old Hall
4 Ganstead Grange
5 Later golf course
6 Later site of lodges
7 Later Manor Farm
8 Turmer Hall

Bilton
1 St. Peter's church
2 Moat
3 Parsonage
4 Later cemetery
5 Later allotment gardens
6 Later site of Church school/vicarage house
7 Later Old Hall Farm
8 Later High Farm
9 Later site of primary school
10 Later site of village halls
11 Later site of vicarage house
12 Later site of pumping station
13 Later site of recreation room and theatre
14 Salts Cottage, later Armitage House
15 Later site of Bilton Grange Farm
16 Later site of Red House Farm

Wyton
1 Wyton Holmes gate
2 Wyton Holmes Farm
3 Wyton Abbey
4 Fish pond
5 Poorhouses
6 Methodist chapel
7 Later Glebe or Manor Farm
8 Lodge, later Wyton Cottage
9 Wyton Lodge
10 Ponds
11 Ice house
12 Later Poplar Grange Farm
13 Wyton Villa, later Red House
14 Later Hall, or Southfield, Farm
15 Wyton Hall
16 Pigeon cote

dramatic society as its theatre in succession to the village hall.[26] Since 1940 a county library has been held in the successive village halls.[27] A youth centre was provided near the primary school c. 1970.[28] Allotment gardens provided by 1908 were still used in 1994.[29]

MANOR AND OTHER ESTATES.
A carucate at *BILTON*, belonging in 1066 to Halfdan, had passed by 1086 to Drew de Bevrère[30] and was later part of the Aumale fee. In 1367 land at Bilton was held by knight's service under Burstwick, the chief manor of that fee.[31]

Drew's undertenant in Bilton in 1086 was Franco,[32] ancestor of the Fauconbergs.[33] W. de Fauconberg, tenant in the mid 13th century, was probably Walter de Fauconberg, later Lord Fauconberg (d. 1304),[34] and the estate in Bilton later descended, as an appurtenance of Rise manor, to the Nevilles.[35] It was held of the Fauconbergs by free tenants,[36] one of whom may have been Sir Walter de Fauconberg of Bilton, evidently a cadet, mentioned in 1341.[37] Another member of the family, John de Fauconberg (d. 1366), held ½ carucate of Walter de Fauconberg's widow Isabel, besides other land of the Aumale fee; John was succeeded by his son (Sir) Walter (d. by 1392).[38]

In 1086 the archbishop of York's church of St. John at Beverley had 3 carucates at Bilton.[39] All were held of the provost of Beverley by Stephen of Marfleet, who granted the estate to his daughter Avice's husband, Walter of Lincoln. It later passed to Walter's son-in-law, William of Bilton, who held it as *BILTON* manor; he and his tenants then occupied 2 of the 3 carucates. William was possibly succeeded by his son Saer of Bilton, and Saer's son Sir John of Bilton was lord in the earlier 14th century. From Lady (Joan) of Bilton, presumably John's widow, the manor descended to her daughter, wife of Sir Walter Fauconberg (fl. 1370s). The Fauconbergs left two children, evidently daughters who married Richard Butler

and William Plessington.[40] In 1391 half of Bilton, Bewholme, in Nunkeeling, and Catwick manors was settled on Butler and his wife Catherine, evidently in her right,[41] and her share clearly descended to Isabel Holme, on whom the so-called manors of 'Bilton' and 'Fauconberg', with part of the land there, were settled in 1463.[42] Isabel Holme's interest probably descended to her son Edward (fl. c. 1480).[43] The Plessingtons' share descended to Sir Henry Plessington (d. 1452), his son William (d. 1457), and William's cousin Isabel, wife of (Sir) John Francis.[44] In 1463 part of the landed estate at Bilton was settled on the Francises' daughter Alice Worsley,[45] later Alice Staveley (fl. 1519). The Staveley share of Bilton and other manors descended to Alice's son George (d. 1525) and then to his son John.[46] Another part of the Plessington estate passed by the marriage of Isabel and Sir John Francis's daughter Jane and Roger Flower to their grandson Roger Flower (d. 1527), who settled it on his son George.[47] The shares of the manor were later bought by Sir William Knowles, who had an estate at Bilton from the 1520s.[48] John Staveley and John Flower sold their shares in or about 1539,[49] and by 1553 Knowles also had Edward Holmes's lands.[50] Knowles (d. 1557 or 1558) was succeeded in the manor by his widow Joan (d. 1571) and then by his son-in-law John Stanhope (fl. 1582). Knowles's grandson, William Alford, may have inherited soon after.[51] Sir William Alford[52] was succeeded by his daughter Dorothy Grantham, who sold the manor to Anthony Bedingfield in 1649.[53] Robert Lowther apparently had it later and then Anthony Lowther,[54] who sold the manor to William Ramsden in 1678.[55] John Ramsden, who bought the rectorial estate at Bilton in 1681, had the manor in 1716[56] and, after him presumably, his daughter Elizabeth Roundell. It certainly later belonged to Elizabeth's daughters Catherine Dawnay (d. 1769)[57] and Mildred Bourchier (d. by 1797).[58] Mrs. Bourchier devised the manor and rectorial estate to her nephew Richard Thompson (d. 1820), with remainders in tail successively for the younger sons of John Dawnay, viscount

[26] Inf. from Miss Jackson.

[27] E.R. Educ. Cttee. *Mins.* 1940–1, 86; 1960–1, 153; 1971–2, 14.

[28] Ibid. 1968–9, 172.

[29] O.S. Map 1/2,500, Yorks. CCXXVII. 9 (1910 edn.); R.D.B., 599/517/423; 1562/329/271.

[30] *V.C.H. Yorks.* ii. 268.

[31] *Cal. Inq. p.m.* xii, p. 86; *V.C.H. Yorks. E.R.* v. 9–10.

[32] *V.C.H. Yorks.* ii. 268.

[33] *Complete Peerage; Early Yorks. Fam.* (Y.A.S. Rec. Ser. cxxxv), 26–7.

[34] *Kirkby's Inquest,* 373; *Cal. Inq. p.m.* iv, p. 357.

[35] *Cal. Inq. p.m.* ix, pp. 176–7; xviii, p. 136; below, Rise, manor.

[36] *Cal. Inq. p.m.* iv, p. 357; ix, pp. 176–7.

[37] *Yorks. Deeds,* viii, p. 17.

[38] *Cal. Inq. p.m.* xii, pp. 86–7; *Cal. Pat.* 1391–6, 254.

[39] *V.C.H. Yorks.* ii. 216.

[40] E.R.A.O., PE/129/150, ff. 3d., 4d., 5; *Cal. Inq. p.m.* iv, p. 146; vii, p. 425; Poulson, *Holderness,* ii. 250.

[41] P.R.O., CP 25(1)/278/145, no. 39; below, Catwick, Nunkeeling, (both) manors.

[42] P.R.O., CP 25(1)/281/162, no. 7.

[43] *Yorks. Deeds,* ix, pp. 40–1.

[44] P.R.O., C 139/148, no. 3; C 139/169, no. 34.

[45] Ibid. CP 25(1)/281/162, no. 7.

[46] Ibid. C 142/45, no. 18; *Cal. Inq. p.m. Hen. VII,* i, p. 456.

[47] P.R.O., C 142/48, no. 92; inaccurate pedigree of Flower in *Visit. Yorks. 1584–5 and 1612,* ed. J. Foster, 618. For possibly another part of the former Fauconberg estate at Bilton, *Yorks. Fines,* i. 23, 50.

[48] *Yorks. Fines,* i. 52–3.

[49] P.R.O., CP 40/1103, Carte rot. 10; Poulson, *Holderness,* ii. 250.

[50] *Cal. Pat.* 1553, 256. One of the sales was confirmed by John Flower in 1558: *Yorks. Fines,* i. 222.

[51] P.R.O., C 142/199, no. 69; B.I.H.R., Prob. Reg. 15B, ff. 353–4; *Yorks. Fines,* ii. 178.

[52] *Yorks. Fines, 1614–25,* 178.

[53] P.R.O., CP 25(2)/612/1649 Trin. [pt. i, no. 12]; CP 25(2)/612/1650 East. no. 63.

[54] Ibid. CP 25(2)/753/17 Chas. II East. [no. 17].

[55] Ibid. CP 25(2)/758/30 Chas. II Mich. [no. 14].

[56] Below, this section; E.R.A.O., CSR/19/10. For the following, Poulson, *Holderness,* ii. 250–1; J. Foster, *Pedigrees of Yorks.* iii, s.v. Dawnay.

[57] R.D.B., U/269/514.

[58] E.R.A.O., QDE/1/6/3.

Downe (d. 1780).[59] Thompson was duly succeeded in turn by the Revd. William Dawnay, later Lord Downe (d. 1846), and his brother Marmaduke Langley (d. 1851). A third brother, the Revd. Thomas Dawnay (d. 1850), had devised his reversionary interest to his great-nephew Lewis Dawnay, who succeeded on his majority in 1867.[60] In 1909 Lewis Dawnay conveyed the Bilton estate, of 1,172 a., to his younger son Alan, who sold it in many lots in 1911. George and William England bought Bilton Grange farm, with 313 a., William England alone c. 220 a., William Ingram 262 a., and J. R. Woods 99 a.[61] George England died in 1922, and his moiety of Bilton Grange farm was later held for his beneficiaries, George and Sarah England, evidently his son and widow.[62] In 1936 George England and Abraham Leonard, presumably heir to the moiety of William England (d. 1932), sold 286 a. of Bilton Grange farm to Hull corporation which used it for a housing estate.[63] William England left the estate he bought alone to his son Frank, who, after several sales in the 1930s, sold High farm, then of 180 a., and a few acres more to Arthur Wastling in 1944.[64] The farm was bought in 1948 by E. M. and G. R. Cooper, who later sold it piecemeal for house-building.[65]

An early, fortified house may have stood at the south end of Bilton on an earthwork later called Swan hill, and a manor house replacing it on the nearby moated site.[66] The manor house was recorded in 1557.[67]

Another provostry tenant was Sir William of Carthorpe (d. by 1296), who held 1½ carucate at Bilton and may have been succeeded by his son John and later by Thomas of Carthorpe.[68]

Swine priory held 2 bovates at Bilton in the Middle Ages.[69] A proposal to grant land at Bilton to North Ferriby priory in 1379[70] may have been ineffective. Ann Watson's charity of neighbouring Sutton bought a few acres in Bilton in 1910, Armitage farm with 64 a. there from Alan Dawnay in 1911, and 46 a. more in 1931.[71] The estate was reduced by small sales in the mid century,[72] Armitage farm was bought by Hull corporation in 1946, and the trust had no land in Bilton in 1995.[73] Trinity House, Hull, bought Red House farm at Bilton with 187 a. in 1927 and sold it in 1952.[74]

The rectorial tithes and dues of Bilton were bought by John Ramsden in 1681,[75] and they later descended with that manor.[76] Payn Dawnay, possibly as agent for his uncle Marmaduke Langley, was awarded a rent charge of £15 in 1848 for the few unmerged tithes at Bilton.[77]

ECONOMIC HISTORY. COMMON LANDS AND INCLOSURE. Later field-names suggest that the open fields at Bilton included North and East fields,[78] and ridge and furrow evidence shows that much of the tillage also lay south of the village.[79] In 1304 there was pasture land in Bilton stinted for 312 sheep,[80] and Low common was named in 1602.[81] Dorothy Grantham's husband Thomas is said to have inclosed at Bilton in the earlier 17th century,[82] and 'new laid ground' was mentioned there in 1666.[83]

MEDIEVAL HOLDINGS. In 1086 thirteen villeins worked two ploughlands on the archbishop's estate at Bilton and four a ploughland on Franco's estate, which also included 10 a. of meadow.[84]

LATER AGRICULTURE. In 1987 of 543 ha. (1,342 a.) returned under Bilton civil parish, 384 ha. (949 a.) were arable land and 152 ha. (376 a.) grassland; nearly 85,000 poultry, some 700 pigs, and more than 500 cattle were then kept.[85]

There were about six farms at Bilton in the 19th and earlier 20th century; in 1851 the four largest were of c. 250–300 a. each, and in the 1920s and 1930s all or most of the holdings were of 150 a. or more. By 1929 British Oil & Cake Mills Ltd. had an experimental farm at Bilton, which later included a poultry department, and in the 1930s one of the larger farms was also a poultry unit.[86] One or two cowkeepers or dairymen at Bilton were recorded in the earlier 20th century, and one of the larger farms there, Red House farm, was used for dairying.[87] In 1987 of 16 holdings returned under Bilton, one was of 100–199 ha. (247–492 a.), four of 50–99 ha. (124–245 a.), five of 10–49 ha. (25–121 a.), and six of under 10 ha.[88]

MILL. There was a windmill at Bilton in the 16th and 17th centuries.[89]

59 H.U.L., DDFA/44/39.
60 E.R.A.O., DDCL/1009.
61 R.D.B., 114/427/395; 131/564/494; 132/37/33; 132/62/56; 132/64/58; 132/66/60; 132/67/61; 132/68/62.
62 Ibid. 408/143/105; 676/384/303.
63 Ibid. 540/650/484; 676/384/303.
64 Ibid. 676/384/303; 678/542/431.
65 Ibid. 798/378/315; 825/246/199; 1158/466/428; 1171/255/226; 1204/130/116; 1694/310/250; 1801/46/37.
66 O.S. Map 1/10,000, TA 13 SE. (1985 edn.); H. E. J. le Patourel, Moated Sites of Yorks. 110.
67 B.I.H.R., Prob. Reg. 15B, f. 353.
68 E.R.A.O., PE/129/150, ff. 3d., 4d., 5; Cal. Inq. p.m. iii, pp. 199–200.
69 E.R.A.O., PE/129/150, f. 3d.
70 Cal. Pat. 1377–81, 374.
71 R.D.B., 127/472/427; 131/371/321; 433/409/318; V.C.H. Yorks. E.R. i. 346.
72 R.D.B., 509/99/79, etc.
73 Ibid. 730/105/84; inf. from Ann Watson's Trust, Sutton, 1995.
74 R.D.B., 346/329/276; 915/546/469.
75 E.R.A.O., DDCC/111/31; above, Swine township, manors (rectory).
76 R.D.B., U/269/514; above, this section.
77 E.R.A.O., PE/104/101.
78 R.D.B., A/48/60; M/282/454.
79 Hull Univ., Dept. of Geog., Fairey Surveys air photographs, run 366c, nos. 1065–6.
80 Cal. Inq. p.m. iv, p. 146.
81 Yorks. Deeds, iv, p. 75.
82 Poulson, Holderness, ii. 250.
83 P.R.O., E 134/18 Chas. II Mich./10.
84 V.C.H. Yorks. ii. 216, 268.
85 Inf. from Min. of Agric., Fish. & Food, Beverley, 1990.
86 P.R.O., HO 107/2365; directories.
87 R.D.B., 346/329/276; directories.
88 Inf. from Min. of Agric., Fish. & Food.
89 P.R.O., CP 25(2)/758/30 Chas. II Mich. [no. 14]; Yorks. Fines, iv. 76; 1603–14, 123; 1614–25, 178.

LOCAL GOVERNMENT. At Bilton 2 people were relieved permanently and 3 occasionally in 1802–3, and there were 4–5 on permanent and 3–4 on occasional relief between 1812 and 1815.[90] Bilton joined Skirlaugh poor-law union in 1837,[91] and the township, later civil parish, remained in Skirlaugh rural district until 1935. As part of the enlarged civil parish of Bilton, it was then included in the new Holderness rural district and at reorganization in 1974 was taken into the Holderness district of Humberside.[92] In 1996 Bilton parish became part of a new East Riding unitary area.[93] Bilton parish council, established in 1932,[94] opened a cemetery south of the church in 1962.[95]

CHURCH. Swine parish evidently included a chapel at Bilton in 1285, when its burial ground was mentioned.[96] The curacy there became perpetual[97] after endowment in 1794, and, following further grants in 1859,[98] the townships of Bilton, Ganstead, and Wyton were taken from Swine parish to form a district chapelry, or parish, in 1867.[99] The benefice was thereafter a vicarage.[1] In 1952 and 1960 parts of Bilton parish scheduled for development as suburbs of Hull were added respectively to the parishes of Marfleet and St. Michael's, Sutton.[2]

In the Middle Ages the chapel contained or comprised a chantry. The chaplain was admitted by the prioress of Swine, apparently after nomination by the provost of Beverley.[3] The first perpetual curate was presented in 1794 by Archbishop Markham, who then transferred the patronage to Mildred Bourchier in return for her benefaction to the living; the right to present later descended with the manor.[4] Lewis Dawnay conveyed the advowson in 1909 to his son Alan, who sold it to F. A. Scott in 1910, and in 1911 Scott transferred it to the archbishop of York, the present patron.[5]

The curate of Bilton chapel had £4 a year in 1525;[6] part may have come from a house, 1 bovate, and a few acres which belonged to the chapel until they were confiscated by the Crown under the Chantries Act,[7] but a stipend paid

from the rectory probably accounted for most of the sum. In the mid 17th century the stipend for serving Bilton chapel was £3 6s. 8d.; the curate was then also said to receive the Easter offerings[8] and his living may have been augmented from Burstwick and Paull rectories in the 1650s.[9] The stipend was later lost, probably at or after the sale of the rectory in 1681.[10] In 1794 the curacy was endowed with £400 granted from Queen Anne's Bounty by lot and another £400 to meet a benefaction of that amount from Mildred Bourchier.[11] The net income averaged £45 a year between 1829 and 1831.[12] In 1859 Lydia Dawnay, the lord of the manor's sister, gave stock of £1,575 and £500, the latter to obtain a grant of £200 Bounty money,[13] and in 1883 the gross income was £259.[14]

Mildred Bourchier had built a house for the curate by 1795, when she devised it and nearly 5 a. adjoining for the living.[15] In 1968 the house was sold, and the converted school building bought instead;[16] that vicarage house was in turn replaced by another on Main Road, bought c. 1975.[17] By 1998 the last house had been demolished, and one of the newly-built houses to the north of Main Road bought for the incumbent.

The augmentations were used to buy 26 a. at Wyton and an adjoining 18 a. at Preston in 1795.[18] A farmhouse built by 1842 was rebuilt in 1898.[19] Glebe farm was sold in 1910,[20] and in 1978 only c. 4 a. of glebe remained at Bilton.[21]

In 1575 sermons were lacking in Bilton chapel.[22] Baptism, marriage, burial, and communion services were held there in the mid 17th century,[23] when the curate, Samuel Sinclair, was a puritan.[24] From the late 16th century the curacy was held with that of neighbouring Wyton chapel, and it was served with Swine vicarage and other Holderness livings in the 17th and 18th centuries.[25] In 1743 there was a service every other Sunday at Bilton, and Holy Communion was celebrated three times a year, with c. 16 communicants.[26] The first vicar, H. K. Quilter (d. 1905), served for 38 years.[27] He provided two Sunday services, celebrated Communion monthly in 1865 and later weekly, and held an evening school from the 1860s until the

90 Poor Law Abstract, 1804, pp. 592–3; 1818, pp. 520–1.
91 3rd Rep. Poor Law Com. 170.   92 Census.
93 Humberside (Structural Change) Order 1995, copy at E.R.A.O.   94 E.R.A.O., CCO/302.
95 R.D.B., 1200/419/361; gravestones.
96 E.R.A.O., PE/129/150, f. 3d.
97 B.I.H.R., TER. H. Bilton 1817 etc.
98 Below, this section.
99 Lond. Gaz. 1 Mar. 1867, p. 1442.
1 Crockford (1872), 706.
2 B.I.H.R., OC. 713, 758; V.C.H. Yorks. E.R. i. 302.
3 E.R.A.O., PE/129/150, f. 2.
4 H.U.L., DDFA/44/39; E.R.A.O., DDCL/1009; Poulson, Holderness, ii. 251; above, manor.
5 B.I.H.R., OC. 481; Crockford (1993–4).
6 Y.A.J. xxiv. 76.
7 Cal. Pat. 1548–9, 37–8; 1 Edw. VI, c. 14; Y.A.J. xliv. 189–90.
8 P.R.O., E 126/9, ff. 294–5; E 134/18 Chas. II Mic./10.
9 Cal. Cttee. for Compounding, iii, p. 2152.
10 B.I.H.R., TER. H. Bilton [1726]; above, manor [rectory]. Cf. B.I.H.R., CP. H. 2516.
11 B.I.H.R., TER. H. Bilton 1809; Hodgson, Q.A.B. pp. clxxvii, cccxliii.

12 Rep. Com. Eccl. Revenues, 918–19.
13 B.I.H.R., TER. H. Bilton 1861; Hodgson, Q.A.B. supplement, pp. xlv, lxxvi.
14 B.I.H.R., V. 1884/Ret. 1.
15 Ibid. TER. H. Bilton 1809; H.U.L., DDFA/44/39.
16 R.D.B., 1539/356/304; 1562/329/271.
17 Inf. from Mr. F. Sharp, Bilton, 1994.
18 R.D.B., BU/595/905.
19 B.I.H.R., TER. H. Bilton 1809, 1861; E.R.A.O., PE/7/23/1; PE/104/99.   20 R.D.B., 120/226/204.
21 E.R.A.O., PE/7/23/3.
22 Abp. Grindal's Visit., 1575, ed. W. J. Sheils, 75.
23 P.R.O., E 134/18 Chas. II Mich./10.
24 R. A. Marchant, Puritans and Ch. Cts. in Dioc. York, 1540–1642, 279.
25 Lamb. Pal. Libr., Carte Misc. XII/9, f. 132v.; P.R.O., E 134/18 Chas. II Mich./10; B.I.H.R., CP. H. 2516; ibid. TER. H. Bilton [1726]–1786; ibid. V. 1764/Ret. 3, no. 66; T.E.R.A.S. iv. 52; Restoration Exhibit Bks. and Northern Clergy 1662–4, ed. W. J. Sheils, 66; Herring's Visit. iii, p. 128.
26 Herring's Visit. iii, p. 128. Service in 1764 was variously said to be weekly and usually fortnightly: B.I.H.R., V. 1764/Ret. 3, nos. 51, 66.
27 Window in church.

1880s; there were usually 16–17 communicants in 1865 and later up to a dozen. The church was for many years 'High Anglican'[28] but by 1994 had become Evangelical.

The church, formerly of *ST. MARY MAG-DALEN* but by 1823 dedicated to *ST. PETER*,[29] was rebuilt by Payn Dawnay, lord of the manor,[30] with, or for, his sister Lydia Dawnay, and re-opened in 1852.[31] The plan and style of the old church, which was of ashlar,[32] was followed by G. T. Andrews's design, which comprises undivided nave and chancel with north vestry and south porch and western double bellcot, all in a 13th-century style. The rich paving of encaustic tiles in the chancel is well-preserved. By 1868 a stone communion rail dividing chancel and nave had been installed,[33] and a stone reredos was added in 1886.[34] Other fittings include an elaborate, wooden, hanging rood with figures of St. Mary and St. John.

There were two bells in 1552 and later.[35] The Dawnays replaced the plate with a silver-gilt service at rebuilding in 1852.[36] The registers of baptisms, marriages, and burials begin in the 1690s but lack entries then and in the earlier 18th century.[37] Transcripts for Bilton and Wyton survive from 1600.[38]

A lich-gate gives access to the churchyard, additions to which were consecrated in 1905 and 1938.[39]

NONCONFORMITY. A house registered for worship by protestants in 1824 may have been at Bilton in the West Riding.[40] The Primitive Methodists used an unlocated house at Bilton from 1848, *c.* 20 attending services on Sunday evenings in 1851.[41] The congregation was mentioned again in 1865,[42] but evidently ceased to meet soon afterwards.

EDUCATION. The curate kept a school at Bilton in 1604,[43] and in 1818 Richard Thompson supported a dame's school with five pupils.[44] The same or another school was attended by 10–20 boys and girls at their parents' expense in 1833.[45] The school was evidently refounded *c.* 1864 as Bilton Church school and run on National lines, and in 1868 the curate shared the teaching with a mistress. Lewis Dawnay built a new schoolroom and master's house in 1869. The school was supported by subscription, school pence, and from 1872–3 by an annual, government grant. Average attendance was 16 in 1865,[46] 22 boys and girls were present at inspection in 1871, including children from Ganstead, Thirtleby, and Wyton,[47] and infants were accommodated by 1877.[48] A classroom was added in 1893,[49] but by 1911, when Alan Dawnay transferred the school to the county council,[50] it was overcrowded with children from outside Bilton ecclesiastical parish, notably from the suburban parish of Sutton, which contributed 28 of the 69 pupils in 1911. Children from Preston had been excluded in 1909, and those from Sutton were refused admittance from 1912.[51] From 50–60 in the early 20th century, average attendance had fallen by the end of the First World War to *c.* 30, but grew again as a consequence of new building to 73 in 1935–6 and 103 in 1938.[52] The inadequacy of the building, which had been further enlarged and altered in 1912,[53] led to the hiring of accommodation in the village hall[54] and the opening on another site of a new school in 1938. The former school was later a centre for instruction in domestic science and joinery,[55] and from the 1960s served as the vicarage house.[56] In 1954 senior pupils at Bilton school were transferred to South Holderness County Secondary School.[57] The primary school was enlarged with two classrooms and a hall in 1964–5, during which work the village hall was used again,[58] and in 1974 it was completed to accommodate 400 pupils.[59] In 1990 there were 309 on the roll.[60]

Evening classes were held at Bilton in the 1940s.[61]

[28] B.I.H.R., V. 1865/Ret. 1, no. 54; V. 1868/Ret. 1, no. 53; V. 1871/Ret. 1, no. 52; V. 1877/Ret. 1, no. 49; V. 1884/ Ret. 1; V. 1912–22/Ret.; V. 1931/Ret.; E.R.A.O., PE/7/ 23/1–2.

[29] *Y.A.J.* ii. 184; Baines, *Hist. Yorks.* (1823), ii. 167.

[30] B.I.H.R., Fac. Bk. 4, pp. 587–9; above, manor.

[31] *Kelly's Dir. N. & E. R. Yorks.* (1872), 326; (1879), 353.

[32] Poulson, *Holderness*, ii. 251.

[33] B.I.H.R., V. 1868/Ret. 1, no. 53.

[34] *Kelly's Dir. N. & E. R. Yorks.* (1893), 377.

[35] *Inventories of Ch. Goods*, 44; Boulter, 'Ch. Bells', 82.

[36] B.I.H.R., TER. H. Bilton 1764, etc.; *Yorks. Ch. Plate*, i. 222–3.

[37] Some entries were copied from the Swine registers, which contain other entries for Bilton: E.R.A.O., PE/7/ 1–3, 6.

[38] B.I.H.R., PRT. Hold. D. Bilton, Wyton.

[39] Ibid. CD. Add. 1905/1; 1938/5.

[40] Ibid. DMH. Reg. 1, p. 469.

[41] P.R.O., HO 129/522/2/1/4.

[42] B.I.H.R., V. 1865/Ret. 1, no. 54.

[43] Ibid. V. 1604/CB. 1, f. 89.

[44] *Educ. of Poor Digest*, 1095; above, manor.

[45] *Educ. Enq. Abstract*, 1096.

[46] P.R.O., ED 7/135, no. 15; B.I.H.R., V. 1865/Ret. 1, no. 54; V. 1868/Ret. 1, no. 53; *Kelly's Dir. N. & E.R. Yorks.* (1872), 326; *Rep. of Educ. Cttee. of Council, 1872–3* [C. 812], p. 510, H.C. (1873), xxiv.

[47] *Returns relating to Elem. Educ.* 472–3.

[48] B.I.H.R., V. 1877/Ret. 1, no. 49.

[49] *Kelly's Dir. N. & E.R. Yorks.* (1897), 408.

[50] R.D.B., 133/43/40; E.R. Educ. Cttee. *Mins.* 1911–12, 57.

[51] E.R. Educ. Cttee. *Mins.* 1909–10, 141; 1911–12, 69–70; 1912–13, 237.

[52] *Bd. of Educ., List 21* (H.M.S.O., 1908 and later edns.).

[53] E.R. Educ. Cttee. *Mins.* 1912–13, 60, 320.

[54] Ibid. 1934–5, 162, 191; 1935–6, 41.

[55] Ibid. 1935–6, 167; 1937–8, 117, 172; 1938–9, 13, 40; R.D.B., 561/419/331.

[56] R.D.B., 1524/271/245; 1539/356/304.

[57] E.R. Educ. Cttee. *Mins.* 1953–4, 145.

[58] Ibid. 1963–4, 86, 138; 1964–5, 8; 1965–6, 123.

[59] Ibid. 1972–3, 140; inf. from the head teacher, 1994.

[60] Inf. from Educ. Dept., Humbs. C.C., 1990.

[61] E.R. Educ. Cttee. *Mins.* 1943–4, 69.

BURTON CONSTABLE

BURTON Constable, seat of the Constable family, lords of Holderness since the 16th century,[62] lies over 5 km. ENE. of Swine village and *c.* 7 km. south-west from the coast at Aldbrough. Apart from the Hall[63] and its outbuildings, there are only a few scattered houses. The common, Anglian name Burton, meaning settlement, was qualified in 1086 with the prefix 'Santri', the significance of which is unknown; in 1190 the name of its previous tenant, Erneburga, was used to differentiate it and from the mid 13th century that of her descendants, the Constables.[64] Burton Constable, containing 1,277 a. (517 ha.),[65] was combined with West Newton hamlet, in Aldbrough parish, as West Newton township, which had 2,068 a. (837 ha.).[66] In 1935 West Newton with Burton Constable civil parish, formerly West Newton township, and that of Marton were united as Burton Constable civil parish. The combined area, of 3,015 a. (1,220 ha.),[67] was reduced slightly by a transfer to Ellerby in 1952.[68] In 1984 some 10 ha. (25 a.) more were transferred to Ellerby, and in 1991 Burton Constable's area was 1,205 ha. (2,978 a.).[69] In 1377 Burton Constable and West Newton together had 105 poll-tax payers,[70] and 16 houses there were assessed for hearth tax in 1672.[71] The two hamlets had 172 inhabitants in 1801, 239 in 1851, but only 147 in 1901 and 141 in 1931. Burton Constable itself contributed 124 to the 1851 total, that number including the family and their visitors at the Hall and the staff of *c.* 40.[72] The combined population of the civil parishes united in 1935 had been 214 in 1931. The new civil parish evidently had 263 inhabitants in 1951, before the loss of *c.* 40 people to Ellerby in 1952. Thereafter the population declined, from 200 in 1961 to 128 in 1981, but it had recovered by 1991, when there were usually 159 residents and 165 were enumerated.[73]

BURTON CONSTABLE hamlet. By the later 18th century there were, apart from the Hall, only half a dozen scattered houses in the township. They included Smithy Briggs Farm, since rebuilt, the later Brickyard House, and a keeper's lodge in Norwood. Another house standing close to the western boundary and near the way to Thirtleby was then called Burton lodge; it had been demolished by the mid 19th century, possibly being replaced by Lodge Farm, which had by then been built across the boundary in Ellerby.[74]

MANOR AND OTHER ESTATES. In 1086 the archbishop of York had 5 carucates at 'Santriburtone', later *BURTON CONSTABLE*, and 3 carucates in the adjoining West Newton.[75] Later the counts of Aumale held 6 carucates in both places as military tenants of the archbishop until their holding passed to the Crown with the honor of Aumale by the death of Aveline de Forz, countess of Aumale, in 1274.[76] Burton Constable manor and its member at West Newton were held of the Crown as ¾ knight's fee in 1336,[77] and Burton Constable alone was reckoned ⅓ knight's fee in the 16th century.[78]

A knight occupying land at 'Santriburtone' in 1086[79] was evidently succeeded by Erneburga of Burton, who married the count of Aumale's constable Ulbert (fl. earlier 12th century). Her son Robert Constable had land at 'Erneburgh Burton' before 1190,[80] and in the 13th century the Constable family was recorded as holding all 6 carucates of the count of Aumale's estate,[81] comprising 3 carucates in each of the two settlements,[82] then called Burton Constable and Newton Constable.[83] In 1231 William Constable and William de Forz, count of Aumale, were in dispute about hunting over the estate.[84] Robert Constable was named as lord of Burton Constable in 1316,[85] and at his death by 1336 the demesne there and at West Newton comprised 1 carucate and almost 100 a.; 3 carucates and 1 bovate and other land were then held by bond tenants, cottars, and a free tenant.[86] Robert's son John Constable (d. 1349) bought 1 carucate and rent at Burton Constable,[87] and more land there had been purchased by the mid 15th century.[88] By the 16th century the estate evidently also included land held of the archbishop.[89] The manor continued to descend, with Halsham, in the Constables, viscounts Dunbar in the 17th and early 18th century, and their heirs, the Tunstalls, Sheldons, Cliffords, and Chichesters, all of whom substituted or added the name Con-

[62] *V.C.H. Yorks. E.R.* v. 9–10.
[63] Below, manor.
[64] *P.N. Yorks. E.R.* (E.P.N.S.), 61; below, manor.
[65] O.S. Map 6″, Yorks. CCXII, CCXXVII (1855 edn.).
[66] *Census*, 1871.   [67] Ibid. 1931 (pt. ii).
[68] Ibid. 1961; E.R.A.O., CCO/464.
[69] *Census*, 1991; E.R.A.O., Holderness (Parishes) Order 1983; O.S. Map 1/2,500, Yorks. CCXII. 6, 10 (1891 edn.).
[70] P.R.O., E 179/202/60, m. 52.
[71] *Hearth Tax*, 60.
[72] P.R.O., HO 107/2365.
[73] *V.C.H. Yorks.* iii. 493; *Census*, 1901–91.
[74] E.R.A.O., DDCC/141/71 (plan of Burton Constable; plan of Ellerby no. 1); DDCC(2)/plan 15; ibid. DDHI, accession 1141 (Flinton inclosure map); T. Jefferys, *Map of Yorks.* (1772); O.S. Map 6″, Yorks. CCXII (1855 edn.).
[75] *V.C.H. Yorks.* ii. 216.

[76] *Feud. Aids*, vi. 41–2; *Yorks. Inq.* ii, p. 107; English, *Holderness*, 53–4.
[77] *Cal. Inq. p.m.* viii, p. 24.
[78] H.U.L., DHO/8/47.
[79] *V.C.H. Yorks.* ii. 216.
[80] *E.Y.C.* iii, pp. 41–2. For Constable fam., see *Early Yorks. Fam.* (Y.A.S. Rec. Ser. cxxxv), 22; J. Foster, *Pedigrees of Yorks.* iii; English, *Holderness*, 90.
[81] *Kirkby's Inquest*, 375; *Cal. Inq. p.m.* iv, p. 357.
[82] Poulson, *Holderness*, ii. 229 n.
[83] *Yorks. Inq.* ii, p. 107.
[84] H.U.L., DHO/16/36.
[85] *Feud. Aids*, vi. 164.
[86] P.R.O., C 135/47, no. 16.
[87] *Cal. Inq. p.m.* x, pp. 321–2.
[88] E.R.A.O., DDCC/18/6.
[89] P.R.O., C 142/65, no. 61; E 150/240, no. 12.

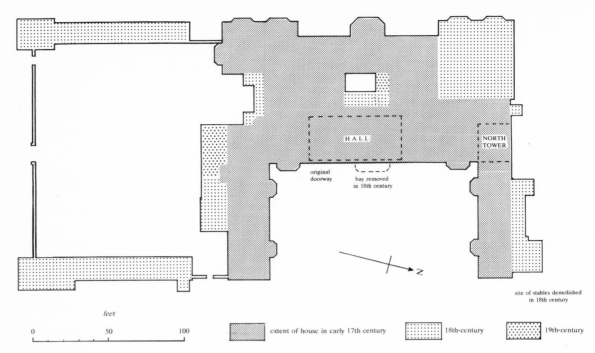

HALL

NORTH
TOWER

original
doorway

bay removed
in 18th century

N

site of stables demolished
in 18th century

feet

0   50   100 | extent of house in early 17th century | 18th-century | 19th-century

FIG. 8. BURTON CONSTABLE HALL. BLOCK PLAN

stable.[90] In 1827 the whole of Burton Constable hamlet was occupied by Sir Thomas Constable, Bt., and his tenants.[91] In 1992 the Chichester-Constable family, in association with the National Heritage Memorial Fund and Leeds City Council, set up the Burton Constable Foundation, and endowed it with the Hall, stable block, and other outbuildings, and 320 a. of parkland. The rest of the Burton Constable estate in Burton Constable and neighbouring villages belonged to Mr. John Chichester-Constable, who had c. 688 ha. (1,700 a.) in 1995, and his daughter, Rodrica Straker, who then owned 485.6 ha. (1,200 a.).[92]

The chief house at Burton Constable, mentioned from 1294,[93] succeeded Halsham as the family's main residence, apparently in the late 15th century.[94] The site may have been moated, a curving ditch running around the north and east of the house until its reduction in the mid 18th century to a fishpond, which remained in 1995.[95] The early structural history of the house is obscure. A length of ashlar wall at the centre of the north elevation forms one side of a nearly-square room, which was later heightened in brick to become a tower. It has a turret staircase at its south-west corner, and both tower and

turret have a possibly 15th-century, brick corbel table below the parapet. The two-storeyed range which abuts the tower on the east appears to be structurally contemporary; that to the south is late 16th-century but replaces an older building from which a disused fireplace survives on the south face of the tower. Those northern and western ranges, together with a southern one, formed a three-sided, courtyard house which was probably still being built in 1578[96] but seems to have been substantially complete by the end of the century. Its principal elevations looked inwards towards the court, which was closed on the east by a wall with a turreted gatehouse.[97] By the early 17th century that was an old-fashioned plan, and a new range was begun along the west side of the house to screen the back of the main range and provide an up-to-date elevation towards the park. It was to be linked to the old building by short ranges separated by one or more small, open courts. The new work, which evidently included a gallery,[98] was left unfinished,[99] perhaps because of the death of Sir Henry Constable in 1607.[1] It seems probable that at the same time as the new work was going on the old, main range was being remodelled, and the great hall and parts of the east front date from the late 16th or early 17th century. The

[90] Ibid. CP 25 (2)/762/24–5 Chas. II Hil. [last but one]; H.U.L., DHO/7/42; DHO/8/47; E.R.A.O., DDCC/111/39, 231; *Feud. Aids*, vi. 273; *Cal. Inq. p.m.* viii, p. 24; ix, pp. 219–20; *Hen. VII*, i, p. 276; ii, pp. 60–2; *L. & P. Hen. VIII*, xiv (1), p. 309; *Yorks. Royalist Composition Papers*, iii (Y.A.S. Rec. Ser. xx), p. 113; *V.C.H. Yorks. E.R.* v. 33; J. Foster, *Pedigrees of Yorks.* iii; [I. Hall] *Burton Constable* (1994), [29–30].
[91] E.R.A.O., DDCC/111/39.
[92] [I. Hall] *Burton Constable* (1994), 1; inf. from Mr. John Chichester-Constable, Burton Constable, 1995.
[93] *Cal. Inq. p.m.* iii, p. 114.

[94] *V.C.H. Yorks. E.R.* v. 33.
[95] E.R.A.O., DDCC(2)/plan 1; DDCC/141/71; Burton Constable Hall, plan of c. 1755; O.S. Map 6″, Yorks. CCXII (1855 edn.).
[96] Burton Constable Hall, DDCC/141/68 (survey), p. 16; microfilm copy at E.R.A.O.
[97] Burton Constable Hall, late 17th-cent. painting, reprod. in *Country Life*, 6 May 1982.
[98] [I. Hall] *Burton Constable* (1994), 12.
[99] Burton Constable Hall, plan of park c. 1755, which shows the north-west corner of the house unbuilt.
[1] P.R.O., C 142/310, no. 79.

two-storeyed hall occupied less than half the elevation, which was more than 130 ft. long. The great bay window was at the centre, on the axis of the gatehouse, and the entrance near the south end, through a relatively modest, Classical doorway with strapwork ornament.[2] Within there was a stone hall screen with similar strapwork ornament.[3] A tower matching the earlier one to the north occupied the corner between the main range and the south wing, which contained the kitchen and service rooms. With its red-brick façades, prominent quoins, and large mullioned and transomed windows, some of them bayed, the house had much of its present appearance by the late 17th century.[4]

A few rooms have reset, early 17th-century panelling, but little structural work seems to have been carried out that century, and only in the early 18th was the gallery panelled. That work appears to have been part of a phase of improvement which included the refitting of the hall, the creation of a cabinet room on the ground floor of the north tower, and the panelling of some adjacent rooms. Externally, two new sash windows and a doorway, all with pediments, were made on the north front. A small addition on the south side of the south wing contains a ground-floor room with an elaborately-moulded cove and above it a room with panelling, overmantel, and rich plasterwork in the style of the 1740s; the rooms suggest the use of the east end of that wing as a self-contained suite—perhaps for the young William Constable or his sister Winefred, who lived at Burton Constable until her death in 1774.[5] When William inherited in 1747, he is said to have considered demolishing the house and rebuilding in a more fashionable style;[6] instead he remodelled it. Dated rainwater heads around the eastern court imply an extensive renovation between 1757 and 1760, and it may have been then that a parapet with windows was substituted for attic dormers on the hall range. Probably in the late 1750s, the large, central, hall bay was removed and replaced by a feature incorporating a doorway,[7] the whole being surmounted, a few years later, by an elaborately-carved achievement of the arms of William Constable, viscount Dunbar (d. 1718).[8] Inside, the hall was refitted in a partly Jacobean-revival style to designs by Timothy Lightoler of York[9] between 1765 and 1769.[10] Before his death in 1769, Lightoler also designed

the dining room, the State Drawing Room, and the staircase hall.[11] In 1772–3 a new service court was formed against the south side of the house from designs by 'Capability' Brown.[12] The northern end of the west range had never been built, and it was not until c. 1770 that Constable completed that elevation; the major interior, now the ballroom, is of 1775 and by James Wyatt. Thomas Atkinson of York designed an adjacent room in 1774, formerly used for billiards but now the chapel, and in 1783 the Blue Drawing Room at the centre of the west front.[13]

Alterations in the 19th century were largely concerned with the remodelling and redecoration of the interior and its gradual elaboration with pictures and furniture by Sir Thomas Constable, Bt. (d. 1870), and his wives. The gallery was restored soon after 1830,[14] and it is now difficult to distinguish the plasterwork of the 17th century, the later 18th-century remodelling, and the 19th-century restoration. The Chinese Room, originally furnished by Thomas Chippendale in 1784, similarly had its decoration enhanced in the style of the Royal Pavilion c. 1840.[15] The billiard room was converted to a chapel with a semicircular sanctuary in 1830 and refitted in 1844,[16] and a theatre made from first-floor rooms at the south end of the house was used in the 1840s and 1850s.[17] Outside, the sash windows which had been installed during the later 18th-century alterations to the west front were replaced by stone mullions and transoms.[18] The house was restored again c. 1910 and by John Chichester-Constable after 1963.[19]

Cuthbert and William Constable assembled an extensive library in the house which was used by, among others, George Poulson for his *History and Antiquities of the Seigniory of Holderness*; William was also a collector of scientific apparatus and exhibits, and a later owner, Sir Thomas Constable, Bt. (d. 1823), was an eminent topographer and botanist. By 1994 most of the remaining collections had been given to Leeds City Art Galleries, which were responsible for their preservation and display in the house.[20]

(Sir) Simon Constable was granted free warren at Burton Constable and West Newton in 1285, and Burton Constable park was recorded from 1367.[21] The medieval park lay to

[2] Burton Constable Hall, late 17th-cent. painting, reprod. in *Country Life*, 6 May 1982. The carved blocks from the doorway were reused in the walls of the cellars below the west front.
[3] [I. Hall] *Burton Constable*, 5. Presumably that referred to in 1715: E.R.A.O., DDCC/140/74 (bill of 2 July 1715).
[4] For descriptions and illus., D. Hey, *Buildings of Britain, 1500–1750, Yorks.* 29–30; Pevsner, *Yorks. E.R.* pl. 64; Pevsner and Neave, *Yorks. E.R.* 371–7, pl. 54; E. Yorks. Georgian Soc. *Trans.* ii (1), p. 22; iv (1), pp. 33–46; *Country Life*, 27 Aug. and 3 Sept. 1932; 22 and 29 Apr. and 6 and 13 May 1982.
[5] Inf. on Winefred Constable from Dr. D. Connell, Burton Constable Foundation, 1996.
[6] [I. Hall], *Burton Constable* (1994), 3.
[7] *Country Life*, 22 Apr. 1982.
[8] [Hall], *Burton Constable*, 3.
[9] *Biog. Dictionary of Brit. Architects, 1600–1840* (1978 edn.), ed. H. Colvin, 520.

[10] Design at Burton Constable Hall, 1996. The screen was not built.
[11] Designs at Burton Constable Hall, 1996.
[12] Colvin, op. cit. 147.
[13] Designs at Burton Constable Hall, 1996; bill of 1774 for design at E.R.A.O., DDCC(2).
[14] *Country Life*, 22 Apr. 1982.
[15] E.R.A.O., DDCC(2)/ bills of 1784 and c. 1840; [Hall] *Burton Constable* [25]; Pevsner and Neave, *Yorks. E.R.* 376.
[16] [Hall], *Burton Constable*, 19–20; Pevsner and Neave, *Yorks. E.R.* 376.
[17] Playbills at E.R.A.O., DDCC/17/13; *Hull Advertiser*, 29 Mar. 1856; [Hall] *Burton Constable*, 15.
[18] [Hall] *Burton Constable*, 3.
[19] Ibid. [2, 30].
[20] *D.N.B.*; *Y.A.J.* xlii. 226–8, 230; [Hall] *Burton Constable*, 1.
[21] *Cal. Chart. R.* 1257–1300, 308; Poulson, *Holderness*, i. 130.

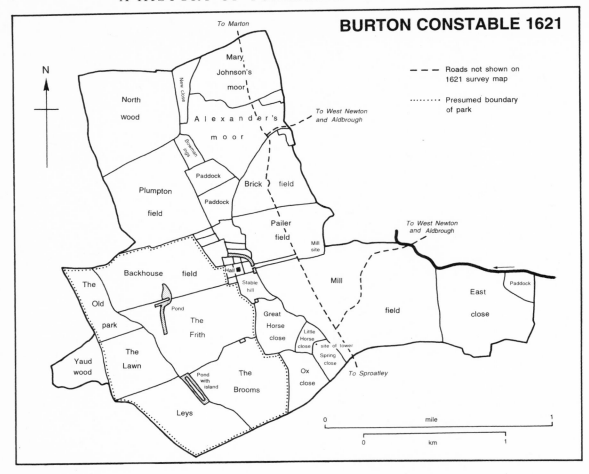

BURTON CONSTABLE 1621

– – – Roads not shown on
1621 survey map

· · · · · · · Presumed boundary
of park

the west of the house, on the boundary with Ellerby, where a 36-a. close was later called Old park.[22] Surviving ridge and furrow testify to the enlargement of the park at the expense of the tillage, and in the 1570s and 1580s Sir John Constable and his son (Sir) Henry also added parts of a pasture in Sproatley.[23] In 1578 there was 385 a. of parkland stocked with red and fallow deer.[24] That park is presumably to be identified with six closes totalling c. 380 a. in 1621. The enlargement of the park brought it closer to the house across a shallow, north-south valley, which by 1621 had been dammed to form ponds, the southernmost of which was a long rectangle enclosing a narrow island. Around the house were brick-walled courts, bounded on the north and east by the irregular ditch.[25] The eastern court was entered through a turreted gatehouse, and by the late 17th century there was a further court with ashlar gate piers.[26] About ½ km. south-east of the house, and outside the

park, a late 16th- or early 17th-century, octagonal, brick tower may have combined a viewing point with a high-level water tank.[27]

Although the main approach to the house was through the eastern forecourts, it could also be reached by a tree-lined track from Thirtleby. Formal avenues leading south, east, and west from the house and north to Norwood had been made by the early 18th century, perhaps as part of a recent landscaping scheme, which also involved the creation of a water garden and a small formal garden, respectively north and west of the house.[28]

It was probably in the garden to the west of the house that William Constable with Thomas Knowlton and Thomas Kyle c. 1758 established a botanical garden with greenhouse and hot walls.[29] In 1763 Constable added at the northern end of the ponds a menagerie, comprising a walled enclosure with small pavilions or houses along its north side and in the southern corn-

[22] Later plan from 1621 survey: E.R.A.O., DDCC(2)/ plan 1.

[23] Cf. Hull Univ., Dept. of Geog., R.A.F. air photographs, run 334A, no. 4141; run 334B, no. 3150. Above, Sproatley, econ. hist.

[24] Burton Constable Hall, DDCC/141/68 (survey), p. 17; microfilm copy at E.R.A.O.; C. Saxton, *Atlas of Eng. and Wales* (1939 facs. edn.).   [25] E.R.A.O., DDCC(2)/plan 1.

[26] Burton Constable Hall, late 17th-cent. painting, reprod. in *Country Life*, 6 May 1982.

[27] A 'water engine' was shown on the site in the later

18th century: E.R.A.O., DDCC/141/71 (plans of Burton Constable); ibid. DDHI, accession 1141 (Flinton inclosure map). The plans are damaged and bear no date but, from the tenants named, it is clear that they were made between 1776 and 1790: cf. ibid. DDCC/141/4.

[28] J. Warburton, *Map Co. York* [1720]; Burton Constable Hall, plan of park c. 1755. The gardens may have been laid out in 1715: bills of 22 May, 20 Aug. 1715 at E.R.A.O., DDCC/140/74.

[29] *Garden Hist.* xxiii (2), 148; I. and E. Hall, *Burton Constable* (1991), 35.

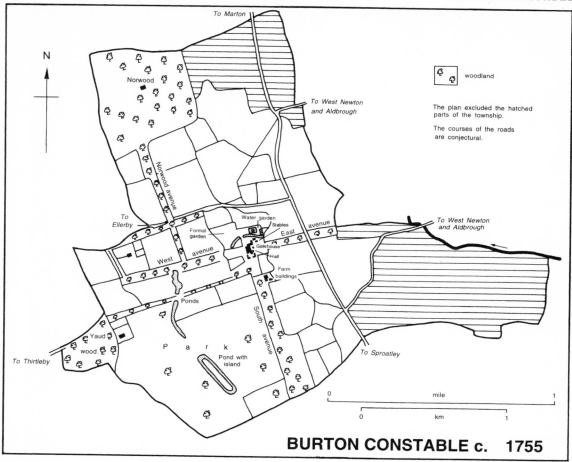

BURTON CONSTABLE c. 1755

ers.[30] The general landscaping of the grounds was apparently undertaken from the 1760s, following the commissioning of designs from 'Capability' Brown, Thomas White, and Constable's architect, Timothy Lightoler.[31] The plan adopted owed as much to White as to Brown, but it was the latter who superintended the work and visited Burton Constable until 1782.[32] Apart from the serpentizing of the ponds, the changes involved the enlargement of the grounds east and north of the house, the felling of the eastern avenue, and much planting of clumps and feature trees around the house. Closer to the house, the gatehouse, walls, and formal gardens were replaced by lawns protected by a ha-ha. In 1774 William Constable had 713 a. in hand, all or most of it occupied as grounds. The Hall and the land within the ha-ha comprised nearly 10 a.; the park, excluding the lakes, was of 152 a., and 148 a. more lay in adjacent closes later added to the park; the Lawn

and Stable Lawn accounted for another 124 a., and two woods together had a similar acreage. There was simultaneously much building within the park, mostly designed by Lightoler. Extensive stables and farm buildings around yards had been built on the site of old farm buildings to the south-east of the house by 1768, and the former stables north-east of the house were demolished.[33] At about the same time, a new kitchen garden was built behind the menagerie replacing that then cleared away from the west of the house.[34] A bridge designed by Brown[35] was built to disguise the dam between the upper and lower lakes, which were being made in 1775,[36] and about that date a pavilion overlooking the upper lake was added in the menagerie enclosure.[37] The bridge became a feature of the southern drive to the house which was completed in 1778[38] and c. 1785 given a Gothick gatehouse, designed by James Wyatt, at the entrance to the park from Sproatley.[39] To

30   [Hall], *Burton Constable* [28]; Burton Constable Hall, plan evidently of *c.* 1767, which also shows the landscaping scheme later followed, including the proposed lake instead of the ponds.   31   Plans surviving at Burton Constable Hall.
32   For Brown's work, see Elisabeth Hall's article in *Garden Hist.* xxiii (2), 145–74. Cf. E.R.A.O., DDCC/17/6; D. [R. J.] Neave and D. Turnbull, *Landscaped Parks and Gardens of E. Yorks.* (E. Yorks. Georgian Soc., 1992), 22–3.
33   Survey of 1774 at E.R.A.O., DDCC(2)/Box 8/4; plans of *c.* 1780: ibid. DDCC/141/71; DDCC(2)/plan 15; Burton Constable Hall, plan of *c.* 1755; *Country Life*, 6 May 1982.
34   E.R.A.O., DDCC(2)/Box 8/4; DDCC(2)/plan 15;

[Hall] Burton Constable [28].
35   Drawing at Burton Constable Hall.
36   Traditional date apparently confirmed by minutes of meetings between Brown and Constable's agent, transcr. in *Garden Hist.* xxiii (2), 157.
37   The pavilion is not on earlier plans of the menagerie: Burton Constable Hall, plans of *c.* 1765, *c.* 1779; plan of *c.* 1780 at E.R.A.O., DDCC/141/71.
38   *Garden Hist.* xxiii (2), 159. The drive was shown on the plan of *c.* 1780: E.R.A.O., DDCC/141/71.
39   *Country Life*, 13 May 1982; Burton Constable Hall, design of 1785.

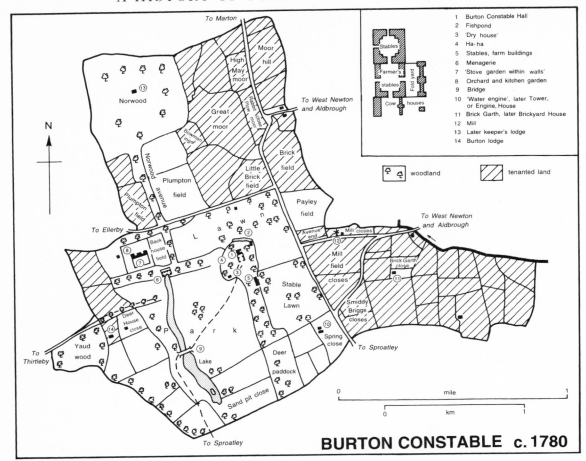

Legend:
1 Burton Constable Hall
2 Fishpond
3 'Dry house'
4 Ha-ha
5 Stables, farm buildings
6 Menagerie
7 'Stove garden within walls'
8 Orchard and kitchen garden
9 Bridge
10 'Water engine', later Tower, or Engine, House
11 Brick Garth, later Brickyard House
12 Mill
13 Later keeper's lodge
14 Burton lodge

woodland   tenanted land

BURTON CONSTABLE c. 1780

the south-west of the house, a 'dry house', or greenhouse,[40] which existed c. 1780, was refaced as an orangery in 1788–9 to designs by Thomas Atkinson.[41]

Norwood was felled at the end of the 18th century, and a private course for horse-racing and steeplechasing had been laid out there by 1838, when the Holderness Hunt meeting was transferred from Beverley to Burton Constable; the meeting remained there until c. 1850.[42] Early in the 19th century, the main farm buildings were converted into additional stables and others were replaced by a covered riding school.[43] The west lawn was then dug up to make formal gardens with topiary and artificial-stone statuary, and a large statue of a stag was placed at the end of a vista from the house c. 1860.[44] On the other side of the house, part of the old east avenue was planted with trees and the clumps

on the Lawn were multiplied and enlarged, while to the north-west Norwood avenue was infilled as another plantation.[45] New buildings included a second lodge, later New Lodge, in a neo-Jacobean style by James Blake which put up across the boundary in Sproatley in the 1860s.[46] Roughly contemporary were a neo-Tudor castellated house, called Tower, or Engine, House, which was built onto the early, octagonal tower south-east of the Hall,[47] and a gas works near the stables.[48] The deer herd, c. 600 strong in 1840, was given up, apparently in the late 19th century, and the deershed in the park was demolished.[49] A beagle pack was however maintained at Skirlaugh into the mid 20th century.[50] A large caravan park was created beside the lake in 1968,[51] and by 1995 a clubhouse had been built there. The grounds were then grazed by cattle, sheep, and horses

40 J. C. Loudon, *Encyclopaedia of Gardening* (1824), 815.
41 E.R.A.O., DDCC/141/71 (the plan is print. in *Garden Hist.* xiv (1), 15); [Hall] *Burton Constable* [28].
42 Race-bills at E.R.A.O., DDCC/17/12; Neave and Turnbull, op. cit. 24; O.S. Map 6", Yorks. CCXII (1855 edn.); below, econ. hist.; J. Fairfax-Blakeborough, *Northern Turf Hist.* ii. 59–60.
43 O.S. Map 6", Yorks. CCXII (1855 edn.).
44 Neave and Turnbull, op. cit. 24; [Hall] *Burton Constable* [28].
45 O.S. Map 6", Yorks. CCXII (1855 edn.). In 1860 a hundred trees were said to have been blown down in the park: E.R.A.O., PE/130/44.
46 Burton Constable Hall, design 1860; O.S. Map 1/2,500, Yorks. CCXXVII. 2 (1891 edn.).
47 [Hall] *Burton Constable*, 27, [28]; O.S. Map 6", Yorks. CCXXVII (1855 edn.); O.S. Map 1/2,500, Yorks. CCXXVII. 3 (1890 edn.).
48 Burton Constable Hall, plan of grounds, watermarked 1862; E.R.A.O., DDCC(2)/ bill for gas works 1860.
49 S. Neave, *Medieval Parks of E. Yorks.* 26; Poulson, *Holderness*, ii. 242, 249. Cf. O.S. Map 6", Yorks. CCXII (1855 edn.); O.S. Map 1/2,500, Yorks. CCXII. 14 (1891 edn.).
50 *Kelly's Dir. N. & E. R. Yorks.* (1929), 615.
51 Inf. from Mr. John Chichester-Constable, Burton Constable, 1995.

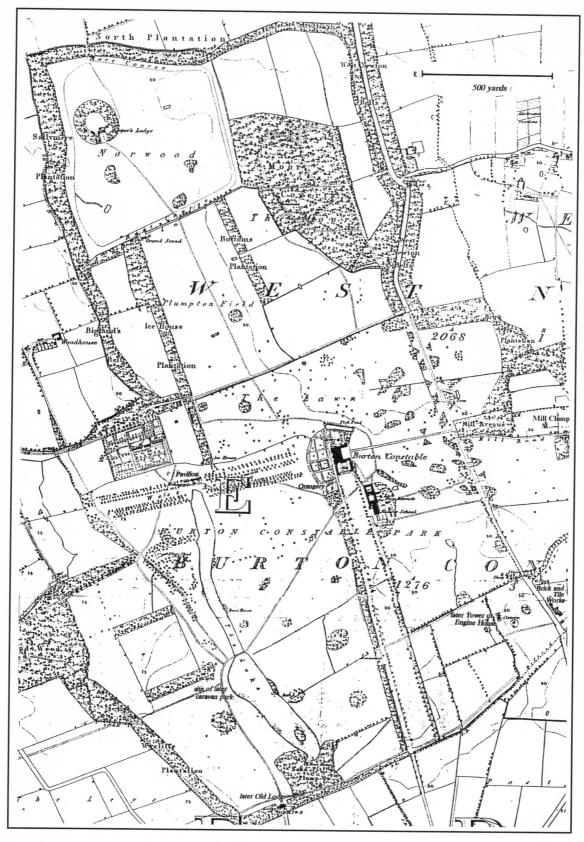

BURTON CONSTABLE IN 1852

associated with a riding school in the stables, but the walled kitchen garden was disused and many of its buildings had been demolished.

By 1190 Robert Constable had given Thornton abbey (Lincs.) a rent at Burton Constable.[52]

The rectorial tithes of Burton Constable were sold by William Thornton to Cuthbert Constable in 1738,[53] and were evidently later merged.

ECONOMIC HISTORY. COMMON LANDS AND INCLOSURE. In 1086 there were five ploughlands at Burton Constable but only one plough was then worked, on the demesne.[54] The open fields of Burton Constable included East field in 1447, and there was evidently also a western field or fields.[55] They had probably been converted to grassland by the 1560s, when evidence from tithe disputes suggests a prevalence of grassland and of pastoral farming there.[56] By 1621 the former East field was almost certainly represented by the 173-a. Mill field, East close, of 85 a., the 10-a. Paddock, and closes called Pailer field and Brick field, each of c. 50 a. Ridge and furrow could be seen throughout the east of the township in the 1940s,[57] and was evident still in the 1990s east of the Hall and on the southern boundary near Tower House. Ridge and furrow north-west of the Hall and elsewhere in the west of the township[58] suggests that the western field or fields had included the almost 400 a. which in 1621 lay in Plumpton field, Backhouse field, the Frith, the Brooms, and the Leys. Most of the western closes had apparently by then been emparked.[59]

In 1447 North, West, and White carrs provided grazing, and North and White carrs also meadow land.[60] Rough grazing may also have been enjoyed on the moor, later the Moors, but that area had evidently been inclosed by 1621, and in 1636 inhabitants of West Newton were presented for taking the lord's furze there.[61]

WOODLAND. A wood recorded from 1294[62] comprised 49 a. of woodland and 11 a. of pasture, all inclosed by a ditch, in 1336, when 7 a. of the underwood was cropped each year.[63] It was probably that wood which was called North-

wood, or Norwood, from the 15th century, when the lord's fisheries were also mentioned there;[64] other woodland, then named Westwood, was presumably that later called Yaud, or Old, wood.[65] The 94 a. of inclosed woodland recorded in 1578 was evidently Norwood, which in the 17th and 18th centuries comprised c. 105 a.; Yaud wood was not mentioned in 1578 but in the later period was of 20–25 a.[66] Much of the business of Burton Constable court from the 16th century was concerned with preventing passage through Norwood and unlicensed wood- and nut-gathering, and in 1611 the taking of eggs, young pheasants, bittern, and heron there was expressly forbidden.[67] Edward Constable sold over 700 ash trees in Norwood in the late 1790s, and there was then little woodland until new plantations were made in the 1820s.[68] By 1852 the area of woodland in the township had been more or less restored by the planting of Moor covert and belts of woodland, notably along the road and around the northern and western boundaries.[69] The woodlands of Burton Constable accounted for most of the 300 a. bearing trees there and in West Newton in 1905, and they were little changed thereafter.[70]

RECENT AGRICULTURE. In 1987 the 1,890 ha. (4,670 a.) returned under Burton Constable civil parish evidently included much land elsewhere, while apparently excluding at least part of the Hall's grounds.[71] Of the area given, 1,558 ha. (3,850 a.) were arable land and 320 ha. (791 a.) grassland; there were then more than 4,000 pigs and 2,000 poultry, and c. 400 sheep and the same number of cattle. The arable land included 75.4 ha. (186 a.) of field vegetables.[72]

In 1774 seven tenants held 530 a. of Burton Constable: one farm was of 224 a., another of 112 a., two of 50–99 a., one of 34 a., and there were two holdings of c. 10 a. each.[73] In the 19th century and earlier 20th most of the land was evidently managed by a bailiff as part of the Burton Constable Hall estate; there were also two farms, of 125 a. and 159 a., in 1851 and later up to five small farms.[74] A firm of nurserymen, also working at Coniston, rented c. 12 a. of gardens and hot-houses at the Hall from about 1880 until c. 1950.[75] A cowkeeper also worked at Burton Constable.[76] There were 15 holdings returned under Burton Constable civil parish in

[52] E.Y.C. iii, pp. 41–2.
[53] E.R.A.O., DDCC/6/8; above, Swine township, manors (rectory).   [54] V.C.H. Yorks. ii. 216.
[55] E.R.A.O., DDCC/18/6; below.
[56] B.I.H.R., CP. G. 1279, 1299.
[57] Hull Univ., Dept. of Geog., R.A.F. air photographs, run 334A, nos. 4138–40.
[58] Ibid. run 334A, no. 4141; run 334B, no. 3150.
[59] E.R.A.O., DDCC(2)/plan 1; above, manor [park].
[60] E.R.A.O., DDCC/18/6.
[61] Ibid. DDCC/18/3, s.v. Apr. 1636; DDCC(2)/plan 1; O.S. Map 6", Yorks. CCXII.SW. (1928 edn.).
[62] Yorks. Inq. ii, p. 160.
[63] P.R.O., C 135/47, no. 16.
[64] E.R.A.O., DDCC/18/1, s.v. 16 Feb. 1438.
[65] Ibid. DDCC/18/6; DDCC(2)/plan 1; O.S. Map 6", Yorks. CCXXVII (1855 edn.); O.S. Map 1/2,500, Yorks. CCXXVII. 2 (1891 edn.).
[66] Survey of 1578 at Burton Constable Hall, DDCC/141/68, p. 17; microfilm copy at E.R.A.O; 1621 plan at

E.R.A.O., DDCC(2)/plan 1; 1774 survey at ibid. DDCC(2)/Box 8/4.
[67] E.R.A.O., DDCC/18/2–3, 7.
[68] Ibid. DDCC/135/70; V.C.H. Yorks. i. 519; Poulson, Holderness, ii. 242.
[69] O.S. Map 6", Yorks. CCXII, XXCCVII (1855 edn.); cf. above, manor [grounds].
[70] Acreage Returns, 1905; O.S. Map 1/10,000, TA 13 NE. (1980 edn.).
[71] Only 2 ha. (5 a.) of woodland were returned, for instance.
[72] Inf. from Min. of Agric., Fish. & Food, Beverley, 1990; above, intro. [area].
[73] E.R.A.O., DDCC(2)/Box 8/4.
[74] P.R.O., HO 107/2365; directories; R.D.B., 1295/284/255.
[75] Bulmer, Dir. E. Yorks. (1892), 520–1; directories; O.S. Map 1/2,500, Yorks. CCXII. 14 (1891 edn.); inf. from Mr. John Chichester-Constable, Burton Constable, 1995.
[76] Directories.

1987, of which four were of 200–499 ha. (494–1,233 a.), one of 100–199 ha. (247–492 a.), four of 50–99 ha. (124–245 a.), and six of 10–49 ha. (25–121 a.).[77]

INDUSTRY. Brick field was named in 1621,[78] bricks for the building works at the Hall were burnt locally in the 18th century, presumably in or near Brick Garth close,[79] and there was a yard on the southern boundary in the mid 19th century.[80]

MILL. A windmill was recorded at Burton Constable in 1294,[81] and from the 17th to the mid 19th century a mill stood close to the eastern boundary. It was evidently demolished soon after 1828, but Mill clump and other place-names mark its site.[82]

LOCAL GOVERNMENT. Court records for Burton Constable manor include rolls for 1433–8, 1546–58, and 1593–1636,[83] a call roll of c. 1730,[84] and presentments from 1704 to 1789.[85] In the 15th century the manor comprised, besides Burton Constable, lands at West Marton, at Etherdwick, Tansterne, and West Newton, all in Aldbrough parish, at Owstwick in Roos, at Grimston in Garton, at Wassand in Sigglesthorne, and in Hilston and Sproatley parishes, but the court was mostly concerned with the agriculture and drainage of Burton Constable and West Newton. Officers elected included four manorial reeves, two wood-reeves, two mill-reeves, two 'gripp-', or dike-, reeves, an aletaster, and a constable for the hamlet. In the mid 16th century the court, which had view of frankpledge, also appointed a bylawman for Burton Constable. There were two meetings a year in the 18th century, when the courts were held at Marton and West Newton.

Burton Constable hamlet joined Skirlaugh poor-law union in 1837.[86] As part of West Newton with Burton Constable civil parish, it remained in Skirlaugh rural district until 1935. With the rest of the enlarged civil parish of Burton Constable, it was then taken into the new Holderness rural district and at reorganization in 1974 was incorporated in the Holderness district of Humberside.[87] In 1996 Burton Constable parish became part of a new East Riding unitary area.[88]

CHURCH. A 'chantry chaplain of Burton' was mentioned in the 1430s and a 'parish priest of Burton Constable' later in the century, and at its dissolution Swine priory was paying a wage to a curate there.[89] There was also said to have been a chapel of Burton Constable, endowed with tithes in that township, presumably by the priory as rector.[90] Although there may have been a chantry associated with the chapel in the Hall, most of this evidence probably relates to nearby Marton chapel.[91]

ROMAN CATHOLICISM. The Constables of Burton Constable were probably the most influential of the Roman Catholic families in Swine parish.[92] Their tenants and servants presumably worshipped in the family's chapel at the Hall until the later 17th century, when a mission was established nearby at Marton for most of them.[93] The chapel at the Hall was very likely one of the two Roman Catholic chapels, each with its own priest, recorded in Swine parish in 1743; it was still used occasionally in 1994.[94]

EDUCATION. Children from Burton Constable have gone to school at Marton, Ellerby, and Sproatley.[95]

CHARITY FOR THE POOR. Little is known of the administration of a charity for the poor of Burton Constable which was created by deed of 1770 and endowed with 12 a. A Scheme obtained in 1982 allowed the charity to be run as a relief in need trust for inhabitants of Burton Constable civil parish with a smaller charity benefiting Sproatley.[96] In 1985–6 the annual income of the two charities was almost £800, but no grants were made and there was a final balance of nearly £4,000.[97]

77 Inf. from Min. of Agric., Fish. & Food.
78 E.R.A.O., DDCC(2)/plan 1.
79 Ibid. DDCC/141/71; Country Life, 22 Apr. 1982.
80 O.S. Map 6″, Yorks. CCXXVII (1855 edn.); Kelly's Dir. N. & E. R. Yorks. (1872), 342.
81 Yorks. Inq. ii, p. 160.
82 E.R.A.O., DDCC(2)/plan 1; H. Teesdale, Map of Yorks. (1828); O.S. Map 6″, Yorks. CCXII (1855 edn.).
83 E.R.A.O., DDCC/18/1–3.
84 Ibid. DDCC/59/4.
85 Ibid. DDCC/18/7.
86 3rd Rep. Poor Law Com. 170.
87 Census.
88 Humberside (Structural Change) Order 1995, copy at E.R.A.O.

89 E.R.A.O., DDCC/18/1, s. vv. 5 Oct. 1433; 16 Feb. 1438; Test. Ebor. iii, p. 279; Miscellanea, ii (Y.A.S. Rec. Ser. lxxiv), p. 100.
90 B.I.H.R., CP. G. 1299; E.R.A.O., DDCC/17/23; Cal. Pat. 1575–8, p. 405.
91 Below, Marton, church.
92 Cal. Cttee. for Compounding, iii, p. 2147; Aveling, Post Reformation Catholicism, 66.
93 Below, Marton, Rom. Cath.
94 Herring's Visit iii, p. 127; iv, p. 217; Aveling, Post Reformation Catholicism, 53–4; local inf.
95 Directories.
96 Review of Char. Rep. 102; Humbs. Dir. of Char. 32; above, Sproatley, charities; Char. Com. reg. no. 810087.
97 E.R.A.O., CCH/116.

CONISTON

CONISTON hamlet lies 2 km. south-east of Swine village. The name was 'Coningesbi' in 1086, and it is uncertain whether it was an Anglian name later Scandinavianized, or the reverse; it may mean 'king's farm'.[98] Coniston, which comprised 602 a. (244 ha.),[99] was united with Thirtleby civil parish in 1935 as the new civil parish of Coniston, with an area of 1,358 a. (550 ha.).[1] In 1984 some 8 ha. (20 a.) of Coniston civil parish was transferred to Bilton, and in 1991 Coniston's area was 540 ha. (1,334 a.).[2] There were 56 poll-tax payers at Coniston in 1377,[3] and 13 houses there were assessed for hearth tax and 2 discharged in 1672.[4] Coniston's population was c. 110 in the 19th and early 20th century, 116 being recorded in 1931, when Coniston and Thirtleby together had 171 inhabitants. The population of the new civil parish increased to 269 in 1951, and 248 of the usual 252 inhabitants were present in 1991.[5]

CONISTON hamlet was built along a street which continued westwards to Swine and south-eastwards to Thirtleby and from which side lanes led to Skirlaugh and Ganstead. A stream flowing southwards through the settlement was formerly fed by a small mere on the north side of the hamlet.[6] Drainage improvements carried out after the inclosure of Coniston in 1790 also included the draining of another, small mere in the northern field.[7] The side lanes of Coniston were later incorporated into the main Hull–Bridlington road, and in the mid 20th century many bungalows and other houses were built alongside the stretch to Ganstead. The main road ran through Coniston hamlet until soon after 1970, when an eastern by-pass was made.[8] The older buildings include one or two 19th-century farmhouses and the newer houses 16 built by Holderness rural district council.[9] North End Farm was built in the later 19th century.[10]

There were one or two licensed houses at Coniston in the later 18th century and in the 1820s one called the Blue Bell.[11] By 1840 that or another house was called the Stag and Hounds; renamed the Blacksmith's Arms c. 1860,[12] it still

traded in 1994. Two acres awarded in 1790 as a gravel pit for road repairs had by 1852 been divided into allotment gardens, which were used until c. 1970.[13] A village hall was built in or shortly before 1951.[14]

MANOR AND OTHER ESTATES. In 1066 Morkar held 4 carucates at Coniston as soke of Mappleton manor; by 1086 the estate had passed to Drew de Bevrère.[15] It was later part of the Aumale fee.

Richard of Ottringham (fl. c. 1140) held land at Coniston of the count of Aumale.[16] It descended, as at Ottringham, to the Lasceles family.[17] In the mid 13th century J(ohn) de Lasceles and William de Lasceles, probably John's son (d. c. 1230) or grandson (fl. 1248),[18] each held 2 carucates at Coniston,[19] and William de Lasceles, either the grandson or his son,[20] was tenant of an indeterminate estate there, wholly occupied by undertenants, in the 1280s. He (d. by 1294) was succeeded by his son John.[21]

Pagan Blussell (Blassell) evidently held nearly 3 carucates at Coniston, practically all of which he gave to Thornton abbey (Lincs.) before 1190; the lordship and the small demesne estate remaining descended to Hugh Blassell (fl. 1280s).[22] As CONISTON manor, the abbey's estate passed to the Crown at the Dissolution.[23] Some land at Coniston formerly belonging to the abbey was granted as concealed land to John and William Marsh in 1576.[24] The manor, which extended into Sutton and Drypool and then included at Coniston houses and lands let for c. £7 a year and court profits of a few shillings, was granted in 1614 to William Whitmore and Edmund Sawyer in fee farm.[25]

It was presumably the same manor which Elizabeth Egleston and others sold to Richard Allanson (Allatson) in 1705[26] and which had descended to his daughter Elizabeth Fysh by 1721.[27] It passed to her son Tristram Fysh (d. by 1742) and then to his sister Catherine Coppinger, who was succeeded by her son Fysh

98 P.N. Yorks. E.R. (E.P.N.S.), 47; G. F. Jensen, Scand. Settlement Names in Yorks. 8, 24.
99 O.S. Map 6″, Yorks. CCXII, CCXXVII (1855 edn.).
1 Census, 1931 (pt. ii).
2 Ibid. 1991; E.R.A.O., Holderness (Parishes) Order 1983; O.S. Map 1/2,500, Yorks. CCXXVII. 6 (1890 edn.).
3 P.R.O., E 179/202/60, m. 37.
4 Hearth Tax, 60.
5 V.C.H. Yorks. iii. 494; Census, 1901–91.
6 E.R.A.O., IA. Coniston; O.S. Map 6″, Yorks. CCXXVII (1855 edn.).
7 Cf. E.R.A.O., IA. Coniston; O.S. Map 6″, Yorks. CCXXVII (1855 edn.).
8 O.S. Map 6″, Yorks. CCXXVII (1855 edn.); E.R.C.C. Mins. 1970–1, 27–8.
9 R.D.B., 854/451/376; 875/188/101; 875/189/102.
10 O.S. Map 1/10,000, TA 13 NE. (1980 edn.); O.S. Map 1/2,500, Yorks. CCXXVII. 1 (1891 edn.).
11 E.R.A.O., QDT/2/7, 9.
12 Ibid. DDPK/11/1; directories; O.S. Map 6″, Yorks.

CCXXVII (1855 edn.); O.S. Map 1/2,500, Yorks. CCXXVII. 1 (1891 edn.).
13 R.D.B., BG/291/39; E.R.A.O., IA. Coniston; O.S. Map 6″, Yorks. CCXXVII (1855 edn.); inf. from Mr. A. D. Richardson, Thirtleby, 1995.
14 R.D.B., 898/131/116.
15 V.C.H. Yorks. ii. 265.
16 E.Y.C. iii, p. 43.
17 V.C.H. Yorks. E.R. v. 77–8.
18 E.Y.C. iii, p. 82; Cur. Reg. R. xv, p. 12; Close R. 1247–51, 30.
19 Kirkby's Inquest, 373.   20 'Meaux Cart.' 466–7.
21 Feud. Aids, vi. 40; Kirkby's Inquest, 244; Cal. Inq. p.m. iii, p. 162; iv, p. 353.
22 E.Y.C. iii, pp. 41–2; Cal. Inq. p.m. iv, p. 356.
23 P.R.O., SC 6/Hen. VIII/2022, m. 80 and d.
24 Cal. Pat. 1575–8, p. 28.
25 P.R.O., C 66/1999, no. 3.
26 Ibid. CP 25(2)/983/4 Anne Trin. no. 13.
27 Ibid. CP 25(2)/1084/7 Geo. I East. no. 7.

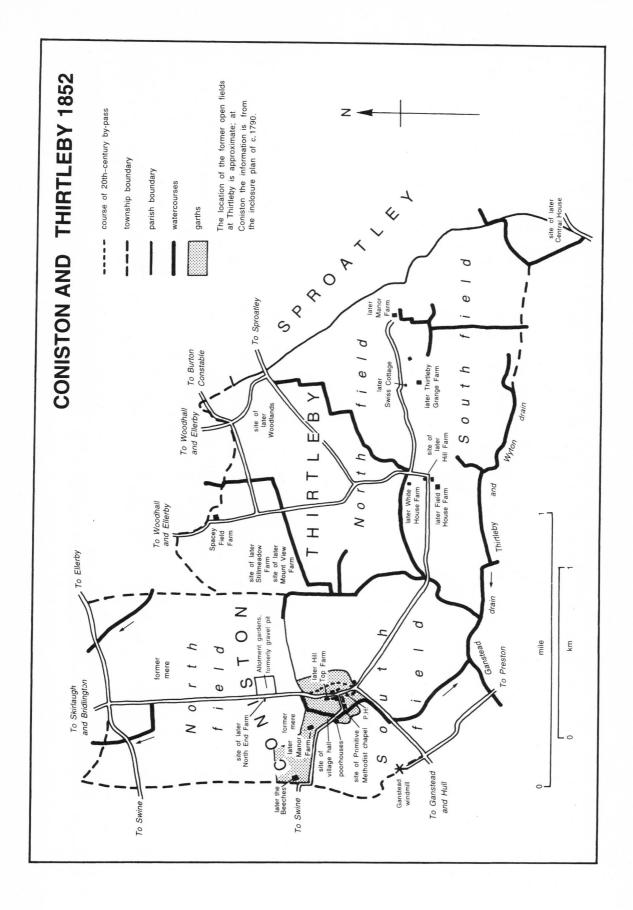

CONISTON AND THIRTLEBY 1852

course of 20th-century by-pass
township boundary
parish boundary
watercourses
garths

The location of the former open fields
at Thirtleby is approximate; at
Coniston the information is from
the inclosure plan of c.1790.

N

To Sproatley

SPROATLEY

To Burton
Constable

later
Manor
Farm

site of later
Central House

To Woodhall
and Ellerby

site of later
Woodlands

North field

later
Swiss Cottage

THIRTLEBY

later Thirtleby
Grange Farm

South field

To Woodhall
and Ellerby

Spacey
Field
Farm

site of later
Stillmeadow
Farm

site of later
Mount View
Farm

site of
later
Hill Farm

Wyton drain

To Ellerby

later White
House Farm

later Field
House Farm

Thirtleby

and

To Skirlaugh
and Bridlington

former
mere

North

field

CONISTON

Allotment gardens,
formerly gravel pit

drain

Ganstead

To Preston

site of later
North End Farm

later Hill
Top Farm

site of
village hall

South

field

former
mere

later
Manor
Farm

poorhouses

site of Primitive
Methodist chapel P.H.

mile

km

later the
Beeches

To Swine

To Swine

Ganstead
windmill

To Ganstead
and Hull

0

1

0

1

0

Coppinger. In 1765 he sold the manor to Robert Wilberforce (d. 1768).[28] Besides rents, the manor then comprised the manor house and another house, 2 carucates and 2 bovates, and c. 40 a. at Coniston and Ellerby.[29] At inclosure in 1790, the lord of the manor was Robert's son William Wilberforce, the philanthropist, who was awarded 304 a. and 73 a. more with Jane Tennyson; his allotments included 13 a. for glebe land, and his mother Elizabeth (d. 1798) also received 104 a. and rents for tithes.[30] From Wilberforce (d. 1833) the estate, which comprised nearly 500 a. in three farms in 1865,[31] descended to W. B. Wilberforce (d. 1913)[32] and then presumably to his son William. In 1920 the Wilberforce trustees sold the estate, comprising a 494-a. farm and several houses, to William England (d. 1932), who left his estate at Coniston and Swine to his son James.[33] House plots and some of the buildings were sold in the 1930s,[34] and in 1944 the farm, remaining buildings, and 487 a., mostly at Coniston, were bought by J. A. Foxton (d. 1954).[35] In 1974 the farm was vested in B. P. Foxton, who had earlier bought the 88-a. Hill Top farm.[36] In 1994 Manor farm and the other land at Coniston were conveyed to Foxton Farmers Ltd.[37]

Other tenants of the Aumale fee at Coniston included the Suttons, who held 1 carucate in the late 13th century,[38] and in the 14th century the Helpstons.[39] Swine priory had land at Coniston worth £2 a year in 1535.[40]

A manor of Coniston sold by Alexander Rishworth and his wife Beatrice to Richard Rogers in 1571[41] may have been elsewhere, and no more is known of it.

The rectorial tithes of Coniston, together with 'Leconby farm', another part of Swine rectory, possibly at Coniston, were bought in 1681 by Thomas Johnson.[42] Compositions were then paid for hay tithes.[43] Some tithes at Coniston were sold in 1773.[44] At inclosure in 1790, the rectorial estate there belonged, like the manor, to the Wilberforces; William Wilberforce was then awarded 13 a. for glebe land and his mother Elizabeth 104 a. and rents totalling £4 17s. 7d. for tithes.[45]

ECONOMIC HISTORY. COMMON LANDS AND INCLOSURE. In 1609 the commonable lands of Coniston included North and South fields and a stinted pasture.[46] The township was inclosed in 1790 under an Act of 1789.[47] By then the tillage had evidently been reduced by the making of closes in the village.[48] Some 570 a. was dealt with. South field then contained 264 a., North field 135 a., and North field, Furlongs, and Whin close 169 a. Whin close, possibly the common pasture recorded earlier, and Furlongs were in the north-east of the township. Besides the 481 a. awarded to William Wilberforce, lord of the manor, Elizabeth Wilberforce, and Jane Tennyson,[49] Robert Burton received 86 a., and there were two small allotments.

LATER AGRICULTURE. In 1987 the area returned under Coniston civil parish was 1,175 ha. (2,903 a.), which evidently included land elsewhere. Arable land accounted for 907 ha. (2,241 a.), grassland for 250 ha. (618 a.), and woodland for 5.4 ha. (13 a.); there were then almost 18,000 poultry, some 4,000 pigs, and more than 800 cattle.[50]

Coniston lay in two to five farms in the 19th and earlier 20th century, only one of which was of 150 a. or more.[51] The augmented area returned under the civil parish in 1987 was divided into 11 holdings: one exceeded 200 ha. (494 a.), another was of 100–199 ha. (247–492 a.), two of 10–49 ha. (25–121 a.), and seven of under 10 ha.[52] A gardener worked at Coniston in 1851; a firm of nurserymen, also active at Burton Constable, had c. 25 a. there in 1892, and in 1905 a Coniston blacksmith specialized in heating apparatuses for greenhouses.[53] In 1987 vegetables were grown on 3.9 ha. (10 a.) of the area returned under Coniston civil parish.[54] There was a cowkeeper at Coniston c. 1930.[55]

NON-AGRICULTURAL EMPLOYMENT has included the digging of a little sand and gravel,[56] and in 1994 Coniston had a garage and a building and joinery concern.

MILL. A maltster of Coniston was recorded in 1690, and a windmill stood in the township's South field in the 18th century.[57]

28 For Wilberforces, Burke, *Land. Gent.* (1952), 2714–16.
29 E.R.A.O., DDX/301/12–13.
30 R.D.B., BG/291/39. An allotment to Wilberforce, shown on the plan but omitted from the award, has been included here: cf. E.R.A.O., IA. Coniston.
31 E.R.A.O., DDPK/11/1.
32 R.D.B., FB/219/236; 99/123/114 (1907); Burke, *Land. Gent.* (1972), 950–3.
33 R.D.B., 224/50/40; 676/384/303.
34 Ibid. *passim.*   35 Ibid. 677/364/294.
36 Ibid. 1070/527/468; 1093/233/204; 1887/525/427.
37 Inf. from Mr. P. Foxton, Coniston, 1995.
38 *Cal. Inq. p.m.* iii, pp. 2–3; iv, p. 355. Cf. H.U.L., DHO/6/101.
39 *Cal. Inq. p.m.* viii, p. 356; ix, p. 425.
40 P.R.O., E 309/3/9 Eliz./6, no. 1; *Valor Eccl.* (Rec. Com.), v. 114.
41 *Yorks. Fines,* ii. 2.
42 E.R.A.O., DDCC/111/31; DDRI/30/1; above, Swine township, manors (rectory).
43 B.I.H.R., CP. H. 4217.
44 P.R.O., CP 25(2)/1460/13 Geo. III Trin. no. 734.

45 R.D.B., BG/291/39; Burke, *Land. Gent.* (1952), 2714–16.
46 P.R.O., LR 2/230, ff. 232–4.
47 29 Geo. III, c. 41 (Priv. Act); R.D.B., BG/291/39; E.R.A.O., IA. Coniston. An allotment shown on the plan but omitted from the award is included here.
48 For ridge and furrow in the garths, Hull Univ., Dept. of Geog., Fairey Surveys air photographs, run 365B, nos. 2140–1.
49 Above, manor.
50 Inf. from Min. of Agric., Fish. & Food, Beverley, 1990.
51 P.R.O., HO 107/2365; directories.
52 Inf. from Min. of Agric., Fish. & Food; above, previous para.
53 P.R.O., HO 107/2365; Bulmer, *Dir. E. Yorks.* (1892), 520–1; O.S. Map 1/2,500, Yorks. CCXXVII. 1 (1891 edn.); directories.
54 Inf. from Min. of Agric., Fish. & Food.
55 Directories.
56 O.S. Map 1/2,500, Yorks. CCXXVII. 1 (1891 edn.).
57 R.D.B., R/238/567; BG/291/39; B.I.H.R., CP. H. 4217.

LOCAL GOVERNMENT. Poorhouses were maintained at Coniston.[58] Permanent relief was given to two people and three were relieved occasionally in 1802–3, and between 1812 and 1815 the township had 4–6 on permanent and 4–7 on occasional relief.[59] Coniston joined Skirlaugh poor-law union in 1837,[60] and the township, later civil parish, remained in Skirlaugh rural district until 1935. As part of the enlarged civil parish of Coniston, it was then included in the new Holderness rural district and at reorganization in 1974 in the Holderness district of Humberside.[61] In 1996 Coniston parish became part of a new East Riding unitary area.[62]

NONCONFORMITY. Most of the houses registered for protestant worship at 'Coniston' in 1793, 1795, 1808, and 1809 were probably at other Conistons.[63] The schoolroom was said to have been used in the early 1800s by an Independent congregation, established after missionary work from Fish Street chapel, Hull.[64] In 1829 the Wesleyan Methodists provided a chapel just over the boundary in Swine township by converting two cottages rented from the Wilberforces; the chapel was almost certainly closed on the opening in the 1890s of Swine chapel,[65] and it has been demolished. The Primitive Methodists built a chapel at Coniston in 1872,[66] and extended it with a schoolroom in 1893.[67] Later the Methodist chapel,[68] it was closed in 1991 and was disused in 1995.[69]

EDUCATION. About 1790 William Wilberforce began a school at Coniston, providing the schoolroom, a master's house, and £10 a year, for which 10 children were taught free. In 1833 the school was attended by 20 boys and girls, all then paid for by their parents.[70] It was evidently closed soon afterwards, and in 1871 children from Coniston attended Swine school.[71] A dame's school for infants was recorded in 1872.[72]

ELLERBY

THE hamlet of Ellerby lies 4 km. north-east of Swine village. Since the Middle Ages there have been subsidiary settlements at Dowthorpe and Oubrough, both c. 1 km. west of the hamlet, at Woodhall, the same distance south, and at Langthorpe, 2 km. to the north. Woodhall was the site of the chief manor and Oubrough and Langthorpe the locations of granges of Swine priory.[73] The opening near Langthorpe of Ellerby station in the 1860s[74] led to the building along the Marton road there of the group of houses now called New Ellerby. The name Ellerby, meaning 'Elfweard's farm', is an Anglo-Scandinavian hybrid; Dowthorpe, 'Dufa's hamlet', and probably also Langthorpe, or 'Lambi's village', are Scandinavian names, and Oubrough, 'the owl-haunted stronghold', is Anglian.[75]

Ellerby contained 2,248 a. (910 ha.) until 1952 when the civil parish was slightly enlarged at the expense of Burton Constable.[76] In 1984 part of New Ellerby lying in Burton Constable civil parish, comprising some 10 ha. (25 a.), was transferred to Ellerby, which in 1991 had 925 ha. (2,286 a.).[77] In 1377 there were 110 poll-tax payers at Ellerby, Dowthorpe, Langthorpe, and Thirtleby.[78] In 1672 Ellerby, evidently including Langthorpe and presumably also Dowthorpe, Oubrough, and Woodhall, had 26 houses assessed for hearth tax.[79] Numbers at Ellerby rose almost uninterruptedly from 151 in 1801 to 358 in 1901, before declining to 323 in 1931. About 40 people were gained from Burton Constable in 1952, and Ellerby's population was 405 in 1961. It fell to 349 in 1971 but had recovered by 1991, when those normally resident numbered 396 and 384 were present.[80]

ELLERBY hamlet mostly straggles down a street running along some of the highest land in the parish, but at its southern end a more coherent group of buildings stands in or near a short side lane, the survivor of a pair of western spurs off the street. There was formerly a green at the south end; it was built on in the 18th century[81] and may also have included later closes to the east of the street, one called Intack in 1820 and the Green in 1852 and the adjoining close used for allotment gardens by the mid 19th century.[82] Most of the c. 40 houses were built in the mid and late 20th century, and they include

[58] Ibid. BG/291/39; O.S. Map 6″, Yorks. CCXXVII (1855 edn.).
[59] *Poor Law Abstract, 1804*, pp. 592–3; *1818*, pp. 520–1.
[60] *3rd Rep. Poor Law Com.* 170.
[61] *Census.*
[62] Humberside (Structural Change) Order 1995, copy at E.R.A.O.
[63] B.I.H.R., Fac. Bk. 3, pp. 9, 466, 524; P.R.O., RG 31/5, nos. 1087, 2263.
[64] C. E. Darwent, *Story of Fish St. Ch., Hull* (1899), 129, 132.
[65] P.R.O., HO 129/522/2/5/2; E.R.A.O., DDPK/11/1; ibid. MRH/1/28; O.S. Map 6″, Yorks. CCXXVII (1855 edn.); O.S. Map 1/2,500, Yorks. CCXXVII. 1 (1891 edn.); above, Swine township, nonconf.
[66] O.N.S. (Birkdale), Worship Reg. no. 21432; datestones.
[67] R.D.B., 54/498/451 (1892); 375/490/404; datestone.
[68] R.D.B., 680/69/56.
[69] D. [R. J.] and S. Neave, *E.R. Chapels and Meeting*

Ho. (E. Yorks. Loc. Hist. Soc.), 48; inf. from the Revd. M. Wilson, Sutton, 1995.
[70] *Educ. Enq. Abstract*, 1096.
[71] *Returns relating to Elem. Educ.* 472–3.
[72] E.R.A.O., SL/106/1, s.v. 18 Oct.
[73] Below, manors (Oubrough, Langthorpe, Woodhall).
[74] Above, general intro. [rlys.].
[75] *P.N. Yorks. E.R.* (E.P.N.S.), 47–8; G. F. Jensen, *Scand. Settlement Names in Yorks.* 26, 57, 62.
[76] E.R.A.O., CCO/464; O.S. Map 6″, Yorks. CCXI, CCXII, CCXXVII (1855 edn.); *Census*, 1961.
[77] *Census*, 1991; E.R.A.O., Holderness (Parishes) Order 1983; O.S. Map 1/2,500, Yorks. CCXII. 6, 10 (1891 edn.).
[78] P.R.O., E 179/202/60, m. 82.
[79] *Hearth Tax*, 60; below, manors (Langthorpe).
[80] *V.C.H. Yorks.* iii. 494; *Census*, 1901–91.
[81] E.R.A.O., DDX/301/30; ibid. DDCC/108/25.
[82] Ibid. DDCC/108/68; O.S. Map 6″, Yorks. CCXII (1855 edn.); O.S. Map 1/2,500, Yorks. CCXII. 14 (1891 edn.).

seven council houses.[83] The pantiled Manor Farm[84] dates from the early 18th century. In the later 18th century one or two houses were licensed at Ellerby, and the Blue Bell, named in the 1820s,[85] still existed in 1994.

At NEW ELLERBY, the Railway inn was trading by 1872[86] and remained in 1994. The c. 25 houses there in 1889, most of them in Gladstone and Granville Terraces, were joined by eight council houses[87] and many others in the mid 20th century, and in 1995 there were nearly 100 houses at New Ellerby. Marton Grange Farm there, of one storey with dormers, probably dates from the 18th century.[88] A childrens' playing field was provided at New Ellerby in the 1970s.[89]

Away from the hamlets, a field west of the main Hull–Bridlington road was used for sports in the mid 20th century.[90] A barn at a garden centre nearby was used c. 1990 for a restaurant, before being re-converted into the Gardeners' Arms.[91]

MANORS AND OTHER ESTATES. A manor of *ELLERBY*, comprising 4 carucates, was said to have been held in 1066 by Fran, Elaf, Mann, Thorbiorn, and Ramkel, but later only Fran son of Thor was named as the tenant. It passed to William Malet and, after his deprivation c. 1070, to Drew de Bevrère, whose undertenant Tibbald occupied it in 1086.[92] It was later part of the Aumale fee, which passed with Burstwick manor to the Crown and its grantees.[93]

Herbert de St. Quintin (d. by 1223) almost certainly had an estate in Ellerby by 1201,[94] and in 1223 and 1224 his widow Agnes claimed dower in c. 10 carucates at Ellerby, Dowthorpe, and Thirtleby from Herbert's son William de St. Quintin.[95] The St. Quintins' holding in those places and Langthorpe was later put at 11 carucates.[96] In 1287 William's son (Sir) Herbert held 5 carucates and 5 bovates in Ellerby and Thirtleby in demesne, and his undertenants held c. 4½ carucates at Thirtleby and Dowthorpe.[97]

The demesne estate then and later formed *WOODHALL* manor, which was held of the Crown as successor to the counts of Aumale as ⅐ knight's fee.[98] Sir Herbert (d. 1302) was succeeded by his grandson (Sir) Herbert, named as lord of Ellerby in 1316.[99] The last Herbert's widow Laura held Woodhall manor in dower in 1350.[1] The St. Quintins' estate later descended with Mappleton to the FitzHughs[2] and their successors, the Fienneses.[3] Anne (d. 1595), widow of Gregory Fiennes, Lord Dacre, made George Goring her executor,[4] and he sold the estate, of just over 1,000 a., in lots.[5] Thomas Darrell bought Woodhall manor and c. 700 a. in 1598 and sold the manor with c. 380 a. to Marmaduke Langdale in 1599.[6] Langdale died in 1611 holding a large estate in the parish, composed of former monastic and other land; besides Woodhall, it included land at Coniston, Dowthorpe, and Langthorpe.[7] He was succeeded by his great-nephew William Langdale (d. 1645) and then by William's son Philip (d. 1648)[8] and grandson (Sir) William Langdale[9] (d. by 1685). Sir William's son Philip inherited Woodhall[10] and sold the manor with c. 320 a. there and at Ellerby to Joseph Fernley, a Hull merchant, in 1700.[11] Fernley (d. 1724) was succeeded in turn by his widow Sarah (d. 1745) and daughter Jane Lazenby (d. c. 1775). The manor then passed to Sarah Fernley's great-nephew Henry Maister (d. 1812). Maister bought more land in Ellerby in 1808 and left the Woodhall estate to his nephew H. W. Maister (d. 1846), whose nephew and others sold it, then comprising 455 a., to Sir Thomas Constable, Bt., in 1849.[12] Constable already had 270 a. in Ellerby.[13] In 1963 the Chichester-Constables' estate in Ellerby included c. 190 a. in Manor and Woodhouse farms;[14] both farms and other properties had been sold by 1995, Manor farm to Foxton Farmers Ltd., but Wood Hall, Wood Hall farm, and parkland there then remained with Mr. John Chichester-Constable's daughter, Rodrica Straker.[15]

The chief house at Woodhall, recorded from 1303,[16] stood on an extensive, moated site; much of the moat, now largely dry, remained in 1995.[17] In 1814–15 H. W. Maister built a new house

[83] R.D.B., 588/494/383; 609/620/484; 1134/271/242.
[84] E.R.A.O., DDCC/141/71 (plan of Ellerby no. 2).
[85] Ibid. QDT/2/7, 9.
[86] O.S. Map 6″, Yorks. CCXII (1855 edn.); *Kelly's Dir. N. & E. R. Yorks.* (1872), 552.
[87] R.D.B., 883/565/487; 923/543/459; O.S. Map 1/2,500, Yorks. CCXII. 10 (1891 edn.).
[88] It was shown c. 1775: E.R.A.O., DDCC/141/71 (plan of Marton). [89] E.R.A.O., charities index slip.
[90] R.D.B., 1523/480/421.
[91] Inf. from the Gardeners' Arms, 1995.
[92] *V.C.H. Yorks.* ii. 167–8, 268, 295.
[93] *V.C.H. Yorks. E.R.* v. 9–10.
[94] Below, Thirtleby, manor.
[95] *Cur. Reg. R.* v. 10; xi, pp. 265, 303, 538–9. For fam., *Early Yorks. Fam.* (Y.A.S. Rec. Ser. cxxxv), 79–80; English, *Holderness,* 150; *Complete Peerage;* J. Foster, *Pedigrees of Yorks.* iii.
[96] H.U.L., DHO/16/38; *Kirkby's Inquest,* 373.
[97] *Cal. Inq. p.m.* iv, p. 357.
[98] Ibid. ix, p. 26; *Cal. Chart. R.* 1257–1300, 328.
[99] *Cal. Inq. p.m.* iv, p. 95; *Feud. Aids,* vi. 164.
[1] *Cal. Inq. p.m.* ix, p. 26; *Cal. Inq. Misc.* iii, pp. 18–19.

[2] P.R.O., C 139/34, no. 45; C 139/151, no. 43; *Cal. Inq. p.m. Hen. VII,* i, pp. 115–16; *Complete Peerage,* s.v. Fitz-Hugh; below, Mappleton, manors.
[3] P.R.O., C 142/56, no. 68.
[4] Ibid. C 142/246, no. 122; *Complete Peerage,* s.v. Dacre.
[5] E.R.A.O., DDCC/35/37–40; DDCC/108/1; *Yorks. Fines,* iv. 59.   [6] E.R.A.O., DDCC/108/2.
[7] P.R.O., C 142/337, no. 81; for the Langdales, *Y.A.J.* xi, facing p. 372.
[8] E.R.A.O., DDCC/108/31; *Y.A.J.* xi. 429–31; *Yorks. Fines, 1603–14,* 202.   [9] H.U.L., DDLA/33/14.
[10] E.R.A.O., DDCC/108/6; DDCC/111/32.
[11] Ibid. DDCC/35/31.
[12] Ibid. DDCC/108/28, 40, 48, 56; Poulson, *Holderness,* ii. 257; M. E. Ingram, *Maisters of Kingston upon Hull 1560–1840,* pedigree facing p. 122.
[13] E.R.A.O., PE/104/105.
[14] R.D.B., 1295/284/255.
[15] Inf. from Mr. John Chichester-Constable, Burton Constable, 1995, and Mr. B. P. Foxton, Langthorpe, 1995.
[16] *Yorks. Inq.* iv, p. 32.
[17] E.R.A.O., DDCC/35/31; O.S. Map 6″, Yorks. CCXII (1855 edn.); Poulson, *Holderness,* ii. 258.

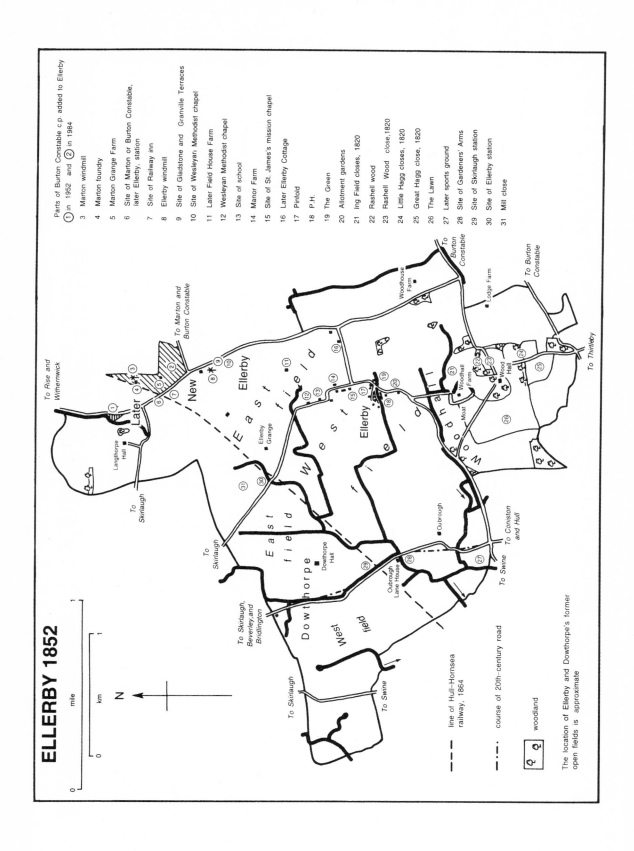

ELLERBY 1852

Parts of Burton Constable c.p. added to Ellerby
① in 1952 and ② in 1984

3   Marton windmill
4   Marton foundry
5   Marton Grange Farm
6   Site of Marton or Burton Constable, later Ellerby, station
7   Site of Railway inn
8   Ellerby windmill
9   Site of Gladstone and Granville Terraces
10 Site of Wesleyan Methodist chapel
11 Later Field House Farm
12 Wesleyan Methodist chapel
13 Site of school
14 Manor Farm
15 Site of St. James's mission chapel
16 Later Ellerby Cottage
17 Pinfold
18 P.H.
19 The Green
20 Allotment gardens
21 Ing Field closes, 1820
22 Rashell wood
23 Rashell Wood close, 1820
24 Little Hagg closes, 1820
25 Great Hagg close, 1820
26 The Lawn
27 Later sports ground
28 Site of Gardeners' Arms
29 Site of Skirlaugh station
30 Site of Ellerby station
31 Mill close

——— line of Hull–Hornsea railway, 1864

—·—·— course of 20th-century road

🌳🌳 woodland

The location of Ellerby and Dowthorpe's former open fields is approximate

300 m. to the south. That house, which is of grey brick and in the Italianate villa style, has an asymmetrical plan with a round tower at one corner and a service wing, now partly demolished, which joins the main block at 45 degrees and formerly terminated in the stable court. An unnamed London architect was said to have built the house or to have superintended its design,[18] and it has been attributed to John Nash[19] and Robert Lugar,[20] as well as to Charles Mountain of Hull.[21] A 58-a. park, later the Lawn, had been made by 1820.[22] The old house, which was rebuilt in the late 18th century, has been used since at least the 19th as a farmhouse.[23]

In 1066 Thorfridh held the 2-carucate *OUBROUGH* manor. It had passed to Drew de Bevrère by 1086, when it was occupied by his undertenant Frumold,[24] and it later formed part of the Aumale fee. Oubrough, with other land in Holderness, was evidently granted by a count of Aumale to his butler.[25] In 1252 the butler's fee was held by Amand the butler's daughter Beatrice de Friboys and John de Surdeval, presumably the heir of Amand's daughter Hawise de Surdeval.[26] As at Benningholme, the butler's fee at Oubrough was evidently bought from Geoffrey Vernon by Simon Constable, who was recorded as the Aumale tenant there in 1284–5.[27] John of Routh (d. by 1311) held an estate at Oubrough under Simon's son Robert.[28]

Swine priory was the demesne tenant of all 2 carucates at Oubrough by 1276,[29] and the 297-a. Oubrough grange was among the dissolved priory's lands granted in 1540 to Sir Richard Gresham and returned to the Crown by exchange in 1544.[30] Oubrough grange was sold by the Crown to Sir John Constable and his son Henry in 1557,[31] by Henry Constable to Thomas Bamburgh in 1582,[32] and by Bamburgh's son Humphrey[33] to John Legard in 1597. It then descended in the Legards of Ganton[34] until 1726, when Sir Thomas Legard, Bt., sold the estate, of *c.* 430 a. in three farms, to the Revd. John Moorhouse.[35] Moorhouse (d. 1740) left a son John (d. 1764),[36] whose heirs were his daughters Mary Bramley and Sarah Brown. In

1791 the so-called manor of Oubrough, the grange farms, and a house and land at Arnold and North and South Skirlaugh, were partitioned: Mrs. Bramley was awarded a moiety of the manor and two of the farms with 232 a. and Mrs. Brown the other moiety, a farm of 216 a., and the house and land at North and South Skirlaugh. Mrs. Brown's share has not been traced further. Mary Bramley (d. 1801) was succeeded in her share of Oubrough by her son Thomas Bramley (d. 1804), whose trustees sold it to C. E. Broadley in 1805. Broadley (d. 1809) already owned 377 a. at Dowthorpe,[37] and in 1836 his son C. B. Broadley sold both estates to John Beadle (d. 1869). They were bought by the Crown in 1870, and later descended with Swine manor.[38] In 1962 the Crown bought the 214-a. Oubrough House farm, evidently the farm awarded earlier to Mrs. Brown.[39] In 1995 the Crown's estate of Dowthorpe Hall comprised 325 ha. (803 a.).[40]

In 1066 Ulf held 3 carucates at *DOWTHORPE* as soke of his manor of Aldbrough; they had passed to Drew de Bevrère by 1086,[41] and were later part of the Aumale fee. Land at Dowthorpe was held of the counts of Aumale by the St. Quintins and of them by the Doles. In 1223 Roger Dole was the tenant of 1½ carucate there, and in 1348 his namesake was said to hold 2 carucates.[42] It may have been the same estate which Sir Robert Tyrwhit held there in 1575 and which his son William sold in 1588 to Marmaduke Langdale.[43] It later descended like Woodhall to William Langdale, who had 364 a. there in 1634, and his successor (Sir) William Langdale.[44] No more is heard of it until 1744, when Dorothy Colston devised a third share in the Dowthorpe estate to her sisters Elizabeth and Ann, who presumably held the other shares. Elizabeth (d. by 1758) evidently succeeded to the whole, which she devised to her neice Elizabeth, wife of Isaac Webster.[45] Webster (d. *c.* 1795) was succeeded by his son Isaac, who sold the 377-a. estate to C. E. Broadley in 1798.[46] Dowthorpe later descended with Broadley's estate at Oubrough.[47] Dowthorpe Hall, named in 1760,[48] was used as a farmhouse *c.* 1840.[49] The

[18] E.R.A.O., DDCC/108/28, 68; Poulson, *Holderness*, ii. 257; Ingram, op. cit. 108, 130.
[19] M. Mansbridge, *John Nash: a complete catalogue* (1991), p. 198.
[20] Pevsner and Neave, *Yorks. E.R.* 400.
[21] Pevsner, *Yorks. E.R.* 373, pl. 92; J. Summerson, *Life and Work of John Nash, Architect*, pl. 12A.
[22] E.R.A.O., DDCC/108/68; O.S. Map 6″, Yorks. CCXII (1855 edn.).
[23] Poulson, *Holderness*, ii. 258; T. Jefferys, *Map of Yorks.* (1772). [24] *V.C.H. Yorks.* ii. 268.
[25] *Kirkby's Inquest*, 373; *Yorks. Fines, 1232–46*, p. 82; above, Benningholme, manors; above, Hilston, manor.
[26] *Yorks. Fines, 1246–72*, p. 88.
[27] *Feud. Aids*, vi. 40; Poulson, *Holderness*, ii. 256.
[28] P.R.O., CP 40/291, rot. 57.
[29] *Yorks. Fines, 1246–72*, p. 88; *Rot. Hund.* (Rec. Com.), i. 107. [30] Above, Swine, manors (priory).
[31] *Cal. Pat. 1555–7*, 300–1.
[32] For the following, P.R.O., CRES 38/2125 (abstract of title, Oubrough). *Yorks. Fines*, iii. 10.
[33] *Visit. Yorks. 1584–5 and 1612*, ed. J. Foster, 85.
[34] J. Foster, *Pedigrees of Yorks.* iii.

[35] R.D.B., I/435/957. P.R.O., CRES 38/2424 (plan of Oubrough Grange, 1756).
[36] P.R.O., CRES 38/2424 (will 1764; deed 1765); Poulson, *Holderness*, ii. 266.
[37] Below, this section (Dowthorpe).
[38] P.R.O., CRES 38/2125 (deed 1870, abstracts of title, Oubrough, Dowthorpe); above, Swine, manors.
[39] P.R.O., CRES 38/2427.
[40] Inf. from Crown Estate Office, London.
[41] *V.C.H. Yorks.* ii. 266.
[42] *Cur. Reg. R.* xi, p. 265, 303; *Cal. Inq. p.m.* ix, p. 27; Burton, *Mon. Ebor.* 253; above, this section (Woodhall).
[43] P.R.O., E 134/17 Eliz. Hil./6; *Yorks. Fines*, iii. 99.
[44] H.U.L., DDLA/7/9; *Y.A.J.* xi. 429–31; Poulson, *Holderness*, ii. 254–5; above, this section (Woodhall).
[45] H.U.L., DDPR/56/7–8; R.D.B., Z/379/890; AB/116/259; Poulson, *Holderness*, ii. 255–6.
[46] R.D.B., BY/535/834; BY/537/836; E.R.A.O., QDE/1/6/9.
[47] Above, this section (Oubrough).
[48] R.D.B., AB/116/259; T. Jefferys, *Map of Yorks.* (1772).
[49] Poulson, *Holderness*, ii. 256.

present house dates from the 18th century but the main front was remodelled in the later 19th.

Part of the Langdales' estate at Dowthorpe was used to endow the charity of Marmaduke Langdale (d. 1611), and the 33 a. remained with the trustees in 1995.[50] Swine priory was given land at Dowthorpe which was probably included in its grange of Oubrough.[51] The Constables also held a little land at Dowthorpe.[52]

LANGTHORPE manor, of 1 carucate, belonged in 1066 to Thor and, possibly in succession to him, to Egfrid. It passed to William Malet and, after his deprivation c. 1070, to Drew de Bevrère, the tenant in 1086.[53] It was later part of the Aumale fee. In the mid 13th century the St. Quintins were the tenants at Langthorpe.[54]

Swine priory had land at Langthorpe by the 1240s, and its grange there was recorded from 1294.[55] After the Dissolution, Langthorpe grange was granted to Sir Richard Gresham and then returned to the Crown, which sold it to Thomas Reeve and George Cotton in 1553; it then comprised two farms, each with 3 bovates.[56] All or much of Langthorpe passed to Marmaduke Langdale (d. 1611)[57] and then descended with Woodhall manor to Sir William Langdale (d. by 1685).[58] He was succeeded in Langthorpe, then called a manor, and lands at North and South Skirlaugh by his son Marmaduke and he (d. 1712 or 1713)[59] by his brother William.[60] From William Langdale (d. 1721),[61] the estate descended to his son William and then to that William's daughter Jane, who married Sir Walter Vavasour, Bt. He (d. 1802) was succeeded by his brother Sir Thomas Vavasour, Bt. (d. 1826).[62] In 1828 Sir Thomas's trustees sold Langthorpe manor with c. 335 a. there and at South Skirlaugh to Thomas Ward[63] (d. by 1830), who was succeeded by his son (the Revd.) Henry Ward.[64] In 1857 the estate was sold to W. V. Norman[65] (d. 1861), who was succeeded in turn by George Norman (d. by 1883) and T. A. Norman (d. 1890).[66] The estate then evidently

descended to Marmaduke Rees-Webbe, whose trustees[67] sold Langthorpe Hall farm, with 333 a. in South Skirlaugh and Ellerby, to William England in 1919.[68] It was bought in 1920 by Abraham Leonard (d. 1947) and in 1948 by George Lockwood (d. 1957), whose administrator, Westminster Bank Ltd., later held it.[69] In 1988 the 323-a. farm was bought by Foxton Farmers Ltd., which later transferred it to B. P. Foxton, the owner in 1995.[70]

The Langdales' seat in the parish was the 'mansion house' at Langthorpe, which had 11 hearths in 1672.[71] William Langdale lived in Hedon by 1764, and Langthorpe Hall was used as a farmhouse by the mid 19th century;[72] it was rebuilt c. 1830 on a large scale, mostly in grey brick.[73] A Tuscan portico was added in 1990–1.[74]

Sir William Gee bought an estate in Ellerby in 1604.[75] It descended to Roger Gee,[76] who sold it to William Bethell in 1766.[77] Comprising a farm of 218 a., it later descended with Rise.[78] W. F. Bethell devised the farm to his son A. J. Bethell, who sold it to Christopher Pickering in 1891.[79] In 1918 it was bought by James Welford (d. 1919), and in 1920 Welford's brother Ralph sold it to John Smith.[80] As Ellerby Grange farm, it passed to the mortgagee, Allison Rodmell (d. 1932), and was held by his trustees until 1955, when they sold it to G. E. Coates. He conveyed the farm in 1966 to G. B. Coates, who still occupied it in 1994.[81]

The rectorial tithes of Woodhall and part of Ellerby were bought by Ann Thompson in 1681[82] and sold that year to Richard Frank (d. by 1693), who left them to his nephew Francis Loveday. In 1707 Loveday sold them to Mark Kirkby, from whom they descended to James Torre,[83] who sold most of them c. 1800. Henry Maister bought the tithes from c. 360 a. at Woodhall and Ellerby in 1799,[84] and his successor H. W. Maister merged tithes from 437 a. there in 1843.[85] Other tithes in Ellerby township were included in the part of Swine rectory bought by

[50]   Below, S. Skirlaugh, charity.
[51]   Poulson, *Holderness*, ii. 203.
[52]   H.U.L., DHO/7/42; DHO/8/47; Poulson, *Holderness*, ii. 254–5.
[53]   *V.C.H. Yorks.* ii. 167–8, 268, 295.
[54]   Above, this section (Woodhall).
[55]   *Yorks. Fines, 1232–46*, p. 151; *Cal. Inq. p.m.* iii, p. 114; *Valor Eccl.* (Rec. Com.), v. 114.
[56]   *Cal. Pat.* 1553, 156; above, Swine, manors (priory).
[57]   P.R.O., C 142/337, no. 81.
[58]   H.U.L., DDLA/33/14; *Y.A.J.* xi. 429–31.
[59]   E.R.A.O., DDCC/111/32; DDRI/2/42; R.D.B., D/137/224.   [60]   E.R.A.O., QDR/2/36.
[61]   Poulson, *Holderness*, ii. 266.
[62]   R.D.B., BY/199/314; CP/100/151; CP/102/152; Burke, *Peerage & Baronetage* (1888), 1400.
[63]   R.D.B., ED/179/205; ED/199/227.
[64]   Ibid. EK/319/362; EO/92/109; Poulson, *Holderness*, ii. 256.
[65]   R.D.B., HP/307/419 (incorrectly as Newman).
[66]   Ibid. II/123/146; KQ/372/497; NU/256/381; 39/155/145 (1890); *Kelly's Dir. N. & E. R. Yorks.* (1879), 656.
[67]   R.D.B., 59/535/493 (1903); 180/498/425; E.R.A.O., NV 1/40.
[68]   R.D.B., 201/590/493.

[69]   Ibid. 211/327/284; 776/384/328; 781/131/110; 1084/123/114; 1633/115/95.
[70]   Inf. from Mr. B. P. Foxton, 1995.
[71]   P.R.O., E 179/205/504; *Y.A.J.* xi. 429–31; *Cal. Cttee. for Compounding*, iii, p. 1924.
[72]   R.D.B., AE/366/694; ED/179/205; Poulson, *Holderness*, ii. 256.
[73]   Sheahan and Whellan, *Hist. York & E.R.* ii. 390; O.S. Map 6", Yorks. CCXII (1855 edn.).
[74]   Pevsner and Neave, *Yorks. E.R.* 400.
[75]   E.R.A.O., DDRI/22/77.
[76]   H.U.L., DDGE/6/19, 22, 38, 61; DDGE/3/146; J. Foster, *Pedigrees of Yorks.* iii.
[77]   E.R.A.O., DDRI/13/2.
[78]   Ibid. DDRI/40/11; book of plans of estates of H. Bethell, at Rise Park Estate Off.
[79]   R.D.B., 47/61/58 (1891).
[80]   Ibid. 187/12/11; 198/342/286; 223/338/280.
[81]   Ibid. 282/220/186; 455/448/372; 630/40/33; 1015/553/500; 1500/400/340; *Reg. of Electors* (1994).
[82]   E.R.A.O., DDCC/111/31; DDRI/30/1; above, Swine, manors (rectory).   [83]   E.R.A.O., DDCC/35/6.
[84]   Ibid. DDCC/35/19; H.U.L., DDCV(2)/66/6; R.D.B., BZ/413/662; CB/46/68; CC/273/419; CC/275/421.
[85]   E.R.A.O., DDCC/108/48.

Arthur Thornton in 1681.[86] Those of Oubrough were sold by William Thornton in 1765 to John Moorhouse's widow Ann.[87] She (d. 1790) left them to her grandchildren Mary and Ann Brown. Ann (d. 1819) married John Williams,[88] and he, Mary Brown, and James Brown were awarded rent charges amounting to £111 for the tithes at commutation in 1841.[89] The tithes of Langthorpe were bought from William Thornton in 1764–5 by William Langdale and were later merged.[90]

Tithes from a further 381 a., at Dowthorpe, were merged by John Beadle in 1843,[91] and by 1849 only 63 a. of Ellerby township remained titheable; the three impropriators were then awarded rent charges totalling £9 2s. for their tithes.[92]

ECONOMIC HISTORY. COMMON LANDS AND INCLOSURE. *Ellerby.* Woodhall and Ellerby evidently shared commonable lands, which were inclosed, at least in part, at the division and sale of Woodhall manor in the 1590s.[93] The tillage then lay in East and West fields, and a 'fallow field ... east of Oubrough' was perhaps a third field, rather than an alternative description of West field. East field extended as far north as Langthorpe and east and south to Marton and Burton Constable. Ridge and furrow survived in grassland to the west of Woodhall Farm in 1994.[94] The common meadows were dispersed throughout the fields.[95] Some of the meadow land probably lay immediately east of Woodhall manor house, where Ing field closes were recorded later,[96] and the new closes staked out in East field in the 1590s included land probably used as meadow called Wandales. Cow pasture, presumably the common pasture, was also mentioned then and was perhaps among the land inclosed. Some common pasture nevertheless remained at 'Green maile', possibly the 'common field' shared by cottagers c. 1840.[97]

Oubrough. Swine priory may have inclosed all or much of Oubrough before the 16th century, when its grange there included 100 a. of pasture in West field.[98]

Dowthorpe. Dowthorpe's open fields lay east and west of the hamlet until Sir Robert Tyrwhit inclosed them shortly before 1575, thereby depriving farmers at South Skirlaugh of inter-

commonage in the fields in winter.[99] By 1634 Dowthorpe lay in a dozen closes, of which East field contained 87 a., Great West field 59 a., Middle field 54 a., and White Hill close 53 a. William Langdale then had 364 a.; the remaining 22 a. of Dowthorpe, comprising 'lands' in most of the closes, belonged to the other two proprietors.[1] By an exchange of 1656, Langdale's successor, (Sir) William Langdale, obtained 20 a. of 'lands', all then laid down to grass, from John Constable, Lord Dunbar.[2] The closes were re-ordered and divided c. 1850.[3]

Langthorpe. Langthorpe had one ploughland in 1086,[4] but its early agricultural arrangements are unknown. Ridge and furrow remaining around Langthorpe Hall in the 1940s marked the former tillage of the hamlet.[5]

WOODLAND. Woodhall was presumably established by assarting. The woodland there may have extended into Thirtleby, where Herbert de St Quintin's wood was mentioned in 1202.[6] In the 1290s Sir Herbert de St. Quintin evidently added 7 a. in Sproatley, obtained by exchange, to his woodland.[7] The wood was recorded as part of the demesne of Woodhall manor in 1303, when some of it was being coppiced,[8] and a forester was employed there in 1364.[9] There was still a large wood called Ellerby wood and c. 20 a. of coppiced woodland in 1598.[10] Most of the old woodland had been felled by the early 19th century, when c. 35 a. of formerly-wooded land lay in adjoining closes called Rashell Wood, Great Hagg, and Near and Far Little Haggs. Remnants of old woods and new plantations then covered c. 40 a.[11] Woodland returned under Ellerby civil parish totalled 3 ha. (7.4 a.) in 1987.[12]

TENURES AND HOLDINGS TO THE 16TH CENTURY. *Ellerby.* In 1086 there were two villeins and three bordars at Ellerby, where only one plough was then being worked on the four ploughlands. The tenants' holdings presumably included shares in the 20 a. of meadow then recorded there.[13] In 1303 the bond tenants of Woodhall manor owed ploughing, carting, and reaping works, and three cottars rendered poultry rents.[14]

Oubrough. The two ploughlands at Oubrough in 1086 were being worked by two ploughs, one on

86 Above, Swine, manors (rectory).
87 P.R.O., CRES 38/2424 (deed).
88 Ibid. /2125 (abstract of title, Oubrough tithe).
89 E.R.A.O., PE/104/98.
90 Ibid. PE/104/105; R.D.B., AE/366/694; AI/287/578.
91 P.R.O., CRES 38/2125 (abstract of title, Dowthorpe).
92 E.R.A.O., PE/104/105.
93 Para. based on E.R.A.O., DDCC/35/25, 37, 39–40; DDCC/108/1.
94 For other ridge and furrow, Hull Univ., Dept. of Geog., R.A.F. air photographs, run 333A, nos. 4199–4200; run 333B, no. 3261; run 334A, nos. 4143–6.
95 P.R.O., C 133/107, no. 25.
96 E.R.A.O., DDCC/108/68.
97 Poulson, *Holderness*, ii. 253.
98 Below, this section.
99 P.R.O., E 134/17 Eliz. I Hil./6. Cf. Hull Univ., Dept.

of Geog., R.A.F. air photograph, run 333A, no. 4204.
1 Poulson, *Holderness*, ii. 254–5.
2 H.U.L., DDLA/7/9; E.R.A.O., DDCC/35/4.
3 P.R.O., CRES 38/2125 (deposition, 1870).
4 *V.C.H. Yorks.* ii. 268.
5 Hull Univ., Dept. of Geog., R.A.F. air photograph, run 333B, no. 3263.
6 *Yorks. Fines, John* (Sur. Soc. xciv), pp. 76–7.
7 P.R.O., E 142/86(2).
8 *Yorks. Inq.* iv, p. 32.
9 *Cal. Pat.* 1361–4, 539.
10 E.R.A.O., DDCC/108/1. Cf. P.R.O., REQ 2/212/43.
11 E.R.A.O., DDCC/108/28, 68.
12 Inf. from Min. of Agric., Fish. & Food, Beverley, 1990.
13 *V.C.H. Yorks.* ii. 268.
14 P.R.O., C 133/107, no. 25.

the demesne and the other by five villeins and three bordars. The tenants presumably also held parts of the 10 a. of meadow then recorded there.[15] Much of the land of the hamlet was later occupied by Swine priory. In the early 1250s the house was disputing William de St. Quintin's claim to enjoy common rights on its estate at Oubrough as an appurtenance of his land in Ellerby.[16] Oubrough grange was still farmed directly by the priory in 1536, when it comprised 24 a. of arable land in Little field, 100 a. of pasture in West field, East leys, probably also grassland, of 140 a., and several grassland closes.[17] About that date, however, a dairyman there leased 20 cows, and presumably pasture, from the priory in return for supplying butter and cheese, and in the 1550s he or another rented a herd of c. 40 cows there.[18]

LATER AGRICULTURE. In 1834 there were 253 a. of arable land and 157 a. of grassland on the Woodhall estate, and c. 1840 Oubrough had 400 a. of arable and 50 a. of grassland.[19] In 1987 of 673 ha. (1,663 a.) returned under Ellerby civil parish, 611 ha. (1,510 a.) were arable land, 50 ha. (124 a.) grassland, and 5.6 ha. (14 a.) orchards; livestock kept then included over 800 pigs.[20]

In the 19th and earlier 20th century Ellerby usually had about 12 farms; in 1851 four were of 200–360 a. each and the largest had 618 a., and three farms of 150 a. or more were recorded in the 1920s and 1930s. By 1937 there were also several smallholdings, at least one of which remained in 1994. One or two cowkeepers or dairymen have worked at Ellerby,[21] and in 1994 a market garden was operated in the hamlet, and a garden centre beside the main road. Six holdings were returned for the civil parish in 1987, of which two were of 100–499 ha. (247–1,233 a.), one of 50–99 ha. (124–245 a.), one of 10–49 ha. (25–121 a.), and two of under 10 ha.[22]

MILLS. A windmill was recorded on the St. Quintins' estate at Ellerby from 1223,[23] and there may have been two mills there in the 16th century.[24] A windmill stood in Ellerby West field in 1596, and it was probably its site, adjoining Dowthorpe, which was commemorated by Mill close, named in 1782.[25] By the 19th century Ellerby windmill stood in the north of the township, close to Marton.[26] It was assisted by steam by 1889 but ceased to grind c. 1930;[27] by 1993 the former mill had been converted into a house.

NON-AGRICULTURAL EMPLOYMENT seems to have been scarce. A motor engineering concern was run in the earlier 20th century.[28]

LOCAL GOVERNMENT. Brief minutes of proceedings in Woodhall manor court survive for 1712, 1786, 1804, and 1823. The court, which had leet jurisdiction, seems by the 18th century to have been concerned mostly with property transactions and minor drainage defects; its officers included two affeerors, a constable each for Ellerby, Thirtleby, and South Skirlaugh, and a pinder at Ellerby.[29] The courts were held at the 'manor house', possibly meaning Woodhall farmhouse, c. 1840.[30]

Poorhouses were maintained at Ellerby.[31] Ten people there were relieved permanently and 4 occasionally in 1802–3, and 24–6 were on permanent and 5–8 on occasional relief between 1812 and 1815.[32] Ellerby joined Skirlaugh poor-law union in 1837,[33] and the township, later civil parish, remained in Skirlaugh rural district until 1935, then became part of the new Holderness rural district, and at reorganization in 1974 was taken into the Holderness district of Humberside.[34] In 1996 Ellerby parish became part of a new East Riding unitary area.[35]

CHURCH. The vicar of Swine provided Sunday and weekday services in the schoolroom at Ellerby from the late 1870s,[36] and in 1889 a mission room was built there to designs by Smith & Brodrick of Hull, and licensed for all services.[37] In 1900 there was a service each Sunday at Ellerby and communion was celebrated there.[38] The brick building is dedicated to *ST. JAMES* and comprises undivided sanctuary and nave with south vestry and south porch. A west bellcot was removed c. 1940,[39] and its bell remained unhung in 1995, when the church, recently renovated under a Government Training Scheme,[40] was still used.

ROMAN CATHOLICISM. Prominent among the Roman Catholics of Swine parish were the Langdales of Langthorpe, who were frequently presented for religious lapses in the later 16th and 17th century and whose household and tenantry probably accounted for most of the 28 Roman Catholics recorded under Ellerby and Langthorpe in the 1660s. In 1735 Ellerby was said to have 14 Roman Catholics.[41] The congre-

---

[15] *V.C.H. Yorks.* ii. 268.
[16] P.R.O., JUST 1/1046, rot. 63d.
[17] Ibid. E 315/401, p. 381. Cf. Hull Univ., Dept. of Geog., R.A.F. air photograph, run 334A, no. 4148.
[18] B.I.H.R., CP. G. 1529, 3402.
[19] E.R.A.O., DDCC/108/28; ibid. PE/104/98.
[20] Inf. from Min. of Agric., Fish. & Food.
[21] Para. based on P.R.O., HO 107/2365; directories.
[22] Inf. from Min. of Agric., Fish. & Food.
[23] *Cur. Reg. R.* xi, p. 265; *Yorks. Inq.* iv, p. 32.
[24] P.R.O., SC 6/Hen. VIII/6135, m. 1d.; *Yorks. Fines,* ii. 146.
[25] E.R.A.O., DDCC/35/40; book of plans of estates of H. Bethell, at Rise Park Estate Off.
[26] O.S. Map 6", Yorks. CCXII (1855 edn.).
[27] Directories.

[28] Ibid.
[29] H.A.O, DDCC/109/1, 4–5, 14.
[30] Poulson, *Holderness,* ii. 257.
[31] R.D.B., BZ/194/303.
[32] *Poor Law Abstract, 1804,* pp. 592–3; *1818,* pp. 520–1.
[33] *3rd Rep. Poor Law Com.* 170.
[34] *Census.*
[35] Humberside (Structural Change) Order 1995, copy at E.R.A.O.
[36] B.I.H.R., V. 1877/Ret. 3, no. 98; V. 1884/Ret. 2; *Kelly's Dir. N. & E.R. Yorks.* (1879), 656.
[37] R.D.B., 30/542/496 (1889); E.R.A.O., PE/104/113; Pevsner and Neave, *Yorks. E.R.* 400.
[38] B.I.H.R., V. 1900/Ret. no. 375.
[39] Local inf.
[40] Description in ch.

gation was presumably served at Langthorpe and later at Marton.[42]

PROTESTANT NONCONFORMITY. At Ellerby a protestant congregation which registered houses in 1808 and 1817 was probably Wesleyan,[43] and in 1838 the Wesleyan Methodists built a chapel there.[44] It was closed in the late 1940s and demolished.[45] In 1888 a Temperance lecture hall and schoolroom at New Ellerby was bought by the Wesleyan Methodists, who may already have been using it as a chapel. Sometimes called Marton chapel,[46] it was replaced by a chapel built nearby in 1909.[47] The new chapel, later the Methodist church, was still used in 1994.

EDUCATION. A mixed school at Ellerby was begun in 1828 and had 10 pupils in 1833, all taught at their parents' expense, and two school-mistresses there were recorded in 1851.[48] There was probably no school there in 1871, when children from Ellerby attended Swine school.[49] In 1876 W. F. Bethell gave a site for a new school with master's house,[50] and a National school for boys and girls was opened in 1877. It was supported by subscriptions, school pence, rent received for Church use of the schoolroom,[51] and from 1879–80 by an annual, government grant.[52] Later accommodating infants,[53] the school had an average attendance of 24 in 1878,[54] c. 30 in the 1900s, but usually 20 or fewer between 1913 and 1938.[55] In 1944 the school was transferred to the county council, which closed it in 1947 because of the inadequate building; most of the children were transferred to Skirlaugh school, the rest to Marton.[56] The former school was a house in 1994.

GANSTEAD

THE hamlet of Ganstead is less than 1 km. north of Hull, to which it is virtually joined by ribbon development, and c. 2 km. south-east of Swine village. The name, possibly meaning 'Gagni's place or landing-place', is an Anglo-Scandinavian hybrid.[57] Of 809 a. (327 ha.),[58] Ganstead civil parish was added to all of Wyton, almost all of Bilton, and a little of Preston civil parishes to form a new civil parish of Bilton in 1935.[59] Ganstead's poll-tax payers in 1377 may have been recorded under Bilton.[60] In 1672 Ganstead had 11 houses assessed for hearth tax and one was discharged.[61] From 58 in 1801, the population fluctuated upwards to stand at 101 in 1911 and 105 in 1931.[62]

GANSTEAD hamlet in the mid 19th century comprised little more than six houses served by a lane which became part of the main Hull–Bridlington road.[63] Many bungalows were strung along the main road and provided with sewerage by the district council in the mid 20th century,[64] and much of the road was replaced by a straighter diversion in 1986.[65] The few buildings dating from before the present century include a single-storeyed cottage with a lobby entrance, of the early 18th century, and Ganstead Grange with its two lodges.[66] There was a beerhouse at Ganstead in the 1750s,[67] and allotment gardens may have been provided in the 1890s.[68] The course of Ganstead Park Golf Club was laid out on part of Old Hall farm and a clubhouse built in 1975, and in the late 1980s the course was enlarged to 18 holes and c. 36 ha. (90 a.).[69]

MANOR AND OTHER ESTATES. In 1066 Fran and Halfdan held GANSTEAD manor; the 4-carucate estate had passed to Drew de Bevrère by 1086, when his undertenant Albert held it,[70] and it was later part of the Aumale fee, which passed to the Crown, as heir to the counts of Aumale, and thereafter to its grantees.[71]

41 E.R.A.O., QDR/2/31, 36; Cal. Cttee. for Compounding, iii, pp. 1923–4; Aveling, Post Reformation Catholicism, 66–7 and passim.
42 Below, Marton, Rom. Cath.
43 B.I.H.R., Fac. Bk. 3, p. 467; ibid. DMH. Reg. 1, p. 14. John Mackee occurs at Skirlaugh as a Wesleyan in 1800: below, S. Skirlaugh, nonconf.
44 P.R.O., HO 129/522/2/7/6; E.R.A.O., MRH/1/39; O.S. Map 6", Yorks. CCXII (1855 edn.).
45 E.R.A.O., MRH/1/32; inf. from Mr. V. Perry, Ellerby, 1995.
46 R.D.B., 24/169/159 (1888); E.R.A.O., MRH/1/28, 40; O.S. Map 1/2,500, Yorks. CCXII. 10 (1891 edn.).
47 R.D.B., 100/457/418 (1907); 131/383/332; O.N.S. (Birkdale), Worship Reg. no. 43802; datestone.
48 P.R.O., HO 107/2365; Educ. Enq. Abstract, 1096.
49 Returns relating to Elem. Educ. 472–3.
50 R.D.B., MF/10/13; O.S. Map 1/2,500, Yorks. CCXII. 10 (1891 edn.).
51 P.R.O., ED 7/135, no. 41; E.R.A.O., SL/34/1; above, church.
52 Rep. of Educ. Cttee. of Council, 1879–80 [C.2562-I], p. 726, H.C. (1880), xxii.
53 E.R.A.O., SL/34/1.
54 P.R.O., ED 7/135, no. 41.
55 Bd. of Educ., List 21 (H.M.S.O., 1908 and later edns.).
56 E.R.A.O., SL/34/3; E.R. Educ. Cttee. Mins. 1943–4, 87; 1944–5, 156; 1945–6, 186.
57 P.N. Yorks. E.R. (E.P.N.S.), 48–9; G. F. Jensen, Scand. Settlement Names in Yorks. 145.
58 O.S. Map 6", Yorks. CCXXVI, CCXXVII (1855 edn.).
59 Census, 1931 (pt. ii).
60 Above, Bilton, intro.
61 Hearth Tax, 60.
62 V.C.H. Yorks. iii. 494; Census, 1901–31.
63 O.S. Map 6", Yorks. CCXXVII (1855 edn.).
64 R.D.B., 1028/185/164; 1586/224/205; 1587/65/58; 1589/19/18.
65 Roadside plaque.
66 Below, manor.
67 E.R.A.O., QDT/2/9.
68 Ibid. CCO/58.
69 Inf. from Mrs. E. Green, Ganstead Park Golf Club, 1994; below, manor.
70 V.C.H. Yorks. ii. 268.
71 V.C.H. Yorks. E.R. v. 9–10.

Ganstead was held of the counts of Aumale and their successors by the Suttons. Richard of Sutton's tenancy was recorded in the mid 12th century, and in 1196 Alan de Scruteville released 2½ carucates there to Richard's nephew, Amand of Sutton.[72] Amand was succeeded by his son Saer (fl. 1208)[73] and he probably by his son Saer (d. perhaps in 1270) and certainly by the last Saer's son Saer (d. by 1290), who was mesne lord of all 4 carucates.[74] Ganstead descended to Saer's son, John Sutton, Lord Sutton (d. by 1338), of whom it was held as ¹⁄₂₀ knight's fee,[75] and from him, with Sutton on Hull, to the family's heirs.[76]

The Suttons' tenants at Ganstead were the Twyers. The estate which William de la Twyer bought there in the mid 13th century[77] was presumably the manor, which Peter de la Twyer (d. by 1304) held; it then included 2¼ carucates of demesne land. Peter was succeeded by his son William,[78] who was named as joint lord of neighbouring Wyton in 1316, presumably for Ganstead.[79] William (d. by 1334) left a son William,[80] but in 1347 the tenant was evidently Robert de la Twyer, who was then granted free warren at Ganstead.[81] William Twyer of Ganstead, esquire, recorded in 1432, presumably had the manor.[82] From Peter Twyer (d. by 1500)[83] it descended to Joan, daughter of a Peter or Robert Twyer, and her husband, William St. Quintin (d. 1529). The St. Quintins' son or grandson John[84] (d. 1572) left the manor house and its closes to his son-in-law Matthew St. Quintin and grandson Gabriel and the rest of the estate to his daughters Margery Monkton, Jane or Joan Dolman, and Margaret Noddall.[85] The manor was partitioned in 1583.[86] Margery's share descended to her son William Monkton,[87] who sold it in lots in the 1590s.[88] The Dolmans' estate descended to William Dolman, who sold it in 1599 or 1600 to his brother-in-law Robert Constable (d. 1637).[89]

In 1606 Gabriel St. Quintin sold his share of the manor, possibly by then increased to a moiety, to Thomas Beverley, who conveyed it

to his son John in 1607.[90] John sold the estate, as Ganstead manor, to Edward Richardson and others in 1624.[91] Richardson died in 1631, and his son William[92] sold the manor to Henry Barnard in 1652.[93] Henry was succeeded by Sir Edward Barnard (d. 1688)[94] and he in turn by his son Edward (d. by 1718) and Edward's heirs, who held undivided shares. Besides the manor, the estate then comprised a 70-a. farm. Edward Barnard's daughter Margaret married Lovelace Gilby,[95] and by the mid 18th century Ganstead manor was divided between the heirs of their daughter Margaret. The manor was reunited by purchases made in 1752, 1763, and 1764 by Jonathan Midgley (d. 1778).[96] His widow Mary sold the manor to Jonathan's sister Margaret Gilby in 1778. Mrs. Gilby (d. 1790) devised it for life to her sister Mary Midgley (d. c. 1810), with remainder to Jonathan's daughters Anna and Mary.[97] Anna died in 1795,[98] and Mary, who married William Beverley, evidently inherited her share.[99] In 1826 the Beverleys' son R. M. Beverley sold the manor and the farm to James Walker,[1] who in 1829, just before his death, settled them on his son James.[2] In 1847 James Walker sold the estate to J. F. Butter (d. 1866), and in 1867 Sarah Dooby bought it, then of 117 a., from Butter's trustees.[3] W. J. Atkinson bought the manor and farm in 1877,[4] and his trustees held the estate until 1965, when the 125-a. Manor farm was sold to Foxton Farmers Ltd., the owner in 1995.[5]

The manor house stood on the west side of the Hull–Bridlington road until its demolition before 1752. A farmhouse had by then been built near the southern boundary on land inclosed in 1602;[6] it was called White House in 1889 and later Manor Farm.[7] Possible earlier chief houses are discussed below.

The Monktons' share of the manor may have included Turmer Hall, which stands near the southern township boundary: in 1595 one of their sales was made to Robert Taylor of Turmer Hall, perhaps the tenant.[8] Turmer Hall evidently belonged to Richard Atkinson in

[72] *Chron. de Melsa* (Rolls Ser.), i. 95–6, 219; *Feet of Fines, 1182–96* (Pipe R. Soc. xvii), p. 95; for the Suttons, *E.Y.C.* iii, p. 86; *Complete Peerage*.
[73] *Yorks. Fines, John* (Sur. Soc. xciv), pp. 119–20.
[74] *Feud. Aids*, vi. 40; *Cal. Inq. p.m.* iv, pp. 353, 355.
[75] *Cal. Inq. p.m.* iii, pp. 2–3; vii, p. 424.
[76] P.R.O., C 142/49, no. 55; C 142/163, no. 36; *Yorks. Inq. Hen. IV–V*, pp. 159–60; *Complete Peerage*, s.v. Sutton; *V.C.H. Yorks. E.R.* i. 471–2.
[77] *Chron. de Melsa* (Rolls Ser.), ii. 95.
[78] *Yorks. Inq.* iv, p. 66. [79] *Feud. Aids*, vi. 164.
[80] *Cal. Inq. p.m.* vii, pp. 424–5.
[81] *Cal. Chart. R. 1341–1417*, 55.
[82] *Cal. Pat. 1429–36*, 275.
[83] *Monastic Chanc. Proc. Yorks.* (Y.A.S. Rec. Ser. lxxxviii), p. 136.
[84] P.R.O., C 142/49, no. 55; *Visit. Yorks. 1584–5 and 1612*, ed. J. Foster, 127, 153; *Monastic Chanc. Proc. Yorks.* p. 137; Poulson, *Holderness*, ii. 192.
[85] P.R.O., C 142/163, no. 36.
[86] Ibid. REQ 2/26/8.
[87] J. Foster, *Pedigrees of Yorks.* iii, s.v. St. Quintin.
[88] *Yorks. Deeds*, iv, pp. 72–4; *Yorks. Fines*, iv. 11, 15, 35, 83, 86.
[89] P.R.O., REQ 2/26/8; ibid. C 142/552, no. 118; *Yorks.*

Fines, iv. 137; *Visit. Yorks. 1584–5 and 1612*, 86.
[90] *Yorks. Deeds*, iv, p. 78; *Yorks. Fines, 1603–14*, 93.
[91] *Yorks. Fines, 1614–25*, 237.
[92] P.R.O., C 142/563, no. 103.
[93] Ibid. CP 25(2)/613/1652 Trin. no. 36; CP 25(2)/615/1657 Mich. no. 43.
[94] Ibid. CP 25(2)/763/33–4 Chas. II Hil. [last]; Burke, *Land. Gent.* (1937), 103 n.
[95] R.D.B., F/148/319; F/449/966; M/53/86.
[96] Ibid. W/142/303; AC/371/18; AC/384/22; AE/340/649; AZ/283/460.
[97] Ibid. AZ/284/461; BP/3/4; E.R.A.O., QDE/1/6/14.
[98] R.D.B., BS/86/124; *Complete Peerage*, s.v. Grantley.
[99] R.D.B., BY/351/536. [1] Ibid. DZ/119/152.
[2] E.R.A.O., DDSA/1045; J. Foster, *Pedigrees of Yorks.* iii, s.v. Walker.
[3] R.D.B., GG/353/423; IY/230/330; KE/89/112.
[4] Ibid. MF/298/326; 61/48/48 (1893).
[5] Ibid. 919/40/36; 1407/175/151; E.R.A.O., NV/1/19; inf. from Mr. P. Foxton, Coniston, 1995.
[6] R.D.B., T/171/318; W/142/303; E.R.A.O., DDCK/35/24; below, econ. hist.
[7] O.S. Map 1/2,500, Yorks. CCXXVII. 5 (1891 edn.); O.S. Map 1/10,560, TA 13 SW. (1969 edn.).
[8] *Yorks. Deeds*, iv, p. 73.

1609,[9] was sold with land in Bilton by Gervase Bosville to Robert Gunby in 1682,[10] and later passed to William Burton[11] (d. 1752) and then in turn to his sons William (d. 1764) and Robert (d. 1802).[12] Henry Burton and others, evidently Robert Burton's devisees, sold Turmer Hall and another farmhouse with 387 a. in Ganstead and 30 a. in Coniston to William Todd, a Hull merchant, in 1832.[13] Todd (d. by 1838) left a life estate to his son W. G. Todd, with remainder to the latter's daughter Helen,[14] who as Helen Pechell had succeeded by 1889. In 1914 Mrs. Pechell sold the 159-a. Ganstead farm to J. R. Woods, who bought Turmer Hall and 263 a. from the Pechells in 1923.[15] Woods died in 1930 and his widow Eliza probably by 1949, when the trustees sold Turmer Hall with 193 a. to J. A. Foxton (d. 1954). In 1964 Foxton's widow Edith and the other executors vested the farm in B. P. Foxton, who still had it in 1995.[16]

The east range of the present Turmer Hall probably dates from the 17th century but the building was enlarged and remodelled with additional, parallel ranges and Tudor-style façades by W. G. Todd in 1840.[17]

By the 17th century much of the manorial estate belonged to John Herron, and his daughter Elizabeth Robinson had houses called Hall Garth and Twyers house and c. 300 a. at Ganstead in 1699.[18] Part of her estate passed to Stephen Oates (d. 1743), who devised Hall Garth and over 170 a. to his great-nephew Robert Bee. Marmaduke Brown bought Bee's estate in 1750,[19] and it evidently descended c. 1785 to Marmaduke Brown the younger and c. 1795 to Thomas Brown, who bought c. 45 a. more in 1803. From Thomas (d. by 1831), the estate passed to another Thomas Brown[20] (d. 1841) and then to that Thomas's sisters Mary and Elizabeth, who married respectively Haddon Trigg and C. S. Parker, both Hull merchants.[21] The 220-a. estate was sold in lots in 1875. Charles Wells, a Hull shipowner and coal merchant, bought Old Hall and 150 a.[22] In 1909 the mortgagees sold the farm to T. H. Perry (d. 1940), a Hull dairy farmer, who was succeeded

by Annie E. Newlove and Emmie Butler as joint tenants. In 1948 Mrs. Newlove sold her interest to Mrs. Butler, from whom Longdales Development Co. Ltd. bought the farm in 1971.[23] Some of the land was later used for a golf course and all still belonged the company in 1994.[24]

Ganstead manor house, named as Ganstead Hall in 1573,[25] presumably stood where Ganstead Old Hall did until its demolition in the late 1980s; an earlier chief house may have stood nearby on a formerly-moated site, part of which survived on the west side of the new road in 1995.[26] Ganstead Hall evidently lost its association with the manor after that estate's fragmentation in the late 16th century.[27] Ganstead Old Hall, known as Hall Garth in the 18th century,[28] was used as a farmhouse by the mid 19th century. It was apparently the Parkers who c. 1847 built near Old Hall a large *cottage ornée* called Ganstead Grange and laid out an ornamental park to the south. Two lodges had been added by 1889.[29] That house and 27 a. were bought by Septimus Marsdin, a Hull shipowner, in 1875 and by W. H. Richardson, a Hull glass merchant, in 1878. In 1995 the owner was Mr. K. North, a Hull timber merchant.[30]

By 1711 Elizabeth Robinson had sold the rest of her estate, comprising Twyers house and 128 a., to William Hydes, a Hull merchant. Hydes's daughter Mary and her husband Richard Burton conveyed it to William Burton in 1746, and it presumably later descended with the Turmer Hall estate.[31]

A bovate at Ganstead, given to Meaux abbey by Richard of Sutton c. 1150, was later returned to his heir Amand of Sutton.[32] St. Sepulchre's hospital, Hedon, had land at Ganstead by 1208,[33] and in 1535 its estate there and at Coniston was valued at £2 a year.[34] The hospital passed to the Constables, who had a house at Coniston and a bovate at Ganstead in 1609.[35] Before their suppression, the Knights Hospitaller also had an estate at Ganstead; the Crown granted it to the restored order in 1558,[36] and it may later have passed to Philip Herbert (d. 1639).[37] Swine priory's estate at the Dis-

9 P.R.O., LR 2/230.
10 H.U.L., DDCV/61/1; E.R.A.O., DDNA/171.
11 R.D.B., U/303/579.
12 Ibid. AS/191/316; E.R.A.O., DDNA/220; *V.C.H. Yorks. E.R.* iv. 24, 117.
13 R.D.B., ER/233/248; KL/103/143; E.R.A.O., QDE/1/6/14.
14 E.R.A.O., PE/104/102; R.D.B., KL/103/143.
15 R.D.B., 159/221/192; 298/496/415; *Kelly's Dir. N. & E. R. Yorks.* (1889), 341.
16 R.D.B., 714/417/356; 820/182/147; 997/394/344; 1361/115/106; inf. from Mr. P. Foxton, Coniston, 1995.
17 *Kelly's Dir. N. & E.R. Yorks.* (1937), 720.
18 E.R.A.O., DDHV/36/2; R.D.B., R/488/1186.
19 R.D.B., R/238/567; S/27/57; U/191/355; U/194/363.
20 Ibid. CE/582/888; FN/104/98; E.R.A.O., QDE/1/6/14.
21 R.D.B., FP/325/338; FQ/395/396; FS/99/114; FT/145/180; KR/299/420.
22 Ibid. LP/352/487; LP/363/503; LQ/412/574; LR/122/172; NK/370/531.
23 Ibid. 68/287/266 (1894); 112/424/392; 642/361/314; 643/176/146; 780/359/317; 1708/314/272.
24 Inf. from Mrs. E. Green, Ganstead Park Golf Club,

1994; above, intro.
25 *Yorks. Fines*, ii. 31.
26 H. E. J. le Patourel, *Moated Sites of Yorks.* 112; O.S. Map 1/10,000, TA 13 SW. (1984 edn.); inf. from Mrs. E. Green, Ganstead Park Golf Club, 1994.
27 Above, this section.
28 R.D.B., R/238/567; U/191/355; O.S. Map 6", Yorks. CCXXVII (1855 edn.).
29 K. J. Allison, 'Hull Gent. Seeks Country Residence 1750–1850' (E. Yorks. Loc. Hist. Ser. xxxvi), 50; O.S. Map 1/2,500, Yorks. CCXXVII. 5 (1891 edn.).
30 R.D.B., LP/363/503; MU/402/611; inf. from Mrs. J. Kirby, Hornsea, 1995.
31 R.D.B., D/11/17; R/488/1186; above, this section.
32 *Chron. de Melsa* (Rolls Ser.), i. 95–6, 219.
33 *Yorks. Fines, John* (Sur. Soc. xciv), pp. 119–20.
34 *Valor Eccl.* (Rec. Com.), v. 110.
35 P.R.O., C 60/525, no. 52; ibid. LR 2/230, f. 226; *Cal. Pat.* 1547–8, 170; 1553, 87–8; *V.C.H. Yorks. E.R.* v. 194; J. Foster, *Pedigrees of Yorks.* iii, s.v. Constable of Constable Burton.
36 P.R.O., SC 6/Hen. VIII/4458, m. 14d.; *Cal. Pat.* 1557–8, 321.
37 P.R.O., C 142/583, no. 33.

solution included land at Ganstead,[38] some of which was bought by the Constables.[39] Ann Watson's charity of Sutton on Hull had 42 a. at Ganstead until 1952, when Hull corporation bought the estate.[40]

The rectorial tithes and dues of Ganstead were bought by Joseph Micklethwaite in 1681.[41] He sold those of Turmer Hall in 1682, and they were evidently later merged in that estate.[42] Micklethwaite's title to the rest of the tithes descended with Swine manor to Cropley Cooper, earl of Shaftesbury, who in 1848 was awarded a rent charge of £15 9s. for the few unmerged tithes there.[43]

ECONOMIC HISTORY. COMMON LANDS AND INCLOSURE. In 1602 the seven proprietors of Ganstead inclosed all or most of the commonable lands. The tillage and some grassland then lay in East, West, and South fields, which had evidently already been reduced by the making of closes. Other areas dealt with were the common meadows, called South and West ings, and the stinted Town's pasture, all occupying the low land in the west of the township. Adjoining West ings was Lord's pasture, which by 1607 lay in three closes.[44] Some stinted pasture may have remained in an area called Cogham.[45] Much of Ganstead was evidently under grass by the late 17th century,[46] and ridge and furrow, presumably of East field, remained in the grounds of Ganstead Grange in 1994.[47]

MEDIEVAL HOLDINGS. In 1086 three ploughs were at work on the four ploughlands at Ganstead, one on the lord's holding and two operated by 7 villeins and 4 bordars. The holdings presumably also included shares in the 20 a. of meadow land then recorded for Ganstead.[48]

MODERN AGRICULTURE. There were 3–5 farmers at Ganstead in the 19th century and earlier 20th; the one or two larger farms included Turmer Hall, of 700 a. in 1851.[49] Market gardening and dairying have been pursued at Ganstead.[50]

MILLS. A ruinous windmill recorded at Ganstead in 1334[51] had evidently been rebuilt by the early 17th century.[52] It probably stood in the north-east of the township in New Mill close, which was recorded in 1602, together with the more southerly Mill close.[53] The modern post mill occupying the north-eastern site ceased to grind in or soon after 1905 and was demolished in 1909.[54]

LOCAL GOVERNMENT. A call roll and a brief note of proceedings in Ganstead manor court, both of 1811, survive; the court had leet jurisdiction and appointed the constable and a pinder.[55]

At Ganstead 2 people were relieved permanently and 3 occasionally in 1802–3, and 10–12 were on permanent and 5–6 on occasional relief between 1812 and 1815.[56] Ganstead joined Skirlaugh poor-law union in 1837,[57] and the township, later civil parish, remained in Skirlaugh rural district until 1935. As part of Bilton civil parish, it was then included in the new Holderness rural district and at reorganization in 1974 was taken into the Holderness district of Humberside.[58] In 1996 Bilton parish became part of a new East Riding unitary area.[59]

CHURCH. St. George's chapel, Ganstead, had been built by 1226, possibly to house the Sutton family's chantry, which in that year and again in 1236 Swine priory agreed to supply with a chaplain, clerk, and all other necessities for daily services there.[60] No later evidence of services in Ganstead chapel has been found, but the ruined building was mentioned as late as 1764.[61]

ROMAN CATHOLICISM. In the 1660s the half dozen papists at Ganstead included members of the Constable family.[62]

EDUCATION. Children from Ganstead attended Bilton and Swine schools in 1871.[63]

[38] Ibid. E 315/401, p. 378; *Valor Eccl.* v. 114; *Cal. Pat. 1560–3*, 515.

[39] Above, Swine, manors (priory); Benningholme, manors [Benningholme grange].

[40] R.D.B., 916/511/438.

[41] E.R.A.O., DDX/31/518; above, Swine, manors (rectory).

[42] H.U.L., DDCV/61/2.

[43] E.R.A.O., PE/104/102; above, Swine, manors (Swine).

[44] P.R.O., C 142/163, no. 36; *Yorks. Deeds*, iv, pp. 73–6, 78. North field, mentioned in 1609, was perhaps part of East field: P.R.O., LR 2/230, f. 232.

[45] P.R.O., C 142/583, no. 33; *Yorks. Deeds*, iv, pp. 78–9.

[46] H.U.L., DDCV/61/1.

[47] For other ridge and furrow, Hull Univ., Dept. of Geog., Fairey Surveys air photographs, run 365B, no. 2143; run 366C, no. 1064.

[48] *V.C.H. Yorks.* ii. 268.

[49] P.R.O., HO 107/2365; directories.

[50] Directories; above, manor [Old Hall farm].

[51] P.R.O., C 135/40, no. 7; *Yorks. Inq.* iv, p. 66.

[52] *Yorks. Fines, 1603–14*, 187.

[53] *Yorks. Deeds*, iv, pp. 75–6, 78.

[54] T. Jefferys, *Map of Yorks.* (1772); O.S. Map 6", Yorks. CCXXVII (1855 edn.); directories; R. Gregory, *E. Yorks. Windmills*, 36–7 (illus.).

[55] H.U.L., DDCV/62/1–2.

[56] *Poor Law Abstract, 1804*, pp. 592–3; *1818*, pp. 522–3.

[57] *3rd Rep. Poor Law Com.* 170.

[58] *Census.*

[59] Humberside (Structural Change) Order 1995, copy at E.R.A.O.

[60] *Yorks. Fines, 1218–31*, p. 97; *1232–46*, p. 43.

[61] B.I.H.R., V. 1764/Ret. 3, no. 66.

[62] Aveling, *Post Reformation Catholicism*, 67.

[63] *Returns relating to Elem. Educ.* 472–3.

MARTON

THE hamlet of Marton lies 6 km. north-east of Swine village and 8 km. west of the coast at Aldbrough. The name, meaning 'farm near the mere', is Anglian and almost certainly alludes to Lambwath mere which extended into Aldbrough and Withernwick parishes.[64] Lambwath stream, which flowed through the mere and formed the northern boundary of Marton, had been diverted near the western boundary by the late 18th century. Of 946 a. (383 ha.),[65] Marton civil parish and that of West Newton with Burton Constable were united in 1935 as Burton Constable civil parish.[66] Marton, which was not recorded separately in 1377, had 14 houses assessed for hearth tax in 1672.[67] In 1801 Marton's population was 127; later it declined to 68 in 1901, recovered to 87 in 1911, and stood at 73 in 1931.[68]

MARTON is loosely built along one side of a street which at its western end joins the Ellerby–Rise road and in the east turns south to Burton Constable and Sproatley. The short Pipers Lane, leading east from the street, existed by the late 18th century, when it was probably continued, as later, by a footpath to Fosham and West Newton, in Aldbrough, and another path then led to Withernwick.[69] The hamlet formerly had distinct east and west 'ends'.[70] Since the 18th century the pattern of settlement has changed little but only one or two of the dozen farm- and other houses have not been rebuilt. New buildings have included White House Farm, added on the west side of the street c. 1800.[71] Close to the southern boundary stand a Roman Catholic church and a former school,[72] where a lending library was run in 1833.[73] A licensed house traded at Marton from the later 18th century; it was last recorded in 1858.[74]

MANORS AND OTHER ESTATES. In 1066 Sven held *MARTON* manor, of 1 carucate; it had passed to Drew de Bevrère by 1086 and was later part of the Aumale fee. Drew's undertenant was Franco,[75] ancestor of the Fauconbergs.[76]

The estate, later put at 2–3 carucates and located at *EAST MARTON*, was held in succession by Peter de Fauconberg,[77] William de Fauconberg (fl. mid 13th century),[78] and by the 1280s by Walter de Fauconberg, later Lord Fauconberg (d. 1304),[79] whose son Walter was named as a lord of Marton in 1316.[80] Free tenants held the land of the Fauconbergs, whose mesne lordship later descended as an appurtenance of their manor of Rise to the Nevilles and the Crown.[81] The demesne of Rise manor later included houses and land at East Marton; with Rise they passed to Roger Bethell (d. 1626), his sons Robert and Hugh, and later to Hugh Bethell (d. 1752).[82] A cottage and c. 10 a. were granted to William Constable in exchange in 1766.[83]

An estate at East Marton, probably regarded as a manor, belonged to the Hedon family, before passing to the Constables.[84]

Drew de Bevrère also succeeded to the 2 carucates at Marton which Ulf had held in 1066 as sokeland of his manor of Aldbrough.[85] In 1284–5 they were held of the Crown, as successor to Drew and the counts of Aumale, apparently as ¼ knight's fee,[86] though later the same estate was perhaps more correctly reckoned as 1/24 fee.[87]

By the 13th century the Constables held the 2 carucates,[88] which were at *WEST MARTON*. William Constable claimed in 1231 that his estate there had been damaged by his overlord, the count of Aumale.[89] In 1294 the land was held by bond and free tenants of Sir Simon Constable,[90] whose son Robert was named as a lord of Marton in 1316.[91] The Constable family later had a demesne estate at Marton; it was said to comprise 352 a. in 1498 and 278 a. in 1578,[92] and was later enlarged by purchase, notably c. 1600. In 1599 Sir Henry Constable bought a farm of c. 80 a. at East Marton[93] and in 1602 a smaller farm at West Marton from Sir William Knowles's heirs, the Alfords.[94] His son Sir Henry and grandson John bought Henry

64 *P.N. Yorks. E.R.* (E.P.N.S.), 49; below, econ. hist.
65 E.R.A.O., DDCC/141/71 (plan of Marton dated 1774); O.S. Map 6″, Yorks. CCXII (1855 edn.).
66 *Census,* 1931 (pt. ii). 67 *Hearth Tax,* 61.
68 *V.C.H. Yorks.* iii. 494; *Census,* 1901–31.
69 E.R.A.O., DDCC/141/71 (plan of Marton dated 1774); O.S. Map 6″, Yorks. CCXII (1855 and later edns.).
70 E.R.A.O., DDCC/18/2, s.v. Oct. 1548.
71 Ibid. DDCC/141/71 (plan of Marton); H. Teesdale, *Map of Yorks.* (1828); O.S. Map 1/10,000, TA 13 NE. (1980 edn.).
72 Below, nonconf.; educ.
73 *Educ. Enq. Abstract,* 1096.
74 E.R.A.O., QDT/2/7, 9; O.S. Map 6″, Yorks. CCXII (1855 edn.); White, *Dir. Hull & York* (1858), 556.
75 *V.C.H. Yorks.* ii. 269.
76 *Complete Peerage; Early Yorks. Fam.* (Y.A.S. Rec. Ser. cxxxv), 26–7.
77 *Yorks. Deeds,* ix, p. 120.
78 *Kirkby's Inquest,* 375; *Cal. Inq. p.m.* ix, pp. 176–7.
79 *Cal. Inq. p.m.* iv, p. 357.

80 *Feud. Aids,* vi. 164.
81 E.R.A.O., DDCC/64/40; *Cal. Inq. p.m.* iv, 357; ix, pp. 176–7; *Yorks. Inq. Hen. IV–V,* pp. 17–18; below, Rise, manor.
82 E.R.A.O., DDRI/26/55; R.D.B., I/447/972; Foster, *Pedigrees of Yorks.* iii, s.v. Bethell; below, N. Skirlaugh, manors; below, Rise, manor.
83 R.D.B., AI/308/624.
84 Poulson, *Holderness,* ii. 259; below, this section.
85 *V.C.H. Yorks.* ii. 266. 86 *Feud. Aids,* vi. 40.
87 *Cal. Inq. p.m.* viii, p. 24; ix, p. 219.
88 *Kirkby's Inquest,* 375; *Feud. Aids,* vi. 40; Poulson, *Holderness,* ii. 229 n., 259.
89 H.U.L., DHO/16/36.
90 *Cal. Inq. p.m.* iii, pp. 114–16; iv, p. 357. For fam., J. Foster, *Pedigrees of Yorks.* iii.
91 *Feud. Aids,* vi. 164.
92 E.R.A.O., DDCC/141/68 (survey), p. 26; microfilm copy at E.R.A.O.; *Cal. Inq. p.m. Hen. VII,* ii, pp. 60–2.
93 E.R.A.O., DDCC/64/27.
94 Ibid. DDCC/64/34; P.R.O., C 142/160, no. 34; *Yorks. Fines, 1603–14,* 27; above, Bilton, manor.

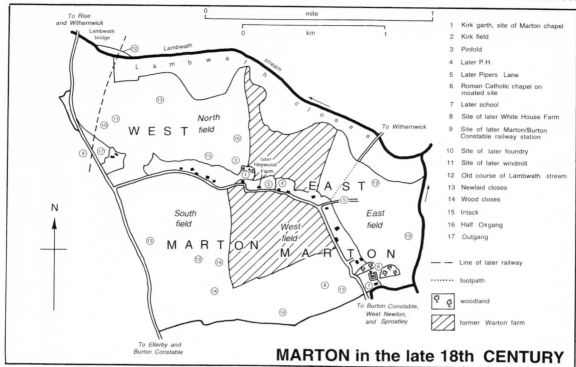

MARTON in the late 18th CENTURY

1   Kirk garth, site of Marton chapel
2   Kirk field
3   Pinfold
4   Later P.H.
5   Later Pipers Lane
6   Roman Catholic chapel on moated site
7   Later school
8   Site of later White House Farm
9   Site of later Marton/Burton Constable railway station
10 Site of later foundry
11 Site of later windmill
12 Old course of Lambwath stream
13 Newlaid closes
14 Wood closes
15 Intack
16 Half Oxgang
17 Outgang

— — —   Line of later railway

· · · · · ·   footpath

woodland

former Warton farm

Hedon's estate at East Marton, comprising East Hall Garth, another three houses, and *c.* 140 a., in 1618.[95] Later reckoned to include manors at East and West Marton, the enlarged estate descended with Burton Constable manor.[96] A 150-a. farm, formerly belonging to the Wartons and their heirs, was bought in 1843 by Sir Thomas Constable, Bt.,[97] who then owned the whole of Marton township.[98] The Chichester-Constables' estate there, of 936 a. in 1963, belonged to Mr. John Chichester-Constable and his daughter, Rodrica Straker, in 1995.[99]

The lordship of Holderness which passed with Burstwick manor to the Crown[1] included a mere at Lambwath.[2] As *LAMBWATH* manor, it was granted in 1538 to Sir John Russell, later baron Russell and earl of Bedford,[3] who sold it to Lady (Joan) Constable and her son (Sir) John Constable in 1549.[4] Most of the mere had evidently gone by the mid 16th century,[5] and in 1609 the manor was described as including 600 a. of meadow ground, of which 341 a. were said in 1693 to be in Withernwick.[6] Lambwath descended in the Constables with the rest of the

family's estate in Marton, in 1719 under the joint description of the manor of Lambwath with Marton.[7] In the late 18th century Lambwath closes at Marton contained 122 a., and in 1827 the Constables had 108 a. of Lambwath closes at Carlton and Fosham, in Aldbrough, and 185 a. in Withernwick.[8]

Other medieval estates at Marton included those of William Hautayn, Amand of Routh, and Walter Whittick, all named as lords there in 1316.[9]

Simon of Marton gave a toft and tillage at East Marton to Meaux abbey, which between 1221 and 1235 granted the land away.[10] Other land at Marton was held of the abbey in the 13th century by descendants of Geoffrey of Bilton.[11]

Swine priory held 4½ bovates at Marton of Sir Simon Constable in 1294.[12] After its dissolution, Sir Thomas Heneage and William Willoughby, Lord Willoughby, bought houses there formerly belonging to the priory in 1548 and sold them to Lady (Joan) Constable in 1549.[13]

95 E.R.A.O., DDCC/64/4. Hedon had sold houses and *c.* 150 a. more in 1616: ibid. DDCC/64/40.
96 P.R.O., CP 25(2)/762/24–5 Chas. II Hil. [last but one]; E.R.A.O., DDCC/111/231; DDCC/141/6; above, Burton Constable, manor.
97 R.D.B., CU/23/26; CU/118/119; FW/377/354; *V.C.H. Yorks. E.R.* vi. 210.
98 E.R.A.O., PE/104/104; Poulson, *Holderness*, ii. 260.
99 R.D.B., 1295/284/255; inf. from Mr. John Chichester-Constable, Burton Constable, 1995.
1 *V.C.H. Yorks. E.R.* v. 9–10.
2 Below, econ. hist.
3 E.R.A.O., DDCC/58/3; *L. & P. Hen. VIII*, xiii (1), p. 412; *Complete Peerage*, s.v. Bedford.
4 E.R.A.O., DDCC/58/4; *Yorks. Fines*, i. 167.

5 Below, econ. hist.
6 H.U.L., DHO/7/42; B.I.H.R., TER. H. Withernwick 1693.
7 H.U.L., DHO/8/47; P.R.O., CP 25(2)/762/24–5 Chas. II Hil. [last but one]; E.R.A.O., DDCC/111/39, 231; DDCC/133/43.
8 E.R.A.O., DDCC/111/39; DDCC/141/71 (plans of Marton and the Lambwath closes dated 1774); cf. R.D.B., 1295/284/255.
9 *Feud. Aids*, vi. 164.
10 *Chron. de Melsa* (Rolls Ser.), i. 415; ii. 103.
11 Ibid. i. 367; ii. 102–5.
12 *Cal. Inq. p.m.* iii. 114–15.
13 P.R.O., E 315/401, p. 379; E.R.A.O., DDCC/64/2; *Valor Eccl.* (Rec. Com.) v. 114; *Cal. Pat.* 1548–9, 118–25.

The rectorial tithes of Marton were sold by William Thornton to Cuthbert Constable in 1738[14] and were later merged in the freehold.[15]

ECONOMIC HISTORY. COMMON LANDS AND INCLOSURE. East and West Marton had separate agricultural systems. The boundary between the two 'ends' was mentioned in the 13th century, and West Marton apparently had its own pinfold in 1610;[16] it was possibly where Marton's pinfold was later.[17] At East Marton, where in 1086 the ploughland on Franco's estate was worked by a villein with one plough and there was 8 a. of meadow land,[18] the open fields lay on the east and west sides of the settlement. Both East and West fields included meadow land, and there was a stinted pasture called le Frithes in 1322.[19] West Marton's tillage evidently lay in North and South fields.[20] An outgang leading north-westwards from the settlement may have given access to pasture of West Marton, either in Lambwath or in Langthorpe, in Ellerby.[21] East Marton's fields had been inclosed at least in part by 1590[22] and those at West Marton evidently by 1616, when Marton included a 53-a. South field close and a North field close of 34 a.[23] Long, curved closes in the north and east of the township locate some of the former open-field land,[24] while close-names recorded in the late 18th century included Intack, Half Oxgang, and several Newlaid closes, all testifying to a probably lengthy process of reorganization.[25]

LAMBWATH MERE. The fishery of William le Gros (d. 1179), count of Aumale, at Withernwick was probably in Lambwath mere, which also lay in Aldbrough parish and Marton.[26] The mere was managed for the lord by a fisherman and warreners, or keepers.[27] Valued for its eels and reeds in 1260,[28] it also supported pike and bream and in 1348–9 a flock of c. 20 swans. The seigneurial right to fowl and other game in the mere may account for a reference to Lambwath park in 1275.[29] Pasture at Lambwath was let and rushes sold from the mid 13th century, but both were claimed by the keeper c. 1350, when the grazing was valued at £3 a year.[30] By the 15th century the fishery, grassland, and rushes were all let; Withernwick farmers, who had earlier

paid for watering rights in the mere, occupied much of the grassland, and tenants of East and West Marton rented the grazing of other parts of the mere. The area of water had evidently been reduced by the 1550s, when Sir John Constable, lord of Lambwath manor, bounded and inclosed Lambwath with a ditch and hedge,[31] and closes had been made there by 1584, when his son (Sir) Henry Constable sold c. 70 a. of Lambwath in Aldbrough and Withernwick parishes.[32] Despite the sales, Lambwath manor still included 600 a. of meadow land in 1609.[33] Unlicensed fishing and fowling in Lambwath were occasionally mentioned in the 16th and 17th centuries[34] but the oversight of the drainage and regulation of the meadows were much more important concerns of the manor court there. Parts of Lambwath, including West Newton's Cottager, or Cotcher, Lambwath, were evidently used in common, pains being laid to ensure that those meadows were mown by all the occupiers before they were opened for grazing.[35] In 1827 the Lambwath closes in Aldbrough parish included Cottagers' Lambwath, of 18 a., and those in Withernwick West and East Cottinger closes, each of c. 7 a. and held by several men.[36]

WOODLAND. The south of Marton township was evidently once wooded, like adjacent ground in Burton Constable; nearly 50 a. of Wood closes were recorded in the late 18th century and c. 5 a. of woodland then remained around the Roman Catholic chapel.[37] By 1849 there was 27 a. of woodland at Marton, and plantations of the Burton Constable estate remain near the southern boundary.[38]

HOLDINGS AND TENURES IN THE 16TH CENTURY. Ploughing and most carting works owed by the Constables' tenants at Marton had been commuted for fowls, eggs, and money rents by the 1540s, when the lord still claimed the right to buy his tenants' farm produce before it was taken to market.[39] There were in the earlier 16th century four farms of 2–3½ bovates each on the estate.[40]

LATER AGRICULTURE. There were usually 6–8 farms at Marton in the 19th and 20th centuries, 3 of which in 1851 and 1–2 in the 1920s

[14] E.R.A.O., DDCC/6/8; above, Swine, manors (rectory).

[15] E.R.A.O., PE/104/104.

[16] 'Meaux Cart.' p. 448; E.R.A.O., DDCC/18/3, s.v. Oct. 1610.

[17] O.S. Map 6″, Yorks. CCXII (1855 edn.).

[18] V.C.H. Yorks. ii. 269.

[19] 'Meaux Cart.' p. 448; E.R.A.O., DDCC/58/1; Yorks. Deeds, ix, p. 121.

[20] Yorks. Deeds, ix, pp. 120–1.

[21] E.R.A.O., DDCC/141/71 (plan of Marton).

[22] Ibid. DDCC/64/25 (a).

[23] Ibid. DDCC/64/40.

[24] Cf. Hull Univ., Dept. of Geog., R.A.F. air photographs, run 333B, nos. 3257–60.

[25] E.R.A.O., DDCC/141/71; O.S. Map 6″, Yorks. CCXII (1855 edn.).

[26] Cur. Reg. R. xiv. 228.

[27] For the following, P.R.O., SC 6/1078/11, 13, 21; SC 6/1079/19; SC 6/1082/7; SC 6/1084/5.

[28] Yorks. Inq. i, p. 79.

[29] Cal. Fine R. 1272–1307, 40.

[30] Cal. Inq. Misc. iii, p. 20.

[31] E.R.A.O., DDCC/139/65; P.R.O., STAC 4/10/11; above, manors.

[32] E.R.A.O., DDCC/58/7–14.

[33] H.U.L., DHO/7/42.

[34] E.R.A.O., DDCC/59/1, s.v. Apr. 1597; DDCC/59/2, s.v. Apr. 1651.

[35] E.R.A.O., DDCC/59/1, s.vv. Oct. 1596, Apr. 1612; DDCC/59/2, s.v. Apr. 1651; DDCC/59/3, s.v. 1721. Undated survey of Lambwath, prob. 17th cent.: E.R.A.O., DDCC/58/17; ibid. DDRI/34/8; DDRI/44/3.

[36] E.R.A.O., DDCC/111/39.

[37] Ibid. DDCC/141/71.

[38] Ibid. PE/104/104; O.S. Map 6″, Yorks. CCXII (1855 edn.); Acreage Returns, 1905.

[39] E.R.A.O., DDCC/18/2.

[40] A fifth farm was unquantified: P.R.O., C 142/65, no. 61; E 150/240, no. 12.

and 1930s were of 150 a. or more. Cowkeeping and nurserying gave employment to a few at Marton in the late 19th century and early 20th, and one or two smallholdings were recorded c. 1930.[41]

MILLING AND INDUSTRY. Robert and Francis Grasby built a windmill at Marton in or soon after 1834. By 1840 they were also working as wheelwrights, and an iron and brass foundry had been added near by by 1846. Milling was apparently abandoned c. 1865 but agricultural engineering continued until c. 1970.[42]

LOCAL GOVERNMENT. The view of frank-pledge and regulation of agriculture at Marton mostly belonged in the 16th and 17th centuries to Burton Constable court. In the mid 16th century 1–2 bylawmen for Marton were elected there and later the constable and an aletaster for the hamlet.[43] The regulation of the meadows alongside Lambwath stream in Marton, Fosham, in Aldbrough, and Withernwick was, however, the chief business of Lambwath manor court, which also had leet jurisdiction. Records of its proceedings survive for 1593–1625, c. 1650, and 1705–89. The court usually met twice a year and regularly appointed 2 ditch supervisors each for east and west Lambwath, and later for the north and south sides instead.[44] Both courts seem to have been held in Marton.[45]

At Marton 2 people were relieved permanently and 10 occasionally in 1802–3, and 5 were on permanent and 1 occasional relief between 1812 and 1815.[46] Marton joined Skirlaugh poor-law union in 1837,[47] and the township, later civil parish, remained in Skirlaugh rural district until 1935. As part of Burton Constable civil parish, it was then included in the new Holderness rural district and at reorganization in 1974 was taken into the Holderness district of Humberside.[48] In 1996 Burton Constable parish became part of a new East Riding unitary area.[49]

CHURCH. Marton chapel was recorded from c. 1240[50] and its dedication to St. Leonard in 1474.[51] Swine priory assigned its rectorial tithes

at Marton, except for those of corn, to the curate as a stipend,[52] and there was also a landed endowment until its confiscation by the Crown at the suppression.[53] In 1525–6 the chaplain's income was £3 6s. 8d. a year.[54] The chapel was served until the end of the 16th century,[55] but by 1650 the building was in disrepair[56] and by the late 17th century the Marton tithes had been annexed to Swine vicarage, presumably because of the abandonment of the cure at Marton.[57] The remains of the chapel were demolished c. 1740 and its yard was later called Kirk Garth.[58] A bell from the chapel was kept in Burton Constable Hall in 1998.[59] After the discontinuance of the chapel, parishioners at Marton were evidently served in Swine church[60] until 1867, when Marton became part of the new parish of Skirlaugh.[61]

ROMAN CATHOLICISM. There may have been c. 30 papists at Marton in the 1630s, and 14 were recorded there in the 1660s and in 1735.[62] Tenants of the Constables at Marton and elsewhere in Holderness probably worshipped in the family's chapel at Burton Constable Hall until the later 17th century, when a mission, partly funded by the Constables, was established at Marton.[63] A house occupying a moated site[64] near the southern boundary was evidently used for the chapel. A small burial ground outside the moat was provided c. 1700.[65] Sometimes called 'Burton' chapel from its proximity to Burton Constable,[66] Marton chapel was very probably one of the two Roman Catholic chapels, each with its own priest, recorded in Swine parish in 1743,[67] and by the mid 18th century the mission was serving the general neighbourhood, including at least part of Hull.[68] The house had been rebuilt early in the 18th century, and in 1788–9 William Constable remodelled the building, adding a purpose-built chapel alongside the house, which was later used as a presbytery. The chapel, designed by Thomas Atkinson of York,[69] comprises a plain, rectangular room, with round-headed windows in the north wall, a shallow, apsidal bay at the east end, and a west gallery. It has been dedicated successively to St. Mary and the Most Holy Sacrament.[70] Memorials there include a Neoclassical wall monument

[41] P.R.O., HO 107/2365; directories; R.D.B., 1295/284/255.
[42] E.R.A.O., DDCC/64/12; O.S. Map 6", Yorks. CCXII (1855 edn.); O.S. Map 1/10,560, TA 13 NE. (1956 edn.); directories; inf. from Mr. H. Sanderson, New Ellerby, 1995.
[43] E.R.A.O., DDCC/18/2–3.
[44] Ibid. DDCC/59/1–3.
[45] Ibid. DDCC/59/2, s.v. 1651; DDCC/59/4.
[46] Poor Law Abstract, 1804, pp. 592–3; 1818, pp. 522–3.
[47] 3rd Rep. Poor Law Com. 170.   [48] Census.
[49] Humberside (Structural Change) Order 1995, copy at E.R.A.O.
[50] Chron. de Melsa (Rolls Ser.), ii. 16. See also above, Burton Constable, church.
[51] Yorks. Deeds, ix, p. 124.
[52] P.R.O., E 318/11/528, m. 10.
[53] Cal. Pat. 1548–9, 37–8.   [54] Y.A.J. xxiv. 76.
[55] B.I.H.R., D/C. CP. 1590/1; Lamb. Pal. Libr., Carte Misc. XII/9, f. 132v.; Inventories of Ch. Goods, 34; Abp. Grindal's Visit., 1575, ed. W. J. Sheils, 73; Lawrance, 'Clergy List', Holderness, 2, p. 152–3.
[56] T.E.R.A.S. iv. 52.

[57] B.I.H.R., TER. H. Swine n.d. etc.; above, Swine, below, S. Skirlaugh, both church sections.
[58] B.I.H.R., TER. H. Swine 1764, 1777; V. 1764/Ret. 3, no. 66; ER. V./CB. 10, f. 77v.; O.S. Map 6", Yorks. CCXII (1855 edn.); Thompson, Swine, 205.
[59] Inf. from Dr. D. Connell, Burton Constable Hall.
[60] Above, this para.
[61] Below, S. Skirlaugh, church.
[62] Aveling, Post Reformation Catholicism, 67. Some seem to have been included from Marton, in Bridlington.
[63] Aveling, op. cit. 54; Herring's Visit. iv. p. 217; above, Burton Constable, Rom. Cath.
[64] H. E. J. le Patourel, Moated Sites of Yorks. 114.
[65] E.R.A.O., DDCC/141/71 (plan of Marton) shows it; J. O. Payne, Old Eng. Catholic Missions, 40.
[66] Aveling, op. cit. 53.
[67] Herring's Visit. iii, p. 127.
[68] Payne, op. cit. 39–40.
[69] Brass plate on door; Burton Constable Hall, drawing 1788; E.R.A.O., DDCC(2)/59, vouchers 20, 21 Apr. 1789.
[70] Sheahan and Whellan, Hist. York & E.R. ii. 392; Bulmer, Dir. E. Yorks. (1892), 508.

to Mary Chichester (d. 1815), and there is a Constable hatchment. The chapel was registered for marriages in 1837,[71] and in 1851 it had a congregation of c. 180.[72] Later in the 19th century there was only a monthly service supplied by a priest from Hedon, but Marton again had a resident priest in the earlier 20th century.[73] Since then the church has been served from Hornsea.[74]

EDUCATION. A non-communicant schoolmaster was recorded at Marton in 1600.[75] St. Mary's Roman Catholic school at Marton was begun by Francis Constable in 1816,[76] probably in the building it later occupied near the chapel.[77] The mixed school had 50–60 pupils in 1833.[78] Separate accommodation for the boys was built in 1839. In 1856 Sir Thomas Constable, Bt., paid the teachers and provided them with their house and 5 a.; the only other income was then from school pence.[79] There were just 18 boys and girls in attendance at inspection in 1871, and the school was evidently closed later in the decade.[80]

A Church school for boys and girls, begun in 1875, took over the building of the former Roman Catholic school. Average attendance was 23 in 1878. The income was entirely from school pence[81] until 1879–80, when an annual government grant was first received.[82] The school, which was run on National lines,[83] was transferred to the county council in 1920, after criticism of the building.[84] Marton school also served, and was rated to, West Newton with Burton Constable civil parish,[85] and it was later called Burton Constable-Marton school. Average attendance between 1906 and the early 1930s was usually 20–30; it had risen to 47 by 1938,[86] about which date the school was enlarged.[87] In 1954 senior pupils were transferred to South Holderness County Secondary School.[88] For the whole of 1984 Marton school was housed at Sproatley primary school because of the dangerous state of the building at Marton. Marton school was officially closed at the end of that year, and the pupils were integrated into the Sproatley school.[89] In 1994 the two-storeyed building, which dates from the late 18th century[90] and has a dentilled eaves course and a pantile roof, was being converted into a house.

CHARITY FOR THE POOR. Land in Fitling, in Humbleton, belonged to the poor of Marton in the 18th and 19th centuries.[91]

NORTH SKIRLAUGH AND ROWTON

THE part of Swine parish which lay in the north division of Holderness comprised North Skirlaugh township and some of Arnold, the rest of which township belonged to the ancient parishes of Long Riston and Rise.[92] North Skirlaugh, c. 4 km. north of Swine village, was formerly the head of Skirlaugh union and remains a centre of local government.[93] The name Skirlaugh is an Anglo-Scandinavian hybrid, meaning 'bright clearing'; Skirlaugh comprised settlements on either side of Lambwath stream which were distinguished from the 13th century by the prefixes North and South. A settlement called Rowton lay ½ km. west of North Skirlaugh; its name is Anglian and means 'rough enclosure'.[94] A stream flowing southwards from Rise to Lambwath stream probably formed the boundary between the two settlements.

In the mid 19th century there were 534 a. (216 ha.) in North Skirlaugh and 671 a. (272 ha.) in Swine parish's part of Arnold township. All 1,680 a. (680 ha.) of Arnold[95] was added in 1885 to North Skirlaugh to form the civil parish later called North Skirlaugh, Rowton, and Arnold,[96] and in 1935 that parish was combined with Long Riston as Riston civil parish.[97] North Skirlaugh and part of Arnold were later transferred to Skirlaugh civil parish.[98] In 1377 there were 132 poll-tax payers at North Skirlaugh, Rowton, and Arnold,[99] and in 1672 the same settlements had 42 houses assessed for hearth tax.[1] The population of North Skirlaugh with Rowton and Swine parish's part of Arnold township rose from 192 in 1811 to 260 in 1821, but had fallen to 210 by 1831. The union workhouse was later built in North Skirlaugh,[2] and 48 inmates

71 Lond. Gaz. 29 Dec. 1837, p. 3386.
72 P.R.O., HO 129/522/2/8/7.
73 B.I.H.R., V. 1912–22/Ret. (s.v. Skirlaugh); Kelly's Dir. N. & E.R. Yorks. (1872), 547; (1889), 457; (1901), 560; Catholic Dir. (1900), 208; (1951), 252.
74 Catholic Dir. (1969), 313; (1992), 283.
75 B.I.H.R., V. 1600/CB. 1B, f. 124v.
76 P.R.O., ED 7/148; Poulson, Holderness, ii. 260.
77 O.S. Map 6″, Yorks. CCXII (1855 edn.).
78 Educ. Enq. Abstract, 1096.
79 P.R.O., ED 7/148.
80 Returns relating to Elem. Educ. 472–3; below, this section.
81 P.R.O., ED 7/135, no. 115; Kelly's Dir. N. & E.R. Yorks. (1889), 457.
82 Rep. of Educ. Cttee. of Council, 1879–80 [C.2562-I], p. 733, H.C. (1880), xxii.
83 E.R. Educ. Cttee. Mins. 1904–5, 210.
84 Ibid. 1907–8, 64; 1919–20, 45, 238; 1920–1, 241.
85 Ibid. 1919–20, 243.

86 Bd. of Educ., List 21 (H.M.S.O., 1908 and later edns.).
87 E.R. Educ. Cttee. Mins. 1936–7, 186, 224; 1937–8, 42, 118; 1938–9, 204.
88 Ibid. 1953–4, 145.
89 Above, Sproatley, educ.; inf. from Mrs. E. Swift, Marton, 1995.
90 Dept. of Environment, Buildings List 1987.
91 Above, Humbleton, manors [Fitling].
92 O.S. Map 6″, Yorks. CCXI, CCXII (1855 edn.).
93 Below, this section.
94 P.N. Yorks. E.R. (E.P.N.S.), 49–51; G. F. Jensen, Scand. Settlement Names in Yorks. 165.
95 Census, 1871; O.S. Map 6″, Yorks. CCXI, CCXII (1855 edn.).
96 Census, 1891.
97 Ibid. 1931 (pt. ii); below, Long Riston, intro.
98 Below, S. Skirlaugh, intro.
99 P.R.O., E 179/202/60, m. 54.   1 Hearth Tax, 62.
2 Below, this section.

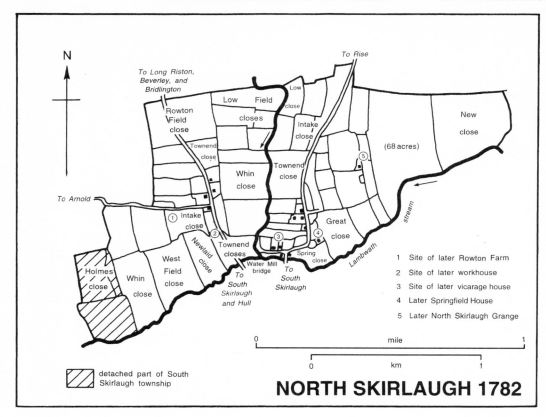

N

To Rise

To Long Riston,
Beverley, and
Bridlington

Low

Low Field

Rowton
Field
close

closes

Low
close

Intake
close

New

close

Townend
close

(68 acres)

⑤

Whin

close

Townend
close

To Arnold

① Intake
close

②

Townend
closes

Newlaid close

③

Whin
close

West
Field
close

Holmes
close

Water Mill
bridge

To
South
Skirlaugh
and Hull

④

Great

close

Spring
close

To
South
Skirlaugh

stream

Lambwath

1   Site of later Rowton Farm
2   Site of later workhouse
3   Site of later vicarage house
4   Later Springfield House
5   Later North Skirlaugh Grange

0   mile   1

0   km   1

detached part of South
Skirlaugh township

NORTH SKIRLAUGH 1782

contributed to the total population of 279 in 1841; the institution's population was still *c.* 50 in the 1880s.[3] Overall, numbers increased to 339 in 1871, before falling to 284 in 1881 and, despite the addition of the rest of Arnold with *c.* 80 people in 1885, to 247 in 1911. There were 292 inhabitants in 1931.[4]

NORTH SKIRLAUGH hamlet. In 1782 the dozen houses of North Skirlaugh mostly stood along both sides of a street which continued northwards to Rise, and at its southern end crossed Lambwath stream into South Skirlaugh. A farmhouse, later North Skirlaugh Grange, then stood to the east of the street amid closes, and there were one or two houses alongside Lambwath stream, in a short side lane which was extended before 1852 to meet the South Skirlaugh to Long Riston road, later part of the main Hull–Bridlington road. At Rowton there were four houses, on either side of the road to Long Riston. One of the farmhouses, later Rowton Farm, had been rebuilt away from the road by the 1850s, when only one other remained there. By then the union workhouse stood beside the road at Rowton,[5] and in 1862 a

terrace of cottages and in 1869–70 a vicarage house were also added,[6] in the lane at North Skirlaugh, later Vicarage Lane. There has been further development along Vicarage Lane and the main road in the 20th century, and there is now little, apart from the stream, separating North Skirlaugh from its larger, southern neighbour. The older buildings include Springfield House[7] and Ivy Cottage, a house with rusticated quoins and window surrounds put up *c.* 1900 by the Bethells,[8] and the newer ones 14 mid 20th-century council houses, built on land earlier used for allotment gardens,[9] and a telephone exchange.[10] A wooden Church hall put up in Vicarage Lane by the 1930s was demolished *c.* 1970.[11]

Skirlaugh union workhouse was built in 1838–9 to serve parishes in mid Holderness.[12] Following the removal to Beverley of the children in 1915 and of the few remaining inmates in 1916, the workhouse became a military hospital.[13] The rural sanitary authority for Skirlaugh union met in the workhouse from 1872 until 1894 and its successor, Skirlaugh rural district council, from then until 1916, when use by the military authorities caused meetings to be

3 E.R.A.O., PUS/1/1.
4 *V.C.H. Yorks.* iii. 495; *Census*, 1811–1931; for Arnold's population see also below, Long Riston, intro.
5 Book of plans of estates of H. Bethell, at Rise Park Estate Off.; O.S. Map 6″, Yorks. CCXI, CCXII (1855 edn.); O.S. Map 1/10,560, TA 14 SW. (1956 edn.); below, this section [workho.].
6 Datestone on cottages; below, S. Skirlaugh, church [vicarage ho.; Chapel Estate].
7 Below, manors.
8 R.D.B., 1554/213/176.

9 Ibid. 720/26/23; O.S. Map 6″, Yorks. CCXI. NE. (1928 and later edns.).
10 R.D.B., 415/537/428; 627/472/373; O.S. Map 1/10,560, TA 13 NW. (1956 edn.).
11 E.R.A.O., PE/88, accession 1561, (insurance policy); inf. from the vicar, 1995.
12 E.R.A.O., DDHE/17/31; *Hull Advertiser*, 14 June 1839.
13 E.R.A.O., PUA/14, p. 337; PUA/15, pp. 49–50, 58, 134, 187, 195–6; PUA/17, pp. 916, 918–19. Min. bks. of the board of guardians of Skirlaugh union survive for 1884–1911: ibid. PUS/1/1–4.

moved to Hull, where they long remained.[14] In 1922 the council bought the redundant workhouse and adjoining land.[15] Parts of the building were later occupied as cottages called Rowton Villas; the rest, and eventually all of the building, served as offices for the council and its successors, Holderness rural district council, Holderness Borough council, and the East Riding council. Designed by J. B. and William Atkinson of York, the former workhouse is of brick with stucco dressings; the two-storeyed front elevation comprises a main block of seven bays with lower, recessed side wings. Prominent pediments crown the larger end bays of the main block, which has another pediment over the central doorway and a mixture of round-headed and rectangular windows. Ranges extending back from the side wings were truncated and the other buildings enclosing the exercise yards removed c. 1975, and between 1988 and 1991 offices and a council chamber were built on the site. A large garage and depot occupies the adjacent land.[16]

MANORS AND OTHER ESTATES. In the Domesday Survey the name 'Skirlaugh' was used without any further distinction, and the land there mentioned cannot thus be identified with later estates in North and South Skirlaugh. In 1066 Skirlaugh comprised 5 carucates and 6 bovates, of which Ulf held 4 carucates as sokeland and 1 carucate as a berewick of his manor of Aldbrough, and Morkar held 6 bovates as soke of his manor of Hornsea. Also soke of Aldbrough were the 2 carucates of Rowton. All of those lands had passed to Drew de Bevrère by 1086,[17] and later were part of the Aumale fee.

Much of the land, lying at Rowton and North Skirlaugh, was held by the Fauconbergs. The first recorded tenant, Peter de Fauconberg,[18] was evidently succeeded by William de Fauconberg, who in the mid 13th century held all 2 carucates at Rowton and 2 carucates at North Skirlaugh, besides land at 'Skirlaugh', later recorded as 2 bovates at South Skirlaugh.[19] The holding descended to Walter de Fauconberg (d. 1304), Lord Fauconberg,[20] and later, as a member of Rise manor, to the Nevilles.[21] The Fauconbergs' demesne estate at Rowton, North Skirlaugh, and Arnold was said in the 1290s to comprise only c. 1 carucate,[22] and in 1349 all 2 carucates at

North Skirlaugh were held of John de Fauconberg, Lord Fauconberg, by freeholders.[23] The estate continued to descend as part of Rise manor, farms in Rowton and North Skirlaugh being held by Roger Bethell (d. 1626), assignee of the Crown's lease of the manor, and then divided among his heirs, one of whom Hugh, later Sir Hugh, Bethell (d. 1679) bought the freehold and reunited the shares.[24] An estate in North Skirlaugh belonging to Hugh's brother John (d. 1651 or 1652) probably also descended later with the rest of the Bethells' estate there.[25] In 1831 Richard Bethell was said to have 478 a. at North Skirlagh and Rowton,[26] and his nephew and later heir, W. F. Bethell, apparently also had 82 a. in the township in 1848.[27] William Bethell's estate at North Skirlaugh and Rowton comprised c. 520 a. in 1915.[28] Land was later sold, but the Bethells still had c. 450 a. in North Skirlaugh and Rowton in 1995.[29]

Springfield House, or an earlier house on the site, existed by 1782.[30] In 1892 it was occupied by William Bethell's land agent.[31] It was sold by the Bethells after 1967.[32]

Two carucates at Rowton, Arnold, and North Skirlaugh were held, presumably under the Fauconbergs, by Simon de Rupella c. 1240, when Meaux abbey acquired his estate. Simon's tenant was then (Sir) Richard of Rowton, whose son Matthew exchanged his holding with the abbey for lands at Riston in 1269 or 1270. Matthew's cousin, Maud of Rowton, had earlier given the abbey 2 bovates at Rowton, and by the 1290s it had 3 carucates and 2 bovates in the three vills, 6 bovates at Rowton held in demesne and the rest of the land occupied by the abbey's tenants. The estate in Rowton, variously called *ROWTON* manor[33] or Rowton grange[34] in the 13th and 14th centuries, was later reckoned part of Meaux abbey's manor of Arnold, and descended with that after the Dissolution to Joseph Micklethwaite and his son John.[35] In 1653 the Micklethwaites exchanged c. 1 carucate with John Dalton, who in 1656 granted that estate, lying in Arnold, Rowton, and North Skirlaugh, to John Anlaby and others.[36] The estate has not been traced further.

The Hildyard family held land belonging to Rise manor in North and South Skirlaugh in the 16th century.[37]

[14] Min. bks.: E.R.A.O., RSSK/1–2; RDSK/1–19.
[15] R.D.B., 247/226/187; 255/523/445.
[16] Plans at E.R.A.O., accession 3053; Min. of Housing and Loc. Govt., *Buildings List* (1965); Dept. of Environment, *Buildings List* (1987); inf. from Devt. Dept., Hold. B.C., 1994.
[17] *V.C.H. Yorks.* ii. 265–6, 326.
[18] *Yorks. Deeds*, viii, p. 4.
[19] *Kirkby's Inquest*, 372–3; *Cal. Inq. p.m.* iv, p. 357.
[20] *Feud. Aids*, vi. 40; *Cal. Inq. p.m.* iv, p. 357; *Complete Peerage.* [21] *Cal. Inq. p.m.* xviii, p. 136.
[22] *Chron. de Melsa* (Rolls Ser.), ii. 214–15; 'Meaux Cart.' pp. 425–9. [23] *Cal. Inq. p.m.* ix, pp. 176–7.
[24] E.R.A.O., DDRI/26/55, 65, 68; Poulson, *Holderness*, i. 402; J. Foster, *Pedigrees of Yorks.* iii, s.v. Bethell; below, Rise, manor.
[25] R.D.B., I/447/972; *Abstracts of Yorks. Wills, Commonwealth* (Y.A.S. Rec. Ser. ix), p. 47.
[26] E.R.A.O., DDRI/40/11.
[27] Ibid. PE/104/100. These figures probably include land in other townships: cf. E.R.A.O., accession 2980, 'Rise Estates 1852'. [28] R.D.B., 170/289/242.
[29] Rise Park Estate Off., 'Rise Settled Estates 1967'.
[30] Book of plans of estates of H. Bethell, at Rise Park Estate Off.
[31] R.D.B., 1525/127/104; Bulmer, *Dir. E. Yorks.* (1892), 506, 509.
[32] Rise Park Estate Off., 'Rise Settled Estates 1967'.
[33] *Chron. de Melsa*, ii. 35, 141–3, 215; iii. 6–7; 'Meaux Cart.' pp. 423–9.
[34] B.L. Cott. MS. Vit. C. vi, f. 221 and v.; *Chron. de Melsa*, ii. 235.
[35] *L. & P. Hen. VIII*, xix (2), p. 78; *Cal. Pat. 1569–72*, p. 453; below, Long Riston, manors.
[36] E.R.A.O., DDRI/2/51; DDRI/35/6.
[37] *Cal. Inq. p.m. Hen. VII*, ii, pp. 419–23; Poulson, *Holderness*, ii. 261.

A house, 1 bovate, and other land at North Skirlaugh were sold as former possessions of Swine priory by the Crown in 1609.[38]

The rectorial tithes of North Skirlaugh, Rowton, and the part of Arnold in Swine parish were bought in 1737 by Hugh Bethell (d. 1752).[39] Those at Arnold were commuted in 1778.[40] At North Skirlaugh and Rowton most had been merged in Richard Bethell's estate by 1848, when he was awarded a rent charge of £18 4s. 8d. for the rest.[41]

ECONOMIC HISTORY. OPEN FIELDS AND INCLOSURE. North Skirlaugh and Rowton may have had separate open fields.

North Skirlaugh. North Skirlaugh was inclosed in 1623 under an Exchequer commission of 1622. Some 195 a. was then allotted to eight tenants of the Crown's manor of Rise, mostly from East field, where a 68-a. close remained undivided in 1782. All of North field, comprising c. 45 a. and butts, and a small area in West field, or West field 'of Rowton', were also awarded.[42]

Rowton. The tillage at Rowton lay in North, South, and East fields in the mid 17th century. In 1658 Hugh, later Sir Hugh, Bethell and the one or two other proprietors at Rowton exchanged more than 80 a. there and at North Skirlaugh, evidently as a preliminary to the inclosure of Rowton.[43] Land from the former North and South fields presumably lay respectively in the 29-a. Rowton Field close and West Field close, of 22 a., in 1782. Many of the closes made in both vills in the 17th century reflected the earlier open-field divisions in their long sinuous shapes. Intake closes recorded in 1782 suggest that there was also some piecemeal inclosure before the 17th century.[44]

COMMONABLE GRASSLAND AND INCLOS-URE. Common meadows and pastures in Arnold township were intercommoned by the farmers of North Skirlaugh, Rowton, and Arnold. Sir Walter de Fauconberg and others overcharged the 200–300 a. of marshland called Arnold and Ryhill carrs in the 1290s, when the capacity of the pasture was put at 8 cattle or horses, 20 sheep, 4 pigs, 5 geese, besides offspring, for each bovate in the vills.[45] The carrs and ings were reached by a way made or confirmed in the 17th century which led westwards from the road at Rowton into Wood House Lane.[46] They were inclosed in 1778.[47]

Another common pasture was Mill Holme. In the earlier 13th century freemen of North Skirlaugh and Rowton had given Swine priory land, including 'Milnehol', and meadow, with power to inclose but reserving certain pasturage rights,[48] and in 1577, after the priory's dissolution, farmers of North Skirlaugh and Rowton successfully defended their right to common pasturage for cattle between August and March in Mill Holme against the tenants of that land.[49] It was then claimed, however, and later accepted, that the land was a detached part of South Skirlaugh, and in 1885 the c. 35 a. (14 ha.) were transferred to Benningholme.[50] In 1657 Hugh Bethell bought Mill Holme close, which evidently comprised North Holmes, adjoining Rowton, South Holmes, next to Benningholme, and a lane called Outgangs. By exchange and lease Bethell obtained common rights in the Holmes and Outgangs in 1658, and the area probably ceased to be commonable soon afterwards.[51]

FARMS. Meaux abbey's grange at Rowton, including a few acres in Benningholme ings, comprised c. 200 a., or 9½ bovates. The abbey had withdrawn from direct exploitation of the grange by the late 14th century, when it was recorded as let for £3 5s. a year, though scarcely worth £1 10s. in an average year.[52]

The Bethells' estate at North Skirlaugh and Rowton comprised most of the township in 1782 and was then occupied as 14 holdings; one farm comprised 161 a., five others c. 40–70 a. each, one 27 a., and two 14 a. each; the other holdings were of an acre or two.[53] By 1852 the 12 holdings in the township included two farms with c. 150 a. each there, two others, one mostly in Riston and Arnold, with c. 60 a. in the township, and three with some 10–24 a. each.[54] In 1915 Rowton farm comprised 297 a., of which 57 a. were in Arnold and Benningholme, and North Skirlaugh Grange 154 a.; 68 a. more in the township were held with a Rise farm and there were nine other holdings, all of 25 a. or less.[55] In the earlier 20th century the farms at North Skirlaugh and Rowton included one or two dairy units.[56]

MILL AND FISHERY. Swine priory's mill at Rowton, recorded in 1241, and its water mill at North Skirlaugh in 1536[57] were probably the

38 P.R.O., C 66/1802, no. 16.
39 R.D.B., O/387/950; above, Swine, manors (rectory).
40 Below, Long Riston, manors.
41 E.R.A.O., PE/104/100.
42 Book of plans of estates of H. Bethell, at Rise Park Estate Off.; P.R.O., E 178/4913.
43 E.R.A.O., DDRI/28/19, 21, 23.
44 Book of plans of estates of H. Bethell, at Rise Park Estate Off.; O.S. Map 6", Yorks. CCXI, CCXII (1855 edn.). Cf. Hull Univ., Dept. of Geog., R.A.F. air photographs, run 333B, nos. 3265–7.
45 *Chron. de Melsa* (Rolls Ser.), ii. 213–17; 'Meaux Cart.' pp. 425–9.
46 E.R.A.O., DDRI/28/23; O.S. Map 6", Yorks. CCXI (1855 edn.).

47 Below, Long Riston, econ. hist.
48 *Yorks. Deeds*, viii, pp. 4–5.
49 E.R.A.O., DDRI/28/2; ibid. DDX/508/28.
50 O.S. Map 6", Yorks. CCXI (1855 edn.); O.S. Map 1/2,500, Yorks. CCXI. 8, 12 (1891 edn.); below, S. Skirlaugh, intro.
51 E.R.A.O., DDRI/28/14–15, 19, 21, 23.
52 B.L. Cott. MS. Vit. C. vi, ff. 221 and v., 230–1.
53 Book of plans of estates of H. Bethell, at Rise Park Estate Off.
54 E.R.A.O., accession 2980, 'Rise Estates 1852'.
55 R.D.B, 170/289/242.
56 Directories; A. Harris, *Milk Supply of E. Yorks. 1850–1950* (E. Yorks. Loc. Hist. Ser. xxxiii), 31.
57 P.R.O., E 315/401, p. 379; *Yorks. Fines, 1232–46*, p. 94.

same; the water mill evidently stood on Lamb-wath stream close to Water Mill bridge.[58] The stream was probably also used for the priory's fishery at North Skirlaugh.[59]

TRADES. Weavers worked at North Skirlaugh in the mid 19th century,[60] and a building firm operated there in 1994.

LOCAL GOVERNMENT. Tenants of Rise manor owed suit to its court, the rights of which in North Skirlaugh, Rowton, and Arnold were said to have been infringed in the early 17th century by officers of the wapentake court.[61]

A poorhouse was maintained at North Skirlaugh.[62] In North Skirlaugh, Rowton, and part of Arnold together 3–5 people were relieved permanently in the early 19th century, and 4–7 were given occasional relief between 1812 and 1815.[63] North Skirlaugh joined Skirlaugh poor-law union in 1837,[64] and the township, later civil

parish, remained in Skirlaugh rural district until 1935. As part of Riston and later of Skirlaugh civil parish, it was included in the new Holderness rural district in 1935 and at reorganization in 1974 was taken into the Holderness district of Humberside.[65] In 1996 Skirlaugh parish became part of a new East Riding unitary area.[66]

EDUCATION. Arnold and North Skirlaugh together had two schools in 1833, possibly one in each place. One of the schools had been begun in 1829 and each was attended by a dozen boys and girls, all of whom, except for a few girls sent by Mrs. Bethell, were paid for by their parents.[67]

CHARITY FOR THE POOR. The poor of North Skirlaugh and Rowton shared in the eleemosynary charity of Marmaduke Langdale (d. 1611).[68]

SOUTH SKIRLAUGH

THE large village of South Skirlaugh lies 4 km. north from Swine village. Its name is discussed above.[69] South Skirlaugh township, later civil parish, was of 1,102 a. (446 ha.) until 1885, when c. 35 a. (14 ha.) were transferred to Benning-holme.[70] Renamed Skirlaugh civil parish in 1935, it was enlarged in 1952 with 627 a. (254 ha.) at North Skirlaugh and Arnold, transferred from Riston civil parish, and 9 a. (3.6 ha.) from Rise civil parish, and the area remains 690 ha. (1,705 a.).[71] South Skirlaugh had 87 poll-tax payers in 1377[72] and 17 houses assessed for hearth tax in 1672.[73] Numbers there grew from 123 in 1801 to 364 in 1861 but had fallen to 261 by 1891. They recovered after 1901 to reach 294 in 1921 but were only 264 in 1931 and little different in 1951. In 1952 some 160 people were gained by the incorporation of North Skirlaugh into the reconstituted parish, which had a population of 522 in 1961, 808 in 1971, 1,575 in 1981, and 1,578 in 1991, when there were usually 1,626 resident.[74]

SOUTH SKIRLAUGH village is mostly built on the valley side of Lambwath stream but a small group of its buildings stands isolated some ½ km. to the south-east. That division of South Skirlaugh into north and south ends probably explains why its chapel was sometimes erroneously recorded under North Skirlaugh.[75]

Formerly South Skirlaugh's main street was probably Church Lane, which continues northwards over the stream into North Skirlaugh and then on to Rise.[76] At its southern end Church Lane joins Hull Road, the present main street. Part of the main Hull–Bridlington road, Hull Road leads north-westwards through North Skirlaugh to Long Riston and eventually to Bridlington and south-eastwards through the south end to Coniston and Hull. From that road, side lanes lead to Benningholme, Ellerby, Langthorpe, and Marton. Since 1852, and notably in the mid and late 20th century, South Skirlaugh has been built-up along Hull Road and in and behind Church and Benningholme Lanes, and similar development in North Skirlaugh has virtually made the two Skirlaughs into one. The rural district council built c. 90 houses, mostly beside Hull Road, in the mid 20th century but the greater part of the modern housing is private;[77] sewerage for the council houses was provided in the 1950s.[78] Another addition was a telephone exchange. Conversely, some village buildings were demolished for the widening of the main road in the early 1960s.[79] At the south end, the dozen houses include a cottage, possibly of the 18th century, and several farmhouses.

Up to four houses were licensed at South Skirlaugh in the later 18th century, and the Sun and the Duke of York were named from the

58 O.S. Map 6″, Yorks. CCXI (1855 edn.).
59 Cal. Pat. 1377–81, 364.
60 E.R.A.O., accession 2980, 'Rise Estates 1852'; P.R.O., HO 107/2365; directories.
61 H.U.L., DDKG/9; Poulson, Holderness, ii. 223.
62 Inf. from Mrs. N. Kemp, N. Skirlaugh, 1995.
63 Poor Law Abstract, 1804, pp. 594–5; 1818, pp. 522–3.
64 3rd Rep. Poor Law Com. 170.
65 Census.
66 Humberside (Structural Change) Order 1995, copy at E.R.A.O.
67 Educ. Enq. Abstract, 1096.
68 Below, S. Skirlaugh, charity.

69 Above, N. Skirlaugh, intro.
70 O.S. Map 6″, Yorks. CCXI, CCXII (1855 edn.); O.S. Map 1/2,500, Yorks. CCXI. 8, 12 (1891 edn.); Census, 1891.
71 E.R.A.O., CCO. 465; Census,, 1931 (pt. ii), 1961, 1991.
72 P.R.O., E 179/202/60, m. 78.
73 Hearth Tax, 61.
74 V.C.H. Yorks. iii. 494; Census, 1901–91.
75 R.D.B., BB/73/13. Cf. T. Jefferys, Map of Yorks. (1772).
76 O.S. Map 6″, Yorks. CCXI, CCXII (1855 edn.).
77 R.D.B., 585/100/77; 1033/424/382; 1222/122/106.
78 Ibid. 1033/424/382.
79 Ibid. 1226/168/156.

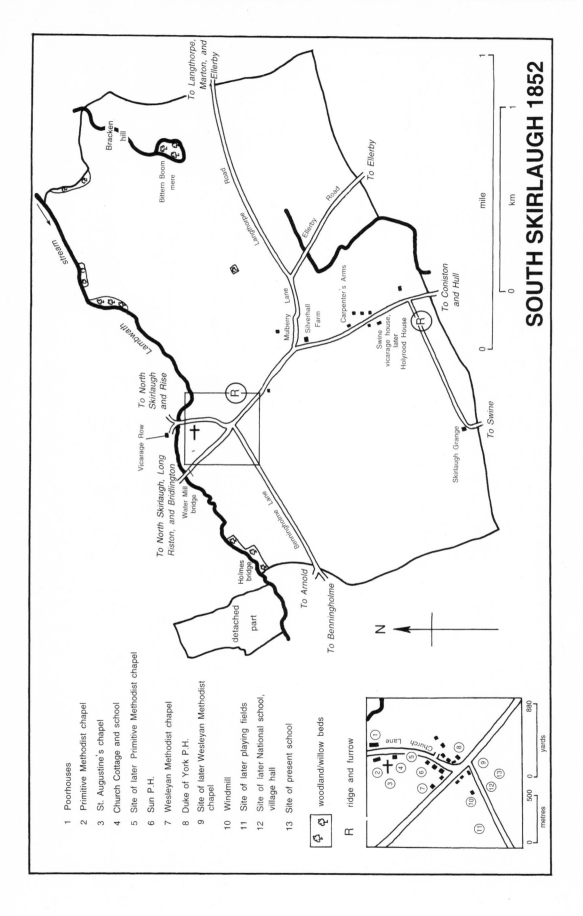

SOUTH SKIRLAUGH 1852

1 Poorhouses
2 Primitive Methodist chapel
3 St. Augustine's chapel
4 Church Cottage and school
5 Site of later Primitive Methodist chapel
6 Sun P.H.
7 Wesleyan Methodist chapel
8 Duke of York P.H.
9 Site of later Wesleyan Methodist chapel
10 Windmill
11 Site of later playing fields
12 Site of later National school, village hall
13 Site of present school

woodland/willow beds

R ridge and furrow

1820s.[80] The latter was briefly called the Royal in the 1840s,[81] and both existed in 1994. A third house, run by a wheelwright from 1840, was presumably the Carpenter's Arms, at the south end; named in 1852,[82] it was closed in or soon after 1968.[83] A lodge of the United Ancient Order of Druids was founded at South Skirlaugh in 1859; it met at the Duke of York and flourished until at least 1938.[84] An annual summer feast was held in the village in the late 19th century.[85]

A reading room and Working Men's Institute for North and South Skirlaugh was opened in 1886 in a former Primitive Methodist chapel;[86] by 1908 it had been removed to an old Wesleyan Methodist chapel,[87] which in the 1960s was demolished for road widening and replaced by a new building nearby.[88] A lending library was recorded in 1892, and later a county library branch was held at the Methodist church until 1960, when it was transferred to the reading room.[89] About 1972 a former school building was adapted for a village hall.[90] Youth clubs have included one held successively in the Church hall, in North Skirlaugh, and the village hall until it was discontinued c. 1990.[91]

The village supported two cricket and two football teams in the earlier 20th century. Football was played successively on grounds behind Church Lane and off the Rise road, in North Skirlaugh, and cricket on fields off Church Lane and at Dowthorpe Hall, in Ellerby, until a village playing field was provided beside Benningholme Lane c. 1970.[92] Allotment gardens have been provided by the parish council on part of the land bought for a cemetery in 1975.[93]

Skirlaugh was the birthplace of Walter Skirlaw, bishop of Durham (d. 1406) and of the topographer John Bigland (d. 1832).[94]

MANORS AND OTHER ESTATES. The 5 carucates and 6 bovates recorded at 'Skirlaugh' in 1086 evidently included land at South Skirlaugh, which, like that at North Skirlaugh, later became part of the Aumale fee.[95]

Most of the Aumale fee at South Skirlaugh was held by the Wytons. Adam of Wyton, the first known tenant there,[96] had been succeeded

by the mid 13th century by W. of Wyton[97] and by the 1280s by Henry of Wyton, whose holding, of 2½ carucates, was wholly held by tenants.[98]

By 1260 Thornton abbey (Lincs.) had been given ½ carucate and a close by Adam of Wyton, and 1 carucate and several tofts by two other donors.[99] The land was later an appurtenance of the abbey's manor of Woodhouse, in Arnold, with which it was granted after the Dissolution to the short-lived Thornton college in 1542.[1] It presumably continued to descend with Woodhouse manor.

Swine priory had land at South Skirlaugh by 1240,[2] and in 1352 it shared the Wytons' holding there with Thornton abbey.[3] Its estate at South Skirlaugh was probably enlarged in or soon after 1415 by grant from bishop Walter Skirlaw's executors,[4] and in 1535 the house had land at North and South Skirlaugh worth £11 a year.[5] After the priory's dissolution, its so-called manor of SOUTH SKIRLAUGH was let in 1541 to Sir Richard Gresham.[6] Part of the estate was granted as concealed land to John and William Marsh in 1576.[7] The Crown later sold 13 houses, nearly 2 carucates, and closes at South Skirlaugh, agents of Sir John Carey, Lord Hunsden, buying most, including the chief house, in 1604 and Edward Bates and Henry Elwes the rest in 1609.[8] Other land at South Skirlaugh, formerly belonging to the priory, was sold in 1609 to Robert Angell and John Walter.[9]

The Constables held land of the Crown in Skirlaugh, possibly as an appurtenance of their lordship of Holderness,[10] and it was perhaps on that account that they and their successors were later reckoned lords of SOUTH SKIRLAUGH manor.[11]

William James (d. by 1723), vicar of Burstwick, endowed his hospital at Cawood (Yorks. W.R.) with a farm of 58 a. at South Skirlaugh, which was sold to Harry and Clive Jackson in 1970.[12]

In 1838 W. V. Norman bought a farm at South Skirlaugh of c. 140 a., formerly part of

[80] E.R.A.O., QDT/2/7, 9.
[81] R.D.B., GF/158/171.
[82] O.S. Map 6″, Yorks. CCXII (1855 edn.); directories.
[83] E.R.C.C. Mins. 1967–8, 243; 1972–3, 162.
[84] D. [R. J.] Neave, E.R. Friendly Soc. (E. Yorks. Loc. Hist. Ser. xli), 67; Bulmer, Dir. E. Yorks. (1892), 508.
[85] Bulmer, Dir. E. Yorks. (1892), 504.
[86] Kelly's Dir. N. & E.R. Yorks. (1889), 456; Bulmer, Dir. E. Yorks. (1892), 505, 508.
[87] R.D.B., 170/137/113; 761/390/320; O.S. Map 1/2,500, Yorks. CCXII. 5 (1891, 1910 edns.).
[88] E.R.C.C. Mins. 1965–6, 225–6.
[89] E.R. Educ. Cttee. Mins. 1959–60, 184; 1967–8, 185; Bulmer, Dir. E. Yorks. (1892), 508.
[90] R.D.B., 1834/392/309; E.R. Educ. Cttee. Mins. 1972–3, 85.
[91] E.R. Educ. Cttee. Mins. 1960–1, 42; inf. from the vicar and Mrs. J. Stott, N. Skirlaugh, 1995.
[92] O.S. Map 6″, Yorks. CCXII. NW. (1929 edn.); inf. from Mrs. N. Kemp, N. Skirlaugh, 1995; inf. from Mr. L. Lowther, S. Skirlaugh, 1995.
[93] B.I.H.R., CD. 902.

[94] D.N.B.   [95] Above, N. Skirlaugh, manors.
[96] Cal. Chart. R. 1300–26, 9–10.
[97] Kirkby's Inquest, 373.
[98] Cal. Inq. p.m. iv, p. 355; x, p. 8.
[99] Cal. Chart. R. 1300–26, 9–10; Cal. Inq. p.m. x, p. 8.
[1] L. & P. Hen. VIII, xvii, pp. 29–30; below, Long Riston, manors (Woodhouse).
[2] Yorks. Fines, 1232–46, p. 86.
[3] Cal. Inq. p.m. x, p. 8.
[4] B.L. Stowe Ch. 482; Cal. Pat. 1413–16, 327; Test. Ebor. i, p. 317; Burton, Mon. Ebor. 253; Poulson, Holderness, ii. 261; below, church.
[5] Valor Eccl. (Rec. Com.), v. 114; above, N. Skirlaugh, manors.   [6] L. & P. Hen. VIII, xvi, p. 723.
[7] Cal. Pat. 1575–8, p. 28.
[8] P.R.O., C 66/1800, no. 7; E.R.A.O., DDX/508/28.
[9] P.R.O., C 66/1802, no. 16.
[10] H.U.L., DHO/7/42; DHO/8/47.
[11] Directories.
[12] R.D.B., HZ/111/134; 1645/326/279; 1677/357/321; E.R.A.O., PE/88/29; Herring's Visit. i, p. 138; V.C.H. Yorks. E.R. v. 13.

the estate attached to Langthorpe Hall, in Ellerby.[13] Another farm, of almost 150 a. and formerly belonging to the Hildyards, was bought in 1846,[14] and the Langthorpe Hall estate in 1857.[15] Mr. Norman (d. 1861)[16] was succeeded in one of the farms at South Skirlaugh by his daughter Elizabeth (d. 1900) and she by Marmaduke Rees-Webbe, who sold Poplar farm in 1919 to R. J. Kirkwood.[17] The other farm passed to Mary Norman (d. by 1898), presumably another daughter, and then in turn to Elizabeth as her devisee and Elizabeth's heir, Marmaduke Rees-Webbe, who sold Silverhall farm to the county council in 1919 for smallholdings.[18]

The Crown's estate in Swine parish included c. 125 a. in South Skirlaugh in the early 20th century.[19]

Rectorial tithes at South Skirlaugh were bought from William Thornton in 1737 by Hugh Bethell (d. 1752), in 1764 by Sir Robert Hildyard, Bt., and in 1765 by William Langdale and John Moorhouse's widow Ann;[20] Thomas Thornton sold others in 1792 to Robert Wood.[21] In 1839 the tithes of the Cawood charity farm were commuted for a rent charge of £4 4s.,[22] and tithes from over 400 a. were merged in 1849.[23]

ECONOMIC HISTORY. COMMONABLE LANDS AND INCLOSURE.

Little is known about the commonable lands of South Skirlaugh. East field was named in 1645.[24] Ridge and furrow remains beside the main road near the southern boundary and at the south end of the village, and the location of other parts of the open fields is suggested by the shapes of some of the later closes.[25] Bracken hill, in the north-eastern corner of the township, and an ill-drained area to its south, may have been used as common pasture.[26] The commonable lands had been inclosed by 1722.[27]

16TH-CENTURY HOLDINGS.

Swine priory had seventeen tenants at South Skirlaugh in 1536; three of the holdings were of over 3 bovates each and four of 1–3 bovates, and there were 10 smaller holdings with little or no open-field land.[28]

LATER AGRICULTURE.

In Skirlaugh chapelry 443 a. was returned as arable land in 1801.[29] Of the 415 ha. (1,026 a.) returned under Skirlaugh civil parish in 1987, 320 ha. (791 a.) were arable land, 88 ha. (218 a.) grassland, and 1 ha. (2.5 a.) woodland; livestock kept in the area then included just over 200 cattle.[30]

There were usually 6–8 farmers at South Skirlaugh in the 19th century and earlier 20th, one or two of whom had 150 a. or more.[31] The Crown let 49 a. at South Skirlaugh from 1909 and two cottages and 75 a. more from 1914 to the county council, which provided ten smallholdings there until the mid 1930s. Other council holdings were made from the 135-a. Silverhall farm, bought in 1919; three of the holdings there, amounting to 39 a., were let that year to Skirlaugh parish meeting. Humberside county council still held the estate in 1995.[32] Up to five market gardeners found employment at South Skirlaugh in the later 19th and early 20th century, and a cowkeeper worked there in the 1870s.[33] In 1987 eight holdings were returned under Skirlaugh civil parish; two were of 100–199 ha. (247–492 a.), one of 50–99 ha. (124–245 a.), three of 20–49 ha. (49–121 a.), and two of under 2 ha. (5 a.).[34]

MILL.

Swine priory had a windmill at South Skirlaugh which was rebuilt in the 1560s and sold by the Crown in 1611.[35] Perhaps the same was the windmill recorded in 1750[36] and the later post mill, off Benningholme Lane, which ground until c. 1910 and was demolished in 1944.[37]

TRADES.

There was small-scale commercial activity in South Skirlaugh village in the 19th and earlier 20th century, c. 30 tradesmen and shopkeepers working there in 1851, for instance, and the two public houses also playing their part. Craftsmen included a weaver in 1851.[38] A motor engineering concern was begun c. 1920, and in 1994 there were two garages beside the main road and a workshop in Church Lane.[39]

LOCAL GOVERNMENT.

Chapelwardens' and churchwardens' accounts survive from 1746 and include details of the Chapel Estate charity.[40] Poorhouses were maintained by South

13   R.D.B., EE/29/41; FF/22/29.
14   Ibid. H/328/680; I/240/545; K/209/421; GF/230/268; H.U.L., DDCV(2)/44/3; J. Foster, *Pedigrees of Yorks*. iii.
15   Above, Ellerby, manors (Langthorpe).
16   R.D.B., II/123/146.
17   Ibid. KQ/370/495; 40/276/265 (1902); 202/199/171; 202/504/431.
18   R.D.B., KQ/367/493; 6/207/185 (1898); 40/276/265 (1902); 202/199/171; below, econ. hist.
19   Below, econ. hist.
20   R.D.B., O/387/950; AI/287/578; H.U.L., DDCV(2)/ 44/20; P.R.O., CRES 38/2424 (deed); above, Swine, manors (rectory).
21   P.R.O., CRES 38/2104.   22   E.R.A.O., PE/88/29.
23   R.D.B., GO/390/437; GO/391/438; P.R.O., CRES 38/2104.
24   E.R.A.O., DDRI/28/10.
25   For other ridge and furrow, Hull Univ., Dept. of Geog., R.A.F. air photographs, run 333A, nos. 4204–7; run 333B, no. 3263.

26   O.S. Map 6″, Yorks. CCXI, CCXII (1855 edn.).
27   R.D.B., H/328/680.
28   P.R.O., E 315/401, pp. 377, 382.
29   Ibid. HO 67/26/394.
30   Inf. from Min. of Agric., Fish. & Food, Beverley, 1990.
31   P.R.O., HO 107/2365; directories.
32   R.D.B., 202/199/171; E.R.C.C. *Mins.* 1909–10, 46, 56–7, 62; 1913–14, 354–5; 1919–20, 194, 215, 402; E.R. Agric. Cttee. *Mins.* 1936–40, 10, 59; inf. from Humbs. C. C., 1995.
33   P.R.O., HO 107/2365; directories.
34   Inf. from Min. of Agric., Fish. & Food.
35   P.R.O., C 66/1902, no. 1; *Cal. Pat.* 1563–6, p. 387. Mill hill and Mill balk were named in 1609: P.R.O., C 66/1802, no. 16.
36   P.R.O., CRES 38/2125 (abstract of title, Oubrough).
37   Directories; R. Gregory, *E. Yorks. Windmills*, 32–4 (illus.); O.S. Map 1/2,500, Yorks. CCXI. 8 (1891 edn.).
38   P.R.O., HO 107/2365; directories.
39   Directories.
40   E.R.A.O., PE/88/19–22.

Skirlaugh.[41] Seven people were relieved there permanently in 1802–3 and 5 occasionally between 1812 and 1815.[42] South Skirlaugh joined Skirlaugh poor-law union in 1837,[43] and the township, later civil parish, remained in Skirlaugh rural district until 1935, then became part of the new Holderness rural district, and at reorganization in 1974 was taken into the Holderness district of Humberside.[44] In 1996 Skirlaugh parish became part of a new East Riding unitary area.[45] Skirlaugh obtained a parish council in 1949.[46] In 1982 a cemetery adjoining the churchyard was consecrated for Skirlaugh and Ellerby civil parishes.[47]

CHURCH. Parishioners of Swine living at North and South Skirlaugh, Arnold, and Rowton were served by the 14th century in South Skirlaugh chapel,[48] sometimes erroneously described as in North Skirlaugh.[49] The curacy was annexed to Swine vicarage by the later 17th century,[50] but in 1867 a separate parish of Skirlaugh was created, comprising North Skirlaugh, South Skirlaugh, Benningholme, and Marton townships, together with the part of Arnold until then in Swine parish. The living was a perpetual curacy in 1867[51] but soon afterwards became a vicarage.[52] Skirlaugh vicarage was united with Long Riston in 1956, when the archbishop of York, the patron since 1867,[53] was given alternate presentations to the united benefice.[54] He obtained the share of the other patron, the Crown, by an exchange of patronages in 1961.[55] In 1989 Skirlaugh parish was reduced by the transfer of its part of Arnold to Riston parish.[56]

Before the mid 14th century Swine priory and the inhabitants of North and South Skirlaugh, Arnold, and Rowton agreed on the maintenance of a chantry in South Skirlaugh chapel. In 1337 a dispute, allegedly occasioned by the priory's withdrawal of the chantry, was settled by the archbishop, who made a new ordination. The priory was to present a chaplain to celebrate daily in the chapel and to pay him £1 13s. 4d. a year, and its earlier assignment to him of 2 bovates at South Skirlaugh and 1d. a year from each

of the priory's bovates at Skirlaugh was ratified. For their part, the inhabitants were to provide all necessities for services and to repair the chapel, 5s. a year, hitherto owed to the priory, being allowed them towards their costs.[57] Walter Skirlaw (d. 1406), bishop of Durham, a native of Skirlaugh and brother of a prioress of Swine,[58] rebuilt the chapel[59] and in 1404 refounded and augmented the chantry to support two chaplains; one was to receive £6 a year as warden and curate and the second chaplain a stipend was £5 6s. 8d. Skirlaw then presented the first incumbents, who included as second chaplain William Skirlaw;[60] thereafter Swine priory was patron.[61] A third chaplain was mentioned in 1525–6.[62] The chantry was recorded in 1535, but had evidently been suppressed by 1542, when pensions were being paid to two chantry priests at Skirlaugh for their lives. There seems only to have been a curate at Skirlaugh in 1546.[63] In 1337 the priory had given land on the north side of the chapelyard as the site for a house for the chantry priest,[64] and in 1576 the Crown sold the chantry house to Andrew Palmer and Alexander King.[65] An almshouse recorded in 1573 may also have been associated with the chantry.[66]

From the 1540s the curate of Skirlaugh, and later the vicar of Swine as curate, received a stipend of £3 6s. 8d. a year from the rectory.[67] By the early 19th century the stipend had been increased by subscription to £26 5s.[68] A curate was deprived in the 1550s,[69] and later the duty seems to have been neglected. There were no sermons in 1575 and 1582,[70] and services were often infrequent in the 18th century.[71] In 1743, however, when the vicar had an assistant curate, a service was held every other Sunday and there were three celebrations of communion, at which c. 50 received.[72]

At the creation of the new parish in 1867 the curate's stipend and an £18 rent charge for tithes at Marton, until then also received by the vicar of Swine, were annexed to Skirlaugh.[73] Two sums of £1,500 each were raised by subscription and met in 1867 and 1876 respectively by annual grants of £46 13s. 4d. and £50 from the Common Fund,[74] and in 1883 the net annual income was £187.[75] A further £6 a year was granted from the Common Fund in 1909.[76] A

41 O.S. Map 6″, Yorks. CCXII (1855 edn.).
42 *Poor Law Abstract, 1804*, pp. 594–5; *1818*, pp. 522–3.
43 *3rd Rep. Poor Law Com.* 170.
44 *Census*.
45 Humberside (Structural Change) Order 1995, copy at E.R.A.O.
46 E.R.A.O., CCO/445.
47 B.I.H.R., CD. 902.
48 Below, this section; *T.E.R.A.S.* iv. 51.
49 R.D.B., BB/73/13.
50 B.I.H.R., TER. H. Skirlaugh, Swine n.d. etc.; *Rep. Com. Eccl. Revenues*, 970–1.
51 B.I.H.R., OC. 262.
52 *Crockford* (1876), 47.
53 B.I.H.R., OC. 262.
54 *Lond. Gaz.* 14 Aug. 1956, pp. 4667–8.
55 B.I.H.R., OC. 762.
56 Below, Long Riston, church.
57 B.I.H.R., Reg. 9A, ff. 395–396v.   58 *D.N.B.*
59 Below, this section.
60 *Reg. Langley*, ii (Sur. Soc. clxvi), pp. 81–90.
61 Lawrance, 'Clergy List', Holderness, 2, pp. 186–7.

62 *Y.A.J.* xxiv. 76.
63 P.R.O., E 318/11/528, m. 10; ibid. SC 6/Hen. VIII/2022, m. 84d.; *Valor Eccl.*(Rec. Com.), v. 118.
64 B.I.H.R., Reg. 9A, f. 396; *Reg. Langley*, ii (Sur. Soc. clxvi), pp. 81–90.
65 *Cal. Pat.* 1548–9, 37–9; 1575–8, p. 31.
66 Ibid. 1572–5, pp. 39–43.
67 P.R.O., E 318/11/528, m. 10; B.I.H.R., TER. H. Skirlaugh n.d. etc.
68 *9th Rep. Com. Char.* 781.
69 A. G. Dickens, *Marian Reaction in Dioc. of York: The Clergy* (St. Anthony's Hall Publ. xi), 34.
70 B.I.H.R., V. 1582/CB. 1, f. 206; *Abp. Grindal's Visit., 1575*, 73.
71 B.I.H.R., TER. H. Swine 1716; ibid. V. 1764/Ret. 3, no. 66.
72 *Herring's Visit.* iii, pp. 127, 131.
73 B.I.H.R., OC. 262; above, Swine, church.
74 B.I.H.R., OC. 262; *Lond. Gaz.* 20 Aug. 1867, p. 4617; 12 May 1876, p. 2924.
75 B.I.H.R., V. 1884/Ret. 2.
76 *Lond. Gaz.* 24 Dec. 1909, p. 9788.

FIG. 9. SKIRLAUGH CHURCH

parsonage for the new parish was built at North Skirlaugh in 1869–70,[77] and that house was designated the parsonage house of the united benefice in 1956.[78]

In 1865 the vicar of Swine provided a weekly service in the chapel, besides another in the workhouse at North Skirlaugh. After the separation from Swine parish, cottage lectures and classes were started at Arnold and Marton and in Skirlaugh school, and by 1871 there were two Sunday services in Skirlaugh church. Holy Communion was quarterly in 1865 and monthly from 1868, with usually up to a dozen communicants in the later 19th century; in 1931, when communion was weekly, five usually received.[79] The congregations of Skirlaugh parish church and of Skirlaugh Methodist church were united in 1982.[80]

The church of ST. AUGUSTINE is largely of ashlar, and has an undivided nave and chancel with north vestry, all of c. 1400, and south porch and west tower of slightly later date.[81] Similar in plan to a college chapel, the nave, chancel, and vestry were built for Walter Skirlaw (d. 1406), bishop of Durham. Of six bays with traceried windows and prominent, pinnacled

buttresses, it is a well-known example of early Perpendicular architecture. Skirlaw's arms occur often in chancel and nave, and their absence from the tower and south porch suggests that they were not part of his gift. The tower is partly built of rubble. The interior of the church was originally fitted with a screen and stalls. The rood loft with images remained in 1567,[82] and the screen survived into the 19th century, being sold c. 1835 with the stalls.[83] The church was repewed in 1819[84] and restored in the late 19th century. Much of the restoration was done by William Botterill & Sons of Hull in 1879–80 and included the removal of a west gallery, the renewal of stonework in the windows and the tower, and reglazing.[85] The chancel was altered and refitted in the mid 1880s,[86] and the church again reseated in 1893.[87] Restoration work in the later 20th century has included the replacement of the original roof by one of lower pitch with a ceiling of timber panels in the 1960s, reglazing and the resetting in the windows of fragments of medieval glass in 1981, and the removal of Victorian panelling and pew platforms in 1990. Over several years Mr. Edward Brown of Skirlaugh repointed all the stonework.[88]

[77] B.I.H.R., NPH. 1869/3; ibid. Ch. Ret. iii; *Lond. Gaz.* 20 Aug. 1867, p. 4617; *Kelly's Dir. N. & E.R. Yorks.* (1889), 456.
[78] *Lond. Gaz.* 14 Aug. 1956, pp. 4667–8.
[79] B.I.H.R., V. 1865/Ret. 2, no. 527; V. 1868/Ret. 2, no. 454; V. 1871/Ret. 2, no. 460; V. 1877/Ret. 3, no. 71; V. 1931/Ret.; *Kelly's Dir. N. & E. R. Yorks.* (1897), 536.
[80] *St. Augustine's Church, Skirlaugh* (1991).
[81] Illus. Poulson, *Holderness*, ii, plates facing p. 265.
[82] J. S. Purvis, *Tudor Par. Doc. of Dioc. York*, 34.
[83] B.I.H.R., ER V./Ret. 2, f. 11; [G. A. Poole], *Illus. of*

Chapel of St. Augustine, Skirlaugh (1855), 50; *Y.A.J.* xxiv. 167–8.   [84] *9th Rep. Com. Char.* 780.
[85] B.I.H.R., Fac. 1878/11; ibid. V. 1884/Ret.2; *Kelly's Dir. N. & E.R. Yorks.* (1889), 456; *Report of Trial ... arising out of Restoration of Skirlaugh Church* (1879) (copy in Beverley Public Libr.).
[86] B.I.H.R., Fac. Bk. 6, pp. 531–3; ibid. Fac. 1884/3.
[87] Ibid. Fac. 1892/28; E.R.A.O., PE/88/24.
[88] E.R.A.O., PE/88/18; *St. Augustine's Church, Skirlaugh* (1991); inf. from the vicar, 1995.

The fabric of the earlier chapel was the parishioners' responsibility in the 14th century,[89] and in 1404 Walter Skirlaw provided for his new chapel by assigning 6*s.* 8*d.* a year of the existing chantry's income to them.[90] By 1623 there was a landed endowment,[91] later the Chapel Estate or Bishop Skirlaw's charity. In the mid 18th century it comprised two houses and *c.* 3 a. at North and South Skirlaugh, rent charges amounting to 9*s.* 4*d.*, and a common right in Arnold carr, for which 8 a. there were allotted at inclosure in 1778.[92] In 1823 the total income was just over £36 a year, of which *c.* £5 was subscribed towards the curate's stipend.[93] Four cottages called Vicarage Row were built at North Skirlaugh in 1862, increasing the income to *c.* £53 a year.[94] By 1930 the income was added to that from Langdale's charity and other sources and spent generally to support the church and its services.[95] The land at Arnold was sold in 1943.[96] In 1963 the income from the Chapel Estate was only £127,[97] but rents were later revised and the site of the Church hall, after the removal of the building in the 1970s, and adjoining land at North Skirlaugh sold for housing. In 1995 the annual income was *c.* £9,000, which continued to be spent on the church and its services.[98]

The chapel was also maintained under the will of Marmaduke Langdale,[99] just over £5 a year being received by the chapelwardens *c.* 1800 and £60 of unspent income being used for repewing in 1819;[1] in the mid 19th century the trustees allowed the church £5–40 a year.[2] By Scheme of 1900 the church was assigned ¼ of the net income of the charity for the fabric, fittings, and services of the church, and *c.* £6–9 a year were received in the earlier 20th century[3] and £30 in 1963.[4]

There were two bells in 1552 and later.[5] The plate includes a paten and a 17th-century cup and cover.[6] The registers of baptisms begin in 1711, of marriages in 1720, and of burials in 1719; baptism entries are lacking for 1712–18 and marriage entries for the 1750s.[7] Transcripts for Skirlaugh and Marton survive, however, from 1600.[8]

The chapelyard, mentioned from the 14th century,[9] was closed partly in 1882 and wholly soon after 1883.[10] Ground adjoining the old yard was bought for an addition in 1883 and then licensed for burials; it was eventually consecrated in 1927, with another addition bought that year.[11]

For his service in Skirlaugh chapel the clerk of Swine parish was entitled to 32 sheaves of wheat from Arnold until inclosure in 1778, when 16*s.* 6*d.* a year was substituted.[12]

ROMAN CATHOLICISM. There were a dozen Roman Catholics at 'Skirlaugh' in the 1660s, some of them possibly connexions of the Langdales of neighbouring Langthorpe, in Ellerby.[13]

PROTESTANT NONCONFORMITY. In 1776 an unidentified, protestant congregation worshipped in a house at 'Skirlaugh'.[14] Wesleyan Methodists registered a house there in 1800 and built a chapel on the east side of the main road at South Skirlaugh in 1821.[15] The chapel had evidently been enlarged by 1869,[16] and in 1893 it was replaced by a new chapel on the other side of the road.[17] The former chapel was later used in succession to one held in an old Primitive Methodist chapel, before being demolished.[18] The new chapel, later the Methodist church, was closed in 1982, when the Methodist and Anglican congregations at Skirlaugh were amalgamated at St. Augustine's. The former church was sold in 1984 and later converted into a house.[19] The Primitive Methodists also built a chapel in 1821, presumably that at the north end of Church Lane attended in 1851 by a congregation of *c.* 55.[20] That chapel was replaced in 1859 by one built further south.[21] The former chapel was a reading room for a few years from 1886;[22] it seems to have been demolished. The Primitive Methodist chapel was closed in or shortly before 1928, when the building was sold, and in 1995 it was used as a motor engineering workshop.[23]

89 Above, this section.
90 *Reg. Langley*, ii (Sur. Soc. clxvi), pp. 81–90.
91 P.R.O., E 178/4913.
92 B.I.H.R., TER. H. Skirlaugh 1749, 1764, 1777; R.D.B., BB/73/13.   93 *9th Rep. Com. Char.* 781.
94 B.I.H.R., TER. H. Skirlaugh 1861, 1865; E.R.A.O., PE/88/18, 21; PE/88 (plan 1863); datestone.
95 E.R.A.O., accession 1681; below, this section.
96 R.D.B., 668/245/210.
97 E.R.A.O., PE/88, accession 1561, (acct.).
98 Inf. from the vicar; above, N. Skirlaugh, intro.
99 Below, charity.   1 *9th Rep. Com. Char.* 780.
2 E.R.A.O., PE/88/24.
3 Ibid. accession 1681; Scheme in possession of the vicar of Skirlaugh, 1995; below, charity.
4 E.R.A.O., PE/88, accession 1561, (acct.).
5 *Inventories of Ch. Goods*, 35; Boulter, 'Ch. Bells', 85.
6 *Yorks. Ch. Plate*, i. 315.
7 E.R.A.O., PE/88/1–2, 5–6.
8 B.I.H.R., PRT. Hold. D. Marton, Skirlaugh.
9 Ibid. Reg. 9A, f. 396.
10 *Lond. Gaz.* 5 May 1882, pp. 2065–7; 31 July 1883, p. 3816.
11 B.I.H.R., CD. 746; E.R.A.O., PE/88/24; R.D.B.,

NU/355/527.
12 B.I.H.R., TER. H. Skirlaugh 1777 etc.; R.D.B., BB/73/13.
13 Aveling, *Post Reformation Catholicism*, 67.
14 B.I.H.R., Fac. Bk. 2, p. 142.
15 Ibid. Fac. Bk. 3, p. 265; ibid. DMH. Reg. 1, p. 546; R.D.B., DL/28/31; O.S. Map 6″, Yorks. CCXII (1855 edn.); T. Allen, *Hist. Co. York*, iv. 274.
16 R.D.B., DL/28/31; KM/330/445.
17 Ibid. 42/143/131 (1891); 57/514/475 (1893); O.N.S. (Birkdale), Worship Reg. no. 34152; datestones.
18 R.D.B., 77/123/119 (1895); 170/137/113; O.S. Map 1/2,500, Yorks. CCXII. 5 (1910 edn.); E.R.C.C. *Mins.* 1965–6, 225–6; below, this section.
19 Inf. from the vicar, Skirlaugh, 1995; *St. Augustine's Church, Skirlaugh* (1991).
20 P.R.O., HO 129/522/2/9/10; O.S. Map 6″, Yorks. CCXII (1855 edn.); T. Allen, *Hist. Co. York*, iv. 274.
21 E.R.A.O., PE/88 (plan 1863); *Kelly's Dir. N. & E. R. Yorks.* (1901), 559.
22 *Kelly's Dir. N. & E.R. Yorks.* (1889), 456; above, this section.
23 R.D.B., 370/358/271; inf. from Mrs. N. Kemp, N. Skirlaugh, 1995.

EDUCATION. There may have been a school at South Skirlaugh before 1582, when it was complained that there was no curate to teach the young,[24] and in 1609, when Marmaduke Langdale (d. 1611) left money for teaching there.[25] There was certainly one in 1615, when a servant of Langdale's heir was teaching without licence.[26] Langdale's school was later held in a schoolhouse on the south side of the chapelyard. The building incorporated a cottage belonging to the Chapel Estate, now called Church Cottage and used for church meetings.[27] In the mid 18th century the Church school had c. 20 pupils, four of them taught free for £2 a year from Langdale's charity;[28] the trustees paid £10 10s. a year for the teaching of 10 boys and girls about 1820,[29] and they supported 17 pupils in 1833, when the other 20 paid school pence.[30] Langdale's charity helped in the building of a new National school with master's house on Benningholme Lane in 1860.[31] It was supported by school pence, subscriptions, including £20 from Langdale's charity,[32] and from 1863–4 by an annual government grant.[33] There were 49 in attendance at inspection in 1871,[34] and infants were accommodated in 1877.[35] Average attendance at the school declined from 115 in 1906–7 to 59 in 1937–8,[36] but c. 20 pupils were received from Ellerby school in 1947[37] and, despite the transfer of the senior pupils to South Holderness County Secondary School in 1954,[38] additional accommodation had to be hired for the school in the 1960s.[39] A new Church school was built nearby and opened in 1968; Swine school was then closed and its pupils transferred to Skirlaugh.[40] There were 268 on the roll at Skirlaugh

in 1990.[41] The old school buildings were used from c. 1972 as a village hall.[42]

By Scheme of 1900 South Skirlaugh school was assigned ¼ of the net income of Langdale's charity and the ½ then allocated for appenticeships might, in their absence, be used to encourage education in the form of prizes and grants. In the earlier 20th century the school's share was £6–9 a year and the trustees spent c. £10 on prizes.[43]

There were evidently also one or two dame schools at South Skirlaugh in the mid 19th century.[44]

CHARITY FOR THE POOR. Marmaduke Langdale (d. 1611) left £100 for the poor of North and South Skirlaugh, Rowton, and Arnold, and £100 to maintain South Skirlaugh chapel and for education. A permanent endowment for the charities, comprising 33 a. at Dowthorpe, in Ellerby, was settled in 1657 and produced an income of £10 a year then, £18 about 1800, and £26 in 1823. The eleemosynary share was intended for marriages and apprenticeships but in 1781 Langdale's bequest was said to be doubtful in its purpose and 'perpetually disputed', and in the early 19th century grants were rare and applications for assistance to marry were discouraged.[45] By Scheme of 1900 half of the clear income was allocated for apprenticeships or in default to education.[46] In the earlier 20th century the gross income was some £30–40 a year, from which grants of up to £10 were made for training and apprenticeship.[47] In 1995 the income was £1,900 a year.[48]

THIRTLEBY

THIRTLEBY hamlet lies 4 km. south-east from Swine village. The name is Scandinavian and means 'Thorkel's farmstead'.[49] Of 755 a. (306 ha.),[50] the civil parish was united in 1935 with that of Coniston as the new civil parish of Coniston.[51] In 1377 poll-tax payers at Thirtleby were recorded with those in Ellerby.[52] Ten houses at Thirtleby were assessed for hearth tax

in 1672.[53] From 44 in 1801, the population of Thirtleby increased to 69 in 1871, fell to 55 in 1881 and 44 in 1891, recovered after 1901 to 75 in 1911, then fell again to 51 in 1921, and was 55 in 1931.[54]

THIRTLEBY hamlet has comprised since the mid 19th century a dozen scattered houses.[55]

[24] B.I.H.R., V. 1582/CB. 1, f. 206.
[25] Below, charity.
[26] Aveling, *Post Reformation Catholicism*, 67.
[27] E.R.A.O., PE/88/18; *9th Rep. Com. Char.* 781; above, church; O.S. Map 6″, Yorks. CCXII (1855 edn.); inf. from the vicar, 1995.
[28] B.I.H.R., V. 1764/Ret. 3, no. 66; *Herring's Visit.* iii, p. 131.
[29] *Educ. of Poor Digest*, 1095; *9th Rep. Com. Char.* 780–1.
[30] *Educ. Enq. Abstract*, 1096.
[31] R.D.B., HZ/111/134; HZ/131/161; E.R.A.O., DDBD/84/37; ibid. SGP. 73.
[32] P.R.O., ED 7/135, no. 170.
[33] *Rep. of Educ. Cttee. of Council, 1863–4* [3349], p. 514, H.C. (1864), xlv.
[34] *Returns relating to Elem. Educ.* 472–3.
[35] B.I.H.R, V. 1877/Ret. 3, no. 71.
[36] *Bd. of Educ., List 21* (H.M.S.O., 1908 and later edns.).
[37] E.R.A.O., SL/34/3.
[38] E.R. Educ. Cttee. *Mins.* 1953–4, 145.
[39] Ibid. 1960–1, 56; 1961–2, 170.
[40] Ibid. 1965–6, 148; 1967–8, 40; inf. from the head

teacher, 1994.
[41] Inf. from Educ. Dept., Humbs. C.C., 1990.
[42] Above, intro.
[43] Scheme in possession of the vicar of Skirlaugh, 1995; E.R.A.O., accession 1681.
[44] P.R.O., HO 107/2365.
[45] B.I.H.R., TER. H. Skirlaugh 1749 etc.; *9th Rep. Com. Char.* 780–1; *Cal. Cttee. for Compounding*, iii, pp. 1925–6; Thompson, *Swine*, 284–99; above, Ellerby, manors (Dowthorpe). Accounts of 1782—1853 are at E.R.A.O., PE/88/28.
[46] Scheme in possession of the vicar of Skirlaugh, 1995; above, educ.
[47] E.R.A.O., accession 1681.
[48] Inf. from the vicar.
[49] *P.N. Yorks. E.R.* (E.P.N.S.), 51–2; G. F. Jensen, *Scand. Settlement Names in Yorks.* 39.
[50] O.S. Map 6″, Yorks. CCXXVII (1855 edn.).
[51] *Census*, 1931 (pt. ii).
[52] Above, Ellerby, intro.   [53] *Hearth Tax*, 61.
[54] *V.C.H. Yorks.* iii. 494; *Census*, 1901–31.
[55] B.I.H.R., TA. 568L; O.S. Map 6″, Yorks. CCXXVII (1855 edn.).

Spacey Field Farm, built *c.* 1800, was demolished in the mid 20th century,[56] and Swiss Cottage, a 16th-century style lodge for Thirtleby Grange, put up by 1852,[57] was taken down in or shortly before 1995. Woodlands, Hill Farm, and Central House were built between 1852 and 1889,[58] and Stillmeadow and Mount View Farms were put up near the site of Spacey Field Farm in the mid 20th century.[59] A beerhouse at Thirtleby was licensed in the 1750s.[60]

MANOR AND OTHER ESTATES. In 1066 Morkar held 4 carucates at Thirtleby as soke of his manor of Mappleton. By 1086 Drew de Bevrère held them,[61] and they were later part of the Aumale fee.

Much of Thirtleby was held of the counts of Aumale by the St. Quintins and later descended as part of their manor of Woodhall, in Ellerby.[62] In 1541 the Woodhall estate included land at Thirtleby let for over £13 a year,[63] and *c.* 260 a. there was sold by George Goring in several lots in the 1590s.[64] Those estates have not been traced further.

About 1200 Herbert de St. Quintin subinfeudated 2 carucates and 2 bovates in Thirtleby to Beatrice wife of William of Rochford as her marriage portion, in return for which the Rochfords quitclaimed Brandesburton to St. Quintin. The estate, mostly held by tenants,[65] descended to Walran of Rochford (fl. 1240), and in 1347 the St. Quintins' tenant was his or another Walran's heir.[66] In 1381–2 Joan Rogerson, probably Sir Walran of Rochford's daughter, sold the estate at Thirtleby, then comprising 2 houses, 1 carucate and 1 bovate, and rent, with the manor of Wold Newton, or Newton Rochford, to Sir Ralph Hastings.[67] As *THIRTLEBY* manor, it descended to William Hastings (d. 1483), Lord Hastings, whose feoffees and executors evidently settled it on Windsor college in support of Hastings's chantry there.[68] Later described as the reputed manor of *EASTHALL GARTH,*[69] the estate seems to have been held by Elizabeth Clough in 1782 and then by Robert Hudson until 1798, both probably lessees of Windsor college. J. B. Tuke, banker and merchant, bought the 249-a. farm from the college, evidently in 1798 or 1799, and divided it into two holdings.[70] Following Tuke's bankruptcy, his estate was sold in lots in 1806, the 100-a. Spacey Field farm being bought by C. E. Broadley and Easthall Garth farm, then of 145 a., by John Stephenson.[71] Stephenson (d. by 1817) was succeeded in turn by Matthew Stephenson (d. by 1827) and Thomas Stephenson.[72] Thomas Stephenson Holland, the last-named or another, had the farm at his death in 1894. G. F. Stephenson Holland succeeded to it, then of 125 a. and called Manor House farm, in 1907 and sold it in 1919 to J. A. Frost (d. 1933) and his wife Margaret.[73] The farm was sold by Mrs. Frost to Joseph and Henry Elliott in 1942, and, as the 100-a. Manor farm, by them to William Gibson in 1953. G. B. Green bought the farm in 1955 and still had it in 1994.[74]

The Constables held a little land at Thirtleby under Woodhall manor *c.* 1600.[75]

Land at Thirtleby belonged to bishop Walter Skirlaw (d. 1406) and was granted by his executors to Swine priory in or soon after 1415.[76] Comprising two houses and 2 carucates, or 195 a., it was held under a Crown lease by Anne Goring in 1609.[77] The estate was evidently later sold by the Crown and in 1704 was held by Edward Graham, viscount Preston, and others who then sold several houses and 419 a. at Thirtleby to Mark Kirkby.[78] Kirkby (d. 1718) devised the estate to his son Christopher[79] (d. *c.* 1733), from whom it passed in turn to his brother Mark (d. 1748) and sister Isabel Collings.[80] Mrs. Collings (d. by 1764) devised part of Thirtleby to her great-nephew the Revd. James Torre and the rest to his son Nicholas Torre.[81]

The Revd. James Torre (d. 1788) was succeeded by his son James (d. 1816) in a farm of *c.* 190 a., which was sold to William Brigham in 1821. Brigham died in 1851 or 1852, and Edward Walker bought the farm in 1853.[82] After Walker's death, 174 a. was sold to Sir Thomas Constable, Bt., in 1865.[83] Later called Thirtleby Grange,[84] the farm remained part of the Burton Constable estate in 1994.

56 R.D.B., CD/461/714; O.S. Map 1/10,560, TA 13 NE. (1956 edn.); O.S. Map 1/10,000, TA 13 NE. (1980 edn.).
57 O.S. Map 6″, Yorks. CCXXVII (1855 edn.).
58 Ibid.; O.S. Map 1/2,500, Yorks. CCXXVII. 2 (1891 edn.); O.S. Map 6″, Yorks. CCXXVII. NW. (1891 edn.).
59 O.S. Map 1/10,560, TA 13 NE. (1956 edn.); O.S. Map 1/10,000, TA 13 NE. (1980 edn.).
60 E.R.A.O., QDT/2/9.
61 *V.C.H. Yorks.* ii. 265.
62 Above, Ellerby, manors.
63 P.R.O., SC 6/Hen. VIII/6135, mm. 1d.–2.
64 E.R.A.O., DDCC/108/1.
65 *Yorks. Fines, John* (Sur. Soc. xciv), pp. 76–7; *Cur. Reg. R.* i. 457; ii. 26, 203; iii. 313; v. 10; *E.Y.C.* xi, p. 354.
66 *Yorks. Fines, 1232–46,* p. 84; *Cal. Inq. p.m.* ix, p. 27.
67 B.L. Add. MS. 26736, f. 120; *Cal. Close, 1381–5,* 124; *Yorks. Deeds,* ix, p. 129; Hist. MSS. Com. 78, *Hastings,* i, p. 195; *V.C.H. Yorks. E.R.* ii. 299.
68 *Test. Vetusta,* i. 368–73; *Complete Peerage,* s.v. Hastings.
69 R.D.B., CA/458/57; CM/173/284.
70 Ibid. BT/451/57; CA/458/57; CB/136/213; CD/461/714; E.R.A.O., QDE/1/6/32.

71 R.D.B., CL/261/427; CM/173/284.
72 E.R.A.O., QDE/1/6/32.
73 R.D.B., 4/442/424 (1885); 70/235/229 (1895); 99/509/476 (1907); 100/16/16 (1907); 194/434/366; 536/635/498.
74 Ibid. 654/223/180; 942/464/410; 1009/219/181.
75 H.U.L., DHO/7/42; DHO/8/47.
76 *Cal. Pat.* 1413–16, 327; *Test. Ebor.* i, p. 317; Burton, *Mon. Ebor.* 254; *Valor Eccl.* (Rec. Com.), v. 114; above, S. Skirlaugh, church.
77 P.R.O., LR 2/230, f. 234. Cf.ibid. REQ 2/212/43, where the estate is differently described.
78 E.R.A.O., DDCK/20/1; *Complete Peerage,* s.v. Preston.
79 R.D.B., G/242/545.
80 H.U.L., DDHO/71/54; above, Roos, manors.
81 H.U.L., DDSY/110/23. For the Torres, R.D.B., U/106/211; J. Foster, *Pedigrees of Yorks.* iii, s.v. Holme.
82 R.D.B., CY/596/886; DM/107/125; GZ/47/18; HB/49/62.
83 Ibid. IS/158/215; IU/48/69; E.R.A.O., DDCC/94/1.
84 O.S. Map 1/2,500, Yorks. CCXXVII. 2 (1891 edn.).

Nicholas Torre's share of Thirtleby seems to have passed to Christopher Torre (d. *c.* 1825), who left the Revd. Henry Torre a farm of some 218 a.[85] It later belonged to the Revd. Henry J. Torre (d. 1904) and then to his widow Hyacinthe (d. 1907), before being sold to Richard Richardson in 1909. Richardson (d. 1929) was succeeded in Field House farm in turn by his son Richard (d. 1964),[86] and grandson Mr. A. D. Richardson, who still occupied it in 1995.[87]

The rectorial tithes and dues of Thirtleby were bought by John Ramsden in 1681,[88] and they later descended with Bilton manor.[89] Some were sold to proprietors and merged,[90] but the rest were commuted in 1842 for a rent charge of £68 18s. 6d. payable to the Revd. William Dawnay, viscount Downe.[91]

ECONOMIC HISTORY. COMMON LANDS AND INCLOSURE. The open fields of Thirtleby evidently lay north and south of the hamlet.[92] Lord FitzHugh converted a few acres of the tillage to pasture before 1517.[93] South field was recorded again in the early 18th century,[94] but at least part of North field had been inclosed by 1750.[95] Large closes, possibly newly-made from the commonable lands, were recorded in 1799: there were 98 a. in Spacey field and 47 a. in Summer pasture, which was soon afterwards divided into three closes.[96] Ridge and furrow remained near Thirtleby Grange in 1994.[97]

LATER AGRICULTURE. There were up to six farmers at Thirtleby in the 19th and earlier 20th century, one or two with 150 a. or more.[98] Market gardening, nurserying,[99] and fruit-farming[1] have also been pursued there. A cattle dealer at Thirtleby was recorded in 1851 and one or two cowkeepers from the late 19th century, and *c.* 1990 cattle- and other livestock-farming there contributed to their prominence in Coniston civil parish.[2]

LOCAL GOVERNMENT. A poorhouse was probably maintained at Thirtleby,[3] where one person was on permanent relief between 1812 and 1815 and up to 9 people were relieved occasionally in the early 19th century.[4] Thirtleby joined Skirlaugh poor-law union in 1837,[5] and the township, later civil parish, remained in Skirlaugh rural district until 1935. As part of Coniston civil parish, it was then included in the new Holderness rural district and at reorganization in 1974 was taken into the Holderness district of Humberside.[6] In 1996 Coniston parish became part of a new East Riding unitary area.[7]

EDUCATION. Children from Thirtleby attended Bilton and Swine schools in 1871.[8]

WYTON

THE hamlet of Wyton, almost 5 km. south-east of Swine village, was formerly favoured for country residence by the well-to-do of Hull, which now lies only *c.* 3 km. away to the south-west. The name Wyton, meaning the 'women's farm', is Anglian.[9] Of 792 a. (321 ha.),[10] Wyton was added to Ganstead and Bilton civil parishes and a little of Preston in 1935 to form a new civil parish of Bilton.[11]

Wyton had 35 poll-tax payers in 1377[12] and 12 houses assessed for hearth tax in 1672.[13] At 86 in 1801, Wyton's population fell in the mid century to 46 in 1871, recovered to 80 in 1881, but then fell to 64 in 1901. Numbers then increased sharply to 105 in 1911 and stood at 111 in 1931.[14]

WYTON hamlet. Professional and commercial families of Hull began to live at Wyton in the 18th century,[15] and by the mid 19th the hamlet comprised half a dozen houses in ornamental grounds grouped along the north side of the Hull–Aldbrough road.[16] Merchants lived in two of the houses and a clergyman's widow in a third in 1891,[17] and the larger houses continued to be occupied mostly by business people from Hull

[85] R.D.B., EF/146/179; EF/147/181; FQ/305/309.
[86] Ibid. 71/529/499 (1904); 76/177/165 (1905); 104/243/226; 111/241/215; 884/248/197; 1404/160/149.
[87] Ibid. 1414/451/397; 1414/454/400; 1614/562/492; 1864/195/167; inf. from Mr. A. D. Richardson, Thirtleby, 1995.
[88] E.R.A.O., DDCC/111/31; above, Swine, manors (rectory).
[89] R.D.B., U/269/514; above, Bilton, manor.
[90] e.g. R.D.B., GB/10/7; P.R.O., CP 25(2)/1460/13 Geo. III Trin. no. 734.
[91] B.I.H.R., TA. 568L.
[92] *Yorks. Fines, John* (Sur. Soc. xciv), pp. 76–7; R.D.B., BC/414/655.
[93] *Trans. R. Hist. S.* N.S. vii. 249.
[94] H.U.L., DDCV(2)/51/6.
[95] Ibid. DDSY/65/1.
[96] R.D.B., CB/136/213; CD/401/621.
[97] For other ridge and furrow, Hull Univ., Dept. of Geog., Fairey Surveys air photographs, run 365B, nos. 2139–40.
[98] This para. based on P.R.O., HO 107/2365; directories.

[99] O.S. Map 1/10,560, TA 13 SE. (1956 edn.); O.S. Map 1/10,000, TA 13 SE. (1985 edn.).
[1] R.D.B., 177/73/60.
[2] P.R.O., HO 107/2365; above, Coniston, econ. hist.
[3] B.I.H.R., TA. 568L.
[4] *Poor Law Abstract, 1804*, pp. 594–5; *1818*, pp. 522–3.
[5] *3rd Rep. Poor Law Com.* 170.
[6] *Census.*
[7] Humberside (Structural Change) Order 1995, copy at E.R.A.O.
[8] *Returns relating to Elem. Educ.* 472–3.
[9] *P.N. Yorks. E.R.* (E.P.N.S.), 52.
[10] O.S. Map 6", Yorks. CCXXVII (1855 edn.).
[11] *Census, 1931* (pts. i–ii).
[12] P.R.O., E 179/202/60, m. 53.
[13] *Hearth Tax*, 61.
[14] *V.C.H. Yorks.* iii. 494; *Census, 1901–31.*
[15] For this para., K. J. Allison, *Hull Gent. Seeks Country Residence 1750–1850* (E. Yorks. Loc. Hist. Ser. xxxvi), 48–9. T. Jefferys, *Map of Yorks.* (1772).
[16] O.S. Map 6", Yorks. CCXXVII (1855 edn.).
[17] P.R.O., RG 11/4787; RG 12/3948.

in 1994.[18] Wyton Lodge, built by Thomas Ward, a Hull merchant, to designs by J. B. and William Atkinson of York in or soon after 1837,[19] is a grey-brick villa with a pedimented entrance and round-headed sashes to the first floor; its gate-house remains as Wyton Cottage. Red House, formerly Wyton Villa, dates from the end of the 18th century but has been greatly altered. Also of the 18th century are Wyton Abbey and Wyton Hall.[20] Most of Wyton was designated a conservation area in 1991.[21] In the mid 20th century the built-up area of Bilton was extended into Wyton by the building of bungalows along the Aldbrough and Preston roads. The district council added a pumping station at Wyton c. 1970.[22]

There was a licensed house at Wyton in the 1770s.[23]

MANOR AND OTHER ESTATES. Four carucates of sokeland at *WYTON* belonging in 1066 to Morkar's manor of Mappleton had passed to Drew de Bevrère by 1086[24] and were later part of the Aumale fee. In the earlier 14th century there was held of the Crown as successor to the counts of Aumale as ¹⁄₂₈ or ¹⁄₃₆ knight's fee.[25]

Most of Wyton was held by a family of that name. Adam of Wyton, tenant of the family's holding at South Skirlaugh,[26] presumably also held Wyton, before W. of Wyton (fl. mid 13th century) and Henry of Wyton, tenant in the 1280s. The estate at Wyton descended from Henry (d. by 1305) to his son John,[27] sole or joint lord of Wyton in 1316,[28] and from John (d. 1349) to his son John (d. 1352). The last John left as heirs his daughters Isabel and Christine. In the mid 14th century the holding at Wyton comprised nearly 2 carucates of demesne and 1¼ carucate held by the Wytons' free tenants.[29] The descent is thereafter uncertain. The estate perhaps passed to the Constables, who were recorded as mesne lords from the 16th century.[30]

The tenants in demesne by the 16th century were the Brighams. Thomas Brigham (d. 1542) was succeeded in Wyton manor by his son George, and George (d. 1576) by his nephew Francis Brigham (d. 1597). In 1543 the estate comprised only 6 bovates and 50 a. and was held of the Constables' manor of Burton Constable as ¹⁄₆ knight's fee.[31] The manor continued to descend in the Brighams,[32] passing to John Brigham (d. 1710), his son Roger[33] (d. by 1742), and Roger's son William[34] (d. 1767). William's widow Ursula and brother Gerard[35] sold Wyton manor with 268-a. in Manor farm to Christopher Bramley, a Leeds salter, in 1768.[36] Bramley (d. in or soon after 1802) left his son Christopher almost 100 a., which he sold to T. E. Upton in 1805 and which was later Wyton Holmes farm.[37] Most of Bramley's estate passed, however, to his grandson Thomas Bramley (d. 1804), who devised his interest to Ann Almond for life.[38] She married Horsfall Scholefield in 1805,[39] and as his widow had a mansion house and c. 220 a., mostly in Wyton, in 1822.[40] She later married John Green (d. by 1825) and Thomas Clubley.[41] Mrs. Clubley (fl. 1853) was probably succeeded by John Bramley.[42] William Raines evidently bought the manor, manor house called Wyton Abbey, and 197 a. at Wyton and 28 a. at Ganstead in 1865.[43] He died in 1874, and Wyton Abbey and the 197 a. were sold to Anthony and Matthias Nornabell.[44] The manor itself remained with Raines's heirs.[45] Susan Nornabell, widow, had succeeded by 1899,[46] and in 1906 H. M. Nornabell sold the estate to Richard Richardson.[47] Richardson (d. 1929) was succeeded in turn by his son W. H. Richardson (d. 1965) and grandson W. H. Richardson, who still had most of the land in 1995.[48]

A hall at Wyton was mentioned in 1352,[49] and the lord of the manor's brother, Henry Brigham, was living in a house with 10 hearths, probably the manor house, in 1672.[50] The house in which William Brigham (d. 1767) lived was evidently rebuilt in the later 18th century, probably by Christopher Bramley; it is of three storeys under a pantiled roof. Ann Scholefield lived there in 1822,[51] but by the mid 19th century it was used as a farmhouse.[52] Called Wyton House in the earlier 19th century and Wyton Abbey by 1865,[53] it was sold with a little land in 1967,[54] and in 1994 was used as a nursing home.

18 Inf. from Mrs. C. Marr, Wyton, 1994.
19 B.I.H.R., Atkinson-Brierley papers 3/2.
20 Below, manor.
21 Inf. from Devt. Dept., Holderness B.C., 1991.
22 R.D.B., 1586/225/206; 1660/239/214.
23 E.R.A.O., QDT/2/9.
24 V.C.H. Yorks. ii. 265.
25 Cal. Inq. p.m. iv, p. 179; ix, p. 291.
26 Above, S. Skirlaugh, manors.
27 Kirkby's Inquest, 373; Cal. Inq. p.m. iv, pp. 179–80, 355.
28 Feud. Aids, vi. 164; above, Ganstead, manor.
29 Cal. Inq. p.m. ix, pp. 291–2; x, p. 8.
30 H.U.L., DDGE/6/19; below, this section.
31 P.R.O., C 142/69, no. 190; C 142/173, no. 51; C 142/250, no. 2; Test. Ebor. vi, pp. 158–9.
32 P.R.O., CP 25(2)/755/21 Chas. II Mic. [14 from end]; Yorks. Fines, 1603–14, 214; Miscellanea, i (Y.A.S. Rec. Ser. lxi), 106. For fam., Visit. Yorks. 1584–5 and 1612, ed. J. Foster, 167.
33 P.R.O., CP 25(2)/896/10 Wm. III Mic. no. 21; CP 25(2)/985/8 Anne Mic. no. 11; Poulson, Holderness, ii. 269.
34 R.D.B., R/69/167; S/210/504.
35 Poulson, Holderness, ii. 269.
36 R.D.B., AI/513/1002; AZ/179/279.
37 Ibid. CH/233/377; DS/130/168; O.S. Map 6″, Yorks. CCXXVII (1855 edn.).
38 R.D.B., CH/21/35; DS/130/168.
39 E.R.A.O., QDE/1/6/36; ibid. PE/185/16, p. 37.
40 R.D.B., DM/312/362.
41 Ibid. DU/207/263; FG/452/23.
42 Ibid. GY/226/267.
43 Ibid. IX/231/306; H.U.L., DDCV(2)/53/9.
44 R.D.B., LN/417/549; E.R.A.O., DDX/287/18.
45 Directories; below, this section.
46 R.D.B., 8/251/239 (1899).
47 Ibid. 88/178/171 (1906).
48 Ibid. 884/246/196; 1439/406/369; 1499/311/283; inf. from Mr. W. H. Richardson, Burstwick, 1995.
49 Cal. Inq. p.m. x, p. 8.
50 P.R.O., E 179/205/504; Visit. Yorks. 1584–5 and 1612, ed. J. Foster, 167. Other Brighams then occupied smaller houses.   51 R.D.B., AI/513/1002; DM/312/362.
52 E.R.A.O., PE/104/99.
53 H.U.L., DDCV(2)/53/9; Baines, Hist. Yorks. (1823), ii. 402; White, Dir. E. & N.R. Yorks. (1840), 273.
54 R.D.B., 1499/311/283.

William Raines had built Wyton Hall by 1788 on land allotted at inclosure in the early 18th century,[55] and in 1794 he enlarged his holding at Wyton to *c.* 130 a. by purchase.[56] He (d. 1798) was succeeded by his son William (d. 1833),[57] who sold the Wyton Hall estate to William Meadley in 1810.[58] Meadley's devisee sold it in 1830 to R. M. Craven,[59] who already owned Red House,[60] and William Raines, son of William (d. 1833), bought both properties in 1852.[61] Raines also bought Wyton Lodge in 1856[62] and the manorial estate and a farm with 182 a. at Wyton in 1865.[63] He (d. 1874) was succeeded by his sisters Fanny Raines (d. 1892) and Anne Atkinson (d. 1896), who held as joint tenants,[64] and then by his cousins Sarah Dunn and Emma Inman (fl. 1904).[65] After the death in 1948 of Maud Dunn, the estate, comprising Wyton Hall, Hall Farm, *c.* 300 a. at Wyton, and some 20 a. in Preston, was sold to T. H. Swift in 1949.[66] Swift (d. 1961) was succeeded by his partner H. A. Swift, who sold Wyton Hall and South-field, formerly Hall, Farm with 98 a. to J. L. Caley in 1971; after a further sale, Mr. Swift retained 134 a. in 1994.[67] Wyton Hall with *c.* 25 a. was bought in 1990 by Charles Marr.[68]

Raines's house was evidently enlarged and remodelled soon after Meadley bought it in 1810, a third storey and a Doric porch being added and stucco applied to the brickwork. Arcaded, red-brick outbuildings, including a stable block, remain at Wyton Hall, as well as the ha-ha of its small park. After standing empty,[69] the house has been restored by Mr. and Mrs. Marr.

By 1190 Thornton abbey (Lincs.) had been given land and grazing at Wyton,[70] and in 1535 a Hedon chantry had land there.[71] Trinity House, Hull, bought the 45-a. Manor, formerly Glebe, farm at Wyton and Preston in 1937 and sold it in 1945.[72] The trustees of Ann Watson's charity of Sutton on Hull bought the 195-a. Wyton Holmes farm in 1924[73] and, apart from small plots sold in the mid century, still owned it in 1994.[74]

The rectorial tithes and dues of Wyton were bought by John Ramsden in 1681,[75] and they later descended with Bilton manor.[76] The Revd. William Dawnay, viscount Downe, was awarded a rent charge of £201 10s. 6d. for the Wyton tithes in 1842.[77]

ECONOMIC HISTORY. COMMON LANDS AND INCLOSURE. Wyton had two open fields, North and South fields,[78] until they were inclosed in or shortly before 1710.[79] A pasture was stinted for cattle in the earlier 14th century,[80] and Wyton Holmes and West croft were recorded as common pastures from the mid 16th, when the Holmes was grazed with the fallow field. Those pastures had evidently once been part of the tillage: West croft included a butt in 1556,[81] and in 1718 eleven 'lands' in Wyton Holmes were conveyed, 'together with the gates, whins, or furze thereunto appurtenant'.[82] In 1717, when the pasture also supported sheep and horses, the stint in Wyton Holmes was, almost certainly anachronistically, tied to the number of bovates held; ½ gate in winter and a whole gate in summer and autumn were then enjoyed for each bovate.[83] Wyton Holmes was inclosed by agreement in 1763. There were then 41 gates in the 69-a. pasture. William Brigham received 42 a. and William Raines 16 a., and two other allotments, of under 10 a., and a rent charge were awarded.[84] Some common pasture may have remained, a cowgate being recorded in West croft in 1768.[85]

WOODLAND. There may have been a wood at Wyton until 1826, when more than 700 trees and saplings lay there awaiting sale,[86] and 9 a. of woodland remained there in 1842.[87]

LATER AGRICULTURE. In the mid and late 19th century Wyton had 5–6 farms, 2 of which in 1851 were of over 150 a. Fewer farmers were recorded *c.* 1900 but there were again 5 in the 1920s and 1930s, 3 of them with larger holdings.[88] Cowkeeping there was recorded from the late 19th century, and Glebe farm was evidently a dairy unit.[89]

TRADES. Non-agricultural employment may have included brickmaking, a Brick close being

55 Ibid. BC/414/655; BN/482/757; H.U.L., DDCV(2)/51/6. If the Raines family earlier had a house called Wyton Hall, as their pedigree asserts, it was evidently elsewhere at Wyton: J. Foster, *Pedigrees of Yorks.* iii.
56 R.D.B., BS/285/438; BS/436/606.
57 J. Foster, *Pedigrees of Yorks.* iii; window in Bilton church.
58 E.R.A.O., DDIV/19/1.
59 R.D.B., EL/214/251.
60 Ibid. DW/266/326; E.R.A.O., DDHE/34, viii, 1–2; O.S. Map 1/2,500, Yorks. CCXXVII. 6 (1890 edn.).
61 R.D.B., GZ/90/72.   62 Ibid. HI/381/471.
63 Ibid. IT/100/148; above, this section.
64 Windows in Bilton church.
65 E.R.A.O., DDX/287/18, 23; R.D.B., 63/431/401 (1904).
66 R.D.B., 797/325/279; 822/330/285; 822/331/286.
67 Ibid. 952/150/138; 1393/159/143; 1712/140/131; inf. from Mr. H. A. Swift, Wyton, 1994.
68 Inf. from Mr. Marr, Wyton, 1994.
69 Dept. of Environment, *Buildings List* (1987); inf. from Mr. Marr.   70 Dugdale, *Mon.* vi. 326.
71 *Valor Eccl.* (Rec. Com.), v. 112; *V.C.H. Yorks. E.R.* v.

183.
72 R.D.B., 569/428/347; 710/212/183; O.S. Map 1/2,500, Yorks. CCXXVII. 6 (1910 edn.).
73 R.D.B., 281/85/72.
74 Ibid. 439/522/418, etc.; inf. from Ann Watson's Trust, 1994.
75 E.R.A.O., DDCC/111/31; above, Swine, manors (rectory).
76 R.D.B., U/269/514; above, Bilton, manor.
77 E.R.A.O., PE/104/99.
78 H.U.L., DDCV(2)/51/3; Poulson, *Holderness*, i. 129.
79 R.D.B., A/351/501; N/195/436; H.U.L., DDCV(2)/51/6; DDCV(2)/62/23.
80 *Yorks. Fines, 1327–47*, p. 168.
81 H.U.L., DDCV(2)/51/1, 4.
82 Ibid. DDCV(2)/51/8.
83 E.R.A.O., DDX/152/20.
84 R.D.B., AC/255/11.   85 Ibid. AI/513/1002.
86 H.U.L., DX/150/16 (15).
87 E.R.A.O., PE/104/99.
88 P.R.O., HO 107/2365; directories.
89 R.D.B., 120/226/204; directories.

recorded in 1733,[90] and there was more recently a joinery workshop[91] and a garage, which was trading in 1994.

MILL. A mill at Wyton was recorded in the 1340s[92] and may have stood north of the hamlet adjoining Thirtleby, where Mill close was named in 1856.[93]

LOCAL GOVERNMENT. Poorhouses were maintained at Wyton,[94] where 3 people were relieved permanently and 1 occasionally in 1802–3, and where 9–16 were on occasional relief between 1812 and 1815.[95] Wyton joined Skirlaugh poor-law union in 1837,[96] and the township, later civil parish, remained in Skirlaugh rural district until 1935. As part of Bilton civil parish, it was then included in the new Holderness rural district and at reorganization in 1974 was taken into the Holderness district of Humberside.[97] In 1996 Bilton parish became part of a new East Riding unitary area.[98]

CHURCH. There was a chapel at Wyton by 1525, when the curate serving it had £4 a year,[99] all or most of which was probably received from the rectory of Swine as a stipend; such a stipend was mentioned in the 1540s and again in the mid 17th century, when its value was £3 6s. 8d.[1]

Until its suppression, there was a chantry in the chapel, endowed with a house and a little land at Wyton.[2] The curacy of Wyton was held from the late 16th century with that of neighbouring Bilton, and in the mid 17th century also with Swine vicarage. Wyton chapel was in disrepair by 1663, when it was closed and parishioners at Wyton ordered to attend Swine church instead. The chapel was demolished soon afterwards;[3] it presumably stood in Chapel close, between Wyton Abbey and the street.[4]

ROMAN CATHOLICISM. The Brighams and up to half a dozen others at Wyton were cited as papists in the 17th century.[5] Henry Brigham of Wyton (d. 1738) was a Benedictine monk, and it was presumably on the family's estate there that the Benedictines conducted a mission early in the 1740s.[6]

PROTESTANT NONCONFORMITY. The Wesleyan Methodists built a chapel at Wyton c. 1840.[7] As Wyton Methodist church, it was extended in or soon after 1957[8] and was still used in 1995.

EDUCATION. In 1871 children from Wyton attended Bilton school.[9]

TUNSTALL

THE village of Tunstall lies 21 km. east of Hull and 500 m. from the sea, which bounds the parish to the east.[10] North of the village land called Monkwith commemorates the hamlet earlier called Monkwick, which has been almost entirely lost to the sea. The name Tunstall, meaning farmstead, is Anglian, as is that of Monkwick, or 'Monks' dairy farm', presumably an allusion to the ownership of the estate by St. John's church at Beverley. Monkwith was called Monk Tunstall in 1367 and Monkwick until the 17th century.[11]

In 1852 the ancient parish contained 1,346 a. (545 ha.) but by 1911 coastal erosion had reduced the area to 1,301 a. (527 ha.).[12] Tunstall civil parish was united with those of Hilston,

Owstwick, and Roos to form a new Roos civil parish in 1935.[13]

There were 126 poll-tax payers at Tunstall, excluding Monkwith, in 1377.[14] In 1672 the parish had 33 houses assessed for hearth tax.[15] There were 32 families in the parish in 1743 and 33 in 1764.[16] The population of Tunstall increased from 145 in 1801 to 172 in 1831 but fell to 144 in 1871; thereafter it declined to 98 in 1901, and was only 102 in 1931.[17]

The parish is largely on boulder clay and mostly lies at over 15 m. above sea level; on a ridge of sand and gravel in the north the ground rises to 25 m., but south of the village it falls below 7 m. Alluvial deposits mark the sites of several meres.[18] The open fields extended south

90 R.D.B., N/195/436.
91 O.S. Map 1/10,000, TA 13 SE. (1970 edn.).
92 *Yorks. Fines, 1327–47*, p. 168.
93 E.R.A.O., DDPK/26/1.
94 Ibid. NV/1/46; ibid. PE/104/99.
95 *Poor Law Abstract, 1804*, pp. 594–5; *1818*, pp. 522–3.
96 *3rd Rep. Poor Law Com.* 170.
97 *Census.*
98 Humberside (Structural Change) Order 1995, copy at E.R.A.O.
99 *Y.A.J.* xxiv. 76.
1 P.R.O., E 318/11/528, m. 10; E 126/9, ff. 294–5.
2 Ibid. C 2/Eliz. I/W 14/47; C 3/34/50; *Cal. Pat. 1575–8*, p. 28.
3 Lamb. Pal. Libr., Carte Misc. XII/9, f. 132v.; P.R.O., E 134/18 Chas. II Mich./10; E 126/9, ff. 294–5 (print. Thompson, *Swine*, 278–83); *T.E.R.A.S.* iv. 52.
4 H.U.L., DDCV(2)/53/9.
5 Aveling, *Post Reformation Catholicism*, 67 and *passim*.

6 *Herring's Visit.* iv, p. 218; H. N. Birt, *Obit Bk. of Eng. Benedictines, 1600–1912*, 91, 362.
7 P.R.O., HO 129/522/1/9/8; R.D.B., FQ/377/371; O.S. Map 6″, Yorks. CCXXVII (1855 edn.).
8 R.D.B., 1075/362/320; illus. in D. [R. J.] and S. Neave, *E.R. Chapels and Meeting Ho.* (E. Yorks. Loc. Hist. Soc.), 60. 9 *Returns relating to Elem. Educ.* 472–3.
10 This article was written in 1990–1.
11 E.R.A.O., DDIV/18/1; Belvoir Castle, near Grantham (Lincs.), Roos ct. roll (1547); *P.N. Yorks. E.R.* (E.P.N.S.), 57; Poulson, *Holderness*, i. 123.
12 *Census*, 1911.
13 O.S. Map 6″, Yorks. CCXXVIII (1855 edn.); *Census, 1931* (pt. ii). 14 P.R.O., E 179/202/60, m. 26.
15 *Hearth Tax*, 61.
16 B.I.H.R., V.1764/Ret. 3, no. 98; *Herring's Visit.* iii, p. 175.
17 *Census*, 1911–31; *V.C.H. Yorks.* iii. 494.
18 Geol. Surv. Map 1″, drift, sheet 73 (1909 edn.).

from the centre of the parish into the lower grounds, which also contained meadow, while the common pastures lay in the north on the higher land. The commonable lands had been reduced by early inclosure by 1779, when those remaining were inclosed.

Tunstall is mostly drained by a stream which forms the southern parish boundary and flows south-west towards the river Humber. Smaller streams flowing south on either side of the village feed the main drain which, as part of Keyingham fleet, was in disrepair in 1367.[19] Keyingham fleet drained 50 a. of Tunstall in 1618, and 78 a. of low ground were assessed to the drainage of the level after 1845;[20] under the Keyingham Level Drainage Acts of 1772 and later the southern boundary stream was improved as Tunstall drain.[21] Other drains insufficient in 1367 were further north; one was that which rises close to the sea in Gills, formerly Gildeson, mere and flows north and then west along the boundary with Roos into Hilston, and the other was probably the drain running along the boundary with Grimston, in Garton.[22] Gills mere survived as an area of marshy ground in 1991. The main drain evidently once flowed from Sandley mere or Sand le Mere, which was itself fed by Spring mere. Coastal erosion has reduced Sandley mere to a hollow depression in the mud cliffs, and already by 1622 a protective bank had been raised there to protect the level from incursions by the sea.[23] The bank was frequently damaged by the sea,[24] which elsewhere in the parish consumed an average of 2 yd. a year during the 19th century.[25] Other meres in Tunstall included Row, sometimes How, mere, Rose mere, and Bramarr.[26]

From Tunstall village minor roads lead north, south, east, and west. That to the east, called Seaside Lane by the 1850s, was once continued by a track to Waxholme, in Owthorne,[27] but that route has been disrupted by erosion and another field road, slightly further inland, now connects Tunstall to Waxholme. The lane to the south led to Thirtle bridge on the road between Roos and Withernsea,[28] which was upgraded in the mid 20th century as part of the Holderness coast road.

The situation of TUNSTALL village on a tongue of high ground closely flanked by converging

streams probably accounts for its linear plan. Most of the houses are loosely strung along both sides of a main street, with the church and a small, triangular green at the centre. Further south the street turns to cross the eastern stream and then continues south-eastwards along the higher ground. By the late 18th century half a dozen houses stood beside the southern lane[29] forming what was called Kiln House Lane in the 1850s.[30] The village buildings mostly date from the 19th and 20th centuries and include several farmhouses. They are largely of brick but several houses and particularly outbuildings incorporate boulder-built walls. Manor Farm was a single-storeyed house of boulders until it was heightened in brick in the early 19th century, and its outbuildings include a boulder-built barn. Also of boulders is Town Farm, of one storey with attics and possibly of the early 18th century. A modern bus shelter is also boulder-built. Tunstall Hall Farm, at the southern extremity of the village, was built in the 18th century and is a sizeable L-shaped house of two storeys with attic.

There were usually two or three licensed houses at Tunstall in the mid 18th century and later one, named the Cock in the 1820s and the King's Arms by 1840; it was closed c. 1970.[31] The Mermaid public house was opened on a caravan site near the sea in 1970.[32] A wooden village hall was put up in 1947,[33] and a branch library used a private house c. 1960.[34]

MONKWITH may already have begun to be eroded by 1360, when Great and Little Monkwick were recorded, and they later comprised two distinct areas separated by land belonging to Tunstall.[35] Monkwith had 28 poll-tax payers in 1377,[36] and in 1517 a house there was reported as decayed and four people had been ejected because of an inclosure;[37] the hamlet was evidently lost by the mid 17th century.[38]

The only outlying farmhouse is Hooks Farm, which was apparently built between 1770 and 1788.[39] High ground in the north was used for a military camp[40] and a beacon c. 1800,[41] and one or two military buildings put up c. 1940 remain close to the sea. A coastguard station with two cottages was built east of the village in 1902 to replace one at Waxholme; it was closed

[19] Poulson, *Holderness*, i. 126.
[20] E.R.A.O., DDCC/54/53; DDPK/3/8.
[21] *V.C.H. Yorks. E.R.* v. 55–7; O.S. Map 6″, Yorks. CCXXVIII (1855 and later edns.).
[22] Poulson, *Holderness*, i. 122–3. For mere, R.D.B., BB/134/17; E.R.A.O., IA. Tunstall.
[23] E.R.A.O., CSR/20/64; ibid. IA. Tunstall; R.D.B., BB/134/17.
[24] E.R.A.O., CSR/4/55, 152, 252; CSR/16/56, 80; CSR/20/23; ibid. DDCK/32/15 (sketch plan of c. 1835); T. Sheppard, *Lost Towns of Yorks. Coast*, 154; O.S. Map 6″, Yorks. CCXXVIII (1855 edn.).
[25] Sheppard, op. cit. 156.
[26] E.R.A.O., DDCC/141/70; ibid. IA. Tunstall.
[27] O.S. Map 6″, Yorks. CCXXVIII (1855 edn.).
[28] R.D.B., BB/134/17; E.R.A.O., IA. Tunstall.
[29] E.R.A.O., IA. Tunstall.
[30] O.S. Map 6″, Yorks. CCXXVIII (1855 edn.); for Kiln Garth earlier, E.R.A.O., DDCC/141/70.

[31] E.R.A.O., QDT/2/7, 9; R.D.B., EU/61/61; directories; O.S. Map 6″, Yorks. CCXXVIII (1855 edn.); inf. from Mrs. P. Kirkwood, Manor Farm, Tunstall, 1991.
[32] Inf. from Mr. A. C. Ellis, Sand-Le-Mere Caravan & Leisure Park, Tunstall, 1991; below, this section.
[33] TS. by G. W. Wilbraham in possession of Mrs. P. Kirkwood, Manor Farm, 1991.
[34] E.R. Educ. Cttee. *Mins.* 1959–60, 86.
[35] E.R.A.O., IA. Tunstall; *Cal. Pat.* 1358–61, 474–5.
[36] P.R.O., E 179/202/60, m. 17.
[37] *Trans. R. Hist. S.* N.S. vii. 246; below, econ. hist.
[38] Below, econ. hist.
[39] H.U.L., DDKE/8/88; R.D.B., BO/580/896; A. Bryant, *Map of E.R. Yorks.* (1829).
[40] E.R.A.O., PE/42/2; Poulson, *Holderness*, ii. 88.
[41] E.R.A.O., LT/9/54; ibid. DDGR/35/38; H. Teesdale, *Map of Yorks.* (1828); R. W. S. Norfolk, *Militia, Yeomanry and Volunteer Forces of E.R. 1689–1908* (E. Yorks. Loc. Hist. Ser. xix), 18, 26.

c. 1970 but the cottages remained in 1991 close to the cliff edge.[42]

A caravan site begun before 1939 was requisitioned during the war and re-established *c.* 1950. Permanent buildings including a shop were built *c.* 1970, and in 1991 the 29½ a. site accommodated some 400 caravans and about 30 residential and holiday chalets.[43]

MANORS AND OTHER ESTATES. In 1066 Morkar held 7 carucates in Tunstall as soke of Kilnsea manor and 1 carucate as soke of Withernsea manor. By 1086 both estates had passed to Drew de Bevrère,[44] and with the manors of Kilnsea and Withernsea they later became part of the Aumale fee and descended like Burstwick manor.[45] The so-called manor of *TUNSTALL* was granted for life in 1522 to Sir Leonard Grey (d. 1541).[46] The estate was, however, later regarded as a mere member of Burstwick manor, with which it passed in 1558 to Henry Neville, earl of Westmorland, and later to the Constables of Burton Constable.[47] Most of the land was held by freeholders and at inclosure in 1779 only 7 a. were awarded as copyhold of Burstwick manor.[48]

The Constable family had a demesne estate in Tunstall from the 15th century.[49] It was perhaps that which, with Garton, was held by Henry Constable (d. 1700) before reverting to the senior line of the family.[50] It comprised a farm of *c.* 80 a. in 1769, when William Constable sold it to William Barron;[51] it has not been traced further.

The Scures family held as undertenants part of the Aumale fee, which passed with Riston to the Hildyards. Sir Robert de Scures was thus succeeded in 4 carucates of the fee by Robert Hildyard by 1287.[52] The estate, described from the 16th century as *TUNSTALL* manor, descended in the Hildyards until the mid 17th century; the land was wholly or very largely held by their undertenants and has not been traced later.[53]

Another part of Tunstall belonged to the Preston family. Roger of Preston was disputing

land there in 1230,[54] and Thomas of Preston (d. by 1246) left as his heir Roger's son William, a minor. The estate evidently later passed to Henry of Preston, possibly Thomas's nephew.[55] It comprised 2 carucates and was said to be held as ¼₄ knight's fee. Henry's estate in Holderness, which also included Waxholme manor, had descended to his grandson John of Preston by the 1280s, when Tunstall was practically all held by undertenants.[56] The mesne lordship and a small demesne estate descended from John (d. by 1334) to his son John, who conveyed the estate to Isabel daughter of John of Preston, presumably his sister, in 1335.[57] Isabel (d. 1349) married Thomas Hautayn and her heir Gillian Stedeman was probably the wife of Thomas Vescy, and the Hautayns and the Vescys evidently granted an interest in Waxholme manor and Tunstall to John del Flete.[58] Flete, who had apparently bought land in Tunstall in 1334,[59] granted Tunstall with Waxholme to Warter priory in or soon after 1350.[60] Occasionally called *TUNSTALL* manor, the estate descended with Waxholme to John Stanhope (fl. 1582), and after his death probably to William Alford.[61] It has not been traced later.

Roger of Grimston was recorded as a mesne lord in Tunstall in 1325. Other members of the family recorded as proprietors included Thomas Grimston in 1275 and Thomas Grimston (d. 1479) of Flinton.[62] The family's estate extended into Monkwick in the 16th century: in 1517 another Thomas Grimston was said to be a freeholder there, and 1 carucate and 1 bovate of copyhold was held in dower by Walter Grimston's widow in 1558.[63] The estate descended with Grimston in the Grimston family from the 16th century. Comprising only a few acres of demesne, it was called *TUNSTALL* manor and was held of Burstwick manor as ¹⁄₁₀₀ knight's fee.[64] In 1779 John Grimston, as lord, was awarded 1 a. for his consent to inclosure, besides a few acres for his commonable lands.[65] In 1918 the family's estate in Holderness included 7 a. in Tunstall.[66]

In the 13th century the Tunstall family held land in Tunstall in serjeanty for acting as bailiff

[42] E.R.A.O., NV/1/28; R.D.B., 48/453/424 (1902); *Kelly's Dir. N. & E.R. Yorks.* (1905), 590; *V.C.H. Yorks. E.R.* v. 88; local inf.
[43] E.R.A.O., PE/42, accession 1218, letters 1940, 1942; R.D.B., 1653/445/386; inf. from Mr. A. C. Ellis, 1991.
[44] *V.C.H. Yorks.* ii. 264–5.
[45] *V.C.H. Yorks. E.R.* v. 9–10, 69, 163.
[46] P.R.O., C 66/639, m. 4; *V.C.H. Yorks. E.R.* v. 191.
[47] E.R.A.O., DDCC/111/21, 23; *Cal. Pat.* 1557–8, 39; *V.C.H. Yorks. E.R.* v. 10.
[48] R.D.B., BB/134/17.
[49] E.R.A.O., DDCC/111/16, 207; DDCC/133/3; Poulson, *Holderness*, ii. 85; J. Foster, *Pedigrees of Yorks.* iii, s.v. Constable of Constable Burton.
[50] E.R.A.O., DDCC/111/231; DDCC/134/17, 23; above, Garton, manors.
[51] R.D.B., AM/112/185.
[52] *Kirkby's Inquest*, 374; *Cal. Inq. p.m.* iv, p. 353; above, Long Riston, manors.
[53] P.R.O., C 142/73, no. 47; C 142/530, no. 155; *Cal. Inq. p.m.* vi, pp. 185–6; *Yorks. Fines*, i. 315; *Yorks. Royalist Composition Papers*, i (Y.A.S. Rec. Ser. xv), pp. 97–104;

J. Foster, *Pedigrees of Yorks.* iii, s.v. Hildyard.
[54] *Close R.* 1227–31, 394.
[55] H.U.L., DHO/16/53.
[56] *Kirkby's Inquest*, 76, 246 n., 374; *Cal. Inq. p.m.* iv, pp. 354, 356; ix, p. 303; *V.C.H. Yorks. E.R.* v. 92.
[57] *Yorks. Fines, 1300–14*, p. 105; *1327–47*, p. 89; *Cal. Inq. p.m.* vii, pp. 413–14.
[58] *Cal. Inq. p.m.* viii, p. 342; ix, pp. 302–3; *Yorks. Fines, 1327–47*, p. 111; *1347–77*, p. 31.
[59] *Yorks. Fines, 1327–47*, p. 70.
[60] *Cal. Pat.* 1348–50, 460.
[61] P.R.O., C 142/160, no. 38; C 142/199, no. 69; *L. & P. Hen. VIII*, xi, p. 207; xvi, p. 325; *Yorks. Fines*, i. 102.
[62] *Cal. Inq. p.m.* vi, p. 364; Poulson, *Holderness*, ii. 85; *Test. Ebor.* iii, p. 251 n.
[63] H.U.L., DDSY/56/1; *Trans. R. Hist. S.* n.s. vii. 246.
[64] P.R.O., C 142/58, no. 27; C 142/160, no. 59; C 142/210, no. 124; C 142/301, no. 65; C 142/401, no. 126; H.U.L., DGN/11/8; R.D.B., H/641/1298; BF/270/465; Foster, *Pedigrees of Yorks.* iii; above, Garton, manors.
[65] R.D.B., BB/134/17.
[66] Ibid. 185/114/93.

in the Tunstall bailiwick of Holderness, which seems to have been named after them.[67] The bailiff was later said to hold a bovate in Bailiff's close, and Bailiff garth was named in 1779.[68]

The largest modern estate in Tunstall was that assembled by the Lorrimar family. In 1779 Edward Lorrimar had c. 150 a.;[69] it was perhaps he who in 1806 was succeeded by Edward Lorrimar[70] (d. 1831), from whom the estate descended to his son Edward (d. 1894).[71] Some 60 a. were bought from Bryan Taylor in 1820,[72] and the Lorrimars later also succeeded to the estate of the North family. William North (d. 1796) left nearly 150 a. to his son William, who sold the estate in 1818 to Philip Hardy (d. by 1829); Hardy devised the land to his niece Frances Lorrimar (d. 1836), wife to Edward (d. 1831), and she also was succeeded by Edward (d. 1894).[73] By the 1890s much of the Lorrimars' estate had passed to the trustees of (Sir) Charles Parsons (O.M., F.R.S., d. 1931) and his wife Katherine, née Bethell (d. 1933), probably by foreclosure of mortgage.[74] Apart from a few acres sold in 1920, the estate, comprising Manor farm with c. 220 a. in Tunstall, descended to the Parsons's daughter Rachel.[75] In 1956 Rachel Parsons sold the farm and 196 a. to Mr. Sidney Kirkwood, who still owned it in 1991.[76]

In 1086 the archbishop of York held the whole of Monkwith (called Monkwick until the 16th century) as a berewick comprising 2 carucates; the estate had by then been assigned to his church of St. John at Beverley,[77] and its overlordship descended after the suppression of Beverley college as part of Beverley Chapter manor.[78]

Monkwith was held of the provost of Beverley by the Ros family. The Ros's also held part of the Aumale fee in Tunstall as a member of Roos manor, and William de Ros was named as the sole lord of Tunstall in 1316.[79] Monkwith comprised 2 carucates and 3 bovates in 1285 and 3 carucates in 1558; in 1363, when it was called *MONKWICK* manor, it was held by the service

of ⅟28 knight's fee.[80] Monkwith was usually, however, regarded as a member of Roos, and with that manor it and the other land in Tunstall descended to the Cecils.[81] The estate was wholly occupied by free tenants and copyholders, and was much reduced by coastal erosion; at inclosure in 1779 only c. 50 a. in Tunstall, mostly in Monkwith, were copyhold of Roos manor.[82]

From 1230 the rectorial estate belonged to the subchanter of York minster.[83] There were 4 bovates of glebe land in Tunstall from the mid 13th century.[84] The rectory, which was worth just over £63 a year gross in 1650, was sold to Matthew Alured in 1651[85] but was recovered by the subchanter at the Restoration. The glebe included a dozen acres in closes,[86] and the subchanter was awarded 59 a. for his commonable lands at inclosure in 1779. The rectorial tithes of the commonable lands were then commuted for 138 a. and those of most of the old inclosures for rent charges amounting to £32 12s. 4d. Of the closes excepted from that commutation of tithes,[87] Long Leys may have been tithed by a modus in the 17th century[88] but was declared to be tithe-free in 1843; by then it had been reduced by erosion to c. 10 a. and it was evidently lost soon afterwards. The remaining tithes, from c. 95 a. in Hall close and the Hooks, had long been paid by moduses; the compositions amounted to just over £2 in 1843, when rent charges of the same sum were substituted for them.[89]

The rectory was let by the 17th century and in the 18th was held by the Barron family.[90] The Ecclesiastical Commissioners, as expectant owners under the Cathedrals Act of 1840, sold their interest to the subchanter's lessee William Barron in 1854; the estate comprised a farm of 183 a., earlier called Tithe farm.[91] Barron (d. 1879) devised it to his son Thomas[92] but by 1897 it evidently belonged to the Revd. Edward Gordon.[93] Gordon sold the farm, then eroded to 165 a., to C. C. Wreathall in 1917.[94] Samuel Marriott bought it in 1919,[95] and sold c. 60 a. in 1921 and 1922 and the house and 102 a. in 1923

[67] English, *Holderness*, 81–3; *Kirkby's Inquest*, 374.
[68] R.D.B., BB/134/17; Poulson, *Holderness*, i. 155.
[69] R.D.B., BB/134/17.
[70] Ibid. CO/399/619; E.R.A.O., PE/42/2.
[71] R.D.B., EO/71/80; EW/278/307; EY/262/270; E.R.A.O., PE/42/7; memorial in church.
[72] R.D.B., DM/309/360.
[73] Ibid. BB/134/17; DC/446/611; DC/447/612; EG/272/337; GX/339/396; GX/399/485; HH/192/210; H.U.L., DRA/545; memorial in church.
[74] R.D.B., MY/94/151; NO/383/557; NS/73/103; 16/424/390 (1899); 98/224/214 (1907); E.R.A.O., NV/1/28; D.N.B., s.v. Parsons.
[75] R.D.B., 223/370/310; 495/194/151.
[76] Ibid. 1038/90/78; inf. from Mr. Kirkwood.
[77] *V.C.H. Yorks.* ii. 216.
[78] P.R.O., E 317/Yorks./17; H.U.L., DDSY/97/16; DDCV/16/1–3; *V.C.H. Yorks. E.R.* iv. 14.
[79] *Feud. Aids*, vi. 163.
[80] H.U.L., DDSY/56/1; *Yorks. Inq.* ii, pp. 32–6; *Cal. Inq. p.m.* xi, p. 401; *Memorials of Beverley Minster*, ii (Sur. Soc. cviii), 322.
[81] P.R.O., C 142/218, no. 52; ibid. E 317/Yorks./17; H.U.L., DHO/7/41; *Cal. Inq. p.m.* viii, pp. 330–42; xi, pp. 400–1; *Test. Ebor.* i, pp. 375–6; *N. Country Wills*, i (Sur.

Soc. cxvi), pp. 184–7; *Yorks. Fines, 1614–25*, 168; above, Roos, manors.
[82] R.D.B., BB/134/17; H.U.L., DDSY/56/1.
[83] Below, church.   [84] *Kirkby's Inquest*, 374.
[85] P.R.O., C 54/3628, no. 5; Lamb. Pal. Libr., COMM/XIIa/18/94–6; *T.E.R.A.S.* iv. 55.
[86] B.I.H.R., TER. H. Tunstall 1716, etc.
[87] R.D.B., BB/134/17.
[88] P.R.O., E 134/28 Chas. II East./4; E 134/29 Chas. II East./7.
[89] E.R.A.O., PE/42/2, terrier 1738; PE/42/12 (tithe award); below, econ. hist.
[90] E.R.A.O., PE/42/12; 17 Geo. III, c. 30 (Priv. Act); B.I.H.R., TER. H. Tunstall 1726; ibid. CC. Succ. 9 Tun. 1; R.D.B., EW/47/58; FM/197/220; Poulson, *Holderness*, ii. 86.
[91] R.D.B., GZ/381/439; 3 & 4 Vic. c. 113, s. 51; Le Neve, *Fasti, 1541–1857*, *York*, 42; A. Bryant, *Map of E.R. Yorks.* (1829).
[92] R.D.B., NA/31/48; 33/458/430 (1889); E.R.A.O., PE/42/7.
[93] B.I.H.R., TER. 79; R.D.B., IK/335/382; LF/215/273; 68/478/454 (1904); E.R.A.O., NV/1/28.
[94] R.D.B., 182/336/280.
[95] Ibid. 196/19/19; 196/20/20.

to Charles Kenington.[96] The mortgagees evidently foreclosed in 1937 and in 1948 sold the farm to Thomas Cook and Thomas Kennington Cook.[97] It was bought by H. E. Brown in 1950, as Westhill farm by F. H. Leckonby in 1956, and by Frank Grassby in 1966, when it had been enlarged to c. 140 a. Mr. Grassby still owned it in 1991.[98] The rectory farmhouse had been rebuilt by 1840.[99]

St. Sepulchre's hospital, Hedon, alienated a toft in Tunstall in the earlier 13th century,[1] but soon afterwards, c. 1240, Sir Walter of Hedon gave the house other land and rent there.[2] By 1326 the hospital had also been given rent and more than 5 bovates by Matthew son of Alexander of Tunstall.[3] After the suppression in 1547 the estate descended with the hospital to Michael Constable (fl. 1630s).[4] It has not been traced further.

Thornton abbey (Lincs.) had land in Tunstall by 1208,[5] and 5 bovates in the mid 13th century.[6] After the Dissolution the land descended as a member of Garton manor to John Eldred and William Whitmore.[7]

Between 1235 and 1249 John Talon gave Meaux abbey 2 bovates, a toft, and rent of 1s. a year, but the land was soon afterwards granted at fee farm to Hugh of Tunstall, serjeant of the count of Aumale,[8] presumably the Hugh Sergeant who later held 4 bovates in Tunstall.[9]

A chantry in Preston church[10] and lights in Roos church were endowed in Tunstall; Roos's endowment was granted to John and William Marsh in 1574, and later passed to the Grimstons.[11] Since the 18th century a few acres in Tunstall have belonged to the fabric of Roos church.[12]

An estate, including half of *TUNSTALL* manor, was bought in the early 16th century by Martin Boynton and used to endow Barmston church and Mount Grace priory (Yorks. N.R.);[13] no more is known of Barmston's endowment, but in 1610 the Crown sold two houses and land in Tunstall formerly belonging to the priory to Edward Bates and Henry Elwes.[14]

ECONOMIC HISTORY. COMMON LANDS AND EARLY INCLOSURE. Tunstall and Monkwith may have had separate common lands in the Middle Ages but after the loss of much of the hamlet to the sea the land remaining was managed with the common lands of Tunstall.[15]

Tunstall. The East field of Tunstall is said to have been named in 1342, and West field was recorded from 1397.[16] Poorly drained parts of both fields were used as common meadow land; Howmarr in West field and Spring and Rose meres in East field were all said in 1750 to be laid out for mowing in strips, a 'gadd', or measure of 7½ ft., being used to determine the breadth of each strip. In the mid 18th century 1 beast gate was enjoyed in East field when it was fallow for each 5 a. held and after it had been harvested for each 3 a.; in West field the stint was 1 gate for 4 a. and 2½ a. respectively.[17]

Tillage evidently once extended into the low ground in the south of the parish. Land at Thirtle Bridge, Thorma green, and 'Ingolspole' was recorded in 1326 as including some arable, besides meadow, turbary, and marsh,[18] and it was there, in the south-west corner of the parish, that South field was later recorded. South field may have been a part of West field, rather than a separate open field, and much of it was probably used as meadow. In 1662 c. 26 a. of meadow were recorded in South field.[19] The field was reduced by piecemeal inclosure: inclosed strips were recorded there in 1637, in 1651 an open-field holding included 8 a. of meadow in a close at 'Thorney' green in South field,[20] and by the later 18th century the commonable land there had been reduced to two small areas called Thorma green and South field. The latter was then flanked by South Field closes, and Intakes along the south side of West field suggest that it too had been encroached upon.[21]

By the 17th century rough grazing and gorse, or whins, for fuel were provided mostly by the common pasture of Hogsey. The pasture seems also to have been formerly part of the tillage and still lay in strips. In 1628 grassland there included 4 a. lying in two former 'lands', and 'ley or whin lands' were recorded in Hogsey in the 18th century.[22] Each proprietor presumably took gorse from his own strips, and the area of the holdings in the pasture was evidently the basis for stinting the grazing there. In 1716 the rector had 18 a. 'containing', probably meaning entitling him to stock, 8 beast gates in Hogsey.[23]

96 Ibid. 241/381/331; 243/594/486; 275/627/490.
97 Ibid. 778/193/172; 784/453/384.
98 Ibid. 845/346/300; 1051/24/23; 1440/338/290; inf. from Mrs. Grassby.   99 Poulson, *Holderness*, ii. 88.
1 *E.Y.C.* iii, p. 46; *V.C.H. Yorks. E.R.* v. 194.
2 Hist. MSS. Com. 78, *Hastings*, i, pp. 162–3.
3 Dugdale, *Mon.* vi. 654–5.
4 P.R.O., C 2/Jas. I/C 3/31; ibid. C 60/525, no. 52; *Valor Eccl.* v. 110; *Cal. Pat.* 1547–8, 170, 250; 1553, 87–8; *Yorks. Deeds*, iv, pp. 76–7; *D.N.B.*, s.v. Stanhope; Foster, *Pedigrees of Yorks.* iii, s.v. Constable of Constable Burton; *V.C.H. Yorks. E.R.* v. 194.
5 *Yorks. Fines, John* (Sur. Soc. xciv), pp. 135–6.
6 *Cal. Chart. R.* 1300–26, 10; *Abbrev. Plac.* (Rec. Com.), 203, 275; *Kirkby's Inquest*, 374.
7 P.R.O., C 66/1903, no. 9; ibid. E 310/27/158, f. 20; E 310/29/169, f. 16; ibid. SC 6/Hen. VIII/2022, m. 79; *L. & P. Hen. VIII*, xvii, pp. 29–30; above, Garton, manors.
8 *Chron. de Melsa* (Rolls Ser.), ii. 23.
9 *Kirkby's Inquest*, 374.

10 *Cal. Pat.* 1334–8, 336; *Valor Eccl.* (Rec. Com.), v. 118; *V.C.H. Yorks. E.R.* v. 199.
11 P.R.O., C 142/401, no. 126; H.U.L., DHO/10/6, feodary's acct.; *Cal. Pat.* 1572–5, pp. 321–5.
12 R.D.B., BB/134/17; E.R.A.O., NV/1/28.
13 P.R.O., CP 40/1014, rot. 141; *T.E.R.A.S.* xix, p. 23; H.U.L., DDWB/2/3; DDSY/56/1.
14 P.R.O., C 66/1882, no. 4.
15 Below, this section.
16 E.R.A.O., DDCC/111/15; Poulson, *Holderness*, ii. 85.
17 The acres were described as 'computed acres': E.R.A.O., DDCC/141/70.
18 Dugdale, *Mon.* vi. 654–5.
19 G. T. J. Miles and W. Richardson, *Hist. Withernsea*, 67–8.
20 P.R.O., C 54/3628, no. 5; C 142/553, no. 30; E.R.A.O., PE/42/2, terrier 1738; H.U.L., DDMC/94/1.
21 E.R.A.O., IA. Tunstall.
22 Ibid. DDIV/18/1; DDCC/141/70; H.U.L., DDCV/166/46.   23 B.I.H.R., TER. H. Tunstall 1716.

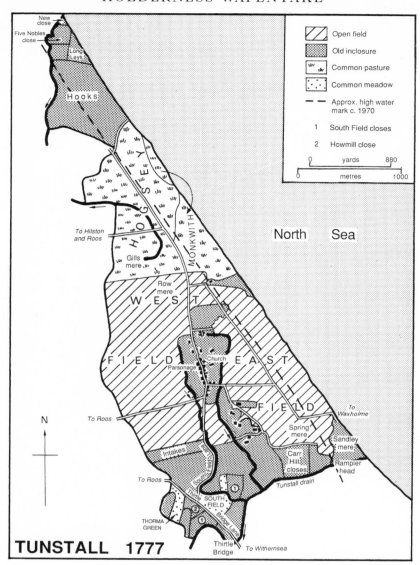

TUNSTALL 1777

A gate might be divided into quarters, or 'feet', each of which comprised 80 perches.[24]

Early inclosures in Tunstall probably also included Tunstall carr, which belonged to Roos manor and was used as meadow in 1285 and pasture in 1558; in the 16th century it contained *c*. 90 a. and was rented by copyholders of the manor for nearly £7 a year.[25] The name Carr Hill located in 1777 suggests that the carr lay in the south-east corner of the parish.[26]

Monkwith. At Monkwith there was land for 2 ploughteams in 1086 but there were then 3, worked by 6 villeins who owed rent of 10*s*.[27] In 1517 one team was reported lost because of an inclosure made at Monkwith, apparently by Thomas Grimston.[28] There were still, however, reckoned to be 3 carucates there in 1558, when

the open-field land was held under Roos manor by 10 copyholders; one holding comprised 1 carucate and 1 bovate and the others 1–2½ bovates each.[29] Coastal erosion may soon afterwards have disrupted agricultural arrangements there. The land remaining was used as common pasture by the mid 17th century, when the grazing was overcharged and a pain was laid against digging there, presumably for turves.[30] The management of the pasture probably reflected earlier arrangements, as in neighbouring Hogsey, and Monkwith was later said to include 25 ley or whin lands carrying an entitlement of 3 gates and 48 perches.[31] Gates in the pasture had been re-ordered by 1670, when 16 beast gates of the old stint were equated with 10⅔ of the new.[32] Monkwith was inclosed as part of Tunstall's commonable grounds in 1779.[33]

[24] Ibid. 1726, 1743; E.R.A.O., DDCC/141/70.
[25] H.U.L., DDSY/56/1; *Yorks. Inq.* ii, pp. 34–5.
[26] E.R.A.O., IA. Tunstall; O.S. Map 6″, Yorks. CCXXVIII (1855 edn.).
[27] *V.C.H. Yorks.* ii. 216.
[28] *Trans. R. Hist. S.* N.S. vii. 246.

[29] One tenant there had no open-field land: H.U.L., DDSY/56/1.
[30] Ibid. DDSY(3)/3/6 (Oct. 1642); DDCV/134/1 (Oct. 1635).
[31] Ibid. DDCV/166/63.
[32] Ibid. DDCV/166/36.   [33] Below, this section.

Hooks. It is not clear what use was made of the extreme north end of the parish. That it was once shared with a neighbouring parish, or parishes, possibly as pasture, is suggested by the inclusion of Hooks, then of 142 a., on a 17th-century map of Garton. Hooks was moreover variously described as part of Grimston[34] or of Hilston, into which parish it clearly extended.[35] Hooks and the adjacent Long Leys close were however titheable to Tunstall.[36] Whatever its use, the land there had been inclosed by the 17th century, when, besides Hooks and Long Leys, New close, of *c.* 20 a., was recorded.[37] Hooks close was later divided, and by 1788 it was occupied as Hooks farm; it had by then been reduced by coastal erosion to just under 100 a.,[38] and Long Leys was lost in the mid 19th century.[39]

PARLIAMENTARY INCLOSURE. The remaining commonable lands in Tunstall were inclosed by an award of 1779 under an Act of 1777.[40] There was 938 a. to be dealt with, besides 356 a. of old inclosures. Allotments made totalled 913 a., and 39 a. of old inclosures were involved in exchanges. There were more than 304 a. in West field, over 214 a. in East field, more than 208 a. in Hogsey, 60 a. in Monkwith, 12 a. in South field, and 7 a. in Thorma Green.[41] The sub-chanter of York as rector received 197 a. for glebe and the tithes of the lands inclosed, and James Smith 126 a.; there were also two allotments of just over 100 a., three of 50–99 a., five of 20–49 a., three of 10–19 a., and seven of under 10 a.

LATER AGRICULTURE. There was said to be 496 a. under crops in Tunstall in 1801,[42] and 878 a. were returned as arable land and 379 a. as permanent grassland in 1905.[43] Arable farming was still predominant in the 1930s. The grassland, which supported a few cowkeepers from the late 19th century, lay mostly west and south of the village alongside the drains.[44] In 1991 many trees were newly planted near Tunstall Hall in the south end of the parish.

There were up to a dozen farmers in Tunstall in the 19th and earlier 20th century, of whom 3 or 4 in 1851 and the 1920s and 1930s had 150 a. or more.[45] A poultry farmer was recorded in the 1930s, when there was a smallholding in the parish.

GRAVEL WORKING. The lord of Holderness took tolls on trade at Tunstall in the 15th cent-

ury, and also then received occasional income from wrecks there.[46] The seigneurial rights over the shore produced income again in the 19th century. Materials for repairing roads were being taken from the beach at Sand le Mere by the 1820s, and the shore was later worked by agents of Sir Thomas Constable, Bt., the lord of Holderness. In 1845 Constable was summoned before the justices in quarter sessions for the removal of gravel from Tunstall beach[47] but he evidently maintained his right. The shore in Tunstall and Waxholme was let to a Tunstall man for 13 years in 1844, and there was much activity in the 1860s, when several Tunstall residents worked as 'gravel catchers'. During the winter of 1868–9 three men took *c.* 400 tons of gravel and 300 tons of cobbles from the beach, and 125 tons of cobbles from elsewhere in Tunstall, for which Constable received nearly £18.[48]

MILL. A mill was recorded in Tunstall in 1246.[49] Place names commemorating mill sites include Howmill close, in the south-west corner of the parish, and Mill hill, north-west of the village.[50]

LOCAL GOVERNMENT. The provost of Beverley successfully maintained his right to waif and stray and wreck of sea in Monkwith *c.* 1350.[51] The hamlet was part of Roos manor and officers appointed in the manor court in the 17th century included 2 bylawmen for Monkwith.[52] Court papers for the Grimstons' manor of Tunstall survive for the mid 19th century. The court had view of frankpledge but its meetings were by then largely concerned with collecting rents. The court was held in the public house and last met in 1869.[53]

Churchwardens' accounts survive for 1799–1914,[54] and extracts from 19th-century constables' accounts have been printed.[55] The parish may have had poorhouses in 1764, when two unendowed almshouses were recorded, and less than 1 a. in Tunstall belonged to the overseers of the poor in 1910.[56] Permanent poor relief was given to 4 people in Tunstall in 1802–3 and to a dozen in 1812–15; up to 6 people were also relieved occasionally in the early 19th century.[57] Tunstall joined Patrington poor-law union in 1836 and remained in Patrington rural district until 1935 when it was taken into Holderness rural district as part of the new civil parish of

34 H.U.L., DDSY/75/6; E.R.A.O., DDCC/42/2.
35 Cf. R.D.B., 992/130/116; O.S. Map 1/2,500, Yorks. CCXXVIII. 7 (1910 edn.). R.D.B., BB/134/17; E.R.A.O., IA. (maps).
36 Above, manors.
37 P.R.O., C 142/708, no. 96; E.R.A.O., DDCC/42/2.
38 H.U.L., DDSY/75/6; DDKE/8/88; R.D.B., BO/580/896.
39 Cf. E.R.A.O., PE/42/12; ibid. DDCC/42/2; O.S. Map 6", Yorks. CCXXVIII (1855 edn.).
40 17 Geo. III, c. 30 (Priv. Act); R.D.B., BB/134/17; E.R.A.O., IA. (maps).
41 The discrepancy in the sum results from rounding.
42 P.R.O., HO 67/26/430.
43 Acreage Returns, 1905.
44 [1st] Land Util. Surv. Map, sheets 33–4; directories.

45 Two paras. based on P.R.O., HO 107/2364; RG 9/3600; directories.
46 H.U.L., DHO/7/42; DHO/8/47; DHO/10/6.
47 E.R.A.O., DDCC/1/62.
48 Ibid. DDCC/136/51, 151–2, 155–7, 179.
49 H.U.L., DHO/16/53.
50 E.R.A.O., DDX/59/27; ibid. IA. Tunstall; R.D.B., MM/37/55; O.S. Map 1/2,500, Yorks. CCXXVIII.11 (1910 edn.).
51 Cal. Pat. 1358–61, 474–5.
52 H.U.L., DDCV/134/1; above, manors.
53 H.U.L., DDCV/167/1–2, 5; Poulson, *Holderness*, ii. 85.
54 E.R.A.O., PE/42/10.
55 Miles and Richardson, *Hist. Withernsea*, 61.
56 B.I.H.R., V. 1764/Ret. 3, no. 98; E.R.A.O., NV/1/28.
57 *Poor Law Abstract, 1804*, pp. 594–5; *1818*, pp. 522–3.

Roos. Roos became part of the Holderness district of Humberside in 1974.[58] In 1996 Roos parish became part of a new East Riding unitary area.[59]

CHURCH. In 1115 Tunstall and other churches in Holderness were given to the priory, later abbey, of Aumale (Seine Maritime),[60] which ceded Tunstall to the archbishop of York in 1228. The church was used to endow the office of subchanter in York minster in 1230 and was later in his peculiar jurisdiction.[61] No vicarage was ordained and Tunstall was later served by curates, who were paid out of the rectory. Following endowment the living became a perpetual curacy in 1752[62] and was declared a rectory in 1867.[63] Tunstall was united with Hilston in 1877 and, on further regroupings of the benefices, with Roos in 1927. Roos with Tunstall and Garton with Hilston were united in 1974.[64]

The patronage of Tunstall passed from Aumale abbey to the archbishop of York in 1228. From 1752 the subchanter of York was patron of the perpetual curacy.[65] Under the Cathedrals Act of 1840 the archbishop became patron again in 1868[66] and presented alternately to the united benefice after 1877.[67] When Tunstall was united with Roos in 1927, the patronage of Roos with Tunstall was declared to belong wholly to the former patrons of Roos, and the archbishop, as former patron of Tunstall, was given one turn in four in the patronage of Garton with Hilston, united at the same time; the other turns were transferred to him in 1956 and 1960.[68] At the further union of 1974 one turn in three was given to the archbishop.[69]

Tithes in the parish worth 15s. a year were given c. 1100 to Sées abbey (Orne), but were evidently resumed soon afterwards and later belonged successively to Aumale abbey and to the subchanter of York.[70]

A stipend paid from the rectory for long comprised the curate's sole income. It was nearly £5

in 1525–6,[71] just over £13 in 1650,[72] and later £20.[73] The living was augmented from Queen Anne's Bounty in 1752, 1800, and 1816, on each occasion with £200.[74] The average annual income was £52 net in 1829–31.[75] Annuities of £12 and £8 were given from the Common Fund in 1853 and 1860 respectively,[76] and a further augmentation, of £250 to meet benefactions of £200, was made from Queen Anne's Bounty in 1863.[77] Tithe rent charges of nearly £35 a year, belonging to the rectory, were granted to the benefice in 1865.[78] The income was £109 net in 1877, when the recently united benefice of Tunstall with Hilston was further endowed.[79]

The augmentations were used to buy 7 a. at Thorngumbald, in Paull, in 1786, 11 a. at East Newton, in Aldbrough, in 1802, and nearly 3 a. at Burton Pidsea in 1822.[80] Most of the land at Burton Pidsea was sold in 1965.[81] The land at East Newton had evidently also been sold by 1978, but 6½ a. then remained at Thorngumbald.[82] There was no house until one was built in 1867, on a site at the north end of the village given by Marmaduke Grimston and enlarged in 1870.[83] The rectory house and nearly 2 a. were sold in 1929 after the union of benefices.[84]

Tunstall church had a lamp dedicated to St. Mary from the 13th century.[85] A house and 1 a. in Tunstall given to the church by the heirs of one Parker passed at the suppression to the Crown, which granted them in 1611 to Francis Morrice and Francis Phillips.[86]

Tunstall was served by a parochial chaplain in 1525–6.[87] In 1567 the parishioners denied that Roman Catholic images and fittings had been retained in Tunstall church.[88] The appointment of curates probably belonged to the subchanter and it was presumably as his grantee that one Hardy nominated in 1660 and 1663.[89] From the 18th century the cure was often served with other parishes and, except in the later 19th and early 20th century, by a non-resident incumbent.[90] An assistant curate was employed c. 1825.[91] Service was weekly in 1743 and in 1764

58 3rd Rep. Poor Law Com. 169; Census.

59 Humberside (Structural Change) Order 1995, copy at E.R.A.O.

60 E.Y.C. iii, pp. 30–1, 35–7; V.C.H. Yorks. E.R. v. 18.

61 Reg. Gray, pp. 22–3, 52–3.

62 B.I.H.R., TER. H. Tunstall 1716, etc.; Rep. Com. Eccl. Revenues, 974–5; Hodgson, Q.A.B. supplement, p. lv.

63 Lond. Gaz. 1 Mar. 1867, p. 1483.

64 B.I.H.R., OC. 880; Lond. Gaz. 11 May 1877, pp. 3076–7; 4 Nov. 1927, pp. 6972–3.

65 Above, this section; R.D.B., IU/195/258.

66 3 & 4 Vic. c. 113, s. 41; Le Neve, Fasti, 1541–1857, York, 42.

67 Lond. Gaz. 11 May 1877, pp. 3076–7.

68 Ibid. 4 Nov. 1927, pp. 6972–3; above, Garton, church; Hilston, church.

69 B.I.H.R., OC. 880.

70 E.Y.C. iii, pp. 27–8; V.C.H. Yorks. E.R. v. 198; above, this section; above, manors.

71 Y.A.J. xxiv. 76.

72 T.E.R.A.S. iv. 55.

73 B.I.H.R., TER. H. Tunstall n.d., etc.

74 Hodgson, Q.A.B. p. cccl.

75 Rep. Com. Eccl. Revenues, 974–5.

76 Lond. Gaz. 16 Sept. 1853, pp. 2536–7; 30 Oct. 1860, pp. 3948–9.

77 Hodgson, Q.A.B. supplement, pp. lv, lxxvi.

78 B.I.H.R., TER. H. Tunstall 1868; R.D.B., IU/195/258; IU/196/259.

79 Lond. Gaz. 11 May 1877, pp. 3076–7; above, Hilston, church.

80 There were evidently 13 a. at East Newton. B.I.H.R., TER. H. Tunstall 1786, 1809, 1825; R.D.B., BL/123/160; CE/505/758; DL/224/255; E.R.A.O., NV/1/40.

81 R.D.B., 1428/567/500.

82 Inf. from York Dioc. Bd. of Finance, 1981.

83 B.I.H.R., TER. H. Tunstall 1865, 1868; R.D.B., IK/325/370; KP/351/462; Rep. Com. Eccl. Revenues, 974–5; Lond. Gaz. 8 July 1870, p. 3312.

84 R.D.B., 391/424/355; Lond. Gaz. 4 Nov. 1927, p. 6972.

85 Chron. de Melsa (Rolls Ser.), ii. 23; Cal. Inq. p.m. v, p. 144.

86 P.R.O., C 66/1908, no. 1; ibid. E 311/35, no. 29.

87 Y.A.J. xxiv. 76.

88 B.I.H.R., V. 1567–8/CB. 1, f. 192v.; Aveling, Post Reformation Catholicism, 67.

89 Poulson, Holderness, ii. 87.

90 B.I.H.R., V. 1764/Ret. 3, no. 98; V. 1884/Ret. 2; Herring's Visit. ii, pp. 219–20; iii, pp. 175–6; Poulson, Holderness, ii. 87; V.C.H. Yorks. E.R. v. 200.

91 B.I.H.R., TER. H. Tunstall 1825; Baines, Hist. Yorks. (1823), ii. 396.

FIG. 10. TUNSTALL CHURCH IN THE EARLIER 19TH CENTURY

during the summer but in the winter only fort-nightly. Communion was then celebrated about four times a year, with usually *c.* 30–40 recip-ients.[92] There was a weekly service from 1865. Communion was celebrated up to nine times a year in the later 19th century, fortnightly *c.* 1920, and on every third Sunday in 1931; there were generally a dozen communicants.[93]

The church of *ALL SAINTS*, so called by 1333,[94] is mostly built of boulders with ashlar dressings and consists of chancel, aisled and clerestoried nave with south porch, and west tower. The chancel has a window and a priest's doorway of the 13th century. Late in the same century the earlier of the three-bayed aisles was added to the north side of the nave. The tower, which is also of the 13th century, was remodelled and heightened in the 14th, when the south aisle was added. A chapel built north of the chancel in the 15th century was later demolished.[95] Other work of the 15th century included the making of new windows in the tower, north aisle, and east wall of the chancel. The south aisle was probably given new windows when the clerestory was added in the early 16th century. The chancel was in disrepair in 1591.[96] The church was repaired in 1802–3 and again in 1844,[97] the brick porch added by 1831,[98] and a west gallery, recorded from the 18th century, removed in the early 1860s.[99] The church was restored *c.* 1875, prob-ably to designs by Smith & Brodrick of Hull; the work included the rebuilding of much of the chancel and parts of the aisles, and the reflooring

and reseating of the whole church.[1] The tower was restored in 1912.[2] The fittings include a font, comprising a 15th-century bowl on a 13th- or 14th-century base, and there is a medieval cross socket in the churchyard.

There were two bells in 1552 and later.[3] The plate includes a cup and paten.[4] The registers of marriages begin in 1567 and of baptisms and burials in 1568; they are complete except for marriages for 1752–61.[5]

Land assigned to church repairs by 1654 pro-duced *c.* £2 a year in 1743.[6] The estate com-prised *c.* 4 a. and grazing rights in 1764, 6 a. after inclosure in 1779,[7] and slightly less by 1910.[8] The income varied from *c.* £7 about 1820 to £20 in the 1860s and stood at £9 in the early 20th century. The holding may later have been administered with a similar estate belonging to Roos church.[9]

NONCONFORMITY. In 1743 the parish had one family of Quakers.[10] A house at Tunstall used for worship by the Primitive Methodists in 1851 was registered the next year, but its use was evidently discontinued by 1865.[11]

EDUCATION. In 1818 there was a school with 18 pupils, of whom 3 were paid for by a gentle-man of the parish and the rest presumably by their parents.[12] It was perhaps the same school in which 20 pupils were taught at their parents' expense in 1833.[13] A dame's school with a dozen pupils was recorded in the 1860s and a school

92 B.I.H.R., V. 1764/Ret. 3, no. 98; *Herring's Visit.* iii, p. 175.
93 B.I.H.R., V. 1865/Ret. 2, no. 556; V. 1868/Ret. 2, no. 509; V. 1871/Ret. 2, no. 515; V. 1877/Ret. 3, no. 126; V. 1884/Ret. 2; V. 1912–22/Ret. (s.vv. Tunstall and Hilston); V. 1931/Ret. 94 York Minster Libr., L2/4, f. 12v.
95 Poulson, *Holderness*, ii. 88.
96 B.I.H.R., V. 1590–1/CB. 1, f. 138.
97 E.R.A.O., PE/42/10.
98 T. Allen, *Hist. Co. York*, iv. 276.
99 B.I.H.R., TER. H. Tunstall 1764, 1861; V. 1865/Ret. 2, no. 556.
1 E.R.A.O., PE/42/2, note in addition to terrier of 1868; PE/42/9; Bulmer, *Dir. E. Yorks.* (1892), 524.

2 *Kelly's Dir. N. & E.R. Yorks.* (1913), 621.
3 *Inventories of Ch. Goods*, 34; Boulter, 'Ch. Bells', 86.
4 B.I.H.R., TER. 534; *Yorks. Ch. Plate*, i. 326–7.
5 Banns are recorded, however, from 1754: E.R.A.O., PE/42/1–2, 4.
6 H.U.L., DDCV/166/3; *Herring's Visit.* iii, p. 175.
7 B.I.H.R., TER. H. Tunstall 1764; R.D.B., BB/134/17.
8 E.R.A.O., NV/1/28.
9 Ibid. PE/42/10; B.I.H.R., TER. 79; above, Roos, church. 10 *Herring's Visit.* iii, p. 175.
11 P.R.O., HO 129/521/1/26/47; O.N.S. (Birkdale), Worship Reg. no. 462; B.I.H.R., V. 1865/Ret. 2, no. 556.
12 *Educ. of Poor Digest*, 1095.
13 *Educ. Enq. Abstract*, 1097.

with 8 pupils in 1871,[14] but by 1877 the children of Tunstall attended school at Roos; most of them were then supported by Snaith's charity, which about 1900 spent c. £4 a year in that way.[15]

CHARITY FOR THE POOR. James Snaith (d. 1870) left £16 a year for the poor of Tunstall, to assist those in the neighbourhood who lost cows, and to apprentice weak or disabled boys.[16] In 1902 part of the income was spent in buying cows for labourers, and in the mid 1920s about £20 of current and accumulated income was spent annually in cash grants to the sick and on coal and other goods.[17] In 1990 the income was being allowed to accumulate.[18]

WAWNE

THE parish of Wawne is situated on the east bank of the river Hull, c. 6 km. north of the centre of the city of Hull.[19] The ancient parish comprised, besides Wawne township, that of Meaux. The town of Beverley stands about 4 km. WNW. from Wawne, relatively inaccessible on the other side of the river, and the former village of Sutton on Hull is c. 3 km. to the south-east. Sutton was Wawne's 'south town', and its grounds, extending south almost to the river Humber and east to Bilton, in Swine, and containing also the settlements of Lopholme and Stoneferry and part of Drypool, lay within a very much larger parish of Wawne until the gradual creation during the Middle Ages of a separate parish of Sutton.[20] Bransholme, perhaps the largest of Hull's council estates, was built in Sutton in the 1960s and 1970s, and extended into the former township of Wawne in the latter decade.[21] The built-up area, which includes several schools, now ends only ½ km. south of Wawne village.[22] Further west, towards the river, another suburb, called Kingswood, was being built in 2000. The northern part of Wawne parish, which lies away from the river, comprised the township of Meaux, known chiefly as the site of a Cistercian monastery founded in 1150 or 1151.[23] The abbey has gone, leaving virtually no visible remains, and the place consists of a few scattered farms, c. 3 km. north of Wawne village.

The name Wawne, recorded as Wagene or Waghene in 1086, Waune in 1230, and Wawne in 1371, is believed to be wholly or partly Anglian and to mean a quagmire.[24] Meaux is thought to be a Scandinavian, or Anglo-Scandinavian, compound word referring to a sandbank in a pool or lake. Its occurrence in 1086, as Melse, weakens the legend in the Meaux chronicle that the place was named by the first Norman tenants of the estate after their native town of Meaux (Seine et Marne), in Latin Meldis. The association of the two names by the monks is, however, thought to have helped the name to shift from Melse, or Melsa,[25] to Meaux, which was in use by 1291.[26]

The boundaries of Wawne, Meaux, and neighbouring settlements were defined soon after the Conquest, and those of Meaux township were described again c. 1400.[27] In the 1520s some maintained that Wawne parish extended as far south as Drypool and east as Bilton and included Sutton and one or two smaller places, but much of that area was then claimed for the emerging independent parish of Sutton.[28] The parish and township boundaries were formed almost entirely by watercourses, chief among them the river Hull which flowed down the western boundary of Wawne township; the river and the lesser drains are discussed in detail below.[29] The boundary between Wawne township and Benningholme, in Swine parish, has since the 1750s been formed by a ditch and bank made then to divide Wawne common.[30]

By 1852 Wawne ecclesiastical parish, no longer including Sutton, contained 5,440 a. (2,201.6 ha.), comprising 3,983 a. (1,611.9 ha.) in Wawne township and 1,457 a. (589.7 ha.) in that of Meaux.[31] Meaux township, later civil parish, included a detached area of former woodland in Routh parish until, apparently in the 1880s, that land was added to Routh, leaving Meaux with 1,409 a. (570.2 ha.). Wawne township was reduced at the same time by 265 a. (107.3 ha.) to 3,718 a. (1,504.7 ha.); the reason is unknown.[32] In 1935 the 5,127 a. (2,074.9 ha.) of Wawne and Meaux civil parishes was added to almost the whole of Sutton on Hull civil parish to form a new civil parish of Wawne, with 7,256 a. (2,936.5 ha.).[33] The extension of the Hull city boundary in 1968 reduced Wawne civil parish by 1,178 ha. (2,911 a.), and re-measurement may account for a further reduction of 7 ha. (17 a.) between 1981 and 1991, leaving Wawne civil parish with 1,751 ha. (4,327 a.).[34]

[14] B.I.H.R., V. 1865/Ret. 2, no. 556; V. 1868/Ret. 2, no. 509; *Returns relating to Elem. Educ.* 472–3.
[15] B.I.H.R., V. 1877/Ret. 3, no. 126; E.R.A.O., accession 1681; below, charity.
[16] East window in church; TS. by G. W. Wilbraham in possession of Mrs. P. Kirkwood, Manor Farm, 1991.
[17] E.R.A.O., accession 1681.
[18] Inf. from the Revd. J. Adey, Roos, 1990.
[19] This article was written in 1999–2000.
[20] B.I.H.R., CP. G. 133; *V.C.H. Yorks. E.R.* i. 305–6. Sutton was regarded as a chaplery of Wawne as late as 1650: *T.E.R.A.S.* iv. 50.
[21] Below, this section.
[22] O.S. Map 1/25,000, TA 03/13 (1994 edn.).
[23] *Chron. de Melsa* (Rolls Ser.), i. 73.

[24] *P.N. Yorks. E.R.* (E.P.N.S.), 44–5.
[25] *Chron. de Melsa,* i. 73–4, 78.
[26] *P.N. Yorks. E.R.* 43–4; G. F. Jensen, *Scand. Settlement Names in Yorks.* 101.
[27] *Chron. de Melsa,* i. 79–81.
[28] B.I.H.R., CP. G. 133; below, churches.
[29] Below, this section [drainage].
[30] Below, econ. hist.; O.S. Map 1/10,560, TA 13 NW. (1956 edn.).
[31] O.S. Map 6″, Yorks. CCXI (1855 edn.).
[32] *Census,* 1891 (pt. ii). The boundaries were unchanged c. 1890: O.S. Map 1/2,500, Yorks. CCXI. 11 (1891 edn.) etc.
[33] *Census,* 1931 (pt. ii).
[34] *Census;* inf. from the Ordnance Survey and the Office of National Statistics, 2000.

Many people in the parish presumably died from plague in 1349, when only 10 of the 50 monks and lay brothers in Meaux abbey survived.[35] There were said to be 100 households in Wawne township c. 1570.[36] Wawne, including a few houses in the liberty of St. Peter's, York, and evidently also those at Meaux, had 77 houses assessed for hearth tax in 1672.[37] There were 43 families in the parish in 1743, and 36 in 1764.[38] The population of Wawne township fell from 299 in 1801 to 250 in 1811. Growth was resumed, however, in the 1850s, and by 1871 there were 353 inhabitants. After a decline in the 1870s, numbers recovered to 317 in 1891 and reached 374 in 1921. In 1931 the civil parish had 335 inhabitants. In Meaux township the population increased more or less steadily during the early and mid 19th century, from 49 in 1801 to 101 in 1881, but then fell to 72 in 1911 and stood at 73 in 1931. As constituted in 1935, the new civil parish of Wawne would have had a total population in 1931 of 604, including 196 in Sutton; in 1951, when a large military depot remained in Sutton, there were 1,097 inhabitants,[39] and 630 were recorded in 1961. The part of Wawne civil parish which remained after the expansion of Hull in 1968 had accommodated 376 people in 1961; that population had grown to 1,142 by 1971, but then fell back, to 1,084 in 1981 and 997 in 1991, of whom 963 were actually counted.[40]

The parish lies mostly between 1.5 m. and 8 m. above sea level. Much of the lowest ground is found on the margins of the parish, beside the river and the main drains, and that is covered with alluvium.[41] Deposits of boulder clay produce a large broken ridge of higher land running north-south through the middle of the parish and reaching 11 m. in the south of Wawne township. The open fields of Wawne were sited on the higher land, which also provided the sites for the settlements of Wawne and Meaux, and for Meaux abbey. More modest rises in level in Meaux overlie sand and gravel deposits there, which have been dug on a small scale.[42] The extensive lower grounds of the parish were used chiefly as meadows and pastures. Inclosure in Wawne township was evidently piecemeal, but much of its commonable ground, including the open fields, seem to have been dealt with in the later 17th or early 18th century.[43]

The parish is drained southwards towards the river Humber, chiefly by the river Hull and the Holderness drain. Flood banks confining the river had evidently been made by the 13th cent-

ury, when a seadike was recorded in Wawne. Land reclaimed from the river by embankment perhaps included that known as Greilak in the 13th century, later as Graylake, and eventually as Grey Legs.[44] The Holderness drain was formerly represented by a stream, or streams, flowing into Old fleet.[45]

The local drainage was evidently much altered by Meaux abbey and other landowners.[46] Between 1160 and 1182 a stream running along the boundary between Routh and Riston and then through Meaux was enlarged or diverted in Wawne as Eschedike, later Ash dike, to give the abbey a navigable link to the river Hull.[47] In the early 13th century, by agreement with Swine priory, some of the water of Lambwath stream was diverted into a new drain, later, as in the case of a near-by watercourse,[48] called Monk dike. Monk dike flowed into the parish along the boundary between Arnold and Benningholme townships, both in Swine parish, and then divided into two channels running north and south of the abbey's woodland before rejoining to fall into Ash dike. The northern branch was evidently intended to supply water to the abbey mill.[49] The southern channel probably later formed the boundary between Meaux and Wawne, and is now represented by Arnold and Riston drain and part of the Holderness drain.[50] The rest of the water from the Lambwath valley flowed into the Hull through the ditches separating Wawne from Swine and Sutton, later called respectively Head or Moor dike and Forge, Forth, or Fore dike, now Foredyke stream and Wawne drain.[51] Forth dike was made or improved to form the boundary between Wawne and Sutton in the earlier 13th century by agreement between Sir Saer of Sutton and other proprietors in Sutton, Peter of Wawne, and Meaux abbey; the ditch was to be navigable and in part comprised two channels.[52]

Other drains recorded in the Middle Ages included those running along the east, west, and north sides of Meaux township. The eastern drain, Wyth, later Monk, dike, was evidently also made or improved by the abbey.[53] Park dike, which flows down the western boundary, was said to have been made by William le Gros, count of Aumale, in the 12th century to enclose one side of his projected park at Meaux; it now forms part of the Holderness drain.[54] Park dike and a continuation flowing along the north-western boundary of Wawne township to the river Hull were known as Skaith, or Double, dike by 1433.[55] The northern boundary drain,

35 *Chron. de Melsa*, iii. 36–7, 77.
36 P.R.O., E 134/14 Eliz. I East./3.
37 Ibid. E 179/205/504, which includes Mrs. Grantham's house at Meaux; below, manors [Alfords].
38 B.I.H.R., V. 1764/Ret. 3, no. 112; *Herring's Visit.* iii, p. 224.
39 *V.C.H. Yorks. E.R.* i. 470.
40 *V.C.H. Yorks.* iii. 494; *Census*, 1911–91.
41 Geol. Surv. Map 1″, drift, sheet 72 (1909 edn.).
42 A. Bryant, *Map of E.R. Yorks.* (1829).
43 Below, econ. hist.
44 B.L. Cott. MS. Otho. C. viii, f. 86 and v.; *P.N. Yorks. E.R.* (E.P.N.S.), 45.
45 J. A. Sheppard, *Draining of Hull Valley* (E. Yorks. Loc. Hist. Ser. viii), 1; O.S. Map 1/25,000, TA 03/13 (1988 edn.).

46 Following based on Sheppard, op. cit. 3.
47 E.R.A.O., CSR/15/4; ibid. DDBV/46/2; *Chron. de Melsa*, i. 160; Poulson, *Holderness*, i. 132; O.S. Map 1/25,000, TA 03/13 (1988 edn.).
48 Below, next para.
49 *Chron. de Melsa*, ii. 82–3; below, econ. hist. (mills).
50 O.S. Map 1/10,560, TA 13 NW. (1956 edn.); *Chron. de Melsa*, i. 356–7; Poulson, *Holderness*, i. 129–30.
51 O.S. Map 1/25,000, TA 03/13 (1994 edn.).
52 *Chron. de Melsa*, i. 356–7, 409–10; ii. 211–12; Poulson, *Holderness*, i. 130.
53 *Chron. de Melsa*, i. 81.
54 Ibid. 77, 79–80; O.S. Map 6″, Yorks. CCXI (1855 edn.).
55 E.R.A.O., CSR/15/4; *V.C.H. Yorks. E.R.* vi. 308; A. Bryant, *Map of E.R. Yorks.* (1829).

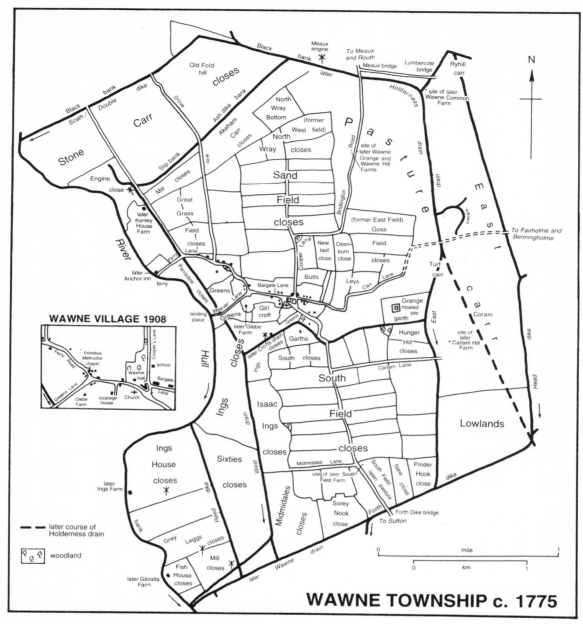

WAWNE VILLAGE 1908

- - - later course of
Holderness drain

woodland

WAWNE TOWNSHIP c. 1775

later the Routh and Meaux drain, had been made or improved by the abbey by 1286.[56]

The drainage of the parish was said to have been injured on occasion by the abbey's works: in the 13th century the abbey allegedly caused flooding in the pasture next to Ash dike and in a meadow near its mill and fishery,[57] and in 1367 Monk dike was said to have been hindered by water being taken in from the river for the mill on Ash dike.[58] In 1436 it was, however, the abbey's neglect of drains in Wawne parish and elsewhere which was given as the reason for flooding in Leven.[59]

The Court of Sewers for the East Parts of the East Riding was responsible for the drainage from the 16th century, when there was apparently a mere south of the village[60] and when much of Wawne and Meaux was said to be frequently under water.[61] In 1580 the court made a new drain, later East drain,[62] through Wawne township linking Monk dike to Forth dike.[63] It was, nevertheless, reckoned in 1650 that 1,800 a. in Wawne was poorly drained.[64] The drainage of the west side of Wawne was improved by Sir Joseph Ashe, lord of Wawne, in 1675. His scheme involved the construction of banks

56 B.L. Cott. MS. Vit. C. vi, f. 13v.; *Chron. de Melsa*, i. 80; ii. 172–3, 212; Poulson, *Holderness*, i. 119; O.S. Map 6″, Yorks. CCXI (1855 edn.); below, Routh, intro. [drainage].
57 *Chron. de Melsa*, ii. 81.
58 Poulson, *Holderness*, i. 130.
59 *Mon. Notes,* i (Y.A.S. Rec. Ser. xvii), p. 9.

60 H.U.L., DDWI/111.
61 P.R.O., E 134/14 Eliz. I East./3; H.U.L., DDWI/116.
62 E.R.A.O., DDBV/46/2.
63 Sheppard, op. cit. 6–7.
64 Poulson, *Holderness*, ii. 282–3.

around the low grounds, notably along the northern side of Wawne lordship where a 'great bank' flanked by dikes called Black, or Stone Carr, bank was made; the cutting of a new drain from the carrs to the outfall of Forth dike into the river, and the building of drainage windmills to assist the new drain, which was consequently called Engine, or West, drain. Ash dike was then also made to flow in a contrary direction, falling into the East drain rather than the river.[65] In the 18th century two wind-powered drainage engines, the 'great' and Kenley engines, were employed in the drainage of Stone carr,[66] and in the 1770s two mills were shown beside West drain, another, the 'Meaux engine', beside the embanked north-eastern boundary, and three others, apparently smaller devices, near the river south of the village.[67] The drainage of Wawne, Meaux, and other parts of the east side of the Hull valley was further improved under the Holderness Drainage Acts of 1764 and later.[68] The area rated to the work of the Holderness Drainage Board in 1775 included 733 a. in Wawne and 502 a. in Meaux,[69] and 682 a. and 640 a. respectively were assessed in 1833.[70] Forth dike was diverted away from the outfall in Wawne by the making of a new course to the river through Sutton c. 1765; the westernmost part of Forth dike was subsequently called Wawne drain.[71] Soon afterwards the Board constructed a new main drain to a lower point in the river Hull. The work in Wawne township was evidently done in, or shortly before, 1779,[72] and involved the cutting of a channel from the northern part of East drain to the south-eastern corner of the parish, where the new Holderness drain was culverted under Forth dike.[73] Despite the improvements, there was flooding in the carrs at Wawne in the 1780s, but in the earlier 19th century the drainage was made more effective by re-routing the main drain to fall directly into the river Humber.[74] Responsibility for the main drains later passed in turn to the River Hull Catchment Board, the Hull and East Yorkshire River Board, and the Yorkshire Water Authority, and in 2000 it belonged to the Environment Agency.[75] The development of the south-western corner of Wawne in the 1990s was accompanied by changes in the drainage there, notably by the culverting of part of Engine drain.

Besides being for long the main drain of the parish, the river Hull was also an important navigation. In 1269 the archbishop of York assigned most of the annual rent he received from Meaux abbey for his land in Wawne to Joan de Stutville, lady of Cottingham manor, in return for her removal from the river of weirs and other barriers to the archbishop's boats going between Beverley and the Humber.[76] Wawne village itself had a landing stage beside the river.[77]

The archbishop of York, or the count of Aumale as his tenant, had a ferry across the river Hull at Wawne, which passed with land there to Meaux abbey in the mid 12th century.[78] In 1584 the Crown leased the river crossing to Lancelot Alford, the Wawne half, with the boat and tolls, as the abbey's successor, and the other half, presumably, as later, from Thearne, in Beverley, as the then owner by exchange of the archbishop of York's manor of Beverley.[79] The ferry from Wawne later belonged, with the manor there, to Sir Joseph Ashe, Bt., and his successors.[80] A new dock was made c. 1780.[81] The river Hull was occasionally shallow enough to be forded at the ferry crossing, the worst barrier in the river, and dredging was undertaken in 1721 and again in the 1880s.[82] By the early 20th century a floating bridge controlled by chains was used for horses and carts, and a punt for foot passengers.[83] The length of the journey to Hull by way of the ferry then prompted suggestions for other crossings in the south of Wawne. In 1913 a floating bridge or ferry boat to Dunswell, in Cottingham, was mentioned, and a new private ferry was then proposed for a site further south, close to the township boundary. During the protracted negotiations with the drainage authorities responsible for either bank and with the river authority, a swing bridge at the existing ferry site was suggested, and the southern scheme was altered from a ferry bridge to a moveable bridge, before being abandoned because of the war and continued official opposition.[84] Wawne ferry ceased to be operated in or shortly before 1947.[85]

Almost the only road in the parish is the minor one running north-south along the higher ground through the two settlements, to Routh and the main Beverley–Bridlington road in the north and to Bransholme, Sutton, and Hull in the south. A short lane, called Ferry Lane in 1639 and later Ferry Road,[86] links the village and the river Hull, and another runs along the Wawne–Meaux boundary to Benningholme, but

65 E.R.A.O., DDBV/46/2; H.U.L., DDWI/78; Sheppard, op. cit. 10.
66 H.U.L., DDWI/38, 78.
67 E.R.A.O., DDBV/46/2; ibid. DDIV/21/3.
68 4 Geo. III, c. 47 (Priv. Act); 6 Geo. III, c. 74 (Priv. Act); 2 & 3 Wm. IV, c. 50 (Private); V.C.H. Yorks. E.R. vi. 278–9.
69 E.R.A.O., DDCC/143/135.
70 Ibid. QDA/12B.
71 V.C.H. Yorks. E.R. i. 475; O.S. Map 6″, Yorks. CCXXVI (1855 edn.).
72 E.R.A.O., DDIV/21/3.
73 Sheppard, op. cit. 13; O.S. Map 6″, Yorks. CCXXVI (1855 edn.).
74 Sheppard, op. cit. 18.
75 Ibid. 22; V.C.H. Yorks. E.R. vi. 279; inf. from Environment Agency, Willerby, 2000.
76 B.L. Lansd. MS. 402, f. 23; Hist. MSS. Com. 54,

Beverley, p. 20; V.C.H. Yorks. E.R. iv. 67–8.
77 E.R.A.O., DDBV/46/2; R.D.B., 122/141/128.
78 E.Y.C. i, p. 48; iii, pp. 94–6.
79 P.R.O., C 66/1260, m. 9; V.C.H. Yorks. E.R. vi. 210.
80 H.U.L., DDWI/25, 78, 101; R.D.B., 139/475/429.
81 E.R.A.O., DDIV/21/3.
82 Ibid. CSR/31/525; Sheppard, op. cit. 10, 21; B. F. Duckham, Inland Waterways of E. Yorks. 1700–1900 (E. Yorks. Loc. Hist. Ser. xxix), 10.
83 P.R.O., MT/10/1868; V.C.H. Yorks. E.R. vi. 297; illus. in G. B. Wood, Ferries and Ferrymen; Yorks. & N. Humbs. Times, 6 Nov. 1981.
84 E.R.A.O., CSR/31/525–6, 528–9; P.R.O., MT/10/1868.
85 E.R.A.O., DDX/328/11; Kelly's Dir. N. & E.R. Yorks. (1937), 783; Yorks. & N. Humbs. Times, 6 Nov. 1981.
86 P.R.O., E 134/15 Chas. I Mich./22; O.S. Map 6″, Yorks. CCXI (1855 edn.).

otherwise the parish depends on field roads. Between Wawne village and Meaux the chief road was called Cooper Lane and Burlington Road in 1734,[87] and later just Cooper's Lane; the part south of Wawne village has been known as Sutton Road.[88] The latter is carried over the southern boundary drain by Foredyke bridge,[89] probably the Forthcross bridge recorded in the 13th century and the 15th-century Forth bridge.[90] The turnpiking of the main road, and of the side road to the ferry which was then to continue over a bridge to join the Beverley–Hull turnpike road in Thearne, was proposed in the later 1760s but came to nothing.[91] The busy road remains relatively unimproved, but a section in Meaux was straightened c. 1970.[92]

WAWNE village was built on higher ground in the middle of the township.[93] The early plan may have comprised two discrete greens with a connecting east-west street, later Bargate Lane, leading through the settlement's open fields. Most of the village, including the church, stood on or around the larger eastern green, which extended south across the shallow valley of a stream, later improved as Crofts drain. The village was clearly extensive by the 12th century, when its buildings included some on the lower southern land. Earthworks excavated there before their destruction in the 1960s revealed several phases of medieval building, and possibly some replanning, but the site was largely abandoned in the 16th or 17th century; the last building was removed in the late 18th century. That field was then called Garths, later Crofts garth, and other closes there and in the west of the village, where similar evidence of medieval occupation and later abandonment was found, were named Greens. The sale of the manor of Wawne in 1651 to (Sir) Joseph Ashe (Bt.) and his subsequent acquisition of tenancies there may account for the reduction in the size of the village.[94] Vestiges of the former greens remained in the shrunken village. Some houses had been said in 1566 to stand 'in a circle near the church',[95] and in the later 18th century there was an open area north of the church, and, further east, 'islands' of houses and garths, almost certainly encroachments on the waste. The former green was then crossed by a lane, probably earlier realigned, leading south-eastwards to the stream,[96] by another leading north to Meaux, and by Bargate Lane, which was continued eastwards into the carrs. At the west end of the village, Bargate Lane divided at the supposed green

there: Ferry Lane or Road led north and west to connect the village to its crossing to Beverley, and Weaver Lane, later Greens Lane, ran south-westwards to the landing place. The street pattern was altered later in the 18th century or in the earlier 19th, when part of Bargate Lane was taken into the grounds of the chief house, later Wawne Hall; the remaining western stretch and part of the southern lane later constituted Main Street, but the eastern end of the lane continued to be called Bargate Lane until the name was changed to Fairholme Lane in the mid 20th century.[97]

It was then that the still small village began to grow. The district council put up eight houses beside the lane to Meaux, formerly Cooper's Lane and now Meaux Road, before the Second World War, and about 1950 it built almost 30 more houses north of Main Street in Oak Square, named after the ancient trees which stand on the central green there.[98] Many private houses were also added by further ribbon development along Meaux Road; by piecemeal infilling of Main Street and Greens Lane;[99] and by the construction of small housing estates off Main Street, that to the north, called Windham Crescent, being built on the site of Wawne Hall in or soon after 1961,[1] and the southern one surrounding the former vicarage house, which was sold in 1963.[2] Wawne Hall and other buildings in the grounds were used during the Second World War as the headquarters of the anti-aircraft batteries along the north bank of the Humber, and later part of the site became the county council's emergency defence and planning centre; a few buildings and radio masts remained behind Windham Crescent in 2000.[3] The district council provided a sewage disposal works beside Crofts drain about 1950, but that was later replaced[4] by a treatment works in Hull, built c. 1965,[5] and pumping stations in Glebe and Sutton Roads.[6]

Most of the buildings date from the 20th century, and, apart from the church, all are of brick. Earlier buildings include farmhouses and their outbuildings, of which No. 4 Main Street, Bamforth Farm, Ferry Road, and Grange Croft, off Sutton Road, may all date from the 18th century.[7] Several houses also remain from the improvements made to Wawne Hall and its surroundings by the chief landowner, the Windham family, in the late 19th and early 20th century. Gate Lodge (No. 32 Main Street) was designed by John Bilson and built in 1904; it has prominent pedimented gables with modillions, and, a

[87] H.U.L., DDWI/78.
[88] O.S. Map 6", Yorks. CCXI (1855 edn.).
[89] O.S. Map 1/25,000, TA 03/13 (1988 edn.).
[90] B.I.H.R., CP. F. 212; Chron. de Melsa, i. 410.
[91] K. A. MacMahon, Roads and Turnpike Trusts in E. Yorks. (E. Yorks. Loc. Hist. Ser. xviii), 27; Beverley Corp. Min. Bks. 1707–1835 (Y.A.S. Rec. Ser. cxxii), 47–9.
[92] R.D.B., 1675/3/3.
[93] The following is based on a plan of Wawne c. 1775 at E.R.A.O., DDBV/46/2; O.S. Map 6", Yorks. CCXI (1855 edn.); C. Hayfield, 'Wawne, E. R. of Yorks.: a case study in settlement morphology', Landscape Hist. vi, 41–65.
[94] Below, manors (Wawne).
[95] H.U.L., DDWI/111.
[96] Hayfield, op. cit. 64.

[97] O.S. Map 1/10,560, TA 03 NE. (1956 edn.); O.S. Map 1/10,000, TA 03 NE. (1984 edn.).
[98] R.D.B., 335/461/375; 609/559/435; 744/226/187; O.S. Map 1/10,560, TA 03 NE. (1956 edn.); O.S. Map 1/10,000, TA 03 NE. (1984 edn.).
[99] R.D.B., 1584/220/171.
[1] Below, manors (Wawne).
[2] R.D.B., 1335/448/414; 1535/231/180.
[3] Inf. from Mr. D. F. Harrison, Wawne, 2000.
[4] R.D.B., 797/89/74; O.S. Map 1/10,000, TA 03 NE. (1989 edn.).
[5] Inf. from Professor Ian Colquhoun, Hull, 2000.
[6] R.D.B., 1730/139/126; inf. from Yorkshire Water, 2000.
[7] For this para. see Dept. of Environment, Buildings List (1989); Pevsner and Neave, Yorks. E.R. 738.

recurring motif in the estate building of the village, diagonal chimney stacks. It was probably then that the adjoining row of single-storeyed 18th-century cottages (now Nos. 34 and 36) and another range behind (Nos. 38 and 40) were remodelled; those fronting the street received most attention, and have Tudor-arched doorways and a flat-tiled crested roof with dormer windows and diagonal chimneys. A semi-detached pair of gabled houses (Nos. 21 and 23 Main Street) are also by Bilson, as may be the single-storeyed Nos. 50 and 52, with bargeboarded eaves, dormer windows, and, once again, diagonal stacks, and Nos. 17–19 Fairholme Lane, which have tile-hung gables. Other houses built on the manorial and rectorial estates are Glebe Farm Cottage (No. 41 Main Street) and the adjoining Glebe Cottage; No. 4 Ferry Road and its neighbour, Rose Cottage, both of one storey with dormers; Nos. 5 and 7 opposite, and the remodelled Smithy Farm, Fairholme Lane.

An alehouse at Wawne was mentioned in the 1590s,[8] and the Plough was named in 1666.[9] Wawne and Meaux each had one or two licensed houses in the later 18th century, but only one was recorded from the 1820s, the Anchor, or Windham Arms, at Wawne, which stood at the river crossing and was kept by the ferryman.[10] It was closed with the ferry in the 1940s,[11] and the building was later used as a farmhouse. The Waggoners Arms, on Sutton Road, was opened in the 1970s[12] and still traded in 2000. A small brick building was provided by the Windhams as a reading room c. 1900, and evidently so used until 1926, when a First World War wooden hut was erected adjoining the room for a village institute. That hut was later replaced by another, and in the later 1980s a new brick-built village hall was put up on the site. The former reading room next door was used for church meetings in 2000.[13] A library was run in Wawne Village Institute by the county council from 1960.[14] Before its 20th-century growth, the village had a cricket field on the south side of Main Street. That was replaced by another pitch, laid out on 1½ a. on the north side of Ferry Road, bought in 1963; in 1971 the parish council enlarged the site by c. ½ a., and in turn made tennis courts and a children's play area there.[15] A pavilion had been added by the 1980s.[16] Land south-east of the church was bought in 1966 for a new vicarage house but was later used instead for allotment gardens.[17]

OUTLYING BUILDINGS. A moated site c. ½ km. east of the church was probably that of Meaux abbey's grange at Wawne, established by 1177;[18] later called Paradise, the site stood in the 1770s in a close called Grange garth. Excavation indicates that occupation ceased c. 1500;[19] by the later 18th century the house later named Grange Croft Farm had been built nearer the village.[20] One or two of the outlying farmhouses in Wawne also occupied old sites. Gibralta Farm probably succeeded a medieval fish house belonging to the abbey,[21] and Ings Farm also existed by the 1770s;[22] both were demolished in the late 20th century. Kenley House Farm was probably named after the Caynglaik family, recorded in 1297: the house was named Kaynglayk in 1396 and Kainglie in the 16th century.[23] Several farmhouses were evidently built in the late 18th or early 19th century, following the completion of inclosure and improvements to the drainage:[24] Wawne Common, South Field, Carlam Hill Farms, and a pair called Wawne Grange Farm and East Field, or Wawne Hill, Farm,[25] had all been put by the 1820s,[26] and Carr House Farm was added soon afterwards[27] and rebuilt in the mid 20th century. South Field Farm was demolished for the development of the North Bransholme estate, and Wawne Hill and Carlam Hill Farms were derelict in 2000. Wawne Lodge had been put up by 1889, possibly for Ashe Windham the younger, who was living there in 1893, before moving to Wawne Hall.[28] It was apparently enlarged by Alexander Alec-Smith in the late 1930s,[29] but was also demolished when Hull's Bransholme estate was extended into Wawne in the 1970s.[30] Foxholme Farm was evidently added in the early 20th century.[31]

MEAUX vill or manor is said to have stood just over 1 km. north-east of the site near the southern township boundary chosen for Meaux abbey in the mid 12th century, and soon afterwards the earlier settlement was replaced by one of the abbey's farms, North grange.[32] A moated site near North Grange Farm, presumably that of the grange, has been excavated.[33] The abbey had another grange in Meaux at Fewsome (Felsam), where there may already have been a

8 B.I.H.R., V. 1595–6/CB. 3, f. 171.
9 P.R.O., E 134/18 Chas. II Mic. 10.
10 E.R.A.O., QDT/2/7, 9; A. Bryant, *Map of E.R. Yorks.* (1829); directories; O.S. Map 6″, Yorks. CCXI (1855 edn.).
11 E.R.A.O., DDX/328/11.
12 Inf. from Miss M. Carrick, Wawne, 2000.
13 Directories; local inf.; Char. Com. reg. no. 700033.
14 E.R. Educ. Cttee. *Mins.* 1959–60, 184; 1965–6, 111.
15 R.D.B., 1306/87/83; 1724/336/290; 1818/473/376.
16 O.S. Map 1/10,000, TA 03 NE. (1984 edn.).
17 B.I.H.R., NPH. 1966/1; local inf.
18 *E.Y.C.* iii, pp. 94–5, 103–4; below, econ. hist.
19 H. E. Jean le Patourel, *Moated Sites of Yorkshire,* 117; C. Hayfield, op. cit. 51.
20 E.R.A.O., DDBV/46/2; A. Bryant, *Map of E.R. Yorks.* (1829); O.S. Map 6″, Yorks. CCXI (1855 edn.); O.S. Map 1/10,000, TA 03 NE. (1989 edn.).
21 Below, econ. hist.

22 E.R.A.O., DDBV/46/2.
23 B.L. Cott. MS. Vit. C. vi, f. 201; P.R.O., E 367/1530; *Yorks. Lay Subsidy, 25 Edw. I* (Y.A.S Rec. Ser. xvi), 119.
24 Above, this section; below, econ. hist.
25 O.S. Map 1/2,500, Yorks. CCXI. 11 (1891 edn.); Dept. of Environment, *Buildings List* (1989).
26 E.R.A.O., DDBV/46/3; H. Teesdale, *Map of Yorks.* (1828); A. Bryant, *Map of E.R. Yorks.* (1829).
27 Bryant, *Map of E.R. Yorks.* (1829); O.S. Map 6″, Yorks. CCXI (1855 edn.).
28 E.R.A.O., PE/146/29; directories.
29 H.U.L., DAS/24/24.
30 Hull Corp. *Mins. Housing Cttee.* 1972–3, 18.
31 O.S. Map 1/2,500, Yorks. CCXI. 14 (1927 edn.) seems to err by not showing it.
32 *Chron. de Melsa,* i. 81.
33 O.S. Map 6″, Yorks. CCXI (1855 edn.); H. E. Jean le Patourel, *Moated Sites of Yorks.* 115; below, econ. hist.

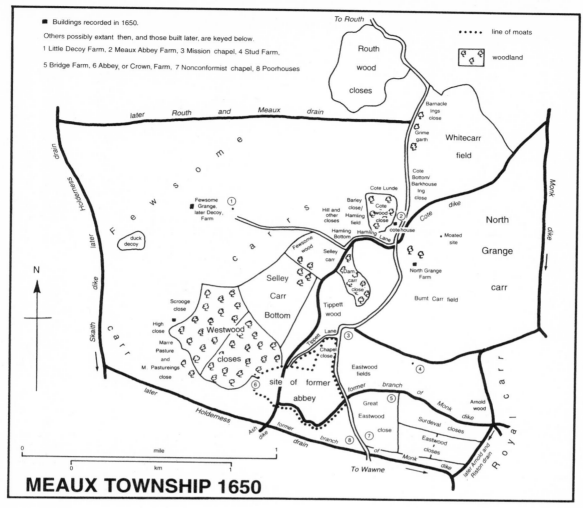

■ Buildings recorded in 1650.

Others possibly extant then, and those built later, are keyed below.

1 Little Decoy Farm, 2 Meaux Abbey Farm, 3 Mission chapel, 4 Stud Farm,

5 Bridge Farm, 6 Abbey, or Crown, Farm, 7 Nonconformist chapel, 8 Poorhouses

• • • • line of moats

woodland

MEAUX TOWNSHIP 1650

farm when Meaux abbey was founded.[34] Apart from the abbey, other early buildings included a chantry chapel on the north side of the monastery.[35] Meaux abbey was demolished in the 1540s,[36] but the derelict Abbey Cottage off Tippett Lane may be a surviving building, or contain stone from the abbey. It is built partly of coursed rubble with some 13th-century stonework, and has a massive brick chimney stack dating from the 16th century.[37] After the abbey's removal, the hamlet comprised a few scattered farmhouses and their cottages. North Grange and Fewsome Grange, later Meaux Decoy Farm, were recorded again in 1650; both were evidently rebuilt later.[38] The present Meaux Decoy Farm may date from the 18th century but was refronted later and reduced and remodelled in the 20th century. Its farm buildings include a pigeon house. Wise's, or Stud, Farm

was presumably one of the three farmhouses bought by Robert Wise in 1810.[39] Meaux Abbey Farm was built on the site of a former abbey sheepcote, evidently in the early 19th century,[40] and Little Decoy Farm had been added by Robert Harrison (d. 1821) or his successor Robert Harrison by 1828.[41] The latter had been abandoned by 2000, when little remained of the buildings. Abbey, later Crown, Farm was built between 1797 and 1828 by the Crown, which in the 1840s or early 1850s also rebuilt Bridge Farm[42] and in 1866 put up two cottages, later Bridge Cottage.[43] A mission chapel and nearby two cottages were added in the 1870s.[44]

The BRANSHOLME estate was built between 1965 and 1983, mostly by Hull corporation as part of its programme of slum clearance and re-housing; its site and other land formerly

34   *Chron. de Melsa*, i. 79–80; below, econ. hist.

35   *Cal. Chart. R. 1226–57*, 233–4; below, church [chant.].

36   Below, manors.

37   Dept. of Environment, *Buildings List* (1989).

38   P.R.O., E 317/Yorks./35; R.D.B., AW/259/447.

39   R.D.B., CS/245/366; H. Teesdale, *Map of Yorks.* (1828); O.S. Map 6″, Yorks. CCXI (1855 edn.).

40   Below, manors (Meaux).

41   R.D.B., CU/309/325; DM/318/370; FT/205/243; GW/379/485; 163/255/215; H. Teesdale, *Map of Yorks.*

(1828), which confusingly calls the house Fewsome Grange; O.S. Map 6″, Yorks. CCXI (1855 edn.); above, Swine, Benningholme, manors [Benningholme grange].

42   Surveys in P.R.O., CRES 35/1899; ibid. MPE 1/538; H. Teesdale, *Map of Yorks.* (1828); O.S. Map 6″, Yorks. CCXI (1855 edn.); O.S. Map 1/10,560, TA 30 NE. (1956 edn.); O.S. Map 1/25,000, TA 03/13 (1994 edn.).

43   P.R.O., LRRO 1/4599; R.D.B., 1535/551/463; 1867/83/67; datestone.

44   P.R.O., CRES 35/1920.

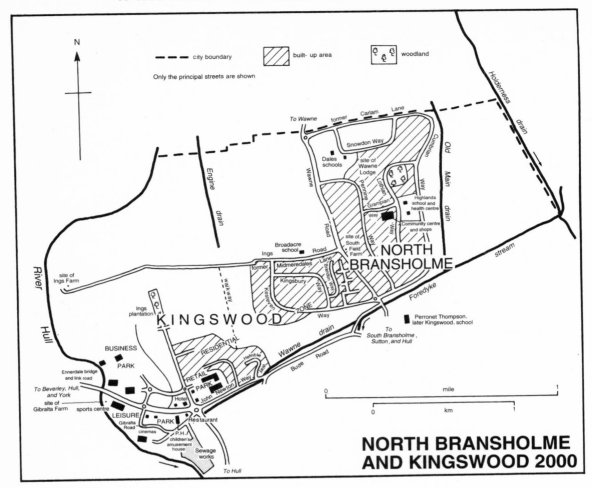

belonging to Sutton and Wawne parishes was transferred to the city in 1968.[45] The southern part of the estate was finished first, North Bransholme being developed on some 500 a., formerly in Wawne parish, from *c.* 1975.[46] The completed estate, very largely made up of council housing, comprised nearly 9,000 dwellings, of which some 2,500 were in North Bransholme. In a wider area comprising Bransholme and the adjacent Sutton Fields estate, more than 13,000 dwellings were built between 1967 and 1983; nearly 11,000 were put up by Hull corporation, some 2,000 by private developers, and about 100 by a housing association.[47] Almost half of the public housing on the Bransholme estate was of new design, much being system-built to plans of the Yorkshire Development Group, but the one- and two-storeyed houses and flats put up in North Bransholme were more traditional in their lay-out and materials.[48] Several schools were built in North Bransholme,[49] and social

facilities were largely associated with them. A temporary building for social events was put up at the Dales schools in 1982, land there was developed by the school for community use in the late 1980s, and the estate as a whole was then provided with a library and sports facilities in the new Perronet Thompson school.[50] Earlier a play area had been laid out for North Bransholme, and in 1980 a prefabricated social hall was opened on Lothian Way;[51] by 2000 that hall had been demolished, and accommodation in the shopping centre opposite was being used for a community meeting place. Licensed premises then included Skippers tavern and the Pennine Rambler. The commercial centre of Bransholme is in the southern part of the estate, but North Bransholme has a small shopping centre off Grampian Way.[52] A temporary surgery was later replaced by a health centre in a redundant school.[53] In the 1990s Bransholme was said to suffer from vandalism, and North Bransholme,

45   Above, this section [area]; Hull City Council, *Housing Strategy for Hull 1995–8*, fact sheet 12; Hull Corp. *Mins. Housing Cttee.* 1966–7, 247–8; 1971–2, 84; inf. from Professor Ian Colquhoun, Hull, 2000.

46   Hull Corp. City Planning Off. *Annual Rep.* 1974–5, 15; 1975–6, 14; Hull Corp. *Mins. Housing Cttee.* 1971–2, 84.

47   Inf. from Professor Colquhoun.

48   Hull City Council, *Housing Strategy for Hull 1995–8*, fact sheet 12; *Hull Area Joint Housing Study: A First Report*, sheet 14; drawings at Hull Corp. Rec. Off., BS 90 AJ, AQ,

AR, AS, AT, AZ, BC; ibid. SP BS 90 (11); illus. *Annual Rep.* 1975–6, 14; Hull Corp. *Mins. Housing Cttee.* 1974–5, 186.

49   Below, educ.

50   Humbs. C.C. *Mins.* 1982–3, B 4171; 1988–9, C 7720, 8039.

51   Hull Corp. *Mins. Housing Cttee.* 1979–80, 464, 523, 557; inf. from Jean Kemp, Highlands health centre, 2000.

52   Hull Corp. *Mins. Housing Cttee.* 1975–6, 216; 1976–7, 85, 205; 1979–80, 423–4.

53   Ibid. 1976–7, 94; below, educ. [Bransholme].

in particular, was classified as an area of social deprivation.[54] Many of the houses in North Bransholme were unoccupied in 2000, some were then being demolished, and the large open areas between them contributed to a bleak aspect.

The corporation's North Bransholme estate extended across to the west side of Wawne Road, where closer-built terraces and semi-detached houses were put up. Development was continued westwards by the building of streets of private houses,[55] roughly parallel to those of the corporation, on land bounded on the south by Kesteven Way and to the north by Ings Road. In the 1990s a new suburb called KINGSWOOD was planned for the large area remaining between North Bransholme and the river Hull. Some 5,000 homes, 3,000 of them privately and 2,000 publicly owned, were proposed for the 320-ha. site, which was expected to take ten to fifteen years to complete.[56] A supermarket was opened in 1996, and the next year a road connecting the area to the Hull–Beverley road was inaugurated, together with its bridge over the river Hull. Soon afterwards a hotel was opened,[57] and by 2000 the retail area comprised about six large shops and an eating house, while on the south side of the new road a leisure park already included a large sports centre, a cinema complex, another restaurant, and a combined public house and children's play house. The residential area was intended to comprise many relatively small and discrete closes, of which Chevening Park and Bushey Park, north and east of the shops, and further east Hunter's Croft, off Kesteven Way, Harvester Court, and Regent's Mead, off Kingsbury Way, were all in progress in 2000. Close to the river the first buildings of Kingswood's business park, four hangars, were also put up in 2000.

MANORS AND OTHER ESTATES. In 1086 the archbishop of York held between 2 and 3 carucates at Wawne as a berewick of his manor of Beverley.[58] The archbishop's holding descended with Beverley, later Beverley Water Towns, manor, passing from the archbishop to the Crown by exchange in 1542, to Sir Michael Warton by sale in 1628, and later belonging to Warton's heirs. The land in Wawne was held of the archbishop and his successors for £5 a year

from the 13th century.[59] The rent from Wawne was sold with Beverley Water Towns manor by Charles Pelham, Lord Yarborough, to Richard Dickson in 1827,[60] and it presumably continued to descend with that estate.

In 1066 Ulf held 7 carucates in Wawne and 2 carucates in Meaux as soke of his manor of Aldbrough; both holdings had passed to Drew de Bevrère by 1086,[61] and they were later parts of the Aumale fee. Sir Basyng of Wawne, mentioned as lord of Wawne after the Conquest,[62] was presumably the tenant under Drew or one of his successors. In 1270 the Aumale fee was said to include WAWNE manor.[63] The counts of Aumale also held the rest of Wawne under the archbishop.[64]

The earliest known tenant at Meaux was Gamel son of Ketel (fl. later 11th cent.). About 1150 Gamel's son or grandson John of Meaux exchanged the holding with his lord, William le Gros, count of Aumale, for Bewick, in Aldbrough. The count intended making a park at Meaux,[65] but soon afterwards he gave the 2 or 3 carucates to Cistercian monks as the site for the abbey of St. Mary at Meaux, together with all his land in Wawne, comprising the 8-carucate Aumale fee and the c. 2 carucates held of the archbishop.[66] The land belonging to the archbishop's fee was resumed by archbishop Roger soon afterwards, only being regained 40 years later c. 1200, and in the 1220s and the later 14th century archbishops unsuccessfully claimed the whole of Wawne as their fee.[67] The abbey's estate in Wawne was enlarged with the smaller gifts of Reiner of Sutton, Robert of Meaux, and Sir Peter of Wawne in the later 12th century,[68] and afterwards by those of, among others, Sir Peter's heirs.[69] In 1294 the Crown granted a 4-bovate farm there as part of the exchange for Wyke and Myton, later Kingston upon Hull. A grant of free warren in Meaux and Wawne, including the lands of North grange and Fish house, had been received in 1293,[70] and in 1316 the abbot of Meaux was recorded as lord of 'Waxan', possibly meaning Wawne.[71] The abbey's manor of WAWNE was referred to later in the 14th century,[72] and in 1535 the house's estate in the parish comprised a reputed manor of MEAUX and the site of the abbey, valued at £24 a year, and lands and houses in Wawne,

[54] Hull City Council, *Housing Strategy for Hull 1995–8*, fact sheet 12.

[55] *Annual Rep.* 1974–5, 15; Hull Corp. *Mins. Housing Cttee.* 1976–7, 104.

[56] Hull City Council, *Housing Strategy for Hull 1995–8*, 27, 31; David Lyons & Associates Ltd., Kingswood brochure (1993), copy at Hull Central Libr.

[57] *Hull Daily Mail*, 21 Nov. 1996, 9 Apr. and 25 June 1997.

[58] *V.C.H. Yorks.* ii. 215, 325.

[59] E.R.A.O., CSR/26/12; H.U.L., DDGE/3/20; DDWI/25; *Yorks. Fines, 1218–31*, pp. 118–19; *Cal. Inq. Misc.* vi, p. 199; *V.C.H. Yorks. E.R.* vi. 210.

[60] R.D.B., EC/136/148.

[61] *V.C.H. Yorks.* ii. 266.

[62] *Chron. de Melsa* (Rolls Ser.), i. 78.

[63] *Cal. Pat.* 1266–72, 478.

[64] *E.Y.C.* iii, p. 96.

[65] Park closes at Meaux were recorded in the 16th cent. and later: P.R.O., C 66/1135, mm. 30–3; R.D.B., CS/245/366. For Park dike, above, intro. [drainage].

[66] *E.Y.C.* i, p. 48; iii, pp. 89, 91–6; *Chron. de Melsa*, i. 77–8, 83, 93; *Yorks. Fines, 1218–31*, p. 118; above, Aldbrough, manors (Bewick).

[67] *Chron. de Melsa*, i. 94–5, 292–6, 407–9; iii. 174–5; *Yorks. Fines, 1218–31*, p. 118; *Mon. Notes* (Y.A.S. Rec. Ser. xvii), i. p. 132.

[68] *E.Y.C.* iii, p. 90, 105–6; *Chron. de Melsa*, i. 159–60.

[69] P.R.O., C 143/420, no. 17; B.L. Cott. MS. Otho. C viii, ff. 86 and v.; *Chron. de Melsa*, i. 83–4, 299, 301–2; ii. 3–5.

[70] *Cal. Chart. R. 1257–1300*, 427, 455; *Chron. de Melsa*, ii. 4, 189; *V.C.H. Yorks. E.R.* i. 1.

[71] *Feud. Aids*, vi. 164. *V.C.H. Yorks. E.R.* v. 93 identifies the place as Waxholme, in Owthorne, and *Kirkby's Inquest*, 305 as Wassand, in Sigglesthorne.

[72] *Chron. de Melsa*, iii. 19.

valued at almost £36 10s.[73] The abbey was surrendered to the Crown in 1539.[74]

Meaux abbey, the history of which is treated elsewhere,[75] was demolished in 1542, much of the stone apparently being used for Henry VIII's contemporary fortification of Hull,[76] and by the 19th century little remained apart from moats and some walling with a gateway. The site was excavated in the 18th century for hardcore for roads[77] and again more sympathetically in the 1830s,[78] c. 1880,[79] and in the earlier 20th century.[80] In 1980 the earthworks were surveyed.[81] A now derelict cottage on the site is partly of ashlar, which may have come from the abbey.[82]

The part of Meaux abbey's former estate which made up *WAWNE* manor remained with the Crown until the earlier 17th century. The net value, composed of rents and court profits, was then c. £105. The manor was pledged as security for the city of London's loan to the Crown in 1625, and in 1628 it was sold in fee farm to the Ditchfield grantees.[83] One of the farms was sold in 1629, and in 1651 Joseph Ashe and his trustees, Edward and Jonathan Ashe, members of a London merchant family, bought the rest of the manor from the city.[84] Joseph Ashe, later Sir Joseph Ashe, Bt., enlarged his estate in Wawne by purchasing several freehold and leasehold estates.[85] Sir Joseph (d. by 1690) was succeeded by his widow Mary and then by their son, Sir James Ashe, Bt.,[86] whose daughter and heir Martha married Joseph Windham. By 1734 the Windhams' estate in the parish had been further enlarged by purchase. Windham, later Joseph Windham Ashe, died in 1746, and was succeeded by John Windham, husband of the Windham Ashes' daughter Mary.[87] John Windham, later John Windham Bowyer, bought c. 100 a. in Wawne from J. C. Crowle in 1776,[88] and died in 1780. He was succeeded by his widow Mary (d. 1789), and then by their son Joseph Windham (d. 1810), who left Wawne to his sister Anne, wife of Sir William Smyth, Bt.[89] Anne (d. 1815) and Sir William (d. 1823) were succeeded by their son Joseph Smyth, who then assumed the name and arms of Windham.[90] In

1846 Joseph Smyth Windham owned c. 3,320 a. of Wawne township.[91] After his death in 1857, Wawne passed in turn to his sons, William Smyth, who took the name Windham and died in 1887, and Ashe, who substituted Windham for Smyth Windham. Ashe (d. 1909) was succeeded by his son, Ashe Windham,[92] who sold almost 2,690 a. in lots in 1912.[93] Some 750 a. of the estate remained to the Windhams in 1915.[94] Wawne Hill farm with 123 a. was sold in 1920, Wawne Lodge with 16 a. to Alexander Smith, later Alec-Smith, a Hull timber merchant, in 1923, and the 482-a. Grange Croft farm in 1935.[95] Ashe Windham (d. 1937) was succeeded by his son, (Sir) Ralph Windham,[96] from whom J. R. Beaulah bought Home farm, of 117 a., in 1951.[97] The 334-a. Ings farm, bought by Ashe Windham in 1932, was left to his wife Cora, who sold it in 1948 to Leonard Smith.[98]

The chief house stood on the north side of Bargate Lane in the 1770s.[99] Later in that century or in the early 19th, the 18th-century house was enlarged as Wawne Hall, and its grounds were extended north and south, encompassing part of Bargate Lane in the process.[1] The Hall was evidently often let, but from the 1890s until the early 1920s the Windhams resided, and the house was then again enlarged and remodelled in a Tudor style.[2] Its grounds extended over 18 a. in 1910.[3] The house was requisitioned during the Second World War, and in 1951 it and 7 a. were bought by the War Office; soon afterwards the house was demolished.[4] In 1961 Sir Ralph Windham repurchased most of the land, and then sold it to Riplingham Estates Ltd. for housing.[5]

Edward Jellett and George Keeble, estate agents, bought some 1,190 a. of the Windham estate in 1912,[6] and then resold much of the land. The largest of their sales was to William Nettleton, who bought 345 a. in Wawne Common and Wawne Grange farms.[7] Jellett and Keeble retained Gibralta and Ings farms with c. 550 a. in 1919, when Keeble bought the 340-a. Carlam Hill farm.[8] The rest of the estate sold in 1912 comprised five farms and almost 1,500 a. The largest of those lots was the 413-a. Kenley House farm, which Thomas Weatherill bought.[9]

73 *Valor Eccl.* (Rec. Com.), v. 108.
74 *V.C.H. Yorks.* iii. 148.
75 *V.C.H. Yorks.* iii. 146–9.
76 *L. & P. Hen. VIII*, xvii, p. 34; *V.C.H. Yorks. E.R.* i. 93, 414.
77 J. Tickell, *Hist. Hull* (1798), 179 (illus.).
78 Poulson, *Holderness*, ii. 314–17 (illus.); White, *Dir. E. & N. R. Yorks.* (1840), 178; *T.E.R.A.S.* xxvi. 136.
79 *T.E.R.A.S.* ii. 1.
80 H.U.L., DDMM/28/26; *Med. Arch.* v. 140; *T.E.R.A.S.* xxii, p. x; xxvi, pp. viii, 108.
81 *Arch. Jnl.* cxli. 46–8.   82 Above. intro.
83 P.R.O., C 54/3636, no. 30; C 66/2220, nos. 20–1; C 66/2351, no. 14, m. 3; C 66/2486, m. 35.
84 London Corp. R. O., RCE deeds 74.15; H.U.L., DDWI/4, 25.
85 H.U.L., DDWI/6, 9, 11, 21; below, this section (rectory) and [Nunkeeling priory].
86 H.U.L., DDWI/15, 75; *9th Rep. Com. Char.* 782.
87 H.U.L., DDWI/73, 75, 78.
88 Ibid. /36; R.D.B., AW/420/714.
89 H.U.L., DDWI/52, 99, 101. For the following, Burke, *Peerage, Baronetage, & Knightage* (1925), 2079.

90 *Lond. Gaz.* 31 May 1823, p. 875.
91 B.I.H.R., TA. 358M.
92 R.D.B., 122/141/128.   93 Below, this section.
94 R.D.B., 139/491/443; 139/488/440; 146/344/288; 167/367/315.
95 Ibid. 221/119/101; 261/184/162; 522/336/259.
96 Ibid. 609/119/85; 609/120/86.
97 Ibid. 897/199/154; 1009/441/382.
98 Ibid. 609/119/85; 609/121/87; 801/32/28.
99 E.R.A.O., DDBV/46/2.
1 A. Bryant, *Map of E.R. Yorks.* (1829); O.S. Map 6″, Yorks. CCXI (1855 edn.).
2 Directories.   3 E.R.A.O., NV/1/59.
4 R.D.B., 897/500/405; Pevsner and Neave, *Yorks. E.R.* 738; illus. in D. [R. J.] Neave and E. Waterson, *Lost Houses of E. Yorks.* (Georgian Soc. for E. Yorks., 1988), 60.
5 R.D.B., 1214/403/359; 1220/508/447.
6 Ibid. 139/480/434; 139/482/435; 139/494/445; 139/497/447; 139/498/448; 146/340/284; 167/558/476.
7 Ibid. 143/346/304.
8 Ibid. 203/174/151; 204/274/242.
9 Ibid. 139/417/376; 139/474/428; 139/475/429; 139/484/436; 143/304/270; 146/284/246; 146/296/254.

The later ownership of those farms has not been traced.

The so called manor of *MEAUX* evidently comprised the abbey site and the demesne, which included North and Fewsome granges, woods, fisheries, and, in Sutton parish, much meadowland and pasture. That part of the abbey's former estate was granted by the Crown in 1550 to John Dudley, earl of Warwick, later duke of Northumberland; forfeited by him in 1553;[10] re-granted to Lord Robert Dudley, later earl of Leicester, in 1561,[11] but returned by him to the Crown in the earlier 1570s.[12] The Crown's estate in Meaux and the other townships, by then reduced by some alienations, was settled on Queen Henrietta Maria in 1629, when its net value was just over £80 a year,[13] and it was later part of the jointure of Charles II's queen, Catherine of Braganza.[14]

Much of the estate in Meaux, Wawne, and Sutton was leased from the Crown by the Alfords in the 16th and earlier 17th century.[15] The Cornwallis family, lessees in the later 17th century,[16] were succeeded in the earlier 18th by the Hampdens and their assignee, Richard Crowle, a London lawyer.[17] Under an Act of 1755, the reversion was conveyed to Crowle's trustees in exchange for his freehold and leasehold near Windsor castle,[18] and in 1776 Crowle's son and heir, J. C. Crowle, divided and sold the former leasehold.

In Meaux township William Kirkby bought Fewsome Grange, or Decoy, farm with 365 a. and the 200-a. North Grange farm from J. C. Crowle in 1776.[19] North Grange farm was quickly re-sold.[20] Kirkby, who also held the lease of the 292-a. of remaining Crown land in Meaux, was succeeded at his death in 1800 by his widow Eliza or Elizabeth,[21] and in 1813 she conveyed both the freehold and leasehold estates to Kirkby's nephew, John Kirkby Picard.[22] Fewsome Grange, or Decoy, farm, then reduced by sales to 288 a., was bought from Picard and his assignees in bankruptcy in 1833 by William Scott (d. 1848 or 1849),[23] and in 1851 Scott's son William Richardson Scott sold the farm to Albert D. Denison, Baron Londesborough.[24] It later passed with Denison's larger estate in Routh to Sir Henry Samman, Bt., who sold the

farm in Meaux, then of 327 a., to G. L. Cullington in 1938.[25] In 1970 Decoy farm was sold by Cullington to the trustees of Leonard Chamberlain's charities in Hull and Sutton on Hull, and they still owned the farm in 2000.[26]

North Grange farm was sold by Kirkby to Thomas Harrison in 1776, and by him in 1778 to William Keeling, who mortgaged the farm to W. S. Wotton.[27] Keeling's creditors seem later to have gained possession.[28] Wotton's interest passed to his brother in law Isaac Mark, who attempted foreclosure in or about 1788, and then, apparently under Wotton's will, to his neice Susannah Mark in 1798.[29] The mortgage was transferred in 1802 by Miss Mark to William Smith the elder (d. by 1815) and younger, and by Smith in 1816 to William Habbershaw (d. 1818 or 1819).[30] The farm was later held by Habbershaw's trustees until 1879, when Robert Habbershaw sold it to William Dale and William Lamplough.[31] In 1907 Dale sold North Grange farm to Aldam Pool (d. 1919).[32] The 185-a. farm was later held by Pool's widow Ada and then by trustees of his will, who in 1937 sold it to Henry, Sydney, and Roland Scales.[33] North Grange farm was bought by T. H. Jackson, a Cottingham fish merchant, in 1942,[34] and in 1952 by Leonard Overend, a market gardener, also of Cottingham. The Overend family still owned the farm in 2000.[35]

In Wawne township c. 100 a., fishing rights, and hen rents were sold by J. C. Crowle to John Windham Bowyer in 1776;[36] they later descended with Wawne manor.

The largely cleared former woodlands of the abbey, amounting to c. 290 a., remained with the Crown after the mid 18th-century exchange with Crowle.[37] The 50-a. Routh wood closes were sold to Henry Samman in 1908,[38] and Crown farm, with much of the remaining land, to the Farnabys in 1977. Bridge farm with 70 a. remained to the Crown in 2000.[39]

Part of the Crown's estate at Meaux, comprising the site of the former abbey and several closes, and accounting in all for £4 of the annual rental of £27 from the demesne, was granted in reversion to Sir Christopher Hatton in 1586.[40] Lancelot Alford, the lessee of the Crown's estate

[10] *Cal. Pat.* 1549–51, pp. 71–3.

[11] Ibid. 1560–3, 189–91; 1569–72, p. 444; *Yorks. Fines,* i. 348.

[12] *Cal. Pat.* 1572–5, pp. 548–9; 1580–2, p. 35.

[13] P.R.O., C 66/2511, no. 6; ibid. E 318/50/16, mm. 7, 9; below, this section [Alford].

[14] P.R.O., E 367/4728.

[15] Ibid. E 315/153, ff. 183–8; *Cal. Pat.* 1560–3, 189–91; 1572–5, 548–9.

[16] E.R.A.O., DDX/316/5, mm. 2–3; H.U.L., DX/75/1.

[17] R.D.B., S/218/524; P.R.O., E 367/4728, 6975.

[18] Ho. of Lords R. O., 28 Geo. II, c. 41 (Priv. Act).

[19] R.D.B., AW/259/447; AW/260/448; BM/93/159; BU/398/603; H.U.L., DDWI/36.

[20] Below, next para.   [21] R.D.B., CC/5/10.

[22] Ibid. CO/96/163; CW/83/126; CW/84/127.

[23] Ibid. CU/309/325; EB/282/296; EC/55/58; EU/212/206; GP/221/232; *Hull Advertiser,* 30 Mar. 1827.

[24] R.D.B., GX/32/35.

[25] Ibid. 92/19/18 (1907); 603/42/33; below, Routh, manors.

[26] R.D.B., 1642/240/214; 1670/381/343; *V.C.H. Yorks. E.R.* i. 338; inf. from the Secretary, Leonard Chamberlain trust, 2000.

[27] R.D.B., AW/296/512; AZ/194/299; AZ/194/300.

[28] E.R.A.O., QDE/1/6/22.

[29] Ibid. DDHB/57/170; R.D.B., BZ/91/125; BZ/92/126.

[30] R.D.B., CE/48/75; CY/503/748; DB/432/605; DE/231/329.

[31] R.D.B., FM/2/3; GA/9/11; MI/128/175; MT/281/419; MT/283/420.

[32] Ibid. 98/511/475 (1907); 206/120/104.

[33] Ibid. 570/5/4; 570/8/5.

[34] Ibid. 652/194/171.

[35] Ibid. 923/47/35; 1476/9/8; inf. from Mr. R. Caley, Meaux, 2000.

[36] Ibid. AW/420/714.   [37] P.R.O., MPE 1/538.

[38] Ibid. LRRO 1/4619; E.R.A.O., NV/1/59; R.D.B., 106/180/160.

[39] Inf. from Mr. Farnaby and Mr. J. Swift, Meaux, 2000.

[40] P.R.O., C 66/1272, mm. 4–22. Cf. ibid. C 66/1135, mm. 30–33; H.U.L., DDWI/116.

at Meaux, is said then to have bought the reversion from Hatton. Alford's uncle, Lancelot Alford (d. 1563),[41] had obtained a 21-year lease of Meaux in 1540; Sir William Cecil's servant Roger Alford bought land in Wawne from Cecil in 1551, and the younger Lancelot Alford was the Crown's lessee at Meaux from 1582.[42] Other land at Meaux, granted in 1587 to Henry Mappleton and Thomas Jones, similarly passed that year to Alford,[43] later Sir Lancelot Alford (d. 1617). His son and successor, Sir William Alford, bought another part of the former abbey's estate in Meaux in 1634; the purchase, rented for nearly £7 a year, had been granted in 1625 to Robert Carey, Lord Carey, and later sold by him to Francis Thorpe and Charles Collins, or Collier.[44] The enlarged estate later descended to William's daughter Dorothy, wife of Thomas Grantham, and their son Thomas (d. 1668).[45] Sometimes called *MEAUX* manor, it was later evidently held by Thomas's widow Frances (fl. 1690), and then in half shares by the Granthams' daughters, Dorothy Holt and Elizabeth Palmer,[46] before falling to the share of Mrs. Holt in 1698. In 1701 or 1702 Meaux passed to Mrs. Holt's daughter Frances and son in law James Winstanley, who sold the estate, then of nearly 500 a. divided between six farms, to Francis Stringer's executors in 1712.[47] Like an estate in Humbleton, Meaux later passed to the FitzWilliams.[48] In 1810 William Wentworth-FitzWilliam, Earl FitzWilliam, sold his 543-a. estate at Meaux to Robert Wise.[49] Wise (d. by 1818)[50] was succeeded by his son Robert (d. 1842),[51] who left the holding to his great-nephew, Robert Wise Richardson.[52] Richardson bought c. 85 a. more in Meaux in 1851.[53] He died in 1914, and in 1917 another Robert Wise Richardson, probably his son, sold Home and Coy farms with 470 a. to George Beaulah.[54] The rest of the Richardsons' estate in Meaux, the 157-a. Stud farm, was sold to Frederick Beaulah in 1952.[55] The trustees of Leonard Chamberlain's charity in Sutton on Hull bought George Beaulah's holding, then comprising Meaux

Abbey farm with 487 a., in 1944, and it still belonged to the trust in 2000.[56]

The Alfords and their successors lived at Meaux from the 16th century: Lancelot Alford's house there was mentioned in the 1550s,[57] Sir William Alford was described as of Meaux in 1617,[58] and Mrs. Grantham, presumably Frances, widow of Thomas (d. 1668), occupied the largest house in the parish, with 16 hearths, in 1672.[59] The Alfords' house was wrongly identified in the 19th century with Meaux Grange,[60] later Meaux Abbey Farm.[61] That house had been built by 1828 on the site of a sheepcot which was still standing in 1797; it was perhaps put up for Robert Wise, the purchaser in 1810 of the Meaux abbey estate.[62] Wise's son Robert lived in the 'neat mansion' in 1840,[63] but his successor, Robert Wise Richardson,[64] gave up the house in the later 19th century, and it became a farmhouse.[65] Meaux Abbey Farm is built of red brick in header bond with a slate roof, and comprises a three-bayed block with single-storeyed side wings. The light of the doorway to the south front has **Y**-tracery, as does the dummy Venetian window in the right wing. Tiled paving taken from the foundations of the abbey church has been reset in the entrance hall, and the garden contains a tombstone and other stonework from the abbey.[66] There are extensive outbuildings around two yards on the north side of the house.

The manor of *WAWNE RECTORY*, occasionally called *PREBEND'S* manor,[67] belonged to the chancellor of York minster from the 13th century.[68] The estate was confiscated during the Interregnum and sold to Matthew Alured in 1651,[69] but the chancellor evidently regained it at the Restoration.

The rectory was leased from the late 14th century to the 16th to Meaux abbey for terms of many years at an annual rent of £20; from the 17th century the leases were for three lives.[70] Members of the Payler family of London were lessees from the late 16th century,[71] Edward

[41] B.L. Harl. Ch. 75. H. 25–6; *Cal. Pat. 1572–5*, pp. 548–9; Poulson, *Holderness*, ii. 315.

[42] H.U.L., DDWI/18; *Cal. Pat. 1560–3*, 189–91; *1572–5*, pp. 548–9.

[43] *Hull Advertiser*, 11 Oct. 1822.

[44] P.R.O., C 142/367, no. 31; C 142/368, no. 103; ibid. E 318/50/16, mm. 7, 9; *Hull Advertiser*, 11 Oct. 1822; Poulson, *Holderness*, ii. 316.

[45] P.R.O., CP 25(2)/615/1657 Mich. no. 117; Poulson, *Holderness*, ii. 316.

[46] H.U.L., DDWI/15; P.R.O., CP 25(2)/894/6 Wm. and Mary Trin. [no. 49].

[47] P.R.O., CP 25(2)/899/10 Wm. III East. no. 6; CP 25(2)/899/13 Wm. III Hil. no. 8; R.D.B., D/68/112; D/70/113.

[48] Above, Humbleton, manors [Humbleton Hall].

[49] R.D.B., CS/245/366.

[50] Ibid. DE/94/132.

[51] Poulson, *Holderness*, ii. 315; floor slab in Wawne church.

[52] H.U.L., DDCV(2)/64/95. For the Richardsons, ibid. DDCV(2)/64/96; R.D.B., ML/376/586; Poulson, *Holderness*, ii. 288; floor slab in Wawne church.

[53] R.D.B., GW/379/485.

[54] Ibid. 163/255/215; 181/37/31.

[55] Ibid. 922/523/458.

[56] Ibid. 683/72/62; 1664/523/449; 1675/3/3; *V.C.H. Yorks. E.R.* i. 338; inf. from the Secretary, Leonard Chamberlain trust, 2000.

[57] P.R.O., STAC 4/10/11.

[58] Ibid. C 66/2114, no. 3.

[59] Ibid. E 179/205/504; Poulson, *Holderness*, ii. 316.

[60] Bulmer, *Dir. E. Yorks.* (1892), 530.

[61] A pavement removed from the abbey to Meaux Grange (Sheahan and Whellan, *Hist. York & E. R.* ii. 396) remains at Meaux Abbey Farm.

[62] P.R.O., E 317/Yorks./35; ibid. MPE 1/538; *Cal. Pat. 1549–51*, 72; H. Teesdale, *Map of Yorks.* (1828); O.S. Map 6", Yorks. CCXI (1855 edn.); above, this section; Dept. of Environment, *Buildings List* (1989).

[63] White, *Dir. E. & N. R. Yorks.* (1840), 178, which gives Wise's forename as John.

[64] Sheahan and Whellan, *Hist. York & E. R.* ii. 396.

[65] Bulmer, *Dir. E. Yorks.* (1892), 530.

[66] J. Tickell, *Hist. Hull* (1798), 179 (illus.); Poulson, *Holderness*, ii, facing 317 (illus.); White, *Dir. E. & N. R. Yorks.* (1840), 178; Pevsner and Neave, *Yorks. E.R.* 613.

[67] H.U.L., DDWI/10–11.

[68] Below, churches. [69] P.R.O., C 54/3628, no. 5.

[70] H.U.L., DDWI/111; *Chron. de Melsa* (Rolls Ser.), iii. 226 n.; Poulson, *Holderness*, ii. 284–5.

[71] J. S. Purvis, *Tudor Par. Doc. of Dioc. York*, 54.

Payler's widow Frances holding the estate, then said to be worth £110 or £125 a year, in 1650.[72] Joseph Ashe, later Sir Joseph Ashe, Bt., lord of the other manor of Wawne, bought up much of the copyhold in the 1650s and 1660s, and from 1665 he and his successors leased the rectory manor from the chancellor. From the mid 17th century the lessee paid an additional rent of £20 a year as an augmentation to the vicar of Wawne.[73]

The tithes of hay, wool, and lambs were reserved to the rector when the vicarage was ordained in 1244,[74] and later his tithes were said to include also those of corn, flax, and rape.[75] The tithes due from Meaux abbey were disputed on several occasions between the 12th century and the 14th; the house's privileges were acknowledged in the late 12th century in return for payment to Wawne church of two pounds of wax a year, but that composition was changed to a rent of £2 a year soon afterwards, and in 1257 a composition of £2 5s. a year was substituted. The last composition was still being paid to the chancellor in the 16th century,[76] but thereafter it fell into abeyance, and in 1822 the rector's attempt to take tithes from Meaux township was resisted by the proprietors, who successfully claimed that their lands were tithe-free.[77] Nunkeeling priory compounded for rectorial tithes due from its estate in Wawne in 1273.[78] In the 16th century the hay tithes were said to be compounded for at the rate of 10d. a 'bovate'.[79] The tithes of Wawne township were commuted by award of 1846 and apportionment of 1847; rent charges amounting to £882 a year, and including £72 from the rectorial glebe, were then awarded to the chancellor for his tithes.[80] The rent charges were transferred to the see of York in 1861, and in 1869 they passed by exchange to the Ecclesiastical Commissioners.[81]

Besides tithes, the rectorial estate comprised 1 carucate and 4½ bovates, 15 houses, and c. 35 a., mostly held by copyholders for some £3 a year; court profits, and 16s. 8d. a year from Wawne church's former chapel at Sutton.[82] As inhabitants of St. Peter's liberty, tenants enjoyed immunity from tolls and other commercial

dues.[83] By a private award of 1825, confirmed by Act of 1826, the rectorial glebe was disentangled from the lessee's own estate, the rectory house and 307 a. then being confirmed as the rector's part.[84] The farm, later comprising 318 a., passed in the mid 19th century to the Ecclesiastical Commissioners for England, but in 1862 it was re-conveyed to the dean and chapter of York.[85] In 1934 the dean and chapter vested the estate in the Ecclesiastical, later the Church, Commissioners, who in 1950 sold it, as Rectory, or Glebe, farm, to Leonard Dixon.[86] Much of the farm was bought compulsorily by Hull corporation in the 1970s for the development of the Bransholme housing estate, and the rest was divided and sold in the 1980s following Mr. Dixon's death.[87]

The rectory house, with three ground-floor rooms in 1649,[88] stood on the south side of the village, at the west end of land called Gild croft.[89] Later called Glebe Farm,[90] the house was greatly remodelled in the late 20th century, following the building of a new farmhouse.[91]

John de Ros held a little land in Wawne of the Scruteville fee in the later 13th century.[92]

About 1240 Peter son of Osbert of Wawne gave 3 bovates, tofts, and 1s. rent in Wawne to Nunkeeling priory.[93] The Crown granted the priory's former estate in Wawne, with the dissolved house, to Sir Richard Gresham in 1540,[94] and it later descended with Nunkeeling manor.[95] In 1671 the half shares in the four farms in Wawne were sold by Thomas Thynne and Leicester Devereux, viscount Hereford, to Sir Joseph Ashe, Bt., and presumably later descended as part of his larger estate in the parish.[96]

About 1200 Osbert of Wawne gave the chapter of Beverley minster a house and land in Wawne, which Meaux abbey eventually acquired in the late 14th century.[97]

A small farm in Wawne was held of Meaux abbey by knight service by Thomas Hildyard (d. by 1322),[98] and it later descended like Riston manor to the Nuthills and then to Elizabeth Suthill and her heirs.[99]

Trinity House, Hull, bought the 482-a.

[72] H.U.L., DDWI/55, 60, 62; *T.E.R.A.S.* iv. 50; Poulson, *Holderness*, ii. 286.
[73] H.U.L., DDWI/11, 26, 62–3, 78, 96, 102.
[74] York Minster Libr., L 2/2(a), ff. 91v.–92.
[75] H.U.L., DDWI/111; B.I.H.R., CP. H. 3841; Poulson, *Holderness*, ii. 286.
[76] York Minster Libr., Torre MSS., Peculiars, p. 495; *Chron. de Melsa*, i. 217–18, 297–8; ii. 76, 291–2; *Valor Eccl.* (Rec. Com.), v. 109.
[77] *Hull Advertiser*, 9 Aug., 11 Oct. 1822.
[78] Poulson, *Holderness*, ii. 284, citing York Minster Libr., Torre MSS., Peculiars, p. 495, where the house is mistakenly given as Bridlington priory.
[79] B.I.H.R., D/C. CP. 1581/2–3.
[80] Ibid. TA. 358M.
[81] Ibid. OC. 282; *Lond. Gaz.* 26 July 1861, p. 3077; 19 Mar. 1869, pp. 1766–7.
[82] H.U.L., DDWI/26, 111. For the payment from Sutton, see York Minster Libr., M 2/3(c), ff. 8v.–9v. (mostly printed in Poulson, *Holderness*, ii. 284 and recited in Blashill, *Sutton*, 129–30). B.I.H.R., CP. G. 189; *Reg. Gray*, pp. 201–2.
[83] H.U.L., DDWI/35.   [84] E.R.A.O., DDX/328/11.
[85] B.I.H.R., TA. 358M; *Lond. Gaz.* 25 July 1862,

pp. 3708–18.
[86] B.I.H.R., OC. 677; R.D.B., 844/596/498.
[87] Inf. from Mr. T. Fisher, Wawne, 2000.
[88] Poulson, *Holderness*, ii. 286.
[89] H.U.L., DDWI/26, 111.
[90] O.S. Map 6", Yorks. CCXI (1855 edn.).
[91] Inf. from Mr. Fisher.
[92] *Kirkby's Inquest*, 373; below, Routh, manors.
[93] B.L. Cott. MS. Otho. C. viii, ff. 86 and v.; *Chron. de Melsa*, ii. 3; *Yorks. Hund. R.* (Y.A.S. Rec. Ser. cli), 37. *Chron. de Melsa*, i. 299 mistakenly gives Osbert as the donor.
[94] P.R.O., SC 6/Hen. VIII/4612, m. 3d.; *L. & P. Hen. VIII*, xvi, p. 95.
[95] Below, Nunkeeling, manors; P.R.O., CP 25(2)/259/12–13 Eliz. I Mich. [pt. 1, last]; CP 25(2)/261/28–9 Eliz. I Mich. no. 1; CP 25(2)/752/12 Chas. II Trin. no. 74; *Cal. Pat.* 1547–8, 331–2; 1575–8, p. 263.
[96] H.U.L., DDWI/68–9; above, this section.
[97] *Chron. de Melsa*, i. 299; iii. 176–7. P.R.O., E 317/Yorks./17.
[98] *Cal. Inq. p.m.* vi, pp. 185–6.
[99] E.R.A.O., DDRI/22/33; DDRI/35/1, 3; P.R.O., REQ 2/1/35, f. 3; *Yorks. Deeds*, iii, p. 100; *Yorks. Fines*, ii. 15; below, Long Riston, manors.

Grange Croft farm in 1935, and the corporation still owned the farm, then reduced to 294 a., in 2000.[1]

ECONOMIC HISTORY. COMMON LANDS AND INCLOSURE IN WAWNE.

Wawne had three open fields. They were called North, South, and East fields in the 13th century. East field then included land called Oxhenburne and part of North field was known as Wragate,[2] and Oxenburn, Wrey gate, and Wray closes were all recorded later.[3] Meaux abbey may have converted tillage to pasture before the mid 13th century,[4] and a reduction in the area tilled is also evident from ridge and furrow in a part of the former carrs used by the 18th century as pasture and later as the site of Wawne Grange farm.[5] North field was known as West field by the mid 16th century,[6] and later perhaps as Sand field. West field was bounded in the 17th century by Akam carr, and South field by the ings, or meadows; the locations of the open fields are otherwise known from the shape of the later closes, which followed the earlier groupings of strips, and from ridge and furrow surviving in the mid 20th century.[7] The common meadows comprised Wawne ings, which extended south-westwards alongside the river from the village to the southern boundary, and Lowlands in the south-eastern corner of the township. In 1639 Wawn ings included pieces of meadowland at Sowerhill, later Sorey, nook, in Fore ings, at Reed's dike mouth, and adjoining the Hull flood bank. In the 17th century Wawne's open fields were said to contain in all 90 bovates,[8] each bovate being equivalent to almost 30 a., possibly including a notional area for pasturage rights; in 1700 a bovate was said to include c. 12 a. divided between the three fields and 7–8 a. in the ings.[9]

There were extensive tracts of marshland, or carr, to the east and north of Wawne village. They were probably intercommoned with neighbouring settlements before the 13th century, when several disputes arose about their use. Early in the century Meaux abbey protested against the digging of turves in the eastern marshes by Swine priory, and at about the same date the marshland of Sutton was separated from that in Wawne by the making of a boundary ditch.[10] Common rights in the eastern marsh were also claimed by Swine priory and other landowners as appurtenant to neighbouring Benningholme, in Swine, the priory's claim being in particular to Lumbercotecarr, in the north of Wawne. By an agreement made by 1235, the western and eastern parts of the marsh, adjoining the arable in Wawne and Benningholme, were assigned to Meaux abbey and Swine priory respectively, with power to inclose, and the middle of the marsh was left common. The pastures in Wawne were surveyed about that date, and the stint set at 15 oxen or horses, 20 sheep, and 2 pigs for each bovate.[11] Possibly in consequence of the earlier agreement, part of East carr lying south-east of the village was divided between Meaux abbey and the freeholders of Wawne c. 1240.[12] Soon afterwards discord over the commonage of marshland in the north-west of the township, adjoining Meaux and Weel in Beverley, was resolved; the archbishop of York and his tenant at Weel were confirmed in their occupation of Weel pasture and were allowed land in the north of Wawne's marsh, then named as Stone carr, the rest of which was to remain to Meaux abbey and the other tenants of Wawne.[13] In the 16th century the eastern carrs included Turf carr, a mile in circumference,[14] and, near Hunger hill, a common called Cow pasture.[15] Another piece of common lay at Pinder hook on the southern boundary in 1610.[16] The chief value of the common pastures was the rough grazing they provided, but the brushwood and other plants growing there were also valuable enough to be regulated through the manor court, which in 1623, for instance, punished the unlawful cutting of thorns.[17]

Wawne seems to have been inclosed piece-meal. About 1570 a proprietor was said to have taken in a small area of South field, thereby infringing the commonable rights of the other inhabitants of the township,[18] and cases of hedge-breaking, recorded in 1623, perhaps reflect later inclosure.[19] The process may have accelerated after the sale of the manor to Joseph Ashe in 1651.[20] By the 1680s flax was being grown in Akam carr, recently improved by Ashe's drainage scheme, and rape was then said to be grown in such quantity in Wawne that the tithes were worth as much as or more than those on the corn and hay crops; in 1683 the rape crop was valued at c. £150.[21] East and West fields had evidently been inclosed by 1734, when Wawne farms included divisions of Sand field, and of Eastfield pasture and Gosfield pasture, both almost certainly parts of the former East field. Some of the common meadows and carrs had also been inclosed: single tenants then held 55 a. divided into two in the ings, 24 a. 'inclosed' there, and halves of Sorey nook, while closes in

1   R.D.B., 522/336/259; inf. from the Secretary, Hull Trinity House, 2000.
2   B.L. Cott. MS. Otho C. viii, f. 86 and v.
3   The rest of the para. is based on P.R.O., E 134/15 Chas. I Mich./22 (a deposition of 1639); H.U.L., DDWI/6, 21 (deeds of 1652, 1669); E.R.A.O., DDBV/46/2 (mid 18th-cent. plan of Wawne).
4   Chron. de Melsa, ii. 81.
5   Hull Univ., Dept. of Geog., R.A.F. air photographs, run 333A, nos. 4215–17; O.S. Map 6", Yorks. CCXI (1855 edn.).
6   H.U.L., DDWI/111.
7   Hull Univ., Dept. of Geog., R.A.F. air photographs, run 333A, no. 4217; run 334A, nos. 4159–61; run 334B, nos. 3165–7; Fairey surveys, run 365B, no. 2145–6.

8   H.U.L., DDWI/42.
9   Ibid. /26.
10 Chron. de Melsa, i. 356–8, 409–10.
11 Ibid. 412–14.
12 Ibid. ii. 5.
13 Ibid. 75–6.
14 P.R.O., C 66/1135, mm. 30–3.
15 Ibid. E 134/14 Eliz. I East./3.
16 Ibid. SC 2/211/143.
17 Ibid. /145.
18 Ibid. E 134/14 Eliz. I East./3; ibid. SP 46/28, f. 231. Cf. H.U.L., DDWI/4.
19 P.R.O., SC 2/211/145.
20 Above, manors (Wawne).
21 B.I.H.R., CP. H. 3841; above, intro. [drainage].

Stone carr and a 'carr close called Sedgham in Lowlands' were also recorded. Parts of the township remained commonable, however. In Midmydale and Sixties meadows and Isaac ings some 170 a. in all was parcelled out among the tenants of Wawne manor, and all or part of South field was occupied as a common pasture containing c. 140 gates.[22] Southfield 'open pasture' was later a 21-a. close at the southern end of the former South field.[23] In 1757 it was let annually to tenants at the rate of £1 a gate; there were then only eight commoners, with probably fewer than 20 gates between them.[24]

Inclosure in the eastern carrs was proposed in the mid 17th century to settle a dispute between Wawne and Benningholme, in Swine parish, over grazing rights there,[25] but it was only achieved in 1751 or 1752, when the two owners of the common rights in Out carr, or Wawne common, William Constable, proprietor of Benningholme Grange farm,[26] and John Windham Bowyer, lord of Wawne, divided the c. 400-a. common between them; a ditch and bank running north-west south-east through the common, made to separate Bowyer's western half from Constable's part, has since also defined the parish and township boundary there.[27] Other parts of the low grounds, including Turf carr, meadow in Lowlands, and a stinted pasture called Royal, or Ryhill, carr, evidently the northernmost part of the eastern carrs extending into Arnold,[28] belonged to the Crown's estate at Meaux.[29] They were wholly or mostly occupied by the lord of Wawne manor in 1734, evidently as sub-lessee,[30] and in 1776 the then lord, John Windham Bowyer, bought them.[31] Those remaining commonable lands were surveyed and inclosed c. 1780, at the same time as the Holderness Drainage Board was improving the drainage of the low grounds.[32] Inclosure involved much hedging and tree planting on Bowyer's estate, 90 fruit trees and 3,500 willow sets being bought, and nurseries planted in Carlam, Coram, and the lane to Lowlands.[33] That some commonable pasture remained in the carrs is indicated by the appointment in Wawne manor court of bylawmen for Out carr, as well as for Southfield open pasture, as late as 1795.[34] In both Meaux and Wawne small pieces of carr remained unimproved into the 20th century.[35]

LAND USE IN MEAUX BEFORE 1800. The location of some of the open-field land at Meaux

was indicated by ridge and furrow remaining near the later Crown Farm and North Grange in the mid 20th century.[36] After the foundation of the abbey, Meaux seems, however, to have been largely given over to grassland and woods. Whitecarr was used as a pasture c. 1300.[37] Much of the abbey's demesne was under grass at the Dissolution: meadow or pasture closes in Meaux then mentioned included the 40-a. Whitecarr field, and Burnt carr, or Burncarr, field, Eastwood field, Barley close, and Marre pasture with Marre pasture ings, all of about 10 a.[38] No arable land was included in the c. 570 a. of former demesne at Meaux surveyed in 1650.[39]

The site chosen for Meaux abbey was said to have included woodland,[40] and the house was later largely enclosed by woods. On the eve of the house's surrender, the abbot proposed cutting down some or all of them, but he was opposed by the Crown, which wanted the timber to repair Bridlington harbour.[41] East and West woods, each reckoned to contain 100 a. in 1540, lay on either side of the abbey precinct, and to the north and north-west there were woods of less than 10 a. each in Selley carr bottom, Dam carr, Friar Tippett wood, and Cote Lunde, or Cote wood. The woodland in Selley carr bottom was then said to consist of alders and underwood. Fewsome wood, of 10 a., lay on the west and north sides of Selley carr,[42] and the 60-a. Routh wood was situated just across the northern boundary in Routh parish.[43] By 1650, when different acreages were recorded, East wood seems to have been cleared and divided into pasture closes. Most of the larger trees, besides coppiced woodland, then grew in West wood, and there were over 100 trees in each of Dam carr and Cote wood.[44] Routh wood seems to have been felled by 1685,[45] and much of the woodland remaining in Meaux was cleared in the 1720s; just over 700 oak trees were then felled in Westwood and Thick Westwood, and c. 100 more in Dam carr and Selley carr.[46] By the 1790s all of the woodland named earlier had been converted to arable or grassland, except for 10 a. in Cote wood, then described as a coppice of oak and ash.[47]

THE DEMESNE AND OTHER FARMS UNTIL THE 17TH CENTURY. There was reckoned to be land for one plough on the archbishop of York's estate at Wawne in 1086, but three ploughs were then worked there by 11 villeins

22 H.U.L., DDWI/78. Cf. note of 1705 in E.R.A.O., PE/146/3.
23 E.R.A.O., DDBV/46/2.
24 H.U.L., DDWI/48–9.
25 Ibid. /42–4.
26 Above, Swine, Benningholme, manors and econ. hist.
27 E.R.A.O., DDCC/6/8; ibid. QDB/4, pp. 132–4; O.S. Map 1/10,560, TA 13 NW. (1956 edn.).
28 P.R.O., E 317/Yorks./35; E.R.A.O., DDBV/46/3; Poulson, Holderness, i. 129.
29 P.R.O., C 66/1135, mm. 30–3; 28 Geo. II, c. 41 (Priv. Act).
30 H.U.L., DDWI/78.
31 R.D.B., AW/420/714; above, manors (Wawne).
32 Above, intro. [drainage].
33 E.R.A.O., DDIV/21/3.
34 H.U.L., DDWI/104.
35 [1st] Land Util. Surv. Map, sheet 33-4; Hull Univ., Dept. of Geog., R.A.F. air photographs, run 334A, no. 4157.
36 Hull Univ., Dept. of Geog., R.A.F. air photographs, run 333A, no. 4219; run 333B, nos. 3278–80.
37 Chron. de Melsa, ii. 213.
38 P.R.O., SC 6/Hen. VIII/4612, m. 1, print. in T.E.R.A.S. i. 40–3.
39 P.R.O., E 317/Yorks./35.
40 Chron. de Melsa, i. 76.
41 L. & P. Hen. VIII, xiii (1), p. 162; V.C.H. Yorks. ii. 32.
42 P.R.O., E 317/Yorks./35.
43 Ibid. SC 6/Hen. VIII/4612, m. 1; ibid. E 315/153, ff. 183–8.
44 Ibid. E 317/Yorks./35.
45 Below, Routh, econ. hist.
46 P.R.O., LR 4/3/12.
47 Ibid. MPE 1/538; 1798 survey in ibid. CRES 35/1899.

and 2 bordars.[48] After Meaux abbey was founded in the mid 12th century, much of its demesne land in the parish, together with some in Sutton, was farmed from granges staffed by the monks or lay brothers.[49] North grange, which replaced the existing settlement of Meaux, was probably the grange next to the abbey recorded in the 1150s,[50] Wawne grange was named in 1177,[51] and Fewsome (Felsa) grange was mentioned from the late 13th century.[52] Pastoral farming was clearly important on Meaux's demesne. The abbey may have converted some of the tillage in Wawne to grazing before the mid 13th century, and the movement of its animals along roads in the parish was then cited as a nuisance.[53] About 1240 a stone building was put up at Wawne to store wool and make cloth for the abbey; skinners were then employed at North grange,[54] and later sheepcots were rebuilt there and at Wawne.[55] Dairy farming and cheese-making were carried on at Fewsome grange, to which the pastures adjoining Weel were assigned.[56] Like much of the demesne, Fewsome grange had been let by 1396. Under his 12-year lease the tenant had the use of most of the grange's land and a herd of 30 cows, and received from the abbey an allowance of bread and ale, fuel, and a robe; in return he was obliged to render all calves born, 80 stones of cheese, and 15 stones of butter, besides feeding the calves at nearby Hamlam House farm.[57]

At Wawne, however, demesne land was tilled, with the help of the abbey's bond tenants. It may have been the whole estate there, comprising the demesne and the tenanted land, which was reckoned at 10 carucates or 60 bovates, 46 of them held by 'brother John', possibly the lay brother then in charge of the grange, and 14 by 'our men', perhaps the tenantry.[58] About 1360, following the Black Death, some of the bondmen witheld their labour and tried unsuccessfully to win their freedom from the abbey.[59] Later in the 14th century the abbey gave up Wawne grange and let it to tenants, removing first stock which included ploughs and oxen.[60] The arable nature of Wawne grange is also evident from the terms of the 12-year lease held by the four tenants in 1396: they were obliged to render each year to the abbey 10 qr. of wheat, 40 qr. of dredge, 20 qr. of oats, 8 pigs, 12 capons, 12 geese, 12 hens, and three cartloads of straw.[61] Another part of the former demesne, comprising pasture closes in the south-western corner of Wawne and 53 a. of common meadowland was then run as a dairy farm. With some fisheries there, the farm was let at will, the allowances, stock, and renders resembling those at Fewsome grange. One differ-ence was the tenant's duty of supplying milk to a sheepcot in Sutton.[62]

The rest of the abbey's estate in Wawne township was held in 1396 by 116 tenants, most holding for life and a few described as serfs or the descendants of serfs.[63] Many of the holdings comprised the tenant's house and garth, sometimes with a few acres of arable land and meadow, but twenty-five included open-field land: five had ½ bovate each, eighteen 1 bovate each, one 1½ bovate, and the largest 2 bovates. Former demesne land probably included the 40 a. of enclosed meadow called Graylak then shared by Thomas Chapman and six others for £3 6s. 8d. a year. In all the money rents from Wawne in 1396 amounted to nearly £63 a year, and 46 cocks and hens, later called 'lake hens',[64] were also rendered by tenants at Christmas. Although some had been commuted for cash payments, most of the tenantry apparently still owed weeding, reaping, and carting services at Wawne grange, and those occupying 12 of the bovates were moreover bound to cart hay to the abbey. Similarly, the tofts of three of the bovaters were held by the duty of serving as reeve. Some demesne in Wawne, including Wawne sheepcot and 63 a. of meadow, was apparently retained by the abbey in the late 14th century, but by 1540 that too had evidently been given up and leased to the tenants, whose number remained almost unchanged.[65] Nearly 53 bovates were then let: nine farms had less than 1 bovate each, eighteen were 1-bovate holdings, and there were seventeen with between 1 and 2 bovates each. The two largest open-field holdings were Ralph Shipwright's 3½ bovates and John Shipwright's 2¾ bovates, which he occupied with Kenley House and other land in Wawne. Other former demesne then let probably included Wawne Grange, Lund, and Upcroft closes, and Carlam pasture, which last was shared among several of the tenants. The total rental then amounted to £107 and some 200 poultry renders, which were commuted at 2d. each. No mention was made of works, which had presumably also been commuted. In 1608 the c. 100 tenants at Wawne included a few freeholders.[66] Forty-seven holdings then contained open-field land: there were ten with less than 10 a. each, twenty-nine of 10–29 a. each, and eight of more than 30 a., the largest holding being Lancelot Brown's with 46 a. of the tillage, besides c. 70 a. of meadow land and the pasture formerly belonging to the abbey's dairy farm.

MILLS. About 1240 Meaux abbey constructed a water mill and millpond at its fishery in the south of Wawne township. The mill was

48 V.C.H. Yorks. ii. 215.
49 Chron. de Melsa (Rolls Ser.), ii. 4.
50 Ibid. i. 81; E.Y.C. iii, pp. 94–5.
51 E.Y.C. iii, pp. 103–4.
52 Cal. Pat. 1374–7, 467.
53 Chron. de Melsa, ii. 81.
54 Ibid. 63–4.
55 Ibid. iii. 225.   56 Ibid. i. 80; ii. 65.
57 B.L. Cott. MS. Vit. C vi, f. 218. For the place name Hamlyn, P.R.O., E 317/Yorks./35.
58 Undated information in B.L. Cott. MS. Vit. C vi, ff. 230 and v., 231v.
59 Chron. de Melsa, iii. 127–42; Cal. Inq. Misc. iii, p. 108; Cal. Pat. 1358–61, 342–3, 481; 1361–4, 67; Y.A.J. xlviii. 107–17.
60 Chron. de Melsa, iii. 126–7, 177, 228.
61 B.L. Cott. MS. Vit. C vi, f. 218.
62 Ibid. For South House cot in Sutton, P.R.O., E 317/Yorks./35.
63 B.L. Cott. MS. Vit. C vi, ff. 201–4.
64 H.U.L., DDWI/4, 78; P.R.O., C 66/1135, mm. 30–3.
65 P.R.O., SC 6/Hen. VIII/4612, mm. 2–3.
66 Some names occur more than once. P.R.O., LR 2/230, ff. 237–72.

out of repair c. 1300, and no more is known of it;[67] its location was later marked by Mill closes.[68] A lack of water to a mill in the abbey precinct led to the building of a second water mill in Wawne in the mid 13th century; it stood on Ash dike near the river Hull. That mill was subsequently also affected by a lack of inland water, and the use of river water instead led to the dike being fouled and complaints being made about flooding upstream.[69] It was presumably that mill which a proprietor in Arnold was seeking to have demolished in the 1290s, but it evidently still existed in 1367.[70] By the mid 13th century Meaux abbey also had a windmill in Stone carr pasture.[71] It was repaired in the 1390s.[72] Probably the same mill, or a rebuilding, was the windmill in Wawne let by the Crown, as successor to the abbey, in 1546,[73] the mill on the north side of the village recorded in 1566,[74] and the corn windmill granted to Edward Ferrers and Francis Phillips in 1612.[75] The hill on which the windmill 'lately stood' was recorded in 1672;[76] the site may have been used for the drainage windmill which stood in Stone carr in the 18th century.[77] One or other of those mills are commemmorated by Mill closes near Kenley House Farm.[78] Part of East field was called Blackmilldale in the 13th century,[79] Millgarth next to East dike was mentioned in the late 14th,[80] and there was a mill at the east end of the village in the 16th century.[81] Besides the windmill, Wawne manor included a mill house in 1608.[82]

As well as the water mill, the abbey site at Meaux is thought to have included a post mill.[83]

FISHING AND FOWLING. By the early 13th century Meaux abbey had a fishery in the south-western corner of Wawne, close to the river Hull,[84] where closes were later named after the abbey's fish house.[85] The fishery had been let by 1396, together with a dairy farm there, and in the 16th century the fish house was evidently being used as the farmhouse of the dairy farm (vaccaria);[86] the area was later called the Fish House Vaccary, and Gibralta Farm probably occupied the site of the medieval fish house.[87] In the early 13th century Meaux abbey allowed other landowners to use nets in the southern boundary ditch in Wawne.[88]

Some of the fishing and fowling of the carrs and meadows of Wawne township passed from the Crown, as Meaux abbey's successor, to Sir Lancelot Alford (d. 1617), and later descended with his estate in Meaux.[89] Other fishing and fowling in Wawne, Meaux, and Routh remained with the Crown, but was leased by the Alfords c. 1600.[90] A duck decoy, described in 1650 as the 'lately-erected fowling place... called the Coy', was made in the carrs at Meaux, to the south-west of Fewsome Grange, later Meaux Decoy, Farm;[91] its use ended with the drainage of the area in the later 18th century.[92] All or some of the Crown's rights were evidently included in the exchange with Richard Crowle, and in 1776 the fishing of Ash and the Stone carr dikes was bought from J. C. Crowle by John Windham Bowyer.[93] Those fisheries, which had been occupied by an earlier lord of Wawne manor, presumably as a sub-lessee, may have been valued chiefly in the 18th century for the crops of reeds, or 'dumbles', grass, and wood growing in and alongside the drains and ponds.[94]

MODERN AGRICULTURE. Since c. 1800 or earlier the parish has been largely given over to arable farming. Wawne and Meaux were reckoned to have 1,497 a. under crops, mostly wheat and oats, in 1801,[95] and in 1846 Wawne township contained 2,405 a. of arable land and 1,088 a. of grassland.[96] The Crown farms at Meaux were also very largely arable in the 1860s.[97] The two townships were said to have 3,207 a. of arable land and 1,679 a. under grass in 1905.[98] The proportions seem to have been more equal in the 1930s, when much of the grassland lay around Wawne village and the former abbey site in Meaux, and in the southern corners of Wawne.[99] In 1987 of 1,364.4 ha. (3,371 a.) returned for Wawne civil parish, 1,043.6 ha. (2,579 a.) were arable land and 292.8 ha. (724 a.) grassland.[1] There has been relatively little woodland in the parish since 1800. In 1846 Wawne township contained 17 a. of woodland,[2] many trees remained on the former abbey site at Meaux,[3] and then and later there were several plantations and shelter belts in both townships.[4] The two townships were said to have 90 a. of woodland in 1905,[5] and

[67] Chron. de Melsa, i. 411; ii. 3, 81, 211; below, this section [fishing and fowling].
[68] E.R.A.O., DDBV/46/2.
[69] Chron. de Melsa, ii. 82–5; Poulson, Holderness, i. 130.
[70] Mon. Notes, i (Y.A.S. Rec. Ser. xvii), pp. 133–4; Poulson, Holderness, i. 130.
[71] Chron. de Melsa, ii. 83.   [72] Ibid. iii. 243.
[73] L. & P. Hen. VIII, xxi (2), p. 441.
[74] H.U.L., DDWI/111.
[75] P.R.O., C 66/1906, no. 1.
[76] H.U.L., DDWI/71.
[77] E.R.A.O., DDBV/46/2; above, intro. [drainage].
[78] E.R.A.O., DDBV/46/2; P.R.O., SC 6/Hen. VIII/4612, m. 2.
[79] B.L. Cott. MS. Otho C. viii, f. 86 and v.
[80] Ibid. Cott. MS. Vit. C. vi, f. 201.
[81] H.U.L., DDWI/111.
[82] P.R.O., LR 2/230, ff. 237–72.
[83] Arch. Jnl. cxli. 48.   [84] Chron. de Melsa, i. 405.
[85] E.R.A.O., DDBV/46/2.
[86] P.R.O., C 1/1339, no. 4; ibid. E 318/42/2263; B.L. Cott. MS. Vit. C. vi, ff. 203v., 218.

[87] E.R.A.O., DDBV/46/2; O.S. Map 6", Yorks. CCXXVI (1855 edn.).
[88] Chron. de Melsa, i. 405.
[89] P.R.O., C 142/367, no. 31; R.D.B., D/68/112; CS/245/366.
[90] P.R.O., C 66/2114, no. 3; ibid. E 315/153, ff. 183–8.
[91] Ibid. E 317/Yorks./35; O.S. Map 6", Yorks. CCXI (1855 edn.).
[92] V.C.H. Yorks. ii. 525–6; above, intro. [drainage]; R. P. Gallwey, Bk. of Duck Decoys, 182.
[93] R.D.B., AW/420/714.
[94] H.U.L., DDWI/78.   [95] P.R.O., HO 67/26/444.
[96] B.I.H.R., TA. 358M.
[97] Survey of 1864–5 in P.R.O., CRES 35/1899.
[98] Acreage Returns, 1905.
[99] [1st] Land Util. Surv. Map, sheet 33–4.
[1] Inf. from Min. of Agric., Fish. & Food, Beverley, 1990.
[2] B.I.H.R., TA. 358M.
[3] Poulson, Holderness, ii. 316.
[4] O.S. Map 6", Yorks. CCXI, CCXXVI (1855 and later edns.); [1st] Land Util. Surv. Map, sheet 33-4.
[5] Acreage Returns, 1905.

14.5 ha. (36 a.) of Wawne civil parish was returned as woodland in 1987.[6] In the south of Wawne, Ash plantation has been incorporated into the landscaping of North Bransholme.

The rotation on the former carrs at Meaux in the 1790s was a fallow crop of rape succeeded by oats and wheat, or two crops of oats.[7] Livestock kept in the parish have included turkeys at Wawne, which were mentioned in 1626.[8] Most of the labourers in Wawne were said in the mid 19th century to have kept a cow until the outbreak of cattle plague,[9] and several people later earned their living by dairying.[10] A cowkeeper was recorded from 1892. When the Windham estate was sold in the 1910s, Ings farm was described as being suitable for a dairy farmer, and a Hull dairyman then bought c. 50 a. elsewhere in Wawne.[11] One of the larger holdings, the riverside Kenley House farm, had been bought by Hull Co-operative Society Ltd. by 1921, primarily for dairying,[12] and by the 1930s three cowkeepers and a dairyman were at work in Wawne. In 1987 there were 500–600 cattle in Wawne civil parish.[13] Sheep were still kept in the mid 19th century, when at least two shepherds were employed in the parish, and a stud farm was then run at Meaux.[14] The sale of Wawne in the 1910s and the proximity to Hull also led to one or two market gardens being established,[15] and there were nurseries beside Ferry Road and at Hilltop farm in the 1980s.[16] A poultry farm was begun in the 1930s, and in 1987 almost 5,000 pigs were kept in Wawne civil parish.[17]

In the 19th century and earlier 20th there were eleven to fourteen farmers in Wawne township; in 1851 ten of the fourteen farms were of 150 a. or more, and the largest holding comprised 500 a. In the 1920s and 1930s there were about eight larger units. In 1851 Meaux township was divided between five farms, of which one had 634 a. and three others 150 a. or more each; there were usually four farms there, all of them larger holdings, in the earlier 20th century.[18] In 1987 the area returned for the civil parish was divided into 19 holdings, of which one was of 200–299 ha. (494–739 a.), five of 100–199 ha. (247–492 a.), three of 50–99 ha. (124–245 a.), five of 10–49 ha. (25–121 a.), and five of less than 10 ha. each.[19]

INDUSTRY, TRADE, AND PROFESSIONAL ACTIVITY. There has been little non-agricultural employment in the parish. Tile mosaic,

evidently for the floor of the abbey church, and roof tiles were made in kilns at North grange in the 13th century.[20] The small village of Wawne had the usual tradesmen and supported one or two shops in the 19th century and earlier 20th, and carriers then provided a regular service between the parish and Beverley and Hull. A corn and flour dealer was recorded in the earlier 20th century, when professionals there included a surgeon and an auctioneer. A gamekeeper was employed at Wawne in the mid 19th century and c. 1900, and one or two worked as gardeners at Wawne Hall and Wawne Lodge.[21] In 2000 the larger village supported two shops, one with a Post Office, and there were two garages, two concerns making furniture, one of them for laboratories,[22] and a kennels.

LOCAL GOVERNMENT. Franchises claimed by the abbot of Meaux in 1293–4 included the profits from the ale assize in Meaux and Wawne.[23] In the late 14th century a dispute between Meaux abbey and Beverley brick- and tile makers over the taking of clay from the banks of the river Hull in Wawne and Sutton was eventually resolved in the abbey's court of Wawne.[24] Estreats of Wawne manor court survive for most years between 1609 and 1633,[25] minutes for 1750–95,[26] and call rolls for 1766–82 and 1788–96.[27] Wawne court met twice a year in the 17th century, annually in the later 18th century, possibly in the steward's house,[28] but only infrequently c. 1840.[29] Its chief concern seems to have been the regulation of agriculture and drainage in the township, although its jurisdiction also included the view of frankpledge and the assizes of bread and ale. Officers included two carrgraves and four bylawmen in the 17th century, and in the 18th the constable, a pinder, two affeerors, two swine ringers, and bylawmen, of whom two were appointed for South field open pasture and two for Out carr.[30]

A court was evidently also held on the rectory manor.[31] It was said in the 19th century to have also had leet jurisdiction, but the court had then long since ceased to meet.[32]

An overseer's account book for Wawne township covering the years from 1760 to 1806 survives.[33] There were stocks at Wawne in 1762. In the 1760s and 1770s about six adults and one or two children were relieved regularly, and about 12 were so supported in 1786, when some 6 were also helped occasionally. Regular out-relief was

6 Inf. from Min. of Agric., Fish. & Food, Beverley, 1990.
7 P.R.O., CRES 35/1899.
8 Ibid. SC 2/211/146.
9 1st Rep. Com. on Employment of Children, Young Persons, and Women in Agric., App. Pt. II [4068-I], p. 369, H.C. (1867–8), xvii.
10 The rest of the para. is based on directories.
11 E.R.A.O., CSR/31/525; R.D.B., 143/90/83.
12 Report of 1921 in H.U.L., DHC/82.
13 Inf. from Min. of Agric., Fish. & Food.
14 P.R.O., HO 107/2359; O.S. Map 6", Yorks. CCXI (1855 edn.).
15 R.D.B., 139/532/478; 157/435/373.
16 O.S. Map 1/10,000, TA 03 NE. (1984 edn.).
17 Inf. from Min. of Agric., Fish. & Food.
18 Para. based on P.R.O., HO 107/2359; directories.
19 Inf. from Min. of Agric. Fish. & Food.
20 Med. Arch. v. 137–68.
21 P.R.O., HO 107/2359; directories.
22 Inf. from Zebracrest, Fairholme Lane, 2000.
23 Yorks. Hund. R. (Y.A.S. Rec. Ser. cli), 247.
24 Chron. de Melsa (Rolls Ser.), iii. 179–81.
25 P.R.O., SC 2/211/28–9, 143–7.
26 H.U.L., DDWI/104.
27 Ibid. /105.
28 Ibid. /38.
29 Poulson, Holderness, ii. 282.
30 Above, econ. hist.
31 H.U.L., DDWI/111.
32 Poulson, Holderness, ii. 282.
33 E.R.A.O., PE/146/19.

given to 16 in 1802–3 and to 30–5 between 1812 and 1815; in the earlier period 6 more were helped occasionally. The township maintained poorhouses, but was evidently also using the local workhouse, presumably that in Sutton,[34] by the early 19th century, a woman being kept there in 1803 and 4–6 people in the 1810s.[35] About 1805 the care of the poor was given to a contractor. In Meaux township, which also had poorhouses,[36] 4–8 were on regular out-relief and 6–8 were helped occasionally in the early 19th century.[37] Wawne and Meaux townships, later civil parishes, joined Beverley poor-law union in 1836,[38] and remained in Beverley rural district, from 1935 as parts of the new civil parish of Wawne, until 1974, when Wawne civil parish was incorporated in the Beverley district, or borough, of Humberside.[39] In 1996 the civil parish became part of a new East Riding unitary area.[40]

Other parochial records include a churchwardens' account book for 1762 to 1877.[41]

CHURCHES. A church at Wawne was recorded from 1115.[42] Since 1244 the living has been a vicarage.[43] The parish formerly included the village of Sutton, but in the Middle Ages a chapel there gradually became independent of Wawne church and its territory was eventually regarded as a separate parish.[44] There were also chapels at Meaux in the Middle Ages.[45] In 1971 the benefice of Wawne was united with that of Sutton, but the two parishes remain distinct.[46]

WAWNE. In 1115 Wawne church was given by Stephen, count of Aumale, to Beauvais abbey (Seine Maritime), evidently as an endowment for its dependency, Aumale priory, later abbey (Seine Maritime).[47] Despite that grant, the church was said also to have been given by William le Gros, count of Aumale, to Meaux abbey at its foundation in 1150 or 1151.[48] Presumably as a result of the double grant, the church was held in halves by two rectors c. 1200.[49] As patron, or co-patron, Meaux abbey then tried to appropriate the church, agreeing to

pay Aumale abbey a pension of £6 13s. 4d. a year for its right in Wawne, but the scheme came to nothing.[50] Baldwin de Béthune, count of Aumale (d. 1212), ignored Meaux abbey's right soon afterwards by presenting his clerk Philip to one of the half shares, and it was presumably from Baldwin that Philip subsequently obtained the other half of the church.[51] In 1227 and 1228 respectively Meaux and Aumale abbeys ceded their interests to the archbishop of York, who in 1230 annexed Wawne church to the office of chancellor in York minster.[52] A vicarage was ordained in 1244, when the chancellor of York presented the first vicar.[53] Wawne was later mostly in the patronage and peculiar jurisdiction of the chancellor.[54] The patronage belonged briefly to the Commonwealth in the mid 17th century,[55] and the dean and chapter collated in 1740, presumably during a vacancy in the chancellorship.[56] By 1869 the archbishop of York was patron.[57] The Crown presented by lapse in 1955, after a long vacancy, and again in 1958.[58] From 1971 the right to appoint the incumbent of the united benefice, known as the rector, belonged to a board comprising the archbishop of York, the archdeacon of the East Riding, the rural dean of Kingston upon Hull, the parochial church councils of Sutton and Wawne, and the former patron of Sutton.[59]

Wawne vicarage was valued at just over £7 a year in 1535[60] and at £12 in 1650.[61] Between 1660 and 1665 Christopher Stone, chancellor of York minster and rector, augmented the vicarage with £20 a year from the rectory,[62] and in 1707 the living was valued at £30 a year.[63] Grants of £200 from Queen Anne's Bounty were made in 1810, 1811, and 1816,[64] but the net income still averaged only £49 a year between 1829 and 1831.[65] Further grants of £200 Bounty money were received in 1841 and 1850, in both cases to meet benefactions of £600 from the chancellor.[66] The vicarage was endowed again in 1856, with £70 a year from the Common Fund,[67] and in 1873, when £33 a year was received from the same source.[68] The net income was £274 a year in 1872, and some £290 in 1883.[69]

Apart from the hay, wool, and lamb tithes,

34 V.C.H. Yorks. E.R. i. 440.
35 Poor Law Abstract, 1804, pp. 594–5; 1818, pp. 522–3.
36 E.R.A.O., NV/1/59; A. Bryant, Map of E.R. Yorks. (1829); O.S. Map 6″, Yorks. CCXI (1855 edn.).
37 Poor Law Abstract, 1804, pp. 592–3; 1818, pp. 522–3.
38 3rd Rep. Poor Law Com. 167.
39 Census.
40 Humberside (Structural Change) Order 1995, copy at E.R.A.O.
41 E.R.A.O., PE/146/20.   42 E.Y.C. iii, p. 30.
43 York Minster Libr., L 2/2(a), ff. 91v.–92.
44 V.C.H. Yorks. E.R. i. 305–6.
45 Below, this section.
46 Copy of Order in Council at E.R.A.O., DDX/447/13; Lond. Gaz. 28 Oct. 1971, p. 11650.
47 E.Y.C. iii, pp. 30, 35–7; V.C.H. Yorks. E.R. v. 18.
48 E.Y.C. iii, p. 96; Chron. de Melsa (Rolls Ser.), i. 73, 83, 296.
49 Chron. de Melsa, i. 217–18, 296–8.
50 Ibid. 218.
51 Ibid. 297.
52 Reg. Gray, pp. 22, 52–3, 158 and n.; Yorks. Fines, 1218–31, pp. 118–19.
53 York Minster Libr., L 2/2(a), ff. 91v.–92.

54 H.U.L., DDWI/26, 111; Lawrance, 'Clergy List', Holderness, 2, pp. 161– 3; Poulson, Holderness, ii. 285–6.
55 T.E.R.A.S. iv. 50.
56 Herring's Visit. iii, p. 225.
57 Clergy List (1869).
58 B.I.H.R., Inst. AB. 35, pp. 391–2; ibid. ADM. 1959/1–2.
59 Copy of Order in Council at E.R.A.O., DDX/447/13; Lond. Gaz. 28 Oct. 1971, p. 11650.
60 Valor Eccl. (Rec. Com.), v. 117.
61 T.E.R.A.S. iv. 50.
62 H.U.L., DDWI/63; B.I.H.R., TER. H. Wawne 1716 etc.; Le Neve, Fasti, 1541–1857, York, 8.
63 B.I.H.R., Bp. Dio. 3, E.R., p. 185.
64 Hodgson, Q.A.B. p. cccl.
65 B.I.H.R., TER. H. Wawne 1861; Rep. Com. Eccl. Revenues, 974–5.
66 The monies granted in 1850 were used for a vicarage house. E.R.A.O., DDX/215/15; Hodgson, Q.A.B. ccxxix, cccl; Supplement, pp. xx, lxxvi.
67 B.I.H.R., OC. 152; Lond. Gaz. 9 Sept. 1856, p. 3035.
68 B.I.H.R., Ch. Ret. iii; Lond. Gaz. 4 Apr. 1873, p. 1828.
69 E.R.A.O., DDX/215/15; B.I.H.R., V. 1884/Ret. 2.

and possibly also those of corn, all the tithes and offerings of Wawne church and Sutton chapel were assigned to the vicar in 1244.[70] The mortuaries of those dying in Sutton and certain customary offerings from that part of Wawne parish were expressly reserved to Wawne church in 1246,[71] and in 1454 the vicar of Wawne was given £1 a year from Sutton college for allowing burial there.[72] The vicar's income in 1535 came almost entirely from tithes.[73] Rape and flax tithes were apparently taken by both the rector and the vicar in the 1680s,[74] and from the early 18th century the latter received a composition of £5 a year for rape, flax, hemp, and other small tithes in Wawne township, besides an old modus of 5s. a year for small tithes at Meaux.[75] The vicarial tithes in Wawne township were commuted by award of 1846 and apportionment of 1847 for rent charges totalling £135 a year, of which £10 was due from the rectorial glebe only when it was not occupied by the rector.[76]

A house east of the church, already used by the priest serving Wawne, was assigned to the vicar at ordination in 1244,[77] but later the vicarage house stood opposite the church.[78] In 1582 the vicar was said to be using the vicarage house as a farm building,[79] and the house was in disrepair in 1649, when it contained four ground-floor rooms.[80] The 'wretched' building was let to two labourers in the 1760s.[81] It was probably rebuilt later, for in 1809 it was described as a brick and tile house with four living rooms and three bedrooms.[82] The house was, nonetheless, classified as unfit c. 1830,[83] and in 1849 it was demolished and a new one built on the small site to designs by the builder, William Hall of Sutton. The cost was met by a grant of £600 from the chancellor and £200 Bounty money to meet his benefaction.[84] That house was sold in 1872, and between then and 1874 another vicarage house was built west of the church to designs by J. B. and William Atkinson of York, largely with a grant from the Common Fund.[85] The vicarage house was sold in 1963,[86] and in 1967 a house in Meaux Road was bought instead.[87] At union in 1971 the house at Wawne was assigned

to one of the vicars of the team ministry, and the parsonage house at Sutton was designated the rector's residence.[88]

Philip of Langbaurgh, rector of Wawne c. 1200, was also the steward of the patron, Baldwin de Béthune, count of Aumale.[89] The vicar in 1412 was licensed to be absent, and later in the 15th century changes of incumbent by resignation or exchange were frequent.[90] In the mid century parishioners served by Sutton college were given the duty of providing a chaplain for the mother church of Wawne, and until his appointment of paying £1 a year to the parishioners at Wawne, perhaps a reflection of the difficulty in staffing the parish church.[91] From the late 17th century Wawne was frequently held by a non-resident vicar, often with the neighbouring poor benefices of Sutton, Drypool, and Marfleet, but George Dixon, vicar from 1827 to the later 1860s, held the more distant benefice of Helmsley (Yorks. N.R.), where he lived.[92] Wawne was served for the vicar by a curate, who usually also lived elsewhere.[93] In the mid 18th century, for instance, the vicar lived in Hull, where he was also vicar of Holy Trinity, and his livings of Wawne, Sutton, and Marfleet were served by a curate also living in Hull. Apart from each eighth Sunday, there was then a weekly service at Wawne, and quarterly celebrations of communion, at which c. 40 usually received.[94] A singing master was paid by the churchwardens in the late 18th and early 19th century.[95] The provision of services increased following the building of a suitable house for the curate in 1849, and by 1871 the vicar was once again resident in the parish.[96] There was still only one Sunday service in 1847, but in 1851 the curate provided two Sunday services at Wawne.[97] Celebrations of communion were held every two months in 1865, once a month by 1868, and fortnightly in the earlier 20th century; about 20 people usually received in the later 19th century, and 10–12 in 1931. The extra provision in the 19th century also included evening classes, which, however, met with little success.[98]

70 York Minster Libr., L 2/2(a), ff. 91v.–92. Cf. Poulson, *Holderness*, ii. 286–7.
71 *Reg. Gray*, pp. 201–2. Cf. B.I.H.R., CP. G. 715.
72 York Minster Libr., M 2/3(c), ff. 8v.–9v., mostly printed in Poulson, *Holderness*, ii. 284 and recited in Blashill, *Sutton*, 129–30. The vicar's payment seems later to have been reduced to 10s. a year: *Cal. Pat.* 1578–80, p. 53. Cf. B.I.H.R., CP. G. 189.
73 *Valor Eccl.* (Rec. Com.), v. 117.
74 B.I.H.R., CP. H. 3578, 3841.
75 Ibid. TER. H. Wawne 1716 etc.; H.U.L., DDWI/78.
76 B.I.H.R., TA. 358M.
77 York Minster Libr., L 2/2(a), ff. 91v.–92.
78 O.S. Map 6″, Yorks. CCXI (1855 edn.).
79 B.I.H.R., V. 1582/CB. 1, f. 206v.
80 Poulson, *Holderness*, ii. 287.
81 *V.C.H. Yorks. E.R.* i. 307–8.
82 B.I.H.R., TER. H. Wawne 1809.
83 *Rep. Com. Eccl. Revenues*, 974–5.
84 Plans and other papers at E.R.A.O., DDX/215/15; B.I.H.R., TER. H. Wawne 1861.
85 Plans and other papers at E.R.A.O., DDX/215/15; R.D.B., KX/35/40; KZ/214/295; B.I.H.R., Ch. Ret. iii; *Lond. Gaz.* 1 Mar. 1872, p. 1270, 12 July 1872, p. 3150; O.S.

Map 1/2,500, Yorks. CCXI. 14 (1910 edn.).
86 R.D.B., 1335/448/414.
87 B.I.H.R., NPH. 1967/5.
88 Copy of Order in Council at E.R.A.O., DDX/447/13; *Lond. Gaz.* 28 Oct. 1971, p. 11650.
89 *Chron. de Melsa*, i. 297–8; English, *Holderness*, 66.
90 Lawrance, 'Clergy List', 2, pp. 161–2.
91 York Minster Libr., M 2/3(c), ff. 8v.–9v., print. in Poulson, *Holderness*, ii. 284. Cf. B.I.H.R., CP. G. 133.
92 E.R.A.O., DDX/215/15; B.I.H.R., V. 1868/Ret. 2, no. 515; V. 1871/Ret. 2, no. 522.
93 *V.C.H. Yorks. E.R.* i. 301. For the curates, see E.R.A.O., PE/146/1 (Fletcher 1836), 6 (Coulson 1810); 20 (Dowbiggin 1765; Thompson 1767–88, Blezard 1826); 29 (Cruddas 1865; Henslowe 1869); B.I.H.R., TER. H. Wawne 1809 (Robinson); *Educ. of Poor Digest*, 1096 (Orman 1818); P.R.O., HO 107/2359 (Kipling 1851).
94 B.I.H.R., V. 1764/Ret. 3, no. 112; *Herring's Visit.* ii. 195–6; iii, pp. 130, 225.
95 E.R.A.O., PE/146/20.
96 Above, this section; B.I.H.R., V. 1871/Ret. 2, no. 522.
97 E.R.A.O., DDX/215/15; P.R.O., HO 129/518/4/4/6.
98 B.I.H.R., V. 1865/Ret. 2, no. 563; V. 1868/Ret. 2, no. 515; V. 1871/Ret. 2, no. 522; V. 1877/Ret. 3, no. 133; V. 1884/Ret. 2; V. 1912–22/Ret.; V. 1931/Ret.

Wawne was served with Routh in the mid 20th century.[99] At the union of Wawne and Sutton in 1971, a team ministry was established to serve an area which was being largely built up as an extension of Hull; the team comprised the incumbent of the united benefice, thenceforward known as the rector, and three other clergy, to be called vicars. The latter were to be chosen jointly by the archbishop of York and the rector, and appointed for fixed terms of up to five years.[1] In 2000 there was a service at Wawne each Sunday, and a monthly celebration of communion.[2]

There was evidently a guild of St. Mary at Wawne by 1462,[3] and it was presumably its house which was later recorded as Lady House. The guild may have also given land near the church its name of Gill or Gild croft.[4] There was also an obit at Wawne endowed with 1s. a year rent.[5]

The church is dedicated to *ST. PETER*, but the alternative attribution of *ST. PETER AND ST. PAUL* was recorded in 1505, and customary donations were owed by parishioners on the feast day of those saints.[6] The building comprises chancel with south vestry, aisled and clerestoried nave of four bays, north porch, and engaged north-west tower. The church is built largely of coursed stone rubble, but the clerestory is of red brick, the vestry of grey brick, and the porch of ashlar. The chancel is lower than the nave, and it is the tall west end with its fine window and three-stage tower which impresses; prominent buttresses, especially on the tower, where they reach the parapet top, add to the sense of the church's tallness. The relatively thick west wall may survive from the nave of an earlier church which was otherwise largely rebuilt in the 13th and 14th centuries, possibly following the chancellor of York minster's acquisition of the church in 1230.[7] The north aisle was added to the wide nave in the early 13th century. There is a lancet window at the west end of that aisle, and above the window outside an early stone head; the arcade has double-chamfered arches, moulded capitals, circular piers, and waterholding bases. The south aisle, which has a similar but more elaborate arcade, was built soon afterwards. The chancel, also wide, is late 13th-century, and has Y-traceried windows, three sedile, and a piscina. Late in the 14th century the south aisle was given a new west window. The tower, whose lower part was constructed within the north aisle, probably before 1300, was given its top stage in the 15th century, presumably in the 1450s, when new bells were mentioned.[8] About

FIG. 11. WAWNE CHURCH

then, too, the best window in the church, the large, five-light, west window, was inserted.[9] Somewhat later, at the end of the 15th or early in the 16th century, the south doorway was renewed, the new entrance having a four-centred arch under a hoodmould with two head stops, and the aisles were largely refenestrated with square-headed windows. The clerestory was perhaps added at the same time, and its late 13th- or early 14th-century windows may have been those displaced from the aisles. Other work possibly included the addition of stone battlements to the aisles to match those on the clerestory, and a brick buttress against the north aisle. Parishioners served by Sutton college were said to owe 1/3 of the cost of maintaining the nave at Wawne, but by the early 16th century some were disputing that burden.[10]

The church was out of repair in the later 16th century.[11] A porch had fallen down or been demolished in 1578, when it was ordered to be rebuilt, unless the rector thought it unnecessary;[12] it was evidently rebuilt later in brick. The church was repewed in the 1820s.[13] By then the tower arches had been filled in; the west end of the south aisle opposite was partitioned off, and the lancet window in the tower had been blocked up.[14] The enclosed part of the south aisle may have been used for the early school, but *c.* 1840 it was a vestry; its chimney remains outside. Most of the ivy-clad church[15] was restored by J. M. Teale of Doncaster in 1874–5. The south side of the clerestory, the porch, and the west

[99] B.I.H.R., Inst. AB. 35, pp. 391–2; ibid. ADM. 1959/1–2; list of rectors in Routh church, 1996; *Crockford*.
[1] Copy of Order in Council at E.R.A.O., DDX/447/13; *Lond. Gaz.* 28 Oct. 1971, p. 11650.
[2] Inf. from the Revd. Carol Fisher-Bailey, Wawne.
[3] P.R.O., SC 6/Hen. VIII/4612, m. 2; *Test. Ebor.* ii (Sur. Soc. xxx), p. 261.
[4] H.U.L., DDWI/11, 26.
[5] *Y.A.J.* xliv. 192.
[6] B.I.H.R., Reg. 18, ff. 346v.–7; York Minster Libr., Torre MSS., Peculiars, pp. 497, 501.
[7] Above, this section.

[8] York Minster Libr., M 2/3(c), ff. 8v.–9v., print in Poulson, *Holderness*, ii. 284.
[9] Illus. in J. C. Cox and C. B. Ford, *Parish Churches*, (1961), 87.   [10] B.I.H.R., CP. G. 133.
[11] Ibid. V. 1567–8/CB. 1, f. 209v.; J. S. Purvis, *Tudor Par. Doc. of Dioc. York*, 34, 54.
[12] B.I.H.R., V. 1578–9/CB. 1, f. 68.
[13] E.R.A.O., PE/146/20, s.v. 1826; Poulson, *Holderness*, ii. 287–8 describes the church before restoration.
[14] E.R.A.O., PE/146/23.
[15] *Kelly's Dir. N. & E. R. Yorks.* (1872), 556; Bulmer, *Dir. E. Yorks.* (1892), 527.

gable were then rebuilt; the nave and aisles were given new roofs, floors, glazing, and seating, and the small vestry was added.[16] The chancel was restored in 1902, the work probably including the re-construction or replacement of the east window.[17]

In the 15th century the church contained an altar dedicated to St. Mary and an image of the Trinity,[18] and in 1567 Roman Catholic survivals included a rood loft with pictures, a gilded and painted altar, and wall paintings of St. Christopher and other saints.[19] The oak chancel screen was kept until the 19th-century restoration.[20] The octagonal font in the south aisle is 14th- or 15th-century, and the altar table is dated 1637. Pieces of a floorstone from the site of Meaux abbey, commemorating Thomas Burton (d. 1437), abbot, are kept in the church.[21] In the chancel there are floor slabs for Robert Wise (d. 1842) and the Richardsons of Meaux; a stained glass window in the south aisle is apparently in memory of William Windham (d. 1887),[22] and there is a mural tablet for Alexander Alec-Smith (d. 1952) and his wife Lucy (d. 1957) in the nave.

New bells were apparently made in the 1450s,[23] and there were three in 1552.[24] The same number was recast or replaced between 1629 and 1638, and later recorded regularly.[25] Apparently in error, Wawne church was said to have four bells by Poulson and later writers.[26] It was, nevertheless, a peal of three bells, including one then recast, which was re-hung during the restoration in the 1870s.[27] In the later 1980s the peal was recast as four bells by Taylor & Co.[28] A clock had been placed in the tower by 1770; it was replaced or reconditioned in the mid 20th century.[29] The plate includes a paten of 1722 and a cup of 1788, apparently acquired in 1814.[30] The registers of baptisms, marriages, and burials begin in 1653; entries for some years in the 17th century are lacking but otherwise the record is complete.[31]

Churchyard extensions given respectively by the Windhams and J. R. Beaulah were consecrated in 1891 and 1961.[32] A small Celtic cross was placed outside the north porch as a War memorial in 1919.[33]

MEAUX. Shortly before 1238 Sir Peter de Mauley built a chapel in woodland to the north of Meaux abbey, had it dedicated to St. Mary, and founded a chantry there for his wife Isabel, who had been a relative of the abbot and was buried in the chapter house. The chantry, which was to be staffed by two chaplains and two clerks, was made the responsibility of the abbey in return for rents, land, and mills granted to it by Sir Peter.[34] Another chapel stood outside the gates of the abbey.[35] No more is known of them.

The vicar of Wawne was lecturing on Sunday evenings in a cottage at Meaux in 1871, and the following year an 80-seat chapel or mission room, dedicated to ST. MARY, was opened there. It was built by Robert Wise Richardson, the Crown, and other proprietors on a site given by Richardson, and was said to have been endowed with £33 a year.[36] A Sunday service was provided for a congregation which in 1884 numbered about 15.[37] Christenings were also conducted there, but marriages and burials continued to take place at the parish church.[38] By the early 20th century the chapel may have been served only in summer, and it was dilapidated in 1912.[39] It was, nevertheless, apparently still used in 1931,[40] but had been closed by 1958, when the building and site were sold. The former chapel was then converted into a house.[41]

NONCONFORMITY. Roman Catholic images were retained in Wawne church after the Reformation and the chancel screen there survived until the 19th-century restoration.[42] Apart from those instances of religious conservatism, and a few cases of non-attendance at services or non-communion in the late 16th and mid 17th century,[43] no evidence has been found that Roman Catholicism or protestant dissent was strong in the parish before the 18th century.

WAWNE. Protestant dissenters obtained the registration for worship of houses in Wawne in 1780, 1792, and 1806,[44] and in 1822 a barn there was licensed.[45] The Primitive Methodists built a chapel in a lane off Ferry Road in 1860;[46] the building was extended in or soon after 1937,[47]

[16] B.I.H.R., Ch. Ret. iii; E.R.A.O., PE/146/22–3; P.R.O., CRES 35/1921; Bulmer, *Dir. E. Yorks.* (1892), 527.
[17] *Kelly's Dir. N. & E. R. Yorks.* (1905), 593.
[18] York Minster Libr., Torre MSS., Peculiars, p. 497; Poulson, *Holderness,* ii. 285.
[19] B.I.H.R., V. 1567–8/CB. 1, f. 209v.; J. S. Purvis, *Tudor Par. Doc. of Dioc. York,* 33–4.
[20] Poulson, *Holderness,* ii. 287; *Kelly's Dir. N. & E. R. Yorks.* (1872), 556.
[21] Illus. in Poulson, *Holderness,* ii. 317.
[22] Wall plaque.
[23] York Minster Libr., M 2/3(c), ff. 8v.–9v., print. in Poulson, *Holderness,* ii. 284.
[24] *Inventories of Ch. Goods,* 40.
[25] B.I.H.R., TER. H. Wawne 1777–[1817]; Boulter, 'Ch. Bells', 86.
[26] Poulson, *Holderness,* ii. 288; note on bells in ch.
[27] B.I.H.R., Ch. Ret. iii.
[28] E.R.A.O., PE/146/20, s.v. 1769; note on bells in ch.
[29] E.R.A.O., PE/146/20, 29.
[30] Ibid. PE/146/20; *Yorks. Ch. Plate,* i. 327.
[31] E.R.A.O., PE/146/1–5, 8. There are transcripts from 1598: B.I.H.R., Chan. PRT. Wawne.
[32] B.I.H.R., CD. Add. 1891/3; 1961/1; R.D.B., 1165/186/165; E.R.A.O., PE/146/24.
[33] B.I.H.R., Fac. Bk. 9, p. 613.
[34] *Cal. Chart. R.* 1226–57, 233–4; *Chron. de Melsa,* ii. 59–61.
[35] *T.E.R.A.S.* i. 3; *V.C.H. Yorks.* iii. 147.
[36] P.R.O., CRES 35/1920; B.I.H.R., Ch. Ret. iii; *Kelly's Dir. N. & E.R. Yorks.* (1893), 502; O.S. 1/2,500, Yorks. CCXI. 7 (1891 edn.).
[37] B.I.H.R., V. 1877/Ret. 3, no. 133; V. 1884/Ret. 2.
[38] P.R.O., CRES 35/1921.
[39] Ibid. /1920; *Kelly's Dir. N. & E.R. Yorks.* (1905), 593.
[40] B.I.H.R., V. 1931/Ret.
[41] R.D.B., 1115/518/465; inf. from Mr. D. Shepherdson, 2000.
[42] Above, churches.
[43] J. S. Purvis, *Tudor Par. Doc. of Dioc. York,* 54; *Depositions from York Castle* (Sur. Soc. xl), pp. 119–21.
[44] B.I.H.R., Fac. Bk. 2, pp. 251, 503; 3, p. 422.
[45] P.R.O., RG 31/5, no. 3710.
[46] R.D.B., 139/480/434; 155/318/287; O.S. Map 1/2,500, Yorks. CCXI. 14 (1910 edn.).
[47] R.D.B., 568/294/228.

and, as the Methodist church, was used until *c.* 1995.[48] The former chapel was later sold, and in 2000 was being converted into a house.

MEAUX. A chapel at Meaux, built by protestant dissenters in 1823,[49] seems later to have been used, separately or jointly, by congregations of Wesleyan Methodists,[50] Independents, and New Connexion Methodists. In 1851, when the Independents held a service there each Sunday, it was described as a preaching station of the East Riding Home Missionary Society.[51] It was associated with the New Connexion Methodists in 1852, when it was named Bethel chapel,[52] and in 1856 Independents and 'Methodists' were said to use the building.[53] It was evidently closed later in the 19th century, and had been demolished by 1889.[54]

EDUCATION. WAWNE. There was a school at Wawne supported by the parents of the *c.* 30 pupils in 1743;[55] its master was usually also the parish clerk.[56] In the 1770s John Windham Bowyer, lord of Wawne manor, paid the schoolmaster £3 3s. a year for teaching eight poor children to read and write,[57] but that subscription was later withdrawn because of the pupils' irregular attendance.[58] The early school may have been held in the church,[59] and in 1781 the churchwardens paid for the painting of the 'schoolhouse'.[60] Wawne Church school was provided with another building, put up in or about 1828, probably by Joseph Smyth Windham, and subsequently used rent free.[61] The school was attended by 9 boys and 13 girls in 1833,[62] and by 20 boys and 15 girls at inspection in 1871.[63] In the 1860s the schoolmistress at Wawne taught the girls until they were twelve years old, but boys were transferred at nine to Sutton school, which had a master.[64] Attendance averaged 29 in 1872. A new schoolroom for Wawne and Meaux, standing on the east side of the lane to Meaux,[65] was built by the inhabitants as an enlargement or replacement of the old room and was opened in 1873. The school was supported then by school pence worth *c.* £15 a year, by subscriptions,

including a sum from the poor's charity for which some children were taught free, and from 1874 by an annual government grant.[66] The accommodation, then comprising a schoolroom and a classroom, was deemed insufficient by the Board of Education in 1903, and, after an unsuccessful attempt to buy the premises from the owner, Major Ashe Windham, the L.E.A. in 1909 bought ½ a. on Greens Lane from him and built a new school accommodating 90 children for the two townships.[67] The old school was closed and the new one opened in January 1910.[68] Average attendance, including that of infants, was usually *c.* 50 in the earlier 20th century, but rose as high as 81 between 1918 and 1927.[69] Senior pupils were transferred to Molescroft County Secondary School in Beverley in 1958.[70] The school was given another classroom and altered in 1960,[71] and later in that decade a larger extension to accommodate 150 pupils was built.[72] Increasing numbers, nevertheless, led to a temporary classroom's being installed in the early 1970s.[73] A playing field laid out in 1963[74] was presumably soon reduced by the building works, for the school used the village playing field from 1966,[75] and 1½ a. was bought for playing fields in 1970.[76] In July 2000 there were 41 juniors and 40 infants on the roll.[77]

By a Scheme of 1878 the Poor's Land charity was divided into an eleemosynary part and the Aske Education Foundation, which was to receive £10 of the annual income, and to give prizes and make payments to encourage attendance at the village school. The charity was in abeyance in the mid 20th century, and by 1980 it had been combined with the eleemosynary charities to form a relief in need trust.[78]

In 1871 those children from Meaux not attending school in Wawne went to Tickton, in Beverley.[79]

An evening school at Wawne was tried unsuccessfully in the 1860s,[80] and another was held in the school three nights a week in winter in the 1870s.[81]

NORTH BRANSHOLME. The first schools built in North Bransholme were a primary

48 D. [R. J.] and S. Neave, *E.R. Chapels and Meeting Ho.* (E. Yorks. Loc. Hist. Soc.), 59; inf. from Mr. H. G. Middleton, Wawne, 2000.
49 B.I.H.R., DMH. Reg. 1, p. 416; A. Bryant, *Map of E.R. Yorks.* (1829).
50 White, *Dir. E. & N. R. Yorks.* (1840), 178.
51 P.R.O., HO 129/518/4/3/5.
52 O.S. Map 6", Yorks. CCXI (1855 edn.).
53 Sheahan and Whellan, *Hist. York & E.R.* ii. 396.
54 Neave, op. cit. 54; O.S. Map 1/2,500, Yorks. CCXI. 11 (1891 edn.).
55 *Herring's Visit.* iii, p. 224.
56 E.R.A.O., PE/146/1, 4; *Educ. of Poor Digest*, 1096.
57 E.R.A.O., DDIV/21/3.
58 *Educ. of Poor Digest*, 1096.
59 Above, church [fabric].
60 E.R.A.O., PE/146/20.
61 P.R.O., ED 7/135, no. 192A.
62 *Educ. Enquiry Abstract*, 1097.
63 *Returns relating to Elem. Educ.* 470–1.
64 *1st Rep. Com. on Employment of Children, Young Persons, and Women in Agric., App. Pt. II* [4068-I], p. 369, H.C. (1867–8), xvii.
65 O.S. Map 1/2,500, Yorks. CCXI. 14 (1910 edn.).

66 P.R.O., ED 7/135, no. 192A; ibid. CRES 35/1919, 1921; below, next para.
67 E.R. Educ. Cttee. *Mins.* 1903–4, 153–4, 226–7; 1908–9, 145, 236–7; 1909–10, 97, 147, 227. The conveyance was dated 1910: R.D.B., 122/141/128.
68 P.R.O., ED 7/135, no. 192A.
69 *Bd. of Educ., List 21* (H.M.S.O., 1908 and later edns.).
70 E.R. Educ. Cttee. *Mins.* 1955–6, 151; *V.C.H. Yorks. E.R.* vi. 256.
71 E.R. Educ. Cttee. *Mins.* 1957–8, 168; 1958–9, 105; 1959–60, 192.
72 Ibid. 1964–5, 102, 144; 1966–7, 129, 156, 176; 1967–8, 37.
73 Ibid. 1971–2, 42, 99.
74 Ibid. 1962–3, 188.   75 Ibid. 1966–7, 6.
76 Ibid. 1970–1, 52.
77 Inf. from the headteacher, Wawne primary school.
78 E.R.A.O., accession 1681; *Humbs. Dir. of Char.* 7; Review of Char. *Rep.* 41; below, charities.
79 *Returns relating to Elem. Educ.* 470–1.
80 *1st Rep. Com. on Employment of Children, Young Persons, and Women in Agric., App. Pt. II* [4068-I], p. 369, H.C. (1867–8), xvii.
81 P.R.O., ED 7/135, no. 192A.

school for 520 pupils from five to nine years old, with a 40-place nursery unit, and a junior high school for 420 children of nine to thirteen, which shared a site on Lothian Way.[82] Opened in 1978, they were named Highlands junior high and primary schools in 1979.[83] Falling numbers and the amalgamation of primary and junior high schools in Hull in 1988,[84] led to the closure then of the junior high school; it was re-opened as a health centre in 1994.[85] In 1999 Highlands primary school had 390 children on its roll, including some in a nursery unit.[86]

Another shared site, on Snowdon Way, was used for The Dales schools, a primary school for 300 or 360 pupils opened in 1979, and a junior high school for 480 which began early in 1980.[87] Reorganized as The Dales primary school in 1988,[88] it was then remodelled to accommodate a 39-place infants' unit.[89] In 1999 there were 290 on the roll, besides the infants. By September 2000 all of the children had been moved into one of the schools, and the other was given over to the youth service.[90]

Broadacre primary school, west of Wawne Road and accommodating 300 children, was opened in 1981.[91] A 39-place nursery unit was added c. 1985.[92] In July 2000 the school had 221 pupils and there were 62 infants in the nursery unit.[93]

Older children attended a comprehensive school, later called successively Perronet Thompson and Kingswood High school, which was built between the northern and southern parts of Bransholme and opened in 1989.[94]

CHARITIES FOR THE POOR. A charity established by Sir Joseph Ashe, Bt., and his widow has been mistakenly attributed to a Sir Joseph Aske, Bt., from the early 19th century or earlier. Ashe's bequest of £50 to the poor of Wawne was apparently altered by his widow, who in 1699 conveyed c. 5 a. in Cottingham to her steward and the vicar, churchwarden, and overseer of Wawne. The Poor's Land comprised 8 a. in the 1820s, when 5 a. was let for £9 9s. a year, and the rest occupied rent-free in return for a contribution from the poor rate which increased the total income to c. £15 a year; the money was then spent on coal.[95] Part of the income was used for education by the 1870s,[96] and under a Scheme obtained in 1878 the charity was divided into separate educational and eleemosynary branches.[97] At the beginning of the 20th century[98] the landed endowment comprised almost 10 a. in Cottingham, rented at £25 a year in 1901 and £30 from 1906. Some 4 a., by then in Hull, was sold to the University college of Hull in 1931,[99] and in 1933 the income of c. £65 a year comprised £15 rent and some £50 from £1,434 stock. The almost 5 a. remaining in Cottingham was sold in 1953,[1] and the following year stock of £2,087 produced an income of about £70. Much of the income remaining for the poor, after the £10 assigned to education had been paid, was spent on coal: £7 in 1901, nearly £13 in the 1920s, £30 in 1933, and £50 in 1954. In the early 20th century about £6 a year was also subscribed to a clothing club, and in the 1930s and 1940s donations amounting to £15 were made to hospitals in Hull. The income, of c. £120 a year about 1980, was then spent mostly or wholly on coal.[2]

By her will dated 1879, and evidently proved the next year, Frances Fletcher of York, widow, left £100 to the vicar of Wawne to provide an income to be spent on coal for the poor of the parish each Christmas.[3] The bequest was invested, and in the earlier 20th century produced an income of c. £2 10s. a year. In the 1900s and 1910s about six people, all or mostly widows, were helped, apparently with cash doles; in 1923 a donation was made to a clothing club and the Sunday school was supported, and c. 1930 the income was spent on coal.[4] A Scheme obtained in 1951 confirmed the original object of providing coal at Christmas, but later the income of c. £4 a year was allowed to accumulate and then spent occasionally on food hampers for pensioners.[5]

By Scheme of 1980 the Wawne charities, including the educational branch, were merged as a relief in need trust for the ancient parish.[6]

---

[82] Humbs. C.C. *Mins.* 1974–5, H 471; Hull Corp. City Planning Off. *Annual Rep.* 1974–5, 18–19.

[83] Humbs. C.C. *Mins.* 1978–9, H 2750; inf. from Jean Kemp, Highlands health centre, 2000.

[84] Humbs. C.C. *Mins.* 1983–4, B 5474; *Educ. in City of Hull* (Humbs. Educ. Cttee. 1984).

[85] Above, intro. [Bransholme]; *Hull Daily Mail,* 26 Jan. 1989; inf. from Jean Kemp, Highlands health centre, 2000; inf. from Highlands primary school, 2000.

[86] Kingston upon Hull Educ. Cttee. *Sch. Prospectus 1999–2000,* 427; inf. from Highlands primary school.

[87] Humbs. C.C. *Mins.* 1975–6, H 1142, 1355; 1978–9, H 2841; 1979–80, H 3057; Hull Corp. City Planning Off. *Annual Rep.* 1975–6, 15; log bk. at E.R.A.O., accession 2490; inf. from Miss M. Carrick, Wawne, 2000.

[88] Humbs. C.C. *Mins.* 1983–4, B 5474.

[89] Ibid. B 5358; 1987–8, C 7416.

[90] Inf. from the headteacher, 2000; inf. from Jean Kemp, Highlands health centre, 2000.

[91] Humbs. C.C. *Mins.* 1976–7, H 1664; 1978–9, H 2632; 1980–1, H 3472; 1981–2, B 3784; inf. from Broadacre primary school.

[92] Humbs. C.C. *Mins.* 1984–5, B 5627.

[93] Inf. from Broadacre primary school.

[94] Humbs. C.C. *Mins.* 1988–9, C 7883. Pevsner and Neave, *Yorks. E.R.* 521–2; inf. from the headteacher, Kingswood high school.

[95] *9th Rep. Com. Char.* 782.

[96] P.R.O., CRES 35/1919.

[97] Review of Char. *Rep.* 41.

[98] Following based on E.R.A.O., accession 1681.

[99] R.D.B., 425/46/39.

[1] Ibid. 935/289/248.   [2] Review of Char. *Rep.* 41.

[3] E.R.A.O., PE/146/13; Review of Char. *Rep.* 41.

[4] E.R.A.O., accession 1681.

[5] Review of Char. *Rep.* 41.

[6] Ibid.; *Humbs. Dir. of Char.* 7; Char. Com. reg. no. 224027.

NORTH DIVISION

ATWICK

THE village of Atwick lies 24 km. NNE. of Hull, 3 km. NNW. of the resort of Hornsea, and c. 500 m. from the coast, which forms the eastern parish boundary.[1] The ancient parish also included the hamlets of Arram, c. 3 km. south-west of the village, and Skirlington, c. 2 km. north. The name Atwick, 'Atta's dairy farm', is Anglian but was not recorded until the 12th century. Arram is a Scandinavian name meaning 'at the shielings', presumably an allusion to pasture there. Skirlington, which may mean 'Scirela's farm', is an Anglian and Scandinavian hybrid. The suffix 'in Holderness' was sometimes used, presumably to distinguish Atwick from Adwick le Street and Adwick upon Dearne (both Yorks. W.R.) and Arram from Arram in Leconfield.[2]

In 1852 the ancient parish contained 2,298 a. (930 ha.), comprising 1,430 a. (579 ha.) in Atwick, 539 a. (218 ha.) in Arram, and 329 a. (133 ha.) in Skirlington.[3] During the 19th century the sea consumed on average 2–3 yd. of the parish each year. By 1911 its area had been reduced to 2,244 a. (908 ha.) and by 1991 to 2,189 a. (886 ha.).[4]

In 1377 there were 103 poll-tax payers in Atwick. Arram was then and later assessed jointly with Bewholme, in Nunkeeling.[5] By 1517 inclosure had resulted in the ejection of 17 people in Atwick.[6] In 1672 there were 25 houses listed in the hearth-tax return for the parish, excluding Arram.[7] There were 35 families in the parish in 1743 and 33 in 1764.[8] From 368 in 1801 the population fell to 286 in 1811 and thereafter fluctuated around 300, standing at 284 in 1901. It was almost the same in 1971 but 360 were counted in 1991, of whom 323 were usually resident.[9]

The parish is largely on boulder clay and much of the ground exceeds 15 m. above sea level. Along the coast the higher ground ends in an unbroken line of steep cliffs, and at Arram, where the land rises to 24 m., it provided the site of the hamlet. Lower land in the west is partly alluvial, and small deposits of lacustrine clay mark the sites of former meres.[10] At Atwick the higher ground north and south of the village was mostly occupied by the open fields and the lower ground in the west by common meadows and pastures; the commonable lands there were inclosed in 1772.

The parish is drained by Stream dike, which flows northwards along the western boundary towards the Skipsea and Barmston drains and eventual outfall into the North Sea. It was evidently Stream dike which was in disrepair in 1367.[11] Tributary streams form part of the southern boundary of Atwick and Arram's eastern boundary. Lesser drains include that which flows west along part of the southern boundary of Arram into Catfoss drain.[12]

The principal road in the parish, from Hornsea to Skipsea, has been upgraded and improved as part of the main Holderness coast road. From the village a minor road leads west to Bewholme, whence others run south and east through Arram to Seaton and Hornsea respectively.

ATWICK village has a linear plan extending across the centre of the parish. The plan was evidently determined by a stream which rises close to the sea and flows through the village to Stream dike. The main village street is that leading west to the church, now comprising Cliff Road and Church Lane. Cross lanes connected it with northern and southern back lanes, the southern one continuing as the Bewholme road. A large irregular green in the centre of the village is crossed both by the main street and one of the side lanes, which forms part of the Hornsea to Skipsea road. The shaft of a medieval cross with a stepped base stands on the green, and there is a pond, named Holy Well, by the Bewholme road. Four council houses were built on Bewholme Road after 1937 and a dozen more, together with a dozen bungalows, in Church Lane in the 1950s and 1960s. Those served to end the isolation of the church and former vicarage house at the west end of the village. The district council also built and subsequently operated a sewage disposal works on Church Lane for the bungalows.[13] In the earlier 20th century the village was also extended by the building on the cliffs of a dozen bungalows and chalets. A caravan site, opened there c. 1945, accommodated c. 30 static caravans in 1992, when there were two smaller sites nearer the village.[14] Most of the village buildings date from the 19th century and are of brick. Boulder construction co-exists with brick in several buildings, among them The Cottage, on Bewholme Road, the former Primitive Methodist chapel, and the outbuildings of Cliff Farm. Atwick Hall, overlooking the green, is a large farmhouse of the 19th century. Conservation areas were designated in Atwick in 1991.[15]

[1] This article was written in 1991.
[2] P.N. Yorks. E.R. (E.P.N.S.), 79–80; G. F. Jensen, Scand. Settlement Names in Yorks. 76, 86, 117, 179, 190, 215.
[3] O.S. Map 6", Yorks. CLXXX, CXCVII (1854–5 edn.).
[4] Census, 1911, 1991; T. Sheppard, Lost Towns of Yorks. Coast, 188.
[5] P.R.O., E/179/202/60, mm. 49, 66. Below, Nunkeeling, intro.
[6] Trans. R. Hist. S. n.s. vi, pp. 288–9; vii, p. 251.
[7] Hearth Tax, 61.
[8] B.I.H.R., V. 1764/Ret. 1, no. 33; Herring's Visit. i,

p. 36.
[9] V.C.H. Yorks. iii. 495; Census, 1911–91.
[10] Geol. Surv. Map 1", drift, sheets 65, 73 (1909 edn.).
[11] Poulson, Holderness, i. 120–1.
[12] E.R.A.O., CSR/31/190–6, 355.
[13] R.D.B., 588/308/227; 892/330/271; 957/405/355; 1413/406/369; inf. from Mrs. B. Vickerton, Atwick, 1992.
[14] Camb., St. John's Coll., MS. SBF2.120; O.S. Map 1/25,000, TA 15 (1953 edn.); inf. from Mr. C. Hornby, Atwick, 1992.
[15] Inf. from Devt. Dept., Holderness B.C., 1991.

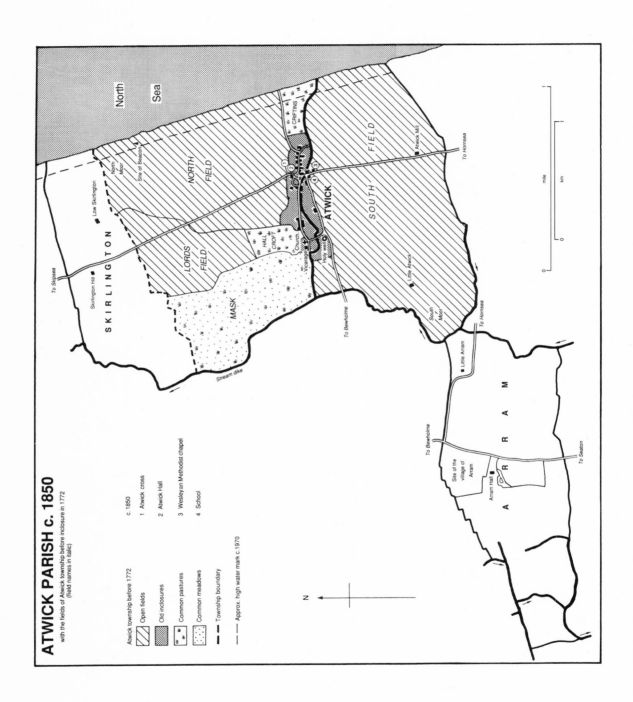

ATWICK PARISH c. 1850
with the fields of Atwick township before inclosure in 1772
(field names in italic)

Atwick township before 1772   c. 1850

Open fields   1 Atwick cross
Old inclosures   2 Atwick Hall
Common pastures   3 Wesleyan Methodist chapel
Common meadows   4 School

— — — Township boundary
—————— Approx. high water mark c.1970

Up to three houses were licensed at Atwick in the later 18th century, and the Black Horse, named in 1822,[16] still traded in 1991. The school, closed in 1960, was later used as a village hall.[17]

ARRAM. At Arram there is thought to have been a medieval settlement, of unknown size, lying north of Arram Hall, which was built in the 17th century and by the mid 18th was the only remaining building.[18] Little Arram Farm, added between 1828 and 1852,[19] was rebuilt c. 1990.

SKIRLINGTON hamlet comprises two farms. High Skirlington Farm, known as Skirlington Hill in 1922, had been built by 1772 and Low Skirlington Farm by 1828.[20] Low Skirlington leisure park, which includes a golf course, was opened in 1965; a caravan park and most of the present buildings date from 1973, and in 1986 a swimming pool was added. About 1990 a Sunday market began to be held on the site, and later large car boot sales were started there. In 1992 the site accommodated c. 800 static caravans.[21]

OUTLYING HOUSES include Little Atwick, also known as Moor House by 1852, and Atwick Mill Farm, both built by 1828 on ground inclosed in 1772.[22] A beacon stood on high ground close to the sea in the late 18th and early 19th century.[23] Land at Atwick was used by the military authorities during both World Wars, and several military buildings put up c. 1940 remain on the cliffs.[24] A gas terminal between Atwick and Skirlington was constructed in 1973–5 and extended in 1983.[25]

MANORS AND OTHER ESTATES. Land at Atwick and Arram was evidently included in Morkar's manor of Hornsea in 1066 and had passed with it to Drew de Bevrère by 1086;[26] it was later part of the Aumale fee. In the mid 13th century William de Ros held 12 carucates at Atwick, which holding descended in the Ros family, later Barons Ros of Helmsley (Yorks. N.R.), and their successors.[27] Robert de Ros was named as undertenant in 1284–5.[28]

In 1300 John of Barton and his wife Joan held 4 carucates at Atwick of Nicholas de Meynell as ⅓ knight's fee,[29] and in 1316 Joan Barton was named as lord of Atwick, together with Richard and Stephen Thorpe, Simon of Goxhill, and Alice of Bushby.[30] In 1318 Joan sold *ATWICK* manor to Sir John Sutton, later Lord Sutton, who held it as ¼ knight's fee from William de Ros, Lord Ros. John (d. by 1338) was succeeded in turn by his sons, John Sutton, Lord Sutton (d. 1356) and Thomas Sutton, Lord Sutton (d. by 1395).[31]

The estate was later divided between Thomas's three daughters. Constance Sutton's second husband, Sir John Godard, held ⅓ of the manor at his death in 1420,[32] and her share passed to the Ughtreds by the marriage of the Godards' daughter Margaret to Thomas Ughtred. That share then descended in the Ughtreds to Sir Robert Ughtred, who in 1527 sold it, as Atwick manor, to Cardinal Wolsey.[33] After Wolsey's attainder the estate was granted to Sir Marmaduke Constable in 1535.[34] It descended in the Constables of Everingham to Sir Philip Constable, Bt., who in 1653 sold the estate, containing c. 120 a., to John Rushworth.[35] That share of the manor has not been traced further.

Another ⅓ share descended to Thomas Sutton's daughter Margery (d. 1391), who married Peter de Mauley.[36] The Mauleys' daughters Constance and Elizabeth married Sir John Bigod (d. 1427) and George Salvan (d. 1418), whose sons Ralph Bigod and John Salvan later held ⅔ and ⅓ shares of the manor respectively.[37] The Bigod share had evidently passed by 1491 to William Babthorp, who sold it to John Pickering that year. In 1510 Pickering's son William sold the estate to John Wensley and Robert White, later the sole owner. It was bought in 1525 by William Longford and others, who conveyed it to St. John's college, Cambridge, in 1527. The college acquired other land in Atwick township as part of Marfleet manor in 1530.[38] It had 238 a. there at inclosure in 1772 and 216 a. in 1910.[39] In 1979 it sold College farm to the Hornby family, the owners in 1991.[40]

From Thomas Sutton's daughter Agnes, wife of Sir Ralph Bulmer (d. 1406) and Sir Edmund Hastings (d. 1448), ⅓ of Atwick manor descended to the Bulmers.[41] Sir Ralph had also

[16] E.R.A.O., QDT/2/6, 9; directories.
[17] *E.R. Educ. Cttee. Mins.* 1962–3, 33; 1972–3, 166; inf. from Mrs. S. Heald, Atwick, 1992.
[18] T. Jefferys, *Map of Yorks.* (1772); below, manors.
[19] H. Teesdale, *Map of Yorks.* (1828); O.S. Map 6″, Yorks. CLXXX (1855 edn.).
[20] R.D.B., 270/512/450; T. Jefferys, *Map of Yorks.* (1772); H. Teesdale, *Map of Yorks.* (1828).
[21] Inf. from Mr. Goodwin, Low Skirlington, 1992 and 2000.
[22] E.R.A.O., PC/14/1; H. Teesdale, *Map of Yorks.* (1828); O.S. Map 6″, Yorks. CLXXX (1855 edn.).
[23] E.R.A.O., LT/9/54; J. Nicholson, *Beacons of E. Yorks.* 28–9; H. Teesdale, *Map of Yorks.* (1828).
[24] Camb., St. John's Coll., MSS. D333.27; SBF2.120; B. Halpenny, *Action Sta.: 4 Military Airfields of Yorks.* 25.
[25] R.D.B., 1879/314/261; 1888/354/308; 1888/356/309; 1888/358/310; inf. from British Gas, 1992.
[26] *V.C.H. Yorks.* ii. 265 and n.; below, Hornsea, manors.
[27] E.R.A.O., DDKP/19/1; *Cal. Inq. p.m.* iv, p. 352; *Kirkby's Inquest*, 372; *Complete Peerage*, s.v. Ros.

[28] *Kirkby's Inquest*, 74.
[29] *Cal. Inq. p.m.* iii, p. 429.
[30] *Kirkby's Inquest*, 303.
[31] P.R.O., CP 25(1)/270/91, no. 26; *Cal. Inq. p.m.* viii, pp. 97–8; x, pp. 259–60; *Cal. Chart. R. 1341–7*, 19; *Cal. Fine R. 1391–9*, 154; *Complete Peerage*, s.v. Sutton.
[32] P.R.O., C 138/48, no. 66; *Cal. Close, 1413–19*, 249–50; *Complete Peerage*, s.v. Sutton.
[33] *Yorks. Fines*, i. 48; *Complete Peerage*, s.v. Ughtred.
[34] P.R.O., C 142/170, no. 31; *L. & P. Hen. VIII*, iv (3), p. 2735; viii, p. 342.   [35] H.U.L., DDEV/24/4.
[36] *Cal. Close, 1413–19*, 249–50; *Complete Peerage*, s.v. Mauley.
[37] P.R.O., C 138/25, no. 14; C 139/29, no. 49; C 139/143, no. 28; *Complete Peerage*, s.v. Mauley.
[38] Camb., St. John's Coll., MSS. D40.3; D63.216–40, 286.
[39] R.D.B., AQ/221/20; E.R.A.O., NV/1/8.
[40] Camb., St. John's Coll., MS. SBF2.120; inf. from Mr. A. Hornby, Atwick, 1991.
[41] *Complete Peerage*, s.v. Bulmer; *Cal. Close, 1413–19*, 249–50.

inherited 2 carucates and 2 bovates, part of the Ros fee at Atwick, from his father Ralph (d. 1366).[42] John Bulmer (d. 1537) forfeited the estate for his part in the Pilgrimage of Grace, but it was restored to his son Sir Ralph (d. 1558). The ⅓ share was divided between his daughters, one of whom, Anne Welbury, sold her interest to George Creswell in 1575.[43] Creswell had bought the shares of the other daughters, Frances Constable, Joan Cholmeley, and Millicent Grey by 1585.[44] At his death in 1592 Creswell's estate at Atwick included 15 houses and evidently comprised land of both the Ros and Aumale fees.[45] In 1613 the estate was divided and sold by George's son Ralph Creswell and Ralph's son George.[46] Part bought by Thomas Acklam may have descended to Jonathan Acklam, who was awarded 140 a. at inclosure in 1772.[47] The Bulmers' share of the manor has not been traced further.

A modern estate at Atwick originated in purchases made by Robert and George Gale (both d. 1824).[48] It comprised c. 180 a. in 1856 when it belonged to G. M. Gale. He (d. 1887) was succeeded by his son, also G. M. Gale.[49] The son already had land in Atwick. In 1863 a half share in a 111-a. farm there had been settled on him, as G. M. Gale the younger, and George Ogle's coheir Mary Ogle shortly before their marriage, and in 1877 the other heir sold her moiety to Gale.[50] He bought 63 a. more in 1903 and at his death in 1916 held c. 350 a. at Atwick.[51] In 1926 the estate was divided and sold in several lots. The 130-a. Cliff farm was conveyed to E. A. Williams and Susannah Gale,[52] and Church farm, of 217 a., was sold to Tom Catton (d. 1950) and Charles Catton (d. 1957).[53] Charles was succeeded by J. B. Catton and his mother Isabella (d. c. 1975), and in 1991 Church farm was owned by J. B. Catton and Son.[54]

In 1066 Thorkil held *ARRAM*, comprising 1 carucate. It had passed by 1086 to Drew de Bevrère, whose tenant Rayner then occupied part of it.[55] Other land at Arram was probably included in Hornsea manor in 1086,[56] and in the mid 13th century 2 carucates at Arram were held by Ralph of Sherburn.[57]

About 1200 donors including Sir Stephen of Arram and Richard son of Peter gave Meaux abbey an estate in *ARRAM*, which was described as a grange by 1202.[58] Comprising 1 carucate and other land, it was granted to Sir Nicholas de Stuteville soon afterwards; Stuteville gave it to John of Meaux and it later passed to his son Peter, who had granted it back to the abbey by 1235.[59] Members of the Skirlington family and others made further gifts during the 13th century, and by 1269 the abbey had more than 1 carucate and 3 bovates in desmesne and 4 bovates held by tenants.[60] After the Dissolution Meaux abbey's manor, then comprising two houses, 1 carucate and 6 bovates, and other land, was granted to Sir Christopher Hatton in 1586. It was bought the same year by Ralph Creswell, who succeeded on his father George's death in 1592 to other land at Arram.[61] In 1618 Creswell sold his estate to Nicholas Waller.[62] Waller's daughter or granddaughter Susan married Gervase Bosville (d. 1621), and their son Thomas sold the manor in 1654 to William Dobson (d. 1666).[63] Dobson's daughter Esther (d. 1716) married Christopher Hildyard (d. by 1685) and the manor later descended in the Hildyards.[64] In 1804 Sir Robert D'Arcy Hildyard, Bt., sold the Arram Hall estate, of c. 490 a., to Thomas Bainton (d. 1842). Bainton was succeeded by his son John (d. 1891) and John by his son Thomas.[65] The mortgagees sold the estate to Thomas Reed in 1899. After Reed's death in 1942, it was bought by Stanley Rhodes in 1944, by Harold Carbutt in 1947, and by George Walton in 1951.[66] In 1954 Walton sold Arram to Lady (Ernestine) Strickland-Constable and it remained part of the Strickland-Constable estate in 1990.[67]

Arram Hall was built in the early 17th century, possibly by Nicholas Waller.[68] It is of red brick with black brick diapering to the upper storey and has shaped end-gables and a two-storied porch with a broken segmental brick pediment to the doorway. The house was enlarged in the 19th or 20th century with two lower wings and bay windows, and the interior has been remodelled. It retains an 18th-century staircase.

In 1066 Morkar held 5 carucates at *SKIRLINGTON* as soke of his manor of Hornsea. The sokeland had passed with the manor to Drew de Bevrère by 1086.[69] Much of Skirlington was granted to Bridlington priory. Simon father

[42] *Cal. Inq. p.m.* xii, p. 97.
[43] P.R.O., E 150/237, no. 28; H.U.L., DHO/7/36; *Yorks. Fines*, ii. 71.
[44] *Yorks. Fines*, ii. 75, 85; iii. 43.
[45] P.R.O., C 142/234, no. 20.
[46] *Yorks. Fines 1603–14*, 198–9, 201–2, 211–12; *Visit. Yorks. 1584–5 and 1612*, ed. J. Foster, 149.
[47] R.D.B., AQ/221/20.
[48] Ibid. BC/177/262; BR/55/76; BU/208/323; BW/170/224; DR/195/224; DR/218/252.
[49] Ibid. HK/9/12; E.R.A.O., PE/32/8/3.
[50] R.D.B., IL/324/412; IL/325/413; IL/326/414; MG/110/167; E.R.A.O., PE/32/8/2.
[51] R.D.B., 53/352/340 (1903); 203/125/108; E.R.A.O., NV/1/8.
[52] R.D.B., 317/327/267; 326/119/98; 330/527/418.
[53] Ibid. 318/359/301; 886/575/478; 1115/232/205.
[54] Ibid. 888/556/466; 1380/495/449; inf. from Mr. J. B. Catton, 1992.
[55] *V.C.H. Yorks.* ii. 267.
[56] Ibid. ii. 265 n.
[57] *Kirkby's Inquest*, 372.
[58] *Chron. de Melsa* (Rolls Ser.), i. 223, 309; G. V. Orange, 'Cart. of Meaux' (Hull Univ. Ph.D. thesis, 1965), pp. 32–3.
[59] *Chron. de Melsa*, i. 369, 376, 423.
[60] Ibid. 369–70; ii. 102, 105; Orange, op. cit. pp. 495–6.
[61] P.R.O., C 142/234, no. 20.
[62] Ibid. C 66/1272, m. 10; E.R.A.O., PE/32/30; PE/32/32 (copy minister's acct.); *Yorks. Fines, 1614–25*, 102.
[63] P.R.O., CP 25(2)614/1654 Mich. [no. 81]; *Dugdale's Visit. Yorks.* (Sur. Soc. xxxvi), 211, 276; M. E. Ingram, *Our Lady of Hull*, 59.
[64] Foster, *Pedigrees of Yorks.* iii, s.v. Hildyard.
[65] R.D.B., CG 405/667; FT/233/271; 46/41/40 (1891).
[66] Ibid. 14/351/330 (1899); 666/571/477; 675/489/421; 753/600/499; 892/150/128.
[67] Ibid. 970/243/209; inf. from W. H. Brown, Agric. Surveyors, Valuers and Land Agents, Northgate Ho., Sleaford, 1990.
[68] Above, this section.
[69] *V.C.H. Yorks.* ii. 265.

of Emma (Emeline) of Skirlington had given 1 carucate there by the mid 12th century, Emma's son Ralph of Skirlington 1 carucate and 2 bovates by 1232, and Ralph's neices 2 bovates by 1229.[70] By the earlier 13th century the priory had also been given land at Skirlington by William d'Oyry and an estate in Arram by Henry le Nayre. It added other land at Skirlington by purchase from Newburgh priory (Yorks. N.R.) and appropriated Atwick rectory.[71] The priory had 5 carucates in Skirlington and Arram by 1285, and in 1290 it was granted free warren in Skirlington.[72] In 1537 the prior was attainted for his role in the Pilgrimage of Grace and the manor was forfeited to the Crown.[73]

The Crown sold Skirlington manor in 1609 to George Salter and John Williams, who then resold it to (Sir) George Etherington (d. 1627). His son George sold the manor in 1631 to Robert Crompton (d. 1646).[74] Crompton devised it to Walter Crompton, possibly his son, who was succeeded in turn by his nephews Walter Crompton (fl. 1742) and William Crompton. William left the estate to Miles Smith, whose son, also Miles, sold it to John Etherington in 1799.[75] The estate was later held by George Etherington (d. 1854), his son Thomas (d. 1868), and then by another Thomas Etherington, possibly the son of Thomas (d. 1868).[76] G. B. Tonge bought Skirlington in 1879 and held it until his death in 1922, when it passed to his daughter Ruth Danby (d. April 1957).[77] Marion Clements (d. Feb. 1957) had also had an interest in the estate, and in 1973 her trustees sold High Skirlington farm to the British Gas Corporation.[78]

The *RECTORY* belonged to Bridlington priory by 1228, when the vicar agreed that the priory should have some of the hay tithes. The rectory evidently also included the 6 bovates given with the church c. 1130.[79] By another agreement, made in 1277, the hay tithes due from Meaux abbey's estate at Arram were compounded for 16d. a year.[80] The rectory was valued at £6 13s. 4d. in 1291 and c. £10 in the early 16th century.[81]

The rectory passed by the priory's forfeiture to the Crown,[82] which granted it to Henry Best

and Thomas Holland in 1600. By 1605 it had evidently been bought by William Green.[83] Green's daughter Elizabeth, wife of Sir John Buck (d. 1648), was named as impropriatrix in 1650; the rectory was then valued at £46 net.[84] It later descended to Robert Buck, whose widow Mary and eldest son John sold the rectory in 1692 to a younger son Robert (d. 1731). Robert's daughter Elizabeth sold the estate in 1768 to Fountayne Osbaldeston (d. 1770).[85] At inclosure in 1772 Osbaldeston's great-nephew Humphrey Osbaldeston received 165 a. for his commonable land and 34 a. for tithes. He (d. 1835) left the estate to Bertram Osbaldeston-Mitford (d. 1842),[86] whose brother Robert and trustees under the Mitford Estate Act of 1854 sold the rectory to J. T. and George Dickinson in 1855.[87] They sold it in 1869 to John Holmes, from whom Harriet Brigham bought it in 1871.[88] It was sold again in 1889 to H. W. Bainton and then passed to Edward Bainton (d. 1945) and to Edward's sister Sybil Bainton.[89] She sold it, as Grange farm, in 1952 to the Vickerton family, the owner in 1991.[90]

There were several small ecclesiastical estates in the parish in the Middle Ages. At Skirlington, Newburgh priory had land in the 12th century and Swine priory was given 2 bovates; both holdings later passed to Bridlington priory.[91] Robert de Scures gave the Knights Templar 70 a. and pasturage there in 1286, and St. Leonard's hospital, York, had 2s. rent at Skirlington in 1535.[92] At the Dissolution the Knights Hospitaller had land at Arram rented for 3s. a year, and in 1558 the refounded order briefly regained that estate.[93]

Trinity House, Hull, bought c. 230 a. at Atwick in 1868–9;[94] sales and coastal erosion had reduced its estate to c. 100 a. by 1991.[95]

ECONOMIC HISTORY. COMMON LANDS AND INCLOSURE. *Atwick.* Atwick village had open fields called North and South fields in 1653.[96] Lord's field, named from 1546, may have been a third field or merely part of North field.[97] The tillage had been reduced by inclosure by 1517.[98] The common meadows lay away from

---

[70] *Bridlington Chart.* ed. W. T. Lancaster, pp. 313–17, 322.

[71] Ibid. 318–20; *Chron. de Melsa*, i. 370; below, this section.

[72] H.U.L., DDWB/20/6; *Kirkby's Inquest*, 75; *Cal. Chart. R. 1257–1300*, 358.

[73] *L. & P. Hen. VIII*, xiii (1), p. 564; *V.C.H. Yorks.* iii. 204.

[74] H.U.L., DRA/336; Poulson, *Holderness* i. 181; *Dugdale's Visit. Yorks.* 322.

[75] R.D.B., Q/458/1136; BZ/312/503.

[76] Ibid. HG/181/227; KP/16/27; MS/250/335; E.R.A.O., PE/32/8/3.

[77] R.D.B., MW/39/61; 270/512/450; 1075/160/135.

[78] Ibid. 1075/136/115; 1879/314/261; above, intro.

[79] *Bridlington Chart.* 312–13.

[80] *Chron. de Melsa* (Rolls Ser.), ii. 152; below, church.

[81] *Tax. Eccl.* (Rec. Com.), 304; *Valor Eccl.* (Rec. Com.), v. 120; *Miscellanea* (Y.A.S. Rec. Ser. lxxx), iii. 18.

[82] *L. & P. Hen. VIII*, xiv (1), p. 158.

[83] P.R.O., C 142/287, no. 8; E.R.A.O., PE/32/19.

[84] *Dugdale's Visit. Yorks.* 70; *T.E.R.A.S.* iv. 63.

[85] R.D.B., AB/261/456; N/401/863; AD/65/159; AL/135/245; H.U.L., DX/42/1; ibid. DDX/187/4; ibid. DDMC/2/1.

[86] R.D.B., AQ/221/20; FT/223/260; *V.C.H. Yorks. E.R.* ii. 231–2; below, Skipsea, manors [Johnson].

[87] R.D.B., HH/184/204; E.R.A.O., DDHB/16/2; Burke, *Land. Gent.* (1937), p. 1607.

[88] R.D.B., KI/402/557; KW/188/225.

[89] Ibid. 29/514/489 (1889); 723/458/389; 834/236/199; inf. from Mrs. B. Vickerton, Atwick, 1992.

[90] R.D.B., 926/3/2; inf. from Mrs. Vickerton.

[91] *Bridlington Chart.* 318–20, 322; *V.C.H. Yorks.* iii. 229; above, this section.

[92] *Cal. Pat. 1281–92*, 243–4; *Miscellanea*, iii. 23.

[93] *Miscellanea*, iv (Y.A.S. Rec. Ser. xciv), 98; *Cal. Pat. 1557–8*, 321.

[94] R.D.B., KD/306/400; KI/47/69.

[95] Ibid. 1888/354/308; 1888/356/309; inf. from Trinity Ho.

[96] Para. based on a deed of 1653: H.U.L., DDEV/24/4.

[97] Ibid. DDEV/4/1–7, 9.

[98] *Trans. R. Hist. S.* N.S. vi, pp. 288–9; vii, p. 251.

the village on the edge of the open fields in 1653, possibly in North and South moors, which were later regarded as parts of North and South fields respectively.[99] Low-lying land west of the village called Mask, perhaps meaning 'marsh', may also have been used for meadow, and part of it was called Ing Mask in 1525.[1] Mask was, however, probably used mostly as rough grazing, stinted pasture there being recorded in 1546, and in the mid 17th century there was another common pasture at Criftins, sometimes regarded as part of South field.[2] Haw croft, called Hawe field in 1546 and known also as Hall croft in the mid 19th century, may once have been part of the tillage but by 1546 it was evidently a common pasture and was then described as containing 2 bovates of tethering ground.[3] In 1653 the appurtenances of a holding of c. 120 a. in Atwick included 27 beast gates in Mask and 3½ in Criftins; the occupier also enjoyed 14 beast gates in Ing Mask, presumably after the taking of the hay, and 11 in the common fields. Early inclosures in Atwick may have included Haver, East, and House fields, all recorded in 1607.[4]

The commonable lands of Atwick village were inclosed by an award of 1772 under an Act of 1769.[5] There were 1,436 a. to be dealt with. Allotments made totalled 1,405 a., and 3 a. of old inclosures were involved in exchanges. Allotments amounting to 472 a. were made from South field, 169 a. from North field, 144 a. from Mask, and 26 a. from Criftins. St. John's college, Cambridge, received 238 a., Humphrey Osbaldeston 199 a., and the Revd. William Mason 163 a. There were also three allotments of 100–149 a., three of 50–99 a., five of 15–49 a., and four of 1 a. each.

Skirlington. Skirlington's West field was named in the 13th century, and there was then stinted pasture for at least 180 sheep.[6] The common lands there were evidently inclosed early, largely perhaps by Bridlington priory for pasture. The priory's estate included a great close by the early 13th century and pastures named Ing close and West field in the 16th century, when grazing worth £5 a year was let.[7]

Arram. The ploughland at Arram was being worked by a plough in 1086.[8] East field was named in 1367 and South field in 1519.[9] The common lands, which still included stinted pasture in the 17th century, were evidently inclosed piecemeal.[10]

LATER AGRICULTURE. In 1801 there was reckoned to be 844 a. under crops in the parish.[11] In the smaller area of Atwick township, 568 a. were arable and 284 a. grassland in 1841;[12] in the parish as a whole, there was roughly the same proportion of arable to grassland in the earlier 20th century, when the grassland lay mostly around the village and close to the farms at Skirlington and Arram. Small plantations of woodland also stood close to Arram Hall.[13] In 1987 some 683 ha. (1,688 a.) were returned as arable land in Atwick parish, 144 ha. (356 a.) as grassland, and 6 ha. (15 a.) as woodland.[14]

In the 19th and earlier 20th century there were usually a dozen farmers in the parish, of whom 6 in 1851 and up to 4 in the 1920s and 1930s had 150 a. or more. From the late 19th century one or two men were also described as cowkeepers.[15] In 1987 of 16 holdings returned for Atwick, one was of 100–200 ha. (247–494 a.), seven were of 50–99 ha. (124–245 a.), and eight were of under 30 ha. (74 a.); more than 3,000 pigs and over 400 sheep were then kept.[16]

INDUSTRY. There has been little non-agricultural employment in Atwick. Lime-burning was carried on around the village in the mid 19th century, and then and later sand and gravel was extracted from the shore. A gravel merchant was recorded at Atwick c. 1920, but in 1925 extraction was prohibited to avoid worsening coastal erosion.[17]

MILLS. A windmill was built at Atwick on former common land between 1772 and 1828; it was assisted by steam by 1889, ceased to be used c. 1900,[18] and was later demolished. At Arram a windmill was recorded on Meaux abbey's estate in the 13th century.[19]

LOCAL GOVERNMENT. In the 15th century breaches of the assize of ale at Atwick were presented in Roos manor court.[20] Constables' accounts for Atwick survive for 1782–1847 and churchwardens' accounts for 1684.[21] An almshouse recorded in 1764 may have been a poorhouse.[22] Regular poor relief was given to 7–10 people in the early 19th century and occasional relief to 1 person in 1803–4 and 29 in 1812–15.[23] The parish joined Skirlaugh poor-law union in 1837.[24] It remained in Skirlaugh rural district until 1935 and then in Holderness rural district until 1974, when it became part of the Holder-

99 R.D.B., AQ/221/20.
1   Camb., St. John's Coll. MS. D63.286.
2   H.U.L., DDEV/4/1; R.D.B., AQ/221/20.
3   H.U.L., DDEV/4/1; B.I.H.R., TER. H. Atwick 1853.
4   B.I.H.R., CP.1607/2.
5   R.D.B., AQ/221/20; E.R.A.O., PC/14/1 (plan); 8 & 9 Geo. III, c. 33 (Priv. Act).
6   *Bridlington Chart.* 321; *Cal. Pat.* 1281–92, 243–4.
7   *Bridlington Chart.* 6, 317; *L. & P. Hen. VIII,* xiii (1), p. 564; *Miscellanea,* iii (Y.A.S. Rec. Ser. lxxx), 11.
8   *V.C.H. Yorks.* ii. 267.
9   H.U.L., DDCV/154/5; Poulson, *Holderness,* i. 120.
10 P.R.O., CP 25(2)/381/15 Jas. I Hil. [no. 55]; CP 25(2)/614/1654 Mich. [no. 81].
11 P.R.O., HO 67/26/27.
12 B.I.H.R., TA. 712s.

13 Acreage Returns, 1905, where figures given exceed the area of the par.; [1st] Land Util. Surv. Map, sheet 28.
14 Inf. from Min. of Agric., Fish. & Food, Beverley, 1990.
15 P.R.O., HO 107/2365; directories.
16 Inf. from Min. of Agric., Fish. & Food.
17 Camb., St. John's Coll., MS. SBF2.120; E.R.A.O., DDCC/136/47, 62; O.S. Map 6", Yorks. CLXXX (1855 edn.); directories.
18 E.R.A.O., PC/14/1; H. Teesdale, *Map of Yorks.* (1828); R. Gregory, *E. Yorks. Windmills,* 38–9 (illus.); directories.
19 *Chron. de Melsa,* ii. 103–4.
20 Burghley Ho., near Stamford (Lincs.), MS. 37/18.
21 E.R.A.O., PE/32/3; ibid. DDX/358.
22 B.I.H.R., V. 1764/Ret. 1, no. 33.
23 *Poor Law Abstract, 1804,* pp. 594–5; *1818,* pp. 522–3.
24 *3rd Rep. Poor Law Com.* 170.

ness district of Humberside.[25] In 1996 Atwick parish became part of a new East Riding unitary area.[26]

CHURCH. Everard de Ros gave Atwick church to Bridlington priory c. 1130. It was evidently then served by a chaplain. By 1228 the priory had appropriated the rectory and a vicarage had been ordained.[27] The advowson of the vicarage remained with the priory until its forfeiture in 1537.[28] The Crown granted the advowson to the archbishop of York in 1558 but that grant was evidently ineffective.[29] The patronage remained with the Crown until 1937, when Atwick vicarage and that of Nunkeeling with Bewholme were united; the Crown and the archbishop of York, the former patron of Nunkeeling, then had the right to present alternately until 1958, when the archbishop gave up his right.[30] In 1972 Atwick was united instead with Hornsea, the Crown becoming the sole patron of the new benefice.[31]

The vicarage was worth £4 6s. 8d. in 1291 and £4 7s. 10d. net in 1535, when the income included an augmentation of £2 from the priory.[32] In 1650 the improved annual value was £30, and in 1829–31 the average net income was £149 a year.[33] The living was augmented in 1837 with £200 from Queen Anne's Bounty to meet benefactions totalling £200 from the vicar and Mrs. Pyncombe's trustees. In 1883 the annual net value was £145.[34]

The vicar had no glebe in the Middle Ages. After dispute with Bridlington priory, it was agreed in 1228 that he should have hay tithes from those parts of the parish where he already enjoyed corn tithes.[35] The vicar also enjoyed wool, lamb, and small tithes from Atwick township. Hay and other tithes were compounded for by the 18th century.[36] At the inclosure of Atwick township in 1772 the vicar received 27 a. and an annual rent charge of £15 for his tithes there.[37] Nearly all of the allotment was sold in 1911.[38] In 1930 the 17-a. Atwick Mill farm was devised to the living, but it was sold later that year and in 1978 less than 2 a. of glebe remained.[39]

In Arram and Skirlington the vicar had all the tithes, except for those from the former estate of Meaux abbey in Arram. The tithes of the hamlets were compounded for only £22 8s. a year in the mid 18th century, but c. 1820 the vicar successfully claimed payment in kind. The tithes of Skirlington and Arram, except for the exempt 490 a. in Arram, were commuted for a rent charge of £210 11s. in 1841.[40]

A vicarage house at Atwick, recorded from 1685,[41] was rebuilt in 1837 to designs by Cresser Hebb of Leven.[42] The house was sold in 1911, and later incumbents lived at Bewholme or Hornsea.[43]

Atwick was frequently served with neighbouring parishes from the 18th century and vicars were often non-resident.[44] Complicated arrangements for doing the duty of the pluralist incumbent of Hornsea, Riston, and Rise involved the curate at Hornsea and Long Riston serving Atwick and the vicar of Atwick taking the services at Long Riston and Rise in 1743.[45] An increase from one to two Sunday services in the 1750s was reversed when the vicar also became curate of Hornsea and a resident there. Communion was celebrated four times a year in the mid 18th century with c. 35 recipients in 1743 and up to 20 in 1764.[46] There were again two Sunday services in the mid and late 19th century; communion was then monthly, with up to a dozen recipients.[47] The former school was used as a mission room c. 1900, presumably in part because of the church's position at the end of the village.[48]

The church of *ST. LAWRENCE* was rebuilt in the 19th century. The earlier building was dedicated to St. Peter in 1295, but the modern dedication was in use by 1461.[49] Before the 19th century, the church comprised chancel, nave with south porch, and west tower.[50] The chancel was in disrepair in 1575.[51] The tower was rebuilt in brick in 1829 and other parts of the building then repaired. The church was rebuilt in 1876 to designs by Hugh Roumieu Gough of London. It is of bright red brick with a red-tile roof, is 13th-century in style, and has an urban character. It comprises chancel, north-east tower with saddleback roof, north vestry, and nave with south porch.[52] Gothic windows at Grebe House (no. 27 Westgate), Hornsea, are said to have come from the old church.[53]

The fittings include a drum-shaped medieval font and a lectern formerly belonging to a Hull church and given in 1959.[54] There were two bells

[25] *Census.*

[26] Humberside (Structural Change) Order 1995, copy at E.R.A.O.

[27] *E.Y.C.* ii, pp. 439–41; iii, 82; *Bridlington Chart.* 312–13.

[28] Poulson, *Holderness*, i. 166–7.

[29] *Cal. Pat.* 1557–8, 420.

[30] B.I.H.R., OC. 651, 745; *Lond. Gaz.* 9 Feb. 1937, pp. 875–6; Poulson, *Holderness*, i. 167; below, Nunkeeling, churches.

[31] B.I.H.R., OC. 854.

[32] *Tax. Eccl.* (Rec. Com.), 336; *Valor Eccl.* (Rec. Com.), v. 116.

[33] *T.E.R.A.S.* iv. 63; *Rep. Com. Eccl. Revenues*, 914–15.

[34] B.I.H.R., V. 1884/Ret. 1; Hodgson, *Q.A.B.* pp. ccxxiii, cccxlii.

[35] *Bridlington Chart.* 312; above, manors.

[36] B.I.H.R., TER. H. Atwick 1685 etc.; *T.E.R.A.S.* iv. 63.

[37] R.D.B., AQ/221/20.

[38] Ibid. 139/43/39; 139/44/40.

[39] Ibid. 405/430/351; 426/173/133; inf. from York Dioc. Bd. of Finance, 1981.

[40] B.I.H.R., TER. H. Atwick 1685 etc.; ibid. TA. 712s.

[41] B.I.H.R., TER. H. Atwick 1685 etc.

[42] Ibid. MGA. 1837/1.

[43] Ibid. OC. 854; *Crockford*; above, this section.

[44] B.I.H.R., TER. H. Atwick 1726; ibid. V. 1764/Ret. 1. no. 33; *Rep. Com. Eccl. Revenues*, 914–15;

[45] *Herring's Visit.* i, pp. 36–7; ii, pp. 88–90; iii, pp. 35–6.

[46] B.I.H.R., V. 1764/Ret. 1. no. 33; *Herring's Visit.* i, p. 36.

[47] B.I.H.R., V. 1865/Ret. 1, no. 28; V. 1868/Ret. 1, no. 26; V. 1871/Ret. 1, no. 26; V. 1877/Ret. 1, no. 25; V. 1884/Ret. 1.

[48] Ibid. V. 1900/Ret. 1; inf. from the vicar, Hornsea, 1992; below, educ.

[49] B.I.H.R., Prob. Reg. 2, f. 462; *Reg. Romeyn*, i, p. 156.

[50] T. Allen, *Hist. Co. York*, iv. 220–1; Poulson, *Holderness*, i. 169–70.

[51] J. S. Purvis, *Tudor Par. Doc. of Dioc. York*, 182.

[52] B.I.H.R., Fac. 1875/2; T. Allen, *Hist. Co. York*, iv. 220–1; Poulson, *Holderness*, i. 169.

[53] Inf. from Dr. J. E. S. Walker, Grebe House, Hornsea, 1998.

[54] Plaque in church.

in 1552 and later; by 1910 there was one.[55] The plate includes a cup made in 1784, two patens, one of 1763, and a flagon of 1848.[56] The registers of baptisms, marriages, and burials date from 1538 and have been printed to 1728. Those of baptisms are complete, marriages largely so, and burials lack only a few years in the mid 17th century and early 18th.[57] Part of the churchyard was closed for burial in 1931.[58]

NONCONFORMITY. Up to 18 Roman Catholics were recorded in Atwick in the early and mid 17th century but very few later. Prominent among them were members of the Constable and Caley families, whose estates were sequestered in the mid 17th century.[59]

The protestant dissenters who registered a house at Atwick in 1802 and a house or chapel there in 1812[60] were presumably Wesleyan Methodists, for they built a chapel in the village in 1821.[61] The Primitive Methodists had a room at Atwick by 1851, and in 1856 they also built a chapel there.[62] It was said in 1865 that almost half of the families in the parish were nonconformist and in 1877 that most of the farmers and all of the labourers were dissenters.[63] The Primitive Methodist chapel had been closed by 1932, when the building was sold;[64] it was later used as a house but was derelict in 1991. The former Wesleyan Methodist chapel was closed in 1987; it stood empty in 1991 but was later converted into a house.[65]

EDUCATION. In 1689 Edward Fenwick gave 1 bovate in Beeford partly for the schooling and apprenticing of a poor boy of Atwick.[66] About 1715 a school was built by subscription beside the village green.[67] Ralph Burton (d. c. 1725) devised ½ bovate in Hornsea partly for teaching poor children and repairing the school.[68] After inclosure, Fenwick's endowment comprised 33 a. and Burton's 14 a.[69]

Atwick school had c. 20 pupils in 1743.[70] About 1820 it was attended by some 35 boys and girls, 22 of whom were taught reading, writing, and arithmetic by the master in return for c. £25 a year from the two charities. The charities then also subscribed to the Sunday school, and Fenwick's provided apprenticeship premiums of about £15 for one or two boys a year.[71] On inspection day in 1871 there were 34 pupils.[72]

A school board was formed in 1876, and a new school on another site was opened in 1877.[73] The board, later council, school was named Etherington school, presumably after Thomas Etherington, the first chairman.[74] It was enlarged in 1910, when the mission room and the Primitive Methodist schoolroom were used as temporary accommodation.[75] Average attendance rose from 43 in 1906–7 to 60 in 1911–12 but later fell steadily to 32 in 1937–8.[76] In 1946 there were 43 on the roll, 18 of them infants and 25 boys and girls of up to fourteen years old, but from 1948 pupils were transferred at eleven to Hornsea primary school.[77] Atwick school was closed in 1961, when most of its 25 pupils were transferred to Bewholme school.[78]

Fenwick's and Burton's charities had been amalgamated by a Charity Commission Scheme of 1878, which assigned ⅔ of the net income to the promotion of the elementary education of the children of Atwick.[79] The old school, and a master's house built in 1822, were sold in 1880;[80] the premises were later used as a church mission room, before being converted to a house, called Bewholme Cottage in 1991.[81] The proceeds of the sale, c. £70, were invested for the Old School and Schoolmaster's House Foundation, created by Scheme of 1879. That charity and the Fenwick and Burton Educational Foundation, established by Order of the Charity Commissioners in 1904, were united under the latter title by Scheme of the Board of Education in 1923. Assisting pupils from Atwick to receive secondary education was made an object of the Foundation, which then had an income of £40 a year.[82] In the earlier 20th century money was spent on fees, prizes, and other benefits for children at Atwick school, on the Sunday school, on grants for secondary education, and the provision of evening classes.[83] The farm at Beeford

55 E.R.A.O., PE/32/12; *Inventories of Ch. Goods*, 52; Boulter, 'Ch. Bells', 82.
56 *Yorks. Ch. Plate*, i. 210–11.
57 E.R.A.O., PE/32/1–8; *Reg. Atwick* (Yorks. Par. Reg. Soc. cxi).
58 E.R.A.O., PE/32/10; *Lond. Gaz.* 13 Feb. 1931, p. 1001.
59 Aveling, *Post Reformation Catholicism*, 42, 44, 56, 68.
60 P.R.O., RG 31/5, nos. 1747, 2662; B.I.H.R., Fac. Bk. 3, pp. 316, 628–9.
61 P.R.O., HO 129/522/4/13. It was apparently registered the next year: P.R.O., RG 31/5, no. 3732.
62 P.R.O., HO 129/522/4/14; datestone illus. in D. [R. J.] and S. Neave, *E.R. Chapels and Meeting Houses* (E. Yorks. Loc. Hist. Soc.), [inside cover].
63 B.I.H.R. V. 1865/Ret. 1, no. 28; V. 1877/Ret. 1, no. 25.
64 R.D.B., 463/322/247; *Kelly's Dir. N. & E.R. Yorks.* (1937), 401.
65 *Hornsea Meth. Circuit Monthly Fam. Mag.* no. 4 (Jan. 1988); inf. from Mrs. T. Heald, Atwick, 1995.
66 *9th Rep. Com. Char.* 753–4.
67 B.I.H.R., V. 1764/Ret. 1, no. 33; O.S. Map 6", Yorks. CLXXX (1855 edn.).

68 B.I.H.R., V. 1764/Ret. 1, no. 33; *9th Rep. Com. Char.* 754.
69 R.D.B., AK/57/6; CI/345/7; *9th Rep. Com. Char.* 753–4; Scheme 1878, Char. Com., Liverpool, 1992.
70 *Herring's Visit.* i, p. 36.
71 *9th Rep. Com. Char.* 753–4; *Educ. of Poor Digest*, 1075. Also B.I.H.R., Fac. Bk. 2, pp. 146–7; *Educ. Enq. Abstract*, 1078.
72 *Returns relating to Elem. Educ.* 472–3.
73 P.R.O., ED 7/135, no. 6; *Lond. Gaz.* 4 Feb. 1876, p. 470.
74 E.R.A.O., SB/1/1.
75 Ibid. SL/3/1, p. 182; E.R. Educ. Cttee. *Mins.* 1909–10, 295, 308; 1910–11, 244, 326, 328.
76 *Bd. of Educ., List 21* (H.M.S.O., 1908 and later edns.).
77 E.R.A.O., SL/3/2, pp. 242, 246.
78 Ibid. p. 258; E.R. Educ. Cttee. *Mins.* 1960–1, 98.
79 Scheme, Char. Com., Liverpool, 1992.
80 R.D.B., NE/15/22.
81 Ibid. 84/318/313 (1896); 524/215/174; 1171/369/324; 1332/263/238; *Reg. of Electors* (1974); inf. from the vicar; above, church.
82 Scheme of 1923 in possession of Mrs. Heald, Atwick.
83 E.R.A.O., accession 1681; E.R. Educ. Cttee. *Mins.* 1921–2, 47; 1922–3, 226–7.

was sold in 1921 and the land at Hornsea in 1930,[84] and more stock was bought. In 1985–6, when the educational branch's share of the net income was £152, twelve grants of £15 each were made.[85]

A Charity Commission Scheme of 1981 established the Atwick Educational Charity to maintain the buildings of the recently-closed school and provide amenities for schools serving Atwick parish. It was to be administered by the Fenwick and Burton trustees.[86] The former school was let for use by a play-group in the 1970s and later as a village hall.[87] The charity had an income of nearly £550, mostly comprising rents, in 1985–6.[88] The master's house was sold in 1991.[89]

A dame school was also recorded in Atwick in 1877.[90]

CHARITIES FOR THE POOR. The charities of Edward Fenwick and Ralph Burton were primarily for education, but Fenwick's might be used to relieve widows and nearly £8 a year of the income of Burton's charity was spent on bread for widows c. 1820. The Poor's Stock, a sum of £10 held by the overseers, was spent about 1810 on inclosing the allotment made for Burton's endowment.[91] The Scheme of 1878 assigned ⅓ of the joint income of Fenwick's and Burton's charities to the poor of Atwick,[92] and another Charity Commission Scheme, of 1921, separated the eleemosynary branch as Fenwick's and Burton's Charities for the Poor.[93] The income was spent in the earlier 20th century on coal, clothing, food, nursing, and Christmas doles.[94] The poor's share of the income was nearly £77 in 1985–6, when nothing was spent.[95]

BARMSTON

BARMSTON village is situated at the southern end of its parish, c. 8 km. SSW. of Bridlington.[96] It extends almost from the south-western parish boundary for c. 750 m. to the North Sea, which forms the eastern boundary. To the north and west the parish was bounded by Earl's dike, an ancient stream which was one of the boundaries of Holderness wapentake, and on the south and south-west by other early streams, partly improved as Barmston Main drain.[97] The name, often recorded as 'Berneston' in the Middle Ages, is probably Anglian, meaning 'Beorn's farm'.[98] The parish also included the settlements of Hartburn and Winkton. Hartburn lay in the north-eastern corner of the parish in the late 12th century, next to Earl's dike and the sea. The name is Anglian or Anglo-Scandinavian and means 'Hart stream'.[99] Coastal erosion was probably the reason that the settlement had been deserted by the 15th century.[1] Winkton, 'Winchetone' in 1086, may be an Anglian name meaning 'Wineca's farm'.[2] It evidently lay in the northern half of the parish,[3] but no evidence has been found to support the traditional site.[4] Winkton seems still to have been inhabited in the 15th century but was evidently abandoned soon afterwards.[5]

In 1851 the ecclesiastical parish of Barmston comprised 2,966 a. (1,200 ha.) of which Barmston township, later civil parish, accounted for

2,418 a. (979 ha.) and 548 a. (222 ha.) lay in the adjoining township of Ulrome; the rest of Ulrome belonged to Skipsea parish, and the history of the township is treated under Skipsea.[6] Measurements taken suggest that the coastline was eroded at an average rate of about 1 yd. a year between the mid 18th and mid 19th century, and Barmston civil parish had been further reduced to 2,391 a. (968 ha.) by 1891 and 2,373 a. (960 ha.) by 1911.[7] In 1935 most of Barmston civil parish, comprising 2,274 a. (920 ha.), was combined with that of Fraisthorpe with Auburn and Wilsthorpe as the new civil parish of Barmston, with a total area of 4,269 a. (1,728 ha.). The remaining 99 a. (40 ha.) of Barmston was then transferred to the new civil parish of Ulrome.[8] Local farmers complained in 1978 that much land was lost by the removal of concrete coastal defences put up during the Second World War,[9] and in 1991 the area of Barmston was 1,695 ha. (4,188 a.).[10]

There were 46 tenants on the manor in 1292.[11] Barmston was omitted from the 1377 poll-tax return. Twenty-six houses were assessed for the hearth tax in 1672, and 8 discharged.[12] There were 27 tenants on the manor at the end of the 17th century, and c. 30 families in the parish in the mid 18th.[13] From 163 in 1801 the population rose to 206 in 1811, increased more gradually in the 1820s and 1830s to stand at 254 in 1841, fell

[84] R.D.B., 233/590/477; 413/430/347.
[85] E.R.A.O., CCH/120.
[86] Scheme in possession of Mrs. Heald, Atwick; Review of Char. Rep. 102.
[87] E.R.A.O., CCH/120; E.R. Educ. Cttee. Mins. 1972–3, 166.
[88] E.R.A.O., CCH/120.
[89] Char. Com. Order 1991 in possession of Mrs. Heald.
[90] B.I.H.R., V. 1877/Ret. 1, no. 25.
[91] 9th Rep. Com. Char. 753–4; above, educ.
[92] Scheme, Char. Com., Liverpool, 1992.
[93] Scheme in possession of Mrs. Heald.
[94] E.R.A.O., accession 1681.
[95] Ibid. CCH/120.
[96] This article was written in 1996–7.
[97] O.S. Map 6″, Yorks. CLXII–CLXIII (1854 and later edns.).

[98] G. F. Jensen, Scand. Settlement Names in Yorks. 253.
[99] P.N. Yorks. E.R. (E.P.N.S.), 83.
[1] Chron. de Melsa (Rolls Ser.), i. 310.
[2] P.N. Yorks. E.R. 83–4.   [3] Below, this section.
[4] O.S. Map 6″, Yorks. CLXIII (1854 edn.).
[5] E.R.A.O., DDCC/4/1; Poulson, Holderness, i. 225; Miscellenea, iv (Y.A.S. Rec. Ser. xciv), 98.
[6] Census, 1871 (pt. ii); O.S. Map 6″, Yorks. CLXII, CLXIII (1854 edn.).
[7] T. Sheppard, Lost Towns of Yorks. Coast, 194; Census, 1891, 1911.
[8] Census, 1931 (pts. i and ii).
[9] Hull Daily Mail, 8 Mar. 1978.
[10] Census, 1991.   [11] P.R.O., C 133/63, no. 20.
[12] Hearth Tax, 61.
[13] E.R.A.O., DDWB/20/61; Herring's Visit. i, p. 109; B.I.H.R., V. 1764/Ret. 1, no. 41.

sharply in the 1850s to 206 in 1861, and was thereafter relatively unchanged, with 198 inhabitants in 1911. Numbers declined to 185 in 1921 but stood at 194 in 1931. At that time 260 lived in the area of the civil parish created in 1935, whose population, 301 in 1951, fell sharply in the 1960s to 236 in 1971. It had recovered by 1981, when 291 were usually resident and holiday visitors increased that number to 320.[14] The population was 314 in 1991.[15]

The landscape of the parish is gently undulating. Most of the land exceeds 8 m. above sea level, rising in the northern half of the parish to over 23 m. at Hamilton hill. As a result, most of the eastern boundary, apart from an area called Low grounds, comprises cliffs. Lower ground borders the boundary streams to north, west, and south. Alongside the streams there are deposits of boulder clay, alluvium, and river gravel, but otherwise the parish lies on a mixture of sand, gravel, and laminated clay.[16] Most of the parish had been inclosed by the end of the 17th century; the remaining commonable lands were dealt with by agreement in 1758 and by Act in 1820.[17]

The parish is now drained into the North Sea by Earl's dike, Barmston Main drain, and smaller streams, but formerly much water was carried south-westwards into the Hull valley. In 1367 Earl's dike and a drain between Barmston and Ulrome, presumably that later improved as Barmston Main drain, were said to be defective.[18] In the west of Barmston the boundary with Gransmoor, in Burton Agnes parish, was described in the later 15th century as comprising ditches belonging to each parish separated by land called a 'broad mere' or 'twenty foot'.[19] In the early 18th century it was marked by a 20-foot bank with a drainage ditch on either side. During a dispute between the tenants of Gransmoor and those of Barmston over drainage c. 1720, it was alleged that the bank dividing the two lordships had been secretly cut, the drains neglected, and water allowed to overflow into Barmston following the inclosure of Gransmoor c. 1700.[20] The drainage was later improved under the Beverley and Barmston Drainage Act of 1798.[21] The principal change made was the diversion of the waters of north Holderness from their accustomed course southwards into the Hull valley to the sea by way of the southern boundary stream of Barmston, then improved as Barmston Main drain. A barrier was made in Beeford to divide the northern and southern sections of the level which were later administered separately. The northern and western boundary

drains were improved by the commissioners as Water Mill beck and Burton drain respectively.[22] Low grounds in Barmston amounting to 340 a. were assessed to the work of the commissioners by the drainage award of 1811.[23] About 1850 the insufficiency of the drainage to the sea resulted in the flooding of c. 300 a.[24] Responsibility for the northern part of the Beverley and Barmston drainage passed from Barmston Drainage Board to North Holderness Drainage Board c. 1970, in 1989 to the National Rivers Authority, and to the Environment Agency in 1996. A long sea outfall was constructed at Barmston c. 1976.[25]

The main road of the parish is that running north-south from Bridlington to Beeford, Hull, and Beverley. From its southern end a minor road, along which Barmston village is built, leads eastwards to the shore, and in the north of the parish another branches from the main road to Fraisthorpe. In the south of the parish the course of the Bridlington road c. 1300 was evidently much the same as at present: mention was then made of the corner by Barmston manor house where the road turns south-westwards as a continuation of the village street towards Lissett, in Beeford.[26] The road was carried over the drain into Lissett by Fisher bridge, named from 1590.[27] Formerly, the chief road to Bridlington was probably that through Barmston village which then continued northwards along the coast. It was included in the White Cross to Bridlington turnpike under Act of 1767; problems caused by erosion have been suggested as the reason for the trust not being renewed, and the route was later abandoned.[28] All traces of the coast road had disappeared by 1996. Another early road was that leading from Lissett to Winkton and Hartburn, over which Bridlington priory was given leave to pass in 1299.[29] It presumably followed the course of the Lissett–Barmston road, before turning northwards to Winkton and then eastwards to Hartburn and the coastal road. From the Hartburn road a side road led north to Fraisthorpe c. 1300, crossing Earl's dike by Fraisthorpe bridge, which was in disrepair in 1367 and was probably that referred to as the 'stone bridge' in 1473.[30] With the failure of the turnpike and the progress of erosion, the chief route to Bridlington became the inland one from Barmston village through Fraisthorpe.[31] That road was later improved as a trunk road. In 1924 it was straightened, bypassing Fraisthorpe village; the new carriageway there crosses Earl's dike by the contemporary New bridge.[32] Barmston bridge, which carries the road over the main drain near the village,

14 Below, this section; below, econ. hist. [caravan park].
15 V.C.H. Yorks. iii. 495; Census, 1911–91.
16 Geol. Surv. Map 1", drift, sheet 65 (1909 edn.).
17 Below, econ. hist.   18 Poulson, Holderness, i. 120.
19 T.E.R.A.S. xix. 70; Y.A.J. xii. 106.
20 E.R.A.O., CSR/4/172; CSR/19/19.
21 38 Geo. III, c. 63 (Local and Personal).
22 E.R.A.O., DDBD/89/4; O.S. Map 6", Yorks. CLXIII (1854 edn.).
23 E.R.A.O., DDBD/89/4 passim; DCBB/4/8; ibid. CSR/26/15–16, 48–9; Beverley & Barmston drainage scheme plans, E.R.A.O., accession 1003; J. A. Sheppard, Draining of Hull Valley (E. Yorks. Loc. Hist. Ser. viii), 15–16, 20–1.
24 E.R.A.O., DDBD/89/4, p. 22.
25 Inf. from Mr. A. Atkin, Environment Agency, 1997; O.S. Map 1/10,000, TA 15 NE. (1983 edn.).
26 Burton, Mon. Ebor. 245.
27 Below, Beeford, intro.
28 Milestones shown on the O.S. map have not survived: O.S. Map 6", Yorks. CLXII, CLXIII (1854 edn.); K. A. MacMahon, Roads and Turnpike Trusts in E. Yorks. (E. Yorks. Loc. Hist. Ser. xviii), 27, 70; V.C.H. Yorks. E.R. ii. 201.
29 Brid. Chart. 301.
30 E.R.A.O., DDCC/3/19; Burton, Mon. Ebor. 245; Poulson, Holderness, i. 120, 225.
31 O.S. Map 6", Yorks. CLXIII (1854 edn.).
32 V.C.H. Yorks. E.R. ii. 201; K. J. Allison, E.R. Yorks. Landscape, 210.

was rebuilt in 1958.[33] Other roads have included a minor road, now a field road, leading westwards from the main road towards Burton Agnes by the mid 18th century.[34] A road to the old inclosures and Hamilton hill was awarded in 1758, and by 1818 it had been extended to the former Hartburn road. A road across South field to Ulrome, used intermittently from the mid 18th century, was confirmed at the inclosure of Barmston in 1820.[35]

BARMSTON village is built east-west along the northern side of a shallow valley through which a stream evidently once flowed.[36] The village is of two parts: the church, former manor house, and one or two other buildings stand at the west end of the street, and the rest of the village c. 500 m. further east. The early houses probably all stood south of the street, but by the mid 18th century a farmhouse at the west end and half a dozen houses further east also stood on its northern side. One of the latter was an almshouse built in 1726, and neighbouring houses occupying long garths may have been recently-made model cottages with allotments; no documentary evidence of such a development has been found, however. At the east end of the village one or two houses had also been built in a southern side lane, later Southfield Lane. By the mid 19th century two farmhouses had been added north of the street, and the earlier cottages there replaced by a school.[37] In the 1920s and 1930s some 30 chalet bungalows were built on the cliff at the end of Sands Lane; most have since been lost to the sea.[38] The name Sands Lane, now applied to the whole village street, appears in the 19th century to have denoted only its eastern continuation to the coast.[39] A large caravan park was also established close to the cliff c. 1960.[40] Other modern houses include half a dozen council houses on the main street, and the same number on Hamilton Hill Road. Sewage pumping stations for the new developments were provided c. 1965. Later in the century, Holly Croft, a private estate of c. 50 houses, was built south of the street on the site of Holly House farm.[41] Boulder construction is found in the churchyard wall and several buildings, but most of the village is of brick.[42] Noteworthy buildings include those formerly used as the

manor house, parsonage (now Barmston House), and an almshouse.[43] Manor Farm is dated 1768, Red Rose Cottage 1788, and No. 51 Sands Lane is a single-storeyed cottage of the 18th century.[44]

There was an alehouse in Barmston in the early 18th century.[45] The Bull and Dog, recorded from 1823, was later variously called the Bull or the Black Bull, the name in 1997. The house was rebuilt in a contemporary, urban style in the 1930s.[46]

A lodge of the Loyal Order of Ancient Shepherds was founded at Barmston in 1842.[47] In 1931 a small cottage was used as a men's reading room,[48] but there was no other meeting place until the Barmston Village Institute Trust, created in 1948, bought land next to Barmston church, and built a village hall for Barmston and Fraisthorpe c. 1955.[49] Nearby land was then leased for a cricket pitch.[50] Allotment gardens were provided on c. 1 a. in the village in the later 20th century.[51]

There was a beacon in Barmston in the mid 16th century. It probably stood on Hamilton hill, where there was a beacon c. 1800.[52] A lifeboat station, owned by the National Lifeboat Institute and manned from Bridlington, stood near the outfall of Barmston Main drain until it was given up in 1898.[53] Eight concrete gun emplacements, set up c. 1940, survive on the cliffs.

MANORS AND OTHER ESTATES. Four manors of *BARMSTON*, comprising 8 carucates, were held in 1066 by Thorkil, Sigeweard, Bonde, and Alfkil. They had passed to Drew de Bevrère by 1086,[54] and were later part of the Aumale fee. The principal estate at Barmston, held as ⅙ knight's fee in 1346,[55] was sometimes regarded as three manors, of Barmston, Hartburn, and Winkton, but at others as a single manor of Barmson, with members at Hartburn and Winkton.[56]

Most of Barmston was held by the Monceaux family.[57] Their tenancy may have originated, as in the case of their land at Boynton, in the grant made by Stephen, count of Aumale, to Alan de Monceaux, possibly in the 1120s,[58] and Alan occurs in the earlier 12th century as the donor of land at Winkton.[59] He (d. after 1161) was suc-

33 E.R.A.O., Bridges reg. 2, bridge 110.
34 Map of 1756, Poulson, *Holderness*, i, facing p. 183.
35 H.U.L., DDWB/2/31-3; DDWB(2)/1/31; DDCV/7/1; R.B.D., DA/59/331.
36 O.S. Map 6″, Yorks. CLXIII (1854 edn.).
37 Map of 1756, Poulson, *Holderness*, i, facing p. 183; O.S. Map 6″, Yorks. CLXIII (1854 edn.).
38 O.S. Map 6″, TA 15 NE. (1956 edn.); Hull Univ., Dept. of Geog., R.A.F. air photographs, run 152, no. 4108.
39 O.S. Map 6″, Yorks. CLXIII (1854 edn.).
40 E.R.A.O., DDX/225/6; O.S. Map 1/10,000, TA 15 NE. (1983 edn.); Hull Univ., Dept. of Geog., R.A.F. air photographs, run 152, no. 4108; Aerofilms A. 241739; below, econ. hist.
41 R.D.B., 600/44/29; 704/539/447; 704/540/448; 1406/12/12; 1406/13/13; 1406/14/14; 1622/384/328 etc.; E.R.A.O., DDX/225/6.
42 E.R.A.O., DDX/225/6; Min. of Housing, *Buildings List* (1965); Pevsner and Neave, *Yorks. E.R.* 274.
43 Below, manor, church, charities.
44 Pevsner and Neave, *Yorks. E.R.* 274.

45 E.R.A.O., QSF/18/C.22.
46 Ibid. QDT/2/6; directories; Pevsner and Neave, *Yorks. E.R.* 274; O.S. Map 6″, Yorks. CLXIII (1854 edn.).
47 D. [R. J.] Neave, *E.R. Friendly Soc.* (E. Yorks. Loc. Hist. Ser. xli), 42.
48 B.I.H.R., V. 1931/Ret.
49 R.D.B., 783/440/360; 997/203/177; 1012/16/13.
50 Inf. from Mr. A. Pitchfork, Barmston, 1997.
51 Inf. from Mrs. A. Wastling, Barmston, 1997.
52 E.R.A.O., LT/9/54; T. Sheppard, *Lost Towns of Yorks. Coast*, 208, 215, 236; J. Nicholson, *Beacons of E. Yorks.* 10, 31-2.
53 Bulmer, *Dir. E. Yorks.* (1892), 104; inf. from Mrs. Wastling.   54 V.C.H. Yorks. ii. 267.
55 *Cal. Inq. p.m.* viii, pp. 409-10.
56 *Yorks. Hund. and Quo Warr. R. 1274-94* (Y.A.S. Rec. Ser. cli), 36.
57 For the Monceauxs, Poulson, *Holderness*, i. 186-8, 258; *Early Yorks. Fam.* (Y.A.S. Rec. Ser. cxxxv), 61-2.
58 *E.Y.C.* iii, p. 50.
59 Below, this section [St. Mary's hosp.].

ceeded by his son Sir Ingram (probably d. by 1205), and Ingram by his son Sir Robert (fl. 1207–8) and supposed grandson Sir Ingram de Monceaux. In 1287 Sir Ingram was said to hold 5 carucates and 6 bovates in demesne at Barmston, Winkton, and Lissett, in Beeford, and his tenants occupied nearly 2 carucates more at Barmston and Winkton.[60] Shortly afterwards, Sir Ingram (d. 1292) gave Barmston manor to his son John (d. by 1297), a minor,[61] who was succeeded by his brother Thomas.[62] From Thomas (d. 1345), the estate descended in turn to his son Sir John (d. 1363) and grandson John (d. 1381).[63] The manor was held by Joan, widow of the last John, in 1410,[64] and in 1428 by Maud, widow of their son John.[65] On the death of Maud's and John's son William in 1446, the manor passed to his sister Maud, wife of Brian de la See, and their son (Sir) Martin de la See had inherited it by 1463.[66] In 1497 Sir Martin's daughter Margaret, wife of Sir Henry Boynton, received all her late father's property in Barmston and Winkton.[67] The Boyntons[68] retained the estate, which comprised 2,375 a. in 1819.[69] After the death of Sir Henry Boynton, Bt., in 1899, Barmston passed to his daughter Cycely, whose husband, Thomas Lamplugh Wickham, added the surname Boynton. Mrs. Wickham-Boynton (d. 1947) was succeeded by her son Marcus, who in 1948 sold the estate, then comprising 2,232 a. in Barmston, to Glendon Estates Co. Ltd., the owner in 1997.[70]

The manor house, mentioned from 1297,[71] occupied a moated site at the west end of the village near the church. It is said to have been rebuilt by Sir Thomas Boynton (d. 1581 or 1582) and his son Sir Francis (d. 1617),[72] but it may have been the work of Francis's successor, Sir Matthew Boynton, Bt. (d. 1647), for Celia Fiennes later called the Barmston house 'newer built' than Burton Agnes Hall, which is of 1601–10.[73] In 1672 the family's heir, William Boynton, lived in the house at Barmston, which then had 10 hearths,[74] but it was later abandoned by the Boyntons and used as a farmhouse. In 1582 the evidently large house had included great, little, old, and garden parlours, many chambers, and a gatehouse and porter's lodge, besides service and farm buildings. In the mid 18th century the house was taken down, except for one wing of two storeys, basement, and

attics, which was later remodelled and survives as part of Old Hall Farm. Materials from the house were said to have been used in building other farmhouses.[75]

William de Forz, count of Aumale, gave 2 carucates and a chief house at Barmston to his chamberlain, Gerard de St. John, c. 1250. Gerard later granted most of the estate to Adam, servant of the rector of Barmston, his wife Agnes, Gerard's daughter, and their heirs. Two bovates had already been granted to Dame Hawise de Monceaux.[76] Gerard was dead by 1287, when 1 carucate and 2 bovates were held in demesne, and the rest of the land was occupied by lay and religious tenants.[77] At least part of the estate descended to Agatha, another of Gerard's daughters,[78] and her sister Alice may also have held a share.[79] It was perhaps one of the daughters' shares, comprising ⅓ of a house and 4 bovates in Barmston, which William Hall (d. by 1353) held of the Crown as successor to the counts of Aumale as 1/96 knight's fee; his heir was his son Amand.[80] No more is known of the St. Johns' estate.

St. Mary's hospital, Bridlington, reputedly a foundation of Bridlington priory, was granted 2 bovates and 2 a. at Winkton by Alan de Monceaux in the earlier 12th century,[81] and c. 5 a. there by Walter Burdon about 1200.[82] The hospital's endowment seems later to have been subsumed in the estate of Bridlington priory in Barmston. That house had been given 1 bovate there by Peter Peto c. 1200,[83] and in 1535 its estate in Barmston was valued at £3 4s. net.[84]

Alan de Monceaux also gave 2 bovates with tofts in Barmston to the Knights Templar.[85] The estate was evidently transferred on the suppression of the Templars in 1312 to the Knights Hospitaller,[86] who held land in Barmston in 1473 and later.[87] After their suppression in the 16th century, their former estate, then also including land at Winkton, was held of the Crown by Matthew Boynton's heirs for 8s. 6d. a year.[88] The land was briefly restored to the Hospitallers in 1558.[89]

Nunkeeling priory is said to have been given 1 bovate in Barmston by Peter de Pettywyn, perhaps the Peter Peto who gave land to Bridlington priory c. 1200.[90] Nunkeeling priory had evi-

60 *Cal. Inq. p.m.* iv, p. 356.
61 Ibid. iii, p. 40; *Abbrev. Plac.* (Rec. Com.), 218.
62 *Cal. Inq. p.m.* iii, p. 278; *Cal. Pat.* 1292–1301, 390; *Feud. Aids*, vi. 162.
63 *Cal. Inq. p.m.* viii, pp. 409–10; xi, p. 54; Poulson, *Holderness*, i. 186.   64 *Cal. Inq. p.m.* xix, p. 256.
65 *Feud. Aids*, vi. 273.
66 E.R.A.O., DDCC/3/22; H.U.L., DDWB/20/27; *Yorks. Deeds*, ix, pp. 39–40.
67 E.R.A.O., DDCC/3/22.
68 For the fam., J. Foster, *Pedigrees of Yorks.* iii; Burke, *Peerage, Baronetage & Knightage* (1937), 350; *Land. Gent.* (1937), 233.
69 R.D.B., DA/59/341.
70 Ibid. 800/595/495; inf. from Mrs. M. Richardson, agent, 1997.
71 *Cal. Inq. p.m.* iii, p. 278.
72 The following is based on Poulson, *Holderness*, i. 213–21 (illus.).
73 *Descriptions of E. Yorks.: Leland to Defoe*, ed. D. [M.]

Woodward (E. Yorks. Loc. Hist. Ser. xxxix), 50; *V.C.H. Yorks. E.R.* ii. 108; Poulson, *Holderness*, i. 198, 200.
74 *Hearth Tax*, 61, 165; Poulson, *Holderness*, i. 198.
75 E.R.A.O., DDX/225/6; Poulson, *Holderness*, i. 213–21; Pevsner and Neave, *Yorks. E.R.* 274.
76 E.R.A.O., DDCC/3/1; *T.E.R.A.S.* xviii. 61–2.
77 *Cal. Inq. p.m.* iv, p. 356.
78 *Cal. Close*, 1346–9, 429; *Cal. Inq. Misc.* ii, p. 504.
79 Poulson, *Holderness*, i. 189.
80 *Cal. Inq. p.m.* ix, p. 358.
81 *Brid. Chart.* 300–1; *V.C.H. Yorks.* iii. 305.
82 *T.E.R.A.S.* xviii. 58–9.
83 Poulson, *Holderness*, i. 191.
84 *Valor Eccl.* (Rec. Com.), v. 45–6.
85 Poulson, *Holderness*, i. 192.
86 *V.C.H. Yorks.* iii. 256.
87 E.R.A.O., DDCC/3/19.
88 *Miscellanea*, iv (Y.A.S. Rec. Ser. xciv), 98.
89 *Cal. Pat.* 1557–8, 321.
90 Burton, *Mon. Ebor.* 386; above, this section.

1. SKIPSEA: CARAVAN SITES AT ULROME IN 1972, LOOKING SOUTH,
SHOWING ALSO THE COASTGUARD COTTAGES

2. SKIPSEA: VILLAGE IN 1989, LOOKING WEST, WITH THE CASTLE SITE (*top*)

3. SKIPSEA: CLIFF-TOP HOUSES IN 1999, LOOKING NORTH

4. HUMBLETON: DANTHORPE HALL, FARM BUILDINGS IN 1999, EAST SIDE OF YARD

5. HILSTON: ADMIRAL STORR'S TOWER IN 1998

6. ATWICK: Cliff Road in the early 20th century, looking west

7. SWINE: the village street in 1998, looking south-east

8. SKIPSEA: the village green in the 1920s, looking west,
showing the reading and recreation room and the Wesleyan Methodist chapel

9. BARMSTON: CHURCH IN 1997, FROM THE SOUTH-EAST

10. ROOS: CHURCH IN 1997, FROM THE NORTH-EAST

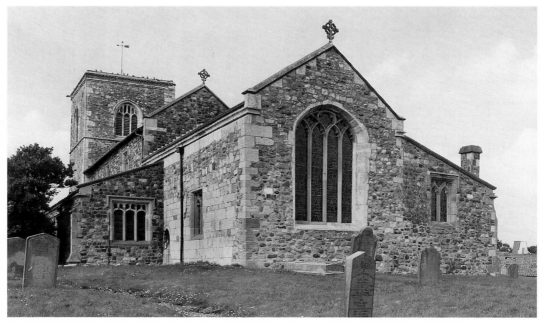

11. ALDBROUGH: CHURCH IN 1997, FROM THE EAST

12. SWINE: CHURCH IN THE EARLY 20TH CENTURY, INTERIOR LOOKING NORTH-WEST

13. NUNKEELING: DISUSED PARISH CHURCH IN 1997, LOOKING EAST

14. GARTON: CHURCH IN THE EARLY 20TH CENTURY

15. GOXHILL: CHURCH IN 1997, FROM THE SOUTH-WEST

16. ATWICK: CHURCH IN THE MID 20TH CENTURY, FROM THE NORTH-EAST

17. HILSTON: CHURCH (REBUILT 1861–2) AND
CHURCH FARM IN THE EARLY 20TH CENTURY

18. HILSTON: CHURCH (REBUILT 1956–7) IN 1986

19. RISE: church in 1997

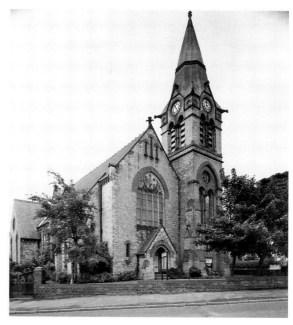

20. HORNSEA: United Reformed church in 1998

21. SWINE: Wyton Methodist church in 1997

22. SKIPSEA: Ulrome Methodist church in 1997

23. HORNSEA: Primitive Methodist chapel
in 1972

24. SKIPSEA: Methodist church, formerly
Wesleyan Methodist chapel, in 1997

25. EAST ELEVATION, *c.* 1680

26. WEST ELEVATION, 1776–7

27. EAST ELEVATION IN 1993

28. WEST ELEVATION IN 1993

SWINE: BURTON CONSTABLE HALL

29. GATEHOUSE BY JAMES WYATT *c.* 1785

30. STABLE BLOCK IN 1993, FROM THE NORTH-WEST

31. ORANGERY IN 1993, FROM THE SOUTH

SWINE: BURTON CONSTABLE HALL

32. NORTH FRODINGHAM: Church End Farm in 1999, from the south-west

33. BARMSTON: Old Hall Farm in 1997, from the north

34. HORNSEA: Old Hall in 1998, from the south

35. ATWICK: Arram Hall in 1997, from the east

36. SWINE: Wyton Hall, rear elevation in 1994, before restoration

37. Wyton Hall, south front in 1997, after restoration

38. SWINE: Benningholme Hall in 1999, garden front

39. SWINE: Wyton Lodge in 1999, from the south

40. SWINE: Wyton Abbey in 1997, from the south-east

41. GARTON: Grimston Garth in 1998, DINING ROOM

42. HUMBLETON: Old Vicarage in 1997

43. LEVEN: White Cross Cottage in 1998

44. RISE HALL: South Lodge in 1998

45. SIGGLESTHORNE: Wassand Hall, West Lodge, *c.* 1998

46. NUNKEELING: Bewholme, Old Vicarage, *c.* 1970

47. GARTON: Blue Hall in 2000, showing
Late 17th-century fittings

48. ROOS: Old Rectory in 1998,
from the North-East

49. Rise Park in 1999, from the south

50. Brandesburton Hall in 1992, from the south-east

51. TUNSTALL: Town Farm in 1997

52. LONG RISTON: terrace of 1871
FROM THE WEST, IN 1998

53. BEEFORD: Alton Farm in 1998,
FROM THE EAST

54. HUMBLETON: Church Cottage in 1998,
FROM THE SOUTH-EAST

55. HORNSEA: Marine Hotel in 1998,
FROM THE SOUTH-EAST

56. HORNSEA: 31 Westbourne Road in 1998,
SHOWING LOCALLY-PRODUCED ACORN TILES

57. HORNSEA: Ristonville, 29 Burton Road, *c.* 1998

58. HORNSEA: Westgate, probably in the early 20th century, looking west, showing Church infants' school of 1848

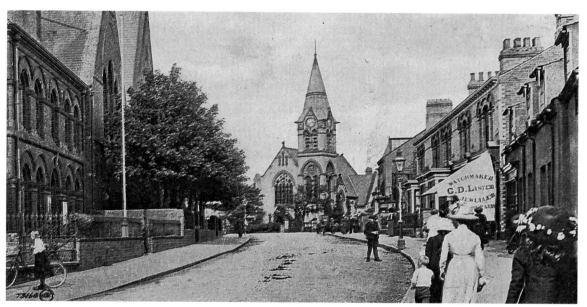

59. HORNSEA: Newbegin, *c.* 1910, looking north-east, showing police station and Wesleyan Methodist chapel (*left*), and the Congregational, later the United Reformed, church (*centre*)

60. HORNSEA: Wilton Terrace in 1998

61. WITHERNWICK: FORMER FORESTERS' HALL IN 1997

62. HORNSEA: FORMER WATERWORKS IN 1998

63. HORNSEA: FORMER RAILWAY BRIDGE IN THE MID 20TH CENTURY

64. HORNSEA: FORMER RAILWAY STATION IN 1998, FROM THE SOUTH

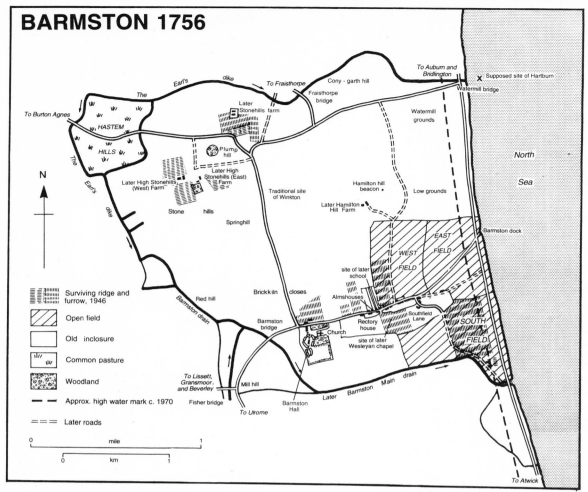

dently been endowed with other land in Barmston, for in the same period it exchanged 2 bovates there for land in Hatfield, in Sigglesthorne.[91] In 1535 Nunkeeling's estate in Barmston was valued at 13s. 4d. a year.[92] The Crown sold land in Barmston and Hartburn formerly belonging to the dissolved house in 1574.[93]

Between 1197 and 1210 Sir Ingram de Monceaux granted Meaux abbey a little land in Hartburn which was evidently later lost to the sea.[94] He also gave a toft with appurtenant common rights in Hartburn to Thornholme priory (Lincs.).[95] Thornton abbey (Lincs.) held land at Winkton of the Monceauxs by 1297,[96] and in the mid 14th century had a house and 4 a. there.[97]

ECONOMIC HISTORY. COMMON LANDS AND INCLOSURE. It is probable that each of the vills had its own common lands, and Winkton field was referred to in 1292.[98] No other docu-

mentary evidence of commonable lands there has been found, but ridge and furrow in the north-west of the parish may indicate the location of Winkton's open field.[99] If Winkton had separate commonable lands, they were evidently inclosed early,[1] or added to Barmston's grounds, in either case perhaps when the settlement of Winkton was abandoned.[2]

Barmston contained 8 ploughlands in 1086, but the land, valued at £3 in 1066, was then said to be waste.[3] South field was recorded in the later 13th century and again in 1416, when North field, lying between the village and Hamilton hill, was also mentioned.[4] Ridge and furrow surviving in the mid 20th century suggest that North field probably extended at least as far as the inland road to Bridlington.[5] By 1473 it was divided into two parts, called East and West fields.[6] The bovates in the fields were made up of the broad and narrow strips noticed elsewhere in Holderness.[7] Meadows adjoining

[91] B.L. Cott. MS. Otho C. viii, f. 77; below, Sigglesthorne, manors (Gt. Hatfield).
[92] *Valor Eccl.* (Rec. Com.), v. 115.
[93] *Cal. Pat.* 1572–5, p. 363.
[94] *Chron. de Melsa* (Rolls Ser.), i. 310.
[95] *Yorks. Deeds*, v, p. 85.
[96] *Cal. Inq. p.m.* iii, p. 278.
[97] *T.E.R.A.S.* xviii. 62.
[98] *Cal. Inq. p.m.* iii, p. 40.

[99] Hull Univ., Dept. of Geog., R.A.F. air photographs, run 152, no. 4108.
[1] Below, this section.   [2] Above, intro.
[3] *V.C.H. Yorks.* ii. 267.
[4] E.R.A.O., DDCC/3/3, 13.
[5] Hull Univ., Dept. of Geog., R.A.F. air photographs, run 152, no. 4108.
[6] E.R.A.O., DDCC/3/19.
[7] Below, Withernwick, econ. hist.

South field in the late 13th century were probably common,[8] and pieces of meadow belonging to strips in North field were recorded in 1434. Part of the village's pasture land was presumably then in the common carr, or marsh, called Tokholme, north of North field.[9] Another common pasture was at Hastem hills, in the north-western corner of the parish; the earlier name, 'Hest Holm', is believed to mean 'horse meadow'.[10] Horse carr near West field was also mentioned in 1590, when there was overstinting of pigs at Barmston.[11] Much of Barmston was evidently used for rough grazing in 1582, when over 900 sheep and more than 150 head of cattle were kept on the demesne; the tillage was then mostly sown with rye.[12]

Early inclosures in the parish may have included a meadow called 'Erlands' and pasture at 'Hest Holm', the latter possibly taken from Hastem hills pasture;[13] both were mentioned as parts of the demesne from the late 13th century.[14] The area of closes was evidently increased at the expense of the commonable lands, and in 1590 many closes, including 'Winton garths', presumably for 'Winkton garths', and South New close, were held by tenants, often in partnership.[15] Among closes named in 1697 were West Field close, Intack closes, Winton Marr close, West New close, East New close, and Great New close.[16] There were said to be some 450 a. of closes in the parish by 1739, all still in joint occupation.[17]

East and West fields were inclosed by agreement of 1757 and award of 1758. The open fields then contained 25½ bovates, of which 23½ belonged to Sir Griffith Boynton, Bt., and 2 to the rector. The two fields were separated by a hedge, and that and furlong boundaries were followed in the making of the closes, several of which had the characteristic long, curving shape of the old selions. There was almost 100 a. in East field,[18] and 91 a. in West field. Boynton was allotted 173 a. and the rector 15 a. South field was described as common pasture in 1758, but it may merely have been lying fallow then, since it was later referred to as an open field.[19] The rest of the commonable lands were dealt with by Act of 1819 and award of 1820.[20] They then comprised South field, of 127 a., the 109-a. Hastem hills pasture, and c. 1 a. of waste plots along the street. Sir Francis Boynton, Bt., was awarded all the land, except for a piece of waste. That, and a small piece of old inclosure, were awarded to the rector in exchange for his rights

of ownership and pasturage in a parcel of coastal land called the Tetherings; he also received 7 a. of old inclosure for his glebe in the lands inclosed.

TURBARIES, FISHING, AND FOWLING. Besides for their rough grazing, the carrs were valued for turves, and the dikes and areas of water in the parish as sources of fish and wild fowl. Turbaries in Hartburn were exploited by the commoners in the later 12th century, and others were recorded later in Barmston and Winkton.[21] In 1299 Thomas de Monceaux granted Bridlington priory exclusive right of fishing in Earl's dike between Fraisthorpe bridge and the sea.[22] In 1590 pains made in the manor court included the prohibition of fishing and fowling in Barmston, presumably because they belonged to the lord.[23]

LATER AGRICULTURE. In the mid 18th century the new husbandry was introduced at Barmston by Benjamin Outram, the Boyntons' steward, and later a five-course rotation of crops, including turnips, rape, and clover, was operated.[24] In 1801 there was 781 a. under crops in the parish.[25] Barmston had 1,924 a. of arable land, 338 a. of grassland, and 12 a. of woodland in 1905.[26] The parish remained predominantly arable in the 1930s, when the grassland was concentrated mainly south-east of the village and on the higher ground of Hamilton hill, High Stonehills, and Red hill.[27] Of the 1,094 ha. (2,703 a.) returned for Barmston civil parish in 1987, 821 ha. (2,029 a.) were arable, 255 ha. (630 a.) grassland, and 6.5 ha. (16 a.) woodland. Nearly 700 cattle were then kept.[28]

There were 7–10 farmers in Barmston during the 19th century, and one or two more in the earlier 20th. Eight of the farms were of 150 a. or more in 1851, and there were nine larger farms in 1948.[29] Of the twelve holdings enumerated in 1987, three were of 100–199 ha. (247–492 a.), eight were of 50–99 ha. (124–245 a.), and one of 40–49 ha. (99–121 a.).[30]

INDUSTRY AND TRADE. There has been little employment in Barmston unassociated with agriculture. Stone and gravel were being taken from the beach at Barmston by the early 19th century, evidently under licence from the Constables, who claimed rights over the shore as lords of the seigniory. Extraction from the beach caused dispute, the rector complaining in

8 E.R.A.O., DDCC/3/3.
9 Ibid. DDCC/3/17.
10 *P.N. Yorks. E.R.* (E.P.N.S.), 84; below, this section.
11 H.U.L., DWB/1/3.
12 Poulson, *Holderness*, i. 221–2.
13 Above, this section.
14 E.R.A.O., DDCC/3/16; *Cal. Inq. p.m.* iii, p. 40; iv, p. 356.
15 H.U.L., DWB/1/3.   16 Ibid. DDWB/20/61.
17 *Diary of Rob. Sharp of S. Cave*, ed. J. E. and P. A. Crowther (Brit. Acad. Rec. of Soc. and Econ. Hist. N.S. xxvi), pp. 351–2.
18 There were one or two, possibly small, parcels near the shore for which no area was given.
19 H.U.L., DDWB/2/31, 33; map of 1756, Poulson, *Holderness*, i, facing p. 183; O.S. Map 6″, Yorks. CLXIII

(1854 edn.); R.D.B., DA/59/318.
20 59 Geo. III, c. 29 (Priv. Act); R.D.B., DA/59/318; E.R.A.O., PR/1767.
21 E.R.A.O., DDCC/3/3; *Yorks. Deeds*, v. 85; *Brid. Chart.* 301.
22 Poulson, *Holderness*, i. 225.
23 H.U.L., DWB/1/3.
24 Ibid. DDWB(2)/1/5; Poulson, *Holderness*, i. 224.
25 P.R.O., HO 67/26/37.
26 Acreage Returns, 1905.
27 [1st] Land Util. Surv. Map, sheet 28.
28 Inf. from Min. of Agric., Fish. and Food, Beverley, 1990.
29 P.R.O., HO 107/2364; E.R.A.O., DDX/225/6; directories.
30 Inf. from Min. of Agric., Fish. & Food.

1814 about the damage done to Barmston's roads, and Sir Francis Boynton, Bt., attempting to restrict access to the parish in 1810 and again in 1817. Francis Constable upheld his rights, however, and the inclosure Act of 1819 was specific in its exception of the shore.[31] In 1843 and 1858 Sir Thomas Constable, Bt., granted 14-year leases of the shore to the Boyntons, allowing the collection of gravel and stone for purposes other than use in cement.[32] Away from the shore, gravel has been dug in the north-west of the parish,[33] and in 1932 about 40 a. near High Stonehills farm was let to an extraction company, Messrs. Maddox and Marlow, which was to pay royalties of 1s. a ton to the Wickham-Boyntons.[34] The quarry was worked by the East Yorkshire Gravel Co. Ltd. in 1948, and later by Harold Needler Quarries Ltd. By 1946 quarrying had removed most of Spring hill, and operations there had ceased by 1957, when the land was returned to the owner for reconversion to agricultural use.[35] Brickmaking near the west end of the village is suggested by 'Bricke Kiln' close, or closes, named from 1697.[36]

A firm of motor engineers was established beside the main road c. 1935, and from the late 1960s boats and caravans were sold on the same site. An agricultural engineering concern was also operated in the village in the mid century.[37]

Barmston began to be visited by holiday-makers in the 1930s, some with caravans, and a permanent caravan park was laid down near the sea cliff c. 1960.[38] Since 1979 the site has been owned by Haven Holiday Group, the proprietor in 1997. There were then bases for up to 400 caravans, as well as a supermarket, entertainments club, and children's playground.[39] Visitors have also been catered for by a café nearby, and by the one or two shops in the village.[40] Another caravan site, behind the Black Bull inn and used since the Second World War, had 23 bases in 1997.[41]

Barmston dock was mentioned in 1683,[42] and a landing beside the coast road to Bridlington was used in the 18th century.[43] The dock seems to have been destroyed by coastal erosion before the end of the 19th century.[44]

MILLS. A water mill at Hartburn, presumably on Earl's dike, was used by Bridlington

priory in 1292, and land next to the drain was later called Watermill grounds.[45] It may have been another water mill which was recorded in the later 16th century[46] and again in 1697, when a location near Fraisthorpe bridge is suggested by the association with the mill of Coney Garth close.[47] A windmill mentioned from the 16th to the early 18th century[48] may have stood on Mill hill in the south-west corner of the parish, near Lissett.[49]

LOCAL GOVERNMENT. About 1280 Sir Ingram de Monceaux claimed the profits of the assize of ale throughout his lands and, as a suitor to the three-weekly wapentake court of Holderness for his four manors of Barmston, Winkton, Lissett, and Hartburn, exemption from the county court.[50] Court rolls for the manor of Barmston survive for 1468 and 1590. Besides the ale assize, the court had view of frankpledge, and its jurisdiction extended to Lissett, in Beeford. In 1468 a constable was appointed for Barmston and Winkton, a dike-reeve for each of the vills, and a general dike-reeve. Other officers of the court included two aletasters, and in 1590 two bylawmen.[51] Rights of wreck and freedom from Admiralty jurisdiction were also claimed by the lord of the manor. In 1528 Dame (Margaret) Boynton had confirmation of those franchises,[52] but the claim to wreck by her descendant, Sir Matthew Boynton, Bt., in 1626 was ultimately rejected, and only flotsam and jetsam allowed to him.[53]

Three people were receiving permanent out-relief at Barmston in 1802–3, and 9–11 between 1812 and 1815; in the early 19th century 2–5 were also helped occasionally.[54] No parochial records from before 1835 survive. Barmston joined Bridlington poor-law union in 1836.[55] It remained in Bridlington rural district until 1974, when it became part of the North Wolds district, later borough, of Humberside. In 1981 the borough's name was changed to East Yorkshire. In 1996 Barmston civil parish became part of a new East Riding unitary area.[56]

CHURCH. The architectural evidence suggests that Barmston church was built in the earlier

[31] E.R.A.O., DDCC/3/34–8; DDCC(2)/41.
[32] Ibid. DDCC/130/150; DDCC/136/60.
[33] O.S. Map 6″, Yorks. CLXIII (1854 edn.).
[34] H.U.L., DDWB(2)/1/16.
[35] E.R.A.O., DDX/225/6; R.D.B., 1066/111/102; 1070/106/87; Hull. Univ., Dept. of Geog., R.A.F. air photographs, run 80, no. 4111.
[36] H.U.L., DDWB/20/61; O.S. Map 6″, Yorks. CLXIII (1854 edn.).
[37] R.D.B., 538/383/293; 1151/72/68; 1268/494/374; 1462/365/327.
[38] Ibid. 1194/393/359.
[39] Inf. from Public Protection Division, E. Riding of Yorks. Council, Bridlington, 1997; inf. from Mr. M. Alston, Barmston Beach Holiday Park, 1997.
[40] E.R.A.O., CCO/10, 338, 487, 597, 670 etc.; directories.
[41] Inf. from Public Protection Division, E. Riding of Yorks. Council.
[42] *Depositions from York Castle* (Sur. Soc. xl), 259.
[43] Map of 1756, Poulson, *Holderness*, i, facing p. 183.

[44] O.S. Map 6″, Yorks. CLXIII (1854 edn.); O.S. Map 1/2,500, Yorks. CLXIII. 14 (1892 edn.).
[45] *Cal. Inq. p.m.* iii, p. 40; O.S. Map 6″, Yorks. CLXIII (1854 edn.).
[46] *Y.A.J.* xii. 106.
[47] H.U.L., DDWB/20/61; O.S. Map 6″, Yorks. CLXIII (1854 edn.).
[48] E.R.A.O., DDCC/3/24; H.U.L., DDWB/2/41; DDWB/20/61.7.
[49] O.S. Map 6″, Yorks. CLXIII (1854 edn.).
[50] *Yorks. Hund. and Quo Warr. R. 1274–94* (Y.A.S. Rec. Ser. cli), 137; *Yorks. Inq.* ii, pp. 39–40.
[51] E.R.A.O., DDCC/4/1; H.U.L., DWB/1/3.
[52] H.U.L., DDWB/2/4.
[53] *Cal. S.P. Dom.* 1625–6, 447, 461, 471; 1627–8, 32; E.R.A.O., DDCC/3/28–9.
[54] *Poor Law Abstract, 1804*, pp. 594–5; *1818*, pp. 522–3.
[55] *3rd Rep. Poor Law Com.* 167.
[56] Boro. of N. Wolds, *Council Proc. and Cttee. Mins.* 1973–4, 4–7; 1980–1, 360; Humberside (Structural Change) Order 1995, copy at E.R.A.O.

12th century.[57] Barmston parish included 548 a. in Ulrome township, most of which lay in the ecclesiastical parish of Skipsea.[58] In 1929 the curacy of Fraisthorpe chapel, then combined with Carnaby vicarage, was united instead with Barmston rectory; the parishes remained distinct until 1979, however, when they were united as the new parish of Barmston with Fraisthorpe. Also in 1979 the benefice of Barmston with Fraisthorpe was united with that of Skipsea with Ulrome.[59]

Possibly soon after it was built, Barmston church was given by Alan de Monceaux to Whitby abbey; his grant was confirmed c. 1170.[60] The details of the patronage are unknown before 1287, when the abbot of Whitby and Sir Ingram de Monceaux were disputing the right of presentation. Monceaux's claim evidently succeeded,[61] the Crown presenting during the minority of John de Monceaux in 1292 and 1295,[62] and in the early 14th century Dame (Emma) de Monceaux, widow of Sir Ingram (d. 1292), holding the advowson as part of her dower.[63] The patronage remained with the Monceaux family until the mid 15th century, and then passed successively, with the manor, to their heirs, the de la Sees and the Boyntons.[64] At the union of Barmston with Fraisthorpe and Skipsea with Ulrome in 1979, the right of presentation was given jointly to the Wickham-Boynton family and the former patrons of Skipsea and Ulrome, the archbishop of York and Dr. Winifred Kane.[65] The Hon. Susan Cunliffe-Lister later succeeded to the Wickham-Boynton interest.[66]

The church was valued at £13 6s. 8d. a year in 1291, and the net value in 1535 was £13 11s. 10d.[67] The improved annual value in 1650 was £123 6s. net.[68] The annual net income averaged £1,065 between 1829 and 1831, and the gross value was given as £900 in 1893.[69]

Most of the income was from tithes, which were valued at some £13 gross in 1535,[70] and in the later 16th century were leased to the lord of the manor for £13 6s. 8d. a year.[71] In 1722 the composition for the tithes from the commonable lands in Barmston was £14 2s. a year; the tithes of the old inclosures were paid for at the rate of 2s. in the pound of the rentable value, and 10s.

was received for the tithes of the manor house and windmill.[72] The tithes of Barmston were commuted at inclosure in 1820 for a rent of £880 a year, reviewable every 14 years. They were worth some £650 c. 1855.[73]

The rectorial tithes of the part of Ulrome township which lay in Barmston parish were valued at £26 gross in 1650.[74] They comprised the corn and hay tithes of the 23½ bovates belonging to Barmston parish, and hay tithes from some of the old inclosures. By 1716 a sum of 15s. 8d. a year was being paid instead of the hay tithes in Ulrome.[75] At the inclosure of Ulrome in 1767 the rector was awarded 75 a. and an annual rent of £19 0s. 9d for his tithes.[76] The allotment evidently included land assigned to the curate of Ulrome for his glebe rights and tithes but awarded in error to the rector of Barmston. An attempt to rectify the error by transferring 32 a. to Ulrome curacy in 1823 was unsuccessful.[77] The land at Ulrome remained unsold in 1978.[78]

In 1535 the glebe was valued at £2 3s. 4d. a year gross.[79] In the early 18th century it comprised 2 bovates, c. 17 a. of closes, and grazing rights.[80] The rector was allotted 15 a. for his land in the open fields at the inclosure of 1758, and a further 7 a., adjoining the rectory house, when the rest of the common lands were inclosed in 1820.[81] Practically all of the glebe land at Barmston was sold between 1948 and 1961, the 36-a. farm being bought by W. N. Harris in 1958.[82]

A parsonage house was mentioned in 1473, and had four hearths in 1672.[83] In 1743 the brick and tile house had been recently rebuilt following a fire, and consisted of four rooms;[84] it may have been remodelled by 1770, when it had eight.[85] William Dade, rector, enlarged the house at 'very considerable expense' in 1776, building a three-storeyed block on the west side, and between 1809 and 1817 the house was further extended to the north.[86] The site was evidently much enlarged during the improvements to the house.[87] The rectory house, later Barmston House, and c. 1 a. were sold in 1961, and a new house was built in another part of the rectory-house grounds.[88] Barmston rectory house was made the residence of the new benefice in 1979.[89]

57 Below, this section.
58 O.S. Map 6″, Yorks. CLXIII (1854 edn.); *Census*, 1871 (pt. ii).
59 B.I.H.R., OC. 593, 955; *V.C.H. Yorks. E.R.* ii. 206.
60 *E.Y.C.* i, pp. 296–7; ii, p. 229.
61 *Reg. Giffard*, i, p. 241; *Reg. Romeyn*, i, pp. 202, 222–3, 236–7; *Reg. Corbridge*, i, pp. 165–6; *Cal. Pat.* 1281–92, 506; 1292–1301, 105.
62 *Cal. Inq. p.m.* iii, p. 40; *Reg. Romeyn*, i, pp. 223, 237.
63 *Reg. Corbridge*, i, pp. 13–14, 177, 188, 198; ii, p. 169.
64 Lawrance, 'Clergy List', Holderness, 1, pp. 8–9; Poulson, *Holderness*, i. 203; R.D.B., 1109/35/28; above, manor.
65 B.I.H.R., OC. 955; *Crockford* (1977–9).
66 *Crockford* (1995–6).
67 *Tax. Eccl.* (Rec. Com.), 304; *Valor Eccl.* (Rec. Com.), v. 115.
68 *T.E.R.A.S.* iv. 59.
69 *Rep. Com. Eccl. Revenues*, 970–1; *Kelly's Dir. N. & E.R. Yorks.* (1893), 360.
70 *Valor. Eccl.* v. 115.
71 B.I.H.R., CP. G. 3086.
72 H.U.L., DDWB/2/31, 41.
73 R.D.B., DA/59/318; P.R.O., HO 129/524/1/17; B.I.H.R., TER. H. Barmston 1861.
74 *T.E.R.A.S.* iv. 59.
75 B.I.H.R., TER. H. Barmston 1716.
76 R.D.B., AH/331/9.
77 Below, Skipsea, churches (Ulrome [glebe]).
78 Inf. from York Dioc. Bd. of Finance, 1981.
79 *Valor Eccl.* v. 115.
80 B.I.H.R., TER. H. Barmston n.d. (c. 1685)–1743; E.R.A.O., DDCC/3/31; H.U.L., DDWB/2/31–3.
81 H.U.L., DDWB/2/33; R.D.B., DA/59/318.
82 R.D.B., 783/440/360; 914/489/435; 997/203/177; 1109/35/28; 1237/483/445; E.R.A.O., PE/6/25.
83 E.R.A.O., DDCC/3/19, f. 6; P.R.O., E 179/205/504.
84 *Herring's Visit.* i, p. 109; B.I.H.R., TER. H. Barmston 1743. 85 B.I.H.R., TER. H. Barmston 1770.
86 Ibid. 1777, 1809, 1817.
87 Map of 1756, Poulson, *Holderness*, i, facing p. 183; O.S. Map 6″, Yorks. CLXIII (1854 edn.).
88 E.R.A.O., PE/6/25; R.D.B., 1237/483/445; B.I.H.R., MGA. 1963/5; *Crockford* (1961–2).
89 B.I.H.R., OC. 955.

Robert de Askeby, rector 1295–1301, was in minor orders at his institution, and in 1298 he was licensed to be non-resident.[90] Amand of Routh, rector 1304–49, was also non-resident, and a parochial chaplain, Robert of Goxhill, was serving Barmston church for him in 1320.[91] Cuthbert Tunstall, a kinsman of the patronal family and later bishop of London and Durham and a high officer of the Crown, was briefly rector in 1506–7.[92] Another non-resident was probably Richard Hildyard, rector 1516–34: in 1525–6 five chaplains were employed in the church, two receiving £4 13s. 4d. a year each and the others £4 each,[93] and from 1528 Hildyard was also rector of Winestead.[94] Thomas Dade, rector 1735–60, also held Burton Agnes vicarage, and lived at both places before 1743, when his assistant curate was fulfilling the residence requirement at Barmston. Two services were then provided every Sunday at Barmston, and Holy Communion was quarterly, with 30 usually receiving.[95] Dade's successor, John Holme, assistant curate from 1735 and rector 1760–75,[96] lived at Brandesburton, where he was also rector, and he similarly employed a curate to do his duty at Barmston and at Ulrome chapel, which then, as later, was held with Barmston. The curate held only one Sunday service at Barmston in 1764 because of the small congregation there.[97] Thomas Dade's son, William, rector 1776–90, was a prominent antiquarian upon whose collections Poulson based his history of Holderness.[98] Griffith Boynton, rector 1859–98, one of three members of the patronal family presented to the rectory, was providing two Sunday services by 1865; communion was monthly in the later 19th century, with on average a dozen communicants.[99] In 1871 Boynton was resident in France, and the church was, once again, in the charge of a curate.[1] In 1931, after union with Fraisthorpe chapel, communion was celebrated there on the first Sunday of every month, and on the others at Barmston.[2] In 1997 a Sunday service was held in rotation at Skipsea, Ulrome, Barmston, and Fraisthorpe, and each place similarly had a monthly communion service.[3]

The church of ALL SAINTS, so called in 1390,[4] is built of rubble and boulders with ashlar dressings, and comprises chancel and nave with south aisle, south porch, and south-west tower. The nave is 12th-century in origin, the thick, north wall being substantially of that period, as also may be a section of walling at the east end of the aisle arcade, which is pierced with a narrow, round-headed arch, possibly the entrance to a former *porticus*. The cylindrical font, decorated with diaper ornament, is also 12th-century. A blocked, ogee-headed doorway in the north wall may be 14th-century, and the south aisle seems to have been added then or early in the 15th century. There is a squint between the aisle and the chancel. John Monceaux requested burial in the aisle, which was dedicated to St. Mary, in 1426.[5] The shouldered-lintel, south doorway may have been reset from the 12th-century nave at the building of the aisle.

A post-medieval remodelling of the church seems to have included the rebuilding of the south arcade and chancel arch, and the addition of the tower and porch. Although the overall style is 15th-century, the east and south windows of the chancel, and those of the tower and nave, have peculiarities of detailing which suggest that they are in fact of c. 1600. A narrow, round-headed, blocked doorway overlapped by the south porch may be 12th-century, reset as an entrance to a screened-off south aisle. The Boyntons continued to use Barmston as their burial place following their removal to Burton Agnes, probably in the later 17th century.[6] The church was repaired and rendered c. 1720,[7] and restoration and refitting was carried out in 1874.[8] In 1938 the nave and aisle were re-roofed at the expense of Lady (Elizabeth) Boynton. The church was repaired by an anonymous benefactor in 1986,[9] when access to it from Sands Lane was also provided.[10]

The chief memorial is in the chancel; it is an alabaster table tomb bearing the effigy of a man in armour, and almost certainly commemorates William Monceaux (d. 1446).[11] In 1996 the tomb was in serious disrepair. Memorials of members of the Boynton family formerly included one for Peregrine (d. 1645), infant son of Sir Matthew Boynton, Bt., from which a table supported by four marble urns survives in the chancel.[12] The outer walls of the aisle and porch contain early 18th-century stone memorials, one with a *momento mori* of skull and cross-bones in the lower panel. Two fragments of medieval glass remain in the south window of the aisle, but most of the windows are filled with modern stained glass; those commemorating members of the Boynton family include the east window of 1965 by L. C. Evetts.[13] Part of a 10th-century hogback monument, supposed to have been

[90] *Reg. Romeyn*, i, p. 237; *Reg. Newark*, p. 206.
[91] Lawrance, 'Clergy List', Holderness, i, p. 10; *Cal. Inq. p.m.* xiii, p. 280.
[92] Lawrance, 'Clergy List', Holderness, i, p. 12; *Test. Ebor.* vi, pp. 36–8; *D.N.B.*
[93] *Y.A.J.* xxiv. 76.
[94] Lawrance, 'Clergy List', Holderness, i, p. 12.
[95] *Herring's Visit.* i, pp. 38, 109, 193; the following is based on a clergy list of 1967 by M. E. Bayldon at E.R.A.O., DPX/57.
[96] *Herring's Visit.* i, p. 110; *Alum. Cantab. to 1751*, 398.
[97] B.I.H.R., V. 1764/Ret. 1, no. 41.
[98] *D.N.B.*; Poulson, *Holderness*, i, p. viii.
[99] B.I.H.R., V. 1865/Ret. 1, no. 39; V. 1868/Ret. 1, no. 37; V. 1877/Ret. 1, no. 37.
[1] Ibid. V. 1871/Ret. 1, no. 38.

[2] Ibid. V. 1931/Ret.
[3] Notice board.
[4] *T.E.R.A.S.* xi. 1.   [5] Ibid. 4.
[6] Above, manors.
[7] B.I.H.R., ER V./Ret. 1, p. 31; ER V./Ret. 2, p. 5.
[8] Ibid. V. 1865/Ret. 1, no. 39; V. 1868/Ret. 1, no. 37; ibid. Ch. Ret. i.
[9] Plaques in church.
[10] *Hull Daily Mail*, 29 Apr. 1986.
[11] Dade and Poulson, among others, make the tomb that of Sir Martin de la See (d. 1497), almost certainly incorrectly: Poulson, *Holderness*, i. 210–11, illus.; *Y.A.J.* xxi. 187–8; xxxvii. 197–200.
[12] A brass copy of the inscription is in the south aisle: Pevsner and Neave, *Yorks. E.R.* 273.
[13] Pevsner and Neave, *Yorks. E.R.* 273.

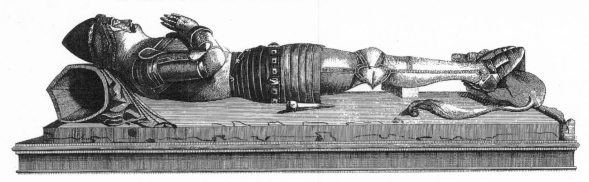

FIG. 12. BARMSTON CHURCH: EFFIGY, PROBABLY OF WILLIAM MONCEAUX (D. 1446)

brought to the rectory house by William Dade, rector,[14] was kept in the church porch in 1996, as was a medieval water stoop. The plate includes a cup of 1724, and a paten and flagon, both given in the earlier 19th century.[15] The registers begin in 1571 and are complete.[16]

NONCONFORMITY. In 1567 the rector was said to be a 'misliker of the new order'.[17] Five parishioners were presented as recusants in 1664, and in 1676 there were said to be 10 protestant dissenters in Barmston.[18] A family described as Anabaptist lived in Barmston or Ulrome in 1743, but dissent was otherwise weak or absent in the 18th century.[19] Unidentified congregations of protestants registered houses in Barmston for dissenting worship in 1824 and 1833, and a barn in 1839.[20] In the last year the Wesleyan Methodists built a chapel on land rented from Sir Henry Boynton, Bt.[21] It was still used in 1997.[22]

EDUCATION. There was evidently a school at Barmston by 1726, when a schoolmaster was recorded.[23] By his will, Sir Griffith Boynton, Bt., (d. 1731) charged his manor of Haisthorpe, in Burton Agnes, with a stipend of £5 a year for a master or mistress to teach the children of Barmston reading and their catechism free of charge. The teacher was also to be provided with a house, the maintenance of which was also a charge on Haisthorpe.[24] Some 20 children were taught in the school in 1743,[25] but by 1764 it seems to have been closed.[26] In 1818 Sir Francis Boynton, Bt., built a new school,[27] which was later evidently supported by the Boyntons, the

rector, and parents.[28] It also took children from Ulrome, and was attended by c. 30 boys and girls in 1833; 16 were counted at inspection in 1871.[29] The school was closed c. 1885, and the children later went to Lissett school.[30] The school building was demolished c. 1947, and the site used for houses.[31]

A private, boarding school for boys was opened at Barmston in the 1760s, but no more is known of it.[32]

CHARITIES FOR THE POOR. In 1726 Sir Griffith Boynton, Bt., built and endowed an almshouse in Barmston for the free accommodation of four poor men from Barmston, Burton Agnes, Haisthorpe, and Roxby (Yorks. N.R.), each of whom was also to receive £3 15s. a year. The maintenance of the house, which comprised four separate dwellings, and the payment of the stipends were charged on the manor of Haisthorpe by his will.[33] Only some of the stipends were being paid c. 1930, and later the income was distributed to the poor of Barmston with Holme's charity. In 1945 twenty people each received doles of 10s. The annual rent charge of £15 which had formerly covered the stipends was transferred from the Haisthorpe to the Burton Agnes estate, before being redeemed, apparently for £1,000, in 1947. By the 1940s three of the almshouses were rented for a total of £36 a year. A Scheme of 1954 allowed income not used for repairs to be spent on the almsmen.[34] The almshouse was sold in 1958 under a further Scheme of 1957, and the proceeds of the sale were also invested. The single-storeyed almshouse, of six bays under attics and a pantile roof, has since been converted into two houses.[35]

[14] J. Lang, *Corpus of Anglo-Saxon Sculpture*, iii. 125, 423–6, illus.   [15] *Yorks. Ch. Plate*, i. 213–14.
[16] E.R.A.O., PE/6/1–9.
[17] Aveling, *Post Reformation Catholicism*, 11.
[18] *Depositions from York Castle* (Sur. Soc. xl), 123; *Compton Census*, ed. Whiteman, 600.
[19] *Herring's Visit.* i, p. 109; B.I.H.R., V. 1764/Ret. 1, no. 41.
[20] P.R.O., RG 31/5, nos. 3864, 3947, 4311, 4454, 4462.
[21] R.D.B., 421/248/207; 834/123/102; commemoration stone on building.
[22] D. [R. J.] and S. Neave, *E.R. Chapels and Meeting Houses* (E. Yorks. Loc. Hist. Soc.), 45; notice board.
[23] B.I.H.R., TER. H. Barmston 1726.
[24] H.U.L., DDWB/25/19.
[25] *Herring's Visit.* i, p. 109.
[26] B.I.H.R., V. 1764/Ret. 1, no. 41.

[27] T. Allen, *Hist. Co. York*, i. 222.
[28] B.I.H.R., V. 1865/Ret. 1, no. 39; *Educ. of Poor Digest*, 1076; Baines, *Hist. Yorks.* ii. 152; *Educ. Enq. Abstract*, 1079; O.S. Map 6″, Yorks. CLXIII (1854 edn.).
[29] *Returns relating to Elem. Educ.* 472–3.
[30] B.I.H.R., V. 1877/Ret. 1, no. 37; V. 1900/Ret. no. 22; V. 1912–22/Ret.; V. 1931/Ret.; directories; below, Beeford, educ. (Lissett).
[31] Inf. from Mrs. A. Wastling, Barmston, 1997.
[32] *York Courant*, 29 Nov. 1768.
[33] H.U.L., DDWB/25/19; datestone.
[34] Above, manor; E.R.A.O., accession 1681; inf. from Char. Com., Liverpool, 1997; Scheme of 1954 in possession of Mr. A. Pitchfork, Barmston, 1997.
[35] R.D.B., 1093/302/226; Pevsner and Neave, *Yorks. E.R.* 274.

The income of the charity, thereafter called the Boynton Almshouses Fund, was to benefit poor men of Barmston, Burton Agnes, Haisthorpe, Roxby, or Rudston.[36] In 1962 four men received £1 10s. each and four married couples £2 10s. each, and eleven people from Barmston benefitted in 1995.[37]

Robert Winter of Bridlington by will dated 1739 bequeathed the interest on £18 to the poor of Barmston, but by the end of the 18th century the charity had become dormant,[38] and it seems later to have been lost.

John Holme, assistant curate from 1735 and rector 1760–75, bequeathed a quarter of the income on £400 of turnpike securities to the poor of Barmston, and £3 7s. 6d. a year was distributed among them c. 1820.[39] Barmston's share of the income was c. £2 in the earlier 20th century. In 1911 payments of 2s. 4d. each were made to 18 recipients, and in 1931 there were seven doles of 5s. and £1 was spent on refreshments at Christmas.[40] Since the 1940s the charity's income has been distributed with that of Boynton's almshouse charity.[41]

BEEFORD

THE large, irregularly-shaped parish of Beeford comprises the village, which is c. 10 km. ESE. of Driffield and 5 km. west of the coast at Skipsea, the hamlet of Dunnington, some 3 km. south-east of the village, and that of Lissett, 4 km. NNE. of Beeford.[42] Beeford is a large village with many of its residents working in nearby towns but the other settlements are very small. The names are Anglian, Beeford alluding to the proximity of a ford, Dunnington, which was Dodinton in 1086 and later Dudinton, meaning 'Dudda's farm', and Lissett probably signifying 'the dwelling near pastureland'.[43]

In 1851 the ecclesiastical parish of Beeford contained 5,747 a. (2,325.8 ha.), of which 3,753 a. (1,518.8 ha.) were in Beeford township, later civil parish, 1,150 a. (465.4 ha.) in that of Lissett, and 844 a. (341.6 ha.) in Dunnington township.[44] In 1935 Beeford civil parish was combined with that of Gembling, in Foston on the Wolds, to form a new civil parish of Beeford with an area of 4,990 a. (2,019.5 ha.). Lissett civil parish was then added to the whole of Ulrome and part of Barmston to form a new civil parish of Ulrome, while Dunnington was combined with Bewholme and Nunkeeling civil parish and that of Bonwick, in Skipsea, as Bewholme civil parish.[45] In 1953 Gembling was transferred to Foston civil parish, leaving Beeford with 3,754 a. (1,519 ha.).[46]

In 1377 there were 162 poll-tax payers at Beeford, 83 at Dunnington with Bonwick, and 84 at Lissett with Little Kelk.[47] At Beeford 63 houses were assessed for hearth tax and 20 discharged in 1672; Lissett then had 17 houses and Dunnnington and Bonwick 12 between them.[48] In 1743 there were said to be 76 families in the parish, that figure possibly including the 13 then returned for Lissett chapelry.[49] The parish had 80 families in 1764.[50] From 378 in 1801 the population of Beeford township rose sharply in the earlier 19th century to 731 in 1831 and 808 in 1851 and 1861; thereafter numbers declined to 648 in 1901, 582 in 1931, and 543 in 1961, before growth was resumed. By 1971 the village had 639 inhabitants and in 1991 there were 874 residents, 845 of whom were then counted.[51]

At Lissett the population fell from 122 in 1801 to 94 in 1811 but then grew, particularly in the 1830s, to stand at 132 in 1841, before declining to 90 in 1881; there were still only 95 there in 1931. From 67 in 1801 the population of Dunnington fluctuated upwards to 86 in 1861 and 98 in 1891; numbers thereafter fell and in 1931 there were only 55 inhabitants.[52]

In Dunnington and the south-east corner of Beeford township most of the land exceeds 15 m. above sea level and a little 23 m.; to the west and north the land shelves down to c. 10 m. at Beeford village and c. 6 m. in the north of Beeford township and in Lissett. Apart from alluvium in the valleys of the main drains and scattered deposits of sand and gravel, on one of which Lissett hamlet was sited, the parish is on boulder clay.[53] The commonable lands of Dunnington were inclosed in the later 17th century and those of Beeford village and Lissett in 1768 and 1772 respectively.

The parish drains westwards into the valley of the river Hull and eastwards to the North Sea. One of the seabound streams, running along the northern boundary of Lissett, was very probably improved long before 1353, when it was called Earl dike.[54] Formerly much water was carried to the river Hull by a stream known by 1768 as Old Howe,[55] which flowed from Skipsea parish along the northern and western boundaries of Beeford township.[56] It was fed by a drain flowing southwards along the eastern boundary of Lissett which was in disrepair in 1367[57] and

36 Scheme in possession of Mr. Pitchfork.
37 Inf. from Mr. Pitchfork.
38 9th Rep. Com. Char. 754.
39 Ibid. 754, 756; B.I.H.R., TER. H. Barmston 1809; Poulson, Holderness, i. 212–13; above, church.
40 E.R.A.O., accession 1681.
41 Above, this section; Review of Char. Rep. 138; inf. from Mr. Pitchfork.
42 This article was written in 1995–6.
43 P.N. Yorks. E.R. (E.P.N.S.), 76–7.
44 O.S. Map 6″, Yorks. CLXII, CLXIII, CLXXIX, CLXXX (1854–5 edn.).
45 Census, 1931 (pt. ii); below, Nunkeeling, intro.; Skip-

sea, intro.
46 Census, 1961–91.
47 P.R.O., E 179/202/60, mm. 43, 83, 87.
48 Ibid. E 179/205/504.
49 Herring's Visit. i, p. 108; ii, p. 163.
50 B.I.H.R., V. 1764/Ret. 1, no. 51.
51 V.C.H. Yorks. iii. 495; Census, 1911–91.
52 V.C.H. Yorks. iii. 495; Census, 1911–31.
53 Geol. Surv. Map 1″, drift, sheets 64–5 (1909 edn.).
54 H.U.L., DDWB/20/10; O.S. Map 6″, Yorks. CLXII (1854 edn.).
55 R.D.B., AK/57/6.
56 T. Jefferys, Map of Yorks. (1772).
57 Poulson, Holderness, i. 120.

by streams in Beeford township. One of the latter skirted the south side of Beeford village and another, flowing from Dunnington, passed through its east end as Beeford beck.[58] The drainage as described at inclosure in 1768[59] was altered under the Beverley and Barmston Drainage Act of 1798.[60] Much of the water carried by Old Howe drain was then made to flow in the contrary direction towards the sea at Barmston through the Lissett boundary drain, a barrier being made in Beeford to separate the truncated Old Howe and the 'new' drain, later Barmston Main drain. The works probably also included the improvement of the sea drain's tributories, among them Earl dike, sometimes called Gransmoor drain.[61] The water which continued to pass through Old Howe drain was, moreover, separated from that of its tributary streams, improved as Pitwherry, Inholms, Braemar, and Sedgemire drains, by the construction of side drains in North Frodingham. Pitwherry drain was a new drain made to carry the water of the stream from Dunnington to a new junction with Old Howe.[62] By the drainage award of 1811 the owners of 269 a. in Beeford were to support the works of the part of the Beverley and Barmston level draining southwards, and 170 a. there and 225 a. at Lissett were similarly assessed to the sea part.[63] The drainage of the rest of the parish remained the responsibilty of the Court of Sewers.[64] Other drains have included one near Moor grange, recorded c. 1230, when its maintenance was the responsibility of Meaux abbey and Nunkeeling priory.[65]

Side lanes leading north to Lissett and south to Brandesburton from the east end of Beeford village later became part of the main Bridlington to Beverley and Hull road. The main road was straightened and diverted away from Lissett hamlet c. 1925 and further improved there c. 1970.[66] The road is carried over Barmston Main drain on the Lissett–Beeford boundary by Lissett bridge, which was rebuilt in 1774, 1929–30, and 1961,[67] and on the Lissett–Ulrome boundary by Lissett New bridge, built in 1924 with the new stretch of road. Near Lissett New bridge part of the replaced main road crosses the drain by Fisher bridge, named in 1590 and rebuilt in 1913[68] and later. Sandwath, or Hull, bridge, described in the late 12th century as in Beeford marsh,[69] is perhaps to be identified with Lissett bridge. Minor roads lead from Beeford

village east to Dringhoe and Skipsea, north to Foston on the Wolds, and south-west to North Frodingham, and others connect Dunnington to the main road and Lissett to Gransmoor, in Burton Agnes. There was formerly a road from Lissett to Gembling.[70] Several roads were given new courses or straightened at inclosure in 1768, ridge and furrow in the verges of the Dunnington road testifying still to its creation in the 1760s.[71] Beeford was connected by omnibus with Beverley, Bridlington, Driffield, and Hornsea from the late 19th century, and there was a service to Hull by 1925.[72]

BEEFORD village extends east-west across the middle of the township for almost its whole width. Most of the buildings lie on or behind a single street, which is crossed near its east end by the main Hull and Beverley to Bridlington road. The eastern part of the main street almost certainly followed a more northerly course until inclosure in 1768, when extensions of the street, later Green and Dringhoe Lanes, were awarded on either side of the Beverley road.[73] The former course of the street would seem to be represented by Church Lane, Breeze Lane, named in the 17th century,[74] and a lane to Crow Garth, in Skipsea, which was discontinued in 1768 and later bordered by former house sites and land called Old Garths.[75] South of the church the village street formerly crossed or skirted a green,[76] and Main Street is still bordered by grass verges. A side lane leading north from the street towards Lissett was formerly called Water Lane, after the beck there;[77] with the southern lane opposite, it has since been incorporated into the main road.

In the mid and late 20th century many new houses were built in gaps in the village street and in small estates behind it, and many of the older houses were remodelled. There was also development alongside the main road, where the new houses included a dozen built by Driffield rural district council.[78] A telephone exchange had been added by 1956, and sewage pumping stations for the new housing were built c. 1960.[79] The older buildings of the largely brick-built village date from the 18th and 19th centuries. They include the single-storeyed Cottage, Bridlington Road, mainly 19th-century but incorporating one of the few surviving mud-walled houses in Holderness, probably of the 18th century. Also 18th-century are the brick and pantile

[58] O.S. Map 6″, Yorks. CLXXIX (1854 edn.).
[59] R.D.B., AK/57/6; E.R.A.O., IA. Beeford. The undated plan evidently incorporates later changes and differs from the award.
[60] 38 Geo. III, c. 63 (Local and Personal).
[61] E.R.A.O., DDBD/89/4; J. A. Sheppard, *Draining of Hull Valley* (E. Yorks. Loc. Hist. Ser. viii), 15–16.
[62] T. Jefferys, *Map of Yorks.* (1772); O.S. Map 1/10,560, TA 15 NW., SW. (1956 edn.); below, N. Frodingham, intro.
[63] E.R.A.O., DCBB/4/2, 8.
[64] e.g. ibid. CSR/31/199.
[65] *Chron. de Melsa* (Rolls Ser.), i. 424.
[66] R.D.B., 281/194/163; 1651/271/216.
[67] Datestone (weathered) on bridge (transcribed at E.R.A.O., PE/114/7); E.R.A.O., Bridges reg. 2, bridge 108.
[68] H.U.L., DWB/1/3; E.R.A.O., Bridges reg. 2, bridge 109; dates on bridges; O.S. Map 1/10,560, TA 15 NW.

(1956 edn.).
[69] *Brid. Chart.* 163; *Chron. de Melsa*, i. 225.
[70] R.D.B., AN/391/27; E.R.A.O., DDX/674.
[71] R.D.B., AK/57/6.
[72] Directories.
[73] This account based on R.D.B., AK/57/6; E.R.A.O., IA. Beeford; O.S. Map 6″, Yorks. CLXXIX, CLXXX (1854–5 edn.).
[74] E.R.A.O., DDX/24/12; P.R.O., C 60/524, no. 6; R.D.B., AO/264/418.
[75] Poulson, *Holderness*, i. 257.
[76] B.I.H.R., TER. H Beeford 1743; below, local govt.
[77] R.D.B., AK/57/6; O.S. Map 6″, Yorks. CLXXIX (1854 edn.).
[78] R.D.B., 522/402/313.
[79] Ibid. 1195/549/485; 1222/14/13; O.S. Map 1/10,560, TA 15 SW. (1956 edn.).

Alton and Town Farms and their barns. The older part of Alton Farm is single-storeyed with a central lobby entrance and a spiral chimney stack. The main block of Town Farm has two storeys with attics and the street range of its L-shaped barns is also of two storeys.[80] Boulder construction in the village is found mostly in the walls of outbuildings but also in Ivy House, dated 1823. In 1996 the remains of a pump survived at the intersection of the street and the main road.

There were up to four alehouses at Beeford in the later 18th century. In 1823 the Ship, the Tiger, and the Black Swan were named, and in the 1840s there were besides three unnamed beerhouses. The Ship was closed after 1937 and the house demolished in 1996. The Black Swan was rebuilt in the earlier 20th century and had been renamed the Yorkshire Rose by 1996, when the Tiger, also standing beside the main road, still traded.[81] A lodge of the Ancient Order of Foresters was founded in 1838 and recorded until 1851. Beeford Friendly Society, founded in 1865, was meeting at the Tiger in 1892; it was perhaps the sick benefit club which held an annual feast day, including a church service, sports, and an evening dance, c. 1930.[82] A former school building at Beeford was bought in 1884 by Catherine Blanche Trevor, the rector's daughter, for a hall and reading room associated with the Church of England Temperance Society. Billiards and other games were later provided there but interest had waned by the 1920s, when the village men were said to go instead to the neighbouring towns for entertainment. The building later became St. Leonard's Church Rooms.[83] The lack of meeting places in the parish was remedied by the use of the schools at Beeford and Lissett for social events in the earlier 20th century.[84] The village had a cricket club in 1931, [85] and playing fields, including areas for bowls and tennis and a children's playground, were later provided on 7 a. north of Main Street, bought in 1949.[86] Beeford Community Centre, built on the other side of the street, was opened in 1989.[87] Among youth groups at Beeford was a girls' club which functioned in the mid 20th century.[88]

A field of 17 a. had been divided into 68 allotment gardens for labourers by 1867, when each garden was let at 8s. 6d. a year,[89] and by the 1890s the Pricketts, the chief landowners, had extended the scheme by setting aside 48 a. of pasture and 36 a. of arable land for letting as ½-a. or 1-a. holdings. The allotment gardens then comprised Hunger Hills, Pannierman Hills, and the 18-a. Spring Gardens.[90] Beeford parish council later administered the smallholdings and allotment gardens, which covered 107 a. in 1914 and 38 a. in 1936.[91] A few allotments remained in Spring Gardens in 1996.[92]

OUTLYING BUILDINGS include several farmhouses put up on land inclosed in 1768.[93] Moorgate House or Cottage may have existed by 1772,[94] Woodhouse Farm, of brick and pantile with stone dressings, is late 18th century,[95] and Rectory Farm was built in 1819.[96] Other post-inclosure farmhouses were Beeford Grange,[97] Northpasture Farm, Westfield Farm, Inholms Farm, and Pinderhill Farm, all built by 1829,[98] and Breeze House, Syke Farm, and Wisefield Farm, added by 1851.[99] Another farmhouse, Moor Grange, was rebuilt in 1813 beside the moated site of an earlier house.[1] Some farmhouses have been rebuilt or replaced in the 20th century. Gas pumping stations stood beside the Frodingham and Dunnington roads in 1996.

LISSETT hamlet stood along both sides of a north-south street, which later formed part of the main Hull and Beverley to Bridlington road until the by-pass was made in the 1920s.[2] By the mid 19th century, when there were 20 houses, one or two buildings, including the newly-built school, also stood in side lanes, called Fisher Lane[3] and Tythe Lane. Later infilling has included the building in the mid 20th century of eight council houses in and off Main Street and four more on the southern side of the new main road.[4] A sewage pumping station was built near the Barmston Main Drain at Lissett in the 1960s.[5] In 1996 the c. 35 houses almost all dated from the 19th and 20th centuries. They included one or two farmhouses but only Manor Farm, which may be 17th-century,[6] was noteworthy. Two cottages in Fisher Lane were perhaps among those built by Joseph Dent soon after his purchase of the manor in 1836.[7] There is boulder walling in the remodelled Old Shop, Main Street, and in a farmyard opposite.

There were one or two licensed houses at Lissett in the later 18th century, and the Board,

[80] Pevsner and Neave, Yorks. E.R. 275; Dept. of Environment, Buildings List (1985).
[81] E.R.A.O., QDT/2/6, 9; directories; O.S. Map 6", Yorks. CLXXIX (1854 edn.).
[82] B.I.H.R., V. 1931/Ret.; Bulmer, Dir. E. Yorks. (1892), 107; D. [R. J.] Neave, E.R. Friendly Soc. (E. Yorks. Loc. Hist. Ser. xli), 42.
[83] E.R.A.O., PE/114/72, 82–5; B.I.H.R., V. 1931/Ret.; below, educ.; O.S. Map 1/2,500, Yorks. CLXXIX. 4 (1892 edn.).
[84] B.I.H.R., V. 1912–22/Ret.; V. 1931/Ret.
[85] Ibid. V. 1931/Ret.
[86] R.D.B., 810/557/453; 810/558/454.
[87] Inf. from Mrs. J. Dawson, Beeford, 1996.
[88] E.R. Educ. Cttee. Mins. 1951–2, 191.
[89] 1st Rep. Com. on Employment of Children, Young Persons, and Women in Agric., App. Pt. II [4068–I], p. 369, H.C. (1867–8), xvii.
[90] Bulmer, Dir. E. Yorks. 104; O.S. Map 1/2,500, Yorks. CLXXIX. 4 (1892 edn.).

[91] R.D.B., 165/202/172; 543/117/94.
[92] Inf. from Mr. J. Welburn, Beeford, 1996.
[93] E.R.A.O., IA. Beeford.
[94] T. Jefferys, Map of Yorks. (1772); A. Bryant, Map of E.R. Yorks. (1829); O.S. Map 6", Yorks. CLXXIX (1854 edn.).
[95] Dept. of Environment, Buildings List (1985).
[96] Below, church [glebe].
[97] Pevsner and Neave, Yorks. E.R. 275.
[98] H. Teesdale, Map of Yorks. (1828); A. Bryant, Map of E.R. Yorks. (1829).
[99] O.S. Map 6", Yorks. CLXXIX (1854 edn.).
[1] Below, manors (Moor Grange).
[2] Above, this section.
[3] P.R.O., HO 107/2367; O.S. Map 6", Yorks. CLXIII (1854 edn.); below, educ.
[4] R.D.B., 599/405/332; 895/193/156; 1149/380/345.
[5] Ibid. 1411/308/275.
[6] Below, manors (Lissett).
[7] Poulson, Holderness, i. 262.

named in 1823, traded until the mid century.[8] A former airfield building served as a village hall c. 1950.[9]

OUTLYING BUILDINGS at Lissett included Tithe Farm, built in 1804,[10] until the Second World War, when much of Lissett was taken over for an airfield.[11] Lissett was opened as a relief landing ground for Catfoss airfield, in Sigglesthorne, in 1942, became a bomber airfield for 158 Squadron in 1943, and was closed in 1945.[12] The disused airfield, of c. 560 a., was sold in 1962.[13] Most of the land has been returned to agriculture but some of the buildings were used industrially in 1996.[14]

DUNNINGTON hamlet stands mostly on the eastern side of the deeply-incised stream which flows north to Beeford village. The settlement was probably once larger, and in 1840 there was said to be evidence of earlier buildings close to the manor house.[15] There were 15 houses in 1851[16] and 9 in 1996. The hamlet was rebuilt in brick in the 19th and 20th centuries, and its buildings, loosely strung along a lane bordered near Dunnington Manor and Dunnington House by clumps of mature trees, include four farmhouses and one or two 'estate' houses. Lodge Farm has a cobble-built, garden wall. Near the northern boundary, isolated from the rest of the houses, stands Dunnington Grange.[17]

An alehouse was recorded at Dunnington in the 1750s.[18]

MANORS AND OTHER ESTATES. In 1066 Ulf had *BEEFORD* manor, comprising 12½ carucates there and 13 carucates and 2 bovates of sokeland in Dunnington, Nunkeeling, and Winkton, in Barmston. By 1086 the manor had passed to Drew de Bevrère,[19] and it was later part of the Aumale fee. Beeford manor comprised over 3,000 a. in the mid 19th century.[20]

In the 12th century Ernald de Montbegon held 6 carucates of the Aumale fee at Beeford and 6 carucates more at Dunnington. His service for the estate was given by a count of Aumale to the Knights Templar, to whom Ernald later granted the land at Beeford for quittance of service at Dunnington.[21] The grant is said to have been made before 1185 and to have included a

chief house and 1 carucate and 4 bovates, possibly Ernald's demesne holding.[22] On the suppression of the Templars in 1312,[23] their estate was transferred to the Knights Hospitaller, who were returned as one of the two lords of Beeford in 1316[24] and retained their manor there until they too were suppressed in the 16th century.[25] In 1544 the Crown granted the order's former estate, as *BEEFORD* manor, to John Bellow and others, who were then licensed to sell it to Richard Empringham.[26] An attempt made in 1558 to restore the estate, including premises at Dunnington, to the Hospitallers at their refoundation[27] had little effect. Possibly in error, Thomas Empringham was said to have the manor in 1558,[28] but Richard Empringham was the tenant at his death in 1559. Then held of the Crown as ¹⁄₂₀ or ¹⁄₂₈ knight's fee, it descended to Richard's son Michael (d. 1578) and grandson Michael.[29] In 1598 Michael Empringham sold the manor to William Green[30] (d. 1600), who was succeeded by his brother Thomas; it then comprised 22 houses and almost 2 carucates.[31] Thomas's son James Green may have had the manor before William Shercliffe, who divided and sold the estate between 1613 and 1616; the manor was bought by Thomas Naylor in 1613–14.[32] Naylor (d. 1627) left the manorial rights to his son Edmund (fl. 1641) and houses and lands at Beeford to each of his other sons, Matthew and Richard; some of the land may have belonged to Naylor's other estate at Beeford.[33] In the mid 17th century the manor once belonging to the Hospitallers was called *ST. JOHN'S* or the *FRANCHISE FEE*, the latter probably because of the testamentary jurisdiction which had descended from the order with that manor. Another manor, then known as the *LAY FEE*, may have been that held by the Creswells; by 1658 it perhaps formed part of the Naylors' estate, and it was certainly later held with the Franchise Fee by the Naylors' successors, the Acklams.[34] A manor of Beeford was sold by Joshua Naylor in 1689 to Peter Acklam, described in 1693 as lord,[35] and his brother Thomas. In 1716 Peter bought 6 bovates and other land at Beeford, and by 1721 he had evidently succeeded Thomas and held a large estate there and at Dringhoe, in Skipsea. In 1724 Peter, as the surviving purchaser, released the manor bought from Naylor to Thomas's son Thomas.[36] The last Thomas (fl. 1750) was suc-

8   E.R.A.O., QDT/2/6, 9; R.D.B., FE/163/155; P.R.O., HO 107/2367; White, *Dir. E. & N. R. Yorks.* (1840), 276; White, *Dir. Hull & York* (1846), 371.
9   R.D.B., 1252/91/83.
10   O.S. Map 6″, Yorks. CLXII (1854 edn.); below, church [tithes].
11   R.D.B., 655/58/46; 824/567/486.
12   B. B. Halpenny, *Action Stations 4: Military Airfields of Yorks.* 131–9.
13   R.D.B., 1252/91/83; 1252/553/499.
14   Below, econ. hist.   15   Poulson, *Holderness*, i. 263.
16   P.R.O., HO 107/2365.
17   Below, manors (Dunnington).
18   E.R.A.O., QDT/2/9.   19   *V.C.H. Yorks.* ii. 267.
20   H.U.L., DDCV/9/10.
21   *Chron. de Melsa* (Rolls Ser.), i. 162; *E.Y.C.* iii., p. 74.
22   Poulson, *Holderness*, i. 246, 248.
23   *V.C.H. Yorks.* iii. 256.
24   *Feud. Aids*, vi. 162.

25   *Cal. Pat.* 1338–40, 125; *Cal. Inq. p.m.* ix, p. 85; *Cal. Inq. p.m. Hen. VII*, iii, pp. 65–6.
26   *L. & P. Hen. VIII*, xix (2), pp. 81, 87.
27   *Cal. Pat.* 1557–8, 318, 321.
28   P.R.O., C 142/111, no. 58.
29   Ibid. C 142/120, no. 79; C 142/182, no. 21.
30   *Yorks. Fines*, iv. 96.
31   P.R.O., C 142/268, no. 133.
32   *Yorks. Fines, 1603–14*, 220; *1614–25*, 3, 7, 65.
33   E.R.A.O., DDX/24/4, 8–10; DDX/152/9; P.R.O., C 142/431, no. 93; C 142/553, no. 49; C 60/524, no. 6; below, this section (Crow grange).
34   P.R.O., C 142/431, no. 93; E.R.A.O., DDX/24/11; R.D.B., H/41/90; below, local govt.; below, this section [Creswell].
35   E.R.A.O., DDX/24/27, A.1.
36   R.D.B., D/401/674; H/41/90; H/679/1382; I/8/12; Poulson, *Holderness*, i. 245. Below, this section (Crow grange); below, Skipsea, manors (Dringhoe).

ceeded by his son Thomas, who was lord of the Franchise Fee manor, and presumably also the Lay Fee, by 1760.[37] He was followed in turn by his sons, Thomas, a minor in 1768,[38] and Peter, lord from 1771.[39] Peter Acklam had c. 650 a. at Beeford in five farms in 1777[40] and bought another farm, of 125 a., in 1802.[41] He (d. by 1805) was succeeded by his son Peter[42] (d. c. 1825), whose trustees sold the manors with c. 550 a., mostly in three farms, to Marmaduke Prickett in 1828.[43] The Pricketts had had a small estate at Beeford in 1768, and before Marmaduke's death in 1837 that had been enlarged to become the 556-a. Beeford Grange farm. Prickett's son Thomas thus succeeded to c. 1,100 a. of Beeford.[44] After Thomas Prickett's death in 1885,[45] the estate was held in undivided shares by members of the Prickett family[46] until its sale in lots in 1914.

T. D. Reed and his brother George bought 874 a., mostly in Beeford Grange and Woodhouse farms, in 1914. George (d. 1923) was evidently succeeded in his share by T. D. Reed (d. 1927), whose widow Alice conveyed the farms in 1935 to their son Charles (d. 1977). In 1996 the farms, managed as C. C. Reed and Co. Ltd., were occupied by Mr. Reed's daughter Diana and her husband David Blanchard.[47]

F. R. Wharram, his wife Jane, and R. S. Wharram bought the 254-a. Manor farm in 1914. After the deaths of Francis and Jane Wharram, R. S. Wharram conveyed the farm to his daughter Mary and her husband J. W. P. Curtis in 1954,[48] and the Curtis family still occupied it in 1994.[49] The farmhouse was rebuilt in the earlier 19th century and by 1851 was called Manor House.[50]

Another part of the Aumale fee at Beeford was held by the Goxhill family. The overlordship of the successors of the counts of Aumale was recorded until 1593.[51] Ralph of Goxhill gave ½ carucate there to Bridlington priory before 1154,[52] and it was presumably another Ralph who was recorded in the late 12th century.[53] Sir Ralph of Goxhill, who bought land at Beeford

c. 1230,[54] was probably succeeded by his brother Giles of Goxhill.[55] From Giles's son Peter of Goxhill (fl. by 1241)[56] the 3 or 4-carucate estate at Beeford descended c. 1280 to his son Ralph[57] and from Ralph (d. by 1294) to his daughter Margaret.[58] Margaret, wife of Philip le Despenser (d. 1313) and John de Ros, Lord Ros of Watton (d. 1338),[59] died in July 1349 and was succeeded in the Goxhills' holdings at Beeford and Dunnington by her son Sir Philip Despenser (d. Aug. 1349) and then by Philip's son Philip Despenser, Lord Despenser of Goxhill (d. 1401). In the mid 14th century the Beeford estate was said to comprise 6 carucates, held as ⅛ knight's fee.[60]

The Goxhills' estate at Beeford was occupied by the family's free tenants,[61] one of the holdings probably having originated in a grant to a junior member of the Goxhill family. John of Goxhill (d. by 1301) was succeeded by his brother Peter in an estate comprising a chief house and c. 1 carucate at Beeford, held as ¼₈ knight's fee of Peter of Goxhill's heir.[62] In the 1340s land at Beeford was held of John of Goxhill,[63] and another John Goxhill of Beeford was a tax commissioner in 1413.[64] Robert Goxhill (d. 1529), grandson of another Robert, was succeeded in the estate at Beeford by his son Henry (d. 1550), whose heirs were his daughters Joan and Gertrude, minors; in 1550 besides the chief house, the carucate, and other land, then said to be held directly of the lord of the Aumale fee as ¼₀ knight's fee, the estate included a further 8½ bovates, of which 2½ were held of the Crown's manor of Beeford as a former possession of Meaux abbey.[65]

Joan Goxhill probably married James Dolman, who, with his wife Joan, sold the Goxhills' estate, then including 11 houses and extending into Dunnington, as a manor of *BEEFORD* to George Creswell in 1579.[66] At Creswell's death in 1592 his estate at Beeford included just over 2 carucates. He was succeeded by his son Ralph,[67] who divided and sold all or much of his estate at Beeford and Dunnington between 1620 and 1623. Purchases included houses and land

[37] H.U.L., DDCV/10/1, 3; R.D.B., U/188/351.
[38] R.D.B., AK/57/6.
[39] Ibid. BD/575/937; BF/219/367; H.U.L., DDCV/10/1, 7.
[40] R.D.B., AT/395/42.
[41] Ibid. CE/475/700.
[42] Ibid. CF/305/492; CH/137/213.
[43] Ibid. ED/153/174; E.R.A.O., DDRI/44/21; H.U.L., DDCV/9/10.
[44] R.D.B., AK/57/6; FD/348/385; directories. For the fam., F. F. Prickett, *Pricketts of Allerthorpe*.
[45] R.D.B., 5/383/370 (1885).
[46] Ibid. KT/111/156; 13/449/425 (1886); 50/37/37 (1902).
[47] Ibid. 165/202/172; 282/177/151; 446/527/425; 448/535/421; 543/115/93; 1774/588/482; inf. from Mr. D. M. Blanchard, Beeford, 1996.
[48] R.D.B., 165/204/173; 897/205/158; 967/123/106; below, Skipsea, manors [Watton priory].
[49] *Reg. of Electors* (1994).
[50] O.S. Map 6″, Yorks. CLXXIX (1854 edn.).
[51] P.R.O., C 142/234, no. 20; *Cal. Inq. p.m.* ix, pp. 192, 194; *Cal. Pat.* 1550-3, 176.
[52] *Brid. Chart.* 2-3; *E.Y.C* iii, pp. 34-5.
[53] *Brid. Chart.* 163; *Chron. de Melsa* (Rolls Ser.), i. 225.
[54] *Chron. de Melsa*, i. 167, 424.
[55] Giles appears under Seaton, in Sigglesthorne, in the

apparently faulty list of fees of the mid 13th century in *Kirkby's Inquest*, 373.
[56] *Brid. Chart.* 343.
[57] Ibid. 326; *Feud. Aids*, vi. 40; *Cal. Inq. p.m.* iv, p. 353; *Cal. Gen.* (Rolls Ser.), i. 370.
[58] *Cal. Inq. p.m.* iii, p. 136; iv, pp. 2-3.
[59] *Complete Peerage*, s.v. Ros.
[60] *Cal. Inq. p.m.* ix, pp. 192, 194; *Complete Peerage*, s.v. Despenser; below, this section (Dunnington). A 15th-century source suggests a much smaller estate at Beeford: P.R.O., SC 6/1077/15; cf. for identification of estate, *Miscellanea*, iv (Y.A.S. Rec. Ser. xciv), 98.
[61] *Cal. Inq. p.m.* iv, p. 353; ix, pp. 192, 194.
[62] Ibid. iv, pp. 2-3. Peter was perhaps Sir Ralph of Goxhill's son Peter, who occurs in 1303: below, this section [Newsham abbey].
[63] *Cal. Inq. p.m.* viii, pp. 258-9; ix, p. 85.
[64] *Cal. Fine R.* 1413-22, 26.
[65] P.R.O., C 142/50, no. 143; C 60/359, no. 7; H.U.L., DHO/7/34; *Cal. Pat.* 1550-3, 176. The Goxhills held some land of the Hospitallers: *Miscellanea*, iv (Y.A.S. Rec. Ser. xciv), 95.
[66] *Yorks. Fines*, ii. 143. For the identification of the estate cf. P.R.O., C 142/234, no. 20; *Cal. Pat.* 1550-3, 176.
[67] P.R.O., C 142/234, no. 20.

at Beeford bought in 1620 by George Acklam, Beeford manor bought by Edward and John Nelthorpe in 1622, and houses and land at Beeford and Dunnington purchased by Ralph Brigham and Anthony Nevill in 1623.[68] The later history of the estate is unknown, but part may have passed to the Acklams.[69]

Between 1160 and 1182 Meaux abbey was given almost ½ carucate on Beeford moor by Osbert of Frismarsh, and a grange had been established there by 1172.[70] Moor grange was later enlarged by grant, purchase, and exchange.[71] A grant of free warren there was received in 1293,[72] and the manor of *MOOR GRANGE* was recorded in the mid 14th century.[73] In 1545 the Crown granted Moor grange to Sir Ralph Ellerker and his male heirs.[74] Ellerker (d. 1546) was succeeded by his son Sir Ralph (d. 1558),[75] and the estate evidently later descended like the Ellerkers' manor of Risby, in Rowley.[76] Ralph Ellerker, a younger son, was dealing with the estate in 1656 and 1676, possibly as trustee for his nephew John Ellerker (d. 1676).[77] Also in 1676 the entail on the estate was removed by an enlarging grant from the Crown,[78] and Moor Grange farm later passed, with Risby, through a daughter to Ellerker Bradshaw (d. 1742) and then to the Mainwaring Ellerkers. Eaton Mainwaring Ellerker received 217 a. at the inclosure of Beeford in 1768.[79] In 1789 the three sisters of Roger M. Ellerker (d. 1775) and the former husband of the fourth sister and co-heir sold Moor Grange with 447 a. and nearly 450 a. across the boundary at Moor Town, in Brandesburton, to George Wood. Later Sir George Wood, he bought c. 315 a. more in 1802 and 1803, and the estate was also enlarged with 120 a. purchased by Thomas Wood in 1810.[80] Sir George (d. 1824) left the entire estate in Beeford, Brandesburton, and North Frodingham to his nephew John Stocks (d. 1872). In 1874 Stocks's trustees sold Moor Grange and Pinderhill farms with 654 a. in Beeford and 38 a. in North Frodingham to John Hotham, Baron Hotham (d. 1907), and the trustees of the Hotham family.[81] Frederick Hotham, Baron Hotham, sold the farms in 1910 to Thomas Broumpton (d. 1915), who was succeeded by Francis Broumpton. St. Andrew's Steam Fishing Co. Ltd. bought the

estate in 1948 and sold Moor Grange farm with 484 a. to J. A. Smith Stafford in 1953.[82] Some land had been sold by 1984, when J. D. T. Megginson bought the house and 268 a. and Nigel Robinson the remaining 138 a.[83] The farmhouse was sold to Gregory Atkin in 1988.[84]

In the Middle Ages Moor Grange farmhouse presumably occupied the moated site which remained there in 1996, but evidently long before the 19th century it was removed to a site outside the moat. In 1813 the existing house was demolished and a new one built by Sir George Wood.[85]

Besides Moor grange, Meaux abbey established another farm at Beeford. Roger of Grimsby had sold ½ carucate to the abbey before 1197, and other parts of his holding, which included mills and extended into Dringhoe, in Skipsea, had been granted to Meaux by 1241 and were used about that date as the site for a grange. Half a carucate at Beeford, presumably Roger of Grimsby's, and 6 bovates at Dringhoe were assigned to the grange, the buildings of which were put up just across the boundary in Dringhoe. The farm was surrounded by many trees and was said to have taken its name Crow grange, occasionally *CROW* manor, from the birds there; later in the Middle Ages a tenant was allowed to cut down the trees expressly to get rid of crows.[86] In 1570–1, after the Dissolution, the Crown granted Crow grange in fee farm to Henry Scrope, Lord Scrope, and he or a succeeding Lord Scrope is said to have sold it to Robert Naylor. Thomas Naylor (d. 1627) was described as of that place,[87] and it was included in Joshua Naylor's sale of Beeford manor to Peter Acklam and his brother Thomas in 1689. Thomas was probably dead by 1721, and in 1724 Peter conveyed Crow Grange farm, with Beeford manor, to Thomas's son Thomas.[88] It evidently later descended with the manor. In 1786 Peter Acklam, grandson of Thomas (fl. 1724), sold Crow Grange farm, with c. 150 a. in Beeford and 13 a. in Dringhoe, and 63 a. more in Beeford to William Jarratt.[89] Jarratt died in or soon after 1823 and Crow Grange was later held in undivided shares by his heirs[90] until 1835, when they sold it to William Crooke and his brother John.[91] In 1842 William Crooke con-

68 *Yorks. Fines, 1614–25*, 153–4, 158, 161, 188, 229; below, this section (Dunnington). For Acklam's estate, *Yorks. Royalist Composition Papers,* iii (Y.A.S. Rec. Ser. xx), p. 75.
69 Above, this section (Lay Fee).
70 *Chron. de Melsa* (Rolls Ser.), i. 163–4; *E.Y.C.* iii, pp. 101–3.
71 e.g. *Chron. de Melsa,* i. 225–6, 309, 424; ii. 106.
72 *Cal. Chart. R.* 1257–1300, 427.
73 *Chron. de Melsa,* iii. 27.
74 *L. & P. Hen. VIII,* xx (1), p. 224.
75 H.U.L., DHO/7/33; P.R.O., C 142/118, no. 43.
76 *V.C.H. Yorks. E.R.* iv. 147; for the Ellerkers, Poulson, *Holderness,* i. 394–6.
77 For this and the following, H.U.L., DDCV(2)/31/41; ibid. DDHO(3)/46/15; ibid. DDKE/8/22; ibid. DDMM/27/1; *Complete Peerage,* s.v. Onslow; below, Brandesburton, manors (Moor Town).
78 P.R.O., C 66/3186, no. 24.   79 R.D.B., AK/57/6.
80 Ibid. CD/462/716; CD/503/778; CG/32/54; CM/5/6; CP/224/336; E.R.A.O., QDE/1/5/4.
81 H.U.L., DDHO(3)/46/12; DDHO(3)/46/16; *Complete*

Peerage, s.v. Hotham.
82 R.D.B., 121/288/263; 678/55/41; 793/68/58; 937/136/120.
83 Inf. from Mr. J. D. T. Megginson, Kirkburn, 1996.
84 Inf. from Mrs. G. Atkin, Beeford, 1996.
85 Datestone; Poulson, *Holderness,* i. 259; O.S. Map 6", Yorks. CLXXIX–CLXXX (1854–5 edn.); H. E. J. le Patourel, *Moated Sites of Yorks.* 114.
86 *Chron. de Melsa* (Rolls Ser.), i. 165, 224; ii. 47–9, 173; iii. 27, 100 n.; English, *Holderness,* 47. Cf. R.D.B., I/8/12. *P.N. Yorks. E.R.* 81, 127 has an alternative explanation of the name.
87 P.R.O., C 66/1080, mm. 41–end; E.R.A.O., DDX/152/1; Poulson, *Holderness,* i. 253, 263; *Complete Peerage,* s.v. Scrope of Bolton.
88 R.D.B., H/41/90; H/652/1322; H/679/1382; I/8/12; Poulson, *Holderness,* i. 245; above, this section (Beeford).
89 R.D.B., BI/436/692; BI/437/693.
90 Ibid. DT/330/360; ED/375/417; EX/234/265; E.R.A.O., QDE/1/5/4.
91 R.D.B., EZ/250/238.

veyed his moiety to John[92] (d. 1848), whose eventual heirs were his two daughters, Jane, who married Albert Iveson, and Priscilla.[93] The Crow Grange estate was later held in moieties. By 1903 it comprised 216 a. in Beeford and Skipsea parishes.[94] Mrs. Iveson's part passed eventually to her son Lancelot.[95] Priscilla Crooke probably married G. W. Harrison, and her moiety descended to Frederick Harrison (d. 1913) and his sister and heir Mabel Weatherill.[96] In 1927 Lancelot Iveson, Mrs. Weatherill, and their trustees sold Crow Grange farm to Thomas Storey.[97] Storey was succeeded in 1950 by William, Thomas, and Beatrice Storey,[98] and the family still had Crow Grange farm in 1994.[99]

Crow Grange was enlarged in 1849 by the building onto the existing house of a new three-bayed front range.[1] Ponds remain from the moat which once enclosed the grange,[2] and whale bones set up at the entrance also survive.[3]

Another part of Meaux's former estate in the parish, comprising the rents of four freeholders and five other tenants holding land at Beeford, was granted by the Crown as BEEFORD manor to John Wells and Henry Best in fee farm in 1595.[4] It was perhaps that manor which was bought by Thomas Crompton and descended to his son Thomas (fl. 1602).[5]

Ralph of Goxhill gave Bridlington priory ½ carucate at Beeford before 1154, and the priory's estate there was later enlarged by smaller gifts.[6] The estate was valued at nearly £2 10s. a year in 1535.[7] Houses and land at Beeford, formerly belonging to the priory and including 3 bovates, were let by the Crown later in the 16th century,[8] and part of its estate was mentioned again in 1745.[9]

Swine priory had been given 2 bovates and other land at Beeford by 1249[10] and retained that estate until the Dissolution.[11]

Nunkeeling priory was granted 1 bovate and other land at Beeford by Ernald de Montbegon and Thomas of Beeford, and in the earlier 13th century the house's estate there was altered by further grant and exchange with Meaux abbey.[12]

In the 16th century the priory had a toft and 1 bovate at Beeford, let for 13s. 4d. a year.[13]

Newsham abbey (Lincs.), founded by Peter of Goxhill in 1143, was given 1 bovate and other land at Beeford by Adam of Beeford before 1291. That gift was apparently confirmed by Ralph of Beeford, perhaps the same as (Sir) Ralph of Goxhill (fl. c. 1230), and in 1303 by Peter son of Sir Ralph of Goxhill.[14] The land was granted, with Newsham, to Charles Brandon, duke of Suffolk, in 1539 and later descended in his heirs.[15]

In 1235 Maud daughter of Henry quitclaimed ½ carucate and tofts in Beeford to Thornton abbey (Lincs.)[16] but no more is known of the estate.

Other estates at Beeford have included the 2 carucates of the Aumale fee which Geoffrey le Breton held in the 12th century and which was later divided among his daughters.[17] The St. Quintins held 1 carucate there in 1275–6, when the Templars occupied it under them.[18] The unidentified Richard de Cotes was returned as the other lord of Beeford in 1316.[19] Henry de Fauconberg was granted free warren there in 1324.[20] For unknown reason, c. 150 a. of Beeford were awarded as copyhold of North Frodingham manor at inclosure in 1768.[21]

The sokeland of Beeford manor included 6 carucates at Dunnington which passed with the manor from Ulf to Drew de Bevrère,[22] and later formed part of the Aumale fee.

In the 12th century a count of Aumale granted the lordship of Dunnington and part of Beeford to the Knights Templar.[23] On the suppression of the order in 1312,[24] the Templars' manor of DUNNINGTON was transferred to the Knights Hospitaller. By their suppression, the lordship passed to the Crown.[25] Two houses, 3 bovates, and other land at Dunnington, formerly belonging to the Hospitallers, were later let by the Crown, and in 1586 were granted in reversion to Sir Christopher Hatton.[26]

In the 12th century Ernald de Montbegon held all 6 carucates at Dunnington of the count of Aumale and later of the Knights Templar as

[92] Ibid. FT/232/270; B.I.H.R., TA. 327s.
[93] R.D.B., KL/41/60; B.I.H.R., Fac. Bk. 6, pp. 845–6; Sheahan and Whellan, Hist. York & E.R. ii. 403–4.
[94] R.D.B., 55/466/443 (1903).
[95] Ibid. II/38/31; KE/152/205; 44/90/67 (1891); 341/389/318.
[96] Ibid. KE/152/206; 55/466/443 (1903); 158/447/400; 161/550/473.
[97] Ibid. 341/586/467; 343/593/491; 706/411/341.
[98] Ibid. 861/127/112.
[99] Reg. of Electors (1994).
[1] Sheahan and Whellan, Hist. York & E.R. ii. 404.
[2] H. E. J. le Patourel, Moated Sites of Yorks. 111; O.S. Map 6″, Yorks. CLXXX (1855 edn.).
[3] N. Redman, 'Whalebones of E. Yorks.', pt. 2', E. Yorks. Loc. Hist. Soc. Bulletin, l. 22.
[4] E.R.A.O., PE/32/28, 32 (copy ministers' accts.); P.R.O., C 66/1435, mm. 37–46.
[5] P.R.O., CP 43/77, Carte rott. 10–11.
[6] Brid. Chart. 325, 343; Chron. de Melsa (Rolls Ser.), i. 226; E.Y.C. iii, pp. 34–5, 73–4; Cal. Inq. Misc. ii, p. 83; Cal. Close, 1318–23, 17.
[7] Valor Eccl. (Rec. Com.), v. 120.
[8] P.R.O., E 310/27/159, f. 80; E 310/30/177, f. 58.

[9] R.D.B., R/335/811.
[10] Chron. de Melsa, ii. 22; Poulson, Holderness, i. 246.
[11] Valor Eccl. v. 114; P.R.O., E 309/1/3 Eliz./5, no. 11; E 309/6/20 Eliz./20, no. 10; E 315/401, p. 379.
[12] B.L. Cott. MS. Otho C. viii, ff. 91v.–92, 95 and v.; Chron. de Melsa, i. 424.
[13] P.R.O., E 310/27/162, f. 79; Valor Eccl. v. 115.
[14] B.L. Harl. Ch. 46 D.37 and 40; Harl. Ch. 47 F.18; Harl. Ch. 50 I.2; Tax. Eccl. (Rec. Com.), 305; V.C.H. Lincs. ii. 199; above, this section [Goxhills].
[15] P.R.O., C 66/1079, mm. 28–33; L. & P. Hen. VIII, xiv (1), pp. 258–60; Complete Peerage, s.v. Monteagle.
[16] Yorks. Fines, 1232–46, p. 31.
[17] Chron. de Melsa, i. 164–7, 370.
[18] Rot. Hund. (Rec. Com.), i. 107.
[19] Feud. Aids, vi. 162.
[20] Cal. Chart. R. 1300–26, 473.
[21] R.D.B., AK/57/6.   [22] V.C.H. Yorks. ii. 267.
[23] Chron. de Melsa, i. 162; E.Y.C. iii, p. 74; above this section (Beeford).
[24] V.C.H. Yorks. iii. 256.
[25] P.R.O., C 142/314, no. 221.
[26] Ibid. E 310/29/172, f. 4; E 311/26, no. 168; C 66/1272, mm. 10–22.

the count's grantees.[27] Much of his estate passed to Ralph of Goxhill (d. by 1294), who was succeeded in 3 carucates and other land at Dunnington by his daughter Margaret.[28] The Goxhills' estate, later held of the Hospitallers and itself reckoned a manor, descended like Little Cowden in Margeret's heirs, the Despensers, and their successors, the Wentworths.[29] In 1539–40 Sir Richard Wentworth's heirs held 2½ carucates of the Hospitallers.[30] Thomas Wentworth, Lord Wentworth, sold Dunnington manor in 1556 to Walter Jobson and Thomas Dalton the younger.[31] Jobson sold his moiety to George Creswell in 1569.[32] Creswell probably also bought land formerly belonging to Meaux abbey in or soon after 1586,[33] and at his death in 1592 he held a chief house, 12 others, and 4 carucates at Dunnington under the Crown's manors of Beeford and East Greenwich. His son Ralph[34] sold part of the estate in 1623.[35] Ralph's son George Creswell (fl. 1659) devised his estate at Dunnington to his wife Catherine (d. c. 1672),[36] and they were succeeded by George's nephew John Brigham.[37] The estate, described as Dunnington manor in 1709, descended from John Brigham (d. 1710) to his son Roger and then to Roger's son William, who sold it in 1745 to Robert Bell (d. by 1759) and his son John.[38] In 1767 James Shutt, cousin and devisee of John Bell, sold Dunnington manor to William Taylor and John Garnett. They bought more land there jointly in 1771 and 1786, and Taylor bought c. 50 a. alone in 1790.[39] After Taylor's death his estate was divided into shares which were bought by Thomas Pearson (Peirson) in 1809, 1810, and 1814.[40] Garnett's heirs similarly sold their interests in 1813, 1817, and 1819 to Pearson (d. by 1819) and his trustees, Robert and George Pearson. The estate then comprised 269 a., including c. 30 a. in Beeford.[41] In 1840 it was conveyed because of George Pearson's incapacity to James Wilkinson and Thomas Richardson.[42] The beneficiary in 1856 was (the Revd.) Thomas Pearson Richardson.[43] In 1868 he, Thomas Richardson, and others conveyed the manor, then comprising 297 a. at

Dunnington and 33 a. at Beeford, to the Revd. John Richardson, who sold it to T. C. Dixon in 1869.[44] Dixon conveyed the estate in 1895 to Robert Dixon (d. 1937).[45] Muriel Dixon and the other trustees sold the chief house in 1946,[46] and in 1955 she sold Dunnington Manor farm, comprising a former hind's house used as a farmhouse and 316 a. in Dunnington and Beeford to R. J. and C. G. Kirkwood.[47] In 1996 Manor farm belonged to R. J. Kirkwood & Son.

The estate of the Goxhills and their heirs at Dunnington included a house from 1294,[48] and the house of eight hearths occupied by John Brigham in 1672 was presumably the manor house.[49] Robert Dixon's trustees sold the chief house, called Dunnington Manor, with the manor and c. 20 a., to Cyril Smith in 1946. The house was bought by Charles Longstaff and his wife in 1948;[50] it was occupied in 1977 by A. C. Longstaff and in 1995 by Robert and Wendy Flood.[51] The present house probably dates from the 18th century but was refronted and enlarged in the 19th.

It was probably another part of the Creswells' estate at Dunnington which Michael Warton (d. 1645) held and which later descended like Beverley Water Towns manor.[52] At the partition of the former Warton estates in 1775, the 312-a. farm at Dunnington fell to the share of Michael Newton (d. 1803).[53] It was sold in 1813 to James Hopkinson.[54] Hopkinson died in 1854 or 1855,[55] and the estate was divided and sold in 1856. George Ansley (d. 1879) bought Dunnington House with 157 a.[56] The farm passed to Ansley's widow Sarah (d. 1897),[57] and in 1930 the trustees of her will sold it to F. J. and J. M. Robinson (d. 1938). It was bought in 1939 by A. E. Saunders (d. 1968) and in 1970 by C. G. Kirkwood. The land was later held with Manor farm by the Kirkwoods.[58]

The second farmhouse built on his estate by James Hopkinson between 1817 and 1853 was perhaps Dunnington House.[59] The large 19th-century farmhouse and a few acres were separ-

---

27 *Chron. de Melsa*, i. 162; *E.Y.C.* iii., p. 74; above this section (Beeford).

28 *Cal. Inq. p.m.* iii, p. 136.

29 *Cal. Close*, 1313–18, 49; P.R.O., C 140/66, no. 35; *Cal. Inq. p.m.* v, pp. 266–7; ix, pp. 192, 194; xviii, p. 132; *Cal. Mem. R.* 1326–7, pp. 302–3; *Cal. Fine R.* 1319–27, 366, 383–4; P.R.O., C 142/50, no. 71; ibid. CP 25(1)/292/68, no. 164; below, Mappleton, manors.

30 *Miscellanea*, iv (Y.A.S. Rec. Ser. xciv), 98. Also P.R.O., SC 6/1077/15.

31 *Yorks. Fines*, i. 193.

32 Ibid. i. 367.

33 Below, this section.

34 P.R.O., C 142/234, no. 20; Poulson, *Holderness*, i. 263.

35 *Yorks. Fines, 1614–25*, 229.

36 E.R.A.O., DDNA/25; Poulson, *Holderness*, i. 263.

37 E.R.A.O., DDNA/28; P.R.O., CP 25(2)/896/10 Wm. III Mic. no. 21; *Visit. Yorks. 1584–5 and 1612*, ed. J. Foster, 149, 167.

38 P.R.O., CP 25(2)/985/8 Anne Mic. no. 11; Poulson, *Holderness*, ii. 269; B.I.H.R., TER. H. Beeford 1726; E.R.A.O., QDR/2/8; QDB/4, pp. 54–8; QDB/5, pp. 118–25.

39 R.D.B., AI/231/469; AO/427/678; BI/476/747; BP/323/532.

40 Ibid. CO/264/424; CO/533/819; CW/435/612.

41 Ibid. CX/524/673; DG/334/429; DG/336/430; DG/339/431.

42 Ibid. FO/66/60.

43 Sheahan and Whellan, *Hist. York & E.R.* ii. 404.

44 R.D.B., KF/380/520; KL/253/335.

45 Ibid. 73/11/10 (1895); 628/550/449; 628/552/450.

46 Below, this section.

47 R.D.B., 1021/191/159.

48 *Cal. Inq. p.m.* iii, p. 136; ix, pp. 192, 194.

49 P.R.O., E 179/205/504.

50 R.D.B., 731/155/130; 797/446/376.

51 Document in Dunnington chapel; *Reg. of Electors* (1995).

52 *Yorks. Royalist Composition Papers*, ii (Y.A.S. Rec. Ser. xviii), p. 93; *V.C.H. Yorks. E.R.* vi. 91, 210.

53 H.U.L., DDHO/48/49–50; E.R.A.O., DDHB/57/152.

54 E.R.A.O., DDBV/55/17; R.D.B., CU/23/26; CY/349/515.　55 R.D.B., HI/1/1.

56 Ibid. HM/187/206; NC/148/244; E. window, Dunnington chapel.

57 R.D.B., 1/118/110 (1898).

58 Ibid. 401/423/360; 401/424/361; 616/517/412; 629/268/200; 1651/41/39; 1655/123/117; above, this section; inf. from Mr. C. G. Kirkwood, Manor Farm, Dunnington, 1996.

59 R.D.B., DB/505/711; HC/90/121.

ated from the rest of the farm by their sale in 1970 to E. A. and A. J. Hickson.[60]

The other part of Hopkinson's estate, comprising the 159-a. Dunnington Grange farm, was bought in 1856 by Jeremiah Lamplugh.[61] Situated in the north of the township and called Collina's Cottage in 1829, Dunnington Grange may have been the chief house of the estate before the 19th century.[62] The house was evidently remodelled then and has a canted bay to the entrance front.

Between 1160 and 1182 Meaux abbey was given 1½ carucate at Dunnington by Isaac of Skeffling, and other land there by Ernald de Montbegon. The land seems to have been farmed as part of Moor grange before being let to tenants.[63] In 1581 Ralph Creswell obtained a lease from the Crown of part of the estate, and in 1586 all the abbey's estate at Dunnington, comprising 1 carucate and 3 bovates, was granted in reversion to Sir Christopher Hatton.[64] It was probably bought soon afterwards by George Creswell, who later held land in Dunnington under the Crown's manor of East Greenwich.[65]

Hawise, countess of Aumale (d. 1214), granted Fulk d'Oyry free warren in Dunnington,[66] and in 1223 he had 2 carucates there.[67] The estate evidently passed to Sir Geoffrey d'Oyry and then to Fulk's grandson Sir William Constable and his successors.[68] In 1282 William's son Sir Simon Constable settled *DUNNINGTON* manor on his son Robert and his wife,[69] and their son Sir John (d. 1349) held a house and ½ carucate there of the Hospitallers by knight service.[70] In 1542 the estate apparently included eight houses.[71] Sir John Constable sold land at Dunnington to George Creswell in 1566, and it presumably descended with the rest of Cresswell's estate there.[72]

Ernulf de Montbegon gave Thornton abbey (Lincs.) ½ carucate in Dunnington before 1190,[73] and in 1396 a rent was being paid to the abbey from Meaux abbey's estate at Dunnington.[74] No more is known of Thornton's estate.

In 1066 Ulf also held *LISSETT* manor, of 3 carucates; like the rest of his estate it passed to

Drew de Bevrère[75] and later became part of the Aumale fee.

The manor evidently passed to the Monceaux family.[76] In the late 12th century (Sir) Ingram de Monceaux acquired ½ carucate in Lissett by exchange,[77] and he was succeeded there by his son Sir Robert and Robert's widow Hawise. Their supposed son, Sir Ingram de Monceaux, held Lissett manor, comprising in 1287 an unquantified area in demesne and 3 carucates more occupied by undertenants.[78] Ingram (d. 1292) was succeeded in turn by his sons John (d. by 1297) and Thomas (d. 1345),[79] who granted the manor to his son (Sir) John and John's wife. In 1353 Sir John settled an estate at Lissett including 1 carucate, besides a little land at Beeford, on his son John (d. 1381) and daughter-in-law,[80] and by 1386 the last John had evidently been succeeded by his son John.[81] From John Monceaux (d. by 1428) Lissett manor descended to his son William[82] (d. 1446) and then to William's sister Maud, wife of Brian de la See. The de la Sees' son Sir Martin de la See[83] left two daughters as heirs, and Lissett manor fell to the share of Joan or Jane (d. 1526), wife of Sir Peter Hildyard,[84] and later descended with Winestead in the Hildyards. In 1527 it was said to comprise 13 houses and 240 a.[85] Sir Christopher Hildyard (d. 1634) settled the Lissett estate on his son Christopher, a Royalist, whose estate was sequestered c. 1645. The restored estate passed after that Christopher's death in 1694[86] to his son Francis (d. by 1703), who had settled parts of it on his brother Gilby and sister Elizabeth Hildyard (d. by 1721).[87] Gilby succeeded to the shares of his brother and sister, and in 1725 he settled the manor, 1 carucate and 2 bovates, and other land at Lissett on his son Christopher (d. 1728) and Christopher's wife Anne.[88] Gilby evidently retained four farms with 7 bovates and other land at Lissett in which he (d. by 1733) was succeeded in turn by his widow Elizabeth (d. 1733) and her brother the Revd. Richard Cressy.[89] After dispute between claimants, the whole manorial estate, with 2 carucates and 1 bovate, was transferred in 1739 to John Saunderson and FitzWilliam White, and in 1766 their sons, John Saunderson and Charles

60   Ibid. 1666/535/469.
61   Ibid. HK/237/247.
62   A. Bryant, *Map of E.R. Yorks.* (1829); above, last para.
63   *Chron. de Melsa* (Rolls Ser.), i. 161, 163–4; below, econ. hist.
64   P.R.O., C 66/1272, mm. 9–22; E.R.A.O., PE/32/32 (copy minister's acct.).
65   Above, this section.
66   English, *Holderness*, 36–7.
67   *Yorks. Fines, 1218–31*, p. 49; *Chron. de Melsa*, i. 424.
68   E.R.A.O., DDCC/111/2; J. Foster, *Pedigrees of Yorks.* iii, s.v. Constable of Constable Burton; *Test. Ebor.* iii, p. 279 n.; Poulson, *Holderness*, i. 262.
69   E.R.A.O., DDCC/133/1.
70   *Cal. Inq. p.m.* ix, pp. 219–20.
71   P.R.O., C 142/65, no. 61; E 150/240, no. 12.
72   *Yorks. Fines*, i. 325; above, this section.
73   *E.Y.C.* iii, pp. 41–2.
74   B.L. Cott. MS. Vit. C vi, f. 207.
75   *V.C.H. Yorks.* ii. 267.
76   The following is based on Poulson, *Holderness*, i. 186–8, 258; *Early Yorks. Fam.* (Y.A.S. Rec. Ser. cxxxv), 61–2.

77   *Doc. illus. of . . . the Danelaw*, ed. F. M. Stenton (Brit. Acad. Rec. of Soc. and Econ. Hist. v), p. 316.
78   *Cal. Inq. p.m.* iv, p. 356; *Feud. Aids*, vi. 41; *Plac. de Quo Warr.* (Rec. Com.), 190.
79   *Kirkby's Inquest*, 244 and n.; *Yorks. Inq.* ii, p. 139 n.; *Cal. Inq. p.m.* viii, pp. 409–10.
80   H.U.L., DDWB/20/10.
81   B.L. Add. MS. 26736, f. 120; P.R.O., JUST. 1/1139, m. 6d.
82   *Cal. Pat. 1429–36*, 275.
83   H.U.L., DDWB/20/27.
84   E.R.A.O., DDCC/3/22.
85   P.R.O., C 142/48, no. 90; C 142/116, no. 55; J. Foster, *Pedigrees of Yorks.* iii, s.v. Hildyard; *V.C.H. Yorks. E.R.* v. 151; *Test. Ebor.* v. pp. 230–1.
86   P.R.O., C 142/530, no. 155; E.R.A.O., DDBC/15/31; *Yorks. Royalist Composition Papers*, i. (Y.A.S. Rec. Ser. xv), pp. 19–22; *Yorks. Ch. Plate*, i. 285.
87   H.U.L., DDCV/103/25, 29, 31, 34–5; Poulson, *Holderness*, i. 261; R.D.B., F/505/1091; F/510/1101.
88   H.U.L., DDCV/103/46; E.R.A.O., PE/115/1.
89   R.D.B., L/54/103; M/376/599; M/382/605.

White, sold it to Jonathan Midgley.[90] In 1771 Midgley also bought estates at Lissett from Hugh Bethell and John Rickaby,[91] and at inclosure in 1772 he received 877 a. there.[92] Midgley (d. 1778) devised his estate at Lissett to his daughter Anna (d. 1795), whose husband William Norton, Baron Grantley, enjoyed it until his death in 1822. Lissett manor then passed to William Beverley, husband of Anna's sister Mary (d. 1802).[93] In 1836 the Beverleys sold the manor to Joseph Dent. The estate then comprised 980 a., mostly in three farms.[94] Dent was succeeded between 1861 and 1878 by his son John Dent Dent (d. 1894)[95] and John by his son J. W. Dent. He sold the estate in 1935 to Samuel Tennant.[96] Some 440 a. were sold to the Air Ministry in 1942 and 1949.[97] The c. 520 a. remaining after those and other sales passed from Samuel Tennant (d. 1955) to Stanley Tennant, who bought c. 560 a. of the disused airfield in 1962.[98] In 1967 he gave Church and Manor farms at Lissett to trustees for his nephew James Tennant, who succeeded in 1974 and still owned the farms in 1996.[99]

Manor Farm probably dates from the late 17th century and has the initials **CH** in tie plates, perhaps for Christopher Hildyard (d. 1728).[1] The Hildyards lived in the chief house in 1725 but by 1840 it was used as a farmhouse.[2]

Part of Lissett, held in 1558 under Lissett manor by service of ¼ knight's fee,[3] was itself occasionally regarded as a manor. The tenant in 1316 was Hugh Moore, who was then returned as lord of Lissett and Little Kelk.[4] His estate at Lissett evidently descended, like Moor Town in Brandesburton, in the Moores and their successors the Ellerkers. Isabel Ellerker (d. 1478) devised it to her son Thomas Ellerker. Later owners were probably Thomas's son Robert Ellerker (d. 1508)[5] and Ralph Ellerker (d. 1543).[6] The heir of Thomas Ellerker (d. 1558) was his son Ralph,[7] presumably the Ralph Ellerker who divided and sold the estate, which included 6 bovates, in the early 1590s. The so-called manor of *LISSETT* was bought in 1593–4 by John Mattison, clerk.[8] Part of the land was resold by Mattison and others in 1648 to John Pearson

(Peirson).[9] The same or another John Pearson held 4 bovates and other land at Lissett in 1674,[10] and the reputed manor later descended from John Pearson (d. by 1718) to his son John, who sold it in 1743 to Hugh Bethell (d. 1752). Bethell's son Hugh sold it to Jonathan Midgley in 1771, and it later descended with Midgley's manor of Lissett.[11]

In the 13th century Sir Ingram de Monceaux's tenants included Ingram son of Sir Geoffrey of Lissett, possibly another member of the Monceaux family.[12]

ECONOMIC HISTORY. COMMON LANDS AND INCLOSURE. *Beeford.* The tillage of Beeford lay separated by the village in North and South fields, named in 1535.[13] Both fields evidently had an infield and an outfield; in the southern field the infield was alternatively known as West field and the outfield as East field. Enlargement of the arable area by the taking in of waste is suggested by the occurrence in North and South fields of forby, or extra, lands, which had no appurtenant meadow or pasture rights.[14] As in other East Riding parishes, the fields contained broad and narrow strips.[15] Three of the bovates were said to have been inclosed c. 1500.[16] Common meadowland lay in Bramer, Reed, later Red, carr, and in Sike meadow, all mentioned in the 17th century.[17]

There was pasture for 300 sheep in the north of the township in the 12th century and more common grazing in the south, on Beeford moor.[18] The moorland grazing was restricted by Meaux abbey's establishment of a grange there in the mid 12th century,[19] and later that which remained was intercommoned with North Frodingham.[20] The pastures were overcharged and turves dug on the moor without licence in the 17th century.[21] Moorheads, Inholms (Inhams, Enholmes), North pasture, and West carr were named as stinted pastures in 1726, when the grazing rights were expressed in gates and divisions of gates called bands.[22] Ridge and furrow evidence suggests that Inholms had once been part of the tillage.[23]

Beeford was inclosed in 1768 under an Act of

90 Ibid. P/305/788; P/306/789; AF/262/11; Poulson, *Holderness*, i. 258–9.
91 R.D.B., AO/441/704. Below, this section.
92 R.D.B., AN/391/27.
93 H.U.L., DDCB/2/8; R.D.B., AZ/283/460; BS/86/124; BY/351/536; *Complete Peerage*, s.v. Grantley.
94 R.D.B., FE/163/155.
95 Memorial in Lissett chapel.
96 R.D.B., HI/360/446; IE/150/205; MS/252/341; MX/202/323; 35/235/227 (1901); 532/322/245; E.R.A.O., DDX/225/1.   97 R.D.B., 655/58/46; 824/567/486.
98 Ibid. 1032/429/386; 1053/520/466; 1252/91/83; 1252/553/499; 1252/555/500.
99 Ibid. 1618/335/292; 1889/475/385; inf. from Mrs. J. Tennant, Fraisthorpe, 1996.
1 Pevsner and Neave, *Yorks. E.R.* 597.
2 H.U.L., DDCV/103/46; Poulson, *Holderness*, i. 262.
3 P.R.O., C 142/116, no. 55.
4 *Feud. Aids*, vi. 162.
5 B.I.H.R., Prob. Reg. 5, f. 127v.; Prob. Reg. 7, f. 47; Poulson, *Holderness*, i. 259, 261, 394–5; below, Brandesburton, manors (Moor Town).
6 *Test. Ebor.* vi, pp. 174–5.

7 P.R.O., C 142/116, no. 55.
8 H.U.L., DDCV/103/3, 6; E.R.A.O., DDCC/112/119; *Yorks. Fines*, iii. 140, 142, 147, 203.
9 P.R.O., CP 25(2)/525/23 Chas. I Hil. [no. 5 from end].
10 H.U.L., DDSY/23/218.
11 E.R.A.O., DDRI/40/8; R.D.B., S/3/5; AP/147/244; J. Foster, *Pedigrees of Yorks.* iii, s.v. Bethell; above, this section.   12 Poulson, *Holderness*, i. 257.
13 P.R.O., E 303/23, no. 473.
14 B.I.H.R., TER. H. Beeford 1726 etc.; R.D.B., M/252/407; AD/282/583.
15 E.R.A.O., DDX/24/13; below, Withernwick, econ. hist.
16 *Trans. R. Hist. S.* n.s. vi. 288–9; vii. 251–2.
17 E.R.A.O., DDX/24/9, 11; O.S. Map 6", Yorks. CLXXIX (1854 edn.). Bramer probably also included arable land and forby lands were later recorded there: R.D.B., H/41/90.   18 *Chron. de Melsa* (Rolls Ser.), i. 163, 309.
19 Below, this section.
20 Below, this section; below, N. Frodingham, econ. hist.
21 E.R.A.O., DDX/24/5–6, 10.
22 B.I.H.R., TER. H. Beeford 1726.
23 Hull Univ., Dept. of Geog., R.A.F. air photographs, run 74A, nos. 3364–6.

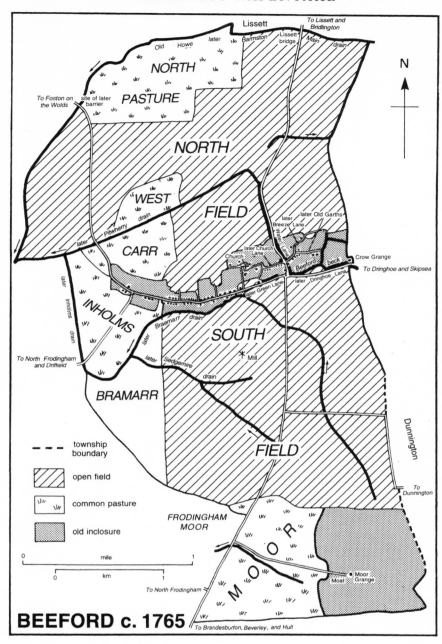

BEEFORD c. 1765

1766.[24] Allotments made totalled 3,397 a., including 186 a. in North Frodingham.[25] South field then contained more than 849 a., North field more than 652 a., and the moor at least 405 a.; North pasture was of at least 97 a. and Inholms of at least 78 a. An allotment of 186 a. was made from the moor to the commoners of North Frodingham for their grazing rights there and evidently continued as a common pasture.[26] Thomas Acklam received 600 a., William Aubrough 415 a., the rector 297 a., and Robert Grimston and Eaton Mainwaring Ellerker 217 a. each. There were also five allotments of 100–199

a., three of 50–99 a., twenty-one of 10–49 a., and the same number of under 10 a.

Lissett. The open fields of Lissett, which included extra, or forby, lands,[27] were named as North and South fields in 1591.[28] Ridge and furrow south and west of the village in the 1940s presumably once belonged to South field.[29] Common meadowland lay in New ings, named in 1353, and the hamlet's rough grazing in two pastures, of which Old pasture was certainly stinted and New pasture probably so.[30] New pasture may have been taken from the tillage,

24   6 Geo. III, c. 28 (Priv. Act); R.D.B., AK/57/6; E.R.A.O., IA. Beeford. A better version of the plan, endorsed 1766, is at H.U.L., DDCV/9/6.   25   Below, this para.
26   Below, N. Frodingham, econ. hist.
27   H.U.L., DDCV/103/2, 46.

28   Ibid. DDCV/103/6.
29   Hull Univ., Dept. of Geog., R.A.F. air photographs, run 83, nos. 4180–2.
30   H.U.L., DDWB/20/10; ibid. DDCV/103/29; R.D.B., AN/391/27; E.R.A.O., DDX/674.

and in 1748 four butts of land there were described as lying in a flatt.[31]

Lissett was inclosed in 1772 under an Act of 1771.[32] Allotments totalled 1,016 a., of which 877 a. were awarded to Jonathan Midgley, 134 a. to the rector of Beeford for tithes, and 4 a. to the only other proprietor. Except for 87 a. from North field and 52 a. from Old pasture, the former locations of the grounds inclosed are not given.

Dunnington. Open-field land was recorded at Dunnington in 1650[33] but the commonable lands were evidently inclosed soon afterwards, it is said by vestry order.[34] Closes called Great and Little West field and North field were recorded there in 1745,[35] two North pasture closes in 1813, and areas called East field, South field, and South pasture in the 1850s.[36] In the mid 20th century ridge and furrow marked the location of much of the settlement's former open-field land,[37] and ridge and furrow was still very apparent near Dunnington House and Dunnington Grange in 1996.

THE DEMESNE AND OTHER FARMS TO THE 16TH CENTURY. *Beeford*.
Only one plough, on the demesne, was recorded in 1086, when there were reckoned to be 12 ploughlands at Beeford. Most of the sokeland was apparently also out of cultivation then, and the manor's value had fallen greatly.[38]

The ½ carucate on Beeford moor given to Meaux abbey in the 12th century was presumably part of Beeford's southern field.[39] Soon afterwards the abbey established a grange on the moor, a development which was opposed by Thornton abbey and the other commoners there.[40] Some of the abbey's tillage may then have been separated from that of the village, and Moor grange was later said to comprise 129 a. in Moor field, 58 a. in the carrs, and 18 a. near the house, presumably in closes. Other land was farmed from the grange, which was also recorded as having 7½ bovates 'in the field of the town called Moor', possibly meaning a remaining share of Beeford's field belonging to Moor grange, 6 bovates in the field of the grange, and apparently also 12 bovates in Dunnington. Another undated record gives the land assigned to the grange as 314 a. of arable land, 58 a. of pasture, and 56 a. of meadow land lying on the moor and in Beeford and Dunnington.[41] Crow, or Dringhoe, grange was said to have had

203 a. of arable land in Dringhoe's open fields, 68 a. in those of Beeford, and a total area of *c.* 320 a.[42] The abbey gave up direct exploitation of its granges in the parish in the later 14th century.[43] In 1396 Crow grange, or manor, with 6 bovates in Dringhoe and 4 in Beeford, and Moor grange were both let to Richard Stopes[44] and his wife for rents of £4 and £4 13s. 4d. a year respectively. Other lands in Beeford, including 2½ bovates, were then occupied by seven tenants for rents amounting to nearly £1 10s., and the 12 bovates at Dunnington by four tenants for rents totalling £3 a year.[45]

In 1539–40 the Hospitallers' estate at Beeford was entirely occupied by freeholders and other tenants for rents amounting to nearly £8 7s. a year.[46]

Lissett. At Lissett, where 3 ploughlands and 30 a. of meadow were recorded, the manor was waste in 1086.[47]

WARREN AND FISHERIES.
Fisheries at Sandwath, or Hull, bridge were mentioned in the late 12th century, Bridlington priory's estate at Beeford also included a fishery,[48] and in 1353 the demesne at Lissett included a rabbit warren and a fishery.[49]

LATER AGRICULTURE.
In 1842 there were 623 a. of arable land, 179 a. of grassland, and 7 a. of woodland in Dunnington, and Moor Grange farm in Beeford included a further 48 a. of plantations.[50] In 1905 Beeford had 2,538 a. of arable land, 1,009 a. of grassland, and 31 a. of woodland, Dunnington 640 a. of arable and 177 a. of grassland, and Lissett 895 a. of arable and 207 a. of grassland.[51] The parish remained mostly arable in the 1930s, with concentrations of grassland around the settlements and on Beeford Grange and Moor Grange farms.[52] In 1987, when the 2,530 ha. (6,252 a.) returned under Beeford civil parish far exceeded its area, 1,887.8 ha. (4,665 a.) were arable land, 580 ha. (1,433 a.) grassland, and 20.3 ha. (50 a.) woodland. More than 27,000 fowls and 22,000 pigs, nearly 1,600 cattle, and 500 sheep were then kept.[53] In the 1990s Manor Farm, Beeford, was the head office of the National Pig Development Co. Ltd. which operated several pig farms in the area.

In the 19th century and the earlier 20th there were generally some twenty farms at Beeford, five at Dunnington, and three or four at

[31] R.D.B., T/103/202.
[32] 11 Geo. III, c. 41 (Priv. Act); R.D.B., AN/391/27; cf. E.R.A.O., DDX/674.
[33] *T.E.R.A.S.* iv. 60.
[34] B.I.H.R., TER. H. Beeford n.d.; Bulmer, *Dir. E. Yorks* (1892), 107; G. Trevor, *Hist. of Our Parish* (*c.* 1886), 98.
[35] E.R.A.O., QDB/4, p. 54.
[36] R.D.B., CY/349/515; O.S. Map 6″, Yorks. CLXXX (1855 edn.).
[37] Hull Univ., Dept. of Geog., R.A.F. air photographs, run 74B, nos. 3288–91; run 75B, nos. 3265–70.
[38] *V.C.H. Yorks.* ii. 267.
[39] Above, manors (Moor Grange).
[40] *Chron. de Melsa*, i. 164.
[41] B.L. Cott. MS. Vit. C. vi, ff. 223v., 230. For ridge and furrow near Moor grange, Hull Univ., Dept. of Geog.,

R.A.F. air photographs, run 75B, nos. 3265–7.
[42] B.L. Cott. MS. Vit. C. vi, ff. 222–3, 230.
[43] *Chron. de Melsa*, iii. 85, 100 n.
[44] Cf. *V.C.H. Yorks.* iii. 149.
[45] B.L. Cott. MS. Vit. C. vi, ff. 206v.–7.
[46] P.R.O., SC 6/Hen. VIII/4458, m. 13d., print. slightly inaccurately in *Miscellanea*, iv (Y.A.S. Rec. Ser. xciv), 95–6.
[47] *V.C.H. Yorks.* ii. 267.
[48] *Chron. de Melsa*, i. 225; *Brid. Chart.* 163, 326.
[49] H.U.L., DDWB/20/10.
[50] B.I.H.R., TA. 336M; TA. 327s; H.U.L., DDCV/9/15; H. Teesdale, *Map of Yorks.* (1828).
[51] Acreage Returns, 1905.
[52] [1st] Land Util. Surv. Map, sheet 28.
[53] Inf. from Min. of Agric., Fish. & Food, Beverley, 1990.

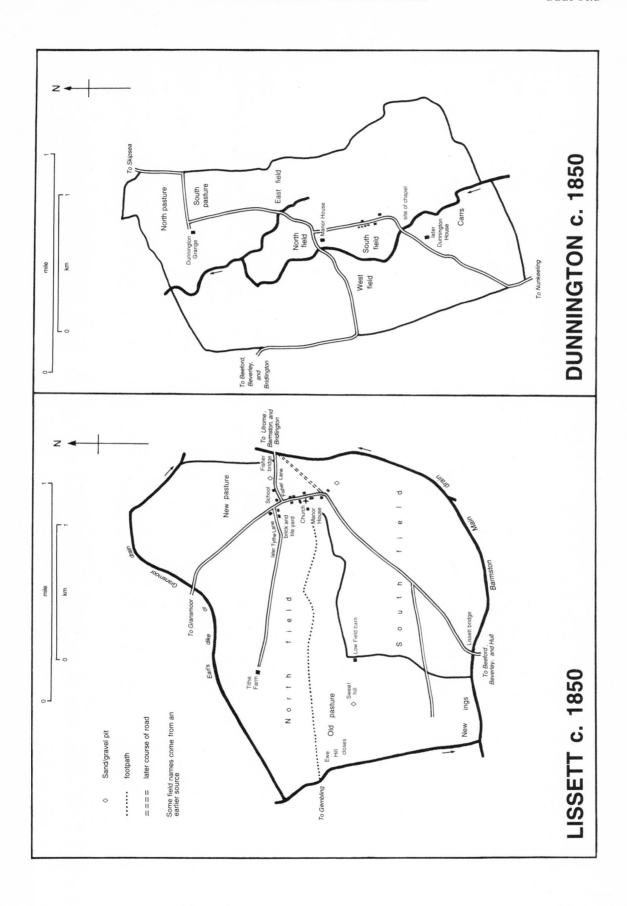

DUNNINGTON c. 1850

LISSETT c. 1850

Lissett.[54] Larger holdings, of 150 a. or more, accounted for nine of the Beeford farms in 1851 and six or seven in the 1920s and 1930s; Dunnington had three larger farms in 1851 and one or two in the 1920s and 1930s, and there were two or three at Lissett. There were also half a dozen smallholdings at Beeford in 1851 and more later;[55] some were probably used by the dozen cowkeepers recorded in 1892 and the four or five market gardeners in 1851 and c. 1910. In 1987 the area returned under Beeford civil parish was divided into 23 holdings; four were of 200 ha. (494 a.) or over, six of 100–199 ha. (247–492 a.), one of 50–99 ha. (124–245 a.), five of 10–49 ha. (25–121 a.), and seven of less than 10 ha.[56] An agricultural feeds concern was run from Manor Farm, Dunnington, in 1996.

TRADE AND INDUSTRY. Tolls were said in 1275–6 to have been increased without warrant at Beeford, apparently by Bridlington priory,[57] and the appurtenances of Beeford Franchise Fee manor, formerly belonging to the Templars and Hospitallers, also included tolls.[58] In the 18th century dues of 4d. from every waggon passing through Beeford, 4d. for each score of sheep, 1d. for every fisherman's horse, and ½d. for each beast were said, possibly mistakenly, to belong to the lord of the seigniory.[59] A fair was held in a field near the church before 1840, but no more is known of it.[60]

Beeford was typical of a large, primarily agricultural village in the number and type of its tradesmen in the 19th century and the earlier 20th, and in 1901 there were a dozen shops. Less usual occupations included rope-making and fish-carrying, both recorded in 1840, and watchmaking in the late 19th and early 20th century.[61] A hiring fair held in November was discontinued c. 1900. Non-agricultural concerns in 1996 included a firm of agricultural engineers, a garage in Main Street, and, beside the main road, another garage and a fish and chip shop.

Bricks and tiles were made at Lissett in the mid 19th century.[62] From the 1950s parts of the former airfield at Lissett were used by a haulage contractor[63] and for a caravan works; the latter premises were sold c. 1980 to a firm making prefabricated agricultural buildings[64] which still operated in 1996. Other concerns, some in former military buildings, then included one making furniture and a garage beside the main road.

MILLS. There were a water mill and a windmill in the late 12th century, both of which were later given to Meaux abbey. The water mill stood close to Crow grange, just across the boundary in Skipsea, and was powered by the stream from Dunnington until its insufficiency in summer caused the mill to fall into decay; the mill had apparently been removed by the 15th century. A replacement had perhaps been built nearby by the 1390s, when a 'Crow mill' was repaired. The windmill was moved by the abbey from Beeford to a higher site in Dringhoe, in Skipsea, partly to secure the tithes for its church of Skipsea, in the late 14th century.[65] The relationship between Meaux's mills and Mill hill, north of the village, and Mill House, on Beeford beck, is unknown.[66] By the late 16th century another windmill had been built in South field at Beeford.[67] A post mill, it was rebuilt as a tower mill in 1820 and ground until c. 1925, since when it has been a farm building. Commercial milling was continued in another building until the late 1960s using an engine powered successively by oil and electricity.[68] At Dunnington a windmill was recorded c. 1300,[69] and there was one at Lissett in 1353.[70]

LOCAL GOVERNMENT. A prison at Beeford in 1304 may have belonged to the Knights Templar.[71] Their successors, the Hospitallers, had testamentary jurisdiction over their tenants, and that right passed after the order's suppression to later lords of Beeford manor, which was presumably on that account called Beeford Franchise Fee. The privilege ceased in the later 18th century. A register of wills and inventories of the peculiar survives for the period from 1561 until 1768.[72] The jurisdiction of the Hospitallers' court evidently also included view of frankpledge in Beeford.[73] Surviving records of the court, or courts, of Beeford manor, by then comprising also the Lay Fee, include estreats of 1626–59, a list of pains of 1648,[74] and brief minutes of proceedings for 1641[75] and years between 1762 and 1782.[76] By the mid 18th century the court of 'Beeford Franchise Fee manor' apparently met only once a year, when 4 bylawmen, 2 affeerors, 2 constables, and a pinder were appointed.

In 1293 Meaux abbey was claiming the profits of the ale assize on its estates at Moor Grange and Dunnington and (Sir) Ingram de Monceaux

54 Para. based on P.R.O., HO 107/2365–7; directories.
55 Above, intro.
56 Inf. from Min. of Agric., Fish. & Food.; above, this section.   57 Rot. Hund. (Rec. Com.), i. 115.
58 E.R.A.O., DDX/24/27, A.1.
59 R.D.B., AY/492/829; Poulson, Holderness, i. 257.
60 Poulson, Holderness, i. 257.
61 Para. based on directories.
62 White, Dir. E. & N. R. Yorks. (1840), 276; White, Dir. Hull & York (1846), 372; O.S. Map 6", Yorks. CLXII (1854 edn.).
63 R.D.B., 881/564/468.
64 Ibid. 1252/91/83; 1341/38/29; 1664/274/233; inf. from A. M. Warkup (Beeford), Lissett, 1996; Hull Daily Mail, 18 Jan. 1977.
65 Chron. de Melsa (Rolls Ser.), i. 165, 224; ii. 47–50; iii. 172, 185, 273; Orange, 'Meaux Cart.', pp. 379–80.
66 O.S. Map 6", Yorks. CLXXIX (1854 edn.).
67 P.R.O., C 142/431, no. 93; Yorks. Fines, iv. 96; 1603–14, 220.
68 T. Jefferys, Map of Yorks. (1772); O.S. Map 6", Yorks. CLXXIX (1854 edn.); directories; R. Gregory, E. Yorks. Windmills, 21, 131; inf. from Mr. Reg. Warkup, Lowthorpe, 1996.
69 Cal. Inq. p.m. iii, p. 136; v, pp. 266–7.
70 H.U.L., DDWB/20/10.
71 Cal. Pat. 1301–7, 229.
72 B.I.H.R., Prob. Reg. Manorial Ct. of Beeford; Index of Wills... in Peculiar of Beeford (Y.A.S. Rec. Ser. lxviii), preface and 213–16. H.U.L., DDCV/10/7; below, this section; Poulson, Holderness, i. 257.
73 E.R.A.O., DDX/24/4; DDX/152/9; Yorks. Fines, iv. 96; 1603–14, 220.
74 E.R.A.O., DDX/24/4–13.
75 Ibid. DDX/152/9.   76 H.U.L., DDCV/10/1.

the same at Lissett.[77] After the Dissolution courts were held at Beeford for tenants on the abbey's former estate in or near Beeford.[78]

At Dunnington the Templars had a court in the 13th century[79] and Sir Philip le Despenser (d. 1401) one which met annually at Michaelmas.[80] View of frankpledge belonged to the Brighams' manor at Dunnington in the early 18th century.[81]

There was evidently a poorhouse at Beeford in which 3–4 were maintained between 1812 and 1815. Out-relief was given to 9–11 people permanently and 3–7 were helped occasionally there in the early 19th century, when 3 at Lissett and 6–8 at Dunnington were on regular or occasional out-relief.[82] At Lissett the overseers were renting five cottages for the poor in 1836,[83] and there may also have been poorhouses at Dunnington.[84] A select vestry was constituted for the parish in 1822 and its minute book survives. Stocks on the green at the east end of the village were joined in or soon after 1842 by a lock-up, built by subscription; the latter was removed c. 1890.[85]

Beeford township, later civil parish, joined Driffield poor-law union in 1836 and remained in Driffield rural district until reorganization in 1974, when it became part of the North Wolds district, later borough, of Humberside. In 1981 the borough's name was changed to East Yorkshire. Lissett joined Bridlington poor-law union in 1836 and remained in Bridlington rural district, after 1935 as part of Ulrome civil parish, until 1974, when Ulrome, too, was incorporated into North Wolds district, later East Yorkshire borough. Dunnington joined Skirlaugh poor-law union in 1837 and remained in Skirlaugh rural district until 1935, when as part of Bewholme civil parish it was taken into the new rural district of Holderness. In 1974 Bewholme civil parish became part of the Holderness district of Humberside.[86] In 1996 Beeford, Ulrome, and Bewholme parishes became part of a new East Riding unitary area.[87] A joint parish council for Lissett and Ulrome had been established by 1997.

CHURCH. There was a church with a priest at Beeford in 1086.[88] An unnamed chapel, apparently at Beeford, was recorded in the 12th century,[89] and the parish includes chapels at

Dunnington and Lissett.[90] In 1977 Beeford rectory was united with the benefices of North Frodingham and Foston on the Wolds to form the benefice of Beeford with Frodingham and Foston.[91]

BEEFORD church was given to Bridlington priory apparently by Ernald de Montbegon between 1157 and 1170 and to Thornton abbey (Lincs.) by Ernald or Ernulf de Montbegon before 1184. After dispute between the two houses, they agreed to share the fruits of the church, and it was probably in connexion with that agreement that c. 1200 Alan de Rowell, evidently the Montbegons' successor, charged the rectory with £4 a year payable to Bridlington and Thornton and bound himself and his heirs not to give the church to any other religious house.[92] Thornton abbey's interest in the church ceased very soon afterwards, possibly by cession to the Knights Templar, lords of Beeford by grant of the Montbegons.[93]

The Montbegons and their successors evidently retained an interest in the patronage after the 12th-century grants of the church to Bridlington and Thornton.[94] Alan, grandfather of Alan Rowell (fl. 1249), presented to the church, and he or another ancestor of Alan the grandson gave the advowson to the Templars as an appurtenance of a landed estate, possibly the manor.[95] In 1200, after dispute with Bridlington priory, the advowson was divided and assigned in half shares to the Templars and the priory, who later presented a rector jointly; by the agreement, which was confirmed by Thornton abbey, the priory and the order were also to receive pensions of 13s. 4d. a year each from the rectory. In 1249, after Alan Rowell had unsuccessfully claimed the right to present,[96] it was ordained that the two patrons should henceforward present alternately.[97] On their suppression in 1312,[98] the Templars' interest was transferred to the Hospitallers, who then presented in turn with the priory or its grantees until the mid 16th century. The dean and chapter of York presented by Bridlington's lapse in 1317, and in the earlier 14th century the Crown tried several times to present to Beeford as the Templars' successor, without effect.[99] In 1543 the Crown, as successor to the priory and the Hospitallers, granted the advowson to the archbishop of York, who had collated in 1539. Nevertheless, the Crown presented three times in the later 16th

77 *Plac. de Quo Warr.* (Rec. Com.), 190, 224.
78 E.R.A.O., PE/32/29.
79 *Cal. Inq. p.m.* iii, p. 136.
80 Ibid. xviii, p. 132.
81 E.R.A.O., QDR/2/8.
82 *Poor Law Abstract, 1804*, pp. 594–5; *1818*, pp. 522–3.
83 R.D.B., FE/163/155.
84 B.I.H.R., TA. 336M.
85 E.R.A.O., PE/114/87; Sheahan and Whellan, *Hist. York & E.R.* ii. 403; *T.E.R.A.S.* iii. 51.
86 *3rd Rep. Poor Law Com.* 167–8, 170; Boro. of N. Wolds, *Council Proc. and Cttee. Mins.* 1973–4, 4–7; 1980–1, 360; *Census.*
87 Humberside (Structural Change) Order 1995, copy at E.R.A.O.
88 *V.C.H. Yorks.* ii. 267.
89 *E.Y.C.* iii. 65, 74.   90 Below, this section.

91 B.I.H.R., OC. 923.
92 *E.Y.C.* iii, pp. 41–2, 74–5; *Brid. Chart.* 323; *V.C.H. Yorks.* iii. 204.
93 Above, manors (Beeford); below, this section [advowson]. That the transfer was by grant of the church to the order by Ernald de Montbegon before 1185 seems mistaken: Poulson, *Holderness*, i. 246, 248.
94 *Brid. Chart.* 323.
95 P.R.O., JUST 1/777, rot. 26; above, manors (Beeford).
96 P.R.O., JUST 1/777, rot. 26; *Yorks. Fines, John* (Sur. Soc. xciv), p. 4; *Reg. Gray*, p. 119; Lawrance, 'Clergy List', Holderness, 1, p. 16; *Brid. Chart.* 323–4.
97 *Reg. Gray*, p. 106; *Yorks. Fines, 1246–72*, pp. 10–11.
98 *V.C.H. Yorks.* iii. 256.
99 B.I.H.R., Reg. 9A, f. 339; Lawrance, 'Clergy List', Holderness, 1, pp. 16–19.

century and again in 1687 and 1811, in most cases apparently because of a vacancy in the see; Michael Empringham exercised a turn in 1576, possibly as the Crown's grantee, and the Commonwealth had the advowson in the mid 17th century.[1] Otherwise the patronage has remained with the archbishop.[2] Since 1977 the archbishop and the Church Society Trust, formerly patron at North Frodingham, have been joint patrons of the united benefice.[3]

In 1291 the church was valued at £20, after payment of the pension of 13s. 4d. to Bridlington priory.[4] In 1535 the annual value was £22 net, the deductions including, besides Bridlington's pension, that of 13s. 4d. paid to the Hospitallers as successors to the Templars. The rector of Beeford then received an annual pension of 10d. from Nunkeeling priory, about which nothing else is known.[5] The improved annual value in 1650 was almost £186 net.[6] Later in the 17th century the rectory was said to be worth £140.[7] The net income was £779 a year between 1829 and 1831 and £675 in 1883.[8] The gross value in 1918 was c. £865.[9]

Most of the value came from tithes. In 1535 the tithes of the whole parish were worth almost £23 a year gross.[10] Those of Beeford township were valued at £110 a year gross in 1650 and at £70 on average in the late 17th century.[11] Pasture gates were thought to have been given at unknown date to the rector for the herbage tithe.[12] At the inclosure of Beeford in 1768 the rector was awarded 192 a. and £80 a year for most of the tithes. The owners of the c. 570 a. in the Moor Grange and Crow Grange estates, as successors of Meaux abbey, owed no tithes when those farms were in hand but when they were let the land was titheable. By award of 1842 and apportionment of 1846 the tithes of the farms, whether let or in hand, were commuted for rent charges of £6 15s. 7d. for Moor Grange and £4 4s. 5d. for Crow Grange.[13]

The tithes of Lissett were valued at £34 a year gross in 1650 and at £24 a year in the late 17th century.[14] Other dues owed to the rector by parishioners at Lissett included a homage halfpenny

and a St. Leonard's penny, both presumably recognitions of their chapelry's dependency on the mother church of Beeford.[15] The tithe on hay growing in the open fields was paid by a modus.[16] At inclosure in 1772 the rector was awarded 134 a. for tithes.[17] A cottage and outbuildings were put up there in 1804, and the house was enlarged in 1855.[18] In 1919 the 139-a. Lissett Tithe farm was sold to the Nettletons.[19] The farmhouse was later demolished when the airfield was made.[20]

In 1650 the tithes of Dunnington were valued at £20 a year gross.[21] By the late 17th century they were being paid by compositions amounting to c. £16 a year, possibly set at inclosure,[22] but c. 1820 the rector successfully applied to the Court of Exchequer for payment in kind. The tithes were commuted for a rent charge of £210 by award of 1842 and apportionment of 1843.[23]

The rectory house and the rest of the glebe at Beeford, including a dozen cottages, were valued at £3 10s. a year gross in 1535 and £16 gross in 1650.[24] In the 17th century the glebe land there comprised 3 bovates, with c. ½ bovate of forby, or extra, land, and c. 6 a. in a close.[25] At the inclosure of Beeford in 1768 the rector received 106 a. for glebe land and his pasture rights, besides the 192 a. for tithes.[26] Farm buildings were put up on the tithe allotment in 1793 and a farmhouse added in 1819.[27] The farm incorporated the glebe land at Dunnington in 1867, when it was called South Grange.[28] In 1919 Rectory farm with 222 a. at Beeford was sold to W. J. Hawkins and other sales made amounting to c. 80 a.[29]

The rectory included cottages and land held by Priesthold tenure, which involved the payment of a fine of one year's rent on each change of tenant or rector.[30] The rents at Beeford amounted to £1 10s. in 1535 and just over £2 a year in the 17th century, when there were twelve cottages.[31] In 1768 at inclosure 23 a. of Priesthold were awarded in Beeford.[32] Also Priesthold was a house at Dunnington.[33]

The glebe at Dunnington was valued at 15s. a year gross in 1535 and at £12 gross in 1650, when it comprised a house, two small closes,

[1] T.E.R.A.S. iv. 60. The Crown also made an ineffective grant of the advowson in 1595: P.R.O., C 66/1435, mm. 37–46.
[2] Poulson, Holderness, i. 251. Lawrance, 'Clergy List', Holderness, 1, p. 20; L. & P. Hen. VIII, xviii (1), p. 128; Yorks. Fines, i. 114–15.
[3] B.I.H.R., OC. 923; below, N. Frodingham, church.
[4] Tax. Eccl. (Rec. Com.), 304.
[5] Valor Eccl. (Rec. Com.), v. 115, 117; above, this section. By 1650 Edmund Naylor had the Hospitallers' pension: T.E.R.A.S. iv. 61.
[6] T.E.R.A.S. iv. 61.
[7] B.I.H.R., TER. H. Beeford n.d.
[8] Ibid. V. 1884/Ret. 1; Rep. Com. Eccl. Revenues, 916–17.
[9] B.I.H.R., TER. 152.
[10] Valor Eccl. v. 117.
[11] B.I.H.R., TER. H. Beeford n.d.; T.E.R.A.S. iv. 60.
[12] B.I.H.R., TER. H. Beeford 1726.
[13] Ibid. 1726, 1849; ibid. TA. 327s; R.D.B., AK/57/6. Also, 'Meaux Cart.', pp. 492–3.
[14] B.I.H.R., TER. H. Beeford n.d.; T.E.R.A.S. iv. 60.
[15] B.I.H.R., TER. H. Beeford 1726.
[16] Ibid.

[17] R.D.B., AN/391/27.
[18] B.I.H.R., TER. H. Beeford 1809; E.R.A.O., PE/114/25/2; H. Teesdale, Map of Yorks. (1828).
[19] R.D.B., 202/204/175.
[20] O.S. Map 1/2,500, Yorks. CLXII. 12 (1892 edn.); 1/10,560, TA 15 NW. (1956 edn.).
[21] T.E.R.A.S. iv. 60.
[22] B.I.H.R., TER. H. Beeford n.d., 1726; G. Trevor, Hist. of Our Parish (c. 1886), 98.
[23] B.I.H.R., TER. H. Beeford 1817, 1825, 1849; ibid. TA. 336M.
[24] Valor Eccl. v. 117; T.E.R.A.S. iv. 60; below, this section.
[25] B.I.H.R., TER. H. Beeford n.d.
[26] R.D.B., AK/57/6.
[27] B.I.H.R., TER. H. Beeford 1809, 1825; A. Bryant, Map of E.R. Yorks. (1829).
[28] E.R.A.O., PE/114/29.
[29] Ibid. PE/114/33; R.D.B., 202/510/436; 202/511/437; 203/375/328; 207/228/202.
[30] B.I.H.R., TER. H. Beeford 1726.
[31] Ibid. n.d.; Valor Eccl. v. 117.
[32] R.D.B., AK/57/6.
[33] B.I.H.R., TER. H. Beeford 1726.

FIG. 13. BEEFORD RECTORY HOUSE 1833–4

and 3 bovates.[34] The commonable lands were evidently inclosed soon afterwards, it is said by vestry order,[35] and later there was *c.* 45 a. of glebe there[36] until it was sold to W. J. Hawkins in 1919.[37] There had evidently been a curacy house at Dunnington before the late 17th century, when the glebe there included a 'vicarage garth' and farm buildings, one of which was later used as a house.[38]

The glebe at Lissett was valued at 4s. a year gross in 1535 and at 11s. gross in 1650, when it comprised two cottages and 3 a.[39] Later in the 17th century the value was given as just over £1.[40] One of the cottages was described later as the 'vicarage house', presumably because it had been used by the curate. By the 17th century it was let to a tenant, and it was perhaps that cottage which was replaced by a new farmhouse in 1818.[41]

The small rectory house, of five bays in 1786 and with four living rooms in 1809,[42] was rebuilt in 1833–4 by Thomas Skelton of Filey.[43] It was much enlarged in 1845, a wing was added in 1863, and the house was extended again in the early 20th century by Brodrick, Lowther, and

Walker of Hull.[44] The south wing was demolished and the north front remodelled by Francis Johnson *c.* 1940.[45] A new house was built in the garden *c.* 1975 and in 1977 was designated the residence of the united benefice. The 19th-century house and outbuildings were demolished in 1995,[46] and in 1998 a new rectory house was being built on the site.

The rectors of Beeford have often been lawyers and theologians with other preferments who did not reside.[47] In their absence, the church and its chapels were served by stipendiaries.[48] The Oxford theologian Richard Ulverston, rector in 1406–7 and 1408–31, was excused in 1409, as a Crown servant, from becoming a priest for seven years and in 1413 he was allowed to hold another benefice with Beeford.[49] Several other rectors were only in minor orders at their presentation. The Marian bishop of Chester, Cuthbert Scott, was rector from 1549 until his deprivation in 1559,[50] and the curate in 1567 was allegedly saying masses for the dead.[51] A puritan, Griffith Briskin, prebendary of Osbaldwick in York minster, was rector 1594–1608. John

34 *Valor Eccl.* v. 117; *T.E.R.A.S.* iv. 60.
35 B.I.H.R., TER. H. Beeford n.d.; G. Trevor, *Hist. of Our Parish* (*c.* 1886), 98.
36 B.I.H.R., TER. H. Beeford 1809, 1849.
37 R.D.B., 202/511/437.
38 B.I.H.R., TER. H. Beeford n.d., 1726, 1764.
39 *Valor Eccl.* v. 117; *T.E.R.A.S.* iv. 60.
40 B.I.H.R., TER. H. Beeford n.d.
41 Ibid. n.d., 1825.
42 Ibid. 1809; E.R.A.O., PE/114/42.
43 B.I.H.R., MGA. 1833/2; Poulson, *Holderness*, i. 257, illus.
44 E.R.A.O., PE/114/25/2; PE/114/30; PE/114/43/1;

B.I.H.R., MGA. 1907/2.
45 E.R.A.O., PE/114/44/2.
46 B.I.H.R., OC. 923; Pevsner and Neave, *Yorks. E.R.* 275; inf. from the rector, 1996.
47 The following is based on Lawrance, 'Clergy List', Holderness, 1, pp. 16–20, 144; Poulson, *Holderness*, i. 251.
48 B.I.H.R., V. 1764/Ret. 1, no. 51; ibid. TER. H. Beeford 1777 etc.; B.L. Harl. Ch. 46 D. 39; *E.Y.C.* iii, pp. 65, 74; J. S. Purvis, *Tudor Par. Doc. of Dioc. York*, 116; *Select Tithe Causes* (Y.A.S. Rec. Ser. cxiv), p. 59; *Restoration Exhibit Bks. and the Northern Clergy, 1662–4*, ed. W. J. Sheils, 68, 70.
49 *D.N.B.*   50 Ibid.
51 B.I.H.R., V. 1567–8/CB. 1, f. 206v.

FIG. 14. BEEFORD CHURCH IN 1784

Neile, chaplain to Charles II and a high officer in York and Durham dioceses, was rector from 1637 until his ejection *c.* 1645 and then again from his reinstatement in 1660 to 1669. The curates in the 1700s were allegedly of ill repute, John Wilkinson being described as 'more fit to be a swineherd than a parson'.[52] William Jackson, rector 1791–1811, was also Regius professor of Greek at Oxford and dean of Bath and Wells and later bishop of Oxford.[53] George Trevor, rector 1871–88, was a High Churchman and canon of York minster.[54]

A cottage and land at Beeford were given to support lights and obits in the church before the mid 16th century.[55] Two Sunday services were held at Beeford *c.* 1750. There were then five celebrations of communion a year, with *c.* 50 receiving at Easter.[56] The parish was better served by resident rectors with assistant curates[57] from the 19th century. An evening school was provided in the mid century but was unsuccessful, and then and later many parishioners were said to attend both church and chapel. Celebrations of communion were once a month by 1865 and weekly by 1877; in the later 19th century 20–30 usually communicated but by 1931 only 5–6.[58]

The church of *ST. LEONARD*, so called by 1407,[59] stands in a large yard planted with

mature trees which was enlarged by ½ a. in 1948.[60] The building comprises chancel with north chapel and vestry, wide, three-bayed nave with north and south aisles, south porch, and west tower. The church is largely built of boulders with stone dressings and later brickwork, but the tower and much of the south porch are of ashlar. There is little evidence of the 11th-century building. The chancel was enlarged in the 13th century, when a pair of windows and a single-seat sedile were made in its south side; a possibly later piscina also survives there. In the 14th century the north doorway to the nave, now reset in the aisle, was made or remade and another window added in the chancel. Much work was done in the 15th century: the tower was built or possibly refaced externally then, the south aisle, and later the south porch, added, and the chancel again remodelled. The square, three-staged tower had a decorative parapet of open, pinnacled niches which was broken and worn away in 1996; it had been renewed by 1998. In a niche on the tower's west face stands a medieval statue of St. Leonard.[61] The fabric was later neglected[62] and 'churchwardenized', the chancel being partly rebuilt in brick in 1719 and some of the church's medieval windows destroyed. A west gallery had been fitted by 1831.[63] The church was enlarged and restored in the mid 19th century. The north aisle, whose

52 Ibid. CP. I. 5, 7, 519.
53 Ibid. Inst. AB. 16, p. 213; *D.N.B*; Poulson, *Holderness*, i. 251–2. 54 *D.N.B*.; list in ch.
55 P.R.O., C 3/34/50; *Cal. Pat.* 1569–72, p. 38.
56 B.I.H.R., V. 1764/Ret. 1, no. 51; *Herring's Visit.* i, p. 108.
57 P.R.O., ED 49/8515; *Rep. Com. Eccl. Revenues*, 916–17; directories.
58 P.R.O., HO 129/523/1/1; HO 129/524/1/5/9;

B.I.H.R., V. 1865/Ret. 1, no. 42; V. 1868/Ret. 1, no. 41; V. 1871/Ret. 1, no. 42; V. 1877/Ret. 1, no. 41; V. 1884/Ret. 1; V. 1900/Ret. 1, no. 24; V. 1931/Ret.; E.R.A.O., PE/114/24.
59 B.I.H.R., Prob. Reg. 3, f. 274.
60 Ibid. TER. H. Beeford 1809; ibid. CD. Add. 1970/1.
61 Pevsner and Neave, *Yorks. E.R.* 274.
62 B.I.H.R., ER. V./CB. 7, f. 2.
63 Poulson, *Holderness*, i. 254–5, illus.; T. Allen, *Hist. Co. York*, ii. 408.

arcade copies that on the south, and a one-bayed extension alongside the chancel to form the chapel were added by H. F. Lockwood at the expense of Mr. Bagge, the rector's son-in-law and curate, in 1846.[64] Other work included the restoration of the east window *c.* 1850,[65] the addition of the vestry in 1859, the refitting of the chancel in 1865 or 1866, and the reflooring and reseating of the nave in 1871.[66] The south aisle windows were evidently also restored. In 1904 the chancel arch was rebuilt and new choir stalls provided there.[67] The roof was given a ceiling and repaired in 1939, when the church was largely re-glazed using clear glass and some of the 19th-century stained glass.[68] The roofs of the chancel and nave were restored in 1953.[69]

An oak chancel screen and stalls were removed in the 1860s,[70] but an octagonal font, probably 15th-century, and Royal Arms of 1814 remain.

The church has a brass commemorating Thomas Tonge, rector 1431–72,[71] a 14th-century effigy of another priest, and memorials to relatives of George Trevor, rector 1871–88 and his son G. W. Trevor, rector 1905–19.[72]

There were three bells in 1552 and later, two being replaced in 1599 and the other in 1675.[73] The plate includes a covered cup of 1562.[74] The registers of burials begin in 1563, baptisms in 1564, and marriages in 1627; those of burials lack entries for some 30 years in the late 16th and early 17th century but the marriage registers are complete and those of baptisms and births more or less so.[75]

The church and its yard were closed for burials in 1883,[76] but extensions of the yard were consecrated in 1884, 1925, and 1970.[77] Robert Dixon of Dunnington (d. 1937) left £50 to maintain the churchyard.[78]

To help defray the cost of repairing the church, the churchwardens had balks in the open fields until inclosure in 1768, when 11 a., later called Church field, was substituted for them. The land was then valued at £3 10s. a year;[79] the income was £19 *c.* 1830 and £24 in 1892.[80] Church field was sold in 1919,[81] and in 1940 the charity had £606 stock. The income was used more generally for church expenses in the earlier 20th century.[82]

The parish clerk was entitled to 3 sheaves of wheat a year from each bovate in Beeford township until 1768, when he was awarded £3 10s. a year instead from the land then inclosed.[83] He was also owed 4d. a year from each inhabited house.[84]

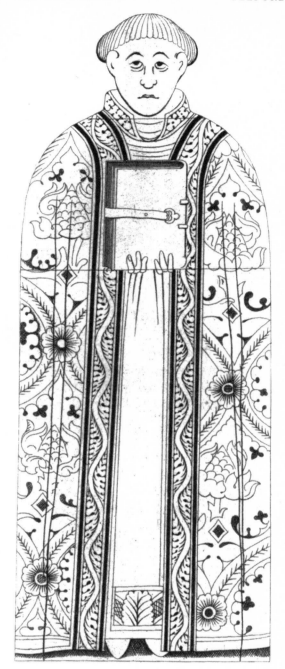

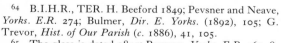

FIG. 15. BEEFORD CHURCH: BRASS OF THOMAS TONGE, RECTOR (D. 1472)

[64] B.I.H.R., TER. H. Beeford 1849; Pevsner and Neave, *Yorks. E.R.* 274; Bulmer, *Dir. E. Yorks.* (1892), 105; G. Trevor, *Hist. of Our Parish* (*c.* 1886), 41, 105.

[65] The glass is dated 1845: Pevsner, *Yorks. E.R.* 167–8.

[66] B.I.H.R., Ch. Ret. i; ibid. Fac. Bk. 6, pp. 19–21; ibid. V. 1868/Ret. 1, no. 41; directories.

[67] B.I.H.R., Fac. 1904/15; E.R.A.O., PE/114/20.; cf. Poulson, *Holderness*, i. 254.

[68] B.I.H.R., Fac. Bk. 12, p. 158; Pevsner and Neave, *Yorks. E.R.* 275.

[69] B.I.H.R., Fac. 1953/2/54.

[70] Poulson, *Holderness*, i. 254; photograph in vestry; Bulmer, *Dir. E. Yorks.* (1892), 105.

[71] Lawrance, 'Clergy List', Holderness, 1, p. 19; for inscription and illus., Poulson, *Holderness*, i. 255.

[72] List of rectors in ch.

[73] *Inventories of Ch. Goods*, 52; Boulter, 'Ch. Bells', 82.

[74] *Yorks. Ch. Plate*, i, pp. 214–15.

[75] E.R.A.O., PE/114/1–5, 9. Transcripts survive from 1609: B.I.H.R., PRT. Hold. D.

[76] *Lond. Gaz.* 25 May 1883, pp. 2734–5.

[77] E.R.A.O., PE/114/30; PE/114/80; PE/114/88/3; B.I.H.R., CD. 724; CD. Add. 1884/2; CD. Add. 1970/1.

[78] E.R.A.O., PE/114/90–1; ibid. accession 1681.

[79] R.D.B., AK/57/6; board in ch.

[80] T. Allen, *Hist. Co. York*, ii. 408; Bulmer, *Dir. E. Yorks.* 105.

[81] R.D.B., 202/509/435.

[82] E.R.A.O., PE/114/92; ibid. accession 1681.

[83] R.D.B., AK/57/6; B.I.H.R., TER. 152; E.R.A.O., AP. Beeford inclosure Act.

[84] B.I.H.R., TER. H. Beeford 1770.

LISSETT. Alan the parson witnessed a Lissett deed in the 13th century,[85] and a chapel there with right of burial was recorded in 1407.[86] The chapel was served separately from the mother church by a curate in the 16th and 17th centuries.[87] In 1650 it was recommended that the existing parish of Beeford be reduced to Lissett chapelry and Beeford township.[88] That plan was not effected, but the chapel was later served from Beeford by the rector or his curate.[89] In the mid 18th century, and evidently for long before, there was only one service a fortnight in the chapel; communion there was then quarterly, with nearly half of the *c.* 30 confirmed members receiving at Easter 1743.[90] The assistant curate paid £108 a year *c.* 1830 probably had charge of Lissett chapel,[91] and a curate was certainly serving it about 1900, when J. W. Dent built a house for him.[92] Service was weekly by 1851[93] and celebrations of communion monthly by 1877, fortnightly *c.* 1920, and monthly again in 1931.[94] In 1996 two services and a celebration of communion were provided each month at Lissett.[95]

The chapel of *ST. JAMES* was so called by 1407 and in 1996 was more fully styled *ST. JAMES OF COMPOSTELLA*.[96] It was built of rubble and boulders with ashlar dressings but has been much rebuilt in brick and largely rendered. The building comprises chancel and nave with south porch and bellcot above the chancel arch. The round-headed south doorway with zigzag decoration and a carved stone above it[97] suggest that the chapel was built in the 12th century. It was evidently remodelled in the 13th, when new windows were made in the chancel and the nave, and a pillar and capital of that period, reset in the chancel, are said to have come from the chancel arch.[98] The chapel was later largely rebuilt, notably after storm damage in 1740.[99] By 1840 a south porch had been added and sashes substituted for tracery in some of the windows,[1] and the building was later said to be in a 'discreditable condition'.[2] It was restored in 1876 by Hugh Roumieu Gough of London for John Dent Dent, lord of the manor, and George Trevor, rector. The work included the rebuilding of the chancel arch, the addition of the bellcot, refenestration, and the paving of the chancel with flowered quarry tiles inspired by the Arts and Crafts movement.[3]

FIG. 16. LISSETT CHAPEL BEFORE RESTORATION IN 1876

The fittings include a 12th-century circular font. Memorials include a stone in the chancel to Christopher Hildyard (d. 1728), the east window and altar rails for John Dent Dent (d. 1894),[4] and a window in the nave and a memorial in the chapelyard commemorating the R.A.F. squadron stationed at Lissett from 1943 to 1945.

Lissett chapel has two ancient bells, one of them, bearing the date 1254, said to be the oldest dated bell in England; they were restored in 1974.[5] Lissett's plate includes a cup and cover, given in 1671 and used in Dunnington chapel after its rebuilding, and a service given at the restoration in 1876.[6] Registrations of burials begin in 1653 and of baptisms in 1679. Marriages are recorded from 1663 but lack entries for a few years in the mid 18th century.[7]

A Christopher Hildyard had left a little land for repairs to Lissett chapel, evidently many years before 1743, when the trust was being fulfilled by his heirs.[8]

DUNNINGTON. Dunnington chapel probably existed by the mid 12th century, a chaplain of Dunnington witnessing the gift of Beeford church to Bridlington priory.[9] It was served by a curate in the 16th century, in 1595–6 with Nunkeeling church. The fabric was decayed in 1575,[10] the chancel was in disrepair in 1623, and in 1663 the chapel was said to be 'quite demolished' for lack of repairs and the parishioners at Dunnington were ordered to attend Beeford church instead. It was then claimed that there had been too few inhabitants to maintain the building;[11] in 1650 it had been proposed to provide the chapel with more support by making a

85 Poulson, *Holderness*, i. 258.
86 B.I.H.R., Prob. Reg. 3, f. 274.
87 Lamb. Pal. Libr., Carte Misc. XII/9; *Test. Ebor.* vi, p. 175; *Inventories of Ch. Goods*, 54; J. Lawson, *Primary Educ. in E. Yorks. 1560–1902* (E. Yorks. Loc. Hist. Ser. x), 4; *Restoration Exhibit Bks. and the Northern Clergy, 1662–4*, ed. W. J. Sheils, 69.   88 *T.E.R.A.S.* iv. 60.
89 B.I.H.R., TER. H. Beeford n.d., 1749.
90 Ibid. V. 1764/Ret. 1, no. 51; *Herring's Visit.* ii, p. 164.
91 *Rep. Com. Eccl. Revenues*, pp. 916–17.
92 *Kelly's Dir. N. & E. R. Yorks.* (1905), 419.
93 P.R.O., HO 129/524/1/5/9; B.I.H.R., V. 1865/Ret. 1, no. 42.
94 B.I.H.R., V. 1877/Ret. 1, no. 41; V. 1912–22/Ret.; V. 1931/Ret.   95 Church notice.
96 B.I.H.R., Prob. Reg. 3, f. 274.
97 *Y.A.J.* xxi. 260–1; J. Lang, *Corpus of Anglo-Saxon Sculpture*, iii. 230.
98 G. Trevor, *Hist. of Our Parish*, 46.

99 B.I.H.R., Reg. 35, ff. 209–10, 216.
1 Poulson, *Holderness*, i. 259–62, illus.
2 B.I.H.R., Ch. Ret. i.
3 Ibid. Fac. 1876/15; ibid. V. 1877/Ret. 1, no. 41; V. 1884/Ret. 1; Pevsner and Neave, *Yorks. E.R.* 597; G. Trevor, *Hist. of Our Parish* (*c.* 1886), 45–6.
4 Brass plate.
5 B.I.H.R., Fac. 1974/18; Boulter, 'Ch. Bells', 84.
6 B.I.H.R., TER. 152; *Yorks. Ch. Plate*, i, pp. 285–6.
7 E.R.A.O., PE/115/1–3, 5. Transcripts survive from 1600: B.I.H.R., PRT. Hold. D.
8 *Herring's Visit.* ii, pp. 163–4.
9 *E.Y.C.* iii, p. 74. Also *Chron. de Melsa* (Rolls Ser.), i. 424.
10 Lamb. Pal. Libr., Carte Misc. XII/9; *Inventories of Ch. Goods*, 50; *Abp. Grindal's Visit., 1575*, ed. W. J. Sheils, 69; J. S. Purvis, *Tudor Par. Doc. of Dioc. York*, 52.
11 B.I.H.R., ER V./CB. 1, f. 76v.; V. 1623/CB. 1, f. 156; V. 1662–3/CB. 1, f. 317v.

parish for it comprising Dunnington and Bon-wick township, in Skipsea parish.[12] 'Small remains' of the chapel, which had had a tower, survived later, and its yard continued to be used for burials. A house was used for services in the early and mid 19th century.[13] After the building of a new chapel, a Sunday service was held there; communion was usually monthly in 1884, fort-nightly c. 1920, and monthly again in 1931.[14] In 1996 service was monthly at Dunnington.[15]

The present chapel of *ST. NICHOLAS* was built in 1879 on the site of the earlier building, possibly to designs by H. Roumieu Gough. The building, which was used from that year, was paid for largely by George Ansley (d. 1879).[16] Of red brick and vaguely 13th-century in style, the chapel evidently comprised an undivided chancel and nave with north porch and bellcot on the western gable. In 1903 H. J. Tebbutt, rector, had the interior remodelled, raising the floor of the chancel and extending it into the nave, and further raising the floor at the east end to mark the sanctuary. Both chancel and sanctuary are tiled.[17] Fittings include a small 19th-century font. There were two bells in 1552 but later only one.[18] Registrations for Dunnington were made in the Beeford registers and a few transcripts also sur-vive from the earlier 17th century.[19]

NONCONFORMITY. In the 17th century about five people were regularly presented as Roman Catholics at Beeford and two at Lissett; at Dunnington, where adherents included the Creswells, numbers rose to 13 about 1640 and, as a papist, Roger Brigham registered his manor there c. 1715.[20] The Ellerkers of Moor Grange suffered as recusants c. 1630.[21]

A Quaker meeting said to have had 100 mem-bers was held in a house at Lissett in 1669.[22] Eleven protestant dissenters were returned for Beeford in 1676,[23] but there were said to be no dissenters in the parish in the mid 18th cent-

ury.[24] Houses were, nevertheless, registered at Beeford by unidentified protestant congrega-tions in 1779, 1787, and 1788.[25]

The missionary efforts of members of Fish Street chapel, Hull, included visits c. 1800 to Beeford and Lissett, and in 1799 the Ind-ependents registered a barn at Beeford.[26] A prea-cher for Beeford, Skipsea, and Patrington was appointed in 1803, and an Independent chapel was built south of the street at Beeford in 1810. In 1851, when the chapel was connected with that at North Frodingham, a congregation of c. 50 attended the service at Beeford chapel on Sunday afternoons.[27] The building was enlarged in 1857[28] and altered in 1880.[29] By the 1890s Beeford Congregational church was united with those at North Frodingham and Skipsea and a manse had been built at Beeford for the minister of the churches.[30] The Congregational church had been closed by 1922[31] and was derelict in 1996.[32]

An unidentified protestant congregation at Beeford which registered a house in 1801 and a chapel in 1802 was probably Wesleyan Method-ist,[33] and there was certainly a Wesleyan chapel by 1823.[34] Standing on the south side of the vil-lage street,[35] it was replaced by a new build-ing further east in 1866. Later the Methodist church,[36] it was still used in 1996.[37]

The Primitive Methodists built a chapel and school on the south side of the street at Beeford in or soon after 1839 and registered the premises in 1842. The site had been greatly enlarged by 1866[38] and other land was added in 1874,[39] fol-lowing the rebuilding of the chapel in an Italianate style by Joseph Wright of Hull in 1873.[40] It was closed in 1964 and stood disused in 1996.[41]

A house at Dunnington was registered for protestant worship in 1807,[42] perhaps by the Wesleyan Methodists, who built a chapel there in 1858.[43] It was closed c. 1970,[44] and in 1996 was used as a storeroom.

12 T.E.R.A.S. iv. 60.
13 B.I.H.R., V. 1764/Ret. 1, no. 51; V. 1877/Ret. 1, no. 41; ibid. TER. H. Beeford 1849; Poulson, Holderness, i. 263.
14 B.I.H.R., V. 1884/Ret. 1; V. 1912–22/Ret.; V. 1931/Ret.
15 Church notice.
16 B.I.H.R., TER. 152; Pevsner and Neave, Yorks. E.R. 393; window in church; G. Trevor, Hist. of Our Parish (c. 1886), 43.
17 B.I.H.R., TER. 152; list of rectors in Beeford church; Kelly's Dir. N. & E. R. Yorks. (1909), 431.
18 Inventories of Ch. Goods, 50; G. R. Park, Ch. Bells of Holderness, 66.
19 Above, this section [Beeford ch., regs.]; B.I.H.R., PRT. Hold. D.
20 E.R.A.O., QDR/2/8; Aveling, Post Reformation Catholicism, 68; Compton Census, ed. Whiteman, 600; Depositions from York Castle (Sur. Soc. xl), 123.
21 P.R.O., C 66/2685, no. 22.
22 G. L. Turner, Orig. Rec. of Early Nonconf. i. 164; B. Dale, Yorks. Puritanism and Early Nonconf. 263.
23 Compton Census, ed. Whiteman, 600.
24 B.I.H.R., V. 1764/Ret. 1, no. 51; Herring's Visit. i, p. 108; ii, p. 163.
25 P.R.O., RG 31/5, nos. 555, 694, 712.
26 B.I.H.R., DMH. 1799/62.
27 P.R.O., HO 129/523/1/1/3; O.S. Map 6", Yorks. CLXXIX (1854 edn.).

28 Bulmer, Dir. E. Yorks. (1892), 106.
29 D. [R. J.] and S. Neave, E.R. Chapels and Meeting Houses (E. Yorks. Loc. Hist. Soc.), 45.
30 B.I.H.R., V. 1884/Ret. 1; R.D.B., 839/49/47; C. E. Darwent, Story of Fish St. Ch., Hull (1899), 128–9, 131, 138.
31 B.I.H.R., V. 1912–22/Ret.
32 Neave and Neave, op. cit. 45.
33 B.I.H.R., Fac. Bk. 3, pp. 286, 315; P.R.O., HO 129/523/1/1/4.
34 Baines, Hist. Yorks. ii. 154.
35 R.D.B., FR/259/272; O.S. Map 6", Yorks. CLXXIX (1854 edn.).
36 R.D.B., IZ/135/162; datestone; O.S. Map 1/2,500, Yorks. CLXXIX. 4 (1892 edn.).
37 Neave and Neave, op. cit. 45; inf. from Mr. S. D. Bales, Driffield, 1996.
38 R.D.B., IZ/345/426; B.I.H.R., DMH. Reg. 2, pp. 127–8; P.R.O., HO 129/523/1/1/2; O.S. Map 6", Yorks. CLXXIX (1854 edn.).
39 R.D.B., LR/22/31.
40 Datestone; Pevsner and Neave, Yorks, E.R. 275.
41 Neave and Neave, op. cit. 45; E.R.A.O., MRD. accession 1036, circuit plans.
42 B.I.H.R., Fac. Bk. 3, p. 449.
43 Datestone; R.D.B., HU/167/200.
44 E.R.A.O., MRH/1/32; Neave and Neave, op. cit. 19 (illus.), 48.

Wesleyan Methodists registered houses at Lissett in 1807 and 1808.[45] Their services were still held in a house in 1851[46] but by 1879 they had been moved to Lissett school.[47]

EDUCATION. BEEFORD. A school may have been held in the church in the mid 16th century.[48] The private school supported by parents recorded under Beeford parish in the mid 18th century was perhaps the same as that held in a schoolhouse in the north-west corner of the churchyard in 1786.[49] A National school supported by subscription and school pence had been established in the village by 1818. It was attended then by 53 children from Beeford and Lissett and in 1833 by 40 boys and 20 girls.[50] A new school had been provided on the south side of Dringhoe Lane in 1816, perhaps by re-modelling an existing building; it may have been used from the outset, as it was later, for the boys.[51] An 'old school' was either continued or re-established in 1823,[52] and it was apparently its schoolhouse which Thomas Prickett, lord of the manor, gave to the trustees of the National school in 1846. Built on waste ground on the north side of Green Lane,[53] it may have been rebuilt soon after the conveyance and was later recorded as the girls' school.[54] The National school also included an infants' department by 1865.[55] In the mid century the school was supported by the rector, subscribers including the lord of the manor, school pence, and an annual government grant, first received in 1866, when the average attendance was 70.[56] The infants' school was apparently then kept in another building but its location is unknown; later the infants seem to have been taught in the girls' school.[57] At inspection in 1871 there were 101 pupils at the school.[58] The site of the boys' school was enlarged by gift of John Stocks in 1870.[59] A new National school for all departments was built in 1880 on land given by the rector on the south side of the street. The building was improved in 1890.[60] The former boys' school and its site were sold in 1883,[61] and in 1884 the former girls' school, 'lately called the infant school', was bought for a reading room.[62] The new school was enlarged in 1902.[63] In 1907–8 average attendance at Beeford Church school was 131, of whom 27 were infants. Numbers had fallen to an average of 113 by 1913–14[64] but the infants' department was then reckoned to be overcrowded and in 1929 the building was altered and enlarged and a playing field was provided.[65] In the 1920s and 1930s there were usually c. 100 pupils in attendance, but by 1937–8 only 86. Senior pupils were transferred to Hornsea County Secondary School in 1958.[66] The primary school site was enlarged by 2 a. in 1965.[67] In 1990 there were 64 on the roll at Beeford.[68]

In 1833 Beeford also had two mixed day schools supported by parents, one begun in 1823 with 20 pupils and the other started in 1826 with 31 in atttendance.[69]

LISSETT. At Lissett a Church school was built c. 1840, probably by Joseph Dent, whose family later owned the premises.[70] The mixed school, supported by subscription and school pence, had 10 pupils at inspection in 1871.[71] An annual government grant was received from 1882–3, when average attendance was 29.[72] The school accommodated infants and children from neighbouring settlements and farms, and in the 20th century it was called Ulrome, Lissett Church school.[73] The schoolhouse was restored by John Dent Dent in 1872,[74] and enlarged by J. W. Dent in 1901.[75] Average attendance at the school was usually c. 45 between 1906 and 1938 but in 1918–19 it was only 22 and in 1931–2 it stood at 58.[76] In 1934 the building and site were vested in the York Diocesan Board of Finance.[77] In 1951 there were 41 pupils aged between five and ten years old.[78] Ulrome, Lissett school was closed in 1968, the pupils then being transferred to a new primary school at Skipsea.[79] In 1996 the much-altered school building at Lissett was used as a house.

45 B.I.H.R., Fac. Bk. 3, pp. 448, 472.
46 P.R.O., HO 129/524/1/5/10.
47 Ibid. ED 7/135, no. 105.
48 H.U.L., DDPR/2/1.
49 B.I.H.R., V. 1764/Ret. 1, no. 51; E.R.A.O., PE/114/42; Herring's Visit. i, p. 108.
50 Educ. of Poor Digest, 1076; Educ. Enq. Abstract, 1079.
51 P.R.O., ED 7/135, no. 11; R.D.B., CY/239/346; O.S. Map 6″, Yorks. CLXXIX (1854 edn.).
52 E.R.A.O., PE/114/87, s.v. Oct. 1823.
53 Ibid. PE/114/93; R.D.B., GF/132/150.
54 P.R.O., ED 7/135, no. 11; O.S. Map 6″, Yorks. CLXXIX (1854 edn.).
55 P.R.O., ED 7/135, no. 11.
56 B.I.H.R., V. 1865/Ret. 1, no. 42; V. 1868/Ret. 1, no. 41; V. 1877/Ret. 1, no. 41; Rep. of Educ. Cttee. of Council, 1866-7 [3882], p. 656, H.C. (1867), xxii.
57 P.R.O., ED 7/135, no. 11; below, this section.
58 Returns relating to Elem. Educ. 472–3.
59 P.R.O., ED 49/8515; E.R.A.O., PE/114/94, 96; R.D.B., KS/24/27.
60 E.R.A.O., PE/114/97; O.S. Map 1/2,500, Yorks. CLXXIX. 4 (1892 edn.); Bulmer, Dir. E. Yorks. (1892), 106.
61 R.D.B., NW/52/84; E.R.A.O., PE/114/99. The Forge, no. 8, Skipsea Road, may be the remodelled building: inf. from Mr. G. Welburn, Beeford, 1996.

62 E.R.A.O., PE/114/82; above, intro.
63 Kelly's N. & E. R. Yorks. (1905), 419.
64 For attendance figures here and below, Bd. of Educ., List 21 (H.M.S.O., 1908 and later edns.).
65 E.R.A.O., PE/114/101–3; E.R. Educ. Cttee. Mins. 1913–14, 246; 1926–7, 36; 1927–8, 184; 1929–30, 160, 207, 210.
66 Ibid. 1955–6, 151; below, Hornsea, educ.
67 R.D.B., 1421/540/467; E.R. Educ. Cttee. Mins. 1964–5, 201–2, 205.
68 Inf. from Educ. Dept., Humbs. C.C., 1990.
69 Educ. Enq. Abstract, 1079.
70 R.D.B., 510/39/33; above, manors (Lissett).
71 P.R.O., ED 7/135, no. 105; Returns relating to Elem. Educ. 476–7.
72 Rep. of Educ. Cttee. of Council, 1882–3 [C.3706-I], p. 761, H.C. (1883), xxv.
73 E.R.A.O., SL/77/1, pp. 231–2, 245; SL/77/2, pp. 365–6; B.I.H.R., V. 1912–22/Ret. (s.v. Barmston).
74 Kelly's Dir. N. & E. R. Yorks. (1889), 326.
75 E.R.A.O., SL/77/1, pp. 324–6.
76 Bd. of Educ., List 21 (H.M.S.O., 1908 and later edns.).
77 R.D.B., 510/39/33.
78 E.R.A.O., SL/77/2, pp. 365–70.
79 Ibid. p. 434 and letter; H.U.L., DX/169/16; E.R. Educ. Cttee. Mins. 1962–3, 113.

Children from Dunnington have gone to school at Bewholme, in Nunkeeling.[80]

CHARITIES FOR THE POOR. Sir George Wood (d. 1824) left an annual rent charge for the poor of Beeford, its value, of £10, being fixed by his executors.[81] The charge had been redeemed by 1901, when the endowment comprised £300 stock and the income of just over £8 was spent on coal. Later some 30 doles were given instead.[82] The charity had been in abeyance for several years in 1980,[83] but in 1985 a Scheme was obtained for the charity.[84]

Robert Dixon of Dunnington by will proved in 1938 left £250 for needy parishioners. The sum was invested in stock, producing an income of c. £8 a year, which was spent on coal and groceries in 1939[85] and about 1980 was used for cash gifts at Christmas.[86]

BRANDESBURTON

THE parish of Brandesburton lies 18 km. north of Hull, 9 km. west from the coast at Hornsea, and is bounded on the west by the river Hull.[87] Brandesburton village is situated towards the southern boundary; 2 km. north is the small settlement of Moor Town and 2 km. WNW. is Burshill hamlet; Baswick, 5 km. to the west, was partly in Leven and its history is dealt with under that parish. The name Brandesburton is an Anglian and Scandinavian hybrid, meaning 'fortified farmstead belonging to Brandr', and Burshill, 'broken hill', is an Anglian name.[88]

In 1851–2 the ancient parish contained 5,185 a. (2,098 ha.), comprising 4,672 a. (1,891 ha.) in Brandesburton township and 513 a. (208 ha.) in that of Moor Town.[89] In 1885 Heigholme, with c. 300 a., was transferred from Hempholme, in Leven, to Brandesburton civil parish, but in 1895 it was added instead to Leven civil parish. Brandesburton contained 4,659 a. (1,885 ha.) by 1901.[90] In 1935 Hempholme civil parish, with 1,048 a. (424 ha.), was united with the civil parishes of Brandesburton and Moor Town to form the new civil parish of Brandesburton, containing 6,220 a. (2,517 ha.).[91] Some 28 ha. (70 a.) of Brandesburton were lost to Bewholme civil parish and about 2 ha. (4 a.) to Seaton civil parish in 1984, but c. 9 ha. (23 a.) were then gained from Seaton.[92] The area of Brandesburton was 2,494 ha. (6,163 a.) in 1991.[93]

There were 271 poll-tax payers in Brandesburton parish in 1377,[94] and 66 houses were assessed for hearth tax and 19 discharged in 1672.[95] The parish had 58 families in 1764.[96] In 1801 Brandesburton township had 432 inhabitants; its population increased steadily to 784 in 1861, fell to 658 in 1871, 604 in 1901, and 568 in 1931. The population of Moor Town rose from 32 in 1801 to 40 in 1811; thereafter it was usually c. 30 until the 1880s when numbers fell to 19 in 1891. There were only 17 people there in 1931. At that date 654 people lived in the area of the civil parish formed in 1935, whose population increased sharply to 1,011 in 1951, reflecting the development of Brandesburton hospital and an R.A.F. camp. The population was about the same in 1971, but had risen to 1,106 in 1981 and in 1991 was usually 1,362, of whom 1,332 were actually counted. That increase was partly due to Brandesburton's development as a dormitory village for Beverley and Hull.[97]

The higher ground in the east reaches 18 m. above sea level, while in the west the land lies at less than 5 m. The northern half of the parish is covered with boulder clay and the south and west with sand and gravel or alluvium. The settlements of Brandesburton and Burshill were sited on the sand and gravel,[98] which has been extensively extracted. The open fields of Brandesburton lay north-east and north-west of the village and the common pastures on the low-lying land to the south and west and on moorland to the north-east. Most of the commonable lands of Brandesburton, Moor Town, and Burshill were inclosed by agreement in 1635 and those remaining in 1847.[99]

The northern half of the parish mostly drains towards the river Hull in Hempholme through Frodingham and Holm drains, which run along the parish boundary, and Catchwater drain. Another drain running along Black bank marks the boundary between Brandesburton and Moor Town.[1] The southern half of Brandesburton was evidently once drained by small streams flowing south into Leven, one of which rose near Burshill and another close to the village. The Burshill stream was later improved as the Burshill and Barf drain and the other streams connected to it by the southern boundary drain, at least part of which, called New drain, was probably man-

---

[80] *Returns relating to Elem. Educ.* 472–3; E.R. Educ. Cttee. *Mins.* 1912–13, 58.

[81] H.U.L., DDCV(2)/31/41; Bulmer, *Dir. E. Yorks.* (1892), 106.

[82] E.R.A.O., accession 1681.

[83] Review of Char. *Rep.* 138.

[84] Char. Com. reg. no. 224191.

[85] E.R.A.O., PE/114/90–1; ibid. accession 1681.

[86] Review of Char. *Rep.* 138.

[87] This article was written in 1993 and later revised.

[88] *P.N. Yorks. E.R.* (E.P.N.S.), 74–5; G. F. Jensen, *Scand. Settlement Names in Yorks.* 135, 143.

[89] O.S. Map 6″, Yorks. CLXXIX, CXCVI (1854–5 edn.). The discrepancy comes from rounding.

[90] E.R.A.O., CCO/23; *Census*, 1891, 1901; below, Leven, intro.

[91] *Census*, 1931 (pt. ii).

[92] E.R.A.O., Holderness (Parishes) Order 1983; O.S. Map 1/2,500, Yorks. CLXXIX. 16, CLXXX. 13, CXCVI. 4 (1891 edn.).

[93] *Census*, 1991.

[94] P.R.O., E 179/202/60, m. 62.

[95] *Hearth Tax*, 61.

[96] B.I.H.R., V. 1764/Ret. 1, no. 85.

[97] *V.C.H. Yorks.* iii. 495; *Census*, 1911–91.

[98] Geol. Surv. Map 1″, sheets 72–3 (1909 edn.).

[99] Below, econ. hist.

[1] O.S. Map 6″, Yorks. CLXXIX (1854 edn.).

made. The alterations to the drainage may have been carried out in the mid 17th century. In the 1630s, just before inclosure, the carrs in Brandesburton were described as 'good grounds . . . continually drowned', and a scheme for their drainage was then agreed with people described as Dutchmen.[2] In 1743, however, despite earlier drainage work, the river was higher than four-fifths of Ing carr, which was regularly flooded.[3] As elsewhere in the Hull valley,[4] effective drainage of the carrs only began to be achieved after the formation in 1764 of the Holderness Drainage Board, which made or improved a drain through the carrs in Brandesburton and, more importantly, provided a new outfall to the Humber in the 1830s. Over 1,000 a. in the west of the parish were rated to the Holderness Drainage in 1775[5] and about the same in the 1830s.[6] The drainage of the parish was also improved under the Beverley and Barmston Drainage Act of 1798, primarily by the making of a new drain along the west bank of the river in Watton parish; 318 a. in Brandesburton and Moor Town were assessed to the work by the award of 1811.[7] Regular flooding of the carrs, neverthelesss, continued until the 1950s, when water levels in the river were reduced by the making of two reservoirs on its west bank.[8] In 1993 the river banks between Baswick and Hempholme were strengthened.[9]

From Brandesburton the principal road of the parish runs north to Beeford and south to Leven. It later became part of the main road connecting Bridlington with Hull and Beverley. Improvements to the road included the building of a bypass, called New Road, along the south-eastern edge of the village c. 1925,[10] and in 1994 a larger bypass for Brandesburton and Leven was opened further east. Minor roads connect the village with Nunkeeling, Catwick, Burshill, and North Frodingham. A road over Brandesburton moor, linking the Beeford and Nunkeeling roads, was made at inclosure in 1847.[11] From Burshill minor roads through the carrs lead to Baswick, Heigholme, and Hempholme; the course to Hempholme was diverted in 1956 to extend sand and gravel workings.[12] The parish's communications have also included the river Hull and there was a landing at Baswick.[13]

BRANDESBURTON. The main street of Brandesburton village bends to make an **L**, one part having an east-west alignment and the other running north-south, and both also forming a

stretch of the old Beeford to Leven road. The church, rectory house, Old Manor House, and school stand north of the eastern arm of Main Street, which formerly had almost no other houses on that side; on the south side, in the angle formed with Boardman Lane, is a small green called Cross Hill, on which stands the shaft of a medieval stone cross with part of the head. Houses were grouped along the southern arm of Main Street and in cross and back lanes. The name Little Burton, formerly given to the west end of the village, is now attached to one of the lanes there. Church Lane, which connected Main Street and a northern back lane, had been stopped up by the late 19th century, and the back lane, earlier and later also called Church Lane,[14] was discontinued in 1994. The buildings are of brick and mostly date from the 19th and 20th centuries. The older houses include Manor House, Brandesburton Hall,[15] and the Black Swan public house, which dates from the mid 18th century. Home Farm, probably rebuilt c. 1700, has a plat band and dentil eaves course; it belonged to George Noel (d. 1701) of Heigholme, in Leven, in the 1730s to his heirs, the Hunters, and in the earlier 19th century to the Revd. W. H. Dixon.[16] About 1975 the 18th-century hall fittings of no. 42 Blanket Row, Hull, including a staircase by George Schonswar, were used in the enlargement of Rectory Cottage.[17] A conservation area was designated in 1977.[18] The growth of the village in the 19th century included the building of a school in Main Street and chapels in Stockwell Lane and Little Burton.[19] In the mid 20th century c. 40 council houses were built at the north end of the village.[20] Later, houses were put up on either side of New Road and estates built at the west and south ends of the village. The district council also provided a sewage works beside New drain c. 1970.[21]

An alehouse called the Anchor was recorded in 1743, two licensed houses later in the 18th century, and the Black Swan and the Cross Keys in 1823.[22] The Cross Keys had been renamed the Dacre Arms by 1872.[23] Both still traded in 1993. A lodge of the Benevolent Society was founded in 1811 and mentioned until 1837. It may have been replaced by the Emanuel Hospital Lodge, founded in 1837 by the Independent Order of Oddfellows; it had 33 members in 1845 but was closed c. 1850. The Franklin Death Brief was founded c. 1844, had 92 members in 1905,[24] and still existed in

[2] Poulson, *Holderness*, i. 274.

[3] J. A. Shepherd, *Draining of Hull Valley* (E. Yorks. Loc. Hist. Ser. viii), 11, citing Lond. Corp. R.O., Emanuel hosp. box 3.10.

[4] *V.C.H. Yorks. E.R.* vi. 278–9.

[5] E.R.A.O., DDCC/143/135 (with map).

[6] Ibid. QDA/12A (map, 1833), 12B, 13 (with map, 1838).

[7] Ibid. DCBB/4/2, 8; 38 Geo. III, c. 63 (Local and Personal).

[8] Inf. from Mr. D. Rhimes, Leven, 1993.

[9] *Hull Daily Mail*, 22 July 1993.

[10] R.D.B., 287/61/49.

[11] E.R.A.O., QAH/1/21; H. Teesdale, *Map of Yorks.* (1828). [12] E.R.A.O., HD/223.

[13] O.S. Map 6″, Yorks. CXCVI (1855 edn.).

[14] Ibid.; O.S. Map 1/2,500, Yorks. CXCVI. 8 (1891

edn.); R.D.B., O/67/150. [15] Below, manors.

[16] R.D.B., O/67/150; CO/431/677; Lond. Corp. R.O., Emanuel hosp. plan, drawer 1, roll 19; plan, M 6b; below, Leven, manors (Heigholme).

[17] Inf. from the late Mr. Antony Blackmore, Brandesburton, 1994.

[18] Inf. from Devt. Dept., Holderness B.C., 1990.

[19] Below, nonconf.; educ.

[20] R.D.B., 590/487/387; 721/271/240; 769/159/133; 811/119/98; 1342/128/114.

[21] Ibid. 1764/338/294.

[22] Lond. Corp. R.O., Emanuel hosp. box 3.10, p. 54; E.R.A.O., QDT/2/6, 9.

[23] Directories.

[24] E.R.A.O., QDC/2/26; H.U.L., DX/26/14; D. [R. J.] Neave, *E.R. Friendly Soc.* (E. Yorks. Loc. Hist. Ser. xli), 45.

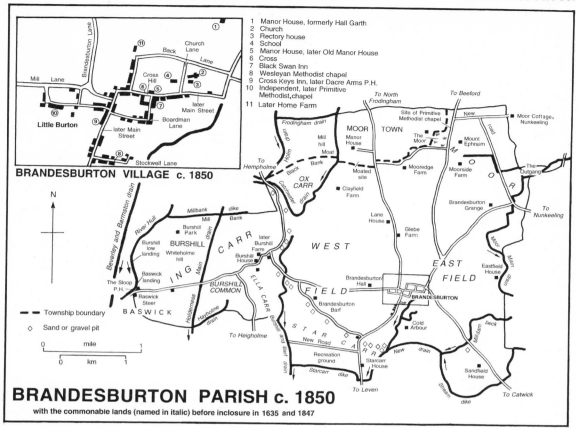

1 Manor House, formerly Hall Garth
2 Church
3 Rectory house
4 School
5 Manor House, later Old Manor House
6 Cross
7 Black Swan Inn
8 Wesleyan Methodist chapel
9 Cross Keys Inn, later Dacre Arms P.H.
10 Independent, later Primitive
    Methodist chapel
11 Later Home Farm

BRANDESBURTON VILLAGE c. 1850

BRANDESBURTON PARISH c. 1850

with the commonable lands (named in italic) before inclosure in 1635 and 1847

1993.[25] A Mutual Instruction, or Improvement, Society, formed in 1852 and with c. 60 members in 1892, operated a reading room and library in the village.[26] Allotment gardens were provided west of the village in the late 19th and early 20th century.[27] Land south-west of the village was allotted to the churchwardens and overseers of the poor at inclosure in 1847 for a recreation ground, which was evidently used until at least the late 19th century.[28] A cricket club played in the grounds of Brandesburton Hall until 1933, when a new recreation ground, named after the donor, Elizabeth Riall, was opened off New Road; it was also used for bowling from 1938.[29] The parish council was given a former R.A.F. building on the Catwick road by the Mewburn family c. 1950 for a village hall,[30] and a football club played on a field opposite it in 1993. The council also provided a children's playground in Mill Lane in 1973.[31] Several businesses have been established to exploit the former gravel workings: Humberside Shooting Ground was opened c. 1975, Billabong Water-sports c. 1980, Dacre Lakeside Park in 1985, and Fosse Hill

Jet Ski Centre c. 1987.[32] Hainsworth Park golf course was opened in 1982 on the former parkland of Brandesburton Hall.[33]

Brandesburton Hall was a hospital for the mentally incapacitated from 1932. The accommodation provided by the Hall and the converted stable block was enlarged by the building of three houses in the grounds in the mid 1930s, and in 1937 there were 192 patients. During the Second World War, the patients were evacuated and the buildings used to house R.A.F. personnel from Catfoss airfield, in Sigglesthorne. Mill Cottage remains from the military occupation, and following the re-occupation of the hospital many other additions were made. The hospital was closed in 1995.[34] A private children's home, opened c. 1935 on the Frodingham road, was later bought for the hospital and used as a children's ward and, by 1993, as staff accommodation;[35] it was sold in 1995. A Special School was opened by the L.E.A. in Brandesburton hospital in 1971; the children went to school in Beverley from 1972 until a new building in the

25 Notice in Dacre Arms, Brandesburton.
26 O.S. Map 1/2,500, Yorks. CXCVI. 6 (1891 edn.); Sheahan and Whellan, Hist. York & E.R. ii. 407; Bulmer, Dir. E. Yorks. (1892), 391.
27 O.S. Map 1/2,500, Yorks. CXCVI. 3 (1891 and 1910 edns.).
28 R.D.B., GI/1/1; O.S. Map 1/2,500, Yorks. CXCVI. 11 (1891 edn.).
29 Inf. from Mr. J. H. Mewburn, Brandesburton, 1993; O.S. Map 1/2,500, Yorks. CXCVI. 3 (1910 edn.).
30 Inf. from Mr. M. L. Hawkins, Brandesburton, 1993,

and Mr. G. Richardson, Beverley, 1998.
31 R.D.B., 1870/576/487.
32 Inf. from Mr. P. Thornton, Brandesburton, 1994; Billabong Water-sports, 1994; Fosse Hill Jet Ski Centre, 1993; Mr. Mewburn.
33 Inf. from Mr. B. Atkin, Brandesburton, 1994.
34 Below, manors [Midgley]; inf. from Mr. D. Robinson, Brandesburton Hall hospital, 1995; R.C.H.M., Report on Brandesburton hosp.
35 Inf. from Mr. G. Richardson, Beverley, 1993, and Mr. Robinson, 1994.

hospital grounds was opened in 1977, but falling numbers led to its closure in the early 1980s.[36]

From 1938 the Air Ministry bought or obtained rights over c. 330 a. in the east of the parish for the enlargement of Catfoss airfield. An associated camp was built at Brandesburton in or soon after 1948. The airfield was finally closed in 1963;[37] the land and buildings in Brandesburton were sold between 1960 and 1970 and have since been returned to agriculture or used industrially.[38]

BURSHILL hamlet comprises half a dozen farmhouses and cottages. Burshill House dates from the 18th century but was enlarged, remodelled, and refitted c. 1830.[39] About six scattered farmhouses make up Moor Town. Other outlying buildings in the parish include Brandesburton Barf, Brandesburton Grange, Glebe Farm, and Lane House, all built by 1772[40] and later remodelled or rebuilt.

Thomas Keith, mathematician (1759–1824), was born at Brandesburton.[41]

MANORS AND OTHER ESTATES. In 1066 seven manors of Brandesburton, comprising 12½ carucates and evidently including Burshill, were held by Sven, Ulfkil (*Ulchil*), Vek (*Waih*), Ketilfrith (*Chilvert*), Earnwig (*Arnui*), and two men called Ulf. Four of the manors and 11 carucates, then described as belonging to Ealdwif, Ulf, Ulf's brother, and Ulfkil, passed to William Malet, who was deprived c. 1070. By 1086 Drew de Bevrère held all 12½ carucates,[42] which were later part of the Aumale fee.

Part of Drew's estate was occupied in 1086 by a knight,[43] and Richard de St. Quintin probably held much of *BRANDESBURTON* in 1166.[44] Richard's son Herbert de St. Quintin had inherited the estate by 1194, and in 1202 William of Rochford and his wife Beatrice released their rights in Brandesburton to him in exchange for land at Thirtleby, in Swine.[45] Herbert (d. by 1223) was succeeded by his son Anselm, who had 9 carucates in Brandesburton.[46] By the mid century Anselm's estate had descended to his

nephew (Sir) Herbert de St. Quintin (d. 1302), who held 7 carucates in Brandesburton and 1 carucate in Burshill.[47] John de St. Quintin was recorded as lord of Brandesburton in 1316.[48] Herbert's grandson and heir Sir Herbert de St. Quintin (d. 1339), later had the manor. It then passed in turn to his son Sir Herbert (d. 1347), that Herbert's relict Margery (d. 1361), later wife of Sir Roger Hussey,[49] and to Herbert and Margery's daughter Laura (d. 1369), wife of Robert Grey[50] and Sir John de St. Quintin (d. 1397). Laura may have been succeeded by her son Herbert de St. Quintin (d. 1398) and certainly was by her daughter Elizabeth Grey (d. 1427), wife of Henry FitzHugh, Lord FitzHugh.[51] The manor descended in the FitzHughs to George FitzHugh (d. 1513), whose heirs were his aunt Alice FitzHugh, wife of Sir John Fiennes, and Sir Thomas Parr, the son of another aunt, Elizabeth FitzHugh.[52] It was evidently assigned to the Fienneses, who held the estate, except during periods of forfeiture in the mid 16th century, until Gregory Fiennes, Lord Dacre, died in 1594.[53] His wife Anne (d. 1595) devised the manor to Emanuel hospital, Westminster, founded under her will.[54] George Goring, Lord Goring, later earl of Norwich, (d. 1663) was the lessee at inclosure in 1635, when he was awarded 1,714 a. for 10 carucates and 2 bovates; he held besides old inclosures at Baswick and elsewhere in the parish. Goring's interest was assigned to his son George Goring (d. 1657), Lord Goring, who was succeeded by his brother Charles (d. 1671), later earl of Norwich.[55] Lessees of London corporation, which was governor of the hospital, later held the manor.[56] It comprised 3,634 a. in 1743 and 3,164 a. in 1910.[57]

In 1920 the Brandesburton estate was sold in many lots.[58] Manor House and Eastfield House farms, together comprising c. 400 a., were bought by Francis Richardson,[59] who sold c. 70 a. in the mid century.[60] After his death in 1955, his executors, F. W. O. Richardson and J. E. S. Richardson, held the estate, and it still belonged to the Richardsons in 1993.[61]

Manor House, on the north-eastern edge of the village, has also been known as Hall Garth and Hall Farm.[62] The present building probably

[36] E.R. Educ. Cttee. *Mins.* 1970–1, 167–9; 1971–2, 213; 1972–3, 58; *Beverley Guardian*, 28 July 1977; inf. from Mrs. Morley, Brandesburton Hall hospital, 1995.
[37] R.D.B., 593/139/113; 593/265/209; 594/171/133; 596/361/285; 607/72/54; 641/20/19; 769/76/69; 775/69/51; 779/3/3; 788/232/188; 790/293/244; 791/568/483; 801/437/351; 801/439/352; 806/119/101; 807/274/228; 812/37/31; 1008/330/291; B. B. Halpenny, *Action Stas.: 4. Military Airfields of Yorks.* 40–1; below, Sigglesthorne, intro. (Catfoss).
[38] R.D.B., 1176/395/339; 1422/171/150; 1422/507/441; 1424/185/167; 1427/555/481; 1428/511/450; 1435/230/209; 1439/444/402; 1538/190/166; 1881/204/188.
[39] Dept. of Environment, *Buildings List* (1985).
[40] T. Jefferys, *Map of Yorks.* (1772).
[41] *D.N.B.* [42] *V.C.H. Yorks.* ii. 267 and n., 295–6.
[43] Ibid. ii. 267.
[44] For the St. Quintins, *Early Yorks. Fam.* (Y.A.S. Rec. Ser. cxxxv), 79–80; *Complete Peerage*; J. Foster, *Pedigrees of Yorks.* iii.
[45] *E.Y.C.* iii, p. 50; xi, p. 354.
[46] *Cur. Reg. R.* xi, p. 265; English, *Holderness*, 150.
[47] *Cal. Inq. p.m.* iv, p. 95; *Kirkby's Inquest*, 373.
[48] *Kirkby's Inquest*, 303.
[49] *Cal. Inq. p.m.* ix, pp. 25–8; xi, p. 68; *Yorks. Fines, 1347–77*, pp. 214–15. [50] *Yorks. Deeds*, vi, p. 10.
[51] P.R.O., C 139/34, no. 45; *Complete Peerage*, s.v. FitzHugh; St. Quintin brass in church.
[52] P.R.O., C 139/151, no. 43; *Cal. Inq. p.m. Hen. VII*, i, pp. 115–16; *Feud. Aids*, vi. 273.
[53] P.R.O., C 142/244, no. 129; *Cal. Pat. 1580–2*, 64; *Complete Peerage*, s.v. Dacre.
[54] P.R.O., C 142/246, no. 122; Lond. Corp. R.O., Emanuel hosp. box 1.2.
[55] P.R.O., C 5/83/37, etc.; Poulson, *Holderness*, i. 270–7; *Complete Peerage*, s.v. Norwich.
[56] Lond. Corp. R.O., Emanuel hosp. box 2.2–3.
[57] Ibid. box 3.10; E.R.A.O., NV/1/24.
[58] R.D.B., *passim*. [59] Ibid. 217/337/300.
[60] Ibid. 507/244/190; 590/487/387; 821/26/20.
[61] Ibid. 1019/423/375; 1090/317/301; *Reg. of Electors* (1993).
[62] Lond. Corp. R.O., Emanuel hosp. box 3.8, 10, 12; box 4.2b; box 5.2; ibid. plan, drawer 1, roll 19; O.S. Map 6", Yorks. CXCVI (1855 edn.); directories.

dates from the early 18th century but was remodelled in the early 19th.[63] The panelled, 18th-century hall retains its original staircase.

Manor farm, of 106 a., was bought in 1920 by John Speed.[64] He sold 23 a. in 1924 and the house and 83 a. in 1934 to Frank Bell.[65] In 1940 Bell sold the farm to George (d. 1944), William (d. 1948), Frank, and Thomas Broumpton.[66] In 1948 Frank and Thomas Broumpton sold most of the land, and in 1954, after their deaths, the farmhouse was sold.[67] The estate has not been traced further. The farmhouse, said to have been rebuilt in 1715 and again in 1818, was called Manor House in the mid 19th century and later Old Manor House.[68] The two-storeyed, brick farmhouse stands on the street facing the village green.

Part of the Fienneses' estate was excepted from the gift to the hospital and passed to George Goring, Lord Goring, who c. 1630 had 6 bovates at *BURSHILL* and 1 bovate at Brandesburton, besides closes and common rights at Burshill.[69] That estate evidently passed with the leasehold to Goring's son Charles Goring (d. 1671), earl of Norwich, whose heirs sold part of it in 1674 to Sir Hugh Bethell (d. 1679) and the rest in 1686 to Bethell's nephew Hugh (d. 1717).[70] The Bethells' estate descended, like Rise, to Richard Bethell, who had 347 a. at Burshill in 1842.[71] A little land was sold in 1932 and the rest after the death in 1941 of W. A. V. Bethell.[72] The largest lot, Burshill farm, of c. 230-a., was bought in 1942 by John Rawson[73] and sold in 1948 to Richard and Kenneth Deighton.[74] The Deightons still farmed it in 1993.[75]

Jonathan Midgley bought a farm at Brandesburton in 1729, and between the 1750s and his death in 1778 he made other purchases there.[76] Midgley built a chief house which he left to his wife Mary; his daughter Mary, later wife of William Beverley, succeeded to most of the land and on her mother's death in 1791 evidently also to the house. In 1837 the Beverleys' son Robert conveyed c. 230 a. to Jonathan Harrison, who had almost 300 a. in Brandesburton in 1842.[77] Harrison (d. 1867) was succeeded by his son

J. S. Harrison, who bought c. 260 a. at Brandesburton in 1869 and 290 a. at Moor Town in 1874.[78] After Harrison's death in 1884, his estate descended to his son James, who had 583 a. at Brandesburton in 1910.[79] James died in 1923, and c. 125 a. was sold in small lots that year and the next.[80] The chief house, known by 1840 as Brandesburton Hall,[81] and 98 a. were bought for a hospital in 1931 by the East Riding and York Joint Board for the Mentally Defective;[82] it later passed to the East Riding Hospital Management Committee and in 1974 to the Humberside Health Authority.[83] The rest of the Harrisons' estate at Brandesburton descended like Moor Town and was sold in 1947;[84] the largest lot, Westfield farm of 271 a., was bought by Richard and John Dore.[85] It has not been traced further.

Jonathan Midgley is said to have built his house in 1772, and it was much enlarged for J. S. Harrison in 1851; of red brick with stone quoins, the house then comprised a main block with two wings.[86] The house was again rebuilt as a large Italianate mansion for Harrison in 1872 by William Hawe of Beverley, who was also responsible for the stable block of 1874 and a new kitchen block to the north, put up in or soon after 1881. Much of the ornamental planting of shrubs and trees around the house remained in 1998. About 1910 Brandesburton Hall was further enlarged with a west wing, comprising a large saloon and additional first-floor rooms, the existing exterior was enriched with more stonework, and the interior was generally refurbished. It was probably then that the several 18th-century fire surrounds, presumably rescued from other houses, were installed. The early 20th-century work for James Harrison was to designs by W. H. Brierley of York, with plasterwork by G. P. Bankart of London.[87] By the late 19th century the Hall stood in a large park.[88] James Harrison travelled in South America, Africa, and the Far East, and between 1905 and 1907 he had half a dozen pygmies from the Ituri forest, Zaire, living in the park.[89] After the Hall was opened as a hospital in 1932, several buildings were added in the grounds.[90]

Herbert de St. Quintin's estate in the parish included land at Moor Town in 1285.[91] It was

63 Dept. of Environment, *Buildings List* (1985).
64 R.D.B., 211/400/346.
65 Ibid. 281/353/298; 493/46/37.
66 Ibid. 634/151/118; 995/14/12.
67 Ibid. 791/568/483; 793/83/67; 941/294/255; 995/14/12.
68 Poulson, *Holderness*, i. 284; O.S. Map 6", Yorks. CXCVI (1855 edn.); directories; datestone.
69 Poulson, *Holderness*, i. 273.
70 E.R.A.O., DDRI/7/13, 15, 18, 21–2, 25; J. Foster, *Pedigrees of Yorks.* iii, s.v. Bethell; *Complete Peerage*, s.v. Norwich; above, this section.
71 B.I.H.R., TA. 853VL; below, Rise, manor.
72 R.D.B., 443/43/35; 655/563/481; 658/175/161; 659/ 12/10.   73 Ibid. 659/61/54.
74 Ibid. 805/32/27.   75 *Reg. of Electors* (1993).
76 R.D.B., L/33/62; Z/349/818; AI/97/201; AM/527/901; AZ/283/460.
77 Ibid. AZ/283/460; BY/351/536; FD/370/409; B.I.H.R., TA. 853VL.
78 R.D.B., KE/370/515; KY/83/111; E. Walford, *Co. Fam.* (1879), 478; below, this section (Moor Town).
79 R.D.B., 3/231/214 (1885); 17/480/474 (1887);

E.R.A.O., NV/1/24.
80 R.D.B., 269/270/228 and *passim*.
81 Poulson, *Holderness*, i. 285.
82 R.D.B., 420/532/433.
83 Inf. from Mr. D. Robinson, Brandesburton Hall hospital, 1994.
84 R.D.B., 769/159/133; 769/273/235; 770/21/18; 770/ 61/32; 770/148/127; 770/444/385; 771/301/252; below, this section (Moor Town).   85 R.D.B., 771/499/421.
86 Above, previous para.; Sheahan and Whellan, *Hist. York & E.R.* ii. 407; H. Teesdale, *Map of Yorks.* (1828); A. Bryant, *Map of E. R. Yorks.* (1829); O.S. Map 6", Yorks. CXCVI (1855 edn.).
87 B.I.H.R., Atkinson-Brierley papers 7/22a.; date on stables. O.S. Map 1/2,500, Yorks. CXCVI. 3 (1891 and 1910 edns.), which show that some of the early 20th-cent. work had been completed by 1909.
88 Bulmer, *Dir. E. Yorks.* (1892), 391; O.S. Map 1/2,500, Yorks. CXCVI. 3–4, 7 (1891 edn.).
89 *Country Life*, 10 Nov. 1977.
90 Above, intro. [Brandesburton hosp.].
91 *Kirkby's Inquest*, 74.

evidently held under the St. Quintins by a family named after the settlement. Robert Moore was granted free warren in the moor in 1309,[92] the manor of *MOOR* next to Brandesburton was settled on the same or another Robert Moore and his wife in 1323, Roger Moore held 1 carucate there of Sir Herbert de St. Quintin in 1347,[93] and another Robert Moore probably had the estate in 1408. It passed to the Ellerkers by the marriage of Isabel, daughter of Sir Robert or Sir John Moore, and John Ellerker. She (d. 1478) was apparently succeeded by her son Ralph Ellerker,[94] but later the estate, called *MOOR TOWN* manor in 1539, descended in the senior line of the Ellerkers, like Risby, in Rowley, passing eventually to the Bradshaws and Mainwaring Ellerkers.[95] In 1789 Roger M. Ellerker's heirs sold the estate of c. 450 a., together with an adjacent holding over the boundary in Beeford parish, to (Sir) George Wood (d. 1824), who devised both to his nephew John Stocks.[96] In 1842 Stocks had c. 500 a. at Moor Town.[97] He died in 1872, and his devisees sold the estate in 1874; the manor and Manor House Farm, of 290 a., were bought by J. S. Harrison of Brandesburton Hall and the rest by the rector, John Hymers, on his own behalf.[98] After James Harrison's death in 1923, his widow Mary (d. 1932) retained the farm at Moor Town.[99] In 1947 James Aconley bought it, and the Aconleys still had it in 1993.[1] The medieval manor house may have occupied one or other of the moated sites to the west and south-east of Manor House Farm,[2] which is a 19th-century building.

In 1086 the archbishop of York had a berewick of 1 carucate at Brandesburton. It was already assigned to his church of St. John at Beverley, which was later patron of Brandesburton church.[3] Land later belonging to Brandesburton rectory may account for part of the archbishop's estate, about which nothing further has been found.

Some of the Aumale fee had evidently passed to the Ros family by 1347. The estate, then 2 carucates, descended as an appurtenance of Roos manor.[4]

In 1371 St. Leonard's hospital, York, was licensed to acquire almost 1 carucate in Brandes-

burton and Seaton, in Sigglesthorne.[5] Nunkeeling priory had land at Burshill,[6] which was worth 10s. a year in 1535.[7]

ECONOMIC HISTORY

COMMON LANDS AND INCLOSURE. The tillage at Brandesburton was divided between East field, named from 1458,[8] and West field.[9] Common meadow land lay in Ing, later Inn, carr,[10] where 'wandales' of meadow were mentioned in 1630, and the ill-drained carrs also provided much rough grazing. Farmers at Moor Town probably shared the commonable lands of Brandesburton, and all parishioners had rough grazing on Brandesburton moor, an unstinted pasture of nearly 500 a.[11] which was probably intercommoned with Nunkeeling.[12] At Burshill at least 6 bovates remained of the hamlet's open fields in 1630; other land there, including desmesne land of Brandesburton manor at Baswick and Whiteholme, was evidently already inclosed. Much of Brandesburton and probably also part of Burshill were inclosed by agreement between 1630 and 1635, when the process was ratified by Chancery decree. West field was said to contain 1,321 a. and East field 1,174 a., Ing carr 307 a., West carr 250 a., and Ox carr 171 a.; North and Ella carrs, also mentioned, may have been parts of the quantified carrs. Star carr, variously put at 58 a. and 173 a., was awarded with an adjacent 90 a. from West field as a common pasture to support c. 120 gates,[13] hitherto enjoyed in Star carr and the open fields.

In 1743 the continuing pastures comprised, besides the moor, Ing carr of 557 a., which supported 240 beast gates and probably represented the former West and Ing carrs, Star carr of 246 a., and 35 a. in Ella carr and Burshill common enjoyed by the tenants of Burshill. Ing carr was then very poorly-drained and liable to flooding from the river Hull,[14] and all or part of Star carr was ploughed in 1749 after an outbreak of cattle plague and only returned to grass in 1754.[15] The inclosure of the remaining commonable lands was delayed partly by the poor drainage of the carrs.[16] Before final inclosure in 1847, the higher ground on Brandesburton moor was described as a 'rough uncultivated spot' on which 'many a thing' died.[17]

An award of 1847 under an Act of 1844 allot-

92 *Cal. Chart. R.* 1300–26, 133.
93 P.R.O., CP 25(1)/271/99, no. 22; *Cal. Inq. p.m.* ix, p. 27.
94 P.R.O., C 140/71, no. 56; H.U.L., DHO/7/19; *Cal. Close R.* 1405–9, 302; Poulson, *Holderness*, i. 259, 394–5.
95 P.R.O., C 142/118, no. 43; H.U.L., DHO/7/33; ibid. DDKE/8/84; DDKE/10/4; E.R.A.O., DDHE/34/111/7; *Yorks. Star Chamber Proc.* (Y.A.S. Rec. Ser. xli), 35 n.; *V.C.H. Yorks. E.R.* iv. 147.
96 R.D.B., BO/100/148; H.U.L., DDCV(2)/31/41; above, Beeford, manors (Moor Grange).
97 B.I.H.R., TA. 159s.
98 R.D.B., LH/417/546; LH/418/547; H.U.L., DDCV(2)/31/41; below, church [services].
99 R.D.B., 763/417/360; memorial in church; above, this section [Midgley].
1 R.D.B., 771/93/75; *Reg. of Electors* (1993).
2 O.S. Map 6", Yorks. CLXXIX (1854 edn.); O.S. Map 1/2,500, TA 1049 (1996–7 edn.).
3 *V.C.H. Yorks.* ii. 216; below, church [adv.].

4 P.R.O., C 142/139, no. 103; C 142/218, no. 52; H.U.L., DDSY/59/1; ibid. DHO/7/41; *Cal. Inq. p.m.* ix, pp. 25–8.
5 *Cal. Pat.* 1370–4, 67.
6 B.L. Cotton MS. Otho. C. viii, f. 88 and v.; Poulson, *Holderness*, i. 375.
7 *Valor Eccl.* (Rec. Com.), v. 115.
8 *Beverley Chapter Act Bk.* ii (Y.A.S. Rec. Ser. cviii), p. civ.
9 Rest of para. based on Poulson, *Holderness*, i. 270–7.
10 R.D.B., GI/1/1.
11 Lond. Corp. R.O., Emanuel hosp. box 3.10.
12 Below, Nunkeeling, econ. hist.
13 P.R.O., C 78/605/3; Lond. Corp. R.O., Emanuel hosp. box 3.4; E.R.A.O., PE/77/51. Confirmation printed in Poulson, *Holderness*, i. 270–7.
14 Lond. Corp. R.O., Emanuel hosp. box 3.10.
15 *Reg. Brandesburton* (Yorks. Par. Reg. Soc. cxlii), 153.
16 Camb., St. John's Coll., D67.80.
17 A. Harris, *Rural Landscape of E.R. Yorks.*, 43–4, 109.

ted 1,324 a. in all and there were *c.* 150 a. of exchanges, including 18 a. at Heigholme, in Leven, and 11 a. at Burshill. There were 549 a. to be inclosed in Ing carr, 457 a. on Brandesburton moor, 242 a. in Star carr, 28 a. in Ella, then Alley, carr, and 5 a. in Burshill common. Emanuel hospital received 814 a., Richard Bethell 126 a., and there were four allotments of 20–99 a., five of 10–19 a., and twenty of less than 10 a.[18] After inclosure 12 tenants of Emanuel hospital occupied 20 a. of 'cottagers' cow pastures', possibly as a continuing common pasture, and much of the land allotted to the hospital in the carrs was parcelled out among its smaller tenants.[19] Part of the moor remained unimproved *c.* 1850.[20]

HOLDINGS TO THE 17TH CENTURY. In 1086 there was land for 12½ ploughteams on Drew de Bevrère's estate at Brandesburton, and 3 teams were then worked, one of them by 6 villeins. One team was worked on the archbishop's estate, which also supported one villein and where 8 a. of meadow were recorded.[21] In 1630, besides the estates of Emanuel hospital and Lord Goring, amounting to over 11 carucates, freeholders held 3 carucates and 2 bovates; one had 1 carucate and 5 bovates and the other six holdings were of 1–4 bovates each.[22]

AGRICULTURE SINCE 1800. In 1801 the parish was said to have 847 a. under crops.[23] In 1842 there were 2,214 a. of arable land and 1,711 a. of grassland in Brandesburton, and 428 a. and 65 a. respectively in Moor Town.[24] Some of the grassland was ploughed after inclosure, and in 1905 the parish had 3,067 a. of arable land and 1,107 a. of grassland.[25] The proportion of arable to grassland was much the same in the 1930s, when most of the grassland was around the settlements and outlying farms.[26] For Brandesburton civil parish 2,091 ha. (5,167 a.) were returned as arable land in 1987 and 568 ha. (1,404 a.) as grassland.[27] Woodland covered 56 a. in 1905, but by 1987 there was only 11 ha. (27 a.) in small plantations.[28]

In the 19th and earlier 20th century there were usually two to three dozen farmers in Brandesburton, of whom 10 in 1851 and half a dozen in the 1920s and 1930s had 150 a. or more. At Moor Town there were 2–4 farmers, one or two of whom had larger farms. One or two cowkeepers, a cattle-dealer, and a market gardener were also recorded in the late 19th and

early 20th century.[29] In 1987 of 35 holdings returned under Brandesburton civil parish, three were of 200–499 ha. (494–1,233 a.), eight of 100–199 ha. (247–492 a.), six of 50–99 ha. (124–245 a.), and eighteen of less than 50 ha.; there were then more than 14,000 pigs, 1,700 sheep, and 1,300 cattle in the parish.[30]

MARKET AND FAIR. In 1286 Sir Herbert de St. Quintin was granted a weekly market on Thursdays and an annual fair on the eve, day, and morrow of the Invention of the Holy Cross (3 May).[31] A market and fair were still held *c.* 1840 but had ceased by the 1890s.[32]

MILLS. A windmill and another mill stood on the St. Quintin estate at Brandesburton in 1223,[33] and a windmill was recorded there until the late 18th century.[34] The location of a water mill is indicated by the name Milldam beck, and that of the windmill perhaps by Mill Lane. There was evidently also a windmill at Moor Town, where Mill hill was recorded.[35]

INDUSTRY. Chicory was dried in a kiln near Brandesburton Hall *c.* 1850.[36] Sand and gravel were dug from small pits in the parish before the 1920s, when larger-scale working was begun.[37] Extraction was continuing in the south-east of the parish in 1993, when some of the water-filled former workings were used for leisure pursuits.[38] There was then a small industrial estate on the Catwick road, and several small businesses, including a motor engineering firm, traded in the village.

LOCAL GOVERNMENT. A bylawman was recorded at Brandesburton in the early 18th century.[39] The village had stocks near the cross.[40]

In Brandesburton township, including Burshill, 12 people in 1802–3 and two dozen in 1812–15 received permanent out-relief; 3 and 15–20 respectively were helped occasionally. Moor Town gave occasional relief to *c.* 20 in 1812–15.[41] Both townships joined Skirlaugh poor-law union in 1837[42] and remained in Skirlaugh rural district until 1935, when, as part of the enlarged civil parish of Brandesburton, they were incorporated in the new Holderness rural district. Brandesburton civil parish was taken into the Holderness district of Humberside in 1974[43] and in 1996 became part of a new East Riding unitary area.[44]

[18] R.D.B., GI/1/1; plan at E.R.A.O., IA. (F5).
[19] Lond. Corp. R.O., Emanuel hosp. box 5.2.
[20] O.S. Map 6″, Yorks. CLXXIX (1854 edn.).
[21] *V.C.H. Yorks.* ii. 216, 267.
[22] Poulson, *Holderness*, i. 270–7.
[23] P.R.O., HO 67/26/27.
[24] B.I.H.R., TA. 159s; TA. 853vl.
[25] Acreage Returns, 1905.
[26] [1st] Land Util. Surv. Map, Sheet 28.
[27] Inf. from Min. of Agric., Fish & Food, Beverley, 1990.
[28] Ibid.; Acreage Returns, 1905.
[29] P.R.O., HO 107/2365; directories.
[30] Inf. from Min. of Agric., Fish & Food.
[31] *Cal. Chart. R.* 1257–1300, 328.
[32] Poulson, *Holderness*, i. 285; Bulmer, *Dir. E. Yorks.* (1892), 390.

[33] *Cur. Reg. R.* xi, p. 265.
[34] R.D.B., G/363/805; H.U.L., DDKE/12/11.
[35] O.S. Map 6″, Yorks. CLXXIX, CXCVI (1854–5 edn.).
[36] O.S. Map 6″, Yorks. CXCVI (1855 edn.).
[37] R.D.B., 336/223/179; 340/184/137; 343/31/24; H.U.L., DDFA(5)/13/434; O.S. Map 6″, Yorks. CLXXIX, CXCVI (1854–5 edn.).
[38] Above, intro. [social institutions].
[39] Lond. Corp. R.O., Emanuel hosp. box 2.4.
[40] *T.E.R.A.S.* iii. 48; Poulson, *Holderness*, i. 285.
[41] *Poor Law Abstract, 1804*, pp. 594–5; *1818*, pp. 522–3.
[42] *3rd Rep. Poor Law Com.* 170.
[43] *Census.*
[44] Humberside (Structural Change) Order 1995, copy at E.R.A.O.

CHURCH. There may have been a church at Brandesburton in 1086, when a clerk was recorded on the archbishop of York's estate,[45] and there was certainly one by 1251, when the first known rector was mentioned.[46] The archbishop's church of St. John at Beverley was patron until its suppression in 1548. Its successor, the Crown, presented in 1603, but evidently later sold the advowson. A dozen men presented between 1603 and the end of the century; some or all of them were exercising turns granted by the owner of the advowson, whose identity is thus obscured.[47] In 1650 Richard Lawson, rector, was said also to be patron,[48] and the advowson evidently passed to his son-in-law the Revd. Samuel Bromsgrove. Bromsgrove sold it in 1707 to Thomas Watson, bishop of St. David's,[49] who gave it to St. John's college, Cambridge, in 1710. A right of nomination in certain circumstances was reserved to Hull corporation until it released its interest to the college in 1909.[50] The college exercised its patronage, except in 1954 and 1988, when the archbishop presented by lapse.[51] The ecclesiastical parish was enlarged by the transfer of Hempholme from Leven in or soon after 1982.[52] In 1997 Brandesburton was united with Leven with Catwick.[53]

The rectory was worth £13 6s. 8d. in 1291, after payment of a pension of £2 to the provost of Beverley, and almost £25 net in 1535.[54] The improved annual value was £150 14s. net in 1650.[55] Between 1829 and 1831 the net income averaged £895 a year, and in 1897 it was £836.[56] In 1635 the tithes of the lands then inclosed and of the old inclosures at Brandesburton and Burshill were compounded for £128 a year; those of Moor Town were already paid by a modus of £12 a year.[57] The tithes of the whole of Brandesburton township were commuted for a rent charge of £993 6s. 6d. by awards of 1842 and 1845 and apportionment of the latter year. Those of Moor Town were extinguished for a rent charge of £90 5s. by award of 1842 and apportionment of 1846.[58]

The glebe land included 4 bovates, for which c. 90 a. were evidently awarded at inclosure in 1635.[59] In 1650 the glebe was valued at £20 gross a year.[60] There were 105 a. of glebe land in 1842.[61] At the inclosure of 1847 the rector received 38 a. more for common rights.[62] Glebe farm was sold in 1930,[63] and in 1978 less than 8 a. of glebe land remained.[64] A rectory house was recorded from 1535.[65] The present house dates mostly from the 18th century, as does its stable building. In the early 19th century the house was enlarged,[66] but in 1958 a wing was demolished.[67] In 1989 a new rectory house was built nearby and the old one was sold.[68]

In the 16th century rectors of Brandesburton often served other cures and were non-resident.[69] In the mid 18th century the resident rector provided two Sunday services and quarterly celebrations of communion for 40–50 recipients.[70] Assistant curates were employed in the 19th century, in the later part of which 7–8 communions were celebrated each year, with two dozen people usually receiving.[71] Hymers college, Hull, was founded in 1889 in fulfilment of the wishes of John Hymers, rector of Brandesburton from 1852 until his death in 1887.[72] A wooden mobile chapel was built in 1888 with the intention of moving it between Burshill and Moor Town, but the difficulty of that operation caused it later to be stationed permanently at Moor Town. Although licensed for baptisms and communion, it was used almost entirely for a fortnightly service on Wednesday evenings until that was discontinued in the mid 20th century. The chapel was given to Brandesburton football club for a changing room in the late 1950s.[73]

The church of *ST. MARY*, so called by 1311,[74] is mostly of boulders and brick with stone dressings; it comprises chancel with north vestry, aisled and clerestoried nave with south porch, and west tower. A 12th-century doorway in the chancel and fragments of similar date rebuilt into the tower and south aisle wall suggest that there was a church on the site at that time. Chancel, arcades, aisles, and tower all seem to be of 13th-century origin. The chancel was remodelled in the 14th century and again early in the 16th, and the aisles were refenestrated in the 15th century, perhaps at the same time as the clerestory was added and the tower altered.[75] A squint and a niche with a crocketed, ogee canopy remain in the chancel and an ogee-

45 *V.C.H. Yorks.* ii. 216.
46 *Cal. Papal Reg.* i. 273.
47 Lawrance, 'Clergy List', Holderness, 1, pp. 21–4; Poulson, *Holderness*, i. 282–3.
48 *T.E.R.A.S.* iv. 61.
49 Camb., St. John's Coll., D67.79.
50 Ibid. D23.12; D67.86.
51 Inf. from the rector, Leven, 1993.
52 E.R.A.O., PE/128/T.93.
53 Inf. from the rector, Leven, 1997.
54 *Tax. Eccl.* (Rec. Com.), 302–3; *Valor Eccl.* (Rec. Com.), v. 119.
55 *T.E.R.A.S.* iv. 61.
56 *Rep. Com. Eccl. Revenues*, 920–1; *Kelly's Dir. N. & E.R. Yorks.* (1897), 412.
57 Camb., St. John's Coll., SBFL.2; Poulson, *Holderness*, i. 273–4.
58 B.I.H.R., TA. 159s; TA. 853vl.
59 Ibid. TER. H. Brandesburton 1685; Poulson, *Holderness*, i. 272.
60 *T.E.R.A.S.* iv. 61.
61 B.I.H.R., TA. 853vl.

62 R.D.B., GI/1/1.
63 Ibid. 404/582/472.
64 Inf. from York Dioc. Bd. of Finance, 1981.
65 B.I.H.R., TER. H. Brandesburton 1685; *Valor Eccl.* v. 119.
66 B.I.H.R., TER. H. Brandesburton 1716 etc.
67 Ibid. MGA. 1958/4.
68 Inf. from the late Mr. Antony Blackmore, Brandesburton, 1994.
69 Lawrance, 'Clergy List', Holderness, 1, p. 23.
70 B.I.H.R., V. 1764/Ret. 1, no. 85; *Herring's Visit.* i, p. 107.
71 Lond. Corp. R.O., Emanuel hosp. box 5.2; B.I.H.R., V. 1865/Ret. 1, no. 75; V. 1868/Ret. 1, no. 73; V. 1871/Ret. 1, no. 72; V. 1877/Ret. 1, no. 68; V. 1884/Ret. 1.
72 *D.N.B.*; *V.C.H. Yorks. E.R.* i. 365.
73 B.I.H.R., TER. 82; ibid. V. 1931/Ret.; Bulmer, *Dir. E. Yorks.* (1892), 392; typescript memories of Mrs. Ena Dean, 1998, communicated by Mr. Andrew Anderson, Brandesburton, 1999; inf. from Mr. G. H. White, Bewholme, 1992.
74 *Beverley Chapter Act Bk.* i (Sur. Soc. xcviii), 285.
75 B.I.H.R., Prob. Reg. 4, f. 185.

FIG. 17. BRANDESBURTON CHURCH AFTER RESTORATION

headed piscina in the south aisle. The tower was decayed in 1600.[76] The north side of the church and the tower were repaired *c.* 1720, when the chancel screen was also removed.[77] In 1892 the church was restored by W. S. Weatherley; the work included the rebuilding of the tower with a staircase turret and the replacement of a south vestry, added in 1857 by John Hymers, by that on the north side of the chancel.[78] New fittings then installed included a carved, wooden reredos.

Memorials in the chancel include a brass for Sir John de St. Quintin (d. 1397) and his wife Laura (d. 1369) and the only example in the East Riding of a 'bracket' brass,[79] commemorating William Darrell, rector (d. 1364). A wall monument to Charles Richardson, rector, and Thomas Richardson (both d. 1755) has a heavy, stone border crowned by a broken pediment and another, pyramidal in shape, commemorates Jonathan Midgley (d. 1778) and his wife Mary (d. 1791). Royal Arms of George IV remain. There were three bells in 1552, but only two from the late 18th century.[80] The plate includes an early 17th-century chalice and a new service given by the rector in 1862.[81] The registers of

baptisms, marriages, and burials date from 1558 and are complete; they have been printed to 1804 for baptisms and burials and to 1753 for marriages.[82] Churchyard additions were consecrated in 1867, 1913, and 1955.[83]

NONCONFORMITY. Several recusants and non-communicants were recorded at Brandesburton in the 16th and 17th centuries,[84] and in 1676 there were said to be 9 recusants in the parish.[85]

Ten protestant dissenters were recorded in 1676,[86] and unidentified protestant congregations registered houses at Brandesburton in 1795 and 1819.[87] Independents, encouraged by Fish Street chapel, Hull, registered a house there in 1805 and built a chapel in the lane called Little Burton in 1809.[88] The chapel was rebuilt in 1842, but its congregation was only *c.* 20 in 1851 and in 1856 it was sold to the Primitive Methodists.[89] That congregation, which had used a house for worship since 1839,[90] enlarged the former Independent chapel in 1863.[91] The Wesleyans built a chapel in Stockwell Lane in

[76] Ibid. V. 1600/CB. 2, f. 127v.
[77] Ibid. ER. V. Ret. 1, f. 30; ER. V. Ret. 2, f. 3.
[78] Ibid. Ch. Ret. i; ibid. Fac. 1889/1.
[79] *Y.A.J.* xii. 203.
[80] B.I.H.R., TER. H. Brandesburton 1764 etc.; *Inventories of Ch. Goods*, 43; G. R. Park, *Ch. Bells of Holderness*, 65.
[81] B.I.H.R., TER. H. Brandesburton 1764 etc.; ibid. TER. 82; *Yorks. Ch. Plate*, i. 226.
[82] E.R.A.O., PE/77/1–9; *Reg. Brandesburton* (Yorks. Par. Reg. Soc. cxlii).
[83] B.I.H.R., CD. Add. 1867/1; 1913/1; 1955/1.

[84] *Depositions from York Castle* (Sur. Soc. xl), 123; Aveling, *Post Reformation Catholicism*, 23, 68.
[85] *Compton Census*, ed. Whiteman, 600.
[86] Ibid.
[87] P.R.O., RG 31/5, nos. 1115, 3330.
[88] Ibid. no. 1975; ibid. HO 129/522/5/8; B.I.H.R., Fac. Bk. 3, p. 406; O.S. Map 6″, Yorks. CXCVI (1855 edn.); C. E. Darwent, *Story of Fish St. Ch., Hull* (1899), 129, 134–5.
[89] P.R.O., HO 129/522/5/8; R.D.B., HO/138/169.
[90] P.R.O., RG 31/5, no. 4465; B.I.H.R., DMH. 1839/23.
[91] Bulmer, *Dir. E. Yorks.* (1892), 391.

1809, registered it in 1810, and restored it in 1888.[92] A new Methodist church was built in Main Street *c.* 1937, after the union of the Methodist congregations,[93] and it was still used in 1993. The former Primitive and Wesleyan chapels were sold in 1938[94] and later used as private houses. At Moor Town the Primitive Methodists built a small chapel in 1870.[95] It was closed in 1976[96] and was derelict until converted into a crematorium for small animals *c.* 1985.[97]

EDUCATION. There was an unlicensed schoolmaster at Brandesburton in 1604,[98] the curate had a school there in 1640, and a boys' school was attended by *c.* 40 pupils from Brandesburton and neighbouring places in the mid 18th century.[99] The school benefited from a bequest of £100 for the teaching of poor children of Brandesburton, made by Frances Barker in 1729. The interest on the sum was paid at first to the schoolmaster as a salary. In the early 19th century the same or another school, then mixed, was held in a room rented from London corporation. By then 11 a. at Sutton had been bought with Barker's bequest, and *c.* 1820 the £25 rental was being used mostly to support pupils; 17 were then paid for, parents supporting the other 53.[1] The boys and girls were taught separately by 1833. The boys' school, with 42 pupils, then received £37 a year from Barker's charity, for which 30 were taught free. At the girls' school about half of the 34 pupils were paid for by London corporation and 3 by donations.[2]

In 1843 the corporation of London built a new school in the village with departments for boys and girls; the brick building is of one storey with a symmetrical, six-bayed elevation. In 1855 a separate building was being used for 42 infants.[3] The former boys' and girls' schools were converted into houses.[4] At inspection in 1871 there were 61 boys and 26 girls at the school,[5] which was enlarged by the building of another block in 1877, possibly to accommodate the infants.[6] Besides the sum from Barker's charity, subscriptions, and school pence, the school was funded by an annual government grant from 1876.[7]

The boys' and girls' departments were amalgamated in 1904, and in 1921 the school was transferred to the county council.[8] Average attendance from 1906 was usually *c.* 90 but fell to 78 in 1932. Numbers recovered with the admittance of pupils from the childrens' home.[9] By 1955 a room in the rectory house was used for a classroom, and in 1960 the school was again enlarged.[10] Senior pupils were transferred to Hornsea County Secondary School in 1958.[11] There were 110 on the roll in 1990.[12] In 1999 the school was extended with three classrooms, a hall, a computer room, and staff rooms.[13]

The income from the Barker charity land was £24 a year in 1901.[14] The land was sold in 1921, and by Scheme of 1923 the School Land Foundation was established to support children from the parish in secondary and further education; *c.* 1980 the income from stock was £152 a year.[15]

Children from Moor Town went to Brandesburton and North Frodingham schools in the 19th century.[16]

CHARITIES FOR THE POOR. The Revd. William Mason (d. by 1720) left the poor £50, for which his daughter Frances and her husband Thomas Barker substituted an annual rent charge of £2 10s. The income was distributed as doles *c.* 1820[17] and in the early 20th century,[18] but the charity was later lost.[19]

John Holme, rector 1755–75, bequeathed a quarter of the income from stock for Christmas doles at Brandesburton, and £3 7s. 6d. a year was distributed *c.* 1820.[20] In 1985 the income of just over £1 was added to an unspent balance of £21.[21]

One Boswell gave £20 in the 1760s for the inclosure of Barker's charity land at Sutton. Interest of £1 a year from an unspent part was being given to the poor by the rector *c.* 1820.[22] John Chapman (d. by 1729) left £10 to the poor of Brandesburton, the income from which was to be distributed annually on May Day.[23] No more is known of either charity.

92 P.R.O., HO 129/522/5/9; ibid. RG 31/5, no. 2410; O.S. Map 6", Yorks. CXCVI (1855 edn.); Bulmer, *Dir. E. Yorks.* (1892), 391.
93 R.D.B., 567/166/124.
94 Ibid. 609/349/268; 610/607/484.
95 Ibid. KN/324/452; Bulmer, *Dir. E. Yorks.* (1892), 391; illus. in D. [R. J.] and S. Neave, *E.R. Chapels and Meeting Houses* (E. Yorks. Loc. Hist. Soc.), 47.
96 *Hull Daily Mail*, 4 June 1977.
97 Inf. from Mr. W. E. Copeland, Moor Town, 1993.
98 B.I.H.R., V. 1604/CB. 1, f. 84.
99 P.R.O., ED 7/135, no. 20; B.I.H.R., V. 1764/Ret. 1, no. 85; *Herring's Visit.* i, p. 107; J. Lawson, *Primary Educ. in E. Yorks. 1560–1902* (E. Yorks. Loc. Hist. Ser. x), 4.
1 *9th Rep. Com. Char.* 755–6; *Educ. of Poor Digest*, 1077.
2 *Educ. Enq. Abstract*, 1080.
3 P.R.O., ED 7/135, no. 20; Lond. Corp. R.O., Emanuel hosp. box 5.2, 5.5; plaque on school; Pevsner and Neave, *Yorks. E.R.* 337.
4 Lond. Corp. R.O., Emanuel hosp. box 5.2.
5 *Returns relating to Elem. Educ.* 472–3.
6 Lond. Corp. R.O., Emanuel hosp. box 5.5; *Hull Daily Mail*, 1 Mar. 1993; Bulmer, *Dir. E. Yorks.* (1892), 391.

7 P.R.O., ED 7/135, no. 20; *Rep. of Educ. Cttee. of Council, 1875–6* [C.1513–I], p. 656, H.C. (1876), xxiii.
8 R.D.B., 227/498/439; E.R. Educ. Cttee. *Mins.* 1904–5, 118; 1921–2, 38.
9 *Bd. of Educ., List 21* (H.M.S.O., 1908 and later edns.); E.R. Educ. Cttee. *Mins.* 1937–8, 117.
10 E.R. Educ. Cttee. *Mins.* 1955–6, 77; 1959–60, 214.
11 Ibid. 1955–6, 151; below, Hornsea, educ.
12 Inf. from Educ. Dept., Humbs. C.C., 1990.
13 *Hull Daily Mail*, 18 May 1999.
14 E.R.A.O., accession 1685.
15 E.R. Educ. Cttee. *Mins.* 1921–2, 47, 112; *Humbs. Dir. of Char.* 82; Review of Char. *Rep.* 102; inf. from Mr. L. Hawkins, Brandesburton, 1993.
16 *Returns relating to Elem. Educ.* 472–3.
17 *9th Rep. Com. Char.* 755–6, 857–8; *Reg. Brandesburton* (Yorks. Par. Reg. Soc. cxlii), 92.
18 E.R.A.O., accession 1685.
19 Review of Char. *Rep.* 102.
20 *9th Rep. Com. Char.* 756–7; memorial in church; *Alum. Cantab. to 1751*, 398.
21 E.R.A.O., CCH/84.
22 *9th Rep. Com. Char.* 756.
23 *Reg. Brandesburton*, 89.

CATWICK

THE parish lies 18 km. NNE. of Hull and 10 km. WSW. of Hornsea, with the small village of Catwick close to the northern boundary.[24] The name Catwick is Anglian and probably means 'the dairy farm of Catta and his people'.[25] In 1851 the ancient parish contained 1,570 a. (635 ha.);[26] its boundary has since remained unchanged.

The number of poll-tax payers at Catwick in 1377 is not known but in 1672 the parish had 24 houses assessed for hearth tax and 9 discharged.[27] There were 18 families in 1743 and 15 in 1764.[28] From 132 in 1801 the population rose sharply in the 1810s to 190 in 1821 and grew again in mid century to 248 in 1861 and 273 in 1871. From the 1880s it fell to 195 in 1901 and thereafter fluctuated around 200, before falling again to 173 in 1961. There were 197 inhabitants by 1981 but only 171 were recorded in 1991, when 174 were usually resident.[29]

The parish is on boulder clay, sand, and gravel, and much of the land exceeds 7 m. above sea level, rising to 15 m. at the eastern boundary.[30] Sand and gravel deposits in the north and west form some of the higher land, including Gildholm hill, Catwick hill, and Westlands hill; much of the gravel north-east of the village has been extracted.[31] Lower, mostly alluvial, land borders the main drains, which flow west into the Holderness drain. The northern boundary is formed by a stream comprising Catfoss drain, Stream dike, and New drain, and another drain, also called Stream dike and then Bowlams dike, runs through the southern half of the parish. The former existence of meres in Catwick is evident from the names Bramer, Star mere, and Great mere, all recorded in 1685.[32] The open fields and common meadows lay east, south, and west of the village, with the common pastures in the north-west and south-east corners of the parish; the commonable lands were inclosed in 1732.

The principal road is that crossing the parish from Beverley and Leven in the west to Hornsea in the east. The western stretch was improved in the 1930s and the eastern part c. 1980.[33] From the Leven–Hornsea road minor roads run south to Long Riston, south-east to Rise, north-west to Brandesburton, and north to Catfoss, in Sigglesthorne. The Long Riston road was diverted in 1811.[34] At the east end of the village the road from Rise formerly crossed the main road and continued north-eastwards to join the Brandesburton road; as a public road that course was discontinued in 1878, but it continued to be used as a field track.[35]

CATWICK village is built along both sides of the principal road, called Main Street, in a southern back lane, and in Little Catwick, lying further south beside the Long Riston road. Most of the buildings are of brick and were built in the 19th and 20th centuries. Older buildings include Catwick House, in Main Street, which dates from the late 18th century and retains a contemporary stable block. Willow Croft Farm, in Little Catwick, was put up in 1792, and its outbuildings include a wheelhouse.[36] Houses stood on the sites of both Manor Farm, on the Long Riston road, and Old Hall at Little Catwick by 1772.[37] The church and former rectory house stand in the back lane, where Wesleyan and Primitive Methodist chapels were added in the mid 19th century.[38] Modern in-filling has included the building in the mid 20th century of half a dozen council houses in Main Street and that part of the back lane called Rowpit Lane. Sewage pumping stations in Rowpit Lane and beside the Brandesburton road were also built and operated by the district council.[39] An alehouse was licensed at Catwick in the later 18th century,[40] but there is no later record of a public house there. A recreation hut, opened c. 1920, was replaced by a village hall built on the same site in 1987.[41] The village formerly included a holy well, named Lady well, in the grounds of Manor Farm. A moated site, north of Catwick House, may have been the site of a medieval manor house.[42]

OUTLYING BUILDINGS include three farmhouses built on land inclosed in 1732: Catwick Mill Farm had been put up by 1772, and Cobble Hall and Catwick Grange date from between 1772 and 1829.[43]

MANORS AND OTHER ESTATES. In 1066 two manors of *CATWICK*, comprising 5 carucates, were held by Sven and Murdoch. Four of the carucates, belonging before or after 1066 to Ealdwif, passed to William Malet, who was deprived c. 1070. By 1086 all 5

---

[24] This article was written in 1992.
[25] *P.N. Yorks. E.R.* (E.P.N.S.), 73.
[26] O.S. Map 6″, Yorks. CXCVI–CXCVII (1854–5 edn.).
[27] *Hearth Tax*, 61.
[28] B.I.H.R., V. 1764/Ret. 1, no. 119; *Herring's Visit.* i, p. 157.
[29] *V.C.H. Yorks.* iii. 495; *Census*, 1911–91.
[30] Geol. Surv. Map 1″, drift, sheets 72–3 (1909 edn.).
[31] O.S. Map 6″, Yorks. CXCVI–CXCVII (1854–5 edn.); below, econ. hist.
[32] B.I.H.R., TER. H. Catwick 1685.
[33] R.D.B, 544/638/496; inf. from Mrs. H. M. Clubley, Catwick, 1993.
[34] E.R.A.O., HD/17.

[35] Ibid. HD/85; O.S. Map 6″, Yorks. CXCVI (1855 edn.); O.S. Map 1/2,500, Yorks. CXCVI. 8, 12 (1891 edn.); O.S. Map 6″, Yorks. TA 14 NW. (1956 edn.).
[36] Datestone.
[37] T. Jefferys, *Map of Yorks.* (1772).
[38] Below, nonconf.
[39] R.D.B., 588/309/228; 694/223/188; 1560/565/480; 1739/235/207.
[40] E.R.A.O., QDT/2/9.
[41] Inf. from Mr. W. H. Brumpton, Catwick, 1992; inf. from Mrs. Clubley.
[42] O.S. Map 6″, Yorks. CXCVI (1855 edn.).
[43] E.R.A.O., IA. (G. 34); Jefferys, *Map of Yorks.* (1772); A. Bryant, *Map of E.R. Yorks.* (1829).

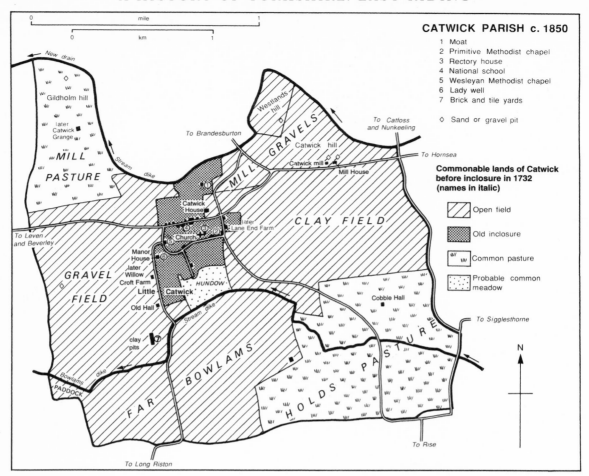

CATWICK PARISH c. 1850

1 Moat
2 Primitive Methodist chapel
3 Rectory house
4 National school
5 Wesleyan Methodist chapel
6 Lady well
7 Brick and tile yards

◇ Sand or gravel pit

Commonable lands of Catwick
before inclosure in 1732
(names in italic)

▨ Open field
▦ Old inclosure
▨ Common pasture
▨ Probable common meadow

carucates were held by Drew de Bevrère and were later part of the Aumale fee. The manors of Catwick were occupied in 1086 by two of Drew's knights.[44]

One of Drew's knights was probably the Ralph who in 1086 held Carlton manor, in Aldbrough, which had also been Sven's, and he or another, as Ralph of Catwick, gave a moiety of Catwick church to Pontefract priory before 1127. Like Carlton, Catwick descended in the Whittick family and then passed apparently to the Meltons and Darcys.[45] Simon Whittick held 3 carucates of the Aumale fee at Catwick in the mid 13th century, and in the 1280s his successor William Whittick had 3½ carucates in demesne.[46] Walter Whittick was named as a lord of Catwick in 1316.[47] John Melton (d. 1458) held the manor.[48] John Darcy, Lord Darcy, was dealing with the manor in the 16th century, and, after his death in 1602, his successor, also John Darcy, Lord Darcy, sold it, then comprising

only 6 bovates, to Robert Escrick the elder (d. 1621) and the younger.[49] Robert Escrick the elder enlarged the estate by purchase in 1608 and 1617. The younger Robert (d. 1643) was succeeded by his sons Robert (d. by 1690) and Ralph (d. 1728).[50] Ralph's heirs sold the manor in 1729 to Hugh Bethell, who already had an estate in the parish, bought in 1654 by his great-uncle Sir Hugh Bethell. Bethell (d. 1752)[51] was awarded 289 a. at the inclosure of Catwick in 1732 and bought 83 a. more in 1746.[52] The estate later descended, like Rise, in the Bethells to William Bethell, who had 422 a. in the parish in 1910.[53] After his death in 1926, Manor farm, comprising 237 a., was sold to James Mewburn in 1929; most of the remaining land was sold in several lots in 1943, and only 14.6 ha. (36 a.) in the parish remained with the Bethells in 1990.[54] From Mewburn (d. 1935) Manor farm passed to his widow and son Robert, who divided and sold the estate in 1948 and 1953, c. 230 a. going to Arthur and Kenneth Newton.[55] The Newtons

44 V.C.H. Yorks. ii. 267, 295–6, 327; Cal. Inq. p.m. iv, p. 355.
45 E.Y.C., iii, p. 46; above, Aldbrough, manors (Carlton); below, church.
46 Cal. Inq. p.m., iv, p. 355; Kirkby's Inquest, 372.
47 Kirkby's Inquest, 304.
48 P.R.O., CP 25(1)/281/161, no. 5; C 139/168, no. 28.
49 Ibid. C 142/273, no. 82; C 142/758, no. 218; E.R.A.O., DDRI/11/61; Yorks. Fines, i. 236.
50 R.D.B., K/618/1318; E.R.A.O., PE/9/1–2; ibid. DDRI/11/67; Yorks. Fines, 1603–14, 93.

51 R.D.B., L/2/3; L/102/105; E.R.A.O., DDRI/11/4; J. Foster, Pedigrees of Yorks. iii, s.v. Bethell.
52 R.D.B., B/57/24; S/304/730.
53 E.R.A.O., NV/1/31; below, Rise, manor.
54 R.D.B., 350/497/415; 400/211/163; 661/310/273; 661/440/381; 667/378/332; 667/379/333; 667/432/378; 667/565/493; 668/314/269; 669/124/108; inf. from Rise Park Estate Off. 1990.
55 R.D.B., 531/443/319; 785/244/197; 938/318/274; 938/510/450.

already owned *c.* 180 a. in the parish and were still the owners of Manor farm in 1992.[56] Manor Farm House, formerly Manor House, was evidently rebuilt in the 19th century.[57]

Drew de Bevrère's second knight in 1086 was evidently succeeded by the Fauconbergs. W. de Fauconberg, who held 2 carucates in Catwick in the mid 13th century,[58] was probably Walter de Fauconberg, later Lord Fauconberg, tenant of the estate at Catwick in the 1280s.[59] It later descended, as an appurtenance of their manor of Rise, in the Fauconbergs, Lords Fauconberg, before passing to the Nevilles.[60]

The Fauconbergs' estate was held by their free tenants,[61] who were apparently cadet members of the Fauconberg family. In 1316 Henry de Fauconberg and Walter son of John de Fauconberg were named as lords of Catwick,[62] and John de Fauconberg (d. 1366) was succeeded by his son (Sir) Walter in 1 carucate there, held of Isabel, dowager Lady Fauconberg, under Rise manor. As a manor of Catwick, the estate evidently later descended like Bilton manor, in Swine.[63] It thus passed in shares from Sir Walter Fauconberg to his heirs, the Butlers and Plessingtons, and from them to the Holmes, Francises, Staveleys, and Flowers.[64] A manor of Catwick being dealt with by Alexander Balam in 1527 was part of the same estate.[65] Part of the manor had been bought by (Sir) William Knowles by the 1540s, when his manor of Catwick was recorded, and that estate descended to his daughter, Mary Stanhope (d. 1567), and son-in-law, John Stanhope (fl. 1582). Knowles's grandson William Alford probably inherited the manor soon after.[66]

One of the half shares in the Fauconbergs' manor evidently passed to the Hildyard family. The Hildyards held 130 a. in the parish under Burstwick, the chief manor of the Aumale fee, by the 15th century,[67] and it was presumably an enlarged estate, then described as including a moiety of the manor, which Christopher Hildyard sold in 1571–2 to Robert Shippabotham. Shippabotham (d. 1579) was succeeded by four sisters.[68]

Nunkeeling priory received an estate in the 12th and 13th centuries from Eustace de Fauconberg, Simon Whittick, Peter of Bilton, and others. It comprised *c.* 1 carucate and was valued at £2 14s. in 1535.[69] After the Dissolution the land was granted in 1541 to Sir Richard Gresham (d. 1549) and later descended, with Nunkeeling manor, to William Thornton and William Hudson, who were jointly awarded 107 a. at inclosure in 1732.[70] Hudson (d. 1734) was succeeded in his half share by his son Joseph. Joseph's nephew John Hudson bought the other moiety from William Thornton in 1761 and conveyed it to Joseph.[71] In 1764 Joseph sold the reunited estate to William Wells, and it had passed by 1787 to Wells's devisees Richard Hood and his brother William (d. 1852).[72] The estate was sold in 1853 to William Norman and in 1862, after Norman's death, to William Wright (d. 1884).[73] Comprising *c.* 110 a., and later identified as Lane End farm, it was sold in 1918 by Wright's trustees to Edmund Broumpton (d. 1938) and vested in 1939 in Broumpton's sister Margaret (d. 1943).[74] The farm was bought in 1944 by Alfred Smith and in 1953 by James Calvert, who enlarged it in 1965.[75] Calvert's daughter Heather and her husband Arthur Clubley succeeded to three quarters of the estate and in 1989 sold most of it in several lots.[76]

Peter de Fauconberg gave Meaux abbey a rent in Catwick in the late 12th century.[77]

The largest modern estate was that of Philip Wilkinson, who was awarded 359 a. at inclosure in 1732.[78] From Wilkinson (d. by 1762) the estate descended to his daughter Jane (d. by 1770) and then in turn to Philip's grandsons John Wilkinson and Henry Wilkinson (d. 1788).[79] Henry's children sold *c.* 220 a. of the estate in 1792 to Marmaduke Constable of Wassand, in Sigglesthorne, who made further purchases *c.* 1800.[80] The estate descended, with Wassand, in the Constables and Strickland-Constables to Frederick Charles Strickland-Constable, who had *c.* 370 a. in the parish in 1910.[81] In 1990 Lady

[56] Ibid. 184/548/471; 756/88/72; 762/579/483; 1214/345/308; inf. from Mrs. M. Newton, Catwick, 1993.
[57] O.S. Map 6″, Yorks. CXCVI (1855 edn.); *Reg. of Electors* (1997); above, intro.
[58] *Kirkby's Inquest*, 372; *V.C.H. Yorks.* ii. 267; *Complete Peerage* s.v. Fauconberg.
[59] *Kirkby's Inquest*, 74.
[60] *Cal. Inq. p.m.* ix, p. 177; xii, pp. 86–7; xviii, p. 136; below, Rise, manor.
[61] *Cal. Inq. p.m.* ix, p. 177.
[62] *Kirkby's Inquest*, 304.
[63] *Cal. Inq. p.m.* xii, pp. 86–7; above, Swine, Bilton, manor.
[64] P.R.O., CP 25(1)278/145, no. 39; CP 25(1)/281/162, no. 7; ibid. C 139/148, no. 3; C 139/169, no. 34; C 142/45, no. 18; C 142/48, no. 92; *Cal. Inq. p.m. Hen. VII*, i, p. 456; inaccurate pedigree of Flower in *Visit. Yorks. 1584-5 and 1612*, ed. J. Foster, 618.
[65] *Yorks. Fines*, i. 50.
[66] P.R.O., C 142/199, no. 69; *Yorks. Fines*, i. 138; ii. 178.
[67] *Cal. Inq. p.m. Hen. VII*, ii, pp. 419–23; *V.C.H. Yorks. E.R.* v. 9.
[68] H.U.L., DDLG/42/6; *Yorks. Fines*, ii. 13.
[69] B.L. Cotton MS. Otho. C. viii, ff. 72v., 73–5; *Valor Eccl.* (Rec. Com.), v. 115; Poulson, *Holderness*, i. 375.
[70] R.D.B., B/57/24; *L. & P. Hen. VIII*, xvi, pp. 95–6; *Cal. Pat.* 1547-8, 331–2; 1569–72, 65; *D.N.B.*, s.v. Gresham; *V.C.H. Wilts.* xiv. 199; below, Nunkeeling, manors.
[71] R.D.B., O/36/76; T/6/6; AD/172/391; AD/173/393; Poulson, *Holderness*, i. 382; below, Nunkeeling, manors.
[72] R.D.B., AB/469/851; E.R.A.O., QDT/1/5/9; ibid. PE/128/10.
[73] R.D.B., HD/34/51; II/123/146; IK/107/131; I/383/338 (1885).
[74] Ibid. 189/176/164; 615/345/271; 626/352/274; 672/264/225; E.R.A.O., NV/1/31.
[75] R.D.B., 674/428/349; 938/217/186; 1400/169/150; 1407/32/27.   [76] Inf. from Mrs. Clubley.
[77] *Chron. de Melsa* (Rolls Ser.), i. 222.
[78] R.D.B., B/57/24.
[79] Ibid. AO/248/398; BQ/538/818; B.I.H.R., PRT. Cleveland D.; E.R.A.O., DDHB/45/174.
[80] R.D.B., BQ/538/818; BW/469/656; CC/495/738; CF/189/293.
[81] E.R.A.O., NV/1/31; below, Sigglesthorne, manors (Wassand).

(Ernestine) Strickland-Constable owned 320 a. in the parish and 132 a. more were held by the Strickland-Constable trustees.[82]

In 1086 the archbishop of York had 1 carucate in Catwick; the holding may already have been assigned to his church of St. John at Beverley, and it later belonged to the provost of Beverley minster. A knight occupied the estate in 1086, and c. 1370 it was held of the provost by Sir Amand of Routh.[83]

ECONOMIC HISTORY. AGRICULTURE BEFORE 1800. In 1086 there was land for 5 ploughteams on Drew de Bevrère's estate at Catwick and 3 teams were then worked, one of them by 2 villeins and 2 bordars; the estate also included 40 a. of meadow. One plough was worked on the archbishop's estate, which also supported 3 villeins and 4 bordars.[84]

East and West fields were named in 1654[85] but their relationship to the four open fields, or parts of open fields, recorded later is uncertain. In 1716 the tillage east and north-east of the village lay in North and Mill fields, all or most of the former West field was contained 'in the field to Leven', and there was a South field.[86] Those areas were differently described at inclosure in 1732. Mill field was then known as Clay field, North field as Mill Gravels, West field as Gravel field, and South field as Far Bowlams;[87] land called 'Bowlands' had earlier been recorded in South field.[88]

The open fields included common meadow-land, South field containing a furlong of eight 'gadds' called Paddock in 1716.[89] Hundow, lying between the village and Stream dike, and the unlocated Mill Holme, recorded in 1685, may also have been meadows.[90] Grazing was probably also provided in the open fields; in Gravel field land called Mask, probably for marsh, may have been permanent pasture.[91] The main common pastures lay, however, in the north-west and south-east corners of the parish. Mill pasture was recorded from 1654, and Hurds, later Holds, pasture from 1685.[92]

The commonable lands of Catwick were inclosed by award of 1732 under an Act of 1731. Allotments totalled 1,417 a. They included 290 a. in Clay field, 286 a. in Gravel field, 278 a. in Far Bowlams, 245 a. in Holds pasture, 129 a. in Mill pasture, 98 a. in Mill Gravels, 22 a. in Westlands, adjoining Mill Gravels, and 20 a. in

Hundow. Philip Wilkinson received 359 a. and Hugh Bethell, lord of the manor, 289 a. There were also three allotments of 100–199 a., three of 50–99 a., four of 10–49 a., and four of less than 10 a.[93]

LATER AGRICULTURE. In 1905 there were 1,078 a. of arable land and 426 a. of grassland. The proportion of arable to grass was much the same in the 1930s, when the grassland lay mostly around the village.[94] The 14 a. of woodland recorded in 1905 lay in a fox cover and small plantations.[95] For Catwick civil parish 709 ha. (1,752 a.) were returned as arable land and 45 ha. (111 a.) as grassland in 1987.[96]

In the 19th and earlier 20th century there were usually a dozen farmers in the parish, of whom 3 in 1851 and 5 in the 1920s and 1930s had 150 a. or more. Two market gardeners were also recorded in 1892.[97] In 1987 eight holdings were returned for Catwick civil parish, one of 200–299 ha. (494–739 a.), two of 100–199 ha. (247–492 a.), one of 50–99 ha. (124–245 a.), and four of less than 50 ha.; there were then over 250,000 fowls and more than 6,000 pigs in the parish.[98]

MILLS. There was a mill at Catwick in 1086.[99] Early mills presumably stood in or near Mill Gravels and Mill pasture. A windmill was recorded on the Hildyard estate in the late 16th century, and the same or another mill stood in Mill Gravels by 1772.[1] Shortly before 1910 the mill fell into disrepair and it was demolished in 1911. The miller replaced the windmill with a steam engine at his house and continued to grind corn until c. 1925.[2]

INDUSTRY AND TRADE. By 1852 bricks and tiles were being made at a yard owned by the Bethells in Little Catwick; it was closed c. 1915.[3] Sand and gravel was dug before the 1850s from small pits in the north-east of the parish, one of which was used as a landfill site from c. 1975 to 1993.[4] Larger-scale extraction, extending into Brandesburton parish, was begun c. 1930, and in 1992 a site near Catwick Grange was being worked by Sandsfield Gravel Co.[5] From c. 1970 motor engineering and haulage firms operated in Catwick, and a Sunday market was begun east of the village in 1989.[6]

LOCAL GOVERNMENT. Surviving parish records include churchwardens' accounts for

82 Inf. from W. H. Brown, Sleaford, 1990.
83 E.R.A.O., PE/129/150, f. 6v.; V.C.H. Yorks. ii. 216.
84 V.C.H. Yorks. ii. 216, 267.
85 E.R.A.O., DDRI/11/4.
86 B.I.H.R., TER. H. Catwick 1716.
87 R.D.B., B/57/24.
88 B.I.H.R., TER. H. Catwick 1716.
89 Ibid.; R.D.B., B/57/24.
90 B.I.H.R., TER. H. Catwick 1685; E.R.A.O., DDRI/11/54; ibid. IA. (G. 34).
91 B.I.H.R., TER. H. Catwick 1685 etc.
92 Ibid.; E.R.A.O., DDRI/11/4.
93 4 Geo. II, c. 16 (Priv. Act); E.R.A.O., IA. (G. 34); R.D.B., B/57/24.
94 Acreage Returns, 1905; [1st] Land Util. Surv. Map, sheet 28.
95 Acreage Returns, 1905; O.S Map 6″, Yorks. CXCVI–

CXCVII (1854–5 edn.).
96 Inf. from Min. of Agric., Fish. & Food, Beverley, 1990.
97 P.R.O., HO 107/2365; directories.
98 Inf. from Min. of Agric., Fish. & Food.
99 V.C.H. Yorks. ii. 267.
1 T. Jefferys, Map of Yorks. (1772); A. Bryant, Map of E.R. Yorks. (1829); Yorks. Fines, ii. 13; directories.
2 Beverley Guardian, 25 Nov. 1911; R. Gregory, E. Yorks. Windmills, 21, 33 (illus.); directories.
3 R.D.B., 63/143/124 (1893); O.S. Map 6″, Yorks. CXCVI (1855 edn.); directories.
4 O.S. Map 6″, Yorks. CXCVI–CXCVII (1854–5 edn.); inf. from Mrs. Clubley.
5 R.D.B., 549/110/84; 563/423/316; 622/557/434; 661/440/381; 712/236/200; 820/173/139; 916/577/489; inf. from Mrs. Clubley.
6 Inf. from Mrs. Clubley.

1722–1807[7] and overseers' accounts for 1773–1838. The parish maintained poorhouses at Catwick in the late 18th and early 19th century.[8] Regular poor-relief was given to two people in 1802–3 and to about ten in 1812–15; one person in the earlier year and up to five a year in 1812–15 were aided occasionally.[9] The parish joined Skirlaugh poor-law union in 1837.[10] It remained in Skirlaugh rural district until 1935 and then in Holderness rural district until 1974, when it became part of the Holderness district of Humberside.[11] In 1996 Catwick parish became part of a new East Riding unitary area.[12]

CHURCH. A church recorded at Catwick in 1086 belonged in moieties to Drew de Bevrère's undertenants and their successors.[13] Pontefract priory was given one of the moieties by Ralph of Catwick before 1127 and the other by Peter de Fauconberg by 1160.[14] The priory successfully defended its right of patronage against Everard of Catwick in 1224[15] but, as a dependency of the alien priory of La Charité-sur-Loire (Nièvre), temporarily lost the advowson to the Crown during the wars with France in the 14th century.[16] The Crown was patron from the Dissolution until 1901, when the advowson passed by exchange to Henry Strickland-Constable.[17] Catwick rectory was united with Long Riston vicarage in 1922 and with Leven rectory instead in 1956; the Strickland-Constables presented alternately from 1922.[18] Leven with Catwick was united with Brandesburton in 1997.[19]

The rectory was worth £7 in 1291 and £14 4s. 10d. gross in 1535; on each occasion a pension of £2 was owed to Pontefract priory.[20] The improved annual value was £53 0s. 2d. net in 1650.[21] The net annual income averaged £149 in 1829–31 and was £170 in 1883.[22] Tithes, worth more than £11 in 1535 and £50 gross in 1650, were mostly commuted at inclosure in 1732 for a rent charge of £90. The remaining tithes, from Catwick mill, were dealt with in 1843, when the rector was awarded 15s. a year for them.[23] The 5 bovates which Pontefract priory held in

Catwick in the mid 12th century may have been glebe. In 1535 the glebe was valued at £2 and in 1650, when it was said to include 4 bovates, at more than £7. In 1732 at inclosure 61 a. were awarded for the commonable glebe.[24] Some 20 a. were sold in 1936 and the rest in 1963 and 1964.[25] The rectory house, recorded in 1650, was in disrepair in 1768, when the outbuildings were rebuilt.[26] The house itself was enlarged c. 1800 and mostly rebuilt in 1862 to designs by George Wilkinson of Hull.[27] Its grounds were enlarged by exchange in 1855.[28] The rectory house was sold in 1954,[29] and the rector later lived at Leven.

In the mid 16th century the rector also served Hornsea, and in the 1560s sermons were lacking at Catwick.[30] In 1743 and 1764, when the rector was also curate of North Frodingham, a service was held weekly and communion was administered four times a year with c. 30 recipients.[31] In the mid and late 19th century, when Catwick was served alone, there were two Sunday services and monthly communion, with usually a dozen recipients.[32]

The church of ST. MICHAEL, so called in 1555,[33] stands on elevated ground. A small stone figure, of the 11th century or early 12th and perhaps representing St. Michael, is set in the north wall of the chancel. The medieval church comprised chancel, nave with transeptal chapels and south porch, and west tower. The chapels were added in the earlier 14th century and the nave partly refenestrated in the 15th.[34] The chancel was neglected in the 16th and 17th centuries.[35] The nave and tower were restored c. 1720,[36] and sash windows had been fitted in the chancel by the 19th century.[37] Except for the tower, the church was rebuilt in 1863 to designs of Mallinson & Healey of Bradford.[38] The new church, of boulders with ashlar dressings, incorporates some of the medieval windows. It largely follows the earlier plan, the probable exception being the addition of a north vestry to the chancel. The external stonework was cleaned in 1992–3.[39]

There were two bells in 1552 and later, cast by Thomas Deacon, probably in Beverley or Hull in the 14th century.[40] The plate includes a

7 E.R.A.O., PE/9/15.   8 Ibid. PE/9/19–21.
9 *Poor Law Abstract, 1804*, pp. 594–5; *1818*, pp. 522–3.
10 *3rd Rep. Poor Law Com.* 170.
11 *Census.*
12 Humberside (Structural Change) Order 1995, copy at E.R.A.O.   13 *V.C.H. Yorks.* ii. 267.
14 *E.Y.C.* iii, pp. 46–8; above, manors.
15 *Cur. Reg. R.* xi, p. 582.
16 *Cal. Pat.* 1348–50, 370; 1374–7, 17; 1388–92, 475; Lawrance, 'Clergy List', Holderness, i, pp. 30–1.
17 B.I.H.R., OC. 437; Lawrance, 'Clergy List', Holderness, i, p. 32; Poulson, *Holderness*, i. 293–4.
18 B.I.H.R., OC. 540, 736; notice in church.
19 Inf. from the rector, Leven, 1997.
20 *Tax. Eccl.* (Rec. Com.), 304, 336; *Valor Eccl.* (Rec. Com.), v. 117.
21 *T.E.R.A.S.* iv. 62.
22 B.I.H.R., V. 1884/Ret. 1; *Rep. Com. Eccl. Revenues*, 924–5.
23 R.D.B., B/57/24; B.I.H.R., TA. 85s.
24 R.D.B., B/57/24; *E.Y.C.* iii, pp. 48–9, 149–52; *Valor Eccl.* v. 117; *T.E.R.A.S.* iv. 62.
25 R.D.B., 563/423/316; 1312/132/118; 1339/109/97.

26 B.I.H.R., Fac. 1787/3; *T.E.R.A.S.* iv. 62.
27 B.I.H.R., TER. H. Catwick 1809, 1865; ibid. MGA. 1862/2; ibid. Ch. Ret. i.
28 B.I.H.R., TA. 121s.
29 R.D.B., 964/18/17.
30 B.I.H.R., V. 1567–8/CB. 1; *Abp. Grindal's Visit. 1575*, p. 72.
31 B.I.H.R., V. 1764/Ret. 1, no. 119; *Herring's Visit.* i, p. 158.
32 B.I.H.R., V. 1865/Ret. 1, no. 107; V. 1868/Ret. 1, no. 103; V. 1871/Ret.1, no. 104; V. 1877/Ret. 1, no. 102; V. 1884/Ret. 1.
33 Ibid. Prob. Reg. 14, f. 71v.
34 Illus. in Poulson, *Holderness*, i. pl. facing p. 294.
35 B.I.H.R., ER V. 1662–3/CB. 1; *Abp. Grindal's Visit. 1575*, p. 72.
36 B.I.H.R., ER V. Ret. 1, f. 35; ER V. Ret. 2, f. 9v.
37 Poulson, *Holderness*, i. 294.
38 E.R.A.O., PE/9/39.
39 Inf. from the rector, 1993.
40 B.I.H.R., TER. H. Catwick 1770 etc.; *Inventories of Ch. Goods*, 54–5; G. R. Park, *Ch. Bells of Holderness*, 65; *V.C.H. Yorks.* ii. 451.

FIG. 18. CATWICK CHURCH BEFORE REBUILDING IN 1863

cup, possibly of the mid 16th century, and a paten of 1766.[41] The registers of baptisms, marriages, and burials date from 1586; baptisms lack entries for 1670–8 and 1712–21, marriages for 1616–78 and a few years in the 18th century, and burials for 1662–78.[42] In 1962 the churchyard was enlarged with glebe land but the extension had yet to be brought into use in 1992.[43]

The parish clerk had beastgates in the common pastures and open fields until their inclosure in 1732, when a yearly rent charge of 18s. 4d. was substituted.[44]

NONCONFORMITY. An unidentified congregation of protestant dissenters used a house at Catwick from 1812.[45] The Wesleyans registered a room there in 1817 and in 1835 built a chapel,[46] which was closed in 1986[47] and stood derelict in 1992. The Primitive Methodists registered a house in 1820 and built a chapel in 1839.[48] The chapel was closed in the 1930s and later converted into a private house.[49]

EDUCATION. A school in the village attended by c. 15 children in 1743 was not mentioned in 1764,[50] and in 1818 Catwick children were taught in an adjoining parish, probably Leven.[51] Hannah Smith (d. by 1792) left £20 for education, and the income was evidently being used in 1833 to support a school attended by half a

dozen boys and girls.[52] It was presumably the same school for which a building was put up in 1847, on land given by the Revd. Charles Constable.[53] It was run on the National plan and was supported with 13s. from the charity, by subscription, and by school pence.[54] An annual government grant was first received in 1859.[55] The school took infants and on inspection day in 1871 was attended by 37 children.[56] The building was enlarged in 1882 and further extended in 1911.[57] Average attendance fell from 48 in 1906–7 to 33 in 1913–14; numbers recovered in the 1920s but later fell to 34 in 1937–8.[58] The school was closed in 1949, the younger of its 33 pupils being transferred to Leven school and the elder ones to Hornsea County School.[59] The former school building at Catwick was sold c. 1960[60] and later used as a private house.

CHARITIES FOR THE POOR. James Young (d. 1768), rector, left £50 for poor widows and other parishioners. In the early 19th century the income of £2 10s. was distributed twice a year. James's wife Mary (d. 1786) left a rent charge of £2 12s. 6d. from a house in Hornsea for the poor at Christmas.[61] In 1902 the joint income of the Young charities was nearly £4 10s. and was distributed in doles.[62]

George Gibson (d. 1774) and an unknown benefactor left £5 and £20 10s. respectively for

[41] B.I.H.R., TER. H. Catwick 1770 etc.; ibid. TER. 529; Yorks. Ch. Plate, i. 235.
[42] E.R.A.O., PE/9/1–7.   [43] B.I.H.R., CD. Conv. 14.
[44] R.D.B., B/57/24.
[45] P.R.O., RG 31/5, no. 2663.
[46] Ibid. HO 129/522/5/5; ibid. RG 31/5, no. 3151; R.D.B., FI/325/319.
[47] O.N.S. (Birkdale), Worship Reg. 1719; inf. from Mrs. T. Heald, Atwick, 1995.
[48] P.R.O., HO 129/522/5/6; ibid. RG 31/5, no. 3383; R.D.B., DQ/406/48.
[49] R.D.B., 645/552/475; E.R.A.O., MRH/3/15.
[50] B.I.H.R., V. 1764/Ret. 1, no. 119; Herring's Visit. i, pp. 157–8.
[51] Educ. of Poor Digest, 1078.

[52] 9th Rep. Com. Char. 757–8; Educ. Enq. Abstract, 1082.
[53] E.R.A.O., PE/9/36.
[54] P.R.O., ED 7/135, no. 30.
[55] Rep. of Educ. Cttee. of Council, 1859–60, [2681], p. 777, H.C. (1859–60), liv.
[56] E.R.A.O., PE/9/24; Returns relating to Elem. Educ. 472–3.
[57] Kelly's Dir. N. & E.R. Yorks. (1889), 364; E.R. Educ. Cttee. Mins. 1911–12, 174.
[58] Bd. of Educ., List 21 (H.M.S.O., 1908 and later edns.).
[59] E.R.A.O. SL/24/1; E.R. Educ. Cttee. Mins. 1949–50, 6.
[60] Inf. from Mrs. Clubley.
[61] E.R.A.O., DDCC/17/26; 9th Rep. Com. Char. 757.
[62] E.R.A.O., accession 1681.

the poor. The town stock thereby created produced an income of £1 5s. 6d. in the early 19th century, when cash doles were given annually.[63] Hannah Smith (d. by 1792) left £20 for education, with the relief of the poor and sick as a secondary object.[64] Her charity was later applied to the elemosynary object. In 1901 the income

was combined with that of the town stock, and cash doles amounting to £1 6s. were distributed.[65]

By a Scheme of 1981 the charities were amalgamated as the Catwick Relief in Need charity, and the rent charge was then redeemed. In 1992 the charity was, however, inactive.[66]

NORTH FRODINGHAM

NORTH Frodingham parish lies in the Hull valley, the river and a tributary called Frodingham beck forming the western boundary of the parish.[67] The other boundaries are mostly formed by lesser drains. North Frodingham village, linear in form, is in the north of the parish, 22 km. north of Hull and some 7 km. south-east of Driffield and WSW. of the coast at Skipsea. The Anglian name Frodingham, meaning the 'settlement of Froda's people', was from the mid 13th century distinguished from South Frodingham, in Owthorne, by the prefix North. Emmotland, comprising half a dozen houses, lies 2 km. south-west of the village, close to the junction of the beck and the river; the name, meaning 'river confluence', was used by 1569.[68] In 1850–1 the ancient parish contained 3,147 a. (1,274 ha.).[69]

North Frodingham had 196 poll-tax payers in 1377,[70] and 64 houses were assessed for hearth tax and 21 discharged in 1672.[71] The parish had c. 70 families in 1764.[72] From 365 in 1801, its population increased markedly in the early 19th century, reaching 711 in 1831 and exceeding 800 in the middle years of the century; numbers fell from the 1860s to stand at 555 in 1901 and remained at that level until the 1970s. In 1981 the population had risen to 647, and in 1991 it was usually 716, of whom 699 were present.[73]

The higher ground in the east of the parish reaches 16 m. above sea level and is covered with boulder clay, while in the west the land lies at less than 7 m. and is mostly alluvial. The farmhouses of Emmotland stand on deposits of sand and gravel,[74] which have been much reduced by extraction. The open fields of North Frodingham lay north, south, and east of the village and its common pastures in the south and south-east of the parish. The common meadows seem to have been in the fields and carrs. The commonable lands were inclosed in 1808.[75]

The parish was mostly drained by the river Hull, Frodingham beck, and the beck's tributary

streams, a drainage system which was improved under the Beverley and Barmston Drainage Act of 1798. The meandering course of Old Howe drain, the stream flowing along the northern and north-western boundary into Frodingham beck, was evidently straightened, and much of Frodingham's water was diverted into new drains made beside Old Howe, the beck, and the river. In North Frodingham and Emmotland 971 a. were assessed by the drainage award of 1811.[76] Despite the changes, and later improvements downstream at Hempholme, in Leven, the carrs remained liable to flooding[77] until the mid 20th century, when the water level in the river was reduced by the construction of reservoirs on the west bank in Watton parish.[78] Land was evidently gained from the watercourses by earlier accretion and drainage improvements, 'new lands' being referred to in 1674 and New ings later.[79] Lesser drains in North Frodingham include Moor drain, which flows into Moor Town, in Brandesburton, and was evidently the drain said to be in disrepair in 1367,[80] and Constable drain leading from the west end of the village towards the beck.

Frodingham beck was navigable in the mid 13th century, when Thornton abbey (Lincs.) was said to have prevented boats from passing up the 'Old Hull', possibly Howe, at North Frodingham and to have removed a bridge there.[81] In the 18th century there was a landing place at Emmotland.[82] Under Acts of 1767 and 1801 Frodingham beck was made a branch of the Driffield navigation. Dredging operations under the latter Act were associated with the improvement of a tributary stream, Foston beck, as a private navigation by the proprietor of mills in Foston on the Wolds. In 1825–6 a new wharf and a swing bridge were built at the junction of the Foston and Frodingham navigations,[83] and coal and lime were carried to Frodingham Bridge until c. 1960.[84]

From North Frodingham the principal road

[63] 9th Rep. Com. Char. 757; E.R.A.O., PE/9/3; directories.

[64] 9th Rep. Com. Char. 757–8; above, educ.

[65] E.R.A.O., accession 1681.

[66] Ibid. MIS. 207, 101 (53); Char. Com. index; Review of Char. Rep. 103.

[67] This article was written in 1994 and revised later.

[68] H.U.L., DHO/16/55; P.N. Yorks. E.R. (E.P.N.S.), 27, 75–6; V.C.H. Yorks. E.R. v. 85–7; Poulson, Holderness, i. 299.

[69] O.S. Map 6″, Yorks. CLXXIX (1854 edn.).

[70] P.R.O., E 179/202/60, m. 79.

[71] Hearth Tax, 61.

[72] B.I.H.R., V. 1764/Ret. 1, no. 200.

[73] V.C.H. Yorks. iii. 495; Census, 1911–91.

[74] Geol. Surv. Map 1″, sheet 64 (1909 edn.).

[75] Below, econ. hist.

[76] E.R.A.O., DCBB/4/2, 8; ibid. IA. (C. 10); 38 Geo. III, c. 63 (Local and Personal).

[77] E.R.A.O., DDBD/89/4.

[78] Inf. from Mr. H. G. McKie, N. Frodingham, 1994; below, Leven, intro.

[79] H.U.L., DDCV/120/5; R.D.B., CI/273/20.

[80] Poulson, Holderness, i. 120.

[81] H.U.L. DHO/16/55.

[82] Poulson, Holderness, i. 307.

[83] 7 Geo. III, c. 97; 41 Geo. III, c. 134 (Local and Personal); B. F. Duckham, Inland Waterways of E. Yorks. 1700–1900 (E. Yorks. Loc. Hist. Ser. xviii), 20–1, 24–6.

[84] Inf. from Mr. McKie.

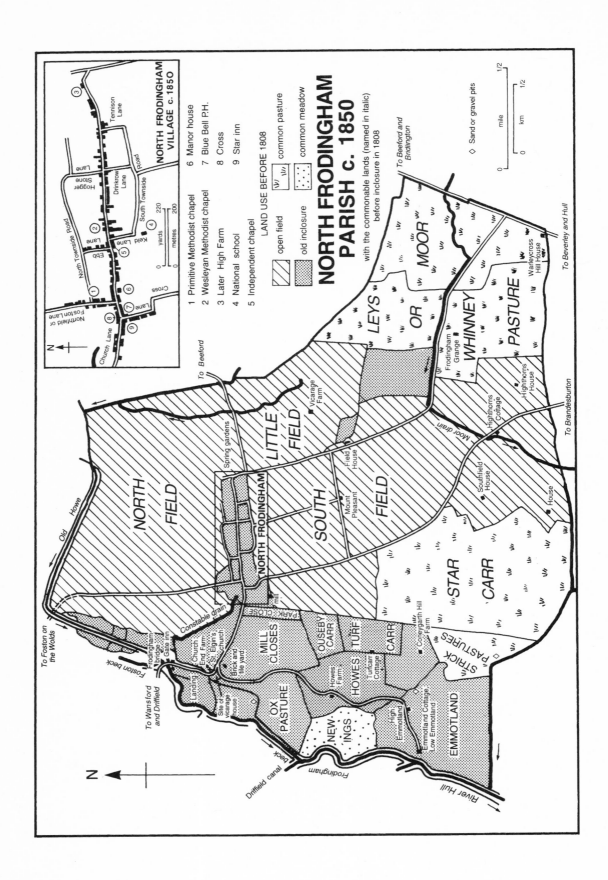

runs east to Beeford and west to Wansford and Driffield. Minor roads lead south from the village to Emmotland, Brandesburton, and the main Hull–Bridlington road, which forms the south-eastern parish boundary. The Emmotland road may formerly have continued to Hempholme, in Leven, the abbot of Thornton being held responsible for an unrepaired road between North Frodingham and 'Holme' in 1362.[85]

NORTH FRODINGHAM village is sited midway across the northern half of the parish, its buildings lining both sides of an east-west main street from which cross lanes lead to northern and southern back lanes. The main street is continued north-westwards by Church Lane and at its end, c. ½ km. from the rest of the village, stand the church and former vicarage house; that location, close to the beck, may have been the original site of the village.[86] A medieval stone cross formerly stood at the junction of the main street and the lane to Brandesburton. It was allegedly destroyed by navvies working on the Beverley and Barmston drains c. 1800, and a replacement cross was set up on the original base in 1811 and given a new shaft in 1991.[87] A 19th-century pump also survives in the main street. The buildings are of brick and include several farmhouses. Church End Farm may be medieval in origin[88] but otherwise the oldest buildings are probably 18th-century and the village mostly dates from the 19th and 20th centuries. Few of the buildings are noteworthy but one or two single-storeyed cottages remain and others are evident in enlarged and heightened houses. In the 19th century a school was built in the southern lane and chapels added to the main street and a northern cross lane.[89] In the 20th century the village has grown to the south and east, the new buildings including two dozen council houses.[90] The district council also provided a sewage works beside Old Howe drain c. 1960.[91]

Half a dozen alehouses were recorded at North Frodingham in the later 18th century, and the Red Lion, Gate, and Star were named in 1823.[92] The Red Lion was closed soon afterwards, or renamed the Blue Bell, which was trading by 1834 and was closed c. 1930. The Gate, at Frodingham Bridge, ceased to trade c. 1915. In 1994 the Star still existed, as did the Blue Post, which had been named since 1910.[93] The village had several friendly societies. The earliest recorded was founded in 1798, had 66 members in 1803, and existed until at least 1852. A lodge of the Independent Order of Oddfellows

was founded in 1837 and had 91 members in 1845; it left the order c. 1850 and no more is known of it. The Driffield branch of a Primitive Methodist preachers' provident society was founded in fact at North Frodingham in 1856, had 27 members in 1866, but was discontinued in 1873. The Ancient Shepherds and Shepherdesses had lodges at North Frodingham c. 1840. The Rising Star Benefit Society, founded in 1869, was recorded until 1926.[94] In the earlier 20th century a reading room was held in a former school, and a Methodist Sunday school was also used for recreation.[95] A prisoner-of-war camp was established during the Second World War beside South Townside Road, and one of the huts was later used as a village hall and the site as a recreation ground. A new village hall was built in or soon after 1972, and the old one has been demolished. A second recreation ground, on the northern edge of the village, was opened c. 1980.[96] At the east end of the village, land named Spring gardens in 1851 was probably already occupied by allotment gardens, as it was c. 1900, when there were other gardens south of the village.[97]

OUTLYING BUILDINGS include the farmhouses of Emmotland, of which High Emmotland Farm existed by 1772 and Low Emmotland and Coneygarth Hill Farm by 1828.[98] Farmhouses built on land inclosed in 1808 include Carr House, Vicarage, later Eastfield, Farm, Field House Farm, Frodingham Grange, Highthorns House, and Southfield House, all put up by 1828.[99]

MANOR AND OTHER ESTATES. In 1066 Ulf had a manor of NORTH FRODINGHAM, comprising 12 carucates; it had passed by 1086 to Drew de Bevrère,[1] and was later part of the Aumale fee.

In the mid 12th century William le Gros, count of Aumale, granted the manor and church of North Frodingham to Thornton abbey (Lincs.),[2] and the abbot was lord in 1316.[3] After the Dissolution the Crown let the manor,[4] before alienating it in 1628 to Edward Ditchfield and others, trustees for the city of London, as security for a loan from the city. It was sold by the city in 1667 to William Harpham and by his nephew, William Harpham, in 1673 to Christopher Wilkinson. Robert Bethell of Hull, merchant, bought the manor in 1674, and it was probably he who, as Robert Bethell the younger of London, mariner, conveyed it in 1680 to his

[85] *Public Works in Medieval Law*, ii (Selden Soc. xl), pp. 309–10.
[86] K. J. Allison, *E.R. Yorks. Landscape*, 81.
[87] Poulson, *Holderness*, i. 306; *Driffield Times*, 9 May 1991; above, this section [drainage]; below, local govt.
[88] Below, manor (rectory).
[89] Below, nonconf., educ.; O.S. Map 6″, Yorks. CLXXIX (1854 edn.).
[90] R.D.B., 605/239/201; 753/439/361; 923/560/473; 1618/345/301.
[91] Ibid. 1205/139/126.
[92] E.R.A.O., QDT/2/6, 9.
[93] Ibid. NV/1/94; R.D.B., 199/207/176; O.S. Map 6″, Yorks. CLXXIX (1854 edn.); directories.

[94] D. [R. J.] Neave, *E.R. Friendly Soc.* (E. Yorks. Loc. Hist. Ser. xli), 53. [95] Below, nonconf., educ.
[96] E.R. Educ. Cttee. *Mins.* 1972–3, 85; inf. from Mr. McKie.
[97] O.S. Map 6″, Yorks. CLXXIX (1854 edn.); O.S. Map 1/2,500, Yorks. CLXXIX. 7 (1892, 1910 edns.).
[98] T. Jefferys, *Map of Yorks.* (1772); H. Teesdale, *Map of Yorks.* (1828).
[99] E.R.A.O., IA. (C. 10); H. Teesdale, *Map of Yorks.* (1828); O.S. Map 6″, Yorks. CLXXIX (1854 edn.).
[1] *V.C.H. Yorks.* ii. 267.
[2] Dugdale, *Mon.* vi. 326.
[3] *Kirkby's Inquest*, 303.
[4] *Cal. Pat.* 1563–6, 158–9, 389, 397; *V.C.H. Lincs.* ii. 164.

uncle, Robert Bethell the elder of Beverley. The last Robert (d. 1689) left the manor to his second cousin, Hugh Bethell of Rise (d. 1717), and it later descended, like Rise, in the Bethells.[5] At inclosure in 1808 Charlotte Bethell was awarded 161 a., and in 1854 Richard Bethell had c. 230 a. at North Frodingham.[6] The Bethells' estate was divided and sold, mostly in 1865, but not until 1877 were the manorial rights sold to Henry Walker. He sold them in 1898 to H. W. Bainton (d. 1907), who devised them to E. C. Bainton (d. 1945) and J. H. Bainton (d. 1951) as tenants in common.[7]

The manor house was recorded from the 16th century.[8] Standing in the main street, it was rebuilt c. 1810.[9] As part of Manor House farm, the house was separated from the manor in 1865.[10]

In 1808 the largest estate at North Frodingham was evidently that assembled by Thomas Duesbery. He was then awarded 672 a. with his wife Sarah and Thomas Hinderwell and 113 a. with other co-tenants.[11] The Duesberys and Hinderwell sold nearly 500 a. to Jonathan Harrison, father and son, in 1810 and 1812;[12] it was presumably the father who already had 140 a. at North Frodingham at inclosure.[13] Parts of the enlarged estate were evidently settled on other members of the Harrison family.[14] The elder Jonathan Harrison died in 1828, leaving c. 150 a. at Emmotland to his son Richard and the rest of his land to his son Jonathan, whose estate later included c. 220 a. of copyhold.[15] Harrison (d. 1867) was succeeded by his son J. S. Harrison, who had bought a 142-a. farm, from W. F. Bethell in 1865 and added 48 a. more in 1870 and c. 76 a. in 1876.[16] He (d. 1884) was succeeded by his son James, who had 637 a. at North Frodingham in 1910.[17] James Harrison bought the 154-a. High Emmotland farm in 1913[18] but in 1918 sold High farm of c. 230 a. and Manor House farm with 80 a. to Thomas (d. 1946) and Annie Rafton.[19] The rest of the land was held after Harrison's death in 1923 by his widow Mary (d. 1932)[20] and was eventually sold off in lots in 1947.[21] After the death of Thomas Rafton's executrix Edith Rafton in 1957, the Manor House estate, then comprising

c. 100 a., was sold in 1958 to William Nicholson.[22] In 1965 Nicholson bought the 104-a. Howes farm, and his family held both farms in 1994.[23]

After the ordination of a vicarage,[24] North Frodingham *RECTORY* remained with Thornton abbey until the Dissolution. The tithes of corn and hay were let with land at North Frodingham in the earlier 16th century.[25] The rectory was sold to Henry Best and Francis Jackson by the Crown in 1600,[26] to George Hunter in 1610, and in 1631 to Christopher Pasley.[27] In 1650 the rectorial tithes and 6 bovates of glebe land were valued at £74 gross.[28] Most of the glebe land seems to have been sold later. Pasley was succeeded by his son Charles (d. by 1685), who devised the rectory and 1 bovate of glebe to his daughter Frances (d. by 1711).[29] The estate then passed to a kinsman, Christopher Blakiston (d. by 1735), who left it to his goddaughter Dorothy Neville (d. 1785). She devised the rectory to Christopher Blakiston's cousin, Philip Saltmarsh (d. 1796). Saltmarsh was succeeded by his great-nephew, Philip Saltmarsh[30] (d. by 1847), and he by his son Philip.[31] At inclosure in 1808 the rectorial tithes were commuted for 360 a. and £1 17s. 9d. a year, and 12 a. were received for the bovate of glebe.[32] The estate comprised the 412-a. Frodingham Grange farm in 1872, when Philip Saltmarsh sold it to the trustees of Beaumont Hotham, Baron Hotham, (d. 1870). It was later transferred to John Hotham, Baron Hotham. He bought 38 a. more in 1874 and died in 1907.[33] In 1910 his successor, Frederick Hotham, Baron Hotham, sold Frodingham Grange farm, then of 454 a., to George Meadley[34] (d. 1928). Meadley was succeeded by his son George (d. 1937) and he in turn by his widow Ann (d. 1957) and their son Philip.[35] The Meadleys still held the farm in 1994.[36]

Church End Farm was formerly the chief house of the rectory. The north-south range incorporates an ashlar building which appears to have been the medieval cross wing to an eastern hall. The house was remodelled in brick for George Hunter in 1619, when two chimney stacks were built up from the original bases on

[5] H.U.L., DDCV/120/1–2, 4–6; DDCV/121/27; J. Foster, *Pedigrees of Yorks.* iii, s.v. Bethell; Poulson, *Holderness*, i. 298; below, Rise, manor.

[6] R.D.B., CI/273/20; valuation at Rise Park Estate Off., 1990.

[7] R.D.B., ME/67/99; 99/31/29 (1898); 539/661/499; 723/458/389; 918/323/286.

[8] P.R.O., SC 6/Hen. VIII/2022, ff. 79v.–80; *Cal. Pat. 1563–6*, p. 389.   [9] Poulson, *Holderness*, i. 306.

[10] Above and below, this section.

[11] R.D.B., CI/273/20; below, econ. hist.

[12] H.U.L., DDCV/121/7, pp. 219, 225, 235, 276–7.

[13] R.D.B., CI/273/20.

[14] H.U.L., DDCV/121/7, pp. 245, 547.

[15] Ibid. DDCV/121/7, p. 562; DDCV(2)/86/49.

[16] Ibid. DDCV/121/8, pp. 1008, 1010; R.D.B., IS/206/283; KS/48/66; LY/177/279.

[17] R.D.B., 3/231/214 (1885); 17/480/474 (1887); E.R.A.O., NV/1/94.

[18] R.D.B., 155/255/228.

[19] Ibid. 186/212/181; 186/323/273; 614/460/369; 753/87/70; 801/514/417.

[20] Ibid. 269/270/228; 763/417/360; plaque in Brandesburton church.

[21] R.D.B., 743/511/441; 769/141/117; 769/455/390; 770/275/242; 771/90/74; 771/335/281; 775/516/444.

[22] Ibid. 1095/360/326; 1098/301/266.

[23] Ibid. 1407/433/382; *Reg. of Electors* (1994).

[24] Below, church.

[25] P.R.O., SC 6/Hen. VIII/2022, ff. 79v.–80.

[26] Ibid. C 66/1539, mm. 16–18.

[27] Ibid. CP 25(2)/520/6 Chas. I Mich. file 1 [no. 2]; *Yorks. Fines, 1603–14*, 143.

[28] *T.E.R.A.S.* iv. 61.

[29] E.R.A.O., DDSA/637, 639.

[30] Ibid. DDSA/641; R.D.B., AE/513/971; Poulson, *Holderness*, i. 300.

[31] E.R.A.O., DDSA/647.

[32] R.D.B., CI/273/20.

[33] Ibid. KY/314/419; ND/296/430; 110/242/223; H.U.L., DDHO(3)/46/16.

[34] R.D.B., 121/403/368.

[35] Ibid. 382/501/415; 606/265/213; 1070/253/223.

[36] *Reg. of Electors* (1994).

the west side.[37] It may have been then that the hall range was demolished; a 19th-century wing now occupies part of its site. Church End Farm was replaced as the chief house by a new farmhouse built on the rectorial allotment soon after 1808 and known successively as Pasture House and Frodingham Grange.[38]

In 1285 William de Lascelles held land at North Frodingham, which had descended to his son John by 1303.[39] No more is known of the estate.

Meaux abbey may have had a small estate in the parish in the 16th century.[40]

ECONOMIC HISTORY. COMMON LANDS AND INCLOSURE. The tillage lay in North, South, and Little fields, all named in 1609. North and Little fields were evidently rotated as one before inclosure in 1808.[41] Enlargement of the fields at the expense of the waste in the Middle Ages may account for the later distinction made between bovates of the old and new tenures.[42] In 1659 copyholders had 5 carucates and 2 bovates, or 462 a., of 'old land' and 5 carucates, or 440 a., of 'new land',[43] and at inclosure in 1808 there were 6 carucates and 7 bovates of 'old land', each bovate of which was charged with a poultry render to the lord of the manor.[44] Common meadowland lay in the fields and the carrs, 'wands' of meadow in Hill carr and hay in West carr being mentioned in 1598, and New ings, beside the beck, being commonable at inclosure. The village's chief common pastures were probably Star carr, which was stinted by the mid 16th century,[45] and a moor, which was intercommoned with Beeford until the inclosure of that township in 1768. An allotment of 186 a. was then made to the commoners of North Frodingham as their share of the moor, and that remained as a common pasture until North Frodingham was inclosed in 1808.[46] Adjoining the moor, commonable land called Leys or Whinney pasture evidently provided more rough grazing, besides whins or gorse, which were taken there without licence in 1660.[47] Milnecroft, in which beast gates were held in the mid 16th century, was presumably another piece of the commonable grazing.[48] Star carr also included a turbary by 1588, and turves were presumably dug from the c. 30-a. Turf carr, which seems to have been inclosed by the mid 16th century, and was then and later occupied in undivided thirds.[49]

Turf carr and much other land near the river and beck was clearly inclosed early, possibly as part of the demesne, and by 1588 the adjoining Howesbie, later Ouseby, carr had been divided, one of the farms in North Frodingham including half of it.[50]

The commonable lands were inclosed by award of 1808 under an Act of 1801.[51] Allotments made totalled 2,303 a., of which 39 a. were from old inclosures; 1,609 a. were copyhold and 694 a. freehold of the manor of North Frodingham. Many allotments were from more than one area, and, apart from New ings, which contained 48 a., only minimum acreages can be calculated for the commonable lands; there were at least 561 a. in North field, 310 a. in South field, 184 a. in Little field, and 38 a. in the moor. The Act accommodated manorial custom by allowing allotments to mortgagees and other co-tenants. Thomas Duesbery, his wife Sarah, and Thomas Hinderwell acquired many holdings before inclosure when they received 672 a.; another allotment, of 113 a. and awarded to Duesbery with Elizabeth Dealtry and William Thompson, was evidently later Duesbery's.[52] Philip Saltmarsh was awarded 372 a. for the rectorial tithes and glebe land, William Dobson and others 252 a., and Charlotte Bethell, lord of the manor, 161 a., which included compensation for the hay of the balks and her right in the soil of the waste. The vicar received 109 a. There was also one allotment of 57 a., twenty-two of 10–49 a., and twenty-seven of less than 10 a.

THE DEMESNE AND OTHER HOLDINGS. In 1086, when there was reckoned to be land for 12 ploughteams and 30 a. of meadow at North Frodingham, one plough was worked on the desmesne and four more by villeins.[53] In 1541–2 the manor was reckoned to be worth nearly £82 a year. All or much of the demesne was then let for £31 a year; the premises included part of Emmotland, tithes, turves, fishing rights, and the 'heybones' and 'heiloodes', presumably works owed by the tenantry. Except for just over £1 from the profits of the manor court, the rest of the value was composed of rents, the largest sums being the £31 and £7 owed respectively as the 'old' and 'new' rents, evidently another reference to some earlier enlargement or re-ordering of land in North Frodingham.[54] Houses and land at Emmotland, and Cow pastures, both then held by a single tenant for rents amounting to £7 a year, and the park, Ouseby carr, and Ox pastures, all in multiple occupation, may have been other parts of the former demesne.[55]

37 Datestone with initials G. and M. H.
38 E.R.A.O., IA. (C. 10); H. Teesdale, Map of Yorks. (1828); O.S. Map 6", Yorks. CLXXIX (1854 edn.).
39 Kirkby's Inquest, 75, 244 n.
40 P.R.O., SC 6/Hen. VIII/2022, ff. 79v.–80.
41 Ibid. LR 2/230, ff. 205–208v.; 41 Geo. III, c. 87 (Priv. Act).   42 H.U.L., DDCV/121/14, folder A, s.v. 1581.
43 Lond. Corp. R.O., Emanuel hosp. box 7.7.
44 R.D.B., CI/273/20. Cf. P.R.O., SC 6/Hen. VIII/2022, ff. 79v.–80.
45 H.U.L., DDCV/121/14, folder A, s.vv. 1574, 1588, 1598, 1599; below, this section.
46 R.D.B., AK/57/6; E.R.A.O., IA. Beeford; below, this section.
47 E.R.A.O., IA. (C. 10); R.D.B., CI/273/20; H.U.L., DDCV/121/1, s.v. Oct. 1660.
48 P.R.O., SC 6/Hen. VIII/2022, ff. 79v.–80.
49 Ibid.; H.U.L., DDCV/121/6, pp. 198, 204; DDCV/121/14, folder A; R.D.B., CI/273/20. Turf carr was partitioned at inclosure: R.D.B., CI/273/20.
50 H.U.L., DDCV/121/14, folder A; E.R.A.O., IA. (C 10); below, this section [demesne].
51 41 Geo. III, c. 87 (Priv. Act); R.D.B., CI/273/20; E.R.A.O., IA. (C 10).
52 H.U.L., DDCV/121/7, p. 562.
53 V.C.H. Yorks. ii. 267.
54 Above, this section (common lands).
55 P.R.O., SC 6/Hen. VIII/2022, ff. 79v.–80.

FISHING, FOWLING, AND RABBIT WARREN. Three fisheries were recorded in 1086,[56] and in 1588 ditches in Star carr were used for fishing.[57] A fishery was sold with the rectory in 1610, and another was recorded at Emmotland in 1659.[58] The carrs and river were also valued for their birds. A swanner of Frodingham was mentioned in 1609, a swannery evidently existed at Emmotland in the 18th century,[59] and two 'lake hens', presumably wildfowl, were owed to the lord of the manor annually from each of 55 bovates until that due was commuted at inclosure in 1808.[60] There seems to have been a rabbit warren at North Frodingham: the 'coneygarth' was let with other demene land there in the 16th century, and it was later commemorated by Coneygarth hill.[61]

LATER AGRICULTURE. In 1801 the parish was said to have c. 490 a. under crops.[62] In 1905 there were 2,284 a. of arable land and 522 a. of grassland in the parish, and the ratio was still much the same in the 1930s, when most of the grassland lay around the settlements and outlying farms.[63] In 1987, when information for only 969.5 ha. (2,396 a.) of North Frodingham was returned, 544 ha. (1,344 a.) were arable land and 414 ha. (1,023 a.) grassland. Over 7,000 pigs and 1,000 cattle, nearly 3,000 poultry, and some 600 sheep were then kept.[64]

In the 19th and the earlier 20th century there were usually one to two dozen farmers in North Frodingham, of whom 4 in 1851 and 7–8 in the 1920s and 1930s had 150 a. or more. A market gardener was also recorded in the late 19th and early 20th century, and a cowkeeper c. 1930.[65] In 1987 of 27 holdings returned under the civil parish, one was of 200–299 ha. (494–739 a.), two of 100–199 ha. (247–492 a.), four of 50–99 ha. (124–245 a.), and twenty of less than 50 a.[66]

TRADE AND INDUSTRY. In the late 19th century North Frodingham had merchants dealing in coal, corn, lime, and stone, presumably from beck-side premises at Frodingham Bridge, and there was a fertiliser works at Emmotland in the early and mid 20th century.[67] Small amounts of sand and gravel had been dug in the west of the parish before the 1940s; larger-scale extraction begun then was ended c. 1960,[68] leaving a string of water-filled pits. Bricks and tiles

were being made at a yard at Church End by the mid 19th century; production seems to have ceased c. 1905.[69] In 1994 small businesses trading in the parish included motor engineering firms in North Frodingham village and beside the main Hull–Bridlington road.

MARKET AND FAIRS. Thornton abbey probably established the market and fairs held later at North Frodingham. The weekly market was removed to Driffield in the mid 18th century.[70] Fairs for haberdashery, held on 24th June and 21st September in the mid 17th century, had been altered, partly in response to the change of calendar in 1752, to 10th July and 2nd October by the mid 19th century; they ceased to be held c. 1900.[71] Tolls were paid at North Frodingham in the late 18th century.[72]

MILL. A windmill, recorded at North Frodingham in the 16th century,[73] probably stood where the later mill did, on the south-west edge of the village. Milling was evidently given up c. 1915,[74] and the mill was later demolished.

LOCAL GOVERNMENT. In 1293 the abbot of Thornton claimed sac and soc and toll and team at North Frodingham.[75] A pillory later stood near the cross and stocks at the end of Cross Lane.[76] Court rolls and papers of North Frodingham manor survive for 1574–1937, with some lost years, notably in the late 17th century. The court, which had view of frankpledge, usually met twice a year from the later 17th century. Officers regularly appointed included 3 affeerors, 2 constables, and, in the late 18th and early 19th century, 4 carr-reeves, two dike-reeves, 4 bylawmen, and a pinder.[77] A custumal of 1569 has been printed.[78]

The East Riding constabulary, established in 1857, had a constable based at North Frodingham.[79]

Regular poor relief was given to 7 people in 1802–3, and about the same number each received regular and occasional relief in 1812–15.[80] Half a dozen poorhouses were recorded at North Frodingham in the mid 19th century.[81] The parish joined Driffield poor-law union in 1837[82] and remained in Driffield rural district until 1974, when it was taken into the North Wolds

[56] V.C.H. Yorks. ii. 267.
[57] H.U.L., DDCV/121/14, folder A.
[58] P.R.O., CP 25(2)/615/1659 Trin. [no. 19]; Yorks. Fines, 1603–14, 143.
[59] Poulson, Holderness, i. 307; ii. 267.
[60] R.D.B., CI/273/20.
[61] P.R.O., SC 6/Hen. VIII/2022, ff. 79v.–80; O.S. Map 6", Yorks. CLXXIX (1854 edn.).
[62] P.R.O., HO 67/26/324.
[63] Acreage Returns, 1905; [1st] Land Util. Surv. Map, sheet 28.
[64] Inf. from Min. of Agric., Fish. & Food., Beverley, 1990.
[65] P.R.O., HO 107/2366; directories.
[66] Inf. from Min. of Agric., Fish. & Food.
[67] R.D.B., 227/319/268; 775/516/444; directories.
[68] R.D.B., 662/400/336; 741/465/382; 743/511/441; 775/516/444; 1241/99/87; O.S. Map 6", Yorks. CLXXIX (1854 edn.); inf. from Mr. H. G. McKie, N. Frodingham, 1994.

[69] O.S. Map 6", Yorks. CLXXIX (1854 edn.); directories.
[70] Sheahan and Whellan, Hist. York & E.R. ii. 410.
[71] Farming and Account Books of Henry Best (Sur. Soc. xxxiii), 113–14; directories.
[72] R.D.B., AY/492/829.
[73] P.R.O., SC 6/Hen. VIII/2022, ff. 79v.–80; ibid. C 66/1539, mm. 13–15.
[74] O.S. Map 6", Yorks. CLXXIX (1854 edn.); directories.
[75] Plac. de Quo Warr. 211–12.
[76] Poulson, Holderness, i. 306; T.E.R.A.S. iii. 48.
[77] H.U.L., DDCV/121/1–11, 14.
[78] Ibid. DDCV/121/21; Poulson, Holderness, i. 298–9. Also H.U.L., DDCV/121/22–3.
[79] A. A. Clarke, Country Coppers: Story of E.R. Police, 18–19.
[80] Poor Law Abstract, 1804, pp. 594–5; 1818, pp. 522–3.
[81] R.D.B., GA/240/307.
[82] 3rd Rep. Poor Law Com. 168.

district, later borough, of Humberside. In 1981 the borough's name was changed to East Yorkshire.[83] In 1996 North Frodingham parish became part of a new East Riding unitary area.[84]

In 1883 a cemetery with a chapel was provided off South Townside Road by a burial board.[85] The old shaft of the village cross was re-erected there in 1991.[86]

CHURCH. A church and a priest were recorded at North Frodingham in 1086.[87] In 1115 Stephen, count of Aumale, gave it to Aumale priory, later abbey (Seine Maritime). The grant was revoked by his son William, who gave it instead to Thornton abbey (Lincs.).[88] The abbey appropriated the church, and by 1292 a vicarage had been ordained.[89] The patronage remained with Thornton until the Dissolution.[90] The Crown granted the advowson to the archbishop of York in 1558, evidently without effect,[91] and sold it in 1600 to Henry Best and Francis Jackson.[92] George Hunter bought the advowson in 1610,[93] and it evidently descended to Samuel Hunter (d. 1729),[94] who was succeeded by his son, the Revd. Samuel Hunter. There were few or no institutions in the 17th century, and in 1768 the Crown presented by lapse.[95] Hunter left the advowson to George Acklam (d. 1793),[96] and later the patronage was sold repeatedly. In 1797 the Revd. John Atkinson and the Revd. Rowland Croxton bought it, Croxton presenting Atkinson in 1799 and Atkinson the Revd. Francis Drake in 1809.[97] Drake bought the advowson in 1810 and in 1832 resigned the living to his son William Drake, who also succeeded his father as patron.[98] The advowson belonged to the Revd. John King before 1856, when the Revd. Henry West bought it and presented himself.[99] He sold the advowson to T. S. and Eliza Upton in 1890, and, after subsequent transfers in the early 20th century, it came in 1919 to the Church Association Trust.[1] In 1977 North Frodingham was united with Beeford and Foston on the Wolds, and the Church Society

Trust, the successor to the Church Association Trust, has since been joint patron with the archbishop of York.[2]

The church was worth £8 in 1291.[3] In 1308 Thornton abbey was cited because of the insufficiency of the vicar's portion, which in 1535 was valued at only £5 net.[4] The living was augmented from Queen Anne's Bounty with £200 in 1777 and £400 in 1786, of which £200 was to meet Christopher Blakiston's benefaction of £20 a year.[5] The net income averaged £96 a year in 1829–31 and was £272 in 1883.[6]

By 1535 the vicar had four beast gates in North Frodingham, but there was no glebe land until 1779, when Bounty money was used to buy 19 a. at Driffield.[7] The wool, lamb, and small tithes belonging to the vicar were valued at £4 6s. 8d. a year net in 1535 and £20 gross in 1650. At inclosure in 1808 he received 94 a. and £1 17s. 9d. a year for them, besides 15 a. for the beast gates.[8] The allotments later comprised Vicarage, afterwards Eastfield, farm, which was sold in 1920. Nine acres at Driffield had been sold in 1919,[9] but the rest remained in 1978.[10]

A vicarage house, recorded in 1535, had been demolished by 1685.[11] A new house was built c. 1860.[12] It was evidently sold before the union of 1977, when the parsonage house of Beeford was designated the residence of the new benefice.[13]

A guild of St. Helen was recorded in 1519 and a guild house in 1581.[14]

There was no vicar at North Frodingham in 1650[15] or in 1743, when the living was served by the rector of Catwick. There was then one service each Sunday at North Frodingham,[16] and in 1764 communion was quarterly with 30–40 recipients.[17] In the later 19th century the then resident vicar provided two Sunday services, and from 1868 there were monthly celebrations of communion, with up to a dozen recipients.[18]

The church was dedicated to *ST. HELEN* in 1519 and 1545, but c. 1700 Torre transcribed wrongly the latter record and his attribution to the otherwise unknown *ST. ELGIN* has been accepted.[19] The medieval church comprised

[83] *Census*; Boro. of N. Wolds, *Council Proc. and Cttee. Mins.* 1973–4, 4–7; 1980–1, 360.

[84] Humberside (Structural Change) Order 1995, copy at E.R.A.O.

[85] *Kelly's Dir. N. & E.R. Yorks.* (1889), 390; O.S. Map 1/2,500, Yorks. CLXXIX. 7 (1892 edn.).

[86] Inf. from Mr. McKie, 1995; above, intro.

[87] *V.C.H. Yorks.* ii. 267.

[88] *E.Y.C.* iii, pp. 30–4; Dugdale, *Mon.* vi. 326; *V.C.H. Yorks. E.R.* v. 18.

[89] *Reg. Romeyne*, i (Sur. Soc. cxxiii), pp. 215, 222–3.

[90] Lawrance, 'Clergy List', Holderness, i, pp. 43–4; *V.C.H. Lincs.* ii. 164.

[91] *Cal. Pat.* 1557–8, 420.

[92] P.R.O., C 66/1539, mm. 16–18.

[93] *Yorks. Fines, 1603–14*, 143.

[94] E.R.A.O., PE/118/3.

[95] Poulson, *Holderness*, i. 301.

[96] E.R.A.O., PE/118/4.

[97] R.D.B., BW/338/468; BX/403/651; Poulson, *Holderness*, i. 301.

[98] R.D.B., CR/500/687; GS/402/509; Poulson, *Holderness*, i. 301.

[99] R.D.B., HE/156/188; HL/381/383; B.I.H.R., Inst. AB. 22, pp. 42, 112.

[1] R.D.B., 40/246/232 (1890); 80/139/132 (1905);

B.I.H.R., BA. TP. 1905/2, 1911/1, 1913/6, /10, 1919/1.

[2] B.I.H.R., OC. 923.

[3] *Tax. Eccl.* (Rec. Com.), 304.

[4] *Reg. Greenfield*, v, p. 226; *Valor Eccl.* (Rec. Com.), v. 116.

[5] B.I.H.R., TER. H. N. Frodingham 1786 etc.; Hodgson, *Q.A.B.* pp. clxxv, cccxlv.

[6] B.I.H.R., V. 1884/Ret.; *Rep. Com. Eccl. Revenues*, 936–7.

[7] B.I.H.R., TER. H. N. Frodingham 1781 etc.; *Valor Eccl.* v. 116.

[8] R.D.B., CI/273/20; *Valor Eccl.* v. 116; *T.E.R.A.S.* iv. 61.

[9] R.D.B., 217/430/386; 197/483/409.

[10] Inf. from York Dioc. Bd. of Finance, 1981.

[11] B.I.H.R., TER. H. N. Frodingham 1685; *Valor Eccl.* v. 116.

[12] B.I.H.R., Ch. Ret. i   [13] Ibid. OC. 923.

[14] Ibid. Prob. Reg. 9, f. 97v.; H.U.L., DDCV/121/14, folder A.

[15] *T.E.R.A.S.* iv. 61.

[16] *Herring's Visit.* i, pp. 158, 224.

[17] B.I.H.R., V. 1764/Ret. 1, no. 200.

[18] Ibid. V. 1865/Ret. 1, no. 196; 1868/Ret. 1, no. 179; V. 1871/Ret. 1, no. 178; V. 1877/Ret. 1, no. 176; V. 1884/Ret.

[19] Ibid. Prob. Reg. 9, f. 97v.; Prob. Reg. 13, f. 45; York Minster Libr., Torre MSS., Parochial Churches, p. 1408.

chancel, nave with north aisle and south porch, and west tower; it was evidently of boulders and rubble with stone dressings.[20] The chancel and nave may have been 12th-century in origin. The north aisle was added in the 14th century and the tower in the 15th. The nave was in disrepair *c.* 1600, and in the early 18th century the chancel was repaired and its screen taken down.[21] By the mid 19th century the church was very decayed, and in 1871 the school was being used for services.[22] The chancel, nave, and north aisle were restored to designs by Hugh Roumieu Gough of London in 1877–8; the tower, then repaired, was heightened in 1891–2 with an ashlar belfry to designs by Temple Moore at the expense of Sir Tatton Sykes, Bt.[23] In 1938 the sanctuary was panelled in oak by Mr. Arwidsson, presumably Adolph Arwidsson, the patron 1913–19, and his wife.[24]

The church contains part of a 10th-century cross, the 'most decorative and stylish... in the East Riding',[25] a fragment of a 14th-century cross depicting Atlas, and a 16th-century parish chest. Outside, a heavily-restored, 14th-century, image niche has been inserted in the nave wall. There were three bells in 1552 and later.[26] The plate includes a cup of 1617 and a modern service given by the Revd. Solomon Isaacson, vicar 1890–1936.[27] The registers of marriages and burials date from 1559 and of baptisms from 1579; the record of baptisms and especially of burials is incomplete before 1677, and marriages lack entries in the mid 17th and earlier 18th century.[28] The churchyard was closed in 1883 and replaced by a cemetery.[29]

The parish clerk had two sheaves of wheat a year for every bovate until inclosure in 1808, when 5 a. were awarded instead.[30]

NONCONFORMITY. Several recusants and non-communicants were recorded at North Frodingham in the late 16th and 17th century,[31] but in 1676 only one papist was returned for the parish.[32]

Ten protestant dissenters were recorded in 1676,[33] and unidentified congregations regis-

tered buildings at North Frodingham in 1779, 1809, 1818, 1819, 1820, and 1826.[34] The missionary efforts of members of Fish Street chapel, Hull, included visits *c.* 1800 to North Frodingham, and the Independents built Bethesda chapel in the main street in 1820 or 1821, when it was registered. In 1827 a chapel at Foston and later Beeford and Skipsea chapels were affiliated to that of North Frodingham, which in 1915 became part of the Driffield pastorate. North Frodingham chapel was altered in 1858, restored in 1878, and closed in 1976; the building was sold in 1979[35] and has been demolished. The Wesleyan Methodists registered a chapel in the main street in 1801, and in 1891 replaced it with a new building nearby, which was still used for services in 1995. The old chapel was later the Sunday school[36] but in 1995 it stood disused.[37] The Primitive Methodists built a chapel in Foston Lane in 1842 and registered it the next year.[38] After union with the Wesleyans, the former Primitive Methodist chapel was closed in 1954 and sold in 1956;[39] part has been demolished and the rest was a workshop in 1994. A Sunday school, built by the Primitive Methodists at the junction of the street and Foston Lane in 1865, was used as a recreation room for the village in the mid 20th century, before being demolished.[40]

EDUCATION. There was probably already a school at North Frodingham in the mid 18th century, when the Revd. Samuel Hunter gave £25 for teaching children there. The school was not held between 1803 and 1807, when unspent income increased the capital to £30, but *c.* 1820 it had 50 pupils, four of whom were taught at reduced rates in return for £1 10s. paid to the schoolmaster from the charity. The endowment was later lost.[41] The mixed school was held in 'North Lane', presumably Northfield Lane or North Townside Road,[42] until 1845, when a new school was built on land on South Townside Road given by the Bethells. Run according to the National plan,[43] the school received an annual government grant from 1856.[44] At

[20] H.U.L., DP/159/7 (illus.); Poulson, *Holderness*, i. 297 (illus.), 302–3.
[21] B.I.H.R., Chancery AB. 13, f. 199v.; ibid. ER. V./CB. 1, f. 84v.; ibid. ER. V./Ret. 1, ff. 29, 117; ibid. ER. V./Ret. 2, f. 3v.
[22] Ibid. V. 1865/Ret. 1, no. 196; V. 1868/Ret. 1, no. 179; V. 1871/Ret.1, no. 178.
[23] Ibid. Fac. 1877/4; drawing in church; Dept. of Environment, *Buildings List* (1985); Pevsner and Neave, *Yorks. E.R.*, 632.
[24] B.I.H.R., BA. TP. 1913/6, 1919/1; inscription.
[25] J. Lang, *Corpus of Anglo-Saxon Sculpture*, iii. 187–9, illus.
[26] Ibid. ER. V./CB. 3, f. 4v.; *Inventories of Ch. Goods*, 56–7; G. R. Park, *Ch. Bells of Holderness*, 66.
[27] B.I.H.R., TER. 475; *Yorks. Ch. Plate*, i. 296; memorials in church.
[28] E.R.A.O., PE/118/1–14. Transcripts from 1600 survive: B.I.H.R., PRT. Hold. D.
[29] *Lond. Gaz.* 31 August 1883, 4271; above, local govt.
[30] R.D.B., CI/273/20.
[31] *Depositions from York Castle* (Sur. Soc. xl), 123; Aveling, *Post Reformation Catholicism*, 68.
[32] *Compton Census*, ed. Whiteman, 600.   [33] Ibid.

[34] P.R.O., RG 31/5, nos. 536, 2313, 3222, 3298, 3392, 4038.
[35] Ibid. no. 3515; ibid. HO 129/523/1/6; E.R.A.O., EC/4/1–3; C. E. Darwent, *Story of Fish St. Ch., Hull* (1899), 128–9, 136, illus. facing p. 136; *V.C.H. Yorks. E.R.* ii. 189; D. [R. J.] and S. Neave, *E.R. Chapels and Meeting Houses* (E. Yorks. Loc. Hist. Soc.), 54; O.S. Map 6", Yorks. CLXXIX (1854 edn.).
[36] P.R.O., HO 129/523/1/8; ibid. RG 31/5, no. 1677; O.S. Map 6", Yorks. CLXXIX (1854 edn.); O.S. Map 1/2,500, Yorks. CLXXIX. 7 (1910 edn.); datestone.
[37] Inf. from Mr. H. G. McKie, N. Frodingham, 1995.
[38] P.R.O., HO 129/523/1/7; ibid. RG 31/5, no. 4559; O.S. Map 6", Yorks. CLXXIX (1854 edn.).
[39] E.R.A.O., accession 1036 (MRD. box 23); R.D.B., 1038/552/483.
[40] E.R.A.O., accession 1036 (MRD. box 23, correspondence 1956); Bulmer, *Dir. E. Yorks.* (1892), 201; inf. from Mr. McKie.
[41] *Educ. of Poor Digest*, 1081; *9th Rep. Com. Char.* 760.
[42] *Educ. Enq. Abstract*, 1085; Poulson, *Holderness*, i. 305.
[43] R.D.B., 1481/270/245; Sheahan and Whellan, *Hist. York & E.R.*, ii. 410; O.S. Map 6", Yorks. CLXXIX (1854 edn.).
[44] *Mins. of Educ. Cttee. of Council, 1856–7* [2237], p. 185, H.C. (1857 Sess. 2), xxxiii.

inspection in 1871 there were 102 in attendance, including children from Moor Town, in Brandesburton.[45] The school was evidently also supported by subscription before 1900, when the vicar complained about the farmers' refusal to contribute.[46] Average attendance in the early 20th century was *c.* 100.[47] In 1915 a new council school on North Townside Road was opened to replace the by then inadequate earlier building.[48] The former school was used as a men's reading room *c.* 1920, later fell into disrepair, and was demolished in 1961; the site was sold for £260 which was invested to benefit the Church Sunday school.[49] Numbers at the council school, which was intended also to accommodate children from Brigham, in Foston on the Wolds, averaged 135 in 1922 but only 92 by 1938.[50] In 1990 there were 48 on the roll.[51]

In 1833 a second village school had 30 pupils, all taught at their parents' expense.[52]

CHARITIES FOR THE POOR. Francis Smith (fl. 1812) bequeathed £10 for bread.[53] The charity had about £17 stock in the early 20th century, when the annual income of *c.* 9*s.* was still applied, some 20 people benefitting at Christmas in 1901. Distribution ceased in 1918 for lack of claimants and the income later accumulated;[54] in 1973 the charity had nearly £27 stock. By will proved in 1936, the Revd. Solomon Isaacson, vicar, gave £100 for coal. An almshouse charity benefitting North Frodingham was created by Charles Alfred Swift's will, proved in 1936, and by Scheme of 1937 for Lily Swift; in 1973 the charity had £1,425 stock and £110 in cash. The three charities were amalgamated as the North Frodingham Church Relief in Need Charity by Scheme of 1973, and in the 1990s the combined income of *c.* £70 a year was used to provide medical services and equipment.[55]

GOXHILL

GOXHILL is the smallest parish in north Holderness. The settlement lies 19 km. NNE. of Hull and less than 4 km. south-west from the coast at Hornsea.[56] The name Goxhill may be an Anglian and Scandinavian hybrid meaning 'cuckoo hill', referring in part to the elevated site.[57] The suffix 'in Holderness' was occasionally used, presumably to avoid confusion with Goxhill (Lincs.). The lost settlement of 'Arnestorp', recorded in 1086, may have lain in Goxhill.[58] In 1852 the parish contained 838 a. (339 ha.). In 1935 it was united with the civil parishes of Great and Little Hatfield to form Hatfield parish with an area of 3,303 a. (1,337 ha.).[59]

In 1377 there were 42 poll-tax payers in Goxhill.[60] In 1588, when Goxhill was visited by sweating sickness, 72 burials were recorded.[61] In 1672 the parish had 10 houses assessed for hearth tax and 3 were discharged.[62] There were 8 families in the parish in 1743 and at least 5 houses in 1764.[63] From 54 in 1801 the population rose to 68 in 1811 and thereafter fluctuated about 60, before increasing to 70 in 1871 and to 83 in 1891. It had fallen to 60 in 1901 and stood at 70 in 1931.[64]

The parish is largely on boulder clay and about half of the land lies more than 15 m. above sea level. A small deposit of sand and gravel occurs near the church and a larger pocket in the south-east corner of the parish.[65] The commonable lands were apparently inclosed in the mid 17th century. Goxhill is drained partly by tributaries of a stream which flows north-westwards to Hornsea mere, one of the lesser streams forming part of the eastern parish boundary. Stretches of the southern boundary are defined by other drains, carrying water southwards into Hatfield.

A minor road from Wassand, in Sigglesthorne, forms part of the western boundary, before turning to run along the axis of the parish to the eastern boundary and then on to Hornsea. A field road leading south to Little Hatfield, in Sigglesthorne, defines the rest of the western boundary, and from the axial road side lanes lead north to the settlement of Goxhill and south to Great Hatfield, also in Sigglesthorne. The Hull-Hornsea railway line, opened in 1864,[66] crossed the parish. A station, known until 1904 as Goxhill station and thereafter as Wassand station, stood close to the settlement; it was closed for passengers in 1953 and entirely in 1960, before the closure of the line in 1965. The track has been lifted but the station house remained in 1992.[67]

GOXHILL village is situated in the eastern half of the parish. In 1663 it comprised a wedge-

45 *Returns relating to Elem. Educ.* 472–3, 874–5.
46 B.I.H.R., V. 1900/Ret. no. 279.
47 *Bd. of Educ., List 21* (H.M.S.O., 1908 and later edns.).
48 E.R. Educ. Cttee. *Mins.* 1912–13, 325; 1913–14, 70, 172; 1914–15, 238; 1915–16, 61.
49 B.I.H.R., V. 1921–2/Ret.; ibid. TER. 475; R.D.B., 1481/270/245; inf. from Mr. McKie, 1995.
50 *Bd. of Educ., List 21* (H.M.S.O., 1922 and later edns.); E.R. Educ. Cttee. *Mins.* 1913–14, 247.
51 Inf. from Educ. Dept., Humbs. C.C., 1990.
52 *Educ. Enq. Abstract*, 1085.
53 *9th Rep. Com. Char.* 760.
54 E.R.A.O., accession 1681.
55 B.I.H.R., TER. 475; Scheme in possession of, and inf. from, Mr. McKie, 1995; above, church [plate].
56 This article was written in 1992.

57 *P.N. Yorks. E.R.* (E.P.N.S.), 66–7; G. F. Jensen, *Scand. Settlement Names in Yorks.* 135, 156.
58 *V.C.H. Yorks.* ii. 265.
59 O.S. Map 6″, Yorks. CXCVII (1854 edn.); *Census*, 1931 (pt. ii).
60 P.R.O., E 179/202/60, m. 41.
61 E.R.A.O., PE/33/1.   62 *Hearth Tax*, 61.
63 B.I.H.R., V. 1764/Ret. 1, no. 217; *Herring's Visit.* ii, p. 13.
64 *V.C.H. Yorks.* iii. 495; *Census*, 1911–31.
65 Geol. Surv. Map 1″, drift, sheet 73 (1909 edn.).
66 K. A. MacMahon, *Beginnings of E. Yorks. Rlys.* (E. Yorks. Loc. Hist. Ser. iii), 18.
67 C. R. Clinker and J. M. Firth, *Reg. Closed Passenger Stas. and Goods Depots* (1971), 145, 186; *Hull Daily Mail*, 30 Apr. 1965.

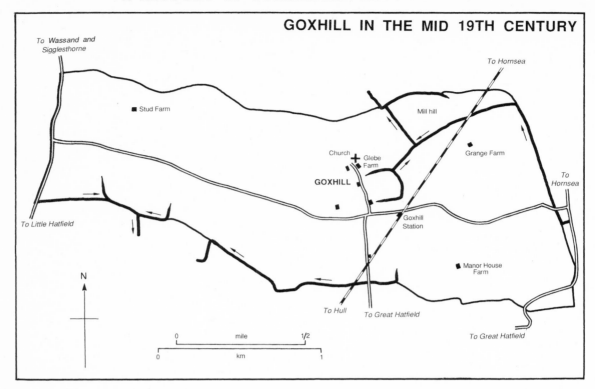

GOXHILL IN THE MID 19TH CENTURY

shaped group of garths and closes, divided by a north-south street and side lanes. The church stood at the northern end of the street, and most of the 20 or so houses then in Goxhill were also built beside it.[68] By the late 20th century only the church and half a dozen houses remained in the village. Apart from the church, the only noteworthy building is the 18th-century Glebe Farm.[69] Outlying buildings include three farmhouses built by the 1820s and since remodelled. One was called Goxhill Grange in 1828 but had been renamed Manor House Farm by 1890; the others were later called Stud Farm and Grange Farm.[70]

MANOR AND OTHER ESTATES. In 1066 Morkar had *c.* 3 carucates at Goxhill and 1½ carucate in 'Arnestorp' as soke of his manor of Mappleton. All the land had passed to Drew de Bevrère by 1086[71] and was later part of the Aumale fee.

Robert of Goxhill (d. by 1287) held in *GOX-HILL* 2 carucates and 3 bovates in demesne and his tenants occupied a further 3 carucates and 5 bovates.[72] The manor later passed, together with the advowson, to the Lelley and Stokes families. By 1289 it may have belonged to Ralph Lelley, who then presented to the

church, and Goxhill evidently descended to his widow Gillian, who was named as lord in 1316.[73] The manor, comprising 3½ carucates in the early 14th century and held as ¹⁄₁₂ knight's fee, later descended from father to son, being held by Ralph Lelley (d. by 1325), Robert Lelley (d. by 1339), Thomas Lelley (probably d. by 1369), and Ralph Lelley (d. by 1412).[74] That Ralph's widow Agnes presumably held the manor, presenting to the church in 1423 and again in 1452, but by 1488 the patronage and evidently also the manor had passed to Robert Stokes (d. 1506). He or another Robert Stokes was succeeded in Goxhill by a daughter Elizabeth (d. 1561), wife of Marmaduke Constable of Wassand and later of one Ashburne. In the 16th century the manor apparently extended into Great and Little Hatfield, and it may also have had appurtenances in Sigglesthorne, which would explain the references to Goxhill as part of the liberty of St. John's, Beverley.[75] It later descended with Wassand in the Constables and Strickland-Constables. The Revd. Charles Constable had 792 a. in the parish *c.* 1840.[76] The estate was enlarged in 1914 by the purchase of *c.* 40 a. of glebe land, and in 1992 it belonged to Lady (Ernestine) Strickland-Constable.[77]

Meaux abbey was given 4 bovates in Goxhill by Peter Tuschett and a close there by another

68   Map to Joseph Osborne's survey of Goxhill at Wassand Hall. Photograph of at E.R.A.O.
69   Below, church.
70   H. Teesdale, *Map of Yorks.* (1828); O.S. Map 1/2,500, Yorks. CXCVII. 11 (1891 edn.).
71   *V.C.H. Yorks.* ii. 265.
72   *Cal. Inq. p.m.* iv, pp. 353, 355; *Kirkby's Inquest*, 371.
73   *Kirkby's Inquest*, 303; Lawrance, 'Clergy List', Holderness, 1, p. 49 and n.

74   *Cal. Inq. p.m.* vi, p. 364; viii, p. 158; Lawrance, 'Clergy List', Holderness, 1, p. 49; Poulson, *Holderness*, i. 308.
75   P.R.O., C 142/48, no. 161; C 142/129, no. 94; *Cal. Pat.* 1338–40, 162; *Cal. Inq. p.m. Hen. VII*, iii, p. 144; Lawrance, 'Clergy List', Holderness, 1, p. 50.
76   B.I.H.R., TA. 618s; Foster, *Pedigrees of Yorks.* iii (s.v. Constable of Flamborough); below, Sigglesthorne, manors (Wassand).
77   Inf. from Wm. H. Brown, Sleaford, 1990; below, church.

donor *c.* 1200 but the land was alienated before the mid 13th century.[78] William Mayne gave Nunkeeling priory a rent in Goxhill in 1498.[79]

ECONOMIC HISTORY. Open fields probably lay on the east and west sides of Goxhill village: a close named Little East field was recorded in 1716, and in 1992 ridge and furrow survived west of the settlement. Rough grazing probably bordered the main drain in the north-east corner of the parish, where Southorpe pasture was mentioned in 1716.[80] The commonable lands were evidently inclosed between 1650, when there were 2 bovates of glebe land, and 1685, when the rector had 36 a. instead; the rest of the land inclosed was presumably allotted to the Constable family.[81] Inclosure had perhaps taken place by 1663, when *c.* 150 a. at the west end of the parish lay in four adjoining closes which had apparently been landscaped with trees, probably by the Constables.[82]

In 1801 the area returned as under crops in the parish was 173 a.[83] There were 573 a. of arable land and 243 a. of grassland in 1839, and 467 a. and 223 a. respectively in 1905.[84] The proportion of arable to grassland was much the same in the 1930s, when the grassland mostly lay around the settlement and the outlying farms.[85] The parish also included 9 a. of woodland in 1905,[86] and several small plantations remained in 1992.

In the 19th and early 20th century there were half a dozen farmers, most of whom had 150 a. or more. A cowkeeper was also recorded from *c.* 1900.[87]

MILL. Mill hill was presumably the site of the windmill recorded in 1325.[88]

LOCAL GOVERNMENT. Regular poor relief was given to two people in 1802–3 and to half a dozen a year in 1812–15; one person was aided occasionally in the earlier year and five a year in 1812–15.[89] Goxhill joined Skirlaugh poor-law union in 1837.[90] It remained in Skirlaugh rural district until 1935, and then, as part of Hatfield civil parish, in Holderness rural district until 1974, when it became part of the Holderness

district of Humberside.[91] In 1996 Hatfield parish became part of a new East Riding unitary area.[92]

CHURCH. A church existed at Goxhill by the early 13th century, when a rector was recorded.[93] The rectory and Hornsea vicarage were united and the two parishes made one in 1939, but in 1972 that union was dissolved and the former parish of Goxhill was annexed instead to Mappleton, thenceforward known as the benefice and parish of Mappleton with Goxhill.[94]

The advowson descended with the manor in the Lelley, Stokes, and Constable families until the later 17th century, when it passed to the Listers.[95] In 1758 William Lister sold the patronage to Thomas Wakefield, then rector, from whom Marmaduke Constable bought it in 1774.[96] It then again descended with the manor until 1901, when Henry Strickland-Constable exchanged the advowon of Goxhill with the Crown. The Crown, which also had the presentation of Hornsea, became the patron of the united benefice in 1939.[97]

The rectory was worth £5 in 1291 and £9 8s. 6d. gross in 1535.[98] The improved annual value was £42 16s. 6d. net in 1650.[99] The net income averaged £284 a year in 1829–31 and in 1883 was £200.[1] Tithes were worth over £7 in 1535 and £30 gross in 1650. They were commuted for a rent charge of £183 13s. in 1839.[2] Glebe land included 2 bovates until 36 a. were evidently substituted for them between 1650 and 1685.[3] In 1914 the glebe, then of *c.* 40 a., was sold to Charles Strickland-Constable.[4]

The parsonage house, recorded from 1535, was rebuilt on the same site *c.* 1745.[5] It was evidently unused by incumbents and *c.* 1830 was returned as 'not fit'.[6] There was erroneously said to be no parsonage house in 1884, when it was let as the glebe farmhouse, together with another cottage; both houses were sold with the glebe in 1914.[7]

The church had a chantry dedicated to St. Mary and founded in 1389 by John of Goxhill, a former rector. Its patronage belonged to the rector in 1425, when the last known chaplain was presented.[8]

There is no evidence for rectors living at

78 *Chron. de Melsa* (Rolls Ser.), i. 308, 367; ii. 32, 102–5.
79 B.L. Cott. MS. Otho. C. viii, f. 75v.
80 B.I.H.R., TER. H. Goxhill 1716.
81 Ibid. 1685; *T.E.R.A.S.*, iv. 65.
82 Map to Joseph Osborne's survey of Goxhill 1663 at Wassand Hall, reprod. in Popham, 'Wassand Estate', pp. 7–8, map 1, copy at E.R.A.O.
83 P.R.O., HO 67/26/179.
84 B.I.H.R., TA. 618s; Acreage Returns, 1905.
85 [1st] Land Util. Surv. Map, sheet 28.
86 Acreage Returns, 1905.
87 P.R.O., HO 107/2365; directories.
88 *Cal. Inq. p.m.* vi, p. 364.
89 *Poor Law Abstract, 1804*, pp. 594–5; *1818*, pp. 522–3.
90 *3rd Rep. Poor Law Com.* 170.   91 *Census.*
92 Humberside (Structural Change) Order 1995, copy at E.R.A.O.
93 G. V. Orange, 'Cart. of Meaux' (Hull Univ. Ph.D. thesis, 1965), pp. 433–4.
94 B.I.H.R., OC. 854; *Lond. Gaz.* 30 May 1939, p. 3638; below, Mappleton, churches.

95 Poulson, *Holderness*, i. 309–10; above, manor.
96 R.D.B., Y/201/29; AT/113/15; Poulson, *Holderness*, i. 310.
97 *Lond. Gaz.* 19 Mar. 1901, pp. 1928–9; 30 May 1939, p. 3638; below, Hornsea, church [adv.].
98 *Tax. Eccl.* (Rec. Com.), 304; *Valor Eccl.* (Rec. Com.), v. 116.
99 *T.E.R.A.S.* iv. 65.
1 B.I.H.R., V. 1884/Ret. 1; *Rep. Com. Eccl. Revenues*, 936–7.
2 B.I.H.R., TA. 618s; *Valor Eccl.* (Rec. Com.), v. 116; *T.E.R.A.S.* iv. 65.
3 B.I.H.R., TER. H. Goxhill 1685 etc.; *T.E.R.A.S.* iv. 65.
4 R.D.B., 163/29/25.
5 B.I.H.R., TER. H. Goxhill 1764; *Valor Eccl.* (Rec. Com.), v. 116.
6 *Rep. Com. Eccl. Revenues*, 936–7.
7 B.I.H.R., TER. H. Goxhill 1764 etc.; ibid. V. 1884/Ret. 1; above, previous para.
8 Lawrance, 'Clergy List', Holderness, i, p. 48.

FIG. 19. GOXHILL CHURCH c. 1830

Goxhill in recent centuries. For much of the 18th century the rector, or in 1764, when he lived at Rowley, his curate, served Goxhill with Mappleton and Withernwick and lived at Great Hatfield. In the mid century a service was held at Goxhill on alternate Sundays and communion was administered there four times a year with 15 recipients in 1743 and 14 in 1764.[9] A curate was employed once more c. 1830.[10] In the 1860s, when the incumbent again also served Mappleton, service was weekly but communion was still only quarterly and there were no more than 8 communicants.[11] Goxhill was served alone c. 1880, when two weekly services and monthly communions were provided, but later the church was again held in plurality, with Hornsea, until the union of 1939, services being provided by the rector and an assistant curate.[12] The church was used only occasionally for services in 1992.[13]

The church of *ST. GILES*, so called in 1412, was in disrepair by the early 18th century and was largely rebuilt in 1786 at the expense of Marmaduke Constable.[14] The tower was replaced in 1817, and in 1840 the Revd. Charles Constable paid for the rest of the church to be rebuilt once again.[15] The church comprises chancel with pentagonal apse, nave, and west tower, and is in a plain, Gothick style.[16] It is built of boulders and brick, but the south sides of the chancel and nave have been faced with stone and the rest of the building rendered. The

slate roofs are prominent and have deep eaves. Inside, the nave roof is borne by beams with large, pendant bosses, and the fittings include 19th-century oil lamps.

Burial at Goxhill ceased in the 1940s.[17] Memorials inside the church include a late medieval, carved floor-stone to Joan Lelley in the chancel, a floor-stone to Marmaduke Constable (d. 1690) in the nave, and a wall tablet to the Constables of Wassand. A restored 12th-century tub font, found at Hornsea,[18] and the stonework of a 15th-century piscina incorporating arms, apparently of the Lelley family,[19] are also preserved in the church. The modern font was removed to West Newton chapel-of-ease, in Aldbrough, in 1939.[20] There were two bells in 1552 but later only one.[21] The plate includes two cups, one of 1827, and a paten of 1830.[22] The registers of baptisms, marriages, and burials date from 1561 and are complete.[23]

NONCONFORMITY. A protestant dissenter was recorded at Goxhill in 1676,[24] but no other evidence of nonconformity has been found.

EDUCATION. The children of Goxhill have gone to school at Sigglesthorne, Hornsea, and Great Hatfield in the 19th and 20th centuries.[25]

CHARITIES FOR THE POOR. None known.

9   B.I.H.R., V. 1764/Ret. 1, no. 217; V. 1764/Ret. 3, no. 140; *Herring's Visit.* ii, pp. 14–15, 223; iii, pp. 225–7.
10   *Rep. Com. Eccl. Revenues*, 936–7.
11   B.I.H.R., V. 1865/Ret. 1, no. 212; V. 1868/Ret. 1, no. 192.
12   Ibid. V. 1877/Ret. 1, no. 189; V. 1884/Ret. 1; V. 1900/Ret. no. 146; *Lond. Gaz.* 30 May 1939, p. 3638.
13   Inf. from Mrs. M. M. Mallison, Goxhill, 1992.
14   B.I.H.R., Reg. 18, f. 22v.; ibid. ER. V/Ret. 2, f. 8; E.R.A.O., PE/27/10; Poulson, *Holderness*, i. 311–12, illus. facing p. 294.
15   E. Yorks. Georgian Soc. *Trans.* v, 34; plaque on church.
16   Pevsner and Neave, *Yorks. E.R.* 439.
17   E.R.A.O., PE/33/7; *Hornsea and Goxhill Monumental*

Inscriptions (E. Yorks. Fam. Hist. Soc.).
18   Notice in church.
19   Poulson, *Holderness*, i. 308 n., 311–13.
20   E.R.A.O., PE/76/19 (2); above, Aldbrough, church [services].
21   B.I.H.R., TER. H. Goxhill 1777 etc.; G. R. Park, *Ch. Bells of Holderness*, 66; *Inventories of Ch. Goods*, 57.
22   *Yorks. Ch. Plate*, i. 255–6.
23   E.R.A.O., PE/33/1–7.
24   *Compton Census*, ed. Whiteman, 600.
25   *Educ. of Poor Digest*, 1081; *Returns relating to Elem. Educ.* 472–3; directories; inf. from Mr. H. A. Robinson, Goxhill, 1992.

HORNSEA

THE town and seaside resort of Hornsea, 20 km. NNE. of Hull, lies between the waters of Hornsea mere and the sea.[26] The medieval town had some importance as a market centre, partly based on fishing and seaborne trade. The market town stood close by the end of the mere, with the seafaring settlement of Hornsea Beck further east; there were outlying hamlets inland at Northorpe and Southorpe and near the sea to the south at Hornsea Burton. The sites of Hornsea Beck and Hornsea Burton were later eroded by the sea, and the other hamlets were also depopulated. The establishment of a seaside resort began in the early 19th century and was quickened by the opening of a railway line from Hull in 1864, which from the first attracted commuters as well as visitors. In 1873 Hornsea was described as 'the quaintest mixture of a small country town and a callow sea bathing place. The better half of it is... little more than a marine suburb of Hull'.[27] Those contrasting elements in its character were never lost.

The name Hornsea, perhaps meaning a peninsula projecting into a lake, is Scandinavian;[28] it may refer to ground called Kirkham or Kirkholme, which projects into the mere close to the town. In 1280 a causeway divided Hornsea mere from Hornsea Burton mere.[29] The mere, which covered 468 a. c. 1700, 361 a. in 1809, and 324 a. in 1890,[30] and its wooded surrounds give a picturesque aspect to the landward side of Hornsea. The belt of trees beside the mere along the Seaton road was planted in the later 19th century.[31] The western end of the mere, which was reserved for their own use by the Strickland-Constables, owners of Wassand Hall, was managed with a concern for wildlife at the end of the 19th century, and about 1910 a cooperative association with the Yorkshire Naturalists Union was begun.[32] A reserve including the mere and adjoining land was established by the Royal Society for the Protection of Birds in 1970; it was given up in the late 1990s.[33]

Hornsea contained 3,332 a. (1,348.5 ha.) in 1852, of which 409 a. (165.5 ha.) were in Hornsea Burton township.[34] In 1894 the civil parish was made an urban district, which existed until 1974.[35] As the result of erosion by the sea, which

accounted for 1–2 yd. a year in the later 19th century,[36] the area of the urban district in 1971 was only 1,332 ha. (3,292 a.). In 1991 it was 1,310 ha. (3,237 a.).[37]

There were 271 poll-tax payers at Hornsea, 264 at Hornsea Beck, 96 at Hornsea Burton and in the southern part of Hornsea Beck, 7 at Northorpe, and 28 at Southorpe in 1377.[38] In 1490 the vicar numbered his cure of souls as 340 at Hornsea, 240 at Hornsea Beck, 50 at Hornsea Burton, 14 at Northorpe, and 30 at Southorpe.[39] Hornsea had 83 houses assessed for hearth tax and 14 discharged in 1672.[40] There were 133 families in the parish in 1743 and 131 in 1764.[41] The population in 1801 was 533, increasing rapidly to 704 in 1811. There was another sharp rise between 1831 and 1841, from 780 to 1,005, although more than 50 holidaymakers were included in the latter figure. Numbers stood at 1,063 in 1861, but after the opening in 1864 of a railway they increased steadily to 1,685 in 1871, 1,836 in 1881, 2,013 in 1891, and 2,381 in 1901.[42] In the 20th century the rate of increase varied: numbers rose to 3,024 in 1911, 4,279 in 1921, 4,450 in 1931, 5,324 in 1951, 5,955 in 1961, 7,031 in 1971, and 7,301 in 1981. In 1991 of 7,934 usually resident only 7,831 were present.[43]

Much of the parish is on boulder clay and lies at between 15 and 25 m. above sea level.[44] It was mostly occupied by the open fields of Hornsea, which were inclosed in 1809; Hornsea Burton township had been inclosed as early as the 1660s. The town itself stands on gravel terraces. Lower-lying alluvial ground adjoins both the mere and Stream dike, which flows from the mere through the town to the sea. A sluice controlled the flow of water along the dike by the late 16th century.[45] Stream dike was straightened and given a more direct outlet in 1846,[46] and in 1979 Yorkshire Water Authority installed a system designed to prevent discharges from the mere into the dike when the water level in the mere fell below 12 ft. above sea level.[47] The modest North and South cliffs peter out to produce the so-called Hornsea Gap near Stream dike.[48] South bridge, which was mentioned c. 1400,[49] may have been that which carried

[26] This article was written mainly in 1989 and revised in and after 1997.

[27] *Spectator*, 27 Sept. 1873, cited by K. L. Mayoh, 'Comparative Study of Resorts on Coast of Holderness' (Hull Univ. M.A. thesis, 1961), 192.

[28] G. F. Jensen, *Scand. Settlement Names in Yorks.* 97.

[29] *Yorks. Fines, 1272–1300*, p. 55.

[30] E.R.A.O., DDSC, accession 4248 (plan of mere); ibid. IA. Hornsea; O.S. Map 1/2,500, Yorks. CXCVII. 7 (1891 edn.). The reduction in the extent of the mere, and the landscape in general, are discussed in Popham, 'Wassand Estate'.

[31] Between 1852 and 1890: O.S. Map 6", Yorks. CXCVII (1854 edn.); 1/2,500, Yorks. CXCVII. 3–4, 7 (1891 edn.). Popham, 'Wassand Estate', p. 32.

[32] Popham, 'Wassand Estate', p. 33.

[33] Inf. from R.S.P.B., Sandy (Beds.), 1989; inf. from R.S.P.B., Bempton, 2000.

[34] O.S. Map 6", Yorks. CXCVII (1854 edn.).

[35] Below, local govt.

[36] T. Sheppard, *Lost Towns of Yorks. Coast*, 166.

[37] *Census*, 1971, 1991.

[38] P.R.O., E 179/202/60, mm. 47, 50, 55, 58, 64.

[39] P. Heath, *Med. Clerical Accts.* (St. Ant. Hall Publ. xxvi), 57.   [40] *Hearth Tax*, 61.

[41] B.I.H.R., V. 1764/Ret. 2, no. 48; *Herring's Visit.* ii, p. 88.

[42] *Census*, 1831–41; *V.C.H. Yorks.* iii. 495; below, this section. After 1841 census day was never in the holiday season.

[43] *Census*, 1911–91.

[44] Geol. Surv. Map 1", drift, sheet 73 (1909 edn.).

[45] E.R.A.O., DDRI/19/2; *Cal. Pat.* 1575–8, p. 493; *Diary of Abraham de la Pryme* (Sur. Soc. liv), 272.

[46] E. W. Bedell, *Acct. of Hornsea* (1848), 54.

[47] Popham, 'Wassand Estate', appendix 5, pp. 4–5.

[48] O.S. Map 6", Yorks. CXCVII (1854 edn.).

[49] *Public Works in Med. Law*, ii (Selden Soc. xl), 356.

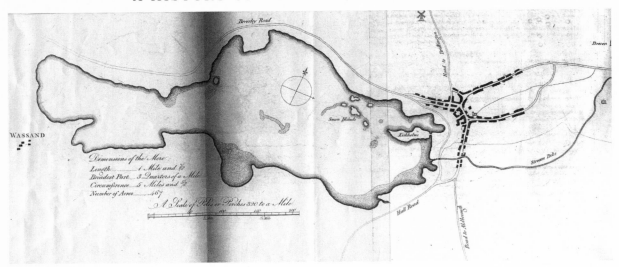

FIG. 20. HORNSEA: MAP OF THE MERE, SHOWING ALSO WASSAND AND HORNSEA TOWN, LATE 18TH CENTURY

Southgate over the dike.[50] The largest of several streams flowing into the mere is Foss dike, which forms the western boundary of Hornsea Burton township; it was recorded in 1682, along with Coye and Lund Wyke dikes.[51]

The main street of the old town, running roughly parallel to the shore of the mere, comprises Westgate, Market Place, and Southgate, the first recorded in 1539 and the last in the 1480s.[52] Behind the west side of the street lie Back Westgate, Mere Side, and Back Southgate, and several small lanes run from the street to join them, including Chambers Lane, Hillerby Lane, and Mere Walk, formerly Strait Lane. Before the inclosure of the common in 1809, the back lane extended to the Hatfield road. From the opposite side of the main street Eastgate and Newbegin, the latter recorded in the 1480s,[53] lead towards the sea. The cul-de-sac known as Football Green, on the east side of Southgate, takes its name from ground mentioned in 1539.[54] Access to the sea shore was formerly provided only by Eastgate and its continuation Sea Road or Sands Lane (later part of Eastgate), which was given a straight new course at inclosure in 1809. Newbegin crossed Sands Lane, and in 1809 a continuation of it northwards was set out as Cliff Lane or Road.[55] It was not until 1848 that New Road was made from Newbegin to the sea front.[56] A medieval cross stood in Market Place until the mid 19th century, when it was moved to Southorpe Hill Farm.[57] In 1898, after eight cottages adjoining the churchyard had been demolished as an improvement to com-

memorate the Diamond Jubilee, the cross was placed in the churchyard;[58] it has been restored with a new top. A second medieval cross stands beside Southgate. Since the late 19th century Newbegin has replaced Market Place as the shopping and service centre of the town.

Of the roads leading out of the parish the chief is that which runs westwards beside the mere to Seaton and on towards Beverley; parts of it are carried over the lowest ground by causeways.[59] Other roads lead northwards to Atwick and Bewholme and southwards to Hatfield and Rolston. Until inclosure in 1809 the Bewholme road left the Atwick road on the edge of the town.[60] The roads to Atwick and Rolston were later upgraded as parts of the main Holderness coast road, and that to Hatfield, formerly called Lelley Lane, became part of the main road to Hull. From the Rolston road the former Mill Lane (later Burton Lane and Hornsea Burton Road) leads to the sea.

The Wade family, Hull timber merchants, played a leading part in securing a railway line and in furthering the development of the town. It was probably no coincidence that John Wade completed his country house in Hornsea in 1846,[61] the year in which the York & North Midland Railway Co. was sanctioned to build a line from Beverley.[62] Wade was succeeded in 1850 by his nephew Richard William Wade (d. 1852),[63] who led unsuccessful efforts to force the company to fulfil its commitments.[64] The Wade estate then passed in turn to Richard's father Abraham (d. 1853) and another of Abraham's

[50] The bridge in Southgate was recorded in 1624: E.R.A.O., PE/30/33, f. [6].

[51] E.R.A.O., DDRI/19/2.

[52] P.R.O., SC 6/Hen. VIII/4595; Heath, *Med. Clerical Accts.* 38.

[53] Heath, op. cit.

[54] P.R.O., SC 6/Hen. VIII/4595; E.R.A.O., PE/30/33, f. 7v.

[55] R.D.B., CI/345/27; E.R.A.O., IA. Hornsea; ibid. DDX/253/1 (undated pre-incl. plan); Hull Pub. Libr., proprietors' and incl. commissioners' mins.; O.S. Map 6", Yorks. CXCVII (1854 edn.).

[56] Below (growth of town).

[57] Bulmer, *Dir. E. Yorks.* (1892), 430–1; O.S. Map 6",

Yorks. CXCVII (1854 edn.); O.S. Map 1/2,500, Yorks. CXCVII. 11 (1891 edn.).

[58] Hornsea U.D.C. Mins. 1896–1906, 63–4 (at E.R.A.O., UDHO); *Kelly's Dir. N. & E.R. Yorks.* (1897), 476; (1901), 498; M. Sewell, *Joseph Armytage Wade* (Hornsea Museum, 1996), 84 (illus.).

[59] Popham, 'Wassand Estate', appendix 5, p. 2.

[60] T. Jefferys, *Map of Yorks.* (1772).

[61] Below (growth of town).

[62] K. A. MacMahon, *Beginnings of E. Yorks. Rlys.* (E. Yorks. Loc. Hist. Ser. iii), 17.

[63] H.U.L., DSJ/35, p. 465; Sewell, op. cit. *passim.*

[64] *Hull Advertiser*, 30 May, 20 June 1851.

sons, Joseph Armytage Wade (d. 1896).[65] It was J. A. Wade who promoted a line from Hull, and the Hull & Hornsea Railway Co. was formed in 1861. It was originally intended that the line should end near the old town, but Wade, as chairman of the company, insisted that it should reach his land near the sea front and a viaduct was therefore needed to carry it across the low ground beside Stream dike, greatly increasing the cost. The line was opened in 1864 with a terminal station near the sea and another station at Hornsea Bridge, where the line crossed the Rolston road. The railway was not a financial success and in 1866 the company was merged with the North Eastern Railway.[66] The viaduct was later replaced by an embankment.[67] The terminus was closed entirely in 1964 and Hornsea Bridge station for passengers in 1964 and for goods the following year.[68] The red-brick terminal station has a porte-cochère of five arched bays and five-bayed side wings with round-headed windows in blank arches; it has been converted to housing. Hornsea Bridge station and the bridge across the road have been demolished. The track has been lifted but its course has been designated a footpath and forms part of the Transpennine trail.[69]

The hamlet of Northorpe stood ½ mile north of Hornsea, where a house beside the Atwick road still bears the name. Its tax assessment was only 13s. 4d. in 1334.[70] Cottages there were recorded in the early 17th century[71] but all the garths were empty in 1809.[72] Southorpe, recorded from 1086,[73] stood close to the south-eastern corner of the mere, where earthworks mark the site. Cottages were recorded in the early 17th century,[74] but a ruinous house was evidently all that remained in 1650[75] and there were no houses in the garths in 1809. The site of Hornsea Beck, which presumably took its name from the watercourse later called Stream dike, has been eroded by the sea. The settlement was mentioned in the early 13th century and rivalled Hornsea itself for size in the late 14th.[76] More men were mustered there in 1539 than at Hornsea.[77] In 1609 it was said that 38 houses had been destroyed since 1547[78] and in 1637 that 20 had gone within living memory;[79] by 1695 all but one or two houses had been washed away.[80] Hornsea Burton, the site of which has also been

eroded, stood a short distance south of Stream dike. It was mentioned from 1086.[81] In 1663 there were still c. 8 houses, lying close to a small common or green,[82] but in 1697 the hamlet was described as wasted by the sea.[83]

GROWTH OF THE TOWN. The old market town lay close to the mere, its houses concentrated mainly in Market Place, Newbegin, Southgate, and Westgate, with a few in Eastgate.[84] It was evidently a place of many but modest dwellings: in 1672, for example, 58 out of 97 households had only one hearth, 34 had only two or three, and a mere 5 had between four and six,[85] while in 1784 there were 46 houses and as many as 82 cottages.[86] A storm in 1732 destroyed 24 houses and 14 barns close to the cross in Market Place.[87]

The surviving early houses are of the 17th century and are mostly single-storeyed with attics.[88] The walls are generally of boulders, with brick used sparingly for offsets, dressings, and tucked gables.[89] A full upper storey occurs only rarely,[90] and, as with single-storeyed houses of brick,[91] may be an indication of a later, that is early 18th-century, date. A feature of the older parts of the town is the use of boulders for garth walls, which often survive although the houses have been rebuilt in the 19th century.

In the earlier 19th century most of the new building in the town took the form of infilling with small houses and cottages in the existing streets.[92] At the same time several larger houses were built, one or two of them by Hull businessmen as country residences. Ivy Lodge, in Eastgate, was built between 1819 and 1831 by George Green of Hornsea.[93] Close by in Eastgate, Hornsea House, later called the Hall, was built in 1845–6 by John Wade (d. 1850), a Hull merchant.[94] The house, now demolished, was designed by Charles Hutchinson of Hull; only its later 19th-century entrance lodges remain.[95] Another house in Eastgate, formerly known as Holme Lea and the Lair and later as Burnside, was probably built by William Conway of Hornsea c. 1800 and enlarged after 1806 by William Whitehead of Hornsea, who sold it in 1819 to William Gibson (d. 1820), a Hull ship-builder; it may have been rebuilt by Gibson's son Edward (d. 1859) and refronted later.[96] In

[65] H.U.L., DSJ/36, pp. 252, 254; DSJ/42, p. 521.
[66] MacMahon, op. cit. 17–18; *Hull Advertiser*, 15 Nov., 6 Dec. 1856.
[67] O.S. Map 1/2,500, Yorks. CXCVII. 7 (1891 edn.).
[68] C. R. Clinker and J. M. Firth, *Reg. Closed Passenger Stas. and Goods Depots*, 67.
[69] Plaque of 1996 behind Hornsea Leisure Centre.
[70] *Lay Subsidy of 1334*, ed. R. E. Glasscock, 366. Earlier refs. (*P.N. Yorks. E.R.* 65) prob. relate to Northorpe in Easington.
[71] E.R.A.O., PE/30/33, f. [7].
[72] Ibid. IA. Hornsea.   [73] *V.C.H. Yorks.* ii. 265.
[74] E.R.A.O., PE/30/33, f. [7].
[75] P.R.O., E 317/Yorks./28.
[76] *Chron. de Melsa* (Rolls Ser.), i. 421.
[77] *L. & P. Hen. VIII*, xiv (1), p. 307.
[78] P.R.O., E 178/4813.
[79] Ibid. E 134/13 Chas. I East./7.
[80] W. Camden, *Britannia*, ed. E. Gibson (1695), 748.
[81] *V.C.H. Yorks.* ii. 265.
[82] H.U.L., DDX/16/214.

[83] P.R.O., E 134/9 Wm. III Mich./45.
[84] E.R.A.O., IA. Hornsea.
[85] P.R.O., E 179/205/504.
[86] E.R.A.O., PE/30/3, inside front cover.
[87] Ibid. PE/30/2, flyleaf.
[88] e.g. nos. 10–12 Eastgate, no. 42 Southgate, and part of the museum in Newbegin.
[89] e.g. no. 36 Southgate.
[90] e.g. no. 41 Southgate.
[91] e.g. nos. 43–4 Southgate.
[92] cf. inclosure map of 1809 (E.R.A.O., IA.) and O.S. Map 6", Yorks. CXCVII (1854 edn.).
[93] H.U.L., DSJ/34, pp. 137, 457.
[94] Ibid. DSJ/35, pp. 79, 465; DSJ/37, p. 322; White, *Dir. Hull & York* (1846), 374; O.S. Map 1/2,500, Yorks. CXCVII. 3–4 (1891 and 1910 edns.); illus. in Sewell, *Joseph Armytage Wade*, 73.
[95] E.R.A.O., DX/138.
[96] H.U.L., DSJ/34, p. 133; DSJ/39, p. 11; ibid. DDCV/82/5, pp. 337, 346, 367; O.S. Map 1/2,500, Yorks. CXCVII. 3–4 (1891 and 1910 edns.).

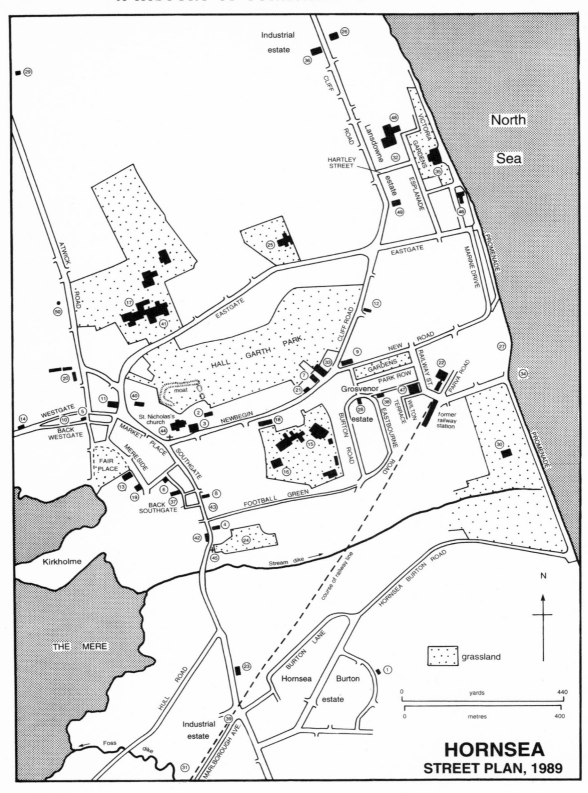

North

Sea

Industrial
estate

HARTLEY
STREET

Grosvenor

Kirkholme

THE MERE

grassland

Foss

dike

Industrial
estate

N

HORNSEA
STREET PLAN, 1989

1 Church hall	11 Former Primitive Methodist chapel	21 Former police station	31 Site of gasworks	41 Site of the Hall
2 Vicarage	12 Christian Scientist meeting room	22 Police station and court house	32 Site of gasworks (Lansdowne estate)	42 White House
3 Parish hall	13 Former National school	23 Fire station	33 Public library	43 Site of Hornsea House
4 Roman Catholic church	14 Former infants' school	24 Cemetery	34 Site of pier	44 Cross (in churchyard)
5 Quaker Cottage	15 Primary school	25 War Memorial Cottage Hospital	35 Floral Hall	45 Cross (Southgate)
6 Former Wesleyan chapel	16 Nursery school	26 Former chidren's convalescent home	36 Former Victoria Picture Theatre	46 Marine Hotel
7 Methodist church	17 Hornsea School (secondary)	27 Site of lifeboat house	37 Former drill hall and ex-sevicemen's club	47 Alexandra Hotel
8 Former Independent chapel	18 Pickering almshouses	28 Former lifeboat house	38 Masonic hall	48 Former Granville Court Hotel
9 United Reformed church	19 Stockdale homes	29 Former waterworks	39 Site of Hornsea Bridge railway station	49 Elim Lodge
10 Site of Primitive Methodist chapel	20 Hart homes	30 Sewage pumping station	40 Old Hall	50 Remains of windmill

Newbegin three houses were built in 1805 by John Bedell, a Hull customs officer.[97] One of them was sold in 1815 to John Marshall (d. 1825), a Hull shipowner, who lived there before moving to another Hornsea House, in Southgate, which he built after 1819.[98] Another of the houses built by Bedell was sold in 1829 to William Bettison, a Hull brewer, who built a folly tower in the garden and kept the house until 1853.[99] Also in Newbegin a house called Marine Villa was built by Thomas E. Collinson of Hull between 1806 and 1813. It was sold in 1827 to George Goodwin (d. 1850), a Hull merchant. Close by Goodwin built Swiss Terrace[1] (nos. 90–100 Newbegin) in a Swiss chalet style.

Early interest in the seaside also resulted in the erection of houses close to the cliffs. The Marine Hotel was built near the end of Eastgate in 1837 by Richard Casson, a Hull surgeon, who sold it in 1842 to Thomas Cunnington of Hull.[2] Further south, two houses, later part of Marine Terrace in Marine Drive, were built in 1835 by Thomas Wilson of Leven and five more in 1845–6 by Ralph Grantham, a Hull builder.[3] Access to Marine Terrace was improved in 1848 when New Road was made, by public subscription, from Newbegin to the shore, replacing a footpath nearby.[4] Away from the town, a *cottage ornée*, later known as Mushroom Cottage, was built near the Wassand boundary in 1812.[5]

The later 19th century saw a continuation of infilling in the main streets and of new building on the edges of the town. Infilling included the building of terraced cottages known as Ocean and Welbourne Terraces, behind Southgate. Westgate House, in Westgate, may have been built by Elizabeth Bainton of Hornsea c. 1865[6] and the originally neighbouring house (nos. 26–8 Westgate, formerly Firbank House) by S. F. Simpson of Hornsea after 1866.[7] Ventnor House (no. 27 Westgate, now Grebe House) was built in the late 1870s,[8] and further out, on the Seaton road, Suffolk Terrace was put up in 1868.[9] Off Leys Lane, the first three houses in Northumberland Avenue were built in 1878–9.[10] In Mill Lane, off the Rolston road, Bank Terrace was erected between 1862 and 1874 by J. A. Wade.[11]

Greater changes took place on the seaward side of the town. During the 25 years after the opening of the railway in 1864 the resort developed in two areas: one around the railway station and New Road, the other further north between Cliff Road and the sea. By 1890 about 70 houses had been erected in the former and some 40 in the latter.[12] Several landowners played a prominent part in laying out streets and building plots, but numerous people, many of them from Hull, shared in the erection of houses. One of the leading figures was J. A. Wade; in 1866–8 he bought nearly 50 a. on both sides of New Road and southwards alongside the sea as far as Stream dike.[13] West of Wade's land on the south side of New Road was a 10-a. site bought in 1865 by Samuel and Thomas Haller, Hull shoemakers,[14] which later became known as the Grosvenor or Oval estate.[15] Beside Cliff Road the largest proprietor was William M. Jackson of Hull, who bought c. 17 a. in 1866–8;[16] it became known as the Lansdowne estate.[17] An attempt to develop land adjoining the sea in Hornsea Burton was made by Pierre H. M. du Gillon of Sheffield, who bought 59 a. there in 1875, but his grandiose plans for the South Cliff estate were not fulfilled.[18]

Houses erected on Wade's land included Alexandra Terrace (nos. 1–4 Railway Street), built in 1869,[19] the Alexandra Hotel (later for a time called the Mere Hotel), built in 1867,[20] Albert Villa, Grosvenor Terrace, and Wilton Terrace. Albert Villa, in Railway Street, later called Brampton House, is a large detached house put up by 1882 for John Hunt, a Hull music-hall proprietor, as his own residence.[21] Grosvenor Terrace, on the north side of New Road, consists of two rows of houses built in the late 1860s and 1870s.[22] Wilton Terrace, near the railway station, which comprises two-storeyed houses with a higher centrepiece, was built by 1868.[23] On the Hallers' estate the early houses included nos. 4–12 New Road[24] and Eastbourne Terrace (nos. 8–16 Eastbourne Road);[25] some of the occupiers had the use of the Grosvenor Garden, fronting New Road.[26] In the late 1870s Alfred Maw of Hull began to be involved in building on the Grosvenor estate; in 1881 he took over the remaining empty plots, c. 90 all told, but in 1886 he conveyed them to a Hull builder, John Emerson.[27] Four pairs of

97 H.U.L., DDCV/82/5, pp. 206, 289, 295.
98 Ibid. DSJ/34, pp. 19, 133; DSJ/35, p. 277.
99 Ibid. DDCV/82/5, p. 503; ibid. DSJ/34, pp. 415, 453, 469; DSJ/35, p. 65; DSJ/36, p. 40; DSJ/37, p. 176.
1 Ibid. DDCV/82/5, pp. 338, 526; ibid. DSJ/34, pp. 357, 555; DSJ/35, p. 559; R.D.B., 135/243/213.
2 H.U.L., DSJ/34, p. 524; DSJ/35, p. 93; *Hull Advertiser*, 2 June 1837.
3 H.U.L., DSJ/34, pp. 522, 534, 593; DSJ/35, pp. 151–81, 215–27, 321.
4 E.R.A.O., HD/53; ibid. PE/30/22, pp. 16–17.
5 *Trans. E. Yorks. Georgian Soc.* v (1), 34.
6 H.U.L., DSJ/37, pp. 258, 275; DSJ/42, p. 50.
7 Ibid. DSJ/37, p. 335; DSJ/41, p. 441; DSJ/42, p. 73; DSJ/45, p. 145; O.S. Map 1/2,500, Yorks. CXCVII. 3–4 (1891 edn.).
8 H.U.L., DSJ/39, pp. 170, 175. Dated plans of 1876–7 in possession of Dr. J. E. S. Walker, Grebe House, 1998. The name Ventnor House is borne by a division of the original house (no. 25 Westgate).
9 R.D.B., KF/42/61; KF/43/62; KI/189/249–50; KI/190/251–2; KI/191/253–4.

10 Ibid. MU/13/22; MX/359/574; MX/360/575; H.U.L., DSJ/40, p. 291.
11 H.U.L., DSJ/36, p. 491; DSJ/38, p. 511.
12 O.S. Map 1/2,500, Yorks. CXCVII. 3–4 (1891 edn.).
13 R.D.B., IX/307/422; KE/96/124; KH/380/451.
14 H.U.L., DSJ/37, p. 185.
15 E.R.A.O., DDX/298/12.
16 R.D.B., IY/187/264; IY/338/485; KG/317/480.
17 E.R.A.O., DDX/298/11.
18 Ibid. DDX/298/8–9; R.D.B., LU/373/553; H.U.L., DDX/16/344.   19 R.D.B., KN/200/279.
20 Ibid. KF/59/74; *Illus. Guide to Hornsea* (1894), 11.
21 R.D.B., KY/157/207; NP/46/67.
22 Ibid. IZ/311/385; KF/301/405; KG/65/106; KG/207/316; KN/112/155; KV/109/138; KY/196/252; LC/330/430; MC/342/527; MT/79/108.   23 Ibid. KF/59/74.
24 H.U.L., DSJ/37, p. 270; DSJ/38, pp. 97, 346; DSJ/39, pp. 70, 296.
25 Ibid. DSJ/37, pp. 205, 214, 223, 232, 241.
26 R.D.B., NA/336/489.
27 Ibid. MP/210/294; MR/138/205; NF/222/348; 12/331/321 (1886).

3-storeyed, semi-detached houses (later nos. 18–32 Eastbourne Road) were being built by Emerson in 1890.[28]

Beside Cliff Road, on the Lansdowne estate, the first streets to be made were Hartley Street and Flamborough Terrace Road (later part of the Esplanade). Houses built in the 1860s and 1870s included Cliff Villas[29] and Carlton Terrace,[30] both in Cliff Road, Flamborough Terrace,[31] and a terrace in Headland View.[32] One much larger house was Elim Lodge, Cliff Road, built in 1871 by Thomas Keyworth of Hull but sold in 1873 to Thomas B. Holmes, a Hull tanner, who lived there himself until his death in 1913.[33] Holmes also bought other land from Jackson and built several houses.[34] Among houses built further north along Cliff Road, beyond Jackson's estate, were Mountain Villa[35] and Cliff Terrace.[36]

Between 1890 and 1908 most of the new building took place in existing streets.[37] In the older part of the town it included several terraces of small houses in Mill Lane, Mount Pleasant, and Eastgate View. St. Bede's College, on the Atwick road, was built in 1895 by Henry Elsom.[38] Near the sea, several new streets were also laid out, like Victoria Avenue, near the Marine Hotel, Carlton and Carrington Avenues and Clifford Street, on the west side of Cliff Road, and Belvedere Park. The more noteworthy new houses include the ornate terraces forming nos. 59–69 Eastgate, nos. 4–14 Esplanade, and nos. 1–8 Victoria Avenue, which were built c. 1900 by T. B. Holmes and G. L. Scott, a Hull builder.[39] The children's convalescent home in Cliff Road was built in 1908.[40] Off the Rolston road, a long terrace of small houses was built in Marlborough Avenue, alongside the existing terrace of Brickyard Cottages.

The houses built in the later 19th century show considerable variety of size, style, and materials. They range from small cottages to large villas, stand singly or in pairs, short rows, or long terraces, and are built of pink, red, white, or yellow brick. Many have brick or wood bay windows to one or two floors, and some have attics or a full third floor; several are adorned with towers or pinnacles. A few have stone dressings or are faced with tiles,[41] and there is much decorative brickwork and woodwork.

Between 1908 and 1925 infilling in and around existing streets included building between Eastgate and New Road which effectively united the two initial areas of resort development. The few new streets which appeared during that period included Clifton Street and Westbourne Road.[42] Soon after 1920 the urban district council built its first houses, in Southgate Gardens.[43] A large hotel known at first as the Imperial Hydro, later Granville Court, was built in the Esplanade in 1914 by John Wilson, a Hull tin can manufacturer who then lived in Hornsea.[44] It had shaped gables and a high domed tower. The building was demolished c. 1990 following a fire.[45] By 1925, too, houses had been built on the Rolston road and near Marlborough Avenue on the Edenfield estate, and further south a few wooden bungalows had been put up in Strawberry Gardens.[46]

By 1938 building had begun on the Hull road, and the first of the wooden bungalows in Pasture Road were built, to be followed by others in Mill Lane, later Hornsea Burton Road. After the war much new building took place on the south side of the town, in Hornsea Burton, and on the north side, off Eastgate, where the Ashcourt Drive estate was developed from 1966. The southern additions included a large council estate in Hornsea Burton, begun in 1946, and Tranmere Park, Lindale Avenue, and Greenacre Park, all of the early 1960s.[47] More recent building includes two large estates of private housing, the Trinity Fields estate off the Rolston road, where work was continuing along Tansley Lane in 2000, and, on the west side of the town, the Cheyne Garth estate. An existing development off Cliff Road was also added to by the district council and housing associations, Sandpiper Court being opened in 1994.[48]

THE RESORT. Visitors were attracted to Hornsea soon after 1800, when two or three bathing machines were provided for them. There were few other attractions, apart from horse races on the beach in July and a chalybeate spring, soon to be choked up and forgotten, near the mere.[49] A dancing or assembly room was built before 1811 by John Bedell near his house in Newbegin.[50] Early in the century public fishing was allowed on the mere but that was soon discontinued.[51] Accommodation, moreover, was limited to lodgings in existing houses and to inns

28 Ibid. 39/213/202 to 39/217/206 (1890).
29 Ibid. KG/318/481; KG/337/507.
30 Ibid. KT/73/95; KT/175/240; MM/273/438.
31 Ibid. KD/269/356.
32 Ibid. KO/154/206; MG/9/13.
33 Ibid. KU/262/363; KU/263/364; LF/318/406; 217/418/374.
34 Ibid. LF/318/407; LF/320/408; LH/136/191; LO/271/380; LO/272/381; MG/9/13.
35 H.U.L., DSJ/38, pp. 141, 342, 374.
36 Ibid. DSJ/39, pp. 105, 442.
37 O.S. Map 1/2,500, Yorks. CXCVII. 3–4, 7 (1910 edn.).
38 H.U.L., DSJ/42, pp. 427, 430.
39 R.D.B., 18/391/355 (1900); 18/475/438 (1900).
40 Date on building.
41 Illus. in Sewell, *Joseph Armtage Wade*, 77.
42 O.S. Map 1/2,500, Yorks. CXCVII. 3–4 (1927 edn.).
43 R.D.B., 198/554/478; 220/394/341; B.I.H.R., V. 1910–22/Ret.; G. L. Southwell, *Hornsea in Old Postcards*, p. [44].

44 R.D.B., 74/343/326 (1905); 80/174/166 (1905); 130/193/169; 135/310/272; 371/26/21; 702/588/498; *Reg. of Electors* (1915); E.R. Licensing Cttee. *Mins.* 1904–23, 223. Illus. in M. and B. Chapman, *Holderness in old picture postcards*, 30; I. and M. Sumner, *Britain in Old Photographs: Holderness*, 39.
45 The dome was removed in 1989. Pevsner and Neave, *Yorks. E.R.* 482; inf. from Mr. M. Sewell, Hornsea, 1997.
46 O.S. Map 6″, Yorks. CXCVII. NE. (1929 edn.). For the Edenfield estate, see R.D.B., 238/137/115; 238/317/266 etc.
47 R.D.B., 691/514/431; Mayoh, 'Resorts of Holderness', 193; inf. from Dr. J. E. S. Walker, Hornsea, 1997.
48 Plaque on Sandpiper Court; inf. from Mr. Sewell, 2000.
49 Bedell, *Acct. of Hornsea* (1848), 97–8; directories. For bathing machines, cf. *Hull Advertiser*, 3 June 1825.
50 H.U.L., DDCV/82/5, pp. 289, 503; ibid. DSJ/34, p. 415.
51 *Hull Advertiser*, 10 Sept. 1814; 8 Aug. to 5 Sept. 1818.

in the old town which could only be 'classed among ordinary public houses'.[52] The half a dozen alehouses of the later 18th century had by the 1820s been reduced to four: the Hare and Hounds (renamed the Rose and Crown by 1840), the Prince of Wales (renamed the Victoria by 1840), and the New Hotel (now the Pike and Heron), all in Market Place, and the Old Hotel in Southgate.[53] At the height of the season in 1834 every lodging house was said to be full.[54]

Lodgings near the sea were available from the mid 1830s, when two houses and the Marine Hotel were built there.[55] In 1836 the Britannia coffee and beer house provided beds and bathing machines.[56] Thomas Cunnington of Hull, who bought the Marine Hotel in 1842, was credited with making Hornsea more widely known, and during the 1840s baths, coffee, and newspapers, besides c. 70 bedrooms, were provided at the hotel; other baths were then available in the town, the Neptune coffee house was opened at Marine Terrace, where more houses were built, a boat was on hand for sea trips, and the number of bathing machines was increased to 18.[57] The natural amenities may have satisfied many visitors: Charlotte Bronte after a visit in 1853 recalled walking on the beach or by the mere.[58] The number of lodging houses rose from 28 in 1840 to 67 in 1846 and 70 in 1851; many of their keepers were part-time, but there were evidently 15 in 1848 who depended upon letting rooms for their livelihood.[59] Coaches running from Hull to Hornsea had been increased from one a day except Fridays in 1823 to four a day in the season in 1846.[60] Few of the visitors were from far afield: of those at the Marine Hotel on 6 September 1844, 50 per cent were from Hull, 33 per cent from the West Riding, and 7 per cent from the rest of Yorkshire.[61]

The opening of the railway from Hull in 1864 induced many Hull businessmen to live in Hornsea, as the vicar remarked in 1867.[62] The retiming of trains for the convenience of commuters was requested in 1869 and again in 1870, when 54 inhabitants held annual season tickets to Hull.[63] In 1873 a visitor commented upon the daily gathering of wives and children at the station to meet their menfolk returning from work.[64] The railway also clearly boosted the popularity of the resort. In 1870 there were seven trains each weekday in both directions and one on Sundays; by 1876 an extra train ran on Sundays during the summer, and in 1890 there

were nine on weekdays and three on Sundays. Special excursions were run, too: on Whit Monday in 1890, for example, 2,000 people travelled to Hornsea.[65]

An additional hotel, the Alexandra, was built near the railway station in 1867;[66] it was later known as the Mere Hotel, before reverting to its original name in the 20th century. In the week ending 7 August 1869 there were 413 visitors staying in 95 lodging houses, in that ending 11 August 1870 there were 512 in 115 houses, and in that ending 10 August 1871 there were 595 in 125 houses.[67] Much lower numbers of lodging houses were recorded in directories, for example, 25 in 1872, and they may have excluded those kept part-time. There were still few facilities or attractions for visitors, although the public rooms opened in 1869 included a concert hall, besides reading and committee rooms.[68] The first steps to protect the cliffs from erosion were taken in 1869, when two groynes and a timber breastwork over 100 yd. long were built by W. M. Jackson to safeguard his estate; the Marine Hotel was also protected, and two groynes were built by J. A. Wade south of the railway station.[69]

A decline in the popularity of the resort in the 1870s is suggested by the numbers of visitors, which fell to 462 in 97 lodging houses in the week ending 12 August 1876 and 265 in 68 houses in that ending 7 August 1880. Numbers increased, however, to 423 in 97 houses in the week ending 9 August 1890.[70] The full-time lodging house keepers recorded in directories remained comparatively few: there were c. 30 in both 1879 and 1889, for example, though they increased to c. 60 in the 1890s.[71] The catchment area was still largely restricted to Yorkshire: in the first week in August in 1876, 1880, and 1890 visitors from Hull accounted for 60–70 per cent and from the West Riding 20 per cent, and of 284 visitors present on 6 August 1887 c. 55 per cent were from Hull, 18 per cent from the West Riding, and 7 per cent from the rest of the county.[72] The amenities provided during those years included a pier. The Hornsea Pier Co. was formed by J. A. Wade c. 1865,[73] but he was handicapped by the failure of the railway to make a profit and was later in conflict with Pierre du Gillon, who formed the Hornsea Pier, Promenade, & General Improvement Co. in 1876.[74] It was the Hornsea Pier Co. which eventually, from 1878, built a pier 1,072 ft. long.

[52] G. Head, *Tour of Manufacturing Districts of Eng.* (1836), 270.   [53] E.R.A.O., QDT/2/6, 9; directories.

[54] *Hull Advertiser*, 18 July 1834.

[55] Above, intro. (growth of town).

[56] *Hull Advertiser*, 5 Aug. 1836.

[57] Ibid. 2 July 1841; 27 Jan., 16 June 1843 (with illus.); Bedell, *Acct. of Hornsea* (1848), 94, 96–7; directories; Sumners, op. cit. 40.

[58] F. R. Pearson, *Charlotte Bronte on E. Yorks. Coast* (E. Yorks. Loc. Hist. Ser. vii), 25–6.

[59] Bedell, *Acct. of Hornsea* (1848), 96; directories.

[60] Directories.

[61] Mayoh, 'Resorts of Holderness', 33; for visitors at the hotel, see *Hull Advertiser*, 25 Aug. 1848; 13 July 1849; 19 Sept. 1857.

[62] *1st Rep. Com. on Employment of Children, Young Persons, and Women in Agric., App. Pt. II* [4068–I], p. 366,

H.C. (1867–8), xvii.

[63] Mayoh, 'Resorts', 66–7.

[64] *Spectator*, 27 Sept. 1873, cited by Mayoh, 'Resorts', 192.

[65] Mayoh, 'Resorts', 134, 136.

[66] Above, intro. (growth of town).

[67] Mayoh, 'Resorts', 66.

[68] H.U.L., DSJ/38, p. 89; Bulmer, *Dir. E. Yorks.* (1892), 428; directories.

[69] Mayoh, 'Resorts', 89–90.

[70] Ibid. 66.   [71] Directories.

[72] Mayoh, 'Resorts', facing p. 128; Bedell, *Acct. of Hornsea* (1848), [at end unpag.].

[73] E.R.A.O., DDCC/51/10–12; for the following, also Sewell, *Joseph Armytage Wade*, 7, 39–48 (illus.).

[74] Ibid. DDCC/51/16–19; R.D.B., LU/373/553; *Abridged Hist. Hornsea Pier Negotiations* (1876) (copy in Hull Pub. Libr.).

Before it could be opened it was hit by a ship during a gale in 1880 and *c.* 300 ft. was lost; the pier and later the truncated part was used as a grandstand on the day of the regatta from 1880 and seems finally to have been opened to visitors in the summer season of 1885. It was last used for the regatta in 1897, but in that year was sold for scrap.[75] Apparently in the 1880s the mere began to be used by the public. By 1887 the Hornsea Mere & Hotel Co. had obtained a lease of the mere for fishing and boating, and by 1892 more than 20 yachts were kept on the eastern part of the mere and there were pleasure boats for hire.[76] A regatta on the sea was held in August from 1876 to 1914, but the horse races on the beach are said to have ended in the 1880s. Other entertainments in the late 19th century included brass band concerts, musical promenades at the Alexandra Hotel and on North Cliff, concerts by vocal and choral societies, and a floral and horticultural show; many events took place in the public rooms.[77]

A simple promenade had been made alongside North Cliff by 1890, but land beside the cliff was bought by a private syndicate and the Promenade, later the Victoria, Gardens were laid out there by public subscription in 1897; they were taken over by the urban district council in 1905[78] and the Floral Hall was built there in 1913.[79] The timber sea defences were seriously damaged by a storm in 1906[80] and as a result three new groynes and a 700-ft. long sea wall were built by the council in 1906–7.[81] There were tennis courts near the boathouse at the mere by 1908,[82] and Hornsea golf club, founded in 1898, had a 9-hole course in Hall Garths and a clubhouse in Newbegin until 1908, when a new, 18-hole course, mostly in Rolston, was opened.[83]

After the First World War new facilities included Hall Garth Park, opened in 1920; a 9-hole golf course was made there two years later and tennis courts were also provided.[84] Moving pictures were first shown in the public rooms in 1900,[85] and by 1925 the building had been converted to the Star Picture Theatre.[86] The former steam laundry in Cliff Road was used as the Victoria Picture Theatre from 1921 to 1928.[87] In 1923 the sea wall was lengthened by 450 ft. on the north side and 1,240 ft. on the south,[88] and in 1930 it was continued southwards across Hornsea Gap to Hornsea Burton.[89] Both the Victoria Gardens and the Floral Hall were enlarged in 1928.[90] There were roundabouts and swings on the beach in the early 20th century, and *c.* 1940 a fair was held beside Hornsea Burton Road.[91] The numbers of full-time lodging house keepers recorded in directories increased to 82 in 1905 but fell to 42 in 1913, 30 in 1925, and 5 in 1937. A large hotel, the Hydro, was built in 1914, and in the 1930s there were two or three private hotels.[92] The inns in the old town all survived, along with the Alexandra and the Marine Hotel, the latter several times altered or rebuilt after erosion and fire.[93]

Cheap excursions attracted many short-term visitors to Hornsea in the 1920s and 1930s, and after the Second World War day-trippers were the main visitors. For those who stayed longer, caravans gradually replaced lodging houses. Most visitors arrived by road, still predominantly from Yorkshire. A sample survey made in 1960 showed that 80 per cent of visitors were day-trippers, that 50 per cent arrived by car and only 25 per cent by train, and that 40 per cent were from Hull and 40 per cent from the West Riding.[94] Entertainments provided for visitors included a boating lake, a 'Go-Kart' track, amusement arcades, a roller skating rink, and a small zoo. Car parks were laid out near the sea front, and among the caravan sites north and south of the town was one provided by the urban district council. Work on the sea walls was carried out in the 1950s and 1960s.[95] It was argued in 1960 that Hornsea did not want day-trippers and that they did not need Hornsea, and commercial exploitation of the sea front aroused opposition among the residential and commuting population of the town.[96] Commuting continued despite the closure of the railway line to passengers in 1964 and a reduction in bus services:[97] in 1921 commuters to Hull accounted for 88 per cent of the inhabitants who worked outside the town, in 1951 for 70 per cent, and for 62 per cent in 1981.[98] The preservation of the character of the town was encouraged by the formation of a civic society in 1966 and the

75 *Hornsea Gaz.* 30 Oct. 1880, cited by Mayoh, 'Resorts', 117; Sewell, op. cit. 39–48 (illus.).

76 Slater, *Royal Nat. Com. Dir. Yorks.* (1887), 106; Bulmer, *Dir. E. Yorks.* (1892), 431; Sumners, op. cit. 28.

77 J. E. Hobson, *Sketch of Hornsea* (1974 edn.), 103–4; Sewell, op. cit. 45.

78 R.D.B., 95/363/336 (1897); 79/372/355 (1905); O.S. Map 1/2,500, Yorks. CXCVII. 3–4 (1891 edn.); *Illus. Guide to Hornsea* (1908), 5.

79 Hornsea U.D.C. Mins. 1913–19, 37 (at E.R.A.O., UDHO).

80 Illus. in G. L. Southwell, *Hornsea in Old Picture Postcards*, nos. 53–5, 68.

81 Hornsea U.D.C. Mins. 1906–12, 5–6, 52; *Illus. Guide to Hornsea* (1908), 5; *Kelly's Dir. N. & E.R. Yorks.* (1909), 529; illus. in Southwell, op. cit., nos. 59–60, 62–3.

82 *Illus. Guide to Hornsea* (1908), 9.

83 Ibid. 21; *V.C.H. Yorks.* ii. 543; *Hall Garth Park, Hornsea*, p. [2] (copy in Beverley Pub. Libr.); A. A. Clarke, *Hornsea Golf Club, 1898–1998.* In 1922 the club bought the course, then comprising 18 a. in Hornsea and 135 a. in Rolston: R.D.B., 245/451/392; 245/452/393. Hall Garths

was later used as pasture and then by the military authorities: inf. from Dr. J. E. S. Walker, Hornsea, 1998.

84 Below, local govt. (public services).

85 Hobson, *Sketch of Hornsea*, 118.

86 *Kelly's Dir. N. & E.R. Yorks.* (1925), 559.

87 R.D.B., 213/148/128; 238/361/299; 364/389/325.

88 *Kelly's Dir. N. & E.R. Yorks.* (1925), 555.

89 Ibid. (1933), 483.

90 Ibid. (1929), 511.

91 Illus. in Southwell, *Hornsea in Old Picture Postcards*, no. 75; inf. from Dr. J. E. S. Walker, Hornsea, 1997.

92 Directories. For the Hydro, above, intro. (growth of town).

93 For the Marine Hotel, see Hobson, *Sketch of Hornsea*, 101, 121.

94 Mayoh, 'Resorts', facing pp. 128, 136, 175; inf. from Dr. Walker, 1997.

95 e.g. E.R.C.C. *Mins.* 1955–6, 228; 1956–7, 112; 1966–7, 418; 1967–8, 111; inf. from Dr. Walker.

96 Mayoh, 'Resorts', 104–7, 195–6.

97 Inf. from Dr. Walker; above [first section].

98 *Census.*

establishment of a conservation area in 1969, which was enlarged in 1976.[99] The entertainments and facilities provided in 1989 were little changed.

SOCIAL INSTITUTIONS. Some institutions, including places of entertainment, have been dealt with above.[1]

The Hornsea Reading and Conversation Society was founded in the 1840s. It had a library of c. 200 books in 1848, took newspapers, and provided lectures.[2] A lending library was opened in the public rooms, Newbegin, in 1872.[3] A branch county library was held in the urban district council offices, Elim Lodge, from c. 1930 until it was moved to Southfield House, Newbegin, in 1938.[4] A new building for the library was opened on the site of the public rooms in Newbegin in 1975.[5] The North Holderness Museum of Village Life was opened in Newbegin, in a converted farmhouse, in 1978.[6] An annual show was held by the Floral and Horticultural Society from 1870 to 1914, and J. A. Wade's efforts resulted in the Holderness Agricultural Show being held in Hornsea in some years from 1885.[7] Another flower show was begun in the ex-servicemen's club in 1938, was moved to the Floral Hall in 1941, and was held c. 1950 in the grounds of Elim Lodge. The ex-servicemen's premises were also used as a site for a Scout hut erected in 1924.[8]

A brass band was formed in the town in 1856.[9] The Vocal Society was formed in 1874 and the Choral Association in 1882.[10]

There have been several friendly societies in the town. An Oddfellows' lodge was founded in 1838; it had been closed or had left the order by 1860 but another lodge existed in 1860. A branch of the Druids was formed in 1862 and another for female Druids in 1912. A lodge of British Workmen was formed in 1873.[11] The former Congregational chapel in Southgate was used as a temperance hall, known as the Temple or the Templars' Hall, from 1874 until 1888.[12] A freemasons' lodge was formed by 1875[13] and a masonic hall was built in Alexandra Road in 1899; a former coastguard store next to the hall was bought c. 1985.[14] A Liberal club was founded in 1880 and was later held in the former Wesleyan chapel in Back Southgate.[15]

The East Yorkshire Artillery Volunteers, which had a battery at Hornsea from c. 1860, built a drill hall in Back Southgate in 1884 and enlarged it in 1890.[16] The E.R. Territorial Army Association allowed the premises to be used rent-free by Hornsea Ex-Servicemen's Club from its foundation in 1920. The club bought the building in 1927 and later enlarged it further.[17]

The *Hornsea Gazette* was founded c. 1863 and published, at Hornsea, until 1901.[18] Less long-lived were the *Hornsea Telegraph* and the *Hornsea Guardian*, mentioned in 1901 and c. 1908 respectively, the *Hornsea and District Bulletin*, which was published in the 1920s and early 1930s, and the *Hornsea Recorder*, which also appeared in the 1930s.[19] From 1982 an edition of the *Holderness Gazette*, published at Withernsea, was issued as a new *Hornsea Gazette*. A free paper, the *Hornsea and District Post*, later the *Hornsea Post*, has been published in the town since 1987.[20]

A cricket club established in 1859 was short-lived but another was set up by the Wade family in the mid 1860s; it was united in 1900 with the town's second cricket club, begun in 1875. A women's tennis club, formed in 1879, played on part of the earlier cricket club's grounds near the railway station. A cycling club was begun in the 1880s, a football club by 1899,[21] and a swimming club in 1904.[22]

Hornsea was twinned with La Grande-Motte (Hérault) in 1981.[23]

MANORS AND OTHER ESTATES. In 1066 Morkar held the manor of *HORNSEA*, comprising 27 carucates but evidently including land at Atwick and Arram. By 1086 the manor had passed to Drew de Bevrère. Soke of the manor comprised 2 carucates at Hornsea Burton, 1½ carucate at Southorpe, 2 carucates and 6 bovates at Long Riston, 6 bovates at North Skirlaugh, in Swine, and 5 carucates at Skirlington, in Atwick.[24] Hornsea passed, like Burstwick, to William I's brother-in-law, Eudes, count of

[99] Hornsea Civic Soc. *Town Walk and Street Map*; inf. from Devt. Dept., Holderness B.C., 1990.

[1] Above, intro. (resort).

[2] Bedell, *Acct. of Hornsea* (1848), 113; *Hull Advertiser*, 24 Mar. 1848.

[3] Hobson, *Sketch of Hornsea*, 118.

[4] Hornsea U.D.C. Mins. 1928–31, 88 (at E.R.A.O., UDHO); E.R. Educ. Cttee. *Mins*. 1936–7, 138, 194; 1937–8, 229.

[5] E.R. Educ. Cttee. *Mins*. 1971–2, 225; Humbs. C.C. *Mins*. 1974–5, H 290.

[6] *Hull Daily Mail*, 26 Apr. 1978; Humbs. C.C. *Mins*. 1980–1, J 729.

[7] Hobson, *Sketch of Hornsea*, 103; Sewell, *Joseph Armytage Wade*, 39.

[8] *Short Story of Hornsea Ex-Servicemen's Club Ltd.* (Hornsea, priv. print. [1951]).

[9] Hobson, *Sketch of Hornsea*, 85–6.

[10] Ibid. 103.

[11] D. [R. J.] Neave, *E.R. Friendly Soc.* (E. Yorks. Loc. Hist. Ser. xli), 56.

[12] Hobson, *Sketch of Hornsea*, 119.

[13] Ibid. 105.

[14] Dates on bldg.; *Kelly's Dir. N. & E.R. Yorks.* (1901), 499; inf. from Dr. J. E. S. Walker, Hornsea, 1997.

[15] R.D.B., 86/403/374 (1906); Sewell, op. cit. 69.

[16] R. W. S. Norfolk, *Militia, Yeomanry, and Volunteer Forces of the E.R. 1689–1908* (E. Yorks. Loc. Hist. Ser. xix), 55; Bulmer, *Dir. E. Yorks.* (1892), 430; Sewell, op. cit. 68.

[17] R.D.B., 355/112/80; *Short Story of Hornsea Ex-Servicemen's Club Ltd.* (Hornsea, priv. print. [1951]).

[18] Files for 1869–1901 (1872–3, 1896 missing) at B.L.: *Cat. Newspaper Libr.* v. 421; copy for 17 Mar. 1877 at Beverley Pub. Libr. *Kelly's Dir. N. & E.R. Yorks.* (1872), 379.

[19] *Kelly's Dir. N. & E.R. Yorks.* (1901), 501; (1937), 480; *Illus. Guide to Hornsea* (1908), 26; inf. regarding the *Recorder* and *Bulletin* from Dr. Walker, 1997.

[20] *Willing's Press Guide*; *V.C.H. Yorks. E.R.* v. 163.

[21] J. Lonsdale, 'Beginnings of Cricket in Hornsea' (TS. in Beverley Pub. Libr. 1989); Sewell, op. cit. 35, 69; Hobson, *Sketch of Hornsea*, 102–3.

[22] E.R.A.O., accession 2043.

[23] Cairn near South Promenade; inf. from Mr. N. Bakes, Hornsea, 1998.

[24] *V.C.H. Yorks.* ii. 265 and n.; above, Atwick, manors.

Champagne,[25] who soon afterwards gave it to St. Mary's abbey, York.[26] It was held by St. Mary's until the abbey was surrendered in 1539.[27]

The manor was retained by the Crown and in 1665 it was assigned to trustees for Queen Catherine.[28] It was often in the hands of Crown lessees, including Hugh and Slingsby Bethell from 1674 and Peter Acklam from 1684.[29] In 1696 the Crown granted the manor to Hans Willem Bentinck, earl of Portland,[30] whose grandson William, duke of Portland, conveyed it in 1743 to Hugh Bethell.[31] The lease remained, however, with the Acklams until 1759.[32] The manor thereafter descended in the Bethell family.[33] In 1760 the Bethell estate comprised 309 a. of inclosed land and 155 a. in the open fields.[34] At inclosure in 1809 Charlotte Bethell was allotted 255 a., including 14 a. of old inclosures.[35] The estate comprised 464 a. in 1852. Almost 120 a. was sold to Henry Strickland-Constable in 1874. The Bethells still had 225 a. in 1915, but the 197-a. Southorpe Hill farm was sold in 1929 and the rest later.[36]

The manor house, with lands that included Hall Garth, was let by the Crown after the dissolution of the abbey.[37] In 1650 the manor house, called the hall, contained three ground-floor and three first floor-rooms and occupied a 2-a. site.[38] The house was not mentioned again, but the site was included in the grant of 1696 and the sale of 1743. Old inclosure called Hall Garths was exchanged by Charlotte Bethell at inclosure in 1809 with Peter Acklam, and later passed to the Constables of Wassand.[39] The moat within which the house presumably stood survived in Hall Garth Park in 1989.

The Acklam family also owned a copyhold estate in Hornsea, including a house in Southgate. A cottage there called Low Close was acquired by Thomas Acklam in 1665 and devised to his son Peter in 1667. In 1675 Peter (d. 1690) surrendered it, together with three cottages described as a house, reserving the garden as a burial place. His sons Peter (d. 1744) and Thomas recovered the house in 1689, and in 1730 Peter's daughter Anna Maria Acklam surrendered four cottages, described as the house where she lived.[40] The house was later called

successively Low Hall, the Old Hotel, and White House.[41] It may have been built by Peter Acklam c. 1670 and was perhaps the house where John Acklam had four hearths in 1672.[42] It is of brick and boulders and has a string course; it retains a staircase and three fireplaces of the 17th century, the overmantels formerly containing contemporary paintings of biblical scenes.[43]

Nearly 1,500 a. of the commonable lands inclosed in 1809 were copyhold.[44] The largest copyhold then awarded was 215 a., along with 19 a. of old inclosures, belonging to Marmaduke Constable. Several other holdings were later acquired by the Constables: thus the Revd. Charles Constable in 1825 bought the allotments and other land of Peter Acklam, amounting in all to c. 120 a., and in 1828 most of the 130 a. awarded to Bryan Taylor; he had also bought 324 a. of the rectorial estate in 1812.[45] The estate descended like Wassand, in Sigglesthorne, and in 1910 F. C. Strickland-Constable owned more than 1,100 a. in Hornsea, in addition to the mere. The 197-a. Southorpe Hill farm was bought in 1929.[46] Many small building plots in the town were later sold but the bulk of the estate remained in 1990, when it included, besides Southorpe Hill farm, Brockholme and Northfield farms.[47]

The township of Hornsea Burton belonged to the fee of Aumale. Giles of Goxhill was the undertenant of 2 carucates there in the mid 13th century.[48] William de Forz, count of Aumale (d. 1260), had 5 carucates and 5 bovates there, much of which the heirs of Gilbert of Mappleton held in 1287 as undertenants;[49] those heirs had held 6 carucates there in 1284–5, and John of Mappleton held the same in 1302–3.[50] John was named as a lord of Hornsea Burton in 1316.[51] Walter son of Gilbert of Mappleton in 1323 granted to Stephen son of John Hautayn the reversion of certain tenements in the township.[52] At his death in 1349 Walter, who then lived at Hornsea Burton, held 1 carucate and 2 bovates and 11 tofts of the Aumale fee there by gift of Stephen Hautayn as 1/36 knight's fee.[53] William de Forz also had 2 bovates which in 1287 were held

25 V.C.H. Yorks. E.R. v. 9.
26 E.Y.C. i, p. 27; iii, p. 26.
27 V.C.H. Yorks. iii. 111.
28 P.R.O., C 66/3080, [no. 1].
29 Ibid. E 159/337, rot. 105; E.R.A.O., PE/30/33.
30 P.R.O., C 66/3386, no. 5.
31 E.R.A.O., DDRI/19/3.   32 Ibid. PE/30/33.
33 Ibid.; H.U.L., DDCV/82-5; ibid. DSJ/34–47; below, Rise, manor. For pedigree, see J. Foster, Pedigrees of Yorks. iii; Burke, Land. Gent. (1969), ii. 46–7.
34 Book of plans of estates of H. Bethell, at Rise Park Estate Off.
35 R.D.B., CI/345/27.
36 Ibid. LH/414/541; 170/289/242; 398/519/428; 408/90/75; valuation of estates of Ric. Bethell, 1852, in E.R.A.O., DDRI/accession 2980, box 2; inf. from Rise Park Estate Office.
37 P.R.O., C 66/2901, no. 21; ibid. SC 6/Hen. VIII/4595; L. & P. Hen. VIII, xv, p. 564; Acts of P.C. 1552–4, 246–7; Cal. Pat. 1575–8, p. 493.
38 E.R.A.O., PE/30/33, ff. 73, 79v., 102v., 104v., 151–2, 281v.; Poulson, Holderness, i. 335; below, prot. nonconf.

39 H.U.L., DDCV/82/5, p. 457; R.D.B., 10/276/261 (1899).   40 P.R.O., E 317/Yorks./28.
41 O.S. Map 6", Yorks. CXCVII (1854 edn.); O.S. Map 1/2,500, Yorks. CXCVII. 7 (1891 edn.); above, intro. (resort).
42 P.R.O., E 179/205/504.
43 Pevsner, York & E.R. 257; below, prot. nonconf.
44 R.D.B., CI/345/27.
45 H.U.L., DDCV/82/5, p. 457; ibid. DSJ/34, pp. 62, 316, 374; below, this section.
46 E.R.A.O., NV/1/8; R.D.B., 398/519/428; below, Sigglesthorne, manors (Wassand).
47 R.D.B., 1589/491/406; 1621/428/341; 1639/462/416; 1747/171/146; 1843/321/265; and passim for sales; inf. from Wm. H. Brown, Agric. Surveyors, Valuers and Land Agents, Northgate Ho., Sleaford, 1990.
48 Kirkby's Inq. 373.
49 Cal. Inq. p.m. iv, pp. 353, 355.
50 Feud. Aids, vi. 40; Kirkby's Inq. 246.
51 Feud. Aids, vi. 163.
52 P.R.O., CP 25(1)/271/98, no. 92.
53 Cal. Inq. p.m. ix, p. 256.

by Walter de Fauconberg, later Lord Fauconberg. They later descended like Rise manor in the Fauconbergs.[54] Hugh Baxter (d. 1346) and Richard Wright (d. 1349) also held small estates in the township of the honor of Aumale.[55]

Two or three small estates were recorded as manors of *HORNSEA BURTON*. Walter of Harome held 2 bovates and 2 tofts in Hornsea Burton and Hornsea Beck in 1302, perhaps as an undertenant of the Aumale fee, and was licensed to have an oratory in his manor of Hornsea Burton the next year. He was still in possession in 1319–20.[56] By 1348 land in Hornsea Burton which had formerly belonged to Geoffrey Henknol was granted by the Crown to William of Metham; in 1393 Richard of Metham lived there, as did Robert of Metham in 1414, when he was said to hold Hornsea Burton manor. John Metham lived at Hornsea Beck in 1436, and Sir Thomas Metham (d. 1498) had lands there to which his son Thomas was heir.[57] Another estate belonged to Isabel Ellerker (d. 1478), Ralph Ellerker (d. 1539), who was said to have Hornsea Burton manor, and Sir Ralph Ellerker (d. 1546).[58]

Meaux abbey built up an estate, mostly in Hornsea Burton township, from many small gifts. John de Lasceles gave a fishery in Hornsea mere between 1210 and 1220. Walter Thorn (*de spineto*) gave 2 bovates and 3 closes in Hornsea Burton and tolls at Hornsea Beck, Amfrey son of William Noble 1 bovate, a close, and a toft in Hornsea Burton, and Roger of Richmond 1 bovate and a close there, all between 1221 and 1235. Walter Thorn added 3 bovates, 2 tofts and crofts, and other property in Hornsea Burton between 1235 and 1249, and Swine priory then assigned lands and rents there to Meaux. Between 1249 and 1269 Meaux exchanged a fishery in Hornsea mere for rents owed to St. Mary's abbey and lost a judicial combat with St. Mary's for a fishery in Hornsea and Wassand meres.[59] In 1293 Meaux had a grant of free warren at Hornsea,[60] and the abbot was named as a lord of Hornsea Burton in 1316.[61] It was found in 1401 that 27 a. of the abbey's land at Hornsea Burton had been lost to the sea.[62] The estate was retained until the Dissolution, and in 1539–40 it comprised 1 carucate and 2 bovates

and several houses, crofts, and closes.[63] In 1544 the former abbey property in Hornsea Burton and elsewhere was granted in fee to Morgan Wolff and others, the grant to be void if the purchase money was repaid within a year.[64]

In 1663 the largest landowner in Hornsea Burton was Marmaduke Constable, with 103 a.[65] The Trinity House, Hull, bought land there from Constable in 1674;[66] in 1843 its estate comprised 86 a.[67] and a further 35 a. were bought in 1867.[68] The House sold 25 a. in 1945, 9 a. in 1950, 36 a. in 1951, 8 a. in 1961, and 21 a. in 1988; 22 a. remained in 1990.[69] Much of the land sold has been used for housing.

After the appropriation of the church in 1423,[70] the *RECTORY* belonged to St. Mary's abbey until 1539. After the Dissolution the rectory was at first let by the Crown,[71] but it was later acquired by Francis Morrice and Francis Phillips, who in 1611 conveyed it to Michael Warton.[72] The rectorial tithes were worth £90 a year in 1650[73] and £95 in 1684, when those of Southorpe and Hornsea Burton contributed £16 each.[74] On the partition in 1775 of the estates of Sir Michael Warton (d. 1725) the rectory fell to the share of Michael Newton. At the inclosure of Hornsea in 1809 Newton's sister Catherine and her husband Philip Blundell were awarded 25 a. for glebe and 324 a. for tithes.[75] Most of the estate was sold to the Revd. Charles Constable in 1812 and descended with the Constables' and Strickland-Constables' other land in Hornsea; the remaining 25 a. were sold to Richard Anderson in 1821.[76]

The tithes of Hornsea Burton passed in or after 1812 to Michael Newton's niece Susannah Houblon.[77] In 1839 the tithes from 35 a. in Hornsea Burton were merged and the rest sold by J. A. Houblon to Benjamin Haworth.[78] Tithes on a further 153 a. were merged in 1840–1.[79] By 1844 the tithes of 355 a. had been merged; those remaining were then commuted for a rent charge of £9 15s. payable to Haworth and another of £15 to the vicar.[80]

The rectory house is said to have been sold by Michael Warton in 1611 to Robert Moore[81] and by Moore in 1651 to Peter Acklam.[82] It may have been the house in which Peter Acklam had six hearths in 1672.[83] When Old Hall, in Market

54 Ibid. iv, pp. 353–4, 357; ix, p. 177; xviii, p. 136; below, Rise, manor.
55 *Cal. Inq. p.m.* ix, pp. 2, 252.
56 P.R.O., CP 25(1)/271/94, no. 85; *Yorks. Fines, 1300–14*, p. 25; *Reg. Corbridge*, i. 195.
57 *Cal. Pat.* 1358–61, 133; *Cal. Fine R.* 1356–68, 106–7; 1391–9, 27; 1430–7, 282; *Yorks. Deeds*, iv, p. 38; *Cal. Inq. p.m. Hen. VII*, ii, p. 113.
58 H.U.L., DHO/7/19, 33; *Yorks. Sta. Cha. Proc.* i (Y.A.S. Rec. Ser. xli), 35 n.
59 *Chron. de Melsa* (Rolls Ser.), i. 369, 420–1; ii. 22, 31, 96–102; English, *Holderness*, 209–10.
60 'Meaux Cart.', pp. 250–1.
61 *Feud. Aids*, vi. 163.
62 *Chron. de Melsa*, iii. 285.
63 P.R.O., SC 6/Hen. VIII/4612.
64 *L. & P. Hen. VIII*, xix (2), p. 78.
65 H.U.L., DDX/16/214.
66 Inf. from the Trinity Ho., Hull, 1989.
67 E.R.A.O., PE/30/31; H.U.L., DOG/5/11.

68 R.D.B., KB/78/105.
69 Ibid. 691/514/431; 854/585/487; 1212/289/254; inf. from the Secretary, the Trinity Ho., Hull, 1990.
70 Below, church.
71 *L. & P. Hen. VIII*, xv, p. 564; *Acts of P.C.* 1552–4, 246; *Cal. Pat.* 1575–8, p. 493; *Cal. S.P. Dom.* 1595–7, 12.
72 P.R.O., CP 43/113, rot. 16.
73 *T.E.R.A.S.* iv. 63.
74 Y.A.S., MS. 661, p. 35.
75 R.D.B., CI/345/27; H.U.L., DDEV/21/123–4; *V.C.H. Yorks. E.R.* vi. 210.
76 R.D.B., CU/93/90; CU/128/123; DN/268/299; above, this section.
77 H.U.L., DDEV/21/124; Burke, *Land. Gent.* (1937), 1182.
78 R.D.B., FK/253/284; FK/254/285.
79 Ibid. FO/11/13; FP/86/85.
80 B.I.H.R., TA. 299s.
81 Poulson, *Holderness*, i. 323.
82 Hobson, *Sketch of Hornsea* (1974 edn.), 23.
83 P.R.O., E 179/205/504.

Place, was sold by another Peter Acklam to the Revd. Charles Constable in 1821, it was described as the mansion house of the rectory, and it may have been the successor of the earlier house. The Strickland-Constables retained it until 1930.[84] Old Hall is a 17th-century **H**-shaped building of brick with shaped gables.[85] A west wing was added in the 18th century and bay windows to the front in the 19th.

Bridlington priory was given 2 bovates in Hornsea Burton by James of Wassand between 1175 and 1185.[86] The Knights Hospitaller had 2s. rent from a toft and croft in Hornsea Burton in 1539–40, and in 1558 their lands and liberties in Hornsea and Hornsea Burton were granted to the briefly refounded order.[87] Swine priory assigned lands and rents in Hornsea Burton to Meaux abbey between 1235 and 1249,[88] but it still had a few shillings rent from the township at the Dissolution.[89] Beverley corporation had land at Hornsea Burton by 1691;[90] it later comprised 18 a. and was sold in 1907.[91]

ECONOMIC HISTORY: AGRICULTURE. There were separate open fields for Hornsea, Southorpe, and Hornsea Burton. The open-field land of Hornsea lay north of the town and from the early 17th to the late 18th century was divided into East and West fields; by 1809 it had been reorganized with North field in addition to the others. South of the mere lay the open fields of Southorpe, East, West, and Far fields,[92] the last of which was apparently used in 1758 and 1809 as pasture.[93] In 1539 the fields of Hornsea and Southorpe included 95 bovates, and in 1650 there were 80 copyhold bovates, besides 5 in demesne.[94] The erosion of North cliff steadily reduced the area of the fields. In 1609 it was alleged that the cliffs had receded 240 yd. since 1547, and the land was said in 1612 to lie daily in waste of the sea; in 1637 it was recorded that 100–200 a. of East field had been lost within living memory.[95]

Common meadows and pastures included the Tetherings, in West field, and ground called the Leys, lying north of the town. The Tetherings was recorded in 1613, when inhabitants were fined for having cows there, and the Leys pasture in 1623.[96] In 1650 the manor included 8 leys in the Leys,[97] which was evidently divided

among the proprietors. In 1764 the vicar had 2 ⅘ horse gates representing a 4-a. share of the Leys, and he also enjoyed a share of meadow in the Tetherings.[98] Between the town and the sea lay other common meadows or pastures called Chrystals, Holmes, and How carr. References to individual 'lands' in Chrystals in the early 18th century suggest that it was then divided among the proprietors.[99] Common pasture also lay around the eastern end of the mere, and another common pasture called Brockhams was mentioned in 1800;[1] Brockhams, Martla Butts, and Mean Piece were dealt with at inclosure in 1809, when they were treated as part of West field and probably lay between the mere and the Seaton road.[2] A pasture called the Hold lay between the site of Southorpe hamlet and the mere.[3]

Old inclosures in the manor comprised c. 230 a. in 1650, many of the closes lying east of the town near Stream dike; the largest close was the 70-a. Lund, on the south side of the mere, which had been mentioned in 1539.[4] In 1668 the manor included four closes which were said to be often flooded by the sea in spring, autumn, and winter.[5] An unsuccessful attempt was made in 1758 to inclose the two open fields called Southorpe fields, together with pastures called Far field and the Hold.[6] Old inclosures were reckoned to comprise 379 a. in 1800.[7]

The copyholders were said in 1612 to make payments in lieu of 24 boons and day works, and later in the century their entry fines were equal to a year's rent.[8]

The remaining commonable land was inclosed by an award of 1809 under an Act of 1801. Allotments were made totalling 2,135 a. They included 409 a. from East field, more than 240 a. from North field, over 153 a. from West field, more than 100 a. from Leys, 34 a. from Mere side, 24 a. from Holmes, 23 a. from Chrystals, and 9a. from How carr. South of the mere, 351 a. were from Southorpe field, 97 a. from Southorpe Far field, and 111 a. from Southorpe field and Southorpe pasture. Charlotte Bethell, lady of the manor, received 241 a., Philip and Catherine Blundell, owners of the rectorial estate, 340 a., and the vicar 68 a. Other large allotments were of 215 a. to Marmaduke Constable, 130 a. to Bryan Taylor, 110 a. to John Kirkus, 104 a. to Peter Acklam, 103 a. to William Whitfield, and 100 a. to Cornwell Wilson.

84 R.D.B., DM/25/35; 419/117/90.
85 One of the shaped gables was added in the 19th cent.: Bedell, *Acct. of Hornsea*, facing p. 116; *Illus. Guide to Hornsea* (1908), facing p. 12; I. and M. Sumner, *Britain in Old Photographs: Holderness*, 32, 36.
86 *E.Y.C.* ii, p. 456.
87 *Miscellanea*, iv (Y.A.S. Rec. Ser. xciv), 98; *Cal. Pat. 1557–8*, 321.
88 *Chron. de Melsa* (Rolls Ser.), ii. 22.
89 *Miscellanea*, iii (Y.A.S. Rec. Ser. lxxx), 98.
90 *Beverley Boro. Rec. 1575–1821* (Y.A.S. Rec. Ser. lxxxiv), 181.
91 E.R.A.O., PE/27/44; R.D.B., 92/301/275.
92 Popham, 'Wassand Estate', appendix 2, p. 7.
93 P.R.O., LR 2/230, ff. 209–10; B.I.H.R., TER. H. Hornsea *passim*; H.U.L., DDCV/155/1; R.D.B., CI/345/27.
94 P.R.O., SC 6/Hen. VIII/4595; ibid. LR 2/230, ff. 209–10.
95 Ibid. E 134/13 Chas. I East./7; E 178/4813; ibid. LR

2/230, ff. 209–10.
96 Ibid. SC 2/211/59.
97 Ibid. E 317/Yorks./28.
98 B.I.H.R., TER. H. Hornsea 1764.
99 H.U.L., DDCV/82/1, e.g. 14 Oct. 1718.
1 Hull Pub. Libr., proprietors' and incl. commissioners' mins.
2 Along the N. side of the road according to Bedell, *Acct. of Hornsea* (1848), 86–7. The Brockholm stone is shown on O.S. Map 6″, Yorks. CXCVII (1854 edn.).
3 H.U.L., DDCV/155/1; O.S. Map 6″, Yorks. CXCVII (1854 edn.).
4 P.R.O., E 317/Yorks./28; ibid. SC 6/Hen. VIII/4595.
5 Ibid. SC 12/36/25.
6 H.U.L., DDCV/155/1.
7 E.R.A.O., IA. Hornsea; Hull Pub. Libr., proprietors' and incl. commissioners' mins.
8 P.R.O., E 134/13 Chas. I East./7; E 317/Yorks./28; ibid. LR 2/230, ff. 209–10.

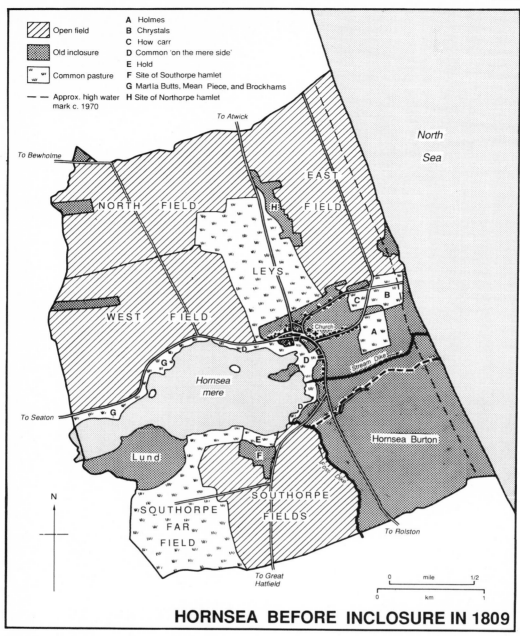

HORNSEA BEFORE INCLOSURE IN 1809

There were also five allotments of 50–99 a., five of 20–49 a., twelve of 10–19 a., and thirty-two of under 10 a. each. The small allotments included a fair ground and watering place beside the mere near the town, a public watering place on the north side of the mere, and a common landing place next to the sea. Apart from the manorial, rectorial, and vicarial allotments, all were copyhold.[9]

The open fields of Hornsea Burton were inclosed in or soon after 1663, when the township was surveyed for the purpose. Marmaduke Constable received 103 a. and William Audas 92 a.; there were also four allotments of 40–70 a. and two of 15–20 a. The 8-a. common was left uninclosed; four landowners had equal shares in it and two others were entitled to take their cattle to the watering place there.[10] The layout of the fields is not known but ridge and furrow survived beside Hornsea Burton Road in 1989.

The scattered farmhouses in Hornsea were built soon after inclosure in 1809.[11] Trinity House farm in Hornsea Burton was leased to the East Riding county council in 1912 for use as smallholdings;[12] the farmhouse there was demolished in the 1980s. There were usually 15–20 farmers in the parish in the 19th and 20th centuries, besides half a dozen cowkeepers and dairymen. Six farmers in 1851 and three in 1933 had 150 a. or more.[13] In 1801 there was 1,059 a.

[9] E.R.A.O., IA. Hornsea; Hull Pub. Libr., proprietors' and incl. commissioners' mins.; R.D.B., CI/345/27; 41 Geo. III, c. 110 (Priv. Act).   [10] H.U.L., DDX/16/214.

[11] A. Bryant, *Map of E.R. Yorks.* (1829).
[12] E.R.C.C. *Mins.* 1911–12, 431.
[13] P.R.O., HO/107/2365; directories.

of arable in the parish,[14] in 1844 there were 315 a. of arable and 90 a. of meadow and pasture in Hornsea Burton township,[15] and in 1905 there were 1,571 a. of arable, 858 a. of permanent grass, and 45 a. of woodland in the parish.[16] Arable land was still predominant in the 1930s.[17] In 1987 some 613 ha. (1,514 a.) were returned as arable and 58 ha. (143 a.) as grassland; of 17 holdings returned, nine were of under 10 ha., four of 10–99 ha. (25–245 a.), and four of 100–199 ha. (247–492 a.); there were 5,870 fowls and 1,378 pigs.[18]

MILLS. Two windmills in Hornsea belonged to St. Mary's abbey before 1539, and East and West mills were mentioned in 1610.[19] A windmill, sometimes called the Beck mill, stood in Chrystals[20] until it was blown down in 1732.[21] Another stood near the Atwick road, close to the town, in 1772.[22] A new windmill was built nearby in 1820–1;[23] it was also worked by steam by 1909 and was mentioned until 1921.[24] Part of the tower remained in 1997. Another windmill, in Hornsea Burton, was mentioned from 1584[25] and stood near Mill Lane, later Burton Lane, in 1663.[26]

FISHING AND SHIPPING. The fishing of the mere belonged to St. Mary's abbey, but its rights there were disputed by neighbouring landholders.[27] The abbey allowed the Ros family to have a fishing boat on the mere in the 12th and 13th centuries,[28] and Meaux abbey also claimed rights of fishery there in the 13th century.[29] In 1343 St. Mary's abbey complained of the illegal taking of swans, fishing, and damage to a fish inclosure in the mere,[30] and in the 1550s the lessee of the fishing and fowling under the Crown was molested by Marmaduke Constable of Wassand.[31] The Crown had granted the fishing and fowling of the mere to John Dudley, earl of Warwick, in 1550, and after his attainder in 1553 it was regranted to Robert Dudley, later earl of Leicester, in 1563.[32] In 1595 Anne, widow of Ambrose Dudley, earl of Warwick, conveyed them and the mere itself to another Marmaduke Constable.[33] In 1682 his successor, also Marmaduke Constable, upheld against tenants of the

manor his exclusive right to the fishing and fowling of the whole of the mere, including the hills and 'batts' or islands where fowl bred, Kirkham alone being excepted.[34] A duck decoy had been made close to the later Decoy plantation by the early 18th century.[35] Since the late 19th century fishing in the mere has been let for public use.[36]

In the Middle Ages fishing and seaborne trade were carried on at Hornsea Beck. Meaux abbey claimed between 1221 and 1235 that Walter Thorn (de spineto) had given it his tolls of merchandise and 'bordtolls' of ships at Hornsea Beck, but that the abbey was unable to enjoy them because north of the beck they belonged to St. Mary's abbey and south of it, in Hornsea Burton, to the lords of Holderness.[37] In 1357 a proclamation was made for the sale of fish at Hornsea, and in 1364 the town was included in a commission concerning oversea traffic.[38] Thefts of fish and wool at Hornsea were reported in the late 14th century, and Robert Ticlot of Hornsea Beck (d. 1390) bequeathed a ship, two small boats, and several nets.[39] Fishermen and shipmen of Hornsea Beck and Hornsea Burton were recorded in the 15th and 16th centuries, and a coble belonging to a fisherman was mentioned in 1528.[40] There was a quay or pier at Hornsea Beck: the abbot of St. Mary's complained in 1537 about the cost of maintaining it.[41] It was declared to be ruinous in 1549, £1,000 was ordered in 1553 to be spent on its repair, in addition to a like sum already used,[42] and by 1556 timber had been fetched from Hull Bridge for the work.[43] In 1555 the farmer of the rectory claimed tithes called quay doles for every fishing voyage that was made from Hornsea Beck. Witnesses alleged, however, that 30–40 years earlier fishermen had promised to make the payments called doles or quay doles to the abbot to encourage him to repair the quay, and that those payments had lapsed.[44] The doles were, nevertheless, included in a lease of the rectory in 1578.[45] Hornsea was still included in a list of ports in 1565,[46] but there is no further evidence of activity there until the 19th century. The loss of the quay was held in the 17th century to have allowed the more rapid destruction of houses at Hornsea Beck.[47]

14   P.R.O., HO 67/26/219.
15   B.I.H.R., TA. 299s.
16   Acreage Returns, 1905.
17   [1st] Land Util. Surv. Map, sheet 28.
18   Inf. from Min. of Agric., Fish. & Food, Beverley, 1990.
19   P.R.O., C 66/1804, [no. 1]; ibid. SC 2/211/59.
20   E.R.A.O., PE/30/33, f. 281v.; PE/30/34, p. 213.; O.S. Map 6″, Yorks. CXCVII (1854 edn.) shows Mill hill.
21   E.R.A.O., PE/30/2, flyleaf.
22   T. Jefferys, Map of Yorks. (1772).
23   H.U.L., DSJ/34, pp. 168, 179, 195.
24   Kelly's Dir. N. & E.R. Yorks. (1909), 532; (1921), 537.
25   P.R.O., SC 2/211/59; Yorks. Fines, iii, 17.
26   H.U.L., DDX/16/214; O.S. Map 6″, Yorks. CXCVII (1854 edn.) shows Mill hill.
27   English, Holderness, 208–10.
28   E.Y.C. iii, pp. 26–9; Yorks. Fines, John, pp. 146–7; Yorks. Fines, 1246–72, p. 96; 1272–1300, pp. 54–5; Cal. Inq. p.m. ii, p. 345.
29   Above, manors.
30   Cal. Pat. 1343–5, 89.
31   P.R.O., STAC 4/1/25.
32   Cal. Pat. 1549–51, 373; 1557–8, 17; 1560–3, 539, 542.

33   Poulson, Holderness, i. 320–1.
34   P.R.O., E 134/31 Chas. II Mich./17; E.R.A.O., DDRI/19/1–2.
35   E.R.A.O., DDSC, accession 4248 (plan of mere); O.S. Map 6″, Yorks. CXCVII (1854 edn.).
36   Above, intro. (resort).
37   Chron. de Melsa (Rolls Ser.), i. 421.
38   Acts of Parl. and Proclamations relating to E.R. Yorks. and Hull, 1529–1800, ed. K. A. MacMahon, 64; Cal. Pat. 1364–7, 77.
39   B.I.H.R., Prob. Reg. 1, f. 8; B. H. Putnam, Proc. before J.P. (Ames Foundation), 439, 442; Poulson, Holderness, i. 327.
40   Cal. Pat. 1436–41, 463; Cal. Close, 1402–5, 190; Test. Ebor. v, pp. 152 n., 237.
41   L. & P. Hen. VIII, xii (2), p. 418.
42   Acts of P.C. 1547–50, 396; 1552–4, 255.
43   E.R.A.O., DDCC/139/65; cf. P.R.O., E 178/160.
44   B.I.H.R., CP. G. 720–2, 3558; Select 16th Cent. Causes in Tithe (Y.A.S. Rec. Ser. civ), 69–71.
45   Cal. Pat. 1575–8, p. 493.
46   Acts of P.C. 1558–70, 289.
47   P.R.O., E 134/13 Chas. I East./7; E 178/4813.

With the advent of visitors in the 19th century there was a new demand for fish. A landing place at the end of Sea Road was allotted at inclosure in 1809.[48] Salmon fishing was begun in 1844, and it was said in 1848 that fishing had been tried but discontinued because the tides posed problems and bait was in short supply.[49] There were only three fishermen at Hornsea in 1851.[50] Another attempt to revive fishing was evidently made after the opening of the railway. Some 10–15 fishermen were recorded in 1871, 1881, and 1892,[51] and there were 12 boats employing 20 men in 1894. Landings in 1896 amounted to 198 cwt. of wet fish, 69,855 crabs, 91 lobsters, and 58 cwt. of other shellfish, and in 1912 the corresponding figures were 269 cwt., 61,700, 2, and 13 cwt. There were only two cobles at Hornsea in 1922. Little wet fish was landed after 1925 but crabbing continued, numbers caught in good years reaching 11,000 in the 1920s and about 25,000 in the early 1930s. Activity then declined and there was little commercial fishing after the war, although a few part-time fishermen supplied local shops with crabs and lobsters.[52] Three cobles were worked full-time from Hornsea in 1990.[53]

MARKETS AND FAIRS. The right to hold a market on Mondays was granted to St. Mary's abbey in 1257.[54] A fair on and about 6 December was presumably that granted to the abbey by 1275; another fair, from 31 July to 2 August, was added in 1358.[55] The fair days in 1650 were 1 August and 6 December.[56] In the later 18th century the fairs were held on 12 August and 17 December, and market day was Saturday.[57] Ground adjoining the mere was allotted for a fair ground and watering place at inclosure in 1809.[58] The market, which was presumably held in Market Place, where there was a bull ring,[59] was said to be disused by 1823, but the cattle fairs continued until late in the century and hirings for servants until the early 20th century.[60] A market in Sands Lane, begun c. 1970, was still held in 1989 on 14 Wednesdays a year and every Sunday between Easter and Christmas.[61]

OTHER INDUSTRY AND TRADE. The seaside resort is discussed above. Gravel-getting from the beach employed three men in 1851.[62] A brickyard in Westgate was mentioned in 1794.[63] A brickmaker at Hornsea Burton was recorded in 1846, and there was a brickworks beside the sea at the southern end of the township in 1848, which was evidently still worked in 1864.[64] J. A. Wade was also described as a brickmaker in 1864,[65] and licence was given in 1865 for a brickworks near the Hull road, south of the railway line, on land which Wade had acquired in 1859. The works were powered by a windmill and later also by steam. A terrace of thirteen cottages was built nearby by 1881.[66] By 1890 the site also housed a hydraulic engineering works which made centrifugal pumps.[67] The brickworks was used until the First World War.[68] Another brickworks, opened near the Seaton road by 1871, was closed in 1881.[69]

Lime was burnt in several kilns in the mid 19th century.[70]

Pottery making at Hornsea was begun by Colin and Desmond Rawson at a house in Victoria Avenue in 1949. They moved to Old Hall, Market Place, in 1951, but in 1953 they bought Edenfield House and adjoining ground, formerly the brick and tile works, in Marlborough Avenue and moved their works there the next year. In 1955 they established the Hornsea Pottery Co. Ltd. The site was later much enlarged. By the mid 1960s nearly 200 people were employed and in the early 1970s nearly 300.[71] Local opposition to the further growth of the pottery caused the firm to open another factory in Lancaster, and commercial problems later resulted in the company going into receivership in 1984 and then changing hands several times before closing in 2000.[72] Various attractions for visitors were provided at the pottery, including in 1989 collections of birds of prey, butterflies, and cars. A shopping village, Hornsea Freeport, was opened on the site in 1994.[73]

A small industrial estate was created in Cliff Road in the later 1960s; another, on part of the former railway near the Rolston road, was established in the 1980s,[74] and two or three small firms were in business on each of them in 1989.

[48] R.D.B., CI/345/27.
[49] Hull Advertiser, 24 May 1844; Bedell, Acct. of Hornsea (1848), 97.
[50] P.R.O., HO 107/2365.
[51] Ibid. RG 10/4803; RG 11/4790; Bulmer, Dir. E. Yorks. (1892), 436.
[52] N.E. Sea Fisheries Cttee. Mins. 1893–4, 6; 1895–6, 35–46; 1913–15, 27; 1923–5, 111; and passim.
[53] Hull Daily Mail, 22 Feb. 1990.
[54] Cal. Chart. R. 1226–57, 463. The grant of a mkt. in 1466 (e.g. recorded by Bedell, Acct. of Hornsea (1848), 66) was only a confirmation: Cal. Chart. R. 1427–1516, 210.
[55] Yorks. Hund. and Quo Warr. R. 1274–94 (Y.A.S. Rec. Ser. cli), 36; Cal. Chart. R. 1341–1417, 157.
[56] P.R.O., E 317/Yorks./28.
[57] K. L. McCutcheon, Yorks. Fairs & Mkts. (Thoresby Soc. xxxix), 174; 1st Rep. Royal Com. Mkt. Rights & Tolls, Vol. i [C.5550], p. 219, H.C. (1888), liii.
[58] R.D.B., CI/345/27.
[59] O.S. Map 6", Yorks. CXCVII (1854 edn.).
[60] Directories.
[61] Local inf.
[62] P.R.O., HO 107/2365; E.R.A.O., DDCC/136/165–6.

[63] E.R.A.O., PE/30/34, p. 129.
[64] White, Dir. Hull & York (1846), 375; Bedell, Acct. of Hornsea (1848), 120 n.; Slater's Royal Nat. Com. Dir. (1864), 205; O.S. Map 6", Yorks. CXCVII (1854 edn.).
[65] Slater's Royal Nat. Com. Dir. Yorks. (1864), 205. Sewell, Joseph Armytage Wade, 36–8, 47, 55 (illus.).
[66] H.U.L., DSJ/37, p. 320; DSJ/43, p. 169; P.R.O., RG 11/4790; illus. in Sewell, op. cit. 52.
[67] O.S. Map 1/2,500, Yorks. CXCVII. 7 (1891 edn.); H.U.L., DSJ/44, p. 100; Sewell, op. cit. 38, 55 (illus.).
[68] Directories.
[69] P.R.O., RG 10/4803; R.D.B., LR/328/488; O.S. Map 1/2,500, Yorks. CXCVII. 3–4 (1891 edn.); Sewell, op. cit. 36.
[70] O.S. Map 6", Yorks. CXCVII (1854 edn.).
[71] R.D.B., 958/74/60; 974/422/381; 1025/395/353; 1350/251/226; 1350/252/227; R. W. Doughty, 'District of Hornsea in Holderness' (Univ. of Reading B.A. dissertation, 1966), 61–2; Story of Hornsea Pottery (1977), [6, 8, 10, 13, 37].
[72] Inf. from Dr. J. E. S. Walker, Hornsea, 1997.
[73] Inf. from Hornsea Freeport, 2000.
[74] Holderness B.C. Mins. 1981–2, no. 545 (copy at E.R.A.O., DCHO); inf. from Dr. Walker, 1997.

LOCAL GOVERNMENT. In the 1270s the abbot of St. Mary's, York, claimed wreck and the assize of bread and of ale at Hornsea; he also had gallows, pillory, prison, and tumbril there.[75] Wreck was still taken by the lord of the manor in the late 17th century.[76]

Estreats for Hornsea manor survive for 1609–11, 1613–14, and 1621–3,[77] and court rolls for 1623–1925.[78] The jurisdiction comprised view of frankpledge with court baron and customary court. In the late 17th century officers appointed included 2 aletasters, 2 constables, 2 leather searchers, and 2 pinders, one for Hornsea common fields and the other for Southorpe fields; 2 surveyors of highways were chosen in 1688. Two affeerors and 4 bylawmen for Hornsea fields and 2 for Southorpe fields were also appointed in the early 18th century; later in the century there were only 2 bylawmen for each set of fields, and in the 19th century only 2 affeerors, 2 constables, and a pinder were chosen.

Surviving parish records for Hornsea include a rate book of 1804.[79] In the early 19th century permanent poor relief was given to 20–30 people and occasional relief to as many as 20 more;[80] the overseers of the poor maintained four parish poorhouses in 1823.[81] Hornsea joined Skirlaugh poor-law union in 1837.[82] A vestry or 'town meeting', the minutes of which survive for 1847–95,[83] met in the vestry or the National school. Churchwardens, overseers, and surveyors were elected, and from 1852 a salaried assistant overseer was appointed. Under the Public Health Act of 1848 and the Local Government Act of 1858 a local board was formed in 1864 with 12 members; it met at first in the National school, and J. A. Wade was chairman until 1889.[84] From 1869 it had a board room and office in the public rooms in Newbegin, but from 1885 it used purpose-built rooms at the cemetery in Southgate.[85] In 1894 the local board was replaced by an urban district council; T. B. Holmes, who had been chairman of the local board from 1890, was chairman of the urban district council until 1906.[86] By 1905 the offices were again in the public rooms, which were bought by the council in 1920,[87] and they remained there until 1927, when Elim Lodge in

Cliff Road was bought for a town hall.[88] In 1974 Hornsea became part of the Holderness district of Humberside, which was granted the title Holderness Borough in 1977,[89] and the town later formed two of the wards in the district. The old offices in Cliff Road were closed and in 1997 Elim Lodge was a nursing home. In 1996 Hornsea became part of a new East Riding unitary area.[90] The former police station in Newbegin, earlier acquired as a local office for the district council,[91] was used by the East Riding council in 1997. Other council offices then included Ravenswood, the former children's home.[92] From 1974 Hornsea had a town council, of 12 members, with the powers and duties of a parish council; its chairman was styled town mayor.[93] The former lifeboat station in Burton Road was used as a town hall.

PUBLIC SERVICES. The town's water was supplied by shallow wells and pumps until 1878, when a waterworks with a deep well and pumping station was built by the local government board on the Atwick road; a few private wells remained in use.[94] The works were several times improved.[95] From 1927 water was supplied to the urban district council from Hull in bulk, using a water tower in Mappleton, and a direct supply from Hull was provided in 1963.[96] The original waterworks building, of red and yellow brick in a Gothic style, was for a time used as a refuse incinerator and later for storage. A former claypit beside it was filled by refuse tipping and was still a civic amenity refuse site in 1989.[97]

The laying of a deep drainage system was carried out by the local board in 1874–5.[98] The sewers were reconstructed and a new outfall provided in 1926–7.[99] Later improvements included the making in the 1970s of a new outfall sewer, with a pumping station in the seafront playing fields.[1]

Gas was supplied to much of the town by a company founded by J. A. Wade in 1864, with works near the Hull road; by 1870 it had 30 street lights.[2] After nationalization in 1948, the works passed to the North Eastern Gas Board; gas production at Hornsea ended in 1966–7 and the works were later demolished. Gas was sup-

[75] *Yorks. Hund. and Quo Warr. R. 1274–94* (Y.A.S. Rec. Ser. cli), 36, 171–3.
[76] P.R.O., E 134/9 Wm. III Mich./45.
[77] Ibid. SC 2/211/59.
[78] E.R.A.O., PE/30/33–4; H.U.L., DDCV/82/1–8; ibid. DSJ/34–49.
[79] E.R.A.O., DDX/665/1.
[80] *Poor Law Abstract, 1804*, pp. 594–5; *1818*, pp. 522–3.
[81] *9th Rep. Com. Char.* 764–5; below, church [last para.]; charities [town stock].
[82] *3rd Rep. Poor Law Com.* 170.
[83] E.R.A.O., PE/30/22, pp. 61 and *passim*.
[84] Ibid. pp. 124, 129–30; Hornsea L.B. Mins. *passim*; *Lond. Gaz.* 3 July 1863, p. 3343; 19 Apr. 1864, p. 2174; Hornsea L.B. *Bylaws* (copy in Hull Pub. Libr.). The board's mins. survive for 1872–8 and 1886–94: E.R.A.O., LBHO.
[85] Bulmer, *Dir. E. Yorks.* (1892), 432; Hobson, *Sketch of Hornsea* (1974 edn.), 102; Sewell, *Joseph Armytage Wade*, 59; below, local govt. (public services).
[86] Mins. survive for 1895–1924, 1928–74: E.R.A.O., UDHO.
[87] R.D.B., 222/282/248; directories.
[88] R.D.B., 352/523/422.
[89] *V.C.H. Yorks. E.R.* v. 180.
[90] Humberside (Structural Change) Order 1995, copy at E.R.A.O.
[91] Humbs. C.C. *Mins.* 1974–5, D 305.
[92] Below, local govt. (public services).
[93] Inf. from town clerk, Hornsea, 1989.
[94] Hornsea L.B. Mins. 1872–8, *passim* (at E.R.A.O., LBHO); E.R.C.C. *Mins.* 1906–7, 383–4.
[95] *Kelly's Dir. N. & E.R. Yorks.* (1897), 476; (1901), 498; E.R.C.C. *Mins.* 1905–6, 44; 1910–11, 388; 1924–5, 369. Illus. in Sewell, *Joseph Armytage Wade*, 59.
[96] Hull Corp. Water Cttee. *Mins.* 1925–6, 10; 1926–7, 27, 49; *V.C.H. Yorks. E.R.* i. 373.
[97] Humbs. C.C. *Mins.* 1975–6, K 469.
[98] Hornsea L.B. Mins. 1872–8, 132; E.R.A.O., accession 2382 (drainage cttee. mins. 1874–7).
[99] E.R.C.C. *Mins.* 1926–7, 170; *Kelly's Dir. N. & E.R. Yorks.* (1933), 483.
[1] Hornsea U.D.C. *Mins.* 1971–2, 197, and *Mins. passim* (at E.R.A.O., UDHO).
[2] *Kelly's Dir. N. & E.R. Yorks.* (1889), 404.

plied from Hull until the town went over to North Sea gas in 1968.[3] A gasworks built by W. M. Jackson in Hartley Street supplied the Lansdowne estate from c. 1870 and 8 of the 57 public lamps in the town in 1892; it was disused by 1899.[4]

Electricity was supplied from 1930 by the South East Yorkshire Light & Power Co. Ltd., taking a bulk supply from Hull corporation.[5] The company was succeeded by the Yorkshire Electricity Board, which used the former steam laundry in Cliff Road as a base for the electrification of much of Holderness until 1964.[6]

In 1655 the lessees of the manor gave a piece of ground on the south side of the churchyard as the site for a prison, and one end of a cottage built there was still described as a prison in 1676.[7] Stocks are said to have stood in Market Place until the early 19th century.[8] The appointment of a policeman was approved by the town meeting in 1848 but was effected only in 1850, after the adoption of the Lighting and Watching Act of 1833. The provisions of the Act were, however, abandoned in 1853.[9] The East Riding constabulary, established in 1857, had a constable based at Hornsea. He evidently lived at no. 16 Westgate.[10] In 1859 the inhabitants petitioned for a lock-up and for the constable's beat to be restricted to Hornsea, on account of the disorderly state of the town.[11] It was not until the late 1870s, however, that a police station was built in Newbegin,[12] manned in 1889 by a sergeant and two constables.[13] From 1923 some meetings of the petty sessional court for North Holderness were held at Hornsea, at first in the public rooms, Newbegin, but from 1927 in the urban district council offices, Cliff Road.[14] A new police station and court house were built in Parva Road and opened in 1973; the latter had been closed by 1997.[15] The old station was converted to offices for Holderness district council.[16]

The urban district council had a fire brigade by 1902; a station in Market Place was replaced by the former lifeboat house in Burton Road, bought for the purpose in 1924.[17] After the Second World War the brigade passed to the East Riding county council, and a new station in Southgate was opened in 1965.[18]

In 1884 the local board bought 2 a. in Southgate and a cemetery was opened there the next year.[19] The site for the Edenfield burial ground, in Marlborough Avenue, was bought by the urban district council in 1953.[20]

Hall Garths were bought by the urban district council in 1919 and opened the next year as a public park, which was later enlarged to comprise c. 24 a.[21] Playing fields west of the Atwick road were given to the town by John and Mary Hollis in 1927 and enlarged in 1947.[22] Near the beach Hornsea Leisure Centre, comprising swimming and other facilities, was provided by Holderness Borough council in 1996.[23]

The War Memorial Cottage Hospital was opened in Eastgate in 1923 with eight beds and was later enlarged. It had 22 beds in 1983.[24] A convalescent home in connexion with the Victoria Hospital for Sick Children, Hull, was opened in a house in Cliff Road in 1885; it was moved in 1904 to a larger house, which was replaced by a new building in 1908. It was closed in 1970 and has been converted into flats.[25] A holiday home for the Port of Hull Society was provided in Cliff Road by Sir James Reckitt, Bt., in 1908.[26] The Hull Guild of Brave Poor Things had a holiday home in Alexandra Road in 1908 but replaced it before 1910 with a new building in New Road, which had been closed by 1973.[27] The East Riding county council bought Ravenswood (no. 12 Cliff Road) in 1950 for use as a children's home, which was closed c. 1980, and in 1967 it built the Willows old people's home in Newbegin, which had also been closed by 1997 and was later demolished. Hull corporation bought Westgate House for the same purpose in 1953;[28] it later passed to Humberside county council. A 'camp school' was built by Wakefield corporation on the Hull road in 1938[29] and still existed in 1989.

Beacons were erected at Hornsea to warn of enemy naval activity. Three were in place in 1588.[30] One was put up in 1746 and removed in

3   N.E. Gas Bd. Ann. Rep. 1966–7, 12; 1968–9, 21.
4   R.D.B., KW/240/300; 22/493/468 (1900); Bulmer, Dir. E. Yorks. (1892), 427.
5   E.R.A.O., DP/283; R.D.B., 410/585/473; Hull Corp. Elect. Cttee. Mins. 1928–9, 28; 1929–30, 97; V.C.H. Yorks. E.R. i. 374.
6   The building was later a U.D.C. depot; it was demolished in 1994. Inf. from Dr. J. E. S. Walker, Hornsea, 1997.
7   E.R.A.O., PE/30/33, ff. 50, 102, 107v.
8   Bedell, Acct. of Hornsea (1848), 116.
9   E.R.A.O., PE/30/22, pp. 13, 20–1, 30, 34–6, 38, 51, 57, 67, 79; Hull Advertiser, 8 Mar. 1850.
10   A. A. Clarke, Country Coppers: Story of E.R. Police, 18–19, 108 (illus.); inf. from Dr. J. E. S. Walker, Hornsea, 1998. The cell door from 16 Westgate is in Hornsea Museum.
11   E.R.A.O., QAP/1/1, s.vv. 11 Feb. 1857; 18 Oct. 1859; P.R.O., RG 9/3604; RG 10/4803.
12   R.D.B., MX/278/450; H.U.L., DDCV/81/18.
13   Kelly's Dir. N. & E.R. Yorks. (1889), 404.
14   E.R.C.C. Standing Joint Cttee. Mins. 1922–5, 161; 1925–8, 98, 237; E.R.C.C. Mins. 1964–5, 122; 1967–8, 108.
15   E.R.C.C. Mins. 1971–2, 352; 1972–3, 333; plaques in bldgs.; inf. from Mr. M. Sewell, Hornsea, 1997.
16   Humbs. C.C. Mins. 1974–5, D 305.
17   Hornsea U.D.C. Mins. 1896–1906, 270; 1919–24, 452;

Kelly's Dir. N. & E.R. Yorks. (1925), 556.
18   E.R.C.C. Mins. 1965–6, 58.
19   R.D.B., NZ/397/358; Bulmer, Dir. E. Yorks. (1892), 430; illus. in Sewell, Joseph Armytage Wade, 67.
20   R.D.B., 934/205/185.
21   Ibid. 202/432/373; 219/538/470; Hall Garth Park, Hornsea (copy in Beverley Pub. Libr.); Kelly's Dir. N. & E.R. Yorks. (1925), 555.
22   R.D.B., 365/244/203; 766/409/341; notice board at playing fields, 1989.   23   Plaques in building.
24   R.D.B., 280/436/378; 623/9/7; E.R.C.C. Mins. 1923–4, 327; Hospitals & Health Services Year Bk. 1985, 81.
25   V.C.H. Yorks. E.R. i. 384; Illus. Guide to Hornsea (1894), 11; G. Patrick, A Plague on You, Sir!, 112–13, 317; inf. from Dr. J. E. S. Walker, Hornsea, 1997.
26   R.D.B., 107/82/79; 119/220/196; Illus. Guide to Hornsea (1908), 20.
27   R.D.B., 112/316/289; E.R.A.O., NV/1/8; Illus. Guide to Hornsea (1908), 20; Hornsea U.D.C. Mins. 1973–4, 37.
28   R.D.B., 859/69/62; 945/410/349; E.R.C.C. Mins. 1948–9, 595; 1966–7, 341; 1967–8, 16; local inf.; inf. from Mr. M. Sewell, Hornsea, 1997.
29   R.D.B., 568/131/97; E.R. Educ. Cttee. Mins. 1938–9, 49.
30   J. Nicholson, Beacons of E. Yorks. 10.

1786, and two were erected in 1794, one in East field and the other in Pennels close; a signal station to communicate with the beacons was recommended for Hornsea in 1803.[31] After the loss of life in shipwrecks the previous year, a lifeboat was provided at Hornsea by subscription in 1852.[32] It was taken over by the Royal National Lifeboat Institution in 1854, and a new boat was presented in 1857.[33] The first boathouse stood on the shore south of New Road[34] but a new one was built in Burton Road in 1878–9. The lifeboat was withdrawn in 1924,[35] and the former boathouse was used as a fire station until 1965, then as a council garage, and in 1989 as a town hall.[36] From 1879 the Board of Trade had a rocket apparatus house in Alexandra Road.[37] A customs officer at Hornsea was recorded from 1720.[38] Tenders for building two cottages, a store place, and a watch room were invited by H.M. Customs in 1828.[39] That was presumably the coastguard station, said to have been provided in 1830, which stood on the shore at the end of New Road.[40] The coastguards later lived in a terrace of five houses in Cliff Road, and a lookout has occupied various sites on the North cliffs.[41]

CHURCH. There was a church at Hornsea in 1086.[42] In the early 12th century it was given by Stephen, count of Aumale, to St. Mary's abbey, York.[43] Licence for the appropriation of the church was granted in 1346 and thrice renewed[44] before the church was eventually appropriated and a vicarage ordained in 1423.[45] The rights of the church extended to the village of Long Riston, presumably because land there was soke of Hornsea manor,[46] and a church built at Long Riston was acknowledged in the 12th century to be subordinate to Hornsea church.[47] The two were held as united livings until Riston was made a separate parish in 1907.[48] In 1939 Hornsea vicarage and Goxhill rectory were united and the two parishes made one, with Hornsea as the parish church. That union was dissolved in

1972, when Hornsea was united instead with Atwick and the former parish of Goxhill was transferred to Mappleton.[49]

Presentations were made by St. Mary's abbey until the Dissolution.[50] A grant of the advowson to the archbishop of York in 1558[51] was evidently ineffectual and the Crown retained the patronage, which was later exercised by the Lord Chancellor.[52]

The rectory was worth £38 6s. 8d. in 1291, including £5 a year payable to St. Mary's abbey.[53] Besides that £5 portion, the abbey also had half of the tithe of sea fish at Hornsea in 1396.[54] When ordained in 1423, the vicarage was assigned glebe and tithes in Hornsea and Riston estimated to be worth £26 13s. 4d.[55] The vicar unsuccessfully sued the abbey for augmentation of his income in 1493, when he alleged that Hornsea was worth only £6 a year and Riston £8.[56] Hornsea vicarage was worth £4 13s. 4d. gross in 1535, when the net value of the joint living was £13 3s. 2d.[57] In 1650 Hornsea vicarage was valued at £14 a year,[58] and c. 1700 the joint living was said to be worth £85.[59] The net income of the joint living averaged £382 a year between 1829 and 1831,[60] and the net value in 1883 was £287.[61]

The vicar was assigned the small tithes, 2 bovates of glebe, and a house in Hornsea in 1423. Tithes there contributed £3 6s. 8d. and the glebe and house £1 6s. 8d. to the value of the living in 1535, and tithes, glebe, and house together were worth £14 a year in 1650. At the inclosure of Hornsea in 1809 the vicar was allotted 68 a. for tithes and glebe;[62] a 4-a. allotment on the cliff top was later reduced by erosion and the remaining 2 a. there was sold in 1926.[63] George Heslop (d. 1929) devised a 65-a. farm in Hornsea Burton to enlarge the glebe; all but 2 a. of it was sold in 1930.[64] The remaining glebe still belonged to the living in 1978.[65]

The incumbent had licence to celebrate divine service in the rectory house in 1397.[66] By the ordination of 1423, a vicarage house was to be

[31] E.R.A.O., PE/30/3, flyleaf; LT/4/18; ibid. QSF/153/D.25; QSF/311/D.5; T. Jefferys, Map of Yorks. (1772); R. W. S. Norfolk, Militia, Yeomanry, and Volunteer Forces of the E.R. 1689–1908 (E. Yorks. Loc. Hist. Ser. xix), 18, 30. Pennels or Beacon close, near Hornsea Beck, was the site of a gibbet where the body of Edw. Pennel, a pirate, was displayed in 1770: E.R.A.O., PE/30/3, p. 47; H.U.L., DDX/16/245.

[32] Hull Advertiser, 3 Oct. 1851; 6 Feb., 5 Mar. 1852.

[33] Bulmer, Dir. E. Yorks. (1892), 432; plaques in church; inf. from R.N.L.I., West Quay Rd., Poole (Dors.), 1989.

[34] E.R.A.O., DP/22.

[35] R.D.B., MR/138/204; 289/573/492; inf. from R.N.L.I., 1989.

[36] Above, this section and loc. govt.; inf. from Dr. J. E. S. Walker, Hornsea, 1997.

[37] R.D.B., MT/174/255; E.R.A.O., NV/1/8.

[38] E.R.A.O., PE/30/33, f. 237v.; below, charities [Rob. Smithson].

[39] Hull Advertiser, 13 June 1828.

[40] Sheahan and Whellan, Hist. York & E.R. ii. 418; O.S. Map 6″, Yorks. CXCVII (1854 edn.).

[41] O.S. Map 1/2,500, Yorks. CXCVII. 3–4 (1891 and later edns.); inf. from Dr. Walker, 1997.

[42] V.C.H. Yorks. ii. 265.

[43] E.Y.C. iii, p. 26.

[44] Cal. Pat. 1345–8, 123; 1396–9, 72; 1399–1401, 252; 1422–9, 94.

[45] B.I.H.R., Reg. 18, ff. 199–201.

[46] Above, manors.

[47] Below, Long Riston, church.

[48] B.I.H.R., OC. 458.

[49] Ibid. 854; Lond. Gaz. 30 May 1939, p. 3638.

[50] Lawrance, 'Clergy List', Holderness, i, pp. 64–9.

[51] Cal. Pat. 1557–8, 420.

[52] B.I.H.R., OC. 854; P.R.O., Inst. Bks.; Cal. Pat. 1557–8, 355; 1558–60, 269; Crockford; Lond. Gaz. 30 May 1939, p. 3638.

[53] Tax. Eccl. (Rec. Com.), 304.

[54] Cal. Papal Reg. v. 2.

[55] B.I.H.R., Reg. 18, f. 201.

[56] P. Heath, Med. Clerical Accts. (St. Ant. Hall Publ. no. xxvi), 5–11, 25–59.

[57] Valor Eccl. (Rec. Com.), v. 116.

[58] T.E.R.A.S. iv. 63.

[59] B.I.H.R., Bp. Dio. 3, E.R., p. 176.

[60] Rep. Com. Eccl. Revenues, 942–3.

[61] B.I.H.R., V. 1884/Ret. 1.

[62] R.D.B., CI/345/27.

[63] Ibid. 339/608/500.

[64] Ibid. 405/431/352; 406/521/432.

[65] Inf. from York Dioc. Bd. of Finance, 1981.

[66] D. M. Smith, Cal. Reg. Waldby, 10.

built by St. Mary's abbey next to the church-yard.[67] The house may not have been wholly habitable in 1614, when the vicar took his meals at an alehouse in the town but used a room in the vicarage house as a study.[68] The house was unroofed by a storm in 1732.[69] A new house was built in 1831;[70] it is of grey brick with a main front of three bays, the central bay recessed, and the low-pitched roof has wide overhanging eaves.

Four guilds in the church, dedicated to Corpus Christi, Holy Trinity, St. Catherine, and St. Mary, were mentioned in 1430 and 1527. St. Mary's altar was also mentioned in 1430.[71] Houses formerly belonging to the guilds were recorded later.[72]

Several rectors in the 14th century held other livings,[73] among them William Melton, 1301–17, later archbishop of York, and three foreigners who held Hornsea by papal provision from 1321 to 1337.[74] By the ordination of 1423, the vicar was to have a chaplain at Riston, and in the late 15th century he had another at Hornsea.[75] There was a chaplain at Hornsea in 1525 and 1554, and a curate at Riston in 1552.[76] Vicars often did not reside at Hornsea. There was said to be no constant preacher in 1650, when Hornsea was considered unfit to be held with Riston because of the distance between them.[77] In the mid 18th century Hornsea and Riston were held with Rise, and the vicar lived at Rise or in York. His curate occupied the vicarage house at Hornsea, whence he also served Atwick church.[78] The vicar resided and employed an assistant curate c. 1840,[79] but in 1848 a curate again officiated at Hornsea, while the vicar lived at a distance.[80] Later in the century the vicar resided at Hornsea; in 1865, 1868, 1877, and 1884 he had an assistant curate at Riston, and in 1871 another at Hornsea. There were two assistants in 1900 but none in 1921 or 1931.[81]

By 1743 two services were held each Sunday and prayers were read on three weekdays; communion was received 7–8 times a year by c. 80 people.[82] There was only one Sunday service in 1764, when communion was celebrated quarterly with 40–50 recipients. Two services were

again held on Sundays by 1865, and there were three by 1877. Communion was monthly by 1865 and weekly by 1877, at first with 50–70 recipients but later with 15–20; in 1931 there were 45–50 recipients.[83]

A parish room was built in Newbegin near the church in 1887;[84] it was replaced on the same site in 1907 by a church institute, which contained club, billiards, and recreation rooms, besides a parish room.[85] The former Congregational chapel in Southgate was used as a mission hall by 1901 and was bought for the church in 1918.[86] It was later used as a parish hall but was closed in 1960 and subsequently sold;[87] thereafter the church institute served as a parish hall. A church hall in the Crescent, on the council housing estate in Hornsea Burton, was built as a Sunday school in 1959.[88]

The church of *ST. NICHOLAS*, so called in 1390,[89] is built mainly of rubble with ashlar dressings and stands on an eminence at the junction of Market Place and Newbegin. It consists of aisled and clerestoried chancel with crypt and north vestry, aisled and clerestoried nave with south porch, and a west tower, which is flanked by continuations of the aisles. The narrow nave and the clasped tower suggest that the plan has early origins, but there are no surviving features earlier than the triple lancets in the aisles. The arcades are of the late 13th century, and the aisles are almost as wide as the nave, suggesting that each may originally have been ridge roofed. There is a blocked arch for a side chapel in the south aisle. The tower is also of the 13th century, but has 14th-century battlements and a 15th-century west window. The line of an earlier nave roof is visible on the east wall of the tower. The clerestory was probably added in the 15th century, when the east end of the chancel was refenestrated. The east and west windows of the aisles are slightly later.

The chancel was out of repair in 1575 and 1615.[90] The tower was ruinous in 1693, and licence to sell lead from it was given in 1699.[91] The wooden spire was blown down in 1714, and the church was unroofed during the storm of 1732.[92] The north aisle of the nave is said to have

[67] B.I.H.R., Reg. 18, f. 201.   [68] Ibid. CP. G. 1023.
[69] E.R.A.O., PE/30/2, flyleaf. The glebe terriers (B.I.H.R., TER. H.) give no indication of rebuilding or burning, as in Sheahan and Whellan, *Hist. York & E.R.* ii. 417; Hobson, *Sketch of Hornsea* (1974 edn.), 113. The ho. was omitted, perhaps in error, from the incl. map of 1809 (E.R.A.O., IA. Hornsea; ibid. DDCK/35/1(j)).
[70] E.R.A.O., PE/30/16; B.I.H.R., MGA. 1831/2.
[71] B.I.H.R., Prob. Reg. 2, f. 629v.; 9, f. 388. Also E.R.A.O., DDCC/139/65.
[72] e.g. in manorial ct. rolls: above, local govt.
[73] *Fasti Dunelm.* (Sur. Soc. cxxxix), 51, 113, 143; *Cal. Papal Reg.* ii. 22; *Cal. Papal Pets.* i. 446.
[74] Lawrance, 'Clergy List', Holderness, 1, pp. 65–6; *Cal. Papal Reg.* ii. 211, 239, 326; iii. 241.
[75] B.I.H.R., Reg. 18, f. 201; Heath, *Med. Clerical Accts.* 7 sqq.
[76] *Y.A.J.* xxiv. 75; *Select 16th Cent. Causes in Tithe* (Y.A.S. Rec. Ser. civ), 59, 69; *Inventories of Ch. Goods*, 55.
[77] *T.E.R.A.S.* iv. 63.
[78] B.I.H.R., V. 1764/Ret. 1, no. 33; Ret. 2, nos. 48, 212; *Herring's Visit.* i, p. 36; ii, pp. 88–90; iii, pp. 35–6; above, Atwick, church.

[79] P.R.O., HO 107/1222; *Rep. Com. Eccl. Revenues*, 942–3.
[80] Bedell, *Acct. of Hornsea* (1848), 99.
[81] B.I.H.R., V. 1865/Ret. 1, no. 255; V. 1868/Ret. 1, no. 229; V. 1871/Ret. 1, no. 229; V. 1877/Ret. 2, no. 36; V. 1884/Ret. 1; V. 1910–22/Ret.; V. 1931/Ret.
[82] *Herring's Visit.* ii, p. 89.
[83] B.I.H.R., V. 1764/Ret. 2, no. 48; V. 1865/Ret. 1, no. 255; V. 1868/Ret. 1, no. 229; V. 1871/Ret. 1, no. 229; V. 1877/Ret. 2, no. 36; V. 1884/Ret. 1; V. 1931/Ret.
[84] *Kelly's Dir. N. & E.R. Yorks.* (1889), 404.
[85] R.D.B., 104/68/66; *Illus. Guide to Hornsea* (1908) 17.
[86] R.D.B., 184/434/375; *Kelly's Dir. N. & E.R. Yorks.* (1901), 499.
[87] R.D.B., 1280/292/258; inf. from Mr. A. H. Croft, Hornsea, 1990.
[88] Inf. from Mr. Croft.
[89] B.I.H.R., Prob. Reg. 1, f. 8.
[90] Ibid. V. 1615/CB. 1, f. 222v.; *Abp. Grindal's Visit.*, 1575, ed. W. J. Sheils, 70.
[91] B.I.H.R., Fac. 1699/4; *Diary of Abraham de la Pryme* (Sur. Soc. liv), 272.
[92] E.R.A.O., PE/30/2, flyleaf.

FIG. 21. HORNSEA CHURCH

been restored in 1845,[93] and the whole church was restored by Sir G. G. Scott in 1866–7, when the pinnacles were added to the tower.[94] The vestry was built in 1902.[95]

The church contains three effigies: two, one of which is said to be that of Sir William Fauconberg (d. 1294), were brought from Nun-keeling church in 1948 and the other from Goxhill church. There is a tomb chest commemorating Anthony St. Quintin, rector (d. 1430).[96] The font is 13th-century.

There was one bell in 1552, another having been sold for the repair of the pier at Hornsea Beck,[97] and still only one, cast in 1634, until two more were added in 1767.[98] A peal of eight was provided in 1919, including recastings of the three earlier bells.[99] By 1860 the tower included a clock, which was replaced by one given as a War memorial by Christopher Pickering in 1921.[1] The plate included a chalice in 1552, another having been sold for the pier work.[2] The church later had two chalices, one given by Leonard Robinson (d. 1655) and the other made c. 1670.[3] The registers of baptisms, marriages, and burials begin in 1654 and are complete.[4]

Lands held for the repair of the church were let for £21 a year in 1743 and 1764, and in the latter year there was a balance in hand of £90–100.[5] The feoffees were allotted c. 58 a. at inclosure in 1809, when they also held several old inclosures.[6] In 1823 the estate comprised two houses and 71 a. of land, producing an annual rent of £102 10s.; four cottages built on the land, partly at the expense of the feoffees, were let to the overseers of the poor for a further £8 8s. rent.[7] The income from rent was £172 in 1901.[8] Several plots of land were later sold.[9] In 1929 the estate comprised 57 a., a house and other buildings in Market Place, and £5,207 stock.[10] The income in 1951 was £402 in rent and £152 interest on £5,767 stock.[11]

ROMAN CATHOLICISM. Up to a dozen recusants and non-communicants were reported in Hornsea with Riston from the late 16th to the late 18th century.[12] Hornsea parish was said to have one popish family in 1743.[13] A Roman Catholic parish of Hornsea was formed in 1928.[14] A temporary building was used for worship in 1931 and a hut in Football Green from 1939.[15] The Church of the Sacred Heart in Southgate was built in 1956,[16] and a church hall behind it was added in 1962.[17]

PROTESTANT NONCONFORMITY. Members of the Acklam family were among recusants reported at Hornsea in 1664, and Quakers were alleged to hold meetings in Peter Acklam's house

93 Bedell, *Acct. of Hornsea* (1848), 111.
94 B.I.H.R., Fac. Bk. 5, p. 152; ibid. Ch. Ret. ii; *Kelly's Dir. N. & E.R. Yorks.* (1872), 378.
95 B.I.H.R., Fac. 1901/22; *Kelly's Dir. N. & E.R. Yorks.* (1909), 529.
96 Notices in church.
97 *Inventories of Ch. Goods*, 53–4.
98 Boulter, 'Ch. Bells', 84.
99 B.I.H.R., Fac. Bk. 9, p. 569; plaque in church.
1 Inf. from Dr. J. E. S. Walker, Hornsea, 1997.
2 *Inventories of Ch. Goods*, 49–50.
3 *Yorks. Ch. Plate*, i. 264–5.
4 E.R.A.O., PE/30/1–4, 7.
5 B.I.H.R., V. 1764/Ret. 2, no. 48; *Herring's Visit.* ii, p. 89.

6 E.R.A.O., CI/345/27.
7 *9th Rep. Com. Char.* 764–5; below, charities [town stock].
8 E.R.A.O., accession 1681.
9 e.g. R.D.B., 330/616/491; 410/585/473; 1149/150/143; 1745/531/450.
10 Ibid. 1743/454/396.
11 E.R.A.O., accession 1681.
12 Aveling, *Post Reformation Catholicism*, 68.
13 *Herring's Visit.* ii, p. 88.
14 *Catholic Dir.* (1988).
15 B.I.H.R., V. 1931/Ret.; O.N.S. (Birkdale), Worship Reg. no. 58992; local inf.
16 *Catholic Dir.* (1988).
17 Stone on bldg.

in 1665.[18] In 1675 Peter Acklam reserved the garden of the later Low Hall, Southgate, as a burial place for him and his children, and his sons similarly reserved it in 1698.[19] Burials are also said to have taken place in the garden of Old Hall.[20] A meeting house licensed in 1711 may have been that mentioned in 1743 and that in a garner in Westgate recorded in 1750; adjoining land was used as a burial ground by 1785.[21] Two Quaker families were reported in the parish in 1743 and one in 1764; seldom more than 4 or 5 people were said to attend the meeting house in 1743 and 10 or 12 in 1764.[22] The meeting house was so described in 1814[23] but was later closed. Quaker Cottage in Back Westgate, presumably the same building, was still owned by the Friends in 1989 and was available for worship.[24]

George Whitfield's house in Hornsea was licensed for unspecified dissenting worship in 1714, John and Samuel Dunn and others obtained the registration of a barn in 1766, and John Dunn's house was licensed in 1777, Samuel Dunn's house in 1778, and Frances Savage's house in 1790.[25]

In the late 18th century Wesleyan Methodists met first in Low Hall, Southgate, and then in another building nearby.[26] A house was licensed for Methodist worship in 1808. A chapel was built in Back Southgate in 1814[27] and replaced by Trinity chapel in Newbegin in 1870.[28] The old chapel was later put to various uses and served as a garage in 1989. A school was built beside the new chapel in 1875.[29] Trinity chapel, which was still used in 1989, was designed by J. K. James of Hull[30] and built of red brick with stone dressings.

Meeting places for unspecified dissenting worship registered by George Whitfield in 1714 and Charles Bondfield in 1716[31] may have been for Presbyterians; one Presbyterian family was reported at Hornsea in 1743.[32] The missionary efforts of members of Fish Street chapel, Hull,

included visits to Hornsea c. 1800.[33] A house was licensed for worship by the Independents in 1807, and Bethesda chapel was built in Southgate and licensed in 1808.[34] The chapel was later enlarged, and a burial ground behind it was acquired c. 1847.[35] A new chapel, designed by Samuel Musgrave of Hull and built of red and yellow brick with stone dressings, was erected in New Road in 1872–4.[36] The old chapel was later used for various purposes and in 1989 was a storehouse. The building in New Road was severely damaged by fire in 1968 and was subsequently remodelled.[37] In 1972 the church became part of the United Reformed Church,[38] and it was still used in 1989. A bequest by Ann Harrison for the Congregational minister produced £6 interest on £206 stock in 1901 and 1931.[39]

A barn near Westgate licensed in 1821, a room in 1824, a building in 1833, and a house in 1835[40] may all have been for the Primitive Methodists, who built a chapel in Westgate in 1835.[41] A new chapel, designed by Joseph Wright of Hull, was built in Market Place in 1864,[42] and the old one was later demolished. A schoolroom was built behind the new chapel in 1897.[43] The chapel remained in use after the Methodist union in 1930, but the two Methodist congregations were united in 1981[44] and the Market Place chapel was closed in 1983;[45] it later had various uses and in 1997 was a Pentecostal church.[46]

In the 1880s the Salvation Army held meetings in several places in the town: the public rooms, Newbegin, and the temperance hall, Southgate, were used from 1881 and the former Wesleyan chapel in Back Southgate from 1883 to 1890.[47]

The Christian Scientists met in the former Wesleyan chapel in Back Southgate from 1908[48] until they acquired a meeting room in Cliff Road in 1922.[49] The room was closed in or soon after 1989, sold in 1994, and later converted into a house.[50]

[18] *Cal. S.P. Dom.* 1664–5, 218–19; *Depositions from York Castle* (Sur. Soc. xl), 123, 129 n.

[19] E.R.A.O., PE/30/33, ff. 104v., 175. There were still memorial stones in the garden in 1989.

[20] Bedell, *Acct. of Hornsea* (1848), 78.

[21] E.R.A.O., QSF/13/D.6; H.U.L., DDCV/82/3, rot. 92; DDCV/82/4, pp. 17, 298; *Herring's Visit.* ii, p. 88.

[22] B.I.H.R., V. 1764/Ret. 2, no. 48; *Herring's Visit.* ii, p. 88.

[23] H.U.L., DDCV/82/5, p. 547.

[24] Local inf.

[25] P.R.O., RG 31/5, nos. 255, 466, 510, 790; B.I.H.R., Fac. Bk. 1, p. 411 (1766); ibid. DMH. 205, 242, 519; E.R.A.O., QSF/26/E.2.

[26] R. A. Loten, 'Hist. Hornsea Wesl. Meth.' (copy in Beverley Pub. Libr.); Bedell, *Acct. of Hornsea* (1848), 112.

[27] P.R.O., RG 31/5, nos. 2159, 2923; ibid. HO 129/522/4; B.I.H.R., Fac. Bk. 3, pp. 472, 727; E.R.A.O., DDIV/35/1–2; O.S. Map 6", Yorks. CXCVII (1854 edn.).

[28] O.N.S. (Birkdale), Worship Reg. no. 19702; *Kelly's Dir. N. & E.R. Yorks.* (1872), 378.

[29] Date on bldg.

[30] Loten, op. cit. [31] P.R.O., RG 31/7, nos. 25, 27.

[32] *Herring's Visit.* ii, p. 88.

[33] C. E. Darwent, *Story of Fish St. Ch., Hull* (1899), 128–9.

[34] P.R.O., RG 31/5, nos. 2070–1; ibid. HO 129/522/4; B.I.H.R., Fac. Bk. 3, pp. 439, 475.

[35] Bedell, *Acct. of Hornsea* (1848), 111.

[36] O.N.S. (Birkdale), Worship Reg. no. 21859; *Kelly's Dir. N. & E.R. Yorks.* (1879), 411; *Hull & E.R. Cong. Mag.* vi (65), pp. lxv–lxxi.

[37] Inf. from Dr. J. E. S. Walker, Hornsea, 1997.

[38] United Reformed Ch. *Year Bk.* (1973–4).

[39] E.R.A.O., accession 1681.

[40] P.R.O., RG 31/5, nos. 3732, 3931, 4313, 4366; B.I.H.R., DMH. Reg. 1, pp. 372, 479, 690; DMH. Reg. 2, p. 16.

[41] P.R.O., RG 31/5, no. 4371; ibid. HO 129/522/4; B I.H.R., DMH. Reg. 2, p. 19; O.S. Map 6", Yorks. CXCVII (1854 edn.).

[42] *Prim. Meth. Mag.* xlvi. 695; date on bldg.

[43] *Illus. Guide to Hornsea* (1908), 19; Hobson, *Sketch of Hornsea* (1974 edn.), 130.

[44] *Hull Daily Mail*, 29 Sept. 1981.

[45] O.N.S. (Birkdale), Worship Reg. no. 17278; inf. from Revd. P. D. Wright, Hornsea, 1989.

[46] Inf. from Mr. M. Sewell, Hornsea, 1997.

[47] O.N.S. (Birkdale), Worship Reg. nos. 25880, 25899, 26753; 27047; E.R.A.O., DDIV/35/7, 12. Groups of 'Salvation Soldiers' competed with the Army followers: Sewell, *Joseph Armytage Wade*, 62.

[48] O.N.S. (Birkdale), Worship Reg. no. 43451; E.R.A.O., DDIV/35/15.

[49] O.N.S. (Birkdale), Worship Reg. no. 48389.

[50] Inf. from Dr. J. E. S. Walker, Hornsea, 1997.

Jehovah's Witnesses met in Westgate from 1941 until 1958 and then on Hull Road until 1959.[51]

EDUCATION. Schoolmasters at Hornsea were recorded in 1698, 1743, 1768, and 1800,[52] and in the 19th century there were several private schools in the town.[53] In 1818 there was one public school with 45 pupils, of whom 10 were taught free by virtue of a gift of £10 10s. a year from Richard Bethell.[54] It was described as a Church school in 1823.[55] In 1833 three schools had 82 pupils all told; in addition a Congregational day school, opened in 1819, and a Methodist day school, opened in 1829, had 15 and 12 pupils respectively.[56]

A National school was built in Mereside on land given by the Revd. Charles Constable and opened in 1845.[57] An annual government grant was first received that year.[58] There were 104 pupils at inspection in 1871.[59] A school board for the parish was formed in 1884.[60] The school was enlarged in 1909.[61] Average attendance was usually c. 200 until the 1920s and stood at 260 in 1931–2.[62] It was necessary to use the church institute as additional accommodation in 1924, and in 1930 the school was said to be full.[63] After the county council opened a new school in 1935, the Mereside building was used for infants. Average attendance was 124 in 1937–8.[64] The infants' school was let by the governors to the county council in 1944. Additional temporary accommodation was in use in 1952, and the parish hall was later used as a canteen. The school was closed in 1959 and the pupils transferred to the school in Newbegin.[65]

A Church of England infants' school was built in Westgate in 1848 at the expense of Lady Strickland.[66] A classroom was added in 1896.[67] Average attendance was usually 50–60 until the early 1920s and then rose to c. 70 in 1926–7.[68] The school was overcrowded in 1930 and was closed in 1935.[69] The building, of boulders and rusticated brick, was later used as a dwelling house, known as Mereton in 1989.

A new school was built by the county council in Newbegin and opened in 1935.[70] It accommo-

dated all children of school age, except for infants, who were duly added in 1959.[71] The school was later enlarged but the Congregational schoolroom had nevertheless to be used as additional accommodation in 1955. It was decided that year to transfer the senior pupils to the county secondary school when it was opened.[72] The primary school had 680 pupils on the roll in 1990.[73]

A county secondary school was built on the site of Hornsea House in Eastgate and opened in 1958 with more than 500 pupils; it included an institute of further education. Additional accommodation was provided in 1970 after the raising of the school leaving age, and in 1971 there were c. 800 pupils. Reorganization as a comprehensive school began in 1971 and it was renamed Hornsea School; at the completion of reorganization there were more than 1,000 pupils. Further additions to the buildings were made in the 1970s and 1980s.[74] There were 1,077 pupils on the roll in 1990.[75]

A county nursery school in the grounds of the primary school in Newbegin was opened in 1973.[76] There were 100 pupils on the roll in 1990.[77]

The Hollis Educational Trust was created in 1938 with an income of £70, which was to be used for contributions towards the fees and expenses of Hornsea boys attending Hull grammar school. When the latter ceased to be a fee-paying school, the charity fell into abeyance. There were substantial balances c. 1980, and new educational purposes were then adopted.[78]

CHARITIES. William Day, by will proved in 1616, charged his land at Hornsea Burton with £2 a year to be given to the poor of Hornsea parish at Easter and Christmas; the money was distributed with the town's stock in 1823.[79] The income was still distributed in 1930,[80] but by 1980 the charity had been in abeyance for many years.[81] Robert Smithson (d. 1731) bequeathed 9s. a year charged on land in Hornsea Burton to be distributed to the poor in bread; in 1823 the money was used as directed.[82] Distributions

[51] O.N.S. (Birkdale), Worship Reg. nos. 59884, 66712.
[52] H.U.L., DDCV/82/5, p. 185; E.R.A.O., PE/30/2, p. 41; PE/30/3, p. 46; PE/30/110, f. 178v.
[53] Directories.
[54] Educ. of Poor Digest, 1084.
[55] Baines, Hist. Yorks. ii. 220.
[56] Educ. Enquiry Abstract, 1087.
[57] E.R.A.O., PE/30/29; Hull Advertiser, 23 May 1845; O.S. Map 6", Yorks. CXCVII (1854 edn.).
[58] Mins. of Educ. Cttee. of Council, 1852–3 [1623], p. 160, H.C. (1852–3), lxxix.
[59] Returns relating to Elem. Educ. 472–3.
[60] E.R.A.O., SB/19/1.
[61] Ibid. SL/54/2, p. 233.
[62] Bd. of Educ., List 21 (H.M.S.O., 1908 and later edns.).
[63] E.R. Educ. Cttee. Mins. 1924–5, 155; 1930–1, 149.
[64] Bd. of Educ., List 21.
[65] R.D.B., 673/180/149; 673/182/150; E.R. Educ. Cttee. Mins. 1935–6, 207; 1944–5, 26; 1952–3, 20; 1954–5, 114; 1958–9, 150; 1959–60, 89.
[66] Bedell, Acct. of Hornsea (1848), frontis., 112; Sheahan and Whellan, Hist. York & E.R. ii. 418; O.S. Map 6", Yorks. CXCVII (1854 edn.).

[67] Kelly's Dir. N. & E.R. Yorks. (1901), 500.
[68] Bd. of Educ., List 21 (H.M.S.O., 1908 and later edns.).
[69] E.R. Educ. Cttee. Mins. 1930–1, 149; 1935–6, 207.
[70] R.D.B., 493/660/474; 512/166/127; E.R. Educ. Cttee. Mins. 1935–6, 168.
[71] Above, this section; inf. from the late Mr. R. R. N. Lowe, head teacher 1953–77.
[72] R.D.B., 745/408/337; E.R. Educ. Cttee. Mins. 1952–3, 20; 1953–4, 49, 51, 190; 1955–6, 77, 151.
[73] Inf. from Educ. Dept., Humbs. C.C., 1990.
[74] R.D.B., 967/275/231; E.R. Educ. Cttee. Mins. 1970–1, 143; Hornsea School, 1958–83 (copy in Beverley Pub. Libr.), 5, 7, 12, 14, 16, 19–20, 37.
[75] Inf. from Educ. Dept.
[76] Local inf.
[77] Inf. from Educ. Dept.
[78] Review of Char. Rep. 107.
[79] B.I.H.R., Prob. Reg. 34A, ff. 92v.–93v.; 9th Rep. Com. Char. 763.
[80] E.R.A.O., accession 1681.
[81] Review of Char. Rep. 106.
[82] E.R.A.O., PE/30/2, s.v. 26 Mar. 1731; 9th Rep. Com. Char. 763.

were still made in 1919,[83] but the charity was not mentioned again. Peter Acklam, by will dated 1758, charged his estate in Hornsea, including Low Hall, with £1 a year payable to the overseers to provide gowns for two poor women; in 1823 three women benefited.[84] Clothes or materials were still given in 1955,[85] but it was found c. 1980 that no such grants had been made for 16 years.[86] Young's charity originated in surrenders made in the 1780s: Robert Byass conveyed a cottage in Hornsea for the free occupation of one or more persons in 1780 and David Austin ground to provide rent to repair the cottage and the walls of the ground in 1784.[87] Mary Young (d. 1786) is said to have bought the cottage and ground and to have settled them for those purposes. In 1823 a poor person occupied the cottage and the ground produced 16s. rent for repairs.[88] By a Scheme of 1898 the income of £4 10s. was to be used to provide a pension for a poor person.[89] In 1911 the same income, deriving from £186 stock, was still given to a pensioner,[90] but by 1980 no payments had been made for many years.[91] The town stock, the origin of which is unknown, comprised £70 which several years before 1823 was used to build four cottages for the parish on church land in Newbegin. Interest on the rent was spent in 1823 with Day's charity.[92] Income of £3 from the Church Land estate was still distributed to the poor in 1922;[93] the income was about £2 from £87 stock in 1980, but it had then not been used for some years.[94] Hannah Duke, by will of 1882, gave £2 10s. a year for flour and coal for the poor at Christmas. In 1885 stock was bought with £100 from the bequest.[95] The same income was still distributed to a dozen recipients in 1930,[96] but the charity had by 1980 been inactive for some years. The Lonsdale charity, of unknown origin, and Payne's charity, governed by a trust declaration of 1931, were intended to provide coal for the poor at Christmas. The joint income of £4.50, from £94

and £82 respectively, was administered by a coal club which was being wound up c. 1980.[97]

By a Scheme of 1980 all of those charities except Smithson's were amalgamated as a modern relief in need trust; there were then accumulated balances of over £700.[98] The Hornsea Relief in Need Charity thus established had an income of £100,[99] but it has since remained dormant.[1]

Christopher Pickering, a Hull trawler-owner who bought Hornsea House in 1897,[2] founded six almshouses on the site of the parish poorhouses in Newbegin. The houses were built in 1908 and settled on trustees, together with £2,000, and they were to be occupied by elderly women or married couples who had lived in Hornsea for not less than 10 years.[3] The income of £167 in 1930 included £5 rent from land behind the houses and £72 from £2,400 stock.[4] The land was sold in 1934.[5] In 1988 the income of £2,122 included £1,842 rent from the occupants of the almshouses. In a separate fund £803 interest was received on a legacy of Elsie M. Watson (d. 1957), who provided that, after the death of her husband, a share of the residue of her estate was to be applied for several charitable institutions, among them the Pickering almshouses; Mr. Watson died in 1981.[6]

Joseph H. Stockdale (d. 1904) left the residue of his estate for charitable purposes at the discretion of his executor.[7] Three almshouses were built in Mereside in 1907 and rebuilt as four flats in 1984.[8] The income in 1949 was £29 rent from two houses in Back Southgate; the houses were sold for £297 in 1952, and the income in 1954 was £4 from £100 stock.[9] In 1988–9 the income was £4,179 in maintenance contributions and £195 from investments.[10]

Herbert W. Hart provided for the building of homes in Atwick Road for middle-class business people of straitened means from Hull or the East Riding; the homes were opened in 1958.[11]

LEVEN

THE parish lies 17 km. north of Hull and 11 km. WSW. from the coast at Hornsea,[12] on the east bank of the river Hull, with which Leven village is connected by an early 19th-century canal.[13] The ancient parish comprised the townships of

Leven and Hempholme. Leven township comprised the village, close to the eastern parish boundary, a large area of low-lying ground further west known as Leven carrs, and part of Baswick hamlet, 4 km. north-west of the village;

[83] E.R.A.O., accession 1681.
[84] 9th Rep. Com. Char. 763.
[85] E.R.A.O., accession 1681.
[86] Review of Char. Rep. 106.
[87] H.U.L., DDCV/82/4, pp. 227, 286.
[88] 9th Rep. Com. Char. 764; cf. H.U.L., DDCV/84/4, p. 315.
[89] Review of Char. Rep. 106.
[90] E.R.A.O., PE/30/27–8; ibid. accession 1681.
[91] Review of Char. Rep. 106.
[92] 9th Rep. Com. Char. 763; O.S. Map 1/2,500, Yorks. CXCVII. 3–4 (1891 edn.).
[93] E.R.A.O., accession 1681.
[94] Scheme of 1980 (copy supplied by Mr. A. H. Croft, Hornsea, 1990); Review of Char. Rep. 106; above, church.
[95] E.R.A.O., PE/30/28.
[96] Ibid. accession 1681.
[97] Review of Char. Rep. 106; Scheme of 1980.

[98] Review of Char. Rep. 106; Scheme of 1980.
[99] Humbs. Dir. of Char. 33.
[1] Inf. from Char. Com., Liverpool, 1990.
[2] H.U.L., DSJ/43, p. 4.
[3] R.D.B., 109/409/387; inf. from secy. to the trustees, 1990.   [4] E.R.A.O., accession 1681.
[5] R.D.B., 512/166/127.
[6] E.R.A.O., CCH/16; inf. from secy. to the trustees, 1990.
[7] Inf. from Mrs. T. M. Stockdale, Hull, 1990.
[8] Plaque in almsho.; inf. from Dr. J. E. S. Walker, Hornsea, 1997.
[9] E.R.A.O., accession 1681; R.D.B., 923/259/218; 924/276/237.
[10] Inf. from Char. Com., Liverpool, 1990.
[11] V.C.H. Yorks. E.R. i. 343–4.
[12] This article was written in 1993.
[13] Below, this section.

the rest of Baswick lay in Brandesburton but its history is treated below. Brackenholme, recorded *c.* 1220,[14] was probably another small settlement. Hempholme township comprised, besides the hamlet, 5 km. NNW. of Leven village, the settlements of Hallytreeholme and Heigholme, respectively 5 km. and 2 km. northwest of Leven. Most of Hempholme township was separated from the rest of Leven parish by Brandesburton, Heigholme alone adjoining Leven township. Neither Heigholme nor Hallytreeholme have ever included more than a few farmhouses. The settlement of 'Luvetotholm', recorded in 1086, may have been in Leven, although Long Riston has also been suggested for its location; Thornholme and Nepeholme, mentioned in the 13th century,[15] were perhaps in Hempholme.

Most of the names allude to the proximity of the river Hull. Leven is an Anglian name meaning 'the slow-moving one', and Baswick, 'the farm near which perch are caught', may also be Anglian. Heigholme, Brackenholme, 'the meadow with or near bracken', and Hallytreeholme, 'the meadow with or near a holy tree', are all Anglo-Scandinavian hybrid names, as is Hempholme, meaning 'hemp field'.[16]

In 1851–2 the ancient parish contained 5,061 a. (2,048 ha.), comprising 3,709 a. (1,501 ha.) in Leven township and 1,352 a. (547 ha.) in that of Hempholme.[17] Heigholme, with *c.* 300 a. (121.4 ha.), was transferred from Hempholme in 1885 to Brandesburton civil parish, but in 1895 it was added instead to Leven civil parish.[18] The area of Hempholme was thus reduced to 1,051 a. (425 ha.) by 1891, and from 1911 it was 1,048 a. (424 ha.); in 1935 Hempholme civil parish was united with those of Brandesburton and Moor Town to form the new civil parish of Brandesburton. Leven's area had been reduced to 3,698 a. (1,496.6 ha.) by 1891, before the addition of Heigholme raised it to 4,009 a. (1,622 ha.); the size of the civil parish remained unchanged in 1991.[19]

There were 159 poll-tax payers in Leven in 1377.[20] In 1672 Leven had 49 houses assessed for hearth tax and 17 discharged, and in Hempholme 17 houses were assessed.[21] The parish had 53 families in 1743 and 37 in 1764.[22] The population of Leven township grew in the earlier 19th century, possibly in consequence of the building of the canal; numbers rose from 411 in 1801 to 574 in 1811 and then sharply in the 1830s to stand at 890 in 1841. The population declined in the late 19th century to 659 in 1901, despite the addition of Heigholme. There were later usually *c.* 700 inhabitants until Leven was developed as a dormitory village for Beverley and Hull; from 683 in 1961, the population grew to 1,504 in 1971, 1,717 in 1981, and 2,036 in 1991, 2,002 of whom were present on census day. The population of Hempholme township rose from 57 in 1801 to 93 in 1821 and 117 in 1851 but had dropped to 95 by 1871. Thereafter it rose again, to 120 in 1881 and 123 in 1891, despite the loss of *c.* 30 inhabitants at Heigholme by the boundary alterations of 1885; the increase may reflect the works then being carried out on the river. Later numbers fell, to 104 in 1901, 76 in 1911, and 69 in 1931.[23]

Much of the parish is covered with alluvium and lies at less than 5 m. above sea level.[24] Deposits of sand and gravel form the higher land, which rises to 8 m. above sea level at Woofel hill, north-west of Leven village, and they provided all the settlements of the parish with their sites. Sand and gravel have been extracted near Leven village and at Hempholme.[25] The open fields of Leven lay on the higher ground north and south of the village, the carrs presumably providing most of the village's grazing. At Hempholme the open fields evidently also lay north and south of the hamlet. The commonable lands of Leven township were inclosed in 1796 and those of Hempholme at an unknown date.[26]

The natural drainage of the parish has been much altered by a lengthy process of improvement and by the construction of the canal. Some of the parish drains into the river, through the westward-flowing Mickley dike, probably the Miklene fleet recorded in the 13th century,[27] and Scurf dike, which drains eastwards. Away from the carrs, however, much of the water is carried southwards. A stream flowing through the middle of the parish close to the village and on between Routh and Long Riston has been improved as the Burshill and Barf drain; it may have been that watercourse which Meaux abbey had by 1200 and the maintenance of which was disputed with the lord of Brandesburton in 1351.[28] A parallel stream further west in the carrs, improved as part of the Holderness drain, is connected with the central stream by cross drains, including one forming the southern boundary. The higher ground east of the village is drained by Catchwater drain, which flows between drains running along the northern and southern township boundaries. In 1436 the provost of Beverley claimed that the abbot of Meaux's failure to repair sewers in Leven had caused 800 a. there to flood,[29] and in 1568 land near the river was flooded and three sewers decayed.[30] There was probably little improvement in the drainage before the late 18th century,[31] when the Holderness Drainage Board, formed in 1764, improved the Holderness drain;[32] over 2,300 a. in Leven and *c.* 200 a. in

[14] *Chron. de Melsa* (Rolls Ser.), i. 413.
[15] *Bridlington Chart.* p. 305; *V.C.H. Yorks.* ii. 295; *V.C.H. Yorks. E.R.* v. 3; below, Long Riston, intro.
[16] *P.N. Yorks. E.R.* (E.P.N.S.), 72–3, 258; G. F. Jensen, *Scand. Settlement Names in Yorks.* 91.
[17] O.S. Map 6″, Yorks. CLXXIX, CXCVI (1854–5 edn.).
[18] E.R.A.O., CCO/23.   [19] *Census,* 1891–1991.
[20] P.R.O., E 179/202/60, m. 61.
[21] *Hearth Tax,* 61.
[22] B.I.H.R., V. 1764/Ret. 2, no. 123; *Herring's Visit.* ii, p. 163.

[23] *V.C.H. Yorks.* iii. 495; *Census,* 1911–91.
[24] Geol. Surv. Map 1″, sheets 64, 72 (1909 edn.).
[25] O.S. Map 6″, Yorks. CLXXIX, CXCVI (1854–5 edn.); below, econ. hist.   [26] Below, econ. hist.
[27] *Bridlington Chart.* p. 305.
[28] 'Meaux Cart.' pp. 416–17, 495.
[29] *Monastic Notes* (Y.A.S. Rec. Ser. xvii), 9.
[30] *Cal. Pat.* 1566–9, pp. 400–1.
[31] E.R.A.O., CSR/4/12.
[32] 4 Geo. III, c. 47 (Priv. Act); 6 Geo. III, c. 74 (Priv. Act); *V.C.H. Yorks. E.R.* vi. 278–9.

Hempholme were rated to the Holderness Drainage in 1775 and 1838.[33] The Beverley and Barmston Drainage Act of 1798 brought some further improvement, chiefly by the making of a new drain on the west bank of the river; 609 a. in Leven and Hempholme were assessed to the work of that system by the award of 1811. The efficiency of the Beverley and Barmston Drainage was, however, compromised by the Driffield navigation trustees, who, also c. 1800, built a lock at Hempholme after straightening the river there.[34] Despite more work to the river in the late 19th century and the installation of a pump at Hempholme,[35] regular flooding of the carrs continued until the 1950s, when two reservoirs were made west of the river in Watton parish.[36]

A 3-mile long canal was made between the village and the river Hull at the promotion of Charlotte Bethell between 1801 and 1805.[37] It carried coal, lime, corn, bricks, and tiles until the 1930s, when competition from road transport forced its closure. One of the warehouses at the village end has been converted to a private house and the other partly demolished. The lock at the river end has been sealed, and in 1993 the canal remained disused.

From Leven village roads lead north to Brandesburton and Bridlington, east to Hornsea, and south to Hull and Beverley. The last road divides in the south-east corner of the parish at a place called White Cross after a medieval stone cross, the shaft of which remained there in 1993. The road between White Cross and Beverley was turnpiked in 1761, and the trusts were continued until 1867. The proposal in 1767 to continue the turnpike from White Cross to Bridlington was ineffective.[38] Improvements were made to the Hornsea road between 1796 and 1828,[39] and to that road, the Bridlington road, and the White Cross junction in the mid 20th century.[40] In 1994 a bypass was opened for Leven and Brandesburton. Minor roads lead west from the village to the carrs and then north to Heigholme, Burshill, in Brandesburton, Hallytreeholme, and Hempholme.

LEVEN. By the late 18th century Leven village stood along a single street, now comprising East and West Streets. In 1796 most of the buildings were on the north side of the street, with a few in side lanes, including those which continued as the Bridlington and Beverley roads. A village green, comprising at least 9 a., then lay mostly on the east side of the Burshill and Barf drain.[41] The western extremity of the main street, beyond that drain and reached across a late 18th-century bridge, is called Little Leven. The early site of the village may have lain 1 km. west of Little Leven where Hall Garth, Leven's manor house, stands close to the site of the medieval church of St. Faith's and St. Faith's well,[42] now filled in.

The buildings in Leven are of brick and mostly date from the 19th and 20th centuries. Earlier houses include no. 3 East Street, built c. 1700, and Leadgate and Lamploughs Farms. After inclosure and the construction of the canal, the village began to be developed along the road to Beverley, there called Barley Gate[43] and later South Street. Among the new buildings were Canal House, the New Inn, and a dozen terraced houses. Further south still Leven Rectory, Rectory Farm, and Leven Grange were built on newly-inclosed land between 1796 and 1828.[44] The village continued to grow in the mid and later 19th century when chapels were built on East and West Streets, a school on the part of the Hornsea road called High Stile, and a new church on South Street.[45] In the 1920s three council houses were added on the Heigholme road,[46] and infilling increased sharply in the mid and late 20th century. New buildings included 48 council houses at the east end of the village and two sewage stations built and operated by the district council.[47] In 1993 several private housing estates were being built at the east and west ends of the village.

A police station with a lock-up and courtroom was built on High Stile in 1852,[48] and when the East Riding constabulary was established in 1857 a superintendant was based at Leven.[49] Petty sessions for North Holderness were held there until 1951.[50] In 1976 a police house and office in East Street were built to replace the station,[51] which was soon after sold and later used for a doctor's surgery.

Up to four alehouses were recorded at Leven in the later 18th century,[52] and c. 1825 the Hare and Hounds, the Minerva, and the Blue Bell were joined by the New Inn.[53] The Minerva and the Blue Bell, both in South Street, were last recorded in the mid and late 19th century respectively,[54] but the Hare and Hounds and the New Inn still traded in 1993. A lodge of the Ancient Order of Foresters was founded in 1838 and had 170 members in 1860; it left the order in 1868 to become Bethell's Benefit Society, rejoined in 1912, and was mentioned until 1920.

33 E.R.A.O., DDCC/143/135 (with map); ibid. QDA/12A (map, 1833), 12B, 13 (with map, 1838).

34 E.R.A.O., DCBB/4/2, 8; ibid. DDBD/89/4; 38 Geo. III, c. 63 (Local and Personal); J. A. Sheppard, Draining of Hull Valley (E. Yorks. Loc. Hist. Ser. viii), 16.

35 Sheppard, Draining of Hull Valley. 21.

36 Inf. from Mr. D. Rhimes, Leven, 1993.

37 B. F. Duckham, Inland Waterways of E. Yorks. 1700–1900 (E. Yorks. Loc. Hist. Ser. xxix), 34–6.

38 K. A. Macmahon, Roads and Turnpike Trusts in E. Yorks (E. Yorks. Loc. Hist. Ser. xviii), 26–7, 70.

39 E.R.A.O., IA. (E. 16); ibid. HD/80; H. Teesdale, Map of Yorks. (1828).

40 R.D.B., 1133/214/193; 1388/342/296; 1576/263/217; 1581/262/202; 1611/432/387.

41 Ibid. BT/182/24; E.R.A.O., IA. (E. 16).

42 O.S. Map 6″, Yorks. CXCVI (1855 edn.).

43 Ibid.

44 E.R.A.O., IA. (E. 16); H. Teesdale, Map of Yorks. (1828); below, church.

45 Below, church, nonconf., educ.

46 R.D.B., 232/239/197.

47 Ibid. 614/580/469; 956/29/27; 1082/449/404; 1154/456/420.

48 E.R.A.O., QAP/5/78.

49 A. A. Clarke, Country Coppers: Story of E.R. Police, 18–19.

50 E.R. Standing Joint Cttee. Mins. 1949–53, 187–8; directories.

51 Humbs. Police Cttee. Mins. 1976–7, pp. 4, 8–9.

52 E.R.A.O., QDT/2/9.   53 Ibid. QDT/2/6.

54 Directories.

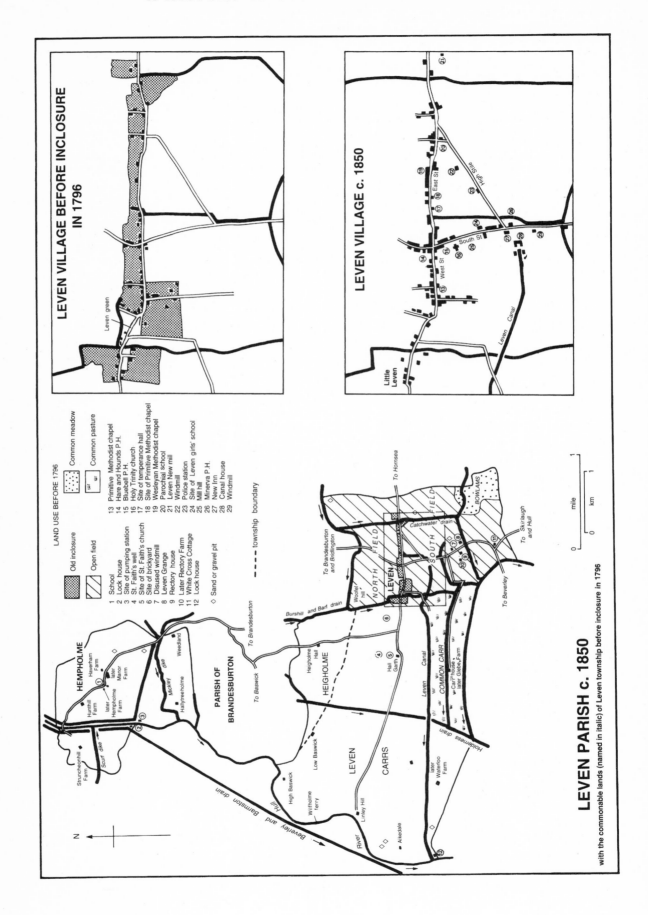

LEVEN VILLAGE BEFORE INCLOSURE IN 1796

LEVEN VILLAGE c. 1850

LAND USE BEFORE 1796

Old inclosure
Common meadow
Open field
Common pasture

1 School
2 Lock house
3 Site of pumping station
4 St. Faith's well
5 Site of St Faith's church
6 Site of brickyard
7 Disused windmill
8 Leven Grange
9 Rectory house
10 Later Rectory Farm
11 White Cross Cottage
12 Lock house
13 Primitive Methodist chapel
14 Hare and Hounds P.H.
15 Bluebell P.H.
16 Holy Trinity church
17 Site of temperance hall
18 Site of Primitive Methodist chapel
19 Wesleyan Methodist chapel
20 Parochial school
21 Leven New mill
22 Windmill
23 Police station
24 Site of Leven girls' school
25 Mill hill
26 Minerva P.H.
27 New Inn
28 Canal house
29 Windmill

◊ Sand or gravel pit
- - - - township boundary

LEVEN PARISH c. 1850

with the commonable lands (named in italic) of Leven township before inclosure in 1796

In 1885 the United Ancient Order of Druids established a lodge, which had 259 members in 1910 and was closed down in 1981. The Order of the Sons of Temperance had a lodge from 1905; it had 71 members when last recorded in 1910. Another friendly society, the Leven Free Gift Society, was founded c. 1860, but no more is known of it.[55] A temperance hall was built in Middle, later East, Street in 1860 and later used as a Wesleyan school[56] and, before the Second World War, for the showing of films and for concerts; it was eventually demolished in the 1960s.[57] A library was run from the Hare and Hounds in the 1850s.[58] An agricultural show is said to have been held at Leven c. 1900.[59] A reading room, north of, and associated with, the church, was run from the early 20th century until c. 1965, when it was demolished.[60] A recreation hall in East Street, opened c. 1920, has been used by the British Legion and the Women's Institute, and from c. 1960 served as a public library; it was renovated c. 1990.[61] A bowling green next to the hall was made c. 1930,[62] and a football club played on land south of High Stile before the Second World War.[63] Leven Playing Field Association provided grounds at the north end of the village c. 1965, and in 1972 built a sports hall there.[64] A youth club on High Stile was opened in 1967, and from 1987 there was a scout and guide hut in West Street.[65] The district council provided allotment gardens at the west end of the village c. 1975.[66]

HEMPHOLME. There were only a dozen scattered buildings, mostly farmhouses, in Hempholme hamlet in the 1850s.[67] A ferry across the Hull from Hempholme to Rotsea, in Hutton Cranswick, was recorded in the 14th century and again in the early 17th.[68] After the change in the river's course c. 1800, one of the farms had to be reached by a swing bridge.[69] A schoolroom, later used as a chapel, was apparently built in 1818,[70] and a pumping station and lock-keeper's house had been added by 1890.[71] There were few other changes until the later 20th century, when two new houses were built.

BASWICK. The settlement of Baswick comprises half a dozen houses. In the mid 19th century it had a landing on the river Hull and a ferry to Wilfholme, in Kilnwick.[72] High Baswick was built before 1772 and later remodelled.[73] The Sloop public house was named in 1823 but had been closed by c. 1890 and was later a private house; it was demolished in 1987.[74]

OTHER OUTLYING BUILDINGS in the parish include Heigholme Hall and the farmhouses of Linley Hill and Hallytreeholme, all existing in 1772 but later remodelled.[75] Evidently built soon after inclosure in 1796 were Glebe Farm[76] and a house at the White Cross junction;[77] the latter has a symmetrical front of three bays, ogee-headed windows, and an embattled parapet.

Hull Aero Club opened a small airfield 3 km. west of Leven village in 1991.[78]

MANORS AND OTHER ESTATES. Edward the Confessor is said to have given *LEVEN* manor to the archbishop of York's church of St. John of Beverley,[79] which in 1086 had the 6-carucate estate.[80] The provost of Beverley was granted free warren in Leven in 1281, and the manor remained with the collegiate church until its suppression in 1548.[81] The manor later descended in the Crown, like Patrington being assigned to trustees for Queen Henrietta Maria (d. 1669) and later Queen Catherine (d. 1705), before being granted in reversion to Hans Willem Bentinck (d. 1709), earl of Portland.[82] Manorial courts were held until 1736 by the lessees, the Micklethwaites and their heir.[83] The manor descended to the earl of Portland's grandson, William Bentinck, duke of Portland, who sold it in 1742 to Hugh Bethell.[84] Bethell bought another estate the same year, called Baswick Hill then but later Low Baswick.[85] At inclosure in 1796 at least 881 a. were copyhold of the manor of Leven.[86] Like Rise, Leven descended in the Bethells,[87] who had c. 2,000 a. in Leven in 1842 and 1910.[88]

[55] D. [R. J.] Neave, *E.R. Friendly Soc.* (E. Yorks. Loc. Hist. Ser. xli), 60; inf. from United Ancient Order of Druids, 1994.

[56] Below, nonconf.

[57] Inf. from Mrs. M. A. Dales, Leven, 1993.

[58] Sheahan and Whellan, *Hist. York & E.R.* ii. 421.

[59] M. and B. Chapman, *Holderness in old picture postcards*, 39.

[60] B.I.H.R., V. 1912–22/Ret.; E.R.A.O., PE/128/74/1.

[61] Inf. from Mr. Rhimes; inf. from librarian, Leven, 1993.

[62] Inf. from Mr. J. Nixon, Leven, 1993.

[63] Inf. from Mr. Rhimes.

[64] R.D.B., 1362/55/47; 1362/56/48; 1630/449/401; 1736/397/330; 1784/137/87.

[65] Inf. from Mrs. S. Etherington, Leven, 1993; inf. from Mrs. J. Richardson, Leven, 1993.

[66] Inf. from Mr. G. Barkworth, Leven, 1993.

[67] O.S. Map 6″, Yorks. CLXXIX (1854 edn.).

[68] P.R.O., LR 2/230, f. 40; *Public Works in Med. Law*, ii (Selden Soc. xl), p. 306.

[69] O.S. Map 6″, Yorks. CLXXIX (1854 edn.); above, this section.

[70] Below, church, educ.

[71] O.S. Map 1/2,500, Yorks. CLXXIX. 14 (1892 edn.);

above, this section.

[72] O.S. Map 6″, Yorks. CXCVI (1855 edn.).

[73] T. Jefferys, *Map of Yorks.* (1772).

[74] O.S. Map 1/2,500, Yorks. CXCVI. 6 (1891 edn.); inf. from Mr. M. Voase, Baswick, 1994.

[75] T. Jefferys, *Map of Yorks.* (1772).

[76] B.I.H.R., TER. H. Leven 1809 etc.

[77] Cf. E.R.A.O., IA.; H. Teesdale, *Map of Yorks.* (1828).

[78] Inf. from Hull Aero Club, Leven, 1992.

[79] Dugdale, *Mon.* ii. 129.

[80] *V.C.H. Yorks.* ii. 216.

[81] *Cal. Chart. R. 1257–1300*, 250; *V.C.H. Yorks. E.R.* vi. 77.

[82] P.R.O., SC 12/37, no. 4; *Cal. S.P. Dom. 1640–1*, 528; 1696, 482; *V.C.H. Yorks. E.R.*, v. 101–2; *Complete Peerage.*

[83] P.R.O., E 317/Yorks./34; H.U.L., DDCV/101/1; Shaftesbury MSS., M 218–19; Poulson, *Holderness*, i. 350; above, Swine, Swine township, manors (Swine).

[84] R.D.B., Q/461/1146; Q/462/1147; *Complete Peerage.*

[85] R.D.B., R/355/810; O.S. Map 6″, Yorks. CXCVI (1855 edn.).

[86] R.D.B., BT/182/24.

[87] J. Foster, *Pedigrees of Yorks.* iii, s.v. Bethell; below, Rise, manor.

[88] B.I.H.R., TA. 80s; E.R.A.O., NV/1/56.

After the death of W. A. V. Bethell in 1941,[89] the estate was sold in several lots. The 535-a. Hall Garth farm was sold in 1949 to Sidney Bays and by him in 1952 to Cecil Taylor (d. 1953).[90] It was thereafter held by Taylor's widow Lilian and son Derek, the owners in 1993.[91] Hall Garth was so named in 1650, when the house was described in detail;[92] it was rebuilt in the mid 18th century and a new wing added in the 19th.

Waterloo farm of 173 a., the 263-a. Aikedale farm, and the 449-a. Linley Hill farm were sold in 1946 to Percy Saul, Thomas Watson, and Albert and Herbert Plaxton respectively.[93] After several changes of ownership,[94] Waterloo farm was bought in 1964 by Charles Pugh,[95] who had purchased Aikedale farm from Thomas Watson in 1963 and who bought Linley Hill from the Plaxtons in 1966.[96] In 1970 the three farms were sold to the Equitable Life Assurance Society,[97] which then bought another part of the former Bethell estate, Low Baswick farm, comprising 494 a.[98] In 1989 Waterloo, Aikedale, and Linley Hill farms were sold to the Electricity Supply Nominees Ltd., the owner in 1993.[99]

Beverley college's estate in Leven included the manor of *HEMPHOLME*, or *HOLME*.[1] In 1309 the demesne tenant was Sir Marmaduke Thwing (d. 1323),[2] from whom the manor evidently descended, like Thwing, in the Thwings and Lumleys to Ralph Lumley (d. 1399 or 1400), Lord Lumley, and John Lumley, Lord Lumley,[3] who sold it in 1577 to Sir Thomas Heneage.[4] Heneage exchanged the manor in 1588 with the Crown,[5] which leased Hempholme in 1661 to Sir Hugh Bethell (d. 1679).[6] In 1866 the Crown sold the estate of *c.* 800 a. to J. S. Harrison (d. 1884), who was succeeded by his son James (d. 1923).[7] The five farms on the estate, later named as Bank, Hempholme, Haverham, Hunthill, and Struncheonhill farms, passed to James's widow Mary (d. 1932) and were sold in 1947.[8] Bank farm, with 65 a. in the parish, was then bought by John Northgraves and sold in 1951 to William and Valerie

Weightman. In 1956, as Manor farm, it was bought by Harold Needler Quarries Ltd. and exchanged with Mark Stamp, who then conveyed it to his son Leonard.[9] In 1969 the farm was bought by Joseph Wright, and the Wrights evidently still had it in 1993.[10] The largest of the other farms sold in 1947, Hunthill farm, comprising 275 a., was bought by Alexander Newton and in 1968 by the Southwell family, the owners in 1993.[11] The 19th-century Manor Farm may have been built on the site of the manor house recorded in 1650.[12]

In the mid 12th century Robert de Scures granted an estate, later variously called the grange or manor of *HEIGHOLME*, to Meaux abbey.[13] In 1187 the abbey recovered the estate from Osbert son of Godfrey and Ranulph of Flinton.[14] The manor was held by the abbey's lessees in the 13th and 14th centuries, and comprised *c.* 200 a. at the Dissolution.[15] It was granted in 1564 to Edward Clinton, later earl of Lincoln, and his son Henry,[16] but later passed to John Ellerker and his son William (d. 1591). William Ellerker was succeeded by his son John (d. 1617), who left a son William.[17] The estate was sold to Arthur Noel in 1636–7[18] and descended to Sir Andrew Noel and George Noel (d. 1701).[19] Called Noel farm, and variously said to comprise 240 a. or 309 a., it was later held in undivided shares by George Noel's three nieces.[20] One third belonged to Dorothy Hunter, whose husband Robert acquired another third in 1738[21] and sold both to Matthew Lister in 1742–3.[22] Lister had already acquired part of the Noel estate, and in 1750 and 1752 he bought the rest.[23] Lister (d. by 1773) was succeeded by James Lister, who in 1780 settled the estate on his son, Richard Humpton Lister.[24] The last named sold the 290-a. estate in 1802 to William Harrison and John Harrison (d. by 1829). John Harrison left his estate to his nephew, John Harrison.[25] He (d. 1872)[26] was succeeded by William Harrison's grandson, William Harrison Preston (d. 1918). Preston's widow Isabel[27] sold

89 R.D.B., 655/563/481.
90 Ibid. 820/536/442; 907/201/166; 954/72/66.
91 Ibid. 1003/154/131; loc. inf.
92 P.R.O., E 317/Yorks./34.
93 R.D.B., 736/50/46; 737/335/272; 738/273/218.
94 Ibid. 771/259/214; 781/555/484; 868/165/149; 1028/143/131.
95 Ibid. 1385/87/83.
96 Ibid. 954/72/66; 1402/376/333; 1479/2/2.
97 Ibid. 1640/161/143.
98 Ibid. 1085/30/30; 1640/156/138.
99 Inf. from the Equitable Life Assurance Soc., 1993.
1   *Beverley Chapter Act Bk.* i (Sur. Soc. xcviii), 239.
2   Ibid.; *Cal. Inq. p.m.* vi, p. 239.
3   *Cal. Pat.* 1553–4, 157–9; *Cal. Inq. p.m.* xviii, pp. 324–5; *V.C.H. Yorks. E.R.* ii. 326; *Complete Peerage.*
4   *Yorks. Fines*, ii. 109.
5   Ibid. iii. 93.
6   *Cal. S.P. Dom.* 1661–2, 70; J. Foster, *Pedigrees of Yorks.* iii, s.v. Bethell.
7   R.D.B., IZ/173/216; 3/231/214 (1885); 17/480/474 (1887); 269/270/228.
8   Ibid. 361/7/5; 763/417/360; 768/570/468; 770/148/127; 770/289/256; 771/349/292; 773/3/2; plaque in Brandesburton church.
9   R.D.B., 770/148/127; 877/361/292; 1036/135/124;

1063/228/209.
10 Ibid. 1631/284/250; *Reg. of Electors* (1993).
11 R.D.B., 771/349/292; 1573/23/16; *Reg. of Electors* (1993).
12 P.R.O., E 317/Yorks./27.
13 *Chron. de Melsa* (Rolls Ser.), i. 96–7.
14 *E.Y.C.* iii, p. 68.
15 *Chron. de Melsa*, ii. 235; iii. 122; Poulson, *Holderness*, i. 354.
16 *Cal. Pat.* 1563–6, 83; *Complete Peerage.*
17 P.R.O., C 142/230, no. 37; C 142/367, no. 12; *Yorks. Fines*, ii. 21.
18 P.R.O., C 5/15/31; C 78/597/6.
19 *Dugdale's Visit. Yorks.* (Sur. Soc. xxxvi), 70; *Reg. Brandesburton* (Yorks. Par. Reg. Soc. cxlii), 136; Poulson, *Holderness*, i. 354–5.
20 R.D.B., K/198/396; K/458/970; M/382/604.
21 Ibid. K/198/396; P/243/632.
22 Ibid. R/170/460; R/278/676.
23 Ibid. M/382/604; O/230/568; U/464/885; W/157/335.
24 Ibid. AU/211/336; BC/591/922; E.R.A.O., QDE/1/5/16.
25 R.D.B., CE/259/402; EI/96/94.
26 Ibid. EI/96/94; LG/277/263; B.I.H.R., TA. 649M; E.R.A.O., PE/128/1.
27 R.D.B., 199/459/407; Bulmer, *Dir. E. Yorks.* (1892), 451.

it, as Home farm, to the Lickiss sisters, from whom John Wood bought it in 1950.[28] The estate was sold in 1978 to J. Thompson and c. 1980 to R. P. Wreathall, whose son T. F. Wreathall was the owner in 1993.[29]

The manor house at Heigholme occupied a moated site. Sir Andrew Noel may have rebuilt the house, but in the mid 19th century the Harrisons demolished it and built Heigholme Hall east of the moat,[30] which survived in 1993. North of Heigholme Hall stands the converted coach house of the former house; built c. 1800, the two-storeyed building has a symmetrical front of three bays, with a central pediment and cupola.[31]

Bridlington priory had been granted an estate at *HALLYTREEHOLME* by the early 13th century, when John of Octon confirmed and enlarged the gift, which included land in Hempholme, Brackenholme, Thornholme, Nepeholme, and Weedland marsh.[32] The priory was granted free warren at Hallytreeholme in 1290 and retained the estate, called a manor in 1523,[33] until the Dissolution. The manor was leased to the Bethell family, it is said by Elizabeth I for 999 years,[34] and Richard Bethell held 168 a. at Hallytreeholme in 1842.[35] The trustees of W. A. V. Bethell (d. 1941) sold the lease in 1943 to Fred Northgraves.[36] It was bought by Nellie Perry in 1949 and in 1968 by Alan and John Aconley, and the Aconleys still farmed the estate in 1993.[37]

Anne Routh (d. by 1722) devised her 41 a. at Baswick to Beverley corporation for an almshouse charity in that town.[38] As High Baswick farm, it was sold in 1918 to John Salvidge and in 1937 first to Henry Mitchell and later to Walter Clayton (d. 1951).[39] Clayton's family conveyed the farm in 1953 to Mary Fewson, who sold it in 1962 to Kenneth Voase.[40] In 1971 he sold it to the West Hartlepool Steam Navigation Co. Ltd., the owners in 1993.[41]

ECONOMIC HISTORY. AGRICULTURE BEFORE 1800. *Leven.* In 1086 the church of Beverley's estate at Leven included four ploughlands; one plough was then worked on the demesne and three others by 15 villeins and a bordar.[42] The tillage of Leven lay on either side of the village in North and South fields, which

were named in 1608. The open fields included commonable meadow and pasture land,[43] but most of the rough grazing was probably in the carrs. Land named Bowlams in the south-east corner of the parish was also used as common meadow; it evidently adjoined meadows in Far Bowlams, one of Catwick's open fields.[44]

The commonable lands of Leven were inclosed by award of 1796 under an Act of 1791.[45] Allotments totalled 1,478 a., 597 a. freehold and 881 a. copyhold. North field then included 410 a., the common carr 383 a., South field more than 278 a., and Bowlams at least 61 a. The rector received 433 a., John Bowman 167 a., and Peter Nevill 124 a.; there were also one allotment of 67 a., twenty-two of 11–49 a., and thirteen of less than 10 a.

Hempholme, Heigholme, and *Hallytreeholme.* At Hempholme, too, the settlement was flanked by North and South fields, named from 1608. Common meadow and pasture lay in the open fields in the 17th century, when common meadow was also found in Ings.[46] Hempholme, Heigholme, and Hallytreeholme were evidently all inclosed early, the last two presumably by Meaux abbey and Bridlington priory respectively.

AGRICULTURE AFTER 1800. In 1842 there were 1,658 a. of arable land and 353 a. of grassland in Leven township,[47] and 970 a. and 300 a. respectively in Hempholme township.[48] Leven parish included 2,794 a. of arable land and 695 a. of grassland in 1905.[49] The proportion of arable to grassland was much the same in the 1930s, when most of the grassland was around the settlements and outlying farms.[50] In Leven civil parish 1,105 ha. (2,730 a.) were returned as arable land and 104 ha. (257 a.) as grassland in 1987.[51] There had also been 32 a. of woodland in 1905, but in the mid 20th century many trees were cut down around Heigholme Hall and by 1987 only 3 ha. (7 a.) of woodland survived, in small plantations.[52]

In the 19th and earlier 20th century there were up to two dozen farmers in Leven and half a dozen in Hempholme, where in 1851 four of the farms were of 150 a. or more. In the 1920s and 1930s there were two larger farms at Hempholme, and one or two at Leven. A cowkeeper and one or two market gardeners were recorded in the late 19th and early 20th century.[53] In 1987

[28] R.D.B., 199/459/407; 280/458/396; 867/27/26.
[29] Inf. from Mr. T. F. Wreathall, Leven, 1993.
[30] Poulson, *Holderness*, i. 355.
[31] Department of Environment, *Buildings List* (1987); Pevsner and Neave, *Yorks. E.R.* 597.
[32] *Bridlington Chart.* p. 305; *Yorks. Deeds*, i. 77.
[33] *Cal. Chart. R.* 1257–1300, 358; *Miscellanea*, iii (Y.A.S. Rec. Ser. lxxx), 16.
[34] Poulson, *Holderness*, i. 357.
[35] B.I.H.R. TA. 649M.
[36] R.D.B., 659/185/156; above, this section.
[37] R.D.B., 814/139/118; 1549/124/104; *Reg. of Electors* (1993).
[38] *V.C.H. Yorks. E.R.* vi. 269.
[39] R.D.B., 189/142/131; 570/83/58; 579/595/478; 895/538/452.
[40] Ibid. 937/567/496; 1258/59/56.

[41] Ibid. 1755/468/378; inf. from the West Hartlepool Steam Navigation Co. Ltd., Hartlepool, 1993.
[42] *V.C.H. Yorks.* ii. 216.
[43] P.R.O., LR 2/230, ff. 83–105.
[44] B.I.H.R., TER. H. Leven 1693 etc.; above, Catwick, econ. hist.
[45] 31 Geo. III, c. 56 (Priv. Act); E.R.A.O., IA. (E 16) (plan); R.D.B., BT/182/24 (award).
[46] P.R.O., LR 2/230, ff. 33–40.
[47] B.I.H.R., TA. 80s.
[48] Ibid. TA. 649M.
[49] Acreage Returns, 1905.
[50] [1st] Land Util. Surv. Map, Sheet 28.
[51] Inf. from Min. of Agric., Fish. & Food, Beverley, 1990.
[52] Acreage Returns, 1905; inf. from Min. of Agric., Fish. & Food; inf. from Mr. Rhimes.
[53] P.R.O., HO 107/2359, 2365; directories.

of 18 holdings returned under Leven civil parish, one was of 500–699 ha. (1,236–1,727 a.), one of 200–299 ha. (494–739 a.), one of 100–199 ha. (247–492 a.), two of 50–99 ha. (124–245 a.), and thirteen of less than 50 ha.; more than 27,000 fowls and 2,000 pigs were then kept in the parish.[54]

FISHING AND FOWLING. The river and carrs in Leven and Hempholme were valued for their reeds and for the fishing and fowling which they provided. In the 12th century Meaux abbey was given fisheries in the river Hull near Heigholme, and c. 1200 Bridlington priory had three river fisheries at Hallytreeholme named Hermeregard, Prestegote, and Micclene.[55] Another fishery in the river at 'Berswyk', recorded in 1364, was presumably at Baswick.[56] Several fisheries remained at Hempholme in the 17th century, and in 1650 the fishing and fowling of Leven manor were valued at £5 a year. Duck decoys made in the carrs[57] included the Coy belonging to Leven manor in 1659.[58] The management of swans on the river was controlled by Hempholme manor court, which was held until at least the 1930s; a list of pains laid in the court in 1708 survives.[59]

MARKET AND FAIR. In 1270 the provost of Beverley was granted a weekly market on his manor of Leven and an annual fair on the eve, feast, and morrow of St. Simon and St. Jude (27–9 October).[60] The grant is elsewhere said to have been of a fair on the eve, feast, and morrow of St. Faith (5–7 October),[61] and those were the days confirmed in the 15th century, when the market day was given as Tuesday.[62] Neither the fair nor the market survived in the late 18th century.[63]

TRADE AND INDUSTRY. Two brewers and maltsters worked at Leven in the early 19th century, and Jane Turnbull brewed behind the New Inn from the 1870s until c. 1920.[64] Merchants dealing in coal and coke, lime and manure, seeds, corn, and flour traded at Leven in the late 19th and early 20th century, presumably from premises at or near the canal.[65] Bricks were made at the west end of the village prior to 1842,[66] and before the mid 20th century sand and gravel had been dug from small pits in the

parish.[67] Larger-scale extraction, begun in the 1940s,[68] had ended by 1993, when several pits, most of them water-filled, remained. Small businesses operating in the village then included a motor engineering firm.

MILLS. In 1172 Meaux abbey had a mill at Heigholme.[69] A windmill recorded at Leven in 1608 possibly stood south of the village on Mill hill.[70] By the later 18th century a windmill occupied another site, also in South field,[71] but that mill was apparently abandoned between 1842 and 1852.[72] Evidently shortly before the making of the canal, another windmill was built on the west side of the Beverley road, close to the intended head of the navigation; it was apparently grinding in 1800, was later assisted by steam, and was closed c. 1890.[73] A windmill north of High Stile is said to have been put up in 1807; also powered partly by steam by the late 19th century, it was used until the early 20th century and demolished in 1919.[74] Leven New mill was built on the Hornsea road, it is said in 1847; later a wind and steam mill, it ceased to operate c. 1900.[75] In 1993 only the stump of Leven New mill remained.

LOCAL GOVERNMENT. Court rolls for Leven manor survive for 1416–17,[76] 1650–60,[77] and 1708–1940. The court, which had view of frankpledge, usually met twice a year from the 17th century; regularly appointed officers included 1–2 penny-graves, 1–2 carr-graves, 2 affeerors, 2 constables, 4 bylawmen, and a pinder. Also mentioned in the mid 17th century were 2 aletasters and a bailiff.[78] Courts were also held for the Rectory manor, for which rolls survive for 1725–1931, and for Hempholme manor.[79]

Permanent out-relief was given in 1802–3 to 10 people at Leven and in 1812–15 to c. 20; 4 people in the earlier year and 12–20 in 1812–15 were aided occasionally. At Hempholme 3 residents received permanent relief in the early 19th century, and 2–3 were helped occasionally in 1812–15.[80] Leven township, later civil parish, joined Beverley poor-law union in 1836[81] and remained in Beverley rural district until 1974, when it was taken into the Beverley district of Humberside at reorganization.[82] Hempholme

54 Inf. from Min. of Agric., Fish. & Food.
55 'Meaux Cart.' pp. 13–15; Yorks. Deeds, i. p. 77.
56 Yorks. Fines, 1347–77, p. 103.
57 P.R.O., C 66/2969, m. 13; ibid. E 317/Yorks./34; Sheppard, Draining of Hull Valley, 12.
58 Abstracts of Yorks. Wills (Selden Soc. ix), p. 163.
59 E.R.A.O., DDX/434; Poulson, Holderness, i. 355–6; directories.
60 Cal. Chart. R. 1257–1300, 156.
61 Poulson, Holderness, i. 349.
62 Cal. Chart. R. 1341–1417, pp. 457–8.
63 1st Rep. Royal Com. Mkt. Rights and Tolls, Vol. i [C. 5550], p. 219, H.C. (1888), liii.
64 O.S. Map 1/2,500, Yorks. CXCVI. 15 (1891 edn.); directories.
65 Directories.
66 B.I.H.R., TA. 80s.
67 H.U.L., DDFA(5)/13/434; O.S. Map 6", Yorks. CLXXIX, CXCVI (1854–5 edn.)
68 R.D.B., 625/104/78.
69 'Meaux Cart.' pp. 13–15.
70 P.R.O., LR 2/230, f. 88; H.U.L., DSJ/50, p. 86; O.S. Map 6", Yorks. CXCVI (1855 edn.).
71 E.R.A.O., IA.; T. Jefferys, Map of Yorks. (1772).
72 E.R.A.O., PE/128/25; O.S. Map 6", Yorks. CXCVI (1855 edn.).
73 E.R.A.O., PE/128/25; ibid. QDP/51; O.S. Map 1/2,500, Yorks. CXCVI. 15 (1891 edn.); directories.
74 E.R.A.O., PE/128/25; O.S. Map 1/2,500, Yorks. CXCVI. 15 (1891 edn.); directories; R. Gregory, E. Yorks. Windmills, 47.
75 Gregory, op. cit. 131; O.S. Map 6", Yorks. CXCVI (1855 edn.); directories.
76 B.L. Lansd. Ch. 402–3.
77 Shaftesbury MSS., M 218.
78 Ibid. M 219; H.U.L., DDCV/101/1; ibid. DSJ/50-7.
79 Ibid. DDCV/102/1; above, econ. hist.
80 Poor Law Abstract, 1804, pp. 598–9; 1818, pp. 522–3.
81 3rd Rep. Poor Law Com. 167.
82 Census.

joined Skirlaugh union in 1837[83] and was in Skirlaugh rural district until 1935, when, as part of the enlarged civil parish of Brandesburton, it was included in the new Holderness rural district. It was taken into the Holderness district of Humberside in 1974.[84] In 1996 Leven and Brandesburton civil parishes became part of a new East Riding unitary area.[85]

CHURCH. Leven church was recorded as part of the estate of St. John's church, Beverley, in 1086,[86] and the collegiate church retained the patronage of Leven until its suppression in the 16th century, after which the Crown or its lessees presented.[87] The advowson had evidently been sold by 1650, when Rowland Eyre was named as patron, and in 1667 Rowland and Anthony Eyre sold it to Michael Warton, who presented in 1669.[88] Thereafter it descended, like Beverley Water Towns manor, in the Wartons and Pennymans. The trustees of Sir James Pennyman, Bt. (d. 1808), sold the advowson in 1813 to Thomas Hull and Samuel Hall,[89] who resold it in 1815 to George Sampson, instituted that year as rector.[90] Sampson sold the patronage in 1838 to George Wray, who presented himself the next year.[91] The advowson was bought from Wray in 1863 by John Leather (d. 1885)[92] and from the trustees of Frederick Leather (d. 1890) in 1908 by Archibald Watts.[93] In 1912 Harold Staveley (d. 1928) and his wife Marion (d. 1945) bought the patronage, and their son Claude was presented as rector in 1933.[94] In 1956 Leven rectory was united with that of Catwick, and the patrons of Leven were given the right of alternate presentation to the united benefice.[95] The following year the Revd. Claude Staveley and his sister transferred the patronage, which had descended to them, to the Simeon trustees,[96] the alternate patrons in 1993. In or soon after 1982 the ecclesiastical parish of Leven was reduced by the transfer of Hempholme to that of Brandesburton.[97] Leven with Catwick was in turn united with the benefice of Brandesburton in 1997.[98]

The rectory was worth £13 6s. 8d. in 1291, after payment of a small pension to the provost of Beverley, and £16 13s. 1½d. net in 1535.[99] The improved annual value was £75 3s. net in

1650.[1] The net annual income averaged £1,190 between 1829 and 1831, and it was £1,050 in 1883.[2] Tithes were worth more than £14 gross in 1535 and almost £66 in 1650. In 1796 at the inclosure of Leven the rector received 233 a. for the tithes of the commonable lands and tithe rents amounting to £1 16s. 6¾d. for those of certain old inclosures.[3] The tithes of the rest of Leven township, comprising Hall Garth, Baswick, and the carr farms, were compounded for £15 16s. in 1764, paid in kind in 1817, and commuted in 1842 for a rent charge of £480.[4] In Hempholme township the tithes of Hallytreeholme and Weedland were paid in 1693 by compositions amounting to 13s. 4d., and 6s. 4d. more was owed for fish tithes. The former estate of Meaux abbey at Heigholme was tithe-free when occupied by the proprietor but tithable when tenanted. In 1764 the tithes of both Hempholme and Heigholme were paid by a composition of £20 13s., but by 1817 those of Heigholme were taken in kind. In 1842 the tithes of Hempholme township, comprising Hempholme, Hallytreeholme, Weedland, and Heigholme, were commuted for a rent charge of £252, almost £80 of which was payable for Heigholme when tenanted.[5]

The glebe was valued at £7 13s. a year gross in 1535, when it included 4 bovates, and at £16 gross in 1650.[6] An allotment of 200 a. was made for glebe land inclosed in 1796, and that and the 233 a. then allotted for tithes were later occupied as three farms.[7] A little land was sold in 1959,[8] the 161-a. Leven Grange farm in 1962, and in 1963 the 85-a. Rectory farm and 139-a. Carr House, or Glebe, farm.[9] The glebe also included a small manor, comprising 2 houses and 3 garths, from which the rector received yearly rents of 10s. 4d. from copyholders in 1849.[10] One of the garths was enfranchised in 1912, and a house was sold in 1931.[11]

A rectory house, recorded from 1535, stood west of the village, near the church.[12] In 1575 the rector lived in the village and the outlying house was occupied by a tenant.[13] The rectory house was demolished in 1817, shortly after a glebe farmhouse south of the village had been substituted for it; at the same time a new farmhouse, later Rectory Farm, was built nearby.[14] The replacement rectory house was enlarged

[83] 3rd Rep. Poor Law Com. 170.

[84] Census.

[85] Humberside (Structural Change) Order 1995, copy at E.R.A.O.

[86] V.C.H. Yorks. ii. 216; above, manors.

[87] Lawrance, 'Clergy List', Holderness, i, pp. 83–5.

[88] H.U.L., DDCB/4/94; T.E.R.A.S. iv. 61; Poulson, Holderness, i. 351.

[89] R.D.B., CX/507/649; V.C.H. Yorks. E.R. vi. 210.

[90] R.D.B., DB/587/816; plaque in church.

[91] R.D.B., FF/156/190; Poulson, Holderness, i. 351.

[92] R.D.B., IN/50/69; 107/347/322.

[93] Ibid. 107/348/323; 107/394/364; 108/107/97.

[94] Ibid. 148/55/51; 373/232/193; 808/9/8; inf. from Mrs. V. Jones, Leven, 1993; plaque in church.

[95] B.I.H.R., OC. 736.

[96] Ibid. BA. TP. 1955/2, 1957/2; R.D.B., 808/9/8; 899/179/143.

[97] E.R.A.O., PE/128/T. 93.

[98] Inf. from the rector, Leven, 1997.

[99] Tax. Eccl. (Rec. Com.), 302; Valor Eccl. (Rec. Com.),

v. 118.

[1] T.E.R.A.S. iv. 61.

[2] B.I.H.R., V. 1884/Ret. 2; Rep. Com. Eccl. Revenues, 950–1.

[3] R.D.B., BT/182/24.

[4] B.I.H.R., TA. 80s; rest of para. based on B.I.H.R. TER. H. Leven 1693 etc.

[5] Ibid. TA. 649M.

[6] Valor Eccl. (Rec. Com.), v. 118; T.E.R.A.S. iv. 61.

[7] B.I.H.R., TER. H. Leven 1849 etc.; R.D.B., BT/182/24.

[8] R.D.B., 1154/456/420; 1156/409/371; 1157/396/366.

[9] Ibid. 1270/308/279; 1293/9/8; 1293/168/154.

[10] B.I.H.R., TER. H. Leven 1744 etc.; Poulson, Holderness i. 353.

[11] R.D.B., 145/252/226; H.U.L., DDCV/102/1.

[12] B.I.H.R., TER. H. Leven 1663 etc.; Valor Eccl. (Rec. Com.), v. 118.

[13] Abp. Grindal's Visit., 1575, ed. W. J. Sheils, 74.

[14] B.I.H.R., Fac. 1816/4; ibid. TER. H. Leven 1849; O.S. Map 1/2,500, Yorks. CXCVI. 2 (1891 edn.).

FIG. 22. LEVEN CHURCH, DEMOLISHED IN THE 19TH CENTURY

soon afterwards and again in the late 19th and early 20th century.[15] Its principal fronts, facing south and west, are in early 19th-century grey brick but the rest of the house is of red brick. It was sold in 1959,[16] and, as Leven House, was an old people's home in 1993. A new rectory was built adjoining Leven House and used until 1985, when it in turn was sold and replaced by a house bought in West Street.[17]

In the mid 18th century the rector lived on his other cure at Cherry Burton, and his service at Leven was performed by a curate. There was then a Sunday service at Leven and quarterly celebrations of communion with *c*. 30 recipients.[18] Two Sunday services were held in the mid and late 19th century, when at monthly celebrations of communion up to 25 received.[19] An assistant curate was employed in the 1870s by the aged incumbent.[20]

The medieval church stood 2 km. from the middle of the present village. It was dedicated in 1538 to *ST. ZITA* (Scytha), a saint popularly associated with rivers and bridges,[21] but *ST. FAITH* seems to have been an alternative dedicatee. Her feast day was chosen for the medieval fair and in 1567 St. Faith's church was recorded.[22] The church was of brick and boulders and comprised chancel, nave with south aisle, porch, and vestry, and west tower.[23] The building was in disrepair in the 16th and 17th centuries, and in 1720 its chancel screen was removed.[24] The distance from the village was noted as an inconvenience in 1743,[25] and in 1844 most of the decayed church was demolished. The chancel was left and used for burial services until the churchyard was closed in 1876; it was pulled down in 1883.[26]

The new church of *HOLY TRINITY* was built in 1843–4 on land in the centre of the village given by Richard Bethell, largely at the expense of George Wray, rector; it was consecrated in 1845.[27] Designed by Robert Chantrell of Leeds[28] in a 13th-century style, the building is of ashlar and comprises chancel, nave with north transept and south aisle and porch, and west vestry and tower.

The new church contains part of a 9th-century cross shaft,[29] a late 13th-century font,[30] and the head of a 15th-century cross from St. Faith's churchyard.[31] There were two bells in 1552, but only one by the early 19th century; a new peal of four bells was given to Holy Trinity in 1845,[32] when new plate was also given by the rector's family.[33] The registers of baptisms, marriages, and burials date from 1653 and are complete, except for marriages between 1673–5.[34] A churchyard for Holy Trinity was consecrated in 1868.[35]

By the early 13th century Bridlington priory had provided a chapel at Hallytreeholme, dedicated to St. Nicholas.[36] In 1871 an unlicensed

[15] B.I.H.R., TER. H. Leven 1825; ibid. MGA. 1937/3; plans in possession of Mrs. B. Etherington, Leven, 1993.
[16] R.D.B., 1156/409/371.
[17] Inf. from the rector, Leven, 1993.
[18] B.I.H.R., V. 1764/Ret. 2, no. 123; *Herring's Visit*. ii, p. 163.
[19] B.I.H.R., V. 1865/Ret. 2, no. 327; V. 1868/Ret. 2, no. 292; V. 1871/Ret. 1, no. 295; V. 1884/Ret. 2.
[20] Ibid. V. 1871/Ret. 1, no. 295; V. 1877/Ret. 2, no. 107.
[21] B.I.H.R., Prob. Beverley Reg., f. 1v.; D. H. Farmer, *Oxford Dict. of Saints*, 418–9; O.S. Map 6″, Yorks. CXCVI (1855 edn.).
[22] B.I.H.R., Prob. Reg. 17, f. 701v.; above, econ. hist.
[23] B.I.H.R., Fac. 1843/3; illus. in Poulson, *Holderness*, i, pl. facing p. 294.
[24] B.I.H.R., V. 1575/CB. 2, f. 154; V. 1582/CB. 1, f. 207;

ER. V./CB. 3, f. 139v.; ER. V. Ret. 1, ff. 28, 30.
[25] *Herring's Visit*. ii, p. 163.
[26] B.I.H.R., Fac. 1843/3; ibid. Fac. Bk. 6, p. 463; *Lond. Gaz*. 29 Oct. 1876, p. 4119.
[27] B.I.H.R., CD. 205, 378; ibid. Ch. Ret. ii.
[28] Ibid. Fac. 1843/3.
[29] J. Lang, *Corpus of Anglo-Saxon Sculpture*, iii, 174, illus.
[30] Illus. in Poulson, *Holderness*, i. 353.
[31] Plaque in church; illus. in Poulson, *Holderness*, i, pl. facing p. 400.
[32] B.I.H.R., TER. H. Leven 1809 etc.; *Inventories of Ch. Goods*, 42; G. R. Park, *Ch. Bells of Holderness*, 62.
[33] *Yorks. Ch. Plate*, i. 285.
[34] E.R.A.O., PE/128/1–11.
[35] B.I.H.R., CD. 378.
[36] *Bridlington Chart*. p. 306; above, manors.

FIG. 23. LEVEN: CAPITAL OF 15TH-CENTURY CROSS FROM ST. FAITH'S CHURCHYARD

schoolroom at Hempholme was used for evening services in summer; it ceased to be used for services in 1962 and was derelict in 1993.[37]

NONCONFORMITY. A few non-communicants and recusants were recorded in the parish in the 16th and 17th centuries.[38]

Unidentified congregations of protestant dissenters registered houses at Leven in 1790, 1795, 1808, 1809, and 1811.[39] The 1809 registration was perhaps by Independents, who were said to have provided themselves with a chapel that year, with encouragement from Fish Street chapel, Hull.[40] The chapel was mentioned again in 1840[41] but no more is known of it. The Primitive Methodist chapel, in West Street, was built in 1836.[42] It was replaced in 1877 by a new building in East Street,[43] later the Methodist church, which was largely rebuilt on the same site in 1967 and was still used in 1993. The former Primitive Methodist chapel was a private house in 1993. The Wesleyan Methodists had

licensed a house at Leven in 1810, and in 1816 they built a chapel in East Street,[44] which was enlarged in 1835 and restored in 1889.[45] The Wesleyans also ran a Sunday school in the temperance hall, East Street, in the early 20th century.[46] After Methodist union, the redundant Wesleyan chapel was sold in 1959.[47]

EDUCATION. LEVEN. A school at Leven had its site enlarged by Marmaduke Constable in 1812; it was presumably that later shown between High Stile and East Street.[48] In 1833 it was attended by 56 boys and girls, all taught at their parents' expense.[49] In 1866 the girls were removed to a new school.[50] The continuing boys' school, supported by subscriptions and run according to the National plan,[51] was attended by 42 at inspection in 1871.[52] The school was rebuilt on an adjacent site in 1873 and reopened in 1874.[53] A new Church school for girls was built in 1866 in South Street at the expense of the rector and his sister Harriet Wray, who

37 B.I.H.R., LDS. 1962/6.
38 *Depositions from York Castle* (Sur. Soc. xl), 123; J. S. Purvis, *Tudor Par. Doc. of Dioc. York*, 58.
39 P.R.O., RG 31/5, nos. 802, 1064, 2137, 2315, 2503.
40 C. E. Darwent, *Story of Fish St. Ch., Hull* (1899), 129.
41 Poulson, *Holderness*, i. 353–4.
42 P.R.O., HO 129/518/6; O.S. Map 6″, Yorks. CXCVI (1855 edn.).
43 Bulmer, *Dir. E. Yorks.* (1892), 451; O.S. Map 1/2,500, Yorks. CXCVI. 15 (1891 edn.).
44 P.R.O., RG 31/5, no. 2388; ibid. HO 129/518/5.

45 Bulmer, *Dir. E. Yorks.* (1892), 450.
46 *Hull Times*, 5 July 1913; above, intro.
47 R.D.B., 1144/410/369.
48 H.U.L., DSJ/52, pp. 119–20; *Educ. of Poor Digest*, 1086; N. Wright, *John Day, a Village Poet*; O.S. Map 6″, Yorks. CXCVI (1855 edn.).
49 *Educ. Enq. Abstract*, 1091.
50 Below, this section.
51 P.R.O., ED 7/135, no. 104.
52 *Returns relating to Elem. Educ.* 468–9.
53 E.R.A.O., SL/76/1; O.S. Map 1/2,500, Yorks. CXCVI. 15 (1891 edn.).

endowed it with 2 a. of land.[54] An infants' room was added in 1896.[55] That school, also run on National lines, was supported by school pence and from 1867 by an annual government grant.[56] At inspection in 1871 there were 41 in attendance.[57] In 1906–7 average attendance there was 47 and at the boys' school 54.[58] In or soon after 1910 the girls' and infants' school was further enlarged and the boys transferred to it.[59] The former boys' school was sold in 1911,[60] and in 1993 was a café. From 145 in 1913–14, average attendance at the mixed school fell to 119 in 1918–19 and 83 in 1937–8.[61] Children from Catwick were transferred to Leven in 1949,[62] and in the early 1950s another classroom was added for infants and temporary accommodation had to be provided in the recreation hall.[63] Senior pupils were removed to Hornsea County Secondary School in 1958.[64] The school was again remodelled and enlarged in 1966,[65] and in 1990 there were 183 on the roll.[66]

By Scheme of 1911 the land given by Harriet Wray was vested in trustees and the income dedicated to the maintenance of the school building. The land was sold c. 1975, and by a Scheme of 1977 the charity became the Wray Educational Trust, which could make grants for

higher education and in support of the Sunday school, the playing fields, or a nursery. In 1993–4 the annual income was £5,196.[67] The Philip Theasby Memorial Fund was set up in 1980, in memory of a former headmaster, to provide school prizes, but in 1993 the income of £45 was used instead to buy books.[68]

A British school was recorded in 1866 and again in 1871.[69] It was perhaps that school which 24 boys attended at inspection in 1871.[70]

HEMPHOLME. A room was built at Hempholme, apparently in 1818, for a school, which was supported by subscription; it had evidently been closed by 1833.[71] On inspection day in 1871 Hempholme children attended North Frodingham school, and the former schoolroom was then and later used for church services.[72] The schoolroom was evidently being used again in 1889, when a National school at Hempholme had an average attendance of 14.[73] No more is heard of the school, and by the 1930s Hempholme children went to Brandesburton.[74]

CHARITY FOR THE POOR. One Wilkinson of Hull (d. by 1764) left £1 a year, but payment was refused and the charity was lost.[75]

MAPPLETON

THE village of Mappleton stands beside the North Sea protected by recently erected defences, 19 km. north-east of Hull and 4 km. south-east of the resort of Hornsea.[76] To the south the parish includes the scattered settlements of Great and Little Cowden and nearly 2 km. north-west the hamlet of Rolston. Little Cowden was formerly a separate parish, but its church had been lost to the sea by the 17th century and the parish was later associated with that of Aldbrough; since the 19th century, however, Little Cowden has been linked for civil purposes with Great Cowden, mostly in Mappleton parish,[77] and its history is thus treated below. Mappleton parish also included detached areas in Great Hatfield and Withernwick, respectively 3 km. west and 4 km. south-west of the village; most of Great Hatfield was in Sigglesthorne parish and the rest of Withernwick in Withernwick parish, and the history of the detached

parts is dealt with under those parishes. The names Mappleton, meaning 'farm by a maple tree', and Cowden, or Colden, probably signifying 'charcoal hill', are Anglian, while Rolston, 'Rolf's farmstead', is an Anglo-Scandinavian hybrid. The prefixes Great and Little were used from the 13th century to distinguish the neighbouring Cowdens, which have also been called North and South Cowden respectively.[78]

In 1852 the ancient parish of Mappleton contained 3,455 a. (1,398 ha.), of which 1,186 a. (480 ha.) were in Mappleton township, 851 a. (344 ha.) in Great Cowden, 767 a. (310 ha.) in Rolston, 518 a. (210 ha.) in Great Hatfield, and 131 a. (53 ha.) in Withernwick. The ecclesiastical parish of Colden Parva contained 728 a. (295 ha.) in 1852, comprising all 500 a. (202 ha.) of Little Cowden and the remaining 228 a. (92 ha.) of Great Cowden hamlet; for civil purposes Little Cowden and all 1,079 a. (437 ha.) of Great

54 Bulmer, Dir. E. Yorks. (1892), 450; O.S. Map 1/2,500, Yorks. CXCVI. 15 (1891 edn.).
55 E.R.A.O., PE/128/39.
56 P.R.O., ED. 7/135, no. 104; Rep. of Educ. Cttee. of Council, 1867–8 [4051], p. 732, H.C. (1867–8), xxv; Bulmer, Dir. E. Yorks. (1892), 450.
57 Returns relating to Elem. Educ. 468–9.
58 Bd. of Educ., List 21 (H.M.S.O., 1908).
59 E.R. Educ. Cttee. Mins. 1910–11, 25, 250.
60 R.D.B., 137/287/257.
61 Bd. of Educ., List 21 (H.M.S.O., 1914 and later edns.).
62 Above, Catwick, educ.
63 E.R. Educ. Cttee. Mins. 1950–1, 18, 51–2; 1951–2, 93, 128; 1953–4, 9, 51; 1954–5, 114.
64 Ibid. 1955–6, 151; above, Hornsea, educ.
65 E.R. Educ. Cttee. Mins. 1965–6, 75.
66 Inf. from Educ. Dept., Humbs. C.C., 1990.
67 Draft Scheme at E.R.A.O.; R.D.B., KH/261/292;

LG/47/65; Review of Char. Rep. 33; inf. from Mrs. D. S. Theasby, Leven, 1993; Char. Com. index.
68 E.R.A.O., Char. Reg. no. 513704; inf. from Mrs. Richardson.
69 E.R.A.O., SL/76/1; Beverley Guardian, 1 Dec. 1866.
70 Returns relating to Elem. Educ. 468–9.
71 Educ. of Poor Digest, 1086; Educ. Enq. Abstract, 1091; weathered date stone.
72 Returns relating to Elem. Educ. 472–3; above, church.
73 Kelly's Dir. N. & E.R. Yorks. (1889), 422.
74 Above, Brandesburton, educ.
75 B.I.H.R., V. 1764/Ret. 2, no. 123.
76 This article was written in 1992.
77 Above, Aldbrough, local govt.; church; below, this section; churches.
78 P.N. Yorks. E.R. (E.P.N.S.), 62–3; G. F. Jensen, Scand. Settlement Names in Yorks. 129, 198.

Cowden then formed Cowdens Ambo town-ship.[79] Mappleton and Rolston townships were later united as a civil parish, and by 1891 coastal erosion had reduced its area to 1,912 a. (774 ha.) and that of Cowdens Ambo to 1,548 a. (627 ha.).[80] In 1935 Mappleton and Rolston civil parish was united with Great and Little Cow-dens civil parish as the new parish of Mappleton; the total area was then 3,424 a. (1,386 ha.).[81] By 1991 erosion had further reduced that to 1,291 ha. (3,190 a.).[82]

In 1377 there were 100 poll-tax payers at Mappleton and 56 at Rolston, and in 1672 they together had 36 houses assessed for hearth tax and 14 discharged. At Great and Little Cowden 86 poll-tax payers were recorded in 1377, and in 1672 there were 28 houses assessed for hearth tax and 8 discharged in the two Cowdens.[83] In 1764 the parish had 64 families.[84] The popu-lation of Mappleton and Rolston rose from 159 in 1801 to 191 in 1811 and 213 in 1861, before falling to 178 in 1881 and 147 in 1911. The Cowdens had 115 inhabitants in 1801, 146 in 1821, and 154 in 1861; probably because of the limitation and eventual prohibition of gravel extraction from the beach, numbers fell sharply in the 1870s to 119 in 1881 and stood at 95 in 1901. Mappleton and Rolston civil parish and Great and Little Cowdens civil parish had a combined population of 265 in 1931. After their union numbers rose to 351 in 1951, the increase probably being due in part to the presence of military personnel. There were 290 inhabitants in 1961, 283 in 1971, and 342 in 1981. In 1991 there were 327 present, 321 of whom were usu-ally resident.[85]

Nearly all of the parish lies on boulder clay.[86] The land is mostly between 15 m. and 23 m. above sea level, ending in the east in an un-broken line of cliffs. Frank hill on the clay at Great Cowden was named by the 13th century.[87] Scattered deposits of sand and gravel provided the site of the village and probably also that of the former hamlet of Great Cowden, besides producing several isolated hills rising above 23 m. Gravel has been extracted in the west of the parish.[88] Lower land, some of it alluvial, lies in the north and west and at Little Cowden, where most of the hummocky ground lies below 15 m. Other deposits of alluvium occur on higher land near the village and may derive from former meres: at Great Cowden in the 13th cent-ury were Eelmere, or 'eel pool', and Broad-mere.[89]

The parish is drained mainly by streams flowing south and west towards Lambwath stream and eventual outfall into the river Hum-ber, the dependence of Mappleton, Rolston, and the Cowdens on Lambwath stream being re-corded in 1367.[90] Much of Mappleton township is served by South drain, which runs across almost its entire width, and West drain, which forms part of the township boundary, while the Cowdens were partly divided by and reliant upon Cowden drain.[91] Rolston and the north-east part of Mappleton township is, however, now mostly drained by Acre dike which flows north, for much of its course beside the main road, into a stream feeding Hornsea mere. The stream draining from Great Cowden to Hornsea mere in 1367 was perhaps a more extensive Acre dike, later disrupted by erosion and diversion.[92]

The sea consumed c. 1 a. a year at Little Cow-den in the late 18th century, and 1–4 yd. a year were lost at Mappleton and the Cowdens in the 19th century. The c. 630 yd. between Mappleton church and the cliff in 1786 had been almost halved by 1956,[93] and in 1991 defensive works comprising cliff walling and granite groynes were built to protect the village. Erosion never-theless continued further south at Great Cowden.[94]

The lower land at Mappleton and Rolston was used as common meadow and pasture and the higher for the open fields. At Great and Little Cowden lower land bordering Cowden drain was probably also used as grassland. Little Cowden was inclosed early, Great Cowden in 1772, Mappleton in 1849, and Rolston in 1860.

Cliff-side and other land in the parish has been much used by the military and other auth-orities. Three beacons were recorded at Mapple-ton in 1588, and one was put up in 1768 at Great Cowden and removed c. 1826.[95] A coastguard was recorded at Great Cowden in 1851, and a rocket life-saving apparatus was operated there c. 1900.[96] In 1953 some 200 a. in the Cowdens were bought for a Royal Air Force practice range, still in use in 1992.[97] At Rolston land was let for an Army camp by 1921, when the hut-ments covered just over 20 a.; the site, bought outright in 1927, was enlarged with c. 55 a. by purchase in 1922. The enlargement was sold in 1935, but the camp was still used by the Ministry of Defence for training in 1992.[98] North of the camp at Rolston, a rifle range had been set up in 1907; it extended over 58 a. in 1921, when the Territorial Army Association of

[79] O.S. Map 6″, Yorks. CXCVII, CCXII, CCXIII (1854–5 edn.); Census, 1871. The discrepancy in the sum results from rounding to the nearest acre.
[80] Census, 1891.
[81] Ibid. 1931 (pt. ii).   [82] Ibid. 1991.
[83] P.R.O., E 179/202/60, mm. 57, 65, 73; Hearth Tax, 61.
[84] B.I.H.R., V. 1764/Ret. 2, no. 140.
[85] V.C.H. Yorks. iii. 495; Census, 1911–91.
[86] Geol. Surv. Map 1″, drift, sheet 73 (1909 edn.).
[87] 'Meaux Cart.', p. 438.
[88] O.S. Map, Yorks. CXCVII (1854 edn.).
[89] P.N. Yorks. E.R., 62; O.S. Map 1/10,000, TA 24 SW. (1981 edn.); 'Meaux Cart.', pp. 434, 438.
[90] Poulson, Holderness, i. 129.
[91] E.R.A.O., IA. Mappleton; O.S. Map 6″, Yorks. CXCVII, CCXII–CCXIII (1854–5 edn.).

[92] For Acre dike, Lamb. Pal. Libr., COMM. XIIa/18/91; Poulson, Holderness, i. 121.
[93] E.R.A.O., PE/27/2; Poulson, Holderness, i. 363, 372; T. Sheppard, Lost Towns of Yorks. Coast, 163.
[94] Plaque on works; Hull Daily Mail, 12 Sept. 1991; 20 Jan., 1 Feb. 1992.
[95] E.R.A.O., LT/9/54; ibid. QSF/240/D.6; QSF/285/D.11; R.D.B., 47/177/169 (1902); J. Nicholson, Beacons of E. Yorks. 10, 42; T. Sheppard, Lost Towns of Yorks. Coast, 80, 210.
[96] P.R.O., HO 107/2365; E.R.A.O., DDHU/17/20; direc-tories; O.S. Map 1/2,500, Yorks. CCXIII. 1 (1891 edn.).
[97] R.D.B., 935/134/112; 935/386/331; 944/38/33; Hull Daily Mail, 15 Oct. 1976; O.S. Map 1/10,000, TA 24 SW. (1981 edn.).
[98] R.D.B., 240/236/203; 259/44/40; 362/248/209; 517/255/201.

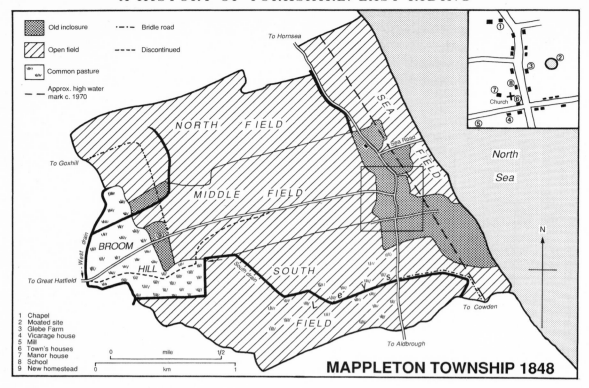

Old inclosure · — · — Bridle road
Open field - - - - Discontinued
Common pasture
- - Approx. high water mark c. 1970

1 Chapel
2 Moated site
3 Glebe Farm
4 Vicarage house
5 Mill
6 Town's houses
7 Manor house
8 School
9 New homestead

To Hornsea
NORTH FIELD
To Goxhill
MIDDLE FIELD
Sea Road
SEA FIELD
BROOM HILL
West drain
To Great Hatfield
South drain
SOUTH FIELD
VALLEYS
North Sea
Church
To Cowden
To Aldbrough
N

0 mile 1/2
0 km 1

MAPPLETON TOWNSHIP 1848

the East Riding bought it. The range had been reconstructed by 1935 because of erosion.[99] In the 1940s the Army also requisitioned land in Great Cowden, removed residents from there, and took over a holiday camp in Mappleton village.[1]

Several camps for young people were begun along the coast in the earlier 20th century. The Y.M.C.A. had a holiday camp in the village from the 1930s. It was requisitioned by the Army during the Second World War, and after its return was used to house boys from the North-East under the British Boys for British Farms scheme. Hungarian refugees were also lodged there before the camp was closed in the 1960s.[2] Hull Young People's Christian and Literary Institute ran a camp at Great Cowden from 1920.[3] Another camp, at Rolston, belonged to Hull Boys' Club by the mid 1930s[4] and from 1939 to another city trust.[5] Hull corporation as an L.E.A. sent children to camp at Great Cowden and Rolston,[6] and in 1950 it took over Rolston camp.[7] The camp passed to Humberside county council in 1974 and to Hull city council in 1989, when it was used by schools and youth groups from Humberside and the West

Riding.[8] Inland at Rolston 135 a. of the Haworth-Booths' estate were let, with a smaller area in Hornsea, to Hornsea golf club, which opened links there in 1908 and bought the course in 1922.[9]

Roads leading from Mappleton north to Hornsea and south to Aldbrough have been up-graded and improved as parts of the Holder-ness coast road. By 1778 the Aldbrough road had been diverted at Little Cowden to run closer to one of the farms there.[10] Side roads connect the coast road with the parallel street of Rolston, c. 200 m. to the west, and the scattered buildings of Great Cowden, one of the side turnings con-tinuing west to Withernwick. At the inclosure of Mappleton in 1849 a road to Great Hatfield was re-aligned and alterations were made to bridle roads to Goxhill and Cowden,[11] while at Rolston a new road to Hornsea, Goxhill, and Great Hatfield was made at inclosure in 1860.[12] A field way continuing Rolston street south to Mappleton in the mid 19th century was later also discontinued.[13]

MAPPLETON village is built along both sides of a street, now part of the main coast road, and

99 Ibid. 229/40/36; NE. Sea Fisheries Cttee. *Mins.* 1907–9, 150; 1933–5, 90.
1 E.R.A.O., MRH/1/38; below, this section.
2 *Hull Daily Mail*, 30 Dec. 1987, 3 May 1989; *Kelly's Dir. N. & E.R. Yorks.* (1937), 500; local inf.
3 R.D.B., 218/371/326; directories.
4 Hull City R. O., TAA 43; *Kelly's Dir. N. & E.R. Yorks.* (1937), 500.
5 R.D.B., 620/553/428; Kingston-upon-Hull, *Mins. Educ. Cttee.* 1934–5, 12; 1938–9, 16; *V.C.H. Yorks. E.R.* i. 339; illus. in M. and B. Chapman, *Holderness in old picture postcards*, 56.
6 Kingston-upon-Hull, *Mins. Educ. Cttee.* 1934–5, 36, 65; 1935–6, 44; 1938–9, 37–8.

7 Kingston-upon-Hull, *Mins. Colleges and Sch. Sub-Cttee.* 1949–50, p. 20; *Mins. Educ. Finance and General Purposes Sub-Cttee.* 1967–8, p. 29.
8 Inf. from Educ. Dept., Humbs. C.C., 1992.
9 R.D.B., 245/451/392; *Illus. Guide to Hornsea* (1908), 21; above, Hornsea, resort.
10 The change was confirmed in 1814–15, soon after the sale of the farm. E.R.A.O., HD. 20; cf. ibid. DDCK/35/5/2.
11 E.R.A.O., IA. Mappleton.
12 Ibid. IA. Rowlston; O.S. Map 6", Yorks. CXCVII (1854 edn.).
13 H. Teesdale, *Map of Yorks.* (1828); O.S. Map 6", Yorks. CXCVII (1854 and later edns.).

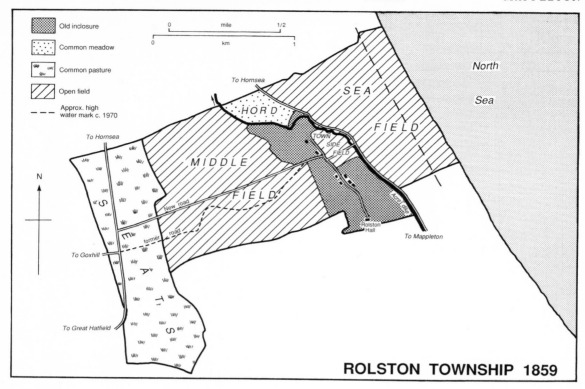

ROLSTON TOWNSHIP 1859

in a cross lane, called Mill Lane west of the street and Cliff Lane to the east.[14] The village buildings are almost all of brick and mostly date from the 19th century. They include terraced cottages in Cliff Lane, half a dozen farmhouses, several bungalows, and eight council houses, built opposite the church c. 1952.[15] Apart from the church, boulder construction occurs mostly in the walls of outbuildings. Seaview Farm, of one storey with attics, has boulder-built walls and a pantile roof; it may date from the 17th century. Also pantiled and with Yorkshire sashes and a dentilated eaves course is Gray's Farm, which was formerly two houses[16] and is believed to date from the early 18th century. There was an alehouse at Mappleton in the later 18th century,[17] and a reading and recreation room was run there in the 1920s.[18] A village institute for Mappleton, Rolston, and Cowden was held in a former Army hut in Cliff Lane from c. 1950 until 1971, when the redundant Methodist chapel replaced it as the village hall.[19] Away from the village, Broom Hill Farm was built by the Haworth family in or soon before 1848.[20]

ROLSTON also had a linear plan with a single street, parallel to, and probably influenced by, Acre dike, with commonable lands to east and west. At its southern end the street enters the wooded grounds of Rolston Hall. A road in the

hamlet was stopped up and appropriated by the Stutvilles c. 1300.[21] The dozen farm and other houses comprising the hamlet mostly date from the 19th and 20th centuries, one or two of the more recent ones standing in a side lane. Boulder construction includes walling in a cottage on the west side of the street which may have been built in the 18th century and raised in brick in the 19th; it retains Yorkshire sashes and a pantile roof. Willow Garth, at the north end of the street, had been built by the Haworth-Booth family by 1921; the tall house with rusticated quoins and carved bargeboards was used as an old people's home in 1992.[22] A waterworks and wind pump were built to serve the Rolston estate c. 1900; the works were bought by Hornsea golf club in 1936 but were disused in 1992.[23] Outlying buildings include Rolston Seats Farm, built on former commonable land in the later 19th century.[24]

GREAT COWDEN was also a linear settlement aligned north-south with its commonable lands to east and west.[25] The choice of site was probably influenced by the springs there, and c. 1900 the western back lane, usually known as Garthends or Garth End Lane, was called Wild Wells Lane. In the mid 19th century the north end of the main street was less than 150 yd. from the cliff edge, the intervening ground forming a

[14] B.I.H.R., TER. H. Mappleton 1825; *Reg. of Electors* (1991).
[15] R.D.B., 929/320/281.
[16] Local inf.
[17] E.R.A.O., QDT/2/9.
[18] B.I.H.R., V. 1912–22/Ret.
[19] R.D.B., 809/415/343; 1746/165/137; inf. from Mrs. J. Hepworth, Rolston, 1992.
[20] R.D.B., GM/310/399.

[21] *Cal. Inq. Misc.* iii, p. 19.
[22] R.D.B., 230/360/303.
[23] Ibid. 240/236/203; 556/356/271; O.S. Map 1/2,500, Yorks. CXCVII. 11 (1910 edn.); O.S. Map 1/10,000, TA 24 SW. (1981 edn.); inf. from Mr. J. Hepworth, Rolston, 1992.
[24] O.S. Map 6″, Yorks. CXCVII (1854 edn.); O.S. Map 1/2,500, Yorks. CXCVII. 11 (1892 edn.); Bulmer, *Dir. E. Yorks.* (1892), 457.
[25] Below, econ. hist.

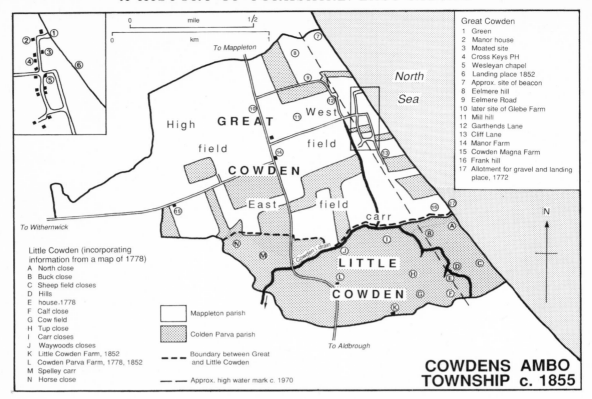

Great Cowden
1 Green
2 Manor house
3 Moated site
4 Cross Keys PH
5 Wesleyan chapel
6 Landing place 1852
7 Approx. site of beacon
8 Eelmere hill
9 Eelmere Road
10 later site of Glebe Farm
11 Mill hill
12 Garthends Lane
13 Cliff Lane
14 Manor Farm
15 Cowden Magna Farm
16 Frank hill
17 Allotment for gravel and landing place, 1772

Little Cowden (incorporating information from a map of 1778)
A North close
B Buck close
C Sheep field closes
D Hills
E house.1778
F Calf close
G Cow field
H Tup close
I Carr closes
J Waywoods closes
K Little Cowden Farm, 1852
L Cowden Parva Farm, 1778, 1852
M Spelley carr
N Horse close

Mappleton parish
Colden Parva parish
Boundary between Great and Little Cowden
Approx. high water mark c. 1970

COWDENS AMBO TOWNSHIP c. 1855

small green, and there was also an eastern back lane named Cliff Lane.[26] The northern end of the street and much of Cliff Lane were washed away in the late 19th and earlier 20th century, and in 1992 Garth End Lane ran along the cliff edge.[27] Several farmhouses were built inland on former common land in the mid 19th century: Cowden Magna, Manor, and Mill Hill Farms were put up between 1829 and 1852 and Glebe Farm between 1852 and 1889.[28] In the earlier 20th century there was more building, in Garth End Lane,[29] where only one or two houses remained in 1992, and away from the cliff, along Eelmere Lane and beside the main road. In Eelmere Lane a dozen chalet bungalows were built, and c. 1943 the Cross Keys, which had traded in the hamlet at least since 1822,[30] was rebuilt at the junction of the lane and the main road; the house still traded in 1992.[31] With the other newer houses, most of them on the main road, the rebuilt hamlet comprises c. 30 houses. A caravan site on Eelmere Lane was opened c. 1950 and in 1992 had room for some 220 vehicles.[32]

LITTLE COWDEN. There were seven houses at Little Cowden in 1401, but an inclosure there

resulted in 24 people being evicted by 1517.[33] The settlement may have occupied high ground later named Hills close. One farm remained there in 1778, when the only other stood further west beside the main road, but by 1852 the site had been abandoned and Little Cowden Farm rebuilt further inland. One or two houses and buildings associated with the practice range have been added in the 20th century.[34]

MANORS AND OTHER ESTATES. In 1066 Morkar held the manor of *MAPPLETON*, which extended into several other parishes; there were 13 carucates at Mappleton, and sokeland of 5 carucates and 2 bovates at Rolston and 3 carucates at Little Cowden. All of the land had passed to Drew de Bevrère by 1086, and later formed part of the Aumale fee.[35] The Crown succeeded to the lands of the Aumale fee, and Mappleton was held of it as ⅙ knight's fee in 1347.[36]

An estate at Mappleton and Rolston was evidently held in 1206 by Peter de Brus (d. 1222), and his grandson Peter de Brus (d. 1272) was the Crown's mesne tenant of 12 carucates in those

[26] R.D.B., 48/421/392 (1902); O.S. Map 6", Yorks. CCXII–CCXIII (1855 edn.); *Reg. of Electors* (1991).
[27] O.S. Map 1/2,500, Yorks. CCXIII. 1 (1891 edn.); O.S. Map 6", TA 24 SW. (1957 edn.); O.S. Map 1/10,000, TA 24 SW. (1981 edn.).
[28] A. Bryant, *Map of E.R. Yorks.* (1829); O.S. Map 6", Yorks. CCXII (1855 edn.); O.S. Map 1/2,500, Yorks. CCXII. 4 (1891 edn.).
[29] R.D.B., 560/572/444; 603/561/428; 646/298/249; 646/299/250.
[30] E.R.A.O., QDT/2/6; H.U.L., DX/150/16 (25);

R.D.B., 22/496/471 (1900); 532/382/285; directories; O.S. Map 6", Yorks. CCXIII (1855 edn.).
[31] R.D.B., 661/329/290.
[32] Inf. from proprietor, Cowden Caravan Park, 1992.
[33] *Cal. Inq. p.m.* xviii, p. 132; *Trans. R.H.S.* N.S. vii. 251.
[34] E.R.A.O., DDCK/35/5/2; ibid. DDHV/6/1; R.D.B., Q/70/142; O.S. Map 6", Yorks. CCXIII (1855 edn.).
[35] *V.C.H. Yorks.* ii. 265; *Cur. Reg. R.* iv. 220; *Yorks. Fines, 1232–46*, p. 162; *Cal. Inq. p.m.* xi, p. 68.
[36] *Cal. Inq. p.m.* ix, p. 26.

places. Part of the Bruses' manor passed by marriage to the Fauconbergs.[37] In 1347 the tenant in demesne was said to hold directly of the Crown, but the Fauconbergs' lordship was recorded in 1408.[38]

In 1206 Alice de Stutville, widow of Roger de Merlay, held the manor of Peter de Brus, and later in the century the Merlays and their successors held it.[39] The manor, evidently including land of the fee in Rolston, was subinfeudated to Alice's sister Agnes, who married Herbert de St. Quintin.[40] From Herbert (d. by 1223) the estate at Mappleton and Rolston descended mostly like Brandesburton in the St. Quintins.[41] The mesne lordship of Rolston apparently descended without interruption from Sir Herbert de St. Quintin (d. 1302) to his grandson (Sir) Herbert (d. 1339), who was recorded as lord there in 1316.[42] Mappleton was held in dower for much of the 14th century. Lucy, probably the widow of Sir Herbert (d. 1302) or of his son Sir Herbert (dead then), married Robert de Cotum, named as lord of Mappleton in 1316, and held the manor until at least 1347.[43] Margery, relict of Sir Herbert de St. Quintin (d. 1347), held ⅔ of the manor at her death in 1361.[44] Mappleton was then assigned to their daughter Elizabeth and her husband Sir John Marmion, but after 1370 it reverted to the descendants of her sister Laura.[45] The manor, of 8 carucates in 1408,[46] and the estate at Rolston again descended with Brandesburton[47] to Thomas Fiennes, Lord Dacre, and William Parr, lords c. 1530,[48] and then to Gregory Fiennes, Lord Dacre (d. 1594). His sister and heir Margaret, Lady Dacre, and her husband Sampson Lennard[49] sold the manor to Hugh Bethell in 1598.[50]

It may have been the same manor which Sir William Gee (d. 1611) held, together with Great Cowden manor. That estate descended in the Gees of Bishop Burton to William Gee (d. 1718),[51] who devised it to a younger son James. By will of 1750 James Gee, who also held the rectory as lessee, left his estate to his son William, the owner in 1757.[52] The Revd. Richard Gee, William's brother, had succeeded by 1764,

and in 1772 he was awarded 75 a. for his commonable lands at Great Cowden.[53] Gee (d. 1815) left his freehold and leasehold to his wife Hannah (d. 1826), with remainder to his nephew Robert Whyte.[54] Whyte, who assumed the name Moyser, died in 1846.[55] Mappleton and Great Cowden manors descended to his son Edward, whose incapacity caused the estate to be committed to his brother, the Revd. J. R. Whyte.[56] In 1850 it comprised 593 a. at Mappleton and 73 a. at Great Cowden.[57] By 1864 Mrs. Florence Whyte, presumably Edward's widow, held the manors as life tenant.[58] The estate later belonged to Whyte's daughter Giva Fantoni, devisee of ⅓ share, and to Constance Incontri and Mary Whyte, probably his other daughters and devisees.[59]

In 1883 Mary Whyte bought the freehold of most of the rectory, and the c. 200 a. of former glebe land at Mappleton and Great Cowden were included in the sales by the Whyte heirs of the manor of Great Cowden in 1883 and of Mappleton in 1898. Benjamin Booth Haworth-Booth (d. 1919) and his wife Margaret bought Mappleton manor with 695 a. there and at Cowden.[60] Mrs. Haworth-Booth sold c. 130 a. in 1920 and 1921.[61] She died in 1939 and her nephew Sir George Kinloch, Bt., and another trustee sold the rest of the estate in 1940 to Hollis Bros. & Co. Ltd.; it then comprised Manor farm with 388 a. and the 76-a. Glebe farm, formerly part of the rectory.[62] Most of Manor farm was bought by Muriel Bird in 1943.[63] B. A. Parkes bought the farm in 1954 and George, Enid, and Brian Basham in 1967, when it was of 324 a.[64] It still belonged to the Basham family in 1992.[65] Manor Farm, west of the church, is of brick and may be a 17th-century house enlarged in the 18th century. Glebe farm, Mappleton, was sold in 1943 to Herbert Clark and in 1957 to Thomas Lofthouse, and in 1973 Stuart Saunt bought most of the land. The farmhouse is discussed below.[66]

At *GREAT COWDEN* the archbishop of York had a berewick of 9 carucates in 1086,[67] his

37 *Cur. Reg. R.* iv. 220; *Yorks. Inq.* i, pp. 201–2; for the Bruses, *E.Y.C.* ii, p. 15.
38 *Cal. Inq. p.m.* ix, p. 26; *Yorks. Inq. Hen. IV–V*, p. 71.
39 H.U.L., DHO/16/91; *Yorks. Fines, 1232–46*, p. 162; *Cur. Reg. R.* iv. 220; v. 14; *Cal. Inq. p.m.* i, p. 200; *Yorks. Inq.* i, pp. 201–2; *V.C.H. Yorks. E.R.* ii. 107; for the Stutvilles and Merlays, *E.Y.C.* ix, pp. 27–34.
40 *Cur. Reg. R.* iii. 39, 177; iv. 220; v. 14.
41 H.U.L., DHO/16/91; *Yorks. Fines, 1232–46*, p. 162; *1347–77*, pp. 214–15; *Cal. Inq. p.m.* i, p. 200; *Yorks. Inq.* i, pp. 201–2; English, *Holderness*, 150; above, Brandesburton, manors. For the St. Quintins, *Early Yorks. Fam.* (Y.A.S. Rec. Ser. cxxxv), 80; *Complete Peerage*; J. Foster, *Pedigrees of Yorks.* iii.
42 *Feud. Aids*, vi. 163.
43 Ibid.; *Yorks. Fines, 1347–77*, 214–15; *Cal. Inq. p.m.* ix, pp. 25–7.
44 *Cal. Inq. p.m.* xi, p. 68. For the life tenancy of Ric. de St. Quintin (fl. c. 1350), ibid. ix, p. 256; *Cal. Inq. Misc.* iii, p. 19.
45 *Yorks. Deeds*, vi, p. 10; *Yorks. Fines, 1347–77*, p. 228.
46 *Yorks. Inq. Hen. IV–V*, p. 71.
47 P.R.O., C 139/34, no. 45; C 139/151, no. 43; C 141/4, no. 45; *Cal. Inq. p.m. Hen. VII*, i, pp. 115–16; *Feud. Aids*, vi. 273; *Complete Peerage*, s.v. FitzHugh.
48 P.R.O., C 142/48, no. 161.

49 Ibid. C 142/244, no. 129; ibid. SC 6/Hen. VIII/6135; *Complete Peerage*, s.v. Dacre; *Cal. Pat.* 1580–2, p. 64.
50 *Yorks. Fines*, iv. 88.
51 P.R.O., C 142/332, no. 165; H.U.L., DDGE/6/19, 22, 30, 51. For the Gees, J. Foster, *Pedigrees of Yorks.* iii.
52 H.U.L., DDGE/3/146, 150; P.R.O., CP 43/697, rot. 281.
53 R.D.B., AQ/61/8; P.R.O., CP 43/724, rot. 221.
54 H.U.L., DDMC/108/36; *V.C.H. Yorks. E.R.* iv. 118. Foster, op. cit., has Rob. as second cousin once removed of Ric.   55 R.D.B., FC/22/21–2; NS/378/559.
56 Ibid. GK/29/37; GO/156/167; NL/207/296.
57 Ibid. GR/180/218; E.R.A.O., IA.
58 E.R.A.O., DDCC/136/171; ibid. CSR/31/369.
59 R.D.B., KF/135/176; LD/76/72; NL/207/296; 6/458/447 (1885).
60 Ibid. 1/99/95 (1898); 197/362/310; 221/487/430; below, this section (rectory).
61 R.D.B., 222/74/67; 223/304/251; 239/176/155 etc.
62 Ibid. 634/343/262; 635/335/267; 635/336/268; E.R.A.O., IA.
63 R.D.B., 664/405/347.
64 Ibid. 991/30/30; 1534/90/84.   65 Local inf.
66 R.D.B., 665/318/271; 1065/300/277; 1833/287/241; below, this section (rectory).
67 *V.C.H. Yorks.* ii. 216.

manor of Cowden was recorded from the later 13th century,[68] and it was evidently for Great Cowden that he was named joint lord of Cowden in 1316.[69] Part or all of the archbishop's estate was held by a knight in 1086, and it was later reckoned as 1 knight's fee. William Cockrell in the earlier 12th century and later Robert Cockrell, probably the benefactor of Meaux abbey or his son (both fl. c. 1215), may have held the whole fee as undertenant,[70] but later the land was divided.[71] It was probably the archiepiscopal manor of Great Cowden which Master William Passemer held in 1267,[72] and John Passemer (d. 1303) held just over 1 carucate. Part of Passemer's holding descended to Sir Robert Sturmy, who was succeeded c. 1400 by his wife Catherine in 2 carucates at Great Cowden held as ¼ knight's fee.[73] Another holding, of c. 2 carucates, belonged to the Hautayns in the mid 14th century.[74] Thomas Brigham (d. 1542) had seven houses and 140 a. at Great Cowden, and Sir John Constable (d. 1542) almost 1 carucate there.[75] As an appurtenance of Bishop Burton manor, Great Cowden was exchanged by the archbishop with the Crown in 1542, although it was not then named, and with that manor it evidently passed to Sir William Gee (d. 1611), and later descended with his estate at Mappleton to the Whytes.[76]

In 1883 the Whyte heirs sold Great Cowden manor with 228 a. there to William Whiting (d. 1889), who devised that and another farm there to his nephews H. K. and Smith Whiting.[77] In 1899 Smith Whiting and his brother's trustee in bankruptcy sold the manor and the 228 a. to G. W. Oldham, who enlarged the estate by piecemeal purchases, including 61 a. of land belonging to North Ferriby vicarage and c. 50 a. more to St. Mary's, Lowgate, Hull, bought respectively in 1904 and 1909.[78] In 1910 he settled the manor and c. 445 a. on his daughter Sarah (d. 1948).[79] Her heirs G. H. and H. H. Oldham sold the 107-a. Glebe farm to Herbert Clark in 1948 and Manor farm with 209 a. to Tom Wells in 1950.[80] Wells died in 1956 and in 1957 his executor sold Manor farm to S. H. and C. D. Norman (d. 1969).[81] In 1974 Sir Francis

Legh and others bought the farm, and in 1992 it belonged to R. H. Leonard.[82]

The manor house, or its site, was mentioned in 1286.[83] The house may have occupied the same site in the 1850s, when it was an old thatched building at the north end of the street. Another house, on a large moated site nearby, was probably a successor to the chief house of one of the larger medieval estates.[84] A new farmhouse, later named Manor Farm, was built inland between 1829 and 1852; the old manor house continued to be recorded until 1895, but its site was later washed away.[85]

(Sir) Robert de Scures held all 3 carucates at *LITTLE COWDEN* by the mid 13th century, and in 1280 he conveyed them to his daughter Joan's husband, Robert Hildyard, who was recorded as tenant of the Aumale fee there in 1284–5.[86] The manor was held in demesne by Giles of Goxhill in the mid 13th century, and by Peter of Goxhill in 1280.[87] Peter's son and heir Ralph had died by 1294, leaving a daughter Margaret. She married Philip le Despenser (d. 1313) and then John de Ros, Lord Ros of Watton (d. 1338), who was returned as joint lord of Cowden in 1316. The Crown briefly confiscated the estate c. 1325 because of John's adherence to the queen's party.[88] From Margaret (d. July 1349) the manor passed to her son Sir Philip Despenser (d. Aug. 1349), to his son Philip Despenser, Lord Despenser of Goxhill (d. 1401), and to that Philip's son Philip (d. 1424).[89] The last Philip's daughter Margery married Roger Wentworth, and Little Cowden later descended in the Wentworths.[90] In 1568 Thomas Wentworth, Lord Wentworth, sold the manor to Wolstan Dixey and (Sir) Stephen Slaney.[91]

One moiety was sold by Slaney to John Thorpe in 1599 and held in turn by Richard Thorpe (d. 1613) and his son John (d. 1640). John left the moiety to his mother Mary Hall for life, with remainder to his half-brother Francis Hall.[92] From Hall (d. by 1693) the share passed to his widow Mary and son Thomas. Thomas (d. by 1739) was succeeded by his

68 *Reg. Romeyne*, ii (Sur. Soc. cxxviii), p. 67; *Feud. Aids*, vi. 261. 69 *Feud. Aids*, vi. 163.
70 *V.C.H. Yorks.* ii. 216; *E.Y.C.* i, pp. 44–5; *Reg. Giffard* (Sur. Soc. cix), p. 17; *Reg. Romeyne*, ii (Sur. Soc. cxxviii), p. 67; *Reg. Greenfield*, v (Sur. Soc. cliii), pp. 161–2; 'Meaux Cart.', pp. 434–8.
71 *Reg. Romeyne*, ii, pp. 260–1; *Kirkby's Inquest* (Sur. Soc. xlix), 413, 420.
72 *Abbrev. Plac.* (Rec. Com.), 167, 173; *Reg. Giffard*, 109.
73 *Yorks. Inq.* iv, pp. 29–30; *Feud. Aids*, vi. 273; *Cal. Papal Reg.* v. 224.
74 *Yorks. Fines, 1327–47*, pp. 110, 146; Poulson, *Holderness*, i. 368.
75 P.R.O., C 142/65, no. 61; C 142/69, no. 190; E 150/240, no. 12.
76 H.U.L., DDGE/3/20, 23; P.R.O., C 142/214, no. 205; *V.C.H. Yorks. E.R.* iv. 4; above, this section (Mappleton).
77 R.D.B., NX/127/180; 30/470/449 (1889); 78/291/269; 78/293/270 (both 1895).
78 Ibid. 12/326/310; 14/363/340 (both 1899); 71/110/106 (1904); 114/366/337; *V.C.H. Yorks. E.R.* i. 295.
79 R.D.B., 133/401/371; 788/430/360.
80 Ibid. 798/243/203; 837/222/184.
81 Ibid. 1045/128/106; 1065/564/498; 1643/203/178.

82 Ibid. 1882/266/207; inf. from Mrs. S. Pile, Manor Farm, 1992.
83 *Reg. Romeyne*, ii, p. 67.
84 O.S. Map 6", Yorks. CCXIII (1855 edn.); Sheahan and Whellan, *Hist. York & E.R.* (1856), ii. 425.
85 R.D.B., 78/291/269 (1895); A. Bryant, *Map of E. R. Yorks.* (1829); O.S. Map 6", Yorks. CCXII (1855 edn.); O.S. Map 1/2,500, Yorks. CCXII. 4 (1891 edn.).
86 *Kirkby's Inquest*, 371; *Feud. Aids*, vi. 40; *Cal. Inq. p.m.* iv, p. 355; Poulson, *Holderness*, i. 369. Hildyard's lordship was challenged by the Crown c. 1285: *Abbrev. Plac.* (Rec. Com.), 209.
87 Poulson, *Holderness*, i. 369; *Kirkby's Inquest*, 371; *Cal. Inq. p.m.* iv, p. 355.
88 *Feud. Aids*, vi. 138, 163; *Cal. Inq. p.m.* iii, pp. 135–8, 324–5; v, p. 266; *Cal. Fine R. 1319–27*, 366; *Abbrev. Plac.* (Rec. Com.), 320; *Complete Peerage*, s.v. Ros.
89 *Cal. Inq. p.m.* ix, pp. 192–3; xviii, p. 132; *Complete Peerage*, s.v. Despenser.
90 P.R.O., C 140/66, no. 35; C 142/50, no. 71; ibid. CP 25(1)/292/68, no. 164.
91 Ibid. CP 40/1270, rot. 405; *Yorks. Fines*, i. 356.
92 H.U.L., DHO/7/44; P.R.O., C 142/609, no. 77; *Yorks. Fines*, iv. 124.

brother Benjamin and then by another brother Joseph (d. by 1755), who devised it to his nephew Thomas Plumer.[93] Plumer (d. by 1784) was succeeded by his son Hall Plumer, who sold the share in 1786 to Oliver Beckett.[94] Beckett was dead in 1813, when his assignees in bankruptcy and the mortgagees sold the moiety to Thomas Duesbery,[95] who bought the other moiety.

Dixey's moiety passed to William Widnell or Wignall, who sold it in 1613 to William Towrie. By will of 1615, Towrie devised the estate to his son Francis (d. by 1624), who may have been succeeded by his half-brother George.[96] It presumably belonged to Tristram Towrie of Cowden, who refused knighthood c. 1630,[97] and it evidently descended to Mary Cooke and Judith Mould, who sold it in 1698 to William Robinson (d. by 1721). Robinson's son Robert conveyed ¼ of the manor to William Cooper in 1721.[98] Cooper (d. 1723) left a full moiety to another William Cooper,[99] from whom it descended to George Cooper (d. by 1764). George devised it to his great-nephew, the Revd. Cooper Abbs (d. by 1800), and Abbs to his son Bryan.[1] In 1813 Thomas Duesbery bought that moiety, thereby reuniting the manor, which then comprised just over 500 a. in two farms.[2]

In 1813 Duesbery sold the manor and one farm with 275 a. to Thomas Whitaker, the elder and younger, and the other farm, of 230 a., to John Foster.[3] The larger estate, later called Cowden Parva farm, had passed to Thomas Price and others by 1824.[4] By 1851 it belonged to Thomas Fairfax, who sold it to Robert Holtby in 1855.[5] Holtby (d. 1889) was succeeded by Anne Holtby, who married Hugh Campbell and died in 1940,[6] when her heirs Dorothy Worssam and Edmond Holtby sold the farm to Hollis Bros. & Co. Ltd. W. S. Barchard bought the farm in 1943,[7] and sold the house and 163 a. to J. W. Wilberforce and his wife in 1953. The reduced Cowden Parva farm was sold to Percy Langthorne in 1960. The farmhouse and 114 a. were bought by R. H. Leonard and C. D. Pugh in 1963. Pugh conveyed his moiety in 1964 to Leonard, who bought a large adjoining estate, including other land in Mappleton, from St. Thomas's hospital, Southwark, in 1972.[8] The

manor house was recorded in the 13th century, and a chief house on the Thorpe family's estate in the 17th.[9] A house standing on the site of Cowden Parva Farm by 1778 was rebuilt in or shortly before 1827.[10]

Fulcher was named as lord of ROLSTON in the early 12th century,[11] and William of Rudston (d. by 1203) held nearly 2 carucates there of the Stutvilles.[12] In 1307 Simon de Stutville held an estate at Rolston by knight service of Herbert de St. Quintin,[13] and John de Stutville was succeeded c. 1325 by his son John (d. by 1329), that John by his wife Agnes, and Agnes by her daughter Isabel of Pickering (fl. 1350).[14] Other tenants at Rolston in the mid and late 13th century were the Scotewayne (or Sotwayn), Pickering, and Preston families.[15] By the 16th century Thomas Mayne is believed to have acquired the manor,[16] which in 1593 was said to be held of Lord Dacre's manor of Mappleton but in 1639 of the Crown as successor to the counts of Aumale.[17] Thomas Mayne's son Christopher and Christopher's son William were dealing with the manor in 1564.[18] William was succeeded in turn by his brothers Marmaduke (d. 1593) and Thomas.[19] Thomas's daughter Alice married Edward Truslove (d. 1639). Edward, whose estate was of nearly 3 carucates, mostly in Mappleton township, and his son Mayne[20] (fl. 1670) enlarged the estate by purchase. It may have descended to another Edward Truslove, for in 1699 his widow Avril, son Edward, and daughters Elizabeth and Mary, wife of John Brough, were dealing with it. Most, including Rolston manor, a dozen houses, and almost 5 carucates in Rolston and Mappleton, was settled on Mary Brough, widow, in 1711; the rest, with another carucate at Mappleton, was then the share of her sister Elizabeth Truslove.[21] The Broughs' son John (d. 1766) bought more land.[22] He was succeeded by his son William (d. 1783), a marshal of the Admiralty court who took part in the trial of Adm. Byng, and William by his widow Susannah in an estate of nearly 8 carucates.[23] Susannah (d. 1822) devised the estate to her niece Theresa Arneman, who married Benjamin Haworth.[24] In 1844 the Haworths had

[93] R.D.B., Q/70/142–3; X/260/589; E.R.A.O., DDHV/6/1.
[94] R.D.B., BH/346/595; BL/315/482.
[95] Ibid. BL/321/487; CW/45/64.
[96] P.R.O., E 134/22 Jas. I Mic./44; Yorks. Fines, 1603–14, 216; Poulson, Holderness, i. 371.
[97] Miscellanea, i (Y.A.S. Rec. Ser. lxi), 106.
[98] R.D.B., A/601/853; H/134/280; P.R.O., CP 25(2)/895/10 Wm. III/Trin. no. 12.
[99] R.D.B., H/525/1064; N/105/223.
[1] Ibid. AE/528/1006; CB/255/411; CU/345/381.
[2] Ibid. CU/345/381.
[3] Ibid. CU/294/315; CU/295/316.
[4] Ibid. ED/279/326; E.R.A.O., QDE/1/5/10; O.S. Map 6", Yorks. CCXII (1855 edn.).
[5] R.D.B., HH/39/45; B.I.H.R., TA. 548s.
[6] R.D.B., 30/293/276 (1889); 56/423/389 (1903); 636/181/146; E.R.A.O., NV/1/2; directories.
[7] R.D.B., 637/172/144; 666/120/100.
[8] Ibid. 939/35/29; 944/38/33; 1181/382/335; 1327/73/66; 1369/542/481; 1402/376/333; below, this section [St. Thos.'s hosp.].
[9] H.U.L., DHO/7/44; Cal. Inq. p.m. iii, p. 136.

[10] E.R.A.O., DDCK/35/5/2; Hull Advertiser, 7 Dec. 1827.
[11] Chron. de Melsa (Rolls Ser.), i. 86.
[12] Cur. Reg. R. iii. 39, 177.
[13] Mon. Notes, ii (Y.A.S. Rec. Ser. lxxxi), p. 31.
[14] Cal. Inq. Misc. iii, p. 19; Cal. Pat. 1327–30, 423; Yorks. Fines, 1272–1300, p. 96.
[15] Kirkby's Inquest, 371; Feud. Aids, vi. 41; Cal. Inq. p.m. iv. 353–6.
[16] For the Maynes and Trusloves, Poulson, Holderness, i. 365.
[17] P.R.O., C 142/236, no. 6; C 142/704, no. 110.
[18] Yorks. Fines, i. 294.
[19] P.R.O., C 142/236, no. 6.
[20] Ibid. C 142/704, no. 110; ibid. CP 25(2)/523/13 Chas. I/East. [no. 27]; Miscellanea, i (Y.A.S. Rec. Ser. lxi), 106.
[21] E.R.A.O., DDBC/15/390; H.U.L., DDEV/20/2; R.D.B., A/407/586; A/519/746; Yorks. Fines, iv. 109.
[22] R.D.B., K/682/1459; K/683/1460; U/377/717; for the Broughs, Poulson, Holderness, i. 366; tomb in ch.
[23] R.D.B., BH/450/767.
[24] Ibid. DO/15/15; for the Haworths and Haworth-Booths, J. Foster, Pedigrees of Yorks. iii; Burke, Land. Gent. (1937), 196.

481 a. at Mappleton and 372 a. at Rolston.[25] The estate was held in undivided shares by Theresa (d. 1880) and her children and grandchildren.[26] A 140-a. farm at Rolston was added in 1902.[27] After the death in 1919 of Benjamin Booth Haworth-Booth, the estate was disentailed[28] and sold in many lots by Sir Francis Haworth-Booth in 1921; it then contained 1,290 a. in Rolston and Mappleton. Newcombe Estates Co. Ltd. bought 535 a., including Broom Hill, Hill, and Middle farms.[29] Part of the purchase, 135 a. occupied by a golf club, was sold in 1922,[30] and in 1943 the company sold the 181-a. Broom Hill farm to W. H. and Frank Fussey.[31]

The manor house, called Rolston Hall by 1711,[32] was bought with 37 a. of grounds by Claire Holme in 1921, sold by the mortgagee in 1922 to Frank Moor, and bought in 1931 by J. B. Upton, who purchased an adjacent farm of 72 a. in 1935.[33] He sold the estate in 1951 to C. F. W. Bilton, who gave it to his son R. F. Bilton in 1954.[34] Some 260 a., including Broom Hill farm, were added in 1958 and 1965, and 178 a. sold in 1972.[35] The Rolston Hall estate belonged to P. F. Bilton in 1992.[36]

Rolston Hall is a two-storeyed house with attics under a pantile roof; it may date from the 17th century but has been largely remodelled in succeeding centuries, an east block being added in the 20th century.[37] Traces of the moat which enclosed the site survive.[38]

In 1230 the *RECTORY* was annexed to the archdeaconry of the East Riding. From 1254 the archdeacon had the tithes of corn, hay, wool, and lambs and 1 carucate of glebe land.[39] He temporarily lost the rectory in the Interregnum; it was, nevertheless, held under his lease by the Remington family c. 1650, when it was worth nearly £138 gross a year, mostly from tithes.[40] At Withernwick, where the rector had only corn and hay tithes from the c. 2 carucates in Mappleton parish, a composition was paid for the hay by the 16th century, and tithes due from Great Hatfield were similarly paid by modus in the mid 17th century.[41] The archdeacon was awarded 122 a. for the rectorial and vicarial tithes due from Great Cowden at the inclosure of that hamlet in 1772.[42] In 1814 at the inclosure of Withernwick he received 85 a. for tithes.[43] The remainder of the great tithes, from Great Hatfield, Mappleton, and Rolston, were commuted for a rent charge of £444 4s. in 1844.[44] In 1849 at the inclosure of Mappleton the archdeacon received 75 a. for his glebe land; 47 a. more were awarded to Edward Whyte, either as owner or as lessee of the archdeacon.[45] In 1883 the Ecclesiastical Commissioners, in whom the rectory had been vested in 1855,[46] sold the freehold to the lessee Mary Whyte; besides tithe rent charges, the Commissioners then conveyed c. 320 a. in Mappleton and Withernwick parishes, including the allotment of uncertain status. The rectory was thus joined with the Whytes' other land in the parish.[47]

The rectory house occupied its site on the east side of the main road by 1663.[48] Then or earlier it may have stood on the island site which survived near the present house in 1992 and which formerly gave the house its name of Moat Farm. The farmhouse, later called Glebe Farm,[49] was rebuilt after 1971.[50]

William, count of Aumale, probably William le Gros (d. 1179), had given Thornton abbey (Lincs.) 1 carucate in Mappleton by 1190,[51] but by the later 13th century most of that land had passed to Sir Simon Constable, who granted it to Nunkeeling priory.[52] Thornton abbey later had land at Cowden, 3 bovates of which lay at Great Cowden.[53] The estate was granted after the Dissolution to Thornton college in 1542, and after the college's suppression to John Eldred and William Whitmore in 1611.[54]

In the later 13th century Sir Simon Constable gave his estate in Mappleton, including 1 carucate and 1 bovate and rent, to Nunkeeling priory in an exchange.[55] The priory may also have received land at Rolston from Robert Franks in 1386.[56] After the Dissolution the Crown let 1 carucate and 1 bovate as formerly belonging to the priory.[57]

[25] B.I.H.R., TA. 638L; E.R.A.O., IA. Mappleton, Rowlston.

[26] R.D.B., HO/208/265; KF/355/486; KN/10/16; 35/83/81 (1890); 37/414/400 (1901).

[27] Ibid. 40/484/466 (1902).

[28] Ibid. 210/166/150; 220/241/215; 221/487/430.

[29] Ibid. 228/373/314; 231/234/189; 240/236/203; 240/264/223 etc.

[30] Above, intro.   [31] R.D.B., 668/357/310.

[32] Ibid. A/407/586.

[33] Ibid. 240/264/223; 240/267/225; 255/293/245; 436/157/123; 518/121/92.

[34] Ibid. 876/94/80; 1000/135/115.

[35] Ibid. 1099/374/336; 1402/532/464; 1804/297/236.

[36] Local inf.

[37] Illus. at E.R.A.O., DDEY/100 (101). Description based on Min. of Housing, *Buildings List* (1965). Access to the house was not obtained.

[38] O.S. Map 6", Yorks. CXCVII (1854 edn.).

[39] B.I.H.R., TER. H. Mappleton 1716; *Reg. Gray*, pp. 52-3, 118; *Kirkby's Inquest*, 371.

[40] The details of the surveys of 1649 (Lamb. Pal. Libr., COMM. XIIa/18/90-2) and 1650 (ibid. COMM. XIIa/17/292-4; *T.E.R.A.S.* iv. 63) are not wholly comprehensible, and the 1650 survey was also erroneously copied. For the Remingtons, E.R.A.O., DDRI/10/3; P.R.O., C 2/Jas. I/R 4/52.

[41] B.I.H.R., TER. H. Withernwick 1749, 1764; ibid. CP. G. 3444; ibid. DC. CP. 1676/1.

[42] R.D.B., AQ/61/8.

[43] Ibid. CQ/245/16.

[44] Agreement confirmed 1838 and apportioned 1844: B.I.H.R., TA. 638L.

[45] E.R.A.O., IA. Mappleton; B.I.H.R., TA. 638L.

[46] *Lond. Gaz.* 23 Mar. 1855, pp. 1175-6.

[47] R.D.B., NL/207/296; NT/313/439; above, this section (Mappleton).

[48] B.I.H.R., TER. H. Mappleton 1662/3; Lamb. Pal. Libr., COMM. XIIa/18/90.

[49] R.D.B., 133/401/371.

[50] Ibid. 1718/530/471.

[51] *E.Y.C.* iii, pp. 41-2.   [52] Below, next para.

[53] *Cal. Inq. Misc.* iii, p. 58; *Cal. Inq. p.m.* x, p. 8.

[54] P.R.O., C 66/1903, no. 9; *L. & P. Hen. VIII*, xvii, pp. 29-30.

[55] B.L. Cott. MS. Otho. C. viii, ff. 77v., 79; E.R.A.O., DDCC/111/4.

[56] H.U.L., DHO/6/120.

[57] P.R.O., E 310/30/181, f. 86; *Valor Eccl.* (Rec. Com.), v. 115.

Between 1210 and 1220 Robert Cockrell gave Meaux abbey 6 bovates, other land, and grazing at Great Cowden. Part of the estate was granted in fee farm to his son Matthew, and the rent was later lost.[58] The rest of the abbey's land had evidently been consumed by the sea by 1401.[59]

Small estates at Great Cowden belonged in the 16th century to the Knights Hospitaller[60] and the Dominicans of Beverley,[61] and Swine priory had land at Mappleton, all or part of which later belonged to the Brough family.[62] Peter Basset had given Kirkham priory his estate at Rolston, including a house and 6 bovates, by 1336, but no more is known of it.[63] Land at Great and Little Cowden belonged to Bewick manor, in Aldbrough, and descended with it to St. Thomas's hospital, Southwark; the sale of the estate in 1972 included c. 50 a. in Mappleton parish.[64]

ECONOMIC HISTORY. COMMON LANDS AND INCLOSURE. Mappleton, Great Cowden, Little Cowden, and Rolston each had their own commonable lands.

Mappleton. Some of the open-field land at Mappleton seems to have been consolidated by the later 13th century, when several of Sir Simon Constable's bovates were described as lying together throughout the whole field *in culturis*.[65] The village's fields were named as East and West fields in the mid 17th century. Both then included common meadow land, that in East field called Maske, possibly for 'marsh'. West field had almost certainly by then been reduced by the making of two closes recorded later near the western parish boundary. Common pasture lay in the Leys and at Broom hill; the stint for a bovate was evidently 1 beast gate at Broom hill and nearly 2 in the Leys. The Leys had been part of the tillage before the 17th century, when it still lay in 'leys' or 'lands', and in 1716 the vicar had 5 lands there for which he might stock 2¾ cow gates.[66] Part of the Leys had been inclosed by 1658, when the ridge and furrow in the pasture extended into an adjoining close.[67] The commonable lands had been reordered by the 19th century, probably because of the loss to the sea of much of East field. Arable and grassland north and east of the village lay c. 1840 in Sea field, presumably virtually all that remained of East field. That much of Sea field was used as grassland is suggested by its altern-

ative name of Cow pasture.[68] The former West field and the Leys, and possibly also the rest of East field, were divided between North, Middle, and South fields. The commonable lands were inclosed under the general Inclosure Acts in 1849. Allotments made totalled 1,105 a. and included 40 a. of old inclosures. South field then contained 337 a., North field 260 a., Middle field 237 a., Sea field 119 a., and Broom hill 112 a. Edward Whyte, lord of the manor and lessee of the rectory, was awarded 548 a., the trustee of Benjamin Haworth and his wife Theresa 472 a., and the archdeacon of the East Riding as rector 75 a. There were three other allotments of under 5 a. each.[69]

Great Cowden. The tillage of Great Cowden lay in East and West fields, and had evidently been enlarged by assarting by the 14th century, when a bovate was called 'Avenham'.[70] The common meadows and pastures were probably in the carr, which formed part of East field;[71] grazing was stinted at the rate of about 4 beast gates a bovate in the early 18th century.[72] The commonable lands were disrupted by erosion and possibly rearranged before the later 18th century, when East field extended across the township to the south of both the hamlet and West field.[73] Great Cowden was inclosed in 1772 under an Act of 1770. Allotments made totalled 957 a. West field then contained more than 305 a., East field over 215 a., and a third field, High field, more than 187 a. The archdeacon of the East Riding received 122 a. for the rectorial and vicarial tithes, Thomas Broadley 81 a., and the Revd. Richard Gee 75 a. There were also five allotments of 50–69 a., seven of 20–49 a., seven of 10–19 a., and four of less than 10 a.[74]

Little Cowden. Little Cowden had been partly inclosed by 1517, when it was reported that John Wentworth had put down four ploughs and converted 100 a. to pasture,[75] and by 1693 all the land lay in closes. Close names then recorded suggest that the former commonable lands included a North field; North Field and High North Field closes may have been those in the north-east of the township called Buck and North closes in 1778.[76] Pasture in the carr, possibly stinted, had been mentioned in the late 13th century,[77] and the low-lying land was probably also used for the common meadows; in the 17th century the closes included Carr Waworth (later Waywoods) close and Carr Half close, on the

[58] *Chron. de Melsa* (Rolls Ser.), i. 366, 420; 'Meaux Cart.', pp. 434–40.
[59] *Chron. de Melsa*, iii. 285, 293.
[60] *Miscellanea*, iv (Y.A.S. Rec. Ser. xciv), 98; *Cal. Pat.* 1557–8, 313, 321.
[61] B.L. Add. Ch. 5798; *V.C.H. Yorks.* iii. 264.
[62] P.R.O., E 310/31/187, f. 78; R.D.B., A/519/746; *Valor Eccl.* (Rec. Com.), v. 114; above, this section (Rolston).
[63] *Cal. Chart. R.* 1327–41, 369.
[64] R.D.B., 1814/495/433; *Y.A.J.* xliii. 106; Hist. MSS. Com. 78, *Hastings*, i, pp. 170–1; *Cal. Close*, 1377–81, 245, 247; above, Aldbrough, manors (Bewick).
[65] B.L. Cott. MS. Otho. C. viii, f. 77v.
[66] B.I.H.R., TER. H. Mappleton 1662/3, 1685, 1716; Lamb. Pal. Libr., COMM. XIIa/18/90–1; E.R.A.O., IA. Mappleton; A. Bryant, *Map of E.R. Yorks.* (1829). For the

location of the Leys cf. E.R.A.O., DDGD/789; DDHB/14/4.
[67] P.R.O., E 134/1658 Mich./1.
[68] B.I.H.R., TA. 638L; E.R.A.O., PE/27/2.
[69] E.R.A.O., IA. (including plan).
[70] 'Meaux Cart.', p. 434; B.I.H.R., TER. H. Mappleton 1685; Poulson, *Holderness*, i. 369.
[71] E.R.A.O., CSR/14/91; Poulson, *Holderness*, i. 369; O.S. Map 6", Yorks. CCXIII (1855 edn.).
[72] R.D.B., G/363/805.
[73] Cf. O.S. Map 6", Yorks. CCXIII (1855 edn.); R.D.B., AQ/61/8.
[74] 10 Geo. III, c. 90 (Priv. Act); R.D.B., AQ/61/8.
[75] *Trans. R.H.S.* N.S. vii. 251.
[76] E.R.A.O., DDHV/6/1; ibid. DDCK/35/5/2.
[77] H.U.L., DHO/9/20.

northern township boundary, and Spelley carr in the west. Other names recorded then and later, like Sheep field and Tup close, suggest the relative importance of animal husbandry in the township.[78]

Rolston. At Rolston East and West fields were recorded in 1653, when both included meadow land. Some of the common meadow land lay north of the hamlet, in an area called the Hode or Hold in 1774 and later the Hord. Land called Seats provided the hamlet's rough grazing; the pasture was stinted by 1653,[79] and in the 18th century the rate was 3 beast gates a bovate.[80] As at Mappleton, the commonable lands had been renamed and possibly rearranged by the 19th century, when East field was represented by Sea field and the small Town Side field,[81] and West field by Middle field. That there had earlier been some loss of tillage by piecemeal inclosure is suggested by ridge and furrow in the garths near Rolston Hall.[82] Rolston was inclosed under the general Inclosure Acts in 1860. Allotments made totalled 675 a.; 237 a. came from Middle field, 197 a. from Sea field, 192 a. from Seats, 22 a. from the Hord, and 15 a. from Town Side field. The Haworths' trustees received 284 a., William Jarratt 215 a., and Thomas Hutton and his wife Sarah 175 a. The only other allotment was of less than an acre.[83]

TENURES AND FARMS TO *c*. 1800. *Mappleton*. In 1086, when there were 13 ploughlands and 100 a. of meadow at Mappleton, Drew de Bevrère had one plough there and another was worked by four villeins.[84]

Great Cowden. At Great Cowden there were then 7 ploughlands but only four ploughs were then worked, one on the holding of an undertenant and three by 12 villeins.[85]

Little Cowden. It was probably the whole or part of Little Cowden manor which was in the Crown's hands in 1289–90. Much of the land, including 1 carucate and 2 bovates of demesne land, was then let to tenants, all or most of them bond tenants or cottars.[86]

LATER AGRICULTURE. Only 820 a. of the parish was returned as under crops in 1801.[87] In 1838 the parish included 1,510 a. of arable land and 790 a. of grassland in Great Hatfield, Map-

pleton, and Rolston,[88] and the proportion of arable land and grassland in Mappleton and Rolston was much the same in 1905, with 1,282 a. and 502 a. respectively.[89] Arable land was predominant in the Cowdens, 387 a. as against 110 a. of grassland being recorded at Little Cowden in 1851,[90] and 1,027 a. and 336 a. respectively at Great and Little Cowden in 1905.[91] In the 1930s much of the grassland was at Rolston, where there was a golf course and rifle range; in Mappleton and the Cowdens the smaller areas of grassland lay around the village and along the coast.[92] In 1987 of 829 ha. (2,049 a.) returned for Mappleton civil parish, 593 ha. (1,465 a.) were arable land and 218 ha. (539 a.) grassland.[93] Most of the 26 a. of woodland recorded in 1838 lay close to Rolston Hall; 6 ha. (15 a.) remained in 1987.[94]

There were half a dozen farms at Mappleton in the 19th and earlier 20th century, of which three in 1851 and two in the 1920s and 1930s were of 150 a. or more. Little Cowden then and earlier lay in two large farms, but Great Cowden was divided into *c.* 10 mostly smaller holdings. At Rolston there were about four farmers, two of whom in 1851 and one in 1937 had larger holdings.[95] In 1898 a dozen smallholdings of ¼ a. to 3 a. lay south of Mappleton village, mostly beside the main road,[96] and a smallholder was later recorded in the parish. One or two cowkeepers or dairymen worked at Great Cowden and Rolston in the late 19th century and the 20th century,[97] and there were poultry farms at Rolston and Mappleton from the 1920s. In 1987 of 15 holdings returned for Mappleton civil parish, three were of 100–199 ha. (247–492 a.), two of 50–99 ha. (124–245 a.), five of 10–49 ha. (25–121 a.), and five of under 10 ha. There were then nearly 38,000 fowls, almost 7,000 pigs, and about 500 each of cattle and sheep in Mappleton.[98] Many pigs were kept in Mappleton and the Cowdens in 1992.

MILLS. A windmill recorded on Mappleton manor in the 17th century was presumably that later standing in South field[99] and in use until *c.* 1905. The tower was derelict in 1992, when the mill house was being restored.[1] There was a mill at Great Cowden in 1303, and that or another mill was recorded in 1337;[2] Mill hill is east of the main road.[3] At Little Cowden a mill mentioned *c.* 1290 was probably the windmill which had been removed by 1401.[4]

[78] R.D.B., AG/149/298; CZ/131/200.
[79] H.U.L., DDEV/24/4, where Seats is 'Seales'; E.R.A.O., DDHV/36/30.
[80] R.D.B., G/363/805; AS/382/632; A. Bryant, *Map of E.R. Yorks.* (1829).
[81] E.R.A.O., DDHV/36/30.
[82] Cf. E.R.A.O., IA. Rowlston; Hull Univ., Dept. of Geog., R.A.F. air photograph, run 77A, no. 4005.
[83] Ibid. IA. Rowlston (and plan).
[84] *V.C.H. Yorks.* ii. 265.   [85] Ibid. 216.
[86] H.U.L., DHO/9/20; *Cal. Inq. p.m.* iii, p. 137; *Yorks. Inq.* ii, p. 168.
[87] P.R.O., HO 67/26/290.
[88] B.I.H.R., TA. 638L.
[89] Acreage Returns, 1905.
[90] B.I.H.R., TA. 548s.
[91] Acreage Returns, 1905.

[92] [1st] Land Util. Surv. Map, sheet 28.
[93] Inf. from Min. of Agric., Fish. & Food, Beverley, 1990.
[94] Ibid.; B.I.H.R., TA. 638L; O.S. Map 6", Yorks. CXCVII (1854 edn.); O.S. Map 1/2,500, Yorks. CXCVII. 11 (1892 edn.); O.S. Map 1/10,000, TA 24 SW. (1981 edn.).
[95] Para. based on directories. P.R.O., HO 107/2365; above, manors (Little Cowden).
[96] E.R.A.O., DDGD/789; cf. *Hull Advertiser*, 7 Jan. 1831.
[97] *Hull Daily Mail*, 12 Sept. 1991.
[98] Inf. from Min. of Agric., Fish. & Food.
[99] P.R.O., C 142/332, no. 165; H.U.L., DDGE/6/51; E.R.A.O., IA. Mappleton.
[1] R.D.B., 76/76/70 (1905); 797/483/400; directories.
[2] *Yorks. Inq.* iv, pp. 29–30; *Yorks. Fines, 1327–47*, p. 110.
[3] O.S. Map 1/10,000, TA 24 SW. (1981 edn.).
[4] H.U.L., DHO/9/20; *Yorks. Inq.* ii, pp. 165–8; *Cal. Inq. p.m.* xviii, p. 132.

INDUSTRY AND TRADE. Mappleton was included in a list of seaports in 1565, and in 1772 at the inclosure of Great Cowden 3 a. were awarded as a landing place and for getting gravel.[5] Gravel was being extracted from the beach there c. 1830,[6] and about eight men were taking cobbles, sand, and gravel in the 1860s. Sir Thomas Constable, Bt., as lord of Holderness, was then in dispute with them and the lady of Mappleton and Great Cowden manors, who also claimed the royalties. Constable evidently maintained his right, and in 1868–9 the Cowden gravel men paid £2–£8 each for a licence. Rolston beach was also exploited by Constable's licensees, who paid him 3d. a ton for cobble and 2d. for sand or gravel.[7] The Board of Trade prohibited extraction before 1892, when the population of Great Cowden was said to have decreased as a result.[8] Lime was also burnt at Great Cowden in the 19th century.[9] There has been little other non-agricultural activity in the parish. A motor haulage firm traded c. 1930, and a garage opened in the village by 1929 was still run in 1992.[10]

LOCAL GOVERNMENT. In 1286 the archbishop exonerated his free tenants at Great Cowden from suit of court there every three weeks on condition that they came when summoned for the hearing of Crown or other pleas.[11] Court perquisites there were valued at 18d. a year in 1388 and £1 in the 16th century.[12] The manor court at Cowden recorded in 1289–90 was probably that of Little Cowden, which was later said to have view of frankpledge.[13] Leet jurisdiction was also claimed for Rolston manor court in 1711.[14]

Residents at Cowden were relieved by the overseers of Aldbrough in the mid 18th century,[15] but later the Cowdens were responsible for their own poor, up to six people there being relieved permanently and one or two occasionally in the early 19th century. At Mappleton and Rolston half a dozen people received regular relief in the early 19th century, and two persons in 1802–3 and up to a dozen in 1812–15 were helped occasionally.[16] There were two poorhouses adjoining the churchyard at Mappleton,[17] and presumably others at Great Cowden, where Poorhouse close was recorded.[18] Mappleton and

Rolston township and that of Great and Little Cowden joined Skirlaugh poor-law union in 1837,[19] and remained in Skirlaugh rural district until 1935, when as the new civil parish of Mappleton they were taken into Holderness rural district. Mappleton became part of the Holderness district of Humberside in 1974,[20] and of a new East Riding unitary area in 1996.[21]

CHURCHES. MAPPLETON. In 1115 Mappleton church was given, with others in Holderness, to Aumale priory, later abbey (Seine Maritime).[22] The abbey ceded it in 1228 to the archbishop of York, who annexed it to the archdeaconry of the East Riding in 1230 and ordained a vicarage in 1254.[23] The vicarage lapsed in the later 17th century,[24] and the church was later served by curates, whose living, augmented from 1809, became a perpetual curacy or vicarage.[25] In 1962 those parts of Mappleton parish which lay in Great Hatfield were annexed to Sigglesthorne parish, those in Withernwick to that parish, and that in Great Cowden to Aldbrough with Colden Parva parish; at the same time detached parts of Aldbrough with Colden Parva parish in Great Cowden were transferred to Mappleton parish.[26] In 1972, however, Great Hatfield and Little Hatfield, also in Sigglesthorne parish, and the former parish of Goxhill were added to Mappleton parish; benefice and parish were then renamed Mappleton with Goxhill.[27] In 1979 Mappleton with Goxhill was further united with the benefices of Aldbrough with Colden Parva and Withernwick.[28]

The advowson was said to have been granted by Aumale abbey to Anselm de Stutville, on condition that the presentee paid the abbey 2½ marks a year. Anselm (d. by 1199) granted the patronage back to Aumale, and in 1212 his sister Agnes and her husband Herbert de St. Quintin confirmed it to the abbey.[29] From 1230 Mappleton was in the patronage and peculiar jurisdiction of the archdeacon.[30] Since 1979 the archdeacon has had one turn in three in the patronage of the united benefice.[31]

The vicarage was worth £4 13s. 4d. net in 1535.[32] The improved annual value was £16 net in 1650.[33] After the vicarage lapsed, Archdeacon Brearey augmented the curate's income with £8

[5] R.D.B., AQ/61/8; Acts of P.C. 1558–70, 289. The landing place was later moved closer to the hamlet: O.S. Map 6″, Yorks. CCXIII (1855 edn.).

[6] H.U.L., DX/150/16 (25).

[7] E.R.A.O., DDCC/136/151, 154, 166–7, 170–1, 177.

[8] Bulmer, Dir. E. Yorks. 456.

[9] O.S. Map 6″, Yorks. CCXIII (1855 edn.); O.S. Map 1/2,500, Yorks. CCXIII. 1 (1891 edn.).

[10] Directories.

[11] Reg. Romeyne, ii (Sur. Soc. cxxviii), pp. 67, 260–1.

[12] H.U.L., DDGE/3/23; Cal. Inq. Misc. v, p. 78.

[13] H.U.L., DHO/9/20; R.D.B., AW/390/675.

[14] R.D.B., A/519/746.

[15] E.R.A.O., PE/76/53.

[16] Poor Law Abstract, 1804, pp. 594–5; 1818, pp. 522–3.

[17] B.I.H.R., TA. 638L; E.R.A.O., IA.; O.S. Map 6″, Yorks. CXCVII (1854 edn.).

[18] R.D.B., 78/291/269 (1895).

[19] 3rd Rep. Poor Law Com. 170.   [20] Census.

[21] Humberside (Structural Change) Order 1995, copy at E.R.A.O.

[22] E.Y.C. iii, pp. 30–3; V.C.H. Yorks. E.R. v. 18.

[23] Reg. Gray, pp. 22, 52–3, 118.

[24] B.I.H.R., TER. H. Mappleton 1685 etc.

[25] Ibid. TA. 638L; ibid. TER. H. Mappleton 1825 etc.; Rep. Com. Eccl. Revenues, 952–3; below, this section.

[26] B.I.H.R., OC. 774.

[27] Ibid. 854.

[28] Ibid. 942.

[29] Poulson, Holderness, i. 359–60; V.C.H. Yorks. E.R. ii. 107; Yorks. Fines, John, p. 169.

[30] Lawrance, 'Clergy List', Holderness 1, pp. 88–9; B.I.H.R., TA. 638L. The inclusion of the advowson in a fine relating to the manor in 1571 was evidently in error: Yorks. Fines, ii. 7.

[31] B.I.H.R., OC. 942.

[32] Valor Eccl. (Rec. Com.), v. 116.

[33] T.E.R.A.S. iv. 63.

a year from the rectory c. 1680.[34] The curacy was endowed in 1809 with £200 from Queen Anne's Bounty and in 1811 and 1822 with parliamentary grants of £300 each, to meet benefactions totalling £400. The living, by then a vicarage again, was further augmented with £172 a year from the Common Fund from 1870.[35] The net value averaged £58 a year in 1829–31 and was £232 in 1883.[36] In 1925 a further grant of £27 a year was made.[37]

The share of the church assigned to the vicar at ordination in 1254 comprised the personal tithes of the parishioners, the tithes of garths, and the tithes of animals, except for those of wool and lambs.[38] The small tithes and offerings still accounted for practically the whole value in 1535 and 1650.[39] In the 18th century the tithes included those of rape and furze, and compositions were then paid for the tithes of calves and herbage.[40] The tithes at Great Cowden were extinguished at inclosure in 1772 for £12 a year, payable from the allotment made to the archdeacon for all tithes.[41] At Withernwick less than an acre was awarded for the small tithes at inclosure in 1814; the allotment was sold in 1945.[42] The rest of the tithes, from Great Hatfield, Mappleton, and Rolston, were commuted in 1844 for a rent charge of £29 5s.[43]

A house south of the church was assigned to the vicar in 1254,[44] and the vicarage house occupied the same site until its decay and demolition in the later 17th century.[45] There was then no house until 1822–3, when benefactions and part of the augmentation were used to build one to designs by Appleton Bennison of Hull on the old site.[46] From 1979 the incumbent of the united benefice lived in the Mappleton house, but c. 1983 a new benefice house was built at Aldbrough.[47] The former vicarage house at Mappleton, a double-pile house with a Venetian window, was sold in 1984.[48]

From the 17th century the glebe comprised one or two acres in the vicarage garth and land and 2¾ gates in the common pasture; c. 1800 the curate was given nearly 4 a. for the gates, and at inclosure in 1849 an allotment of like amount was substituted.[49] Six acres at Great Cowden,

bought with the augmentation in 1810, were sold in 1912.[50] Some 5 a. remained unsold in 1978.[51]

A chaplain of Mappleton, recorded in 1320, may have assisted in the church.[52] Nicholas Jackson, vicar from 1563, denied charges made in 1567 that he had abandoned his cure for two years and set a bad example by quarrelling, drinking, and gaming, but he resigned shortly afterwards.[53] In 1596 it was presented that the rector had failed to provide sermons 'this last year'.[54] In the early 1640s William Davison, vicar, fled his cure and served in the Royalist army; he had evidently returned to Mappleton by 1649, was made a prebendary of York at the Restoration, and was still vicar in 1663.[55] No vicar was instituted later and the living was served by curates,[56] who usually held other Holderness livings.[57] For much of the 18th century Mappleton was served with Goxhill and Withernwick from Great Hatfield. Service was only fortnightly at Mappleton in the mid 18th century, when Holy Communion was celebrated five times a year, with 30 recipients at Easter being returned in 1764.[58] The antiquary W. H. Dixon was curate from 1819.[59] In the 1860s, when Mappleton was again served with Goxhill, there was a weekly service, and there were two from the 1870s. Communion was celebrated quarterly in the 1860s, monthly from the 1870s, and weekly by the earlier 20th century, with generally 10–20 communicants throughout the period.[60] The parish church was said to be 'very poorly attended' in the 1960s.[61]

The church of *ALL SAINTS*, so called in 1454,[62] occupies an elevated site and comprises chancel with north vestry, nave with north aisle and south porch, and west tower with spire. It is mostly of boulders with ashlar dressings. The building was extensively restored in 1855–6, when most of the architectural features were renewed or removed.[63] There was formerly a 12th-century south doorway[64] but the width of the nave suggests that that part of the church was remodelled at a later date. The chancel was altered or rebuilt in the 13th century. Much

34 B.I.H.R., TER. H. Mappleton 1685 etc.; Le Neve, *Fasti, 1541–1857, York*, 18.

35 Hodgson, *Q.A.B.* pp. clxxxv, cxcviii, cccxlvii; E.R.A.O., DDX/215/7; ibid. PE/27/2; *Lond. Gaz.* 10 Feb. 1871, p. 494; Le Neve, *Fasti*, iii. 144, 332.

36 B.I.H.R., V. 1884/Ret. 2; *Rep. Com. Eccl. Revenues*, 952–3.

37 E.R.A.O., PE/27/19.   38 *Reg. Gray*, p. 118.

39 *Valor Eccl.* (Rec. Com.), v. 116; *T.E.R.A.S.* iv. 63.

40 B.I.H.R., TER. H. Mappleton 1743, 1749, 1764.

41 R.D.B., AQ/61/8; 76/74/69 (1905).

42 Ibid. CQ/245/16; 690/342/275.

43 B.I.H.R., TA. 638L.

44 *Reg. Gray*, p. 119.

45 B.I.H.R., TER. H. Mappleton 1662/3; ibid. V. 1693–4/CB. 1, f. 49; Lamb. Pal. Libr., COMM. XIIa/18/93; *Valor Eccl.* v. 116; *T.E.R.A.S.* iv. 63.

46 E.R.A.O., DDX/215/7; ibid. PE/27/2; B.I.H.R., TER. H. Mappleton 1716, 1825.

47 B.I.H.R., OC. 942; above, Aldbrough, church.

48 Inf. from Mr. R. R. Kirke, Mappleton, 1992.

49 P.R.O., E 134/1658 Mic./1; E 134/1658 Mic./10; B.I.H.R., TER. H. Mappleton 1716 etc.; E.R.A.O., IA. Mappleton.

50 B.I.H.R., TER. H. Mappleton 1825; R.D.B., 144/38/34.

51 Inf. from York Dioc. Bd. of Finance, 1981.

52 *Kirkby's Inquest* (Sur. Soc. xlix), 413.

53 Lawrance, 'Clergy List', Holderness 1, p. 89; J. S. Purvis, *Tudor Par. Doc. Dioc. York*, 33.

54 B.I.H.R., V. 1595–6/CB. 1, p. 288.

55 Lamb. Pal. Libr., COMM. XIIa/18/93; B.I.H.R., TER. H. Mappleton 1662/3; *Miscellanea*, i (Y.A.S. Rec. Ser. lxi), 156; *T.E.R.A.S.* iv. 63; *Walker Revised*, ed. A. G. Matthews, 392.

56 B.I.H.R., TER. H. Mappleton 1685 etc.

57 E.R.A.O., PE/27/10, s.v. 1786.

58 B.I.H.R., V. 1764/Ret. 2, no. 140; V. 1764/Ret. 3, no. 140; *Herring's Visit.* ii, pp. 14–15, 223; iii, pp. 129–30, 225–7.

59 *D.N.B.*; B.I.H.R., Bp. Dio. 3, E.R., p. 191.

60 B.I.H.R., V. 1865/Ret. 2, no. 343; V. 1868/Ret. 2, no. 305; V. 1871/Ret. 2, no. 308; V. 1877/Ret. 2, no. 121; V. 1884/Ret. 2; V. 1912–22/Ret.; V. 1931/Ret.

61 B.I.H.R., MRD. 1/6/3 (closures 1966–9).

62 York Minster Libr., Reg. of Wills 1 (L 2/4), f. 277.

63 Below, this para.

64 For the earlier fabric, Poulson, *Holderness*, i. 361–2, pl. facing p. 390.

FIG. 24. MAPPLETON CHURCH IN THE EARLIER 19TH CENTURY

work was done in the 15th century, when the north aisle and arcade and the three-stage tower were added. It was perhaps then that the nave was enlarged. In 1590 the chancel was in disrepair,[65] and by the earlier 19th century there were sash windows in both nave and chancel. The broach spire was added at the mid 19th-century restoration, which was by Mallinson & Healey of Bradford.[66] The north aisle and arcade were then rebuilt, and the chancel was refenestrated in 14th-century style and the nave in that of the 15th century. The spire is of stone said to have been obtained from a local shipwreck.[67] Hannah Duke (d. 1882) left £100 for the maintenance of the church, and c. 1910 the income of £4 a year was used for church expenses.[68] The glass in eight windows was destroyed by enemy action in 1940; the east window was replaced and others reglazed c. 1955.[69]

The church contains an octagonal font of the 14th or 15th century bearing coats of arms[70] and a large marble tomb chest and a hatchment, both commemorating the Broughs of Rolston. There were two bells in 1552 but later only one, which was recast at York in 1708.[71] The plate includes a cup and a paten, the latter made in 1734.[72] Apart from some entries of baptisms for 1682, the registers begin in 1684; those of baptisms are complete, but marriages and burials lack a few years, chiefly in the 1690s.[73]

The wages of the parish clerk included a sheaf of wheat paid annually from each bovate,[74] for

which a rent charge of £1 7s. 2d. a year and 1½ a. were awarded at the inclosures of Great Cowden in 1772, Mappleton in 1849, and Rolston in 1860.[75] At Withernwick, where two sheaves were owed from each of two bovates, the clerk was awarded a few shillings a year at inclosure in 1814.[76] The land at Mappleton and Rolston remained unsold in 1978.[77]

LITTLE COWDEN. Until it was lost to the sea in the 16th or 17th century, there was a church at Little Cowden, the dedication being given variously as *ST. JOHN THE EVANGELIST* and *ST. JOHN THE BAPTIST*.[78] It was perhaps originally a chapel of either Aldbrough or Mappleton, both of which were given to Aumale abbey with their dependencies. The church was sometimes called a chapel, and in the 15th century it was said to be in Aldbrough parish;[79] by 1291, moreover, Aumale abbey had a pension from it, payable to the abbey's cell, Burstall priory (in Skeffling), and the prior of Burstall presented c. 1310.[80] The Crown presented in 1349, presumably because of the war with France. A share in the patronage, described as the advowson but possibly rather the right of nomination, had belonged to the lord of the manor, Ralph of Goxhill (d. by 1294),[81] and his heirs, the Despensers, successfully claimed the patronage from the Crown in the mid 14th century, when the abbey's right was in abeyance. In 1396 Aumale abbey sold the advowson and the

[65] B.I.H.R., V. 1590–1/CB. 1, f. 131v.

[66] Ibid. V. 1865/Ret. 2, no. 343; ibid. Ch. Ret. ii; E.R.A.O., PE/27/14–15.

[67] Notes in ch.

[68] R.D.B., NQ/80/113; E.R.A.O., PE/27/19; ibid. accession 1681; window in ch.

[69] B.I.H.R., Fac. 1954/1/39; inscription in ch.; cf. Poulson, *Holderness*, i. 362.

[70] *Y.A.J.* xxvi. 237.

[71] B.I.H.R., TER. H. Mappleton 1777 etc.; ibid. ER. V./CB. 1, f. 84; *Inventories of Ch. Goods*, 56; G. R. Park, *Ch. Bells of Holderness*, 68.

[72] *Yorks. Ch. Plate*, i. 289–90.

[73] E.R.A.O., PE/27/1–3, 6. They include marriages at Goxhill and burials at Great Hatfield. Transcripts survive

from 1600: B.I.H.R., ER. PRT.

[74] Ibid. TER. H. Mappleton 1764, 1777.

[75] E.R.A.O., IA. Mappleton, Rowlston; R.D.B., AQ/61/8.

[76] B.I.H.R., TER. H. Mappleton 1777; Withernwick 1764 etc.; R.D.B., CQ/245/16.

[77] Inf. from York Dioc. Bd. of Finance, 1981.

[78] B.I.H.R., Reg. 22, f. 92; Reg. 29, f. 121v. (Evangelist). Ibid. Reg. 18, f. 15v.; ibid. Bp. Dio. 3, E.R., p. 169, and later sources (Baptist).

[79] B.I.H.R., Reg. 22, f. 28; *Reg. Wickwane*, p. 114; *Cal. Pat. 1391–6*, 585.

[80] *Tax. Eccl.* (Rec. Com.), 304; *Reg. Greenfield*, v, p. 236. The account of the patronage is based on Lawrance, 'Clergy List', Holderness, 1, pp. 34–5.

[81] *Cal. Inq. p.m.* iii, pp. 135–7.

pension to Kirkstall abbey,[82] but Robert Despenser nevertheless presented in 1408. Kirkstall presented from 1420 until the Dissolution, when the Despensers' heirs, the Wentworths,[83] evidently maintained their right to present. The advowson later descended with the manor,[84] but the last presentations were made by the Crown, in 1608 by lapse[85] and in 1639 as guardian of John Bernard.

The church was worth £5 a year, after payment of the pension, in 1291, but only £2 13s. 4d. in 1535.[86] The poor living, called a rectory from the 14th century,[87] was held with Humbleton in the earlier 16th century.[88] By the 17th century the church and much land at Little Cowden had been lost to the sea;[89] the last known institution to Little Cowden alone was in 1639, and Little Cowden was described as 'anciently' a parish in 1650. Its area, comprising Little Cowden hamlet and part of Great Cowden, was regarded then and usually later as in Aldbrough parish,[90] to which the rectory of Little Cowden was annexed.[91] Hay tithes at Great Cowden had been compounded for an annual payment of 4d. a garth by 1685, and they remained uncommuted in 1857. Little Cowden was said to be tithe-free in 1650, and the rector had only surplice fees there in 1716. He later claimed the tithes,[92] and before 1830 accepted a lump sum of £500 from a landowner at Little Cowden for them; that agreement was disallowed by the Tithe Commissioners, who commuted the tithes in 1851 for £84 a year payable to the rector.[93]

NONCONFORMITY. One or two Roman Catholics were recorded in the 17th and 18th centuries,[94] and a Quaker family lived in the parish in 1764.[95] In the early 19th century the Scotch Baptist congregation in Beverley included members from Mappleton.[96] A house at Mappleton was registered by protestant dissenters in 1823[97] and an Independent chapel built there in 1838. The Wesleyans also used

the chapel by 1840,[98] and they rebuilt it on an enlarged site in 1890.[99] Sunday services ceased to be held in 1966, the chapel was closed in 1967, and the building was sold for a village hall in 1971.[1]

Missionary visits were paid by members of Fish Street chapel, Hull, to Cowden c. 1800,[2] and protestant dissenters registered a house at Great Cowden in 1813.[3] The Wesleyans built a chapel on waste land there in 1835 and had transferred it to the Primitive Methodists by 1877.[4] It was closed in 1942 by the military authorities, to whom the building was then sold because of the probability of its future destruction by the sea.[5]

EDUCATION. There was a school at Mappleton in the mid 17th century and c. 1800.[6] In 1818 the parish clerk kept a school in which c. 20 children were supported by Susannah Brough,[7] and it was probably for his school that a schoolhouse was built north of the church in 1820.[8] In 1833 there were 51 pupils, 21 paid for by subscription and the rest by their parents; two other schools were then recorded in Mappleton, both newly opened and together attended by 24 children.[9] It was probably the school of 1820 which was later recorded as a Church school; it was attended by 30–40 boys and girls in 1865 and on inspection day in 1871 by 56 children, including infants and children from the Cowdens.[10] In 1873 a new school was built at the junction of the street and Cliff Lane, on land given by Florence Whyte.[11] By 1872 the school's income included £6 6s. a year from a charity established by Mrs. Gee, probably Hannah Gee (d. 1826), an annual government grant was received from 1872–3, and the Ecclesiastical Commissioners had given £3 a year from the rectory by 1889.[12] Average attendance at the school, which also took private pupils, was usually 20–30 between 1906 and 1938, but only 16 in 1918–19 and 37 in 1926–7.[13] The school was closed in 1947 and its c. 15 pupils transferred to Hornsea County

[82] Cal. Pat. 1391–6, 585; Cal. Inq. Misc. vi, p. 52. Pension mentioned in P.R.O., E 134/12 Jas. I Hil./5.
[83] Complete Peerage, s.vv. Despenser, Wentworth.
[84] R.D.B., HH/39/45; Yorks. Fines, 1603–14, 216.
[85] P.R.O., E 134/22 Jas. I Mich./44.
[86] Tax. Eccl. (Rec. Com.), 304; Valor Eccl. (Rec. Com.), v. 119.
[87] Lawrance, 'Clergy List', Holderness, i, p. 34; Valor Eccl. v. 119.
[88] Lawrance, 'Clergy List', Holderness, i, pp. 35, 72.
[89] B.I.H.R., Bp. Dio. 3, E.R., p. 169.
[90] E.R.A.O., DDCC/1/1, s.v. 1674; R.D.B., AQ/61/8; Lawrance, 'Clergy List', Holderness, i, p. 35; T.E.R.A.S. iv. 51, 63; Census, 1871; above, intro.
[91] B.I.H.R., Bp. Dio. 3, E.R., p. 169; ibid. V. 1868/Ret. 1, no. 13.
[92] Ibid. TER. H. Aldbrough 1685 etc.; T.E.R.A.S. iv. 51.
[93] B.I.H.R., TA. 548s.
[94] Ibid. Bp. Dio. 3, E.R., p. 191; Depositions from York Castle (Sur. Soc. xl), p. 123; Aveling, Post Reformation Catholicism, 68.   [95] B.I.H.R., V. 1764/Ret. 2, no. 140.
[96] V.C.H. Yorks. E.R. vi. 243.
[97] P.R.O., RG 31/5, no. 3788.
[98] E.R.A.O., MRH/1/28; P.R.O., HO 129/522/4/1/2; Poulson, Holderness, i. 364; O.S. Map 6", Yorks. CXCVII (1854 edn.).

[99] R.D.B., 75/348/333 (1895); datestone.
[1] B.I.H.R., MRD. 1/6/3 (closures 1966–9); R.D.B., 1746/165/137.
[2] C. E. Darwent, Story of Fish St. Ch., Hull (1899), 128.
[3] B.I.H.R., Fac. Bk. 3, p. 666.
[4] E.R.A.O., MRH/1/28; P.R.O., HO 129/522/3/5/8; O.S. Map 6", Yorks. CCXIII (1855 edn.); O.S. Map 1/2,500, Yorks. CCXIII. 1 (1891 and later edns.).
[5] E.R.A.O., MRH/1/38.
[6] P.R.O., E 134/1658 Mic./1; N. Wright, John Day, a Village Poet.
[7] Educ. of Poor Digest, 1086.
[8] Baines, Hist. Yorks. (1823), 365; O.S. Map 6", Yorks. CXCVII (1854 edn.).
[9] Educ. Enq. Abstract, 1092.
[10] B.I.H.R., V. 1865/Ret. 2, no. 343; P.R.O., ED 7/135, no. 112; Returns relating to Elem. Educ. 472–3.
[11] B.I.H.R., Ch. Ret. ii; E.R.A.O., SGP. 54; R.D.B., LF/72/94; Bulmer, Dir. E. Yorks. (1892), 455. Kelly's Dir. N. & E.R. Yorks. (1889), 425 has 1871 in error.
[12] Kelly's Dir. N. & E.R. Yorks. (1872), 520; (1889), 425; Rep. of Educ. Cttee. of Council, 1872–3 [C.812], p. 519, H.C. (1873), xxiv; for Mrs. Gee, above, manors (Mappleton).
[13] B.I.H.R., V. 1912–22/Ret.; Bd. of Educ., List 21 (H.M.S.O., 1908 and later edns.).

School.[14] The building was sold in 1950[15] and was used as a house in 1992.

CHARITIES FOR THE POOR.

Robert Brown (d. by 1795) bequeathed £100 for fortnightly distributions of bread worth 2s. and Christmas doles; William Ake gave £100 with the same objects in 1848,[16] and Hannah Duke (d. 1882) left £100 for fuel at Christmas.[17] The three charities were administered together. In the early 20th century the combined annual income was c. £10, and half a dozen people received bread weekly and doles at Christmas for coal or flour.[18] The charities were evidently later inactive and, after Christmas doles totalling £20 had been made to widows from the combined income of nearly £28 in 1985, £142 of accumulated income remained unspent.[19] Town stock of nearly £7 was recorded in 1786 but later lost.[20]

NUNKEELING

THE parish lies 22 km. NNE. of Hull, extending east–west for about 5 km. over some of the highest ground in Holderness.[21] It focuses on two distinct settlements. At the west end was the parish church and the priory founded in the mid 12th century, which gave parish and settlement the first element of their name. The earlier name Keeling was Anglian, meaning the place of 'Cylla and his people'.[22] Since the Dissolution the settlement of Nunkeeling seems to have been very small, and in the 17th century it was called Little Keeling.[23] Larger, but still not large, is the hamlet of Bewholme, 2 km. east, where a mission church became the parish church in 1928.[24] The name Bewholme is Scandanavian and is believed to refer to bends in a river,[25] presumably Stream dike which forms the eastern parish boundary.

In 1851 the ancient parish contained 2,315 a. (937 ha.).[26] The civil parish, called Bewholme and Nunkeeling, had the same area. In 1935 the civil parish was united with those of Dunnington, in Beeford, and Bonwick, in Skipsea, to form the new civil parish of Bewholme, with a total area of 3,934 a. (1,592 ha.).[27] In 1984 c. 28 ha. (70 a.) were transferred to Bewholme from Brandesburton civil parish and about 1 ha. (3 a.) lost to Seaton civil parish.[28] In 1991 Bewholme comprised 1,619 ha. (4,001 a.).[29]

In 1377 there were 130 poll-tax payers in Nunkeeling, Bewholme, and Arram, in Atwick. At the Dissolution the priory housed 12 nuns, and c. 25 other people lived or worked there.[30] In 1672 Bewholme, Arram, and presumably also Nunkeeling, had 40 houses assessed for hearth tax.[31] The parish had 26 families in 1743 and 22 in 1764.[32] From 173 in 1801 the population rose to 291 in 1841, but had fallen to 217 by 1911 and stood at 224 in 1931, when the area later included in the new civil parish of Bewholme

had 303 inhabitants. The population was 267 in 1951 and 235 in 1991, when 246 were usually resident.[33]

The parish is largely on boulder clay. Scattered alluvial deposits occur on the lower land, and there is a pocket of sand and gravel near the southern boundary.[34] The land lies mostly more than 15 m. above sea level, rising in the middle and north of the parish to over 23 m. and to 30 m. north of the priory site. The parish is drained chiefly by Stream dike which flows north towards the Skipsea and Barmston drains and eventual outfall into the North Sea. It was evidently Stream dike which was in disrepair in 1367.[35] Lesser streams carry water from the middle of the parish into a sewer in Dunnington, and others bounded the ancient parish on the west and south.[36] At Nunkeeling the tillage lay north and south of the settlement and was evidently inclosed early, along with the other commonable lands. In Bewholme township the tillage apparently occupied the ground on either side of the settlement, with common meadows and pastures on lower ground in the east and south-west of the parish; Bewholme's commonable lands were inclosed in 1740.

The principal road is that crossing the parish between Brandesburton in the west and Atwick in the east. Other minor roads from Bewholme lead north to Skipsea and south to Seaton, in Sigglesthorne, and Hornsea. From Nunkeeling roads lead north to Dunnington, west to Brandesburton, and south and south-east to the principal road. The road south was made in 1796 to replace a way which evidently ran along the western parish boundary.[37]

NUNKEELING. Since the mid 19th century Nunkeeling has comprised only a dozen scattered houses, half of them farmhouses. The

[14] E.R. Educ. Cttee. *Mins.* 1946–7, 245; 1947–8, 114, 131.
[15] R.D.B., 851/380/312.
[16] *9th Rep. Com. Char.* 767–8; boards in ch.
[17] R.D.B., NQ/80/113; E.R.A.O., PE/27/19; *Kelly's Dir. N. & E.R. Yorks.* (1893), 461; window in ch.
[18] E.R.A.O., accession 1681.
[19] Ibid. CCH/68; Review of Char. *Rep.* 108.
[20] *9th Rep. Com. Char.* 768.
[21] This article was written in 1992.
[22] *P.N. Yorks. E.R.* (E.P.N.S.), 79.
[23] B.I.H.R., CP. H. 1098.
[24] Below, churches [services].
[25] *P.N. Yorks. E.R.* (E.P.N.S.), 77–8; G. F. Jensen, *Scand. Settlement Names in Yorks.* 77, 90.
[26] O.S. Map 6″, Yorks. CLXXX (1855 edn.).

[27] *Census,* 1931 (pt. ii).
[28] E.R.A.O., Holderness (Parishes) Order 1983; O.S. Map 1/2,500, Yorks. CLXXIX. 16, CLXXX. 13, CXCVI. 4 (1891 edn.).
[29] *Census,* 1991.
[30] P.R.O., E 179/202/60, mm. 66, 72; *Miscellanea* iii (Y.A.S. Rec. Ser. lxxx), 101, 105–6.
[31] *Hearth Tax,* 61.
[32] B.I.H.R., V. 1764/Ret. 2, no. 176; *Herrings's Visit.* ii, p. 203.
[33] *V.C.H. Yorks.* iii. 495; *Census,* 1911–91.
[34] Geol. Surv. Map 1″, drift, sheets 65, 73 (1909 edn.).
[35] Poulson, *Holderness,* i. 120–1.
[36] O.S. Map 6″, Yorks. CLXXX (1855 edn.).
[37] E.R.A.O., HD/4; ibid. QSF/353/B.2.

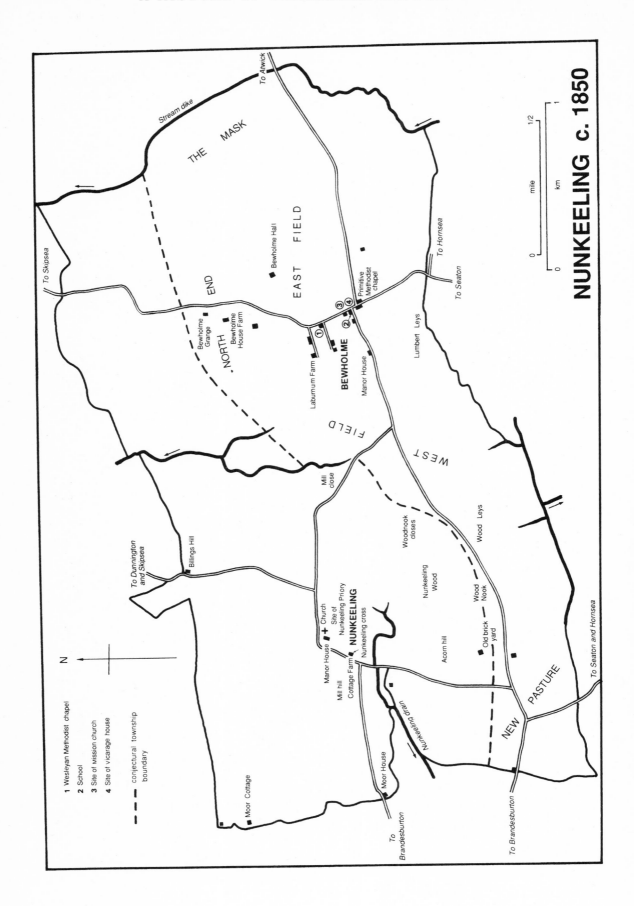

NUNKEELING c. 1850

1 Wesleyan Methodist chapel
2 School
3 Site of mission church
4 Site of vicarage house
– – – conjectural township
          boundary

manor house, called Nunkeeling Priory, dates from c. 1700.[38] In front of Magdalen Cottage, formerly Nunkeeling Cottage Farm, is the shaft of a stone cross inscribed 1718.

BEWHOLME. At Bewholme the settlement lies in two distinct groups, one near the junction of the Brandesburton-Atwick and Skipsea-Seaton roads, the other a group of farmhouses to the north known as North End. The buildings near the junction lie along the two intersecting roads and in side lanes running west from the Skipsea road. The 18th-century manor house[39] was built on the north side of the Brandesburton road. In the 19th century new buildings on the Skipsea-Seaton road, close to the junction, included the vicarage house, dissenting chapel, and school. Later building included the mission church of 1900 and 14 council houses.[40] Most of the buildings are of brick, but on one of the side lanes and beside the Brandesburton and Seaton roads there are several with boulder walls. Numbers 3 and 4 Front Row comprise a boulder-built, lobby-entry cottage, probably of the 18th century, which was extended and divided in the 19th. Two conservation areas in Bewholme were designated in 1991.[41] A 19th-century water pump survives opposite the school.

One or two houses at Bewholme were licensed in the later 18th century, and there was a beer-house there in the mid 19th century.[42] A former chapel-of-ease at Bewholme was used c. 1920 as a reading room and general parish meeting place, and a hut north of the church has been used as a recreation room since 1921.[43]

OUTLYING BUILDINGS include Moor Cottage in the north-west corner of the parish; it was run as a private lunatic asylum by the Beal family from 1821 to 1851, housing up to 29 private and pauper inmates.[44] Billings Hill Farm, north-east of the settlement of Nunkeeling, and Bewholme Grange, part of North End, existed by 1772, and Bewholme Hall from c. 1800.[45]

Between 1938 and 1949 the Air Ministry bought or obtained rights over c. 120 a. in the south-west corner of the parish for use as part of Catfoss airfield, which was mostly in Sigglesthorne.[46] The airfield was closed to flying in 1945 and completely in 1963;[47] the land in Nunkeeling was sold in the 1960s and has since been returned to agriculture or used industrially.[48]

MANORS AND OTHER ESTATES. In 1066 two manors of Keeling, comprising 4 carucates, were held by two men called Ketilfrith, and 5 carucates and 6 bovates in three manors of Bewholme by Norman, Ketilfrith, and Thorkil. All of the land had passed by 1086 to Drew de Bevrère and was later part of the Aumale fee. Drew's undertenants were then Baldwin in Keeling and Manbodo in Bewholme. In 1066 Ulf held 2 carucates in Keeling as soke of Beeford manor, and they too had passed to Drew by 1086.[49]

Herbert de St. Quintin (fl. early 12th century) evidently held a large part of the Aumale fee in the parish. Herbert's relict Agnes de Arches, or of Catfoss, used much of the estate to found Nunkeeling priory c. 1150. Agnes's gift, which was confirmed by her stepson Richard de St. Quintin, comprised Nunkeeling church, 3 carucates at Nunkeeling, and land and rights in Bewholme wood.[50] Other donors included her sons William and Hugh Foliot, her daughter Alice de St. Quintin, and her son Walter de Fauconberg.[51] In the mid 13th century the priory held half of Bewholme, comprising 3 carucates, and by 1276 it had 5 carucates at Nunkeeling and Bewholme together. In 1316 the prioress was named sole lord of Nunkeeling; at Bewholme one of the lords was then given as the prior of Bridlington, evidently in error for the prioress of Nunkeeling.[52] The priory was surrendered in 1540, and its site and the lands at Nunkeeling and Bewholme were granted that year to Sir Richard Gresham.[53]

Gresham (d. 1549) gave a moiety of *NUNKEELING* manor to his daughter Christine and her husband Sir John Thynne (d. 1580). That share descended from father to son, being held in turn by Sir John Thynne[54] (d. 1604), Sir Thomas Thynne (d. 1639), Sir Thomas Thynne (d. by 1671), and Thomas Thynne (d. 1682), before being sold in 1683 and 1684 to Edward Howard, later viscount Morpeth.[55] Edward's son Charles Howard, earl of Carlisle, sold his half of the manor to John Hudson in 1707. Hudson was succeeded by his brother William (d. 1734), who devised the share of Nunkeeling to his son Benjamin.[56] At the inclosure of Bewholme in 1740 Benjamin Hudson was awarded 279 a. jointly with the proprietor of the other half of Nunkeeling for the commonable lands of the manor.[57] Hudson (d. 1761) left the estate to

38 Below, manors (Nunkeeling).
39 Ibid. (Bewholme).
40 R.D.B.,   664/557/476;   809/89/73;   892/333/274; 1064/338/296.
41 Inf. from Devt. Dept., Holderness B.C., 1991.
42 E.R.A.O., QDT/2/9; directories.
43 B.I.H.R., V 1912–21/Ret; inf. from Mr. G. H. White, Bewholme, 1992; below, churches.
44 J. A. R. and M. E. Bickford, *Private Lunatic Asylums of the E.R.* (E. Yorks. Loc. Hist. Ser. xxxii), 19–22.
45 R.D.B., CF/225/350; T. Jefferys, *Map of Yorks.* (1772).
46 R.D.B., 596/507/398; 636/590/483; 775/69/51; 779/3/3; 802/584/498; 805/571/473; 806/119/101; 819/258/202.
47 B. B. Halpenny, *Action Stas.: 4. Military Airfields of Yorks.* 40–1; below, Sigglesthorne, intro. (Catfoss).
48 R.D.B., 1176/395/339; 1428/228/200; 1428/511/450; 1435/230/209; 1453/130/116; 1538/190/166; below, econ. hist. (ind.).

49 *V.C.H. Yorks.* ii. 267; *Cal. Inq. p.m.* iv, pp. 354, 356–7.
50 *E.Y.C.* iii, pp. 53–5; *Early Yorks. Fam.* (Y.A.S. Rec. Ser. cxxxv), 79; *V.C.H. Yorks.* iii. 119–20.
51 B.L. Cott. MS. Otho. C. viii, ff. 67, 69v., 70–2, 76; *E.Y.C.* iii. pp. 55–9; *Early Yorks. Fam.* 27, 79.
52 *Rot. Hund.* (Rec. Com.), i. 107; *Kirkby's Inquest*, 303, 372.
53 *L. & P. Hen. VIII*, xvi, pp. 95–6; *V.C.H. Yorks.* iii. 121.
54 P.R.O., C 142/195, no. 118; *Cal. Pat.* 1547–8, 331–2; *D.N.B.*, s.v. Sir Ric. Gresham; for the Thynnes, *Staffs. Pedigrees 1664–1700* (Harl. Soc. lxiii), 222; *Complete Peerage*, s.v. Weymouth.
55 P.R.O., C 142/765, no. 47; H.U.L., DDWI/68; *V.C.H. Wilts.* xiv. 199; Poulson, *Holderness*, i. 382; below, this section (rectory).
56 R.D.B., O/36/76; T/6/6.
57 Ibid. B/131/41.

his son John, who later reunited the manor by purchase.[58]

The other half of Nunkeeling manor evidently descended in turn to Sir Richard Gresham's sons Sir John (d. by 1563) and Sir Thomas (d. 1579).[59] In 1586–7 Thomas's widow Anne settled it on her son Sir William Read's son Sir Thomas (d. 1595), with remainder to Anne (d. 1596). Sir William Read (d. 1621) succeeded his mother.[60] Read's estate was shared after his death between his granddaughters, Jane Withypoole, Elizabeth Berkeley, Lady Berkeley, and Bridget Feilding, countess of Desmond.[61] Jane's share had descended by 1646 to her daughter Elizabeth, wife of Leicester Devereux, later viscount Hereford (d. 1676), and he bought the other shares in 1660.[62] In 1681 Devereux's executors sold his half of the manor to Arthur Thornton (d. after 1683). From Thornton the estate descended in turn to his son Sir William (d. by 1715) and grandson William Thornton. At the inclosure of Bewholme in 1740 Thornton was awarded 279 a. jointly with Benjamin Hudson, the owner of the other half of the manor, and in 1761 he sold his half to Benjamin's son and successor, John Hudson.[63]

Hudson died in 1772 and his Nunkeeling estate was sold in several lots between 1773 and 1775. Thomas Carter bought c. 350 a. in a farm, later known alternatively as Church or Manor farm, from Hudson's trustees in 1774 and c. 140 a. more the following year from John Burrill.[64] The manorial rights were, however, retained by Hudson's trustees and c. 1840 they belonged to Henry Hudson.[65] Carter (d. 1795) was succeeded by his daughter Rosamond (d. 1837), wife of Robert Dixon (d. by 1827), and they in turn by their son Thomas (d. 1850) and grandson T. C. Dixon.[66] The estate was enlarged in 1894 with c. 70 a. in Moor House and Cottage farms at Nunkeeling.[67] It passed after Dixon's death in 1899 to his son T. C. B. Dixon, who had previously bought c. 110 a. in Laburnum farm, Bewholme, and in 1906 added Bewholme Manor farm, later Bewholme Manor House farm, of c. 200 a.[68]

T. C. B. Dixon (d. 1906) was succeeded by his brother Robert Dixon, who had c. 880 a. in the parish in 1910.[69] After Dixon's death in 1937, most of the estate was partitioned between two of his daughters. In 1939 Elizabeth Ken-

nedy received Bewholme House farm, comprising c. 210 a., and Muriel Dixon c. 300 a., mostly in Church and Nunkeeling Cottage farms.[70] Elizabeth Kennedy (d. 1952) was succeeded in Bewholme House farm by her children, the Revd. Francis Kennedy and Kathleen Molz, and Kathleen and Mr. Kennedy's son Andrew were the joint owners in 1992.[71] Muriel Dixon died in 1968, and in 1973 her farms, together with Manor House and Laburnum farms at Bewholme, were vested in the Revd. Francis Kennedy and Kathleen Molz who later sold much of the estate in separate lots.[72] Laburnum farm was bought by R. L. Kirkwood in 1983,[73] Church and Nunkeeling Cottage farms, then comprising c. 260 a., by the Arnott family in 1987,[74] and c. 85 a., formerly part of Bewholme Manor House farm, by R. W. Elliott c. 1990. The Dixon heirs retained c. 125 a. in 1992.[75]

The chief house at Nunkeeling, formerly Manor House,[76] was built in the later 17th or early 18th century, although it incorporated some fragments of medieval walling from the nunnery. It served as the farmhouse for Church farm until 1967, when the house was separated from the land by sale; it has since been remodelled and renamed Nunkeeling Priory.[77]

After the appropriation of the church in 1409 the RECTORY also belonged to Nunkeeling priory. It was valued at £8 at the Dissolution.[78] In 1544 the Crown granted the rectory to Sir Richard Gresham, who had previously obtained the priory's landed estate, Nunkeeling manor. The rectory descended with the manor and was held in the same shares.[79] In 1650 the impropriators were given as George Feilding, earl of Desmond, husband of Bridget Feilding, presumably representing Read's heirs, and Sir Thomas Thynne. The rectory was then valued at £71.[80] At the inclosure of Bewholme in 1740 the two impropriators, Benjamin Hudson and William Thornton, were awarded a rent charge of £36 for the rectorial tithes; 9 bovates of their land were then tithe-free,[81] presumably as former demesne of the priory.

Much of the Aumale fee at Nunkeeling was held in the mid 13th century by Simon Whittick, who had 3 carucates there, and in 1284–5 by William Whittick.[82] No more is known of the estate.

---

[58] Below, this section.

[59] P.R.O., C 142/93, no. 50; ibid. C 3/77/44; D.N.B. s.v. Sir Thos. Gresham; Cal. Pat. 1547–8, 332.

[60] P.R.O., CP 25(2)/261/28–9 Eliz. I. Mich., no. 1; ibid. C 142/249, no. 57; C 142/396, no. 137.

[61] P.R.O., C 142/396, no. 137; rest of para. based on Poulson, Holderness, i. 380–2.

[62] Complete Peerage, s.vv. Desmond, FitzWalter.

[63] R.D.B., B/131/41; AD/172/391; E.R.A.O., DDRI/30/1.

[64] Hudson Estate Act, 13 Geo. III, c. 74 (Priv. Act); R.D.B., AS/235/398; AS/324/551; AS/325/552; AS/326/553; AS/327/554; AS/328/555; AS/364/590; E.R.A.O., PE/82/1.

[65] Poulson, Holderness, i. 384.

[66] R.D.B., BW/235/323; EC/346/389; FC/395/404; FC/396/406; FD/166/187; E.R.A.O., PE/31/1; PE/31/4/2; stone in churchyard.

[67] R.D.B., 69/301/285 (1894).

[68] Ibid. 47/318/295 (1891); 50/99/95 (1902); 86/292/70; 86/293/271 (both 1906).

[69] Ibid. 86/61/60 (1906); E.R.A.O., NV/1/18; inf. from Mr. White.

[70] R.D.B., 592/598/471; 628/540/443; 628/542/444; 628/594/485; inf. from Mr. D. A. D. Kennedy, Bewholme, 1992.

[71] Ibid. 926/133/112; 1085/438/385; inf. from Mr. Kennedy.

[72] Ibid. 1568/202/185; 1830/533/432; 1845/290/233; 1845/291/234.

[73] Inf. from Mr. A. C. T. Proctor, Bewholme, 1992.

[74] Inf. from Mr. R. W. A. Todd, Nunkeeling, 1992.

[75] Inf. from Mrs. C. Elliott, Bewholme, 1992.

[76] O.S. Map 6", Yorks. CLXXX (1855 edn.).

[77] Inf. from Mr. Todd.

[78] Valor Eccl. (Rec. Com.), v. 115; Miscellanea, iii. 101–2; below, churches (1st para.).

[79] E.R.A.O., DDCC/111/208; above, this section.

[80] T.E.R.A.S. iv. 62; Complete Peerage, s.v. Desmond.

[81] R.D.B., B/131/41; E.R.A.O., DDRI/4/1.

[82] Kirkby's Inquest, 75, 373.

It was probably part of the St. Quintin estate at Nunkeeling which Anne Fiennes, Lady Dacre (d. 1595), devised to Emanuel hospital, London. Comprising c. 50 a. in 1910, it descended with a larger estate in Brandesburton.[83]

The St. Quintins' estate at *BEWHOLME* had by 1278 descended to Herbert de St. Quintin, who then partitioned 2 carucates and 5 bovates and other land there with Walter de Fauconberg, later Lord Fauconberg.[84] In 1287 Herbert held 1 carucate and 2 bovates of the Aumale fee in demesne at Bewholme, and he was granted free warren there in 1286.[85] The St. Quintins' estate had evidently been granted away by the mid 14th century. John Moore, named as a lord of Bewholme in 1316, was presumably a tenant of the St. Quintins, and on the death of Herbert de St. Quintin in 1347 his only estate at Bewholme was apparently the 4 bovates held of him by Roger Moore.[86] The purchaser from the St. Quintins may have been Sir William de la Pole (d. 1366), who held 1 carucate and 6½ bovates at Bewholme under Burstwick, the chief manor of the Aumale fee.[87] From William's widow Catherine (d. 1382) the estate, later called Bewholme manor, descended to Edmund de la Pole, earl of Suffolk (d. 1513).[88]

Bewholme manor was evidently held of the de la Poles by the Butlers and Plessingtons, probably as heirs of Sir Walter Fauconberg. In 1391 a half share of Bewholme manor and those of Bilton, in Swine, and Catwick was settled on Richard Butler and his wife Catherine, evidently in her right.[89] Like Bilton, that share of Bewholme manor seems to have passed to Isabel Holme (fl. 1463), while the other moiety descended in the Plessingtons and their heirs, the Francises, Staveleys, and Flowers.[90] The whole or part of a manor of Bewholme being dealt with by Alexander Balam in 1510 and 1527 belonged to the same estate.[91]

Much of Bewholme was held by the Fauconbergs. In 1202 Parnel, widow of Stephen de Fauconberg (d. 1199), released to Stephen's brother Walter and his wife Agnes, her sister, land of the Fauconbergs at Bewholme which she presumably held in dower.[92] Walter and Agnes were succeeded by William de Fauconberg, who held half of Bewholme, comprising 3 carucates,

in the mid 13th century.[93] His successor, Walter de Fauconberg, later Lord Fauconberg, who partitioned land at Bewholme with Herbert de St. Quintin in 1278, held 1 carucate and 2 bovates of the Aumale fee there in 1287.[94] The estate, held by free tenants and said to comprise 6 carucates in the 14th and 15th centuries, descended as an appurtenance of the Fauconbergs' manor of Rise to their successors, the Nevilles and later the Crown.[95]

Bewholme was evidently settled on descendents of Stephen de Fauconberg. William de Fauconberg (d. 1294) held a wood in Nunkeeling, perhaps at Bewholme, of Walter de Fauconberg, Lord Fauconberg, and it was presumably William's grandson who, as Walter son of John de Fauconberg, was named as a lord of Bewholme in 1316.[96] John de Fauconberg (d. 1366) was succeeded in 1 carucate at Bewholme, held of Lady Isabel de Fauconberg's manor of Rise, by his son (Sir) Walter. That estate probably descended with Walter's other land in Bewholme,[97] and it seems to have been the same which Hilary Constable (d. 1571) held.[98]

It was presumably all or part of Walter de Fauconberg's estate which the Hopper family held under Rise manor in the early 17th century. A manor house, and evidently also land, descended from William Hopper to his son Walter (d. 1658)[99] and from Walter to his daughter Susanna, who married Robert Johnson in 1659.[1] The manor was later shared between the Johnsons' daughters, of whom Susanna married Simon Grindall. The Grindalls' son Simon bought another ⅕ share from William Piper in 1728 and was awarded 58 a. at inclosure in 1740.[2] He was dead by 1742, when his widow Priscilla bought another ⅕ from Elizabeth Burton, granddaughter of Robert Johnson.[3] Priscilla was dead by 1748, and in 1761 her daughter Priscilla Grindall sold the estate to William Acklam (d. 1789).[4] It then descended from father to son, being held by William Acklam (d. 1804), Thomas Acklam (d. 1811), and William Acklam (d. 1865).[5] The executors of William's widow Ann (d. 1873) sold the estate, of 205 a., in 1875 to John Bainton (d. 1891).[6] Bainton's son John sold it, as Bewholme Manor farm, in 1906 to T. C. B. Dixon and it later descended with the Dixon family's larger estate in the parish.[7]

Bewholme Manor House is an early 18th-

[83] E.R.A.O., NV/1/18; *Complete Peerage*, s.v. Dacre; above, Brandesburton, manors; Mappleton, manors.

[84] *Yorks. Fines, 1272–1300*, pp. 14–15; *Complete Peerage*, s.v. Fauconberg.

[85] *Cal. Chart. R. 1257–1300*, 328; *Cal. Inq. p.m.* iv, p. 357; *Kirkby's Inquest*, 74; *Yorks. Inq.* iv (Y.A.S. Rec. Ser. xxxvii), pp. 32–3.

[86] *Cal. Inq. p.m.* ix, p. 27; *Kirkby's Inquest*, 303.

[87] *Cal. Inq. p.m.* xii, p. 55; *Cal. Close, 1346–9*, 10; *V.C.H. Yorks. E.R.* v. 9.

[88] E.R.A.O., DDCC/112/119; *Cal. Inq. p.m.* xv, p. 232; *Cal. Inq. p.m. Hen. VII*, i, p. 456; *Cal. Pat. 1388–92*, 208–9; 1494–1509, pp. 259–61; *Cal. Close, 1447–54*, 215; *Complete Peerage*, s.v. Suffolk.

[89] P.R.O., CP 25(1)/278/145, no. 39; above, Swine, Bilton, manor; above, Catwick, manors.

[90] P.R.O., CP 25(1)/281/162, no. 7; ibid. C 139/148, no. 3; C 139/169, no. 34; C 142/45, no. 18; C 142/48, no. 92; *Cal. Inq. p.m. Hen. VII*, i, p. 456; *Yorks. Deeds*, viii, p. 132.

[91] *Yorks. Fines*, i. 23, 50.

[92] *Yorks. Fines, John* (Sur. Soc. xciv), pp. 12–14; *E.Y.C.* iii, p. 49.   [93] *Kirkby's Inquest*, 372.

[94] *Yorks. Fines, 1272–1300*, pp. 14–15; *Kirkby's Inquest*, 74; *Cal. Inq. p.m.* iv, p. 357; *Complete Peerage*, s.v. Fauconberg.

[95] P.R.O., C 142/583, no. 27; *Cal. Inq. p.m.* ix, p. 177; xviii, p. 136; *Complete Peerage*, s.vv. Fauconberg, Westmorland; below, Rise, manor.

[96] *Cal. Inq. p.m.* iii, pp. 159–60; *Kirkby's Inquest*, 303; *Complete Peerage*, s.v. Fauconberg of Cuckney.

[97] *Cal. Inq. p.m.* xii, pp. 86–7; above, previous para.

[98] P.R.O., C 142/160, no. 43.

[99] Ibid. C 142/583, no. 27; E.R.A.O., PE/31/1.

[1] R.D.B., P/338/870; E.R.A.O., PE/29/1.

[2] R.D.B., B/131/41; K/395/817; P/338/870; E.R.A.O., PE/29/1.   [3] R.D.B., Q/382/979; R/61/144.

[4] Ibid. S/514/1253; AD/195/432; E.R.A.O., PE/31/4/1.

[5] R.D.B., IS/117/153; E.R.A.O., PE/31/4/1.

[6] R.D.B., LI/74/93; LR/63/88; 46/41/40 (1891).

[7] Above, this section (Nunkeeling).

century building which was enlarged and re-modelled in the mid 19th century. It has extensive farm buildings of the 18th and 19th centuries.

Another manor of Bewholme was sold by Edmund Lloyd in 1709 to John Hudson, who also bought part of Nunkeeling manor and rectory.[8] Hudson devised it to his brother William (d. 1734) and he to his son Thomas, who was awarded 358 a. at inclosure in 1740.[9] Thomas Hudson (d. by 1764) left the manor to his nephew William Hudson (d. by 1810),[10] and William's wife and daughter sold most of the estate in 1810–16.[11] The largest part, comprising c. 315 a. and including shares previously sold to others, passed to Thomas Ward (d. by 1830).[12] He was succeeded by his son Thomas (d. by 1868), who enlarged the estate at Bewholme to c. 370 a.[13] Ward's trustees sold it in several lots in 1891, 220 a. going to Samuel Haldane (d. 1910).[14] As Bewholme Hall farm, it was sold in 1910 to W. S. Hoe and in 1911 first to Walter Stickney and then to Edmond Richardson (d. 1915) and Francis Richardson.[15] In 1938 the farm was vested in Francis (d. 1955) and F. W. O. Richardson, and it still belonged to the Richardsons in 1992.[16]

ECONOMIC HISTORY. AGRICULTURE BEFORE 1800. Nunkeeling and Bewholme probably each had their own fields and commons.

Nunkeeling. At Nunkeeling in 1086 there was land for 4 ploughteams and 16 a. of meadow land.[17] Part of the tillage there lay north and south of the priory, where ridge-and-furrow survived in 1992. The commonable lands of the settlement were presumably inclosed early by the priory. The house and its tenants evidently also enjoyed grazing rights on Brandesburton moor, a funnel-shaped outgang followed by the parish boundary linking the village and the moor.[18]

Bewholme. At Bewholme in 1086 there was 1 ploughland and 20 a. of meadow.[19] The open fields there were recorded as East and West fields in 1562,[20] and ridge-and-furrow survived on either side of the village in 1992. The fields were said to include meadow land and pasture, some of the grassland in East field probably lying in Mask.[21] On the eve of inclosure in 1740, East field contained 37 and West field 35 narrow

bovates, and each field had 12 broad bovates. Rough grazing was then also provided by New pasture, which adjoined West field. When West field was fallow, it was grazed in summer with New pasture, 10 beast gates being enjoyed in the field and pasture for each broad bovate in West field and 4 gates for each narrow bovate. When East field was fallow, New pasture was grazed in summer at the rate of 20 gates for each broad and 2 gates for each narrow bovate in East field; the stint in East field itself was 2 gates for each of the 49 bovates from March to May, and 4 gates in summer. After harvest, the pasture in West field was stinted at the rate of 10 gates for each broad bovate and 6 gates for each narrow one there; in East field the rate was 8 gates a bovate, broad or narrow. Householders and cottagers also enjoyed beast, sheep, and geese gates in the fallow and harvested fields.

The commonable lands of Bewholme were inclosed by an award of 1740 under an Act of that year. Allotments made totalled 1,043 a. They comprised 491 a. in East field, 418 a. in West field, and 134 a. in New pasture. Thomas Hudson received 358 a., and William Thornton and Benjamin Hudson 279 a. jointly. There was also one allotment of 114 a., three of 50–79 a., four of 10–29 a., and two of under 5 a.[22]

Woodland. Much of the parish was formerly wooded. In 1086 woodland 3 furlongs long and 1 furlong broad was recorded at Bewholme,[23] and c. 1150 Agnes de Arches gave Nunkeeling priory the use of her wood at Bewholme for the repairing of its ploughs and harrows.[24] Later it was stipulated that the timber be taken on four days each year under the supervision of a forester.[25] The woodland evidently lay mostly south of the priory, where later field-names have included Acorn hill, Wood nook, Woodnook closes, and Nunkeeling wood. It was reduced by assarting, which probably created New pasture, Wood leys, and Lumbert leys.[26] By 1851 the only woodland was that in several small plantations, and in 1987 no more than 12 a. (5 ha.) of woodland were returned for Bewholme civil parish.[27]

LATER AGRICULTURE. In 1801 there was said to be 645 a. under crops in the parish.[28] In 1905 there were 1,499 a. of arable land and 824 a. of grassland, and the proportion of arable to grass was much the same in the 1930s, when the grassland lay mostly around Bewholme village and the settlement of Nunkeeling.[29] In Bew-

[8] R.D.B., A/142/205; above, this section (Nunkeeling, rectory).

[9] R.D.B., B/131/41; O/36/76; Poulson, *Holderness*, i. 382.

[10] R.D.B., AE/477/907; CR/141/174; CZ/527/792.

[11] Ibid. CR/141/174; CR/141/175; CR/142/176; CR/142/177; CR/143/178; CR/143/179; CY/55/81; CZ/36/61.

[12] Ibid. CZ/527/792; DF/122/173; DO/59/65; EL/248/295; EM/92/90.

[13] Ibid. EM/92/90; KF/62/78.

[14] Ibid. 47/4/4; 47/5/5; 47/60/57; 47/62/59; 47/73/70; 47/318/295 (all 1891); 124/439/391.

[15] Ibid. 127/44/43; 136/358/297; 136/359/298; 607/106/83.

[16] Ibid. 607/106/83; 1019/423/375; 1057/120/114; inf. from Mr. F. W. O. Richardson, Bewholme, 1992.

[17] *V.C.H. Yorks.* ii. 267.

[18] Above, Brandesburton, econ. hist.

[19] *V.C.H. Yorks.* ii. 267.

[20] E.R.A.O., DDBV/4/1.

[21] Ibid. DDRI/4/1; O.S. Map 6″, Yorks. CLXXX (1855 edn.).

[22] 13 Geo. II, c. 16 (Priv. Act) at E.R.A.O., DDRI/4/1; R.D.B., B/131/41.

[23] *V.C.H. Yorks.* ii. 267.

[24] *E.Y.C.* iii, p. 53.

[25] Burton, *Mon. Ebor.* 386.

[26] O.S. Map 6″, Yorks. CLXXX (1855 edn.).

[27] Ibid.; inf. from Min. of Agric., Fish. & Food, Beverley, 1990.

[28] P.R.O., HO 67/26/324.

[29] Acreage Returns, 1905, where the figures exceed the area of the par.; [1st] Land Util. Surv. Map, sheet 28.

holme civil parish 1,231 ha. (3,042 a.) were returned as arable land and 190 ha. (469 a.) as grassland in 1987, when more than 8,000 pigs and 1,200 sheep were kept.[30]

In the 19th and earlier 20th century there were usually a dozen farmers in Nunkeeling parish, half of whom had 150 a. or more. Two men also worked as cowkeepers from the late 19th century.[31] In 1987 of 23 holdings returned for the civil parish, one was of 200–299 ha. (494–739 a.), four of 100–199 ha. (247–492 a.), six of 50–99 ha. (124–245 a.), and twelve of under 50 ha.[32]

MILLS. Nunkeeling priory had a mill at Bewholme,[33] and former mill sites are commemorated by Mill hill and Mill close.

INDUSTRY. There has been little non-agricultural employment in Nunkeeling parish. Bricks were made in the south-west of the parish before 1852.[34] In 1968 Belmont Caravan Co. bought c. 40 a. of the former Catfoss airfield, mostly in Nunkeeling, and in 1992 its successor, A. B. I. Caravans Ltd., maintained a storage site for c. 3,000 vehicles there.[35] A light engineering workshop was established at Bewholme in 1973, moved to Nunkeeling in 1984, and was still operated in 1992.[36]

LOCAL GOVERNMENT. Regular poor relief was given to 7 people in 1802–3 and to c. 20 in 1812–15, when about 10 were helped occasionally.[37] Bewholme and Nunkeeling joined Skirlaugh poor-law union in 1837[38] and remained in Skirlaugh rural district until 1935, when, as part of Bewholme civil parish, they were incorporated into the new rural district of Holderness. In 1974 Bewholme civil parish became part of the Holderness district of Humberside.[39] In 1996 Bewholme parish became part of a new East Riding unitary area.[40]

CHURCHES. Agnes de Arches gave Nunkeeling church c. 1150 to the priory which she then founded there. The priory appropriated the church in 1409;[41] no vicarage was ordained, and the cure was later served by stipendary chaplains supplied by the priory.[42] After the Dissolution the living was styled a perpetual or donative curacy until it became a vicarage following augmentation in the 19th century. A chapel-of-ease was then provided at Bewholme.[43] The benefice, later called Nunkeeling with Bewholme, was united with Atwick in 1937, with Sigglesthorne instead in 1972, and also with Rise in 1974.[44]

The advowson was granted in 1544, with the rectory, to Sir Richard Gresham. The patronage later belonged to the proprietors of the halves of Nunkeeling manor and rectory until 1761 and thereafter descended with the reunited estate.[45] In 1935 Robert Dixon transferred the advowson to the archbishop of York.[46] From 1937 the archbishop had the right to present alternately to the united benefice until 1958, when he ceded his right to the other patron, the Crown. The Crown remained the sole patron after the further unions of 1972 and 1974.[47]

From the 17th to the 19th century the sole income was the curate's stipend of c. £20 a year paid from the rectory.[48] The living was augmented from Queen Anne's Bounty with grants of £200 in 1807, 1811, and 1825, and a parliamentary grant of £200 was received in 1817.[49] In 1829–31 the average net income was £55 a year.[50] A further augmentation of £100 from Queen Anne's Bounty was made in 1859 to meet a like benefaction from Mrs. Pyncombe's trustees,[51] and in 1889 the net value was said to be £80 a year.[52]

The augmentations were used to buy 7 a. at Great Cowden, in Mappleton, in 1810, 5 a. in Aldbrough in 1812, and 5 a. in Atwick in 1821.[53] The land at Aldbrough was sold in 1968, that at Atwick c. 1975, and the holding at Great Cowden by 1978.[54] The monies granted in 1859 were used that year to build a parsonage house on land at Bewholme given by Thomas Ward. The house, too grand for the poor living, was designed by William Burges, but probably built under the supervision of William Foale, who was also recorded as its architect; it is of red brick with prominent, slate roofs and has two storeys with attics, a seven-bayed front, and a projecting stair tower. The deep, overhanging eaves with bargeboards are supported by large, flying brackets, of painted wood, and the windows have decorative stone heads.[55] The house was sold in 1961, and the incumbents later lived at Hornsea or Sigglesthorne.[56]

Nunkeeling was served with other Holderness parishes from the 18th century and curates were

30 Inf. from Min. of Agric., Fish. & Food.
31 P.R.O., HO 107/2365; directories.
32 Inf. from Min. of Agric., Fish. & Food.
33 B.L. Cott. MS. Otho C. viii, f. 69v.
34 O.S. Map 6″, Yorks. CLXXX (1855 edn.).
35 R.D.B., 1538/190/166; 1541/97/83; inf. from A. B. I. Caravans, Beverley, 1992.
36 R.D.B., 1840/168/133; inf. from Mr. W. Acomb, Catfoss, 1992.
37 Poor Law Abstract, 1804, pp. 594–5; ibid. 1818, pp. 522–3.
38 3rd Rep. Poor Law Com. 170.   39 Census.
40 Humberside (Structural Change) Order 1995, copy at E.R.A.O.
41 E.Y.C. iii, p. 53; Miscellanea, ii (Sur. Soc. cxxvii), 180 and n.
42 B.I.H.R., Bp. Dio. 3, E.R., p. 178.
43 Ibid. TER. H. Nunkeeling 1685 etc.; Rep. Com. Eccl. Revenues, 958–9; directories; below, this section.

44 Lond. Gaz. 9 Feb. 1937, pp. 875–6; 30 May 1972, p. 6506; 24 Oct. 1974, p. 9834.
45 R.D.B., AD/172/391; E.R.A.O., DDCC/111/25; Cal. Pat. 1569–72, p. 65; 1575–8, p. 263; above, manors (rectory).
46 Lond. Gaz. 22 Feb. 1935, pp. 1259–60.
47 B.I.H.R., OC. 651, 745, 854, 881.
48 Ibid. TER. H. Nunkeeling 1685 etc.
49 Hodgson, Q.A.B. p. cccxlviii.
50 Rep. Com. Eccl. Revenues, 958–9.
51 Hodgson, Q.A.B. supplement, pp. xliv, lxxvi.
52 Kelly's Dir. N. & E.R. Yorks. (1889), 434.
53 E.R.A.O., PE/31/17–19.
54 R.D.B., 1578/509/403; inf. from Mr. White; inf. from York Dioc. Bd. of Finance, 1981.
55 B.I.H.R., Ch. Ret. ii; R.D.B., HX/57/70; E.R.A.O., DDX/215/10; The Ecclesiologist, xxi. 41; Pevsner and Neave, Yorks. E.R. 323–4.
56 R.D.B., 1228/430/376; B.I.H.R., OC. 854; Crockford.

FIG. 25. NUNKEELING CHURCH IN 1784

usually non-resident; in 1743 the curate lived at Sproatley, where he was rector. In the mid 18th century service was weekly in summer and fortnightly in winter; communion was celebrated three times a year, with up to 26 recipients in 1743 and 1764.[57] At the parish church, which was remote from most of the houses, a Sunday service was held only in summer by 1865. Bewholme school had been licensed for services in 1857, and in 1865 weekly services were being held there throughout the year.[58] In the later 19th century up to 10 people usually received at the monthly celebrations of communion, which were presumably held in the parish church.[59] William Burges designed a church for Bewholme in 1860,[60] but it was not built and c. 1875 the vicarage coach house there was converted to serve as a chapel-of-ease.[61] In 1895 adjacent land was consecrated as a burial ground, and on it a mission church, dedicated in 1900, was built to replace the chapel-of-ease and licensed for all services, except marriage.[62] In 1928 services were discontinued at Nunkeeling and the mission church became the parish church, receiving a licence for marriages in 1929.[63]

NUNKEELING. The parish church was evidently dedicated to *ST. MARY MAGDALEN AND ST. HELEN* at the foundation of the priory c. 1150.[64] Unusually, but as at Swine,[65] the parish church later stood east of, and adjoining, the priory church, which was removed after the Dissolution. The medieval parish church comprised chancel and nave with north aisle. The aisle was added in the 13th century, and a remodelling of the chancel then is evident from its former windows. Presumably after the Dissolution, the aisle was removed and its windows refixed in the blocked arcade. The building fell into disrepair, and by the end of the 18th century the chancel was roofless.[66] The church was rebuilt in 1810 at the expense of Robert Dixon.[67] The new church, of boulders and brick with stone dressings, comprised chancel and nave with west bell turret.[68] Some materials from the medieval building were reused, principally the north arcade which was rebuilt as a triple chancel arch. Nunkeeling church ceased to be used in 1928 and fell into disrepair; the walls of the unroofed building were consolidated by the parish council in 1987.[69] In 1992 it was unused.

The medieval church evidently had a Norman font and stone effigies thought to commemorate the Fauconberg family, all of which were refixed after rebuilding in the 19th-century church. The font was removed to a Hull church in 1939[70]

57 B.I.H.R., V. 1764/Ret. 2, no. 176; *Herring's Visit.* ii, p. 204.
58 B.I.H.R., V. 1865/Ret. 2, no. 387; ibid. LDS. 1857/5.
59 Ibid. V. 1865/Ret. 2, no. 387; V. 1868/Ret. 2, no. 345; V. 1871/Ret. 2, no. 348; V. 1877/Ret. 2, no. 165.
60 *The Ecclesiologist,* xxi. 189–90.
61 E.R.A.O., PE/31/28.
62 B.I.H.R., CD. 541; ibid. Inst. AB. 28, p. 25; R.D.B., 72/148/144 (1895); directories.
63 E.R.A.O., PE/31/7/1; PE/31/21; PE/31/26.

64 *E.Y.C.*, iii, p. 53; *V.C.H. Yorks.* iii. 119–20.
65 Above, Swine, church.
66 B.I.H.R., V. 1615/CB. 5, ff. 214v., 215; ibid. ER. V. Ret. 1, f. 33; ER. V./Ret. 2, f. 7; *Y.A.J.* ix. 209–11; illus. in Poulson, *Holderness,* i, pl. facing p. 386.
67 B.I.H.R., TER. 85; Poulson, *Holderness,* i. 386; inf. from Mr. I. Harness, Bewholme, 1992.
68 T. Allen, *Hist. Co. York,* iv. 229.
69 E.R.A.O., PE/31/7/1; inf. from Mr. White.
70 B.I.H.R., Fac. Bk. 12, p. 165A.

and the memorials to Hornsea church in 1948.[71] Since 1552 there has been one bell, which was rehung in 1908 and later removed to Bewholme. The plate formerly included a cup, perhaps made in 1765.[72]

BEWHOLME. The small, mission church of *ST. JOHN THE BAPTIST* at Bewholme was built in or soon before 1900 to designs by W. S. Walker.[73] It is of red brick and comprises undivided chancel and nave with south porch and west bell turret. The pitch-pine fittings include benches and chancel and vestry screens. It has one bell, formerly in Nunkeeling church, and a modern service of silver-gilt.[74]

The registers of baptisms date from 1607, of marriages from 1656, and of burials from 1559. They are complete, except for marriages from 1689–94.[75]

NONCONFORMITY. Up to 33 Roman Catholics were recorded in Nunkeeling in the 17th century, but there were very few later.[76] Prominent among them were Ralph Creswell, who employed a papist tutor in 1604, and George Acklam, who compounded for his estate in 1653.[77]

One protestant dissenter was recorded in 1676.[78] In the mid 18th century two families in the parish were Presbyterian, and in 1764 a few Presbyterians were said to meet monthly in a house licensed for worship.[79] The Independents registered a house at Bewholme in 1805, and it seems to have been the same congregation which obtained a licence for another house there in 1812.[80] The Wesleyan Methodists built a chapel there in 1831.[81] The chapel was disused by 1893, was reopened c. 1905, but was closed finally and sold in 1924.[82] It was later a house.[83] The

Primitive Methodists built a chapel at Bewholme in 1839.[84] It was largely rebuilt in 1863,[85] and in 1868 almost all of the labourers were said to be members of that congregation.[86] That chapel became the Methodist church and was still used for services in 1992.

EDUCATION. A school opened at Bewholme in 1824 had 6 pupils in 1833, and another, begun there in 1832, had 14 pupils; both were supported by the parents.[87] A school was built at Bewholme in 1848.[88] At inspection in 1871 the Church school had 27 children in attendance, including some from Dunnington, in Beeford.[89] The building was enlarged in 1875.[90] The school was transferred in 1910 to the county council,[91] which enlarged the premises the next year; the children were taught temporarily in the parish room during the alterations.[92] From 1906 until 1938 the average attendance was usually 40–50.[93] Senior pupils were removed to Hornsea County Secondary School in 1958.[94] Pupils from Atwick were received by the primary school in 1961, and in 1990 there were 31 on the roll at Bewholme.[95]

CHARITIES FOR THE POOR. In 1630 George Acklam gave £5 as a town stock and directed that the annual income of 6s. 8d. be distributed to the poor of the parish. He, or another George Acklam, apparently replaced the gift later with 5s. a year charged on a house at Bewholme. Payment was refused after 1812 and the charity was lost.[96]

Ann Acklam (d. 1873) devised £100, the income to be distributed at Christmas. The income was £5 in the earlier 20th century but had fallen to c. £2 by 1992, when the charity had been inactive for many years.[97]

[71] *Y.A.J.* xxxvii. 4; above, Hornsea, church [monuments].
[72] Ibid. TER. H. Nunkeeling 1764 etc.; ibid. TER. 85; G. R. Park, *Ch. Bells of Holderness*, 68; *Inventories of Ch. Goods*, 51; *Yorks. Ch. Plate*, i. 298; below, this section.
[73] Pevsner and Neave, *Yorks. E.R.* 323; above, this section [services].
[74] B.I.H.R., TER. 878; inf. from Mr. White.
[75] E.R.A.O., PE/31/1, 3–7.
[76] Aveling, *Post Reformation Catholicism*, 68.
[77] *Cal. Cttee. for Compounding*, iv, pp. 3, 111; J. T. Cliffe, *Yorks. Gentry*, 194–5.
[78] *Compton Census*, ed. Whiteman, 600.
[79] B.I.H.R., V. 1764/Ret. 2, no. 176; *Herring's Visit.* ii, p. 203.
[80] B.I.H.R., Fac. Bk. 3, pp. 408, 604.
[81] P.R.O., HO 129/522/5/2/2.
[82] Circuit plan of 1905 at E.R.A.O., accession 1474; directories; inf. from Mr. White.
[83] D. [R. J.] and S. Neave, *E.R. Chapels and Meeting Houses* (E. Yorks. Loc. Hist. Soc.), 46.
[84] P.R.O., HO 129/522/5/2/3. It was registered apparently in 1841 and certainly in 1842: B.I.H.R., DMH. 1841/17; 1842/24; R.D.B., 3/256/239 (1885).

[85] Illus. in Neaves, op. cit. 46; *Nonconformist Chapels and Meeting Houses in N. of Eng.* (Royal Com. Hist. Monuments, 1994), 192.
[86] B.I.H.R., V. 1868/Ret. 2, no. 345.
[87] *Educ. Enq. Abstract*, 1093. Also *Educ. of Poor Digest*, 1087.
[88] Sheahan and Whellan, *Hist. York & E.R.* ii. 426.
[89] *Returns relating to Elem. Educ.* 472–3; above, Beeford, educ.
[90] Bulmer, *Dir. E. Yorks.* (1892), 462.
[91] R.D.B., 130/246/215; E.R. Educ. Cttee. *Mins.* 1909–10, 290; 1910–11, 197.
[92] E.R. Educ. Cttee. *Mins.* 1910–11, 72; 1911–12, 57, 169, 321.
[93] *Bd. of Educ., List 21* (H.M.S.O., 1908 and later edns.).
[94] E.R. Educ. Cttee. *Mins.* 1955–6, 151; above, Hornsea, educ.
[95] Inf. from Educ. Dept., Humbs. C.C., 1990; above, Atwick, educ.
[96] *9th Rep. Com. Char.* 768–9; R.D.B., CT/102/76; E.R.A.O., PE/31/1.
[97] E.R.A.O., PE/31/23; ibid. accession 1681; *Review of Char. Rep.* 102; inf. from Mr. Harness; above, manors (Bewholme).

RISE

THE small village of Rise lies *c.* 11 km. east of Beverley and NNE. of Hull and 7 km. south-west of the coast at Hornsea.[98] Close by, on the edge of Rise park, stand Rise Hall and Rise Park, former and present seats of the Bethell family.[99] The parish is relatively well-wooded for Holderness and the former significance of its woodlands is evident from the Scandinavian name, meaning 'amongst the brushwood'.[1]

In 1852 the ancient parish contained 2,040 a. (826 ha.), of which 6 a. (2.4 ha.) lay in Arnold township and the rest formed Rise township, later civil parish.[2] Possibly in error, the area of Rise civil parish was recorded as 2,041 a. (826 ha.) from 1891.[3] It was reduced by 9 a. (3.6 ha.) transferred to Skirlaugh civil parish in 1952 and was thereafter given as 2,033 a. (823 ha.).[4] In 1984 some 10 ha. (25 a.) were added from Riston,[5] and in 1991 Rise was said to comprise 830 ha. (2,051 a.).[6]

There were 87 poll-tax payers at Rise in 1377,[7] and 25 houses were assessed for hearth tax and 5 discharged in 1672.[8] The parish had 33 families in 1743 and 25 in 1764.[9] From 155 in 1801 the population of Rise increased to 203 in 1811 and 221 in 1821, fell to 164 in 1831, then recovered gradually to 206 in 1871, before declining again, notably in the 1890s, to 132 in 1901.[10] Between 1911 and 1931 it stood at *c.* 160 but then declined to 132 in 1961 and 95 in 1971; 92 of the 100 usually resident were counted in 1991.[11]

Much of the parish lies on boulder clay but deposits of sand and gravel help to produce a broad band of higher ground, 15–25 m. above sea level, which runs from north to south through the centre of the parish, providing the village with its site.[12] Lower ground is found in the east and west of Rise and to the south, where the land falls to 8 m. in the valley of Lambwath stream. Formerly Lambwath stream ran along much of the southern parish boundary but as a result of its diversion before 1762 the stream and the boundary now coincide hardly at all.[13] The south of the parish is drained by Lambwath stream and the north by a stream flowing northwards into Sigglesthorne and thence into the Hull valley; both were recorded as insufficient

drains in 1367.[14] Lambwath stream in Rise was repaired and cleansed as part of William Chapman's drainage scheme for Withernwick carried out *c.* 1810.[15]

From Rise minor roads lead north to Sigglesthorne and Hornsea, south-east to Withernwick, south to Skirlaugh, and west to Long Riston. The Sigglesthorne and Long Riston roads, and a field road called Folly, or Oak Tree, Lane, run along parts of the parish boundary, which was formerly also marked by Huddle cross.[16] In 1762 the Sigglesthorne road diverged from the boundary, joined a way from Little Hatfield, in Sigglesthorne, and continued southwards to Rise village and the Withernwick road. Soon afterwards, possibly in connexion with inclosure in Long Riston, a new road was made continuing the Sigglesthorne road along the boundary and the road from Little Hatfield, later called Mill Lane, was straightened; in 1824 part of the old Sigglesthorne–Rise road was stopped up.[17] Field roads mark another former road, to Catwick.[18]

RISE VILLAGE. In 1762 the buildings of Rise village lay along two streets, one leading east from the church past the manor house to join the second, longer street, which was aligned north-south. A stretch of the latter street, which continued to Sigglesthorne and Withernwick, faced the park and most of its houses stood on the east side. In 1774 William Bethell had the east-west street diverted away from his house to a more northerly course which added the church and its yard and half a dozen houses to the buildings south of the street.[19] Except for the church, parsonage, and manor house, the southern buildings were later removed and their sites used to extend the park and woods. Other houses close to the enlarged grounds were also demolished. The village was rebuilt some 200 m. north of the new road and beside the new Sigglesthorne road, *c.* 500 m. north-west of the old settlement, where half a dozen cottages on smallholdings and a school comprised New Rise by the 1850s.[20] Much of the rebuilding, including the creation of New Rise, was done by Richard Bethell in the early and mid 19th century.[21] The *c.* 25 houses and estate yard buildings

98 This article was written in 1994–5.
99 Below, manor.   1 *P.N. Yorks. E.R.* 22, 70.
2 O.S. Map 6″, Yorks. CXCVII, CCXI, CCXII (1854–5 edn.); *Census,* 1871 (pt. ii).
3 The part of Arnold township in Rise ecclesiastical parish seems to have been included in the transfer of that township to North Skirlaugh in 1885 but may also have been added to Rise civil parish by mistake: *Census,* 1891 (pt. ii); above, Swine, N. Skirlaugh, intro.; below, Long Riston, intro.
4 E.R.A.O., CCO. 465; *Census,* 1951–71.
5 E.R.A.O., Holderness (Parishes) Order 1983; O.S. Map 1/2,500, Yorks. CCXII. 1 (1891 edn.).
6 *Census,* 1991.   7 P.R.O., E 179/202/60, m. 70.
8 *Hearth Tax,* 61.
9 B.I.H.R., V. 1764/Ret. 2, no. 212; *Herring's Visit.* iii, p. 35.
10 *V.C.H. Yorks.* iii. 495.   11 *Census,* 1921–91.
12 Geol. Surv. Map 1″, drift, sheet 73 (1909 edn.).
13 E.R.A.O., accession 2980, 1762 plan.

14 Poulson, *Holderness,* i. 121, 129.
15 E.R.A.O., PE/81/70.
16 Poulson, *Holderness,* i. 414–15; A. Bryant, *Map of E.R. Yorks.* (1829); O.S. Map 6″, Yorks. CXCVII (1854 edn.); O.S. Map 1/2,500, Yorks. CXCVII. 13 (1891 edn.).
17 E.R.A.O., HD. 25; 1762 plan in book of plans of estates of H. Bethell, at Rise Park Estate Off.; T. Jefferys, *Map of Yorks.* (1772); O.S. Map 6″, Yorks. CXCVII (1854 edn.); below, Long Riston, intro., econ. hist.
18 T. Jefferys, *Map of Yorks.* (1772); O.S. Map 6″, Yorks. CXCVII (1854 edn.).
19 1762 plan in book of plans of estates of H. Bethell, at Rise Park Estate Off.; E.R.A.O., QSF. Christ. 1775, E.1.
20 O.S. Map 6″, Yorks. CCXII (1855 edn.); H. Teesdale, *Map of Yorks.* (1828).
21 E.R.A.O., DDRI/40/11; ibid. HD. 25; E.R.A.O., accession 2980, 'Rise Estates 1852'; *1st Rep. Com. on Employment of Children, Young Persons, and Women in Agric., App. Pt. II* [4068-I], p. 365; below, manor.

at Rise and New Rise are of brick and date from the 19th and 20th centuries. Among the oldest is the Smithy, which was built in the early 19th century. At New Rise a terrace of cottages with a taller, pedimented centre is dated 1847. By the mid 20th century accommodation had been reduced by the remodelling of cottages,[22] but six council houses were then built in the village.[23] The noteworthy buildings are Rise Hall and its outbuildings and Rise Park, formerly the rectory house.[24]

An alehouse was licensed at Rise in the mid 18th century.[25] The school was used occasionally for meetings in the earlier 20th century, and after its closure in 1948 became the village hall;[26] in 1995 it was being used by a playgroup. A room provided as a First World War memorial was perhaps the mid 20th-century meeting room formerly standing opposite East Lodge.[27]

OUTLYING HOUSES. Except for Park Farm, all of the six farmhouses away from the village existed by the mid 18th century.[28] Rebuildings of the 19th century include Rise Grange and Mill House Farm, of c. 1845.[29] Park Farm, with bargeboarding to its many gables, was added in 1880.[30] Two lodges were put up at or soon after the rebuilding of Rise Hall: Round House is a T-shaped building with canted corners and Tudor hoodmoulds, and South Lodge, formerly Wood Cottage, a stuccoed cottage with rustic verandahs, ogee-headed doorway, Tudor hood-moulds, and some of its original leaded lights. Other houses built by the estate include Oak Cottages, on the Withernwick boundary, which had been put up by 1840.[31]

It may have been William Bethell, owner of the winner of the 1780 St. Leger, who laid out a circular course for training horses on 60 a. at Farnton hill, just across the parish boundary in Long Riston; the track was still used in 1995.[32] He also kept a pack of hounds and hunted from Rise, and in the earlier 20th century the East Holderness foxhounds were kennelled there.[33]

MANOR AND OTHER ESTATES. *RISE* manor, variously said to comprise 5½ or 7½

carucates, was held by Knut[34] in 1066, then passed to William Malet and, after his deprivation c. 1070, to Drew de Bevrère by 1086. The estate, which was later part of the Aumale fee, was held in 1086 by Drew's undertenant Franco de Fauconberg.[35] Rise was evidently later the chief manor of the Fauconberg fee in Holderness, in 1624 including holdings at Arnold, Bilton, Marton, Rowton, and North Skirlaugh, all in Swine parish, Catfoss, Great Hatfield, and Seaton, in Sigglesthorne, Bewholme, in Nunkeeling, South Frodingham, in Owthorne, Ulrome, in Skipsea, and Southcoates, in Drypool, and in the parishes of Catwick, Hornsea, and Sutton. The appurtenances of Rise manor outside the parish were regarded as a separate manor, of *RISE OUT TOWNS*, in the 18th century.[36] Walter de Fauconberg was lord of Rise c. 1200.[37] The manor descended almost certainly to Sir Peter de Fauconberg (fl. earlier 13th century)[38] and by 1264 belonged to his son Walter de Fauconberg, later Lord Fauconberg (d. 1304).[39] It was recorded as ½ or ⅛ knight's fee in the 14th century[40] and in 1304 included a demesne of 2½ carucates, 90 a., and a park; 2 carucates and 3 bovates more were held by Fauconberg's bond tenants.[41] In 1316 the lord was Fauconberg's son, Walter, Lord Fauconberg (d. 1318), whose widow Alice, later wife of Sir Ralph Bulmer, succeeded to Rise[42] but apparently released it to her stepson, John de Fauconberg, Lord Fauconberg (d. 1349).[43] John's son Walter, Lord Fauconberg, died in 1362, and his widow Isabel later held the manor as her jointure. The reversion was sold in 1372 by Walter's son Sir Thomas Fauconberg to Sir John Neville (d. 1388), whose son Ralph Neville, earl of Westmorland, duly succeeded to the manor on Isabel's death in 1401. Neville (d. 1425) was succeeded in turn by his widow Joan (d. 1440)[44] and their son Richard Neville, earl of Salisbury. Rise was forfeited to the Crown in 1459 and 1460 by the attainder of Neville (d. 1460)[45] but then descended to his son Richard Neville (d. 1471), earl of Warwick and Salisbury, 'the kingmaker'. At the partitioning of Warwick's estates in 1475, Rise and other Yorkshire manors were assigned to Warwick's son-in-law, Richard Plantagenet, duke of Gloucester,[46] later Richard III. The

22   Rise Park Estate Off., 'Rise Settled Estates 1967'.
23   R.D.B., 782/264/228.
24   Below, manor; church.
25   E.R.A.O., QDT/2/9.
26   B.I.H.R., V. 1912–22/Ret.; Rise Park Estate Off., 'Rise Settled Estates 1967'; below, educ.
27   *Kelly's Dir. N. & E.R. Yorks.* (1933), 701; O.S. Map 1/10,560, TA 14 SE. (1956 edn.); inf. from Rise Park Estate Off., 1995.
28   E.R.A.O., accession 2980, 1762 plan; T. Jefferys, *Map of Yorks.* (1772).
29   E.R.A.O., accession 2980, 'Rise Estates 1852'.
30   Ibid. 'Rise Settled Estates 1967'.
31   Poulson, *Holderness*, i. 416; Pevsner and Neave, *Yorks. E.R.* 659; O.S. Map 6", Yorks. CCXII (1855 edn.).
32   H.U.L., DDX/16/244, pp. 28–9; Poulson, *Holderness*, i. 416; O.S. Map 6", Yorks. CXCVII (1854 edn.); inf. from Rise Park Estate Off., 1995.
33   H.U.L., DDX/16/244, pp. 28–9; *Kelly's Dir. N. & E.R. Yorks.* (1933), 701.
34   Knut may have been the son of Carl, who killed Earl Aldred in 'Rise wood', and grandson of Thorbrand: *Y.A.J.*

iv. 391; *V.C.H. Yorks.* ii. 145.
35   *V.C.H. Yorks.* ii. 167–8, 268, 295; *Feud. Aids*, vi. 40. For Franco and his successors, *Chron. de Melsa* (Rolls Ser.), i. 78; *Complete Peerage.* s.v. Fauconberge; *Early Yorks. Fam.* (Y.A.S. Rec. Ser. cxxxv), 26–7.
36   H.U.L., DDKG/9; R.D.B., BZ/448/719.
37   *Chron. de Melsa* (Rolls Ser.), i. 303.
38   *Yorks. Deeds*, ix, p. 11; below, church.
39   *Yorks. Deeds*, viii, p. 74;, *Kirkby's Inquest* (Sur. Soc. xlix), 372; *Feud. Aids*, vi. 40; *Cal. Inq. p.m.* iv, p. 357.
40   *Cal. Inq. p.m.* vi, p. 112; ix, p. 176.
41   *Yorks. Inq.* iv, pp. 63–4.
42   *Feud. Aids*, vi. 163; *Cal. Inq. p.m.* iv, p. 137; vi, p. 112; *Cal. Pat.* 1317–21, 272.
43   *Cal. Inq. p.m.* ix, p. 176.
44   Ibid. xi, p. 262; xviii, p. 136; *Complete Peerage*, s.v. Westmorland; *Cal. Close, 1422–9*, 238–9; *Feud. Aids*, vi. 272–3.
45   *Complete Peerage*, s.v. Salisbury; *Cal. Pat.* 1452–61, 578; *Cal. Fine R.* 1452–61, 274.
46   *Cal. Pat.* 1467–77, 483, 486–7; *Rot. Parl.* vi. 100–01; *Complete Peerage*, s.vv. Gloucester, Warwick.

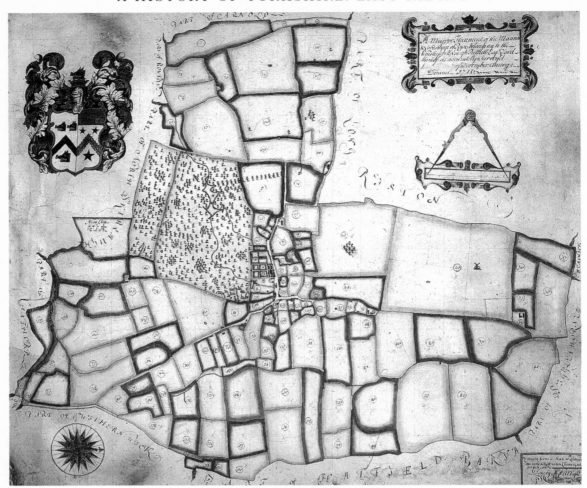

FIG. 26. RISE PLAN, 1716 (NORTH TO THE RIGHT)

Crown retained Rise, later accounted part of Sheriff Hutton (Yorks. N.R.) lordship and the duchy of York,[47] until 1628, when the manor and *c.* 120 a. of woodland at Rise were alienated to the Ditchfield grantees as security for the city of London's loan to the Crown.[48] In 1639 William Raven and Michael Evans bought the estate from the grantees, evidently for William Burgess and Francis Braddock.[49] The freehold was sold in 1646 to Thomas Bacon and Christopher Beckwith, for Hugh, later Sir Hugh, Bethell, who simultaneously bought an existing long lease of the estate.[50]

The Bethells or ap Ithells had moved into the East Riding from Herefordshire in the later 16th century[51] and from that period held Rise by assignment or sub-lease from the Crown's lessees. Queen Elizabeth's servant Blanche Parry, lessee of the manor and woods from *c.* 1570, bequeathed her terms to Hugh Bethell and

Francis Vaughan, the Crown's chief steward in the East Riding, before 1591, when Vaughan released his interest to Bethell, afterwards Sir Hugh. Later Crown leases of the manor, to John Overton and George Haxby in 1605, and for their lives to George Kirke and his wife in 1627, were also enjoyed by the Bethells.[52] Sir Hugh Bethell (d. 1611 or 1612) was succeeded in his leasehold by his brother Roger (d. 1626).[53] The estate was later divided between Roger's heirs, one of whom, his grandson Hugh, later Sir Hugh, Bethell, the purchaser of the manor, reunited the leasehold by purchase *c.* 1650.[54]

In the mid 17th century, before and after the purchase of the manor in 1646, the Bethells bought three small farms,[55] and practically all of the township belonged to Sir Hugh Bethell at inclosure in 1660.[56] He (d. 1679) was succeeded in Rise manor by his nephew Hugh Bethell and Hugh (d. 1717)[57] by his son Hugh (d. 1752) and

47 *Cal. Pat.* 1476–85, 457; 1566–9, pp. 52–3; 1572–5, p. 80; *L.& P. Hen. VIII*, iii (2), p. 866.

48 E.R.A.O., DDRI/26/21; P.R.O., E 318/53/Chas. I/146, mm. 1, 25; above, N. Frodingham, manor.

49 E.R.A.O., DDRI/26/29–30.

50 Ibid. DDRI/26/33–4, 44.

51 Poulson, *Holderness*, i. 408 (Bethell pedigree); J. Foster, *Pedigrees of Yorks.* iii, s.v. Bethell.

52 E.R.A.O., DDRI/26/9, 11–12, 22–3; *Cal. Pat.*

1566–9, pp. 52–3; 1572–5, p. 80; 1578–80, p. 179.

53 E.R.A.O., DDRI/26/18; ibid. PE/80/1; H.U.L., DDKG/9.

54 E.R.A.O., DDRI/26/23, 60–1, 63–5, 68; DDRI/40/1.

55 Ibid. DDRI/26/28, 31, 36.

56 Below, econ. hist.

57 E.R.A.O., DDRI/26/49. For the following, J. Foster, *Pedigrees of Yorks.* iii, s.v. Bethell; Burke, *Land. Gent.* (1952), 170–1.

FIG. 27. RISE HALL, REMODELLED 1815–20

grandsons Hugh (d. 1772) and William (d. 1799) in turn.[58] In 1762 Hugh Bethell, later M.P. for Beverley, had *c.* 1,840 a. of Rise township.[59] William Bethell left the estate to his widow Charlotte (d. 1814), with remainder to a kinsman Richard Bethell, M.P. for the East Riding in the 1830s. Bethell (d. 1864) was succeeded by his nephew W. F. Bethell (d. 1879) and he by his son William.[60] Including 1,955 a. at Rise in 1915, the estate descended in turn from William Bethell (d. 1926) to his son W. A. V. Bethell (d. 1941) and grandson R. A. Bethell, who in 1973 vested Rise in his son H. A. Bethell.[61] The Bethells still owned practically the whole of Rise civil parish in 1995.[62]

The manor house was recorded in the earlier 14th century,[63] but by the early 16th the medieval house of the Fauconbergs had gone and several other buildings apparently then stood on its site. The extensive earthworks which survive in Blackhall close, west of the village, have since 1624 been identified with the Fauconbergs' house. The chief house in 1624 was probably that with 8 a. adjoining it, occupied by Roger Bethell's son Hugh,[64] and in 1672 it was the 13-hearth house of Sir Hugh Bethell.[65] In 1716 the house was on the site of the later Rise Hall and had an **E**-plan north front, approached by a

central path, and formal gardens to the south and west.[66] The house was also shown about that date with three gables to the front and what seems to have been a walled forecourt.[67] By 1762 most of the house had been rebuilt as a long **U** plan, open to the east,[68] and in 1773 William Bethell gave the house a new front, apparently almost 180 ft. long, and then or soon after refurbished the interior. Fabric of the earlier house was incorporated at the east end, where 16th- or 17th-century walling is evident inside on the first floor, abutting the mainly 18th-century, red-brick service court, and possibly along the north side, where the main range and inner court together have much the same length as the late 18th-century house. Between 1815 and 1820 Richard Bethell extensively remodelled the house;[69] his architects were almost certainly Watson & Pritchett of York.[70] The present house, which has been known successively as Rise Hall, Rise Park,[71] and now Rise Hall once again, is in Greek-revival style and is faced with fine ashlar. The plan is irregular, no doubt to accommodate the pre-existing fabric. The north range is of seven bays between deep, end projections of one wide bay; the south range has a nine-bayed centre, with the middle three bays broken forward under a pediment, and wide,

58 R.D.B., F/434/942; BZ/448/719.
59 E.R.A.O., accession 2980, 1762 plan and survey; *Hist. Parl., Commons, 1754–90*, ii. 89.
60 R.D.B., MO/156/241; NA/39/63; E.R.A.O., DDRI/40/11; J. Markham, *Nineteenth-Cent. Parl. Elections in E. Yorks.* (E. Yorks. Loc. Hist. Ser. xxxvii), 44.
61 R.D.B., 170/289/242; 350/497/415; 655/563/481; 661/240/221; 1847/146/95.
62 Rise Park Estate Off., 'Rise Settled Estates 1967'.
63 P.R.O., C 134/63, no. 2; C 135/96, no. 4; *Yorks. Inq.* iv, p. 64.
64 H.U.L., DDKG/9; H.U.L., DDX/16/244, p. 7.
65 P.R.O., E 179/205/504.

66 Rise Park Estate Off., 1716 plan; E.R.A.O., accesssion 2980, 1762 plan; E.R.A.O., QSF. Christ. 1775, E.1; J. Warburton, *Map Co. York* [1720]; O.S. Map 6″, Yorks. CCXII (1855 edn.).
67 B.L. Lansd. MS. 911 (iv), f. 430; *Sam. Buck's Yorks. Sketchbk.* 328.
68 Rise Park Estate Off., book of plans of estates of H. Bethell.
69 E.R.A.O., DDGR/42/29; Poulson, *Holderness*, i. 415–16, pl. facing p. 416.
70 Pevsner and Neave, *Yorks. E.R.* 658–9.
71 H.U.L., DDLG/46/26; O.S. Map 6″, Yorks. CCXII (1855 edn.); *Kelly's Dir. N. & E.R. Yorks.* (1872), 537.

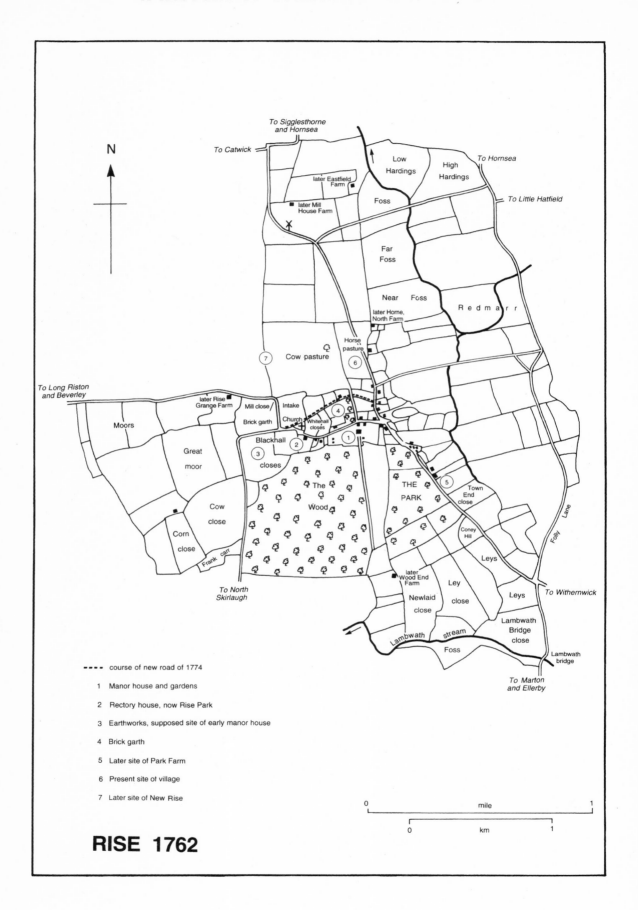

N

To Sigglesthorne
and Hornsea
To Catwick

Low
Hardings
High
Hardings
To Hornsea

later Eastfield
Farm

To Little Hatfield

later Mill
House Farm

Foss

Far
Foss

R e d m a r r

Near Foss

later Home,
North Farm

To Long Riston
and Beverley

Horse
pasture

7 Cow pasture

6

later Rise
Grange Farm

Mill close

Intake

Moors

Brick garth

Church

Whitehall
closes

4

Blackhall

2

1

Great

3 closes

moor

THE
PARK

The
Wood

Town
End
close

Cow

5

close

Coney
Hill

Corn

Leys

close

Frank carr

later
Wood End
Farm

Ley
close

Leys

To North
Skirlaugh

Newlaid
close

Lambwath
Bridge
close

Folly Lane

To Withernwick

Lambwath stream

Lambwath
bridge

Foss

To Marton
and Ellerby

- - - - course of new road of 1774

1   Manor house and gardens

2   Rectory house, now Rise Park

3   Earthworks, supposed site of early manor house

4   Brick garth

5   Later site of Park Farm

6   Present site of village

7   Later site of New Rise

0   mile   1

0   km   1

RISE 1762

shallowly-projecting ends, one being the south end of the west range, which contains the entrance. Here a pedimented, Ionic portico leads into a top-lit, off-axis spine of staircase hall, galleried inner hall, and service stair. The principal, south-facing rooms open off that spine: the library fills the south end of the west range, followed by three, linked rooms in the centre, and a smoking room in the eastern projection. The neoclassical decoration is restrained but some rooms were remodelled in the late 19th or early 20th century, the dining room in the Adam style. Along the north range, smaller rooms linked by their own corridor were probably used as upper servants' and business rooms: the lay-out may reflect a previous arrangement, as rooms in the north-east wing fit awkwardly behind the early 19th-century stone skin. The 18th-century brick, service end was remodelled to integrate it with the new house and extended east to form an additional court. North-east of the house a late 18th-century stable yard is enclosed by three two-storeyed, red-brick ranges and a fourth, detached range, which may have been partly domestic; behind the yard there is a barn, originally open-sided. Stone-faced lodges with Ionic columns flanking the main entrance gates to Rise Hall and its park are contemporary with the rebuilding of the house, and are probably by Watson & Pritchett.[72] The brick East Lodge, on the Withernwick road, was built to replace a smaller house there in the later 19th century.[73] The Bethells gave up the house in or by 1946, when they bought the former rectory house, later called Rise Park.[74] Their former seat, thereafter Rise Hall, was let from 1946 to the Canonesses Regular of St. Augustine, who ran a Roman Catholic boarding and day school for girls there, in succession to the order's schools at Hull and Boynton, until 1989 and in 1995 were using the house as an occasional educational centre. A gymnasium and a dining room were added c. 1980.[75] The former dining room became the chapel.[76] The house stood empty in 1998.

Sir Peter de Fauconberg had a park at Rise in the earlier 13th century and his son Walter was granted free warren there in 1292.[77] The park was mentioned again in the early 14th century and c. 1380, when it was allegedly broken into.[78] The medieval park may later have been reduced or even extinguished by the making of closes. It was not mentioned in the 1624 survey, in 1716 deer were kept in the demesne woods rather than a park, and in 1762 the area between those woods and the Withernwick road included 65 a. in four Park closes and 10 a. nearby in Coney hill close.[79] It was probably soon afterwards, in the 1770s, that a new, larger park was made from Park and other closes, adjoining woodland, and garths then added to the grounds by the diversion of one of the village streets. In 1716 the woods had included a lake, and another was added and both Old and New Ponds given small islands as part of the landscaping.[80] The 'improvements' may have been to plans for Rise made by 'Capability' Brown in 1775 but now unknown.[81] About 1840 some 300 deer were kept in the park, where New pond was drained, or silted up, between 1852 and 1889.[82] In 1915 the park was of 138 a., and there were also 32 a. in Old park close, c. 130 a. of woodland, and c. 4 a. of water.[83] The herd of fallow deer was killed at the start of the Second World War and the park was ploughed;[84] it has since been returned to grass. An ice-house near the lakes remained in 1995.[85]

In 1086 the archbishop of York had ½ carucate at Rise, which may already have been assigned to his church of St. John at Beverley.[86] The land was perhaps used to endow Rise church, which was later in the jurisdiction of the provost of Beverley; the glebe land in 1650 included four bovates.[87] An archiepiscopal 'manor of Rise', recorded in 1399, was perhaps on the provost's estate, but nothing else is known of it.[88]

Other estates included that which Herbert de St. Quintin held in 1284–5 of the Crown as successor to the counts of Aumale; it was then held of St. Quintin in alms or free tenure.[89]

A small estate at Rise descended like Tansterne manor, in Aldbrough, in the Rouths and their successors, falling in 1614 to the share of Sir Richard Michelbourne, whose sons Abraham and Francis sold it in 1646 to Hugh Bethell the younger, later Sir Hugh (d. 1679).[90]

In 1553 the Crown granted Giggleswick (Yorks. W. R.) grammar school five bovates and other land formerly belonging to a chantry at Rise.[91] At inclosure in 1660 the school had c. 90 a. at Rise.[92] The farm was sold to Richard Bethell in 1863.[93]

72   Pevsner and Neave, *Yorks. E.R.* 659.

73   O.S. Map 6″, Yorks. CCXII (1855 edn.); O.S. Map 1/2,500, Yorks. CCXII. 1 (1891 edn.).

74   Below, church.

75   R.D.B., 1554/213/176; *Catholic Dir.* (1951), 252; *V.C.H. Yorks. E.R.* i. 363; *Hull Daily Mail*, 18 Nov. and 12 Dec. 1988; inf. from the community, Rise Hall, 1995.

76   Rise Park Estate Off., plan of St. Philomena's convent, Rise, 1972.

77   English, *Holderness*, 148–9; *Cal. Chart. R.* 1257–1300, 426.

78   P.R.O., C 134/63, no. 2; *Yorks. Inq.* iv, p. 64; *Cal. Pat.* 1377–81, 363, 465.

79   H.U.L., DDKG/9; Rise Park Estate Off., 1716 plan; 1762 plan and survey in book of plans of estates of H. Bethell, at Rise Park Estate Off.

80   Rise Park Estate Off., 1716 plan; B.I.H.R., TER. H. Rise 1770, 1777; H. Teesdale, *Map of Yorks.* (1828); O.S. Map 6″, Yorks. CCXII (1855 edn.); above, intro. [village].

81   D. Stroud, *Capability Brown* (1950), 172.

82   Poulson, *Holderness*, i. 416; O.S. Map 6″, Yorks. CCXII (1855 edn.); O.S. Map 1/2,500, Yorks. CCXII. 1 (1891 edn.).

83   R.D.B., 170/289/242.

84   S. Needham, 'E.R. Deer Parks' (Hull Univ. B.A. dissertation, 1987), 127.

85   O.S. Map 6″, Yorks. CCXII (1855 edn.); inf. from Rise Park Estate Off., 1995.

86   *V.C.H. Yorks.* ii. 216.   87   Below, church.

88   Hist. MSS. Com. 54, *Beverley*, p. 147.

89   *Feud. Aids*, vi. 40; *Cal. Inq. p.m.* iv, p. 357.

90   E.R.A.O., DDRI/26/31; DDRI/35/33; P.R.O., C 142/48, no. 161; C 142/214, nos. 205, 221; *Cal. Inq. p.m. Hen. VII*, iii, pp. 589–90; *Suss. Arch. Colln.* l. 78; above, Aldbrough, manors.

91   *Cal. Pat.* 1553, 68–9; below, church.

92   E.R.A.O., DDRI/26/40.

93   R.D.B., IO/32/38.

Between 1235 and 1249 Peter Ash gave arable land in Rise to Meaux abbey[94] but no more is known of it.

ECONOMIC HISTORY. COMMON LANDS AND INCLOSURE.

East field was named from the 13th century and West field from the 14th.[95] The tillage apparently included an area called Maxwelldale, where the tenants' grazing rights after harvest were disputed in 1577.[96] The common meadows may have included 'grounds or closes' called Fosse, Frank carr, and Small Hills, from which hay was taken in 1613. Two meadows called Fosses contained at least 18 a. in 1624, when Frank carr was again mentioned as a 10-a. meadow close and 8 a. more of meadow land called Redmarr lay 'open to East field'.[97] Most of the commonable grazing in 1624 was evidently in a stinted pasture called Great leys, but there were also a few gates in each of Hedon leys, West leys, and Hardings. Except for Hardings, the location of those pastures is unknown. Great leys may, however, have lain immediately north of the village, at the end of an outgang from the street, where closes called Cow Pasture, Horse Pasture, and Intake, the last perhaps taken from the pasture, together contained just over 100 a. in 1762.[98] By the early 17th century much of Rise was already in closes, particularly in the west and south where the demesne land was concentrated. In 1624, besides c. 135 a. of woodland, some 440 a. of demesne land was recorded, much of it inclosed; closes then named included Blackhall closes, Mill close, Corn croft, perhaps the later Corn close, Cow close, Frank Carr close, and several moor closes.[99] The remaining commonable lands were inclosed in 1660 by an Exchequer decree confirming an agreement made in 1655 between Hugh, later Sir Hugh, Bethell, lord of the manor, and the only other proprietors, Giggleswick school and the rector. The school was then allotted 79 a. and the rector c. 50 a.; the rest of the township was evidently Bethell's share.[1]

THE DEMESNE AND OTHER HOLDINGS.

Six ploughlands were recorded at Rise in 1086, when there were two ploughs on the demesne and a third worked by seven villeins and six bordars; the manor then included 30 a. of meadow land.[2] In 1304 the manor was valued at just over £35 a year, the park and other demesne lands contributing about half of that sum and the rest coming from the rents of free and bond tenants.[3]

The manor also included fisheries in streams in Rise but they were disused by the 17th century.[4] Another fishery in Rise belonged in 1345 to the Crown, presumably as lord of Holderness, and may have been in Lambwath stream.[5]

Apart from the nearly 600 a. of demesne,[6] the manor was occupied by three freeholders and c. 35 other tenants in 1624; one man held nearly 80 a., twelve between 20–40 a., seven 8–19 a., and almost 20 under 5 a. each.[7] In 1762 Hugh Bethell had 510 a. in hand at Rise; the rest of the estate there was held by 28 tenants, one of whom had 324 a., three 150–220 a., four 50–90 a., eleven 5–49 a., and nine under 5a. each.[8] In the 19th and 20th centuries there were, besides the Bethells' home farm, half a dozen others; smaller holdings presumably included those on which worked the one or two cowkeepers then recorded.[9] The area in hand was much the same in 1852, when the tenanted farms comprised two of c. 70 a., one of 186 a., and four of over 200 a. Cottages and garths accounted for most of the other 22 holdings, but there were also half a dozen smallholdings of 3–29 a.[10] In 1967 there were two small farms and five with more than 200 a. each, the 384-a. Park farm which was combined with a farm in Withernwick having a total area of 551 a. Nearly 800 a. in Rise were then exploited directly by the Bethells, including 334 a. in Wood End farm, 88 a. in Mill House farm, a dairy unit, c. 140 a. of parkland, and c. 135 a. of woodland.[11]

WOODLAND.

Rise had included c. 40 a. of pasturable woodland in 1086, woodland grazing were again recorded in 1349,[12] and in the later 16th century there were two woods, Rise wood, of 100 a., and, along its southern edge,[13] the 20-a. Launde. The woods were then let on 21-year terms, the Crown reserving timber and larger trees, prohibiting more than two fellings a term, and requiring the lessee to enclose and protect the regrowth from animals. In 1572 most of Rise wood had an underwood of thorn and hazel which were usually cropped at 20-year intervals, but the remaining 26 a. had been neglected and provided insufficient wood to maintain its fence, while the Launde was said to be 'thin set' with underwood.[14] Some of the woodland was again decayed in 1624, when all was said to be being damaged by the lessee, Roger Bethell; the Crown had by then sold the larger trees in Rise wood, leaving c. 900 younger trees and thick underwood.[15] In 1762, before the expansion of the park, the woods covered just

94 *Chron. de Melsa* (Rolls Ser.), ii. 36.

95 H.U.L., DDKG/9; E.R.A.O., DDRI/26/7; *Chron. de Melsa* (Rolls Ser.), ii. 36; Poulson, *Holderness*, i. 405.

96 P.R.O., E 123/5, f. 318.

97 B.I.H.R., CP. H. 1069; H.U.L., DDKG/9; for locations, E.R.A.O., accession 2980, 1762 plan.

98 H.U.L., DDKG/9; E.R.A.O., accession 2980, 1762 plan and survey.

99 The demesne total apparently excludes the park: H.U.L., DDKG/9.

1 E.R.A.O., DDRI/26/40, 45; B.I.H.R., TER. H. Rise 1716 etc.   2 *V.C.H. Yorks.* ii. 268.

3 P.R.O., C 133/112, no. 9.

4 *Cal. Pat.* 1377–81, 363, 465; H.U.L., DDKG/9.

5 *Cal. Pat.* 1343–5, 586; *V.C.H. Yorks. E.R.* v. 10.

6 Above, this section.

7 H.U.L., DDKG/9. Location in Rise has been assumed where no place was specified.

8 E.R.A.O., accession 2980, 1762 plan and survey. One of the larger holdings included land in N. Skirlaugh.

9 P.R.O., HO 107/2365; directories.

10 E.R.A.O., accession 2980, 'Rise Estates 1852'; for smallholdings, Poulson, *Holderness*, i. 416; above, intro. [New Rise].   11 E.R.A.O., 'Rise Settled Estates 1967'.

12 P.R.O., C 135/96, no. 4; *V.C.H. Yorks.* ii. 268.

13 Rise Park Estate Off., 1716 plan; E.R.A.O., accession 2980, 1762 plan and survey; Poulson, *Holderness*, i. 415.

14 P.R.O., E 310/29/170, f. 88; E.R.A.O., DDRI/26/9, 11–12; *Cal. Pat.* 1572–5, p. 80.

15 H.U.L., DDKG/9; E.R.A.O., DDRI/26/70.

over 200 a.[16] The area of woodland was put at 184 a. in 1838 and 135 a. in 1905.[17] In the 20th century Rise wood, comprising the former Launde, contained just over 100 a. and there were also c. 30 a. of plantations in Rise.[18] The estate works probably included a saw mill by 1762, when a wood yard was recorded, and the mill was still operated in 1995.[19]

LAND USE FROM THE 18TH CENTURY. In 1720 many of the closes in Rise were occupied as grassland.[20] Only 357 a. of the parish was returned as under crops, mostly corn, in 1801.[21] In 1838 there were 898 a. of arable and 931 a. of grassland,[22] and in 1905, when the figures evidently also included land from another parish, there were said to be 1,123 a. of arable and 833 a. of grassland.[23] In the 1930s much of Rise, notably in and around the park, was used as grassland and woodland, arable land predominating in the east and west of the parish.[24] In 1987 Rise civil parish seems to have been covered by the agricultural returns made for neighbouring Riston which are treated under that parish.[25]

NON-AGRICULTURAL EMPLOYMENT. Bricks were evidently made in or close to the village before 1762, and prominent earthworks remain there. A century later there was a brick field in the south-eastern corner of the parish.[26] The Bethells' estate also provided non-agricultural employment: in 1851, for instance, residents at Rise included two gamekeepers, four gardeners, and a staff of over 20 at the Hall.[27] By the 1880s the estate works also included a private gasworks.[28]

MILLS. A mill at Rise was recorded in 1086,[29] a water mill and a windmill in the earlier 14th century,[30] and a windmill in 1624.[31] A post mill in the north of the parish was grinding by the early 18th century; 'in middling repair but rather old' in 1852, it was given up c. 1860 and demolished.[32] Before 1762 another mill presumably stood in Mill close at the west end of the village.[33]

LOCAL GOVERNMENT. In the early 17th century the jurisdiction of Rise manor court, which included view of frankpledge, was allegedly infringed by officers of the wapentake court.[34] No more is known of the court at Rise and its records do not seem to have survived. Apart from an account book of the overseers of the poor for 1833–7, there is also little record of parochial administration. A cottage and 2 a. were used for the poor of the parish, perhaps before the 1830s when the overseers were receiving a rent.[35] Permanent poor relief was given to seven people and the same number were helped occasionally at Rise in 1802–3; in 1812–15 the numbers were respectively 10–11 and 6–7.[36] Rise joined Skirlaugh poor-law union in 1837[37] and remained in Skirlaugh rural district until 1935. It was then included in the new Holderness rural district and at reorganization in 1974 was taken into the Holderness district of Humberside.[38] In 1996 Rise parish became part of a new East Riding unitary area.[39]

CHURCH. Rise church existed by 1221, when Peter de Fauconberg's claim to be patron was disputed by the provost of Beverley,[40] in whose peculiar jurisdiction the church lay.[41] Fauconberg nevertheless presented, as Sir Peter de Fauconberg, in 1250 or 1251,[42] and the advowson later descended in the Fauconbergs and their successors as lords of Rise, passing in the 15th century to the Crown.[43] The living was shared by the rector and his vicar in the 13th century but, at the institution of the rector in 1250 or 1251, it was ordained that when the incumbent vicar died his portion should be consolidated,[44] and since the later 13th century the living has consequently been a rectory.[45] In 1974 Rise rectory was united with the benefice of Sigglesthorne with Nunkeeling and Bewholme; the patronage of the united benefice belonged to the Crown and was thereafter exercised alternately on its behalf by the Prime Minister and the Lord Chancellor.[46]

Rise rectory was worth £5 in 1291 and £10 os. 4d. net in 1535.[47] The improved annual value in 1650 was £78 net.[48] The annual net income

[16] E.R.A.O., accession 2980, 1762 plan and survey; above, manor [park].
[17] B.I.H.R., TA. 656s; Acreage Returns, 1905.
[18] R.D.B., 170/289/242; 1554/213/176; Rise Park Estate Off., 'Rise Settled Estates 1967'; inf. from Rise Park Estate Off., 1995.
[19] E.R.A.O., accession 2980, 1762 plan and survey.
[20] R.D.B., F/434/942.
[21] P.R.O., HO/67/26/349.
[22] B.I.H.R., TA. 656s.
[23] Acreage Returns, 1905.
[24] [1st] Land Util. Surv. Map, sheet 28.
[25] Below, Long Riston, econ. hist.
[26] Ibid. 1762 plan and survey; O.S. Map 6", Yorks. CCXII (1855 edn.).
[27] P.R.O., HO 107/2365.
[28] O.S. Map 1/2,500, CCXII. 1 (1891 edn.).
[29] V.C.H. Yorks. ii. 268.
[30] P.R.O., C 134/63, no. 2; C 135/96, no. 4; Yorks. Inq. iv, p. 64.
[31] H.U.L., DDKG/9.
[32] Rise Park Estate Off., 1716 plan; E.R.A.O., accession 2980, 'Rise Estates 1852'; O.S. Map 6", Yorks. CXCVII

(1854 edn.); O.S. Map 1/2,500, Yorks. CXCVII. 13 (1891 edn.); directories.
[33] E.R.A.O., accession 2980, 1762 plan.
[34] H.U.L., DDKG/9.
[35] E.R.A.O., PE/80/14; R.D.B., IO/367/531.
[36] Poor Law Abstract, 1804, pp. 594–5; 1818, pp. 522–3.
[37] 3rd Rep. Poor Law Com. 170.
[38] Census.
[39] Humberside (Structural Change) Order 1995, copy at E.R.A.O.
[40] Cur. Reg. R. x. 161–2.
[41] Tax. Eccl. (Rec. Com.), 303; Memorials of Beverley Minster, ii (Sur. Soc. cviii), p. 309; V.C.H. Yorks. iii. 85.
[42] Reg. Gray, p. 265.
[43] Yorks. Inq. iv, p. 64; Cal. Close, 1422–9, 238–9; Cal. Inq. p.m. ix, p. 176; Lawrance, 'Clergy List', Holderness, 2, pp. 115–16; Poulson, Holderness, i. 411; above, manor.
[44] Reg. Gray, p. 265.
[45] Tax. Eccl. 303; Valor Eccl. (Rec. Com.), v. 116; Rep. Com. Eccl. Revenues, 962–3.
[46] B.I.H.R., OC. 881.
[47] Tax. Eccl. 303; Valor Eccl. v. 116.
[48] T.E.R.A.S. iv. 62.

averaged £550 in 1829–31[49] and was £498 in 1851 and £449 in 1883.[50]

Tithes and offerings were valued at nearly £11 a year gross in 1535[51] and £70 net in 1650.[52] Tithes had allegedly been compounded for by the early 17th century,[53] and at inclosure in 1660 it was agreed that £30 a year be paid for those of the commonable lands.[54] The tithes from old inclosures were later mostly paid by a modus of 2s. in the pound of the rentable value, but some lesser tithes continued to be taken in kind. The rector was also entitled to tithes from 42 a. in Arnold township until its inclosure in 1778, when 6 a. were awarded instead.[55] The tithes of Rise were commuted for £549 7s. 4¾d. a year in 1838.[56]

The rectory house and glebe land were valued at £1 6s. 8d. a year gross in 1535[57] and £8 a year net in 1650, when the glebe included four bovates.[58] Before and after inclosure in 1660 there were c. 55 a. of glebe land, to which 6 a. were added for the tithes at Arnold in 1778.[59] Some land was sold with the rectory house in 1946, but c. 55 a. in Rise and Arnold remained in 1978.[60]

The rectory house had four hearths in 1672,[61] and in 1716 it comprised an east-west range with a small, north-east wing, which probably included the kitchen.[62] It was enlarged by Dr. Jaques Sterne, rector 1722–59, who added the north-west wing which includes a panelled dining room of the mid 18th century,[63] and again by Nicholas Torre, later Holme, rector 1782–1833. Torre is credited with rebuilding the house in 1809 but the present structure includes 18th-century brickwork and some of the details of the new work are similar to Rise Hall, built 1815–20.[64] His contribution was evidently rather the refacing of the old south front, the redecoration of the principal rooms behind it, and probably also the addition on the east side of the house of a new service wing.[65] The remodelled south front has a central entrance with a pedimented, stone doorcase, giving onto an apsidal-ended hall. The eastern service wing was rebuilt to designs by F. S. Brodrick of Hull in the 1870s[66] and reconstructed c. 1950, and the area between the northern wings was remodelled in 1993.[67] The gardens are mostly to the south and

included on the axis of the central doorway a short, 18th-century canal, now represented by a dry depression in the grass.[68] In 1946 the rectory house and nearly 6 a. were sold to the trustees of the Rise estate and R. A. Bethell, and, as Rise Park, it has since been the Bethells' seat in Rise, instead of the 19th-century chief house, Rise Hall.[69]

In 1525–6, besides the rector, there were two chaplains in Rise church, one of them probably serving the chantry there.[70] The church may have been neglected by Thomas Langdale, rector 1558–87, who was also rector of Patrington and lived there and elsewhere, serving Rise by a curate.[71] Robert Johnson, D.D., rector from 1628, may also have held Bainton, and in 1650 Rise was being served by John Bronson, who was instituted as rector in 1662.[72] Jaques Sterne, LL. D. (d. 1759), rector for 36 years, was a nonresident pluralist, whose preferments also included Riston and Hornsea. His duty at Riston and Rise was done by the vicar of Atwick, who may have lived at Long Riston, and the two churches were again served together, by the then-resident rector of Rise, in 1764. In the mid 18th century there was only one Sunday service. Holy Communion was quarterly, with usually c. 20–35 receiving.[73] Nicholas Torre, later Holme, who served as rector for 51 years and vicar of Aldbrough for nearly 40 until his death in 1833, employed an assistant curate.[74] In the later 19th century there were two Sunday services and monthly communions, usually with fewer than 20 communicants.[75] W. J. Whately, sometime canon of York, succeeded his brother, Charles Whately, rector since 1840, in 1850 and held the living until 1894.[76] From 1945 until the 1970s Rise was served with Withernwick, where the rector lived; since the union of 1974 the incumbent has lived in Sigglesthorne Rectory.[77]

By 1366 a chantry dedicated to St. Thomas the Martyr had been founded at Rise, almost certainly by the Fauconbergs who presented the chaplain.[78] At the suppression there was a chantry in the church dedicated to St. Mary, perhaps the earlier Fauconberg foundation. In 1535 it was endowed with a house, five bovates, closes, and rent, worth in all £4 a year, which estate

49 Rep. Com. Eccl. Revenues, 962–3.
50 P.R.O., HO 129/522/2/13/14; B.I.H.R., V. 1884/ Ret. 2.   51 Valor Eccl. (Rec. Com.), v. 116.
52 T.E.R.A.S. iv. 62.   53 B.I.H.R., CP. H. 1069.
54 E.R.A.O., DDRI/26/40.
55 B.I.H.R., TER. H. Rise 1716 etc.; R.D.B., BB/73/13.
56 B.I.H.R., TA. 656s.
57 Valor Eccl. (Rec. Com.), v. 116.
58 T.E.R.A.S. iv. 62.
59 B.I.H.R., TER. H. Rise n.d, 1716 etc.; E.R.A.O., DDRI/26/40; ibid. PE/80/13; R.D.B., BB/73/13.
60 Inf. from York Dioc. Bd. of Finance, 1981; below, next para.
61 P.R.O., E 179/205/504; Lawrance, 'Clergy List', Holderness, 2, p. 116.
62 Rise Park Estate Off., 1716 plan; B.I.H.R., TER. H. Rise 1716.
63 Poulson, Holderness, i. 411, 415.
64 Ibid. 411, 416; stone to Nic. Holme in churchyard; above, manor [Rise Hall].
65 B.I.H.R., TER. H. Rise 1764, etc.; E.R.A.O., PE/80/13.

66 B.I.H.R., MGA. 1877/6.
67 Inf. from Rise Park Estate Off.; plaque on building.
68 B.I.H.R., TER. H. Rise 1716; E.R.A.O., accession 2980, 1762 plan; E.R.A.O., PE/80/13.
69 R.D.B., 726/41/36; above, manor [Rise Hall].
70 Y.A.J. xxiv. 64, 71–2; below, next para.
71 B.I.H.R., V. 1582/CB. 1, f. 205v.; ibid. HC. CP. 1571/1; Lawrance, 'Clergy List', Holderness, 2, p. 115; J. S. Purvis, Tudor Par. Doc. of Dioc. York, 33, 115.
72 Lawrance, 'Clergy List', Holderness, 2, pp. 115–16.
73 B.I.H.R., V. 1764/Ret. 2, no. 212; Herring's Visit. i, pp. 36–7; ii, pp. 88–90; iii, pp. 35–6; memorial to Sterne recorded in Poulson, Holderness, i. 413.
74 Rep. Com. Eccl. Revenues, 962–3; Poulson, Holderness, ii. 9; stone in Rise churchyard.
75 P.R.O., HO 129/522/2/13/14; B.I.H.R., V. 1865/Ret. 2, no. 426; V. 1868/Ret. 2, no. 377; V. 1871/Ret. 2, no. 382; V. 1877/Ret. 2, no. 200; V. 1884/Ret. 2.
76 Memorial in church.
77 B.I.H.R., OC. 881; Crockford (1965–6), 559; (1971–2), 780; (1980–2), 445.
78 P.R.O., C 54/204, m. 11d.; B.I.H.R., Reg. 5A, f. 223.

FIG. 28. RISE CHURCH BEFORE 1844

was granted by the Crown to Giggleswick (Yorks. W. R.) grammar school in 1553, together with tithes belonging to an Aldbrough chantry.[79] Rise church also included lights endowed with land in Rise and Riston.[80]

A chapel at Rise was mentioned c. 1200, before the first known record of the church, and again in 1420.[81] It was presumably the same which was granted to a chaplain for life in 1491 as the free chapel called 'le Dawinte'. It may have been demolished soon afterwards, for Chapel garth beside the Withernwick road was by 1535 merely a close belonging to St. Mary's chantry.[82]

The church of ALL SAINTS, formerly ST. MARY'S,[83] was rebuilt in the mid 19th century. The medieval church comprised a chancel and a nave with south porch and western bell turret. A blocked, round-headed doorway in the north side of the nave suggests that it was of 12th-century origin although most of the features were said to be 14th-century. In the north wall there was evidence of a former arcade for an aisle. By the 19th century it was a 'small, dilapidated, ancient structure' with modern, wooden frames in all but the west window. It evidently then also included a side chapel or vestry.[84] The old church was demolished and a new one built in 1844–5 by Richard Bethell to designs by R. D. Chantrell.[85] The new church is built of fine ashlar in a plain 13th-century style and comprises chancel with north vestry, nave with south porch, and west tower with a broach spire. Some

13th-century stonework was reused in the chancel arch. In or soon after 1928 the chancel was repaved and refitted and the pulpit and reading desk renewed.[86] Both the church and its yard, which was extended in 1845,[87] contain many memorials to the Bethell family; they include brass plates and four 17th- and 18th-century mural tablets from the earlier church.[88]

There were two bells from 1552 until 1845 when three were cast for the new church.[89] A new peal of five bells was given by William Bethell in 1904.[90] A silver cup and cover, bought in 1633, were replaced after 1830 by a new service.[91] The registers begin in 1559 but are deficient, notably in the 17th century.[92]

The parish clerk received £2–3 a year as wages from parishioners in the 19th century.[93]

NONCONFORMITY. A requiem mass was celebrated at Rise in the 1560s,[94] but later there was little nonconformity or its expression was discouraged by the Bethells. In 1868 there was said to be an 'inclination to Dissent' in the parish but there were no chapels at Rise and any nonconformists there must have belonged to neighbouring congregations.[95]

EDUCATION. In 1743 there was a school at Rise attended by c. 25 children. It was then said to be supported by the parishioners,[96] but later the mixed school was run largely at the expense of the Bethells, who probably also supplied the

79 Valor Eccl. (Rec. Com.), v. 117; Cal. Pat. 1553, 68–9; above, manor; above, Aldbrough, manors (rectory); church [chant.].
80 E.R.A.O., DDRI/26/7; Cal. Pat. 1575–8, pp. 486–7.
81 E.R.A.O., DDRI/26/1–2; above, this section.
82 Cal. Pat. 1485–94, 344; O.S. Map 6″, Yorks. CCXII (1855 edn.); Valor Eccl. v. 117.
83 Y.A.J. ii. 188.
84 E.R.A.O., DDHE/31/B.26; Baines, Hist. Yorks. ii. 382; Poulson, Holderness, i. 412–13, pl. facing p. 390.
85 P.R.O., HO 129/522/2/13/14; B.I.H.R., Ch. Ret. ii; ibid. CD. 207; Pevsner and Neave, Yorks. E.R. 658.
86 B.I.H.R., Fac. 1928/1/26.

87 R.D.B., DQ/442/55; B.I.H.R., Ch. Ret. ii; ibid. CD. 207.
88 B.I.H.R., Fac. 1928/1/26.
89 Ibid. TER. H. Rise 1764, 1853; Inventories of Ch. Goods, 39; Boulter, 'Ch. Bells', 85.
90 B.I.H.R., TER. 749.
91 Ibid. TER. H. Rise 1764, 1853; Yorks. Ch. Plate, i. 303.
92 E.R.A.O., PE/80/1–4, 6. Some of the missing years are covered by B.I.H.R., PRT. Hold. D.
93 B.I.H.R., TER. H. Rise 1817, 1853.
94 Ibid. V. 1567–8/CB. 1, f. 205.
95 Ibid. V. 1868/Ret. 2, no. 377.
96 Herring's Visit. iii, p. 35.

building.[97] By 1824 the school was being held in a building beside the Sigglesthorne road at New Rise.[98] Average attendance was 20 about 1865, when pupils were taken from under six years old to thirteen,[99] and 21 boys and girls were present at inspection in 1871.[1] The school was then run on National lines.[2] A new Church school, built by William Bethell in the main part of the village, was opened in 1910;[3] the former school was later demolished. Between 1906 and 1938 average attendance continued to be about 20,[4] but by 1947 there were only seven on the roll, and early in 1948 the remaining pupils were transferred to Skirlaugh school, Rise school being closed officially later that year.[5] The former schoolhouse was later used as a village hall.[6]

CHARITIES FOR THE POOR. Sir Hugh Bethell by will of 1679 left £2 a year from Rise manor for the poor of the parish.[7] Legacies of £50 from Hugh Bethell (d. 1717) and £20 from Elizabeth Bethell, possibly his daughter, were used in 1737 with parish funds to buy a house and land at Withernwick; some of the land had been charged with £2 a year for the poor of Withernwick[8] and that sum was paid from the Rise charity until its redemption in 1980.[9] The Poor's Estate was let for £4 a year in 1764 and £12 in 1823, when the £10 belonging to Rise were distributed at Christmas with Bethell's rent charge.[10] The estate in Withernwick comprised c. 8 a. in 1910.[11] Rise's share of the Poor's Estate was £8–9 in the early 20th century; grants of 6s. to £1 each were then made from that charity and Sir Hugh Bethell's to c. 20 parishioners.[12] Nearly 2 a. were sold in 1963 and 1970[13] and the proceeds invested. In 1985 the rent of the remaining land, interest on balances, and income from stock produced just over £187, from which five grants of £20 were made.[14]

LONG RISTON

THE village of Long Riston, lying on the edge of the Hull valley 14 km. north of Hull and 9 km. ENE. of Beverley, has been favoured since the Second World War as a commuter settlement for those towns.[15] The name, sometimes recorded as 'Ruston' or 'Reston' and perhaps meaning the 'farmstead near the brushwood' or 'inclosure overgrown with brushwood', is Anglian. The prefix, appropriate for such a straggling village, was used from the early 17th century, presumably to distinguish Riston from Ruston Parva.[16] The township of Arnold, south of the village, was divided between the ancient parishes of Long Riston, Rise, and Swine, but its history is dealt with here. The name, also Anglian, may mean 'Arna's nook of land'.[17] The settlements of 'Chenecol' or 'Chenuthesholm' and 'Luvetotholm', recorded in 1086, may have lain in Riston[18] but no more is known of them. In 1851 Long Riston parish contained 2,837 a. (1,148 ha.), comprising 1,834 a. (742 ha.) in Riston township and 1,003 a. (406 ha.) in Arnold; Arnold township also included 671 a. (272 ha.) in Swine and 6 a. (2.4 ha.) in Rise.[19] In 1885 the whole of Arnold was added to North Skirlaugh, in Swine, to form the civil parish later called North Skirlaugh, Rowton, and Arnold.[20] In 1935 that civil parish and Long Riston were united as Riston civil parish, with a total area of 4,047 a. (1,638 ha.), but in 1952 the new civil parish was reduced to 3,420 a. (1,384 ha.) and was made roughly coextensive with the old townships of Riston and Arnold.[21] In 1984 some 10 ha. (25 a.) were transferred to Rise civil parish. In 1991 the area was 1,374 ha. (3,395 a.).[22] Henceforth, to avoid ambiguity, the name Long Riston is used in this article for the village and Riston for the ancient parish.

There were 96 poll-tax payers at Riston in 1377,[23] and Long Riston had 39 houses assessed for hearth tax in 1672.[24] In both years Arnold was recorded with North Skirlaugh, in Swine.[25] In 1743 there were 49 families in the parish.[26] The population of Long Riston and Riston's part of Arnold township together was 269 in 1801; it rose to 403 in 1841 and 417 in 1871.

97 P.R.O., ED 7/135, no. 142; Poulson, *Holderness*, i. 415; *Educ. of Poor Digest*, 1089; *Educ. Enq. Abstract*, 1094; White, *Dir. Hull & York* (1846), 380.

98 E.R.A.O., HD. 25; O.S. Map 6″, Yorks. CCXII (1855 edn.). It was later erroneously said to have been built c. 1843: P.R.O., ED 7/135, no. 142.

99 B.I.H.R., V. 1868/Ret. 2, no. 377; *1st Rep. Com. on Employment of Children, Young Persons, and Women in Agric.*, *App. Pt. II* [4068-I], p. 365, H.C. (1867–8), xvii.

1 *Returns relating to Elem. Educ.* 472–3.

2 *Kellys Dir. N. & E. R. Yorks.* (1872), 537.

3 P.R.O., ED 7/135, no. 142; H.U.L., DDLG/46/26; *Kelly's Dir. N. & E. R. Yorks.* (1913), 599.

4 *Bd. of Educ., List 21* (H.M.S.O., 1908 and later edns.).

5 E.R. Educ. Cttee. *Mins.* 1947–8, 52, 114; 1948–9, 3.

6 Rise Park Estate Off., 'Rise Settled Estates 1967'; inf. from Rise Park Estate Off., 1995.

7 *9th Rep. Com. Char.* 773.

8 B.I.H.R., V. 1764/Ret. 2, no. 212; E.R.A.O., DDRI/34/20–1; Poulson, *Holderness*, i. 409.

9 Below, Withernwick, educ., charities.

10 B.I.H.R., V. 1764/Ret. 2, no. 212; *9th Rep. Com. Char.* 773.

11 E.R.A.O., NV/1/76.   12 Ibid. accession 1681.

13 Ibid. MIS. 207; R.D.B., 1355/69/66.

14 E.R.A.O., CCH/65.

15 This article was written in 1989.

16 *P.N. Yorks. E.R.* (E.P.N.S.), 70.

17 Ibid. 50.

18 *V.C.H. Yorks.* ii. 267, 295.

19 O.S. Map 6″, Yorks. CXCVI, CCXI (1855 edn.); *Census*, 1871.

20 *Census*, 1891 (pt. ii).

21 E.R.A.O., CCO/465; *Census*, 1931 (pt. ii); 1961; above, Swine, N. and S. Skirlaugh, intros.

22 E.R.A.O., Holderness (Parishes) Order 1983; O.S. Map 1/2,500, Yorks. CCXII. 1 (1891 edn.); *Census*, 1991.

23 P.R.O., E 179/202/60, m. 60.

24 *Hearth Tax*, 61.

25 Above, Swine, N. Skirlaugh, intro.

26 *Herring's Visit.* ii, p. 89; no figure for Riston was given in 1764.

Separate figures were not always given for the two settlements, but the Riston part of Arnold contributed 59 to the total in 1811, 58 in 1841, and 84 in 1851, and that part of Arnold had *c.* 80 inhabitants at the boundary change of 1885. Swine parish's part of Arnold had a population of 76 in 1811, 96 in 1841, and 108 in 1851. The population of Long Riston alone was 271 in 1881, rising to 299 in 1911 but falling to 266 in 1931. The population of Long Riston and Arnold, in the civil parish as reconstituted in 1952, was 415 in 1951, rising to 467 in 1961, and again in the 1980s to 527 in 1991, when those usually resident numbered 535.[27]

The eastern half of the parish is on boulder clay, the ground lying at 7–12 m. above sea level around the settlements and rising to over 15 m. near Farnton hill, which is capped with sand and gravel. In the west much of the low-lying ground in the Hull valley is alluvial, with some sand and gravel.[28] The open fields of Long Riston and Arnold occupied the higher ground, with common meadows and carrs further west; the commonable lands were inclosed in 1778.

The natural drainage of the low grounds was southwards, but from the early 13th century water from Riston was carried westwards by Monk dike, which had been constructed by Meaux abbey, and discharged into the river Hull by Eschedike, between Weel and Wawne. Neglect by Thornton abbey (Lincs.) of the part of Monk dike from Woodhouse to Rowton in 1368 caused Meaux abbey's land to be flooded, and neglect by Meaux was found in 1377 to have caused flooding on Peter Hildyard's land.[29] In the late 16th century the commissioners of sewers evidently restored drainage southwards along a channel which later formed the western boundary of Riston parish and bore the name Monk dike; water reached the river by Forthdike, between Wawne and Sutton on Hull. Under an Act of 1764 all the low grounds east of the river Hull were removed from the jurisdiction of the Court of Sewers for the East Parts of the East Riding and a new Holderness Drainage Board was formed. By the consequent award made in 1775 *c.* 152 a. of low grounds in Long Riston and others in Arnold were rated to the drainage.[30] Within the parish a new drain across the carrs, later called the Arnold and Riston drain, was made at inclosure in 1778, and an overseer was ordered to be chosen to raise an assessment and maintain the drain and certain banks and bridges.[31] Under an Act of 1832 a new main drain west of Riston, the Holderness lowland drain, was made to carry water from the Hull valley to the river Humber; the old drain,

of which Monk dike formed part, became the upland drain and continued to carry water from Holderness to the river Hull. By the award made in 1838 under the 1832 Act, the low grounds in Riston rated to the drainage amounted to 157 a. and those in Arnold, Rowton, and North Skirlaugh to 516 a., most of them in Arnold.[32] The work of the Holderness Drainage Board was taken over in 1941 by the River Hull Catchment Board, the responsibility of which had passed by 1989 to the Yorkshire Water Authority and in 2000 belonged to the Environment Agency.[33]

Roads leading from Long Riston north to Leven and south to South Skirlaugh, in Swine, became part of the main road from Hull to Bridlington in the 20th century, and a bypass west of the village was opened in 1986.[34] Minor roads lead northwards to Catwick, eastwards to Rise and Sigglesthorne, and southwards through Arnold to Swine. Before inclosure one of the roads from Rise evidently ran north of Long Riston village and joined the Leven road; it was presumably diverted into the village in 1778.[35]

LONG RISTON VILLAGE AND ARNOLD HAMLET. Most of the older houses in Long Riston are strung out for *c.* 1 km. along Main Street, with a few in a short cul-de-sac on the west side of the street named after the Lauty family. The church stands isolated in the fields near the north end of the village, approached by footpaths and by a carriage road set out at inclosure in 1778 and overgrown by 1989.[36] The hamlet of Arnold lies a short distance west of the main road and close to Long Riston village, to which it is linked by a pedestrian roadway under the bypass. Few of the houses in either settlement are noteworthy. Those in Long Riston include the single-storeyed Whinns Cottage, formerly called Overseer's Cottage,[37] a terrace of small, 19th-century cottages, another terrace of four Gothic-style houses dated 1871, and 24 council houses built on a site acquired in 1945.[38] Infilling with new houses was continuing in 1989.

In both Long Riston and Arnold there were one or two licensed houses in the later 18th century, and the Traveller's Rest in the former and the Bay Horse in the latter have existed at least since the 1820s.[39] A beerhouse in Long Riston was also mentioned from 1840 and known as the Board by 1909; it was closed in 1913.[40] An Oddfellows' lodge was founded at Long Riston in 1836 and still existed in 1981.[41] A reading room was established in the village in 1881.[42] A 4-a. playing field was laid out on land bought in 1954–5,[43] and a village hall was built there in 1976 on the site of a Women's Institute hall.[44]

[27] *V.C.H. Yorks.* iii. 495; *Census*, 1851, 1881–1931, 1961–91.
[28] Geol. Surv. Map 1″, drift, sheets 72–3 (1909 edn.).
[29] *Monastic Notes* (Y.A.S. Rec. Ser. xvii), 136; *Public Works in Med. Law*, ii (Selden Soc. xl), pp. 345–6.
[30] E.R.A.O., DDCC/143/135.
[31] R.D.B., BB/73/13; H.U.L., DSJ/62, pp. 112 sqq.; O.S. Map 6″, Yorks. CCXI (1855 edn.).
[32] E.R.A.O., QDA/13.
[33] Para. based on J. A. Sheppard, *Draining of Hull Valley* (E. Yorks. Loc. Hist. Ser. viii), *passim*; *V.C.H. Yorks. E.R.* vi. 278–9. For the channels made by Meaux abbey, below, Wawne, intro. Inf. from Environment Agency, Willerby, 2000.

[34] Humbs. C.C. *Mins.* 1979–80, F 2113; plaque at underpass.
[35] T. Jefferys, *Map of Yorks.* (1772).
[36] R.D.B., BB/73/13.
[37] Ibid. 1030/268/249.   [38] Ibid. 699/480/402.
[39] E.R.A.O., QDT/2/6, 9; directories.
[40] Directories; E.R. Licensing Cttee. *Mins.* 1904–23, 187.
[41] D. Neave, *E.R. Friendly Soc.* (E. Yorks. Loc. Hist. Ser. xli), 65.
[42] Bulmer, *Dir. E. Yorks.* (1892), 487.
[43] R.D.B., 970/168/142; 970/169/143; 999/5/4.
[44] 'Some Hist. Notes' (copy in church, 1989), 3; O.S. Map 6″, Yorks. CCXI. NE. (1928 edn.).

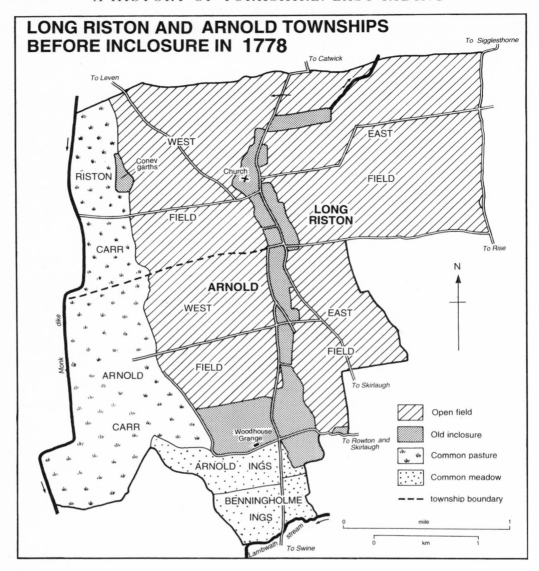

LONG RISTON AND ARNOLD TOWNSHIPS BEFORE INCLOSURE IN 1778

	Open field
	Old inclosure
	Common pasture
	Common meadow
	township boundary

OUTLYING HOUSES in Long Riston include Riston Grange[45] and half a dozen other farmhouses, all built after inclosure in 1778;[46] that called Criftins, north of the village, takes its name from ground recorded from the mid 12th century. Several of the farmhouses in Arnold were also built after inclosure, but Woodhouse Farm existed earlier and was presumably near the site of the monastic grange recorded from *c.* 1300.[47] A group of houses called New Rise stands on a minor road forming the eastern boundary of Riston but most of them are in Rise parish. At Farnton hill nearby there has been a training course for horses since the 19th century.[48]

MANORS AND OTHER ESTATES. In 1066 Morkar had 2 carucates and 6 bovates at Riston

as soke of the manor of Hornsea; by 1086 they belonged to Drew de Bevrère.[49] The manor of *RISTON* thereafter formed part of the Aumale fee and was held by the Scures family as undertenant. From Ansketil de Scures it had passed by 1130 to his son Alan, who was succeeded in turn by his son Robert, by another son William by 1166, and later by William's sister Maud. She was succeeded by her cousin Walter and he by his son Sir Robert de Scures.[50] In 1278 Sir Robert sold Riston to his daughter Joan and her husband Sir Robert Hildyard.[51] Robert held 1½ carucate of the Aumale fee in Riston in 1287.[52] After Joan's death *c.* 1295, the manor descended successively to her son Robert Hildyard and that Robert's son Thomas, who was named as lord of Riston in 1316 and had died by 1322. Thomas was succeeded by his daughter Catherine, who

45 Below, manors.
46 A. Bryant, *Map of E.R. Yorks.* (1829).
47 E.R.A.O., DDRI/accession 2980, map with incl. award; T. Jefferys, *Map of Yorks.* (1772); below, manors; econ. hist.
48 O.S. Map 6", Yorks. CXCVII (1854 edn.); above,

Rise, intro.
49 *V.C.H. Yorks.* ii. 265.
50 *Early Yorks. Fam.* (Y.A.S. Rec. Ser. cxxxv), 82–3; *Chron. de Melsa* (Rolls Ser.), i. 97.
51 *Yorks. Fines, 1272–1300*, p. 13.
52 *Cal. Inq. p.m.* iv, p. 352.

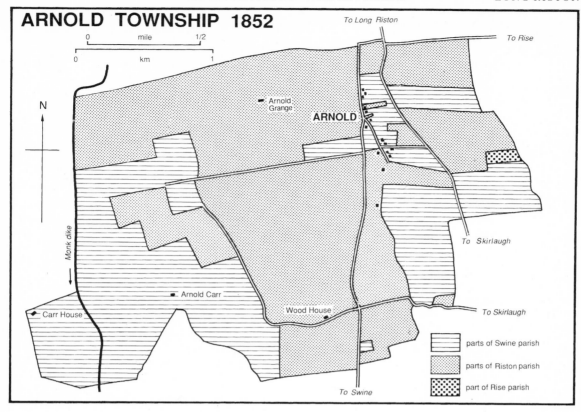

ARNOLD TOWNSHIP 1852

parts of Swine parish

parts of Riston parish

part of Rise parish

married Sir Peter Nuthill.[53] It was perhaps the same Catherine who settled Riston manor on herself and her then husband, Sir John Chaumon, in 1370.[54]

The manor had descended by the late 14th century to the Nuthills' son Peter, and it was perhaps that Peter's son Thomas who was described as lord of Riston in 1427 and, as Thomas Nuthill of Riston, was named on royal commissions between 1428 and 1446.[55] Thomas was succeeded by his son Sir Anthony Nuthill who was attainted in 1461.[56] The manor was granted by the Crown to George Plantagenet, duke of Clarence, in 1465,[57] but in 1477 it was restored to Sir Anthony's sister Elizabeth, wife of Henry Suthill.[58] Peter Hildyard of Winestead (d. 1502) held 4 tofts and 60 a. in Riston of Elizabeth Suthill.[59] The reversion of the manor was settled in 1478 on Elizabeth's daughters Agnes, wife of John Barnby, and Isabel, wife of John Frechwell (Frechvyll).[60]

The Frechwell share belonged to Peter Frech-

well by 1572.[61] In 1602 he or another Peter Frechwell conveyed his share of the manor to Thomas Barnby, who was probably the great-great-grandson of John and Agnes Barnby and who the same year sold both shares to William Gee of Hull and William Gee of Beverley.[62] Riston descended in the Gee family[63] until 1712, when William and Thomas Gee sold it to Hugh Bethell; it then included a dozen bovates and c. 15 closes.[64] The Bethells bought several other holdings, including 1 carucate and 2 bovates, in the 17th and 18th centuries,[65] and the enlarged estate descended in that family.[66] At inclosure in 1778 William Bethell was allotted 905 a. in Riston.[67] The estate in Long Riston and Arnold together comprised 1,996 a. in 1782 and 1,924 a. in 1852; in Long Riston alone the Bethells had 1,023 a. in 1930.[68] Many small plots in Long Riston were later sold, together with a farm of 131 a. in 1972, but the Bethells still owned c. 800 a. in 1990.[69]

The Hildyards had a chief house in Riston in

53 Chron. de Melsa, i. 97–8; Yorks. Inq. iii, pp. 26–7; Cal. Inq. p.m. vi, p. 185; vii, p. 385; Feud. Aids, vi. 163.
54 E.R.A.O., DDRI/22/33.
55 Ibid. DDRI/35/1; B.L. Add. Ch. 5421; Cal. Fine R. 1422–30, 220; 1445–52, 39; Chron. de Melsa, i. 97–8. Cf. the slightly different descent of Nuthill manor in V.C.H. Yorks. E.R. v. 11.
56 W.Y.A.S., Spencer-Stanhope MS. 66; Rot. Parl. v. 476–83.
57 Cal. Pat. 1461–7, 454; 1467–77, 457–8.
58 Ibid. 1476–85, 72; Rot. Parl. vi. 175–6.
59 Cal. Inq. p.m. Hen. VII, ii, p. 421.
60 W.Y.A.S., Spencer-Stanhope MS. 50; P.R.O., C 1/291/49; ibid. REQ 2/1/35; V.C.H. Yorks. E.R. v. 11 (where the name is given as Fretwell).

61 Yorks. Fines, ii. 15.
62 E.R.A.O., DDRI/22/65, 70, 73. For Barnby pedigree, see Visit. Yorks. 1584–5 and 1612, ed. J. Foster, 339.
63 For pedigree, see J. Foster, Pedigrees of Yorks. iii.
64 E.R.A.O., DDRI/22/100, 124.
65 Ibid. DDRI/22/96–7, 101, 114, 121, 148, 150, 161, 166, 169–70, 178, 187, 202; DDRI/35/21.
66 For pedigree, see Burke, Land. Gent. (1969), ii. 46–7.
67 R.D.B., BB/73/13.
68 Ibid. 170/289/242; 408/90/75; book of plans of estates of H. Bethell, at Rise Park Estate Off.; valuation of estates of Ric. Bethell, 1852, in E.R.A.O., DDRI/accession 2980, box 2.
69 R.D.B., 1813/436/364; inf. from Rise Park Estate Off. 1990.

1296 and 1322; it was called Hall Garth in 1602 and 1712.[70] The house may have stood south-east of the church, where earthworks survived in 1989. By the 19th century a house nearby in Catwick Lane was known as Manor House.[71]

Apart from the manor, the largest modern estate in Long Riston was that based on Riston Grange. At inclosure in 1778 Peter Nevill was allotted 228 a., together with old inclosures called Coney garths given in exchange for certain houses and garths.[72] He devised the estate in 1807 to Peter Jackson,[73] who left it in 1831 to John Jackson and he in 1865 to his brother Hugh W. Jackson.[74] Hugh (d. 1874) was succeeded by his sons Bryan B. (d. 1892) and Thomas B. Jackson (d. 1918).[75] In 1921 the Jacksons' trustees sold the 251-a. estate to Henry King; it was bought from King in 1939 by Francis L. C. Plummer and from him in 1952 by his son-in-law Robert W. Brown. Most of the land was sold to T. H. Caley and Sons in 1977 and later farmed from Routh.[76]

The large brick house known as Riston Grange was built by Peter Nevill in 1773.[77] By 1952 part of it was converted to a separate dwelling called East House.[78] Riston Grange was separated from the farm by a sale of c. 1985.[79]

The Jacksons also owned the c. 130-a. Criftins farm. At inclosure in 1778 it had been allotted to Joseph Williamson (d. 1785), whose devisee William Williamson sold it in 1809 to Peter Jackson.[80] It was conveyed in 1824 to Jackson's son the Revd. Peter Jackson, who in 1852 conveyed it to Hugh W. Jackson. It descended with Riston Grange, and in 1918 was sold by Thomas B. Jackson to Walter Kirkwood (d. 1929).[81] The estate was later held by Kirkwood's executor before being sold in 1962 to Kirkwood's grandson, Walter T. Kirkwood, the owner in 1998.[82]

Besides the Scures, other undertenants of the Aumale fee in the parish included the Ros and Fauconberg families. Robert de Ros confirmed gifts at Arnold to Meaux abbey in the early 13th century, and another Robert de Ros held an estate there in 1284–5. Walter de Fauconberg was a benefactor of Meaux abbey in Riston c. 1200. Another Walter de Fauconberg held in demesne 1 bovate in Riston and 4 bovates in Arnold of William de Forz, count of Aumale (d. 1260); he was perhaps Walter de Fauconberg, later Lord Fauconberg, who held land in Arnold

as an appurtenance of his manor of Rise in 1284–5, and had a grant of free warren in Long Riston and Arnold in 1292. Fauconberg (d. 1304) was succeeded by his son, also Walter de Fauconberg, Lord Fauconberg, who was named as a lord of Arnold in 1316, along with Nicholas of Reddings, Richard of Thorpe, and Thornton abbey (Lincs.).[83]

An estate in Arnold was held in demesne by a branch of the Hildyard family, which acquired numerous small holdings in the 13th and 14th centuries and lived at Arnold. The first known representative was Peter Hildyard, brother of Sir Robert Hildyard who acquired the manor of Riston in 1278. After Peter's death, his widow married Nicholas of Reddings, who was named as one of the lords of Arnold in 1316. The estate later belonged to Peter Hildyard's son Robert, Robert's son John, and John's son Peter. It was described as the manor of *ARNOLD* in 1457 and descended with Winestead manor, which Sir Robert Hildyard of Arnold acquired in the earlier 15th century.[84] Peter Hildyard (d. 1502) held 2 houses, 4 tofts, and 110 a. in Arnold of the Fauconberg fee and 3a. there of Thornton abbey.[85]

Peter Hildyard had a chief house at Arnold in 1341. It presumably occupied the moated site at the north end of the hamlet which was destroyed when the bypass was built.[86]

Meaux abbey had confirmation between 1210 and 1226 of the gifts of 5 a. in Arnold by Robert son of Osmund and the site of its grange there by Richard of Arnold; both were held of the Ros fee. Other small gifts in Arnold were made to the abbey, which had a grant of free warren there in 1293[87] and whose manor of *ARNOLD* was mentioned from the 14th century. In Long Riston the abbey was given 4 bovates, a toft, and 2s. rent by Walter de Fauconberg c. 1200. A bovate given by Henry de Scures between 1210 and 1220 was later exchanged for a holding in Arnold. Other parcels of land were given to the abbey by Stephen Ward and Simon the clerk c. 1230. The abbey exchanged its 4 bovates in Long Riston for land in Rowton, in Swine, in 1269 or 1270.[88] In 1535 the land at Arnold and Rowton was worth nearly £13 a year, and 8s. 4d. rent was owed in 1539 for a house, a close, and c. 5 a. in Long Riston. The abbey also had land at Benningholme, in Swine, worth £1 in

70 E.R.A.O., DDRI/22/65, 96; *Yorks. Inq.* iii, p. 26; *Cal. Inq. p.m.* vi, p. 185.
71 O.S. Map 6", Yorks. CXCVI (1855 edn.).
72 R.D.B., BB/73/13.
73 Ibid. CN/117/186; E.R.A.O., PE/89/2.
74 R.D.B., FP/227/233; IU/326/450; E.R.A.O., PE/89/7.
75 R.D.B., LP/36/51; 57/251/237 (1893); 191/470/399; H.U.L., DDX/16/123.
76 R.D.B., 240/378/320; 618/510/343; 914/494/439; inf. from Mrs. Caley, Church Farm, Routh, and Mr. W. T. Kirkwood, Criftins Farm, Long Riston, 1998.
77 Poulson, *Holderness*, i. 348.
78 R.D.B., 914/494/439.
79 Inf. from Mrs. Caley, Routh, 1998.
80 R.D.B., BB/73/13; BL/223/339; CO/347/541; E.R.A.O., PE/106/3.
81 R.D.B., EP/56/70; GX/334/389; 184/285/239; 399/

286/235.
82 Ibid. 1232/177/165; inf. from Mr. W. T. Kirkwood, Long Riston, 1998.
83 *Cal. Inq. p.m.* iv, pp. 354, 357; *Cal. Chart. R.* 1257–1300, 426; *Feud. Aids*, vi. 40, 163; below, this section [Meaux abbey]; *Complete Peerage*, s.v. Fauconberge; above, Rise, manor.
84 E.R.A.O., DDHI, 'Leaguer bk.'(Hildyards of Arnold, *passim*); Poulson, *Holderness*, ii. 220–1; *Chron. de Melsa*, ii. 218; *Feud. Aids*, vi. 40.
85 *Cal. Inq. p.m. Hen. VII*, ii, p. 419.
86 E.R.A.O., DDHI, 'Leaguer bk.'; O.S. Map 6", Yorks. CCXI (1855 edn.); above, intro.
87 'Meaux Cart.', pp. 32, 152, 250–1, 421, 570.
88 Ibid. pp. 418–19; *Chron. de Melsa* (Rolls Ser.), i. 303, 365, 419; ii. 94, 141–2, 218; iii. 6–7; *Cal. Chart. R.* 1257–1300, 427.

1535,[89] and that and the land at Rowton were later recorded as appurtenances of Arnold manor. In 1544 after the Dissolution the manor was granted to Morgan Wolff, Robert Trappes, and others.[90] Francis Trappes had the estate in 1572,[91] Francis Trappes Byrnand and Sir John Egerton and their wives were dealing with it in the 1600s,[92] and in 1634 Robert Trappes and Ursula Proud sold it to Joseph Micklethwaite and his son John. The manor was conveyed to Christopher Hildyard of Ottringham and his son Christopher in 1639, and it was probably the son who, as Christopher Hildyard of Routh, re-conveyed it to Joseph Micklethwaite in 1647.[93] It was evidently the same estate which John Blount and his sons Samuel and William sold to Hugh Bethell in 1695; it then included c. 275 a. and 4½ bovates in Arnold.[94]

Besides their possible acquisition of the Hild-yard estate and Meaux abbey's former estate,[95] in the later 17th and 18th century the Bethells bought several other holdings in Arnold.[96] At inclosure in 1778 William Bethell was allotted 852 a. in Arnold, besides land and a rent for tithes.[97] The family had 1,653 a. in Arnold, Rowton, and North Skirlaugh in 1930, much of it in Arnold; many small plots were later sold but the Bethells still had c. 1,100 a. in 1990.[98]

The rectorial tithes of the part of Arnold in Swine parish were granted in 1546 with Swine rectory to Sir Richard Gresham,[99] and desc-ended with that rectory to William Thornton, who sold them to Hugh Bethell in 1737.[1] At inclosure in 1778 William Bethell was allotted 48 a. and £30 11s. 6d. a year for tithes there.[2]

By the early 14th century Thornton abbey (Lincs.) had a grange at WOODHOUSE, in Arnold.[3] William de Ros, Lord Ros, enlarged the abbey's estate with a house and 3 bovates in Arnold, given c. 1310,[4] and in the 1540s the grange, or manor, including land in Withern-wick and Skirlaugh, was leased for £21 a year.[5] As Woodhouse manor, the abbey's former estate was granted to the short-lived Thornton college in 1542.[6] In 1553 the Crown granted Woodhouse grange, including a house, to Ralph Constable,[7] and it later descended in the Constables of St.

Sepulchre's Garth to Michael Constable (fl. c. 1630).[8]

A house called Woodhouse Grange, together with both closes and open-field land, was dev-ised by Charles Robinson (d. 1695) to his wife Elizabeth, who conveyed it to Mark Kirkby.[9] Extending into Benningholme, in Swine, the estate was devised by Kirkby (d. 1718) to his son Richard,[10] who was succeeded in turn by his brother Mark (d. 1748) and sister Isabel Collings. Mrs. Collings by will proved in 1764 left it to Mann Horsfield.[11] At inclosure in 1778 Horsfield was allotted 125 a.; his devisees sold 90 a. to Robert C. Broadley in 1797, including old-inclosed land at Woodhouse, and the same year they sold Woodhouse Grange, with old inclosures and the rest of Horsfield's allotment, to William Taylor.[12] Broadley had already acquired, in 1792, the farmhouse and land of James Moore, who was allotted 75 a. at inclosure in 1778.[13] Broadley (d. 1812) left his estate in Arnold to his nephew John Broadley (d. 1833), whose devisees sold it in 1835 to Jane Williamson and Thomas Whitaker; it later passed to Thomas's son the Revd. Robert Whitaker.[14] William Taylor (d. by 1799) was succeeded by his son John (d. c. 1829), whose devisees con-veyed Woodhouse Grange and 176 a. to John's brothers Robert and William in 1830. The Taylors sold the estate to Jane Williamson and Thomas Whitaker in 1837.[15]

The Broadley and Taylor estates were added to other land in Arnold already belonging to the Whitakers. In 1778 an allotment of 141 a. had been made to the representatives of Daniel Whitaker (d. by 1774),[16] and it evidently passed to his son Thomas and then, by 1813, to Thomas's sons Charles and Thomas: Charles conveyed his half to his brother Thomas in 1838.[17] Thomas Whitaker sold 154 a. to Robert and William Billaney in 1857, and Woodhouse Grange and 176 a. to William Wright in 1858; the Revd. Robert Whitaker's trustees sold 175 a. to Wright in 1859.[18] William, later Sir William, Wright died in 1884, and the estate was held by trustees until 1918, when Woodhouse Grange, another farmhouse, and 369 a. were sold to Thomas Jackson.[19] In 1937 Jackson sold the estate, then reckoned at 374 a., to Hilda, wife of Arthur Walgate, and in 1944 the Walgates

89 P.R.O., SC 6/Hen. VIII/4612; *Valor Eccl.* v. 108.
90 *L. & P. Hen. VIII*, xix (2), p. 78.
91 *Cal. Pat.* 1569–72, p. 453.
92 *Yorks. Fines*, iv. 170; *1603–14*, 46–7.
93 E.R.A.O., DDRI/35/6; *Yorks. Royalist Composition Papers*, ii (Y.A.S. Rec. Ser. xviii), p. 11.
94 E.R.A.O., DDRI/2/33, 37.
95 Above, this section.
96 E.R.A.O., DDRI/2/17, 21, 23, 26, 32, 46, 49, 51, 54.
97 R.D.B., BB/73/13. For the tithes, below, next para.
98 R.D.B., 170/289/242; 408/90/75; and *passim*; inf. from Rise Park Estate Off. 1990.
99 *L. & P. Hen. VIII*, xxi (1), pp. 573–5.
1 E.R.A.O., DDRI/2/46; above, Swine, Swine town-ship, manors (rectory).
2 R.D.B., BB/73/13.
3 *Chron. de Melsa*, ii. 217; *Cal. Chart. R.* 1300–26, 9.
4 *Cal. Pat.* 1301–7, 524; 1307–13, 449.
5 P.R.O., SC 6/Hen. VIII/2022, m. 79.
6 *L. & P. Hen. VIII*, xvii, pp. 29–30.

7 *Cal. Pat.* 1553, 87. Some land at Woodhouse was kept by the Crown: ibid. 1580–2, pp. 6–7.
8 H.U.L., DDMC/78/1; P.R.O., C 2/Jas. I/C 3/31; ibid. C 60/525, no. 52; J. Foster, *Pedigrees of Yorks.* iii, s.v. Constable of Constable Burton.
9 H.U.L., DDCV/152/1–2.
10 R.D.B., G/242/545; above, Roos, manors.
11 H.U.L., DDSY/108/3, 5; DDSY/110/23; *V.C.H. Yorks. E.R.* v. 12, 90.
12 R.D.B., BY/133/209; BY/134/134.
13 Ibid. BB/73/13; BR/124/190.
14 Ibid. CS/519/726; EZ/89/78; HK/285/294; HT/77/97; Burke, *Land. Gent.* (1937), s.v. Harrison-Broadley.
15 R.D.B., EG/373/443; EK/246/271; FD/354/391; E.R.A.O., QDE/1.
16 R.D.B., AU/77/115; BB/73/13.
17 Ibid. FH/384/408; FH/386/411; E.R.A.O., QDE/1.
18 R.D.B., HQ/197/250; HT/77/97; HW/219/263.
19 Ibid. LZ/57/78; 1/383/338 (1885); 167/236/210; 188/519/477.

conveyed it to Ann Watson's charity trustees, who still owned it in 1994.[20]

Several other religious houses owned small estates in Long Riston and Arnold. Swine priory had property in Long Riston by the late 13th century, and its right to 3 bovates in Arnold was acknowledged in 1240.[21] Its estate in Long Riston and Arnold was worth c. £5 a year in 1535. In 1553 the Crown granted John Green and Ralph Hall a house and a close called North grange and 1 bovate in Riston, formerly belonging to Swine, and in 1609 it granted another part of the priory's former estate there, including c. 7 bovates, to Edward Bates and Henry Elwes.[22]

Nunkeeling priory was given 1 bovate in Long Riston and other land there and in Arnold by Sir Andrew Fauconberg in the 13th century, and its estate in both places may have been enlarged by gift of Robert Franks in 1386. In 1535 the priory's land in Long Riston and Arnold was worth c. £2 a year.[23] A toft and croft in Arnold, formerly belonging to Nunkeeling, were granted by the Crown in 1553 to John Green and Ralph Hall.[24] Bridlington priory was given 4 bovates in Long Riston by Ansketil de Scures.[25] Fountains abbey (Yorks. W.R.) evidently also had property in Long Riston.[26] A croft in Arnold, held of the chapter of Beverley, was given to Meaux abbey in 1308, and part of Long Riston lay within the liberties of the chapter and the provost of Beverley in 1334. Two houses and c. 50 a. were held of the provost by Peter Hildyard (d. 1502).[27] By 1191 the Knights Hospitaller had 2 bovates in Long Riston,[28] and Peter Hildyard (d. 1502) held 50 a. of them. The estate included 7 houses and cottages and 2 bovates, worth 5s. 6d. a year, in 1539. It was briefly regranted to the refounded order in 1558.[29] St. Leonard's hospital, York, was given 1 a. and common of pasture in Long Riston by Robert de Scures c. 1150. In 1609 the Crown granted Edward Bates and Henry Elwes a cottage there formerly belonging to the hospital.[30]

Anne Routh, by will proved in 1722, devised 26 a. in Arnold as part of the endowment of her hospital in Beverley; the charity was administered by Beverley corporation, which was allotted 24 a. at inclosure in 1778,[31] and later by Beverley Consolidated Charities, which sold 12 a. in 1966 and 14 a. in 1968.[32]

A manor of CHENECOL, comprising 1 carucate and held in 1066 by Gamel, was presumably the same as that of CHENUTHESHOLM, also of 1 carucate. The latter had passed from Knut to William Malet, who was deprived c. 1070, and in 1086 both belonged to Drew de Bevrère. Another carucate formed LUVETOTHOLM manor; it had belonged to Luvetote before passing in turn to Malet and Bevrère.[33] No more is known of them.

ECONOMIC HISTORY. COMMON LANDS AND INCLOSURE. Long Riston and Arnold each had its own open fields. Those at Long Riston, called East and West fields, together with Little fen, the marsh, meadow in North carr, and a pasture right in the Frith, were mentioned in the 13th century,[34] when a rabbit warren there belonging to the Hildyards was also recorded.[35] Criftins was mentioned in the mid 12th century.[36] In 1771 East field at Long Riston included ground called Ox pasture and West field had parts called North carr and Criftins; the open-field land at Arnold was also divided into East and West fields, and there was common meadow land called the ings, Arnold ings, or Benningholme ings. Each of the townships had a carr or common. Common rights in Arnold were attached to 44 houses there and in North Skirlaugh and Rowton.[37]

Old inclosures in Long Riston included pastures called Angram and Thurkelholm, which were evidently inclosed by Robert Hildyard after eight freeholders had granted him their rights there in 1278.[38] A close there called North grange, formerly belonging to Swine priory, was mentioned in 1553.[39] Both Meaux and Thornton abbeys had inclosed land at their granges in Arnold.[40] In the mid 13th century Swine priory was granted rights in a meadow in Arnold, with freedom to inclose, sow, and improve it, provided that the donors retained commonage there after harvest and before sowing or the next inclosure.[41]

The remaining commonable lands in Long Riston and Arnold were inclosed in 1778 under an Act of 1771; the award also dealt with some adjoining grounds in Benningholme (in Swine).[42] Allotments were made totalling 1,634 a. in Long Riston, 1,412 a. in Arnold, and 95 a. in Benningholme. In Long Riston they comprised more

[20] Ibid. 572/472/376; 673/543/450; inf. from Ann Watson's Trust, 1994.
[21] W.Y.A.S., Spencer-Stanhope MS. 22; *Yorks. Fines, 1232–46*, p. 86.
[22] P.R.O., C 66/1800, no. 7; *Valor Eccl.* (Rec. Com.), v. 114; *Cal. Pat.* 1553, 215. For Crown leases before 1553, see *Yorks. Mon. Suppression Papers* (Y.A.S. Rec. Ser. xlviii), 157; *L. & P. Hen. VIII*, xvi, p. 723.
[23] W.Y.A.S., Spencer-Stanhope MS. 33; H.U.L., DHO/6/120; B.L. Cott. MS. Otho C. viii, ff. 79v.–81; *Valor Eccl.* v. 115.
[24] *Cal. Pat.* 1553, 216.
[25] *Bridlington Chart.*, p. 225.
[26] *Memorials of Fountains*, i. (Sur. Soc. xlii), 401, 409–10.
[27] 'Meaux Cart.', pp. 152, 422; *Lay Subsidy of 1334*, ed. R. E. Glasscock, 368; *Cal. Inq. p.m. Hen. VII*, ii, p. 421.
[28] E.R.A.O., DDRI/22/1; W.Y.A.S., Spencer-Stanhope MS. 11.

[29] *Cal. Inq. p.m. Hen. VII*, ii, p. 421; *Miscellanea*, iv (Y.A.S. Rec. Ser. xciv), 75, 99; *Cal. Pat.* 1557–8, 321.
[30] P.R.O., C 66/1800, no. 7; *E.Y.C.* ii, pp. 64–5.
[31] R.D.B., AA/73/13; *V.C.H. Yorks. E.R.* vi. 269.
[32] R.D.B., 1440/457/391; 1548/200/173.
[33] *V.C.H. Yorks.* ii. 267, 295.
[34] W.Y.A.S., Spencer-Stanhope MSS. 14, 15, 18; E.R.A.O., DDRI/22/5, 28; *Chron. de Melsa*, i. 305.
[35] W.Y.A.S., Spencer-Stanhope MSS. 19, 52; *Cal. Inq. p.m.* vi, p. 185.
[36] *Chron. de Melsa*, i. 81.
[37] Long Riston and Arnold Incl. Act, 11 Geo. III, c. 92 (Priv. Act).
[38] W.Y.A.S., Spencer-Stanhope MS. 16.
[39] *Cal. Pat.* 1553, 215. [40] Above, manors.
[41] *Yorks. Deeds*, viii, pp. 4–5.
[42] E.R.A.O., DDRI/accession 2980, award with plan; 11 Geo. III, c. 92 (Priv. Act).

than 714 a. from East field, over 579 a. from West field, and 211 a. from the carr; in Arnold 327 a. came from East field, 424 a. from West field, 131 a. from Arnold ings, and 528 a. from the carr, together with 4 a. in an outgang. In Long Riston William Bethell was allotted 905 a., Peter Nevill 228 a., Joseph Williamson 137 a., and the rector 129 a.; there were four allotments of 30–80 a. and five of up to 10 a. In Arnold, Bethell was allotted 900 a., representatives of the late Daniel Whitaker 141 a., Mann Horsfield 125 a., and the rector 51 a.; there were three other allotments of 20–80 a. and seven of up to 12 a.

LATER AGRICULTURE. In 1801 there was said to be 486 a. under crops in Riston, and 1,128 a. of arable, 620 a. of grassland, and 18 a. of woodland were recorded in 1905.[43] There was still much meadow and pasture in the 1930s, especially around the villages, although most of the parish was then arable.[44] In the 19th and earlier 20th century there were usually c. 8 farmers in Long Riston, of whom 2 in 1851 and 4–5 in the 1930s had 150 a. or more, and c. 6 in Arnold, 2 in 1851 and 3 in the 1930s with larger holdings. The number of cowkeepers in the parish rose from 1 in the 1850s to 9 in 1909, and there were still 5 in the 1930s.[45] In 1987 the area returned under Riston civil parish, 1,979 ha. (4,889 a.), may have included holdings that extended into Rise; 1,686.7 ha. (4,168 a.) were arable and 225.3 ha. (557 a.) grassland. Of the holdings returned, five were of under 10 ha. (25 a.), two of 100–199 ha. (247–492 a.), and one of over 700 ha. (1,729 a.); there were then 3,776 pigs and 1,904 sheep.[46]

MILLS. Peter the miller was recorded at Long Riston in the 13th century,[47] the Hildyards had a windmill in 1322,[48] and in the 1540s the former Fountains abbey estate included a derelict windmill.[49] There was a windmill in 1602, but in 1670 the mill hill was let with licence to remove the mill.[50] A windmill in Arnold was recorded in 1588.[51]

LOCAL GOVERNMENT. In the early 19th century permanent poor relief was given to 4–5 people and occasional relief to 2–8 others. There were then four cottages for the poor.[52] Long Riston and Arnold joined Skirlaugh poor-law union in 1837[53] and remained in Skirlaugh rural

district until 1935. They were then taken into Holderness rural district as part of the new civil parish of Riston, which in 1974 was included in the Holderness district of Humberside.[54] In 1996 Riston parish became part of a new East Riding unitary area.[55]

CHURCH. A church was built at Long Riston by Alan de Scures, and c. 1170 his son William acknowledged it to be subordinate to the church at Hornsea.[56] Thereafter Riston rectory and Hornsea vicarage were held as united livings. Riston was separated from Hornsea in 1907 and made a perpetual curacy, though it was later usually called a vicarage.[57] It was united with Catwick in 1922[58] and with Skirlaugh instead in 1956.[59] That part of Arnold which was anciently in Swine parish was transferred for ecclesiastical purposes to Skirlaugh parish at its creation in 1867 and to Riston parish in 1989.[60]

The advowson belonged like that of Hornsea to St. Mary's abbey, York, and later to the Crown, for whom it was exercised by the Lord Chancellor.[61] After 1922 the Lord Chancellor presented alternately with the Strickland-Constable family and from 1956 with the archbishop of York,[62] who obtained the Crown's share by an exchange of patronages in 1961.[63]

The vicar of Hornsea alleged that Riston was worth £8 a year in 1493.[64] It contributed £12 9s. a year gross to the value of the united livings in 1535,[65] and in 1650 the annual, improved value of Riston was £75 net.[66] At the ordination of Hornsea vicarage in 1423, it was provided that there should be 2 bovates of glebe at Long Riston.[67] By 1650 there was only 1 bovate, along with two closes; together with the parsonage house, the glebe was then worth £6 a year. From 1685 the glebe also included ½ bovate in Arnold and common rights in both Long Riston and Arnold. Tithes from Long Riston were worth £54 and from Arnold £20 a year in 1650.[68] At inclosure in 1778, the incumbent was allotted 28 a. for glebe and 101 a. for tithes in Long Riston and 10 a. and 42 a. respectively in Arnold, besides rents in lieu of tithes totalling £118 12s.[69] Nine acres in Arnold was sold in 1972, but there was still 172 a. of glebe in 1978.[70] By the ordination of 1423, a parsonage house at Long Riston was to be provided by St. Mary's abbey. A house was recorded from 1535; by 1781 a new one, later called Rectory Farm, had been built on land allotted at inclosure and the old

43 P.R.O., HO 67/26/266; Acreage Returns, 1905.
44 [1st] Land Util. Surv. Map, sheets 28, 33–4.
45 P.R.O., HO 107/2365; directories.
46 Inf. from Min. of Agric., Fish. & Food, Beverley, 1990.
47 W.Y.A.S., Spencer-Stanhope MS. 14; E.R.A.O., DDRI/22/15.
48 Cal. Inq. p.m. vi, p. 185.
49 Memorials of Fountains, i. 401, 410.
50 E.R.A.O., DDRI/22/73, 123.
51 Yorks. Fines, iii. 96.
52 Poor Law Abstract, 1804, pp. 594–5; 1818, pp. 522–3.
53 3rd Rep. Poor Law Com. 170.
54 Census.
55 Humberside (Structural Change) Order 1995, copy at E.R.A.O.
56 E.Y.C. iii, p. 66.
57 B.I.H.R., OC. 458; Crockford; directories.
58 Lond. Gaz. 17 Mar. 1922, p. 2226.
59 Ibid. 14 Aug. 1956, p. 4667.
60 Inf. from the vicar, 1990; above, Swine, S. Skirlaugh, church.
61 Yorks. Fines John, p. 4; above, Hornsea, church.
62 Crockford. 63 B.I.H.R., OC. 762.
64 P. Heath, Med. Clerical Accts. (St. Ant. Hall Publ. xxvi), 58.
65 Valor Eccl. (Rec. Com.), v. 116.
66 T.E.R.A.S. iv. 62.
67 B.I.H.R., Reg. 18, ff. 199–201.
68 Ibid. TER. H. Long Riston 1685 etc.; T.E.R.A.S. iv. 62.
69 R.D.B., BB/73/13.
70 Ibid. 1811/226/185; inf. from York Dioc. Bd. of Finance, 1981.

FIG. 29. LONG RISTON CHURCH BEFORE 1855

house demolished.[71] In 1778 the rector of Rise was allotted 6 a. for the tithes of that part of Arnold which lay in his parish.[72]

From 1423 Riston was usually served by a curate, who was sometimes resident there.[73] In the late 19th century he lived in the 'parsonage house', perhaps meaning Rectory Farm. It may have been in 1907, when Riston was made a separate living, that a vicarage house in Catwick Lane was provided, evidently by the Bethells. After its disuse, it was sold by Richard Bethell in 1943. From 1922 the incumbent lived elsewhere.[74] In the Middle Ages and later parishioners of Swine at Arnold were served in South Skirlaugh chapel.[75]

In 1743 a service was held each Sunday and Holy Communion was celebrated quarterly with c. 45 recipients.[76] By 1865 there were two services each Sunday; c. 10 people then received at the monthly communions. In 1884 there were sometimes three services on Sundays, and by 1919 communion was fortnightly.[77]

The church of ST. MARGARET, so called in 1434,[78] is built largely of boulders with ashlar dressings, but has been patched with brick; it comprises chancel with north vestry, nave with south porch, and west tower. The thick walls and the proportions of the nave suggest the church's 12th-century origin, although both surviving doorways are of the 14th century and the windows are 15th-century and much renewed. The tower was added in the 14th century. There is now no evidence of the aisle which

was reported to be in ruins in 1663. The outer walls were ordered to be repaired in 1720,[79] and the buttresses against the south wall are probably of that date. A restoration of the church in 1855 included the moving of the porch from the centre to the westernmost bay of the nave and the building of the vestry.[80] The chancel and chancel arch were probably also rebuilt at that time. The tower was restored in 1881.[81]

There were two bells in 1552 and later; one was replaced by a bell made by Samuel Smith of York in 1665.[82] Under a faculty of 1897, one bell was recast and a third bell made by Taylor & Co. of Loughborough.[83] The plate included a chalice in 1552 and later; it was replaced by another presented by Peter Nevill in 1785.[84] The registers date from 1653 and are nearly complete.[85]

An unknown person at an unknown date devised a 4-a. close in Long Riston to provide rent for the repair of the church.[86] The income was £8 a year in the early 20th century[87] and £120 in 1990.[88]

The churchyard was enlarged in 1891.[89]

At inclosure in 1778 the parish clerk was awarded rents totalling £7 19s. 5d. for his sheaves of wheat at Arnold and Long Riston.[90]

NONCONFORMITY. Missionary visits to Long Riston were paid by members of Fish Street chapel, Hull, c. 1800, and a barn was fitted up for worship in 1803. The house licensed there

[71] B.I.H.R., Reg. 18, ff. 199–201; ibid. TER. H. Long Riston 1781; *Valor Eccl.* v. 116.
[72] R.D.B., BB/73/13; above, Rise, church.
[73] Above, Hornsea, church.
[74] R.D.B., 667/469/411; directories; *Crockford.*
[75] *Yorks. Mon. Suppression Papers* (Y.A.S. Rec. Ser. xlviii), 156–7; above, Swine, S. Skirlaugh, church.
[76] *Herring's Visit.* ii, p. 90.
[77] B.I.H.R., V. 1865/Ret. 2, no. 427; V. 1884/Ret. 1; V. 1920–1/Ret.
[78] Ibid. Prob. Reg. 3, f. 395.
[79] Ibid. ER. V./CB. 1, f. 12.
[80] Bulmer, *Dir. E. Yorks.* (1892), 486. For meeting to approve restn. (1853) and assessment prior to restn. (Mar.

1854), see E.R.A.O., PE/89/13. For illus. before restn., see Poulson, *Holderness*, i, facing p. 294.
[81] Bulmer, *Dir. E. Yorks.* (1892), 486.
[82] B.I.H.R., TER. H. Long Riston 1764 etc.; *Inventories of Ch. Goods*, 56; Boulter, 'Ch. Bells' 85.
[83] B.I.H.R., Fac. 1897/36.
[84] Ibid. ER. V./Ret. 1, f. 6; ibid. TER. H. Long Riston 1764; *Inventories of Ch. Goods*, 56; *Yorks. Ch. Plate*, i. 303.
[85] E.R.A.O., PE/89/1–3.
[86] Ibid. accession 1681; char. bd. in vestry, 1989.
[87] Inf. from the vicar, 1990.
[88] E.R.A.O., PE/89/21.
[89] B.I.H.R., CD. Add. 1891/2; R.D.B., 29/58/50 (1889).
[90] R.D.B., BB/73/13.

in 1803 perhaps comprised the barn.[91] An Independent chapel was built in Lauty Lane, Long Riston, in 1837.[92] It was sold to the Wesleyan Methodists in 1872,[93] and services were held there until 1920;[94] it was used as a storehouse in 1989. A Primitive Methodist chapel was built in Main Street, Long Riston, in 1836[95] and closed in 1977;[96] it was derelict in 1989.

EDUCATION. There may have been a school in 1636, when a testator is said to have left 1*d*. to each schoolchild in Long Riston.[97] In 1801 Peter Nevill placed 1 a., with a house and smithy, in trust for the education of poor children;[98] in 1818 the income of £10 14s. was used to support 16 children at a school in the parish which had an average attendance of 40.[99] In 1833 the endowment was enjoyed by a school attended by 30 boys in summer and 60 in winter; a second school was then attended by 25 girls taught at their parents' expense.[1] The parish school, in Main Street,[2] was one of two schools which had a joint attendance of 44 at inspection in 1871.[3] The endowment passed to a National school at Long Riston which was built and opened in 1873 and otherwise supported by subscriptions and school pence; the mixed school accommodated infants and that year had an average attendance of 40. An annual government grant was received from 1874–5. In 1907 the endowment income was £14 14s.[4] Average attendance at Riston Church school in the early 20th century was 50–70.[5] The school was granted Controlled status in 1950. The senior pupils were transferred to the secondary school at Hornsea at its opening in 1958. The Women's Institute hall was hired as additional accommodation for the remaining children in 1963,[6] and a temporary classroom was provided in 1978.[7] There were 24 pupils on the roll in 1990.[8] By 1987 the endowment consisted of stock, yielding in 1989–90 an annual income of more than £8,000, which was used to make grants for the benefit of young people, including the maintenance of facilites in the village used by them.[9]

CHARITIES FOR THE POOR. The charity of Frances Fletcher, who left £100 to provide coal at Christmas, was created by will in 1879. The income of £2 11s. from £102 stock was distributed to 7–8 widows in the 1920s; a similar sum was still distributed *c*. 1980, at the incumbent's discretion, but not thereafter.[10]

The poor of Arnold shared in the eleemosynary charity of Marmaduke Langdale (d. 1611).[11]

ROUTH

THE parish of Routh is situated in the valley of the river Hull, *c*. 3 km. ENE. from Beverley; 7 km. south is the city of Hull and 11 km. ENE. the coast at Hornsea.[12] The name Routh, sometimes also Ruda or Rue in the Middle Ages, is Scandinavian and seems to describe the location as a clearing or a tract of rough ground;[13] the formerly wooded nature of the parish is clear from the considerable remains of trees dug out of the carrs in the 19th century, as well as from the evidence of woods in the Middle Ages.[14] The boundaries with Meaux were defined by a jury of Holderness in the 13th century.[15] In 1851–2 the parish contained 2,385 a. (965 ha.). Meaux abbey, in neighbouring Wawne parish, had been given *c*. 50 a. of wood and marshland in the 12th century[16] and, as Routh wood, the land later formed a detached part of Meaux township and Wawne parish.[17] In the 1880s Routh civil parish, which was coterminous with the ecclesiastical parish, was enlarged by 53 a., possibly by the transfer of Routh wood from Meaux civil parish.[18] The area was thereafter 2,438 a. (987 ha.) until it was reduced slightly to 985 ha. (2,434 a.) after 1981.[19]

There were 134 poll-tax payers at Routh in 1377,[20] and 37 houses there were assessed for the hearth tax and 8 discharged in 1672.[21] The parish had *c*. 20 families in the mid 18th century.[22] Standing at 115 in 1801 and 119 in 1831,

---

[91] P.R.O., RG 31/5, no. 1762; B.I.H.R., Fac. Bk. 3, p. 324; C. E. Darwent, *Story of Fish St. Ch., Hull* (1899), 128–9.

[92] R.D.B., FI/349/347; P.R.O., HO 129/522/2/13; stone on building.

[93] R.D.B., KY/102/130.

[94] E.R.A.O., MRH/1/2, esp. pp. 167, 169; MRH/1/17; MRH/1/21.

[95] R.D.B., DQ/338/25; P.R.O., HO 129/522/2/12; stone on building.

[96] O.N.S. (Birkdale), Worship Reg. no. 13144.

[97] W. K. Jordan, *Char. of Rural Eng. 1480–1660*, 340 (the will cannot be traced at B.I.H.R.).

[98] R.D.B., CD/51/63; *Par. Doc. of Archd. of E.R.* (Y.A.S. Rec. Ser. xcix), 118–19.

[99] *Educ. of Poor Digest*, 1089.

[1] *Educ. Enq. Abstract*, 1094.

[2] O.S. Map 6", Yorks. CCXI (1855 edn.).

[3] *Returns relating to Elem. Educ.*, 472–3.

[4] P.R.O., ED 7/135, no. 108; ED 49/8573; *Rep. of Educ. Cttee. of Council, 1874–5* [C. 1265-I], p. 445, H.C. (1875), xxiv.

[5] *Bd. of Educ., List 21* (H.M.S.O., 1908 and later edns.).

[6] E.R. Educ. Cttee. *Mins.* 1955–6, 151; 1963–4, 98; above, Hornsea, educ.

[7] Humbs. C.C. *Mins.* 1978–9, F 928.

[8] Inf. from Educ. Dept., Humbs. C.C., 1990.

[9] Inf. from the vicar, 1990; inf. from Char. Com., Liverpool, 1990.

[10] E.R.A.O., accession 1681; Bulmer, *Dir. E. Yorks.* (1892), 487; Review of Char. *Rep.* 108; inf. from the vicar, 1990.

[11] Above, Swine, S. Skirlaugh, charity.

[12] This article was written in 1996.

[13] *P.N. Yorks. E.R.* (E.P.N.S.), 71; G. F. Jensen, *Scand. Settlement Names in Yorks.* 79, 102.

[14] Poulson, *Holderness*, i. 400; below, econ. hist.

[15] *Chron. de Melsa* (Rolls Ser.), i. 79; ii. 39.

[16] Below, manors.

[17] O.S. Map 6", Yorks. CXCVI, CCXI (1855 edn.).

[18] *Census*, 1891 (pt. ii), which records a loss of 48 a. from Meaux.

[19] Ibid. 1921–91.   [20] P.R.O., E 179/202/60, m. 67.

[21] *Hearth Tax*, 61.

[22] B.I.H.R., V. 1764/Ret. 2, no. 221; *Herring's Visit.* iii, p. 34.

the population of Routh rose sharply to 178 in 1841 but later fluctuated downwards to 159 in 1901.[23] Numbers increased in the 1910s to reach 183 in 1921 but then fell to 140 in 1931 and 97 in 1981. In 1991 there were 113 residents, 108 of whom were then counted.[24]

Most of the land lies below 8 m. above sea level, falling to *c.* 2 m. in the former carrs in the south and west of Routh. Alluvium covers land alongside the boundary drains in the north, east, and south, but otherwise the parish is mostly on boulder clay. Deposits of sand and gravel occurring north of the village have been exploited commercially. The higher ground in the middle of the parish was occupied by the village and open fields and the peripheral carrlands by meadows and pastures. Routh was inclosed *c.* 1675.[25]

The parish is almost entirely bounded by drains. The natural drainage may mostly have been southwards through streams feeding Old fleet, which eventually flowed into the river Humber.[26] Later much of the water seems to have been diverted westwards to the river Hull but the insufficiency of the Hull as an outfall eventually resulted in the construction of modern drains again leading southwards to the Humber. Meaux abbey, sited in the neighbouring parish of Wawne, altered the existing drainage in the late 12th or 13th century: the eastern and northern boundary drain, later known as Wyth dike or Monk dike, was evidently then made or improved by the abbey, and by 1286 the abbey had made a new drain leading westwards from the Routh–Meaux road along the southern boundary. The southern drain, in 1685 comprising Meaux sewer dike and further west Mempit dike, is now represented in part by the Routh and Meaux drain and the northern drain is called Cross drain.[27] Other drainage works carried out by the abbey in the 13th century included the enlargement of the ditch around Routh wood. In 1389 the south-eastern boundary was re-made as a ditch to prevent cattle from Routh marsh from straying into North grange, in Meaux township.[28] The southern boundary drain was insufficient in 1367,[29] and later in the 14th century and in the 15th Meaux abbey was alleged to have neglected the boundary drains and thereby to have caused flooding in neighbouring parishes.[30] Flooding at Routh and elsewhere in the level led in 1690 to the diversion of water into the Humber,[31] and in 1693 Sir James

Bradshaw built a drainage windmill near Monk dike in the south-eastern corner of the parish.[32] The drainage of the east side of the Hull valley was much improved under the Holderness Drainage Acts of 1764 and later.[33] The area of Routh contributory to the work of the Holderness Drainage Board was 1,316 a. in 1775 and 1,329 a. in 1838.[34] The duties of the Holderness Drainage Board passed in 1941 to the River Hull Catchment Board, in 1950 to the Hull and East Yorkshire River Board, which widened the Routh and Meaux drain in 1960, and later to the Yorkshire Water Authority.[35]

Roads from Routh village lead southwest to Tickton, Hull Bridge, and Beverley and northeast towards Leven and Long Riston. The only other road runs south from the village to Meaux, Wawne, and Sutton on Hull. It was probably for the maintenance of the Beverley–Leven road that Sir William of Routh (? fl. *c.* 1230) provided by giving a toft and pasture rights to support a road mender, who was to be chosen by himself or his heirs jointly with Meaux abbey,[36] and its repair was certainly the object of an indulgence in the late 13th century.[37] The road crosses Monk dike by Monk bridge, mentioned as Routh bridge from the 13th century.[38] By the mid 13th century Meaux abbey had made a causeway to Routh wood, later presumably part of the southern road, and between 1249 and 1269 it built another stretch, connecting Routh church and the Beverley–Leven road.[39] The Beverley–Leven road and the side road to Wawne were both in disrepair in 1367, and in 1433 Meaux abbey was held responsible for the insufficiency of Routh bridge.[40] The road to Leven may have been realigned at inclosure *c.* 1675, when it was called White Cross Lane, after a roadside cross just over the boundary in Leven. The Wawne road was then known as Suddenby, later Southenby, Lane, but since the later 19th century it has been Meaux Lane.[41] The road between Beverley and White Cross was turnpiked in 1761, and the trust was continued until 1867.[42] A toll house formerly stood at the junction of the turnpike and the Wawne roads,[43] and two milestones still stand. The former turnpike road was upgraded and improved in the 20th century as part of the Beverley to Bridlington road.[44]

ROUTH village mostly stands along the northwestern side of a street which formed part of the

[23] *V.C.H. Yorks.* iii, 495.

[24] *Census,* 1911–91.

[25] Geol. Surv. Map 1″, drift, sheet 72 (1909 edn.); below, econ. hist.

[26] For this para. generally, J. A. Sheppard, *Draining of Hull Valley* (E. Yorks. Loc. Hist. Ser. viii), *passim.*

[27] B.L. Cott. MS. Vit. C. vi, f 13v.; E.R.A.O., CSR/15/4; B.I.H.R., TER. H. Routh 1685; *Chron. de Melsa,* i. 304; ii. 36–7, 172–3, 212.

[28] *Chron. de Melsa,* ii. 37, 92, 172; iii. 172.

[29] Poulson, *Holderness,* i. 119.

[30] E.R.A.O., CSR/15/4; *Mon. Notes,* i (Y.A.S. Rec. Ser. xvii), pp. 9, 136; *Chron. de Melsa,* iii. 172; *Public Works in Med. Law,* ii (Selden Soc. xl), pp. 345–7.

[31] E.R.A.O., CSR/4/12, 47.

[32] Sheppard, op. cit. 10. It was shown in 1782: E.R.A.O., DX/132.

[33] 4 Geo. III, c. 47 (Priv. Act); 6 Geo. III, c. 74 (Priv.

Act); 2 & 3 Wm. IV, c. 50 (Private); *V.C.H. Yorks. E.R.* vi. 278–9.

[34] E.R.A.O., DDCC/143/135; ibid. QDA/12A (plan), 12B; 13; R.D.B., FC/311/318.

[35] R.D.B., 1178/536/491; *V.C.H. Yorks. E.R.* vi. 279; Sheppard, op. cit. 22.

[36] 'Meaux Cart.', p. 263; *Chron. de Melsa,* ii. 92.

[37] *Reg. Romeyn,* i, p. 11 n.

[38] *Chron. de Melsa,* i. 304; ii. 37.

[39] Ibid. ii. 37, 92. Also ibid. 212.

[40] E.R.A.O., CSR/15/4; Poulson, *Holderness,* i. 119–20.

[41] B.I.H.R., TER. H. Routh 1685; E.R.A.O., DX/132; above, Leven, intro.; O.S. Map 1/2,500, Yorks. CCXI. 2 (1893 edn.).

[42] K. A. MacMahon, *Roads and Turnpike Trusts in E. Yorks.* (E. Yorks. Loc. Hist. Ser. xviii), 26–7, 70.

[43] H.U.L., DDFA/15/59; O.S. Map 6″, Yorks. CXCVI (1855 edn.).   [44] Below, next para.

Beverley–Leven road until much of it was by-passed by straightenings of the main road *c.* 1970.[45] A short distance away from the main group of buildings, the church and a few houses, including two farms, are loosely strung along the southern side lane leading to Wawne, and more outlying farmhouses stand back from the main road. On the north side of the Wawne lane a close called Garths in 1782 and near-by earth-works known as Butt hills suggest that there were formerly more buildings there. A small site, probably once moated but now enclosed by wide, dry ditches, also survives south of the church but its previous use is unknown. Most of the farmhouses were evidently rebuilt in the former open fields between their inclosure in the later 17th century and 1782. Low Barn, later Carr House, was added in the earlier 19th century.[46] Routh was again largely rebuilt in brick in the later 19th century by the Denisons, Lords Londesborough.[47] Park Farm and Rycote House both bear Londesborough ciphers, and the Denisons were evidently responsible for all of the other farms and several cottages, besides adding the school.[48] Cleveland House, formerly the rectory house, was also rebuilt and later remodelled in the 19th century.[49] Early in the 20th century the Sammans built four pairs of cottages, and more recent buildings include six prefabricated houses put up by the rural district council in or soon after 1950.[50]

The Nag's Head at Routh has traded at least since the later 18th century and was so named by the 1820s.[51] A reading room provided in the parsonage by 1900 was evidently moved to the former school building, which was also used for village meetings.[52] A larger village hall, adjoining the reading room, was built by the parishioners in 1935; its site was given by Sir Henry Samman, Bt., and the two buildings were later called Samman Hall. During the Second World War the hall served as a billet for men from Catfoss airfield, in Sigglesthorne. Later it was little used and was sold in 1968 for conversion to a house; it has since become a nonconformist church.[53] In the mid 20th century the county council ran a library at Routh, at first in the village hall and later in a private house.[54]

OUTLYING BUILDINGS in the parish have included a medieval hospital; it was recorded in the 13th and 14th centuries and its location, near the eastern boundary on the road to Leven, was later commemorated in the name Spittle ings.[55] The 'old raceground' shown in 1855 near Low Farm was presumably for horse-racing,[56] and hare-coursing was a feature of the village's social life until the early 1930s.[57] It is not known why Castle park, in the south-west of the parish,[58] is so called. A decoy airfield called Routh aero-drome was operated *c.* 1940 to protect Lecon-field.[59]

MANORS AND OTHER ESTATES. In 1086 the archbishop of York's church of St. John at Beverley had 1 carucate and 7 bovates at Routh. The church may have held another carucate there and was then said to have had 2 carucates taken away by Drew de Bevrère.[60] William de la Mare, one of the two lords of Routh in 1316,[61] presumably held the Beverley minster estate. A kinsman of archbishops Melton and Thoresby, he was provost of Beverley 1338–60[62] and from the 1320s treasurer and a prebendary of York.[63] After the suppression of the collegiate church in 1548, Routh manor was held of the Crown and succeeding lords of Beverley Chapter manor.[64]

A family named from their land in the parish held all or part of the provost's estate there as a manor of *ROUTH*. Sir Simon of Routh, the first recorded member of the family, presumably held the manor, and land adjoining it was bought from Meaux abbey by Simon's grandson Sir William or by William's son Sir Amand (fl. later 13th and early 14th century).[65] The manor was settled on Sir Amand's son, (Sir) John of Routh in 1306.[66] Later the estate mostly desc-ended like Tansterne, in Aldbrough, in the Rouths[67] and their successors, the Cutts[68] and the Michelbournes.[69] About 1370 Sir Amand of Routh held 1 carucate and 6 bovates of the prov-ost.[70] Another Sir John Routh's son John (fl. earlier 15th cent.) had the estate before his brother and heir Brian,[71] at whose death in 1483 the untenanted estate comprised, besides the

45 E.R.C.C. *Mins.* 1965–6, 129; 1967–8, 130, 351; R.D.B., 1522/515/471; 1678/122/103; 1694/323/258.
46 E.R.A.O., DX/132; O.S. Map 6", Yorks. CXCVI, CCXI (1855 edn.); O.S. Map 1/10,560, TA 04 SE. (1956 edn.).
47 Below, manors. For Routh before rebuilding, E.R.A.O., DX/132; H. Teesdale, *Map of Yorks.* (1828); A. Bryant, *Map of E.R. Yorks.* (1829).
48 Sale catalogue of 1938 with photographs at H.U.L., DDX/16/351; below, educ.   49 Below, church.
50 H.U.L., DDX/16/351; R.D.B., 839/372/300; Beverley R.D.C. *Mins.* 1949–50, 67, 159.
51 E.R.A.O., QDT/2/6, 9. Cf. H.U.L., DDFA/15/59; R.D.B., GR/330/400.
52 B.I.H.R., V. 1900, no. 314; V. 1931/Ret.; H.U.L., DDX/16/351; directories.
53 R.D.B., 621/101/79; 1551/384/343; Review of Char. *Report,* 35; below, nonconf.; inf. from Mr. D. F. Hall, Routh, 1997.
54 B.I.H.R., V. 1931/Ret.; inf. from Mr. Hall.
55 *Chron. de Melsa,* ii. 92; Poulson, *Holderness,* i. 120; O.S. Map 6", Yorks. CXCVI (1855 edn.).
56 O.S. Map 6", Yorks. CXCVI (1855 edn.).
57 Inf. from Mr. Hall, 1997.

58 B.I.H.R., TER. H. Routh 1685.
59 Hist. inf. board in Routh, 1996; B. B. Halpenny, *Action Stations 4: Military Airfields of Yorks.* 100.
60 *V.C.H. Yorks.* ii. 216, 326; below, this section [Morkar].   61 *Feud. Aids,* vi. 163.
62 *Beverley Minster Fasti* (Y.A.S. Rec. Ser. cxlix), 8–9; *Mon. Notes,* i (Y.A.S. Rec. Ser. xvii), p. 8.
63 Le Neve, *Fasti, 1300–1541, Northern Province,* 13, 71, 84, 92.
64 P.R.O., C 142/214, no. 205; ibid. E 317/Yorks./17; e.g. H.U.L., DDCV/16/5; *V.C.H. Yorks. E.R.* vi. 77, 211.
65 E.R.A.O., PE/129/150, ff. 5v.–6v.; *Chron. de Melsa,* ii. 39, 92, 172; *Reg. Corbridge,* i, p. 200. For the Rouths, *Chron. de Melsa,* ii. 39; *Yorks. Fines, 1300–14,* p. 57.
66 *Yorks. Fines, 1300–14,* p. 57.
67 E.R.A.O., PE/129/150, f. 7v.; *Yorks. Fines, 1347–77,* pp. 201–2; *Cal. Pat. 1358–61,* 68; *Cal. Chart. R. 1341-1417,* 301; *Feud. Aids,* vi. 273; above, Aldbrough, manors (Tansterne). For the Rouths, also E.R.A.O., PE/147/26–7.
68 P.R.O., C 142/48, no. 161; *Yorks. Fines,* i. 140.
69 P.R.O., CP 40/1154, Carte rot. 15; ibid. C 142/214, nos. 205, 221.   70 E.R.A.O., PE/129/150, f. 6v.
71 P.R.O., C 1/9/440; *Cal. Close, 1461-8,* 321–2; *Y.A.J.* xii. 225.

manor, only a house and five crofts.[72] Thomas Michelbourne (d. 1582) was probably succeeded in his share of Routh manor by his son Lawrence, who by will of 1600 left his lands to his brother Thomas.[73] In 1614, on the partition of the Michelbournes' estates, Routh manor fell to the share of Sir Richard Michelbourne (d. 1638).[74] His sons sold the manor in 1647 to Thomas Chatt (d. by 1661). Chatt's son John[75] exchanged Routh manor with 2 bovates for Fitling manor, in Humbleton, with Henry Hildyard in 1662.[76] The estate descended with Hildyard's other land in Routh.[77]

The manor house of Sir Amand of Routh included an oratory in 1301.[78]

In 1066 Morkar's manor of Mappleton included 4 carucates of sokeland at Routh; in 1086 Drew de Bevrère may have held all 4 carucates or 3 of them, St. John's church, Beverley, having the remaining carucate. Drew's holding, moreover, seems to have included 2 carucates which he was said to have taken from St. John's church.[79] As elsewhere in Holderness, Drew's holding passed to the counts of Aumale and descended with their honor of Holderness to the Constables.[80] In 1574 and again c. 1615 the Constables were disputing the service owed to them from the manor.[81]

It was almost certainly part of the Aumale fee at Routh which the Scrutevilles held. Richard de Scruteville was settled at Routh soon after the Conquest, and c. 1150 Alan de Scruteville exchanged some of his land there with William le Gros, count of Aumale, for an estate at Ringbrough, in Aldbrough.[82] Alan was probably succeeded in the rest by his son Sir William de Scruteville, and William's son Alan was lord of Routh c. 1215. Alan was followed by his son William (fl. c. 1230),[83] but later in the mid 13th century the Scruteville holding in Routh, of 4 carucates and 1 bovate, passed to John de Ros, husband of Sir William de Scruteville's daughter Emma.[84] He was perhaps succeeded by his son Richard de Ros, who certainly presented

to Routh church in 1273.[85] The estate, then described as a manor of *ROUTH*, was held by the overlord, the countess of Aumale, in the 1270s and 1280s by reason of the minority of Richard's son (Sir) John de Ros.[86] Described as of Gedney (Lincs.) or of Ringbrough, he was one of the two lords of Routh in 1316[87] and dying by 1319 was succeeded by his son (Sir) Richard (d. 1351); in the 14th century the manor was held as 1/12 knight's fee and included a chief house and c. 2 carucates and another 2 carucates held of the Roses by free tenants owing military services and rents. Routh evidently descended to Richard's son William (d. by 1378)[88] and then to one or more John Roses.[89] From John Ros, esquire (d. 1451 or 1452), the manor probably passed to Thomas Ros (d. by 1463) and was certainly held by Thomas's son John (d. by 1515). John's son Edward[90] had died by 1558, leaving as heirs Christopher Kendall, Catherine Cholmeley, and his nephew George Brigham. Brigham apparently succeeded to the whole estate and in 1565 sold the reversion of the manor after his death and that of his wife (both fl. 1570) to (Sir) Christopher Hildyard and his heirs.[91] Hildyard bought land at Routh in 1568.[92] Routh manor, in 1635 said to include 24 houses and just over 1,000 a., descended with Winestead in the Hildyards to Henry Hildyard (d. by 1674).[93]

Hildyard's estate, comprising the advowson and two manors of Routh, one called Chatt's farm or Michelbourne's manor,[94] was evidently held by Lady Anne Hildyard, his widow, in 1679 and passed to Sir James Bradshaw in 1681 or 1682.[95] The Bradshaws of Risby, in Rowley, later held it as one manor.[96] Sir James Bradshaw (d. by 1710) was succeeded by his son Ellerker, whose estate at Routh was then of at least 703 a.[97] Ellerker Bradshaw (d. 1742) devised his estates in tail male to Eaton Mainwaring, who added the name Ellerker and died in 1771.[98] His son Roger (d. 1775) left as coheirs four sisters, Elizabeth, Charlotte, Arabella, and Harriet Mainwaring Ellerker, who later held the

[72] P.R.O., C 141/4, no. 45.

[73] Ibid. C 142/214, no. 221; for the Michelbournes, *Suss. Arch. Colln.* l, 67–101.

[74] E.R.A.O., DDRI/35/29, 33; P.R.O., E 317/Yorks./17; *Yorks. Fines, 1614–25,* 11.

[75] P.R.O., CP 25(2)/525/23 Chas. I Trin. [no. 18]; E.R.A.O., DDRI/35/50; H.U.L., DDMC/6/1.

[76] P.R.O., CP 25(2)/752/14 Chas. II Mic. nos. 41, 80; Poulson, *Holderness,* i. 393.

[77] Below, this section. [78] *Reg. Corbridge,* i, p. 66.

[79] *V.C.H. Yorks.* ii. 216, 265, 326.

[80] *V.C.H. Yorks. E.R.* v. 9–10.

[81] E.R.A.O., DDCC/111/213; DDCC/112/120; DDCC/139/5.

[82] *Chron. de Melsa,* i. 78, 83; *E.Y.C.* iii, p. 91; above, Aldbrough, manors (Ringbrough).

[83] *Chron. de Melsa,* i. 363–4, 418; *Yorks. Fines, 1218–31,* pp. 153–4; *Cur. Reg. R.* xii, p. 191. For the Scrutevilles and their heirs, the Roses, *Chron. de Melsa,* ii. 38–9; *Yorks. Fines, 1218–31,* p. 154 n.

[84] *Chron. de Melsa,* ii. 38, 92; *Kirkby's Inquest,* 373; E.R.A.O., DDCC/112/120.

[85] Lawrance, 'Clergy List', Holderness, 2, p. 122.

[86] P.R.O., SC 6/1078/17, m. 3; SC 6/1079/4 (the latter account identifies the holding); *Feud. Aids,* vi. 40; *Cal. Inq. p.m.* iv, p. 356; *Chron. de Melsa,* ii. 212.

[87] *Feud. Aids,* vi. 163.

[88] P.R.O., C 135/112, no. 37; *Cal. Inq. p.m.* vi, p. 98; ix, p. 440; Lawrance, 'Clergy List', Holderness, 2, p. 123.

[89] *Yorks. Deeds,* viii, p. 108; ix, pp. 38–9; *Chron. de Melsa,* iii. 172.

[90] P.R.O., C 142/30, no. 66; *Test. Ebor.* ii, pp. 159–60; iii, pp. 181 n., 238 n., 337.

[91] E.R.A.O., DDCC/112/120; P.R.O., C 3/119/14; C 142/111, no. 67; B.I.H.R., CP. G. 1182; *Yorks. Fines,* i. 304; *Visit. Yorks. 1584–5 and 1612,* ed. J. Foster, 167. Brigham's relationship is variously given in the sources. For the Cholmeleys, *Yorks. Fines,* i. 264; P.R.O., C 66/1525, mm. 10–19, and the Kendalls, *Cal. S.P. Dom.* 1598–1601, 484–5.

[92] *Yorks. Fines,* i. 360.

[93] P.R.O., C 142/530, no. 155; ibid. CP 43/330, rot. 37d.; *Yorks. Fines,* iv. 21; *Yorks. Royalist Composition Papers,* i (Y.A.S. Rec. Ser. xv), pp. 97–8, 104; J. Foster, *Pedigrees of Yorks.,* iii, s.v. Hildyard.

[94] E.R.A.O., DDHI, mortgage 1678; above, this section [Routh, Scruteville].

[95] E.R.A.O., PE/147/24; J. Foster, *Pedigrees of Yorks.* iii, s.v. Hildyard.

[96] P.R.O., CP 25(2)/987/5 Anne Trin. [no. 1]. For the following, also *V.C.H. Yorks. E.R.* iv. 147.

[97] R.D.B., A/276/396; A/325/461; G/298/657.

[98] H.U.L., DDKE/8/84; DDKE/10/4.

Yorkshire estate in undivided shares.[99] In 1787 it included, besides Routh manor and the advowson of Routh church, almost 2,340 a. there, virtually the whole parish.[1] In 1792 the shares of Arabella (d. 1782), formerly wife of Thomas Onslow, later earl of Onslow, and Charlotte, wife of George Ellerker (formerly Townshend), earl of Leicester, were settled respectively on Elizabeth and Harriet.[2] Under a resettlement of 1816 Elizabeth's moiety passed at her death in 1831 to Harriet (d. 1842), who was succeeded in the whole estate as life tenant by her nephew Edward Mainwaring Onslow, from 1843 Edward Mainwaring Mainwaring Ellerker Onslow. In 1851 Routh was sold to Albert D. Denison, Baron Londesborough, and the Denison trustees, who then also bought a neighbouring farm at Meaux, in Wawne.[3] He was succeeded in 1860 by his son W. H. F. Denison (d. 1900), Baron Londesborough, later earl of Londesborough, and grandson W. F. H. Denison, earl of Londesborough. The last named sold the whole estate, then of 2,691 a., in 1907 to Henry Samman, a Hull shipowner.[4] Samman bought 50 a. more in 1908.[5] Later Sir Henry Samman, Bt., he died in 1928 and the estate was divided and sold by his son Sir Henry Samman, Bt., in 1938.[6] The manor was bought by protestant bodies for the advowson associated with it and was not conveyed until 1940.[7] Manor House farm, of 377 a., and the 293-a. Low farm were bought by Marjorie Mackrill.[8] The Goodlass family bought Low farm from Mrs. Mackrill in 1962, and c. 1985 her heir sold Manor House farm to the Sinklers, the present owners.[9]

In 1672 Henry Hildyard had a house with 10 hearths at Routh,[10] and it was perhaps the same which was recorded as Hall Garth in 1685 and the manor house from 1710.[11] By 1782 there was a house on the site of Manor House Farm[12] which was rebuilt in the 19th century.

William le Gros, count of Aumale, had given Meaux abbey a wood and adjoining marshland at Routh, later said to comprise 50 a., by 1151.[13] Philip the chaplain of Routh with his brother Robert and sister Agnes, children of a rector of Routh, added ½ carucate there in the early 13th

century, and the abbey then bought 3 bovates more from Herbert de St. Quintin. Later gifts included another bovate, granted between 1235 and 1249.[14] The abbey was granted free warren at Routh in 1293,[15] and its estate there was called *ROUTH* manor c. 1340.[16] In 1600 the Crown sold the dissolved abbey's manor of Routh to Henry Best and Robert Holland; it then comprised a manor house and 14 other houses, 1 carucate and 3 bovates, and closes and crofts, all held by a freeholder and other tenants.[17] The manor with much of the land was evidently resold soon afterwards and belonged by 1616 to Sir Christopher Hildyard (d. 1634); comprising seven houses, 1 carucate, and other land, all occupied in 1635 by Hildyard's tenants, the estate descended to Sir Christopher's youngest son Christopher, who may have sold it after 1646.[18] The manor was evidently later part of the estate of the Mainwaring Ellerkers.[19]

Before 1157 Walter of Routh gave Bridlington priory 2 bovates at Routh, parts of which were exchanged with William de Scruteville for other land there c. 1190.[20]

Land at Routh was also held by the St. Quintins, as tenants of the Scrutevilles and their heirs,[21] and by Lady Agnes of Kelk, who succeeded, as at Aldbrough, by William of Sunderlandwick.[22] Land in or adjoining Routh was held by Amand de Surdeval in the 13th century and by his namesake in the 1370s.[23]

Routh hospital was endowed with 1½ bovate in the parish in the 13th century.[24]

ECONOMIC HISTORY. COMMON LANDS AND INCLOSURE. There seem to have been three or four open fields in the 17th century, North, East, and West fields, and one variously called Hill field, (Old) Mill Hill field, or Old Mill field, which may merely have been a part of East field.[25] As elsewhere in the East Riding, the fields contained both broad and narrow lands.[26] The tillage was surrounded by extensive carrs which provided common meadowland and pastures. North and east of the village meadow-

99 R.D.B., AS/66/111; AS/500/841; AY/337/553.
1 H.U.L., DDFA/15/59.
2 R.D.B., BR/75/104; BR/77/105. For the Onslows, Burke, *Peerage, Baronetage, & Knightage* (1937), 1837–8, and Townshends, *Complete Peerage*.
3 R.D.B., FB/168/183; FZ/332/389; GR/330/400; GT/71/85; GX/32/35; Mainwaring Ellerker Estate Act, 8 & 9 Vic. c. 14 (Private).
4 R.D.B., 92/19/18 (1907); *Complete Peerage*, s.v. Londesborough; Burke, *Peerage, Baronetage & Knightage* (1931), 2090.
5 R.D.B., 106/180/160.
6 Ibid. 594/485/385; 603/42/33; 603/229/167; 603/443/334; 604/43/33; H.U.L., DDX/16/351.
7 Below, church [patronage].
8 R.D.B., 602/598/471; 602/599/472; 602/600/473.
9 Ibid. 1249/250/226; inf. from Mrs. Sinkler, Routh, 1996.
10 P.R.O., E 179/205/504.
11 R.D.B., A/325/461; B.I.H.R., TER. H. Routh 1685.
12 E.R.A.O., DX/132; O.S. Map 1/2,500, Yorks. CCXI. 2 (1893 edn.).
13 *E.Y.C.* iii. pp. 91, 93–4; *Chron. de Melsa*, i. 83; *Yorks. Fines, 1218–31*, pp. 153–4.

14 E.R.A.O., DDCC/112/120; *Chron. de Melsa*, i. 362–5, 418–19; ii. 38, 40.
15 *Cal. Chart. R. 1257–1300*, 427.
16 *Chron. de Melsa*, iii. 11.
17 P.R.O., C 66/1525, mm. 10–19.
18 Ibid. C 142/530, no. 155; E.R.A.O., DDCC/139/5; *Yorks. Royalist Composition Papers*, ii (Y.A.S. Rec. Ser. xviii), pp. 11–12; J. Foster, *Pedigrees of Yorks.* iii, s.v. Hildyard.
19 Above, this section.
20 *E.Y.C.* ii, pp. 442–4; iii, p. 70; *Chron. de Melsa*, i. 365; ii. 40–1; *Bridlington Chart.* ed. W. T. Lancaster, 307; *Valor Eccl.* (Rec. Com.), v. 120.
21 *Chron. de Melsa*, i. 362; ii. 290; *Cur. Reg. R.* xii, p. 191.
22 *Chron. de Melsa*, ii. 40; above, Aldbrough, manors (Thorpe).
23 *Chron. de Melsa*, ii. 172; *Public Works in Med. Law*, ii (Selden Soc. xl), pp. 345–7.
24 E.R.A.O., DDCC/112/120; above, intro.
25 The following is based on B.I.H.R., TER. H. Routh n.d., 1685; cf. plan of 1782 at E.R.A.O., DX/132; O.S. Map 6", Yorks. CXCVI, CCXI (1855 edn.).
26 Below, Withernwick, econ. hist.

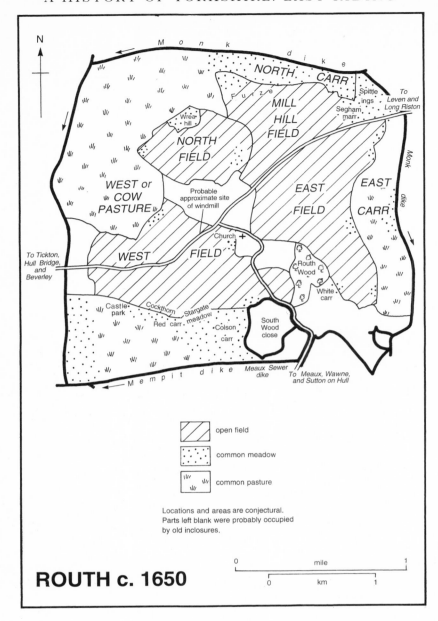

ROUTH c. 1650

land was mentioned in areas called the Furze, Wrea, later Ray, hill, Segham marr, and Spittle ings, as well as in the eastern carrs; other meadows lay close to the southern boundary at Cockthorn and Colson, in or adjoining Red, possibly Reed, carr,[27] and nearby was Stargate meadow. Much of the meadowland bordered the open fields, which contained other, probably smaller, pieces of meadow. Part of the eastern carrs, described as Routh marsh, was evidently being used as a common pasture in 1389,[28] and in the 17th century there were two there, East and Deep carr pastures. The village's third pasture, sometimes called Cow pasture, occupied low-lying ground west of the village.

Routh was inclosed c. 1675[29] but the agreement and other records seem not to have sur-

vived. The earlier layout in the open fields was followed in the making of the new closes, which long after retained the characteristic narrow, curved shape of inclosed selions.[30] Some of the allotments evidently remained undivided after inclosure: in 1699 a North field close apparently contained 96 a., and 85 a. lay in West pasture close in 1782, when the 44-a. Whin hill and some other carrland were still unimproved rough grazing.[31]

MEDIEVAL HOLDINGS AND TENURES. In 1086 there were 7 villeins with 2 ploughs on St. John's estate at Routh, which included 12 a. of meadow. Two carucates formerly belonging to the church were then said to be waste.[32] William de Scruteville had an intake at Routh c. 1190,[33]

27 R.D.B., A/325/461.
28 *Chron. de Melsa*, iii. 172.
29 B.I.H.R., TER. H. Routh 1716.
30 E.R.A.O., DX/132; O.S. Map 6″, Yorks. CXCVI,

CCXI (1855 edn.).
31 R.D.B., A/276/396; E.R.A.O., DX/132.
32 *V.C.H. Yorks.* ii. 216.
33 *E.Y.C.* iii, p. 70.

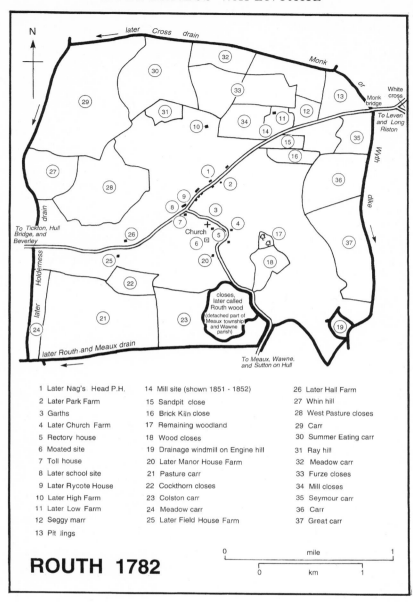

1 Later Nag's Head P.H.
2 Later Park Farm
3 Garths
4 Later Church Farm
5 Rectory house
6 Moated site
7 Toll house
8 Later school site
9 Later Rycote House
10 Later High Farm
11 Later Low Farm
12 Seggy marr
13 Pit lings

14 Mill site (shown 1851 - 1852)
15 Sandpit close
16 Brick Kiln close
17 Remaining woodland
18 Wood closes
19 Drainage windmill on Engine hill
20 Later Manor House Farm
21 Pasture carr
22 Cockthorn closes
23 Colston carr
24 Meadow carr
25 Later Field House Farm

26 Later Hall Farm
27 Whin hill
28 West Pasture closes
29 Carr
30 Summer Eating carr
31 Ray hill
32 Meadow carr
33 Furze closes
34 Mill closes
35 Seymour carr
36 Carr
37 Great carr

ROUTH 1782

and the carrs were reduced by the making of closes, primarily perhaps by Meaux abbey which established a grange at Routh in the 13th century. The abbey exchanged a close of woodland and other land for part of Routh carr between 1235 and 1249,[34] and had closes there called Carr dales *c.* 1300. Those closes and others belonging to Scruteville's successor, Sir John de Ros, were used as meadows but after mowing all were intercommoned by both proprietors.[35] Meaux abbey's grange, or manor, at Routh was said to comprise 9½ bovates, or 150 a. of arable land and more than 35 a. of meadow. By 1396 most of it had been leased to one man, who held 1 carucate and other land for nearly £4 10s. a year; fourteen other holdings producing less than 10s. each brought the abbey's total

rental at Routh to just over £7 a year. Two of the tenants also owed works at North grange, in Meaux, and later rents included renders of poultry.[36] The manor of the Roses included no or little demesne in the late 13th century, when all or part of the holding was let during a minority for £23 a year. Tenants on that manor then owed chevage.[37]

TURBARIES, FISHING, AND FOWLING. Besides rough pasture, the carrs provided turves, fish,[38] and wildfowl. In the mid 13th century William de Scruteville was using Monk dike to carry turves dug from his land alongside the drain in Routh marsh, and a turbary of 2 a. mentioned in 1277–8 was probably on the same estate.[39] Meaux abbey also had turbaries in the

34 *Chron. de Melsa*, i. 365; ii. 36, 172.
35 Ibid. ii. 213.
36 B.L. Cott. MS. Vit. C. vi, ff. 205 and v., 221v.–2, 230v.; P.R.O., C 66/1525, mm. 10–19.

37 P.R.O., SC 6/1078/17, m. 3; SC 6/1079/4; above, manors.   38 *Test. Ebor.* iii, p. 143.
39 P.R.O., SC 6/1078/17, m. 3; *Chron. de Melsa*, ii. 37; above, manors.

marsh, and turbary rights in Routh were mentioned again in 1662.[40] A fishery in the carr recorded in 1277–8 probably belonged to the Roses.[41] Meaux abbey's fisheries were allegedly trespassed upon in the 1370s,[42] and the Crown as successor to the abbey let fisheries in Routh carrs in the 16th and 17th centuries.[43] In 1570, when ownership of the fishing and fowling of Deep carr was disputed, it was said to belong to George Brigham's manor, and the fishing of another piece of carr called Castle park to the Michelbournes' manor.[44] The rector had a net in Deep carr in 1685.[45]

WOODLAND. It is not certain when the woodland remaining in Routh in the Middle Ages was cleared. The largest wood was perhaps that of c. 50 a. given to Meaux abbey in the 12th century,[46] but William de Scruteville apparently also had inclosed woodland in Routh in the 13th century, and it was probably to the value of his successor's estate that sales of wood and woodland grazing contributed in 1277–8.[47] The abbey's wood, called Routh, or South, wood, had probably been felled by 1685, when it was described simply as a close; it had been divided into three closes by 1782. In 1685 there was another wood, on the opposite side of the road to Meaux, but by 1782 only 5 a. of that woodland remained.[48] Woodland covered less than 40 a. of Routh later.[49]

LATER AGRICULTURE. The parish has been predominantly arable in the 19th and 20th centuries: there were 1,967 a. of arable land and 350 a. of grassland in 1843, 1,844 a. and 449 a. respectively in 1905, and c. 1,815 a. and 560 a. in 1938. In the 1930s the grassland lay around the village and outlying farms.[50] In 1987, when the area returned for Routh, 1,475.9 ha. (3,647 a.), evidently included land outside the parish, there were 1,326.2 ha. (3,277 a.) of arable land and only 76.5 ha. (189 a.) of grassland. The only livestock kept in any numbers were pigs, of which there were 1,970.[51]

In 1787 there were 7 farms at Routh, the largest of 474 a. and the others with 200–399 a. each, and a few small holdings of 15 a. or less.[52] That pattern of landholding remained virtually un-

changed during the 19th and early 20th centuries.[53] One or two cowkeepers also earned a living in Routh from the late 19th century, a smallholder was mentioned as well in 1937, and there was later a nursery.[54] In 1987 the area including Routh was in seven farms, the largest of which had over 500 ha. (1,236 a.), two 100–499 ha. (247–1,233 a.), two 50–99 ha. (124–245 a.), and two less than 5 ha. (12 a.).[55]

INDUSTRY AND TRADE. Sand and gravel was dug from small pits in the north-east of the parish before the 20th century, and bricks had evidently been made there before 1782.[56] Larger-scale extraction started in 1988 on 194 a. of Low farm, the house of which was demolished; in 1996 an adjacent area was being worked and it was then hoped to continue operations until the year 2000. Most of the quarried area had been landscaped around a lake, or returned to agriculture, by 1996.[57]

The estate joiner established his own business in 1873 and the concern was still carried on in 1997,[58] and a pottery business was conducted from the former rectory house in the 1960s and 1970s.[59] A garage and motor engineering workshop, opened in the 1920s,[60] had by 1996 been enlarged with a café and village stores.

MILLS. A mill at Routh in 1277–8 was probably the windmill recorded on the manor of the Ros family and their successors between the 14th and 17th centuries.[61] Another mill standing on Sir Amand of Routh's manor in the mid 14th century was mentioned again, as a windmill, in the 17th century.[62] The mills presumably stood north-east and south-west of the village, but neither existed in 1782.[63]

LOCAL GOVERNMENT. In 1277–8 court profits added just over £1 to the value of an estate at Routh, probably the Roses', and the court of their manor was mentioned in 1351.[64] Meaux abbey, which also held a court on its manor at Routh, was claiming the profits of the ale assize there in 1293,[65] and in the 1330s tenants of the provost at Routh were found, presumably in his court at Beverley, to have

[40] P.R.O., CP 25(2)/752/14 Chas. II Mic. no. 80; *Chron. de Melsa*, i. 365.
[41] P.R.O., SC 6/1078/17, m. 3; above, manors.
[42] *Mon. Notes*, i (Y.A.S. Rec. Ser. xvii), p. 136.
[43] P.R.O., C 66/1135, mm. 30–3; E 315/153, ff. 183–8.
[44] Ibid. C 3/119/14; C 142/30, no. 66. Also ibid. CP 25(2)/752/14 Chas. II Mic. no. 80; *Yorks. Fines*, i. 119; ii. 87.
[45] B.I.H.R., TER. H. Routh 1685.
[46] *Chron. de Melsa*, i. 79; ii. 173; above, manors [Meaux abbey].
[47] P.R.O., SC 6/1078/17, m. 3; *Chron. de Melsa*, ii. 36; above, manors.
[48] B.I.H.R., TER. H. Routh 1685; E.R.A.O., DX/132; O.S. Map 1/2,500, Yorks. CCXI. 3 (1891 edn.).
[49] B.I.H.R., TA. 657L; H.U.L., DDX/16/351; Acreage Returns, 1905.
[50] B.I.H.R., TA. 657L; H.U.L., DDX/16/351; Acreage Returns, 1905; [1st] Land Util. Surv. Map, sheet 28.
[51] Inf. from Min. of Agric., Fish. & Food, Beverley, 1990.
[52] H.U.L., DDFA/15/59.
[53] Ibid. DDX/16/351; B.I.H.R., TA. 657L; R.D.B., 92/19/18 (1907); P.R.O., HO 107/2359.

[54] Directories; inf. from Mr. D. F. Hall, Routh, 1997.
[55] Inf. from Min. of Agric., Fish. & Food; above, this section.
[56] E.R.A.O., DX/132; O.S. Map 6″, Yorks. CXCVI (1855 edn.); O.S. Map 1/2,500, Yorks. CXCVI. 14–15 (1891 edn.).
[57] Inf. from Tarmac Quarry Products (Eastern) Ltd., Matlock, 1996; *Hull Daily Mail*, 13 Nov. 1995.
[58] Board on business; inf. from Mr. Hall, 1997.
[59] R.D.B., 1172/505/455; 1883/258/214.
[60] Ibid. 604/47/34; directories.
[61] P.R.O., C 135/112, no. 37; C 142/530, no. 155; SC 6/1078/17, m. 3; *Cal. Inq. p.m.* vi, p. 98; *Yorks. Fines*, i. 298, 304; above, manors.
[62] E.R.A.O., PE/129/150, f. 7v.; P.R.O., CP 25(2)/752/14 Chas. II Mic. no. 80.
[63] B.I.H.R., TER. H. Routh 1685; E.R.A.O., DX/132; O.S. Map 6″, Yorks. CXCVI (1855 edn.).
[64] P.R.O., C 135/112, no. 37; SC 6/1078/17, m. 3; above, manors.
[65] P.R.O., C 66/1525, mm. 10–19; *Plac. de Quo Warr.* (Rec. Com.), 224.

breached the assize of bread.[66] It was probably because of the Crown's lordship in both places that a constable for Routh was sworn in Leven manor court in 1650.[67]

Surviving parish records include church-wardens' accounts from 1737 to 1851.[68] Overseers' accounts for 1679–83 reveal that 4–5 people were then relieved by the parish,[69] which maintained poorhouses at Routh in the 18th[70] and early 19th century.[71] Two people at Routh were on permanent out-relief in 1802–3 and 12 between 1812 and 1815; occasional help was given to 4 in the earlier period and to 5–10 in the later one.[72] Routh later also supported paupers in the parochial workhouse at Beverley,[73] and in 1836 it joined Beverley poor-law union.[74] Routh remained in Beverley rural district until 1974, when it became part of the Beverley district, or borough, of Humberside.[75] In 1996 Routh parish became part of a new East Riding unitary area.[76] The parish council had lapsed before 1967, when a new one was set up for Routh and Tickton together.[77]

CHURCH. There was evidently a church at Routh by the late 12th century.[78] The living has remained a rectory but the last institution was in 1959 and since 1963 the church has been entrusted to a curate in charge.[79]

Richard de Ros presented to Routh in 1273 and the advowson later descended with their manor in the Ros family, the Crown presenting during minorities in 1354 and 1378 and grantees of the Roses in 1477 and 1559.[80] The right to present continued to descend with the manor in the Hildyards,[81] Bradshaws, Mainwaring Ellerkers, Onslows, and Denisons.[82] In 1907 both were sold by W. F. H. Denison, earl of Londesborough, to Henry Samman, later Sir Henry Samman, Bt.,[83] who presented a relative, A. H. Samman, rector 1907–32.[84] In 1938 Samman's son, Sir Henry Samman, Bt., sold the advowson and the manor to Adolph Arwidsson, acting for two Evangelical bodies, the Church Association

Trust, later the Church Society Trust, and the Incorporated Trinitarian Bible Society Trust, whose share of the patronage passed c. 1990 to the Reformation Church Trust.[85] In 1958 the Crown presented to Routh by lapse.[86]

Routh rectory was valued at £6 13s. 4d. in 1291[87] and £8 1s. 5d. net in 1535.[88] The improved annual value in 1650 was almost £67 net.[89] The value, probably gross, c. 1700 was £100 and in 1787 it was put at over £120 a year.[90] The annual net income averaged £470 between 1829 and 1831[91] and was said to be the same in 1883.[92]

Tithes and other dues contributed over £8 and the glebe lands £1 9s. to the gross annual income in 1535.[93] Apart from a few acres around the parsonage house, the glebe land comprised 2 bovates with appurtenant meadow grounds[94] until inclosure c. 1675, when the rector accepted an annual rent charge for his commonable land and most of the tithes; the sum was £66 12s. in 1716, £60 in 1743, and £63 in 1770. The tithes of the old inclosures and small tithes remained payable in kind, and 'old' compositions amounting to nearly 11s. for the tithes from land called Castle park and those of fish and rushes, or dumbles, remained in force.[95] In 1815 tithe rents were said to bring in nearly £384.[96] The rent charge and compositions were replaced in 1843, when all the tithes were commuted for a new rent charge of £540.[97]

A house with four hearths was occupied in 1672 by a Mr. Hildyard, possibly Christopher Hildyard, rector.[98] In 1716 the gardens of the rectory house were being laid out, and in 1764 it was said to have 12 rooms.[99] The building was very dilapidated by the early 19th century, when the incumbent lived in Beverley. Appleton Bennison of Hull rebuilt it in 1818–19 as a two-storeyed house in red and white brick with four principal rooms.[1] A cottage was added between 1827 and 1849.[2] The house was evidently let c. 1840,[3] and in 1865 it was extended and remodelled and its offices rebuilt by Ewan Christian of London, a three-storeyed bay in cream brick being then added to the south front.[4] The house,

[66] E.R.A.O., PE/129/150, f. 6v.
[67] Shaftesbury MSS., M 218; above, manors; above, Leven, manors.
[68] E.R.A.O., PE/147/22.
[69] Ibid. PE/147/24.
[70] B.I.H.R., V. 1764/Ret. 2, no. 221; H.U.L., DDFA/15/59; Herring's Visit. iii, p. 34.
[71] Overseers' accts. 1804–36: E.R.A.O., PE/147/25.
[72] Poor Law Abstract, 1804, pp. 594–5; 1818, pp. 522–3.
[73] E.R.A.O., PE/147/25; V.C.H. Yorks. E.R. vi. 192.
[74] 3rd Rep. Poor Law Com. 167.
[75] Census.
[76] Humberside (Structural Change) Order 1995, copy at E.R.A.O.
[77] E.R.A.O., CCO/768; inf. from Mr. D. F. Hall, Routh, 1997.
[78] Below, this section [incumbents].
[79] Lists of rectors and curates in Routh church, 1996.
[80] Para. based on Lawrance, 'Clergy List', Holderness, 2, pp. 122–5. Above, manors.
[81] Yorks. Fines, iv. 21.
[82] P.R.O., CP 25(2)/987/5 Anne Trin. [no. 1]; R.D.B., AS/66/111; GR/330/400; Poulson, Holderness, i. 397.
[83] R.D.B., 92/19/18 (1907); B.I.H.R., BA. TP. 1907/2; above, manors.

[84] B.I.H.R., Inst. AB. 28, pp. 447–8; Inst. AB. 32, p. 281.
[85] B.I.H.R., BA. TP. 1940/1; R.D.B., 638/136/114; above, manors; Ch. of Eng. Yr. Bk. (1962), pp. 295–6; (1976), p. 285; Crockford (1989–90, 1991–2).
[86] B.I.H.R., ADM. 1959/1–2.
[87] Tax. Eccl. (Rec. Com.), 304.
[88] Valor Eccl. (Rec. Com.), v. 115.
[89] T.E.R.A.S. iv. 62.
[90] H.U.L., DDFA/15/59; B.I.H.R., Bp. Dio. 3, p. 170.
[91] Rep. Com. Eccl. Revenues, 962–3.
[92] B.I.H.R., V. 1884/Ret. 2.
[93] Valor Eccl. (Rec. Com.), v. 115.
[94] Reg. Giffard, pp. 298–9.
[95] B.I.H.R., TER. H. Routh n.d.[later 17th cent.]–1849.
[96] Ibid. MGA. 1815/4. [97] Ibid. TA. 657L.
[98] P.R.O., E 179/205/504; below, this section [incumbents].
[99] B.I.H.R., TER. H. Routh 1716, [1764].
[1] Ibid. MGA. 1815/4; Acct. of Benefices ... 1810–16, H.C. 5, p. 206, (1818), xviii.
[2] B.I.H.R., TER. H. Routh 1825, 1849; Poulson, Holderness, i. 397.
[3] Directories; memorial in chancel.
[4] B.I.H.R., MGA. 1865/4; dated rainwater heads at ho. The brickwork was painted in the later 20th cent.

later called Cleveland House, cottage, and c. 2½ a. were sold in 1956, and a field of 1½ a. remained in 1978.[5]

A hermitage was founded in Routh by Meaux abbey and endowed with a little land there. Part of the endowment, an acre or two of meadow land called Church ings, was occupied by the churchwardens in the late 16th and mid 17th century.[6]

Thomas, the first known rector, evidently held the church late in the 12th century before resigning it and marrying the mother of his children.[7] In 1303 the church was apparently being served by a curate for the aged incumbent.[8] In 1309 the Ros family presented Hervey of Winchcomb, acolyte, who was licensed to be absent for three years for study in 1310 and in 1313 was further excused as a servant of Master Nicholas de Ros, a royal clerk and York prebendary.[9] His successor in 1324 was John de Ros, also in minor orders and a licensed absentee; he was indicted in 1338 with Sir Richard de Ros and others for the death of Sir Amand of Routh's son[10] and had resigned the living by 1347. The church was exchanged four times between 1354 and 1378, when incumbents were again licensed to be absent. Another connexion of the patronal family, which had an estate at Gedney (Lincs.), was Master Thomas Gedney, rector 1475-7, and Robert Brandesby, nominated by John Ros (d. by 1515) to pray for him in the church for five years,[11] was presented as rector in 1523. Thomas Griffith, rector 1581-1612, was among the incumbents who in 1594 disobeyed an order, probably from the Council in the North, to attend the classes in Beverley of the puritan Thomas Whincop, curate of the minster.[12] Christopher Hildyard, a member of the patronal family, was rector from 1661 to 1712.[13]

In the mid 18th century there was at least one service each Sunday, a second being provided in summer when there was likelihood of a congregation. There were then three celebrations of Holy Communion a year, at which 10-20 usually received in 1743.[14] Routh was later served by curates[15] for non-resident incumbents like Charles Hall, rector for nearly 40 years from 1827, who lived at Terrington (Yorks. N.R.) where he was also rector.[16] In 1865 the curate

was holding two Sunday services and celebrating communion seven times a year. A resident rector was instituted later that year, and communion was monthly by 1868 and weekly in the earlier 20th century; a dozen people usually received in the later 19th century but only 5 in 1931.[17] In the mid 20th century Routh was served with Wawne,[18] and since 1963 it has been the responsibility of the incumbent of Beverley minster.[19] There was each Sunday at Routh either a service or the monthly celebration of communion until 1996, when the provision was reduced to one service and one communion a month.[20]

Lands at Routh were given for lights in the church and by Edward Ros to support a priest to pray for him.[21]

The church was dedicated to *ALL SAINTS*, or *ALL HALLOWS*, by 1451.[22] The building comprises a long chancel, nave with south porch, and small, west tower. A window of the 13th century survives in the nave, and both the chancel and nave were evidently refenestrated in the 14th century. The church was of ashlar until, probably in or soon after the 15th century, brick was used for the rebuilding of the chancel, the addition of the south porch, and the extensive rebuilding of the tower; the brickwork is covered mostly by later pebble-dashing. The fabric was neglected c. 1300 and again in the later 17th and early 18th century, the chancel being in disrepair in 1663 and the tower c. 1680.[23] About 1830 the nave was reroofed and its south wall rebuilt.[24] The church was further restored in the 1860s, the nave being reseated and repaved in 1864 and the chancel reroofed and the east window reglazed in 1869.[25] Another, more radical, restoration was carried out in 1905 by Brodrick, Lowther, & Walker of Hull, the main work being the rebuilding of the tower. The low, embattled tower was rebuilt in ashlar in a pinnacled, 15th-century style, incorporating earlier stonework and the 15th-century west window. The chancel was also refitted, and it was presumably then that its floor was raised to be higher rather than lower than that of the nave.[26]

Fittings include a late medieval, octagonal font, and an 18th-century pulpit. There was

5 O.S. Map 1:10,000, TA 04 SE. (1974 edn.); R.D.B., 1045/443/394; inf. from York Dioc. Bd. of Finance, 1981.
6 P.R.O., E 310/27/159, f. 100; ibid. C 142/530, no. 155.
7 He was perhaps Thos. clerk of Routh who witnessed a deed c. 1190 and whose son Phil. fl. in the early 13th century: *Chron. de Melsa*, i. 363-4; *E.Y.C.* iii. 106; 'Meaux Cart.', pp. 437-8.
8 *Reg. Corbridge*, i, pp. 185-6.
9 Le Neve, *Fasti, 1300-1541, Northern Province*, 71, 92; *Cal. Pat.* 1307-13, 280.
10 *Cal. Close*, 1339-41, 490-1.
11 *Test. Ebor.* iii, pp. 181 n., 337.
12 Lawrance, 'Clergy List', Holderness, 2, pp. 122-4; *V.C.H. Yorks. E.R.* vi. 79; J. S. Purvis, *Tudor Par. Doc. of Dioc. York*, 96.
13 Lawrance, 'Clergy List', Holderness, 2, p. 125; Poulson, *Holderness*, ii. 498.
14 B.I.H.R., V. 1764/Ret. 2, no. 221; *Herring's Visit.* iii, pp. 34-5.
15 B.I.H.R., TER. H. Routh [1809].
16 Ibid. V. 1865/Ret. 2, no. 433; ibid. Inst. AB. 23, p. 10;

R.D.B., FC/311/318; P.R.O., HO 129/518/4/2/4; *Rep. Com. Eccl. Revenues*, 962-3; directories.
17 B.I.H.R., V. 1865/Ret. 2, no. 433; V. 1868/Ret. 2, no. 383; V. 1871/Ret. 2, no. 388; V. 1877/Ret. 2, no. 206; V. 1884/Ret. 2; V. 1912-22/Ret.; V. 1931/Ret.
18 B.I.H.R., Inst. AB. 35, pp. 391-2; ibid. ADM. 1959/1-2; list of rectors in Routh church, 1996; *Crockford*.
19 List of curates in charge in Routh church, 1996; *Crockford*.
20 Notice in church porch; *Beverley Minster Par. Mag.* (June 1996).
21 *Cal. Pat.* 1572-5, pp. 39-43; 1575-8, p. 486-90.
22 E.R.A.O., PE/147/11; *Test. Ebor.* ii, p. 159.
23 B.I.H.R., ER. V./CB. 1, f. 89v.; ER. V./CB. 4, f. 139v.; ER. V./CB. 5, f. 154v.; ER. V./CB. 12, f. 79v.; *Reg. Corbridge*, i, p. 172.
24 E.R.A.O., PE/147/22. For the church before restoration, Poulson, *Holderness*, i. 398-9, illus. facing 390.
25 B.I.H.R., Ch. Ret. ii; inscription in window.
26 A proposed vestry was not built: B.I.H.R., Fac. 1904/20; E.R.A.O., PE/147/11; Poulson, *Holderness*, i. 399.

formerly glass bearing the arms of the Ros and Routh families,[27] fragments of which remain. In the chancel earlier 15th-century brasses commemorate Sir John Routh and his wife Agnes,[28] a mutilated, cross-legged, stone effigy an unknown knight, and a wall tablet by T. Hayes of Beverley Matilda Smith (d. 1844).

There were two bells in 1552[29] but later only one, cast in 1732.[30] A clock was added to the tower as a war memorial in 1919.[31] The plate formerly included a silver cup and cover which were replaced by a plated set between 1825 and 1849.[32] The registers of baptisms begin in 1639, of marriages in 1632, and burials in 1631; there is no marriage register for 1754–1815, and the mid 17th-century registrations of marriages and burials lack entries for a few years.[33]

An extension to the churchyard, which was enclosed by a ditch in 1840,[34] was consecrated in 1987.[35]

In 1777 the parish clerk was said to receive £1 1s. a year from the parishioners, 6d. from each house, and a peck of wheat from each farmer; by 1825 his wages were £4 and 6d. from each parishioner.[36]

The proceeds of the sale of Samman Hall in 1968[37] were spent partly on the provision of a bus shelter and the improvement of the church's heating. The balance of almost £140 was invested. Later grants were made towards reroofing the church and extending its yard. A Scheme was obtained from the Charity Commission in 1983 establishing the Samman Community Trust for Routh, and in 1997 the income was being allowed to accumulate.[38]

NONCONFORMITY. One person was recorded as a papist and three others as non-communicants at Routh in 1663,[39] and a protestant dissenter was returned in 1676.[40] There is later little evidence of nonconformity but in 1868 a few dissenters were said to meet in a cottage on Sundays.[41] Samman Hall, comprising buildings formerly used as a school and a village hall,[42] was bought in 1995, remodelled, and opened as a church in 1996 by a Christadelphian congregation which formerly worshipped in Hull and Skidby. In 1996 three services a week were held for members from as far afield as Bridlington and North Cave.[43]

EDUCATION. There was no school at Routh in the mid 18th century, although some children there were then taught occasionally at their parents' expense, probably by the rector,[44] and in 1818 children from the parish went to school in Beverley or a neighbouring village.[45] A National school was built by W. H. F. Denison, Baron Londesborough, in 1864[46] and supported by him and the rector.[47] At inspection in 1871 it was attended by 10 boys and girls.[48] The school was attended only by infants in 1900 and was closed soon afterwards: in 1905 children from Routh went to school at Tickton, in Beverley, and Leven, and the school building at Routh was disused in 1907.[49] The building was later used as a reading room and in 1996 as part of a nonconformist church.[50]

CHARITY FOR THE POOR. None known.

SIGGLESTHORNE

THE village of Sigglesthorne lies nearly 18 km. NNE. of Hull and 5½ km. from the sea.[51] The large ancient parish included the townships of Catfoss, Little Hatfield, Seaton, Sigglesthorne, and Wassand, together with part of Great Hatfield, the rest of which lay in Mappleton parish. The hamlets of Catfoss, Little Hatfield, and Wassand have always been small, though Catfoss was enlarged with houses built at a former military airfield; Wassand consists of a few estate houses standing among the woods and parkland surrounding Wassand Hall, at the western end of Hornsea mere. The names of most of the settlements are Anglian, though those of Hatfield and Sigglesthorne were Scandinavianized; Sigglesthorne means 'Sigel's thorn tree', Catfoss 'Catta's ditch', Hatfield 'heath land', and Seaton 'farmstead near the lake'. Wassand, the 'sandy ford', is Scandinavian. From the 13th century the two Hatfields were sometimes distinguished by the prefixes East and West or Great and Little.[52]

27 Poulson, *Holderness*, i. 399.
28 *Y.A.J.* xii. 223–4, illus.; Poulson, *Holderness*, i. 399 and illus.   29 *Inventories of Ch. Goods*, 51.
30 Boulter, 'Ch. Bells', 85. B.I.H.R., ER. V./CB. 10, f. 86v.
31 B.I.H.R., Fac. Bk. 9, p. 553; plaque on tower.
32 B.I.H.R., TER. H. Routh [1764]–1849; *Yorks. Ch. Plate*, i. 305, which errs in the identification of the donor of the modern set.
33 E.R.A.O., PE/147/1–4. There are transcripts from 1600: B.I.H.R., PRT. Holderness D. Routh.
34 Poulson, *Holderness*, i. 399.
35 B.I.H.R., CD. Add. 1987/3.
36 Ibid. TER. H. Routh 1777, 1825.
37 Above, intro.
38 Review of Char. *Report*, 35; Char. Com. index; inf. from County Archivist, Beverley, 1996; inf. from Mr. D. F. Hall, Routh, 1997.
39 Ibid. ER. V./CB. 1, f. 89v.
40 *Compton Census*, ed. A. Whiteman, 600.
41 B.I.H.R., V. 1868/Ret. 2, no. 383.
42 Above, intro.; below, educ.
43 *Hull Daily Mail*, 9 May 1995; 8 Jan. 1996; inf. from Mr. J. Maunder, Beverley, 1996.
44 B.I.H.R., V. 1764/Ret. 2, no. 221; *Herring's Visit.* iii, p. 34.   45 *Educ. of Poor Digest*, 1089.
46 Bulmer, *Dir. E. Yorks.* (1892), 492; *Kelly's Dir. N. & E. R. Yorks.* (1893), 481; datestone on former school; O.S. Map 1/2,500, Yorks. CXCVI. 14 (1891 edn.); *Complete Peerage*, s.v. Londesborough.
47 B.I.H.R., V. 1868/Ret. 2, no. 383.
48 *Returns relating to Elem. Educ.* 470–1.
49 B.I.H.R., V. 1900/Ret. no. 314; R.D.B., 92/19/18 (1907); *Kelly's Dir. N. & E. R. Yorks.* (1905), 568; E. R. Educ. Cttee. Mins. 1903–4, 154; 1914–15, 233–4.
50 Above, intro., nonconf.
51 This article was written in 1990.
52 *P.N. Yorks. E.R.* (E.P.N.S.), 62–3, 67–9; G. F. Jensen, *Scand. Settlement Names in Yorks.* 77, 107, 134–5, 157, 164.

The area of the parish in 1852 was 5,807 a. (2,350.1 ha.), comprising 1,032 a. (417.7 ha.) in Sigglesthorne, 1,084 a. (438.7 ha.) in Catfoss, 971 a. (393 ha.) out of a total of 1,489 a. (602.6 ha.) in Great Hatfield, 976 a. (395 ha.) in Little Hatfield, and 1,744 a. (705.8 ha.) in Seaton and Wassand together.[53] Seaton and Wassand were later combined as a civil parish for local government purposes. In 1935 Catfoss civil parish and that of Seaton and Wassand were combined to form a new civil parish of Seaton, with an area of 2,831 a. (1,146 ha.), and all of Great Hatfield civil parish was added to those of Little Hatfield and Goxhill as Hatfield civil parish, with a total area of 3,303 a. (1,337 ha.).[54] In 1984 Seaton civil parish lost c. 9 ha. (23 a.) to Brandesburton civil parish but acquired some 4 ha. (10 a.) from Bewholme and Brandesburton; Seaton's area was 1,141 ha. (2,819 a.) in 1991. The area of Sigglesthorne civil parish remains c. 417 ha.[55]

There were at least 266 poll-tax payers in the parish in 1377,[56] 92 houses were recorded in 1672,[57] and there were said to be 105 families in 1743 and 70 in 1764.[58] The population of the parish was 510 in 1801 and 796 in 1901.[59] The larger area comprised in Sigglesthorne, Hatfield, and Seaton civil parishes had a population of 949 in 1981 and 992 in 1991, of whom 979 were present on Census day.[60]

At Sigglesthorne village there were 84 poll-tax payers in 1377, and in 1672 it had 17 houses assessed for hearth tax and 10 discharged. The population of Sigglesthorne was 135 in 1801, rising to 228 in 1871 and standing at 222 in 1901; it fell to 202 in 1931 but rose to 274 in 1961 and 315 in 1981. In 1991 of 300 present 299 were usually resident.

In 'Hatfield' there were 106 poll-tax payers in 1377, and the two Hatfields had 21 houses assessed and 8 discharged in 1672. The population of Little Hatfield was 24 in 1801, usually 25–40 during the rest of the century, 41 in 1901, and 44 in 1921. At Great Hatfield there were 127 inhabitants in 1801, rising to 171 in 1861 but falling to 137 in 1901; there were 154 in 1921. In 1931 the two Hatfields and Goxhill, the area of the civil parish created in 1935, had a combined population of 280; numbers fell to 221 in 1971 but recovered to 258 in 1981 and 285 in 1991, of whom 274 were then present.

The number of poll-tax payers at Catfoss is not known, but 9 houses were assessed there in 1672. Its population was 46 in 1801, usually 40–60 during the rest of the century, 45 in 1901, and 57 in 1921. There were 76 poll-tax payers at Seaton and Wassand in 1377, and 20 houses were assessed and 7 discharged in 1672. The

population of Seaton and Wassand was 178 in 1801; it rose to 443 in 1861 but had fallen to 351 by 1901 and was 357 in 1921. In 1931 Catfoss and Seaton and Wassand, later combined as one parish, together had a population of 629; numbers fell to 471 in 1951 and 351 in 1971 but recovered to 376 in 1981 and 408 in 1991, of whom 405 were counted.

The parish is bisected by a shallow valley in which Carr dike flows westwards towards the river Hull and Croftings drain eastwards into Hornsea mere. Other streams flow westwards across Catfoss and from Little Hatfield across Sigglesthorne township, but a large part of the Hatfields is drained southwards towards Lambwath stream.[61] Along the valley the ground falls to less than 15 m., in places less than 7 m., above sea level, and much of Catfoss, Great and Little Hatfield, and Wassand townships also lie below 15 m. In the valley a narrow strip of alluvium is bordered on both sides by sand and gravel. A larger area of alluvial ground occupied by Low wood indicates the former extent of Hornsea mere, which now barely reaches into Sigglesthorne parish.[62] Parts of the water were sometimes described as Seaton and Wassand meres.[63] In the rest of the parish the ground lies between 15 and 25 m., and away from the valley it consists mostly of boulder clay, although there are several patches of sand and gravel, including the sites of both the Hatfields. The parish was mostly inclosed early and at unknown dates; the only parliamentary inclosure was that of Sigglesthorne township in 1781.

The main road from Beverley to Hornsea runs along the valley, crossing Carr dike by Leas Lane bridge, and Seaton hamlet lies beside it. In Sigglesthorne township part of the main road was called Gott Gate.[64] Minor roads lead northwards from Seaton towards Bewholme, in Nunkeeling, and Nunkeeling, and another runs through Catfoss, also towards Nunkeeling. Other minor roads from the main road lead southwards towards Rise, one of them forming the main street of Sigglesthorne village, while another runs south-eastwards through the Hatfields and on towards Withernwick. From Sigglesthorne the Wassand road leads eastwards to Wassand and Goxhill, and from Great Hatfield another road runs eastwards towards Mappleton. Other formerly minor roads in Great Hatfield have been upgraded since the Second World War to become part of the road from Hull to Hornsea. The Hull–Hornsea railway line, opened in 1864,[65] crossed the parish, with a station known as Hatfield until 1874, when it was renamed Sigglesthorne. The station was closed for goods in 1963 and entirely in 1964,

53 O.S. Map 6″, Yorks. CXCVII (1854 edn.). The boundary between Seaton and Wassand is shown in B.I.H.R., TA. 77s and 674L, which give the area of Seaton as 1,164 a. and that of Wassand as 534 a.

54 Census, 1931 (pt. ii).

55 E.R.A.O., Holderness (Parishes) Order 1983; O.S. Map 1/2,500, Yorks. CXCVI. 4 (1891 edn.); Census, 1991.

56 P.R.O., E 179/202/60, mm. 59, 69, 71.

57 Ibid. E 179/205/504 (for Hatfields); Hearth Tax, 61–2.

58 B.I.H.R., V. 1764/Ret. 3, no. 24; Herring's Visit. iii, p. 124.

59 V.C.H. Yorks. iii. 495.

60 Census, 1911–91.

61 For Lambwath stream, see below, Withernwick, intro.

62 Geol. Surv. Map 1″, drift, sheet 73 (1909 edn.). The mere and the landscape in Wassand are discussed in detail in Popham, 'Wassand Estate'.

63 e.g. P.R.O., E 134/31 Chas. II Mich./17.

64 O.S. Map 6″, Yorks. CXCVII (1854 edn.); below, this section and local govt.

65 K. A. MacMahon, Beginnings of E. Yorks. Rlys. (E. Yorks. Loc. Hist. Ser. iii), 18.

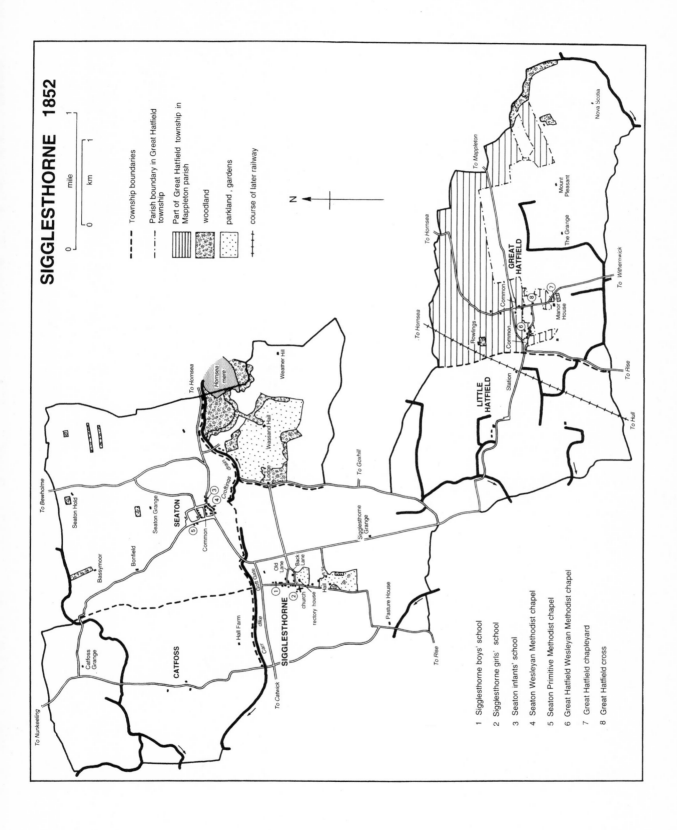

SIGGLESTHORNE 1852

mile

km

- - - - Township boundaries

- · - · - Parish boundary in Great Hatfield township

Part of Great Hatfield township in Mappleton parish

woodland

parkland, gardens

course of later railway

1 Sigglesthorne boys' school
2 Sigglesthorne girls' school
3 Seaton infants' school
4 Seaton Wesleyan Methodist chapel
5 Seaton Primitive Methodist chapel
6 Great Hatfield Wesleyan Methodist chapel
7 Great Hatfield chapelyard
8 Great Hatfield cross

before the closure of the line;[66] the track has been lifted and the buildings converted into housing.

SIGGLESTHORNE. The older buildings in Sigglesthorne village all lie along Main Street, and the church, on its west side, stands on one of the highest points in the parish. Back Lane and Old Lane run east from the street and join to form the Wassand road. The street has wide, grass verges, the large churchyard contains many trees, and the former rectory, Manor House, and Hall all have large, ornamental grounds.[67] A conservation area for the village was formed in 1986.[68] Gothic Terrace, in Back Lane, consists of four early 19th-century houses with a central pediment and pointed windows. Twenty-eight council houses were built in Main Street and on the Seaton road in the 1950s, and 23 more on the Wassand road c. 1970.[69] Other modern houses include an estate in Old Lane under construction in 1990 in fields where earthworks indicated old house sites.[70] An alehouse on Gott Gate was mentioned in 1724, and there was a beerhouse at Sigglesthorne in the mid 19th century.[71] A well dedicated to St. Lawrence formerly lay north of the Beverley road.[72] Two isolated farmhouses in the township were built between inclosure and 1829.[73]

CATFOSS hamlet consists of half a dozen houses on the Nunkeeling road, among them a farmhouse known as Catfoss Manor. Isolated to north and south are Catfoss Grange and Catfoss Hall Farm. There were only four houses by 1730.[74] Earthworks recorded in 1852 in garths beside the road may have marked the sites of other houses.[75] A camp was built at Catfoss by the R.A.F. on land bought in 1928.[76] The airfield was enlarged in 1939–40, the additions including land in Bewholme and Brandesburton. It was closed to flying in 1945 but was used as a missile site from 1959 to 1963.[77] It was sold in separate lots, mainly in 1965,[78] and a dozen houses built as married quarters, all in Catfoss, were later acquired by the district council.

GREAT HATFIELD. Most of the houses in Great Hatfield hamlet lie on the Sigglesthorne–Withernwick road. At the east end of Main Street stands the carved shaft and base of a medieval cross.[79] Small areas of common land lying beside the Mappleton and Sigglesthorne roads in the mid 19th century[80] were later inclosed. Houses built in the 20th century include 14 council houses.[81] There was usually one

FIG. 30. GREAT HATFIELD CROSS

licensed house in the later 18th century. The Black Bull beerhouse was recorded in 1851 and an unnamed beerhouse in 1858. The Holderness Hunt inn was mentioned from 1879 until c. 1900, when it was renamed the Wry Garth; it still existed in 1990.[82] There are half a dozen scattered farmhouses in the township. The outlying houses formerly included one built in a close called Seats, near the boundary with Mappleton, by 1593.[83]

LITTLE HATFIELD. In 1717 Little Hatfield hamlet comprised six houses standing beside the road from Sigglesthorne to Great Hatfield, but later there were only two or three; one isolated farmhouse was built after inclosure that year.[84]

SEATON. The houses of Seaton hamlet stand on the Beverley–Hornsea road, which forms Main Street, beside the Nunkeeling road, known in the hamlet as Breamer Lane, and in two back lanes. Small commons or greens adjoin Breamer Lane. The hamlet was said to have been much improved by John Maw (d. 1883) of Seaton House, who built several new cottages,[85] and further improvements were made by his successor W. P. Maw.[86] A children's playground was provided, a reading room was established in 1885, 33 cottage gardens were made available in 1886 and 11 allotments later, and public rooms

66 C. R. Clinker and J. M. Firth, *Reg. Closed Passenger Stas. and Goods Depots* (1971), 127, 182; above, Hornsea, intro.; *Hull Daily Mail*, 30 Apr. 1965.
67 Below, manors (Sigglesthorne).
68 Inf. from Devt. Dept., Holderness B.C., 1990.
69 R.D.B., 810/58/47; 810/59/48; 1015/292/260; 1444/261/220.
70 Humbs. C.C., Arch. Unit, N. Holderness Survey, *Bull.* iii.
71 E.R.A.O., PE/144/23; directories.
72 O.S. Map 6″, Yorks. CXCVII (1854 and later edns.).
73 A. Bryant, *Map E.R. Yorks.* (1829).
74 E.R.A.O., DDRI/accession 2980, map of Catfoss, 1730.
75 O.S. Map 6″, Yorks. CXCVII (1854 edn.).

76 R.D.B., 375/316/258; *Kelly's Dir. N. & E.R. Yorks.* (1933), 537. For photos., see A. T. G. Hall, scrapbk. ii. 17–19 (in Hull Pub. Libr., 1989).
77 B. B. Halpenny, *Action Stas.: 4. Military Airfields of Yorks.* 40–1.
78 e.g. R.D.B., 1407/213/186.
79 Illus. at H.U.L., DX/51/5.
80 O.S. Map 6″, Yorks. CXCVII (1854 edn.).
81 R.D.B., 798/114/93; 1000/14/9.
82 E.R.A.O., QDT/2/9; P.R.O., HO 107/2365; directories.
83 P.R.O., C 142/247, no. 12.
84 H.U.L., DDLG/22/22.
85 R.D.B., NZ/349/497.
86 Directories; below, manors [Seaton].

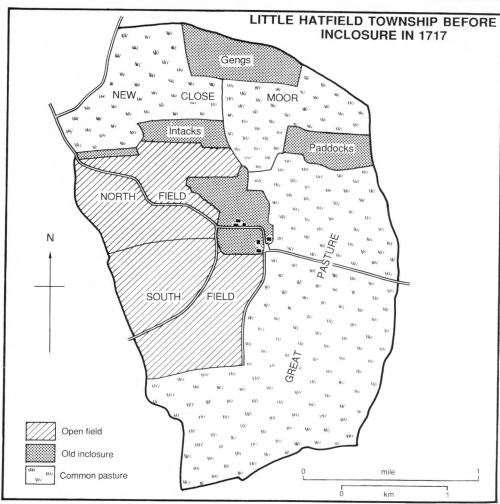

LITTLE HATFIELD TOWNSHIP BEFORE INCLOSURE IN 1717

were built in 1887.[87] Several ornate houses had also been built on the Hornsea road by the Strickland-Constables by 1890.[88] A conservation area in Seaton was designated in 1991.[89] There has been much infilling in the hamlet in the 20th century, and other houses have been built along the Sigglesthorne road, where a sewage pumping station was erected c. 1970.[90] There were usually one or two licensed houses at Seaton in the later 18th century; the Barrel was recorded in the 1820s, and the Swan or the White Swan has existed since at least 1839.[91] The White Swan lodge of the Oddfellows was established in 1869 and still existed in 1940.[92] A wooden, recreation hall was erected on a site in Main Street provided by the Strickland-Constables in 1935.[93] The former infants' school was used as a men's institute in the 1950s and 1960s.[94] There are half a dozen scattered farmhouses in the township.

WASSAND. The approach to Wassand Hall from the Beverley–Hornsea road is partly along

a raised causeway across the low-lying ground at the end of Hornsea mere. The small park made around the 17th-century house was improved and considerably enlarged after the building of the new house in the early 19th century.[95] Tree planting was also carried on outside the park, notably on land left by the receding mere: a plantation running along the boundary with Hornsea, north of the main road, was made c. 1812; the later Low wood, of c. 30 a., and Decoy plantation, both already enclosed with trees in 1809, had been planted by the middle of the century, and the planting of the northern edge of the mere was complete by the late 19th century. Other changes made when Wassand Hall was built included the reduction of the two farmsteads near by to one and the building of a new farmhouse, Weatherhill Farm, to the east of the park in 1814. A *cottage ornée*, Mushroom Cottage, had been built just over the Hornsea boundary in 1812, West Lodge towards Sigglesthorne was added in 1815 and in 1830 East

[87] *Kelly's Dir. N. & E.R. Yorks.* (1889), 453; (1893), 487; Bulmer, *Dir. E. Yorks.* (1892), 496.
[88] O.S. Map 1/2,500, Yorks. CXCVII. 6 (1891 edn.).
[89] Inf. from Devt. Dept., Holderness B.C., 1991–2.
[90] R.D.B., 1656/179/149.
[91] E.R.A.O., QDT/2/6, 9; *Hull Advertiser*, 15 Mar. 1839;

directories.
[92] D. [R. J.] Neave, *E.R. Friendly Soc.* (E. Yorks. Loc. Hist. Ser. xli), 66.   [93] R.D.B., 527/350/272.
[94] H.U.L., DX/169/35; E.R. Educ. Cttee. *Mins.* 1952–3, 240; 1967–8, 128.
[95] Below, manors (Wassand).

Lodge towards Seaton, and in the mid 19th century three cottages were put up on the Hornsea road, opposite the northern entrance to the Hall.[96]

MANORS AND OTHER ESTATES. Except for Sigglesthorne, all of the townships were held in 1086 by Drew de Bevrère and later became part of the Aumale fee.[97]

In 1086 the archbishop of York held a berewick of 8 carucates at Sigglesthorne; by then the estate had been assigned to his church of St. John at Beverley,[98] and the provost of Beverley was granted free warren in *SIGGLES-THORNE* manor in 1314.[99] Tenants of the provost *c.* 1370 included Sir Amand of Routh, who held 1 carucate of the fee in Sigglesthorne.[1]

After the suppression of Beverley college in 1548 the Crown granted 4 bovates in Sigglesthorne, formerly belonging to the provost, to Christopher Estoft and Thomas Doweman or Dolman,[2] and in 1614 William Whitmore and Edmund Sawyer were granted the provost's former manor of Sigglesthorne.[3] The manor later passed to the Ingrams, and in 1633 Sir Arthur Ingram, Sir William Ingram, and John Ibson conveyed it, then including 5 bovates of demesne and 2 carucates of other land, to Henry Blashall and George Gibson the elder. The next year the manor was divided in moieties, Blashall taking 7 bovates and rents from 6 bovates and Gibson 5 bovates and rents from 5 bovates.[4]

In 1689 Blashall conveyed his half of the manor to Ralph Rand. The latter soon after sold it to Matthew Gibson,[5] who was one of the lords of the manor in 1705.[6] After Gibson's death his son Robert sold the moiety in 1731 to Hugh Bethell.[7] Bethell had bought 5 bovates which had belonged to the Constables of Catfoss in 1726, and in 1733 he acquired another 5 bovates from Arthur Smithson, together with several smaller holdings in the township.[8] At inclosure in 1781 William Bethell was allotted 254 a., and he bought a further 102 a. from Wakefield Simpson in 1793.[9] The estate descended in the Bethell family, who had 371 a. in Sigglesthorne in 1852 and 424 a. in 1915; the 129-a. Manor farm was sold in 1929 to Frederick Bird, but the Bethells still had *c.* 250 a. in 1990.[10]

A mansion house in which Matthew and Robert Gibson lived was mentioned in 1711.[11] Manor Farm, later called Manor House, is said to have been built near the site of the old house.[12] A depression at the roadside may be the remains of a moat.

George Gibson's share of the manor evidently passed to his grandson George Gibson the younger, who was the other lord of the manor in 1705.[13] Another George Gibson was allotted 99 a. at inclosure in 1781, and he increased his holding in Sigglesthorne in 1787.[14] The estate was devised by George Gibson (d. 1809) to his brother Matthew T. Gibson (d. 1833), who left it to George Gibson Richardson; it comprised a mansion house and 156 a. in 1837, when it was mortgaged by Richardson, along with another 46 a. In 1850 Richardson sold the whole estate to William, later Sir William, Wright (d. 1884).[15]

The Wrights sold Sigglesthorne Hall and 18 a. adjoining to R. V. S. Riall in 1888, and the nearby Hall Farm and 130 a. to John Haggas in 1889.[16] The Hall was sold twice in 1892, by Riall to Henry Strickland-Constable and by him to G. R. Bethell, who bought a further 46 a. from the Wrights in 1898.[17] After Bethell's death in 1919 his executors sold the estate in 1920 to David C. Smith,[18] who bought Hall farm in 1936.[19] Smith died in 1971, and the following year his executors sold the farm to John L. Spooner and the Hall to John E. and Jennifer A. Townend, who were still the owners in 1990.[20]

The Hall was built by Matthew T. Gibson early in the 19th century, when it comprised a 3-bay, central block with small, single-storeyed wings. It was enlarged in the early 1850s by William Wright, who raised the wings, added canted bays and a new north front, and remodelled the interior, under the supervision of Cuthbert Brodrick.[21] The house is of grey brick with stucco dressings. It contains some 18th-century fittings from the former Red Hall at Winestead.[22] There is an early 19th-century stable block.

The chapter of St. John's college evidently had an interest in the archbishop's estate in Sigglesthorne, and after the suppression fee farm rents in the township formed part of the

96 Popham, 'Wassand Estate', pp. 19, 21, 25–7, 28, 30, 32; figure 3; O.S. Map 1/2,500, Yorks. CXCVII. 6 (1891 edn.); *Trans. E. Yorks. Georgian Soc.* v (1), 34; D. [R. J.] Neave and D. Turnbull, *Landscaped Parks and Gardens of E. Yorks.* (E. Yorks. Georgian Soc., 1992), 9.
97 Below, this section.
98 *V.C.H. Yorks.* ii. 216; *Early Yorks. Families* (Y.A.S. Rec. Ser. cxxxv), 59; *Monastic Notes*, i (Y.A.S. Rec. Ser. xvii), 8; *Cal. Pat.* 1358–61, 474–5; 1377–81, 415; *Beverley Chapter Act Bk.* ii (Selden Soc. cviii), 312, 322, 327.
99 *Cal. Chart. R.* 1300–26, 241.
1 E.R.A.O., PE/129/150, f. 6v.
2 *Cal. Pat.* 1550–3, 254.
3 P.R.O., C 66/2002, no. 2.
4 E.R.A.O., DDRI/27/3.
5 Ibid. DDRI/27/33.
6 Ibid. DDRI/27/3.
7 Ibid. DDRI/27/41.
8 R.D.B., A/475/687.
9 E.R.A.O., DDRI/10/50, 52; DDRI/27/51, 60, 64–5.
10 Ibid. DDRI/27/25; R.D.B., BB/264/32; valuation of

estates of Ric. Bethell, 1852, in E.R.A.O., DDRI/accession 2980, box 2; inf. from Rise Park Estate Off.
11 R.D.B., 756/172/143; 1336/300/280; 1381/403/367; 1384/160/147.
12 Sheahan and Whellan, *Hist. York & E.R.* ii. 432.
13 E.R.A.O., DDRI/27/3.
14 Ibid. QDE/1; R.D.B., BB/264/32.
15 R.D.B., FE/10/10–11; GS/88/91; GS/91/92; 1/383/338 (1884); tablets in church.
16 R.D.B., 26/402/360 (1888); 30/256/242 (1889).
17 Ibid. 50/527/478 (1892); 52/138/133 (1892); 98/26/26 (1898).
18 Ibid. 209/582/492; 221/440/389.
19 Ibid. 298/208/169; 552/538/428.
20 Ibid. 1782/437/348; 1787/154/133; 1800/55/45; 1800/56/46.
21 Sheahan and Whellan, *Hist. York & E.R.* ii. 431. For illus. of the earlier ho. dated 1834, see *Trans. E. Yorks. Georgian Soc.* v (1), frontispiece.
22 R. A. Alec-Smith, 'Winestead' in *Trans. E. Yorks. Georgian Soc.* i (3), 30–1.

manor of Beverley Chapter, which was made up of former college property.[23] A small estate in Sigglesthorne also belonged to St. Mary's abbey, York. Sir Robert Constable (d. 1488) held 3 bovates there of the abbey.[24] Land at Sigglesthorne belonged to a chantry in the chapel at Great Kelk, in Foston on the Wolds,[25] and Henry of Weighton was licensed in 1336 to give land in Sigglesthorne to sustain a chaplain in the chapel at Gardham, in Cherry Burton.[26]

In 1066 Knut held 6 carucates comprising *CATFOSS* manor. The estate evidently passed to William Malet, who was deprived *c.* 1070. By 1086 it was held by Drew de Bevrère's man Franco, ancestor of the Fauconbergs,[27] and in the 1280s Walter de Fauconberg, later Lord Fauconberg, was recorded as the undertenant. Catfoss had evidently been granted to a cadet of the family before 1295, when William de Fauconberg was found to have held by knight service of Walter de Fauconberg 4 carucates and 3 bovates in demesne and 1 carucate and 7 bovates more occupied by his tenants. William was then succeeded by his son John, who granted Catfoss to his brother Henry.[28] Henry had a grant of free warren at Catfoss in 1324.[29] Sir Henry Fauconberg, perhaps the same, is said to have released his right in the manor in 1329–30 to Fulk Constable, who had married Henry's daughter Agnes.[30] Catfoss thereafter descended in the Constable family of Catfoss, which held it of the Fauconbergs and their successors as an appurtenance of Rise manor.[31] The heirs of Sir Robert Constable (d. 1720) sold the estate to Hugh Bethell in 1726, when it comprised *c.* 410 a.[32]

The Bethells had 1,051 a. in Catfoss in 1730 and 1839[33] and 1,079 a. in 1915; part of Grange farm was sold in 1928, the rest, comprising 332 a., to Arthur F. Hainsworth in 1943, and the 296-a. Manor farm, to Frank Smith, in 1947. The Bethell estate still included *c.* 300 a. in Catfoss in 1990.[34]

A chief house was mentioned in 1295.[35] The manor house is said to have been rebuilt by Mary, wife of John Constable (d. 1659),[36] and it had 10 hearths in 1672.[37] Catfoss Hall, as it was sometimes called, was included in the sale to

Bethell in 1726.[38] It is said to have been demolished in 1815 and the outbuildings converted to a farmhouse,[39] which was itself later called Catfoss Hall.

At unknown date part of the estate was separated from the rest. Sometimes called North Catfoss manor, it belonged to Richard Remington (d. by 1616), who was succeeded in turn by his son Richard and, by 1649, his grandson Sir Thomas; it comprised *c.* 500 a. in 1639.[40] It was sold by Sir Thomas and Richard Remington in 1672 to Richard Bethell, who conveyed it to Hugh Bethell in 1683.[41]

Nunkeeling priory had land in Catfoss worth 16*s.* a year in 1535.[42]

In 1066 Redhe held 2 carucates and 3 bovates comprising the manor of *GREAT HATFIELD*, and Morkar 2 carucates and 6 bovates there as soke of his manor of Mappleton. In 1086 the manor was held by Drew de Bevrère's man Walter.[43] In the 1280s the manor was held by Geoffrey Berchaud's heir as undertenant, and other estates there by William de Chestrunt and Walter de Fauconberg, later Lord Fauconberg.[44] In 1316 Walter of Hatfield and Walter de Fauconberg, Lord Fauconberg, were named as lords of Great Hatfield and its members.[45] Fauconberg's estate evidently continued to descend like Rise manor, passing eventually to the Crown.[46]

The manor descended in the Hatfield family until the early 16th century, when Maud, daughter and heir of John Hatfield, married William Constable.[47] The estate was evidently enlarged with the land of Robert Stokes (d. 1506).[48] The manor was held by the Constables of Hatfield, in 1572 it was said of the Crown's manor of Hampton (Mdx.) in socage,[49] until 1632, when Christopher Constable settled it on his daughter Jane upon her marriage to John Lister.[50] In 1700 another John Lister and his wife conveyed it to William Dickinson (d. 1702), who devised it to his granddaughter Sarah, widow of Hugh Bethell (d. 1717).[51]

The Bethell family's estate in Great Hatfield comprised 688 a. in 1767, slightly more *c.* 1840, and 780 a. by 1915.[52] Three farms were sold in

[23] H.U.L., DDCV/16/5 sqq. For Beverley Chapter manor, see *V.C.H. Yorks. E.R.* vi. 211.

[24] *Cal. Inq. p.m. Hen. VII*, i, pp. 151, 527.

[25] *V.C.H. Yorks. E.R.* ii. 187.

[26] *Cal. Pat.* 1334–8, 333.

[27] *V.C.H. Yorks.* ii. 167, 267, 295; *Complete Peerage*.

[28] *Feud. Aids*, vi. 40; *Kirkby's Inq.* 372; *Cal. Inq. p.m.* iii, pp. 159–60; iv, pp. 354, 357; *Yorks. Inq.* iii, p. 5; *Cal. Pat.* 1292–1301, 140.

[29] *Cal. Chart. R.* 1300–26, 473.

[30] Poulson, *Holderness*, i. 436–7.

[31] e.g. *Cal. Inq. p.m.* iii, p. 305; above, Rise, manor. For pedigree, see J. Foster, *Pedigrees of Yorks.* iii.

[32] E.R.A.O., DDRI/10/36, 47, 50, 52.

[33] Ibid. DDRI/accession 2980, map of Catfoss, 1730; B.I.H.R., TA. 254M.

[34] R.D.B., 170/289/242; 375/316/258; 408/90/75; 662/48/34; 771/293/246; inf. from Rise Park Estate Off. For pedigree, see J. Foster, *Pedigrees of Yorks.* iii; Burke, *Land. Gent.* (1969), ii. 46–7.   [35] *Cal. Inq. p.m.* iii, p. 160.

[36] P.R.O., E 179/205/504.

[37] Poulson, *Holderness*, i. 435–6.

[38] E.R.A.O., DDRI/10/43.

[39] Sheahan and Whellan, *Hist. York & E.R.* ii. 432.

[40] P.R.O., C 142/353, no. 9; E.R.A.O., DDRI/10/1–4.

[41] E.R.A.O., DDRI/10/26–7, 34–5, 57.

[42] B.L. Cott. MS. Otho. C. viii, f. 76; *Valor Eccl.* (Rec. Com.), v. 115. For leases, see *Cal. Pat.* 1563–6, p. 397; 1580–2, p. 6.

[43] *V.C.H. Yorks.* ii. 265, 268. The manor was put at 2⅔ carucates in the Summary: ibid. 327.

[44] *Cal. Inq. p.m.* iv, pp. 353, 355–6; *Feud. Aids*, vi. 40–1.

[45] *Feud. Aids*, vi. 163.

[46] P.R.O., C 142/160, no. 43; above, Rise, manor.

[47] J. Foster, *Pedigrees of Yorks.* i (s.v. Hatfield).

[48] *Cal. Inq. p.m. Hen. VII*, iii, p. 144; *L. & P. Hen. VIII*, Add. i (1), p. 305.

[49] P.R.O., C 142/160, no. 43.

[50] E.R.A.O., DDRI/15/1; J. Foster, *Pedigrees of Yorks.* iii, s.v. Constable of Flamborough.

[51] E.R.A.O., DDRI/15/11, 14; ibid. PE/66/2; J. Foster, *Pedigrees of Yorks.* iii, s.v. Bethell.

[52] E.R.A.O., DDRI/15/18; B.I.H.R., TA. 522S, TA. 638L; R.D.B., 170/289/242.

1930, including the 107-a. Manor farm to Cecil E. Appleyard, and nothing remained after the sale in 1942 of the 292-a. Mount Pleasant farm to L. A. North and the 252-a. Grange farm to John R. Rawson.[53]

The chief house of the manor was mentioned in 1632.[54] Its remains are said to have been converted to a farmhouse,[55] later called Manor Farm. The present Manor Farm is a brick and pantile house, possibly of the 18th century.

William de Chestrunt's estate in Great Hatfield evidently passed, like Holmpton, to Bolton priory (Yorks. W.R.) in 1310.[56]

A holding in Great Hatfield built up by the Midgley family in the earlier 18th century[57] passed at the death of Jonathan Midgley in 1778 to his widow Mary (d. 1791), and then to their daughter Mary, wife of William Beverley.[58] In 1837 R. M. Beverley sold a 248-a. farm in Great Hatfield and Cowden to Jesse Bowlby, from whose trustees W. H. Harrison-Broadley bought it in 1870.[59] In 1920 J. B. Harrison-Broadley sold the farm to William W. North (d. 1937), and it was later called Wood farm.[60]

Meaux abbey was given 1½ bovate and a close in Great Hatfield by William Tele and Baldwin Tyrrell, but sold them c. 1215. Simon de Rupella gave the service of Gilbert de Monceaux from 1 carucate in the township, but the service was released by the abbey c. 1240.[61] Nunkeeling priory was given land and tenants in Hatfield, probably Great Hatfield, by William of Anlaby and Simon de Rupella's relict, Beatrice, wife of Amand the butler.[62]

A chief house, several cottages, and 7 bovates of land in Great Hatfield held by Roger Kirkby (d. 1593) were said to have formerly belonged to St. Mary's chantry in Burstall church, in Skeffling.[63]

In 1066 Ketilfrith and Ramkel held 3 carucates comprising *LITTLE HATFIELD* manor; by 1086 they were occupied by Drew de Bevrère's man Rayner.[64] Little Hatfield was later held by the Areins family as undertenant. It belonged c. 1200 to William de Areins, who was

succeeded in turn by his sons Arnold, Thomas, and Bernard, and then by Bernard's son Thomas, who held it in the 1280s. Thomas gave his estate in the township to Sir Robert Tilliol,[65] who held it at his death c. 1320; when Robert's widow Maud died in 1343, it descended to Robert's son Peter. Maud Tilliol's first husband had been Sir William Hilton,[66] and the estate had evidently come to Maud's great-grandson Sir Robert Hilton by the late 14th century. Little Hatfield later descended, like Swine, from the Hiltons to the Meltons and so to the Darcy family.[67]

Little Hatfield manor was held by Dorothy Darcy (d. 1557) and her husband George (d. 1558), Lord Darcy,[68] whose great-grandson John Darcy (d. 1635), Lord Darcy, conveyed it in 1606 to William Hustler.[69] Hustler was succeeded by his son William in 1644,[70] and in 1694 Sir William Hustler sold the manor to Robert Greame.[71] The estate, which comprised the whole township apart from the glebe land, amounted to 931 a. in 1842.[72] It descended in the Greame, later the Lloyd Greame, family until 1921, when Yarburgh Lloyd Greame sold one holding of 582 a., later called Middle farm, to James Swales, and another of 366 a., later called Manor farm, to Frederick Nettleton.[73]

A chief house was mentioned in 1687.[74]

Meaux abbey was given 5 bovates in Little Hatfield by William de Areins c. 1200, 2 bovates by his grandson Thomas, 1 carucate by members of the Routh family, who had acquired them from the Areinses, and 3 bovates by John de Ousefleet.[75] The abbey had a grant of free warren in Hatfield in 1293.[76] Its estate there was worth £3 5s. a year in 1535.[77]

In 1066 Svartgeirr and Ulf held 6½ carucates comprising two manors of *SEATON*; in 1086 Drew de Bevrère's man Robert occupied all or part of the land.[78] In the 1280s Seaton was held by William de Lasceles and William Whittick as undertenants.[79] In 1316 Richard of Tharlesthorpe and Walter de 'Whityng', presumably for Whittick, were named as two of the lords of Seaton and its members,[80] and in 1339 land in Seaton was held of William Whittick.[81] About 1350 most of Seaton was said to belong to Sir Walter de Fauconberg as of the Lasceles fee.[82]

53 R.D.B., 399/170/142; 399/199/167; 400/389/312; 658/154/144; 659/60/53; inf. from Rise Park Estate Off.
54 E.R.A.O., DDRI/15/1.
55 Sheahan and Whellan, *Hist. York & E.R.* ii. 433.
56 *V.C.H. Yorks. E.R.* v. 50.
57 R.D.B., B/56/23; B/245/45.
58 Ibid. AZ/283/460; BQ/369/577; BR/83/114; E.R.A.O., QDE/1; *Brandesburton Monumental Inscriptions* (E. Yorks. Fam. Hist. Soc.), 35.
59 E.R.A.O., DDHB/14/6–7, 12, 17–18.
60 R.D.B., 206/271/230; 573/494/378; 1307/298/273.
61 *Chron. de Melsa* (Rolls Ser.), i. 353, 366; ii. 32. For the Monceaux fam. at Hatfield, see *Yorks. Deeds*, viii, p. 74.
62 B.L. Cott. MS. Otho. C. viii, ff. 76v.–77.
63 P.R.O., C 142/247, no. 12.
64 *V.C.H. Yorks.* ii. 268.
65 *Chron. de Melsa*, i. 306–7; *Cal. Inq. p.m.* iv, pp. 353, 355; *Feud. Aids*, vi. 40.
66 *Cal. Inq. p.m.* vi, p. 166; viii, pp. 292–3; Poulson, *Holderness*, ii. 197–8.

67 Shaftesbury MSS., M 220 (acct. 33–4 Hen. VI); *Chron. de Melsa*, i. 307; ii. 219; above, Swine, Swine township, manors (Swine).
68 P.R.O., C 142/116, no. 57.
69 Ibid. CP 25(2)/3, [no. 38]; Burke, *Peerage* (1959), 610.
70 P.R.O., C 142/774, no. 4.
71 H.U.L., DDLG/22/11.   72 B.I.H.R., TA. 549s.
73 R.D.B., 231/580/482; 234/88/81; 793/244/209; 872/90/84; for the fam., see *V.C.H. Yorks. E.R.* ii. 95.
74 H.U.L., DDLG/22/9.
75 *Chron. de Melsa*, i. 306–7, 367; ii. 24, 32–3, 39, 96, 219.
76 *Cal. Chart. R. 1257–1300*, 427.
77 *Valor Eccl.* (Rec. Com.), v. 108.
78 *V.C.H. Yorks.* ii. 267.
79 *Cal. Inq. p.m.* iv, pp. 353, 355–6.
80 *Feud. Aids*, vi. 163. 'Marlesthorp' is presumably in error for Tharlesthorpe: cf. *Cal. Pat. 1343–5*, 89.
81 *Cal. Inq. p.m.* viii, p. 158. For the Whitticks, above, Aldbrough, manors (Carlton).
82 *Cal. Pat. 1358–61*, 474.

The many small estates in the township in the 18th century included that of William Leake, which passed to his brother, the Revd. Thomas Leake (d. 1786 or 1787), and then to their nephew William Moxon (d. by 1854). The estate was sold in 1859 to George Taylor; it then comprised 171 a. and included 29 a. later known as Manor farm.[83] Taylor was described as lord of Seaton in 1879.[84] He died in 1880, and his 146-a. estate, including Manor farm, passed to his brother Richard Taylor and his nephew Harry T. Bateson; it was sold to Henry Strickland-Constable of Wassand in 1894.[85] The Constables had 275 a. in Seaton in 1843, and by 1910 the estate of the Strickland-Constables included c. 515 a. there.[86] The holding was much the same in 1990, and then included Bassymoor, Buttercup, and Seaton Hold farms, besides Manor farm.[87]

In 1843 John Maw, a Hull draper, bought a house at Seaton which had been built c. 1825, and was known as Seaton House or Hall in the 1840s; a curate lived there in 1846 but Maw himself by 1858.[88] He died in 1883 and was succeeded by William P. Maw.[89] The estate comprised the house and 161 a. in 1902, when it was conveyed to Herbert F. Milvain. It was divided and sold later, some lots before Milvain's death in 1937 but 86 a. in 1958.[90] Seaton House, of grey brick, has a three-bayed centre with a Doric porch, flanked by deeply recessed wings of one bay.

Meaux abbey received many gifts in Seaton. William de Areins gave 3 bovates and William son of Godfrey of Seaton 6 a. c. 1200; John de Lasceles a close c. 1215; Stephen of Thorpe 5s. rent from 2 bovates, Richard Lorrimer 1 carucate and 2 bovates, Robert son of Odo of Seaton 5 a., Amfrid the noble a toft and croft, Peter son of Robert of Seaton 2 selions, and various benefactors 6 selions and other parcels of land c. 1240, and Peter son of Robert of Seaton a toft, a croft, and 1 a. and Nicholas son of Albreda of Seaton ½ bovate c. 1260. The estate in Seaton was farmed as part of the abbey's grange of Wassand.[91]

Nunkeeling priory was also given land and rents in Seaton.[92]

The provost of Beverley had an estate at Seaton which his heir, the Crown, held as a manor in 1572.[93]

In 1066 Sven held 2 carucates comprising the manor of *WASSAND*; in 1086 it was occupied by Drew de Bevrère's man Thorsten.[94] In 1287 Wassand was held as mesne lord by Geoffrey Berchaud's heir.[95] By the early 13th century the Wassand family held at least part of the manor in demesne, and in 1252 Roger of Wassand and Robert son of James of Wassand had estates there.[96] In 1316 Robert of Wassand was named as one of the lords in Seaton and its members, and by 1346 Thomas of Wassand had been succeeded by John of Wassand.[97]

The manor later belonged to Sir John Godard (d. 1420), from whom it evidently descended, like a share in Atwick manor, to the Ughtreds.[98] Sir Robert Ughtred (d. 1472) held ⅓ of Wassand manor, and Sir Henry Ughtred (d. 1510) all of it.[99] Sir Henry's son Sir Robert Ughtred later conveyed it to Robert Hodgson, subject to the payment of £13 6s. 8d. a year, for which Hodgson compounded in 1524.[1] Hodgson sold the manor in 1529 to Joan, widow of Sir William Constable of Caythorpe, in Rudston, and her son Marmaduke.[2] The manor, sometimes called Great Wassand, descended in the Constables of Wassand, who in 1841 had 506 a. in the township.[3] On the death in 1852 of the Revd. Charles Constable the estate passed to Sir George Strickland, Bt., who had married Constable's daughter Mary. Their son Henry took the additional surname Constable in 1863, and thereafter Wassand descended in the Strickland-Constable family. Sir Henry Marmaduke Strickland-Constable, Bt. (d. 1975), was succeeded in the estate by his widow, Lady (Ernestine) Strickland-Constable (d. 1995), and she by trustees including her and Sir Henry's great-nephew Rupert Russell.[4] The estate comprised c. 520 a. in Wassand in 1910,[5] and much the same in 1990, when it included Home and Weatherhill farms, besides the park and woodlands.[6]

A manor house is said to have been built by Mary, wife of Philip Constable (d. 1618),[7] and the Constables had a house with 10 hearths in 1672.[8] The building, which had a **U**-shaped plan

[83] E.R.A.O., QDE/1; R.D.B., BM/129/209; BW/564/808; HF/194/254; HS/143/173; HW/15/16.
[84] *Kelly's Dir. N. & E.R. Yorks.* (1879), 647.
[85] E.R.A.O., PE/144/17; R.D.B., NF/54/85; NF/55/86; 67/227/209 (1894).
[86] B.I.H.R., TA. 674L; E.R.A.O., NV/1/36. Cf. E.R.A.O., DDSC, accession 4248 (plan of Wassand and Seaton 1809).
[87] R.D.B., 1589/493/407; 1639/462/416; inf. from Wm. H. Brown, Agric. Surveyors, Valuers and Land Agents, Northgate Ho., Sleaford, 1990.
[88] R.D.B., FX/210/259; directories; *Hull Advertiser*, 15 Oct. 1841.
[89] E.R.A.O., PE/144/17; R.D.B., NY/331/490; NZ/345/493; NZ/349/497.
[90] R.D.B., 45/415/396 (1902); 838/568/479; 1091/236/211.
[91] *Chron. de Melsa*, i. 308–9, 369; ii. 43–4, 96–7; below, this section [Wassand].
[92] B.L. Cott. MS. Otho. C. viii, f. 75 and v.
[93] P.R.O., C 142/160, no. 43.

[94] *V.C.H. Yorks.* ii. 268.
[95] *Cal. Inq. p.m.* iv, pp. 353, 355.
[96] P.R.O., CP 25(1)/264/43, no. 44; below, this section [Meaux abbey].
[97] *Feud. Aids*, vi. 163, 210.
[98] *Yorks. Inq. Hen. IV–V*, pp. 159–60; above, Atwick, manors (Atwick).
[99] P.R.O., C 140/42, no. 47; C 142/25, nos. 122–3; E.R.A.O., DDKP/19/1; *Complete Peerage*, s.v. Ughtred.
[1] P.R.O., C 54/392, no. 12.
[2] Poulson, *Holderness*, i. 430.
[3] B.I.H.R., TA. 77s; J. Foster, *Pedigrees of Yorks.* iii, s.v. Constables of Flamborough, etc.
[4] Foster, op. cit. iii, s.v. Strickland; Burke, *Peerage* (1959), 521–3; *Debrett's Peerage & Baronetage* (1985), B. 214, P. 34–5; Popham, 'Wassand Estate', pp. 33–4.
[5] E.R.A.O., NV/1/36.
[6] R.D.B., 1621/428/341; 1639/462/416; inf. from Wm. H. Brown, 1990.
[7] Poulson, *Holderness*, i. 431, 435.
[8] P.R.O., E 179/205/504.

FIG. 31. WASSAND: WATERCOLOUR OF FORMER MANOR HOUSE

FIG. 32. WASSAND: WEST ELEVATION OF WASSAND HALL BY THOMAS CUNDY, BUILT BETWEEN 1813 AND 1815

with gabled wings,[9] was renovated in the 1770s. The Revd. Charles Constable built a new house further south to designs by Thomas Cundy between 1813 and 1815, when the old house was demolished, and between 1821 and 1823 the service accommodation of the new house was extended by Watson & Pritchett of York. Wassand Hall is of white brick with stone dressings. The original three-bayed entrance front, to the west, had a Tuscan porch which was removed in the late 19th century. In 1947–8 the north elevation of the Hall was remodelled, the southern and western fronts were restored, and the greater part of the service wings was removed. A new stable block was built in the early 19th century with the house, an icehouse was made in 1818, and c. 1820 a later demolished *cottage ornée* was erected on Lady Island in the mere.[10]

The early house had a small park made from former open-field land. Some tree planting seems to have been done in the earlier 18th century, but there was much more a century later, following the building of Wassand Hall and the extension of the park westwards, which more than doubled its area.[11]

By the mid 12th century St. Mary's abbey, York, had been given 1 carucate at Wassand by Jocelin,[12] and its estate there was mentioned again in the mid 13th century.[13] Great Wassand manor was said to be held of the abbey by the Ughtreds, and at the death of Marmaduke Constable in 1568 it was believed to have belonged formerly to the abbey.[14]

Henry of Wassand gave Meaux abbey 2 bovates and a toft in Wassand and Robert Stanere

another bovate c. 1200, and Robert of Wassand added a close and 3 a. there c. 1215.[15] Meaux was granted free warren at Wassand in 1293.[16] The abbey's grange of Wassand included its land in Seaton, and in 1535 the estate in both places was worth £7 5s. 9d. a year.[17] The Crown granted 3 bovates, a house, a croft, and 2 closes in Wassand, formerly belonging to the abbey, to John Brown and Thomas Wood in 1557.[18] They later became part of Wassand manor.

ECONOMIC HISTORY. COMMON LANDS AND INCLOSURE. All the townships presumably had their own open fields, and from early times some of the low-lying ground was used as meadow land: there was meadow, varying from 6 a. to 30 a., in each township in 1086.[19]

Sigglesthorne. The open fields of Sigglesthorne were called East and West fields in 1650, when they included furlongs known as East and West Gravels and East and West Pastures,[20] suggesting that some of the township's common pasture was then in cultivation. Men were appointed in 1711 to investigate means of getting rid of water so as to keep the two open fields as dry as possible; it was also agreed to stint the common pasture at 1½ gates for each bovate, the same rate as the previous year.[21] In 1718 East field contained 335 a., West field 284 a., Gravels 112 a., the Pasture 228 a., and Mill hill 6 a.;[22] Gravels, the land use of which is uncertain, lay north of the village and the Pasture occupied the southern end of the township.[23]

The remaining commonable land in Sigglesthorne township was inclosed by an award of 1781 under an Act of 1772.[24] The award dealt

[9] Photograph of lost watercolour taken from a negative at Wassand Hall, reprod. in Popham, 'Wassand Estate'. E.R.A.O., DDSC, accession 4248 (plan of Wassand 1809).

[10] Popham, 'Wassand Estate', pp. 17, 23, 27–8, 33, illus.; *Trans. E. Yorks. Georgian Soc.* v (1), 32–8, with illus.

[11] Popham, 'Wassand Estate', pp. 7, 10, 25, 30; E.R.A.O., DDSC, accession 4248 (plan of Wassand 1809); J. Tuke, *Map of Yorks.* (1787); O.S. Map 6″, Yorks. CXCVII (1854 edn.).

[12] *E.Y.C.* i, pp. 269, 274; iii, p. 29.

[13] *Yorks. Assize R. John and Hen. III* (Y.A.S. Rec. Ser. xliv), pp. 71–3.

[14] P.R.O., C 142/150, no. 147; Poulson, *Holderness*, i. 430.

[15] *Chron. de Melsa* (Rolls Ser.), i. 308, 368.

[16] *Cal. Chart. R.* 1257–1300, 427.

[17] *Chron. de Melsa*, i. 308; *Valor Eccl.* (Rec. Com.), v. 108.

[18] *Cal. Pat.* 1555–7, 393–5.

[19] *V.C.H. Yorks.* ii. 216, 267–8.

[20] P.R.O., E 317/Yorks./30.

[21] E.R.A.O., PE/144/23.

[22] Ibid. PE/144, accession 1202 (rector's acct. bk. 1710–34).

[23] O.S. Map 6″, Yorks. CXCVII (1854 edn.).

[24] R.D.B., BB/264/32; 12 Geo. III, c. 63 (Priv. Act).

with 934 a. and the commissioners allotted a total of 899 a. The minimum areas of the grounds inclosed were 233 a. in West field, 182 a. in East field, 104 a. in West pasture, 90 a. in Gravels, and 47 a. in East pasture. The rector received 101 a. for glebe and tithes, William Bethell 254 a., William Smith's executors 105 a., George Carrick's executors 102 a., and George Gibson 99 a. There were also ten allotments of 10–39 a. and eleven of under 10 a., including a 2-a. common allotment for gravel digging.

Other townships. Catfoss, Great Hatfield, and Wassand were inclosed at unknown dates, Seaton in 1657,[25] and Little Hatfield in 1717. The whole manor of Catfoss was in closes in 1639.[26] The East field of Great Hatfield, recorded in 1601, may then have been inclosed. An estate there in 1593 had included several closes, including Great Mask and Seats, and in 1632 closes called West field and Intacke were part of the manor.[27] At Wassand the commonable lands included ground called North green, near the mere.[28] Roger of Wassand and Alan le Ros were found *c.* 1250 to have inclosed *c.* 10 a. of pasture at Wassand, depriving Robert of Staverne of common rights there.[29] The remaining commonable land at Wassand may have been inclosed in the mid 17th century, and ridge and furrow lying west and south of the Hall later marked the location of some of the settlement's tillage.[30] At Little Hatfield there was already more than 100 a. of old inclosures, including East and West Gengs, Great and Little Intacks, and East and West Paddocks, in 1717; practically the whole township then belonged to John Greame, and the remaining commonable land was divided among his three tenants and the rector of Sigglesthorne. The allotments comprised 137 a. from South field, 108 a. from North field, 395 a. from Great pasture, 79 a. from the Moor, and 101 a. from New close.[31] The last mentioned close existed by 1698[32] but was evidently not held in severalty, for both before and after 1717 the rector held lands and gates in it.[33]

MEDIEVAL HOLDINGS. Meaux abbey set up a grange at Wassand, including its land at Seaton, *c.* 1200, and it also had a grange at Little Hatfield.[34]

WOODLAND. Nunkeeling priory was granted the right to take wood at Catfoss in the 13th century.[35]

FISHING. Meaux abbey claimed fishing rights in that part of Hornsea mere which lay in

Seaton and Wassand, but in the mid 13th century it was forced to surrender them to St. Mary's abbey, York, the owner of the rights in the rest of the mere.[36]

LATER AGRICULTURE. In 1809 the estate of the Constables comprised 534 a. in Wassand, 275 a. in Seaton, and 7 a. in Sigglesthorne; there were then three farms, one of 222 a. and the others of 195 a., and six holdings of 6–13 a.[37] In the 19th and 20th centuries there were usually 4–5 farmers in Sigglesthorne, 3 in Catfoss, 7–10 in Great Hatfield, 2 in Little Hatfield, a dozen in Seaton, and 1 or 2 in Wassand; in the whole parish at least 12 in 1851 and *c.* 10 in the 1920s and 1930s had 150 a. or more. There were also 4 or 5 cowkeepers, 1 or 2 market gardeners, and 3 or 4 poultry farmers in the parish.[38] In 1987 of 37 holdings returned for Hatfield, Seaton, and Sigglesthorne civil parishes five were of 100–299 ha. (247–739 a.), ten of 50–99 ha. (123–245 a.), and twenty-two of under 50 ha.[39]

There was 1,549 a. under crops in the parish in 1801.[40] In Sigglesthorne, Catfoss, and Seaton and Wassand there were 2,430 a. of arable, 1,529 a. of grassland, and 86 a. of woodland, and in the Hatfields 1,575 a. of arable, 807 a. of grassland, and 20 a. of woodland in 1905.[41] In the 1930s much of the parish was arable, but there were large areas of grassland around the settlements, alongside Carr dike, and in Catfoss and Wassand townships.[42] In 1987 in Hatfield, Seaton, and Sigglesthorne civil parishes together 1,391 ha. (3,435 a.) were returned as arable and only 357 ha. (882 a.) as grassland, along with 12 ha. (30 a.) of woodland. There were then nearly 13,000 pigs, well over 8,000 poultry, and almost 700 each of cattle and sheep.[43]

FAIR. The provost of Beverley was granted a fair at Sigglesthorne in 1314, to be held on the eve, feast, and morrow of St. Lawrence (9–11 August), and his right to its tolls was upheld *c.* 1350.[44] He was receiving the profits from the fair *c.* 1420,[45] but no more is known of it.

INDUSTRY. Bricks were made at Wassand in the mid 18th century, and several pits remain there, either from that activity or the digging of sand.[46] The only other industrial activity recorded in the parish was the commercial digging of gravel in Catfoss in the mid 20th century.[47]

MILLS. The holding of Sir Amand of Routh in Sigglesthorne included a mill *c.* 1370.[48] Windmills were recorded at Great Hatfield in

25 E.R.A.O., PE/144/24; PE/144, accession 1202 (rector's acct. bk. 1710–34).   26 E.R.A.O., DDRI/10/2.
27 P.R.O., C 142/247, no. 12; E.R.A.O., DDRI/15/1; B.I.H.R., DC. CP. 1601/6.
28 *Chron. de Melsa*, i. 368–9; ii. 220.
29 *Yorks. Assize R. John and Hen. III*, pp. 71–3.
30 Popham, 'Wassand Estate', pp. 5, 7, figure 1.
31 H.U.L., DDLG/22/19, 22.
32 Ibid. DDLG/22/16.
33 B.I.H.R., TER. H. Sigglesthorne 1685 etc.
34 *Chron. de Melsa*, i. 308; ii. 219.
35 English, *Holderness*, 202.
36 *Chron. de Melsa*, i. 369; ii. 97–101.
37 Popham, 'Wassand Estate', pp. 19–20.
38 P.R.O., HO 107/2365; directories.
39 Inf. from Min. of Agric., Fish. & Food, Beverley, 1990.
40 P.R.O., HO 67/26/371.
41 Acreage Returns, 1905.
42 [1st] Land Util. Surv. Map, sheet 28.
43 Inf. from Min. of Agric., Fish. & Food.
44 *Cal. Chart.R.* 1300–26, 241; *Cal. Pat.* 1358–61, 474.
45 Sheffield City Libr., Lindsay Coll. 69.
46 Popham, 'Wassand Estate', p. 13; appendix 2, pp. 5, 10; figure 1.
47 O.S. Map 6″, Yorks. CXCVII. NW. (1951 edn.). Land was bought by Hoveringham Gravels Ltd. in 1965 and 1968: R.D.B., 1430/555/489; 1586/64/58.
48 E.R.A.O., PE/129/150, f. 6v.

1264 and 1632,[49] at Little Hatfield in 1343, 1454–5, 1606, and 1687,[50] and at Sigglesthorne in 1600 and 1650.[51] There was also a mill at Seaton in the Middle Ages.[52]

LOCAL GOVERNMENT. The provost of Beverley, lord of Sigglesthorne, was said c. 1350 to have claimed liberties in four tenements in Seaton.[53] He received profits from a court at Sigglesthorne c. 1420.[54] In the 17th century the occupant of a house on Gott Gate was obliged to provide a room in which the manorial court of Sigglesthorne could be held.[55] Two affeerors were appointed in the manorial court c. 1610[56] and again in 1740, when its other officers included 2 bylawmen, a constable, and a pinder.[57] Stocks and a whipping post in Sigglesthorne were replaced in 1828 by new stocks, which by the 1890s had also been removed.[58] Courts were held on the Meltons' manor at Little Hatfield in the 15th century.[59]

In 1730 the rector stated that there were usually 16 poor people in the parish, to each of whom he gave a bushel of wheat in winter and who all dined with him at Christmas; those in Sigglesthorne township also had daily and weekly charity from him, which he claimed was almost complete support for them.[60] In 1802–3 permanent out-relief was given to 26 people; half of them lived in Seaton township, where another 17 received occasional relief. In 1812–15 about 50 people were relieved permanently and c. 20 occasionally, about half of each group living in Seaton.[61] Sigglesthorne and the other townships, later civil parishes, joined Skirlaugh poor-law union in 1837, and a cottage formerly used to house the poor was sold in 1863.[62] The civil parishes were later part of Skirlaugh rural district, which was replaced in turn by Holderness rural district in 1935 and in 1974 by the Holderness district of Humberside.[63] In 1996 Sigglesthorne, Seaton, and Hatfield parishes became part of a new East Riding unitary area.[64]

CHURCH. There was a church at Sigglesthorne in 1086.[65] It was evidently assigned to St. John's college, Beverley, along with the arch-

bishop's estate in Sigglesthorne, and it was later in the peculiar jurisdiction of the college.[66] The benefice was united with Nunkeeling and Bewholme in 1972[67] and also with Rise in 1974.[68] A chapel of Wassand within a house was mentioned in 1252.[69] A medieval chapel of Great Hatfield and a mission church built there in 1890 are discussed below.[70] Those parts of Mappleton parish which lay in Great Hatfield were annexed to Sigglesthorne parish in 1962, but both Great and Little Hatfield were transferred to Mappleton in 1972.[71]

The advowson belonged to the provost of Beverley until the suppression of the college in 1548, and thereafter to the Crown. After 1974 the patronage of the united benefice also belonged to the Crown, for whom the Lord Chancellor and the Prime Minister presented alternately.[72]

The church was worth £28 13s. 4d. a year in 1291[73] and £29 14s. 5d. in 1535.[74] The improved value in 1650 was £145 net,[75] and c. 1700 the church was worth £180.[76] Net income averaged £685 a year between 1829 and 1831,[77] and it was £773 in 1883.[78] Tithes and offerings contributed £32 2s. 8d. to the gross value in 1535 and £144 in 1650. At the inclosure of Seaton in 1657 a rent charge of £34 was awarded to the rector for tithes, and in the 18th century the tithes of all the townships but Sigglesthorne were generally paid by composition.[79] When Sigglesthorne was inclosed in 1781, an allotment of 55 a. and a rent charge of £44 9s. 0 ½d. were awarded for tithes.[80] The tithes of Catfoss, Great and Little Hatfield, and Seaton and Wassand were commuted between 1839 and 1843 by separate awards for rent charges totalling £711 15s. 6d.[81] Glebe land and the parsonage house were worth £1 13s. 4d. a year in 1535 and £8 in 1650, when the glebe included a cottage, 3 closes, and 4 bovates in Sigglesthorne. At inclosure there in 1781 the rector was allotted 46 a. for glebe.[82] The rector also had several parcels of land and pasture gates in Little Hatfield; at inclosure in 1717 the glebe comprised 5 a. and gates in certain closes, but by 1842 there were 13 a., still in several parcels.[83] The rector sold 81 a. of glebe in Sigglesthorne and 13 a., by then consolidated, in Little Hat-

49 P.R.O., CP 43/200, rot. 15; *Yorks. Deeds*, p. 74.
50 P.R.O., CP 25(2)/3, [no. 38]; H.U.L., DDLG/22/9; Shaftesbury MSS., M 220 (acct. 33–4 Hen. VI); *Cal. Inq. p.m.* viii, p. 292.
51 P.R.O., C 142/261, no. 5; E 317/Yorks./30.
52 B.L. Cott. MS. Otho. C. viii, f. 75.
53 H.U.L., DCC/2/43; *Cal. Inq. Misc.* iii, pp. 18–20; *Cal. Pat.* 1358–61, 474.
54 Sheffield City Libr., Lindsay Coll. 69.
55 E.R.A.O., DDRI/27/33.
56 P.R.O., SC 2/211/124.
57 H.U.L., DDCV/147/1.
58 *T.E.R.A.S.* iii. 49.
59 Shaftesbury MSS., M 220 (acct. 33–4 Hen. VI).
60 E.R.A.O., PE/144, accession 1202 (rector's acct. bk. 1710–34).
61 *Poor Law Abstract, 1804*, pp. 594–5; *1818*, pp. 522–3.
62 R.D.B., IO/367/532; *3rd Rep. Poor Law Com.* 170.
63 *Census*.
64 Humberside (Structural Change) Order 1995, copy at E.R.A.O.
65 *V.C.H. Yorks.* ii. 216.

66 Lawrance, 'Clergy List', Holderness, 2, p. 126.
67 B.I.H.R., OC. 854.   68 Ibid. OC. 881.
69 P.R.O., CP 25(1)/264/43, no. 44.
70 Below, this section.
71 B.I.H.R., OC. 774, 854.
72 Ibid. OC. 854, 881; ibid. Bp. Dio. 3, E.R., p. 174; Lawrance, 'Clergy List', Holderness, 2, pp. 126–8; P.R.O., Inst. Bks.; *Crockford*.
73 *Tax. Eccl.* (Rec. Com.), 303.
74 *Valor Eccl.* (Rec. Com.), v. 119.
75 *T.E.R.A.S.* iv. 64.
76 B.I.H.R., Bp. Dio. 3, E.R., p. 174.
77 *Rep. Com. Eccl. Revenues*, 966–7.
78 B.I.H.R., V. 1884/Ret. 2.
79 Ibid. TER. H. Sigglesthorne; E.R.A.O., DDX/162/1; ibid. PE/144, accession 1202 (rector's acct. bk. 1710–34).
80 R.D.B., BB/264/32.
81 B.I.H.R., TA. 77s (Wassand), 254M (Catfoss), 522s Gt. Hatfield), 549s (Little Hatfield), 674L (Seaton).
82 R.D.B., BB/264/32.
83 B.I.H.R., TER. H. Sigglesthorne; ibid. TA. 549s; H.U.L., DDLG/22/19, 22.

field in 1921.[84] There was still 20 a. unsold in Sigglesthorne in 1978.[85] The parsonage house, which had been described as in decay in 1623, had 9 hearths in 1672.[86] A large, new house was built nearby in 1767, and the ornamental grounds were later enlarged to cover 5 a. The house consists of a seven-bayed front range and rear wings. It was replaced by a new rectory house in 1969[87] and was sold that year.[88]

A guild priest in the church was mentioned in 1538, and property in Catfoss formerly belonging to the Lady guild in Sigglesthorne church was granted to John and William Marsh in 1576.[89] A cottage given for an obit in the church was granted to Francis Morrice and Francis Phillips in 1609.[90]

A chapel of St. Helen at Great Hatfield was recorded in 1492.[91] It was in decay in 1595–6 and only one sermon had been given there the previous year. Soon after that it fell down. In 1650 it was recommended that the chapel be rebuilt and Great and Little Hatfield made a separate parish,[92] but nothing was done. Ruins remained in 1764,[93] and the former chapel yard, on the Withernwick road, was still used for burials in 1990.

The incumbents of Sigglesthorne have included several with other preferments who lived elsewhere. Robert Monceaux, rector in 1418, was a non-resident student in minor orders and Fulk Birmingham, rector c. 1438, a royal servant who held many Church offices.[94] In 1535 a Dr. Trafford was rector but his duty was done by a deacon, whom he paid £1 6s. 8d. a year; it was probably the stipendiary who was referred to as the curate in 1538.[95] Thomas Law, rector from 1657, was ejected in 1662.[96] Two assistant curates were employed in the 1860s and one c. 1890.[97]

By 1743 services were held twice on Sundays, and communion was celebrated six times a year with 50–60 communicants.[98] Some 25 received at the monthly communions in the later 19th century and c. 40 at the weekly celebrations in the 1920s.[99] The boys', girls', and infants' schools were licensed for services in 1848, when the church was being restored.[1]

A mission church, comprising chancel, nave, porch, and bell turret, was opened in Main Street at Great Hatfield in 1890, and in 1892 a service was held there each Sunday.[2] The church was used until 1952 and then again, after refitting with furnishings from the bomb-damaged Christ Church, Hull, from 1961[3] until 1980. A monthly Anglican service later held in the Methodist chapel ceased early in 1990.[4] The former mission church has been converted to a house.

The church of *ST. LAWRENCE*, so called in 1393,[5] is built of boulders with ashlar dressings, and has been much repaired with brick. It consists of chancel with north vestry, aisled and clerestoried nave with south porch and south chapel, or transept, and west tower. Much of the fabric dates from the 13th century, when the church comprised chancel, nave with transepts and narrow, three-bayed aisles, and west tower. The porch is the only later-medieval addition.

The chancel was said to be in decay in 1575 and was substantially rebuilt in brick soon after that. One of the aisles was in disrepair in 1595–6,[6] and about that date the brick clerestory was probably added. The tower was restored in 1676, and battlements were added to the south aisle in 1714.[7] Repairs to the tower in 1763 were so expensive that steps were taken to oblige parishioners living in Great Hatfield to pay church rates, a burden which they had hitherto avoided.[8] A gallery was erected in 1822, replacing a loft of 1712. The north aisle was rebuilt in 1827;[9] the work involved the demolition of the transept, which is probably to be identified with the chapel of the Constables of Catfoss.[10] The tower was strengthened in 1842, and restoration of the church by J. L. Pearson in 1847–8 included new seating and the insertion of lancet windows. The tower was again restored in 1920.[11] A medieval, altar slab survives in the churchyard.

[84] R.D.B., 235/568/479.
[85] Inf. from York Dioc. Bd. of Finance, 1981.
[86] B.I.H.R., V. 1623/CB 1; P.R.O., E 179/205/504.
[87] B.I.H.R., Fac. 1767/1B; MGA. 1969/8; TER. H. Sigglesthorne; E.R.A.O., PE/144, accession 1202 (terriers of 1910, 1966, 1972); Sheahan and Whellan, *Hist. York & E.R.* ii. 431.
[88] R.D.B., 1638/291/246; inf. from the rector, 1990.
[89] *N. Country Wills*, i (Sur. Soc. cxvi), p. 159; *Cal. Pat. 1575–8*, pp. 25, 28.
[90] P.R.O., C 66/1810, no. 1.
[91] *Test. Ebor.* v, p. 1.
[92] B.I.H.R., V. 1627/CB. 1, f. 311; J. S. Purvis, *Tudor Par. Doc. of Dioc. York*, 55; *T.E.R.A.S.* iv. 64.
[93] B.I.H.R., V. 1764/Ret. 3, no. 24.
[94] Lawrance, 'Clergy List', Holderness, 2, pp. 127–9; *Test. Ebor.* iii, p. 172 n.; *Abp. Grindal's Visit. Dioc. York, 1575*, ed. W. J. Sheils, 75; Purvis, *Tudor Par. Doc.*, 56. For Birmingham, Le Neve, *Fasti*, i. 637; ii. 66, 140, 197, 369, 375; iii. 194.
[95] *Valor Eccl.* (Rec. Com.), v. 119; *N. Country Wills*, i, p. 159.
[96] E.R.A.O., PE/144/1, s.v. 1662; Lawrance, 'Clergy List', Holderness, 2, p. 129.
[97] B.I.H.R., V. 1865/Ret. 2, no. 487; V. 1868/Ret. 2, no. 443; *Kelly's Dir. N. & E.R. Yorks.* (1889), 454; (1897), 532.
[98] *Herring's Visit.* iii, p. 124.
[99] B.I.H.R., V. 1764/Ret. 3, no. 24; V. 1865/Ret. 2, no. 487; V. 1868/Ret. 2, no. 443; V. 1871/Ret. 2, no. 450; V. 1877/Ret. 3, no. 61; V. 1884/Ret. 2; V. 1921–2/Ret.; V. 1931/Ret.
[1] Ibid. LDS. 1848/8.
[2] Bulmer, *Dir. E. Yorks.* (1892), 496, which gives 1888 as the date of opening; *Kelly's Dir. N. & E.R. Yorks.* (1893), 487 and later dirs. give 1890.
[3] E.R.A.O., PE/144/19–22; B.I.H.R., LDS. 1962/5; N. Wright, *Hist. Sigglesthorne*, 55.
[4] E.R.A.O., PE/27/45; local inf.
[5] B.I.H.R., Reg. 14, f. 39.
[6] *Abp. Grindal's Visit. 1575*, ed. Sheils, 75; Purvis, *Tudor Par. Doc.* 56.
[7] E.R.A.O., PE/144/23, s.v. 1714; date 1676 on tower. The battlements were removed later: Poulson, *Holderness*, i, facing p. 422.
[8] E.R.A.O., DDRI/27/17; date on tower.
[9] E.R.A.O., PE/144/1 (memo. at back); PE/144/23, s.v. 1712; White, *Dir. E. & N.R. Yorks.* (1840), 286; stone in N. aisle.
[10] Sheahan and Whellan, *Hist. York & E.R.* ii. 431. For the church before restoration, Poulson, *Holderness*, i. 422–3.
[11] B.I.H.R., Ch. Ret. iii; E.R.A.O., PE/144/24, s.vv. 1847–8; Pevsner, *Yorks. E.R.* 339; tie-rod heads on tower (1842); stone on porch (1848); tablet in nave (1920).

FIG. 33. SIGGLESTHORNE CHURCH IN THE EARLIER 19TH CENTURY

There were three bells in 1552 and later; they were recast in 1785 by James Harrison of Barrow on Humber (Lincs.).[12] The plate included a chalice in 1552 and a chalice with cover and a paten in 1720, when that chalice was replaced with another.[13] A new service was given by W. H. E. Bentinck, rector, in 1838; the flagon, made in 1639, was later lost but recovered. An alms-dish was given in 1894.[14] The registers of baptisms, marriages, and burials begin in 1562 and are complete.[15]

An addition to the churchyard was consecrated in 1909.[16]

NONCONFORMITY. A few recusants and non-communicants were recorded in the parish from the late 16th to the 18th century, among them Christopher and John Constable at Hatfield in 1580–1.[17] In 1664 there were 4 recusants from Seaton, 2 from Hatfield, and 1 from Sigglesthorne, and the parish was said to include 2 popish and 8 other dissenters in 1676, and 6 papists in 1706.[18] Wassand Hall was registered for worship by Quakers in 1718, and a house in Seaton in 1740,[19] and there was one Quaker family in the parish in 1743 and 1764.[20]

At Seaton houses were licensed for noncon-formist worship in 1758 and 1808. A Wesleyan Methodist chapel was built there in 1810 and enlarged in 1878, and a Primitive Methodist chapel was put up in 1837.[21] The Primitive Methodist chapel, later the Methodist church, was still used in 1990, when it had been recently enlarged. The former Wesleyan chapel was deregistered in 1949[22] and later demolished.

A house at Great Hatfield was licensed for nonconformist worship in 1822.[23] A Wesleyan Methodist chapel was built there in 1838 and sold, after the 'failure of the cause', in 1885.[24] It was converted to a house but later demolished.[25] The Primitive Methodists licensed a building at Great Hatfield in 1860 and built a chapel there in 1862; it was enlarged, in red and yellow brick, in 1901[26] and was still used by the Methodists in 1990.

EDUCATION. SIGGLESTHORNE. John Garnett, rector, paid a master to teach at Sigglesthorne in a schoolhouse which he had built, perhaps in 1723; in 1731 he pulled down the building because it was so wet, and the use of a rented house instead lasted for only a few years.[27] There was, however, a school in 1788, when John Day became master; he gave up the post in 1803 because the remuneration was too small but returned in 1812, when Marmaduke Constable left £400 for the education of children at Sigglesthorne or Seaton. Day enjoyed a local reputation as a poet.[28] A National school was built in 1813 and attended by 18 boys in 1818.[29]

12 B.I.H.R., TER. H. Sigglesthorne 1764; E.R.A.O., PE/144/24, s.v. 1785; *Inventories of Ch. Goods*, 55; Boulter, 'Ch. Bells', 85.

13 B.I.H.R., ER. V./Ret. 1, ff. 8v., 36v.; *Inventories of Ch. Goods*, 55.

14 B.I.H.R., TER. H. Sigglesthorne; E.R.A.O., PE/144, accession 1202 (terriers of 1910, 1966); *Yorks. Ch. Plate*, i. 312–13.

15 E.R.A.O., PE/144/1–3, 7–8.

16 Ibid. PE/144, accession 1202 (terrier of 1910).

17 Ibid. PE/144/23, s.v. 1667; Aveling, *Post Reformation Catholicism*, 68.

18 B.I.H.R., Bp. Dio. 3, E.R., p. 174; *Depositions from York Castle* (Sur. Soc. xl), 123; *Compton Census*, ed. A. Whiteman, 600.

19 P.R.O., RG 31/5, no. 14; RG 31/7, no. 32; B.I.H.R., Fac. Bk. 1, p. 53.

20 B.I.H.R., V. 1764/Ret. 3, no. 24; *Herring's Visit.* iii, p. 124.

21 P.R.O., RG 31/5, nos. 98, 2199, 2411, 4492; HO 129/522/4/5/4–5; B.I.H.R., Fac. Bk. 3, pp. 474, 557; *Kelly's Dir. N. & E.R. Yorks.* (1893), 487.

22 O.N.S. (Birkdale), Worship Reg. no. 1717.

23 P.R.O., RG 31/5, no. 3734.

24 Ibid. HO 129/522/4/5/7; E.R.A.O., MRH/1/49.

25 R.D.B., LP/306/421; 55/206/190 (1892); 1220/41/31; O.S. Map 6", Yorks. CXCVII (1854 edn.).

26 O.N.S. (Birkdale), Worship Reg. no. 9322; stones on building.

27 E.R.A.O., PE/144/23, s.vv. 1723, 1731, 1734.

28 P.R.O., ED 49/8592; N. Wright, *John Day, a Village Poet*.

29 E.R.A.O., PE/144/24, s.v. 1813; Baines, *Hist. Yorks.* (1823), ii. 387; *Educ. of Poor Digest*, 1093.

The master received *c.* £19 from Constable's bequest in 1818, and 15 of his pupils were taught free in 1823.[30] In 1833 there were 40–50 boys in attendance, and the income was £14 a year.[31] An annual parliamentary grant was received from 1859.[32]

A National school for girls was built in the churchyard at Sigglesthorne in 1818 by Mrs. Bentinck, the rector's wife, and supported by her; in 1833 the school's income came from subscriptions and the school pence of its 40–50 pupils.[33]

The boys' and girls' schools were replaced by a mixed school in Sigglesthorne, built in 1867.[34] The former boys' school was later demolished; that for girls was used as a nursery school in 1990 and still stood in 1998. The attendance of 48 on inspection day in 1871 included children from Goxhill.[35] The school benefited from Constable's charity and from that of W. H. E. Bentinck, rector (d. 1868), who left £1,700 for the education of children at Sigglesthorne and Seaton. In 1906 the income of Constable's bequest was £9 a year from £379 stock and of Bentinck's £47 from £1,826 stock.[36] The school was enlarged in 1894, and after amalgamation with an infants' school at Seaton in 1924 a classroom was added later that year.[37] Average attendance from 1906 to 1932 was usually 70–90; from 1935 to 1938 it was *c.* 55.[38] The senior pupils were transferred to the secondary school at Hornsea in 1958,[39] and in 1990 there were 54 pupils on the roll at Sigglesthorne.[40]

SEATON. One of the parish cottages at Seaton was used as a school in 1840,[41] perhaps for infants. A new infants' school was built there that year. It was supported by voluntary contributions, income from Bentinck's charity, and school pence, and in 1865 had an average attendance of 50.[42] From 1906 to 1922 average attendance was usually 30–40.[43] The school was amalgamated with the junior school at Sigglesthorne in 1924.[44] The former school was used as a storehouse in 1990.

In 1940 the endowment of Bentinck's charity comprised 2¼ a. at Seaton, the school playing field at Sigglesthorne, and £1,826 stock, producing an income of £51 a year. Land at Seaton was sold in 1960 and 1963, and that adjoining

Sigglesthorne school to the county council in 1965.[45] The income from Bentinck's charity in 1989–90 was £310, from which payments totalling £249 were made, mainly to school funds and for student transport; the income from Constable's charity was then £13, but no payments were made.[46]

GREAT HATFIELD. A school was opened in 1894 in the mission church at Great Hatfield.[47] From 1906 to 1938 average attendance was usually 30–40.[48] In 1952 the village hall was rented as additional accommodation,[49] but in 1959 the school was closed and its pupils were transferred to Hornsea.[50] The building was later converted to a house.

CHARITIES FOR THE POOR. William Hopper, by will dated 1658, left 4s. a year from his house at Seaton, and Thomas and Mary Egglerton, by deed of 1676, gave 4s. a year from the same house, the monies in both cases to be distributed to the poor of Seaton and Wassand at Christmas. The income was so used in 1823. In the early 20th century the 8s. rent charge was used to make payments to a dozen people each year; the charity was still active in 1943[51] but no more is known of it.

Three acres of common land at Seaton called the Whinn was assigned to the poor of the township for collecting fuel at inclosure in 1657;[52] it is not known what became of it.

William Day in 1616 gave £2 a year to the poor of Great Hatfield from land there. The income was distributed by the overseers in 1823. In the early 20th century the money was used to make payments to 2–6 people each year. The charity was wound-up *c.* 1990.[53]

Matthew T. Gibson, by will proved in 1833, left £400 for the poor. The income was £10–11 a year from £390 stock in the early 20th century, when the money was distributed to 20–30 people each year. In 1989–90 the same income was received and £10 was distributed at Christmas. W. H. E. Bentinck, rector (d. 1868), made a bequest for the upkeep of his grave and for the poor which produced £1 income in the early 20th century, when payments were occasionally made to 1 or 2 people. Income of £2 was received in 1989–90 but no payments were made.[54]

30 *9th Rep. Com. Char.* 774–5; *Educ. of Poor Digest,* 1093.
31 *Educ. Enq. Abstract,* 1095.
32 *Rep. of Educ. Cttee. of Council, 1859–60* [2681], p. 792, H.C. (1860), liv.
33 Baines, *Hist. Yorks.* ii. 387; *Educ. Enq. Abstract,* 1095; stone on building.
34 B.I.H.R., Ch. Ret. iii.
35 *Returns relating to Elem. Educ.* 472–3.
36 P.R.O., ED 49/8592–3.
37 *Kelly's Dir. N. & E.R. Yorks.* (1897), 531; E.R. Educ. Cttee. *Mins.* 1924–5, 35, 213; below, this section.
38 *Bd. of Educ., List 21* (H.M.S.O., 1908 and later edns.).
39 Wright, *Hist. Sigglesthorne,* 48.
40 Inf. from Educ. Dept., Humbs. C.C., 1990.
41 B.I.H.R., TA. 674L.
42 P.R.O., ED 7/157; ED 49/8592; stone on building.
43 *Bd. of Educ., List 21.*
44 E.R. Educ. Cttee. *Mins.* 1924–5, 35.

45 R.D.B., 639/452/367; 1200/410/352; 1295/87/84; 1436/507/459; E.R. Educ. Cttee. *Mins.* 1962–3, 192.
46 E.R.A.O., CCH/41; Review of Char. *Rep.* 111; inf. from Mr. D. A. Wilkinson, Seaton, 1990.
47 E.R.A.O., SL/47/1.   48 *Bd. of Educ., List 21.*
49 E.R. Educ. Cttee. *Mins.* 1952–3, 95.
50 E.R.A.O., SL/47/2; E.R. Educ. Cttee. *Mins.* 1955–6, 151; 1958–9, 85; 1959–60, 89; above, Hornsea, educ.
51 Tablet in church; E.R.A.O., accession 1681; *9th Rep. Com. Char.* 775.
52 Tablet in church; *9th Rep. Com. Char.* 775.
53 Tablet in church; B.I.H.R., Prob. Reg. 34A, ff. 92v.–93v.; E.R.A.O., accession 1681; *9th Rep. Com. Char.* 775; Wright, *Hist. Sigglesthorne,* 44; Review of Char. *Rep.* 104; inf. from Mr. H. A. Robinson, Goxhill, 1992.
54 E.R.A.O., CCH/41; ibid. accession 1681; tablet in church (Gibson); Review of Char. *Rep.* 112; inf. from Mr. Wilkinson, 1990.

SKIPSEA

THE large, coastal parish of Skipsea comprises, besides Skipsea village, known for the extensive earthworks of its 11th-century castle, the village of Ulrome and the hamlets of Bonwick, Dringhoe, Skipsea Brough, and Upton.[55] There is a church at Ulrome, which is now a separate parish[56] but in the mid 19th century belonged mostly to the ecclesiastical parish of Skipsea[57] and is therefore treated here. Two other settlements, Cleeton and Newhithe, have been lost to the sea,[58] which has continued to reduce the area of the parish.[59]

In 1852 the ecclesiastical parish of Skipsea contained 5,118 a. (2,071.3 ha.), of which Skipsea township, later civil parish, comprised 1,593 a. (644.7 ha.), that of Dringhoe, Upton, and Brough 1,705 a. (690 ha.), and Bonwick township 774 a. (313.2 ha.). The rest of the parish was in Ulrome township, where 1,046 a. (423.3 ha.) belonged to Skipsea and 548 a. (221.8 ha.) to Barmston parish.[60] By 1891 erosion had reduced the area of Skipsea to 1,566 a. (633.8 ha.) and of Ulrome to 1,589 a. (643 ha.).[61] In 1935 Skipsea civil parish, then further reduced to 1,524 a. (616.8 ha.), and that of Dringhoe, Upton, and Brough were combined as the new civil parish of Skipsea. Its area had decreased to 1,279 ha. (3,160 a.) by 1991. A new parish of Ulrome was formed in 1935 from the existing civil parish, then of 1,576 a. (637.8 ha.), the 1,152-a. (466.2-ha.) Lissett civil parish, in Beeford, and 99 a. (40 ha.) of Barmston civil parish. Land was later lost and in 1991 Ulrome contained 1,129 ha. (2,790 a.). Bonwick civil parish was added to those of Bewholme and Nunkeeling and Dunnington, in Beeford, to form the new parish of Bewholme in 1935.[62] In this article Dringhoe, Upton, and Brough, the boundaries between which are unknown, will sometimes be referred to shortly as Dringhoe, and, unless otherwise said, the name Ulrome will mean the township, chapelry, or ecclesiastical parish, rather than the enlarged civil parish.

Skipsea village is situated 7 km. NNW. of Hornsea, 14 km. ESE. of Driffield, and 1 km. west from the North Sea, which forms the eastern boundary of much of the parish. Ulrome village is 2 km. north of that of Skipsea but has been extended southwards by recent cliff-top development. Evenly strung along a road leading west from Skipsea village to the parish boundary 3 km. away are successively the ham-

lets of Skipsea Brough, Dringhoe, and Upton, and c. 2 km. south of the village is the shrunken settlement of Bonwick.

The chief settlement in the parish in 1086 was Cleeton.[63] The name, meaning 'clay farm' or 'clay village', was Anglian.[64] Cleeton became less important after the development of a new settlement at Skipsea.[65] From the late 13th century it was Skipsea, not Cleeton, which was named in taxation and other government records,[66] although the name Cleeton continued to be used for the manor.[67] Cleeton is supposed to have stood a little more than a mile ESE. from Skipsea village, on land lost to the sea c. 1800.[68] The position of Clayton Hill Farm, now Far Grange,[69] supports that location, but the name Cleeton, borne since the the 19th century or earlier by a lane leading north-eastwards from Skipsea village, suggests that the traditional site is incorrect.[70]

The name Skipsea occurs from the 12th century and is a Scandinavian or Anglo-Scandinavian description of the former mere there, meaning literally a lake navigible by ships. The mere and the sea were probably, then as later, connected by a drain.[71] Evidence of early habitation in or near the mere includes platforms for huts constructed it is believed in the Stone and Bronze Ages and discovered beside the western boundary drain of Ulrome in the 19th century.[72] A castle and a church had been built in the mere by the end of the 11th century,[73] and then or later a village grew up there. The relationship of Skipsea village to the unsuccessful town of Skipsea Brough, or borough, is obscure. The borough of Skipsea castle, recorded between 1160 and 1175,[74] was perhaps founded by William le Gros, count of Aumale (d. 1179). It was presumably laid out south of the castle precinct, where the defensive bank is interrupted by the beginning of Skipsea Brough's street. No charter is known. Markets and fairs granted in the 13th and 14th centuries were variously for Skipsea town, Skipsea manor, and Skipsea Brough manor, presumably all the same and possibly by then meaning Skipsea village.[75]

Ulrome was recorded as Ulfram or Ulreham in 1086 and is believed to be an Anglian name altered by Scandinavian influence meaning 'Wulfhere's or Wulfwaru's homestead'. Dringhoe, in 1086 Dringolme, would seem to be a Scandinavian name denoting a hillock occupied

---

55   This article was written in 1996–7.
56   Below, churches.
57   Below, this section.
58   Below, this section [Cleeton, Newhithe]; econ. hist. (Cleeton).
59   P.R.O., E 134/8 & 9 Chas. I Hil./4; *Chron. de Melsa* (Rolls Ser.), iii. 97 n., 98 n.; T. Sheppard, *Lost Towns of Yorks. Coast*, 190, 193.
60   O.S. Map 6″, Yorks. CLXIII (1854 edn.), CLXXX (1855 edn.); *Census*, 1871 (pt. ii).
61   *Census* 1891 (pt. ii). Rest of para. based on *Census*, 1931 (pt. ii) and later years.
62   Above, Beeford, Nunkeeling (both intro.).
63   Below, manors.
64   *P.N. Yorks. E.R.* (E.P.N.S.), 82.

65   Below, this section; below, manors.
66   *Yorks. Lay Subsidy, 1297* (Y.A.S. Rec. Ser. xvi), 129; *Lay Subsidy of 1334*, ed. R. E. Glasscock, 358; *L. & P. Hen. VIII*, xiv (1), p. 309.
67   Below, manors.
68   Cf. E.R.A.O., IA. Skipsea; O.S. Map 6″, Yorks. CLXXX (1855 edn.).
69   Below, this section (outlying buildings).
70   P.R.O., HO 107/2367.
71   *P.N. Yorks. E.R.* 82; below, this section [drainage].
72   *Archaeologia*, lxii (2), 593–610; O.S. Map 1/2,500, Yorks. CLXIII. 13 (1892 edn.).
73   Below, manors (Cleeton).
74   *E.Y.C.* iii, p. 72.
75   Below, this section (Skipsea Brough); econ. hist.

by one or more young men or free tenants known as 'drengs'. Upton and Bonwick are Anglian names meaning respectively the 'upper farm' and either 'Buna's dairy farm' or the 'dairy farm near the reeds'.[76]

Newhithe, or New Hide, whose Anglian name meant the 'new landing place', may have been intended as the port of Skipsea, and Skipsea and 'Hyda' were assessed together in 1334.[77] Comprising 10 tofts in 1260, Newhithe was losing land to the sea by the 1330s and by the early 15th century much or all of the settlement had been carried away.[78]

In 1377 there were 95 poll-tax payers at Skipsea and Brough, 42 houses were recorded at Skipsea in 1439,[79] and in 1672 Skipsea had 43 houses assessed for hearth tax and 26 discharged. At Dringhoe and Upton there were 74 poll-tax payers, and 27 houses were recorded at Upton, which probably also comprised Brough and Dringhoe, in 1672.[80] Bonwick was combined with Dunnington, in Beeford, the two settlements having a total of 83 payers in 1377 and 12 houses in 1672.[81] Skipsea parish as a whole was said to have 80 families in 1743 and 67 in 1764.[82] The population of Skipsea township rose from 220 in 1801 to 290 in 1811, 386 in 1831, and 435 in 1851, but then declined to 394 in 1871, 341 in 1891, and 288 in 1901. Numbers fluctuated in the early 20th century and in 1931 stood at 295. Dringhoe, Upton, and Brough township had 122 inhabitants in 1801; numbers rose to 190 in 1841 but then fell, to 163 in 1851 and 113 in 1911. There were 128 inhabitants in 1931. After the union of Skipsea and Dringhoe, Upton, and Brough in 1935 the population of the new civil parish of Skipsea increased to 472 in 1951, then fell to 396 in 1971 before rising again. There were 515 usually resident in 1981 and 647 in 1991, visitors inflating the numbers counted to 548 and 649 respectively.[83]

The population of Bonwick township was 31 in 1801 and 1861 but then fell to 20 in 1871 and 14 in 1901. There were 26 there in 1921 and 24 in 1931.[84]

At Ulrome there were 63 poll-tax payers in 1377, and 32 houses there were assessed for hearth tax and 14 discharged in 1672.[85] By 1743 Ulrome chapelry apparently had 29 families, 6 of them living in the part of Ulrome which belonged to Barmston parish.[86] Thirty-five families were recorded at Ulrome in 1764[87] and 143 people in 1801. The population rose, notably in the 1830s, to stand at 220 in 1841 but later fell, to 194 in 1881 and 157 in 1911. In 1931 the population was 153. The area comprised in the new civil parish of Ulrome had 254 inhabitants in 1931, including 6 in Barmston. Numbers grew to 383 in 1961 but then fell. There were usually 249 residents in 1981 and 254 in 1991 but visitors resulted in 263 and 286 respectively being counted.[88]

Skipsea and Ulrome lie mostly on boulder clay, with alluvium alongside the main streams and deposits of sand and gravel which produce small hills, notably to the south of Skipsea village.[89] From less than 8 m. above sea level beside the main drains in Ulrome, Dringhoe, and Skipsea, the land rises to c. 25 m. in the southern half of Skipsea. The rolling ground ends in the east in a virtually uninterrupted line of crumbling cliffs and its rises and hilltops were used as the sites of most of the settlements and farms.

For most of their drainage Skipsea and Ulrome depend on Barmston Main drain which carries water into the North Sea. The drain was made from ancient streams flowing along the northern and western boundaries of Ulrome and the northern limit of Dringhoe; they carried some of the water into the sea, as now, but the rest formerly drained westwards and southwards into the valley of the river Hull.[90] The stream between Barmston and Ulrome and its continuations across the north-west corner of Ulrome and down the boundary between Lissett and Ulrome and Dringhoe were all mentioned as insufficient in 1367.[91] That drainage pattern was changed radically c. 1800 by the Beverley and Barmston Drainage commissioners, appointed under an Act of 1798; they improved the streams as the Barmston Main drain and diverted all of the water into the sea at Barmston. According to the drainage award of 1811, the improvements benefited 249 a. in Skipsea and Dringhoe and 120 a. in Ulrome.[92]

Barmston Main drain is fed by Skipsea drain, part of a lengthy watercourse called Stream ditch or dike which formed the boundary between Dringhoe and Ulrome and further south between Bonwick and Skipsea. As well as draining much of the parish, Stream dike also collected water from the higher grounds to its south. Stream dike has also been known as the Scurf in Ulrome, which is separated from Skipsea by a tributary stream called Sewer dike.[93] Sewer dike was recorded in the later 16th century as Ulrome or New dike, which then flowed between Ulrome and Skipsea from the mere to the sea.[94] Stream dike, which evidently also fed the mere around the castle, was insufficient in 1367, especially to the south of Skipsea village.[95] It was mentioned again as the ditch or 'little

[76] P.N. Yorks. E.R. 80–1, 84; G. F. Jensen, Scand. Settlement Names in Yorks. 93, 150.

[77] P.N. Yorks. E.R. 82; Lay Subsidy of 1334, ed. R. E. Glasscock, 358.

[78] P.R.O., SC 11/730, m. 6; ibid. SC 6/1081/1, m. 2 and d.; SC 6/1084/5, m. 8 and d.

[79] P.R.O., C 139/93, no. 44, m. 4.

[80] For the early association of Dringhoe, Upton, and Brough, L. & P. Hen. VIII, xiv (1), p. 309.

[81] P.R.O., E 179/202/60, mm. 43, 63, 74; Hearth Tax, 61.

[82] B.I.H.R., V. 1764/Ret. 3, no. 36; Herring's Visit. iii, p. 129.

[83] V.C.H. Yorks. iii. 495; Census, 1911–91.

[84] V.C.H. Yorks. iii. 495; Census, 1911–31.

[85] P.R.O., E 179/202/60, m. 56; Hearth Tax, 61.

[86] Herring's Visit. i, p. 109; iii. 177.

[87] B.I.H.R., V. 1764/Ret. 3, no. 100.

[88] V.C.H. Yorks. iii. 495; Census, 1911–91.

[89] Geol. Surv. Map 1″, drift, sheet 65 (1909 edn.).

[90] E.R.A.O., CSR/22/1, f. 22.

[91] Poulson, Holderness, i. 120.

[92] E.R.A.O., DCBB/4/2, 8; ibid. DDBD/89/4; 38 Geo. III, c. 63 (Local and Personal); above, Beeford, intro.

[93] R.D.B., AF/180/9; O.S. Map 6″, Yorks. CLXIII, CLXXX (1854–5 edns.); O.S. Map 1/10,000, TA 15 NE., NW., SE. (1983 edn.).

[94] E.R.A.O., DDCC/85/1, s. vv. 1562, 1585.

[95] Poulson, Holderness, i. 120–1.

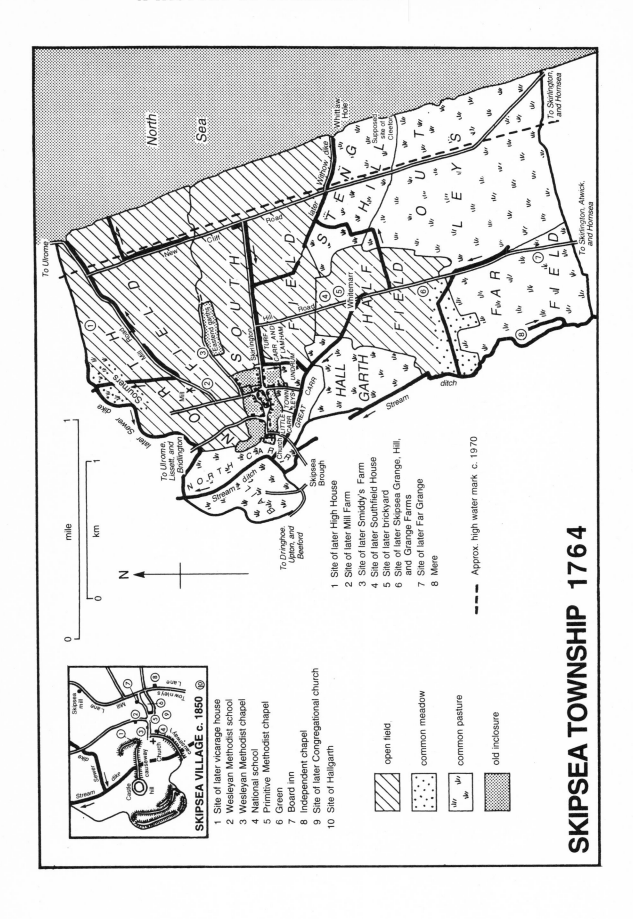

SKIPSEA TOWNSHIP 1764

SKIPSEA VILLAGE c. 1850

1 Site of later vicarage house
2 Wesleyan Methodist school
3 Wesleyan Methodist chapel
4 National school
5 Primitive Methodist chapel
6 Green
7 Board inn
8 Independent chapel
9 Site of later Congregational church
10 Site of Hallgarth

1 Site of later High House
2 Site of later Mill Farm
3 Site of later Smiddy's Farm
4 Site of later Southfield House
5 Site of later brickyard
6 Site of later Skipsea Grange, Hill, and Grange Farms
7 Site of later Far Grange
8 Mere

— — — Approx. high water mark c. 1970

open field

common meadow

common pasture

old inclosure

river' flowing east of the castle site in 1546.[96] The course of Stream dike across the low grounds near the village was later embanked, perhaps either about the date of inclosure in 1765, when drains awarded included a new one south of the village, or *c.* 1800 by the Beverley and Barmston Drainage commissioners.[97] Skipsea mere evidently disappeared during the Middle Ages, but another mere remained beside Stream dike in the south-western corner of Skipsea in the 1760s.[98]

The chief roads in Skipsea and Ulrome connect those villages to the road from Beverley and Hull to Bridlington which is carried over the main drain in the north-western corner of Ulrome by Lissett New bridge.[99] One road leads westwards from Skipsea through Dringhoe and Upton to join the Bridlington road at Beeford, the other north-westwards by way of Ulrome to meet the main road near Lissett. The stretch from Ulrome included a part called Allison Lane, named in 1760, and the junction there is known as Allison Lane End.[1] The road through Ulrome was widened in the mid 20th century.[2] From Allison Lane End a minor road, formerly part of the main road, continues to Lissett.[3] Another road, Hornsea Road, leads east from Skipsea and then south to Atwick and Hornsea, lesser roads run south from Skipsea Brough to Bonwick, Bewholme, and Dunnington, and eastern lanes connect both villages to the sea and to each other. The Skipsea to Atwick road was one of several in Skipsea and Ulrome which were made, or given straighter courses, at inclosure in the 1760s, and one of the eastern lanes, Mill Road, later Lane, was then given a new entry into Ulrome, further inland. A coastal road made then later comprised Cliff and Green Lanes.[4] Apart from the route by Allison Lane End, Ulrome village has been connected to Barmston by one or two field roads since the 18th century.[5] In the 1870s omnibus services ran to Bridlington, Driffield, and Hornsea, and there were carriers to those towns and Hull and Beverley.[6]

SKIPSEA village was built *c.* 300 m. east of the castle, with which it was connected by a causeway across the mere.[7] From the church at its western end, the main street leads eastwards, probably in the Middle Ages into a funnel-shaped green used for the village's markets and fairs.[8] The green had been reduced by building before 1471,[9] and by the 18th century most of that space was occupied by an island of houses and garths, separating the street from a northern back lane. It may have been the back lane which was recorded in 1577 as Finkle Street.[10] The small green which remains formerly included a pond called the Weir.[11] Side lanes from the street lead north to Ulrome and south, one formerly giving access to the village's meadows, and the other crossing low ground by another causeway to Brough and Beeford.[12] The village seems to have had an east end, an isolated group of old inclosures a short distance from the village being known as Eastend garths. They stood south of a lane which formerly ran along the northern edge of the village, possibly joining at its western end the causeway road from the castle; in 1997 the lane was represented by Cleeton Lane and a disused, sunken course to the west of Mill Lane. In the 20th century the village has been extended eastwards by the building of houses on Hornsea Road and along Cleeton Lane,[13] much piecemeal infilling of the older streets has taken place, and small, private housing estates have been developed behind Main Street and Hornsea Road.

The village buildings include several farmhouses. There are about ten boulder-built cottages[14] and cobble walling is also found in the outbuildings of the farms and around gardens but otherwise the village is of brick. The older buildings mostly date from the 19th century, and the newer include *c.* 30 council houses.

In the later 18th century up to four houses were licensed at Skipsea, but there was only one there by the 1820s, the Board, which still traded in 1997.[15] There were several friendly-society branches at Skipsea. The Independent Order of Rechabites' Teetotalers Victory Tent, founded in 1838, had closed or left the order by 1851, and an Oddfellows' lodge established in 1839 was dissolved in 1848. Skipsea Benevolent Friendly Society, also called the Poor Man's Friendly Society, was begun in 1865 or 1866. It met at the Board inn,[16] and held an annual feast day in the village, before being wound up *c.* 1950.[17] The Rechabites seem to have used part of the Independent chapel in Leys Lane, apparently added for them and the Sunday school in

[96] *L. & P. Hen. VIII*, xxi (1), p. 485.

[97] Above, this section.

[98] R.D.B., AF/180/9. 'Skipsea Bail marre', mentioned in 1661, was probably a mere place-name and the source may anyway be anachronistic: E.R.A.O., CSR/22/1, f. 22.

[99] Above, Beeford, intro. [roads].

[1] R.D.B., AB/321/574; O.S. Map 6", Yorks. CLXIII (1854 edn.). Allison was 'Aleysholm' in 1352, 'Allisholme' in 1626, and 'Allisham' in 1762: P.R.O., C 142/425, no. 71; R.D.B., AD/531/1068; *Cal. Inq. p. m.* x, p. 16. No mention was made of the road between Ulrome and Skipsea at inclosure, presumably because it ran entirely through old inclosures: Poulson, *Holderness*, i, facing p. 242; cf. Skipsea incl. plan, E.R.A.O., IA. Skipsea.

[2] R.D.B., 522/407/316; 1460/469/418; E.R.C.C. *Mins.* 1934–5, 251, 256.

[3] Above, Beeford, intro. [roads].

[4] R.D.B., AF/180/9; AH/331/9; E.R.A.O., IA. Skipsea; map of Ulrome print. Poulson, *Holderness*, i, facing p. 242; O.S. Map 6", Yorks. CLXIII, CLXXX (1854–5 edn.).

[5] H.U.L., DDWB(2)/1/31; map of Ulrome in Poulson, *Holderness*, i, facing p. 242; O.S. Map 6", Yorks. CLXIII (1854 edn.); A. Bryant, *Map of E.R. Yorks.* (1829).

[6] *Kelly's Dir. N. & E.R. Yorks.* (1872), 545.

[7] The following is based on the inclosure plan, E.R.A.O., IA. Skipsea, and O.S. Map 6", Yorks. CLXXX (1855 edn.).

[8] Below, econ. hist.   [9] P.R.O., SC 6/1084/5, m. 8.

[10] E.R.A.O., DDCC/85/1.

[11] Ibid. DDCC(2)/83, vol. iv, s.v. 15 July 1915.

[12] Ibid. DDCC/85/1, s.v. 1592.

[13] O.S. Map 1/10,560, TA 15 NE. (1956 edn.).

[14] Poulson, *Holderness*, i. 456.

[15] E.R.A.O., QDT/2/6, 9. The house was recorded as the Hare and Hounds in 1872. *Kelly's Dir. N. & E.R. Yorks.* (1872), 545; (1879), 648.

[16] B.I.H.R., V. 1931/Ret.; D. [R. J.] Neave, *E. R. Friendly Soc.* (E. Yorks. Loc. Hist. Ser. xli), 67; Bulmer, *Dir. E. Yorks.* (1892), 503.

[17] Inf. from Mrs. D. Statters, Skipsea, 1997.

1839.[18] After the chapel's replacement, the whole building evidently came to be called the schoolroom or the Tent.[19] It was used in the late 19th century as a reading room and later by a youth club, the W.I., and other groups; it was demolished after 1952 and houses have been built on the site.[20] A house and shop at the west end of the green bought in 1904 and neighbouring properties acquired in 1915 and 1920 were evidently rebuilt or remodelled to serve as a reading and recreation room.[21] The room fell into disrepair but was restored and in 1991 re-opened as a village meeting hall.[22] Another meeting place is the pre-fabricated building put up beside Cleeton Lane by Skipsea Arts Group in the 1950s and sold in 1960 for use as the village hall.[23] In the mid 20th century the county council provided a library in the reading room and the village hall, then called Windsor Hall, and the former was also used by a bank.[24] Two acres on the north side of Cleeton Lane, awarded to the lord of the manor at inclosure for the pasture rights enjoyed by his pennygrave, or rent-collector, were used with 9 a. south of the lane as allotment gardens from the late 19th century until c. 1940. Their common use probably accounts for the larger plot, later used for council housing, being called Pennygraves and the smaller the Half Pennygraves.[25]

OUTLYING BUILDINGS. Away from the village, farmhouses were built on the former commonable lands after inclosure in 1765; High, or Cliff, House, Mill Farm, Smiddy's Farm, Southfield House, Skipsea Grange, Hill Farm, Grange Farm, and Far Grange, or Clayton Hill Farm, had all been put up by the 1820s.[26] Recent additions include a group of farms just over the boundary with Ulrome.[27]

Skipsea began to be developed as a seaside village in the 1930s, when many shacks were put up along Cliff and Green Lanes, and tea rooms and a cliff-top café were opened.[28] The more intensive development of the cliff in Ulrome extends into the north-east of Skipsea,[29] while near the southern boundary a large caravan park, a leisure centre, and a 9-hole golf course had

also been established by 1997. Far Grange caravan park could then accommodate almost 1,000 static and touring caravans.[30]

Three beacons stood in Skipsea and Ulrome in the 16th century,[31] and South beacon at Skipsea was mentioned in 1594.[32] An aerial firing and bombing range at Skipsea, established by the Air Council in the late 1920s, was sold in 1961.[33]

ULROME village has a plan typical of Holderness, being built along a single street which extends east-west for over 1 km. From its western end, side lanes leading to Lissett and Skipsea now form part of the Bridlington-Hornsea road, isolating the end of the street which is known as Bugg Lane. The village's buildings were grouped at either end of the street, possibly reflecting the early division of Ulrome between two manors. Those at West End include the church, the former vicarage house,[34] Manor House,[35] and Ulrome Hall. West End was evidently built around a green, one part of which remains next to the village pond, and others perhaps in the grass verges of Bugg Lane. There was probably also a green at East End, where a tiny triangle of grass survives at the junction of the main street and a side lane. Mention of former garths and crofts in 1793 suggest that the village had declined by that date.[36] Until its inclosure in 1767 the southern open field extended up to the village street,[37] and the south side remains relatively unbuilt.

Most of the buildings are of brick and date from the 19th and 20th centuries. Besides the church, older buildings may include a single-storeyed cottage and the outbuildings of several farms, all boulder-built. The Old Joiner's Shop, comprising a house and converted barn, is mostly of brick and pantiles with some cobble walling to the barn; it may date from the mid 18th century.[38] Prefabricated houses put up by the rural district council c. 1950 were demolished about 1985, and in 1997 the site was being used for private houses. The council also built eight other houses, which remain,[39] besides making the usual improvements to the sewage system.[40]

[18] Poulson, *Holderness*, i. 456; below, nonconf.
[19] Cf. E.R.A.O., DDCC(2)/83, vol. iv, s.v. 30 Mar. 1868; R.D.B., 928/385/345.
[20] R.D.B., 928/385/345; Bulmer, *Dir. E. Yorks.* (1892), 502, which calls the library established there a 'parish library'; O.S. Map 1/2,500, Yorks. CLXXX. 2 (1892 edn.); inf. from Mrs. D. Statters, Mrs. M. Newton, Skipsea, 1997.
[21] E.R.A.O., DDCC(2)/83, vol. iv, s.v. 6 Apr. 1904, 15 July 1915; R.D.B., 1228/381/336; deeds in possession of Mrs. M. Newton, Skipsea, 1997. The 1920 purchase may have included the site of the war memorial. Illus. in I. and M. Sumner, *Britain in Old Photographs: Holderness*, 13.
[22] *Hull Daily Mail*, 4 Nov. 1991; *Driffield Times*, 29 Sept. 1983. Illus. in M. and B. Chapman, *Holderness in old picture postcards*, 60.   [23] R.D.B., 965/79/71; 1196/24/22.
[24] E.R. Educ. Cttee. *Mins.* 1958–9, 18; 1964–5, 19; inf. from Mrs. M. Newton, Skipsea, 1997.
[25] R.D.B., AF/180/9; E.R.A.O., IA. Skipsea; O.S. Map 1/2,500, Yorks. CLXXX. 2 (1892 edn.); O.S. Map 1/10,560, TA 15 NE. (1956 edn.); inf. from Mrs. D. Statters, Skipsea, 1997.
[26] H. Teesdale, *Map of Yorks.* (1828); A. Bryant, *Map of E. R. Yorks.* (1829); O.S. Map 6", Yorks. CLXIII, CLXXX (1854–5 edn.); Poulson, *Holderness*, i. 455; Dept. of Environment, *Buildings List* (1987).

[27] O.S. Map 1/10,560, TA 15 NE. (1956 edn.); O.S. Map 1/10,000, TA 15 NE. (1983 edn.).
[28] R.D.B., 511/314/231; 626/265/205; O.S. Map 1/2,500, Yorks. CLXXX. 2 (1910 edn.); O.S. Map 1/10,560, TA 15 NE., SE. (1956 edn.); *Kelly's Dir. N. & E.R. Yorks.* (1937), 533.
[29] Below, this section (Ulrome).
[30] Inf. from Public Protection Division, E.R. of Yorks. Council, Bridlington, 1997.
[31] T. Sheppard, *Lost Towns of Yorks. Coast*, 208–10, 212; J. Nicholson, *Beacons of E. Yorks.* 34, 54.
[32] E.R.A.O., DDCC/85/2.
[33] E.R. Agric. Cttee. *Mins.* 1926–9, 228; R.D.B., 376/458/381; 382/591/492; 392/230/196; sale particulars in possession of Mrs. F. Davies, Skipsea Grange, 1997.
[34] Below, churches (Ulrome).
[35] Below, manors (Ulrome).
[36] R.D.B., BR/544/882.
[37] Map of 1766 print. Poulson, *Holderness*, i. facing p. 242.
[38] Dept. of Environment, *Buildings List* (1987); below, manors (Ulrome [Manor Ho., Ulrome Hall]; Pevsner and Neave, *Yorks. E.R.* 728.
[39] R.D.B., 583/513/397; 712/174/147; 917/283/253; inf. from Mrs. Joan Thornton, Ulrome, 1997.
[40] R.D.B., 1409/508/465; 1409/509/466; 1554/283/211.

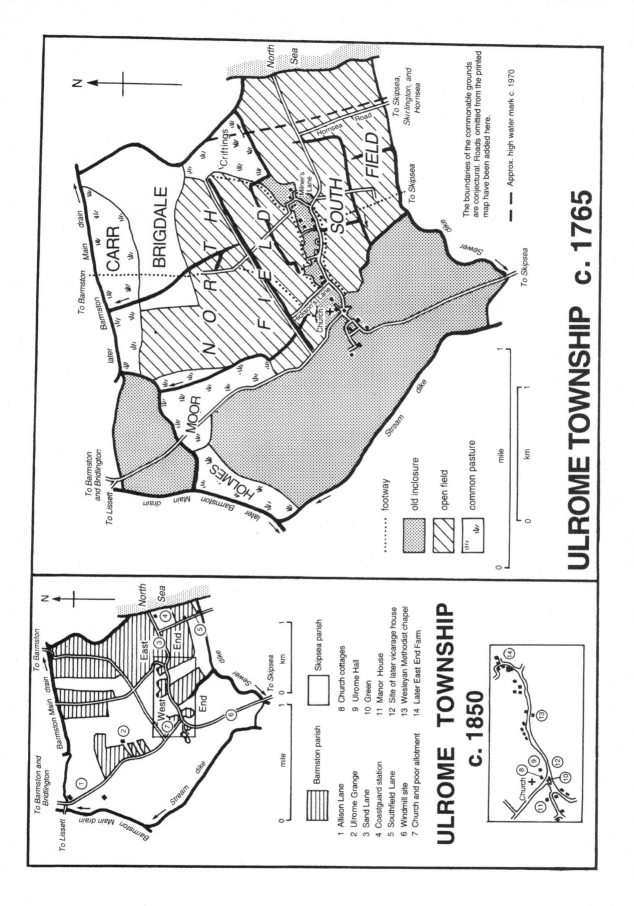

ULROME TOWNSHIP c. 1765

The boundaries of the commonable grounds are conjectural. Roads omitted from the printed map have been added here.

– – – Approx. high water mark c. 1970

.... footway
old inclosure
open field
common pasture

ULROME TOWNSHIP c. 1850

Barmston parish
Skipsea parish

1 Allison Lane
2 Ulrome Grange
3 Sand Lane
4 Coastguard station
5 Southfield Lane
6 Windmill site
7 Church and poor allotment
8 Church cottages
9 Ulrome Hall
10 Green
11 Manor House
12 Site of later vicarage house
13 Wesleyan Methodist chapel
14 Later East End Farm

One or two alehouses had been licensed at Ulrome in the later 18th century,[41] but none were mentioned later. Allotment gardens made from land belonging to the poor and the church by the late 19th century were used until the mid 20th.[42] Other land, adjoining the village pond and possibly taken in from the green, was similarly used in the mid 20th century under the name Wyre gardens.[43] A village hall for Ulrome, called Rickaby Hall, was built in 1952.[44]

OUTLYING BUILDINGS. After inclosure in 1767 former open-field land was used for the sites of Ulrome Grange and one or two houses beside Southfield Lane, all apparently built c. 1840.[45]

In the mid 20th century caravan parks were laid out at the east end of the village, and by 1997 the cliff-top parks and buildings serving them stretched southwards more or less without a break along both sides of Southfield Lane into Skipsea.[46] The facilities of the largest concern there, Skipsea Sands Holiday Village, then included swimming pools and a licensed house, the Sportsman, which, together with the nearby Skipsea Beach social club, was opened c. 1940.[47] The parks in Ulrome and Mill Lane, Skipsea, had room for c. 1,890 static and mobile caravans in 1997.[48]

A coastguard station had been built at the end of Sand Lane, which continued the village street to the sea, by 1829. After 1890 it was rebuilt further inland, at the junction of Sand Lane and Southfield Lane, the cliff road, together with 4 cottages.[49] Five coastguards were employed in the mid 19th century, three or four c. 1900, but later only one or two, and the station was evidently closed about 1930. The cottages remained in 1997. There was also a rocket life-saving apparatus at Ulrome manned by volunteers c. 1900.[50] Troops were stationed in Ulrome in the First World War,[51] and buildings put up by the military authorities c. 1940 remain near the cliff in both Ulrome and Skipsea.

SKIPSEA BROUGH, DRINGHOE, AND UPTON. The alignment of Skipsea Brough's street with an entrance into the bailey of Skipsea castle and two long, narrow garths on the street's east side substantiate its probable origin as a 12th-century planned town.[52] Dringhoe and Upton were probably also built along single streets.

The line of house sites and closes following the higher ground was broken in Dringhoe and between that settlement and Upton by the shallow valleys of streams, and some of the lower ground formed a green at the east end of Dringhoe. Upton lay on either side of the Skipsea-Beeford road in Forker garths and east of Low Upton Farm but those sites were largely abandoned after inclosure. In 1997 earthworks marked the sites of some of the former buildings.[53] The streets of all three hamlets may together have formed the early road between Skipsea and Beeford, but by the mid 18th century Dringhoe's street had evidently been superseded by a more direct road further south connecting Brough to Upton, and at inclosure in 1763 two lanes running between the garths at Dringhoe from the northern to the southern field were also stopped up. A footpath from Upton to Dringhoe awarded at inclosure may have followed the line of the old road.[54] Crow Garth, or Grange, Dringhoe Hall, Dringhoe Manor House, Dringhoe Grange, Happy Lands, and Low Upton all occupied garths in 1762, but Field House Farm, then shown on commonable land in South field, was almost certainly a recent addition. By 1829 Upton House, or Park Farm, and Tithe Farm, later Low Fields, had also been built on land inclosed in 1763.[55] Happy Lands Farm was re-fronted by Jeremiah Lamplugh in 1810;[56] he also built a windmill and probably the mill house, now Southfield House.[57] Manor Farm, Dringhoe, was added in 1882.[58] Field House Farm, Low Upton Farm, Low Fields, and Dringhoe Grange had all been rebuilt by 1997, when the rebuilding of Dringhoe Manor House was almost complete; older outbuildings remained on the farms. More recent houses include two council houses, built on the Beeford road at Dringhoe in the mid 20th century.[59] In contrast to the scattered farms of Dringhoe and Upton, Skipsea Brough comprises a dozen closely-built houses. They are of brick and mostly date from the 19th and 20th centuries.

There was an unlicensed alehouse at Dringhoe in 1756. At Skipsea Brough there was usually one licensed house in the later 18th century, and the Ship was recorded in the 1820s;[60] it was perhaps the same house which later traded mostly as the Buck inn until its closure c. 1910.[61] Unused parts of a plot of land at Skipsea Brough acquired for a burial ground have been let as

[41] E.R.A.O., QDT/2/9.
[42] Below, charities.
[43] Inf. from Mrs. Joan Thornton, Ulrome, 1997.
[44] R.D.B., 833/432/339; datestone.
[45] H. Teesdale, *Map of Yorks.* (1828); A. Bryant, *Map of E. R. Yorks.* (1829); O.S. Map 6", Yorks. CLXIII (1854 edn.).
[46] O.S. Map 1/10,000, TA 15 NE. (1981 edn.).
[47] Inf. from Mrs. M. Newton, Skipsea, 1997.
[48] Inf. from Public Protection Division, E.R. of Yorks. Council, Bridlington, 1997.
[49] E.R.A.O., NV/1/82; A. Bryant, *Map of E.R. of Yorks.* (1829); O.S. Map 6", Yorks. CLXIII (1854 edn.); O.S. Map 1/2,500, Yorks. CLXIII. 14 (1892 edn.); Poulson, *Holderness*, i. 241.
[50] Directories; Sheahan and Whellan, *Hist. York & E.R.* ii. 439; Bulmer, *Dir. E. Yorks.* (1892), 280.
[51] E.R.A.O., DDX/215/19.
[52] Ibid. IA. Dringhoe; above, this section.

[53] E.R.A.O., IA. Dringhoe; O.S. Map 6", Yorks. CLXXX (1855 edn.). For the house sites, and adjoining early inclosure from the tillage, see also Hull Univ., Dept. of Geog., R.A.F. air photographs, run 74A, no. 3359; run 85, nos. 4100–1.
[54] R.D.B., AC/178/9; E.R.A.O., IA. Dringhoe; O.S. Map 6", Yorks. CLXXX (1855 edn.).
[55] E.R.A.O., IA. Dringhoe; A. Bryant, *Map of E.R. Yorks.* (1829); O.S. Map 6", Yorks. CLXIII, CLXXX (1854–5 edn.); O.S. Map 1/2,500, Yorks. CLXIII. 13, CLXXX.1 (1892 edn.); below, manors [Watton priory].
[56] Datestone; below, manors (Dringhoe).
[57] O.S. Map 6", Yorks. CLXXX (1855 edn.); below, econ. hist. (mills).
[58] Below, manors. [59] R.D.B., 587/468/363.
[60] E.R.A.O., QDT/2/6, 9.
[61] O.S. Map 6", Yorks. CLXXX (1855 edn.); directories. In 1881 it was called the Blacksmith's Arms: P.R.O., RG 11/4797.

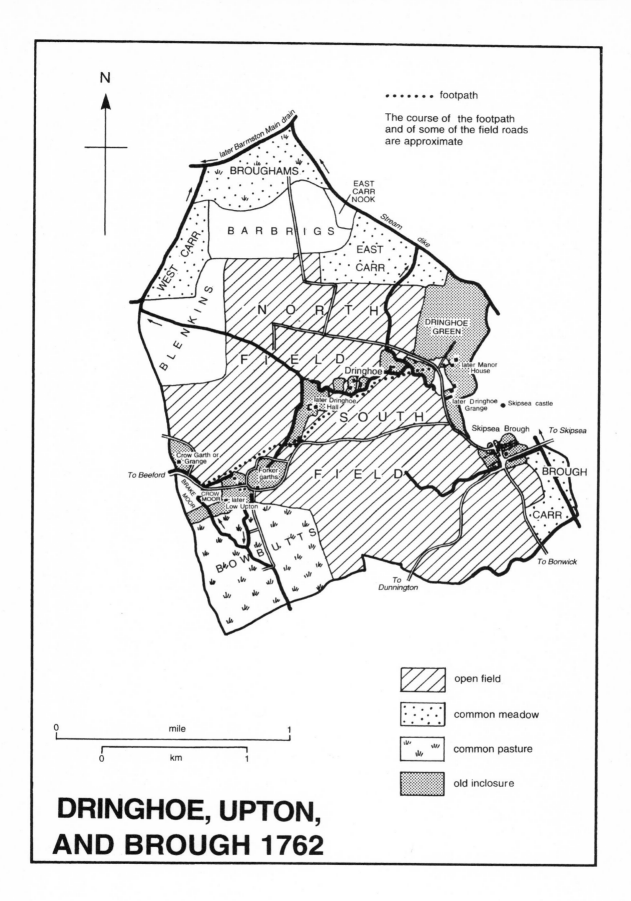

N

•••••••• footpath

The course of the footpath
and of some of the field roads
are approximate

BROUGHAMS

later Barmston Main drain

EAST
CARR
NOOK

BARBRIGS

WEST CARR

Stream dike

EAST
CARR

BLENKINS

NORTH

DRINGHOE
GREEN

FIELD

Dringhoe

later Manor
House

later Dringhoe
Hall

SOUTH

later Dringhoe
Grange

Skipsea castle

Crow Garth or
Grange

FIELD

Skipsea Brough

To Skipsea

To Beeford

Forker
garths

BROUGH

BRAKE MOOR

CROW
MOOR

later
Low Upton

CARR

BOW BUTTS

To Bonwick

To
Dunnington

	open field
	common meadow
	common pasture
	old inclosure

0 ——— mile ——— 1

0 ——— km ——— 1

DRINGHOE, UPTON,
AND BROUGH 1762

allotment gardens since the 1920s; in 1997 there were 16 gardens and a small field rented to a farmer.[62]

MANORS AND OTHER ESTATES. In 1066 Earl Harold had the manor of *CLEETON*, comprising 28 carucates and 1½ bovate there, 5½ carucates of sokeland at Dringhoe and Upton, and a berewick of 2 carucates at Wilsthorpe, in Bridlington. By 1086 Drew de Bevrère held the manor.[63] Cleeton evidently descended like Burstwick, of which it was accounted a member by the 14th century.[64] It thus passed from Drew de Bevrère in turn to the counts of Aumale,[65] the Crown,[66] and its grantees. The last included Geoffrey le Scrope who briefly held Cleeton manor by grant of 1335.[67] By the attainder in 1521 of Edward Stafford, duke of Buckingham, heir to one of the 14th-century grantees, the former Aumale fee in the parish, with the rest of the lordship of Holderness, was forfeited to the Crown, which granted Cleeton manor to Sir Anthony Browne in 1530.[68] It was bought back in 1537[69] but in 1544 was sold to Robert Raynolde, Robert Whetstone, and other citizens of London.[70] In 1546 the other purchasers quit-claimed the manor, held of the Crown as ¹⁄₂₀ knight's fee,[71] to Whetstone,[72] who also purchased land at Dringhoe and Skipsea. He (d. 1557) was succeeded by his son Robert,[73] who sold Cleeton manor with appurtenances in Dringhoe, Upton, and Brough to Ralph Bosville and his son Henry in 1565–6.[74] Henry Bosville had succeeded his father by 1581, and in 1589 he sold the manor to Tristram Conyers. Conyers (d. 1619)[75] was evidently followed by his widow Elizabeth, and by 1623 his nephew William Conyers had Cleeton manor. In 1628 he sold it to John Wright for Henry Constable, viscount Dunbar, and the manor later descended, with Skipsea manor, in the Constables.[76] Courts were, nevertheless, held by the Wrights until 1662, and between 1674 and 1694 by Sir Ralph Warton and Vincent Grantham, presumably also Constable trustees.[77]

SKIPSEA manor was evidently at first merely part of Cleeton manor. It was called a manor in 1276[78] but its relationship to Cleeton manor was still uncertain in the 1330s.[79] Soon afterwards Skipsea was again recorded as a separate manor,[80] and the manor of Skipsea Brough, mentioned in 1343, was presumably the same.[81] By the late 14th century Skipsea was clearly the more important of the two manors, Cleeton sometimes being regarded as a mere appurtenance of Skipsea manor, rather than a separate manor.[82] Skipsea castle was the head of the honour of Aumale in Holderness[83] before the 13th century, when it was succeeded as the administrative centre of Holderness by Burstwick.[84] Skipsea descended with Cleeton, its fellow member of Burstwick.[85] Arnulf de Montgomery (deprived 1102) apparently held Skipsea castle,[86] and in 1316 Margaret de Gavaston, countess of Cornwall, probably held Cleeton manor as well as its members of Skipsea and Newhithe, of which she was then recorded as lady.[87] When the Crown alienated Cleeton manor in 1530,[88] it retained Skipsea manor and its appurtenances in Ulrome and Dringhoe, and they continued to descend with the lordship of Holderness, passing by Crown grant in 1558 to Henry Neville, earl of Westmorland,[89] by sale of 1560 to his son-in-law Sir John Constable,[90] and thereafter in Constable's successors, of whom Henry Constable, viscount Dunbar, re-united Cleeton manor with the rest of the fee by purchase in 1628.[91]

It was claimed that Cleeton manor was wholly or largely occupied as demesne until the mid 15th century; the copyholders at Skipsea were then said to have leased the demesne, adding it to their bond holdings and, in the 16th century, taking advantage of stranger lords to secure admissions to the former demesne land as copyhold. John Wright's claim *c.* 1630 to the land at Cleeton as his freehold seems to have been unsuccessful,[92] and later the only land held by the Constables and their heirs, lords of Skipsea and Cleeton manors, was the 2-a. allotment awarded to William Constable at the inclosure

[62] B.I.H.R., CD. 761; below, loc. govt.; inf. from Mrs. M. Newton, Skipsea, 1997.

[63] *V.C.H. Yorks.* ii. 150, 265, 269; *V.C.H. Yorks. E.R.* ii. 105.

[64] *Cal. Chart R.* 1327–41, 446–7; *V.C.H. Yorks. E.R.* v. 9–10.

[65] *Cal. Inq. p.m.* i, p. 132.   [66] Ibid. iv, p. 354.

[67] *Cal. Chart. R.* 1327–41, 328–9, 446–7; *Cal. Pat.* 1354–8, 13, 185; *Cal. Close*, 1377–81, 178; *Cal. Inq. Misc.* vi, p. 202.   [68] E.R.A.O., DDCC/23/1.

[69] Ibid. DDCC/139/7; P.R.O., SC 6/Hen. VIII/4302; Poulson, *Holderness*, i. 460–1.

[70] P.R.O., E 318/23/1296; *L. & P. Hen. VIII*, xix (2), p. 315, which incorrectly has 'Whelstone'.

[71] P.R.O., C 142/111, no. 34.

[72] E.R.A.O., DDCC/23/3.

[73] Ibid. DDCC/24/1; P.R.O., C 142/111, no. 34; *Yorks. Fines*, i. 162; *Cal. Pat.* 1557–8, 359.

[74] E.R.A.O., DDCC/23/7; *Yorks. Fines*, i. 303; *Cal. Pat.* 1563–6, p. 264. Other Whetstones released their rights in 1573: E.R.A.O., DDCC/23/8.

[75] E.R.A.O., DDCC/23/11–12; DDCC/24/1; *Yorks. Fines*, ii. 184; iii. 112; *Cal. Pat.* 1580–2, p. 279; Poulson, *Holderness*, i. 461. Other parts of the estate were sold earlier: *Yorks. Fines*, iii. 41, 98.

[76] E.R.A.O., DDCC/23/13–15, 21–2; above this section.

[77] E.R.A.O., DDCC/24/2–5.

[78] *Abbrev. Plac.* (Rec. Com.), 190.

[79] *Cal. Chart. R.* 1327–41, 328–9; *Cal. Pat.* 1338–40, 193, 286–7.   [80] *Cal. Chart. R.* 1327–41, 470–1.

[81] *Cal. Pat.* 1343–5, 141.

[82] Ibid. 1396–9, 281.

[83] It was so described retrospectively in 1338: H.U.L., DHO/5/58.

[84] English, *Holderness*, 173.

[85] *Cal. Chart. R.* 1327–41, 328–9, 446–7, 470–1; *Cal. Pat.* 1354–8, 13, 185; 1396–9, 281; 1399–1401, 152–3; 1422–9, 59–60; *Cal. Close*, 1377–81, 178; *Cal. Inq. Misc.* vi. 202; *Cal. Inq. p.m.* i, p. 132.

[86] *E.Y.C.* iii, pp. 27–8.

[87] *Feud. Aids*, vi. 162; *Cal. Chart. R.* 1327–41, 328–9.

[88] Above, this section (Cleeton).

[89] *Cal. Pat.* 1557–8, 39.

[90] H.U.L., DCC/2/63.

[91] E.R.A.O., DDCC/85/1–8; DDCC/141/6; *V.C.H. Yorks. E.R.* v. 10; below, this section (Cleeton). For the Constables, J. Foster, *Pedigrees of Yorks.* iii; Burke, *Land. Gent.* (1952), 514.

[92] Ibid. DDCC/139/7; P.R.O., E 134/8 & 9 Chas. I Hil./4; ibid. SC 6/Hen. VIII/4302.

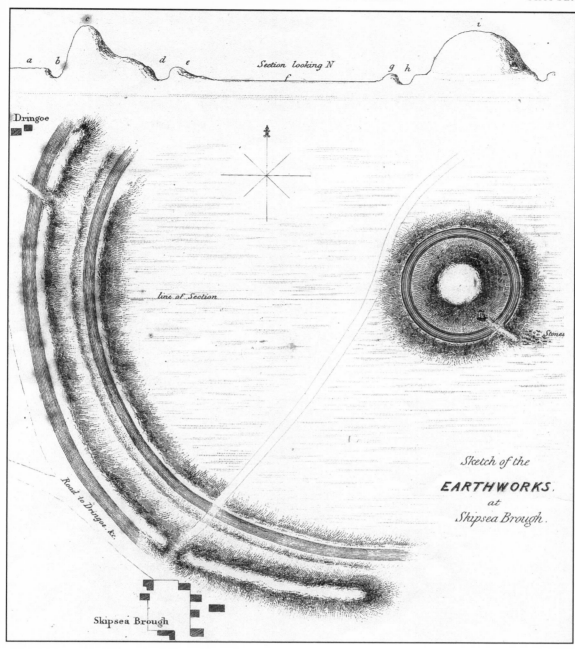

FIG. 34. SKIPSEA CASTLE EARTHWORKS

of Skipsea in 1765 for the pasture rights of his pennygrave, or rent-collector. Copyhold allotments in Skipsea belonging to Cleeton manor then totalled 770 a. and those of Skipsea manor 612 a.,[93] and the latter manor included c. 18 a. more of copyhold at Brough.[94] Some 200 a. was enfranchised in Skipsea c. 1780,[95] about 60 a. in 1890,[96] and 153 a. in 1908.[97] The rest of the land was freed in the 1920s and 1930s.[98]

A motte and bailey castle was built at Skipsea soon after the Conquest, it is said by Drew de Bevrère.[99] It was recorded but not named c. 1100 with its church.[1] Military tenants on the Aumale fee held land by the service of guarding the castle[2] but that obligation was later commuted to a money rent.[3] Skipsea castle is believed to have been disused by the early 13th century,[4] and in 1221 it was ordered to be destroyed

93 R.D.B., AF/180/9; 232/171/146; Poulson, *Holderness*, i. 447.
94 R.D.B., AC/178/9.
95 E.R.A.O., DDCC/111/38; ibid. DDHE/33, f. 24; R.D.B., AW/21/41.
96 R.D.B., 37/296/279 (1890).
97 E.R.A.O., DDCC(2)/82 (vol. ii).

98 R.D.B., 363/127/106; 559/435/348; 592/413/335; 670/182/157.
99 *Chron. de Melsa* (Rolls Ser.), i. 89.
1 *E.Y.C.* iii, p. 27; below, churches.
2 *E.Y.C.* iii, pp. 109–10.
3 English, *Holderness*, 173–4; *Cal. Inq. p.m.* iv, p. 137, etc.
4 English, *Holderness*, 173.

because of William de Forz's rebellion.[5] Presumably anachronistically, the castle continued to be recorded into the 15th century.[6] Wapentake courts may have been held occasionally at Skipsea castle until the mid 13th century, and the sheriff's tourn for the North division of Holderness was held at Skipsea or Skipsea Brough c. 1600.[7] After the demolition of the castle, its site of nearly 20 a. was used for pasture.[8] It seems to have been encroached upon, and in 1397 the 'castle' was said to be waste and of no net value.[9] The surviving earthworks comprise the motte, a conical mound c. 90 m. in diameter at the base and c. 12 m. high with a ditch around it, and lower banks enclosing a crescent-shaped bailey on higher ground to the west of the motte.[10] A bank also remains on the east side of the castle site but otherwise the complex was evidently protected by the mere, fed by streams flowing close to the motte and along the western side of the bailey.[11] The only evidence of building is a stretch of cobble walling on the side of the motte.

After the demolition of the castle, the counts of Aumale may have lived in Cleeton manor house,[12] and during the Crown's possession of Holderness the king evidently stayed there.[13] The manor house was presumably Hallgarth, situated on a small hill just south of Skipsea village. The site may have been moated.[14] The chapel, hall, and great or high chamber of the house were mentioned in the 13th and 14th centuries,[15] but by the 16th only the brick foundations remained.[16]

One of the larger copyhold estates in Skipsea belonged to the Johnsons. Francis Johnson (d. by 1658) was succeeded by his son James in 1 carucate and 1½ bovate and several houses.[17] James Johnson, who also held land in Ulrome, and his wife Mary sold a house and 1 carucate and 5 bovates to John Pockley in 1673.[18] Pockley (d. 1679 or 1680) was succeeded in 1680 by his nephew, George Pockley, but in 1682 John's widow Mary (prob. d. c. 1710) was also admitted. Robert Pockley, probably the son of John

Pockley's nephew Thomas, had the estate from 1712 until 1743, when he sold it to his brother-in-law Fountayne Osbaldeston. Osbaldeston bought other land in 1758,[19] and at inclosure in 1765 he was awarded 240 a.[20] The estate descended under the will of Osbaldeston (d. 1770) in turn to his great-nephew Humphrey Brooke, later Humphrey Osbaldeston (d. 1835), Bertram Mitford, later Bertram Osbaldeston-Mitford (d. 1842), great-grandson of Fountayne Osbaldeston's sister Mary Mitford, and then to Bertram's brother Robert Mitford.[21] Under the Mitford Estate Act of 1854,[22] Skipsea Grange farm with 151 a. and an 83-a. farm were sold in 1855 to William Hornby[23] (d. 1871). In 1889 Hornby's heirs released the estate to the trustees of the mortgagee, Sir James Walker, Bt. (d. 1883).[24] The farms were enfranchised in 1908.[25] In 1912 Sir Robert Walker, Bt., divided and sold the estate at Skipsea, Mary Simpson buying Skipsea Grange farm with 179 a.[26] Mrs. Simpson (d. 1919) was evidently succeeded by Susannah Nattriss (d. 1926) and Susannah's brother J. H. Nattriss. The Air Council bought 122 a. in 1928, and John Rafton the farmhouse and 52 a. in 1929. Skipsea Grange farm descended to Mary Rafton (d. 1967), whose successor was Joan Wray; it still belonged to the Wrays in 1997.[27]

Land at Skipsea Brough belonging to the Aumale fee was held in the 14th century by the Lorrimer family in return for their service at the wapentake court.[28]

In 1066 Thorkil and Thorsten held two manors of *ULROME* with 2½ carucates. They passed to Drew de Bevrère[29] and were later part of the Aumale fee. Ulrome was later reckoned to contain 4 carucates.[30]

In 1086 Drew's estate at Ulrome was held by Erenbald.[31] Most of the Aumale fee there was later held by a family named from the place. Its members may have included an abbot of Meaux and the 14th-century artist-monk John of Ulrome.[32] The first-known tenant of the 3-carucate holding at Ulrome was Adelin, who was

5 *Rot. Litt. Claus.* (Rec. Com.), i. 474.
6 *Cal. Pat.* 1232–47, 258; 1340–3, 89; 1396–9, 281; 1422–9, 59–60.
7 E.R.A.O., DDCC/112/6; *V.C.H. Yorks. E.R.* v. 4–5; English, *Holderness*, 112.
8 P.R.O., SC 6/1079/15, m. 8; SC 6/1081/1, m. 2.
9 *Cal. Inq. Misc.* iii, p. 20; vi, pp. 201–2.
10 Pevsner and Neave, *Yorks. E.R.* 686; Poulson, *Holderness*, i. 458–9 (illus.); *V.C.H. Yorks.* ii. 37–9 (illus.); *Y.A.J.* xxiv. 260–2 (illus.); K. J. Allison, *E.R. of Yorks. Landscape*, pl. 10; Humber Archaeology Partnership, 'Survey of Skipsea Castle Earthworks, 1987–8'. The earthworks were placed in the guardianship of the Commissioners of Works and Public Buildings in 1911: B.I.H.R., CC. Ab. 10 Skips.
11 O.S. Map 6", Yorks. CLXXX (1855 edn.).
12 *E.Y.C.* iii, p. 52 n.; *V.C.H. Yorks.* iii. 204.
13 *Cal. Inq. p.m.* viii, p. 258; *Cal. Inq. Misc.* i, p. 447.
14 O.S. Map 6", Yorks. CLXXX (1855 edn.); Poulson, *Holderness*, i. 455; H. E. J. le Patourel, *Moated Sites of Yorks.* 116.
15 P.R.O., SC 6/1078/12, m. 6; SC 6/1079/15, m. 8; SC 6/1082/5, m. 6.
16 Ibid. E 134/8 & 9 Chas. I Hil./4; E.R.A.O., DDCC/139/7.

17 E.R.A.O., DDCC/24/2, s.v. 19 Apr. 1655; DDCC/85/3, s.vv. 19 Apr. 1655; 12 Oct. 1658.
18 Ibid. DDCC/24/2, s.v. 15 Oct. 1673; DDCC/85/4, s.v. 15 Oct. 1673.
19 Ibid. DDCC/24/2–4; DDCC/85/4–5; DDCC(2)/83 (vol. i); for the Osbaldestons, Brookes, and Mitfords, Burke, *Land. Gent.* (1898), i. 517–18, 1039–40; for the Pockleys, Poulson, *Holderness*, i. 240–1.
20 R.D.B., AF/180/9.
21 E.R.A.O., DDX/187/4.
22 17 & 18 Vic. c. 18 (Private), copy at E.R.A.O., DDHB/16/2.
23 E.R.A.O., DDCC(2)/82 (vol. i), 83 (vol. iii).
24 Ibid. DDCC(2)/82 (vol. ii); 83 (vol. iv).
25 Ibid. DDCC(2)/82 (vol. ii); DDCC(2)/83 (vol. iv).
26 R.D.B., 140/554/497; 140/555/498; 141/206/184; 141/208/185; Burke, *Peerage & Baronetage* (1970), 2735.
27 R.D.B., 198/291/250; 361/45/29; 376/458/381; 383/391/332; 1532/2/2; inf. from Mrs F. Davies, Skipsea Grange, 1997.
28 *Cal. Fine R.* 1327–37, 334; *Cal. Inq. p. m.* vii, p. 336.
29 *V.C.H. Yorks.* ii. 267.
30 *Kirkby's Inquest*, 372.
31 *V.C.H. Yorks.* ii. 267.
32 Poulson, *Holderness*, i. 231.

succeeded by his son Ralph of Ulrome between 1150 and 1170; a rent of 30s. a year payable to the count of Aumale from the estate was assigned by the count to Bridlington priory soon afterwards, when the tenant was named as Robert of Ulrome, perhaps Ralph's son.[33] Robert's son Ralph occurred in the late 12th century,[34] and another (Sir) Robert of Ulrome had the estate in the mid 13th.[35] The 3 carucates may have been partitioned in the 13th century for the rent owed to Bridlington priory from the Ulrome family's part was later only 15s.[36] About 1260 Adam of Hornsea held 1½ carucate and William of Buckton the same.[37] (Sir) Adam of Ulrome, perhaps the same as Adam of Hornsea, was, nevertheless, given as the tenant of all 3 carucates in 1284–5,[38] but in 1302–3 the holding was shared between (Sir) William of Buckton and John of Ulrome, probably in succession to his father, Hugh of Carlisle.[39] John of Ulrome was recorded as one of the two lords of Ulrome in 1316, and in 1322 after his death he was found to have held ULROME manor of William de Ros, Lord Ros, and Bridlington priory. His son Hugh inherited the manor.[40] Part of the land was settled for life on John of Ulrome, another of John's sons. Hugh (d. 1352) was succeeded in almost 2 carucates at Ulrome by his son William,[41] who further divided the holding by grant of a moiety to Geoffrey St. Quintin and his wife Constance. The part remaining to William of Ulrome's son William in 1367 comprised four houses, a mill, 1 carucate and 3½ bovates, and pasture land.[42] Land of the Ros fee, and possibly other land, passed from the Ulromes to the Grimston family, tenants at Ulrome in the 1530s,[43] and later to six freeholders of Roos manor.[44] Their holdings have not been traced.

The Bucktons' share of Ulrome evidently descended to Constance de Shulton (d. 1349). It then comprised 1 carucate and 2 bovates and ten tofts, held of the Crown as successor to the counts of Aumale as ¼₀ knight's fee and by payment of 15s. a year to Bridlington priory, 3 bovates held of the Roses, and the same of the Greystokes. Her son Sir Richard de Shulton[45] and William of Buckton's son John settled it on Shulton for life in 1356, and in 1359 John of Buckton granted the reversion to John of

Wallewyk, his wife Margaret, and their heirs.[46] It was apparently that estate which the Goxhills had in the 16th century. Comprising 1 carucate and 2 bovates, houses, and meadow land held under the Crown's manor of Burstwick as ¼₅ knight's fee and a house and 2 bovates belonging to the Ros fee, it descended from Robert Goxhill (d. 1529) to his son Henry (d. 1550), who left two infant daughters Joan and Gertrude.[47] The Goxhills' estate was said to have passed to Leonard Robinson[48] and presumably descended with his other land in Ulrome.[49]

The Fauconbergs held 1 carucate at Ulrome. Walter de Fauconberg endowed Nunkeeling priory with land there c. 1200.[50] W. de Fauconberg, recorded as the tenant in the mid 13th century,[51] was perhaps Walter de Fauconberg, later baron Fauconberg, who held the estate at Ulrome by the 1280s.[52] The land later descended with the Fauconbergs' estate at Dringhoe and with Rise manor to Ralph Neville (d. 1425), earl of Westmorland, and his successors.[53] In 1624 three freeholders, including Leonard Robinson's heirs and Christopher Hartas, held 4 houses, 6 bovates, and other land as appurtenances of Rise manor.[54]

Land in Ulrome held by the Brus family may have passed to the Roses as coheirs.[55] William de Ros, later Lord Ros of Helmsley (Yorks. N.R.), held 1 carucate of the Aumale fee there in 1287.[56] The estate descended as a member of Roos manor in the Roses, Lords Ros,[57] and their successors, the Manners family, earls of Rutland, and the Cecils, earls of Exeter.[58] A rental of Roos manor dated 1558 almost certainly includes later details and exaggerates the size of the Ros fee there.[59]

The relationship of William de Wyvill, named as the second lord of Ulrome in 1316, with the preceding estates is unknown.[60]

Thomas Lacy (d. 1525) held part of the Ros fee as a manor of ULROME. He was succeeded in turn by his son Robert (d. 1556) and grandson Brian (d. 1579). Brian's widow Elizabeth and sons William and Robert[61] sold the manor, together with the advowson of Ulrome chapel,

[33] E.Y.C. iii, pp. 106–7; Bridlington Chart. p. 103.
[34] E.Y.C. v, p. 344; ix, p. 133.
[35] Yorks. Fines, 1218–31, p. 79; Kirkby's Inquest, 372. Poulson, Holderness, i. 189, dated by English, Holderness, 77.
[36] Cal. Inq. p.m. x, p. 16.
[37] P.R.O., SC 12/17/43.
[38] E.R.A.O., DDML/5/2(a); Feud. Aids, vi. 41.
[39] E.R.A.O., DDML/5/2(a); Kirkby's Inquest, 245; Cal. Inq. Misc. iii, p. 18.
[40] Feud. Aids, vi. 162; Cal. Inq. p.m. vi, p. 225; viii, pp. 342–3.
[41] Cal. Inq. p.m. vii, p. 336; x, p. 16.
[42] P.R.O., C 44/5/3; H.U.L., DHO/16/16.
[43] L. & P. Hen. VIII, xiv (1), p. 309; Valor Eccl. (Rec. Com.), v. 109.
[44] H.U.L., DDSY/56/1. The problems of this source are discussed below, this section [Ros fee].
[45] Cal. Inq. p.m. x, pp. 70–1.
[46] H.U.L., DHO/16/16; Cal. Pat. 1354–8, 422; 1358–61, 302.
[47] P.R.O., C 142/50, no. 143; H.U.L., DHO/7/34.

[48] H.U.L., DDSY/56/1. For the source, below, this section [Ros fee].
[49] Below, this section [Lacy].
[50] B.L. Cott. MS. Otho. C. viii, f. 94; Complete Peerage, s.v. Fauconberge.   [51] Kirkby's Inquest, 372.
[52] Feud. Aids, vi. 40; Cal. Inq. p.m. iv, p. 357.
[53] P.R.O., C 142/584, no. 57; Cal. Inq. p.m. ix, pp. 176–7; xviii, p. 136; below, this section (Dringhoe).
[54] H.U.L., DDKG/9; above, below, this section [Robinson, Hartas].
[55] Below, this section (Dringhoe).
[56] Cal. Inq. p.m. iv, pp. 352, 354; Feud. Aids, vi. 39.
[57] Cal. Inq. p.m. vi, p. 225; viii, pp. 331, 341–3; x, p. 16; Complete Peerage.
[58] P.R.O., CP 25(2)/527/7 Chas. I Mic. [no. 13]; N. Country Wills, i (Sur. Soc. cxvi), p. 186; Yorks. Fines, 1614–25, 168; above, Roos, manors.
[59] H.U.L., DDSY/56/1.
[60] Feud. Aids, vi. 162.
[61] P.R.O., C 142/44, no. 153; C 142/109, no. 44; C 142/189, no. 55.

to Leonard Robinson the elder in 1582–3.[62] Robinson's estate at Ulrome evidently included other land.[63] When Leonard Robinson, perhaps the purchaser, died in 1600, he was said, probably inaccurately, to have held the manor with nearly 4 carucates under Rise manor as ¹⁄₂₀ knight's fee. Ulrome manor later evidently descended from father to son in Leonard Robinsons of Newton Garth[64] until 1657, when it and the advowson were said to have been bought by George Hartas.[65] John and William Hartas had, however, been dealing with part of the estate, and the advowson, as early as 1600–01,[66] and George's father, Christopher Hartas (d. 1626), had held a free rent, the advowson of Ulrome chapel, eight houses, over 1 carucate of open-field land, and many closes in the township.[67] George Hartas (fl. 1663)[68] was probably succeeded by his son Joseph. By the marriage of Joseph's sister Alathea to Thomas Shipton, or by a sale of 1699, the Ulrome estate passed to Shipton.[69] After his death the manor was sold in 1717 to Giles Rickaby, a Bridlington merchant. It then comprised a farm with 3½ bovates, and other houses and closes.[70] Rickaby (d. 1729) and his son John enlarged the estate by piecemeal purchases, one, of 1762, including 4 bovates.[71] John Rickaby (d. 1785) was succeeded by his nephew John Rickaby (d. 1813),[72] and he by his brother Charles (d. 1838) and Charles's son John. The estate comprised c. 460 a. at Ulrome in 1843.[73] From John Rickaby (d. 1860) it descended to his son, also John, who in 1925 conveyed c. 540 a., mostly in Manor and two other farms, to two sisters, Catherine and Charlotte Rickaby, as common tenants. After Charlotte's death in 1931, Catherine was the sole owner.[74] Many small sales were made in the earlier 20th century, reducing the estate[75] to c. 490 a. by 1954.[76] Catherine Rickaby died in 1964, and in 1966 her executors vested the estate in William Isherwood and his wife Grace.[77] In 1967 Manor House, the farmhouse of Manor farm, was sold to Robert Punt, and the farmland added to Ulrome Grange farm, which Robert Watson bought c. 1980. That farm had been divided and sold by 1997.[78]

The manor house was said to have been rebuilt in the mid 17th century by George Hartas, who had a house with five hearths in 1672, and again in 1785.[79] It is built on a lobby-entry plan, with brown brick walls and a pan-tiled roof.[80]

James Johnson evidently sold land in Ulrome, with his estate in Skipsea, to John Pockley in 1673,[81] and both later descended in turn to George and Robert Pockley. The latter (d. 1744) was succeeded in Ulrome by his daughter Theodosia, her husband Gabriel Brooke (d. 1781), and their son Humphrey.[82] At inclosure in 1767 Gabriel and Humphrey Brooke received 220 a. for their commonable land.[83] Humphrey Brooke duly succeeded also to the Skipsea estate, and took the name Osbaldeston instead of Brooke.[84] He died in 1835 and was succeeded in Ulrome by his daughter Theodosia Osbaldeston, later Theodosia Brooke (d. 1850),[85] and then by his granddaughter Jane Robson, later Jane Brooke (d. 1871). A grandson of Humphrey Osbaldeston's sister Mary Firman, Humphrey Brooke Firman (d. 1868), had an interest in the estate from 1856, however, and his son, also Humphrey Brooke Firman, is said to have succeeded Jane Brooke in 1871. In 1880 Firman had two farms in Ulrome with 362 a.[86] In 1919 Old Hall farm with 205 a. was sold to Maria Watson, and East End farm, of 153 a., to Charles Washington.[87] In 1942 Old Hall farm was vested in Mrs. Watson's children, Francis, Tom, and Mary Watson, and it remained with the family, trading as F. S. Watson & Sons, which in 1970 bought the 102-a. Heron's farm in Skipsea and Ulrome and 51 a. in Dringhoe.[88] In 1997 the farmland of Hall farm belonged to Francis Watson's grandson Geoffrey Watson, and the outbuildings to Geoffrey's cousin Derrick Watson; the farmhouse had by then been sold.[89]

In 1672 James Johnson had a house with 10 hearths at Ulrome, presumably that later called Ulrome Hall. The house may have been rebuilt by the Pockleys, and comprised a house with two wings until, before 1840, the centre block was demolished and the west and east wings left as the farmhouse and a barn respectively.[90]

The trustees of Timothy Woolfe's charity benefiting the poor of Bridlington had 31 a. at Ulrome from 1760.[91]

[62] *Yorks. Fines*, ii. 195. Cf. H.U.L., DDSY/56/1, which is discussed above, this section [Ros fee].
[63] Above, this section [Goxhill, Fauconberg].
[64] P.R.O., C 142/261, no. 14; C 142/587, no. 5; Poulson, *Holderness*, ii. 179; *V.C.H. Yorks. E.R.* v. 118.
[65] Poulson, *Holderness*, i. 228–9
[66] *Yorks. Fines*, iv. 159.
[67] P.R.O., C 142/425, no. 71; C 142/554, no. 72.
[68] B.I.H.R., ER. V./CB. 1, ff. 95v.–97v.; Poulson, *Holderness*, i. 232.
[69] H.U.L., DDSY/56/8; ibid. DDFA(2)/2/46; B.I.H.R., Bp. Dio. 3, E.R., p. 183; Poulson, *Holderness*, i. 229.
[70] R.D.B., F/98/215.
[71] Ibid. G/263/586; G/423/916; L/45/85; Q/178/432; X/470/1098; Z/41/92; AD/531/1068; AU/9/16.
[72] Ibid. BR/544/882; CS/374/528.
[73] Ibid. DC/370/504; FH/124/119; FW/70/65; FX/397/474. For the Rickabys, Poulson, *Holderness*, i. 229–30.
[74] R.D.B., 301/402/307; 627/298/236; 663/466/415.
[75] Ibid. 233/503/406; 869/422/355, etc.
[76] Ibid. 1064/214/190.

[77] Ibid. 1406/396/364; 1443/267/235.
[78] Ibid. 1514/109/93; inf. from Mrs. Houghton, Ulrome, 1997.
[79] P.R.O., E 179/205/504; Poulson, *Holderness*, i. 240.
[80] Dept. of Environment, *Buildings List* (1987).
[81] Above, this section [Skipsea, Johnson]; Poulson, *Holderness*, i. 232, 240.
[82] P.R.O., E 134/2 Anne Trin./16; R.D.B., U/45/95; for the Pockleys, Brookes, and Firmans, Burke, *Land. Gent.* (1898), i. 517–18.
[83] R.D.B., AH/331/9.
[84] Above, this section [Skipsea, Johnson].
[85] E.R.A.O., DDX/187/4; DDX/325/5; B.I.H.R., TA. 581s.
[86] R.D.B., MZ/5/8; NA/265/421; 108/298/268.
[87] Ibid. 198/151/125; 198/296/255.
[88] Ibid. 655/513/435; 1126/446/387; 1391/263/231; 1657/256/219; 1680/84/76.
[89] Inf. from Mrs. Joan Thornton, Ulrome, 1997.
[90] P.R.O., E 179/205/504; Poulson, *Holderness*, i. 240.
[91] E.R.A.O., NV/1/82; *V.C.H. Yorks.* ii. 81.

Peter de Brus (d. 1272) held 5 carucates of the Aumale fee in Dringhoe and Ulrome.[92] His heirs included his sisters Margaret de Ros and Agnes, wife of Walter de Fauconberg, later baron Fauconberg.[93] The Fauconbergs inherited land at Dringhoe, where their son, Walter de Fauconberg, baron Fauconberg (d. 1318), was recorded as one of the two lords in 1316.[94] His son, John de Fauconberg (d. 1349), baron Fauconberg, held 2 carucates and 3 bovates in Dringhoe. As a member of the Fauconbergs' manor of Rise, the estate descended to Ralph Neville, earl of Westmorland (d. 1425).[95]

The estate at Dringhoe and Ulrome was probably held of the Bruses by the Stutvilles as an appurtenance of their manor of Burton Agnes, before passing to the Merlays by the marriage of Alice de Stutville (d. 1219) and Roger de Merlay.[96] Their grandson Roger de Merlay (d. 1265) certainly held it with Burton Agnes of Peter de Brus. The Merlays' estate at Dringhoe and Ulrome was evidently subinfeudated, like Mappleton, to Alice de Merlay's sister Agnes de Stutville and her husband Herbert de St. Quintin (d. by 1223), and in 1279 the tenant was given as their grandson Herbert de St. Quintin. Other tenants had, however, been named at Dringhoe in 1266, and no more is heard of the St. Quintins' interest. Roger de Merlay's daughter Mary, wife of William de Greystoke,[97] evidently succeeded to Dringhoe and Ulrome on the partition of her father's lands, and the 5 carucates were later held by her son, Sir John de Greystoke, baron Greystoke (d. 1306),[98] before passing to his cousin, Sir Ralph Fitz-William. He was returned as the other lord of Dringhoe in 1316,[99] and in 1317 the estate at Dringhoe and Ulrome was held of his son, Robert FitzRalph, as ⅛ knight's fee.[1] The estate, said to have been enlarged by purchase in the early 14th century,[2] later descended in Robert's heirs, the Greystokes, barons Greystoke.[3] By the marriage of Elizabeth Greystoke, Lady Greystoke, and Thomas Dacre, Lord Dacre of Gilsland, the estate passed to the Dacres,[4] and then to Elizabeth, sister and co-heir of George Dacre, Lord Dacre and Greystoke (d. 1569), and her husband William Howard, Lord Howard.

Comprising three farms in the 16th century[5] and then and later called *DRINGHOE* manor, it was sold by the Howards, with appurtenances in Ulrome, to William Shawe in 1608.[6] In 1618 Shawe, Robert Booth, and their wives sold the manor to Thomas and John Pearson, and another part of the estate at Dringhoe was then sold by the Shawes alone to William Lister.[7] Thomas and John Pearson added to their holding in Dringhoe by purchase.[8] Thomas Pearson alone was lord in 1637.[9] John Pearson (d. by 1718) had Dringhoe manor before his son, also John, who sold it in 1743 to Hugh Bethell. The estate, which extended into Upton and Brough, then included 2 carucates and 2½ bovates,[10] and at inclosure in 1763 Bethell's son, also Hugh, was awarded 326 a.[11] Comprising c. 385 a. in all, Dringhoe manor later descended in the Bethells with Rise manor.[12] In 1882 a new farmhouse, later Manor Farm, Dringhoe, was built c. ¾ km. west of the manor house.[13] The estate, then of 401 a., was sold in 1891 to Christopher Pickering (d. 1920), who devised it to Edward Cartwright (d. 1937).[14] Cartwright's representative sold 121 a. in 1946, and in 1947 vested the rest of Manor farm, then of 250 a., in Elsie Watson (d. 1957).[15] In the 1980s the farm was sold to N. D. Robinson, who added some of the land to Happy Lands farm; the rest was mostly sold soon afterwards to another farmer, and the farmhouse and a little land to R. N. and S. Kirke.[16]

The old manor house of Dringhoe was being rebuilt in 1997 but its outbuildings remained then. The site may once have been moated.[17]

About 1165 William le Gros, count of Aumale, gave Giles the falconer, nephew of Geoffrey de Cauz, 2 carucates at Dringhoe in tail by the service of being his falconer; Giles was to provide a second man and three horses but would receive an allowance from the count.[18] Giles was probably succeeded in the estate by Robert de Cauz, benefactor of Meaux abbey in the late 12th century,[19] in the later 13th century by Robert son of Gilbert de Cauz,[20] and in the early 14th century by one or two Robert Cauces.[21] Robert Cauce (d. by 1342) held part of the Aumale fee in Dringhoe, including a

[92]   In the mid 13th century there were mistakenly said to be 9 carucates at Dringhoe, all part of the Brus fee: *Kirkby's Inquest*, 372.
[93]   *Cal. Inq. p.m.* iv, p. 354; *Yorks. Inq.* i, pp. 201–2; for the Bruses, *E.Y.C.* ii, p. 15.   [94]   *Feud. Aids*, vi. 162.
[95]   *Cal. Inq. p.m.* ix, pp. 176–7; xviii, p. 136; for the Fauconbergs, *Complete Peerage*; above, Rise, manor.
[96]   For the Stutvilles and Merlays, *E.Y.C.* ix, p. 30. Cf. *Cal. Pat.* 1216–25, 343; *E.Y.C.* ix, p. 29.
[97]   *Cal. Inq. p.m.* i, p. 200; *Yorks. Inq.* i, pp. 99–102, 201–2; *E.Y.C.* ix, p. 32; *Complete Peerage*, s.vv. Greystoke, St. Quintin; above, Mappleton, manors.
[98]   *Chron. de Melsa* (Rolls Ser.), ii. 46.
[99]   *Feud. Aids*, vi. 162.
[1]   *Cal. Inq. p.m.* vi, pp. 26, 29–30.
[2]   Below, this section [Thos. of Dringhoe].
[3]   *Cal. Inq. p.m.* vi, pp. 303–4, 306–8; x, pp. 70–1, 420–1; xiv, pp. 29–30; *Cal. Close.* 1402–5, 343–4.
[4]   *Yorks. Fines*, i. 300.
[5]   Notes from an unlocated survey at H.U.L., DDKG/143(a). No examination of the original record, which is probably at Castle Howard, was possible because of a temporary closure of that archive.

[6]   *Yorks. Fines*, iii. 67; 1603–14, 73, 97; *Complete Peerage*, s.vv. Carlisle, Dacre of Gilsland. It was erroneously included in a later settlement on the Howards: P.R.O., CP 25(2)/527/9 Chas. I Hil. no. 13.   [7]   *Yorks. Fines, 1614–25*, 105, 115.
[8]   Ibid. 169, 200.   [9]   P.R.O., C 142/554, no. 72.
[10]   R.D.B., F/187/410; S/3/5.
[11]   Ibid. AC/178/9; J. Foster, *Pedigrees of Yorks.* iii, s.v. Bethell.
[12]   E.R.A.O., DDRI/40/11; ibid. accession 2980, 'Rise Estates 1852' and plan of 1853; above, Rise, manor.
[13]   Brick bearing date: inf. from Mrs. S. Kirke, Dringhoe, 1997.
[14]   R.D.B., 46/348/330 (1891); 232/30/28; 232/431/357; 590/436/350.
[15]   Ibid. 718/552/442; 755/368/312; 1064/444/394.
[16]   Inf. from Mr. and Mrs. N. D. Robinson, Mrs. S. Kirke, Dringhoe, 1997.
[17]   O.S. Map 1/2,500, Yorks. CLXXX. 1 (1892 edn.).
[18]   *E.Y.C.* iii, p. 114.
[19]   *Chron. de Melsa* (Rolls Ser.), i. 223.
[20]   Poulson, *Holderness*, i. 463.
[21]   P.R.O., CP 25(1)/270/92, no. 21; CP 25(1)/272/101, no. 108; *Cal. Pat.* 1324–7, 154.

house and ½ carucate, by knight service and the falconry duty, then involving the keeping of two falcons at Cleeton manor during the king's visits, taking 3s. a day in allowances. He also held nearly 1 carucate more there, mostly of William de Greystoke, baron Greystoke. His son Edmund (d. 1348) was succeeded by a daughter Isabel (d. 1349), whose heir was her uncle John Cauce.[22] No more is known of the estate.

A large estate at Dringhoe and Ulrome was held by Thomas of Dringhoe, who gave over 1 carucate of it to Meaux abbey c. 1200.[23] The rest of his holding, together with the rent owed by the abbey, descended to his daughter Mazelina, wife of Thomas of Meaux, and then to their son John, as John of Dringhoe recorded as the tenant there in 1284–5.[24] John's estate was partitioned between his daughters, Maud, wife of John de Stutville's son William, and Mazelina, probably the wife of John of Paull. In 1317 William de Stutville and John of Paull held ⅑ knight's fee at Dringhoe and Ulrome of Robert FitzRalph.[25] Between 1318 and 1320 the Stutvilles sold Maud's share, including almost 1 carucate in Dringhoe, Ulrome, and Lissett, together with her half of the rent owed by Meaux abbey.[26] Mazelina and her then husband, John son of John of Ulrome, sold almost ½ carucate and other land in Dringhoe and Ulrome in 1325.[27] Her share of the abbey's rent was said to have been sold to the overlord, possibly with other land, and it was perhaps that estate of the Greystokes and their successors which came to be called the manor of Dringhoe.[28]

Margaret de Ros (d. July 1349) held 1 carucate and 1 bovate at Dringhoe of the Crown as successor to the counts of Aumale as 1/48 knight's fee, perhaps as heir to the Goxhills or to Peter de Brus. As at Little Cowden, in Colden Parva, her estate descended in the Despensers and Wentworths.[29] In 1555 Thomas Wentworth, Lord Wentworth, sold lands in Dringhoe and Upton to John Holme and John Goldwell.[30]

Later, the larger estates included that of a branch of the Acklam family. One or more Thomas Acklams held land at Dringhoe in the earlier 17th century. Another Thomas Acklam (probably d. by 1721) was succeeded in Dring-

hoe and Upton by his son, also Thomas. In 1724 the estate comprised, besides Acklam's house and three others, 1 carucate and 1 bovate, closes, and 6 bovates more in Crow Grange farm.[31] It evidently descended, like Beeford manor, to Peter Acklam,[32] who in 1785 and 1786 sold nearly 450 a. in Dringhoe, Upton, Brough, and Beeford in lots. Jeremiah Lamplugh (Lamplough) bought a 98-a. farm in 1785,[33] and in 1805 he or a namesake purchased Dringhoe Hall and c. 115 a. from Peter Acklam's son, also Peter.[34] Lamplugh, whose estate extended into Skipsea, Brough, and Bonwick, died in or shortly before 1835. He devised Dringhoe Hall and c. 120 a., with other land, to his son Jeremiah (d. 1857), who was succeeded by his son George.[35] George Lamplugh bought c. 50 a. in Upton in 1878, and after 1892 William Lamplugh, probably George's son, inherited some 165 a.[36] William Whitlam Lamplugh, who had the estate at Dringhoe and Upton by 1921, sold Dringhoe Hall with 189 a. to Charles Reed in 1940.[37] Like Beeford Grange farm, Dringhoe Hall farm later descended to the Blanchards.[38]

Dringhoe Hall may once have been moated.[39] The present house, of red brick with a pantiled roof, is thought to date from the 17th century but has been much altered.[40] It was named as Dringhoe Hall in 1779, when it was used as a farmhouse.[41] The house was sold to C. G. Kirkwood, the present owner, in 1983.[42]

For unknown reason, North Frodingham manor included nearly 40 a. of copyhold in Dringhoe, Upton, and Brough and 16 a. at Ulrome in the mid 18th century.[43]

The Aumale fee included land at Bonwick, where William le Gros (d. 1179), count of Aumale, gave 6 carucates as ½ knight's fee to Thomas son of Uvieht; he is perhaps to be identified with Thomas son of Ulviet, a York alderman and moneyer, whose work in Yorkshire may have included the coins issued from the count's new town of Hedon.[44] The Bonwick estate was held with land in Moreby, in Stillingfleet, throughout the Middle Ages. In 1205 or 1206 Agnes, widow of Thomas beyond the Ouse, claimed dower in both places against Thomas's son William.[45] Thomas of Merston held the estate at Bonwick[46] before 1268, when his son

[22] *Cal. Inq. p.m.* viii, pp. 258–9; ix, pp. 85, 290–1.
[23] Following based on *Chron. de Melsa* (Rolls Ser.), ii. 45–6, 289–90. Below, this section [Meaux abbey].
[24] *Feud. Aids*, vi. 41.
[25] *Cal. Inq. p. m.* vi, pp. 26, 29–30.
[26] P.R.O., CP 25(1)/270/91, no. 39; CP 25(1)/270/92, nos. 21, 39; CP 25(1)/271/94, no. 71; E.R.A.O., DDCC/30/1.
[27] P.R.O., CP 25(1)/272/101, nos. 108, 117. Land and rent at Ulrome being dealt with in 1323 by John, his father's widow, and Mazelina seems to have belonged to Mazelina rather than the Ulromes: P.R.O., CP 25(1)/271/99, no. 10.
[28] Above, this section (Dringhoe).
[29] *Cal. Inq. p.m.* ix, pp. 190–4; xviii, p. 132; above, Mappleton, manors (Little Cowden). Cf. P.R.O., SC 6/1077/15; cf. for identification of estate, *Miscellanea*, iv (Y.A.S. Rec. Ser. xciv), 98.
[30] *Yorks. Fines*, i. 189.
[31] E.R.A.O., DDX/152/8, 13; R.D.B., G/459/983; H/652/1322; H/679/1381–2; I/8/12; Poulson, *Holderness*, i. 464. For para., cf. above, Beeford, manors (Beeford, Crow).

For Acklams, below, this section (Bonwick).
[32] R.D.B., U/188/351; AT/395/42; BC/19/21.
[33] Ibid. BI/353/551; BI/436/692; BI/437/693; BI/444/707; BI/479/754.
[34] Ibid. BU/376/575; CH/173/261.
[35] Ibid. EX/269/304; HR/58/59; HR/59/68; E.R.A.O., DDCC(2)/83, vol. iv, s.v. 27 Oct. 1858.
[36] R.D.B., MR/123/181; NQ/382/497; E.R.A.O., NV/1/109; P.R.O., RG 11/4797; Bulmer, *Dir. E. Yorks.* (1892), 502–3.
[37] R.D.B., 233/60/47; 637/496/418.
[38] Above, Beeford, manors (Beeford).
[39] O.S. Map 6", Yorks. CLXXX (1855 edn.).
[40] Pevsner and Neave, *Yorks. E.R.* 687; Department of Environment, *Buildings List* (1987).
[41] R.D.B., BC/19/21.
[42] Inf. from Mr. Kirkwood, 1997.
[43] R.D.B., AC/178/9; AH/331/9.
[44] *Y.A.J.* xxxix. 341–2; English, *Holderness*, 158–9, 216.
[45] *Rot. de Ob. et Fin.* (Rec. Com.), 312–13.

William subinfeudated it to John of Carlton; apart from 6⅔ bovates, most of the land was then held by Thomas of Merston's widow and another woman, presumably also a dowager, for life and had thus to be granted to Carlton in reversion. It was presumably in connexion with Carlton's acquisition of Bonwick that a rent there was released to him the next year.[47] It was perhaps another John of Carlton who had 2 carucates and 2 bovates at Bonwick in demesne in 1287, and whose tenants then occupied 3 carucates and 4 bovates more.[48] He settled Bonwick on Alexander of Carlton in 1302,[49] and Alexander was one of the two lords of Bonwick and its members in 1316.[50] In or soon after 1323 he granted almost all his estate, comprising a house, 6 tofts, 2½ carucates, and rents in Bonwick, to Robert of Moreby and his heirs.[51] The Morebys had had an interest in Bonwick as early as 1269.[52] In 1333 free warren at Bonwick was granted to Moreby and his son William, who as Sir William of Moreby had inherited by 1367.[53] In 1378 Sir William settled 3 carucates and 6 bovates and 22 houses at Bonwick on his sister Mary, relict of Sir William Acklam and then wife of Sir William Percy,[54] and *BONWICK* manor later passed, like Moreby, to the Acklams.[55] John Acklam (d. 1551) was succeeded in Bonwick by his grandson William (d. 1567), and William by his son John[56] (d. 1611) and grandson Sir William Acklam.[57] Sir William evidently enlarged his estate by purchase from Sir Richard Michelbourne in 1616.[58] Sir William (d. 1637) was succeeded by his son John (d. 1644), and he by his daughter Elizabeth,[59] who married Sir Mark Milbanke, Bt. (d. 1680).[60] Bonwick manor descended in turn to Elizabeth Acklam's son Sir Mark Milbanke, Bt. (d. 1698) and grandsons Sir Mark Milbanke, Bt. (d. 1705) and Sir Ralph Milbanke, Bt., who sold it and land in Dunnington, in Beeford, to Dr. Henry Johnson in 1722.[61] Johnson was succeeded by his daughters, Judith, Martha, Frances, and Elizabeth, Elizabeth selling her undivided ¼ share to her sisters in 1751. Martha, Frances, and Judith (d. by 1782) Johnson bought c. 80 a. in Bonwick from Robert Grimston in 1771. The reversion of the whole estate was settled on the Revd. Major Dawson,

son of Mary Dawson, in 1782.[62] Inheriting c. 1790, Dawson (d. 1829 or 1830)[63] was evidently succeeded by another Major Dawson, who had the manor and nearly 700 a. in High and Low Bonwick farms in 1862.[64] Edmund Dawson, recorded as the owner from 1879, had apparently been succeeded by 1892 by a Mrs. Dawson,[65] and by 1895 by Mary Johnston (d. by 1910), whose trustees later held the farms.[66] In 1921 High Bonwick farm, with 395 a., was sold to William Rafton, and the 318-a. Low Bonwick farm to Frederick and John Towse. In 1937 George Wreathall bought High Bonwick from the mortgagee.[67] Wreathall (d. 1970) was succeeded by Robert Wreathall, who gave High Bonwick farm to his wife Suzanne in 1973.[68] The Wreathall family still had the farm in 1997.[69]

The manor house was alternatively called a farmhouse in 1722.[70]

The other lord of Bonwick and its members in 1316 was William de Ros's son John,[71] but no more is known of that estate.

Tenants at Bonwick have also included the Cauce family, which held a small part of the Aumale fee there by knight service in the mid 14th century.[72]

Brian Routh (d. 1483) held 40 a. in Bonwick of the Knights Hospitaller. The land descended mostly like Tansterne manor, in Aldbrough. At partition in 1614 between Sir Richard Michelbourne and Thomas Michelbourne who had half shares in a considerable estate in Holderness, the land at Bonwick fell to Sir Richard.[73] He evidently sold it to Sir William Acklam in 1616.[74]

Skipsea *RECTORY* belonged to Meaux abbey, which in the earlier 14th century was apparently successful in claiming withheld fish tithes from the lord of Cleeton manor, and wool and lamb tithes.[75] Part of the glebe, comprising tofts and crofts in Skipsea and Newhithe, and in Ulrome 1 bovate and the small tithes, was let to tenants in the late 14th century.[76] In 1535 the rectory was valued at £31 14s. 4d. gross. The glebe then comprised 1 carucate, two closes,

[46] *Kirkby's Inquest*, 372.
[47] *Yorks. Fines, 1246–72*, pp. 156–7, 171.
[48] *Cal. Inq. p.m.* iv, pp. 353, 356; *Feud. Aids*, vi. 41.
[49] *Yorks. Fines, 1300–14*, p. 21.
[50] *Feud. Aids*, vi. 163.
[51] *Cal. Pat. 1321–4*, 235; *Cal. Mem. R. 1326–7*, p. 137. Cf. *Cal. Pat. 1324–7*, 154.
[52] *Yorks. Fines, 1246–72*, p. 171. Cf. E.R.A.O., DDNA/9.
[53] *Cal. Chart. R. 1327–41*, 302; *Yorks. Fines, 1347–77*, p. 124.
[54] P.R.O., CP 25(1)/277/140, no. 16. Cf. *Yorks. Fines, 1347–77*, pp. 165, 179–80.
[55] For the Acklams, *Visit. Yorks. 1584–5 and 1612*, ed J. Foster, 109; *V.C.H. Yorks. E.R.* iii. 106.
[56] H.U.L., DDBH/3/78, 80; *Cal. Pat. 1553*, 137–8.
[57] P.R.O., C 142/337, no. 114; *Yorks. Fines, 1614–25*, 27.
[58] E.R.A.O., DDNA/15; below, this section [Routh].
[59] P.R.O., C 142/559, no. 139; C 142/776, no. 53.
[60] J. Foster, *Pedigrees of Yorks.* iii, s.v. Milbanke.
[61] E.R.A.O., DDNA/13–14. Milbanke Estate Act, 8 Geo. I, c. 7 (Priv. Act) at ibid. DDNA/55.

[62] Ibid. DDNA/17, 20–1.
[63] Ibid. QDE/1/5/6; R.D.B., EK/386/443.
[64] R.D.B., IG/57/81.
[65] Bulmer, *Dir. E. Yorks.* 502.
[66] R.D.B., 73/426/400 (1895); 19/302/285 (1900); E.R.A.O., NV/1/22; directories.
[67] R.D.B., 237/33/28; 242/270/218; 359/476/390; 588/436/335.
[68] Ibid. 1793/179/142; 1888/21/20.
[69] *Reg. of Electors* (1997).
[70] E.R.A.O., DDNA/14.
[71] *Feud. Aids*, vi. 163.
[72] *Cal. Inq. p.m.* viii, p. 258; ix, pp. 85, 291.
[73] P.R.O., C 141/4, no. 45; C 142/48, no. 161; C 142/214, nos. 205, 221; ibid. CP 40/1154, Carte rot. 12; E.R.A.O., DDRI/35/29, 33; *Yorks. Fines*, i. 25, 140; above, Aldbrough, manors (Tansterne).
[74] E.R.A.O., DDNA/15; above, this section (Bonwick).
[75] *Chron. de Melsa*, ii. 288–9; Orange, 'Meaux Cart.', pp. 335–43.
[76] B.L. Cott. MS. Vit. C. vi, f. 217.

pasture gates, and a cottage, valued at £6 a year; the rest of the value came from tithes and oblations, evidently including some at Ulrome.[77] The rest of the rectorial tithes at Ulrome belonged to the rector of Barmston.[78] In 1545, after the Dissolution, the Crown granted the rectory to the archbishop of York,[79] who temporarily lost it during the Interregnum. In 1650, when the impropriator was Sydenham Lukins, probably the archbishop's lessee, the gross, annual value was £199, of which £36 came from tithes in Ulrome.[80] Most of the tithes were commuted at the mid 18th-century inclosures: the archbishop received 92 a. and £37 10s. a year for those in Dringhoe, Upton, and Brough in 1763, 90 a. and £50 a year at Skipsea in 1765, and 57 a. and £25 a year for his share in the tithes of corn, wool, and lambs at Ulrome in 1767.[81] The tithes of Bonwick township, apparently worth only £1 6s. 8d. in 1832,[82] were commuted in 1842 for a rent charge of £25 5s. 3d.[83] At the inclosure of Skipsea in 1765 allotments totalling 114 a. were also made to the archbishop for his carucate of glebe land there.[84] Lessees of the rectory included the Acklam family in the 18th century, and in the early 19th John Gilby, curate of Ulrome.[85] In 1861 the archbishop's estate in the parish comprised a 186-a. farm and garths at Skipsea, 90 a. at Dringhoe, and 57 a. at Ulrome.[86] Nearly 70 a. at Skipsea were sold in the 1920s and 1930s[87] and the 113-a. farm to W. H. Watts in 1958. Church, or Glebe, farm was divided and sold in 1963, the farmhouse and 83 a. being bought by Charles Warkup. The Warkup family still owned the farm in 1997.[88] The estate at Ulrome, then comprising 61 a., was sold to Robert and Louisa Watson in 1951.[89] Ernest Smith bought the Dringhoe farm, then of 95 a., in 1949.[90] In the 1980s the farm, variously known as Tithe, Low Fields, or Goose Island farm, was bought by the present owners, Mr. and Mrs. N. D. Robinson, who sold the farmhouse and added the land to Happy Lands farm.[91]

The rectory house at Skipsea, later Glebe or Church Farm, was mentioned from the 16th century.[92]

Between 1182 and 1197 Robert de Cauz gave Meaux abbey two tofts and 6 bovates at Dringhoe, and Simon of Wainfleet then added other land there.[93] It was perhaps Cauz's gift which was later incorporated in the abbey's Crow grange; the farm extended into Beeford parish and is treated there.[94] Thomas of Dringhoe (d. by 1223), son of Gualo, gave the abbey 1 carucate and two tofts in Dringhoe, with his tenants there, and Thomas's nephew Simon added 1 bovate and another two tofts. The lordship of Thomas's estate was later partitioned between two heirs, and in the earlier 14th century Robert Tothe released to Meaux his half share in the rent owed by the abbey.[95] Meaux abbey's estate at Dringhoe was enlarged by other gifts of land and rent, including one from Thomas of Dringhoe's son-in-law, Thomas of Meaux.[96] A grant of free warren there was received in 1293.[97] In the later 16th century Meaux's successor, the Crown, let a 4-bovate farm for £1 5s. 6d. a year and 3 bovates for 18s., both at Dringhoe, another farm with 3 bovates at Upton for £1 2s., and 1 bovate and other land there for 9s.[98] Part of the estate belonged to Samuel Burrill c. 1750; it has not been traced further.[99]

Meaux abbey also had 1 a. at Skipsea, by grant of Edward I in 1293,[1] and a farm at Ulrome with 4½ bovates.[2] Most of the land at Ulrome was included in Christopher Hartas's estate in 1626.[3]

Bridlington priory was given land at Skipsea Brough by Odo Friboys between 1160 and 1175, and more land and a rent there by the Dunsley family in the late 13th century.[4] A cottage at Skipsea formerly belonging to the priory was let by the Crown in the later 16th century.[5] In Ulrome the priory was given a rent of £1 10s. a year by William le Gros, count of Aumale, c. 1170,[6] and land there by Henry de Lascy in the 12th or 13th century.[7]

Nunkeeling priory was given 2 bovates in Ulrome by Walter de Fauconberg c. 1200, 1 bovate and a tenant at Bonwick by Hawise, countess of Aumale, shortly before her death in 1214, and 1 bovate and a toft in Dringhoe by Robert of Arundel.[8] In 1535 the estate at Bonwick was valued at £1 11s. a year, and land at

77 P.R.O., E 318/10/400, f. 6H; *Valor Eccl.* (Rec. Com.), v. 108, 117; below, this section.

78 R.D.B., AH/331/9; above, Barmston, church.

79 *L. & P. Hen. VIII*, xx (1), pp. 214–15.

80 *T.E.R.A.S.* iv. 60; Poulson, *Holderness*, i. 232.

81 R.D.B., AC/178/9; AF/180/9; AH/331/9.

82 E.R.A.O., QDE/1/5/6.

83 B.I.H.R., TA. 585s.   84 R.D.B., AF/180/9.

85 Ibid. I/125/276; B.I.H.R., TER. H. Skipsea 1786, 1809, 1825; Poulson, *Holderness*, i. 237.

86 *Lond. Gaz.* 26 July 1861, p. 3077; R.D.B., HM/313/379.

87 R.D.B., 240/275/231; 382/591/492; 511/314/231; 626/265/205.

88 Ibid. 1105/370/315; 1307/79/72; 1310/312/282; 1337/172/155; *Reg. of Electors* (1996–7).

89 R.D.B., 890/240/201.

90 Ibid. 824/122/107; 1802/482/412; 1835/17/14; *Reg. of Electors* (1973).

91 O.S. Map 6″, Yorks. CLXIII (1854 edn.); O.S. Map 1/2,500, Yorks. CLXIII. 13 (1892 edn.); inf. from Mr. and Mrs. N. D. Robinson, Dringhoe.

92 P.R.O., E 318/10/400, f. 6H; B.I.H.R., TER. H. Skipsea 1716, 1726; *T.E.R.A.S.* iv. 60; *Herring's Visit.* iii,

p. 129; O.S. Map 1/2,500, Yorks. CLXXX. 2 (1892 edn.).

93 *Chron. de Melsa* (Rolls. Ser.), i. 223–4.

94 Ibid. ii. 48; above, Beeford, manors (Crow).

95 *Chron. de Melsa*, ii. 45–7, 289–90; *Cur. Reg. R.* xi, p. 26; xii, p. 17; *Bracton's Note Bk.* iii, pp. 114–15; above, this section [Thos. of Dringhoe].

96 *Chron. de Melsa*, i. 371; ii. 47, 105, 220–1.

97 *Cal. Chart. R. 1257–1300*, 427.

98 P.R.O., E 310/27/159, f. 80; E 310/27/163, ff. 13, 103, 119; E 310/30/179, f. 11.

99 Ibid. E 310/27/163, f. 103; R.D.B., A/281/402; A/322/458; S/195/472; U/60/120.

1 *Cal. Chart. R. 1257–1300*, 430.

2 P.R.O., E 310/27/163, f. 119; E 310/30/179, f. 11; E.R.A.O., PE/32/28; *Valor Eccl.* (Rec. Com.), v. 108.

3 P.R.O., C 142/425, no. 71.

4 *Cal. Inq. p.m.* viii, p. 259; *E.Y.C.* iii, p. 72; *Bridlington Chart.* ed. W. T. Lancaster, p. 302; English, *Holderness*, 76; Burton, *Mon. Ebor.* 240.

5 P.R.O., E 310/31/187, f. 64.

6 Above, this section (Ulrome); *Cal. Inq. p.m.* vi, p. 225; x, pp. 16, 70.   7 *Bridlington Chart.* pp. 302–3.

8 B.L. Cott. MS. Otho. C. viii, ff. 94–5; *Kirkby's Inquest*, 372; *Complete Peerage*, s.v. Fauconberge.

Upton, perhaps part of that earlier recorded under Dringhoe, at less than 2s.[9] The 2 bovates with tofts at Ulrome were let by the Crown for £1 4s. a year in the later 16th century.[10]

Hawise, countess of Aumale, also gave St. Sepulchre's hospital, Preston, a toft and 1 bovate at Bonwick, together with a tenant there.[11] The land at Bonwick was worth 6s. a year in 1535, when the hospital also had less valuable holdings in Ulrome and Upton.[12] The land at Upton was said to have been given by Thomas Castle in the late 12th century.[13] All passed with the suppressed hospital to Sir Michael Stanhope in 1547, and to Ralph Constable in 1553.[14]

Watton priory was given ½ carucate at Dringhoe by Simon of Wainfleet, probably in the late 12th century, and 1 bovate by Robert de Chant.[15] In the 1270s the priory was said to hold 1 carucate and 5 bovates of the Brus fee there.[16] Following the priory's dissolution, Robert Holgate, archbishop of York, held the land at Dringhoe by grant of the Crown from 1540 until his death in 1555.[17] In 1581 the former priory and its lands were let by the Crown to Sir Thomas Heneage, who in 1582 sub-let the estate in Skipsea, comprising a house and 7 bovates in Dringhoe or Upton, to Matthew Grimston.[18] As two tenements in Upton and Dringhoe, the premises were included in Charles I's alienation of 1628 to the Ditchfield grantees as security for the city of London's loan, were sold by them to Thomas Heneage and others in 1629, and in 1650 came to Heneage Finch, earl of Winchilsea, from whom Marmaduke and Francis Grimston bought the estate in 1652.[19] The former Watton priory estate may have continued to descend in the Grimstons. Land at Dringhoe and Upton, together with property at Brough and Bonwick, was settled by John Grimston on his nephew Robert Grimston, both then of Bridlington, in 1741.[20] Robert Grimston (d. 1756) left a son Robert,[21] who in 1772 bought John Hudson's estate in Dringhoe, comprising c. 330 a., and in 1775 had c. 650 a. in Dringhoe and Upton in three farms.[22] In 1785 the estate was sold, Henry Booth buying c. 400 a. and Francis Taylor a farm of nearly 250 a.[23] Booth also bought 103 a. of the Acklam estate in 1786.[24] Ann Booth (d.

1827 or 1828) devised a 246-a. farm at Upton to Thomas Beilby and his wife Jane; including land probably once part of Meaux abbey's Crow grange, the farm descended to Jane Beilby's five daughters, the survivors of whom sold it, then of c. 200 a., to George Hopper in 1878.[25] The farm was later held by Hopper's executors, probably for his brother Thomas, who occupied Upton House farm in 1892.[26] In 1912 the executors sold the farm to F. R. Wharram (d. 1928) and R. S. Wharram, who bought 121 a. of Dringhoe Manor farm in 1946. After R. S. Wharram's death in 1961, the enlarged farm, by then called Park farm, passed to his daughter Mary Curtis.[27] It still belonged to the Curtis family in 1997.

Ann Booth left the other part of her estate in Dringhoe and Upton to John Frost and his wife Mary, and it later descended in the Frosts.[28] Comprising c. 340 a. in 1910,[29] the estate has not been traced further.

Thornton abbey (Lincs.) had a bovate at Ulrome in 1353,[30] and its successor, Thornton college, held land in Dringhoe.[31]

At their suppression the Knights Hospitaller had an estate in Ulrome, which was briefly returned to the restored order in 1558.[32] In 1560 it comprised or included a close occupied by Brian Lacy.[33]

ECONOMIC HISTORY. CLEETON AND SKIPSEA. COMMON LANDS AND INCLOSURE.
Post-medieval evidence shows that the grounds of Cleeton, as opposed to those which had become attached to Skipsea, were mostly in the south of the township, in areas later called Hallgarth, after the presumed manor house there, Half field, Far field, and Out leys; the only other land was the castle site, known as the Bail. All or most of the tillage at Cleeton was probably in Half field.[34] Ploughing in 'Hawe' field was presented as a misdemeanor in 1555, perhaps because the field was then fallow, and it was probably the same which was later variously called Hall field, Haufield, and Half field.[35] Several areas of ridge and furrow survived later from the former Half field.[36] Part of 'Hall field'

9 *Valor Eccl.* (Rec. Com.), v. 115.
10 P.R.O., E 310/27/158, f. 64. Cf. ibid. C 142/584, no. 57.
11 Dugdale, *Mon.* vi. 654–5.
12 *Kirkby's Inquest*, 372; *V.C.H. Yorks. E.R.* v. 194; *Valor Eccl.* (Rec. Com.), v. 110.
13 Poulson, *Holderness*, i. 465.
14 *Cal. Pat.* 1547–8, 170, 250; 1553, 87.
15 B.L. Cott. MS. Otho. C. viii, ff. 94v.–95; above, this section [Meaux abbey]; *Cal. Inq. p.m.* viii, p. 259; Poulson, *Holderness*, i. 464.
16 *Yorks. Hund. and Quo Warr. R.* (Y.A.S. Rec. Ser. cli), 37.
17 *Cal. Pat.* 1550–3, 117–18.
18 E.R.A.O., DDWR/13/1; Poulson, *Holderness*, i. 453.
19 E.R.A.O., DDWR/13/3; H.U.L., DDCV(2)/53/1.
20 R.D.B., Q/435/1079; Q/436/1080; Q/436/1081.
21 Ibid. AL/290/516.
22 Ibid. AR/2/3; AU/408/683.
23 Ibid. BI/162/262; BI/115/187.
24 Ibid. BI/444/707.
25 Ibid. EF/32/43; HT/399/479; MC/274/419; MO/190/289; MQ/377/560; MR/123/181; E.R.A.O., DDJA/47.

26 E.R.A.O., NV/1/109; P.R.O., RG 11/4797; Bulmer, *Dir. E. Yorks.* (1892), 502, 504.
27 R.D.B., 147/346/307; 378/399/330; 718/552/442; 1281/552/490; 1395/124/101; 1395/481/432; inf. from Mrs. D. Statters, Skipsea, 1997.
28 R.D.B., EG/290/354; FI/295/279; 274/497/421; E.R.A.O., DDJA/48/1; Sheahan and Whellan, *Hist. York & E.R.* ii. 435.
29 E.R.A.O., NV/1/109.
30 *Cal. Inq. p.m.* x, pp. 70–1.
31 E.R.A.O., DDWR/13/2.
32 P.R.O., SC 6/Hen. VIII/4458, m. 14; *Cal. Pat.* 1557–8, 313, 321.
33 P.R.O., E 318/47/2483, f. 7; the sale seems not to have been made.
34 E.R.A.O., DDCC/139/7; above, manors (Cleeton, Hallgarth). The court rolls (ibid. DDCC/24/1–2) support the identification of Cleeton's lands.
35 P.R.O., E 134/8 & 9 Chas. I Hil./4; E.R.A.O., DDCC/139/7; ibid. DDCC/24/1, s.vv. 1555, 1592; DDCC/24/2, s.vv. 1638, 1675.
36 Hull Univ., Dept. of Geog., R.A.F. air photographs, run 74A, nos. 3353–4; run 85, nos. 4104–5.

was also used as meadow, and in 1681 'Half field' included meadows on its boundary with Far field.[37] Far field was a stinted pasture in 1588, and references to pasture and overcharging in the Bail, Out leys, and Hallgarth in the 16th and 17th centuries suggest that those grounds, too, were then used wholly or frequently as common pastures. By the 1760s Half field also seems to have been under grass.[38]

Cleeton manor also comprised lands at Skipsea and Newhithe.[39] The lands of Skipsea were organized and managed separately from those of Cleeton, and ditches divided the two systems physically.[40] Skipsea's open-field land lay in North and South fields.[41] The fields had been enlarged by the late 13th century, when rents for forland were being charged.[42] The arable land evidently lay in the broad and narrow strips found elsewhere in the area.[43] As usual, the fields also included areas of meadow-land, like that lying beside the boundary dike in North field at Sowmer, later Soumers.[44] Another meadow named was West leys, presumably the later Town leys, immediately south of the vil-lage.[45] The largest of the village's common pas-tures was that at Steng hill.[46] Steng hill was stinted by the 1590s, when the lessee of the rect-ory was said to have eight beast gates there in lieu of agistment tithes in Skipsea and Cleeton.[47] There was also pasture land at Sowmer and, close to the village, in Undrum, West leys, and North carr. Grazing at 'mere side' may have been in North carr or perhaps in the carrlands south of the village which were presumably also used mainly as pasture land.[48] The grazing of pastures by beasts from outside the parish, evident earlier at Cleeton,[49] continued in both Skipsea and Cleeton in the 16th[50] and 17th cen-turies, when attempts were made to restrict the letting of pasture gates to outsiders and other-wise conserve the grazing.[51] Overcharging of the commonable lands seems, however, to have been common.[52] Besides grazing, Steng hill provided crops of furze,[53] and turves were evidently dug from Turf moor, presumably the later Turf carr.[54]

Both Skipsea and Cleeton were inclosed by award of 1765 under Act of 1764,[55] allotments totalling 1,591 a. being made from c. 15 loca-tions. Allotments from more than one area were common, making it impossible to state precisely the size of the various grounds. Of the larger areas, North field was of more than 312 a. and South field of over 148 a., while Out leys and Far field included at least 206 a. and 120 a. respectively. Fountayne Osbaldeston received 240 a., the archbishop of York as rector 204 a., John Hobman 133 a., Jonathan Acklam 104 a., and Sarah Acklam 66 a. There were also six allotments of 50–99 a., fourteen of 10–49 a., and twelve of less than 9 a.

CLEETON MANOR AND OTHER HOLDINGS. In 1086 there were 28 ploughlands at Cleeton but only three ploughs were then used, two on Drew's demesne and a third worked by six vil-leins, and the value of the manor, including its soke, was said to have fallen from £32 before the Conquest to £6. Grassland on the manor then included 100 a. of meadow land.[56] Much of the land at Cleeton was occupied as demesne.[57] About 1260 the demesne of Cleeton manor was said to comprise c. 350 a. of arable land, some 85 a. of meadow, and pasture worth £2 a year,[58] but the area of tillage given then may have excluded fallow and ley land.[59] In 1330–1 there were 646 a. of arable land, 110 a. of meadow, and 61 a. of pasture, but only 137 a. was then sown and much of the land was let for grazing. Livestock feeding on the demesne in 1330–1 included a flock of c. 340 sheep, and in 1347–8 Bridlington priory kept a flock at Cleeton and nearly 390 a. in Cleeton leys was let as sheep pasture. Other pastures mentioned in the mid 14th century were Withowcarrside, Hall carr, Manor close, Red carr leys, of c. 30 a., and the 18-a. castle site. Over 40 a. of meadow land then lay in Cleeton holmes; other parcels were in Red carr and Whitemoor, presumably the later Whitemarr.[60] The demesne farm was worked in the later 13th and earlier 14th century by 4–8 ploughmen, 1–2 carters, 1–2 shepherds, and a hayward; it seems also to have included a rabbit warren in the charge of a warrener. The services of the bond tenants[61] had evidently by then been commuted for money rents, and agricultural work on the demesne was done by the perm-anent staff assisted by hired labourers. Over 200

37 E.R.A.O., DDCC/24/1, s.v. May 1584; DDCC/24/2, s.vv. Oct. 1638, Apr. 1681.
38 Ibid. DDCC/24/1, s. vv. May 1584, Oct. 1586, Apr. 1588; Apr., Oct. 1597, Sept. 1600; DDCC/24/2, s.vv. Oct. 1637, Apr., Oct. 1651, Oct. 1674; R.D.B., AF/180/9; below, next para.
39 Below, this section (Cleeton manor).
40 E.R.A.O., DDCC/139/7; P.R.O., E 134/8 & 9 Chas. I Hil./4.
41 E.R.A.O., DDCC/85/2, s.v. 1606.
42 P.R.O., SC 6/1079/15, m. 8.
43 E.R.A.O., DDCC/24/1, s.v. Sept. 1601; DDCC/85/2, s.v. 1606; for broad lands, see below, Withernwick, econ. hist.
44 E.R.A.O., DDCC/85/2, s.v. 1594; DDCC/85/3, s.v. 1625; O.S. Map 6", Yorks. CLXIII (1854 edn.).
45 E.R.A.O., DDCC/85/3, s.v. 1625; ibid. IA. Skipsea; R.D.B., AF/180/9.
46 E.R.A.O., DDCC/85/2, s.v. 1606. P.N. Yorks. E.R. (E.P.N.S.), 83.
47 B.I.H.R., CP. G. 2891, 3093.
48 E.R.A.O., DDCC/85/1, s.v. 1581; ibid. IA. Skipsea; O.S. Map 6", Yorks. CLXIII (1854 edn.).

49 Above, this section.
50 B.I.H.R., CP. G. 2891, 3093.
51 E.R.A.O., DDCC/24/1, s.v. 1550; DDCC/85/1, s.vv. 1590, 1593.
52 Many instances in E.R.A.O., DDCC/24/1–2; DDCC/85/1–4.
53 E.R.A.O., DDCC/85/2, s.v. 1622; DDCC/85/3, s.v. 1637.
54 E.R.A.O., DDCC/85/3, s.v. 1626; ibid. IA. Skipsea; R.D.B., AF/180/9.
55 4 Geo. III, c. 17 (Priv. Act); R.D.B., AF/180/9; E.R.A.O., IA. Skipsea.
56 V.C.H. Yorks. ii. 265.
57 E.R.A.O., DDCC/139/7.
58 P.R.O., SC 11/730, m. 6, print. Yorks. Inq. i, pp. 82–3; ibid. SC 12/17/43.
59 For the following, P.R.O., SC 6/1078/11, m. 8 and d.; SC 6/1081/1, m. 2 and d.; SC 6/1082/3, m. 5; SC 6/1082/5, m. 6; SC 6/1082/6, m. 1.
60 O.S. Map 6", Yorks. CLXXX (1855 edn.). For Withow carr, below, this section (fisheries).
61 Below, this section.

sheep were kept in 1343–4, but the dairy herd was then let. By 1397 direct exploitation of the demesne had been abandoned altogether, and the land and stock were then let to a tenant for £32 10s. a year.[62]

Besides the demesne, Cleeton manor comprised land occupied by tenants at Skipsea and Newhithe. In Skipsea 5 carucates were held by 25 bondmen of Cleeton c. 1260, 15 of the holdings being of 2 bovates and 10 of 1 bovate each. The bondmen held each bovate by payment of 1s. 6 ½d. a year, by doing works, including malt-making, and by rendering hens at Christmas and merchet and tallage. Thirteen or fourteen cottars occupied tofts there in return for agricultural services, or money rents in lieu, and eight other holdings were perhaps freely held and also at Skipsea. Newhithe evidently then comprised only 10 tofts rented to customary tenants of Skipsea for 2s. each.[63]

The 14th-century lessee of the Cleeton demesne may have been the nominee of the tenants at Skipsea, who in the 15th century were said to have been granted the lease of the manor, the castle site, and a windmill partly to compensate them for the wasting of their lands by the sea.[64] The copyholders later succeeded in merging the demesne in their bond holdings. By the 1630s, when the lord of Cleeton manor attempted to reclaim the former demesne, some land had been lost by erosion; it was presumably the remainder of the demesne tillage, comprising c. 1 carucate at Cleeton, which ten copyholders then shared.[65]

FISHERIES. Much of the fishing of Skipsea and Cleeton belonged to the counts of Aumale and their successors as lords of Cleeton manor and Holderness. Their chief fisheries were in Skipsea mere and Withow mere or carr, which seem also to have been called the castle fishery and Turf hall carr respectively.[66] Withow dike and Withow hole, later shown south-east of Skipsea village, indicate the location of Withow carr.[67] A third fishery lay near Bonwick, apparently in Stream dike. Most of the catch of eels and fish seems to have been sold, nearly £10 10s. being produced by such sales in 1296–7.[68] Unlicensed fishing was alleged in the earlier 14th century,[69] when Meaux abbey also complained of the breach of its fisheries in Skipsea.[70] In 1343–4 the eels were let for 13s. 4d. a year and fish sales were worth less than £3,[71] and in 1470–1 the fishing and fowling, said formerly to

have been worth £3, were let to the tenants at Skipsea for under £1.[72]

DRINGHOE, UPTON, AND BROUGH.

COMMON LANDS AND INCLOSURE. Dringhoe, Upton, and Brough were evidently sharing open fields and other commonable lands by the early 17th century.[73] North and South fields, and the broad and narrow lands into which they were divided, had been recorded in the mid 16th century.[74] Ridge and furrow evidence makes it clear that some or all of Barbriggs was also used as arable, perhaps as part of the adjoining North field, and that land along the eastern boundary, later taken into the closes, was also tilled, perhaps as part of South field.[75] The common meadowland of the hamlets then lay in Burgham, Wye Peto, Wandams, and West carr meadows, and in the 'short meadow called East carr' in North field. They were apportioned in 15ft.-long 'gadds', two gadds being allotted for each broad land held in the fields and one for a narrow land. The stint in the fields and meadows was 10 sheep for each bovate held, and for 4 bovates 5 cattle. In the 18th century meadow dales were mentioned in Brough carr and Brougham close, presumably the earlier Burgham or Brougholme; Bow Butts, and perhaps also Brougham, were used as pasture.[76]

The commonable lands of Dringhoe, Upton, and Brough were inclosed by award of 1763 under Act of 1762.[77] They then comprised 1,484 a. lying in 13 locations, including North and South fields; the other grounds, some of which were small, were probably all under grass. Allotments from more than one area make it impossible to calculate the size of most of the grounds. Hugh Bethell, lord of Dringhoe, received 326 a., and Thomas Acklam, Thomas Hudson, and Robert Grimston were also awarded over 300 a. each. There were also two allotments of 50–99 a., two of 15–19 a., and five of less than 9 a.

MEDIEVAL TENURES AND FARMS. Part of the 5½ ploughlands at Dringhoe and Upton in 1086 was presumably used by the villein with two oxen then also recorded there.[78] Meaux abbey farmed some of its land in Dringhoe and Upton from Crow grange in Beeford;[79] the rest, including 10½ bovates and a windmill, was occupied in 1396 by eight tenants for rents of just over £4 a year in all.[80]

[62] Cal. Inq. Misc. vi, pp. 202–3.

[63] P.R.O., SC 11/730, m. 6; SC 12/17/43. Cf. Cal. Pat. 1292–1301, 434–5.

[64] P.R.O., SC 6/1083/10; SC 6/1084/5, mm. 8, 11.

[65] Ibid. E 134/8 & 9 Chas. I Hil./4; E.R.A.O., DDCC/139/7.

[66] Chron. de Melsa (Rolls Ser.), ii. 288–9; Orange, 'Meaux Cart.', pp. 335–7; for the following, P.R.O., SC 6/1078/11, m. 8 and d.; SC 6/1080/3, m. 1; SC 6/1081/1, m. 2 and d.; SC 11/730, mm. 6–7; SC 12/17/43. Cf. Y.A.J. lvi. 17–22.

[67] E.R.A.O., IA. Skipsea; O.S. Map 6", Yorks. CLXXX (1855 edn). P.N. Yorks. E.R. (E.P.N.S.), 82.

[68] P.R.O., SC 6/1079/15, m. 8.

[69] Cal. Pat. 1292–1301, 624; 1343–5, 586; 1348–50, 386.

[70] Ibid. 1321–4, 251.

[71] P.R.O., SC 6/1082/5, m. 6.

[72] Ibid. SC 6/1084/5, m. 10d. Cf. L. & P. Hen. VIII, xxi (1), p. 485.   [73] E.R.A.O., DDWR/13/2.

[74] The following based on H.U.L., DDKG/143(a) [notes from a survey (probably at Castle Howard)]; for broad and narrow lands and bovates, below, Withernwick, econ. hist.

[75] Hull Univ., Dept. of Geog., R.A.F. air photographs, run 83, nos. 4180–1; run 84B, no. 3107; cf. E.R.A.O., IA. Dringhoe.

[76] E.R.A.O., DDX/152/8; R.D.B., H/652/1322; I/8/12; I/45/99; U/59/119.

[77] 2 Geo. III, c. 45 (Priv. Act); R.D.B., AC/178/9; E.R.A.O., IA. Dringhoe.   [78] V.C.H. Yorks. ii. 265.

[79] Above, Beeford, manors (Crow), econ. hist.

[80] B.L. Cott. MS. Vit. C. vi, ff. 206v.–7; Orange, 'Meaux Cart.', p. 651.

BOROUGH AND MARKET. Cleeton manor included land at Skipsea Brough.[81] References to the borough in the 13th-century surveys[82] and in ministers' accounts do not show whether the term was then attached to Skipsea Brough or Skipsea village. In 1296–7 the rents of the borough and of Newhithe were charged separately from the customary rents of Skipsea,[83] but in 1343–4 there was one consolidated entry, apparently for the 'borough of Skipsea and Newhithe'.[84] Three or four burgage plots were recorded on the manor in 1260,[85] and about that date the 'borough' was let for 8s. 4d. a year. A market to be held on Skipsea manor each Wednesday was granted in 1272,[86] and the borough's tolls were valued at £1 13s. 4d. in the later 13th century.[87] In 1338 a grant in favour of 'Skipsea town' altered the market day to Thursday, and added two fairs, one to be held on All Saints Day and the three days following (1–4 November) and the other on the Translation of St. Thomas the Martyr and the next three days (7–10 July).[88] The Wednesday market was restored and the fair days were altered to the eve and feast day of All Saints (31 October–1 November) and the four days after Whitsunday by a grant for Skipsea Brough manor made in 1343.[89] The tolls, charged at £2 10s. in 1347–8,[90] were let for £2 in 1470–1 but were then worth only £1, it was said because of the exemption of tenants of the Hospitallers at Beeford and of Thornton abbey at Emmotland, in North Frodingham.[91] It is not known when markets and fairs ceased at Skipsea, but tolls on traffic through the village were collected into the 19th century.[92]

SKIPSEA, DRINGHOE, UPTON, AND BROUGH. LATER AGRICULTURE. In 1801 Skipsea parish was said to have 1,290 a. under crops.[93] At Skipsea and Dringhoe there were 1,935 a. of arable land and 967 a. under grass in 1905.[94] The predominance of arable over grassland was less pronounced by the 1930s, when the grassland included the site of the former mere adjoining Skipsea village and, in the south of Skipsea alongside the coast, the bombing range.[95] In 1987 of the 951.2 ha. (2,350 a.) returned for Skipsea civil parish, 818.9 ha. (2,024 a.) were arable land and 126.7 ha. (313 a.) grassland. Livestock kept then included nearly 6,300 pigs and 500–600 each of cattle and sheep.[96]

Skipsea and Dringhoe, Upton, and Brough had twenty to thirty farms in the 19th and earlier 20th century.[97] Nine were of 150 a. or more in 1851, and about five in the 1920s and 1930s; the larger holdings were mostly at Dringhoe and Upton. There were several smallholdings at Skipsea by the late 19th century,[98] and nine more were provided by the county council on c. 150 a. there, mostly on Clement's farm, bought in 1920. A cowkeeper had been recorded in 1851 and six in 1892, and some of the smallholdings, which remained with the county council in 1997, have been used for dairying.[99] Twenty-one holdings were returned for Skipsea in 1987; three were of 100–199 ha. (247–492 a.), two of 50–99 ha. (124–245 a.), ten of 10–49 ha. (25–121 a.), and six of under 10 ha.[1]

MILLS. Cleeton manor included a windmill c. 1260 and later.[2] The medieval mill seems to have been replaced c. 1550 by a mill built in North field,[3] presumably on the site beside Mill Lane later occupied by Skipsea mill.[4] The mill was closed c. 1895, and demolished soon afterwards.[5] The names Watermill holme and Old Windmillhill dale, recorded in the earlier 14th century, presumably commemorate other mills at Cleeton.[6]

Meaux abbey had a water mill at Crow grange,[7] and a windmill which it moved from Beeford to Dringhoe in the late 14th century, in part to gain the tithes for its church of Skipsea.[8] Another mill stood on the Cauce estate at Dringhoe in 1325,[9] and the Whetstones and their successors, the Bosvilles, had a windmill at Dringhoe in the 16th century.[10] Jeremiah Lamplugh built a windmill north of the Beeford road at Dringhoe c. 1800;[11] it was given up soon after 1905,[12] and has been demolished. A second windmill stood near Park Farm, Upton, in the 1820s.[13]

81 P.R.O., SC 11/730, m. 6 (s.v. Thos. of Dunsley); above, manors (Bridlington priory).
82 P.R.O., SC 11/730, mm. 6, 17; SC 12/17/43.
83 Ibid. SC 6/1079/15, m. 8.
84 Ibid. SC 6/1082/5, m. 6.
85 Ibid. SC 11/730, m. 6.
86 Cal. Chart. R. 1257–1300, 179.
87 P.R.O., SC 6/1079/15, m. 8; SC 12/17/43.
88 Cal. Chart. R. 1327–41, 444.
89 Cal. Pat. 1343–5, 141.
90 P.R.O., SC 6/1082/6, m. 1.
91 Ibid. SC 6/1084/5, m. 8d.; SC 6/Hen. VII/1028; above, N. Frodingham, manor.
92 H.U.L., DHO/7/42; E.R.A.O., DDCC/111/39; Poulson, Holderness, i. 447.
93 P.R.O., HO 67/26/393.
94 Acreage Returns, 1905.
95 [1st] Land Util. Surv. Map, sheet 28; above, intro. (mere, bombing range).
96 Inf. from Min. of Agric., Fish. & Food, Beverley, 1990.
97 Following based on P.R.O., HO 107/2367; directories.
98 P.R.O., RG 11/4797.
99 R.D.B., 240/275/231; Bulmer, Dir. E. Yorks. 503; E.R.

Smallholdings and Allotments Cttee. Mins. 1913–20, s. vv. 11 Mar., 19 Apr., 11 Oct. 1920; E.R. Agric. Cttee. Mins. 1936–40, 155; E.R. Smallholdings Cttee. Mins. s.v. 7 July 1952; inf. from county archivist, Beverley, 1997.
1 Inf. from Min. of Agric., Fish & Food.
2 P.R.O., SC 6/1081/1, m. 2 and d.; SC 6/1083/10, m. 3d.; SC 11/730, mm. 6, 17; SC 12/17/43.
3 Ibid. C 142/111, no. 34; E.R.A.O., DDCC/139/7; L. & P. Hen. VIII, xxi (1), p. 485; Cal. Pat. 1572–5, pp. 321–2.
4 E.R.A.O., IA. Skipsea; O.S. Map 6", Yorks. CLXXX (1855 edn.).
5 Directories; T. Sheppard, Lost Towns of Yorks. Coast, 190.
6 P.R.O., SC 6/1081/1, m. 2 and d.; SC 6/1082/5, m. 6.
7 Above, Beeford, econ. hist. (mills).
8 Chron. de Melsa (Rolls Ser.), iii. 185.
9 Cal. Pat. 1324–7, 154.
10 P.R.O., C 3/8/63; Yorks. Fines, iii. 41.
11 R.D.B., CT/495/702; E.R.A.O., IA. Dringhoe; O.S. Map 6", Yorks. CLXXX (1855 edn.).
12 R.D.B., 259/378/310; directories.
13 Baines, Hist. Yorks. ii. 198; H. Teesdale, Map of Yorks. (1828).

ULROME. COMMON LANDS AND INCLOS-
URE. There is little evidence about the settlement's commonable lands in the Middle Ages.
The tillage would seem to have been divided
between two open fields, East field[14] and West
field. Bovates in West field were recorded until
the mid 17th century,[15] but the field was evidently inclosed soon after: in the 1760s a bovate
in Ulrome was said to have been inclosed many
years before and converted to grassland, the
western half of the township was by then almost
entirely in closes, and several of the bovaters
had continuing common rights in 'West field'.[16]
Areas of ridge and furrow which survived west
and south of the village had presumably once
been parts of West field.[17] By the 18th century
the remaining tillage was usually described as
lying in North and South fields.[18] The common
meadow land was evidently in the open fields.
Stinted pasture was provided by the moor, the
carr, and an area called Holmes, or Westholmes,
as well as in Criftings, where Spring gates were
recorded.[19]

Ulrome comprised 6 carucates of open-field
land before inclosure in 1767 under Act of
1765.[20] John Rickaby, lord of the manor, had 1
carucate and 7 bovates, and Gabriel Brooke and
his son Humphrey 1 carucate and 5 bovates;
there was another holding of 5 bovates, six of
2 bovates each, and four of ½–1 bovate. Seven
tenants had no open-field land. Rickaby received
256 a. and the Brookes 220 a. Three other allotments were of 50–99 a., eight of 10–49 a., and
eleven of less than 9 a. The allotments totalled
945 a., and were made from North and South
fields and five other locations. Mixed allotments
prevent the calculation of the full extent of the
individual grounds: South field had been of
more than 216 a., North field of at least 149 a.,
and the moor of more than 28 a. Ridge and
furrow of the former South field survived beside
Sand Lane in 1997.

MEDIEVAL TENURES AND FARMS. At
Ulrome there were 2 ploughlands in 1086, but
only one plough was then used. Two bordars
and 22 a. of meadow land were also recorded on
the estate, whose value had been reduced from
£2 to 10s. since the Conquest.[21]

LATER AGRICULTURE. Ulrome was reckon-
ed to have 597 a. under crops in 1801,[22] and in

1905 there were 1,122 a. of arable land and 352 a.
under grass.[23] There seems to have been more
grassland by the 1930s, when, besides the land
close to the village, much of the west of Ulrome
was under grass.[24] The area returned in 1987
under Ulrome, 1,276.8 ha. (3,155 a.), evidently
included some land outside the civil parish. It
included 1,129.5 ha. (2,791 a.) of arable land,
126.1 ha. (312 a.) of grassland, and 3.7 ha. (9 a.)
of woodland. Over 5,000 pigs were then kept
and nearly 1,500 sheep.[25]

There were usually about 10 farmers at
Ulrome in the 19th and earlier 20th century, up
to three of whom had 150 a. or more. One or
two small holdings were also recorded in 1851.[26]
In 1987 of 12 holdings returned for Ulrome,
three were of 200–499 ha. (494–1,233 a.), one
of 100–199 ha. (247–492 a.), two of 50–99 ha.
(124–245 a.), one of 10–49 ha. (25–121 a.), and
five of under 10 ha. (25 a.).[27]

MILLS. In the 14th century the estate of the
Ulrome family included a mill.[28] A windmill
recorded at Ulrome in 1717 had been demolished by 1765.[29] Its site in the south of the township was shown later.[30]

BONWICK. AGRICULTURE. The location of
the former open fields at Bonwick is evident from
the ridge and furrow which survived into the
earlier 20th century,[31] but nothing else is known
of the hamlet's early agricultural arrangements.
Inclosure had evidently taken place by the 17th
century.[32] The township had 381 a. of arable land
and 355 a. of grassland c. 1840,[33] and 409 a. and
267 a. respectively in 1905.[34] It lay in two farms
in the 19th and earlier 20th century, both of
which were of over 300 a. in 1921.[35]

SKIPSEA AND ULROME. INDUSTRY,
TRADE, AND PROFESSIONAL ACTIVITY. There
has been little employment unconnected with
agriculture in Skipsea and Ulrome. A weaver of
Skipsea Brough was recorded in the 16th century,[36] and in 1590 a pain was laid in Skipsea
manor court about the bleaching of cloth.[37]
About fifteen people were employed in the usual
trades and as shopkeepers at Skipsea and Skipsea
Brough in the later 19th century.[38] Bricks and
tiles were made at a works near Southfield House

[14] E.R.A.O., DDML/5/2(c); R.D.B., AD/531/1068.
[15] P.R.O., C 142/584, no. 57; Poulson, *Holderness*, i. 230.
[16] R.D.B., AD/531/1068; AH/331/9; map of 1766, print.
Poulson, *Holderness*, i, facing p. 242.
[17] Hull Univ., Dept. of Geog., R.A.F. air photographs,
run 83, nos. 4181–3; run 84B, nos. 3107–8.
[18] Below, this section. Those fields had evidently by then
been reduced by the making of closes adjoining the village:
cf. map of 1766, print. Poulson, *Holderness*, i, facing p. 242;
Hull Univ., Dept. of Geog., R.A.F. air photographs, run
83, nos. 4182–4.
[19] R.D.B., AH/331/9; H.U.L., DDSY/38/28; DDCV/
103/33; P.R.O., C 142/425, no. 71. For Criftings, *P.N.
Yorks. E.R.* (E.P.N.S.), 70–1.
[20] 5 Geo. III, c. 9 (Priv. Act); R.D.B., AH/331/9; map
of 1766, print. Poulson, *Holderness*, i, facing p. 242.
[21] *V.C.H. Yorks.* ii. 267.   [22] P.R.O., HO 67/26/433.
[23] Acreage Returns, 1905.

[24] [1st] Land Util. Surv. Map, sheet 28.
[25] Inf. from Min. of Agric., Fish. & Food, Beverley, 1990.
[26] P.R.O., HO 107/2367; directories.
[27] Inf. from Min. of Agric., Fish. & Food.
[28] H.U.L., DHO/16/16.
[29] R.D.B., F/98/215; AG/143/281.
[30] A. Bryant, *Map of E.R. Yorks.* (1829); O.S. Map 6",
Yorks. CLXIII (1854 edn.).
[31] Hull Univ., Dept. of Geog., R.A.F. air photographs,
run 74A, nos. 3355–6; run 74B, nos. 3285–8; run 75B, nos.
3270–1; run 85, nos. 4103–4.
[32] P.R.O., C 142/776, no. 53.
[33] B.I.H.R., TA. 585s.
[34] Acreage Returns, 1905.
[35] Directories; above, manors (Bonwick); A. Bryant,
Map of E. R. Yorks. (1829).
[36] H.U.L., DDPR/2/1.
[37] E.R.A.O., DDCC/85/1.   [38] Directories.

in the mid 19th century, production evidently ceasing in the 1870s.[39] Brick-making seems also to have been pursued at Upton.[40] Since the 1930s motor and agricultural engineers have also worked at Skipsea,[41] and in 1997 concerns in the village included a garage on Hornsea Road, a firm of builders in Cleeton Lane, and, in part for the seaside visitors, tea rooms and a fish and chip shop.

In the early 19th century gravel was taken from the beach at Withow Hole for road repairs in Skipsea and neighbouring villages by licence of the Constables, who had rights over the shore as lords of the seigniory, and later in the century Sir Thomas A. C. Constable, Bt., let the right to take gravel and stone from the beaches of Skipsea and Ulrome.[42] Gravel dealers were recorded at both places in the late 19th and earlier 20th century.[43] A kiln, perhaps for the burning of chalk imported by sea, was operated at Withow Hole in the earlier 19th century.[44]

At Ulrome an unlicensed physician and surgeon was practising in 1663.[45] There was a tanner there in the 18th century,[46] a weaver in 1851,[47] and in the 19th and earlier 20th century a few also found employment as shopkeepers and tradesmen. A pottery was established at Ulrome in the mid 20th century.[48] The beaches of Ulrome and Skipsea attracted visitors in the earlier 20th century, and later mostly seasonal employment was provided by the caravan parks and the associated shops, cafés, and places of amusement.[49]

LOCAL GOVERNMENT. Skipsea and Cleeton manors evidently had a single court in the Middle Ages. Nine meetings were held in 1347–8 and four in 1470–1.[50] A court roll of 1502–3 for 'Skipsea' survives but it records only the two leet courts held that year; 2 constables, 2 aletasters, and 4 bylawmen were elected, besides a pennygrave for Cleeton.[51] Separate courts for Cleeton manor began to be held in 1530, following its alienation to Sir Anthony Browne.[52] Surviving records include court rolls for 1550–1925[53] and a custumal of 1586.[54] Leet jurisdiction was claimed for the court from 1530 but that was challenged c. 1630, presumably as an infringement of the jurisdiction of Skipsea manor court,[55] and Cleeton was later reckoned a customary or baron court.[56] There were usu-

ally two meetings a year. In the late 16th century the Bail, part of Skipsea castle, was said to have been the venue,[57] but Cleeton Hallgarth, the probable manor-house site,[58] was used in 1637. Officers appointed by Cleeton manor court included 4 bylawmen, 2 dike-reeves, 2 constables, and 1–2 pinders. The record is virtually a copyhold register by the late 17th century, and much business came to be done outside the formal meetings. Later combined meetings were held for Skipsea and Cleeton manors.[59]

Court rolls for Skipsea manor survive for 1562–1925.[60] The court's jurisdiction included view of frankpledge, the ale assize, and civil pleas, such as debt, but agricultural regulation and drainage were probably its major concerns. In the 1620s tenants were also fined for infringing the lord's rights over the shore by taking wreckage.[61] By the late 17th century little was recorded apart from property transfers. Officers elected in the court included 4 bylawmen, 2 constables, 2 surveyors of highways, 2 aletasters and dike-reeves, and a pinder. Meetings were held at least twice a year until the mid 19th century but thereafter annually or less frequently at Skipsea with supplementary meetings elsewhere. Skipsea court may have met in a guild hall which the tenants were ordered to repair in 1568; the 'building' of a court house at Skipsea, perhaps rather the repairing of the guild hall, was proposed in 1572.[62] By the mid 18th century the courts of Skipsea and Cleeton manors met on the same day, and the Cleeton court was probably then, as later, adjourned to the house in which Skipsea manor court was held; in 1925 the Board inn was the venue for the combined meeting.[63]

Stocks formerly stood opposite the church at Skipsea.[64] The East Riding constabulary, established in 1857, had a constable based at Skipsea.[65]

A court was kept on Ulrome manor c. 1600, when officers chosen there included the bylawmen of the township.[66]

Meaux abbey was claiming the profits of the ale assize on its estate at Dringhoe in the 1290s.[67] The manorial court at Dringhoe, which had leet jurisdiction there, was mentioned in the mid 16th century.[68] A brief minute of its proceedings in 1762 records the swearing in of 4 bylawmen,

39 O.S. Map 6″, Yorks. CLXXX (1855 edn.); O.S. Map 1/2,500, Yorks. CLXXX. 2 (1892 edn.); *Kelly's Dir. N. & E.R. Yorks.* (1872), 545.
40 E.R.A.O., DDJA/47.
41 R.D.B., 1738/197/156; directories.
42 E.R.A.O., DDCC/136/13, 30, 47, 49, 57, 59; O.S. Map 6″, Yorks. CLXXX (1855 edn.).
43 Directories.
44 J. Greenwood, *Map of N. Division of Holderness,* print. in Poulson, *Holderness,* i, facing p. 163.
45 B.I.H.R., ER V./CB. 1, f. 97v.
46 R.D.B., X/215/485.
47 P.R.O., HO 107/2367.
48 R.D.B., 1655/263/235.
49 E.R.A.O., CCO/373, 487 etc.; above, intro. (Skipsea, Ulrome).
50 P.R.O., SC 6/1082/6, m. 1; SC 6/1084/5, m. 10d.
51 E.R.A.O., DDCC/15/18.
52 Ibid. DDCC/139/7; above, manors (Cleeton).

53 E.R.A.O., DDCC/24/1–6; DDCC/85/6; DDCC(2)/82 (vols. i–ii); DDCC(2)/83 (vols. i–ii).
54 E.R.A.O., DDCC/23/11; cf. Poulson, *Holderness,* i. 446.
55 E.R.A.O., DDCC/112/148.
56 Cf. H.U.L., DX/30/1.
57 P.R.O., E 134/8 & 9 Chas. I Hil./4.
58 Above, manors (Cleeton).
59 Below, this section.
60 E.R.A.O., DDCC/85/1–8; DDCC(2)/83 (vols. i–iv).
61 Ibid. DDCC/85/2, s.v. 1622; DDCC/85/3, s.v. 1625.
62 Ibid. DDCC/85/1.
63 Ibid. DDCC/85/78; H.U.L., DX/30/1–2.
64 *T.E.R.A.S.* iii. 48.
65 A. A. Clarke, *Country Coppers: Story of E.R. Police,* 18–19.
66 P.R.O., E 134/14 Jas. I Mic./3.
67 *Yorks. Hund. and Quo Warr. R.* (Y.A.S. Rec. Ser. cli), 247.
68 H.U.L., DDKG/143(a).

2 constables, and a pinder.[69] It was evidently held in the manor house.[70]

The regulation of the agriculture and drainage of townships in the north division of Holderness was also the business of the bailiwick courts.[71]

Surviving parish records for Skipsea include churchwardens' accounts from 1813.[72]

Paupers at Skipsea were allowed to glean on their neighbours' lands in the 17th century.[73] In the late 18th and early 19th century some of them, and probably the poor from the other townships too, were maintained in Hunmanby workhouse.[74] Skipsea and Dringhoe together had 15 people on permanent out-relief in 1802–3, the area presumably comprising also Upton and Brough.[75] In 1812–15 in Dringhoe, Upton, and Brough township c. 15 were on permanent out-relief, one person was maintained in a workhouse, and 16–18 more were helped occasionally; at Skipsea up to 5 were then given permanent out-relief and one person occasional relief.

Ulrome maintained poorhouses.[76] Its poor were relieved from the rents of open-field balks until inclosure in 1767, when a 5-a. allotment was awarded instead.[77] Three people from Ulrome were supported in a workhouse in 1802–3, and up to 5 were given permanent out-relief in the early 19th century. In Bonwick township there were then 3 on permanent out-relief.

In 1836 the townships of Skipsea, Ulrome, and Dringhoe, Upton, and Brough joined Bridlington poor-law union.[78] They remained in Bridlington rural district, from 1935 as the new civil parishes of Skipsea and Ulrome, until 1974, when they became part of the North Wolds district, later borough, of Humberside. In 1981 the borough's name was changed to East Yorkshire.[79] Bonwick township joined Skirlaugh poor-law union in 1837, and remained in Skirlaugh rural district until 1935. As part of Bewholme civil parish, it was then included in the new rural district of Holderness, and in 1974 it was taken into the Holderness district of Humberside.[80] In 1996 Skipsea, Ulrome, and Bewholme parishes became part of a new East Riding unitary area.[81]

Most of Bridlington rural district was supplied with water by Bridlington corporation from the 1930s,[82] and corporation standposts remain near Skipsea village green, in Bugg Lane at Ulrome, and at Skipsea Brough.

Part of a burial ground at Skipsea Brough for Skipsea, Dringhoe, Upton, Brough, and Bonwick was dedicated soon after its purchase in 1925, and was in use by 1928; ½ a. more, designated as a Church burial ground, was consecrated in 1930.[83] A joint parish council for Lissett and Ulrome had been established by 1997.

CHURCHES. Skipsea church was recorded as the church of the castle, evidently of Skipsea, c. 1100.[84] The living was a rectory until 1310, when, by ordination of the previous year, the church was appropriated to Meaux abbey and a vicarage was established.[85] There was a chapel at Ulrome, and its territory, for long part of Skipsea and Barmston parishes, eventually became a separate parish.[86] The vicarages of Skipsea and Ulrome were united in 1925, and in 1979 Skipsea with Ulrome and Barmston with Fraisthorpe were combined. The parishes of Skipsea and Ulrome have, however, remained distinct.[87]

SKIPSEA. In 1115 Stephen, count of Aumale, gave Skipsea church, with others in Holderness, to Beauvais abbey, and it was later assigned to Aumale priory (Seine Maritime), then a dependency of Beauvais but itself an abbey from 1130.[88] The patronage of Skipsea church, like that of Easington and Keyingham, was shared between the counts of Aumale, who nominated the rector, and Aumale abbey, which presented him.[89] The archbishop collated by lapse in 1228. Later the Crown, as heir to Aveline de Forz, countess of Aumale (d. 1274), seems to have had the whole right at Skipsea, presenting thrice in the 1290s.[90] Meaux abbey may have held Skipsea church in 1291,[91] and in 1293 it obtained the 'advowson' from the Crown,[92] which in 1305 repeated its grant and licensed appropriation.[93] The abbey presented a rector in 1306,[94] and in 1309–10 secured appropriation and the ordination of a vicarage.[95] Aumale abbey later formally released its right as patron and accepted the appropriation.[96]

Vicars were appointed by the rector before the ordination of a perpetual vicarage in the 14th century;[97] in 1226 the appointment had the assent of the count and abbey of Aumale,[98] but

69   Ibid. DDCV/44/1.
70   Poulson, *Holderness*, i. 465.
71   E.R.A.O., DDCC/112/6 etc.
72   Ibid. PE/137/18.
73   Ibid. DDCC/85/3, s.v. 1625.
74   *V.C.H. Yorks. E.R.* ii. 241.
75   *Poor Law Abstract, 1804*, pp. 594–5; *1818*, pp. 522–3.
76   Poulson, *Holderness*, i. 241.
77   R.D.B., AH/331/9; below, churches (Ulrome); charities.   78   *3rd Rep. Poor Law Com.* 167.
79   Boro. of N. Wolds, *Council Proc. and Cttee. Mins.* 1973–4, 4–7; 1980–1, 360; *Census*.
80   *3rd Rep. Poor Law Com.* 170; *Census*.
81   Humberside (Structural Change) Order 1995, copy at E.R.A.O.   82   *V.C.H. Yorks. E.R.* ii. 64.
83   R.D.B., 390/40/34; B.I.H.R., CD. 761.
84   *E.Y.C.* iii, p. 27.

85   *Reg. Greenfield*, iii, pp. 154–7, 166–8.
86   Below, this section (Ulrome).
87   *Lond. Gaz.* 10 Feb. 1925, pp. 960–1; B.I.H.R., OC. 955.
88   *E.Y.C.* iii, pp. 30, 35–6; *V.C.H. Yorks. E.R.* v. 18.
89   *Cal. Inq. p.m.* i, p. 132; *V.C.H. Yorks. E.R.* v. 29, 63.
90   Lawrance, 'Clergy List', Holderness, 2, pp. 138–9.
91   *Tax. Eccl.* 304.   92   *Cal. Chart. R. 1257–1300*, 430.
93   *Cal. Pat. 1301–7*, 332.
94   Lawrance, 'Clergy List', Holderness, 2, p. 139.
95   *Reg. Greenfield*, iii, pp. 154–7, 166–8; *Chron. de Melsa* (Rolls Ser.), ii. 232–5.
96   *Chron. de Melsa*, iii. 116–19; Orange, 'Meaux Cart.,' pp. 199–202.
97   Lawrance, 'Clergy List', Holderness, 2, p. 139. Stephen 'chaplain of Skipsea' is also recorded: *Bridlington Chart.* ed. W. T. Lancaster, p. 321.
98   *Reg. Gray*, p. 8.

in 1269 the countess of Aumale challenged the rector's right by presenting her own candidate.[99] At appropriation in 1309–10 the archbishop reserved the collation of vicars to his see,[1] and he, or the chapter in his stead, exercised the patronage thereafter, except in 1721 when the Crown presented by lapse.[2] The patronage was shared between the existing patrons at the union of 1925, the archbishop receiving two turns out of every three.[3] By the further union of 1979 the right to present was given jointly to the archbishop and the patrons of Barmston, Fraisthorpe, and Ulrome.[4]

Arnulf de Montgomery gave Sées abbey (Orne) tithes worth £1 a year belonging to Skipsea church c. 1100 but they were evidently resumed on his deprivation in 1102.[5] Skipsea church was valued at just over £23 net in 1291. Outgoings included an annual pension of £1 6s. 8d., formerly paid to Aumale abbey, but then received by its priory at Burstall, in Skeffling.[6] A 'new pension' was added in 1361 in return for Aumale's formal release of its rights as patron, bringing the value to £2, and the whole was paid after 1396 to Kirkstall abbey (Yorks. W.R.), the purchaser of Aumale's English possessions.[7]

Evidently also excluded from the net value of the church in 1291 was the vicar's share.[8] That had been ½ carucate tithe-free, 2 tofts, and all offerings except wool and lamb tithes in 1226.[9] Later in the 13th century the vicar's portion was worth c. £5 a year.[10] By the ordination of 1309–10 he was to receive a stipend of £10 a year out of the rectory.[11] That salary remained unchanged[12] until 1696, when Archbishop Sharp raised it to £15.[13] Sharp also gave £200 for which £200 Bounty money was received in 1715;[14] the interest on the £400 added £16 a year to the living's value until land was bought with it in 1769.[15] The living was further augmented with £200 Bounty money by lot in 1808, and in 1821 with a £1,000 Parliamentary grant.[16]

Between 1829 and 1831 the annual net income of Skipsea vicarage was £96.[17] Another £200 Bounty money was received in 1853 to meet £300 from the archbishop.[18] A grant of £186 a year was made from the Common Fund in 1865, and another, of £9, was paid from 1866.[19] In 1866, when somewhat inflated by temporary grants, the value was £395; it was c. £300 in 1872.[20]

A house previously assigned to the vicar was confirmed to him at appropriation in 1309–10.[21] The vicarage house had gone by 1721, when an evidently unsuccessful attempt was made to have it rebuilt.[22] In 1851 the vicar was living in Mill Lane, presumably in a rented house.[23] A parsonage was finally built in or soon after 1866 to designs by James Fowler of Louth with help from the Ecclesiastical Commissioners.[24] The grounds of the new house included Vicarage garth, presumably the site of the earlier parsonage.[25] The large house has prominent gables and a hipped, slate roof with a decorative ridge. It was designated the residence of the united benefice in 1925[26] but in 1959 it was sold after replacement by the former vicarage house at Ulrome.[27]

The only glebe land c. 1700 was Vicarage garth or close, north of the church; of c. 1 a., it was then rented for £1 a year.[28] The vicar also enjoyed pasture in Skipsea by gift of the parish,[29] which right was let for £1 6s. in 1764 and exchanged for 4 a. at inclosure in 1765. In 1817 the allotment and Vicarage garth produced £13 a year.[30] In 1865 the allotment was exchanged for a smaller piece of land, which was required as the site of the new parsonage and adjoined Vicarage garth.[31] Beyond the township, the augmentation money was used to buy 8 a. in Southcoates, near Hull, in 1769,[32] and 5½ a. at Atwick in 1821. The land at Southcoates was let for £14 a year in 1786, £26 in 1817, and £32 in 1865,[33] and in 1851 the total glebe was worth

[99] Reg. Giffard, p. 53.

[1] Reg. Greenfield, iii, p. 155.

[2] B.I.H.R., Bp. Dio. 3, E.R., p. 182; Lawrance, 'Clergy List', Holderness, 2, pp. 140–1; Poulson, Holderness, i. 451–2. The Crown's grant of the rectory to the archbishop of York in 1545 erroneously included the advowson: L. & P. Hen. VIII, xx (1), pp. 214–16.

[3] Lond. Gaz. 10 Feb. 1925, pp. 960–1; Crockford (1930), 785.

[4] B.I.H.R., OC. 955; V.C.H. Yorks. E.R. ii. 206; below, this section (Ulrome [adv.]); above, Barmston, church.

[5] E.Y.C. iii, pp. 27–8.

[6] Reg. Gray, pp. 22–3; Tax. Eccl. (Rec. Com.), 304. Accounts for the church during a vacancy in 1267–8 survive: P.R.O., SC 6/915/3, m. 1d.

[7] Chron. de Melsa (Rolls Ser.), ii. 235–6; iii. 116–19; Orange, 'Meaux Cart.', pp. 199–202; Valor Eccl. (Rec. Com.), v. 109; V.C.H. Yorks. E.R. v. 133; E.Y.C. iii, pp. 31–2.

[8] Tax. Eccl. 304; Cal. Inq. Misc. i, p. 530; above, this section. [9] Reg. Gray, p. 8.

[10] Reg. Giffard, p. 53; Tax. Eccl. 304. Cf. Cal. Inq. Misc. i, p. 530.

[11] Reg. Greenfield, iii, p. 156.

[12] Chron. de Melsa (Rolls Ser.), iii. 31; Valor Eccl. (Rec. Com.), v. 109, 116; T.E.R.A.S. iv. 60.

[13] B.I.H.R., Bp. Dio. 3, E.R., p. 182; ibid. TER. H. Skipsea 1716 etc. The condition that the parish find another £5 was perhaps met by the gift of pasture rights: below, this section.

[14] Hodgson, Q.A.B. cxxx, cccxlix. B.I.H.R., Bp. Dio. 3,

E.R., p. 182 and ibid. ER. V. Ret. 1, f. 4 give 1718, apparently in error.

[15] B.I.H.R., TER. H. Skipsea 1726 etc.; below, this section.

[16] Hodgson, Q.A.B. cccxlix.

[17] Rep. Com. Eccl. Revenues, 966–7.

[18] Hodgson, Q.A.B. xxviii, lxxvi.

[19] Lond. Gaz. 4 Apr. 1865, pp. 1869–70; 14 May 1867, p. 2765.

[20] B.I.H.R., MGA/1866/6; Kelly's Dir. N. & E.R. Yorks. (1872), 545.

[21] Reg. Greenfield, iii, p. 156.

[22] B.I.H.R., ER. V./Ret. 1, f. 117; ER. V./Ret. 2, f. 6; ibid. Bp. Dio. 3, E.R., p. 182; ibid. V. 1764/Ret. 3, no. 36; Rep. Com. Eccl. Revenues, 966–7.

[23] P.R.O., HO 107/2367.

[24] B.I.H.R., MGA/1866/6; Lond. Gaz. 8 Aug. 1865, pp. 3885–6; 6 Feb. 1866, pp. 663–4.

[25] Below, this section.

[26] Lond. Gaz. 10 Feb. 1925, pp. 960–1.

[27] R.D.B., 1159/198/181; E.R.A.O., PE/137/21; below, this section (Ulrome [glebe]).

[28] B.I.H.R., TER. H. Skipsea 1716 etc.; ibid. Bp. Dio. 3, E.R., p. 182.

[29] Above, this section [augmentations].

[30] R.D.B., AF/180/9; B.I.H.R., TER. H. Skipsea 1726–1817.

[31] E.R.A.O., PE/137/T. 22; above, this section.

[32] R.D.B., AM/171/285.

[33] B.I.H.R., TER. H. Skipsea 1770–1865.

nearly £43 a year.[34] The 8 a. near Hull was sold in 1906,[35] and c. 3 a. with Skipsea vicarage house in 1959.[36] The land at Atwick was evidently sold between 1973 and 1978.[37]

A house was let to St. Mary's guild in 1296–7, and in 1347–8 the 'guild house' and some land were charged with the maintenance of two lights in Skipsea church.[38] The house may later have been used for holding manorial courts.[39] The church had lights dedicated to St. Mary, St. James, St. Thomas, St. Nicholas, St. Catherine, and St. Margaret in 1407, and in the 16th century one light there was endowed with land and others with cows.[40]

Under the appropriation of 1309–10, Meaux abbey was charged with supplying books and customary ornaments for services at Skipsea.[41] The cure was evidently neglected by a non-resident rector in the later 13th century, and in 1311 the vicar was censured for an unspecified offence with a woman.[42] Thomas Glede, vicar 1361–1407, was followed by his relatives, John Selow, 1407–15, and his brother Roger, 1415–51, possibly sons of Alice Selow, Glede's servant.[43] A parochial chaplain was assisting the vicar in the earlier 16th century.[44] Sermons were lacking at Skipsea c. 1570.[45] Women of Skipsea and Ulrome were accused of witchcraft in 1578 and 1650.[46] Ralph Cornwall, minister in 1650, continued to serve Skipsea after the Restoration, together with Burton Pidsea; he may have been replaced c. 1665 for drunkeness, brawling, and other offences but continued to live at Skipsea until at least the 1680s.[47] In the mid 18th century the non-resident vicar served the poor living of Skipsea with others in the vicinity, in 1764 by employing the curate of Beeford to do his duty at Skipsea for £13 a year and the fees. There was then one service each Sunday at Skipsea and quarterly celebrations of communion at which usually c. 50 received.[48] Better provision resulted from the augmentation of the living: by the 1860s the resident incumbent was holding two Sunday services, celebrating communion monthly, with usually c. 12 receiving, and attempting an evening school in winter, which, as usual in the area, met with little success.[49] Communion was weekly in the early 20th century.[50] A parish room

and Sunday school was built on the site of a former school at Skipsea and opened in 1902; the Sunday school and other meetings were held there until c. 1970, and the disused building still stood in 1997.[51] The weekly service and celebration of communion provided in the united benefice in 1997 were rotated among the four churches, including Skipsea.[52]

Skipsea church stands at the west end of the village on a bluff overlooking the former mere. The dedication to *ALL SAINTS* or *HALLOWS* was recorded c. 1500.[53] The church comprises chancel with north vestry, aisled and clerestoried nave with south porch, and west tower. Except for the south aisle and the vestry, which are of ashlar, and the brick porch, it is built of boulders with ashlar dressings. The church seems to have been rebuilt in the 14th century, following appropriation. The four-bayed arcades between the nave and aisles and the east window are of that period, and at the end of the century Meaux abbey certainly added a north window or windows to the chancel.[54] In the 15th century the clerestory was made and the church almost entirely refenestrated, and it was probably then that the building was embattled. The tower, which includes some low, lancet windows, was also evidently rebuilt then. The rendered brick porch, with an elaborate gabled front, may date from c. 1700. After appropriation in 1309–10, Meaux abbey and later the archbishop or his lessees were responsible for the chancel; the rest of the church was repaired by the townships, Skipsea and Dringhoe paying ⅓ each and Ulrome and Bonwick ⅙ each.[55] The chancel and other parts of the building were neglected in the 16th century[56] and later, and an engraving made c. 1800 showed the chancel without a roof.[57] In 1824 the Revd. John Gilby, lessee of the rectory, rebuilt the chancel, and the nave was re-roofed in 1827.[58] Nevertheless, the building was 'almost ruinous' before 1865 and 1866 when it was more or less rebuilt in a similar, 15th-century style to designs by James Fowler of Louth. The church was also then refitted and the chancel restored, and in 1874 the vestry was added, apparently replacing an earlier chapel or vestry.[59] The tower was

34 P.R.O., HO 129/524/1/8/15.
35 R.D.B., 85/378/356; 85/379/357 (both 1906).
36 Ibid. 1159/198/181.
37 B.I.H.R., TER. 856; inf. from York Dioc. Bd. of Finance, 1981.
38 P.R.O., SC 6/1079/15, m. 8; SC 6/1082/6, m. 1; SC 6/1084/5, m. 8d.   39 Above, loc. govt.
40 B.I.H.R., Reg. 5A, f. 337; Prob. Reg. 6, f. 66; *Y.A.J.* xliv. 193.
41 *Reg. Greenfield*, iii, p. 156.
42 Lawrance, 'Clergy List', Holderness, 2, pp. 137–41.
43 B.I.H.R., Reg. 5A, f. 337; Lawrance, op. cit. 140.
44 B.I.H.R., Prob. Reg. 6, f. 66; *Y.A.J.* xxiv. 76.
45 J. S. Purvis, *Tudor Par. Doc. of Dioc. York*, 33; *Abp. Grindal's Visit., 1575*, ed. W. J. Sheils, 71.
46 B.I.H.R., V. 1578–9/CB. 1, ff. 67v., 68v.; *Depositions from York Castle* (Sur. Soc. xl), p. 38 n.
47 B.I.H.R., CP. H. 4994, 5535; Lawrance, 'Clergy List', Holderness, 2, p. 141; E.R.A.O., DDCC/24/2, s.v. 1680; DDCC/85/3, s.v. 1669.
48 B.I.H.R., V. 1764/Ret. 3, no. 36; *Herring's Visit.* ii, pp. 14–15, 223; iii, pp. 36, 129–30, 177–8.

49 B.I.H.R., V. 1865/Ret. 2, no. 495; V. 1868/Ret. 2, no. 451; V. 1871/Ret. 2, no. 457.
50 Ibid. V. 1912–22/Ret.
51 E.R.A.O., PE/137/21, T. 46; B.I.H.R., TER. 88; O.S. Map 1/2,500, Yorks. CLXXX. 2 (1910 edn.); inf. from Mrs. M. Newton, Skipsea, 1997.
52 Notices in Skipsea church.
53 B.I.H.R., Prob. Reg. 6, f. 66; *N. Country Wills*, i (Sur. Soc. cxvi), p. 272. *ST. NICHOLAS* was given, evidently in error, in 1851: P.R.O., HO 129/524/1/8/15.
54 *Chron. de Melsa* (Rolls Ser.), iii. 225, 273.
55 B.I.H.R., TER. H. Skipsea 1770, 1857; *Reg. Greenfield*, iii, p. 156.
56 B.I.H.R., V. 1578–9/CB. 1, f. 69; V. 1590–1/CB. 1, ff. 133v., 134; ER V./CB. 1, f. 90v.; J. S. Purvis, *Tudor Par. Doc. of Dioc. York*, 59.
57 B.I.H.R., ER. V. Ret. 1, f. 32; H.U.L., DP/159/4.
58 B.I.H.R., TER. H. Skipsea 1825; Poulson, *Holderness*, i. 452 n.; Sheahan and Whellan, *Hist. York & E.R.* ii. 435.
59 Rainwater heads of 1866; B.I.H.R., V. 1868/Ret. 2, no. 451; ibid. Fac. 1865/6; Fac. Bk. 5, pp. 98–105; ibid. Ch. Ret. iii; Sheahan and Whellan, *Hist. York & E.R.* ii. 435.

restored in 1893 and 1932.[60] In 1986 Skipsea church was repaired by an anonymous benefactor.[61]

Until 1720, when it was taken down, there was a chancel screen.[62] 'High Church' fittings, including a medieval statue of the Virgin and Child, were added in the mid 20th century, but the interior was very plain in 1997.[63] Memorials include a damaged gravestone, engraved with chalice-like motifs and therefore believed to commemorate a priest, and a wall tablet of c. 1830 by John Earle of Hull. Outside is a sundial incised in the stonework of the south aisle.

There were three bells in 1552 and 1973,[64] but only one in 1997. The plate includes a silver cup made in 1725.[65] The registers of baptisms and burials begin in 1720 and of marriages in 1721; the record of marriages between 1755 and 1812 seems not to have survived.[66] There are transcripts from 1599 for Skipsea and from 1600 for Ulrome.[67]

Besides 4d. from each house in the parish, the parish clerk was entitled to three sheaves of wheat from each bovate in Dringhoe, two sheaves per bovate in Skipsea manor and one sheaf a bovate in Cleeton manor, for which annual rents of £2 from Dringhoe and £1 10s. from Skipsea township were substituted at the inclosures of 1763 and 1765 respectively.[68] The clerk's dues were being refused in 1910.[69]

ULROME. A chapel had been built at Ulrome, perhaps by the Ulrome family, by 1226.[70] The area it came to serve lay in the parishes of Skipsea and Barmston,[71] and tithes belonging to those churches in Ulrome were evidently assigned in support of the chaplain there.[72] Ulrome chapel acquired a measure of independence, and the chapelry was sometimes called, and eventually in the mid 19th century became, a separate parish.[73] The living was called a vicarage from the 16th century.[74] Institutions to the chapel were, however, few, and it was frequently served from the 17th century by licensees,[75] and also described as a curacy.[76] After endowment in the late 18th century the living was reckoned

to be a perpetual curacy,[77] and it has been a vicarage since augmentation in 1863.[78] Burial was generally at Skipsea or Barmston until the right to bury at Ulrome was obtained, apparently in 1878.[79] In 1925 Ulrome was united with Skipsea, and in 1979 that united benefice was enlarged to include Barmston and Fraisthorpe.[80]

The right to present to Ulrome chapel belonged to Robert of Ulrome in 1226, when he released it to William de Forz, count of Aumale.[81] The history of the patronage later in the Middle Ages is not known but it probably descended with the manor. The chapel seems to have been suppressed under the Chantries Act of 1547 but in 1560 Brian Lacy, lord of Ulrome manor, held it as the Crown's tenant,[82] and it evidently survived. The advowson was sold with the manor in 1582–3 to Leonard Robinson the elder,[83] and later passed from the Robinsons to John and William Hartas.[84] The Crown presented in 1626 for its ward William Hartas,[85] and in 1650 the patrons were given as another Leonard Robinson and George Hartas.[86] Robinson was said to have conveyed his right to George in 1657.[87] With Ulrome manor, the right of appointing the curate later passed from the Hartases to the Shiptons and from them to the Rickabys.[88] The Crown presented again, by lapse, in 1721.[89] In 1744 Sir Griffith Boynton, Bt., bought the patronage.[90] The Boyntons were succeeded in it by John Lockwood (d. 1827),[91] whose executors presented his son J. W. K. Lockwood in 1833. The advowson was bought in 1850 by Mary Armistead,[92] in 1857 by Gregory Bateman, vicar 1862–8, and in 1868 by E. A. Tickell, vicar 1868–96.[93] The patronage later belonged to Tickell's trustees.[94] After the union of Skipsea and Ulrome in 1925, E. J. Tickell had one of three turns in presenting to the united benefice.[95] At the further union of 1979 Dr. Winifred Kane, in right of Ulrome, was made one of the joint patrons of the new benefice.[96]

Ulrome vicarage was valued at £3 19s. net in 1535,[97] and in 1650 the annual, improved value

60 Kelly's Dir. N. & E. R. Yorks. (1897), 534; (1933), 539.
61 Plaque in Barmston church.
62 B.I.H.R., ER. V. Ret. 1, f. 32.
63 E.R.A.O., PE/137/21; B.I.H.R., Fac. 1959/2/42; TER. 856.
64 B.I.H.R., TER. H. Skipsea 1764 etc.; TER. 856; Inventories of Ch. Goods, 53; Boulter, 'Ch. Bells', 85.
65 Yorks. Ch. Plate, i. 314.
66 E.R.A.O., PE/137/1–2, 5.
67 B.I.H.R., PRT. Hold. D.
68 Ibid. TER. H. Skipsea 1764; R.D.B., AC/178/9; AF/180/9; E.R.A.O., PE/137/21.
69 B.I.H.R., TER. 88.
70 Yorks. Fines, 1218–31, p. 79.
71 Above, intro.
72 Below, this section.
73 Valor Eccl. (Rec. Com.), v. 117; Lond. Gaz. 10 Feb. 1925, pp. 960–1; directories.
74 B.I.H.R., TER. H. Ulrome 1726; Valor Eccl. (Rec. Com.), v. 117; Herring's Visit. iii, p. 178.
75 Poulson, Holderness, i. 237.
76 B.I.H.R., TER. H. Ulrome 1716.
77 Ibid. TER. H. Ulrome 1809; below, this section [income].
78 Lond. Gaz. 28 July 1863, pp. 3744–5.

79 E.R.A.O., PE/6/9; PE/137/8; PE/141/3; Poulson, Holderness, i. 239.
80 Lond. Gaz. 10 Feb. 1925, pp. 960–1; B.I.H.R., OC. 955.
81 Yorks. Fines, 1218–31, p. 79.
82 P.R.O., E 318/47/2483, f. 7.
83 Yorks. Fines ii. 195.
84 Ibid. iii. 41; iv. 159; above, manors (Ulrome).
85 B.I.H.R., Bp. Dio. 3, E.R., p. 183.
86 T.E.R.A.S. iv. 59–60.
87 Bulmer, Dir. E. Yorks. (1892), 280.
88 B.I.H.R., Bp. Dio. 3, E.R., p. 183; R.D.B., F/98/215.
89 Poulson, Holderness, i. 237.
90 R.D.B., AH/331/9; H.U.L., DDWB/25/25; Poulson, Holderness, i. 229.
91 R.D.B., DR/305/373.
92 Ibid. GY/48/61; H.U.L., DDCV(2)/48/1; Poulson, Holderness, i. 237.
93 R.D.B., HO/292/365; KH/304/346; E.R.A.O., PE/141/1; B.I.H.R., Inst. AB. 23, p. 87.
94 E.R.A.O., DDX/215/19; R.D.B., 317/470/379; Kelly's Dir. N. & E.R. Yorks. (1901), 569.
95 Lond. Gaz. 10 Feb. 1925, pp. 960–1; Crockford (1930), 785.
96 B.I.H.R., OC. 955.
97 Valor Eccl. (Rec. Com.), v. 117.

was £17 2s. 1d. net.[98] The living was augmented
with £200 Bounty money by lot in 1780,[99] and
between 1829 and 1831 the income of Ulrome
averaged £71 a year net.[1] Sums of £200 were
granted from the Common Fund to meet
benefactions of like amount in 1863 and 1864,[2]
and in 1873 tithe rents in the township amounting to £25, formerly belonging to the archbishop
of York as rector, were conveyed to the living,
which had by then received benefactions totalling £600.[3] The net value in 1883 was £132.[4]

In 1396 the small tithes of Ulrome were let to
a chaplain, who presumably served the chapel
there,[5] and tithes of Ulrome township belonging
to Skipsea and Barmston churches were later
enjoyed by the curate at Ulrome. In 1535 hay
and small tithes and offerings accounted for
most of the chapel's value.[6] In the 18th century
the curate's share of the tithes comprised the
hay tithes from the 24 bovates belonging to
Skipsea parish and from some of the old inclosures, wool and lamb tithes from 13 bovates, and
the small tithes. The hay tithes of closes in the
Barmston part of the township were by then
paid by compositions totalling 17s. a year.[7] At
the inclosure of Ulrome in 1767 the curate
was awarded £15 a year for some of his tithes
there; land should have been received for others
but that was mistakenly awarded to Barmston
rectory.[8] The remaining tithe at Ulrome, a
render of a hen from each house at Christmas,[9]
was commuted for a rent charge of 15s. a year
in 1843.[10]

Glebe land and a dovecot were worth 16s. a
year in 1535.[11] In the mid 18th century the
curate had just over 20 a. of closes, pasture gates,
and the right to gorse, or whins, from the
common.[12] At inclosure in 1767 it was clearly
intended to give the curate land for his gates,
whins, and some tithes, but in error that compensation was combined with the land allotted
to the rector of Barmston for his tithes in
Ulrome, and the whole 75 a. was awarded to
John Holme, curate of Ulrome and rector of
Barmston, as rector of Barmston alone.[13] By
deed of 1823 John Gilby, also rector and curate,
attempted to correct the mistake by assigning
to Ulrome curacy 32 a. from the allotments.[14]
Bounty money was used to buy 7 a. at Thorn-

gumbald, in Paull, in 1786.[15] The glebe's value
in 1851 was £35 a year.[16] In 1978 there remained
unsold 21 a. at Ulrome and the 7 a. at Thorngumbald.[17]

A parsonage at Ulrome was used little or
never by those serving the chapel in the 18th
and earlier 19th century, when they rented
another house or lived outside Ulrome.[18] The
mud and thatch cottage[19] was rebuilt as a two-
storeyed brick and tile house by William Dade,
curate, in 1781, shortly after being blown down.
The house was evidently let, in 1839 as two cottages[20] and by 1887 as three; Church Cottages
were sold in 1972, and by 1997 they had been
re-converted into a single house.[21] A fit residence
was built in 1864 with contributions from the
Ecclesiastical Commissioners and the incumbent.[22] It was sold in 1925 on the union with
Skipsea; later called Harbrook Lodge and
Ulrome House, it was re-purchased in 1959 and
became the residence of the united benefice in
place of the Skipsea house.[23] The house at
Ulrome was sold again in 1977 following the
incumbent's move to Barmston Rectory, which
was duly designated as the parsonage house at
the union of 1979.[24]

Ulrome chapel included a chantry, which
Meaux abbey administered and had possibly
once served; in 1368 the abbey granted a life
term in a house and 1 bovate at Ulrome, lately
held by the preceding chaplain, to his replacement, subject to the payment of a rent to the
abbey.[25]

William the chaplain was paid for serving
Ulrome chapel in 1267–8, and John of Ulrome,
chaplain, who held land and the small tithes of
the village from Meaux abbey in 1396 was presumably also curate there.[26] In the 18th century
Ulrome was served with neighbouring livings,
among them Skipsea and Barmston.[27] In 1764,
for instance, the curate of Ulrome, John Holme,
was also rector of Brandesburton and Barmston,
and he employed a curate to live at Barmston
and do his duty there and at Ulrome. There was
then a service each Sunday at Ulrome, and quarterly celebrations of Holy Communion, with
usually c. 30 communicants.[28] Services remained
few in the 1860s, when the incumbent was again

98 T.E.R.A.S. iv. 60.   99 Hodgson, Q.A.B. cccl.
1 Rep. Com. Eccl. Revenues, 974–5.
2 Lond. Gaz. 28 July 1863, pp. 3744–5; 12 July 1864,
pp. 3492–3.
3 Ibid. 11 July 1873, p. 3291; above, manors (rectory).
4 B.I.H.R., V. 1884/Ret. 2.
5 B.L. Cott. MS. Vit. C. vi, f. 217.
6 Valor Eccl. (Rec. Com.), v. 117.
7 B.I.H.R., TER. H. Ulrome 1716, 1726.
8 R.D.B., AH/331/9; below, this section [glebe].
9 B.I.H.R., TER. H. Ulrome 1770.
10 Ibid. TA. 581s.
11 Valor Eccl. (Rec. Com.), v. 117.
12 B.I.H.R., TER. H. Ulrome 1764.
13 R.D.B., AH/331/9.
14 Ibid. DR/305/373; B.I.H.R., TER. H. Ulrome 1825.
Later terriers for Ulrome and Barmston and Barmston's
ownership in the 20th century suggest that the correction
had little effect: B.I.H.R., TER. H. Ulrome, Barmston; inf.
from York Dioc. Bd. of Finance, 1981.
15 B.I.H.R., TER. H. Ulrome 1809; R.D.B., BL/125/163.
16 P.R.O., HO 129/524/1/6/11.

17 Inf. from York Dioc. Bd. of Finance, 1981.
18 Below, this section.
19 B.I.H.R., V. 1764/Ret. 3, no. 100; ibid. TER. H.
Ulrome 1764, 1770; Herring's Visit. iii, p. 177.
20 B.I.H.R., TER. H. Ulrome 1786; Poulson, Holderness, i. 241.
21 B.I.H.R., TER. H, Ulrome 1887; R.D.B., 1762/60/51.
22 E.R.A.O., PE/141/1; ibid. DDX/215/19; B.I.H.R.,
Ch. Ret. iii; Rep. Com. Eccl. Revenues, 974–5.
23 E.R.A.O., PE/137/21; R.D.B., 317/470/379; 974/152/
134; 1137/400/360; above, this section (Skipsea [glebe]).
24 B.I.H.R., OC. 955; inf. from Mrs. Bayley, The Old
Vicarage, Ulrome, 1997.
25 E.R.A.O., DDCC/98/1; B.L. Cott. MS. Vit. C. vi,
f. 217.
26 P.R.O., SC 6/915/3, m. 1d.; B.L. Cott. MS. Vit. C.
vi, f. 217.
27 B.I.H.R., Bp. Dio. 3, E.R., p. 183; Poulson, Holderness, i. 205, 237, 451.
28 B.I.H.R., V. 1764/Ret. 3, no. 100; Herring's Visit. ii,
pp. 14–15; iii, pp. 36, 129–30, 177–8; Alum. Cantab. to
1751, 398.

non-resident, and Ulrome was served by a licensed curate. Ten people on average then communicated.[29] Improvement followed the augmentation of the living in the 1860s and 1870s, and the acquisition of a resident vicar:[30] by 1871 there were two Sunday services, communion was monthly by 1877, and a night school was also attempted. Communion was later weekly.[31] In 1997 a service and a celebration of communion were provided at Ulrome once a month, in rotation with the other three churches of the united benefice.[32]

The church of *ST. ANDREW*, so-called in 1420,[33] stands on a small hill at the west end of Ulrome village. Before its rebuilding in the 19th century, the church was mostly built of boulders, and comprised chancel, nave with south porch, and west tower.[34] Two circular-headed doorways, perhaps of the 13th century, and a 15th-century window then remained in the 'churchwardenized' building; one of the doorways and the window have since been re-used. Later work probably included the addition of the porch and an upper part to the tower, both of brick. The chancel was rebuilt after storm damage in 1778, presumably by the inhabitants of the chapelry who were responsible for the whole building.[35] Repairs were done in the 1860s,[36] and in 1876 the chancel and nave were rebuilt and a north vestry added, all in a 13th-century style by Armfield & Bottomley of Middlesbrough and Whitby. The rebuilding was executed in boulders with brick banding and ashlar dressings; the interior is of brick. It was paid for partly by the Ecclesiastical Commissioners and the incumbent, E. A. Tickell.[37] The boulder-built tower was heightened and given a short, pyramidal roof in 1904 to designs by Brodrick, Lowther & Walker of Hull as a memorial to E. A. Tickell, vicar 1868–96,[38] and a clock was installed in 1914.[39]

Fittings formerly included a chancel screen, removed or reduced in 1720 and replaced in 1753.[40] The font, comprising a large, circular cup on an octagonal shaft, may be 12th-century. Mural memorials include one to William Tomlin, vicar from 1721,[41] and his family, and

another of slate and marble to Mary Robinson (d. 1890).

The plate includes a silver cup of 1729.[42] Registers of baptisms at Ulrome begin in 1813 and of marriages in 1837.[43] There were two small bells in 1552, and later one bell.[44]

Church repairs were said in 1743 to be funded from the sale of furze growing on the common,[45] but at inclosure in 1767 the churchwardens had £1 a year for that purpose from the rents of open-field balks which were also spent on the poor. An allotment of 5 a. was then substituted for the balks,[46] and the church continued to receive £1 of the annual income until 1981, when its share was raised to £6.[47]

The parish clerk of Ulrome was awarded an acre at inclosure in 1767, presumably for some remuneration then extinguished.[48] He also received either 4d. or 1s. from most of the houses in Ulrome.[49]

NONCONFORMITY. There is little evidence of Roman Catholicism in the parish.[50] Protestant nonconformity, on the other hand, seems to have been strong. Failure to attend church and hatwearing on Sundays were recorded at Skipsea c. 1580.[51] George Fox and William Dewsbury visited Skipsea and Ulrome in the early 1650s,[52] and Friends evidently accounted for most or all of the 25 recusants recorded in the parish in 1664 and the 28 protestant dissenters of 1676. Friends at Skipsea included Thomas Thompson[53] and at Ulrome George Hartas, lord of the manor and patron of the chapel there.[54] A burial ground for Friends at Ulrome was obtained in 1682,[55] and a meeting house there was registered in 1711.[56] There were later reputed to have been two burial grounds, one of which, in the grounds of the Hartases' manor house, lay close to the apparent site of a former building, perhaps the meeting house.[57] Registration was being sought for another meeting house, 'lately built' at Skipsea, in 1713,[58] but in 1743 the Friends seem to have had only one meeting house, perhaps the one at Skipsea, and that disused and without a teacher. There was a family of Quakers at Skipsea then, but in 1764 there were said to be

29 B.I.H.R., V. 1865/Ret. 2, no. 559; V. 1868/Ret. 2, no. 511.
30 Above, this section.
31 B.I.H.R., V. 1871/Ret. 2, no. 518; V. 1877/Ret. 3, no. 129; V. 1884/Ret. 2; V. 1912–22/Ret.
32 Notices in Skipsea church.
33 *Test. Ebor.* i, p. 398.
34 This para. based on Poulson, *Holderness*, i. 238–9.
35 B.I.H.R., TER. H. Ulrome 1764.
36 Ibid. V. 1865/Ret. 2, no. 559; V. 1868/Ret. 2, no. 511.
37 Ibid. Ch. Ret. iii; ibid. V. 1877/Ret. 3, no. 129; E.R.A.O., PE/141/5.
38 Plaque on tower.
39 E.R.A.O., PE/141/1; B.I.H.R., Fac. 1903/34; *Kelly's Dir. N. & E.R. Yorks.* (1909), 601.
40 B.I.H.R., ER V./Ret. 1, f. 31; ER V./Ret. 2, f. 5v.; Poulson, *Holderness*, i. 239.
41 *Herring's Visit.* iii, p. 178.
42 *Yorks. Ch. Plate*, i. 327.
43 E.R.A.O., PE/141/1–2. Registers from the 18th century have been noticed but their whereabouts are unknown: Lawton, *Rer. Eccl. Dioc. Ebor.* 419; *Par. Doc. of Archd. of*

E.R. (Y.A.S. Rec. Ser. xcix), 146.
44 B.I.H.R., TER. H. Ulrome 1764; *Inventories of Ch. Goods*, 51; Boulter, 'Ch. Bells', 86.
45 *Herring's Visit.* iii, p. 177.
46 R.D.B., AH/331/9; above, loc. govt.; below, charities.
47 E.R.A.O., accession 1681; below, charities.
48 R.D.B., AH/331/9.
49 B.I.H.R., TER. H. Ulrome 1764, 1887.
50 Aveling, *Post Reformation Catholicism*, 68.
51 B.I.H.R., V. 1578–9/CB. 1, f. 68v.; E.R.A.O., DDCC/85/1.
52 Fletcher, 'Quakerism in E. Yorks.' (Hull University, B.A. dissertation, 1985), 6.
53 H.U.L., DFF/2/11.
54 B.I.H.R., ER V./CB. 1, ff. 90–1, 95v.–97v.; E.R.A.O., DDCC/24/2, s.v. Oct. 1668; *Depositions from York Castle* (Sur. Soc. xl), pp. 121, 123; *Compton Census*, ed. Whiteman, 600; Bulmer, *Dir. E. Yorks.* (1892), 280; above, manors (Ulrome); churches (Ulrome [adv.]).
55 H.U.L., DQR/17/47.
56 P.R.O., RG 31/7, no. 13.
57 Poulson, *Holderness*, i. 240.
58 E.R.A.O., QSF/22/D.2.

no dissenters at either Skipsea or Ulrome.[59] The meeting house at Skipsea is reputed to have fallen down by 1779,[60] but there was later a house called Quakers, or Quaker, House on the south side of the village street;[61] in 1997 it was used as a shop and tearoom. There was then believed to be a burial ground behind it.[62]

The missionary efforts of members of Fish Street chapel, Hull, included visits c. 1800 to Skipsea and Bonwick.[63] Services were held in a farmhouse until 1801, when a converted building in Leys Lane, Skipsea, was opened as an Independent chapel. Later associated with Hornsea,[64] the chapel was rebuilt on another site, to the south of Main Street, in 1875 or 1876 to designs by J. Stork.[65] The old chapel, which seems to have been enlarged in 1839 to accommodate the Sunday school and the Rechabites' Teetotalers Victory Tent,[66] was later used as a reading room and meeting place.[67] The new chapel, later the Congregational church, was by the 1890s united with Beeford and North Frodingham, and served from Beeford.[68] The church was closed in 1954, and c. 1970 the building was demolished and houses were built on the site.[69]

The Wesleyan Methodists have worshipped at Skipsea since the early 19th century. Their meeting place was described in 1822 as a house used as a chapel; it was presumably the same building which had been registered as a chapel in 1812.[70] The chapel is elsewhere said to have been 'erected', possibly meaning converted, in 1815.[71] It was rebuilt in 1836,[72] and again in 1910; the building, of red brick with terracotta dressings in a 15th-century style, is by Samuel Dyer.[73] Wesleyanism was very strongly supported in the earlier 20th century,[74] and the Methodist church was still used in 1997.

A Primitive Methodist chapel built west of Skipsea village green in 1845 was evidently

closed c. 1875.[75] Corner House is believed to incorporate, or occupy the site of, the former chapel.[76]

Unidentified protestants registered a house at Ulrome in 1776, 1805, and 1821,[77] and in 1848 a Wesleyan Methodist chapel was built on the south side of the street there.[78] That chapel was replaced in 1905 by a new one on the opposite side of the street;[79] as Ulrome Methodist church, the yellow brick and terracotta building by Samuel Dyer[80] was still used in 1997. The old chapel, sold in 1936[81] and later used as a garage,[82] still stood in 1997.

EDUCATION. SKIPSEA. A school seems to have been kept in the church at Skipsea in the 16th century,[83] and in the mid 18th parishioners hired a teacher for their children.[84] In 1818 a school for boys and a girls' school at Skipsea together had 60 pupils.[85] There were three schools there in 1833, attended by 46 boys and 22 girls, almost all of them paid for by their parents. The Independents then ran a Sunday school for boys and the Wesleyan Methodists one for girls,[86] and in 1845 the Wesleyans put up a day school beside the road to Ulrome.[87] The day school was supported by subscriptions, collections, and school pence, and in 1869 it took boys, girls, and infants and had an average attendance of 38.[88] At inspection in 1871 it was attended by 48 boys and 21 girls, including children from Dringhoe, Upton, and Brough.[89] Soon afterwards Skipsea Wesleyan school was enlarged, re-opening in 1873[90] and receiving an annual government grant from 1873–4.[91] A school district for Skipsea, Dringhoe, Upton, and Brough, Ulrome, and Bonwick was formed in 1875, and the school was later also supported by a voluntary rate.[92] Average attendance was

59 B.I.H.R., V. 1764/Ret. 3, nos. 36, 100; *Herring's Visit.* iii, pp. 129, 177.

60 D. [R. J.] and S. Neave, *E.R. Chapels and Meeting Houses* (E. Yorks. Loc. Hist. Soc.), 57.

61 R.D.B., 450/226/178; E.R.A.O., DDX/295/9.

62 Inf. from Mr. M. Wilson, Skipsea, 1997.

63 For the following, C. E. Darwent, *Story of Fish St. Ch., Hull* (1899), 128–9, 131–3.

64 P.R.O., RG 31/5, nos. 1539, 1755; ibid. HO 129/524/1/8/13; E.R.A.O., DDCC(2)/83, vol. ii, s.v. 1 Mar. 1803; vol. iv, s.v. 30 Mar. 1868; ibid. DDX/7/33; O.S. Map 6″, Yorks. CLXXX (1855 edn.).

65 O.N.S. (Birkdale), Worship Reg. no. 23626; *Kelly's Dir. N. & E.R. Yorks.* (1889), 455; Bulmer, *Dir. E. Yorks.* (1892), 501; O.S. Map 1/2,500, Yorks. CLXXX. 2 (1892 edn.).

66 Poulson, *Holderness*, i. 456; the datestone was kept in a house nearby in 1997: inf. from Mrs. M. Newton, Skipsea, 1997.

67 Above, intro.

68 Above, Beeford, nonconf.

69 R.D.B., 928/385/345; O.N.S. (Birkdale), Worship Reg. no. 30672; inf. from Mrs. M. Newton, Skipsea, 1997.

70 E.R.A.O., DDCC(2)/83, vol. ii, s.v. 28 Oct. 1822; P.R.O., RG 31/5, no. 2689.

71 E.R.A.O., MRQ/1/31. P.R.O., HO 129/524/1/8/16 dates the building of the chapel to c. 1800.

72 Bulmer, *Dir. E. Yorks.* (1892), 501; O.S. Map 6″, Yorks. CLXXX (1855 edn.).

73 Datestone; O.N.S. (Birkdale), Worship Reg. nos. 2385, 44360; Neaves, op. cit. 57, 62 (illus.); Pevsner and Neave, *Yorks. E.R.* 686; illus. in M. and B. Chapman,

Holderness in old picture postcards, 60.

74 B.I.H.R., V. 1900/Ret. no. 357; V. 1912–22/Ret.; V. 1931/Ret.

75 P.R.O., HO 129/524/1/8/14; O.N.S. (Birkdale), Worship Reg. no. 595; *Kelly's Dir. N. & E.R. Yorks.* (1872), 545; (1879), 648; O.S. Map 6″, Yorks. CLXXX (1855 edn.).

76 Inf. from Mrs. D. Statters, Skipsea, 1997.

77 B.I.H.R., Fac. Bk. 2, p. 146; P.R.O., RG 31/5, nos. 1927, 3560.

78 P.R.O., HO 129/524/1/6/12; ibid. RG 31/5, no. 4678; R.D.B., GK/2/2; O.S. Map 6″, Yorks. CLXIII (1854 edn.).

79 O.S. Map 1/10,560, TA 15 NE. (1956 edn.); G.R.O., Worship Reg. nos. 2382, 41308; Neaves, op. cit. 58 (illus.).

80 Pevsner and Neave, *Yorks. E. R.* 727.

81 E.R.A.O., MRQ/1/39, p. 17.

82 Neaves, op. cit. 59.

83 E.R.A.O., DDCC/24/1, s.v. 25 Sept. 1556.

84 B.I.H.R., V. 1764/Ret. 3, no. 36.

85 *Educ. of Poor Digest*, 1093.

86 *Educ. Enq. Abstract*, 1095.

87 E.R.A.O., DDCC(2)/83, vols. iii, s.v. 19 Nov. 1845; iv, s.v. 14 Mar. 1863.

88 P.R.O., ED 7/135, no. 161; B.I.H.R., V. 1868/Ret. 2, no. 451; O.S. Map 6″, Yorks. CLXXX (1855 edn.).

89 *Returns relating to Elem. Educ.* 474–7.

90 E.R.A.O., MRQ/1/37; O.S. Map 1/2,500, Yorks. CLXXX. 2 (1892 edn.);

91 *Rep. of Educ. Cttee. of Council, 1873–4* [C.1019-I], p. 446, H.C. (1874), xviii. An earlier grant seems to have been made in 1849–50: *Mins. of Educ. Cttee. of Council, 1849–50*, [1215], p. cxlv, H.C. (1850), xliii.

92 Bulmer, *Dir. E. Yorks.* (1892), 501.

c. 60 in the 1870s[93] and 87 in 1889.[94] Skipsea Wesleyan, later Skipsea Methodist, school was altered in 1905.[95] In the early 20th century attendance was usually *c.* 60 but in the mid 1930s it stood at 42.[96] The school was granted Controlled status in the early 1950s.[97] Senior pupils were transferred to Hornsea County Secondary School in 1958.[98] Skipsea Methodist primary school was closed in 1968, when a new county primary school built on Hornsea Road to serve Skipsea, Ulrome, and Lissett, in Beeford, was opened.[99] The former school building was later used as a pottery[1] and in 1997 as a house. In 1990 the new school had 73 on the roll.[2]

There was said to be a 'good parish school' in 1840,[3] and in 1845 a National school for Skipsea and Ulrome was built by the parishioners on land opposite Skipsea church belonging to the archbishop as rector.[4] Supported by school pence, subscriptions, and from 1862–3 by an annual government grant, the mixed school had an average attendance of 46 in 1862.[5] The school was closed in 1870, and the building was used later as a farm outbuilding before being rebuilt in 1902 as a parish room and Sunday school.[6] It was intended to build a new National school in 1869, when the archbishop gave a site for it at the junction of Hornsea Road and Cross Street in the east of the village.[7] The Wesleyan school was, however, the only one in the village in 1875,[8] and, apart from an apparently erroneous reference to a Church school in 1900,[9] no evidence has been found for a second National school.

ULROME. A schoolmaster lived at Ulrome in 1851,[10] and in 1871 there was a Church school for infants attended by 7 boys and 8 girls; older children presumably went then, as later, to school in Skipsea. The school was probably held in a house until 1874, when a schoolhouse is said to have been built.[11] The school was supported by school pence and donations from the vicar and others, and in 1877 it had an average attend-

ance of 27.[12] A new Church, or National, school, built in 1897 to commemorate the Diamond Jubilee on a site given by the vicar, was opened in 1898.[13] The mixed school evidently also took older children, and the transfer of pupils from the Wesleyan school at Skipsea to the new school at Ulrome was said to have led to protracted disputes.[14] Average attendance was *c.* 20 in the early and mid 20th century.[15] Pupils of eleven to fourteen years old were probably transferred, like those at Atwick, to Hornsea primary school in the late 1940s, and eleven year olds later left to attend Hornsea County Secondary School, presumably from its opening in 1958.[16] Ulrome primary school, which by then had Controlled status, used the village hall for some activities by the 1950s.[17] There were 30 pupils in 1961.[18] The school was closed in December 1966, and in January 1967 its former pupils began to attend the soon to be replaced school at Skipsea.[19] The old school at Ulrome was later converted to a house.[20]

In DRINGHOE, UPTON, AND BROUGH township there was a school in which ten girls were taught at their parents' expense in 1833.[21]

CHARITIES FOR THE POOR. John Holme, curate of Ulrome 1745–75,[22] left a quarter of the income from securities for distribution by later incumbents to the poor of the chapelry at Christmas. Ulrome's share *c.* 1820 was about £3 5*s.*[23] In the earlier 20th century the income of *c.* £2 a year was given in doles ranging from a shilling or two to well over £1, 16 people benefiting in 1902 and 8 in 1930.[24]

The income from 5 a. allotted at the inclosure of Ulrome in 1767 belonged mostly to the poor of the township.[25] It was £6 a year in 1862.[26] By the late 19th century the land had been divided into ¼-a. plots and let for gardens. The rents amounted to £7 a year in the early 20th century, when £4 or £5 were distributed in doles of 1*s.*–10*s.* to some 18 people.[27] The gardens were

93 E.R.A.O., MRQ/1/37.
94 *Kelly's Dir. N. & E. R. Yorks.* (1889), 455.
95 E.R.A.O., MRQ/1/58; E.R. Educ. Cttee. *Mins.* 1905–6, 61, 222; 1934–5, 119.
96 *Bd. of Educ., List 21* (H.M.S.O., 1908 and later edns.).
97 E.R. Educ. Cttee. *Mins.* 1953–4, 22.
98 Ibid. 1955–6, 151; above, Hornsea, educ.
99 Letter in E.R.A.O., SL 77/2; E.R.A.O., MRQ/1/59; E.R. Educ. Cttee. *Mins.* 1966–7, 36–7, 40; 1967–8, 118; 1968–9, 19; above, Beeford, educ.
 1 R.D.B., 1655/263/235.
 2 Inf. from Educ. Dept., Humbs. C.C., 1990.
 3 Poulson, *Holderness,* i. 456.
 4 P.R.O., ED 7/135, no. 186; ED 49/8596; E.R.A.O., PE/137/T. 46; O.S. Map 6″, Yorks. CLXXX (1855 edn.).
 5 P.R.O., ED 7/135, no. 186; B.I.H.R., V. 1865/Ret. 2, no. 495; V. 1868/Ret. 2, no. 451; *Rep. of Educ. Cttee. of Council, 1862–3* [3171], p. 522, H.C. (1863), xlvii.
 6 P.R.O., ED 49/8596; E.R.A.O., PE/137/21, T. 46; B.I.H.R., TER. 88; above, churches (Skipsea [church life]).
 7 B.I.H.R., SS. 1869; P.R.O., ED 49/8596.
 8 E.R.A.O., MRQ/1/37.
 9 B.I.H.R., V. 1900/Ret. no. 357.
10 P.R.O., HO 107/2367.
11 *Returns relating to Elem. Educ.* 476–7; *Kelly's Dir. N. & E.R. Yorks.* (1872), 554; (1889), 466.

12 B.I.H.R., V. 1877/Ret. 3, no. 129; V. 1884/Ret. 2.
13 Datestone; E.R.A.O., SL/110/1–3.
14 B.I.H.R., V. 1900/Ret. no. 396; E.R.A.O., PE/141/1; ibid. DDX/215/19; O.S. Map 1/2,500, Yorks. CLXIII. 13 (1910 edn.).
15 *Bd. of Educ., List 21* (H.M.S.O., 1908 and later edns.).
16 E.R.A.O., SL/110/1, p. 208; SL/110/2, pp. 217–22, 235, 242; above, Atwick, educ.; Hornsea, educ.
17 E.R. Educ. Cttee. *Mins.* 1955–6, 151; 1956–7, 212; 1958–9, 5.
18 E.R.A.O., SL/110/2, pp. 217–22.
19 E.R. Educ. Cttee. *Mins.* 1966–7, 57; E.R.A.O., SL/110/2, p. 252.   20 R.D.B., 1599/196/175.
21 *Educ. Enq. Abstract,* 1095.
22 *Alum. Cantab. to 1751,* 398.
23 *9th Rep. Com. Char.* 754–5, 757; *Poor Law Abstract, 1818,* 522–3; above, Barmston, Brandesburton, charities; *V.C.H. Yorks. E.R.* v. 134.
24 E.R.A.O., accession 1681; Review of Char. *Rep.* 155.
25 R.D.B., AH/331/9; above, loc. govt.; above, churches (Ulrome).
26 Correspondence held by County Archivist, Beverley, 1997.
27 E.R.A.O., accession 1681. Cf. map of Ulrome 1766, print. Poulson, *Holderness,* i, facing p. 242; O.S. Map 1/2,500, Yorks. CLXIII. 13 (1892 edn.).

given up in the mid century, and in 1980 a farmer held the land for £40 a year. The Christmas doles had then been discontinued for two years.[28]

By Scheme of 1981 the two charities were united. The rent of the allotment had by then been raised to £138. Apart from £6, which was assigned to church repairs, the net income from the allotment was to be used, with that of Holme's charity, for the relief of needy persons of Ulrome.[29]

WITHERNWICK

THE village of Withernwick lies 14 km. north-east of Hull and 4 km. from the coast.[30] The southern parish boundary is formed by Lamb-wath stream, an ancient boundary which formerly also separated the middle and northern divisions of Holderness wapentake.[31] The name Withernwick may be an Anglo-Scandinavian hybrid, meaning 'dairy farm near a thorn tree'.[32] In 1852 Withernwick township contained 2,822 a. (1,142 ha.), comprising all 2,691 a. (1,089 ha.) of the ecclesiastical parish of Withernwick and detached parts of Mappleton parish amounting to 131 a. (53 ha.).[33] The township, later civil parish, was enlarged in 1885 by the transfer of Scarshaws, of 39 a. (15.8 ha.), from Aldbrough parish, and the civil parish still has 1,157 ha. (2,859 a.).[34]

There were 145 poll-tax payers at Withernwick in 1377,[35] and 56 houses were assessed for hearth tax in 1672.[36] The parish had 48 families in 1743 and 61 in 1764.[37] The population of Withernwick rose from 292 in 1801 to 356 in 1811 and 513 in 1851. Numbers declined from the 1870s, to 449 in 1881 and 365 in 1891, recovered in the first decade of the 20th century, but then fell again to 345 in 1951 and 312 in 1961. The village later grew, notably in the 1970s, when the population increased from 325 to stand at 435 in 1981. In 1991 the usual population was 440 of whom 436 were actually counted.[38]

The parish is largely on boulder clay, and practically all of the land lies below 15 m. above sea level, falling from about 14 m. in the centre of the parish, close to the village, to under 7 m. in the south, alongside Lambwath stream. Land over 15 m. is found only at the eastern boundary, in the north-west corner of the parish, and as several small hills formed by the sand and gravel deposits which provided both the village and its northern outlier with their sites. The low-lying alluvial land in the south was mostly occupied by old inclosures, almost certainly as grassland, and the higher ground on either side of the village by the open fields.[39] The commonable lands were inclosed in the early 19th century, the long drawn-out process being confirmed by award in 1814.[40]

Withernwick is drained by Lambwath stream, which was recorded as defective in 1367,[41] and by tributaries flowing southwards across the parish. Withernwick beck was the main tributary until largely replaced in the early 19th century; a scheme to improve the drainage of the low grounds adjoining Lambwath stream in Withernwick and neighbouring parishes was then designed by William Chapman and carried out in 1812 as part of the inclosure process. Two new, embanked drains were made, one, known later as Catchwater drain, to carry water from the north and centre of the parish south-westwards to a new outfall into Lambwath stream close to the western boundary, and the other flowing westwards close to Lambwath stream.[42] Lambwath stream was later transferred to Keyingham Level Drainage Board, which still existed in 1998. Despite the improvements, the land alongside Lambwath stream remained liable to flooding.[43]

From the village minor roads lead north to Great Hatfield, in Sigglesthorne, west to Rise and Beverley, and east to join the main Holderness coast road near Aldbrough village and also at Great Cowden, in Mappleton. The roads were improved at inclosure, that to Rise and Beverley being described in 1809 as a new road.[44] A lane runs along the western parish boundary from Rise to Marton, in Swine, over Lambwath bridge, which was mentioned in 1367;[45] the southern part is called Lambwath Lane and the northern stretch, now only a bridleway, Folly, formerly Oak Tree, Lane.[46] Another minor road, confirmed in 1814 as the Hull–Hornsea road,[47] crosses the west end of the parish, and there was formerly a side road from it leading to Folly Lane.[48] The Hull–Hornsea railway, opened in 1864, ran through the parish with a station 2 km. west of the village beside the Rise road at Whitedale.[49] The station was closed for passen-

[28] Correspondence held by County Archivist, Beverley, 1997.
[29] Scheme and correspondence held by County Archivist, Beverley, 1997; Review of Char. *Rep.* 155.
[30] This article was written in 1992–3.
[31] English, *Holderness*, 111.
[32] *P.N. Yorks. E.R.* (E.P.N.S.), 26–7, 69; G. F. Jensen, *Scand. Settlement Names in Yorks.* 260–1.
[33] O.S. Map 6″, Yorks. CCXII (1855 edn.); *Census*, 1871.
[34] *Census*, 1891–1991.
[35] P.R.O., E 179/202/60, m. 45.
[36] Ibid. E 179/205/504.
[37] B.I.H.R., V. 1764/Ret. 3, no. 140; *Herring's Visit.* iii, p. 225.
[38] *V.C.H. Yorks.* iii. 495; *Census*, 1911–91.
[39] Geol. Surv. Map 1″, drift, sheet 73 (1909 edn.).

[40] Below, econ. hist.
[41] Poulson, *Holderness*, i. 129.
[42] R.D.B., CQ/245/16; O.S. Map 6″, Yorks. CCXII (1855 edn.).
[43] O.S. Map 1/2,500, Yorks. CCXII. 6, 7 (1910 edn.); inf. from Environment Agency, Hull, 1998.
[44] B.I.H.R., TER. H. Withernwick 1809.
[45] Poulson, *Holderness*, i. 129.
[46] A. Bryant, *Map of E.R. Yorks.* (1829); O.S. Map 6″, Yorks. CCXII (1855 edn.).
[47] R.D.B., CQ/245/16; T. Jefferys, *Map of Yorks.* (1772).
[48] 1763 plan in book of plans of estates of H. Bethell, at Rise Park Estate Off.
[49] K. A. MacMahon, *Beginnings of E. Yorks. Rlys.* (E. Yorks. Loc. Hist. Ser. iii), 31; O.S. Map 6″, Yorks. CCXII (1855 edn.).

gers in 1964 and entirely on the closure of the line in 1965.[50] The track has been lifted and its course designated as a footpath; the station buildings were used as private houses in 1992.

WITHERNWICK village. The pattern of garths suggests that Withernwick village had a linear plan running north–south down the middle of the parish. Its buildings formed three groups, the church and most of the houses occupying a small hill overlooking the Lambwath valley, with other buildings standing c. 500 m. away on another eminence at North End and a few more, closer to the village centre, at South End. Earthworks at North End suggest that it may once have been larger. It was possibly also less separate from the rest of the village; c. 1800 two buildings stood between it and the main part of the village on land later called Old Garths.[51] Conversely, South End, named in 1630,[52] and the rest of the village have virtually been joined by recent building. The village is mostly built along a winding street, incorporating Main Street and parts of the Beverley and Aldbrough roads; in a western back lane, comprising East and West Lambwath Roads but formerly also known at least in part as South Lane; and beside Church Lane, which connects the street and back lane. There was a second cross lane south of Church Lane c. 1800, when the northern part of the street was called Leaper's Lane and a side lane continuing it eastwards Townside Road, later Chapel Lane and now High Street. High Street and a path continuing it northwards to North End, known since the early 19th century as Butcher Lane, may formerly have been parts of the main village street.[53]

Except for the church, the village is built of brick. The oldest surviving houses include 18th- and 19th-century cottages in Church Lane and the later 18th-century Withernwick Hall, formerly North End House, an **L**-shaped farmhouse of two storeys with a pedimented entrance.[54] Elm Tree House, formerly Cottage, in West Lambwath Road, was evidently built soon after 1855 by John Taylor.[55] It has a three-bayed façade of white brick under a slated and hipped roof; a pedimented doorcase is set in a shallowly projecting central bay which rises through both storeys to an eaves pediment. Other 19th-century houses include farmhouses and terraced cottages. In the 1960s and 1970s the district council built an estate of c. 50 houses north of the church,[56] and then and later there was much piecemeal building in the village. Private houses were being added in East Lambwath Road in 1992 and in West Lambwath Road in 1998. The council provided a sewage treatment works near Lambwath stream for the new housing c. 1970.[57]

Two or three houses were licensed at Withernwick in the mid 18th century but later and in the early 19th century only one, called the Gate.[58] It stood in High Street and was recorded, together with a beerhouse, until 1889, when it was called the Gate Hangs Well inn. The successor house, the Falcon, Main Street, was trading by 1892 and still existed in 1992.[59] A lodge of the Ancient Order of Foresters was founded in 1839 and had 160 members by 1895, when it left the order and became the Withernwick Foresters' Society. It rejoined the order in 1912 and was mentioned until 1948.[60] The Foresters built a hall in Main Street in 1890 and in 1910 also owned half a dozen houses in the village. The hall was used for the monthly lodge meetings and rented out for other gatherings.[61] It was sold in 1948 and converted to a house; the façade was copied for a craft shop, built beside it in 1987.[62] Withernwick in 1892 boasted, besides the friendly society, a church institute, a cricket club, and a Conservative association.[63] The cricket club played on a ground near Withernwick Hall until at least 1937, a football club on land south of Westlands Farm during the 1920s, and a tennis club near Prospect House Farm in the 1920s and 1930s.[64] Village sport later declined, but c. 1985 the parish council bought land on the Aldbrough road mostly for recreation.[65] A wooden building was put up in Main Street on land rented from the Poor's Land charity for the Women's Institute in 1939 and was later used as the village hall.[66] A branch library was held in the Methodist schoolroom in the 1970s.[67] Allotment gardens were provided about 1900 on land awarded as a sand pit at inclosure in 1814 and on part of the Bethell estate beside the Beverley road; they were still used in the 1940s.[68]

OUTLYING BUILDINGS. Houses away from the village include Whitehill, formerly Wheat Hill, Farm, built by 1772.[69] Westlands Farm was apparently built c. 1805 during the process of

50   C. R. Clinker and J. M. Firth, *Reg. Closed Passenger Stas. and Goods Depots* (1971), 151; *Hull Daily Mail*, 30 Apr. 1965.
51   E.R.A.O., IA. (C. 31); O.S. Map 6″, Yorks. CCXII (1855 edn.).
52   E.R.A.O., DDBV/51/1.
53   Ibid. IA.; ibid. NV/1/76; R.D.B., CQ/245/16; H. Teesdale, *Map of Yorks.* (1828); O.S. Map 1/2,500, Yorks. CCXII. 7 (1910 edn.).
54   E.R.A.O., IA.; A. Bryant, *Map of E.R. Yorks.* (1829).
55   R.D.B., HH/123/146; 74/90/85 (1895); 173/170/142; P.R.O., RG 10/4802 (s.v. Sarah Taylor); Bulmer, *Dir. E. Yorks.* (1892), 542.
56   R.D.B., 1360/438/401; 1416/251/228; 1723/580/493.
57   Ibid. 1533/57/54; 1544/576/490; 1547/433/381.
58   E.R.A.O., QDT/2/6, 9.
59   Directories; O.S. Map 6″, Yorks. CCXII (1855 edn.).
60   R.D.B., 775/299/250; D. [R. J.] Neave, *E.R. Friendly Soc.* (E. Yorks. Loc. Hist. Ser. xli), 71.
61   E.R.A.O., NV/1/76; datestone on hall; Bulmer, *Dir. E. Yorks.* (1892), 541; *Kelly's Dir. N. & E. R. Yorks.* (1893), 509.
62   R.D.B., 775/299/250; inf. from Mr. C. Young, Withernwick, 1993.
63   Bulmer, *Dir. E. Yorks.* 541.
64   Directories; O.S. Map 6″, TA 14 SE. (1956 edn.); inf. from Mr. S. O. Would, Withernwick, 1993.
65   Inf. from Mr. Would; below, local govt.
66   E.R.A.O., MIS. 207; inf. from Mrs. J. Fryer, Withernwick, 1993.
67   E.R. Educ. Cttee. *Mins.* 1970–1, 77.
68   R.D.B., CQ/245/16; E.R.A.O., IA.; O.S. Map 1/2,500, Yorks. CCXII. 7 (1891, 1910 edns.); *Hull Times*, 12 July 1913; inf. from Mr. J. E. Beeton, Kirkella, 1993.
69   T. Jefferys, *Map of Yorks.* (1772); O.S. Map 6″, Yorks. CCXII (1855 edn.).

inclosure, and Withernwick Grange had been put up by 1828, probably to replace the house nearby shown in 1812. Other new farmhouses in the late 1820s were Ruddens, Whitedale, Homer House, and Little West Hill Farms.[70] Glebe Farm was added in 1899.[71]

MANORS AND OTHER ESTATES. In 1066 Morkar had 6 carucates at Withernwick as soke of his manor of Mappleton, and Thor had a manor of Withernwick containing 1 carucate. By 1086 both estates had passed to Drew de Bevrère, whose tenant Wazelin held all or part of Thor's manor,[72] and they were later part of the Aumale fee. The lordship of the Aumale fee passed to the Crown and later to its grantees,[73] and in 1362 the tenant in demesne held *WITHERNWICK* of Edward III's daughter Isabel as ⅓ knight's fee.[74]

William le Gros, count of Aumale (d. 1179), was said to have given 8 carucates in Withernwick to Peter de Fauconberg, whose son Walter had inherited by 1202 and whose grandson (Sir) Peter de Fauconberg defended his title in 1231.[75] The Fauconbergs, Lords Fauconberg from the late 13th century,[76] retained the estate, usually called a manor but sometimes reckoned part of the neighbouring manor of Rise.[77] Much of the land had apparently been alienated by c. 1300, when Walter, Lord Fauconberg, (d. 1304) held in Withernwick c. 2 carucates in demesne and had bond tenants with 1½ carucate.[78] In 1316, in the lifetime of his son Walter, Lord Fauconberg, (d. 1318), the lords of Withernwick were said to be Anastasia, widow of that Walter's son Sir Walter (d. 1314), and John de Fauconberg, presumably Sir Walter's brother and later Lord Fauconberg (d. 1349).[79] From the death of John's son Walter, Lord Fauconberg, in 1362 his widow Isabel held the manor until her death in 1401; it then comprised 2½ carucates in Withernwick, and 3 carucates more there and in Great Hatfield, all apparently in the hands of tenants. In 1372 Walter's son Sir Thomas Fauconberg sold the reversion to Sir John Neville (d. 1388), whose son Ralph Neville, earl

of Westmorland, (d. 1425) duly succeeded in 1401.[80] He evidently gave the manor to his son William Neville, who married Sir Thomas Fauconberg's daughter Joan and was later held to be Lord Fauconberg. Neville died, as earl of Kent, in 1463, and his relict held the manor until she died in 1490. Withernwick then fell to the share of the Nevilles' grandson Sir James Strangways,[81] whose descendant James Strangways sold it to (Sir) Richard Gresham in 1530.[82] In 1546 Gresham granted the manor in exchange to the Crown.[83] Withernwick manor then comprised some 17 carucates held by freeholders and tenants at will.[84] At least part of Withernwick was still held by the Crown in 1598.[85]

Part of the manor, including the manor house and 7 bovates, was let in 1576 to William Knowles,[86] and it was perhaps that holding which was later regarded as the manor. Marmaduke Langdale (d. 1611) held a 7-bovate manor, together with c. 1 carucate more in Withernwick, bought by him in the 1590s.[87] His estate descended like Woodhall, in Swine, to Sir William Langdale (d. by 1685),[88] who was succeeded in Withernwick by his son Marmaduke.[89] Marmaduke sold the manor in 1703 to Hugh Bethell (d. 1717).[90] It then descended, once again with Rise manor, in the Bethells.[91] The estate was of nearly 600 a. c. 1790, and was evidently enlarged later.[92] Charlotte Bethell, widow of William (d. 1799), sold part of the estate in 1809.[93] The Withernwick estate comprised 669 a. in 1831, and 699 a. in 1852.[94] W. F. Bethell bought the 241-a. Withernwick Grange farm and c. 20 a. more from the Alders in 1865, and a further 118 a. in 1872.[95] In 1915 William Bethell had 985 a. in Withernwick.[96] The 189-a. Manor farm was sold to William Bulson in 1930;[97] Straits farm, of 160 a., was sold in 1942, and in 1943 the 187-a. Whitedale farm and c. 250 a. in Withernwick Grange farm were also disposed of. The 132 a. then remaining unsold, mostly in Ruddens farm, was vested in R. A. Bethell in 1943,[98] and the slightly enlarged farm was transferred in 1973 to his son, H. A. Bethell, who still owned it in 1995.[99] William Bulson (d. 1962)

[70] E.R.A.O., IA.; H. Teesdale, *Map of Yorks.* (1828); A. Bryant, *Map of E.R. Yorks.* (1829).

[71] Below, church.   [72] *V.C.H. Yorks.* ii. 265, 268.

[73] *V.C.H. Yorks. E.R.* v. 9–10.

[74] *Cal. Inq. p.m.* xi, p. 262.

[75] *Curia Regis R.* xiv, pp. 227–8; *Yorks. Fines, John* (Sur. Soc. xciv), pp. 12–13.

[76] *Complete Peerage.*

[77] *Plac. de Quo Warr.* (Rec. Com.), 193; *Cal. Inq. p.m.* xviii, p. 136.

[78] P.R.O., C 133/112, no. 9; *Cal. Inq. p.m.* iv, pp. 354, 357.

[79] *Kirkby's Inquest,* 303.

[80] *Cal. Inq. p. m.* ix, pp. 176–7; xi, p. 262; xviii, p. 136; *Cal. Fine R.* 1399–1405, 112–13; *Complete Peerage,* s.vv. Neville; Westmorland.

[81] P.R.O., C 140/11, no. 33; C 142/79, no. 160; *Cal. Inq. p.m. Hen. VII,* i, pp. 250–1; *Complete Peerage,* s.vv. Fauconberge; Kent.

[82] *Yorks. Fines,* i. 58; *D.N.B.* s.v. Gresham.

[83] *L. & P. Hen. VIII,* xxi (1), p. 573; *Yorks. Fines,* i. 124.

[84] P.R.O., E 318/11/528, m. 2.

[85] E.R.A.O., DDRI/42/2.

[86] P.R.O., E 310/31/185, f. 10; *Cal. Pat.* 1575–8, p. 118.

[87] P.R.O., C 142/337, no. 81; *Yorks. Fines,* iii. 143; iv. 85.

[88] H.U.L., DDLA/33/10, 14; E.R.A.O., DDCC/108/6; *Yorks. Fines, 1603–14,* 202; *1614–25,* 152; *Yorks. Royalist Composition Papers,* iii (Y.A.S. Rec. Ser. xx), p. 112; above, Swine, Ellerby township, manors (Woodhall). For the Langdales, *Y.A.J.* xi, facing p. 372.

[89] E.R.A.O., DDCC/111/32.

[90] Ibid. DDRI/34/9. For the Bethells, J. Foster, *Pedigrees of Yorks.* iii; Burke, *Land. Gent.* (1952), 170–1.

[91] R.D.B., I/447/972; E.R.A.O., DDRI/40/11; above, Rise, manor.

[92] Terriers in book of plans of estates of H. Bethell, at Rise Park Estate Off.; below, this para.

[93] Below, this section.

[94] E.R.A.O., DDRI/40/11; ibid. accession 2980, plan 1851, 'Rise Estates 1852'.

[95] R.D.B., IS/270/374; KX/263/341.

[96] Ibid. 170/289/242.

[97] Ibid. 399/340/285; 408/90/75.

[98] Ibid. 655/564/482; 659/59/52; 659/270/227; 661/119/110; 661/240/221.

[99] Ibid. 1847/146/95; Rise Park Estate Off., 'Rise Settled Estates 1967'.

was succeeded in Manor farm by his widow Vera and sons Geoffrey and J. C. Bulson. The farm was sold in lots c. 1990.[1]

A chief house, recorded from 1304, was called Hall Garth in 1576.[2] It may have stood at South End on the site of the later Manor House or Farm, which was built or rebuilt c. 1840.[3]

A cadet branch of the Fauconbergs held 1 carucate and 2 bovates in Withernwick, which by 1325 Walter de Fauconberg, possibly Lord Fauconberg (d. 1318), had granted to Thomas de Fauconberg.[4] Thomas (d. 1349) was succeeded by his son Walter,[5] and he, who died in or soon after 1360, possibly by his son John.[6] It was presumably the same estate, then described as a manor of *WITHERNWICK* and including 22 houses and 260 a., which Roger Fauconberg (d. 1455) held of the duke of Buckingham, and which in 1460 was ordered to be partitioned between Roger's nephew Walter Nuthill and sister Isabel Suthill.[7] The estate has not been traced further.

The archbishop of York had 1 carucate in 1086.[8] Part at least belonged later to the provost of the archiepiscopal church of St. John at Beverley (Beverley Minster), and c. 1370 Sir Amand of Routh was recorded as holding 2 bovates at Withernwick of the provost.[9]

A small estate was held of the Ros family in the mid 14th century, and that lordship later descended as part of their manor of Roos to the Cecils and the Kirkbys, who had it in the 18th century.[10]

The *RECTORY* was annexed to the prebend of Holme in York Minster in 1230, and from 1259 the prebendary had the glebe land, the rents of the church's tenants, and the corn tithes and a few hay tithes. About 1295 the landed estate comprised a house and 2½ bovates, and 6s. 6d. was received from two tenants.[11] The rectory was briefly lost during the Commonwealth. In 1650, when Susanna Moore held it as prebendal lessee, the glebe land and tithes in Withernwick were valued at £56 net.[12] In the later 17th century the glebe land comprised 2 broad bovates and c. 50 a. of inclosed ground.[13]

By 1693 compositions were paid for the corn tithes of South End field;[14] the rate was 8s. 10½d. a year for each broad bovate and 6s. 8d. for a narrow one in 1802, when tithes of old inclosures were similarly paid by composition. At inclosure in 1814, the rector was awarded 110 a. and rent charges of £3 5s. 0½d. for his tithes, and 36 a. for the glebe.[15]

In 1864 the Ecclesiastical Commissioners, as expectant owners of the prebendal estate under the Cathedrals Act of 1840, sold the reversion of the 201-a. farm to the lessees Thomas Woodward, Thomas Harrison, and William Green in undivided thirds. Green's share was to revert to Thomas Harrison Green,[16] and in 1865 the Greens bought the other thirds from Harrison and Woodward. By 1883 Sarah Green (d. 1890) and Mary Harrison Green owned the farm.[17] In 1891 T. C. B. Dixon (d. 1906) bought the farm, named later as Prospect House farm, and in 1909 his executor Robert Dixon sold it to William Northgraves.[18] J. W. Croft, who bought the farm in 1947, gave it in 1967 to Mr. D. W. Croft and his other children.[19] Mr. Croft bought the other shares in 1974, and in 1993 he and his wife, Mrs. M. A. Croft, owned the farm.[20]

The rectory house was mentioned c. 1295, as the prebendary's manor house,[21] and again from 1649.[22] The large Prospect House Farm dates from c. 1800 but has been much remodelled.

George Alder acquired an estate during the protracted inclosure process. He bought a farm of c. 175 a. from Ann Edwards in 1803, 23 a. more in 1806, and nearly 200 a. from Charlotte Bethell in 1809,[23] besides exchanging land with several proprietors. When the award was eventually made in 1814, he received 573 a., far more than the other allottees.[24] Alder sold 174 a. to William Lee in 1826,[25] and died c. 1845. His son John and another George Alder offered the estate, again of c. 600 a., for sale in 1864, and the next year they sold the 241-a. Withernwick Grange farm and just over 100 a. more, mostly to W. F. Bethell.[26] In 1870 George Alder sold Whitehill farm, of 247 a., to Sir William Wright.[27]

Hugh son of Walter of Withernwick gave Meaux abbey 2s. rent from ½ bovate in With-

[1] R.D.B., 1338/287/260; 1547/433/381; inf. from Mr. J. C. Bulson, Withernwick, 1993.
[2] P.R.O., C 133/112, no. 9; *Cal. Pat.* 1575–8, p. 118.
[3] E.R.A.O., accession 2980, 'Rise Estates 1852', plan 1851; O.S. Map 1/2,500, Yorks. CCXII. 7 (1891 edn.); O.S. Map 1/10,000, TA 14 SE. (1983 edn.).
[4] *Complete Peerage*, s.v. Fauconberge; *Cal. Pat.* 1324–7, 156.
[5] *Cal. Inq. p.m.* x, p. 225.
[6] Withernwick was not then named. *Cal. Inq. p.m.* x, p. 549; *Cal. Fine R.* 1356–68, 269.
[7] P.R.O., C 139/178, no. 51; *Cal. Fine R.* 1452–61, 262. For the Nuthill and Suthill fam., *V.C.H. Yorks. E.R.* v. 11.
[8] *V.C.H. Yorks.* ii. 216.
[9] E.R.A.O., PE/129/150, f. 6v.
[10] H.U.L., DDSY/56/1; DDSY/107/1, f. 158; ibid. DHO/7/41; *Cal. Inq. p.m.* viii, pp. 342, 350–1; *Yorks. Fines, 1614–25*, 168; above, Roos, manors.
[11] E.R.A.O., DDCC/107/11; B.I.H.R., D/C. CP. 1613/7; *Miscellanea*, iv (Y.A.S. Rec. Ser. xciv), 26–7; below, church.

[12] P.R.O., C 54/3624, no. 20; *T.E.R.A.S.* iv. 64; Lamb. Pal. Libr., COMM. XIIa/17/169–72.
[13] B.I.H.R., TER. H. Withernwick 1662/3, 1693.
[14] Ibid. 1693.   [15] R.D.B., CQ/245/16.
[16] B.I.H.R., CC. P./Hol. 10, Wit. 1–3; 3 & 4 Vic. c. 113, s. 51; Le Neve, *Fasti, 1541–1857, York*, 42.
[17] R.D.B., IT/215/310; NU/239/355; 6/239/230 (1885); E.R.A.O., PE/81/10/1.
[18] R.D.B., 43/470/430 (1891); 86/61/60 (1906); 115/249/228.   [19] Ibid. 750/509/415; 1571/205/181.
[20] Inf. from Mr. D. W. Croft.
[21] *Miscellanea*, iv. 27.
[22] Lamb. Pal. Libr., COMM. XIIa/17/169; B.I.H.R., TER. H. Withernwick 1693.
[23] R.D.B., CF/519/822; CK/392/651; CO/187/299.
[24] Ibid. CQ/245/16.
[25] Ibid. DY/193/235.
[26] Ibid. IS/270/374; IU/60/85; H.U.L., DDCV(2)/53/8; K. J. Allison, *'Hull Gent. Seeks Country Residence' 1750–1850* (E. Yorks. Loc. Hist. Ser. xxxvi), p. 41.
[27] R.D.B., KO/17/22.

ernwick between 1221 and 1235, but it was evidently later lost.[28] Peter de Fauconberg had given Thornton abbey (Lincs.) 1 carucate in the parish by 1190.[29] After the Dissolution the land was granted to the short-lived Thornton college in 1542.[30] It was later granted to George Salter and John Williams, and sold by them to Roger and Peter Watson.[31] By the 15th century the Hospitallers had an estate in Withernwick which passed to the Crown at their suppression.[32] St. Thomas's hospital, Southwark, was awarded 32 a. at inclosure in 1814 in exchange for land at Bewick, in Aldbrough.[33] It bought 13 a. more in 1865, and the 43-a. Little Westhill farm in 1949;[34] the 88 a. in Withernwick was sold to the Leonards as part of the Bewick estate in 1972.[35]

Lambwath manor lay partly in Withernwick but it is treated under Marton, in Swine.

ECONOMIC HISTORY. COMMON LANDS AND INCLOSURE. North and South Ends at Withernwick had their own open fields, but by the 17th century they were evidently managed together.[36] North End field and South End field were recorded from 1541.[37] Each End had in fact two fields, to the east and west. In 1545 the manor thus included 1 carucate 'in both fields', and other land in East and West fields.[38] The tillage was further divided between an infield and an outfield: South End field included an infield bovate in 1657, and in 1682 both Ends may have had an eastern infield.[39] The outfield had been reduced by the making of closes by the mid 17th century, a 27-a. close being recorded in 1641 and another outfield close, of c. 50 a., adjoining the poorly drained Lambwath grounds in 1663.[40] Land in ridge and furrow in the south-eastern corner of the parish may have been part of the outfield. By the mid 16th century arrangements within the fields had probably been changed by the division and consolidation of strips: there were then several small plots, or odd lands, besides broad and little bovates.[41] A broad bovate was later said to comprise c. 16 a., and a narrow one c. 12 a.[42] The description of a bovate as broad or narrow is believed to refer to the width of the lands which composed it, broad lands in the East Riding being usually twice as wide as narrow lands.[43]

Twenty-six acres of meadow land was recorded at Withernwick in 1086,[44] and in the 14th century there was meadow adjoining and belonging to the tillage.[45] Leys were recorded later in the fields,[46] and in 1715 it was agreed that strips amounting to a 7 ft. breadth in each narrow bovate, and proportionately more for a broad bovate, should be lain down as meadow.

The common pastures were evidently stinted at 2 beast gates for a bovate in 1304.[47] By the later 17th century there were two common pastures at North End, Criftins, and New, later North End Field, pasture.[48] It is not clear whether they were intercommoned by the farmers of South End. In the late 17th and early 18th century the stint for a bovate was about 2 gates in the winter pasture, 2–3¼ gates in the fallow, and 4–6 gates in the harvested field and pastures in autumn. Grazing was evidently scarce: twenty houses no longer having gates were listed in the 1670s, and injunctions against letting pasturage rights to outsiders were frequent. There may nevertheless have been substantial numbers of sheep in the 18th century, when a village shepherd was waged and bylaws were made to restrict the grazing of the pastures by sheep.[49] The cropping of gorse in the pastures was also regulated by bylaw, labourers and others without rights to it being forbidden to cut it in 1713.

Early inclosures were made at unknown date in the south-east corner of the parish and at its western end, where the name Ruddens means 'cleared land'.[50] the rest of Withernwick was inclosed under an Act of 1801–2, the lengthy process being confirmed by award in 1814.[51] Allotments from the commonable lands totalled 1,506 a., and c. 140 a. of old inclosures in Withernwick and 36 a. more in Bewick, in Aldbrough, were involved in exchanges.[52] There were then more than 476 a. in North End field, over 359 a. in South End field, more than 84 a. in North End Field pasture, over 65 a. in Criftins and Hills, and 12 a. at Mill hill. George Alder was awarded 573 a., Charlotte Bethell 278 a., the rector 146 a., and John Leaper 116 a. There were also five allotments of 50–99 a., seven of 10–49 a., and twelve of under 5 a. The lesser allotments included those of the archdeacon of the East Riding as rector of Mappleton and the incumbent of that church for their tithes in Withernwick township.

FARMS BEFORE 1700. In 1086 four villeins worked a plough on the archbishop's estate,[53]

[28] *Chron. de Melsa* (Rolls Ser.), i. 419.
[29] *E.Y.C.* iii, pp. 41–2.
[30] *L. & P. Hen. VIII*, xvii, pp. 29–30; *Cal. Pat.* 1580–2, pp. 6–7. [31] B.I.H.R., D/C. CP. 1613/7.
[32] P.R.O., C 141/4, no. 45; C 142/48, no. 161; C 142/214, no. 205.
[33] R.D.B., CQ/245/16; above, Aldbrough, manors (Bewick).
[34] R.D.B., IW/125/176; 828/208/180.
[35] Ibid. 1814/495/433.
[36] The account of the commonable lands before inclosure is based on a bylaw book (1673–1809): E.R.A.O., PE/9/53.
[37] Ibid. DDRI/44/3; B.I.H.R., D/C. CP. 1541/1.
[38] E.R.A.O., DDBV/51/1; DDRI/34/14; P.R.O., E 318/11/528.
[39] E.R.A.O., DDRI/44/2–3; ibid. PE/9/53, s.vv. 1674, 1682.

[40] Ibid. DDRI/44/2; B.I.H.R., TER. H. Withernwick 1662/3.
[41] P.R.O., E 318/11/528. [42] R.D.B., CQ/245/16.
[43] A. Harris, '"Land" and Oxgang in the E.R. of Yorks.' *Y.A.J.* xxxviii. 529–35.
[44] *V.C.H. Yorks.* ii. 216, 268.
[45] P.R.O., C 133/112, no. 9.
[46] E.R.A.O., DDRI/42/2.
[47] P.R.O., C 133/112, no. 9.
[48] Below, this section.
[49] E.R.A.O., PE/9/53, s.vv. 1757, 1759, 1782.
[50] Ibid. IA. Withernwick; *Chief Elements in Eng. P.N.* (E.P.N.S.), 39, s.v. *hryding*; above, this section.
[51] 42 Geo. III, c. 86 (Private and Personal, not printed); R.D.B., CQ/245/16; E.R.A.O., IA. (C. 31).
[52] Two closes were exchanged twice.
[53] *V.C.H. Yorks.* ii. 216.

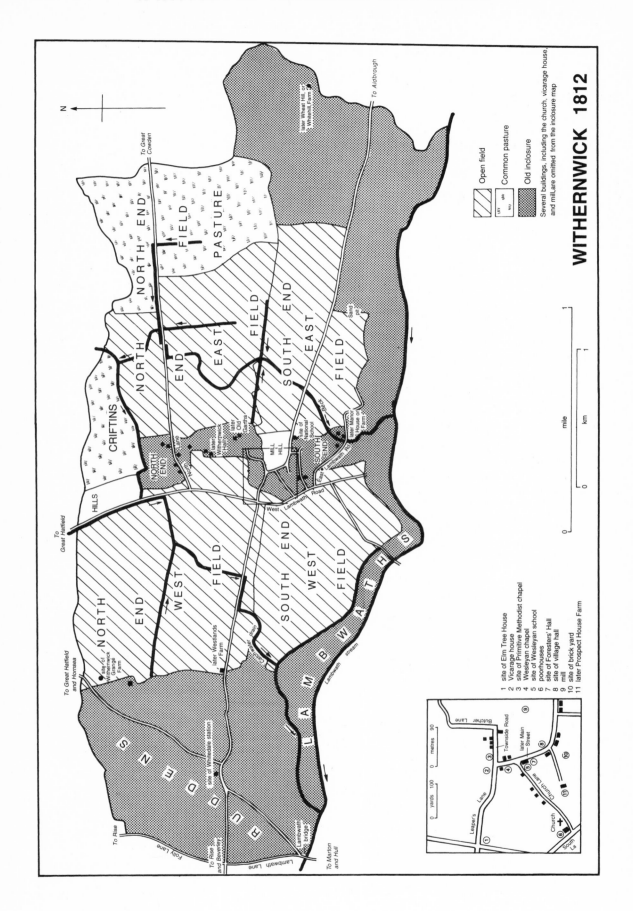

WITHERNWICK 1812

Open field

Common pasture

Old inclosure

Several buildings, including the church, vicarage house,
and mill, are omitted from the inclosure map

1 site of Elm Tree House
2 Vicarage house
3 site of Primitive Methodist chapel
4 Wesleyan chapel
5 site of Wesleyan school
6 poorhouses
7 site of Foresters' Hall
8 site of village hall
9 mill
10 site of brick yard
11 later Prospect House Farm

and two bordars were recorded on the manor formerly belonging to Thor. The latter holding had land for one ploughteam, but it then seems to have been only half cultivated, and the value of the manor had been halved since 1066.[54] In the mid 16th century free tenants of Withernwick manor held nearly 4 carucates, and tenants at will 12 carucates and 7 bovates; there were then 38 holdings, one of which was of 3 carucates, another of 2 carucates and 2 bovates, eight of 6–9 bovates each, seven of 4 bovates each, and four of 2 bovates or less. The 17 remaining holdings, comprising houses and plots of land, were evidently small.[55] In 1682 of 49 holdings in Withernwick, 24 each included less than three pasture gates in the fields, 12 had from three to nine gates each, and 13 had ten or more each.[56]

LATER AGRICULTURE. Experiments with the new husbandry were made before final inclosure. In 1785 it was agreed that each narrow bovate in the East fields should be sown with 1 stone of clover seed, and in 1792 the West fields were sown with clover at the rate of 4 lb. for each pasture gate held there, or 5 lb. if the gate were stocked with sheep.[57] Only 814 a. was returned as under crops in Withernwick in 1801.[58] In 1905 there were 1,652 a. of arable land and 843 a. of grassland,[59] and arable land was still predominant in the 1930s, when the grassland lay mostly around the village and alongside Lambwath stream.[60] Some of the grazing was used by half a dozen cowkeepers from the mid 19th century, and later a little of the arable area by one or two market-gardeners.[61] In 1987 of 1,146 ha. (2,832 a.) returned for Withernwick civil parish, 963 ha. (2,380 a.) were arable and 156 ha. (386 a.) grassland, ⅕ of it rough grazing. Woodland then occupied 5 ha. (12 a.).[62]

There were c. fifteen farms in Withernwick in the 19th and earlier 20th century, of which seven in 1851 and over half in the 1920s and 1930s were of 150 a. or more. In the latter period they also included one or two poultry farms and smallholdings.[63] In 1987 of 21 holdings returned for the civil parish, one was of 200–299 ha. (494–739 a.), two of 100–199 ha. (247–492 a.), six of 50–99 ha. (124–245 a.), ten of 2–29 ha. (5–72 a.), and two of under 2 ha. There were then over 9,000 pigs, c. 300 head of cattle, and 100 sheep in Withernwick.[64]

At the end of the 19th century an annual horse

show and a hiring fair in November were held in Withernwick.[65]

TRADE AND INDUSTRY. In the mid and late 19th century 'very good bricks' and tiles were made from the red clay near Lambwath stream, and later at a yard off Main Street,[66] where lowered ground and ponds remained in 1992. A garage was operated in the village c. 1925, and another, beside the railway station at Whitedale, has been run since the 1930s.[67] In 1992 fitted furniture was made in a workshop on the Aldbrough road.

MILLS. William le Gros, count of Aumale, (d. 1179) had a mill in Withernwick, probably driven by the beck or Lambwath stream.[68] A windmill was recorded on the manor from 1304.[69] The Crown sold the mill to Edward Ferrers and Francis Phillips in 1610,[70] but it was evidently resold soon afterwards, and later belonged, with the manor, to the Langdales and the Bethells.[71] The mill was perhaps rebuilt before or after the sale, a 'new windmill' existing by 1612.[72] The old mill may have stood west of the village, where the site of a former mill was mentioned in 1763; the mill then in use, presumably the earlier 'new' mill, stood on the eastern edge of the village.[73] A post mill, it ceased to grind in the 1890s,[74] and was soon afterwards demolished.[75] The mill house, south of the Aldbrough road,[76] remained in 1993.

LOCAL GOVERNMENT. Great courts for the view of frankpledge were held twice a year and small courts every three weeks on Roger Fauconberg's manor in the 15th century.[77] Courts were held on the Bethells' manor in the earlier 19th century.[78] Surviving parish records include churchwardens' accounts and assessments from 1748 to 1853[79] and a bylaw book of 1673–1809. The bylaws seem to have been made primarily for North End but were often extended to the whole township by agreement; in 1789 one man was said to have signed 'the top town agreements and not the bottom'. The pains were mostly concerned with agricultural regulation, including drainage and fencing, but in 1711 it was agreed that parish officers not rendering an account were to pay a fine to the poor.[80] Regular poor relief was given to 14 people in 1802–3, and in each year between 1812 and 1815

54 Ibid. 268.
55 P.R.O., E 318/11/528, m. 2.
56 E.R.A.O., PE/9/53.
57 Ibid.
58 P.R.O., HO/67/26/461.
59 Acreage Returns, 1905.
60 [1st] Land Util. Surv. Map, sheets 28, 33–4.
61 Directories.
62 Inf. from Min. of Agric., Fish. & Food, Beverley, 1990.
63 P.R.O., HO 107/2365; directories.
64 Inf. from Min. of Agric., Fish. & Food.
65 *Hull Times*, 12 July 1913; directories.
66 Poulson, *Holderness*, i. 475; White, *Dir. Hull & York* (1846), 384; (1858), 570; Bulmer, *Dir. E. Yorks.* (1892), 540; A. Bryant, *Map of E.R. Yorks.* (1829); O.S. Map 6″, Yorks. CCXII (1855 edn.).
67 Directories; inf. from Mr. B. D. H. Spencer,

Withernwick, 1993.
68 *Curia Regis R.* xiv, p. 228.
69 P.R.O., C 133/112, no. 9; *Yorks. Fines*, i. 58.
70 P.R.O., C 66/1871, mm. 25–36.
71 Ibid. C 142/337, no. 81; R.D.B., I/447/972.
72 B.I.H.R., D/C. CP. 1613/7.
73 Terrier in book of plans of estates of H. Bethell, at Rise Park Estate Off.; E.R.A.O., IA.; O.S. Map 6″, Yorks. CCXII (1855 edn.).
74 Directories.
75 O.S. Map 1/2,500, Yorks. CCXII. 7 (1910 edn.); *Hull Times*, 12 July 1913.
76 O.S. Map 1/2,500, Yorks. CCXII. 7 (1891 edn.).
77 P.R.O., C 139/178, no. 51.
78 Poulson, *Holderness*, i. 470.
79 E.R.A.O., PE/81/44.
80 Ibid. PE/9/53; *Y.A.J.* xxxv. 35–60.

some 30 inhabitants were relieved regularly and up to 12 occasionally.[81] Poorhouses adjoined the churchyard until their removal, probably in 1857 soon after the rebuilding of the church.[82] Withernwick joined Skirlaugh poor-law union in 1837[83] and remained in Skirlaugh rural district until 1935, when it became part of the new Holderness rural district. It was taken into the Holderness district of Humberside at reorganization in 1974.[84] In 1996 Withernwick parish became part of a new East Riding unitary area.[85]

About 1985 the parish council bought a piece of land on the Aldbrough road and later used it as a playing field; in 1993 it was proposed to consecrate part as a cemetery.[86]

CHURCH. There was a church at Withernwick by 1115, when it was given with others in Holderness to Aumale priory, later abbey, (Seine Maritime).[87] In 1228 the abbey ceded the church to the archbishop of York, who annexed it to the prebend of Holme in York Minster in 1230.[88] A vicarage ordained in 1259 was in the gift of the prebendary, who had peculiar jurisdiction.[89] Under the Cathedrals Act of 1840 the archbishop became patron again in 1868.[90] The parish was enlarged by the transfer to it of the detached parts of Mappleton parish in 1962,[91] and in 1979 the benefice was united with those of Aldbrough with Colden Parva and Mappleton with Goxhill. The archbishop has one turn in three in the patronage of the united benefice.[92]

In 1535 the vicarage was valued at £6 7s. net, after the deduction of a small pension to the rector.[93] The improved annual value was £30 net in 1650, when the vicar was charged with the repair of the chancel.[94] By 1674 an augmentation of £5 a year had been granted from the rectory.[95] An annuity of £39 from the Common Fund was received from 1868 and another, of £43, from 1871,[96] and in 1883 the living was valued at c. £280 net.[97]

Practically all of the income came from tithes and offerings. The hay tithes were paid by an annual composition, set or confirmed by award of 1589, those from the open fields at the rate of 8d. each for most of the bovates and the tithes of Lambwath meadows at 6d. an acre.[98] In 1716 the hay tithes of the Lambwaths contributed £20, the hay tithes from the fields £2, and wool, lamb, and other small tithes c. £4 to an income of £35.[99] At inclosure in 1814, the vicar received 93 a. and rent charges totalling £4 19s. 6d. for tithes.[1] Those remaining, on c. 210 a. mostly belonging to the Constables, were commuted in 1843 for rent charges totalling £42 17s.[2] The allotment for tithes and the farmhouse built on it, probably in 1899, were sold as Glebe farm in 1920.[3]

In 1259 a house, or a site for one, was assigned to the vicar, who was to pay a rent for it to the rector.[4] A vicarage house and adjoining close were recorded north of the street from 1535, when 2s. paid to the rector as a pension may in fact have been the rent.[5] The house was rebuilt between 1749 and 1764, and in the earlier 19th century it was divided into three cottages and let. The building was demolished shortly before 1860, when a new house was built to designs by Mallinson and Healey of Bradford on the site, which had been enlarged by purchase.[6] The vicarage house was sold in 1978,[7] and the incumbent of the united benefice later lived at Mappleton or Aldbrough.[8]

In the 15th century the poor living was often resigned and exchanged by incumbents, two of whom were defamed c. 1480. Withernwick was held with Stillington (Yorks. N.R.) in 1567 and by a puritan, Henry Thurscross, in the 1590s.[9] For many years in the 18th century the vicar lived at Great Hatfield, in neighbouring Sigglesthorne parish, whence he served, besides Withernwick, the churches of Goxhill and Mappleton. A service was held weekly at Withernwick in the mid century and communion was celebrated five times a year, with 50–100 recipients.[10] The vicar was probably often nonresident in the early and mid 19th century, when a curate was employed to do the duty; in the

[81] Poor Law Abstract, 1804, pp. 594–5; 1818, pp. 522–3.
[82] B.I.H.R., TER. H. Withernwick 1809–57; O.S. Map 6", Yorks. CCXII (1855 edn.).
[83] 3rd Rep. Poor Law Com. 170.
[84] Census.
[85] Humberside (Structural Change) Order 1995, copy at E.R.A.O.
[86] Inf. from Mr. S. O. Would and Mr. B. D. H. Spencer, Withernwick, 1993.
[87] E.Y.C. iii, pp. 30, 35–6; V.C.H. Yorks. E.R. v. 18.
[88] Reg. Gray, pp. 22, 52.
[89] E.R.A.O., DDCC/107/11; Lawrance, 'Clergy List', Holderness, 2, pp. 176–8; R.D.B., CQ/245/16.
[90] 3 & 4 Vic. c. 113, s. 41; Le Neve, Fasti, 1541–1857, York, 42.
[91] B.I.H.R., OC. 774.   [92] Ibid. OC. 942.
[93] Valor Eccl. (Rec. Com.), v. 117.
[94] Lamb. Pal. Libr., COMM. XIIa/17/173; T.E.R.A.S. iv. 64. Later the lessees and purchasers of the rectory were liable for the chancel: B.I.H.R., CC. P./Hol. 10, Wit. 1–3; ibid. Wet. 6; R.D.B., 750/509/415.
[95] B.I.H.R., CC. P./Hol. 10, Wit. 1–3; ibid. Wet. 1; R.D.B., 750/509/415.
[96] Lond. Gaz. 13 Apr. 1869, p. 2237; 1 March 1872, p. 1269.
[97] B.I.H.R., V. 1884/Ret. 2. No return was made for 1829–31.
[98] Ibid. D/C. CP. 1590/1; ibid. TER. H. Withernwick 1693, etc.
[99] Ibid. TER. H. Withernwick 1716; Valor Eccl. v. 117; T.E.R.A.S. iv. 64.
[1] R.D.B., CQ/245/16.
[2] B.I.H.R., TA. 280s.
[3] Ibid. MGA. 1898/1; R.D.B., 222/263/232.
[4] E.R.A.O., DDCC/107/11.
[5] B.I.H.R., TER. H. Withernwick 1662/3, 1693; Valor Eccl. v. 117; Lamb. Pal. Libr., COMM. XIIa/17/173.
[6] B.I.H.R., TER. H. Withernwick 1749–1861; ibid. MGA. 1860/2; E.R.A.O., PE/81/51; Lond. Gaz. 13 Apr. 1869, p. 2236; O.S. Map 6", Yorks. CCXII (1855 edn.); O.S. Map 1/2,500, Yorks. CCXII. 7 (1891 edn.).
[7] Inf. from Mr. I. Jackson, Withernwick, 1993.
[8] B.I.H.R., OC. 942; Crockford (1989–90); above, Aldbrough, church; Mappleton, churches (Mappleton).
[9] B.I.H.R., D/C. AB. 1, ff. 199v., 222; ibid. V. 1567–8/CB. 1, f. 204v.; Lawrance, 'Clergy List', Holderness, 2, pp. 176–7; R. A. Marchant, Puritans and Ch. Courts in Dioc. York 1560–1642, 284.
[10] B.I.H.R., V. 1764/Ret. 3, no. 140; Herring's Visit. ii, pp. 14–15, 223; iii, pp. 225–7.

FIG. 35. WITHERNWICK CHURCH BEFORE REBUILDING IN THE 1850S

1880s the vicar, then resident, had an assistant curate.[11] By the 1860s there were two Sunday services; then and later in the century c. 20 people usually received at the 10 or so celebrations of communion held each year. Communion was weekly by the mid 20th century but in 1931 the average number of communicants was only nine.[12]

The 'God's love bede' to which Agnes Constable left a cloth in 1521 may have been a poorhouse.[13] About 1 a. in Withernwick was given to support a light, presumably in Withernwick church.[14]

The church of *ST. ALBAN*, a dedication recorded in the earlier 16th century,[15] is built of boulders and rubble dressed with ashlar and banded with red brick; it comprises chancel and nave with north vestry, south aisle, and south porch. It was largely rebuilt c. 1854.[16] Reset 12th-century chevron voussoirs in the nave may have come from the north doorway of the earlier church.[17] The eastern bays of the arcade are 14th-century. On the north side of the nave there was formerly a medieval chapel, perhaps the St. Mary's aisle (*angulo*) mentioned in 1521,[18] which was later replaced in turn by a schoolroom and the present vestry. The east window was 15th-century.[19] In 1722 a brick tower was built into the west end of the nave in place of a belfry (*pyramis*).[20] The nave was given a west gallery and in 1806 a new roof, but by

then the appearance of the building was marred by brick patching and in 1840 the windows were 'more fitted for shops than a church'.[21] The rebuilding of the 1850s was generally in a 14th-century style to designs by Mallinson and Healey. The plan was retained except that the tower was demolished, the space being returned to the nave, and a bellcot was placed over the chancel arch instead.[22] In or shortly after 1954 a chapel was formed from the east end of the aisle.[23] By 1972 over £1,100 had been bequeathed for the upkeep of the church and churchyard,[24] much of which was spent in renewing the west window c. 1985.[25]

There are wall tablets to Matthew Topham (d. 1773), vicar, and his sons. There were two bells in 1552,[26] but a broken bell was sold in the 1720s[27] and the remaining bell was replaced by two others at the rebuilding.[28] Also renewed then was the plate, which includes a service made in 1854 and given by the vicar.[29]

The registers of births and baptisms begin in 1652, and of marriages and burials in 1655; marriages are apparently lacking for some years but the registers are otherwise complete. There are transcripts from 1601.[30]

The base of a cross survives in the churchyard,[31] which had been closed for burials by 1993.[32]

The parish clerk received three sheaves of wheat a year from each broad and two from each narrow bovate in the parish until inclosure in

[11] P.R.O., HO 129/522/3/1/1; B.I.H.R., V. 1884/Ret. 2; ibid. Ch. Ret. iii; *Educ. of Poor Digest*, 1097.

[12] B.I.H.R., V. 1865/Ret. 2, no. 600; V. 1868/Ret. 2, no. 557; V. 1871/Ret. 2, no. 561; V. 1877/Ret. 3, no. 173; V. 1884/Ret. 2; V. 1912–22/Ret.; V. 1931/Ret.

[13] *Test. Ebor.* v, pp. 137–8; above, local govt.

[14] P.R.O., E 311/35, no. 29.

[15] B.I.H.R., Prob. Reg. 11A, f. 228; *Test. Ebor.* v, pp. 137–8.   [16] Below, this section.

[17] For the church before rebuilding, Poulson, *Holderness*, i. 469 (illus.), 472–3.   [18] *Test. Ebor.* v, p. 137.

[19] Poulson, *Holderness*, i. 472.

[20] B.I.H.R., D/C. Fac. 1721/1; Poulson, *Holderness*, i. 472.

[21] Plaque in porch; T. Allen, *Hist. Co. York*, ii. 416; Poulson, *Holderness*, i. 472.

[22] B.I.H.R., Ch. Ret. iii; ibid. V. 1865/Ret. 2, no. 600; Pevsner and Neave, *Yorks. E.R.* 763.

[23] E.R.A.O., accession 1436; ibid. PE/81/30.

[24] B.I.H.R., TER. 750.

[25] Inf. from Mr. B. D. H. Spencer, Withernwick, 1993.

[26] *Inventories of Ch. Goods*, 57.

[27] B.I.H.R., D/C. Fac. 1721/1.

[28] Ibid. TER. H. Withernwick 1809–57; G. R. Park, *Ch. Bells of Holderness*, 71.

[29] B.I.H.R., TER. H. Withernwick 1809–57; ibid. TER. 90, 751; *Yorks. Ch. Plate*, i. 335.

[30] E.R.A.O., PE/81/1, 3; B.I.H.R., Hol. PRT.

[31] Poulson, *Holderness*, i. 473; O.S. Map 1/2,500, Yorks. CCXII. 7 (1891 edn.).

[32] Inf. from the vicar.

1814, when £6 5s. 10d. was substituted. He was also entitled to 1s. 2d. from each house and 4d. from each cottage annually. The payments were again recorded in 1861.[33]

NONCONFORMITY. There were generally few recusants and non-communicants in Withernwick in the 17th and 18th centuries,[34] but 17 papists were recorded there in 1706 and c. 1720 William Langdale, of neighbouring Langthorpe, in Swine, and three other papists registered estates in Withernwick.[35]

In 1676 there were said to be two protestant dissenters in Withernwick.[36] In 1783 Thomas Thompson, a leading Hull Methodist, and others registered a house there,[37] and in 1811 the Wesleyans built a chapel in Main Street, which was enlarged in 1843 and 1850 and rebuilt in 1914.[38] The Wesleyans also built a Sunday school in Main Street in 1845.[39] The Primitive Methodists put up a chapel in High Street in 1843 and enlarged the building with another schoolroom c. 1880.[40] About 1920, when half a dozen families were Wesleyan, only a dozen people attended the Primitive chapel,[41] which was then closed; the building was sold in 1923, used as a builder's store in 1993,[42] and had been demolished by 1998, when a house called Chapel Bricks stood on the site. Services were still held in the Methodist church, formerly the Wesleyan chapel, in 1993, but the Sunday schoolroom was then mostly used as a village meeting place.[43]

EDUCATION. Matthias North (d. 1713)[44] charged land in Withernwick with £2 a year for schooling or apprenticing children of Withernwick. The land was bought for the poor of Rise in 1737,[45] and the rent charge was later received from the Rise charity.[46] There was evidently a schoolmaster at Withernwick c. 1770,[47] and the village school was held in the church in the early

19th century.[48] In 1818 it was attended by 30 boys and girls[49] and in 1833 by 24; the school was supported by subscriptions, school pence, and £1 a year from the charity,[50] for which four poor children were taught free in 1823.[51] The other £1 a year from North's charity was then spent occasionally in apprenticing a child.[52] By the mid century 17 children were being taught free, all or most of them at the expense of Richard Bethell (d. 1864), who left £15 a year for the school.[53] A building for the school, which by 1844 was a National school, was put up in 1846 and enlarged with an infants' room in 1858, and in 1865 a master's house was added by W. F. Bethell.[54] Average attendance was 70 in winter and 40 in summer c. 1865. About that date the master ran a night school for some 15 farm boys but gave it up as a financial burden, and a night school attempted later by the vicar was also unsuccessful.[55] An annual government grant was received from 1869, and the school was occasionally also assisted by a rate.[56] On inspection day in 1871 the school was attended by 48 children, including some from Ellerby, in Swine.[57] In 1892 a school board was formed and the school transferred to its management.[58] After the county council assumed control, it set about remedying the 'very unsatisfactory' building; alterations were carried out in 1906, and in 1910 the school was enlarged to include a new infants' room.[59] Average attendance at the council school in the early 20th century was c. 80, but numbers later fell to about 50 in the mid 1920s and 34 in 1937–8.[60] Senior pupils were transferred to Hornsea County Secondary School in 1958.[61] The primary school had 30 pupils on the roll in 1990.[62] The master's house was sold in the 1980s.[63]

A second school in Withernwick in 1833 was attended by 22 fee-paying boys and girls.[64]

CHARITIES FOR THE POOR. A landed endowment, of unknown origin, belonged to the

33 R.D.B., CQ/245/16; B.I.H.R., TER. H. Withernwick 1764–1861.
34 Aveling, *Post Reformation Catholicism*, 57, 68; *Depositions from York Castle* (Sur. Soc. xl), p. 123; *Compton Census*, ed. Whiteman, 600; *Herring's Visit.* iii, p. 226.
35 B.I.H.R., Bp. Dio. 3, E.R., p. 190; E.R.A.O., QDR/2/36, 60, 62; *Herring's Visit.* iii, p. 225.
36 *Compton Census*, ed. Whiteman, 600.
37 B.I.H.R., DMH. 1783/10, 12; *V.C.H. Yorks. E.R.* i. 313–14.
38 P.R.O., HO 129/522/3/1/3; Sheahan and Whellan, *Hist. York & E.R.* ii. 439; datestone, which erroneously has 1810 for the building; O.S. Map 6″, Yorks. CCXII (1855 edn.).
39 Datestone; Sheahan and Whellan, *Hist. York & E.R.* ii. 439; O.S. Map 6″, Yorks. CCXII (1855 edn.); illus. in D. [R. J.] and S. Neave, *E.R. Chapels and Meeting Ho.* (E. Yorks. Loc. Hist. Soc.), 41.
40 P.R.O., HO 129/522/3/1/2; R.D.B., FX/130/160; LZ/225/343; 264/188/156.
41 B.I.H.R., V. 1912–22/Ret.; V. 1931/Ret.
42 R.D.B., 264/188/156; inf. from Mr. B. D. H. Spencer, Withernwick, 1993.
43 Local inf.
44 E.R.A.O., PE/81/1.
45 Ibid. DDRI/34/21; DDRI/44/8; *Herring's Visit.* iii, p. 226.
46 *9th Rep. Com. Char.* 773, 783–4.
47 N. Wright, *John Day, a Village Poet*.

48 T. Allen, *Hist. Co. York*, ii. 416; above, church [fabric].
49 *Educ. of Poor Digest*, 1097.
50 *Educ. Enq. Abstract*, 1099.
51 *9th Rep. Com. Char.* 783; *Poor Law Abstract, 1818*, pp. 522–3.   52 *9th Rep. Com. Char.* 783–4.
53 B.I.H.R., V. 1865/Ret. 2, no. 600; White, *Dir. Hull & York* (1846), 384; J. Foster, *Pedigrees of Yorks.* iii.
54 Sheahan and Whellan, *Hist. York & E.R.* ii. 439; Bulmer, *Dir. E. Yorks.* (1892), 541. The poor's land may have been intended as the site but was not used: R.D.B., GA/189/233; O.S. Map. 6', Yorks. CCXII (1855 edn.); below, charities.
55 B.I.H.R., V. 1877/Ret. 3, no. 173; *1st Rep. Com. on Employment of Children, Young Persons, and Women in Agric., App. Pt. II* [4068-I], p. 365, H.C. (1867–8), xvii.
56 B.I.H.R., V. 1877/Ret. 3, no. 173; *Rep. of Educ. Cttee. of Council, 1869–70* [C. 165], p. 679, H.C. (1870), xxii.
57 *Returns relating to Elem. Educ.* 472–3.
58 E.R.A.O., SB/38/1; *Kelly's Dir. N. & E.R. Yorks.* (1893), 509.
59 P.R.O., ED 49/8621; E.R. Educ. Cttee. *Mins.* 1904–5, 150; 1906–7, 224, 288; 1910–11, 167, 245; 1911–12, 64.
60 *Bd. of Educ., List 21* (H.M.S.O., 1908 and later edns.).
61 E.R. Educ. Cttee. *Mins.* 1955–6, 151; above, Hornsea, educ.
62 Inf. from Educ. Dept., Humbs. C.C., 1990.
63 Inf. from Mr. Spencer.
64 *Educ. Enq. Abstract*, 1099.

poor by 1752, when it was let for £2 13s. a year.[65] It comprised a garth of c. 1 a. and a piece of open-field land, for which ¼ a. was awarded at inclosure in 1814. In 1823 the rents of the Poor's Land, amounting to just over £6, were added to rent charges of £2 from farms in the parish, comprising the Withernwick Doles charity, and the combined income was spent on clothing for widows of the parish and in cash doles given at Easter.[66] The Doles charity, which was later lost,[67] may have been created under the will of William Day (d. 1616), who charged an estate in Withernwick with £2 a year for the poor of the parish.[68] By 1901 the income from the Poor's Land and the £2 rent charge originally given for education[69] together produced just over £10,

which was given as doles of 3s. 6d. to 7s. 6d. to 45 people; in 1921, when the joint income was just over £8, doles of 13s. 6d. each were given to 12 widows and widowers.[70] In 1980 the £2 rent charge was redeemed for £27, which was invested in the name of the Withernwick Poor's Estate charity, and that charity and the Poor's Land, with an income of £15 in 1979,[71] continued to be administered together. In 1985 the combined income of nearly £19 was given to the village Darby and Joan club.[72] In 1993 it was proposed to amalgamate the eleemosynary charity and the village hall trust, to provide a village meeting place and recreational facilities and to give help to the old.[73]

[65] E.R.A.O., PE/9/53.
[66] Ibid. PE/81/44; ibid. IA.; R.D.B., CQ/245/16; 9th Rep. Com. Char. 783.
[67] Review of Char. Rep. 114.
[68] B.I.H.R., Prob. Reg. 34A, ff. 92v.–93v.
[69] Above, educ.
[70] E.R.A.O., accession 1681.
[71] Ibid. MIS. 207.
[72] E.R.A.O., CCH/28.
[73] Notice on hall, 1993.

INDEX

NOTE. Page numbers in bold-face type are those of the principal reference. A page number followed by *n* is a reference only to the footnotes of that page. An italic number denotes an illustration on that page.

The following abbreviations are used in the index: Alex., Alexander; Alf., Alfred; And., Andrew; Ant., Anthony; abp., archbishop; Art., Arthur; Benj., Benjamin; bp., bishop; Cath., Catherine; Chas., Charles; Chris., Christopher; ctss., countess; Dan., Daniel; dau., daughter; d., died; Edm., Edmund; Edw., Edward; Eliz., Elizabeth; fam., family; f., father; fl., flourished; Fred., Frederick; Geo., George; Geof., Geoffrey; Gilb., Gilbert; grdf., grandfather; grds., grandson; Hen., Henry; Herb., Herbert; Humph., Humphrey; Jas., James; Jos., Joseph; jr., junior; Leon., Leonard; Ld., Lord; Marg., Margaret; Marm., Marmaduke; m., married; Mat., Matthew; Mic., Michael; Nic., Nicholas; neph., nephew; Pet., Peter; Phil., Philip; Reg., Reginald; Ric., Richard; Rob., Robert; Rog., Roger; Sam., Samuel; sr., senior; Sim., Simon; s., son; Steph., Stephen; Thos., Thomas; Vct., Viscount; Vctss., Viscountess; Wal., Walter; wid., widow; w., wife; Wm., William.

A. B. I. Caravans Ltd., 327
Abbs:
  Bryan, 313
  Revd. Cooper, 313
Acklam:
  Ann, wid. of Wm. (d. 1865), 325, 329
  Anna Maria, dau. of Pet. (d. 1744), 282
  Eliz., m. Sir Mark Milbanke (d. 1680), 389
  Geo. (fl. 17th cent., one or more), 228, 329
  Geo. (d. 1793), 267
  John (d. 1551), 389
  John (d. 1611), 389
  John (d. 1644), 389
  John (fl. 1672), 282
  Jonathan (fl. 1760s), 208, 392
  Mary, *see* Moreby
  Pet. (d. 1690), 282–3, 292–3
  Pet. (d. 1744), 226, 228, 282
  Pet. (fl. 1758), 295
  Pet. (d. by 1805), 227–8, 388
  Pet. (d. *c.* 1825), 227, 282, 284, 388
  Sarah, 392
  Thos. (fl. earlier 17th cent., one or more), 208, 388
  Thos. (fl. 1665, ?the same), 282
  Thos. (d. by 1721), grds. of last, 226, 228, 282, 388
  Thos. (fl. 1750), s. of last, 226, 228, 388
  Thos. (fl. 1760), s. of last, 227
  Thos. (d. by 1771), s. of last, 227
  Thos. (fl. 1763, one of the above), 393
  Thos. (d. 1811, another), 325
  Sir Wm. (d. by 1378), 389
  Wm. (d. 1567), 389
  Sir Wm. (d. 1637), 389
  Wm. (d. 1789), 325
  Wm. (d. 1804), 325
  Wm. (d. 1865), 325
  fam., 226, 228, 282, 292, 388–91
Aconley:
  Alan, 301
  Jas., 250
  John, 301
  fam., 250, 301
Adam (fl. 13th cent.), 216
  his w., *see* St. John, Agnes
Adelin (fl. earlier 12th cent.), 384
Admiralty, 219, 313
Adwick le Street (Yorks. W.R.), 205
Adwick upon Dearne (Yorks. W.R.), 205
affeerors, 21, 75, 90, 114, 147, 198, 236, 266, 288, 302, 370
Africa, 249
Agnes, sister of Philip the chaplain, 353
agriculture, 3–4; *and see* cattle; common fields; common meadows; common pastures; crops, rotation; crops and livestock; horses; inclosure; market gardening; pig farming; poultry farming; rabbit warrens; sheep farming; waste or woodland; *and see under local government sections for regulation of*

agricultural engineers, machine makers, 4, 21, 74, 219, 236, 396; *and see* Blenkin; Caley, Edw.; Caley & Ayre; Caley & Townsend; Grasby, Francis *and* Rob.; Holderness Plough Co. Ltd.; Seward Agricultural Machinery Ltd.; Stamford, John; Stephenson, Wm.
Air Council, Ministry, 13, 232, 248, 323, 378, 384
Aire, Wal., 31
airfields, 4; *and see* Catfoss; Leconfield; Lissett; Second World War
Ake, Wm., 321
Alan the parson, 242
Albert (fl. 1086), 148
Aldbrough:
  Agnes of, *see* Beverley
  John of, *see* Beverley
  Reynold of, *see* Beverley
Aldbrough, 1, **5–27**, *6*, *8*, 36–7, 76, 95, 152, 306, 317, 319–20, 327, 353, 405
  advowson, 22–3, 317, 412
  Aldbrough Hall, 9
  almshouses, 26
  bridges, 7
  castle, 7
  chantries, 18, 23, 53, 339
  chapels, medieval, 22–4, 319
  chapels, nonconformist, 25–6
  charities, 9, 12, 22–3, 25–7, 67
  church, 7, 14 *n*, 17–18, 22–5, 27, 53; *plate 11*
  church hut, *see* village halls
  common fields, 7, 19, 23
  common meadows, 7, 19, 154
  common pastures, 7, 17, 19
  courts, 21–2
  curates, 24, 37
  domestic architecture, 7, 9–10, 27
  drainage, 7, 109
  Druids' lodge, 9
  fair, 20–1
  guilds, 23
  inclosure, 7, 10–14, 17, 19, 23, 26–7
  industry, 7, 21
  inns, 9
  manor house, Manor Farm, 11–12
  manors, 1, 10–12, 14, 20–2, 52–3, 62, 88, 119, 121, 144, 152, 158, 189
  market, 7, 20–1
  Oddfellows' lodge, 9
  parish council, 9, 22, 27
  parish officers, 22, 25, 27, 317
  playing field, 9
  poor relief, 9, 22, 26–7, 317
  population, 5
  protestant nonconformity, 25
  rectors, 12, 24; *and see* Lucy, Godfrey
  rectory, 12, 14, 17–19, 23
  rectory house, 17
  resort, 9
  roads, 3, 7, 41, 58, 60, 95–6, 109, 123, 169–70, 308, 406
  Roman Catholicism, 25

  schools, 24–6
  Thorpe Garth (or Thorpe, Thorpe next to Aldbrough, Thorpe in Aldbrough, ?Totele), 5, 10–11, 13, 18, 20, 22, 52–3, 88, 121
  tithes, 14, 17, 19, 23–4
  Tymperon's hospital, 9, 27
  vicarage, 18, 22–3, 317, 412
  vicarage houses, 9, 23, 318, 412
  vicars, 9, 20, 23–4; *and see* Browne, John; Fenwick, John; Hutton, John; Mooke; Torre, Nic.
  village halls, church hut, 9, 24
  Wentworth House, 9, 23
  windmills, 21
  and see Bewick; Carlton; Etherdwick; Fosham; Lambwath; Newton, East *and* West; Ringbrough; Tansterne
Aldbrough (Yorks., ?another), 11 *n*
Aldbrough Floral and Horticultural Society, 9
Aldbrough Newton, *see* Newton, East
Alder:
  Geo. (d. *c.* 1845), 408–9
  Geo. (fl. 1865), 408
  John, 408
  fam., 407
Aldred, Earl (fl. 11th cent.), 331 *n*
Alec-Smith:
  (formerly Smith), Alex., 186, 190, 202
  Lucy, w. of Alex., 202
aletasters, bread-tasters, 21–2, 36, 75, 90, 122, 137, 155, 219, 288, 302, 396
Alfkil (fl. 1066), 215
Alford:
  Dorothy, m. Thos. Grantham, 125–6, 192
  Lancelot (d. 1563), 192
  (Sir) Lancelot (d. 1617), 184, 191–2, 197
  Rog., 192
  Sir Wm., 125, 174, 192, 257
  fam., 152, 191–2, 197
Allanson (or Allatson):
  Eliz., m. — Fysh, 138
  Ric., 138
allotment gardens and smallholdings, 9, 20, 27, 35, 46, 49–50, 59, 74, 95, 97, 102, 122, 125, 138, 141, 147–8, 155, 157, 162–3, 178, 186, 215–16, 225, 236, 247, 263, 299, 316, 330, 336, 356, 362, 378, 380, 382, 394, 404, 406, 411
Almond, Ann, m. 1 Horsfall Scholefield, 2 John Green, 3 Thos. Clubley, 170
Alured, Mat., 175, 192
almshouses, hospitals, *see* Aldbrough; Atwick; Barmston; Beverley; Brandesburton; Bridlington; Cawood; Emanuel hospital; Garton; Hornsea; Hull, Kingston upon; Humbleton; Owstwick; poorhouses; Preston; Routh; St. Thomas's hospital; Savoy hospital; Skirlaugh chapelry; Tunstall; York; *and see* nursing; surgeons

schools, 123, 127–8, 151, 169, 172
tithes, 126
vicar, see Quilter
vicarage, 127
vicarage houses, curacy house, 127–8
village halls, 123, 125, 128
windmill, 126
Bilton (Yorks. W.R.), 128
Bird:
  Fred., 364
  Muriel, 311
Birmingham, Fulk, rector of Sigglesthorne, 371
Birney, Sarah, 62
Blake, Jas., 134
Blakiston, Chris., 264, 267
Blanchard:
  David, 227
  Diana, see Reed
  fam., 388
Blashall, Hen., 364
Blassell, see Blussell
Blenkin, Jas., 90
Blount:
  John, 345
  Sam., 345
  Wm., 345
Blundell:
  Cath., see Newton
  Phil., 283–4
Blussell (or Blassell):
  Hugh, 138
  Pagan, 138
Bolton:
  John, rector of Hilston, 54
  Mic., vicar of Burton Pidsea, 39
Bolton priory (Yorks. W.R.), 366
Bonde (fl. 1066), 215
Bondfield, Chas., 293
Bonwick (in Skipsea), 223, 243, 321,
    374–5, 388–91, 393, 395, 397,
    399, 403
  common fields, 395
  drainage, 375
  inclosure, 395
  manor, 389
  manor house, 389
  poor relief, 397
  population, 223, 375
  protestant nonconformity, 403
  rectory, 390
  road, 377
  tithes, 390
Booth:
  Ann, 391
  Hen., 391
  Rob., 387
Boston Deep Sea Fisheries Ltd., 16, 43
Bosville:
  Gervase (d. 1621), 208
  Gervase (fl. 1682), 150
  Hen., 382
  Ralph, 382
  Susan, see Waller
  Thos., 208
  fam., 394
Boswell, —, 254
Botterill:
  Wm., 37
  Wm., & Sons, 165
boulders, buildings of, 3, 7, 24, 28, 30,
    38, 48, 55, 77, 79, 92, 165, 173,
    178, 180, 205, 215, 221, 225–6,
    240, 242, 252, 259, 268, 272, 275,
    282, 294, 304, 309, 318, 323, 328,
    348, 371, 377–8, 384, 399, 402,
    413
Bourchier:
  Eliz., see Tilney
  John, Ld. Berners, 16
  Mildred, see Roundell
Bouwens, Bethell, 14
Bower:
  Edw., 16
  Frances, m. Ric. Smith, 11
  John (fl. 1696), 16
  John (fl. 1719, ?the same), 16
  Priscilla, m. John Dowbiggin, 11

Sam., 11
Wm. (fl. 1656), 16
Wm. (fl. 1696, ?another), 16
Bowes:
  Eliz., 12–13
  Dorothy, 13
  Sir Jerome, 11
  Ralph, 11
Bowlby, Jesse, 366
bowling, 225, 247, 299
Bowman, John, 301
Boynton:
  (later Wickham-Boynton), Cycely, m.
    Thos. Lamplugh Wickham, 216
  Eliz., wid. of Sir Griffith (d. 1937),
    221
  Sir Francis (d. 1617), 216
  Sir Francis (d. 1832 or 1833),
    218–19, 222
  Sir Griffith (d. 1731), 222–3
  Sir Griffith (d. 1761), 218, 400
  Griffith, rector of Barmston, 221
  Sir Hen. (fl. c. 1500), 216
  Sir Hen. (d. 1854), 222
  Sir Hen. (d. 1899), 216
  Marg., see See
  Martin, 176
  Mat. (d. 1540 or 1541), 216
  Sir Mat. (d. 1647), 216, 219, 221
  Peregrine, 221
  Sir Thos. (d. 1581 or 1582), 216
  Wm., 216
  fam., 216, 218–22, 400
Boynton, 215, 335
Brackenholme (?in Leven), 296, 301
Braddock, Francis, 332
Bradford (Yorks. W.R.), 259, 319, 412
Bradshaw:
  Ellerker, 228
  Sir Jas., 350, 352
  K. F., 12
  M. F., 12
  fam., 250, 352, 357
Bramley:
  Chris. (?d. 1802), 170
  Chris. (fl. 1805), 170
  John, 170
  Mary, see Moorhouse
  Thos., 144, 170
Bramston, Edm., 89
Brandesburton, 168, 221, 228, **245–54,**
    247, 296, 303, 321, 325, 360, 362
  advowson, 250, 252
  Benevolent Society lodge, 246
  Brandesburton Hall, 246–7, 249–50;
    plate 50
  Brandesburton moor, 245–6,
    250–1, 326
  chapels, nonconformist, 246, 253–4
  charities, 254
  church, 246, 250, 252–3, *253*
  common fields, 245, 250
  common meadows, 250
  common pastures, 245, 250–1, 326
  cross, 246, 251
  curates, assistant curates, 252, 254
  domestic architecture, 246, 248–9
  drainage, 245–6, 250
  fair, 251
  Franklin Death Brief, 246
  hospital, 245, 247–9; *and see*
    Brandesburton Hall
  inclosure, 4, 245–8, 250–2
  industry, 4, 248, 251, 258
  inns, 246
  Manor House, Old Manor House,
    246, 248–9
  manors, 248, 250, 296, 311
  market, 251
  mill, 251
  Oddfellows' lodge, 246
  parish council, 247
  parish officers, 247
  park, 247, 249
  playing fields, 247
  poor relief, 251, 254
  population, 245
  protestant nonconformity, 253–4

R.A.F. camp, 245, 247–8
rectors, 252–4; *and see* Darrell, Wm.;
    Holme, John; Hymers; Lawson;
    Richardson, Chas.
rectory, 250, 252, 259, 303
rectory houses, 246, 252, 254
roads, 224, 246, 255, 263, 297, 321
Roman Catholicism, 253
schools, 246–8, 254, 306
tithes, 252
village hall, 247
water mill, 251
windmill, 251
woodland, 251
and see Burshill; Moor Town
Brandesby, Rob., rector of Routh, 358
Brandon, Chas., duke of Suffolk, 229
Bransby, John, rector of Sproatley and
    Settrington, master of Sutton
    college, 104
Bransholme, North (in Wawne), 186,
    188, 188–9, 193, 198, 203–4
  hall, 188
  health centre, 188, 204
  play area, 188
  public houses, 188
  schools, 181, 188, 203–4
  shopping centre, 188
  and see Hull, Kingston upon; Sutton
bread-tasters, *see* aletasters
Brearey, Wm., archdeacon of the East
    Riding, 317
Bret, Wm. le, 44
Breton, Geof. le, 229
brewing, brewers, 21, 30, 35, 302
brickmaking, tilemaking, brickmakers,
    4, 7, 21, 35, 46, 74, 90, 102, 114,
    137, 171, 198, 219, 236, 258, 266,
    287, 302, 327, 337, 356, 369,
    395–6, 411
Bridlington, 3, 215, 223
  architect, 55
  charity, 386
  communications, 3, 109, 138, 142,
    148, 157, 160, 184, 214, 219,
    224–5, 246, 263, 266, 297, 341,
    350, 377–8
  corporation, 397
  harbour, 195
  inhabitants, 359, 386, 391; *and see*
    architect
  poor relief, 386
  St. Mary's hospital, 216
  and see Marton; Wilsthorpe
Bridlington poor-law union, 219, 237,
    397
Bridlington priory, 2, 68, 99, 100,
    102–3, 193 n, 208–11, 214, 216,
    218–19, 227, 229, 234, 236–8, 242,
    284, 301–2, 304, 346, 353, 385,
    390, 392
  prior, 209, 323
Bridlington rural district, 215, 219,
    225, 237, 377–8, 380, 397
Brierley, W. H., 249
Briggs, Eliz., *see* Bewe
Brigham:
  Francis, 170
  Geo., 170, 352, 356
  Gerard, 170
  Harriet, 209
  Hen. (fl. 1672), 170
  Hen. (d. 1738, ?another), 172
  John (fl. 1672), 230
  John (d. 1710, ?the same), 170, 230
  Ralph, 228
  Rog., 170, 230, 243
  Thos. (d. 1542), 170, 312
  Ursula, wid. of Wm. (d. 1767), 170
  Wm. (d. 1767), 170–1, 230
  Wm. (d. 1851 or 1852), 168
  fam., 170, 172, 237
Brigham (in Foston on the Wolds), 269
Brighton (Suss.), Royal Pavilion, 131
Briskin, Griffith, prebendary of
    Osbaldwick, rector of Beeford, 239
British Gas Corporation, 209
British Legion, 123, 299

INDEX

Hull, Kingston upon, 109, 158, 198, 204, 246, 308, 398–9
aldermen, *see* Dobson, Wm. (d. 1666); Wood, Ric.
architects, builders, 37–8, 43, 49, 78, 93, 98, 103–6, 144, 147, 165, 180, 239, 243, 259, 275, 277–8, 293, 318, 338, 357–8, 402
banker, 64
bell-founder, 259
boundaries, 1, 3, 123, 181–2, 188
Bransholme estate, 181, 186–8, 193, 203–4
brewer, 277
charities, 67, 87, 191
churches, 211, 328, 359
   Christ Church, 371
   Holy Trinity, vicar of, 105, 200
   St Mary's, Lowgate, 312
communications, 2–3, 7, 9, 58, 95–6, 109, 123, 138, 142, 148, 157, 160, 169, 184–5, 189, 214, 224–5, 246, 263, 266, 273–5, 277, 279–80, 297, 341, 360, 377, 405–6; *and see* Hull & Hornsea Railway Co.
corporation, city council, 123, 126, 151, 187–8, 189, 193, 252, 289, 308
customs officer, 277
dormitory settlements, 2, 3, 95, 245, 273, 279–80, 296, 340
draper, 367
electricity supply, 289
Fish Street chapel, 118, 141, 243, 253, 268, 293, 305, 320, 348, 403
fort, 190
gas supply, 288–9
Guild of Brave Poor Things, 289
hospitals, 204
Hymers college, 252
inhabitants, 2, 9, 24–5, 31, 33, 39, 102, 105, 150, 169–70, 198, 200, 275, 277–80, 295, 306, 343
merchants, 32, 34, 63, 66, 142, 150, 169–70, 190, 263, 274–5, 277
Methodism, 25, 414
mills, 36
music-hall proprietor, 277
parliamentary forces at, 54
population, 123
Port of Hull Society, 289
Roman Catholicism, 155
rural dean, 199
schools, 181, 188, 204, 294, 335; *and see* Hymers college
sculptors, monumental masons, 39, 80, 400
shipbuilders, shipowners, 150, 275, 277, 295, 353
shoemakers, 277
silver-making, 39
suburbs, 107, 123, 126–8, 148, 181, 201; *and see* Bransholme; Kingswood
surgeon, 277
tanner, 278
tin can manufacturer, 278
trade, 110; *and see* carriers
Trinity House, 126, 171, 193–4, 209, 283, 285
University college, 204
Victoria Hospital for Sick Children, 289
water supply, 185, 288
and see Myton; Wyke
Hull, river, valley, 1, 3–4, 107–8, 181–6, 189, 194, 197–8, 214, 223, 245–6, 250, 261, 266, 295–7, 299, 302, 330, 340–1, 349–50, 360, 375
Hull Royal Infirmary, 19
Hull Young People's Christian and Literary Institute, 308
Humber, river, 1, 7, 28, 41, 50, 58, 83, 95, 107–9, 173, 181–2, 184–5, 246, 307, 341, 350
Humberside (county):

council, 163, 185, 289, 308
   smallholdings, 163
and see Beverley Borough district; Holderness Borough district; North Wolds Borough district
Humberside Health Authority, 249
Humbleton (or Humeltone), 1–2, 15, 24, 37, 48, *56*, **56–82**, 192
advowson, 36, 76
almshouse, 82
bridges, 58
chantry, 77
chapel, nonconformist, 80
charities, 59, 76, 81–2
church, 38, 58, 61, 76–81, *78*
common fields, 70
common meadows, 70
common pastures, 70
court, 75
curates, 76–7, 79, 81–2; *and see* Browne, John (fl. 1743) *and* (d. 1787); Fenwick, John
domestic architecture, 58–9, 62, 77
drainage, 58
Hallgarth, 61
Humbleton Grange, 59, 70, 74 *n*
Humbleton Hall, 58–9, 61–2, 68
Humbleton House, 59, 62
Humbleton moor, 58–9, 70
inclosure, 58–9, 70
industry, 74
inn, 59
manor, 1–2, 45, 58, 61–2, 67–70, 73, 75, 78, 81
manor house, 58, 61, 80; *and see* Old Hall
Manor House or Farm, 58, 61–2
market, 74
moated site, 58, 61
Old Hall, 62 *n*
parish officers, 75–6, 79, 82
playing field, 59
poor relief, 75, 82
population, 57
protestant nonconformity, 80
rectory, 68–70, 76
roads, 41, 58, 60–1
Roman Catholicism, 80
schools, 58–9, 81–2; *plate 54*
tithes, 68–71, 76–7
vicarage, 36–7, 76, 79, 320
vicarage house, 37, 59, 76–7; *plate 42*
vicars, 61, 71, 76–9; *and see* Brook; Dixon, Jonathan; Jadis; Mysyn
village hall, 59, 81
water mill, 74
windmill, 74
woodland, 73–4
and see Danthorpe; Elstronwick; Fitling; Flinton; Foston
Hungary, 308
Hunmanby, 397
Hunsden, Ld., *see* Carey, John
Hunt, John, 277
Hunter:
   Geo., 264, 265 *n*, 267
   Rob., and his w. Dorothy, 300
   Sam., 267
   Revd. Sam., s. of last, 267–8
   fam., 246
hunting, hare-coursing 97, 102, 111, 129, 134, 331, 351; *and see* East Holderness Hunt; Holderness Hunt; *see also* fishing; fowling; horse-racing
Hussey:
   Margery, *see* St. Quintin
   Sir Rog., 248
Hustler:
   Wm. (fl. 1606), 366
   Wm. (fl. mid 17th cent.), s. of last, 366
   Sir Wm. (fl. 1694, ?the same), 366
Hutchinson:
   Chas., 275
   Isabella, 31
   Wm., 104

Hutton:
   John:
      John of (fl. 1391), 63
      John (fl. 17th cent.), vicar of Aldbrough, 24
      Thos. (fl. 1708), 62
      Thos. (fl. 1860), and his w. Sarah, 316
Hutton Cranswick, *see* Rotsea
Hutton, Sheriff (Yorks. N.R.), 332
Hydes:
   Mary, m. Ric. Burton, 150
   Wm., 150
Hymers, John, rector of Brandesburton, 250, 252–3

Ibson, John, 364
inclosure, 4; *and see under places*
Incontri, Constance, *see* Whyte
Incorporated Society for the Building of Churches, 104
Incorporated Trinitarian Bible Society Trust, 357
Independents, Congregationalists, 118, 141, 203, 243, 253, 268, 281, 293–4, 305, 320, 329, 349, 377, 403
industry, trades *see* bell-founders; brewing; brickmaking; caravan manufacture; chicory-drying; corn milling; engineering; furniture manufacture; hides; lime-burning; malting; pottery making; ropemaking; sand and gravel extraction; straw-bonnet making; watchmaking; weaving; wood carving; *and see under places under* industry
infangthief, 90
Ingilby:
   Sir John, 100
   fam., 100
Ingram:
   Sir Art. (d. 1642), 61, 364
   Sir Wm. (fl. 1633), 364
   Wm. (fl. 1911), 126
   fam., 364
Inman, Emma, 171
Isaacson, Solomon, vicar of North Frodingham, 268–9
Isabella of France, queen of Edw. II, 312
Isherwood, Wm., and his w. Grace, 386
Iveson:
   Albert, 229
   Eliz., 72 *n*
   Jane, *see* Crooke
   Lancelot, 229

Jackson:
   Bryan B., 344
   Clive, 162
   Francis, 264, 267
   Harry, 162
   Hugh W., 344
   John, 344
   Nic., vicar of Mappleton, 318
   Pet. (fl. earlier 19th cent.), 344
   Revd. Pet. (fl. 1824), s. of last, 344
   Messrs. Ralph, & Sons, 21
   Ralph, 21
   T. H.(fl. 1942), 191
   Thos. B. (fl. 1918), 344
   Thos. (fl. earlier 20th cent., ?the same), 345
   Wm. (fl. 1808), 45
   Wm. (d. 1815), rector of Beeford, dean of Bath and Wells, bp. of Oxford, 240
   Wm. M. (fl. later 19th cent.), 277–9, 289
   fam., 344
   trustees, 344
Jadis, John, vicar of Humbleton, 77
Jamaica, 9
James:
   Hen., 89
   J. K., 293
   Wm., vicar of Burstwick, 162

CORRIGENDA TO PREVIOUSLY PUBLISHED VOLUMES

See also corrigenda published in *V.C.H. Yorks. E.R.* ii. 365; iv. 187; v. 223; vi. 337.

City of York, page 549, *for* 'Bolton (W.R.), Abbey of' *read* 'Bolton (W.R.), priory'

Volume I

page 466, line 31, *for* 'setate' *read* 'estate'

Volume II

page 140b, 8–9 lines from bottom, *delete sentence*
page 140b, note 91, *substitute* 'Not used.' for reference

Volume III

page xvi, line 19, *for* 'Yorkshire Archaeological Society, Record Series,' *read* 'Surtees Society,'

Volume IV

page xvi, line 32, *for* 'Yorkshire Archaeological Society, Record Series,' *read* 'Surtees Society,'

Volume V

page xv, line 2 from end, *delete* 'to Orders... xii' *and substitute* '*relative to the Expense and Maintenance of the Poor*, H.C. 82 (1818), xix'
page xvi, line 2, *for* 'Holdnerness' *read* 'Holderness'
page xvi, line 30, *for* 'Yorkshire Archaeological Society, Record Series,' *read* 'Surtees Society,'
page 23, *transpose and renumber notes 2 and 3*
page 50, line 29, *for* 'abbey' *read* 'priory'
page 50, line 35, *for* 'abbey' *read* 'priory'
page 50, line 38, *for* 'abbey' *read* 'priory'
page 51, line 12, *for* 'abbey' *read* 'priory'
page 53b, line 3, *for* 'abbey' *read* 'priory'
page 131b, lines 12 and 13, *for* 'Wilkinson' *read* 'Wilkin'
page 144b, line 20 from bottom, *for* 'abbey' *read* 'priory'
page 181, line 22, *after* '1837' *add a stop and delete* 'and ... Humberside.'
page 181, note 13, *substitute* 'Not used.' *for* reference
page 204, *for* 'Bolton abbey' *read* 'Bolton priory'
page 221, *delete* 'Wilkinson, Edw., 131' *and add* 'Wilkin, Edw., 131'

Volume VI

page xvii, line 4 from end, *for* 'Yorkshire Archaeological Society, Record Series,' *read* 'Surtees Society,'
page 188, *transpose the first two lines*